The English Flower Garden and Home Grounds; Design and Arrangement Shown by Existing Examples of Gardens in Great Britain and Ireland, Followed by a Description of the Plants, Shrubs and Trees for the Open-air Garden and Their Culture

THE ENGLISH FLOWER GARDEN
AND HOME GROUNDS.

First Edition, *November* 1883
Second   ,,   *February* 1889
Third   ,,   *May* 1893
Fourth   ,,   *June* 1895
Fifth   ,,   *June* 1896
    Reprinted, February 1897
Sixth Edition, *May* 1898
    Reprinted, November 1898
Seventh Edition, *May* 1899
Eighth   ,,   *June* 1900
    Reprinted, December 1900
        ,,   *May* 1901
        .,   *June* 1902
        ,,   *June* 1903

THE ENGLISH
FLOWER GARDEN
AND HOME GROUNDS

Design and Arrangement shown by existing
examples of Gardens in Great Britain and Ireland
followed by a Description of the Plants
Shrubs and Trees for the Open-air Garden
and their Culture By W. ROBINSON
Author of ' The Wild Garden '
Illustrated with many Engravings on Wood
Eighth Edition

" You see, sweet maid, we marry
A gentler scion to the wildest stock,
And make conceive a bark of baser kind
By bud of nobler race this is an art
Which does mend nature, change it rather, but
The art itself is nature "—*Shakespeare*

London John Murray Albemarle Street

m.dccciii

RICHARD CLAY AND SONS LIMITED,
BREAD STREET HILL, E C, AND
BUNGAY, SUFFOLK

To my Friend

Mons. B. LATOUR-MARLIAC

WHO, BY HIS PATIENT EXPERIMENTS, HAS ADDED THE

CHARM OF VARIED COLOUR TO THE HARDY WATER LILIES

OF THE NORTH, THIS NEW EDITION OF THE

"ENGLISH FLOWER GARDEN"

is Dedicated

" *Laying out grounds, as it is called, may be considered as a liberal art, in some sort like poetry and painting, and its object, like that of all the liberal arts, is, or ought to be, to move the affections under the control of good sense   If this be so when we are merely putting together words or colours, how much more ought the feeling to prevail when we are in the midst of the realities of things , of the beauty and harmony, of the joy and happiness of living creatures , of men and children, of birds and beasts, of hills and streams, and trees and flowers, with the changes of night and day, evening and morning, summer and winter, and all their unwearied actions and energies* "—WORDSWORTH

FOREWORDS TO NEW EDITION.

THIS book is the muster of various once forlorn hopes and skirmishing parties now united with better arms and larger aims, and its beginnings may have an interest for others I came to London just when the Royal Horticultural Society's garden at Kensington was being laid out, a series of elaborate patterns set at different levels, and the Crystal Palace, in its glory, was described by the Press of the day to be the most wonderful instance of modern gardening—water-temples, water-paths, vast stone basins and all the theatrical gardening of Versailles reproduced in Surrey.

There was little or no reason admitted into garden design . the same poor imitation of the Italian garden being set down in all sorts of positions If the place did not suit the style, the ground had to be bolstered up in some way so that the plan might be carried out—a costly way to get an often ridiculous result The great writers of the past had laughed the carpenter's rule out of the parks of England, and pictures arose where they were once impossible ; but the ugliness of the garden about the house was assumed to be an essential part of the thing itself, removing that for ever from the sympathies of artistic people.

The flower garden planting was made up of a few kinds of flowers which people were proud to put out in thousands and tens of thousands, and with these, patterns, more or less elaborate, were carried out in every garden save the very poorest cottage garden It was not easy to get away from all this false and hideous " art," but I was then in the Botanic Gardens, Regent's Park, where there was at that time a small garden of British plants, which had to be kept up, and this led me into the varied country round London, from the orchid-flecked meadows of Bucks to the tumbled down undercliffs on the Essex coast, untroubled by the plough; and so I began to get an idea (which should be taught to every boy at school) that there was (for gardens even) much beauty in our native flowers and trees, and then came the thought that if there was so much in our own island flora, what might we not look for from the hills and valleys of the countries of the northern and temperate world ?

From thoughts of this kind if I turned to actual things, I saw the flower-gardener meanly trying to rival the tile or wall-paper men, and throwing aside with contempt all the lovely things that through their height or form did not conform to this idea (so stupid as to life), and this too the rule, not only in the villa garden, but in our great public and private gardens   There was, happily, always the beauty of the woods and lanes and the lovely cottage gardens in the country round London, and here and there, though rare, a quiet garden with things as the great mother made them and grouped them   And so I began to see clearly that the common way was a great error and the greatest obstacle to true gardening or artistic effects of any kind in the flower-garden or home landscape, and then, made up my mind to fight the thing out in any way open to me.

The English Flower Garden consists of two parts   the first dealing with the question of design—the aim being to make the garden a reflex of the beauty of the great garden of the world itself, and to prove that the true way to happiest design is not to have any stereotyped style for all flower gardens, but that the best kind of garden should arise out of its site and conditions as happily as a primrose out of a cool bank.

The second part includes most of the trees and plants, hardy and half-hardy, for our flower gardens and pleasure grounds, and it is illustrated with a view to show the beauty of the things spoken of, as few know the many shrubs and trees worth a place in our open-air gardens, and it is of little use to discuss arrangement if the beauty of the flowers is hidden from us   No stereotyped garden of half-a-dozen kinds of plants will satisfy any one who knows that many beautiful aspects of vegetation are possible in a garden in spring, summer, and autumn

This is not a botanical book, as should be clear from its title ; but some may expect in the book technical terms which I wish to keep out of it   Although the debt of the gardener to Botany is great, the subordination of the garden to Botany has been fruitful of the greatest evil to artistic gardening. The way of arranging a garden like a book, and a very ugly book, as in the French botanic gardens (Caen, Angers, Rouen), in which one sees a sea of showy labels, where one might look for the life and peace of a garden, is a blinding obstacle to beautiful gardening, and the Garden of Plants, in Paris, may be cited as one having had for ages a disastrous effect in the gardening of France It is the spirit of natural beauty we should seek to win into the garden, and so get away from the set patterns on the one hand, and labelled "dots" on the other

English names are given where possible—as it is best to speak of things growing about our doors in our own tongue, and the practice of using in conversation long Latin names, a growth of our own century, has done infinite harm to gardening in shutting out people who have a heart for a garden, but none for the Latin of the gardener There is no more need to speak of the plants in our gardens by their Latin names than to speak of the dove or the rabbit by Latin names, and where we introduce plants that have no good English names we must make them as well as we may   Old English books like Gerard were rich in English names, and we should follow their ways and be ashamed to use for things in the garden a strange tongue—dog Latin, or as it may be. Every plant grown in gardens should have an English name, among the many reasons for this being the frequent changes that Latin names undergo in the breaking down of the characters which are supposed to separate genera   For instance, Azalea and Rhododendron are now one genus , such changes are even more troublesome when they occur in less well-known plants , and one of the most beautiful plants of our gardens, the Irish Heath (Daboecia, now Boretta), will not be found now by its hitherto recorded name in the London Catalogue of British Plants.   But if we have a good English name, these ceaseless botanical changes are of less consequence.   It is impossible for gardeners and nurserymen to keep up with such changes, not always indeed accepted even by botanists themselves   The fact that in speaking of plants we use English names does not in the least prevent us from using the Latin name in its right place, when we have need to do so   The systematic nomenclature followed is that of the Kew list, wherever use does not compel us to adhere to old names like Azalea

For the second part of this book the storehouse of information in *The Garden* has been taken advantage of, but articles have been specially written where necessary, and the following are the names of the writers whose contributions are embodied in the second part of the book, and frequently marked by their initials :—

J. Allen
J. Atkins
P. Barr
W. J. Bean
J. Birkenhead
J. Britten
W. Brockbank
F. W. Burbidge
G. A. Champion
Latimer Clarke
E. T. Cook
J. Cornhill
Mons. H. Correvon
Rev. Harpur Crewe
A. Dean
R. Dean
D. Dewar
Rev. C. Wolley Dod
Rev. H. H. Dombrain
J. Douglas
J. Dundas
Rev. Canon Ellacombe
H. J. Elwes
Rev. H. Ewbank
W. Falconer
D. T. Fish
Dr. M. Foster
P. Neill Fraser
O. Froebel
T. W. Girdlestone

W. Goldring
P. Grieve
J. Groom
W. E. Gumbleton
T. Hatfield
W. B. Hemsley
I. Anderson-Henry
A. Herrington
T. H. Archer-Hind
E. Hobday
Rev. F. D. Horner
Miss F. Hope
C. M. Hovey
E. Jackson
Miss G. Jekyll
Miss R. Kingsley
A. Kingsmill
Max Leichtlin
H. Selfe-Leonard
E. G. Loder
R. I. Lynch
J. M'Nab
B. Latour-Marliac
R. Marnock
G. Maw
F. W. Meyer
A. B. Freeman-Mitford
H. G. Moon
F. Moore
G. Nicholson

J. C. Niven
Miss C. M. Owen
A. Perry
J. T. Bennett-Poë
R. Potter
A. Rawson
The Very Rev. The Dean of
   Rochester
A. Salter
C. R. Scrase-Dickens
C. W. Shaw
J. Sheppard
J. Simpson
J. Smith
T. Spanswick
J. Stevens
Rev. Canon Swayne
W. Thompson
W. P. Thomson
G. Van Tubergen, Junr.
Rev. F. Tymons
Maurice L. de Vilmorin
Dr. A. Wallace
W. Watson
J. Weathers
W. Wildsmith
Miss Willmott
G. F. Wilson
J. Wood
E. H. Woodall

W. R.

CONTENTS.

PART I

PART II

THE

ENGLISH FLOWER GARDEN

PART I

ART IN THE GARDEN. DESIGN AND PLANS IN RELATION
TO THE HOUSE AND HOME LANDSCAPE. VARIOUS KINDS
OF FLOWER GARDENS WITH A VIEW TO ARTISTIC EFFECT
AND GOOD CULTIVATION. ARTISTIC USE OF THE GREAT
GROUPS OF PLANTS FOR THE OPEN AIR GARDENS IN THE
BRITISH ISLES. ALPINE, ROCK AND BORDER PLANTS,
CLIMBERS, ANNUALS AND BIENNIALS, FLOWERING TREES,
SHRUBS, AND EVERGREENS; WATER AND BOG PLANTS,
HARDY FERNS, FINE-LEAVED, BEDDING AND HALF-HARDY
PLANTS, ROSES, SPRING, SUMMER, AUTUMN AND WINTER
GARDENS, HARDY BULBS; ORCHARD BEAUTIFUL THE
WILD GARDEN, FLOWERS FOR CUTTING, COLOUR AND
FRAGRANCE. LABOURS FOR GOOD OR EVIL. LAWNS AND
PLEASURE GROUNDS. ILLUSTRATED FROM EXISTING
EXAMPLES OF BRITISH GARDENS ENGRAVED ON WOOD.

" An unerring perception told the Greeks that the beautiful must also be the true, and recalled them back into the way. As in conduct they insisted on an energy which was rational, so in art and in literature they required of beauty that it too should be before all things rational"
—Some Aspects of the Greek Genius.

THE
ENGLISH FLOWER GARDEN.

CHAPTER I.

ART IN RELATION TO FLOWER-GARDENING AND GARDEN DESIGN

THERE is no reason why we should not have true art in the garden, but much why we should have it, and no reason why a garden should be ugly, bare, or conventional The word "art" being used in its highest sense here, it may perhaps be well to justify its use, and as good a definition of the word as any perhaps is "power to see and give form to beautiful things," which we see shown in some of its finest forms in Greek sculpture and in the works of the great masters of painting.

But art is of many kinds, and owing to the loose, "critical" talk of the day, it is not easy to see that true art is based on clear-eyed study of and love for Nature, rather than invention and the bringing of the "personality" of the artist into the work, of which we hear so much The work of the artist is always marked by its fidelity to Nature, and proof of this may be seen in the greatest art galleries now open to all, so that there is little to hide evidence as to what is said here about art in its highest expression. But as a number of people write much about art in the magazines and papers, while blind as bats to its simple law, there is infinite confusion in many minds about it, and we may read essay after essay about art without being brought a bit nearer to the simple truth, but on the other hand get the false idea that it is not by observing, but by inventing and supplementing, that good work is done. The strong man must be there, but his work is to see the whole beauty of the subject, and to help us to see it, not to distort it in any way for the sake of making it "original" This is often a way to popularity, but in the end it means bad work. It may be the fashion for a season, owing to some one quality ; but it is soon·found out, and we have to return to the great masters of all ages, who are always distinguished for truth to Nature, and who show their strength by getting nearer to her.

The actual beauty of a thing in all its fulness and subtlety is almost the whole of the question, but the critics of the day will not take the trouble to see this, and write essays on art in which many long words occur, but in which we do not once meet with the word *truth.* " Realism " and " idealism " are words freely used, and bad pictures are shown us as examples of " realism," which leave out all the refinement, subtlety, truth of tone, and perhaps even the very light and shade in which all the real things we see are set.

There are men so blind to the beauty of the things set before their eyes in sky, sea, or earth, that they would seek to idealise the eyes of a beautiful child or the clouds of heaven ; while all who see natural beauty in landscape know that no imagining can come near to the beauty of things seen, art being often powerless to seize their full beauty, and the artist has often to let the brush fall in despair.   There are more pictures round the year in many a parish in England than all the landscape painters of Europe could paint in a century.   Only a little, indeed, of the beauty that concerns us most— that of the landscape—can be seized for us except by the very greatest masters.   Of things visible—flower, tree, landscape, sky, or sea—to see the full and every varied beauty is to be saved for ever from any will-o'-the-wisp of the imaginary.

But many people do not judge pictures by Nature, but by pictures, and therefore they miss her subtleties and delicate realities on which all true work depends.   Some sneer at those who " copy Nature," but the answer to such critics is for ever there in the work of the great men, be they Greeks, Dutchmen, Italians, French, or English.

It is part of the work of the artist to select beautiful or memorable things, not the first that come in his way.   The Venus of Milo is from a noble type of woman—not a mean Greek.   The horses of the Parthenon show the best of Eastern breed, full of life and beauty.   Great landscape painters like Crome, Corot, and Turner seek not things only because they are natural, but also beautiful ; selecting views and waiting for the light that suits the chosen subject best, they give us pictures, working always from faithful study of Nature and from stores of knowledge gathered from her, and that is the only true path for the gardener, all true art being based on her eternal laws   All deviation from the truth of Nature, whether it be at the hands of Greek, Italian, or other artist, though it may pass for a time, is in the end—it may be ages after the artist is dead—classed as *debased* art

Why say so much here about art? Because when we see the meaning of true "art" we cannot endure what is ugly and false in art, and we cannot have the foregrounds of beautiful English scenery daubed with flower gardens like coloured advertisements. Many see the right way from their own sense being true, but others may wish for proof of what is urged here as to the true source of lasting work in art in the work of the great artists of all time. And we may be as true artists in the garden and home landscape as anywhere else.

There is no good picture which does not image for us the beauty of natural things, and why not begin with these and be artists in their growth and grouping?—for one reason among others that we are privileged to have the living things about us, and not merely representations of them.

So far we have spoken of the work of the true artist, which is always marked by respect for Nature and by keen study of her. But apart from this we have a great many men who do what is called "decorative" work, useful, but still not art in the sense of delight in, and study of, things as they are—the whole class of decorators, who make our carpets, tiles, curtains, and who adapt conventional or geometric forms mostly to flat surfaces. Skill in this way may be considerable without any attention whatever being paid to the greater art that is concerned with life in all its fulness

This it is well to see clearly; as for the flower gardener it matters much on which side he stands. Unhappily, our gardeners for ages have suffered at the hands of the decorative artist, when applying his "designs" to the garden, and designs which may be quite right on a surface like a carpet or panel have been applied a thousand times to the surface of the much enduring earth. It is this adapting of absurd "knots" and patterns from old books to any surface where a flower garden has to be made that leads to bad and frivolous design— wrong in plan and hopeless for the life of plants. It is so easy for any one asked for a plan to furnish one of this sort without the slightest knowledge of the life of a garden

For ages the flower-garden has been marred by absurdities of this kind of work as regards plan, though the flowers were in simple and natural ways. But in our own time the same "decorative" idea has come to be carried out in the planting of the flowers under the name of "bedding out," "carpet bedding," or "mosaic culture." In this the beautiful forms of flowers are degraded to the level of crude colour to make a design, and without reference to the natural form or beauty of the plants, clipping being freely done to get the carpets or patterns "true." When these tracery gardens were made, often by people without any knowledge of the plants of a garden, they were found to be difficult to plant; hence attempts to do without the

A Devonshire Cottage Garden, Cockington, Torquay. Engraved from a photograph
by S. W. Fitzherbert.

gardener altogether, and get colour by the use of broken brick, white sand, and painted stone, as in Nesfield's work at South Kensington and Sir C. Barry's at Shrubland. All such work is wrong and degrading to the art of gardening, and in its extreme expressions is ridiculous

Why are such designs bad ? The good sense of all is the final court of appeal for even artistic things, and to many people these remarks need not be made, but the stereotyped gardens that abound in many places show us that the fight against the ugly garden has only begun. The modern garden is often no more interesting than an oilcloth pattern, because instead of beautiful form and colour we see emphasis given to pattern-work and plants robbed of all their grace But while the artist may be driven from the common bedding garden, he will perhaps go to rest his eyes on a cottage garden, and make a picture of it, as the cottage garden is itself often a picture. Why should the cottage garden be a picture when the gentleman's garden is not ? Here is an engraving of a small cottage garden in Devonshire : an artistic garden in its simplest expression. There was very little in this beyond Roses and a few Pansies, and yet it was right and beautiful, and there are many as good in every county in England. May the large gardens be as good in proportion to the money spent upon them and their size as this little cottage garden ? Certainly · the gardens shown in this book prove it, although it is rarely nowadays that a large garden shows anything like the charm of simplicity that many cottage gardens do.

The gardener should follow the true artist, however modestly, in his love for things as they are, in delight in natural form and beauty of flower and tree, if we are to be free from barren geometry, and if our gardens are ever to be pictures. The gardener has not the strenuous work of eye and hand that the artist has, but he has plenty of good work to do :—to choose from ten thousand beautiful living things , to study their nature and adapt them to his soil and climate , to get the full expression of their beauty ; to grow and place them well and in right relation to other things, which is a life-study in itself, in view of the great numbers of the flowers and flowering trees of the world. And as the artist's work is to see and keep for us some of the beauty of landscape, tree, or flower, so the gardener's should be to keep for us as far as may be, in the fulness of their natural beauty, the living things themselves. The artist gives us the fair image : the gardener is the trustee of a world of fair living things, to be kept with care and knowledge in necessary subordination to the conditions of his work. And as there is other and higher design than that of the decorator of flat surfaces with patterns, so there is an absolute and eternal difference between conventional form as he expresses it, and the true forms of cloud or hill, vale, stream, path, oak, palm and vine, reed and lily   And the first duty of all who care for the garden as a picture is to see these noble natural forms in every part of life and nature, and once they see them they will never mistake decorative patterns for art and beauty in a garden.

In some writings on garden design, it is assumed as a truism that the landscape and naturalistic view of that design was the invention of certain men, and a mere passing fashion, like many that have disfigured the garden.   This is a serious error, as it was based on observation of the landscape beauty which has existed ever since the eyes of men were first opened to the beauty of the earth, whether on wild mountain woodland, or in the forest plain, apart altogether from man's efforts, as seen in the parks of England from Alnwick to Richmond , and in either case it is too lovely a lesson to forget so long as man has any eyes to see beauty.   If all the works of man in landscape planting were swept away, there would still be beautiful landscape on vast areas in many lands.   There are ten thousand grassy lawns and glades among the mountain Pines of Switzerland, as there are on the mountains of California and Cashmere, and, indeed, the many other woody mountain lands of the world ; and many of these are suggestive of all that is most beautiful in planting.

Apart from the planning of ground and its form, there is the question of the arrangement of all the beautiful things of earth— flower, shrub, or tree in right or wrong ways.   Here there are always lessons to be learned in nature . lovely colonies of Bird's-eye Primrose in the bogs of Westmoreland ; and of Gentian by the alpine streams, islets of wild Heath, lakes of wild Hyacinth, and wood carpets of Primrose ; groups of Venetian Sumach cropping out of the hot southern rocks ; and of May on the hill, the stately groves of the lowland forest, and the Grey Willows of the marsh land.   In planting in like ways we are simply taking a lesson from Nature, and not dabbling in a mere fashion.   Even the creatures of earth and air are held together beautifully—wild birds in the air, delicate brown flocks of them by the cold northern sea, as well as many groups of nobler birds on the banks of the Nile and southern rivers ; the cattle on a thousand hills : in no other way could their forms or colours be so well seen.   And so it must ever be in the garden where natural grouping is the true and artistic way.

The expression of these ideas may seem to some to imply that the garden generally is to be a tangled wilderness. But having plants in natural forms does not in the least prevent us from making a straight walk along a straight wall, or from having the necessary wall protection for our gardens. A straight line is often the most beautiful that can be used , but its use by no means implies that we are not to group our plants or bushes naturally alongside it.

Town-Garden, The Broadway, Worcestershire. From a picture in possession of the author.

As I use the word "artistic," in a book on the flower-garden, it may be well to say that as it is used it means right and true in relation to all the conditions of the case, and the necessary limitations of our art and all other human arts. A lovely Greek coin, a bit of canvas painted by Corot with the morning light on it, a block of stone hewn into the shape of the dying gladiator, the white mountain rocks built into a Parthenon—these are all examples of human art, every one of which can be only fairly judged in due regard to what is possible in the material of each—knowledge which it is part of the artist's essential task to possess. Often a garden may be wrong in various ways, as shown by the conifers spread in front of many a house—ugly in form, not in harmony with our native or best garden vegetation; mountain trees set out on dry plains and not even hardy; so that the word inartistic may help us to describe many errors And again, if we are happy enough to find a garden so true and right in its results in many ways as to form a picture that an artist would be charmed to study, we may call it an artistic garden, as a short way of saying that it is about as good as it may be, taking everything into account.

The Fallacy as to "Matters of Taste."

The man behind the counter often tells us that "it is a matter of taste" if we say a word as to the ugliness of some of his wares, and many other people have the same false idea that obscures all issues about artistic things. If it were confined to the ignorant it would do little harm, but we hear it expressed by men of education. To take a recent instance, the author of "Pages from a Private Diary" (1898) protests against

making a religion of what is purely a matter of taste Weeds are as natural as flowers. A lawn left to Nature would soon become a meadow. A hedge left to Nature would become monstrous and useless, because pervious. A well-grown Yew tree is undoubtedly a beautiful object, but a Yew clipped intelligently is quite as beautiful; and if a tree will clip, it is not unnatural to clip it

Here we have some common ideas written by a man of wit, but who in this instance has not thought of what he writes about; and if we find these notions in such men, how are we to blame the many who with fewer advantages have to study the question of garden design or planting? For this and all artistic questions are only "matters of taste" to those who have not thought of them. The merit of a portrait by Rembrandt and the first Academy daub is not a matter of taste, but of very serious fact So also we may compare an Elizabethan house with one of the carpenter's Gothic of our century, the sculptures of the Parthenon with the statues in our squares; a symphony by Beethoven with the " Maiden's Prayer ; " an English cottage garden, quite simple in plan and full of flowers in their natural forms, with the imitations of very bad carpets (vile in colour and without form) which we now see in French and German watering places (mosaiculture)!

So far from its being true that good or bad garden design or planting are merely matters of taste, the very first thing we should teach to every one who has to think of it is that they are matters of fact, truth and observation   The assumption in the paragraph that any one advised leaving hedges, &c., to Nature does not surely need a reply ; but that a Yew clipped intelligently is quite as beautiful "as a well and naturally grown Yew tree" is a statement that could hardly be made save in jest by any one who has thought the least about tree beauty or natural form of any kind   For here it is not a difference of degree we have to deal with, but a difference in kind, because a clipped tree is a thing without any true form, light or shade, motion or voice. Vast as are the differences above named, between none of them is there so great and hideous a difference as between the divinely given form of the northern evergreen tree, whether of the tree-fringed mountain lawns of Jura, the mountains of the Pacific coast of North America, or the rocks of Scotland, and the ridiculous results of the distortion of forest trees by man.

Yet the fact that garden design or planting is a matter of knowledge of the natural forms, harmonies and colours of things does not mean that this writer or any one is not to do what he pleases in his garden.   But when he tells us that the judgment which enables us to distinguish a good picture from a bad one is to abandon us before the absurdities seen in our gardens, and too often marring the foregrounds of the home landscape of our country houses, he is leading all who trust him into error.   Moreover, individual likes and dislikes are wholly separate from the problem of what is best in a given situation as to design and planting.

The question, like so many others, is made needlessly hard for the student by the *writing without knowledge*, which, unhappily, is devoted to it.   To practice an art without any knowledge of it is bad enough, but when men *write* about an art dealing with so many living things as planting, when clearly they have given no heed to its simplest elements, they do infinite harm in spreading the false idea that it is all " a matter of taste."   Of such quotations as the above, in which every phrase is an error or a false assumption, a volume might easily be put together.

One of the commonest and grossest errors is to take the worst possible work, abuse it, and say nothing about the better way.

Deception is a primary object of the landscape gardener.   Thus to get variety, and to deceive the eye into supposing that the garden is larger than it is, the paths are to wind about in all directions and the lawns are not to be left a broad expanse, but dotted about with Pampas Grasses, foreign shrubs, or anything else that will break up the surface. As was said by a witty Frenchman, " Nothing is easier than to lay out an English garden ; one has only to make one's gardener drunk and follow him about."- THE FORMAL GARDEN

There is not a word said here of the plain fact that we may have true and artistic ways, as well as stupid ones, of forming paths and getting fine variety of surface by planting, without dotting lawns with Pampas Grass, or of the equally plain fact that we can make walks through lawn or wood or by river in lines of easiest gradation and most convenient access without going through any of the antics above described or in any way violating good sense.   There is not a word in the above paragraph which is true of good work in landscape planting.

That bad and ignorant work is done we can no more deny than the existence of the barrel-organ or the Victorian villa, but a man must be blind to the truth who writes thus without knowledge, as there are innumerable instances in every county of picturesque plant-ing without deception of any kind.   The true work of the landscape gardener is wholly different ; it is to study the natural forms of the ground and keep to the best of them , to have keen eyes for every charm of natural growth and to save it for the future beauty of the place ; to know also all the trees of the northern world fitted to adorn it ; to make living pictures, in fact—easy to those who have eyes and hearts for the work, but impossible otherwise.

Another like statement of the writer on clipping trees that wearies us by its want of knowledge of Nature is this :—

A clipped Yew tree is as much a part of Nature—that is, subject to natural laws, as a forest Oak ; but the landscapist, by appealing to associations which surround the personification of Nature, holds up the clipped Yew tree to obloquy as something against Nature   So far as that goes, it is no more unnatural to clip a Yew tree than to cut grass.

The answer is that we mow turf to walk upon ; for the pleasure to the eye of short turf, or for the pleasure of walking on it in the hot days, or for the relief and repose it gives ; for by cutting grass short we disfigure nothing, throw no naturally beautiful things into grotesque or ugly forms offensive to the artist, and all who care for true form   Moreover, short turf is *not* an artificial thing, as there are many natural lawns on the mountains of Europe, short and crisp as ever lawn was seen , set, too, with alpine flowers and guarded by outposts of stately mountain trees.

LANDSCAPE PAINTING AND GARDENS —There are few pictures of gardens, because the garden beautiful is rare   Gardens around country houses, instead of forming, as they all might, graceful foregrounds to the good landscape views, disfigure all, and drive the artist away

Cawdor, showing effect of Garden with natural Forms.

in despair. Yet there may be real pictures in gardens; it is not a
mere question of patterns of a very poor sort, but one of light and
shade, beauty of form, and colour. In times when gardens were
made by men who did not know one tree from another, the matter
was settled by the shears—it was a question of green walls only
Now we are beginning to see that there is a wholly different and
higher order of beauty to be found in gardens, and we are at the
beginning of a period when we may hope to get much more pleasure
and instruction out of this art than ever before.

We have seen in Bond-street a variety of picture exhibitions
devoted to gardens, generally of the trifling stippled water-colour
order   The painters of these pictures, for the most part ten-minute
sketches, have one main idea—that the only garden worth picturing is
the shorn one, and pictures of such places are repeated time after
time ; a clipped line of Arbor-vitæ, with a stuffed peacock stuck by
the side of it, is considered good enough for a garden picture.   Work
of this kind, which is almost mechanical, is so much easier than the
drawing of a garden with the elements of varied beauty in it.   In
the work of Alfred Parsons and a few others we see the beginning of
things of beauty in the painting of gardens, but it is for us gardeners
to commence by first being artists ourselves, and opening our eyes to
see the ugly things about us

Artists of real power would paint gardens and home landscapes if
there were real pictures to draw ; but generally they are so rare that
the work does not come into the artist's view at all.   Through all
the rage of the " bedding-out " fever, it was impossible for an artist
to paint in a garden like those which disfigured the land from Blair
Athol to the Crystal Palace.   It is difficult to imagine Corot sitting
down to paint the Grande Trianon, or the terrace patterns at Versailles,
though a poor hamlet in the North of France, with a few willows
near, gave him a lovely picture.   Once, when trying to persuade
Mr. Mark Fisher, the landscape painter, to come into a district
remarkable for its natural beauty, he replied : " There are too many
gentlemen's places there to suit my work," referring to the hardness
and ugliness of the effects around most country seats, owing to the
iron-bound pudding-clumps of trees, railings, capricious clippings and
shearings, bad colours, and absence of fine and true form, with, almost
certainly, an ugly house in the midst of all.   But we ought to be able
to do better than be makers of garden scarecrows to the very men
who would enjoy our work most, and delight in painting it, rich as
we are in the sources of all beauty of tree or flower, and the three
illustrations in this chapter prove at least that in both cottage, town,
and castle garden, we can get away from geometrical form into
freedom of grace and leaf, flower and tree

CHAPTER II.

DESIGN AND POSITION—AGAINST STYLES, USELESS STONEWORK, AND STEREOTYPED PLANS—TIME'S EFFECT ON GARDEN DESIGN—ARCHITECTURE AND FLOWER GARDENS—DESIGN NOT FORMAL ONLY—USE IN THE GARDEN OF BUILDERS', AND OTHER DEGRADED FORMS OF THE PLASTIC ART.

ONE aim of this book is to uproot the idea that a flower garden must always be of set pattern placed on one side of the house. The wants of flowers can be best met, and their varied loveliness best shown, in a variety of positions, and the first thing to do is to consider the effect of arraying all our flowers in one spot under the same conditions, as such a plan can never give us a tithe of the beauty which our gardens may afford. The settled way has too often been to regard one spot with the same soil and aspect—with every condition alike, in fact—as the only home for open-air flowers, though near at hand there may be positions, each favourable to different groups of flower

For all that concerns us in this artistic question there are laws which will guide us if we seek for them. The laws here meant are Nature's laws—not merely landmarks set out by man for his convenience. Only they are not laws that bind with weary fetters, but as infinite in delightful change as the restless clouds on the hills We shall never settle the most trifling question by the stupid saying that it is "a matter of taste," and if the reader will come with me through these early chapters, I hope to convince him that flower-gardening is "a matter of reason." The laws of all true art can only be based on the eternal laws of Nature, and these are the source from which all our guidance should come

One of the first things we have to do is to get a clear idea of the hollowness of much of the talk about "styles" that forms a great part of what has been written in books about laying out gardens, and there are many dissertations on the several styles, the authors going even to China and to Mexico for illustrations. The first thing every writer on this subject does is to puzzle his readers with words about "styles," but when all is read, what is the result to anybody who looks from words to things? That there are two styles : the one strait-laced, mechanical, with much wall and stone, with water-squirts, plaster-work, and absurd sculpture ; the other natural—in most cases, once free of the house accepting the ground lines of the earth herself as the best, and getting plant beauty from its natural source—the flowers and trees arranged in picturesque ways.

There are positions where stonework is necessary, but the beautiful terrace gardens are those that are built where the nature of the ground required them ; and there is nothing more melancholy than the walls, fountain basins, clipped trees, and long canals of places like the Crystal Palace, not only because they fail to satisfy the desire for beauty, but because they tell of wasted effort, riches worse than lost There are, from Versailles to Caserta, a great many ugly gardens in Europe, but at Sydenham we have the greatest modern example of the waste of enormous means in making hideous a fine piece of ground This has been called a work of genius, but it is the fruit of a poor ambition to outdo another ugly extravagance—Versailles. But Versailles is a relic of the past, and was the expression of such knowledge of the gardening art as men then possessed. As Versailles has numerous tall water-squirts, the best way of glorifying ourselves was to make some taller ones at Sydenham ! Instead of confining the terrace gardening to the upper terrace, by far the greater portion of the ground was devoted to a stony extravagance of design, and nearly in the centre were placed the vast and ugly fountain basins The contrivances to enable the water to go down-stairs, the temples, statues, dead walls, all costly rubbish, praised by the papers as the marvellous work of a genius. When a private individual indulges in such fancies, he may not injure many but himself ; but in this public garden—set up as an example of all that is admirable—we have, in addition to wasteful outlay, what is hurtful to the public taste

Many whose lawns were, or might readily have been made, the most beautiful of gardens have spoiled them for sham terraced gardens, and there is a modern castle in Scotland where the embankments are piled one above another, till the whole looks as if Uncle Toby with an army of corporals had been carrying out his grandest scheme in fortification The rude stone wall of the hill husbandman, supporting a narrow slip of soil for olive-trees or vines, became in the garden of the wealthy Roman a well-built one; but it must be remembered that, even where the wall is necessary, the beauty of the true Italian garden depends on the life of trees and flowers more than on the plan of the garden, as in the Guisti garden at Verona

Arundel. Example of ground requiring terracing, showing also picturesque disposition of the trees to compare with clipped walls of trees near French château.

c

whereas in our sham examples of the Italian garden all is as flat and lifeless as a bad mosaic.

TERRACED GARDENS, allowing of much building (apart from the house), have been much in favour with architects who have designed gardens. The landscape gardener, too often led by custom, falls in with the notion that every house, no matter what its position, should be fortified by terraces, and he busies himself in forming them even on level ground, and large sums are spent on fountains, vases, statues, balustrades, useless walls, and stucco work, where these are out of place. By the extensive use of such materials many a noble lawn is cut up; and often, as at Witley Court, the " architectural " gardening is pushed so far into the park as to curtail and injure the view. If the cost of the stone and stucco ornament lavished on the garden were spent on its legitimate object—the house—how much better it would be for architecture, as well as for gardening!

The best effect is to be got not by carrying architectural features into the usually small level town garden, but by the contrast between the garden vegetation and its built surroundings. This contrast should be got, not by the sham picturesque, with rocks, cascades, and undulations of the ground, but mainly by the simple dignity of trees and the charm of turf. It was said that none but an Italian garden would suit South Kensington, and we had an elaborate garden there carried out with the greatest care, yet the result, as everybody knows, was miserable. There are many private gardens in European cities, with as formal surroundings as those of South Kensington, which are as beautiful as it was stiff and ugly.

Elaborate terraced gardens in the wrong place often prevent the formation of beautiful lawns, though a good lawn is the happiest thing in a garden. For many years past there has been so much cutting up, geometry and stonework, that it is rare to find a good lawn left, and many a site cut up would be vastly improved if changed into a large, nobly fringed lawn. A very common, poorly built house with a fine open lawn has often a better effect than a fine one with a rectilineal garden and terraces in front of it, though there are cases where walls would be the way to a good result.

A style of garden " design " that for a long time has had an injurious effect on many places is the " railway embankment " phase of landscape gardening madness—one in which we see a series of sharply graded grass slopes, exactly like well-smoothed railway embankments. It is curious that any one should imagine that such a plan, marring the whole landscape, should give pleasure to any human being, or do anything but make the foreground of the house wearisome to the last degree. In this variety we often find several sharp banks falling one below the other without a protecting wall

Haddon. Old English garden with terracing essential owing to use and nature of ground.

at the top, and the sharp green angles cutting horrible capers from various points of view, and this perhaps in the face of a beautiful landscape. Of this there was, until lately, an instance at Verdley Place, in the midst of one of the most beautiful landscapes in England, and many others might be named in almost every county.

A beautiful house in a fair landscape is the most delightful scene of the cultivated earth, all the more so if there be an artistic garden—the rarest thing to find! The union between the house beautiful and the ground near it—a happy marriage it should be—is worthy of more thought than it has had in the past, and the best way of effecting that union artistically should interest men more and more as our cities grow larger and our lovely English landscape shrinks back from them. We have never yet got from the garden and the home landscape half the beauty which we might get by abolishing the needless patterns which disfigure so many gardens. Formality is often essential to the plan of a garden but never to the arrangement of its flowers or shrubs, and to array these in rigid lines, circles, or patterns can only be ugly wherever it may be!

After we have settled the essential approaches and levels around a house, the natural form or lines of the earth itself are in nearly all cases the best to follow, and it is often well to face any labour to get the ground back into its natural grade where it is disfigured by ugly or needless banks, lines, or angles. But in the true Italian garden *on the hills* we have to alter the natural line of the earth, or "terrace it," because we cannot otherwise cultivate the ground or stand at ease upon it, and in such ground the strictly formal is as right as the lawn is in a garden in the Thames valley. But the lawn is the heart of the true English garden, and as essential to it as the terrace to the gardens on the steep hills, and English lawns have been too often destroyed for plans ruinous both to the garden and the home landscape. Sometimes on level ground the terrace walls cut off the landscape from the house, and, on the other hand, the house from the landscape!

We may get every charm of a garden and every use of a country place without sacrificing the picturesque or beautiful; there is no reason, either in the working or design of gardens, why there should be a false line in them; every charm of the flower garden may be secured by wholly avoiding the knots and scrolls which subordinate all the plants and flowers of a garden, all its joy and life, to a wretched conventional design. The true way is the opposite. With only the simplest plans to insure good working, we should see the flowers and feel the beauty of plant forms, and secure every scrap of turf wanted for play or lawn, and for every enjoyment of a garden

Time and Gardens.—Time's effect on gardens is one of the main considerations. Fortress-town and castle moat are now without

Garden with picturesque planting, Thrumpington Hall, Derbyshire.

further use, where in old days gardens were set within the walls   To keep all that remains of such gardens should be our first care—never to imitate them now.   Many are far more beautiful than the modern gardens, which by a wicked perversity have been kept bare of plants or flower life.   At one time it was rash to make a garden away from protecting walls ; but when safety came from civil war, then arose the often beautiful Elizabethan house, free from all moat or trace of war.

In those days the extension of the decorative work of the house into the garden had some novelty to carry it off, while the kinds of evergreens were very much fewer than now.   Hence if the old gardeners wanted an evergreen hedge or bush of a certain height, they clipped a Yew tree to the form and size they wanted   Notwithstanding this, we have no evidence that anything like the flat monotony often seen in our own time existed then.   To-day the ever-growing city, pushing its hard face over our once beautiful land, should make us wish more and more to keep such beauty of the earth as may be still possible to us, and the horrible railway embankments, where once were the beautiful suburbs of London, cry to us to save all we can save of the natural beauty of the earth.

Architecture and Flower Gardening.[1]—The architect is a good gardener when he makes a beautiful house.   Whatever is to be done or considered afterwards, one is always helped and encouraged by its presence ; while, on the other hand, scarcely any amount of skill in gardening softens the presence of an ugly building   No one has more reason to rejoice at the presence of good architecture than the gardener and planter, and all stonework near the house, even in the garden, should be dealt with by the architect.

But when architecture goes beyond the strictly necessary round the house, and seeks to replace what should be a living garden by an elaborate tracery on the ground, then error and waste are at work, and the result is ugliness   The proof of this is at Versailles, at the Crystal Palace in great part, in the old gardens in Vienna, and at Caserta, near Naples, where there is a far from beautiful stone garden. One may not so freely mention private places as public ones, but many ugly and extravagant things have been done by trying to adapt a mode of garden design essential in a country like Italy, where people often lived for health's sake on tops of the hills, to gardens in the plains and valleys of England.   I know a terrace in England built *right against the house,* so as to exclude the light from, and make useless, what were once the reception rooms.   That deplorable result came about by endeavouring to adapt Italian modes to English conditions, and was the work of Sir Charles Barry.   To any one

[1] Read before the Architectural Association on Friday, December 16, 1893

Longleat. English country house with picturesque planting.

deeply interested in the question, one of the best places to consider it is the upper terrace at Versailles, looking from the fine buildings there to the country beyond, and seeing how graceless and inert the whole vast design is, and how the clipped and often now dying, because mutilated, Yews thrust their ugly forms into the landscape beyond and rob it of all grace. To those who tell me this sort of work is necessary to "harmonise" with the architecture I say there are better ways, and that to rob fine buildings of all repose by a complex geometrical "pattern in the foreground is often the worst way.

Cost and care of stonework in gardens.—Where stone or stucco gardening is done on a large scale, its cost and maintenance are monstrous. Even with the wealth of France, the repair of elaborate stonework in gardens is a hopeless task, as any one may see at Versailles or at the Crystal Palace. Is it in the interest of architecture that noble means should be so wasted? As the cost and difficulties of the finest work in building increase, the more the need to keep it to its true and essential uses, especially in face of the fact that half the houses in England require to be rebuilt if our architecture generally is to prove worthy of its artistic aims.

I delight in walls for my Roses, and build walls, provided they have any true use as dividing, protecting, or supporting lines. To take advantage of these and sunny sheltered corners in and about our old or new houses, and make delightful little gardens in and near them, as at Drayton or Powis, is quite a different thing from cutting off the landscape with vast flat "patterns" and scroll-work, as on the upper terrace at Versailles and at Windsor and many gardens made in our own day.

"Design" not formal only.—I find it stated by writers on this subject that "design" can only concern formality—an error, as the artistic grouping and giving picturesque effect to groups and groves of Oak, Cedar, or Fir are far higher design than putting trees in lines. There is more true and subtle design in Richmond Park and other noble parks in England, where the trees are grouped in picturesque ways and allowed to take natural forms, than in a French wood with straight lines cut through it, which the first carpenter could design as well as anybody else In our own day a wholly different order of things has arisen, because we have thousands of beautiful things coming to us from all parts of the temperate and northern world, and those who know them will not accept a book pattern design, instead of our infinitely varied garden flora. The trees of North America and Asia form a tree garden in themselves, and it is impossible to lay out gardens of any size or dignity without a knowledge of those and all other hardy trees, not only in a cultivated but in a wild state. If anything demands special study, it is that of garden design

with our present materials. If that art is to be mastered, the work of a life must be given to it—more than that, a life's devotion, and no less is the sacrifice his own art requires of the architect.

No one "style" right.—There is no such thing as a style fitted for every situation ; only one who knows and studies the ground well will ever make the best of a garden, and any "style" may be right where the site fits it. I never see a house the ground around which does not invite plans for itself only. A garden on the slopes about Naples is impossible without much stonework to support the earth, while about London or Paris there is usually no such need. But these considerations never enter into the minds of men who plant an Italian garden in one of our river valleys, where in nine cases out of ten an open lawn is often the best thing before the house, as at Bristol House, Roehampton ; Greenlands, Henley-on-Thames , and in many gardens in the Thames valley And there are right and wrong ways where we cannot have a lawn garden —Haddon, simple, right, and charming on the one hand, and Chatsworth on the other , Knole and Ightham and Rockingham without a yard of stonework not absolutely needed for the house and its approaches, and others with a fortune spent in vast display of costly stonework, only effective in robbing the foreground of a fine landscape of all repose.

The idea that the old style of building in England was always accompanied by elaborate terrace gardening is proved to be erroneous by many beautiful old houses. The Elizabethan house had often an ample lawn in front or plenty of grass near, and such houses are quite as delightful in effect as the old houses and castles where terracing was necessary and right, owing to the ground, such as Berkeley, Powis, and Rockingham. The mosaic in flower-planting is a modern idea, and had nothing to do with old gardens, which, however planned, had their flowers planted in simple ways.

The idea that trees must be clipped to make them "harmonise" with architecture is a mere survival. In the old days of garden design, when in any northern country there were few trees in gardens, these trees were slashed into any shape that met the designer's view. But now that many beautiful trees and shrubs are coming to us from many countries, the aim of true gardening is, so far from mutilating them, to develop their natural forms. In by far the greater number of beautiful places in England, from Knole to Haddon, and from the fine west-country houses to the old border castles, there are many of the fairest gardens where the trees are never touched with shears. Sutton Place, near Guildford, built in 1521, is one of the most beautiful old houses in the home counties, and its architecture is none the less delightful because the trees near show their true

Sutton Place. Example of Elizabethan house without terracing.

natural forms. It is also an example of a fine old house around which there is no terraced gardening.

It would be as hopeless to design a building without knowing anything of its uses or inhabitants as to design a garden without full knowledge of its nobler ornaments—trees and the many things that go to make our garden flora vary so much in form, habits, and hardiness according to soils, situations, and districts. Errors of the most serious kind arise from dealing with such things without knowledge, and any attempt to keep the gardener out of the garden must fail, as it did in our own day in the case of the broken brick and stone flower beds at South Kensington. Except for what is mostly a very small area near the house, the architect and garden-designer deal with distinct subjects and wholly distinct materials They should work in harmony, but not seek to do that for which their training and knowledge have not fitted them

On the Flower-Garden as a Show-Ground for Builders' Sculpture and other Debased Forms of the Plastic " Art."—" In the last century there was a manufactory of garden images in Piccadilly ; in fact, there were four. Mr John Cheece, the owner, did a splendid trade in cast lead figures—gods and goddesses, nymphs and shepherds, Pan with his pipes, Actæon with his hounds, mowers, shepherdesses, and Father Time with his scythe ; these sweet suggestive figures still linger rarely in old-world gardens, almost living by associations of the many that have loved them."—R. Blomfield (*Art and Life,* p 205)

It is clear from the above that there are men who think of the garden, not as a living picture of beautiful natural forms, but as a place to show off one of the most worthless phases of human art In a northern country like ours a statue of any high merit as a work of art deserves to be protected by a building of some kind. The effect of frost and rain in our climate on statuary out-of-doors is very destructive, and the face of a statue of some merit put up only a few years ago opposite the Royal Exchange is now rotted away The scattering of numerous statues of a low order of merit, or of no merit at all, which we see in some Italian gardens, often gives a bad effect, and the dotting of statues about both the public gardens of Paris and London is destructive of all repose. If a place be used for the exhibition of sculpture, well and good ; but let us not in that case call it a garden. In Britain statues are often of plaster material, and those who use a garden as a place to dot about such "works of art" do not think of the garden as the best of places to show the work of Nature, and as one in which we should see many fine natural forms

The earliest recollection I have of any large garden or country seat was one strewn with the remains of statues, but as my evidence as to effect and endurance might not be thought impartial, we may call as a witness Victor Cherbuliez, of the French Academy.

" It was one of those classical gardens the planners of which prided themselves upon as being able to give Nature lessons in good behaviour, to teach her geometry and the fine art of irreproachable lines ; but Nature is for geometers a reluctant pupil, and if she submits to their tyranny she does it with an ill grace, and will take her revenge.   . . . .   The large basin no longer held any water, and the dolphins which in days gone by spouted it from their throats looked as if they asked each other to what purpose they were in this world   But the statues had suffered most ; moss and a green damp had invaded them, as if some kind of plague or leprosy had covered them with sores, and pitiless Time had inflicted on them mutilations and insults   One had lost an arm, another a leg ; almost all had lost their noses   There was in the basin a Neptune whose face was sadly damaged, and who had nothing left but his beard and half his trident, and further on a Jupiter without a head, the rain water standing in his hollowed neck "

As to the artistic value of much of our sculpture, Lord Rosebery, in his speech at Edinburgh in 1896, said—

"If those restless spirits that possessed the Gadarene swine were to enter into the statues of Edinburgh, and if the whole stony and brazen troop were to hurry and hustle and huddle headlong down the steepest place near Edinburgh into the deepest part of the Firth of Forth, art would have sustained no serious loss "

The *Pall Mall Gazette*, commenting on this speech, wishes for a like rush to the Thames on the part of our " London monstrosities," and yet this is the sort of rubbish that some wish us to expose in the garden, where there is rarely the means to be found to do even as good work as we see in cities.   If the politician and the journalist ask to be delivered from the statues with which the squares and streets of our cities are adorned, our duty as lovers of Nature in the garden is clear.

In its higher expression nothing is more precious in art than sculpture , in its lower and debased forms it is less valuable than almost any form of art.   The lovely Greek sculpture in the Vatican, Louvre, or British Museum is the work of great artists, and those who study it will not be led astray by either Piccadilly goddesses in lead or New Road nymphs in plaster.   If we wish to see the results of sculpture in the architect's own work we have but to look at the public buildings in London where it is used, mostly to spoil any architectural grace such buildings should possess, as in the National Portrait Gallery, the Natural History Museum, and the Home Office buildings, and then we may better judge how far we may go in our gardens with such art.

Real artists in sculpture are not concerned with garden design, and sculpture is not the business of the builder or landscape gardener.   A statue or two of any artistic value may be placed in a garden with good effect, never, however, forgetting that a garden is a place for beautiful life, not death.   It is not that we despise other arts than our own, they may charm and even help us, as in the case of a landscape painting by a man of genius or even serious student of the actual beauty of things.   Even a drawing of a tree or flower may be a lesson in form and beauty , but all debased "art" is as harmful in the garden as it is anywhere else.

CHAPTER III

VARIOUS FLOWER GARDENS, MAINLY CHOSEN FOR THEIR
BEAUTY; COTTAGE GARDENS IN KENT AND SOMERSET,
MOUNT USHER; GREENLANDS, GOLDER'S HILL, PENDELL
COURT, RHIANVA, SHEEN COTTAGE; DRUMMOND CASTLE,
PENSHURST; COMPTON WINYATES, KETTON COTTAGE, POWIS;
COTEHELE; EDGE HALL, SHRUBLAND; CHILLINGHAM,
BULWICK; OFFINGTON, WILTON, STONELANDS, AND OTHERS

THESE gardens should help us to get the most precious lesson as
to design—that the best-laid-out garden is that which is best
fitted for its situation, soil and climate, and without much consideration as to any "style" Once we make a rule and say, this is the best
and only way, it is not only the good architect, and that still rarer
being, the good landscape gardener, who will carry it out, but anybody who has any influence in building or gardening will do the same
thing in all sorts of positions with any kind of material, including the
"young man in the office" and other persons who have never even
given the slightest thought to any kind of artistic planting, let alone
any serious study of garden design. Of the expression of this
inartistic ruling we see painful evidence everywhere in the terraces
like railway banks out of place and rampant through the land. On
these stereotyped ideas is based another leading to greater evil,
which is that, once you have got your patterned plateau, you cannot
have your flowers in artistic or picturesque ways on it, and so the poor
gardener has to go on trying to adapt ugly patterns in flowers to the
ugly plan that is given him. The second idea is false too, as flowers
may be arranged in right and natural ways in any garden, but that
fact has not killed the common error that we cannot throw formality .
overboard in arranging flowers.

The really artistic way is to have no preconceived idea of any
style, but in all cases to be led by the ground itself and by the many
things upon it Why should we in the plains or gentle meadows of

England not give effect to the beautiful lines of the landscape, and make our gardens harmonise with them? The right way is, to carry no style in one's head or pocket, and then, before saying much, go over the ground and see it from every point of view, with a view to getting the best that the site, soil, and surroundings will give. If the idea of the bastard Italian garden were the truest that could be expressed by man, it must inevitably lead to monotony and to stereotyping of the garden, and it is only by respecting the site itself and letting the plan grow out of it that we can get gardens free from monotony, and suggestive also, as they should often be, of the country in which they occur. If all our efforts only go to stereotyping the home landscape, it is hardly worth while going for a change from the Midlands into Devon. Why should we not in these islands of ours, where there are so many different kinds of landscape and characteristics of soil and climate, have gardens in harmony, as it were, with their surroundings? Also the taste of the owner ought to count. Why should he be bound to the conventional style? As no one is so likely to know the conditions of soil and climate, and the capabilities of a district as one who has lived amidst them, if we come to the aid of such an owner with an open mind as to style, we shall be much better able to give effect to his views in the shape of artistic and distinct results.

Everywhere the ugliest things are seen, especially in the larger places, but here and there one sees gardens that are beautiful, and nothing will help us so well to a clear view of what is best in the flower-garden as the consideration of such places, but we may first say something of the new and wrong way of having no flowers near the house.

Those who notice the ground round country seats find now and then a house without any flower garden, and with the turf running hard into the walls—the site of a flower garden without flowers. This unhappy omission we may suppose to result from the ugliness in summer, and nakedness in winter, of the common way of planting a flower garden.

But it is a mistake to suppose that the only alternatives to such nakedness are coarse perennials and annuals, that flower a short time and are weedy the rest of their days, or the ordinary summerplanting. Many delightful things may be grown near a house; fragrant plants, too, plants beautiful not only in summer but in colour even in winter. The ceaseless digging about of the beds also may prejudice people against flowers in the garden, as the bedding plants set out in June were taken away in autumn and replaced by spring-flowering things. These had a short period of bloom in spring, and were, in their turn, pulled up leaving bare beds

Cottage garden at Mattingley, near Winchfield, Hants.

until the summer flowers were planted, sometimes very late , so that in June, when we ought to have flowers or, at least, pleasant colour wholly over the ground, there was nothing but grave-like earth, but the spring flowers round a country house should be grown in a different way. They may be naturalised in multitudes, grown in borders, in special little gardens for bulbs, and in various other ways without in the least disturbing the beds near the house, which should for the most part be planted permanently, so that the greatest amount of beauty may be had throughout the fine months, without disfiguring the beds during those months.

But the permanent flowers should be hardy, and of the highest order of beauty, and such as require more than a few weeks or months for development , though here and there blanks might be filled with good, tender plants, like Heliotrope Many of the hardy flowers, too, should be fragrant—Tea Roses, Carnations, and tufted Pansies ; all those, grown in large groups, give off a grateful odour round a house. What is the soil in these gardens for ? Why do people make them ?   Surely it is not to have them laid down to grass in a country like ours where grass in park, meadow, lawn, and playground is seen on all sides? The objection to the bare surface of beds in such gardens is a just one , but it is easily got rid of by permanent planting ; and if the ground in the early state of the bed or from any other cause is bare below the flowers, it is quite easy to surface the beds with small rock and other plants of good colour nearly all the year.

ENGLISH COTTAGE GARDENS are never bare and seldom ugly. Those who look at sea or sky or wood see beauty that no art can show ; but among the things made by man nothing is prettier than an English cottage garden, and they often teach lessons that "great" gardeners should learn, and are pretty from Snowdrop time till the Fuchsia bushes bloom nearly into winter. We do not see the same thing in other lands. The bare cottages of Belgium and North France are shocking in their ugliness ; even in Ireland and Scotland we do not see the same charming little gardens, nor are they so good in some parts of England ; as in Surrey, Kent, and the southern counties.   I often pass a small cottage garden in the Weald of Sussex never without a flower for nine months in the year. It is only a square patch, but the beauty of it is far more delightful than that of the large gardens near, and it is often pretty when they are bare.

What is the secret of the cottage garden's charms ? Cottage gardeners are good to their plots, and in the course of years they make them fertile, and the shelter of the little house and hedge· favours the flowers But there is something more and it is the·

absence of any pretentious "plan" which lets the flowers tell their story to the heart. The walks are only what are needed, and so we see only the earth and its blossoms.

A COTTAGE GARDEN IN KENT.—Driving on one of the sunny days of autumn through the Weald of Kent from Charing to Ashford—a country strewn with pretty houses and gardens—an old house set in flowers was seen to the left just after passing the pretty village of Charing and the big woods above it. We turned from the

A west-country cottage with small open lawn. Engraved from a photograph sent by Mr. E. Brightman.

main road, and, looking over the low garden wall, were asked in to see the pretty old house, oak-panelled, and to stroll about the small garden, little more than a cottage garden in its simplicity of planting. No pretentious plan to consider, only the yellow Sunflowers of the season massed in their own way and running about inside the little wall, and by their profusion giving an unity as well as richness of colour. One lesson of these little gardens, that are so pretty, is that one can get good effects from simple materials, and the absence of complexity and pretence of "design" aids these pictures very much.

D

Many things are not needed for good effect, and very often we see gardens rich in plants, but not artistic because too much cut up into dots. There is no reason why gardens should not be rich in plants and pictures too, but such are rare. A precious thing in a garden is a beautiful house, and this, with its pretty, brown-tiled roof and oak-timbered walls, is an example of many in the Weald of Kent which have braved several hundred winters and are so beautiful in colour.

Old mill-house garden at Mount Usher, Wicklow.

If these cottage gardens are beautiful from such simple materials, how much more might we get by good hardy flower gardening round old country houses with lovely backgrounds and old walks. The Somersetshire cottage garden is in a milder climate than this, and in Somerset things seem to do so well, and in all that delightful west-country. In Kent we must trust to the hardy things of which there are so many that no cottage garden can contain half of them; but in Somersetshire we may have many things which seldom thrive on the eastern side—Myrtle, Bay, and Passion-flower, tall Fuchsias, and even things in the open air in winter which in many other districts we have to put in the greenhouse.

MOUNT USHER, A WICKLOW GARDEN —A quaint creeper-laden mill-house at Ashford, with an acre or two of ground, partly wooded, through which the silvery Vartry River flows, gentle as it falls over its little rocky weirs in summer, but swollen and turbid after wintry storms. The place is really an island at the bottom of a valley ; the hilly country around is beautifully diversified, and is graced by the finest of native timber trees. The garden is quite unlike any other garden I have seen, and to see it in the time of Lilies, Roses, Pæonies, Poppies, and Delphiniums is to see much lovely colour amongst the rich greenery of the rising woodlands In autumn the colour is less brilliant, but equally satisfying as the eye wanders from the Torch Lilies and Gladioli to the blue Agapanthus, and thence to the Pine and Fir-clad hills.

An old Ivy-covered wall makes a good background for the brilliant Tropæolum speciosum, which everywhere runs wild about the place, throwing its soft green wreaths over twig and branch, their tips scarlet with blossoms, or heavily laden with turquoise-blue berries Here also the soft rosy Hydrangeas bloom, and may be seen the big scarlet hips on the great Apple Rose of Parkinson (Rosa pomifera), with its large glaucous leaves scented like those of the Sweet Brier. Mount Usher is a charming example of the gardens that might be made in river valleys, especially those among the mountains and hills. In such places there is often delightful shelter from violent winds, while the picturesque effect of the mountains and hills around offers a charming prospect from the gardens There is a distinct charm about many Irish gardens, and the country also is excellent, at least in the shore districts, for the growth of many plants that soon perish out of doors in most parts of England

GREENLANDS is an example of a garden in which the river front of the house is a simple sloping lawn. Originally laid out by Mr. Marnock for Mr. Majoribanks, it has long been a garden showing good work. There are no terrace gardens, and one passes easily from the house to a pleasant lawn and the well-planted grounds around, studded with many fine trees, among which are beautiful groups of Cedars. A flower garden in front of the house is here avoided ; but at a little distance there are various flower gardens within easy reach, and this plan keeps the lawn immediately in front of the house unbroken, instead of, what it too often is, patched with brown earth or, not always happy, masses of flowers. It would not be the best plan to follow in every case ; the more variety the greater the charm, and there are ways of delightful flower-gardening in which no bare earth can be seen, while there are many cases where the sunny and secluded sides of the house afford the best of sites for the flower garden

D 2

Cottage and garden near Charing, Kent. Engraved from a photograph sent by Miss Vinall.

PENDELL COURT.—It will be seen here that even where it is desired to have the flower garden, in part, against the house, it is by no means always necessary that the ground should be made "architectural." It is a great pleasure to see a beautiful old house, with no impedimenta to keep one away from the door. There are three good views of it: first, that of the lawn in front of the house, which was a flowery meadow yet uncut, with no beds or other obstructions to the view of the house, and with a fine group of trees on either hand. It was a poem in building and in lawn. Quite on the other side a border of flowers and a wall of climbers ran from the house. Looking along this border to the house, a shower of white climbing Roses was seen falling from the wall, and a quaint gable and a few windows and glistening rich Ivy behind formed a lovely picture. Another view of the house from across the water, showing its west end, is also very beautiful. There is a Wild Rose bush on the right and a tuft of Flag leaves on the left, before you, the water and its lilies, then a smooth, gently rising lawn creeping up to the windows, which on this side are all wreathed with white climbing Roses. All these views of the same house, although distinct, show no frivolous patterns, fountains, statues, and such objects, which often destroy all repose. The view from the house to the left is also free and charming—a wide meadow climbing up the hill through groups of trees, and in the woody part reminding one a little of Alpine pastures

RHIANVA.—We have not only to deal with ugly gardens, made in the wrong places, but with a false idea that all the flowers must be set out as smooth and as "hard" as tin plate, and that terraced gardens are not suited for our beautiful hardy flowers But one may here and there see a better way, and at Rhianva, the free growth of evergreens and climbers, and the delightful interlacements of hardy flowers, ferns, and creepers, make the garden beautiful. Again, I remember, the garden at Ockham Park in Dr. Lushington's time was formal and yet beautiful, through the freedom of the vegetation. So again in Italy, the stiffness of the stone is soon softened by the graceful forms of trees, shrubs, and trailers as at Verona and in many Italian gardens

Fifty years ago the site of Rhianva, on the banks of the Menai Straits, was a steep field, with the large gray rocks so characteristic of Anglesey, and was crossed by a small stream which lost itself in marshy ground by the shore, where stood a couple of old Apple and Thorn trees and a little white-washed cottage The extreme steepness of the rocky ground made the site difficult to deal with, and a number of supporting walls were built to form terraces, and, by the help of a protecting sea-wall, the flowers were carried down to the very edge of the water.　Facing a little to the south-east, the garden was protected from the violence of the

View of lawn garden at Pendell Court.

westerly gales, while the more tender plants were sheltered from the east winds of spring by the larger shrubs and trees.　The climate is

mild in winter, and the garden being on a southern slope the trees
and shrubs grew with great rapidity ; so that hedges of red Fuchsias
and of blue and pink Hydrangeas soon hid the stone walls Myrtles
and Camellias, and some Acacias, were found to thrive out of
doors ; and at the present time the only difficulty is to prevent the
shrubs from injuring each other, through their rapid growth. In
summer the luxuriant abundance of the Roses, climbing from bush
to bush, the Cypresses, the Tamarisk and the Vines , and the sea,
and the purple mountains in the background, seem to belong rather
to the Lake of Como than to Anglesey. All the borders are mossed
over with small green plants , large, hardy exotic Ferns are spread
into groups ; and a lacework of Ivy, Vine, and creepers is seen in
many parts. A mixed order of planting is pursued, but in many
cases the shrubs and plants are allowed to spread as they will, and
the climbers take picturesque shapes. Rhianva is an example of the
error of the notion that a terraced garden should only be arranged
as a "bedded-out" garden. We have here a terraced garden in a
position that called for it, namely, a rocky slope, in which the only
way of making a garden was by terracing the ground, but it is a
garden that shelters every treasure of our garden flora, from the
Cyclamen to the Tea Rose.

It has been said that, however valuable the more beautiful hardy
flowers, their place is not the parterre, but some out-of-the-way spot.
Not only may any terrace garden be embellished with hardy flowers,
but it is the best place for them. The odd notion that our fairest
flowers must not show themselves in the flower garden might lead
one to suppose that there never was anything in the flower garden
before bedding-out was invented. Is it well to devote the flower beds
to one type of vegetation only, whether it be hardy or tender? We
have been so long accustomed to forming flat surfaces of colour in
flower beds that few think of better ways of filling them. In Nature
vegetation in its most beautiful aspects is rarely a thing of one effect,
but rather a union or mingling of different types of life often succeeding each other in bloom. So it might often be in the garden
The most beautiful effects must be obtained by combining different
forms so as to aid each other, and give us a succession of pictures
If any place asks for permanent planting it is the precious spot
of ground near the house , for no one can wish to see large, grave-
like masses of soil frequently dug near the windows. It is easy to
form beds that would look well in all seasons by the use of choice
shrubs of many kinds—Rhododendron, Azalea, Dwarf Cypress, Heath,
Clematis, Honeysuckle, Weigela, Hydrangea, Skimmia, Rock Rose,
Tamarix, Daphne, Yucca, Tree Peony. Why should we not use
beautiful Andromedas or Kalmias or fine evergreen Barberries in the

flower garden in the same way as Camellias or Acacias or Tree
Ferns in the winter garden to break and vary the surface?

Gilbert White's garden at Selborne, engraved from sketch by A. Parsons, flowers mostly on the outer fringes of lawn in borders and around beds of "peat shrubs."

The shrubs should be arranged in an open way, the opposite to the
crowding of American shrubs common in our beds. In these all

individual character and form are crushed away in the crowd, yet there is scarcely a shrub that has not a charm of form it will show if allowed room. One good plan is to allow no crowding, and to place the *finest hardy flowers in groups between the free untortured shrubs.* Thoroughly prepare the beds; put in the choicest shrubs, which, without being high enough to obscure the view, adorn the earth all the winter as well as all the summer, and give us a broken surface as well as a beautiful one, and, far from leading to monotony, this would lead to an infinite and varied succession of beauty.

We should not then have any set pattern to weary the eye, but quiet grace and verdure, and little pictures, month by month. The beds, filled with shrubs and garlanded with evergreens and creepers, would everywhere afford nooks and spaces among the shrubs where we could grow some of the many fine hardy Lilies with the Gladioli, Phlox, Iris, tall Anemone, Peony, and Delphinium. The choice shrubs suited for such beds are not gross feeders, like trees, but on the other hand encourage the finer hardy bulbs and flowers. They also relieve the plants by their bloom or foliage, and when a Lily or Cardinal Flower fades after blooming it is not noticed as it might be in a stiff border. In this way we should not need the wretched and costly plan of growing a number of low evergreens in pots, to " decorate " the flower garden in winter.

To get artistic effects in such a flower garden we must not by any means adopt the usual close pattern beds, because no good effect can be got from beds crowded on each other like tarts on a tray. Repose and verdure are essential. Before making the change from the dwarf plants only, be they hardy or tender, it would be well to see that there is ample repose or room for the full expression of the beauty of each bed or group, and no complication or crowding, no complex or angular beds. *The contents of the beds and not their outlines are what we should see.* By this way of planting with beautiful flowering summer or evergreen shrubs, with abundant space for flowers to grow between, we might see beauty in our terrace garden beds on the dullest day in winter. Between the low bushes we could have evergreen carpets of Alpine plants and tiny hill shrubs, and through these the autumn, winter, and spring flowering bulbs could bloom, untarnished by the soil splashing of the ordinary border Shelter, as well as the best culture, could be thus secured for many a fair flower, which, once well planted, would there come up year after year. Among the flowering shrubs we have many lovely wild and garden Roses to help us with our plans

SHEEN COTTAGE.—The late Sir Richard Owen's garden is one of the most charming and simple in the neighbourhood of London. Many a visitor to Richmond Park enjoys the view of his cottage, as it nestles on the margin of the sweep of ground near the Sheen gate, but it is from the other or the garden side that the picture

Rhianva, Anglesey. A terraced garden with picturesque planting.

is best. A lawn, quite unbroken, stretches from near the windows to the boundary, and is fringed with numerous hardy trees. Here and there are masses of flowering shrubs and an odd bed of Lilies, while numerous hardy flowers are seen among the Roses and Rhododendrons. There is in the main part of the garden only one walk, which takes one round the whole, and does not show, as it glides behind the outside of the groups which fringe the little open lawn Instead of coming quite close to the house it is cut off from it by a deep border of evergreen shrubs, intermingled with Lilies and hardy plants, and their flowers look into the windows Instead of looking out of the window, as usual, on a bare gravel walk, the eye is caught by Rhododendrons or Spiræas, with here and there a Lily, a Foxglove, or a tall Evening Primrose From the other side of the garden the effect of the border is quite charming, and the creeper-covered cottage seems to spring out of a bank of flowers. The placing of a wide border with Evergreens against the house is a pleasant change from the ordinary mode of laying out little gardens. Another agreeable feature of this garden is the grass walks, which ramble through a thick and shady plantation. Even in our coolest summers there is many a day on which such shady walks, carpeted with grass, are the most enjoyable retreats one can find. And their margins form capital situations for naturalising many beautiful hardy plants—Daffodils, hardy Ferns, Scillas, the tall Harebells, Snowdrops, and Snowflakes.

CAWDOR CASTLE —The view of Cawdor shows the good of having some form and variety of shape in a garden, be the garden large or small The trees, shrubs, and bushes give the light and shade and variety of form which is so often absent from our gardens. The hard effect which the ordinary garden shows results from the want of all mystery or variety of surface or form In the case of Cawdor the beds are simple, so that we are less concerned with pattern or plan than with the flowers This is as it should be. It is not a model to be followed everywhere, but such freedom and variety is greatly to be desired in gardens. After all considerations of plan have been settled, we ought to abolish the too common practice of excluding all things of a bushy, upright nature from our flower gardens.

DRUMMOND CASTLE.—A house on a rock, graced with many Ferns and Ivy, and wild flowers natural to the spot It would not be easy to find a more graceful example of " natural " rock gardening. It is only, however, on going to the south side of the house, where the ground falls rapidly and is supported by terrace walls, that all gloom is dispelled by the brightest array of blossoming climbers that ever clad gray stones with beauty To fancy one's self in some fairyland of sun-bathed flowers a thousand miles south in a lap of the mountains would be easy. No Italian gardens could probably show the same high beauty at the end of summer, whatever they might do earlier, and the very coolness encourages and prolongs the bloom. The shelter of the terrace, with the house behind, helps many things ; but, beyond training, there is little artificial help. It is our privilege of growing so many plants from other countries that makes our open-air gardens so beautiful in the fall of the year . here, when the leaves begin to colour, and when even the Harebell is past its best on the banks, we have a very paradise of flowers. The fact that this fine plant beauty may be enjoyed by all who have a patch of ground and a wall makes it a precious gift, and the plants that here give most flowers are nearly all as easily grown as our common Honeysuckle.

Loveliest of all the climbers here is the Flame Nasturtium (Tropæolum speciosum), which drapes these stately walls, as it does those of many a cottage in Scotland. Admirable for walls as is this fragile and brilliant plant, it is seen to even greater advantage when a delicate shoot runs over a Yew-hedge, with its arrows of colour, and near it on the walls are many flowers of the older and once better-known Tropæolums ; showy, climbing Nasturtiums of gardens grow high on the walls, and add to the rich glow of colours Nothing could surpass the rich purple of the Clematis here—waves of colour, and flowers of great size, the cool hill air suiting them so well.

In the warm or temperate south, in Madeira or the Riviera, the garden lover sometimes makes a pretty hedge of Oak-leaved Geraniums ; but, as one does not see them in the South of England, it is a surprise to see them happy on the walls here in Scotland, growing from four feet to seven feet high, with fresh foliage and many flowers Their spicy fragrance and pretty foliage make them worth the trouble of storing in the winter, and placing in the open air in early summer. All the winter they are kept in the house on trellises, and, carefully trained in summer against the warm wall, soon make fresh growth and are in good bloom late in September.

Large borders of the common river Forget-me-not remind us of its value as compared with the wood and Alpine Forget-me-nots usually grown in gardens It is beautiful in moist borders, flowering long through summer and autumn. The charm of the place almost ceases with the terraces, for below them is one of those wonderful displays of "bedding out" in its cruder forms, which attains its greatest "glory" near large Scottish houses,—plants in squares, repeated by thousands, and walks from which all interest is taken by the planting on each side being of exactly the same pattern.

STEPS AND TERRACE IN THE OLD PARK, AXMINSTER.—This engraving is instructive as regards the bare state of many gardens. For many years past the rule in some of the most pretentious geometrical gardens has been to allow no vegetation on the walls or balustrades, but the older and graceful way is to garland all wall surfaces with beautiful life, and not to wholly hide them in doing so.   Dividing

A west country garden. Selwood Cottage, near Frome.   Rough wall in foreground covered with rock and wall plants.

lines and walls may do their work without being as bare as if in a stonemason's yard.

The idea of the terrace garden came from the steep slopes of Italy and Greece. The rough wall of the peasant, which prevented the earth from being washed away, and gave a little depth on the stony hillside, became, in the garden of the wealthy man, the built terrace,—structurally right, and necessary whether men gardened for pleasure or for profit. Having got their ground level through terracing, it was the rule to plant with beautiful things—Olive-trees for profit, and Cypress for shade. If anybody will compare such effects with the common debased English planting of the flower-garden, where everything is hard and flat and nothing is allowed on the walls, he will at once see a vital difference.

PENSHURST.—There is no more essential charm for a garden than that it should be itself in character and not be a copy of gardens near it or elsewhere. This merit belongs to Penshurst, and the network of orchard trees and tall summer flowers beneath them which make up much of the flower gardening there. Much of the ground between the kitchen garden and the house is thrown into squares and strips, which shelter and divide the space, and most of this space between the hedges is planted with fruit trees, and walks—very often Grass walks—running between them. The remaining spaces are planted with flowers, from beds of Carnations to mixed borders of tall herbaceous plants and Lilies Foxgloves are at home here, and in rather broad masses under the trees their effect is charming—the shade and mystery of the overhead growth give them something of the look they have in woods The lines of border after border are broken by the trees, and the effect is very soft and different from what it so often is, while the colour tells splendidly in the case of masses of Orange Lily. The growth is free, and there is no such thing as primness, which greatly helps the effect. Groups of Acanthus look well here, and Delphinium, Meadow Sweet, giant Scabious, and many a hardy flower are refreshing to see.

But Penshurst is an example of the many gardens (new and old) where the reaction from the hardness of bedding out and the winter bareness of it have led people to do away with flower beds near the house. It is not the old way to clear everything away but shaven Grass near a beautiful old house, nor is it the true way, but it is now a common one, and it gets rid of much of the ugliness of beds.

But there are ways of putting flowers in charming modesty about a house as well as that of digging up in early summer ugly grave-like beds for them. In the old days flowers clustered round the house, and were the better for its shelter, warmth, and colour. Long before the massing system, with all its garishness, was discovered, flowers were planted for many generations in quiet ways about old English houses. It is right that the main entrance and park side of a great house should be frank and open, but to make the house bare all round for the sake

Manor House garden, Stonelands, Sussex.

of bare Grass, and to lose all the advantage of shelter and seclusion, is not the best way by far. Bays and warm corners, and high walls and their shelter and variety of aspect, are delightful for flowers— flowers such as could not injure any building ; not even a suspicion of the injury that comes from Ivy betimes could attach to borders of Fern or Iris. 'If we lived in a country where close turf was not seen in the park, or hills, or fields, there would be a reason for having nothing but turf under the windows. In the park the short nibbled turf is often fringed by Bracken, Foxglove, and Wild Rose ; whereas, near the house, the way too often now is to let the turf run hard and straight into the walls, and the winds of heaven strike the house un- tempered by the breath of a Violet.

The question of some degree of seclusion about country houses is bound up with this. Nothing is worse than planting that hides sun and air from a beautiful house, but dividing lines and little sheltered gardens are often needed. There are so many ways of screening off such precious spaces, too—Vine, Sweet Verbena, Winter Sweet, and Jasmine for low walls ; Rose, Sweet Brier, and Honeysuckle for fragrant or blossoming hedges ; Clematis, Wistaria, and climbing Rose for arch or pergola   The very lines for shelter or privacy might be gardens of the most fragrant and beautiful things we have, from the winter Jasmine to the climbing Tea Rose. No, the Grass alone is not and never can be the artistic way on all sides of a house, and the common French way of a waste of gravel all round a house is still worse. The gray of the Carnation is welcome in winter seen from the windows, and there are many evergreen rock plants that take their deepest hues of green in winter, and they are a long way better, even for their green, than the winter-worn turf. It is often well, too, to see a glimpse from the windows of the way the Crocus opens its heart to the sun—brilliant forerunner of crowds of fair blossoms.

COMPTON WINYATES.—Compton Winyates is one of the dearest of the old houses jewelled over the land of England, the most charming of countries for its houses. There are graceful old climbers and trees near, but not much showy gardening—almost none. There is also very little of what is called pleasure ground in the ordinary sense ; but that is too stereotyped a thing to make one regret it in the presence of such a beautiful home. None the less is it pleasant to wander over the high fields near and along the deep slopes of the coombe, especially in the autumn time with the tree leaves rich in colour, and the Barberry laden with a thousand coral boughs. Compton Winyates is one of the old houses not surrounded by terraces, but sits quietly on the turf, and tells us, as other of our finest old houses do, that each situation demands its own treatment as regards the surroundings of the house

KETTON COTTAGE.—This is one of the Elizabethan farmhouses common in the villages round Stamford, with some recent additions. It stands in the village, a short distance from the beautiful church of St. Mary, a few yards from the little river Chater, which, coming down from Leicestershire, falls into the Welland a mile or two below Ketton and as far above Stamford. As the position is sheltered from rough winds, the small space of ground between the road and the river has proved a home for such of the hardy shrubs and flowers planted in it during the last thirty years as find the lime in both soil and water congenial to them.

The banks of the stream are in places fringed with Royal Fern and the large American Ferns, all of which bear patiently the floods which sometimes in summer and often in winter pass over their heads, lasting now and then for several weeks. All these Ferns thrive in a bed of rough leaf-mould, 6 inches or 8 inches above and below the usual water level, partly coated in the course of years with earth from the floods, and partly denuded by the action of the water, which is prevented in the exposed portions from washing away the roots by a covering of heavy stones, between which there is just room for the crowns to appear. These conditions prevent the growth of seedling Royal Ferns, but the old plants are, after more than twenty years, as vigorous as their kindred in the Norfolk marshes, the fronds of some in the shade being more than 6 feet in length. In a place rather more sheltered from the force of the stream the American Royal Ferns thrive equally well, as also on a somewhat higher level a certain number of other strong Ferns which do not suffer by floods.

On an open part of the bank a quantity of purple Loosestrife makes a good background for the Ferns, and a patch of Meadow Rue gives variety and a distinct autumn colour. For the rest the engraving shows the distinct and very happy effect of the garden, which is a home for many and beautiful hardy flowers. H.

POWIS CASTLE.—Of the many gardens I have seen, very few gave me the pleasure of Powis: first, because of its noble drive through great Oaks with breaks of Fern between, so unlike the dark mono-tonous avenue which spreads gloom over so many country seats. The light and shade and the noble forms of the trees make the picture more beautiful than any primly set-out avenue. The flower garden is beautiful, partly owing to its position, which is that of a true terrace garden—*i e.* the ground falls so steeply, that terracing is neces-sary. These terraces were wreathed with Clematis and beautiful with shrub, and flower, and life, a picture of what a flower garden should be.

As the original name, "Castell Coch," signifies, the castle is built of red sandstone, and stands on the same rock, and the terraces are

Ketton Cottage. Garden framed in trees showing their natural forms. Engraved from a photograph by Mr. J. T. Hopwood, Ketton Hall

hewn out of this, which forms the walls, for the most part unaided by masonry. Glancing over a balustrading from the castle level on to the terraces beneath, the scene is charming, and we are struck at once with the harmonious blending of the flowers and their surroundings. A happy idea is carried out in regard to colours by the three terraces having each its predominating colour—viz. the lowest white, the middle yellow, and the highest purple, not that other colours are excluded, but these prevailing tones are maintained. A charm of this terrace has been for years a number of trellises, 8 feet to 10 feet high, covered with Clematis. Here and there the Flame Nasturtium suspends graceful festoons of brightest colour. Pyramids, Sweet Peas, good perennials and choice annuals are used ; the stiffness of hard lines being quite broken by the Clematis, Roses, Sunflowers, Hollies, Japanese Maples, and Tree Pæonies The walls of the terrace are covered with Roses, Clematises, Pears, Peaches, Nectarines, Pomegranate, which flowers freely every season, Magnolia, and Wistaria.

COTEHELE, CORNWALL —This is one of the finest old houses in the west of England, and the quaint old terraces are laid out in old-fashioned beds and borders filled with hardy flowers Very little masonry is seen in the formation of the terraces, and the old walls are mantled with various creepers, Vines, Myrtle, Clematis, Magnolia, Jasmines, and Ivy.

The engraving gives a faithful representation of one side of the house, looking east. It is situated on the summit of a high hill on the Cornish side of the river Tamar, with views of its winding course, also of the distant ranges of hills in both Devon and Cornwall. The picturesque freedom of the planting is delightful, the house being prettily covered.

SHRUBLAND PARK.—Shrubland Park, in Suffolk, illustrates the recent history of English flower-gardening, as it was the great bedding-out garden, the "centre" of the system, and which provided many examples for other places in England The great terrace garden in front of the house was laid out in scrolls and intricate beds, all filled with plants of a few decided colours, principally yellow, white, red, and blue, and edged with Box. In every spot in this garden the same rigid system of set beds was followed, and not a creeper was permitted to ramble over the masonry and stonework of the various terraces. Every bit of Ivy that tried to creep up the walls and cover the stonework had to be removed, to leave the stone in its first bareness. Where some particular colour was wanted in a certain spot, coloured stones were freely used—yellow, red, and blue— and in the summer, when the hedgerows and meadows are full of flowers, there were no flowers in this large garden to cut for the

house! A few years ago, when Shrubland passed into the hands of
the Hon. James Saumarez, the elaborate designs were swept away,
and the terrace-garden planted with the flowers that every one loves—
Roses, Lavender, and among them many of what are called common
things, and climbers of many kinds clothed the walls. The self
Carnation and the Tea Rose are the glory of this garden—the flowers
filling the air with fragrance, the silvery hue of the large groups of
fragrant Lavender, the broad masses of Carnations, and the groups
of monthly Roses, make a delightful picture.

Powis Castle, Welshpool.

Of the Tea Rose, all the finest kinds for our climate are planted.
There is an idea that it succumbs to the first frost, but all the varieties
at Shrubland, and they include, we believe, every good kind in cultivation, passed unharmed through 20 degrees of frost, and this without
shelter. One of the most interesting spots of Shrubland is the Bamboo
walk, a straight walk, planted at one time with smooth ribbon
borders. These were swept away, and Bamboos and tall Lilies now
fill their place, and we have never seen Bamboos make finer growth.
There are fine hardy plants to relieve the foliage of the Bamboos,
and the Plume Poppy with its feathery plumes : Lilies, Funkias, or
Plantain Lilies, and Evening Primroses.

CHILLINGHAM CASTLE.—Chillingham is on a ridge of land nearly 1,000 feet above the sea in a rocky moorland district, intersected by deep and beautifully wooded glens. The illustration shows but a small part of the handsome terrace garden, with its beautiful retaining wall 120 yards in length, the wall a picture, with Clematises hanging in festoons, with Ivies, Vines, the climbing Hydrangea, and Pyracantha, in front of the wall a long border was planted with some of the best hardy flowers. The flower beds, although somewhat too angular, are of sufficient size to permit of bold grouping, and this is so well done that the form of the beds is less seen, and the blending of the colours of the many flowers is well carried out. Many hardy plants are here well grown, wild Roses and hardy Fuchsias give height and boldness to the arrangement, and the terrace on summer and autumn days is gay with fine colour. The wall at the end of the terrace, which is partly overhung with trees, has its face in a great part hidden by a lovely veil of maiden hair spleenwort From here, ascending a flight of rough Moss-covered steps, Grass slopes adorned with trees make pleasant shade, and we pass on to the south front of the castle, which has a broad gravel walk in the foreground and a lawn that merges into the park and the adjoining pastures.

WILTON.—One of the glories of Wilton is its fine Lebanon Cedars, the tree having been extensively planted here at the time of its first introduction, and although later years have witnessed a great thinning of its ranks, enough remain to form the most prominent feature of the place. The Wilton Cedars are older than those at Goodwood or Warwick, and although mighty ones have fallen, some still remain, whilst numerous young ones are growing up to take the place of those that fall victims to the storms. Whilst the present wise policy of frequent planting is continued, there will be no break in the history of this tree at Wilton. The finest old specimen has a grand bole about 15 ft. up to the point of branching and of fairly even diameter throughout its length of main stem, which girths fully 24 ft. A stem of greater girth entirely enshrouded in Ivy stands near by, the tree having perished in a storm some years ago. A noble evergreen Oak near the Cedars has a stem that girths 19 ft, and at one time it had a head of branches spreading quite 100 yards in circumference, but a giant Cedar in its fall broke away a large portion of this Oak on one side It is a magnificent tree in perfect health, and bids fair to grow out of its present disfigured state. Near this tree, and on the west side or library front of the house, is an Italian garden, and beyond it a long vista terminated by a stone structure called Holbein's Porch. A fine Chamærops Fortunei stands near, this also being a plant out of the first introduced batch. It has been outside for seventy years, is not so tall as some younger specimens we have seen, but its stem is unusually thick and denotes great age

Cotehele, Cornwall. Engraved from a photograph by Mr. Hayman Launceston.

The view shown is that of the south front of the house, showing a little garden of stone-edged beds set in gravel. Beyond, adorned only by the grand trees on it, the lawn spreads away to the river bank, the river itself being spanned by the " Palladian Bridge," built of stone and having a roof supported by rows of columns on either side. This leads to the deer park, in which the ground rises upwards to a considerable elevation, whilst along this slope another informal avenue of Lebanon Cedars is a fine feature amid the great beauty of native trees in abundance and of large size. An interesting fact gathered in regard to the Cedars is that on an average once in ten years they ripen a batch of good seed, which is sown for future planting about the place

Looking eastwards from the house, the ground stretches away almost as flat as a table, but this flatness has been delightfully broken up by a series of well-arranged groups, chiefly of coniferous or evergreen trees and shrubs margined in a pretty way with graceful masses of Savin. A broad gravel walk at right angles to the east front of the mansion, with lawn and fine trees on either side of it, extends for 300 yards, and is terminated by a seat hedged round with Yew. This bold walk and the shrub groups that break up the flatness of and give distance to the fine expanse of lawn that extends to the waterside are from the designs of Sir Richard Westmacott, who assisted the Countess of Pembroke in planning the grounds.

The second engraving shows well that portion of the house commanding the view of this broad walk, with its lawn and distant water, whilst between the trees in the distance is seen the spire of Salisbury Cathedral. Near the river a statue of Venus on the top of a column stands in the centre of a little square formed by trees of the Italian Cypress. The red Cedar was charming in some of the groups, its branches laden with glaucous fruits, that appeared as a silvery sheen cast over the tree. Yews, Hollies, and Evergreen Oaks, numerous and fine, give perennial verdure to the grounds Coniferous trees in sheltered breaks and nooks are equally fine, a tree of Picea cephalonica especially so, being nearly 100 ft high, whilst many are growing with great vigour. H.

OFFINGTON.—Offington is a very instructive garden, richly stored and pretty too. Large collections are rarely in the hands of those who have any thought for general effect, and no garden is more likely to be inartistic than the one rich in plants, and it is rare to find a pretty garden which is so full of beautiful things as this is It is one of those shore gardens in which there is much gain in point of warmth and other conditions which allow the growing of plants we have no chance of keeping in inland districts The southern and seashore district in one gives us all the conditions we could

Chillingham. Border castle garden with old-fashioned beds.

desire for growing many more plants than are hardy in our country In this garden Major Gaisford has gathered together a host of rare and beautiful trees, shrubs, and plants which, favoured by a genial climate, give to the garden a distinct aspect. There is here an entire absence of that conventional gardening which lays down hard, geometric patterns where we should see the free and graceful forms of shrubs and flowers. The house is nearly hidden by climbing plants, and a grand old Ivy-embowered Walnut standing on an airy lawn

BULWICK —Rambling about Northamptonshire, and delighted with its beautiful old houses, many of them, unfortunately, as bare of flower-gardening as a deserted ship, it was pleasant to come to a real garden at Bulwick, full of Carnations and many open-air flowers arranged in various pretty ways, even the house being full of large basins of Carnations some of them of one self-coloured kind—a rare pleasure. The flower garden was not one of those places which astonish us by a showy display, but modest at first sight as regards flower-gardening in immediate relation to the house, and the chief charm of the place was rather in various little side gardens and long and pretty borders backed with Holly and other hedges, and giving an opportunity for growing a great number of hardy flowers which bloom in the autumn. These formed picture vistas, of which the effect is very often better than a flower garden of the usual type. But, more than this, the excellent plan was followed here by the late Lady Henry Grosvenor of having what I do not think any garden can be right without, namely, a "square" or reserve garden in which things are grown well without reference to effect. It was a large square of the kitchen garden thrown into 4-feet beds, with little beaten alleys between, in which many thousand Carnations were grown in simple masses. One sees at once how much more beauty and variety can be got in such ways than where all the effort goes to help one scheme for effect in front of one's windows. What is the secret of beauty in such a garden, and what the lesson to be learnt from it? It is that no one plan will give us a garden beautiful for any length of time even in the fine season, as any one way is so liable to failure from the weather or other causes, that the main source of success is to have various ways with flowers, as there were at Bulwick. Hardy plants in beds and borders apart from the flower garden proper (that, too, being pretty) are the source of the charms of this garden—the variety of situation, the variety of plants, but of handsome, well-chosen and well-grown plants, and even variety of level in the various gardens, such as occurs at Bulwick, are all good aids, and the nearness of an interesting kitchen garden with sheltering walls is a source of beauty and variety.

EVERSLEY.—In the late Charles Kingsley's rectory garden at

Eversley, we get to see a modest, and simple as charming, type of garden. The walls and borders are full of flowers, while the Grass clothes the central space. When Canon Kingsley became rector of

Steps and terrace, "The Old Park," Axminster. Terrace garden not stiffly planted. From a photograph by Miss Dryden, Canons Ashby.

Eversley, in 1844, he found the garden at the rectory in as unsatisfactory a state as was, in other respects, the rest of his parish; but its capabilities he used to the utmost. On the sloping lawn between the house and the road stood, and still stands, a noble group of three

Scotch Firs, planted about the time that James I —who was just then building the grand old house of Bramshill, hard by, as a hunting box for Prince Henry—planted the Scotch 'Firs in Bramshill Park, and the clumps on Hartford Bridge Flats and Elvetham Mount. Most of the garden consisted then of a line of ponds from the glebe fields, past the house, down to the large pond behind the garden and churchyard The rector at once became his own landscape gardener, and the ponds were drained. Plane trees, which threatened in every high gale to fall on the south end of the house, were cut down, and masses of shrubs were planted to keep out the cold draughts, which even on summer evenings streamed down from the bogs on the edge of Hartford Bridge Flats. What had been a wretched chicken yard in front of the brick-floored room used as a study was laid down in Grass, with a wide border on each side, and the wall between the house and stable was soon a mass of creeping Roses, scarlet Honey-suckles, and Virginian Creeper Against the south side of the house a Magnolia (M. grandiflora) was trained, filling the rooms with its fragrance. Lonicera and Clematis montana, Wistaria, Gloire de Dijon and Ayrshire Roses, and variegated Ivy hid the rest of the wall with a veil of sweetness In front of the study window, on the lawn, an immense plant of Japanese Honeysuckle grows, and next to this the pride of the study garden lay in its double yellow Brier Roses These grew very freely, and in June the wall of the house and garden was ablaze with the golden blooms, the rooms being decorated for two or three weeks with dishes of the yellow Roses. From the low, damp situation of the rectory, none but the hardiest plants could be grown out-of-doors ; but the borders were always gay with such plants as Phloxes, Delphiniums, Saxifrages, Pinks, Pansies, and, above all, Roses and Carnations One bay in front of the house was well covered with Pyracantha, in which a pair of white-throats built un-disturbed for many years. Rhododendrons grew in the greatest luxuriance, and the neighbours always came to see the rector's garden when two beds, on either side of the front, were in blossom. An ancient Yew tree, and a slight hedge of Laburnum, Hollies, Lilac, and Syringa divide the rectory garden from the churchyard, and here, again, the rector turned his mind to making the best of what he had. The church, a plain red brick structure, was gradually covered with Roses, Ivy, Cotoneaster, Pyracantha, &c, and, in order that his parishioners should look on beautiful objects when they assembled in the churchyard for their Sunday gossip before service, the older part of the churchyard was planted with choice trees, flower-ing shrubs, Junipers, Cypress, Berberis, and Acer Negundo, and the Grass dotted with Crocuses where it was not carpeted with wild white Violets

Wilton, looking from house.

Wilton, another view.

EDGE HALL garden is one of those in which the hardy flowers of
the northern world are grown in numbers for the owner's delight and
the good of his friends, and it is in such large collections that charming
novelties for our gardens often make their appearance   Such gardens
in our own day carry on the traditions, so to say, of very interesting
English and Scottish gardens of the past, in which numbers of beautiful open air things were grown—among those I have had the happiness to see were the late Mr Borrer's at Henfield in Sussex, a garden
museum of beautiful hardy plants and of rare British forms of plants and
trees ; the Ellacombes' garden at Bitton , Mr Leeds' garden at Man-
chester ; Stirling's at Edinburgh ; Comely Bank, a home for the rarest
and most beautiful plants ; the Rev. Harpur Crewe's ; Mr Atkins's
garden at Painswick ; Sir George McLeay's at Pendell Court; Major
Gaisford's at Offington, and many other delightful gardens. The riches
of the collection in such gardens are a source of danger as to effect, the
very number of plants often leading to a neglect of breadth and
simplicity of effect ; but there is no real reason why a garden, rich
in many plants, may not also be beautiful in its masses, airiness and
verdure. A mile to the east the well-wooded and well-heathered range
of the Broxton Hills gives shelter, whilst from the south-west to the
north-west the horizon is formed by Welsh mountain ranges   A sunk
fence of sandstone, easily jumped by a fox or a hare, and in other parts
a line of movable hurdles, well wired against rabbits, separate three
acres for house and garden from the surrounding grass fields and from
a small park of eighty acres. About 200 yards from the house the
sand rock comes through, forming a long terrace with an escarpment
towards the west. The woods in spring are carpeted first with Primroses and wood Anemones, then with wild Hyacinths and Pink
Campion, whilst later there is a tall growth of Campanula latifolia
and large breadths of Japanese Knotwort, which have been planted to
supersede Nettles, while overhead is abundance of Hawthorn, Crab
and wild Cherry. The hall stands on the side of a hollow watercourse
worn in the stiff clay, which in Cheshire often lies over the sand
rock. Down this watercourse runs a torrent in heavy rains, but it is
quite dry in summer. On the sloping banks of this, close above the
house, there formerly stood ranges of cow-houses and pig-sties, which
drained into a stagnant pond in the bed of the watercourse within
twenty yards of the bedroom windows. Twenty-five years ago it was
drained, the watercourse confined within a covered culvert ; and the
whole space is now covered all summer with a dense forest of herbaceous
plants—every good kind which will thrive in the cold soil on which
the house stands being cultivated there.

STONELANDS, SUSSEX.—It is pleasant to get out of the conventional and there are many ways of doing so but gardens are often out

of all sympathy with the surrounding country, whereas the landscape and sylvan beauty of a pretty country might often be reflected, so to say, in the home landscape. It might indeed often tell us what to do as regards grouping, and kinds of trees and the natural character of the ground even give hints as to ground work in gardens. Stonelands is characteristic of the small manor house of the woodland district of Sussex, with its groups of Scotch Firs behind the house and in intimate connection with the farm buildings near The house, too, is of a good Sussex kind with bright sunny windows, stone, pretty in colour, big chimneys, and there is a small terrace necessary from the lie of the ground, which also cuts off the house from the road to the farm buildings near.

GOLDER'S HILL.—Places where there are simple conditions for beauty in design and planting are rare, and it is all the more pleasing to meet with an example of artistic treatment of a garden almost in London, on the western border of Hampstead Heath. As regards design and views, it is the prettiest of town gardens, and the conditions of its beauty are so simple that there is little to be said about them , an open lawn rolling up to the house, groups of fine trees, and wide and distant views over the country, the whole suggestive of good effect from simple hardy materials both in trees and flowers, but the elevation is such that no half hardy exotics are likely to succeed, and therefore hardy things give us our best chances of success.

A sunken fence separates the lawn from some park-like meadow with fine Oaks and Firs ; and beyond, the country north of London opens up, without any building visible on either side or in the foreground. From almost every other point of view these trees seem to form a picturesque group, and afford a welcome shade in summer. In front of the house is an open lawn, which one can get on to at once from any point. Being on a gentle rise, some would no doubt have urged this as a reason for making some kind of fortification in the shape of walls, which would have destroyed the repose, verdure, and the freedom of the spot. Now the only drawback—if drawback it be to such perfect freedom and breadth of airy foreground—is the fact that it offers a temptation to unthinking people to dot it over with shrubs, or evergreen trees, and many places, well laid out, are spoiled by this thoughtless dotting about of objects of poor form. The question of flowers is the greatest difficulty, because people are so well accustomed to have all their flowers gathered in front of the house, that if abundant provision is not made for them elsewhere, the carpet is apt, some day or other, to be dissected into a number of ugly flower-beds. The best way to guard against this in lawn gardens is to provide abundance of simple beds elsewhere which, half seen peeping through the trees, or met with in groups here and there at no great

distance from the house, may afford better effects than if all the beds
are under the windows. Thus where the foreground is a pleasant
lawn it is often well to have another site for the flower garden ; and
good large beds or groups of beds, in which fine things can be grown.
To have in one spot a group of large beds, simple in outline
with Roses and smaller plants surfacing the ground ; next in some
isolated nook, large beds of Lilies, separated by a group of low shrubs
and flowering Yuccas from a few beds of hardy flowers ; then a varied
flower garden partially cut off and embowered by trees—these and the
like are in certain situations likely to give that variety of treatment
which it is the aim of this chapter to secure.

Lawn garden, Offington, Worthing. Engraved from a photograph by Miss Gaisford.

TOTLEY HALL, NEAR SHEFFIELD, YORKS.—This fine old country
house stands beside the old coach road from Sheffield to Chatsworth
and Haddon Hall, on an elevation with good and extensive views.
Over the front door is the date 1623, about the time when Gerard's
Herbhal was published, and six years before Parkinson's *Paradisus*
of 1629. Built in such a flower-loving epoch it seems fitting that
it should be a flowery place to-day. Inside the entrance hall there
is some fine old oak carving and staircase, and there was formerly
a quaint old gallery around the hall, but new additions necessitated its removal. The flower garden slopes rather suddenly from

Rectory garden at Eversley.

the fringe of the front lawn and is rich in well-grown Daffodils and other choice flowers, sheltered by winding hedges There is a fine range of hills terminated by a bluff or headland in front of the house, and to the right are vast stretches of moorland. The elevated character and breezy freshness of the place are suggestive of the sea

Here, in spring, appear in great profusion the chaste flowers of the Daffodils, for Totley Hall is a home of the Daffodil. Standing at the lower end of the long flower borders—confined within hedges of Hollies, intersected by a winding path fringed with seedling Auriculas —there is seen a host of Daffodils.

As one gazes upon them, with their delicate and fragile heads waving gently to and fro in the soft westerly breeze, there rush involuntarily to one's mind Wordsworth's words on his sudden view of the wild Daffodils at Ullswater—

> —— then my heart with pleasure fills
> And dances with the Daffodils.

The deep golden yellows glow with a warmth that suggests the absorption of the sun's rays at their brightest moments The chaste and beautiful whiteness of others appears as if they had quietly appropriated, in the stillness of the night, the silvery moonbeams that softly kissed their fragile petals, whilst the paler tints of cream, sulphur and primrose are suggestive of the soft-coloured mantle spread o'er the skies by the lingering rays of the setting sun. The Daffodil— fit emblem of spring—is here in all its forms and colours.—F. W. B.

THE KEEP GARDEN AT FARNHAM CASTLE.—In our own day when it has been stated that the only garden worthy the name is one within four square walls, it interests me to come upon gardens of wholly different character, which show the folly of rules about a subject which admits of so much variety of position, form, and detail as a flower garden does. One of the most interesting I have lately seen is the little flower garden on the top of the old keep at Farnham Castle, which is as picturesque in situation and informal in outline as a garden can be, while it is extremely pretty with the broken walls on all sides clad with Ivy and Clematis, and in the centre many flowers. The variety of form from the walls surrounding it and the various climbers give it a singular charm. The hardiest flowers are grown, as is most fitting for such a garden—Irises in masses and evergreen perennials, which help to keep some grace in the garden towards the end of the year, and Tea and other Roses also help. Although I saw it on the verge of winter, it even then had much beauty of leaf and flower

It should be clear that in any such situation it is only possible through flower gardening of the free and picturesque kind to get a good

F

Edge Hall, Malpas, Cheshire. Lawn garden with hardy flowers in beds and groups. Engraved from a photograph sent by Rev. C. Wolley-Dod.

result, and, happily, there are so many treasures in our gardens now, that while growing things for their beauty of form or flower of fragrance, we may have much variety as to contents, grouping, and succession of bloom in such a garden.

ELDERFIELD.—In Miss Yonge's garden we are again away from convention and free to enjoy the charm of trees and shrubs among the flowers, as in many beautiful British gardens somewhat larger than cottage gardens, but keeping the unstamped grace and variety of the cottage garden One of the good points of such gardens is the freedom enjoyed to do or undo at any time of the year—there is always pleasant work to do and no violent effort at any one time—as is the case with gardens that depend on tender flowers only. The true flower-garden is one in which there is, as in nature and life, ceaseless change. " Elderfield has always looked an ideal home for an authoress A little low white house—nothing but a cottage she calls it herself—covered with creepers, which keep up a succession of bloom to peep in at the windows There is a very old Myrtle to the right, shorn of much of its height since the very cold winter of 1895 , and round Miss Yonge's drawing-room window (the upper one to the left) a Banksian and a summer Rose are ever looking in at her as she writes steadily every morning at the writing table drawn close up to the window, or tapping at the glass when the curtains are drawn and they are in danger of being forgotten   M ACTON "

ENGLISH GARDENS ABROAD AND THEIR LESSONS —Some of the most beautiful flower gardens are to be seen in the homes of English people living in Madeira, the Riviera, Algeria, and countries generally permitting of beautiful flower gardening during the winter and with a season of many flowers throughout the spring , real gardens varied and full of beautiful colour, yet without any trace of the barren monotony characteristic of most gardens at home The generally picturesque nature of the ground, the presence of graceful fruit and other trees, and the absence of any pretentious attempt to conform the whole to one set idea, lead to the simple and artistic garden. The garden of Mr Arkwright at Mustapha, near Algiers, is a good example of the English garden in other lands, a garden full of beautiful things, and these so placed that pictures are seen at every turn Noble Tea Roses like Chromatella are fountains of bloom, sometimes running up a tapering Cypress, and sending out of it far overhead graceful shoots laden with flowers. Lamarque, the noblest of white Roses, grows and blooms about as freely as the Elder bush does at home Many Tea Roses of all sizes are here ; sometimes kinds are superb that rarely open well with us at home, such as Cloth of Gold. But it is not only the climate makes the garden beautiful, as the way of planting is the main source of beauty here.

Lawn garden at Golder's Hill.

Borders are thick set with the foliage of the Iris in many forms, and particularly the winter-flowering Iris, which has its home in Algeria. The Pelargoniums are in lovely bushes in light or shade, while Datura, Palm, Jasmine, Acacia, Fig, Lemon, and Magnolia are happy in the sun, with masses of Cineraria here and there in half-shade, with many Violets, and even wild flowers of the country Bougainvilleas and handsome Bignonias grace the walls in free and pretty ways, while here and there the Algerian Ivy is seen, a noble climber, the fine qualities of which are not in the least affected by the hot sun in the summer here it ascends to high parts of the mountains there, which look arid enough and are terribly hot in summer No one need despair of gracing a dry bank with a fine thing who takes the Algerian Ivy for that purpose, and it may be its long sojourn in so dry a country has prepared it better for growth in the sun than the forms of the Ivy from the cooler northern woods of our Islands Some of the most beautiful garden effects I have seen were here, all the finer from the background of high cliffs above clad with evergreen Oak, Pine, and wild Olive, but the best lesson is not from the varied life in the garden so much as from the happy and natural way the whole is disposed

In this way also we have variety as well as pictures—as much variety as may be wished, of which there is an example in Mr. Hanbury's well-stored garden at La Mortola, in the Italian Riviera

The variety is not in itself so much worth seeking as beauty, which is just what we lose when we commit ourselves to any one way of flower gardening. To be free to add or plant at almost any time of the year is a great advantage , whereas in the pattern flower garden the whole is set out and taken up at fixed times. The result is a dreadfully fixed one too, and if any beautiful bush, or bulb, or flower happens to come in our way that does not fit into the wretched system, so much the worse for it

The fear of anything like a bush or low tree that governs the idea of many flower gardens at home at present does not exist here, so that we have light and shade, many bushes and even low trees that give chances for surprises and changes. This is partly owing to the warmth which allows of the growth of many pretty bushes that may well grace a flower garden, but, once free from the idea that a flower garden must be a flat surface seen at a glance, there would be no real difficulty in carrying out like ways of planting in our climate in which so many lovely bushes grow if we give them a chance. One minor charm of these English gardens abroad arises from the fact that any necessary stone-work is done in a simple way by the garden men. As the ground is often steep, steps and little walls or protecting corners are often wanted , but whenever the native gardener wants

The flower garden in the ruined keep at Farnham Castle, Surrey.

anything of this kind, he does not go through a circumlocution bureau for inspiration and drawings to scale, but builds what he wants in a simple ready way with the stone nearest at hand, and the result is much better from a gardening point of view than more elaborate and costly work The island of Madeira is very instructive too in the variety of its gardens ; every one I remember was distinct, and this was owing to the owners being free to do as the ground invited them, instead of following any fixed idea as to style, or leaving it to men who are ready with similar plans for all sorts of positions. In France, England, or Germany this could never happen, because owing to conformity about style and the use of book plans, we can usually tell beforehand what sort of garden we are to see [1]

Miss Yonge's garden at Elderfield.

CHAPTER IV.

BORDERS OF HARDY FLOWERS.

WE now come to the flowers that are worthy of a place in gardens, and to consider ways of arranging them. Their number and variety being almost without limit, the question is, how the garden lover is to enjoy as many of these treasures as his conditions allow of. As during all time a simple border has been the first expression of flower garden-ing, and as there is no arrangement of flowers more graceful, varied, or capable of giving more delight, and none so easily adapted to almost every kind of garden, some ideas of the various kinds of borders of hardy flowers mainly deserve our first consideration.

COST AND ENDURANCE. — The difference in cost of growing hardy flowers or tender should be thought of. The sacrifice of flower gardens to plants that perish every year has often left them poor of all the nobler plants. We must take into account the hothouses, the propagation of plants by thousands at certain seasons, the planting out at the busiest and fairest time of the year—in June, the digging up and storing in autumn, the care in the winter.

Perhaps the most striking effects from individual plants ever seen in England were Japanese Lilies grown for years in the open air by Mr M'Intosh among his Rhododendrons at Weybridge Heath. And not only Lilies; but many noble flowers may be grown in the same simple way. A few years ago we saw only dense masses of Rhodo-dendrons; now the idea of growing this shrub with the finer hardy plants has spread   It means more room to show the form of the shrubs, and more light and shade, mutual relief of shrub and plant, colonies and groups of lovely plants among the shrubs.   Good preparation and some knowledge of plants are needed, but no neces-sity whatever for any system that may not be called permanent

There are a number of things which, given thorough preparation at first, it would be wise to leave alone for some years at a time—as, for example, groups or beds of the various Tritomas, Irises, Lilies, Pæonies, the free-flowering Yuccas, Narcissi—these and many more, either grouped with others or in families. When all these exhaust the ground or become too crowded, by all means move them and replant, but this is a very different thing from moving all the plants in the flower garden twice a year.

It would be better every way if, so far as the flower garden is concerned, gardeners were to see what could be done unaided by the hothouse; but meanwhile the wise man will reduce the expense of glass, labour, fire, repairs, paint, pipes, and boilers to something like reasonable proportions. In presence of the wealth of our hardy garden flora, the promise of which is now such as men never expected

Flower-borders with grass path between. From a photograph by Mrs. Martin, Bournbrook Hall, Birmingham.

a few years ago, no one need doubt of making a fair flower garden from hardy plants alone.

THE TRUE WAY to make gardens yield a return of beauty for the labour and skill given them is the permanent one. Choose some beautiful class of plants and select a place that will suit them, even as to their effect in the garden landscape. Let the beds be planted as permanently and as well as possible, so that there will remain little to do for years. All plants may not lend themselves to this permanent plan, but such as do not may be grown apart—for instance, the Poppy

Anemones, Turban and Persian Ranunculuses, Carnations, Stocks, Asters, and the finer annuals. But a great many delightful plants can be planted permanently, and be either allowed to arrange themselves, to group with others, or to grow among peat-loving shrubs which, in many places, are jammed into pudding-shaped masses void of form or grace, or light and shade.

One of the best reforms will be to avoid the conventional pattern plans, and adopt simple beds and borders, in positions suited to the plants they are to grow These can best be filled permanently, because the planter is free to deal with them in a bolder and more artistic way than if he has to consider their relation to a number of small beds In this way, also, the delight of flowers is much more keenly felt as one sees them relieved, sees them at different times, and to more advantage than the flowers stereotyped under the window. Roses — favourites with everybody — grouped well together, and not trained as standards, would lend themselves admirably to culture with other things—moss Roses growing out of a carpet of double Primroses, and Tea Roses with Carnations. Then there are many groups made by the aid of the finer perennials themselves, such as the Delphiniums and Phloxes, by choosing things that would go well together. Other plants, such as Yuccas, of which there are now various beautiful kinds, are often best by themselves ; and noble groups they form, whether in flower or not The kinds of Yucca that flower very freely, such as Y. recurva and Y flaccida, lend themselves to grouping with Flame Flowers (Tritoma) and the bolder autumn plants.

No plan which involves expensive yearly efforts on the same piece of ground can ever be satisfactory. All garden plants require attention, but not annual attention. The true way is quite different—the devotion of the skill and effort to fresh beds and effects each year It does not exclude summer " bedding," but includes lovely and varied aspects of vegetation far beyond that attainable in summer " bedding," and attempts to make the garden artistically beautiful It also helps to make the skill of the gardener effective for lasting good, and prevents its being thrown away in annual fireworks. There can be no gardening without care , but is there not a vast difference between some of these beds and borders and those with flowers which disappear with the frosts of October, and leave us nothing but bare earth ?

The main charm of bedding plants—that of lasting in bloom a long time—is really a drawback. It is the stereotyped kind of garden which we have to fight against ; we want beautiful and changeful gardens, and should therefore have the flowers of each season. Too short a bloom is a misfortune ; but so is too long a bloom, and numbers of hardy plants bloom quite as long as can be desired

There is nothing whatever used in bedding out to be compared
in colour, form, or fragrance with many families of hardy plants
There is no beauty among bedding plants at all comparable with that
of Irises, Lilies, Delphiniums, Evening Primroses, Pæonies, Carnations,
Narcissi, and a host of others.   Are we to put aside or into the background all this glorious beauty for the sake of a few things that merely
give us flat colour?   No one who knows even to a slight extent what
the plants of the northern and temperate world are can admit that
this sort of gardening should have the first place.   There is nothing
among "carpet" plants equal to Windflowers in many kinds, flowering
in spring, summer, and autumn ; Torch Lilies, superb in autumn ·
Columbines ; Harebells , Delphiniums ; Day Lilies , Everlasting Peas ;
Evening Primroses ; Pæonies ; Phloxes ; Ranunculus, double and single,
and the many fine species ; all the noble autumn-blooming, Daisy-
like flowers , Scabious ; plumy Spiræas ; Globe Flowers , Lilies, in
noble variety ; Polyanthus ; Primroses ; Auriculas ; Wallflowers ;
Meadow Saffrons ; Crocuses, of the spring and autumn ; Scillas ;
Gladioli , Snowflakes ; Grape Hyacinths ; Narcissi, in lovely variety ,
Tulips, the old florists' kinds, and many wild species ; Yuccas ; Carnations and Pinks ; Dielytras ; Cornflowers ; Foxgloves ; Stocks ; Starworts ; great Scarlet and other Poppies ; Christmas Roses, both of the
winter and spring ; Forget-me-nots , Pansies and many of the rock
plants of the mountains of Europe—from the Alps to the hills of
Greece, cushioned with Aubrietia, and skyblue Wind-flowers—all hardy
as the Docks by the frozen brooks

FLOWER BORDERS FRINGING SHRUBBERIES —A frequent way
in which people attempt to cultivate hardy flowers is in what is
called the "mixed border," often made on the edge of a shrubbery,
the roots of which leave little food or even light for the flowers
The face of a shrubbery should be broken and varied , the shrubs
should not form a hard line, but here and there they should come
full to the edge and finish it   The variety of positions and places
afforded by the front of a shrubbery so arranged is tempting, but
it is generally best to use plants which do not depend for their
beauty on high culture—which, in fact, fight their way near shrubs
—and there are a great many of them, such as the evergreen Candytufts, the large-leaved Rockfoils, Acanthus, Day Lilies, Solomon's
Seal, Starworts, Leopard's Banes, Moon Daisies, and hardy native
Ferns.

A scattered, dotty mixed border along the face of a shrubbery
gives a poor effect, but a good one may be secured by grouping
the plants in the open spaces between the shrubs, making a careful
selection of plants, each occupying a bold space. Nothing can be
more delightful than a border made thus , but it requires knowledge

of plants, and that desire to consider plants in relation to their surroundings which is never shown by those who make a "dotty" mixed
border, which is the same all the way along and in no place pretty.
The presence of tree and shrub life is a great advantage to those who
know how to use it. Here is a group of shrubs over which we can
throw a delicate veil of some pretty creeper that would look stiff and
wretched against a wall; there a shady recess beneath a flowering
tree: instead of planting it up with shrubs in the common way,
cover the ground with Woodruff, which will form a pretty carpet
and flower very early in the year, and through the Woodruff a few
British Ferns; in front of this use only low plants, and we shall

A flower-border at Fillingham Castle, Lincoln.

thus get a pretty little vista, with shade and a pleasant relief. Next
we come to a bare patch on the margin. Cover it with a strong
evergreen Candytuft, and let this form the edge. Then allow a group
of Japan Quince to come right into the grass edge and break the
margin; then a large group of broad-leaved Saxifrage, receding under
the near bushes and trees; and so proceed making groups and
colonies, considering every aid from shrub or tree, and never using a
plant of which we do not know and enjoy the effect.

This plan is capable of much variety, whether we are dealing
with an established and grown shrubbery, or a choice plantation of
flowering Evergreens. In the last case, owing to the soil and the
neat habit of the bushes, we have excellent conditions in which
good culture is possible. One can have the finest things among

them—if the bushes are not jammed together. The ordinary way of planting shrubs is such that they grow together, and then it is not possible to have flowers between them, nor to see the true form of the bushes, which are lost in one solid leafy mass. In growing fine things—Lilies or Cardinal Flowers, or tall Evening Primroses —among open bushes we may form a delightful garden, we secure sufficient space for the bushes to show their forms, and we get light and shade among them. In such plantations one might have in the back parts "secret" colonies of lovely things which it might not be well to show in the front of the border, or which required shade and shelter that the front did not afford

BORDERS BY GRASS WALKS IN SHADE OR SUN —It is not only in the flower garden where we may have much beauty of flower, but away from it there are many places better fitted for growing the more beautiful things which do not require continual attention. Unhappily, the common way of planting shrubberies has robbed many Grass walks of all charm. The great trees, which take care of themselves, are often fine, but the common mixed plantation of Evergreens means death to the variety and beauty of flower we may have by Grass walks in sun or shade   The shrubs are frequently planted in mixtures, in which the most free-growing are so thickly set as soon to cover the whole ground, Cherry Laurel, Portugal Laurel, Privet, and such common things frequently killing all the choicer shrubs and forming dark heavy walls of leaves. Some of these Evergreens, being very hungry things, overrun the ground, rob the trees, and frequently, as in the case of the Portugal Laurels, give a dark monotonous effect while keeping the walks wet, airless, and lifeless.

Light and shade and the charm of colour are impossible in such cases with these heavy, dank Evergreens, often cut back, but once one is free of their slavery what delightful places there are for growing all hardy flowers in broad masses, from the handsome Oriental Hellebores of the early spring to the delicate lavenders of the Starworts in October. Not only hardy flowers, but graceful climbers like the wild Clematis, and lovely corners of light and shade may be made instead of the walls of sombre Evergreens. If we want the ground green with dwarf plants, we have no end of delightful plants at hand in the Ivies and Evergreens like Cotoneaster. There is no need for the labour and ugliness of clipping. I have seen places with acres of detestable clipped Laurels, weary and so ugly! With all these grubbed and burnt, what places, too, for such beautiful things as the giant Fennels with their more than Fern-like grace, and all our strong, hardy Ferns which want no rocks, with Solomon's Seal and Foxgloves among them. Such walks may pass from open spaces into half-shady ones or through groves of old Fir or other trees, and so give us picturesque variety apart from their planting with flowers.

FLOWER BORDERS AGAINST WALLS AND HOUSES.—In many situations near houses, and especially old houses, there are delightful opportunities for a very beautiful kind of flower border. The stone forms fine background, and there are no thieving tree roots. Here we have conditions exactly opposite to those in the shrubbery; here we can have the best soil, and keep it for our favourites; we can have Delphiniums, Lilies, Pæonies, Irises, and all choice plants well grown. Walls may be adorned with climbers of graceful growth, climbing Rose, Wistaria, Vine, or Clematis, which will help out our beautiful mixed border. Those must to some extent be trained, although they may be allowed a certain degree of abandoned grace even on a wall. In this kind of border we have, as a rule, no back-

Flower border against wall at Sidbury Manor.

ground of shrubs, and therefore we must get the choicest variety of plant life into the border itself and we must try to have a constant succession of interest. In winter this kind of border may have a bare look when seen from the windows, but the variety of good hardy plants is so great, that we can make it almost evergreen by using evergreen rock-plants. Where walls are broken with pillars, a still better effect may be obtained by training Vines and Wistaria along the top and over the pillars or the buttresses.

THE FLOWER BORDER IN THE FRUIT OR KITCHEN GARDEN. —We have here a frequent kind of mixed border often badly made, but which may be excellent. A good plan is to secure from about eight to ten feet of rich soil on each side of the walk, and cut the borders off from the main garden by a trellis of some kind from seven feet to nine feet high. This trellis may be of strong iron wire, or, better

still, of simple rough wooden branches.   Any kind of rough permanent
trellis will do, on which we may grow Climbing Roses and Clematis
and all the choicer but not rampant climbers.   Moreover, we can
grow them in their natural grace along the wires or rough branches,
or up and across a rough wooden trellis—Rose and Jasmine showing
their grace uncontrolled.   We fix the main branches to the supports,
and leave the rest to the winds, and form a fine type of flower
border in this way, as we have the graceful climbing plants in contrast
with the flowers in the border.

General borders may be made in various ways ; but it may be well
to bear in mind the following points : Select only good plants ; throw
away weedy kinds, there is no scarcity of the best.   See good collections.   Put, at first, rare kinds in lines across four-feet nursery
beds, so that a stock of plants may be at hand.   Make the choicest
borders where they cannot be robbed by the roots of trees ; see that
the ground is good and rich, and that it is at least two and a half
feet deep, so deep that, in a dry season, the roots can seek their
supplies far below the surface.   In planting, plant in naturally disposed groups, never repeating the same plant along the border at
intervals, as is so often done with favourites.   Do not graduate the
plants in height from the front to the back, as is generally done, but
sometimes let a bold plant come to the edge ; and, on the other hand,
let a little carpet of a dwarf plant pass in here and there to the back,
so as to give a varied instead of a monotonous surface.   Have no
patience with bare ground, and *cover* the border with dwarf plants ; do
not put them along the front of the border only.   Let Hepaticas and
double and other Primroses, and Saxifrages, and Golden Moneywort
and Stonecrops, and Forget-me-nots, and dwarf Phloxes, and many
similar plants cover the ground among the tall plants betimes—at the
back as well as the front.   Let the little ground plants form broad
patches and colonies by themselves occasionally, and let them pass into
and under other plants.   A white Lily will be all the better for having
a colony of creeping Forget-me-nots over it in the winter, and the
variety that may be thus obtained is infinite.

Thoroughly prepared at first, the border might remain for years
without any digging in the usual sense   When a plant is old and
rather too thick, never hesitate to replant it on a wet day in the
middle of August any more than in the middle of winter.   Take it
up and put a fresh bold group in fresh ground ; the young plants
will have plenty of roots by the winter, and in the following spring
will flower much stronger than if they had been transplanted in
spring or in winter.   Do not pay much attention to labelling, if a
plant is not worth knowing, it is not worth growing ; let each good
thing be so bold and so well grown as to make its presence felt.

MR. FRANK MILES ON THE FLOWER BORDER.—Among the first to see the merits of effectively carpeting borders, and who made the border suggested in my *Hardy Flowers*, was the late Frank

Flower border against house.

Miles, the artist, and an excellent flower gardener. His own account of his work I give here.

If we are to have mixed borders of herbaceous plants, one thing is quite certain—we can never go back to the borders of our ancestors in which every

G

plant had a bare space of ground round it In the spot where once a plant had
bloomed, there was an end for the year of any flowers.   Now a yard of ground
should have bloom on it at least eight months in the year, and this applies to
every yard of ground in a really good mixed border I am certain that, once a
border is well made, it need not be dug up at all. But the question is—what is
a well-made border? I think a border is not well made, or suitable for growing
the most beautiful plants to perfection, unless it is as well made as a Vine border
in a vinery. Why we should not take as much trouble with the garden border as
the border of a conservatory I cannot imagine, seeing that Lilies will grow 11 feet
high in the open air, not less than 10½ inches across the flower, and Irises little
less than that. The more I garden the deeper I get my drainage, and the fuller
of sand and fibre my soil. I consider, first, that a border must have a bed of
broken bricks or other drainage, with ashes over that, to prevent the drainage
from filling up ; secondly, that that bed of drainage must have 2 feet of light
soil over it ; thirdly, that that soil must have equal parts of sand, soil, and vegetable matter. A soil of these constituents and depth is never wet in winter and
never dry in summer. During the dry weather I found soil like this, in which
quantities of auratum Lilies were growing, to be quite moist an inch below the
surface, and I know in winter it always appears dry compared with the natural
garden soil

But, for all practical intents and purposes, every 6 inches of ground could
contain its plant, so that no 6 inches of bare ground need obtrude on the eye
Almost any kind of bare rock has a certain beauty, but I cannot say bare ground
is ever beautiful Well, supposing the back of the border filled with Delphiniums,
Phloxes, and Roses, pegged down, and other summer and autumn-blooming plants,
and supposing the border to be made as I have described it, I should carpet the
ground at the back with spring-blooming flowers, so that when the Roses are bare
and the Delphiniums and Phloxes have not pushed above ground, the border should
even then be a blaze of beauty. Crocuses, Snowdrops, Aconites, and Primroses
are quite enough for that purpose. The whole space under the Roses I should
cover with the Common Wood Anemone, and the golden Wood Anemone, and
early Cyclamens, and the earliest Dwarf Daffodils. And among the Roses and
Pæonies and other medium-sized shrubs I would put all the taller Lilies, such
as require continual shade on their roots ; and such as pardalinum and the
Californian Lilies generally, the Japanese, Chinese, and finer American Lilies
Now we come more to the front of the border, and here I would have combinations, such as the great St. Bruno's Lily and the delicate hybrid Columbines,
Primroses planted over hardy autumn Gladioli, so that when the Primroses are at
rest the Gladioli should catch the eye : Carnations and Daffodils, planted so that
the Carnations form a maze of blue-green for the delicate creams and oranges of
the Daffodils When the Daffodils are gone there are the Carnations in the
autumn A mass of Iberis correæfolia happens to have been the very best thing
possible for some Lilium Browni to grow through, for the Iberis flowered early
and then made a protection for the young growth of the Browni, and then a
lovely dark green setting for the infinite beauty of the Lily flowers. As for saying that this cannot be done, I say that it is nonsense, for the Iberis flowered
beautifully under such circumstances, and the Lilies too. If once you get it into
your head that no bit of ground ought ever to be seen without flowers or immediate
prospect of flowers, heaps of combinations will immediately occur to those con-
versant with plants and the deep-rooting habits of most bulbs and the surface
rooting of many herbaceous plants—for instance, Colchicums and Daffodils, with
a surface of Campanula pusilla alba The big leaves of the Colchicum grow in
spring, and there would be nothing but leaves were it not for the masses of

Daffodils. By and by the leaves of the Colchicums and Daffodils are dry enough to pull away, and then the Campanula, be it pusilla, pusilla alba, or turbinata alba, comes into a sheet of bloom. Before the bloom has passed away the Colchicum blooms begin to push up, and as some of my Colchicums are 5 inches across, of the richest rose colour, I do not exactly feel that this is a colourless kind of gardening, and as I have a hundred different kinds of Daffodils, this little arrangement will not be without interest in spring.

THE DAFFODILS and Colchicums root deeply and grow mostly in winter, requiring water then, and not in summer, when the Campanula carpet is taking it all. There are some, however, which one must be careful about—the common white Lily, for instance, which wants exposing to the sun in the autumn. I do not mind the exquisite French Poppies among these candidum Lilies, because the Poppies die about August, and then the Lilies get their baking and refuse to show the bare earth, soon covering it all with their leaves. For the extreme front of the border hundreds of combinations will occur—Pansies over Daffodils, Portulacas over Central Asian bulbs, Christmas Roses and Hellebores over the taller

Flower border in fruit garden at Dunrobin Castle, N.B.

Daffodils, with Gladioli, Tritomas, and giant Daffodils, Hepaticas, and autumn-blooming and spring-blooming Cyclamens, with Scillas and Snowdrops. When Anemone japonica is low, up come the taller Tulips, sylvestris for instance, and higher still out of the dark green leaves come the bejewelled Crown Imperials.

As for the cultural advantages, I can imagine this system in the hands of a skilful gardener to be the best of all. In the first place, the plants suffer much less from drought, because there is so much less surface exposed to sun and wind. Examine, not right under the root, but under the spreading part of a Mignonette, and see if, on a broiling hot day, the ground is not much cooler and moister than on the bare ground. Irises are almost the only plants I know of that do require the soil bare about their rootstocks, but then Irises are a carpet of green always, and a few clumps of Tiger Lilies or Tiger Irises will not seriously injure their flowering prospects. And what cannot be done with an herbaceous border edge when that edge is the green Grass? Crocuses and Crocuses all the autumn and winter and spring in the Grass. The tiniest Scillas and Hyacinths, and Daffodils, and Snowdrops are leading into the border without any break. So I believe, and I think many others will believe by and by, that every bulbous plant ought to be grown in combination with something else, as Amaryllis Belladonna, for instance, which I plant with Arum italicum pictum In spring the Arum comes up extremely early and its leaves protect the far more delicate leaves of the Amaryllis till they are growing freely and the Arum dies down The ground is surfaced with Violets, so that the Belladonnas are now coming into bloom, not with the bare ground but with a setting of Violet leaves in beautiful contrast with their pink blossoms. Christmas Roses of all kinds would probably be a more beautiful setting still, but the Belladonnas want a good deal of summer drying up, which the Hellebores could not stand so well.

WE CAN NEVER GO BACK to the mixed border of our ancestors ; we have been spoilt for such blank, flowerless spaces as they had by the gorgeousness of bedding out But we have now a wealth of hardy plants, especially bulbs, which they never had, and this combination of bulbous plants and herbaceous plants will certainly lead to a preparation of the borders which has been hardly dreamt of by people who do not care what they spend on tropical flowers ; for it seems to be forgotten that we have Irises as big as a plate and Lilies as tall as a tree, all hardy and requiring little attention when once they have been properly planted. The time that used to be spent year after year in digging acres of borders might now be spent in properly making or re-making a few yards of border, till the whole outdoor borders are as exactly suited for the growth of plants to the utter-most perfection—as many as possible being put in the given space—as the borders of a large conservatory. It is in such a border as this that we attain the utmost variety, unceasingly beautiful, every yard different, every week varying, holding on its surface at least three times the value of plant life and successional plant beauty of any ordinary garden The chief enemy to the system is the slug ; but while the Belladonna Delphinium, which is usually half eaten by slugs in most gardens, grows 6 feet high with me, I am not going to give up my system.

The way so well described by Mr F. Miles, and which he carried out admirably in his father's garden at Bingham—one of the few really lovely mixed borders I have seen—is to some extent that carried out in many pretty cottage gardens, owing to the plots being stored with all sorts of hardy flowers ; those are the cottage gardens where one often sees a charming succession of flowers and no bare ground

One of the prettiest garden borders I know is against a small house Instead of the walk coming near the windows, a bed of choice shrubs, varying from 9 feet to 15 feet in width, is against the house Nothing in this border grows high enough to intercept the view out of the windows on the ground floor, from which were seen the flowers of the border and a green lawn beyond. Among the shrubs were tall Evening Primroses, and Lilies, and Meadow Sweets, and tall blue Larkspurs, which after the early shrubs have flowered bloom above them. The ground is always furnished, and the effect is good, even in winter.

EVERGREEN BORDERS OF HARDY FLOWERS.—The plants of the older kind of mixed border were—like the Grasses of the meadows of the northern world—stricken to the earth by winter, and the border was not nearly so pretty then as the withered Grass of the plain or copse. But since the revival of interest in hardy and Alpine flowers, and the many introductions of recent years, we have a great number of beautiful plants that are evergreen in winter and that enable us to make evergreen borders. The great white blanket that covers the north and many mountain ranges in winter protects also for months many Alpine plants which do not lose their leaves in winter, such as Rockfoils, Stonecrops, Primroses, Gentians, and Christmas Roses. The most delicate of Alpine plants suffer, when exposed to our winter, from excitement of growth, to which they are not subject in their own home, but many others do not mind our winters much, and it is easy

Border of hardy flowers on open margin of lawn. (Newton Don, Kelso, N.B.).

by good choice of plants to make excellent borders wholly or in greater part evergreen.

These are not only good as evergreens, but they are delightful in colour, many being beautiful in flower in spring, and having also the charm of assuming their most refreshing green just when other plants are dying in autumn. Along with these rock and herbaceous plants we may group a great many shrublets that come almost between the true shrub and the Alpine flower—little woody evergreen creeping things like the dwarf Partridge Berry, Canadian Cornel, hardy Heaths, and Sand Myrtles, often good in colour when grouped.

Among these various plants we have plenty for evergreen borders, and this is important, as, while many might object to the bare earth of the ordinary border of herbaceous plants near the house or in other

Border of Delphiniums in the garden at Hall Green, showing effect of grouping hardy flowers instead of "dotting." Engraved from a photograph.

favourite spots, it is different with borders of evergreen plants, which may be charming and natural in effect throughout the year.

Of garden pictures, there are few prettier than Crocus, Snowdrops, or Scilla coming through the green, moss-like carpets in these ever-green borders, far prettier to those who love quiet and natural colour than more showy effects   Often narrow evergreen borders are the best things that can be placed at the foot of important walls, as the way of allowing Grass to go right up to the walls is a foolish one, and often leads to injury to the wall trees.   A narrow border (18 inches will do), cut off with a natural stone edging from the Grass or walk, is best   even a border of this size may have many lovely things, from early Cyclamen to the rarer Meadow Saffrons in the autumn.   Besides the flowers already named, we have Violets, Periwinkles, Yuccas, Carnations, Pinks, white Rock Cress, Barren-worts, charming in foliage, purple Rock Cresses, Omphalodes, Iris, Acanthus, Indian and other Strawberries, Houseleeks, Thymes, Forget-me-nots, Sandworts, Gentianella, Lavender, Rosemary, hardy Rock Roses, and many native and other hardy evergreen Ferns in all their fine variety , Bamboos, Ruscus and Dwarf Savin, these are an essential aid in the making of evergreen borders

HARDY BORDER FLOWERS FOR BRITISH GARDENS.

From this list all families not pretty hardy in Britain are ex-cluded : whatever we may do with flower beds, mixed borders should be mainly of hardy plants, and we ought to be able to plant or refresh them at any time through the autumn or winter months.   Well planned mixed borders, covered as they mostly should be with rock plants forming green carpets, should have few gaps in early summer, but where these occur they may be filled up with half-hardy plants as the stock of plants may permit, or with good annuals.   It is important in making borders to use the finest species in each genus

Acanthus	Aubrietia	Convolvulus	Eutoca	Hollyhock
Achillea	Bartonia	Coreopsis	Fritillaria	Hyacinthus
Acis	Bellis	Corydalis	Fuchsia	Iberis
Aconitum	Bocconia	Crocus	Funkia	Iris
Adonis	Brachycome	Cyclamen	Gaillardia	Ixiolirion
Agapanthus	Brodiæa in var	Cypripedium	Galanthus	Kniphofia
Agrostemma	Calendula	Delphinium	Galtonia	Lathyrus
Allium	Calla	Dianthus	Gentiana	Lavatera
Allysum	Calliopsis	Dielytra	Geranium	Lavendula
Alstrœmeria in var	Calochortus	Digitalis	Geum	Leucojum
Amaryllis	Caltha in var	Dodecatheon	Gladiolus	Lilium
Amberboa	Campanula	Doronicum	Godetia	Linaria
Anemone	Carnations	Dryas	Gypsophila	Linum
Anthericum	Catananche	Echinops	Helenium	Lobelia
Antirrhinum	Centaurea	Epilobium	Helianthemum	Lupinus
Arabis	Cerastium	Epimedium	Helianthus	Lychnis
Arenaria	Cheiranthus	Eremurus	Helichrysum	Lythospermum
Argemone	Chelone	Erigeron	Helleborus	Lythrum
Armeria	Chionodoxa	Erodium	Hepatica	Malorpe
Arnebia	Chrysanthemum	Eryngium	Hesperis	Malva
Arum	Colchicum	Erythronium	Heuchera	Meconopsis
Aster	Convallaria	Eschscholtzia	Hieracium	Megasea

Border Flowers for British Gardens—continued.

Michauxia	Papaver	Ramondia	Senecio	Trillium
Mimulus	Pæonia	Rhodanthe	Sidalcea	Triteleia
Mirabilis	Pancratium	Rockets	Sparaxis	Tritonia
Monarda	Pansy	Rudbeckia	Spiræa	Trollius
Montbretia	Pentstemon	Ranunculus	Statice	Tropeolum
Muscari	Phlomis	Salpiglossis	Sternbergia	Tulipa
Myosotis	Phlox	Salvia	Stocks	Veratrum
Narcissus	Physalis	Saponaria	Sweet Pea	Verbascum
Œnothera	Portulacca	Saxifraga	Sweet William	Veronica
Onosma	Polemonium	Scabiosa	Symphytum	Viola
Orchis	Potentilla	Schizostylis	Thymus	Waldsteinia
Ornithogalum	Plumbago	Scilla	Tiarella	Wallflower
Orobus	Primula	Sedum	Tigridia	Zephyranthes
Omphalodes	Puschkinia	Sempervivum	Tradescantia	Zinnia
Oxalis	Pyrethrum			

Borders : The Grove, Wishaw.

English Iris.

CHAPTER V.

THE RESERVE AND CUT-FLOWER GARDENS.

NOTHING is worse in gardening than the way in which plants of all kinds are huddled together without regard to fitness for association in stature, in time of blooming, or in needs of culture. The common scene of confusion is the shrubbery border, into which Carnations, annuals, Alpine flowers, and rampant herbs are often thrown, to dwindle and perish. There is no shrubbery border that could not be made beautiful by carpeting it with wood and copse plants of the northern world in broad groups, but many of our favourite flowers are not wood plants, and many—for example, Carnations—cannot maintain the struggle against the bushes and trees. *Hardy plants should be divided into two broad series at least—those which thrive in and near woody growth, and those which must perish there.* Solomon's Seal and the blue Apennine Anemone are types of plants that one may grow in any shady place: Carnation, Pink, Auricula are among the flowers which must have good soil and be kept away from tree roots, and though good borders, away from shrubby growth, grow many plants well, a further division of the work will be found wise in many places.

One good plan that all can follow is the growing of certain plants without heed to their place in any design, but not in any kind of "mixed border" or in other mixed arrangements. Many hardy flowers are worthy of special culture, and good results cannot often be got without it, whether we grow Carnations, Pinks, Pansies, Phloxes, Lilies, Stocks, double Wallflowers, Cloves, or scarlet Lobelias. Even a choice annual, such as Rhodanthe, or a beautiful Grass, it is not easy to succeed with unless it has a fair chance, away from the crowding of the ordinary mixed border.   This special culture of favourite flowers may be best carried out in a plot of ground set aside for beds of the choicer flowers, in a piece of ground in or near the kitchen garden or any other open position, sheltered, but not shaded.   Such ground should be treated as a market gardener would treat it—well enriched, and open, and thrown into four-foot beds, the little pathways need not be gravelled or edged, but simply marked out with the feet.   With the aid of such a division of the garden, the cultivation of many fine hardy plants becomes a pleasure.   When any plant gets tired of its bed, it is easy to make the Carnation bed of past years the bulb one for the next year, and so on.   It would be easy to change one's favourites from bed to bed, so that deep-rooting plants should follow surface-rooting kinds, and thus the freshness of the garden would be kept up   If any edging is used, it should be of natural stone sunk in the earth, as such edgings are not ugly or costly ; but the abolition of all edgings, beyond one or two main lines, would tend to simplify the work   Such a plot is excellent for giving cut flowers in quantity, and is also a great aid as a nursery, while it would also be a help to exchanges with friends or neighbours, in the generous way of all true gardeners.   The space occupied by it will depend upon the size and wants of the place, but, wherever the room can be spared, an eighth of an acre might be devoted to the culture in simple beds of favourite flowers, and even the smallest garden should have a small plot of this kind

WHAT TO GROW IN THE RESERVE GARDEN.—Among the fair flowers which in this way may be cultivated, each separately and well, are the delightful old Clove Carnations—white, crimson, and scarlet, as well as many other kinds, tall Phloxes, so fair in country gardens in the autumn, scarlet Lobelias, splendid in colour ; Pinks of many kinds ; Persian and Turban Ranunculus ; bright old garden Anemones, and the finer species of Anemone, Lilies, and as many as possible of the splendid kinds introduced into our gardens within the past dozen years from California and Japan, tall perennial Delphiniums, with their spikes of blue ; double Rockets, beautiful Irises, English, Spanish, Japanese, and German ; Pansies in great variety, Tiger Flowers ; the Columbine, including the lovely blue Columbine of the Rocky Mountains ; Pyrethrums, Chinese Pinks, Scabious, Sweet Williams ; Stocks of many kinds, Wall-flowers, double and single, the annual Phloxes, Zinnias, which, if grown as grown abroad—that is to say, well and singly grown—are fine in colour, China Asters, quilled and others, the Sweet Sultan, in two or three forms, showy tricolour Chrysanthemums, Grasses for cutting in winter ; Grape Hyacinths, rare Narcissus ; Meadow Saffrons, Lilies of the Valley, Crocuses, the autumnal as well as the vernal kinds, Dahlias, cactus and single ; Pæonies ; Primroses, double and single ; Pentstemons ; Polyanthus ; Oxlips ; Tulips, many early and late kinds ; 'Sweet Violets ; American Cowslips ; Gladioli ; Christmas Roses ; and, lastly, Everlasting Flowers, which may be grown with the pretty Grasses, and, like them, be gathered for the house in winter. All these fair flowers deserve care in the gardens, and should not be trusted to the too often ill-cultivated slips called " mixed borders," and many other plants which we wish to increase or take good care of.

In these special plots for hardy flowers are included the various hardy florists' flowers. The term " florists' flowers " was once applied to flowers supposed to be popular with amateurs and florists, but it had never any clear meaning. A Rose is a florist's flower; but it is more—

Christmas Roses in bed in reserve garden. (Durie, Fife, N.B.).

it is everybody's flower, and we call it a Rose, having no use for any other term. The reserve garden is a good place to grow flowers for cutting for the house. The enemy in the way of plenty of cut flowers has hitherto been the gardener; but he was limited in his cutting operations to glass-houses, which he naturally wished to keep gay. A supply equal to that of a dozen plant houses can be got from an open square in the kitchen garden or any piece of good ground. For eight months there is a procession of open-air flowers, which can easily be grown in sufficient quantity to allow the cutting of plenty for every want. A bed or a few lines of each favourite in a plot of good soil would give a great number of flowers, and these, aided by the Roses and other bush and tree flowers about the garden, would yield all the flowers that a large house would require, and many besides for hospitals and for those who have not gardens. Flowers grown for cutting should be carefully selected as regards odour, form, and colour, and the gardener should do all he can to carry out an idea tending so much to give people pleasure at home, and the smallest country place can afford a plot of ground to grow flowers for cutting.

DOUBLE CROPPING OF BEDS —We have had evidence of the good way in which inter-cropping suits plants in nursery beds, and there is reason to believe that the presence in rich ground of two plants wholly different in their nature is a good plan   A collection of Narcissi, with lines between of Delphiniums and hardy Fuchsias, that is to say, two lines of each in a 4ft. bed, will thrive.   The same is true of other hardy spring bulbs, which may be alternated with the choicer perennials that bloom in autumn ; and this way is a good one for people who live in their gardens chiefly in spring and autumn, as it secures two distinct seasons of bloom in the same ground   This applies to store beds as distinct from the regular flower garden, though some kind of inter-cropping would give an excellent result in the flower garden also ; as, for instance, if we have beds of Roses, we might have them carpeted with early bulbs, and be none the worse for it, and so also with Pæonies and many other flowers.   It wants some care to find out which go best together , but, given that, all is easy enough

GARDENS OF ONE FLOWER

Apart from the reserve garden, with its flowers in close masses, we may have gardens of a favourite flower and its forms, for the purpose of studying a family or adding to it by collecting or cross-breeding Such gardens now and then owe their existence to the difficulty of cultivating a flower, as was the case of a charming garden of the lovely forms of our native Primrose formed by a friend of mine, who thus describes it ·—

"A PRIMROSE GARDEN.—No flower better deserves a garden to itself than the Primrose.   It is so old a favourite, and has been cultivated into so many forms, that any one determined to have a Primrose garden may choose the kind he likes best, and set to work accordingly. There are the single-stalked Primroses, the earliest of all, flowering from the middle of March onwards, while some may be had in bloom as soon as the end of February.   They range in colour from pure white to deep primrose, and from palest pinky-lilac through strong red-purples to a colour nearly approaching blue, and there are also rich reds of many shades   There is not as yet any Primrose of a true pink colour, nor, though the type colour is yellow, are there as yet any strong yellows of the orange class   There are also double Primroses in nearly all the same colourings.   The Polyanthus, with its neat trusses of small flowers, though beautiful in the hand and indis-

Gardens of one flower: A Primrose garden in Surrey.

pensable in the good garden of hardy flowers, is not a plant for
the Primrose garden, as it makes no show in the mass. The grand
Primroses for garden effect are the large bunch-flowered kinds, white,
yellow, and orange-coloured, red, crimson, and rich brown ; of infinite
variety in form, texture, habit, and colouring, easy to raise to any
amount by seed, as also by division of the older plants. A Primrose
garden (part of which is here illustrated), that for some years has
been an ever-increasing source of pleasure and interest to its owners,
was formed a few years ago by making an opening about 70 yards
long, and varying from 10 yards to 15 yards wide, through a wild
copse of young Birch trees. The natural soil was very poor and
sandy, so it was prepared by a thorough trenching and a liberal
addition of loam and manure, which has to be renewed every year
No formal walks are made, but one main track is trodden down
about 2 feet wide near the middle of the space, dividing into two here
and there, where a broader clearing makes it desirable to have two
paths in the width. The older divided plants are put into groups
of a colour together, from twenty to fifty of a sort. The groups
of seedlings are of necessity more various, though they are more or
less true to the parent colour, so that a patch of a hundred seedlings
—from yellows, for instance—will give a general effect of yellow
throughout the group   The whites and yellows are kept at one end
of the garden, and the reds at the other ; the deepest yellows next to
the reds. Seen from a little distance, the yellow and white part of the
Primrose garden looks like a river of silver and gold flowing through
the copse. The white stems of the Birches and the tender green of
their young leaves help to form a pretty picture, which is at its best
when the whole is illuminated by the evening sunlight."

Some of the Plants for Reserve Garden and for Cutting Flowers.

Carnations	Pyrethrum	Grasses, the more	Campanula	Polyanthus
Phloxes	Schizostylis	graceful kinds	Chrysanthemums	Oxlips
Scarlet Lobelias	Chinese Pinks	Zinnias	Meadow Saffrons	Tulips
Pinks	Scabious	Sweet Sultan	Roses	Violets
Double Rockets	Blue Cornflower	Ranunculus	Crinum	American Cowslips
Iris	Sweet Williams	Anemone	Crocus	Gaillardia
Pansies	Stocks	Lilies	Dahlia	Gladiolus
Alstrœmeria	Wallflowers	Delphiniums	Pæonies	Everlastings
Tigridia	Grape Hyacinths	Narcissus	Pentstemon	Christmas Roses
Columbines		China Asters	Primroses	Lenten Roses

CHAPTER VI.

HARDY BULBOUS AND TUBEROUS FLOWERS, AND THEIR GARDEN USE.

AT no distant time lists of these things were mostly looked at for the sake of getting a few bulbs to force, but that day is past, at least, for all who now see the great part which hardy bulbous and tuberous plants must take in the outdoor gardens of the future. Since those days the hills of California and of Japan alone have given us a noble lily garden, and the plants of this order in cultivation now form a lovely host. We are not nearly so likely to want novelties as knowledge of how to make effective use of the nobler plants, such as the Narcissus, the glory of the spring, as the Lily is of the summer garden.

We may indeed be often tempted with Zephyr flowers, and Ixias and other plants, beautiful in warmer countries than ours, but delicate here, and only living with us as the result of care which is quite needless, but there are so many lovely things from the mountains and plains of the northern world, and from the mountains in all parts, as hardy as the wild Hyacinths of British woods, that our search will be more for the nobler materials and how to make artistic use of them than in quest of novelty as such.

LILIES.—It would be fair to begin with the Snowdrop, but we will take the plants in the order of their value; and, having regard to past service and the present beauty of the Lilies, they should take the first place among hardy bulbs. Who of those who remember the Orange and White Lilies of all English and Irish gardens would have looked for the splendid Lilies that have come to us within less than a generation? For size, and form, and lovely colour they surpass all we had ever dreamt of even among tropical flowers. The variety is so great that a volume would be required to describe them; the catalogues give us many of their names. The main thing for all who care for them is how to possess their beauty with the least amount of care and disappointment; and, happily, the question has been solved for many handsome kinds by planting them in the peat beds that were made at first wholly in the interest of the American shrubs. Some of the finest Lilies thrive admirably in these, and by adding here and there deep leaf-mould, rotten cow manure, and the like, other kinds may be grown, for some Lilies thrive best in such soil.   Nor need we neglect the mixed borders because we have new ways for our Lilies, as several of the European Lilies thrive perfectly in ordinary borders.   They may be naturalised too, or some of them, in deep moist peat bottoms ; for example, the American swamp Lily (L. superbum).   The mania for draining everything might even lead to evil in the case of some Lilies which inhabit the cold northern woods, and which do with a very different degree of moisture from that required by the Lilies of California, where the soil in summer is as road dust on a dry hill.   Lilies are so varied in their nature and stature that they may adorn almost any aspect in sun or shade.   The new and rare among them will have special beds or borders, and we have Lily men and even Lily maniacs who will have Lily gardens   And as these lovely flowers tumble into our lap, as it were, from the woods and hills of Western China, Japan, and California, untouched by man until he found them made to his hand a few years ago, it is reasonable to suppose that some of them would take care of themselves, if trusted in likely spots, with us.   I put some of the Panther Lily deep in a leafy hollow in a Sussex wood, just to see if it would survive in such conditions.   Whether owing to a series of cold wet seasons and the want of the glorious sun of the hills in Nevada County, California, where I found it, we know not, but after the first season it did not come up.   I thought no more of it, but a friend going into the same wood some years afterwards found a colony of it in bloom   So that we must not always cry out if Lilies do not come up, as they have a way of resting for a year now and then.

NARCISSUS —Next to the Lily in value as an outdoor flower is the Narcissus, though when we know the Iris better it may find a high place.   But the wondrous development of the garden forms of Narcissus during recent years, and their fitness for our climate, give it great value.   Mountain plants in origin, for the most part they are as hardy as riverside rushes, and those few southern forms that will only live in dry banks and at the foot of warm walls need not concern us who look for pictures of Narcissi in the open air.   We have not to ask where the Narcissi will grow, as there are few places they will not grow in with the usual garden culture, and in some cool, loamy soils they take to the turf as ducks to water.   Hence it is easy

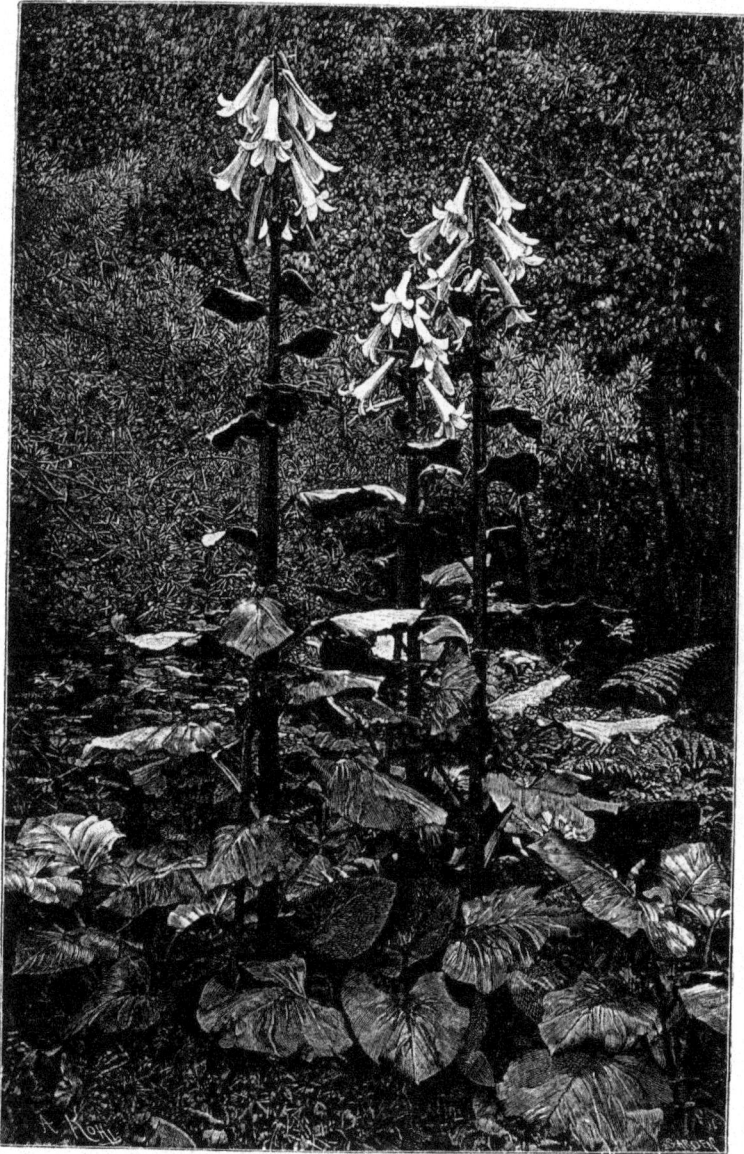

Group of Giant Indian Lilies in half-shady place (Surrey).

on many soils to have a spring garden of these flowers, naturally grouped and massed, set in turf, and giving us many flowers for the house as well as pictures in lawn and meadow. For this purpose what is chiefly wanted is that the bulb growers should offer the best hardy sorts for the wild garden by the thousand at low rates. These precious early flowers will also have their place in the garden for cut flowers or the nursery bed, where the many new forms of Narcissi raised in England must take their place until they become plentiful. The true hardiness of the flower allows of its being enjoyed in all parts of these scattered islands, from Scilly, where it is grown in quantities for the markets, to the north of Scotland. In Ireland the Narcissus is at home, and there are excellent collections in the College Botanic Gardens at Dublin and also at Glasnevin, while there

Narcissus princeps at St. Nicholas House, Scarborough.

is a very well-grown one at Cork, and Miss Currie, of Lismore, grows many of the most precious kinds. In old days the white Narcissi grown in the gardens spread here and there into orchards and fields, and so it happens that now we have to seek in Ireland some of the graceful white Narcissi.

IRIS.—The Iris is one of the oldest of our garden flowers, in many forms too, but, like the Lily, it has come to us in greater novelty and beauty of recent years, and as districts in Central Asia and Asia Minor are opened to collectors, we must have our Iris gardens too. And what so fair as an Iris garden? They are the Orchids of the north, many of them as hardy as reeds, and with more richness of colour than Orchids. The old Irises of our gardens are usually of the Germanica class; there is much variety among these groups, and they are very hardy and precious, and excellent for the adornment of gardens and even walls and thatched roofs, as we see in France, the Iris of this great group having a valuable power of thriving on such surfaces as well as on good' soil.

There is a group of waterside and water-loving Iris, much less seen in our gardens than the above, and some of them not yet come to us, but of great value   They are allied to the common yellow Iris of our watercourses, but are taller and richer in colour, the golden Iris (Aurea), Monnieri, and Ochroleuca being the best known so far, and very free, hardy, and beautiful plants they are, thriving, too, almost anywhere, but best in rich, moist soil   And we have the distinct gain of the splendid Japanese Iris, in its many strange forms, the Japanese surpassing all waterside Irises in its wide range of colour, though most beautiful perhaps in its simple forms, white and purple. This plant, though its beauty suggests that of the tropics, will grow side by side with our great water dock by any lake side, or even in a clay ditch, where only the coarsest weeds live. The Siberian Iris and the forms near it are very graceful beside streams or ponds, either in open or copsy places, and far more graceful and charming in such positions than in set borders. All these water-loving Irises will do for the wild garden in bold groups when we can spare them.

Then there are the brilliant purple and gold Iris reticulata and its allies, little bulbous Irises, for the spring garden, early and charming things, many beautiful , Irises that flower in winter and early spring, like the Algerian Iris , others happy in Britain on warm soils and warm corners, and some for the rock garden, like the crested Iris ; and the many pretty forms of Iris pumila, of some of which edgings were made in old gardens. The foliage of the evergreen Iris is so graceful and usually so nice in colour that artistic use may be made of it in that way. The most novel of all the groups of Iris, however, are the Cushion Irises, which promise much beauty, but are yet too little known to see how far that beauty may be preserved in our gardens   The old Iris Susiana has been known for many years, and some of its allies, like I. Lorteti and the Wolf Iris, seem more hardy and not less beautiful

TULIPS —The old garden Tulip, a favourite for generations, grown in the so-called florist varieties, and the source once of severe mania, is but one of a large number of wild Tulipa, many of which have come to us of late years from Central Asia   The old Tulips are the forms of an Italian species (T. Gesneriana), and these varieties are worthy of all the attention they ever had; but the wild form is as good as any of its varieties for splendid effect, and a selection should be made of its simpler colours, including a good white and yellow. The bedding Tulips, which are earlier in blooming, are forms of T scabriscapa though useful, are not nearly so valuable for their effect as the late tulips The new species coming from Central Asia and other lands promise to be very valuable, too, for their effect, though our climate may not suit all of them, as it does the fine hardy Gesneriana. The colour of these tulips is too fine to be missed, and, as the bloom is too short-lived to give beds under the windows to it, the best way is to plant them in borders, and, when scarce, in the nursery , when plentiful in the wild garden I put some in new hedgerow banks a few years ago, and also the wood tulip in a meadow regularly mown, and now have a splendid bloom every spring. As wild tulips abound in the south of Europe travellers might often get many roots which could be tried in this and other ways Some of the bedding tulips have very ugly slaty colours, and there is much waste in planting them. The Dutch bulb raisers care more for variety than beauty of colour, but the aim in our gardens should be to get more of the fine simple colours, and the wild kinds planted so far as we may in effective ways, a few trials in that way will show that it is a much more effective one than setting out the plants in tile or other patterns The later these wild tulips come into bloom the better, as it brings their nobler colour in when the harsh changes of the spring are nearly over, and in the north they will come in with the early summer days. These ideas of the more picturesque planting of the hardier Tulips need not take from the lover of the old florist kinds his Tulip garden, which was very charming with its long beds of good soil, and at its best in some sheltered—hedged in or walled—garden.

CROCUS.—If the Crocus has any fault it is courage in coming so early that it has to face every trouble of the spring, and green winters induce it to open too early Yet what promise it brings us of the many-blossomed spring in border and in lawn ; for, in addition to the old and good way in garden borders, the Crocus, at least all the forms and series and the hardy and vigorous European kinds, is easily naturalised in lawns or meadow turf, and others even under Beech trees as in Crowsley Park. As regards this question, it should be remembered that the Crocus is wild in rich meadow grass in various parts of England, at Nottingham and in Essex The autumnal kinds may be naturalised too, but they ask perhaps for a warmer soil than the vernal kinds. Recent years have brought us many new Crocuses The effect of the old kinds is not surpassed, but their beauty may be more fully shown than in lines and dots by scattering them in natural-looking groups in grassy places among trees or in the open turf.

SNOWDROP AND SNOWFLAKE.—The old Snowdrop gives as good an effect as any other, but the many new varieties give the Snowdrop more value. Whether these new forms are species or varieties matters little , their value as garden plants is the only question that concerns

Tulip garden at the Castle Dingwall.

flower-gardeners. Who would have thought a few years ago that our Snowdrop was only one of a large number taking care of themselves in the mountains of Asia Minor and other regions? Others are coming, and when these increase in our gardens we shall have fresh aids to make our spring gardens more beautiful. As these new kinds are mostly plants from cool regions, they will probably be easily naturalised in many soils. The snowflake must not be forgotten—few spring flowers are more free than the vernal and late Snowflakes

SCILLAS, HYACINTHS, AND LIKE PLANTS—The lovely early group of plants allied to our Wood Hyacinth—Scilla, Chionodoxa, and Hyacinthus (the more tiny and dwarf wild species are referred to here under this last name)—ask for some thought as to their artistic use. The Scillas are well known, but the newer forms of Chionodoxa give an unlooked-for loveliness of blue very early in the spring, and show a pretty variety in their delicate colours, and yet there is no more lovely thing among them than the Taurian Scilla, a large form of the long-neglected Scilla bifolia. It is so early and so deep a blue that one may get rich effects with it very early. The more tiny and select of all these plants are alpine, delightful for rock-gardens, and all the more so if we can use them in visible groups. The stouter kinds, such as the larger Chionodoxa, are coming in such numbers that we may try their effects in many ways, it is impossible to omit them from whatever kind of spring gardening we adopt.

The common Hyacinth—in its double forms at least—is so stiff that we take little interest in it for the flower garden; but the simpler colours of the single kinds deserve a place. Would it not be worth while growing the single Hyacinth provincialis from which these all come? Hyacinths will come up year after year in flower beds, and throwing away the roots after once blooming is a mistake.

OTHER LILIES—Apart from the true Lilies there are certain plants to which the name is also given betimes, such as the Torch Lily (Kniphofia), the Day Lily (Hemerocallis), the Peruvian Lily (Alstrœmeria), the African Lily (Agapanthus), the Belladonna Lily (Amaryllis), the Cape Lily (Crinum), the Plantain Lily (Funkia), the Wood Lily (Trillium), the Mariposa Lily (Calochortus), besides other Lilies that do not come under our present heading, or which do not ask for thought as regards their effective use.

The Torch Lilies are brilliant in colour, and have been added to of recent years, but severe winters have thinned them, and they will always be best in dry soils and in sunny positions, protected in winter. They are best kept apart from flowers more refined in colour, such as the Tea Rose. The Day Lilies are a really hardy race, and most of them will grow anywhere. With their fine leaves and showy, well-formed flowers, they may be used with good effect in various ways. The Peruvian Lily is valuable, but far more beautiful on warm soils. If on cool soils—and in cool districts it fails—we must prepare beds for it, but the best way in gardening is always to grow the flowers that thrive without great labour in the soil we have   The Belladonna Lily can be grown in no more effective way than the old one of planting it under south walls   The Cape Lilies have increased of late years from hybrids and otherwise, and are worth attention in deep soil in warm corners near walls that protect them from the north   The African Lily is most important for its unrivalled blue, but, save in the warmest parts of the south, where it may live in the open air protected, it is essential to give it greenhouse or like protection in winter.   It is one of the plants for which the expense of tubs or large pots is worth indulging in, and there are new and handsome kinds, which make the culture more interesting.   The Wood Lilies are valuable because they give us effects both distinct and beautiful in peat borders or bog gardens   Shade is not essential, though we think the best effects are attained in half-shady spots.

The Mariposa Lilies are beautiful indeed, some of them almost surpassing any flowers of the old world ; but they come from one of the best climates and warmest soils in the world, and one can hardly hope that they will thrive in our climate without special care   Yet such charming flowers will always have a place in curious gardens, where they will thrive in frames and warm corners   Such plants, however, cannot be depended on for much effect in the open garden, though new kinds are being brought from Western America which may thrive in our climate, and help to show us the beauty of these singularly lovely things

ANEMONES AND RANUNCULUS.—The Poppy Anemone has been a welcome flower in our gardens for hundreds of years, and it should never be forgotten, save in cold soils where it dwindles   Many now grow it well from seed, but the old way of planting the tubers of favourite kinds and colours should be carried out in the flower garden in Rose beds or in any beds to spare.   The Scarlet Anemone and its varieties is also precious , the Star Anemone, so charming in Italy and Greece in spring, is rarely seen happy in our gardens which are too cold for it, no doubt, so it may well be left out in favour of the hardier sorts.   Valuable as the brightest Anemones are, the old Turban and Persian Ranunculus, and other forms were once a great charm of the flower garden, and should not be forgotten in warm soils, where they thrive, but they perish in severe winters, and require some care.

VARIOUS—The old Dog's-Tooth Violet of the mountains of Europe has been joined in our gardens of recent years by a number of its American relations, graceful plants for peat borders, but as yet not so valuable as the European kind in its various forms, which are among the prettiest early spring flowers. They are, moreover, true wild garden plants, which thrive in turf, coming up every year even more faithfully than Crocus or Snowdrop. The Snake's-head, too (Fritillaria), is a charming wild garden plant, thriving in grass in rich or wet meadows, where not native it may well be introduced. The new yellow Fritillaries give a greater interest to this group of plants, some of which are fitted for the wild garden, but we never could see the charms of the Crown Imperials, with their offensive odour. The Stars of Bethlehem (Ornithogalum) thrive in grass, and are pretty in it. Unfortunately the handsome Arabian kind is not hardy. The Montbretias are plants of somewhat recent appearance in our gardens, and they have a vigour and hardiness we do not look for in Cape plants, and a tenacious way of growing and increasing even in cold poor soil, and are, therefore, valuable where we wish to have close tufts of graceful leaves and gay blossoms below flowering shrubs not set too closely on the ground. Grape Hyacinths (Muscari) are often very pretty, and nearly always hardy. I use them freely in grass, where their blue is very pretty in spring. The choicer newer kinds will find a place in the nursery beds or rock-garden till more plentiful.

Among the new plants we have one of fine distinction in the Giant Asphodels (Eremurus), plants of noble port and vigour, but which, though here and there grown and flowered well, are not as yet proved for our climate, with its often open, snowless winters. We must find out the kinds really hardy and that bloom handsomely with us before we can judge of their value in the flower garden.

The old tiger flowers (Tigridia) should not be forgotten, especially on limestone or other warm soils, where they are most at home. There are several new kinds, which make the family of more value. Plants that give much pleasure from their good colours are the Triteleia and Brodiœa. Some new and pretty effects will be given by the best of these as soon as plentiful.

So noble a plant as the Gladiolus should not, perhaps, have been left to the end, but the fact that the finest class are only half hardy, and require care, makes them less important in our country than Lilies and Narcissi, that give so much beauty with little or no care. The years pass so swiftly, and are so full of cares, that things demanding two important attentions yearly—*i e.*, taking up and planting— must take a minor place, except in the case of growers who make a special care of them. The groups known as Lemoinei and Saundersi hybrids, being hardier, give better results, but generally our climate is against the older Gladioli, and disease very often comes with any large attempt to grow them.

HARDY BULBS FOR CUT FLOWERS.—The special or reserve garden includes beds for hardy bulbs—a very good way of growing them, and for supplying flowers for the house.   A curious habit of the flowers of bulbs is that, cut from the plants when just opening and put into water, they get larger than they would if left on the plants out of doors, and this should lead us to encourage many lovely flowers among hardy bulbs that are among the best for our rooms.   Hitherto the horror of the gardener has been cutting flowers for the house ; but if cutting prolongs his bloom, strengthens his plants, and gives all who care for his flowers a fuller enjoyment of them, we may secure his powerful aid.   Consider what one may escape in storms, frosts, and other dangers if a flower, cut just on arriving at maturity, lasts

Bed of Italian Narcissus.

longer indoors than out, and actually, as in the case of the Narcissus, gets larger ! Narcissi, through their hardiness and drooping heads, endure our climate better than any other flowers, and yet severe storms will beat them about and destroy flowers that might have lived for days in the house.   Large showy flowers like Tulips, suffer with every heavy shower.   Anything which makes it easier to have flowers in the house is a real gain ; their exquisite forms are best seen, and tell their story best when brought near to the eye.   A flower of our yellow wood Tulip opening and closing, and showing its changing form in a room, gives ideas of beauty which cannot be gleaned by glancing at a bed of bulbs.   A variety of hardy bulbs should therefore be grown for their value as cut flowers, apart from their use in the garden.

HARDY BULBS AMONG CHOICE SHRUBS.—One of the most

marked improvements is the planting of handsome bulbs in masses of Rhododendrons and like bushes. These beds, as usually planted, are interesting only when in flower, and not always then, owing to the flat surface into which the shrubs are pressed, Lilies, therefore, and the finer bulbs may with great advantage be placed among the shrubs. In many cases where this plan has been carried out, it has almost changed the entire aspects of gardens, and given various beautiful types of life instead of only one, and many fine rare bulbs find a home in such beds, which should be sacred from the spade In placing choice, peat-loving shrubs, give the bushes room to fully attain their natural forms, and plant the interspaces with finer bulbs Light and shade, relief and grace, are among the merits of this mode of planting Beds of the smaller shrubs will do admirably for the smaller and more delicate bulbs, the shelter of low shrubs being an advantage to many little bulbs whose leaves are apt to suffer from cold winds In this way we get relief, variety, and longer bloom, and the shrubs show their forms better when they have free play of light and air about them.

BULBS IN BEDS ON TURF.—Bold beds of Lilies and the taller bulbs are admirable for the lawn, and for quiet corners of the pleasure-ground.   The showy beds of bulbs which are to be seen in public and other gardens, and which come so largely into spring gardens, are familiar to all.   The beds suggested here are of a higher and more permanent nature, and are intended to be placed where they will be let alone.   At Moulton Grange some years ago I saw on the turf in a quiet corner a bed of Tiger Lilies which had no other flowers near to mar its beauty It was a large oval bed, and the colour of the finely grown Lilies was brilliant and effective seen through the trees and glades In point of colour alone, nothing could be better ; the mass of bloom was profuse, and the plants, about 6 feet high, told well in the garden landscape.   The plants had a great advantage in habit, form, and colour over the usual dwarf type of showy "bedding" plant Many hardy flowers of the highest beauty would have as effective colour if we took equal pains with them Colour on a 6-foot plant is usually more effective than on a plant 6 inches or 12 inches high, and some hardy Lilies are well over 6 feet high.   This Lily bed was on one of those little strips of turf which occur by most shrubberies, and within a few yards of a walk, so that it could be easily seen Among the most lovely beds are those of the nobler Lilies, while Iris, and many beautiful Day Lily, Pæony, Gladiolus, and Cape Hyacinth may be grouped with them or near them.   It may be as well to note that what is meant here is not wild gardening with bulbs, but very good cultivation of them, and surfacing and edging the beds with spring flowers.

Some Hardy Bulbous and Tuberous Plants for British Flower Gardens.

Acis	Calochortus	Gladiolus	Narcissus	Scilla
Agapanthus	Chionodoxa	Galtonia	Orchis	Sparaxis
Allium	Colchicum	Hyacinthus	Ornithogalum	Sternbergia
Alstrœmeria	Convallaria	Iris	Oxalis	Tigridia
Amaryllis	Crocus	Ixiolirion	Pæonia	Trillium
Anemone	Cyclamen	Leucojum	Pancratium	Triteleia
Anthericum	Erythronium	Lilium	Puschkinia	Tritonia
Arum	Fritillaria	Montbretia	Ranunculus	Tropæolum
Calla	Galanthus	Muscari	Schizostylis	Tulipa

Iris border (at Bulwick).

CHAPTER VII.

ANNUAL AND BIENNIAL PLANTS, AND HALF-HARDY PLANTS ANNUALLY RAISED FROM SEED.

WHATEVER we may do with perennials, shrubs, or hardy bulbs, the plants in this class must ever be of great value to the flower-gardener; and among the most pleasant memories of flower-garden things are often those of annual or biennial plants : tall and splendid Stocks in a farmhouse garden on a chalky soil, seen on a bright day in early spring ; Wallflowers in London market gardens and in cottage gardens, when not cut down by cruel winters; Snapdragons on old garden walls, and bright Marigolds everywhere; Hollyhock lines, Sweet Pea hedges, and Mignonette carpets; Evening Primrose, Poppies, Sweet Scabious, and Sweet-williams. However rich a garden may be in hardy flowers or bedding plants, it is wise in our climate to depend a good deal upon annuals. Although they do not last so long in bloom, and are not so fine in quality as Lilies or Roses, yet they can generally be depended upon for a very handsome show of flower in early autumn, particularly in northern and cool districts. In some cases it would not be wise to sacrifice the summer garden for autumnal flowering plants, but where people do not much enjoy their garden except in autumn, it is essential to make good use of those treated of herein.

Where the choicest flowers are grown in beds near the house, or in what should be the flower garden, autumnal annuals are not so good as more enduring plants, although useful as an aid In many cases the best way would be to grow the annuals in separate borders, even in borders in the kitchen garden, as they are very well grown at Campsey Ash Like most other plants, they enjoy fresh ground, and where they are grown in borders by themselves it is easy to enrich the ground, and make it fitted for them, easier than when grown among perennials, Roses and the like. With this precaution the culture is very simple ; in the south some attention to watering is essential in dry years, in the north the moist cool climate gives the best results

In wet seasons and in wet northern districts annuals surprise us by their vigour and beauty In warmer counties the effect of the heat may in the case of the hardy kinds be met by autumn-sowing in good rich ground The autumn sowings are the best The plants not only flower much sooner, but, where the soil and climate suit them, they are stronger and more beautiful The reason why they are so often seen in poor condition is that they are sown on hungry soil and are crowded.

Concerning crowding, "Salmoniceps" writes —" I have just measured a plant to-day (October 4) of Nemophila insignis, sown more than a year ago It has been in flower since May, and measures now 4 feet by 3 feet 10 inches. It would take a long time to count the blossoms, although they are not so large as the earlier ones The plant grows in a new and rich border According to the ordinary way of sowing annuals, this single plant occupies the space which is usually allotted to a whole packet of seed "

In nature, annuals are usually autumn-sown and gather strength in the winter In growing a number of annuals from various countries, we must remember that our winters can be faced by the hardy ones only, such as the Sweet Pea, Cornflower, Silene, Nemophila, Viscaria, Limnanthes, Larkspur, Poppy, and Scabious Annuals are best in masses or groups, and they are never perhaps so full of colour and beauty as on an old rich vine border.

In considering the best kinds we will look more at the important groups of plants, as there is a great number of curious kinds that might be named here, but they are not so important for effect

Among annual and biennial flowers we have the lovely Everlastings of Australia, which have an order of beauty quite distinct from those we see in gardens into which annuals do not enter Carefully gathered, they have the additional charm that they may adorn our houses during the winter. The Pimpernels, which with their pretty blue flowers were once made charming use of in gardens, are much neglected. The Mexican Poppy is a pretty flower and quite distinct. Among annuals we find plants of fine foliage or habit, such as the Hemp, Castor Oil Tree and other Mallows, Maize and other grasses, Cotton and Blessed Thistles. The annual Chrysanthemums of Southern Europe and Northern Africa, and indeed of our own fields, are charming in effect. The annual Convolvuli are pretty, and in southern gardens may be used charmingly The annual Larkspurs are so little used in gardens that it is only in seed farms that we have the pleasure of seeing them now and then in all their beauty. The annual Chinese Pinks are very charming grown in sunny beds and good soil Our native Foxglove, which takes such good care of itself in many of our woodlands, breaks in the hands of the gardener into beautiful varieties well worth growing, if not in the garden, in shrubberies and in copses and woods. It is a good plan, when any ground is broken up for fence-making or rough planting, to scatter a few seeds of the white and other pretty kinds and leave them to take care of themselves There are many graceful grasses which may be treated as annuals, and their flowers, like the Everlasting flowers, be in bloom through the winter. The night-smelling Stocks will appeal to some, but are rather too strong in odour for others. The annual Hibiscus when well grown are effective plants, and the same may be said of the Hollyhock, for which probably the best way is to raise it from seed, as in that way we can fight better against the fungus which destroys it. The Single Hollyhock is worthy of much care and is often very effective. The Flaxes are very pretty annuals, red and blue, and even the common cultivated Flax is a beautiful plant. The beauty of the Ice plants, of which we see so little in our country, is fairly shown by the little annual one. In our day quite a series of beautiful forms of Mignonette have come to add to the charms of that always welcome plant. The annual and biennial Evening Primroses are often extremely valuable and showy.

The Sweet Scabious are pretty and varied in colour and so fragrant. Of Sweet Peas there is a delightful series in our own day, when so many kinds have been raised that one could easily make a garden of them. No words can exaggerate their value, either in mixed or separate colours, and they should be both autumn and spring sown, so as to get a chance of those fine tall hedges of Sweet Peas which come where we sow in autumn and get the plants safely through the winter, and they are doubly valuable owing to the many beautiful new kinds. Zinnia is extremely fine in colour, but in our country it wants warm soils and the best positions in order to do well In Italy, Austria, and South Germany they are much more beautiful and vigorous than with us.

Some annual plants, like the Cornflower, Sweet Sultan, Sweet Pea, Scabious, are precious for cutting for the house, and may be grown

White Foxglove.   Engraved from a photograph by H. Hyde of a self-sown plant in shrubbery
at Gravetye Manor.

with the hardy flowers for this purpose where there is room for it , others are good for trellis-work, and others for surfaces we wish to adorn with pretty climbers, such as Canary Creeper, Maurandya, Adlumia, Gourds, Convolvulus.

The various French and African Marigolds, and the prettier forms of the pot Marigold, are very showy plants, and, for those who love much colour, are almost essential, and the same may be said of the various annual Calliopsis   The China Aster used to be grown much better than it is generally now, and there is no doubt, where people do not get much colour from other plants, such as Roses and the finer perennials, the China Aster in its many forms is useful.   But more important by far are the various kinds of Stock, which have the added charm of fragrance, and which do so well in many gardens with light and warm soils in the north and in Scotland   Cosmos are pretty plants worthy of a place, and the best of the annual kinds of Datura are picturesque and distinct.   Chinese Pinks are very beautiful and charming in variety.   The Gaillardias, which are such poor perennials in many soils, are in some cases better raised as annuals, and there are annual kinds of value.   The Gilias are very pretty, varied, and hardy, and some very dwarf, forming a carpet for taller plants.

The Godetias, allied to the Evening Primroses, are handsome when well grown, especially the white and simple coloured kinds, and where they live over the winter, from autumn sowing, they are very strong and handsome the following year.   The many varieties of the annual Ipomæ are graceful, there being much charming variety among the blooms, and with these may be named the various kinds of Convolvulus minor, which does not climb.   Lavatera and Malope are handsome plants in the autumn garden, as are the Lupins, well grown, and the new Nemesia from the Cape is charming.   The white Tobacco and the true Tobacco are handsome in warm soils.   We think the various Nigellas very interesting, while every one should have the annual Phloxes, now to be had in such good colours, and the Portulacas, which are so showy on warm borders.   The Salpiglossis is a beautiful plant, especially where we take the trouble to select the simpler colours, the amber coloured one being very fine   The Sweet Scabious has charming varieties, and is often very fine in colour, though not so good on heavy and cool soils

The Sweet Sultans are pretty, and useful for cutting for the house, and Love-lies-bleeding (Amaranthus) and its allies are quaintly effective.   The Snap-Dragons, which are often treated as annuals, are frequently excellent when grown in their simple colours, the striped kinds not being nearly so good in effect.   The annual Poppies are essential where a good display is hoped for from annuals, also the

Mexican and Californian Poppies. Such handsome plants as the varieties of Tropæolum are also many of them beautiful annuals. Among plants of, perhaps, less importance than some of the preceding, the following may be mentioned : Bartonia, Brachycome, Calandrinia, Cosmidium, Nolana, Didiscus, Kaulfussia, Linum, Lobelia, Martynia, Mesembryanthemum, Nycterinia, Platystemon, Saponaria, Senecio, Stenactis, and Xeranthemum, as affording some good plants for those interested in flower gardening with annual and biennial plants.

HALF-HARDY PLANTS TREATED AS ANNUALS.—It is not every one who has the means to winter a large number of tender bedding

Bed of " China Asters," showing effect of well-grown annual plants in garden.]

plants, and the keeping of a large stock involves much work, and takes up space that might be better occupied.. But a garden may be made very gay in summer with half-hardy plants raised from seed, and without keeping a single plant over the winter in the greenhouse. In seedlings there may be differences in habit and colour, but this should be no objection. There are a few plants which come from seed true to the type through many generations, like Verbena venosa. Seedling Verbenas make a handsome bed, and usually do much better so grown than from cuttings. Balsams, again, are not half so much used for open-air decoration as they deserve to be, and those who have only seen them starving in small

I

pots cannot form an idea of their beauty when planted out in good open soil, away from trees and in warm soils   Take the border Pansies in various shades of purple, yellow, and white.   Varieties may be raised in the early spring for planting out the same summer, and so of the Verbena, Pelargonium, Pyrethrum, Salvia patens, S. argentea, Heliotrope, and Snapdragons, which should be sown in heat in January ; to the Petunia, Phlox Drummondi, Dianthus, Indian Pink, Ageratum, and Lobelia, which in February should be sown in pans in heat, and, if kept growing, will be ready for planting out in May.   Begonias for bedding may be grown from seed in the same year, but are more effective if raised during the preceding year, selected according to colour, and stored in winter ready for bedding out early in summer.   Fuchsias sown in January flower well in August.   Of fine-leaved plants which can be raised from seed for use in the open-air the same year, there are Amaranthus, Celosia, Centaurea, Cineraria, Humea, Cannà, Chamæpeuce, Nicotiana, Ricinus, Solanum, and Wigandia.

Old plants of Verbenas and like plants kept through the winter harbour the eggs of vermin always ready to eat up the collection if it is neglected for a week, but, starting with clean houses and frames, and with seeds in early spring, the gardener makes a better fight against his many insect enemies.   As regards the plants one would like to raise in this way, seedsmen should select and fix distinct colours of different races of plants.   It would not be difficult to select a bluish or purple Verbena which one might count on as coming pretty true from seed   We have so much relied upon cuttings and old plants that the raising of fine seedlings has seldom had fair attention.   Many raise seeds, but few give the early thinning, the light, the sturdy growth, and the unchecked culture that seedlings require , but now, when we may raise not only the annual pure and simple, but the half-hardy flower-garden plants, and the nobler hardy plants like Carnations and Hollyhocks, seed-raising for the flower-garden deserves much attention.

BIENNIAL PLANTS are usually such as make their growth in one year and flower the next, but the line between biennial and annual is not a strict one, because in their native countries annual plants often spring up in one year, and flower the next In countries with open winters and hot summers, annuals do so naturally, and begin to grow in the first rains through the winter, and flower strongly the next year—these often being kinds sown in spring in gardens.   Hollyhocks, Foxgloves, Chimney Campanula, and Sweet Williams come under this head, but in some cases early raising in spring gives us a chance of blooming some of them the same year as they are sown.   In any case it is better for simplicity's sake to group all annual and biennial plants together, and with them the half-hardy plants raised from seed for use in the flower garden, as the work of raising all is, to a great extent, the same.

Some of the more important Families of Annual and Biennial Plants, and of Half-hardy Plants raised from Seed for the Flower Garden.

Acroclinium	Centranthus	Hedysarum	Mesembryan-	Ricinus
Adlumia	Cheiranthus	Helichrysum	themum	Salpiglossis
Agathæa	China Aster	Heliophila	Mignonette	Salvia
Ageratum	Chrysanthemum	Heliotrope	Mimulus	Saponaria
Agrostemma	Clarkia	Hesperis	Mirabilis	Scabious
Alonsoa	Clintonia	Hibiscus	Myosotis	Schizanthus
Alyssum	Convolvulus	Hollyhock	Nemesia	Schizopetalon
Amaranthus	Coreopsis	Iberis	Nemophila	Senecio
Amberboa	Cosmidium	Impatiens	Nicotiana	Silene
Ammobium	Cosmos	Ionopsidium	Nierembergia	Solanum
Anagallis	Crepis	Ipomæa	Nigella	Sorghum
Antirrhinum	Cuphea	Ipomopsis	Nolana	Specularia
Arctotis	Datura	Isotoma	Nycterinia	Sphenogyne
Argemone	Delphinium	Kaulfussia	Œnothera	Stenactis
Artemisia	Dianthus	Lasthenia	Onopordon	Stocks
Bartonia	Didiscus	Lavatera	Oxalis rosea	Sweet Peas
Begonia	Digitalis	Leptosiphon	Oxyura	Sweet William
Boerkhausia	Erysimum	Leptosyne	Papaver	Tagetes
Brachycome	Erythræa	Limnanthes	Pelargonium	Tropæolum
Calandrinia	Eschscholtzia	Linaria	Pentstemon	Verbascum
Calceolaria	Eucharidium	Linum	Petunia	Verbena
Calendula	Eutoca	Loasa	Phacelia	Viola
Calliopsis	Fuchsia	Lobelia	Pharbitis	Virginia Stock
Campanula	Gaillardia	Lophospermum	Phlox	Viscaria
Cannabis	Gilia	Lupin	Platystemon	Waitzia
Cape Marigold	Glaucium	Maize	Podolepis	Whitlavia
Catananche	Godetia	Malope	Polygonum	Zea
Celosia	Gourds	Malva	Portulaca	Zeranthemum
Celsia	Grasses	Martynia	Pyrethrum	Zinnia
Centaurea	Gypsophila	Maurandya	Rhodanthe	

Zea : Knockdolian, Colmonell, N.B.

I 2

CHAPTER VIII.

FLOWERING SHRUBS AND TREES, AND THEIR ARTISTIC USE.

SPRING comes to us wreathed in Honeysuckle, and summer brings the Wild Rose and the May bloom, and these are but messengers of a host of lovely shrubs and low trees of the hills and plains of northern and temperate regions, and also of the high mountains of countries like India, where there are vast alpine regions with shrubs as hardy as our own, as we see in the case of the white Clematis that covers many an English cottage wall with its fair white bloom. If we think of the pictures formed in thousands of places in England, Scotland, and Ireland, by the May alone, we may get an idea of the precious beauty there is in the American, Asiatic, and European kinds, some of which flower later than our own and make the May bloom season longer. Nothing is lovelier among flowering trees than a group of the various Thorns, beautiful also in fruit, and the foliage of some kinds is finely coloured in autumn. The Thorns are but one branch of, perhaps, the most important order of flowering trees, embracing the Apples (a garden in their varied flowers alone); Pears, wild and cultivated, Crabs, pretty in bloom and bright in fruit, Quinces, Medlars, Snowy Mespilus, Almonds, Double Cherries, Japan Quinces, Plums (including Sloe and Bullace), not to speak of a number of less important families. Among these, the larger and more important branches of this great order of plants, there is some likeness in habit and size, which allows of similar use.

The Double Peaches are among the most precious of trees of this order, but for some reason we rarely see them in any but a miserable state in England. In France they are sometimes lovely not only in the flower, but in the mass of colour from healthy growth. It may be that the failure of the shoots to ripen in our cool climate is owing to some weakness through grafting on a bad stock. There is such a great and noble variety among these trees that there is room for distinct effects. An excellent point in favour of trees like Thorns, Crabs, Almonds, and Bird Cherries is that, in their maturity, they, in groups or single specimens, stand free on the turf—free, too, from all care, and it is easy to see how important this is for all who care for English tree-fringed lawns—a long way more beautiful than any other kind of tree garden.

It is not only the flowers on the trees we have to think of, but also in the house—as cut flowers gathered when the buds are ready to open —gathering the branchlets and long twigs before the flowers are quite out and placing them in vases in rooms. In very bad weather this way will prolong the bloom for us, or even save it in the case of very hard frost, and in a cold spring it will advance the bloom a little, the warmth of the house giving a few days' gain in time of opening. As to the kinds of shrubs that may be cut for the house in this way, there are many of the same race, from the Sloe to the beautiful kinds of Apple. There is a good deal in putting them into the right sort of glass. The Japanese are very clever in fitting the flowers into vases so that each may show its form and beauty best. Mr Alfred Parsons says he noticed that flowers seem to last longer in bronze, in which, it may be, the action of the light is less than in an ordinary vessel.

While such trees as the Almond or Crab will usually be in the more distant parts of the garden picture, the variety of flowering shrubs is so great that we may choose from among them for the most precious of flower garden beds. Take an ordinary flower garden under the windows of the house, often with the beds in winter as bare as oilcloth. What beautiful groups of flowering evergreens we might plant in them! Mountain Laurels (Kalmia), Japan and American Andromeda, Azaleas, choice Evergreen Barberries, alpine Cotoneaster, Evergreen Daphne, Desfontainea, in the south; the taller hardy Heaths, Escallonia, Ledum, alpine and wild forms of Rhododendron, Sweet Gale, Star bush, and various Laurustinus, leaving out not a few which thrive only in the warmer districts   Charming gardens might be made of such bushes, not lumped together, but in open groups, with the more beautiful American hardy flowers between them, such as the Wood Lily and Mocassin flower, many rare Lilies, and beautiful bulbous flowers of all seasons   The light and shade and variety in such beds of choice evergreens and flowers mingled are charming, and the plan would be a permanent one as it would tend to abolish the never-ending digging in the flower garden. Beds of flowering shrubs in the flower garden are not always so well suited for small gardens , but in bold ones, now naked in winter, it would make them sightly even at that season, and much easier to deal with in early summer

The Rhododendrons of the hybrid sorts are too much used, and, as they are nearly always grafted, the common stock that bears them in the end kills the plant it should support, and so we too often see the common pontic kind   Yet there are many beautiful things among these hybrids   The good colours are well worth picking out from them, and the aim of the planter should be to show the habit and form of the plant.   This does not mean that they may not be grouped or massed just as before, but openings of all sizes should be left among them for light and shade, and for handsome herbaceous plants that die down in the winter, thus allowing the full light for half the year to evergreens.

In the south and west the various Arbutus are charming for lawns and ravines, and for sheltering the flower garden, as is also the sweet Bay Laurel, but the common Cherry Laurel and the Portugal should not be planted near anything precious.

The hardy Azaleas are, considering their great number and variety, perhaps the most precious flowering shrubs we have , they are fine in form of bush, even when they get little freedom, and superb in colour, the foliage in autumn, too, being rich in colour in sunny places.   The Hydrangeas are noble plants in warm valleys, and on soils where they are not too often cut down by the winter , not only the common one of the markets, which, in soils where it turns blue, is so effective in the garden, but a variety of good kinds, among which should always be the oak-leaved Hydrangea, as old plants of it are so handsome. As these are plants that cannot be grown everywhere, this is a good reason why they should be made much of where the climate suits them.   There are few garden sights more interesting than groups of Hydrangeas well grown and placed, and it is one we rarely see

The Brooms have many effective plants and none more so than the common and the Spanish Brooms, which should be massed on banks, or where they will come into the picture, and some of the smaller Brooms are excellent for rock-gardens.   The Furze in all its obtainable forms is just as precious, as it blooms so early, it will grow almost anywhere, and it brightens up a landscape as no other plant does. We have only to place it in any rough spots to enjoy it without care. Native shrubs should not be neglected , the wild single Guelder Rose is as pretty a shrub as any from across the sea, while all the hardy kinds may give us good and bold effects grouped with or near such bushes as Deutzias, Weigelas, Mock Oranges—all plants of high value and much variety.

From an artistic point of view nothing is better than groups of our hardy Heaths in any open place where room can be found for them, including white heather and all other strong varieties of heather, as well as all other kinds of hardy Heaths. After planting they give little trouble, and they are good in colour even in winter, being generally happiest out of the garden proper, where any other wild plants may be allowed to grow among them. No doubt, the choicest and smallest of these Heaths deserve careful garden culture, but for effect the forms of our common Heather, the Cornish and Irish Heaths, are the best, and in bold masses not primly kept, but, once well rooted, allowed to mingle with any pretty wild plants We might even assist this idea by sowing or planting other things, such as Foxgloves, Harebells, or the small Furze, among the Heaths When Heaths are grown in this way their bloom is charming from the first peep of spring, when the little rosy Heath of the mountains of central Europe begins to open, till the autumn days, and even the mild winter ones, when the delicately tinted Portuguese Heath (E. codonodes) blooms in the south and west of England.

We take little notice of such minor things as the Fire-bush, so lovely in Cornwall, and pretty also in other seashore districts, as it may not be enjoyed in the country generally, and we also leave out some others, like the Witch and Japan Hazels, the Winter-sweet, and the Allspice bushes, which, though pretty seen near at hand, do not give us those definite effects in the garden landscape which it is well to seek if we wish to get out of the fatal jumble of the common shrubbery. The Escallonias, though very precious in seashore gardens and in the south on warm soils, are apt to go into mourning after hard winters elsewhere So many of our island gardens are near the sea that we must not undervalue these shrubs, but a constant source of waste is the planting of things not really hardy in districts where they perish in hard winters, such as the Arbutus about London and in the midlands And, even where things seem hardy, some of them, like Fuchsias, never give the charming effects we get from them in the west of Ireland, in Wales, and in warm coast gardens, whatever care we take Such facts should not discourage, because they only emphasise the lesson that the true way in a garden is for each to do what soil and climate allow of, and in that way we arrive at the most important artistic gain of all, *i e* that each garden has its own distinct charms.

A very lovely group is the Lilacs, much enriched of recent years by the introduction of new species and many charming varieties of the common old Lilac—lovely plants, worthy of the finest days of our English spring. Few of the forms found in France seem to thrive in our gardens, owing to grafting on the Privet, which often, after a year or two's poor bloom, kills the plant and begins to take care of itself How much evil has been done to English ideas of flowering shrubs by thrusting this Privet everywhere! Lilacs, being hardy in all parts of Britain, deserve our best care, and should always be grouped together in the open sun They should always be bought from nurserymen who raise them from layers or suckers in the good old way, and should be, once grown up, always kept a little open and free by simple pruning, so that we may get handsome trusses With these, too, must be grouped such lovely things as the Snow-drop tree, the Stuartias, and bush Magnolias. The Magnolias have recently become more numerous, and it will be easy soon to have a Magnolia garden, at least in favoured places. The tree Mag-nolias should come among the taller flowering trees in the distant parts of our flower grove—Horse Chestnuts, Buckeyes, Tulip Trees, Laburnums, Catalpa, and Yellow Wood. The Alpine Laburnum, so very beautiful in bloom, becomes a tall slender tree where not overcrowded, and the flowering Ash (Ornus) must not be forgotten among the taller flowering trees. For the Paulownia, so beautiful in France and Italy in spring, our climate is not warm enough to secure full size or health, save in the most favoured places in the south.

Some shrubs of modest charm as to their flowers give very pretty effects in well-placed groups, such as the flowering Currant, Tamarix, and Ceanothus on walls But none are more charming than the wild Roses in summer, the Sweet Briar being taken as representing our native wild Roses, the Glossy Rose (R. lucida), the American wild Roses ; the many-flowered Rose (Polyantha), and the Japanese (R. rugosa). These and others I have planted in hedgerows and rough fences, and have never planted anything that has given a more beautiful return.

The Judas Tree is neglected in England, and rarely planted in an effective way. In the Parc Monceau in Paris there is a beautiful grove of it in which trees of various ages form one family party, so to say, showing some differences in colour and earliness. Such slight but often valuable differences arise when we raise trees from seed and do not slavishly follow the habit of grafting one thing on another This is one of the gains of following a more natural mode of

The White Indian Azalea (A. Indica), in a wood at Coolhurst, Sussex.

increasing trees than is usual in nurseries, as those raised from seed
have a chance of interesting variations, whereas grafting from the
same identical form shuts out all chance of it. It is curious that a
tree so effective in bloom, and so distinct in habit as the Judas Tree is,
should be so little planted with us, and, when planted, so often left to
the scant mercy of the shrubbery border   All such trees have their
own ways and wants, and should not be jumbled up in the common
crowded and ignorant way of planting.

I have never seen anything with greater pleasure than a bush of
Citrus Trifoliata which I saw in the School Garden at Versailles
—a sheet of large and beautiful flowers—on April 19. I had previously
no idea that any Citrus could have borne such a beautiful and distinct
bloom in the open air, and yet this was borne by a hardy shrub
standing for years among Crabs, Almonds, and trees of that degree of
hardiness

Of Indian Azaleas in the open air Mr. C. R. Scrase-Dickens
writes : " The hardy Azaleas of the American races are very popular,
but few know the value of the white Indian Azalea for the open
garden in the south of England   Few plants give so little trouble
when once established, even though the late frosts may now and
again spoil the beauty of the flowers. When planted out and left
alone, it is not much more than three or four feet in height, dense
and spreading   The engraving shows a bush over ten feet across
with a shadow thrown over the upper part by a tree of Magnolia
which grows at the side. It gets shelter from cold winds and
from too fierce a sun on the flowers   Any one who intends
to plant this Azalea should remember that it flowers naturally
at a time when there may still be late frosts and cold winds
hovering about, and that it would be a mistaken kindness to
choose any place, such as under a south wall, which would
tend to make the blossoms open earlier in the season. We
have some plants under a north wall which do admirably, but
they seem to like association with other things. The variety
which does best here is the old typical white. Overgrown plants of
other colours from the greenhouse have been turned out sometimes,
but they do not seem so happy or produce so good an effect."

If one-tenth the trouble wasted on " carpet-bedding " plants and
other fleeting and costly rubbish had been spent on flowering shrubs,
our gardens would be all the better for it. There are no plants so
much neglected as flowering shrubs, and even when planted they are
rarely well grown, owing to the " traditions " of what is called the
shrubbery. The common way is to dig the shrubbery every winter,
and this is often carried out as a matter of form without giving the
soil any manure, while much harm is done by mutilating the roots of

the shrubs. The labour and time wasted in this way, if devoted to the proper culture of a portion of the ground each year, would make our gardens delightful indeed. Many shrubs, as fair as any flower requiring the shelter of glass, have been introduced into this country; but for the most part they have been destroyed by the muddle "shrubbery."

The idea of the murderous common shrubbery is so rooted in the popular mind that it is almost hopeless to expect much change for the better. The true way is to depart wholly from it as a mass of *mixed* shrubs, for beautiful families should be grouped apart. Each family or plant should have a separate place, free from the all-devouring

Spiræa (Belmont, Carlow).

Privet and Laurel, and each part of the shrubbery should have its own character, which may easily be given to it by grouping instead of mixing, which ends in the starvation of the choice kinds. We do not allow stove and green-house plants to be choked in this way, yet no plants are more worthy of a distinct place and of care than hardy shrubs. Low flowering trees, like Hawthorns, group admirably on the turf, but the finer kinds of flowering shrubs should be planted in beds. The shrubbery itself need no longer be a dark dreary mass, but light and shade may play in it, its varied life be well shown, and the habits

_124_

and forms of each thing may be seen   Shrubs of high quality or rare deserve to be well grown.   Any one who thinks how much less trouble is given by hardy plants than by pot plants will not begrudge attention to outdoor things, and some may even consider a garden of beautiful shrubs as a conservatory in the open air, no kind of flower gardening being more delightful or enduring.   We have often to re-arrange vigorous herbaceous plants, and constantly to work with the lovable Carnation, but shrubs give us little trouble

It is not only flowers that suffer from being stuck in lines and patterns , our beautiful flowering shrubs are injured in the same way.   The Rhododendron and the Azalea, and what are commonly called American plants, are often put in such close masses that their forms cannot be seen   We may get the flowers to some extent, but they are not so enjoyable as when the plants are allowed to show their individual forms

There is not the slightest reason why we should not have all the force of colour, too, because it is quite possible to have a number of beautiful Rhododendrons and other flowering shrubs together without putting them in the serried mass in which they are usually seen.

So, without going into varieties or touching upon all the treasures within our reach, it is clear how much those who care to adorn their gardens in the most enduring way have to gain by planting flowering shrubs after their own tastes   Those who have given a fair chance to one half the groups of plants referred to in this chapter need not care much about garden coal bills, hot-houses, "contrasts of colour," and the many other considerations, as the beauty of the flowering trees and shrubs will come year after year as certainly as the wind through the Cherry-blooms.

Some Flowering Trees and Shrubs Hardy in British Gardens

Abelia	Chionanthus	Exochorda	Leycesteria	Rhodora
Æsculus	Cladrastis	Fabiana	Liriodendron	Rhodotypos
Akebia	Clematis	Forsythia	Lonicera	Ribes
Amelanchier	Clethra	Fothergilla	Lupinus	Robinia
Amygdalus	Colletia	Garrya	Magnolia	Rosa
Andromeda	Colutea	Gaultheria	Mahonia	Rubus
Aralia	Comptonia	Genista	Malus	Sambucus
Arbutus	Cornus	Gleditschia	Mespilus	Sophora
Arctostaphylos	Corylopsis	Halesia	Olearia	Spartium
Asimina	Cotoneaster	Hamamelis	Ononis	Spiræa
Azalea	Cratægus	Hibiscus	Ornus	Staphylea
Azara	Cydonia	Hypericum	Ozothamnus	Stauntonia
Berberidopsis	Cytisus	Hydrangea	Paulownia	Stuartia
Berberis	Daphne	Illicium	Pavia	Styrax
Bignonia	Desfontainea	Indigofera	Pernettya	Syringa
Buddleia	Desmodium	Jasminum	Philadelphus	Tamarix
Calycanthus	Deutzia	Kalmia	Phlomis	Ulex
Camellia	Edwardsia	Kerria	Piptanthus	Veronica
Caragana	Embothrium	Kœlreuteria	Prunus	Viburnum
Catalpa	Erica	Laburnum	Pterostyrax	Virgilia
Ceanothus	Escallonia	Ledum	Pyrus	Weigela
Cerasus	Euryphia	Leiophyllum	Raphiolepis	Wistaria
Cercis	Euonymus	Lespedeza	Rhododendron	Xanthoceras
Chimonanthus				

*** Some of the evergreens, though thriving long in the southern and shore lands, may perish in severe winters in cold inland districts.

CHAPTER IX.

CLIMBERS AND THEIR ARTISTIC USE.

THE splendid squadrons of the Pine, with crests proud in alpine storm and massed in serried armies along the northern mountains :—the Oak kings of a thousand winters in the forest plain are lovely gifts of the earth mother, but more precious still to the gardener are the most fragile of all woody things that garland bush and tree with beautiful forms and blossoms, like Clematis, Jasmine and Honeysuckle, and the many lace-workers of the woods and brakes. It is delightful to be able to turn our often ugly inheritance from the builder almost into gardens by the aid of these, from great yellow Roses to Ivy in many lovely forms ; but it is well to take a wider view of these climbing and rambling bushes and their places in the garden and in the pleasure-ground. It is for our own convenience we go through the labour of nailing them to walls, and though it is a charming and necessary way of growing them it is well to remember that many climbers may be grown in beautiful ways without such laborious training. The tendency to over-pruning of the climbers on walls ends often in a kind of crucifixion, and the more freely things are trained the better. Proof of this is in the handsome masses of climbers on the high walls of the Trinity College Gardens at Dublin and in many private places where climbers have been liberally and well planted on walls.

But it should never be forgotten that many of these plants will grow by themselves, like the Honeysuckles, which, while pleasant to see on walls, are not less so on banks, or even on the level ground. Pretty fences and dividing screens may also be easily formed by hardy climbers. The wild kinds of Clematis are charming, and, apart from their use in the garden, they should be encouraged for trees and banks

The Ivy of our northern woods has broken into a number of beautiful varieties often distinct in form and even in colour, they deserve far more attention for evergreen bowers, evergreen fences, and dividing lines, apart from their growth on walls and trees   The bush forms of these may make broken hedge-like garlands 2 feet to 3 feet high round little isolated flower gardens   Almost equally beautiful plants in form of leaf are the Green Briers (Smilax), some of which are hardy in England, but seen in few gardens, and rarely treated in an artistic way, though excellent for walls and rocks.   In the eastern counties they may be seen doing well in the open ground, as in Cambridge

Of the beauty of the Jasmine of all climbers there is least need to speak, yet how rarely one sees the old white Jasmine made good use of in large gardens   It should be in bold wreaths or masses where it thrives, and so also the winter Jasmine, which is a precious thing for our country, should not be put in as a plant or two in bad conditions, but treated as a fine distinct thing in masses round cottages and outhouses.   The finest of hardy climbers, the Wistaria, is much more frequently and rightly planted in France than in our gardens, though it thrives in the Thames valley as well as in the Seine valley. It should be, in addition to its use on walls and houses, made into bold covered ways and bowers and trained up trees, and even along Oak fences

VIGOROUS CLIMBERS ON TREES —It is not only that stout climbers are more beautiful and natural, and show their form better growing amongst trees, but it is the best way that many of them can be grown with safety owing to their vigour.   The way the common Ivy wreaths the trees in rich woods, and the wild Clematis throws ropes up trees on the chalk hills, shows what the larger hardy climbers do over trees or rough or open copses, or even now and then in hedgerows   Some vigorous climbers would in time ascend the tallest trees, and there is nothing more beautiful than a veil of Clematis montana running over a tall tree   Besides the well-known climbers, there are species of Clematis which have never come into general cultivation, but which are beautiful for such uses, though not all showy   The same may be said of the Honeysuckles, wild Vines, and various other families with which much of the northern tree and shrub world is garlanded.   Occasionally one sees a climbing Rose rambling over a tree, and perhaps among our garden pictures nothing is more lovely than such a Rose when in flower. By a selection of the hardiest of climbing Roses very beautiful pictures might be formed in our pleasure grounds and plantations, and we might often see as the result

Climbers on the Vicarage, Odiham.

of design what is now mainly an accident, as a number of wild Roses grow "freely" among trees and large shrubs.

CLIMBERS OF CLASSIC BEAUTY OR RARITY are often found a

home for on walls, and in our country some variety of wall surface is
a great gain to botanic gardens and private gardens like Offington, in
which a great variety of shrubs from all countries is grown.   In the
milder districts of the country and in favoured spots round the coast
some of the finest exotics, such as Lapageria, and some greenhouse
plants of great beauty, like Clianthus, which about London can only
be enjoyed in a greenhouse, may be grown on walls in the open air
Some of the fine plants of Chili also may be grown on walls of
various aspects   Abelia, Lardizabala, Berberidopsis and Rhyncho-
spermum are among the plants sometimes so grown, but there is
no limit as to selection.   Many who have visited our best gardens
will probably have stored away in their memories some of the
pictures they have seen given by noble wall plants well grown in this
way—as, for example, the New Zealand Edwardsia at Linton, so fine
in form and colour, and the handsome Fremontia.   Hard winters
settle the fate of many beautiful things among these, but, happily,
some of the loveliest things are hardy, like the Winter Sweet, Bignonia,
Magnolia, and sometimes the splendid colour of the Pomegranate
buds is seen among them

It may be noted here that among the unfortunate attempts of
certain architects who designed gardens to get rid of the gardener and
his troublesome plants were instructions that no climbers were to be
allowed on walls   There was not a single spray of any climber
allowed to grow on the house or extensive terrace walls at Shrubland, some years ago, as if in a garden death were better than
life.

FRAGILE CLIMBERS ON SHRUBS—Apart from the vigorous
climbers that we may trust in shrubberies, woods, and on rough
banks, and which, when fairly started, take care of themselves, there
are fragile things which deserve to be used in rather a new way as far
as most gardens are concerned, namely, for throwing a delicate lacework of flowers over the evergreen and other choice shrubs grown in
our gardens—Rhododendron, Kalmia, Andromeda, Azalea, and even
taller shrubs   A group of Hollies will not look any the worse for
wreaths of fragrant Clematis in autumn.   Often stiff, unbroken
masses of Rhododendrons and Evergreen flowering shrubs will be
more varied if delicate flakes of Clematis (white, lavender, or claret-
red) or the bright arrows of the Flame Nasturtium come among them
here and there in autumn   The great showy hybrid Clematises of
our gardens are not so good for this use as the more elegant wild
Clematises of N America, Europe, and N Africa, such as the Hairbell
and others of the less vigorous Clematis   These are so fragile in
growth that many of them may be trusted among groups of choice
shrubs like Azaleas, training themselves and throwing veils over the

bushes here and there.   Among these nothing is better than the various forms of Clematis Viticella, and there is also a number of not very showy plants which might be used in this way, such as Apios and even the climbing Fern of N. America, and some Bomareas and the wild Nasturtiums.   Two lovely twining shrubs must never be left out in any scheme of this kind, the Atragene or Alpine Clematis of the mountains of Europe, hardy as the Oak and tender in colour as the dove, and in all the warmer districts the winter-flowering Clematis of the islands of the Mediterranean and the North African coasts, where it garlands with the Smilax millions of acres of hyena- and jackal-haunted scrub.

A Trumpet Flower (Bignonia grandiflora).   Engraved from a photograph by Miss Willmott.

ROSES AS CLIMBERS.—It would be difficult to overpraise the value of the Rose in all arrangements of climbing plants.   Many of the more vigorous Wild Roses of the northern world are naturally almost climbing plants, and some of them are seen 20 ft. high or so among trees.   In gardens many varieties might be mentioned which in past years were a great source of beauty and gave a very showy effect when well used, but, in our own time, and within the past generation or two, since the raising of Gloire de Dijon, a noble series of climbing Roses, wholly distinct from the old climbing kinds, has been raised in France, the most precious flowers that have ever adorned the Rose-garden.

K

The old Climbers and Garland Roses were almost too vigorous for the garden, and their bloom did not last long enough to justify their getting a place there; but now, with the great climbing Tea Roses we have for the southern parts of these islands, we may count on a bloom for months. Hence we have in these Roses, where they thrive the best, the most precious of all ornaments for walls of houses, trellis work, pergolas. In southern parts of the country we even get fine results from these Roses on the north side of walls, where some Roses flower better than on the south side. Also, we can grow them in the open on trellises or away from walls, but in the northern parts of the country, where these great climbing Tea Roses may not thrive so well, walls come in to help us more and more by their shelter and warmth, and the encouragement they give to early bloom.

Apart from these great Roses of garden origin, which will long be among the most precious, some Wild Roses are of the highest importance in warm districts and good soils, particularly the Indian R Brunonis and the many-flowered Roses (R. polyantha) of Japan; but in the presence of the need of so much wall space for the garden Roses these Wild Roses will usually be best in the shrubbery or some place apart, where they may be let alone, and no good can arise from choice, garden ground being given to Roses like R. polyantha which are even more vigorous than our own wild Dog Rose.

In Europe perhaps the country that pleases one most by its fitness for Rose culture is that along the shores of the Mediterranean, where the Banksian and other more delicate Roses may be seen up trees, forming hedges, and arranging themselves in other delightful ways I remember being very much struck with the beauty of the single Banksian Rose in such positions, and often wondered why it was not secured for our own gardens, even though it might not grow so freely as there.

VINES FOR THEIR BEAUTY OF FORM.—Going back some thousands of years to the earliest sculptured remains of some of the oldest peoples, we see evidence that the Grape Vine was in common use, and it is no doubt much older than the monuments of Assyria. Among the Kabyle villages of North Africa I passed many Vines of great age trailing over very old Olive trees in the little orchard fields. In such countries there was the value of the fruit, but even in ours, where the Grape ripens rarely out of doors, the charm of the plant is so great that we see many cottages in Surrey and Norfolk set deep in Vine leaves The Grape Vine, however, is but one of a large family, and, though we may not see in our country its garlands from tree to tree purple with fruit, we may see much of its fine forms of leaf. The wild Vines are too vigorous for use on walls, though excellent for banks and trees and for any place outside the flower garden. I have seen them clambering up forest trees, spreading into masses of fine foliage on the ground, and sending out long arms in search of the nearest trees—strong and handsome climbers, hardy, vigorous, and soon covering dry banks, rocks, and trees.

To the Vines (Vitis) have now been joined by the botanists Virginian Creepers (Ampelopsis), and between the two groups it need not be said what noble things they offer for garlanding trees, walls, bowers, rocks, and banks. It cannot be said that we neglect these Virginian and Japanese creepers, but the Vines are so far seldom well used with us, although easy of cultivation.

Wooden Pergola, with Clematis and other hardy Climbers.

PERGOLAS.—Though our summer is often not sunny, there are seasons when shaded walks may be enjoyed, and numbers of free-growing climbing plants give an abundant and lovely choice of living drapery for them, Aristolochia, Wistaria, Virginian Creeper, rambling Roses, Honeysuckles, Jasmines and the free Clematises doing well over such. In Italy and warm countries one often sees in gardens the pergola—as the creeper-shaded walk is called—serving the two-fold purpose of supporting Grape Vines and giving pleasant coolness during the summer heat. As a rule, these pergolas are rude trellis-work structures of wood, sometimes supported by stone posts where these are at hand.   In the gardens in the neighbourhood of Rome, Naples, and Florence there are beautiful examples of the pergola— stately structures, the supports of which are massive columns of stone covered and festooned with Banksian Roses, Wistaria, Periploca, Clematises, Honeysuckles, Passion Flowers, scarlet Trumpet Flowers, and other climbers which form cool retreats in the hot days.   But such pergolas seldom occurred outside the gardens of the great villas, and near humbler dwellings the pergola was usually a simple struc- ture made for the purpose of supporting the Grape Vine, and nearly always pretty

These creeper-clad covered ways should usually lead to somewhere and be over a frequented walk, and should not cut off any line of view nor be placed near big trees, especially such trees as the Elm, whose hungry roots would travel a long way to feed upon the good soil that the climbers should be planted in   A simple structure is the best. The supports, failing the Italian way of making posts of stone—also seen, by the way, in gate-posts in Northern England—should be Oak tree stems, about 9 inches in diameter, let into the ground about 2 feet ; the better if on a bed of concrete.   The posts must be connected and firmly secured to each other by long pieces along the sides, while the top may be formed of smaller pieces to make a firm structure. On no account let the "rustic" carpenter begin to adorn it with the fantastic branchings he is so fond of

TREES SUPPORTING CLIMBERS —Instead of trusting to wire and ugly posts or the many artificial ways for supporting climbers, why should we not do as the Italians and people of south Europe do, use living trees to carry the vine or climber.   Weeping trees of graceful leaf and form might be used in this way with fine effect   Abroad they take for this purpose any kind of tree which happens to be near and keep it within bounds, and those who know our garden flora may select trees which, while beautiful themselves, will not be much trouble to keep in bounds, like the weeping Cherry, weeping Aspen, some Willows even, and any light leaved weeping tree would be charming for its own sake as well as for what it might carry   Some of them might even be beautiful in flower, and there would be no trouble in getting creepers to run over them.

LIGHT ARCHES OVER WALKS. — When a quiet walk leads from one part of the garden to another, and that walk is spanned at intervals with slender iron or other light arches clothed with Honeysuckle, Clematis, or Jasmine, it gives an added grace to the walk   This also is a delightful way of framing, so to say, a flower border, the light arches springing up from the line of the trellis, which should be used to cut off the borders from the kitchen garden.

ANNUAL AND HERBACEOUS CLIMBERS —However rich we may

Pergola in Mrs. Eden's garden at Venice.

be in perennial and shrubby climbers, we must not forget the climbing
things among annual and like plants to help us, especially in the
smaller class of gardens and those on which we depend more on
annual flowers. Hedges of Sweet Peas there are few things to equal ;
the fragile annual Convolvuli in many colours are pretty for low
trellises, the vigorous herbaceous Bindweeds for rough places outside
the flower garden   Most showy of all annual climbers are the many
Gourds, which, treated in a bold way, give fine effects when trained
over outhouses, sheds, or on strong stakes as columns. The showy
annual climbing Tropæolums, as well as the brilliant herbaceous and
tuberous rooted kinds, are most precious, and Apios, Adlumia, Eccremocarpus, Maurandya and Cobæa in mild districts are among the
plants that help us to make walls into gardens   Nor must we forget
the Hop, a vigorous, graceful, herbaceous climber, of much value where
well placed. Among these climbers we may place the Passion Flower,
because so often short-lived in the cold and more inland parts of our
islands   It is best for sheltered and sea-coast places and is not quite
hardy there in our coldest seasons ; still, if its base be sheltered with
some dry Fern, it will spring up again

COVERED WAYS OF FRUIT TREES.—This way of growing fruit
trees and shading walks is not often seen, though few things would be
prettier or more useful in gardens if fruit trees of high quality were chosen
Although in our gardens the shaded walk is not so necessary as it is
in Italy and Southern France, in hot seasons shade is welcome in
Britain ; and, as in many gardens we have four times as many walks as
are needed, there is plenty of room for covering some of them with fruit
trees which would give us flowers in spring, fruit in autumn, and light
shade   The very substance of which walks are made is often good for
fruit, and those who know the Apricot district of Oxfordshire and the
neighbouring counties may see how well fruit trees do in hard walks.
It is not only in kitchen and fruit gardens that their shade might be
welcome, but in flower gardens, if we ever get out of the common
notion of a flower garden which insists on everything being seen at one
glance and the whole as flat and hard as oilcloth

PLASHED ALLEYS—In some old gardens there was a way of
"plashing" trees over walks—trees like the Lime, which grew so
vigorously that they had to be cut back with an equal vigour, this
leading in the end to ugliness in the excessive mutilation of the trees
One result of the frequent cutting was a vigorous summer growth of
shoots, which cast a dense shade and dripped in wet weather. The
purpose of such walks would be well fulfilled by training fruit trees
over them, as they are trees which much more readily submit to
training and give the light and airy shade which is best in our
country   The fruit trellis, whatever it is formed of, need not be

confined to fruit trees only, but here and there wreaths of Clematis or other elegant climbers might vary the lines.

EVERGREENS AS CLIMBERS.—Those who live in sheltered valleys on warm soils, or among pleasant hills above the line of hard frosts, may be so rich in evergreens that they will keep their walls for the fairest of true climbers. But in cold, exposed, and inland parts people are often glad to have good evergreens on walls, even bushes not naturally climbers in habit, such as Garrya elliptica, the choicer evergreen Barberries, Camellias on the north sides of walls, Azara, Escallonia, Cotoneaster, and evergreen Euonymus. The Laurustinus, too, is charming on many cottage walls in winter and may escape there when it would suffer in the open ; the Myrtle is happy on walls in southern districts, and even the Poet's Laurel may be glad of the shelter of a wall in the north. The evergreen Magnolia, which in warmer Europe is a standard tree, in our country must usually be grown on walls, even in the south, and there is no finer picture than a good tree of Magnolia on a house. The beautiful Ceanothus of the Californian hills often keep company with these evergreens on walls ; but even in the warmer soils of the home countries they are tender, and their delicate sprays of flowers are much less frequently seen

Wistaria on covered way.

with us than in France, although we cannot resist trying them on sunny walls, and on chalky and sandy soils they have better chances.

Apart from true shrubs used as evergreens, so frequently seen in Britain, we have some natural evergreen climbing plants for walls, first of all being our native Ivy, in all its beautiful forms, and of varied use for walls, houses, borders, screens, and even summer-houses and shelters. How much better to make bowers in the garden of Ivy, as a living roof, than of rotten timber, straw, or heath! If we make a strong and enduring framework, and then plant the Ivy well, we soon get a living roof, which, with little care, will last for many years and always look well.

SOME CLIMBING, TWINING, AND WALL PLANTS FOR BRITISH GARDENS.—There is scarcely any limit to the different uses that plants of a climbing or rambling habit may be put to, for many of them are extremely beautiful when employed for the draping of arbours, pergolas, or even living trees, while for hiding unsightly fences or clothing sloping banks, the more vigorous kinds are well adapted. For draping buildings or furnishing walls there is a great variety of plants, either quite hardy or sufficiently tender to need the protection of a wall in order to pass through an ordinary winter without much injury. The majority of those enumerated below are hardy enough to succeed as wall plants in any part of England, while a few are adapted only for particularly mild districts.

Those plants marked with an asterisk are either half-hardy or require some slight protection in cold districts or special care in some cases.

Abelia	Celastrus	Exochorda	Lycium	Ribes
Abutilon	Chimonanthus	Exogonum	Magnolia	Rosea
Actinidia	Choisya	Forsythia	*Mandevilla	Rubus
Adlumia	Clematis	Fremontia	Maurandya	Schizandra
Akebia	Cocculus	Fuchsia	Menispermum	Solanum
*Aloysia	Clianthus	Garrya	*Mitraria	Schizophragma
Apios	Convolvulus	Grevillea	Muhlenbeckia	Smilax
Aristolochia	Cotoneaster	Hedera	Myrtus	*Sollya
Azara	Cratægus	Illicium	Paliurus	Stauntonia
Berberis	Cydonia	Indigofera	*Passiflora	Stuartia
*Berberidopsis	Desfontainea	Jasminum	Periploca	*Thunbergia
Bignonia	Eccremocarpus	Kerria	Physianthus	Tropæolum
Buddleia	Edwardsia	*Lapageria	Piptanthus	Vitis (now including
Calystegia	*Embothrium	*Lardizabala	*Pittosporum	Ampelopsis)
Camellia	Escallonia	Leptospermum	Pueraria	Wistaria
*Carpenteria	Eucryphia	Lonicera	*Punica	Xanthoceras
Ceanothus	Euonymus	Lophospermum	Rhus	

Akebia quinata

CHAPTER X.

ALPINE FLOWER- ROCK- AND WALL GARDENS.

IT was a common idea that the exquisite flowers of alpine plants could not be grown in gardens in lowland regions, and it was not confined to the public, but propagated by writers whenever they have had to figure or describe alpine flowers. So far from its being true, however, there are but few alpine flowers that ever cheered the traveller's eye that cannot be grown in these islands.

Alpine plants grow naturally on high mountains, whether they spring from sub-tropical plains or green northern pastures. Above the cultivated land these flowers begin to occur on moorland and in the fringes of the hill woods; they are seen in multitudes in the broad pastures with which many mountains are robed, enamelling their green, and where neither grass nor tall herbs exist; where mountains are crumbled into slopes of shattered rock by the contending forces of heat and cold; even there, amidst the glaciers, they spring from the ruined ground, as if the earth-mother had sent up her loveliest children to plead with the spirits of destruction.

Alpine plants fringe the fields of snow and ice of the mountains, and at such elevations often have scarcely time to flower before they are again buried deep in snow. Enormous areas of the earth, inhabited by alpine plants, are every year covered by a deep bed of snow and where tree or shrub cannot live from the intense cold, a deep mass of down-like snow falls upon alpine plants, like a great cloud-borne quilt, under which they rest safe from alternations of frost and biting winds with moist and spring-like days as in our green winters.

But these conditions are not always essential for their growth in a cool northern country like ours   The reason that alpine plants abound in high regions is because no taller vegetation can exist there ; were these places inhabited by trees and shrubs, we should find fewer alpine plants among them ; on the other hand, were no stronger vegetation found at a lower elevation, these plants would often there appear.   Also, as there are few hard and fast lines in nature, many plants found on the high Alps are also met with in rocky or barish ground at much lower elevations.   Gentiana   erna, for example, often flowers very late in summer when the snow thaws on a very high mountain ; yet it is also found on much lower mountains, and occurs in England and Ireland   In the close struggle upon the plains and low tree-clad hills, the smaller species are often overrun by trees, trailers, bushes, and vigorous herbs, but, where in far northern and high mountain regions these fail from the earth, the lovely alpine flowers prevail

Alpine plants possess the charm of endless variety, and include things widely different ·—tiny orchids, tree-like moss, and ferns that peep from crevices of alpine cliffs, often so small that they seem to cling to the rocks for shelter, not daring to throw forth their fronds with airy grace , bulbous plants, from Lilies to Bluebells ; evergreen shrubs, perfect in leaf and blossom and fruit, yet so small that a finger glass would make a house for them , dwarfest creeping plants, spreading over the brows of rocks, draping them with lovely colour ; Rockfoils and Stonecrops no bigger than mosses, and, like them, mantling the earth with green carpets in winter, and embracing nearly every type of the plant-life of northern lands

In the culture of these plants, the first thing to be remembered is that much difference exists among them as regards size and vigour. We have, on the one hand, a number of plants that merely require to be sown or planted in the roughest way to flourish—Arabis and Aubrietia, for example ; and, on the other, there are some kinds, like Gentians and the Primulas of the high Alps, which are rarely seen in good health in gardens and it is as to these that advice is chiefly required.   And nearly all the misfortunes which these little plants have met with in our gardens are due to a false conception of what a rock-garden ought to be, and of what the alpine plant requires.   It is too often thought that they will do best if merely raised on tiny heaps of stones and brick rubbish, such as we frequently see dignified with the name of " rockwork "   Moun-

tains are often " bare," and cliffs devoid of soil ; but we must not
suppose that the choice jewellery of plant-life scattered over the ribs
of the mountain lives upon little more than the air and the melting
snow   Where else can we find such a depth of stony soil as on the
ridges of shattered stone and grit flanking some great glacier, stained
with tufts of crimson Rockfoil?   Can we gauge the depth of that
chink from which peep tufts of the beautiful little Androsace helvetica,
which for ages has gathered the crumbling grit, into which the roots
enter so far that we cannot dig them out ? And if we find plants growing from mere cracks without soil, even then the roots simply search
farther into the heart of the flaky rock, so that they are safer from
drought than on the level ground.

We meet on the Alps plants not more than an inch high firmly
rooted in crevices of slaty rock, and by knocking away the sides from
bits of projecting rock, and laying the roots quite bare, we may find
them radiating in all directions against a flat rock, some of the
largest perhaps more than a yard long.   Even smaller plants descend
quite as deep, though it is rare to find the texture and position of the
rock such as will admit of tracing them.   It is true we occasionally
find in fields of flat hard rock hollows in which moss and leaves have
gathered, and where, in a depression of the surface, without an outlet
of any kind, alpine plants grow freely, but in droughts they are
just as liable to suffer from want of water as they would be in
our plains   On level or sloping spots of ground in the Alps the
earth is of great depth, and, if it is not all earth in the common
sense of the word, it is more suitable to the plants than what we
commonly understand by that term   Stones of all sizes broken
up with the soil, sand, and grit prevent evaporation , the roots lap
round them, follow them down, and in such positions they never
suffer from want of moisture   It must be remembered that the
continual degradation of the rocks effected by frost, snow, and
heavy rains in summer serves to "earth up," so to speak, many
alpine plants

In numbers of gardens an attempt at "rockwork" has been made ,
but the result is often ridiculous, not because it is puny when compared with Nature's work, but because it is generally so arranged
that rock-plants cannot exist upon it   The idea of rockwork first
arose from a desire to imitate those natural croppings-out of rocks
which are often half covered with dwarf mountain plants.   The conditions which surround these are rarely taken into account by those
who make rock-gardens.   In moist districts, where rains keep porous
stone in a humid state, this straight-sided rockwork may support a
few plants, but in the larger portion of the British Isles it is useless
and ugly.   It is not alone because they love the mountain air

that the Gentians and such plants prefer it, but also because the
great elevation is unsuitable to coarser vegetation, and the alpine
plants have it all to themselves.   Take a patch of Silene acaulis,
by which the summits of some of our highest mountains are sheeted
over, and plant it 2,000 feet lower down in suitable soil, keeping
it moist and free from weeds, and it will grow well ; but leave it to
Nature, and the strong herbs will soon cover it, excluding the light
and killing it.

Although hundreds of kinds of alpine flowers may be grown without a particle of rock near them, yet the slight elevation given by
rocky banks is congenial to some of the rarest kinds   The effect of a
well-made rock-garden is pretty in garden scenery.   It furnishes a
home for many native and other plants which may not safely be put
in among tall flowers in borders , and it is important that the most
essential principles to be borne in mind when making it should be
stated.   The usual mistake is that of not providing a feeding-place
for the roots of the plants.   On ordinary rockwork even the coarsest
British weeds cannot find a resting-place, because there is no body of
soil for the roots to find nourishment sufficient to keep the plant fresh
in all weathers

POSITION FOR THE ROCK-GARDEN.—The rock-garden should
never be near walls ; never very near a house ; never, if possible,
within view of formal surroundings of any kind, and it should be in an
open situation.   No efforts should be spared to make all the surroundings, and every point visible from the rock-garden, graceful and
natural as they can be made.   The part of the gardens around the
rock-garden should be picturesque, if possible, and, in any case, be
a quiet airy spot with as few jarring points as may be.   No tree
should be in the rock-garden , hence a site should not be selected
where it would be necessary to remove favourite trees.   The roots of
trees would find their way into the masses of good soil for the
alpine flowers, and soon exhaust them.   Besides, as these flowers
are usually found on treeless wastes, it is best not to place them
in shaded places

As regards the stone to be used, sandstone or millstone grit
would perhaps be the best ; but it is seldom that a choice can be
made, and almost any kind of stone will do, from Kentish rag to
limestone. soft and slaty kinds and others liable to crumble away
should be avoided, as also should magnesian limestone   The stone of
the neighbourhood should be adopted, for economy's sake, if for no
other reason.   Wherever the natural rock crops out, it is sheer
waste to create artificial rockwork instead of embellishing that which
naturally occurs.   In many cases nothing would be necessary but to
clear the ground, and add here and there a few loads of good soil,

with broken stones to prevent evaporation, the natural crevices and crests being planted where possible. Cliffs or banks of chalk, as well as all kinds of rock, should be taken advantage of in this way: many plants, like the dwarf Harebells and Rock Roses, thrive in such places. No burrs, clinkers, vitrified matter, portions of old arches and pillars, broken-nosed statues, etc., should ever be seen in a garden of alpine flowers. Never let any part of the rock-garden appear as if it had been shot out of a cart. The rocks should all have their bases buried in the ground, and the seams should not be visible; wherever a vertical or oblique seam occurs, it

Passage in rock-garden.

should be crammed with earth, and the plants put in with the earth will quickly hide the seam. Horizontal fissures should be avoided as much as possible. No vacuum should exist beneath the surface of the soil or surface-stones, and the broken stone and grit should be so disposed that there are no hollows. Myriads of alpine plants have been destroyed from the want of observing this precaution, the open crevices and loose soil allowing the dry air to destroy the alpine plants in a very short time, and so one often sees what was meant for a "rock-garden" covered with weeds and brambles, and forgotten!

In all cases where elevations of any kind are desired, the true way is to obtain them by a mass of soil suitable to the plants, putting a "rock" in here and there as the work proceeds; frequently it would be desirable to make these mounds of earth without any strata. The wrong and usual way is to get the elevation by piling up ugly masses of stones, vitrified bricks, and other rubbish.

No very formal walk—that is to say, no walk with regularly trimmed edges—should come near the rock-garden. This need not prevent the presence of good walks through or near it, as by allowing the edges of the walk to be broken and stony, and by encouraging Stonecrops, Rockfoils, and other little plants to crawl into the

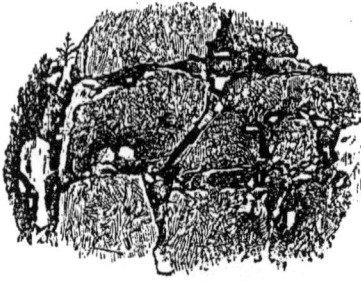

Wrong way of forming rock-garden.

Right.

Alpine Plants growing at the bottom of a sloping ridge.

Alpine Plant on border surrounded by half-buried stones.

Corner of a ledge of natural rock
with Alpine Plants.

Steps from deep recess of Rock-garden, mossed over with
Alpine Flowers.

Ledge of Alpine Flowers (a Garden Sketch.

walk at will, a pretty margin will result. There is no surface of this kind that may not be thus adorned. Violets, Ferns, Forget-me-nots, will do in the shadier parts, and the Stonecrops and many others will thrive in the full sun The whole of the surface of the alpine garden should be covered with plants as far as possible, except a few projecting points. In moist districts, Erinus and the Balearic Sand-wort will grow on the face of the rocks ; and even upright faces of rock will grow a variety of plants. Regular steps should never be in or near the rock-garden Steps may be made quite picturesque, and even beautiful, with Violets and other small plants jutting from every crevice , and no cement should be used

In cases where the simplest type of rock-garden only is attempted, and where there are no steps or rude walks in the rock-garden, the very fringes of the gravel walks may be graced by such plants as the dwarfer Stonecrops The alpine Toadflax is never more beautiful than when self-sown in a gravel walk. A rock-garden so made that its miniature cliffs overhang is useless for alpine vegetation, and all but such wall-loving plants as Corydalis lutea soon die on it The tendency to make it with overhanging " peaks " is often seen in the cement rock-gardens now common

SOIL.—The great majority of alpine plants thrive best in deep soil In it they can root deeply, and when once rooted they will not suffer from drought, from which they would quickly perish if planted in the usual way. Three feet deep is not too much for most kinds, and in nearly all cases it is a good plan to have plenty of broken sandstone or grit mixed with the soil Any free loam, with plenty of sand and broken grit, will suit most alpine plants But peat is required by some, as, for example, various small and brilliant rock-plants like the Menziesia, Trillium, Cypripedium, Spigelia, and a number of other mountain and bog-plants Hence, though the body of the soil may be of loam, it is well to have a few masses of peat here and there. This is better than forming all the ground of good loam, and then digging holes for the reception of small masses of peat The soil of some portions might also be chalky or calcareous, for the sake of plants that are known to thrive best on such formations, like the Milkworts, the Bee Orchis, and Rhododendron Chamæcistus Any other varieties of soil required by particular kinds can be given as they are planted.

It is not well to associate a small lakelet or pond with the rock-garden, as is frequently done. If a picturesque piece of water can be seen from the rock-garden, well and good , but water should not, as a rule, be closely associated with it Hence, in places of limited extent, water should not be thought of.

In the planting of every kind of rock-garden, it should be

remembered that *all* the surface should be planted. Not alone on slopes, or favourable ledges, or chinks, should we see this exquisite plant-life, as many rare mountain species will thrive on the less trodden parts of footways; others, like the two-flowered Violet, seem to thrive best in the fissures between steps; many dwarf succulents delight in gravel and the hardest soil.

In cultivating the very rarest and smallest alpine plants, the stony, or partially stony, surface is to be preferred. Full exposure is necessary for very minute plants, and stones are useful in preventing evaporation and protecting them in other ways.

Few have much idea of the number of alpine plants that may be grown on fully exposed ordinary ground. But some kinds require care, and there are usually new kinds coming in, which, even

Steps in a rock garden at Coneyhurst.

if vigorous, should be kept apart for a time. Therefore, where the culture of alpine plants is entered into with zest, there ought to be a sort of nursery spot on which to grow the most delicate and rare kinds. It should be fully exposed, and sufficiently elevated to secure perfect drainage.

ILL-FORMED ROCK GARDENS.—The increased interest in rock gardening of recent years has led to much work of this kind being done throughout the country, and without good results from an artistic point of view. The rock gardens are not right in structure nor good for growing plants. If they were good for the life of plants one might pass over their other defects, but when made, as they often are, of cement, and even of natural stone so that the plants grow with great difficulty, owing chiefly to the stones overhanging so as to leave dry and dusty recesses, the result is bad. No doubt rocks do in nature often have such recesses, but they very often come out of the ground in ways that the flowers and moss grow well on them.

In the present state of the art of garden design, rock gardens are formed mainly by nurserymen , these are not men who, as a rule, by the very nature of their business, can give much attention to the study of rocks in natural situations, or learn how the different strata crop out in the ways most happy for vegetation, without which study we think no good work in this way is possible.   The work we see now is often done better than the ugly masses of scoria and various rubbish of the earlier "rock works," but it is still a very long way from what is artistic   Simplicity is rarely thought of, or of the rock coming out of the ground in any pretty way, of which we may see numerous examples in upland moors in England, even without going to the· mountains or the Alps.   On the contrary, we see pretentious rickety piles of stone on stone, with pebbles between to keep the big ones up, and forty stones where seven would be enough.

A characteristic of these elaborate failures is a rocky depression, often an ugly one, in the ground   This is by no means the most likely thing in Nature to give the prettiest effects. If alpine and rock plants wanted shelter, we could see some meaning in these depressions, but the conditions that suit such plants are quite the opposite and a rock garden should be for the most part made on a fully exposed rocky knoll.

The fact that such bad work is usual is, however, no proof that we cannot get nearer to the truth, and there is a good opening for one who would devote himself to going on the hills and seeing the ways in which rocks and flowers meet.   He would not have to study only the more imposing aspects of that charming subject, but also the simpler ones, because in gardens in all that concerns the rocks we can get only simple effects, and on a small scale.   One of the commonest mistakes is piling stone upon stone in such a way that there is no room for grouping anything   If one were to take five or six of the stones one sees in a rock garden, and simply lay them with the prettiest and most mossy sides showing out of the bank in the right kind of earth, one would get a better place for plants than a rock garden made, it may be, of hundreds of tons of stone could give, because then we should have room to group and mass them, without which no good effect is possible.

The common "rockery," like the common mixed border, is an incoherent muddle, and can scarcely be anything else so long as the present plan is followed   The plants hate it, and in effect it is very like the rows of false teeth in the dentists' shops in St. Martin's-lane We should seek gardens of alpine flowers, with here and there a mossy stone showing modestly among them—not limiting one's efforts to

Sections on level ground, showing also mowing instead of "dotting" alpine plants. (Figure to give scale.)

any one idea, but beginning at least with simplicity of effect. Then groups and carpets of rock plants would be easy to form, and their culture would be easier in every way

REFUSE BRICK " ROCKERIES "—Whoever started the idea of the use of the refuse of the brickyard to form the rock-garden was no friend of the garden, as alpine flowers do not thrive on masses of vitrified brick rubbish And these brick rubbish horrors are put up with overhanging brows so that a drop of moisture cannot get to the plants, and a dry wind can sweep through them as easily as through a grill. If the practice were confined to cottages near brickfields it would not much astonish us ; but in Dulwich Park several thousand tons of it have been put about under the pretence of making rock-gardens, and also at Waterlow Park, Highgate, which was once a pretty and varied piece of ground. If the County Council waste money in this way, we cannot perhaps wonder so much at the owners of villas doing it, but in any case it is ugly and disgraceful in a garden, though we see it freely used in many large country gardens. No other ignoble materials should be seen in any rock garden, in which even stumps of trees are out of place. With some people any broken-nosed statue or other stony or vitrified rubbish is used in what should be the most beautiful and natural of all gardens—the alpine garden If we have not rock in its natural position, or cannot secure some pieces of natural rock to use even on a small scale, it is far better to grow the rock plants in simple ways, even on the level earth on which many of them thrive

It would be well to ask the cost of such a disfigurement in public and large gardens where it is done on as large a scale as this ; the mere price of cartage would have made a model rock garden of natural stone. When these villainous banks of brick-yard refuse were first erected, anything more hideous in a public garden was not to be seen, but by piling on them common shrubs, evergreens, Tobacco, Stonecrops, China Asters, Begonias, Chrysanthemums, Beetroot, Heath, Elder, and higgledy-piggledy verdure of this nature, a sort of brick-rubbish salad was the result, and the effect of the brick is less seen It is not only the ugliness of this in itself that is bad , it is such an injustice to the gardener, who has to adorn at all seasons such structures, to expect him to get any good results from the kind of thing a Brentford cobbler who happens to live near a brickyard makes a little " rockwork " of in his garden.

MISPLACED ARTIFICIAL ROCK —Artificial rock is formed now and then in districts where the natural rock is beautiful, as in the country round Tunbridge Wells Though why anybody should bring the artificial rockmaker into a garden or park where there is already fine natural beautiful rock it is not easy to see. Also, in certain

In the rock-garden at Batsford.

districts, it is a mistake to place this artificial rock under conditions where rock of any kind does not occur in nature. It would be much better, as far as alpine and rock plants are concerned, to dispense with much of this ugly artificial rockwork, and take advantage of the fact that many of these plants grow perfectly well on raised borders and on fully exposed low banks

ALPINE PLANTS IN GROUPS.—Many vigorous alpine flowers will do perfectly well on level ground in our cool climate, if they are not overrun by coarser plants. Where there are natural rocks or good artificial ones it is best to plant them properly , but people who are particular would often be better without artificial " rockwork " if they wished to grow these plants in simpler ways. There is not the slightest occasion to have what is called "rockwork" for these flowers. I do not speak only of things like the beautiful Gentianella, which for many years has been grown in our gardens, but of the Rockfoils, the Stonecrops, and the true alpine plants in great numbers. Then, for the sake of securing the benefits of the refreshing rains, it would often be best, in the south of England at least, to avoid the dusty pockets hitherto built for rock flowers. In proof of what may be done in this way there is a little alpine garden, made in quite a level place in the worst possible soil for growing the plant, the hot Bagshot sand, where the soil is always fit for working after heavy rain, but in hot summer is almost like ashes. By making the soil rather deep, and by burying a few stones among the plants to prevent dryness, this flower, which naturally thrives in loamy soil, grew well, and the plan suits many alpine plants

The next point is the great superiority of natural grouping over the botanical or labelled style of little single specimens of a great number of plants. In a few yards of border, in the ordinary way, there would be fifty or more kinds, but nothing pretty for those who have ever seen the beautiful mountain gardens. Many rightly contend that, in a sense, Nature includes all, and that therefore the term "natural" may be misapplied, but is a perfectly just one when used in the sense of Nature's way of arranging flowers as opposed to the lines, circles, and other set patterns so commonly followed by man. Through bold and natural grouping we may get fine colour without a trace of formality. But most gardeners find it difficult to group in this natural way, because so used to setting things out in formal lines. But a little attention to natural objects will help us to get away from set patterns, and let things intermingle here and there and run into each other to form groups such as we may see among the rocks by alpine paths. After a little time the plants themselves begin to help us, and an excellent way is, if a number of plants are set out too formally—as in most cases they are—to pull up a number here and there replanting them on the outer fringes of the groups or elsewhere.

WALL GARDENS.—Those who have observed alpine plants must have noticed in what arid places many flourish, and what fine plants may spring from a chink in a boulder. They are often stunted and small in such crevices, but longer-lived than when growing upon the ground. Now, numbers of alpine plants perish if planted in the ordinary soil of our gardens from over-moisture and want of rest in winter. But if placed where their roots are dry in winter, they may be kept in health. Many plants from countries a little farther south than our own, and from alpine regions, will find on walls, rocks, and ruins that dwarf, sturdy growth which makes them at home in our climate. There are many alpine plants now cultivated with difficulty in frames that may be grown on walls with ease.

The Cheddar Pink, for example, grows on walls at Oxford much better than I have ever known it do on rockwork or on level ground. A few seeds of this plant, sown in an earthy chink and covered with a dust of fine soil, soon grow, living for years on the wall and increasing.

In garden formation, especially in sloping or diversified ground,

Pansy on dry brick wall.

what is called a dry wall is often useful, and may answer the purpose of supporting a bank or dividing off a garden quite as well as masonry. Where the stones can be got easily, men used to the work will often make gently "battered" walls which, while fulfilling their object in supporting banks, will make homes for many plants which would not live one winter on a level surface in the same place. In my own garden I built one such wall with large blocks of sandstone laid on their natural "bed," the front of the stones almost as rough as they come out, and chopped nearly level between, so that they lie firm and well. No mortar was used, and as each stone was laid slender rooted alpine and rock plants were placed along in lines between with a sprinkling of sand or fine earth enough to slightly cover the roots and aid them in getting through the stones to the back, where, as the wall was raised, the space behind it was packed with gritty earth. This the plants soon found out and rooted firmly in. Even on old walls made with mortar rock plants and small native ferns very often establish themselves, but the "dry" walls are more congenial to rock plants, and one may have any number of beautiful alpine plants in perfect health on them.

One charm of this kind of wall garden is that little attention is required afterwards. Even on the best rock gardens things get over-run by others, and weeds come in ; but in a well-planted wall we may leave plants for years untouched beyond pulling out any interloping plant or weed that may happen to get in. So little soil, however, is put with the plants that there is little chance of weeds. If the stones were stuffed with much earth weeds would get in, and it is best to have the merest dusting of soil with the roots, so as not to separate the stones, but let each one rest firmly on the one beneath it.

Androsace. Chaddlewood, Plympton.

Among the things which do well in this way almost the whole of the beautiful rock and alpine flowers may be trusted, such things as Arabis, Aubrietia, and Iberis being among the easiest to grow ; but as these can be grown without walls it is hardly worth while to put them there, pretty as some of the newer forms of the Aubrietia are. Between these stones is the very place for mountain Pinks, which thrive better there than on level ground ; the dwarf alpine Harebells, while the alpine Wallflowers and creeping rock plants, like the Toad Flax (Linaria), and the Spanish Erinus, are quite at home there.

The gentianella does very well on the cool sides of such walls, and we get a different result according to the aspect   All our little pretty wall ferns, now becoming so rare where hawkers abound, do perfectly on such rough walls, and the alpine Phloxes may be used, though they are not so much in need of the comfort of a wall as the European alpine plants, the Rocky Mountain dwarf Phloxes being very hardy and enduring in our gardens on level ground.   The advantage of the wall is that we can grow things that would perish on level ground, owing to excitement of growth in winter, or other causes   The Rock-foils are charming on a wall, particularly the silvery kinds, and the little stone covering sandwort (A. balearica) will run everywhere over such a wall.   Stonecrops and Houseleeks would do too, but are easily grown in any open spot of ground   In many cases the rare and somewhat delicate Alpines, if care be taken in planting, would do far better on such a wall than as they are usually cultivated   Plants like Thymes are quite free in such conditions, though it may be too free for the rare kinds ; also the Alpine Violas, and any such pretty rock creepers as the blue Bindweed of North Africa

There is in fact no limit to the beauty of rock and alpine flowers we may enjoy on the rough wall so often and most easily made about gardens in rocky and hilly districts, dressed or expensive stone not being needed   In my own garden there are three wholly different kinds of walls thick set with plants ; and the easiest way to the enjoyment of the most interesting and charming of the mountain flowers of the north is by the aid of walls.

ALPINE AND ROCK-PLANTS FOR BRITISH GARDENS.

Where the name of a large and varied family is given, as in Phlox, Iris, Rhododendron, Pentstemon, Salix, Antirrhinum, it is the alpine, or dwarf mountain kinds, that are meant.

Acæna	Chimaphila	Globularia	Myosotis	Sanguinaria
Acantholimon	Colchicum	Helianthemum	Narcissus	Saponaria
Achillea	Cornus	Helleborus	Nertera	Saxifraga
Acis	Coronilla	Houstonia	Œnothera	Scilla
Æthionema	Crocus	Hutchinsia	Omphalodes	Sedum
Alyssum	Cyclamen	Hyacinthus	Ononis	Sempervivum
Andromeda	Cypripedium	Iberis	Onosma	Senecio
Androsace	Daphne	Iris	Ophrys	Silene
Anemone	Dianthus	Isopyrum	Orchis	Smilacina
Antennaria	Diapensia	Jasione	Orobus	Soldanella
Anthyllis	Dodecatheon	Leiophyllum	Oxalis	Spigelia
Aquilegia	Draba	Leontopodium	Papaver	Statice
Arabis	Dracocephalum	Leucojum	Parnassia	Thalictrum
Arenaria	Dryas	Linaria	Petrocallis	Thlaspi
Armeria	Epigæa	Linnæa	Phlox	Thymus
Asperula	Erigeron	Linum	Polemonium	Trientalis
Astralagus	Erinus	Lithospermum	Polygala	Trillium
Aubrietia	Erodium	Loiseleuria	Potentilla	Triteleia
Bellis	Erpetion	Lychnis	Primula	Tulipa
Bryanthus	Erysimum	Lycopodium	Puschkinia	Tunica
Bulbocodium	Erythronium	Mazus	Pyrola	Vaccinium
Calandrinia	Galanthus	Meconopsis	Pyxidanthera	Veronica
Campanula	Gaultheria	Menziesia	Ranunculus	Vesicaria
Cardamine	Genista	Mertensia	Rhexia	Viola
Cerastium	Gentiana	Muscari	Rhododendron	Waldsteinia
Cheiranthus	Geranium			

Poet's Narcissus in the grass at Belmont, Ireland. From a photograph sent by Mr. J. H. Thomas.

CHAPTER XI.

THE WILD GARDEN.

O universal Mother, who dost keep
From everlasting thy foundations deep,
Eldest of things, Great Earth, I sing of thee.

IN a rational system of flower-gardening one of the first things to do is to get a clear idea of the aim of the "Wild Garden." When I began to plead the cause of the innumerable hardy flowers against the few tender ones put out in a formal way, the answer sometimes was, "We cannot go back to the mixed border"—that is to say, to the old way of arranging flowers in borders. Thinking, then, much of the vast world of plant beauty shut out of our gardens by the "system" then in vogue, I was led to consider the ways in which it might be brought into them, and of the "Wild Garden" as a home for numbers of beautiful hardy plants from other countries which might be naturalised, with very little trouble, in our gardens, fields, and woods—a world of delightful plant beauty that we might make happy around us, in places bare or useless. I saw that we could grow thus not only flowers more lovely than those commonly seen in what is called the flower garden, but also many which, by any other plan, we should have little chance of seeing.

The term "Wild Garden" is applied to the placing of perfectly hardy exotic plants in places where they will take care of themselves It has nothing to do with the "wilderness," though it may be carried out in it It does not necessarily mean the picturesque garden, for a garden may be picturesque and yet in every part the result of ceaseless care. What it does mean is best explained by the winter Aconite flowering under a grove of naked trees in February ; by the Snowflake abundant in meadows by the Thames ; and by the Apennine Anemone staining an English grove blue Multiply these instances by adding many different plants and hardy climbers from countries as cold as our own, or colder, and one may get some idea of the wild garden. Some have thought of it as a garden allowed to run wild, or with annuals sown promiscuously, whereas it does not meddle with the flower garden proper at all.

I wish the idea to be kept distinct from the various important phases of hardy plant growth in groups, beds, and borders, in which good culture may produce many happy effects , from the rock-garden or borders reserved for choice hardy flowers ; from growing hardy plants of fine form , from the ordinary type of spring garden In the smaller class of gardens there may be little room for the wild garden, but in the larger gardens, where there is often ample room on the outer fringes of the lawn, in grove, park, copse, or by woodland walks or drives, new and beautiful effects may be created by its means.

Among reasons for advocating this system are the following .— 1. Because many hardy flowers will thrive better in rough places than ever they did in the old border. Even small ones, like the Ivy-leaved Cyclamen, are naturalised and spread all over the mossy surface of woods. 2. Because, in consequence of plant, fern and flower and climber, grass, and trailing shrub, relieving each other, they will look infinitely better than in stiff gardens. 3. Because no ugly effects will result from decay and the swift passage of the seasons. In a semi-wild state the beauty of a species will show in flowering time , and when out of bloom they will be succeeded by other kinds, or lost among the numerous objects around 4 Because it will enable us to grow many plants that have never yet obtained a place in our " trim gardens "—multitudes that are not showy enough to be considered worthy of a place in a garden. Among the plants often thought unfit for garden cultivation are a number like the coarser American Asters and Golden Rods, which overrun the choicer border-flowers when planted among them. Such plants would be quite at home in neglected places, where their blossoms might be seen in due season. To these might be added plants like the winter Heliotrope, and many others, which, while interesting in the garden, are apt to spread so rapidly as to become a nuisance 5. Because in this way we may settle the question of spring flowers, and the spring garden, as well

as that of hardy flowers generally; and many parts of the grounds
may be made alive with spring flowers, without in the least interfering
with the flower garden itself. The blue stars of the Apennine
Anemone will be seen to greater advantage when in half-shady places,
under trees, or in the meadow grass, than in any flower garden, and
this is but one of many of sweet spring flowers that will succeed in
like ways.

Group of Mullein, near Scotch Firs, in Surrey Heath.

Narcissi in the Wild Garden.—Perhaps an example or two of
what has already been done with Daffodils and Snowdrops may serve
to show the way, and explain the gains of the wild garden, and there
is no more charming flower to begin with than the Narcissus, which,
while fair in form as any Orchid or Lily of the tropics, is as much at
home in our climate as the Kingcups in the marsh and the Primroses
in the wood. And when the wild Narcissus comes with these, in the
woods and orchards of Northern France and Southern England it

has also for companions the Violet and the Cowslip, hardiest children
of the north, blooming in and near the still leafless woods   And this
fact should lead us to see that it is not only a garden flower we have
here, but one which may give glorious beauty to our woods and fields
and meadows as well as to the pleasure grounds.

In our country in a great many places there is plenty of room to
grow them in other ways than in the garden proper, and this is not
merely in country seats, but in orchards and cool meadows.   To
chance growth in such places we owe it already that many Narcissi
or Daffodils which were lost to gardens, in the period when hardy
plants were wholly set aside for bedding plants, have been preserved
to us, at first probably in many cases thrown out with the garden
refuse.   In many places in Ireland and the west of England Narcissi
lost to gardens have been found in old orchards and meadows

There is scarcely a garden in the kingdom that is not disfigured
by vain attempts to grow trees, shrubs, and flowers that are not
really hardy, and it would often be much wiser to devote attention to
things that are absolutely hardy in our country, like most Narcissi
to which the hardest winters make no difference, and, besides, we
know from their distribution in Nature how fearless they are in this
respect.   Three months after our native kind has flowered in the
weald of Sussex and in the woods or orchards of Normandy, many
of its allies are beneath the snow in the mountain valleys of Europe,
waiting till the summer sun melts the deep snow.   On a high plateau
in Auvergne I saw many acres in full bloom on July 16, 1894, and
these high plateaux are much colder than our own country generally.
Soils that are cool and stiff and not favourable to a great variety
of plants suit Narcissi perfectly.   On the cool mountain marshes and
pastures, where the snow lies deep, the plant has abundance of
moisture—one reason why it succeeds better in our cool soils.   In
any case it does so, and it is mostly on dry light soils that Narcissi
fail to succeed.   Light, sandy or chalky soils in the south of England
are useless, and Narcissus culture on a large scale should not be
attempted on such soils.   We must not court failure, and however
freely in some soils Narcissi grow in turf, there is no law clearer than
that all plants will not grow in any one soil, and it is a mercy, too,
for if all soils were alike, we should find gardens far more monotonous
than they are now   Gardening is an art dealing with living things,
and we cannot place these with as little thought as those who arrange
shells, or coins, or plates.   At the same time we may be mistaken as
to failures which now and then arise from other causes than the soil.
I planted years ago some Bayonne Daffodils on the northern slope of
a poor field, and thought the plants had perished, as so little was seen
of them after the first year.   Despairing of the slope, it was planted

Narcissus in turf at Warley Place.

with Alder, a tree that grows in any cool soil. Years afterwards,. walking one day through the Alder, I found the Bayonne Daffodil in. perfect bloom. The roots had doubtless been weak and taken time to recover

Ten years ago I planted many thousands of Narcissi in the grass,. never doubting that I should succeed with them, but not expecting I should succeed nearly so well. They have thriven admirably,. bloomed well and regularly; the flowers are large and handsome, and in most cases have not diminished in size In open rich, heavy bottoms, along hedgerows, banks, in quiet open loamy fields, in every position they have been tried. They are delightful seen near at hand,. and also effective in the picture. The leaves ripen, disappear before mowing time, and do not in any way interfere with the farming. The harrowing and rolling of the fields in the spring hurt the leaves a little, but the plants are free from this near wood walks, by grass walks and open copses and lawns which abound in so many English country places.

As to the kinds we may naturalise with advantage, they are almost without limit, but generally it is better to take the great groups of Star Narcissi, the Poet's, and the wild Daffodil, of which there are so many handsome varieties. We can be sure that these are hardy in our soils , and, moreover, as we have to do this kind of work in a bold and rather unsparing way, we must deal with kinds that are easiest to purchase. There is hardly any limit except the one of rarity, and we must for the most part put our rare kinds in good garden ground till they increase, though we have to count with. the fact that in some cases Narcissi that will not thrive in a garden will do so in the grass of a meadow or orchard.

The fine distant effect of Narcissi in groups in the grass should not be forgotten. It is distinct from their effect in gardens, and it is most charming to see them reflect, as it were, the glory of the spring sun. It is not only their effect near at hand that charms us, but as we walk about we may see them in the distance in varying lights, sometimes through and beyond the leafless woods or copses. And there is nothing we have to fear in this charming work save the common sin—overdoing. To scatter Narcissi equally over the grass everywhere is to destroy all chance of repose, of relief, and of seeing them in the ways in which they often arrange themselves. It is almost as easy to plant in pretty ways as in ugly ways if we take the trouble to think of it. There are hints to be gathered in the way wild plants arrange themselves, and even in the sky. Often a small cloud passing in the sky will give a very good form for a group, and be instructive even in being closer and more solid towards its centre, as groups of Narcissi in the grass should often be The regular

Snowdrops in grass, Straffan, Kildare.

garden way of setting things out is very necessary in the garden, but it will not do at all if we are to get the pictures we can get from Narcissi in the turf, and it is always well to keep open turf here and there among the groups, and in a lawn or a meadow we should leave a large breadth quite free of flowers.

SNOWDROPS NATURALISED —The illustration is from a photograph taken by Mr. John McLeish at Straffan, Co. Kildare, and from it one may gain a glimpse of the pretty and natural way in which these flowers have grouped themselves on the greensward beneath the red-twigged Limes and on the soft and mossy lawns.   Originally no doubt the Snowdrops were planted, but they have seeded themselves so long that they are now thoroughly naturalised, and one of the sights to see at Straffan Gardens is the Snowdrops at their best under the leafless trees.   The common single and double forms are still the best for grouping in quantity and for naturalisation everywhere. There are finer varieties, but none grow and increase so well in our gardens as do these northern kinds   The best of the eastern Snowdrops are very bold and beautiful, they are unsurpassed for vigour of leafage and size of bloom if carefully cultivated, but they do not grow and increase on the grass as do G. nivalis and all its forms

For solid green leafage and size and substance of flower, G. Ikariæ when well grown is, as I believe, the finest of all Snowdrops, but it is from Asia Minor, and does not really love our soil and climate, nor is it likely to naturalise itself with us as G nivalis has done.   The best of all the really hardy and truly northern Snowdrops is a fine form of G. nivalis, leaning to the broad-leaved or G. caucasicus group, which was found in the Crimea in 1856 and introduced from the Tchernaya valley to Straffan   It is called G. nivalis grandis, or the Straffan Snowdrop, or G caucasicus var grandis, and to see it at its best is a great pleasure.   It is really a tall, vigorous-habited, and free-flowering form of the wild Snowdrop (G nivalis) as found in the Crimea.   The flowers are very large and pure in colour, and being borne on stalks a foot or more in length they bunch better than do those of the common type.   G plicatus is also from the Crimea, but is, as I have said, quite different, having much broader plicate leaves and smaller flowers

Snowdrops generally like deep, moist soils and half shade, as their flowers wither and brown quickly on dry, light soils in full sunshine In damp woods, copses, and hedgerows they seem most at home, and, like Narcissi and many other early-flowering bulbs, they rather enjoy flooding or occasional irrigation after root and top growth have begun At Straffan the lawn lies low down near the river Liffey, and it is sometimes submerged for a day or two after the snow melts in early spring or after heavy rains.   From May until September, however, the bulbs are dry among the tree roots with the dense canopy of Lime leafage overhead, as are also the roots of the sky-blue Apennine Anemone that bear them company. We are beginning to perceive that, as a broad rule, some bulbous plants enjoy growing amongst the roots of other plants, or of trees and shrubs, or in the grass of lawn or meadow. The wild Daffodil and Bluebells do this as well as the Snowdrop, and those who have tried to dig up bulbs of any kind abroad with a knife or even with a botanical trowel, will remember how tightly wedged they frequently are in roots of various kinds, or jammed tightly in both roots and stones.   F. W. B.

How to Plant.—I usually plant Narcissi in grass by turning back the sod, making two cuts with the spade at right angles, and then pressing up and back the sod, laying it back on a hinge, as it were, putting in a few bulbs, mostly round the sides of the hole, turning the sod back and treading firmly upon it. The question is largely one of convenience and the ground one has to plant   If one could improve the subsoil it would be better for some soils, no doubt, but if the work is done in a bold way and there is much other planting going on, it is not easy to get time to plant things in the grass with care. Sometimes in breaking new ground or carrying out changes one gets a chance of throwing in some bulbs before the surface is levelled up   Once in planting Grape Hyacinths in an uneven grassy slope they were placed on the turf in the hollows and then levelled up with earth, and both grass and bulbs soon came through. Once some bullocks passed an evening where they "didn't ought to" in a grassy enclosure near the house, and their footmarks suggested a group of the Apennine Windflower, and a few of its roots were put in and the holes filled up   A wily man will see odd ways now and then of getting bulbs or seeds in.   When the men are making sod banks for the only true field fence—a live one—is a very good time to put in Sweet Briars in the bank   In certain soils seeds may be sown betimes—seeds of Foxglove, Evening Primrose, and stout biennials. Fragile bulbs will want more care and less depth than the bolder Narcissi. Many ways are good, though far more important than any way of planting is thought as to the wants of the thing we plant, not only as to soil, but association with the things that will grow about it in grass, in hedgerows and rough places, for plants are not all garotters like the great Japanese Knotworts and the big Moon Daisies ; and little ducks must not be left among barn rats or we may not see them again.

All planting in the grass should be in natural groups or prettily fringed colonies, growing to and fro as they like after planting. Lessons in this grouping are to be had in the woods, copses, heaths, and meadows, by those who look about them as they go.   At first many will find it difficult to get out of formal masses, but they may

M

be got over by studying natural groupings of wild flowers. Once established, the plants soon begin to group themselves in pretty ways

The Secret of the Soil.—In the cultivation of hardy plants and especially in wild gardening the important thing is to find out what things really do in the soil, without which much good way cannot be made. Many people make errors in planting things that are notoriously tender in our country and very often fail in consequence ; but apart from such risky planting perfectly hardy plants may disappear owing to some dislike of the soil. They flower feebly at first and afterwards gradually wane in spite of all our efforts. I have made attempts to establish spring Snowflakes in grass, none of which succeeded, owing to the cool soil, yet one of the Snowflakes in the Thames Valley grows with the vigour of a wild plant. I have put thousands of Snowdrops in places where I could hardly see a flower a few years later, yet in some places it establishes itself in friable soil by streamlets and in many other situations. So it is with the Crocus. I find it difficult to naturalise, taking but slowly and gradually diminishing, and yet I have seen it in places cover the ground. The Narcissus, which is so free and enduring in cool damp soil does little good on warm, light or chalky soil. What will do or will not do is often a question of experience, but the point is when we see a thing doing well to take the hint. People often complain of the texture of the grass as a cause of failure, yet I have thousands of the Tenby Daffodil for ten years in rich and rank masses of Cocksfoot and other coarse grasses in coverts—never mown or the old grass taken away at any time, and the Narcissus gets better year by year. So it is a question of finding out the thing the soil will grow, and we shall perhaps only arrive at that knowledge after various discouragements. Some things are so omnivorous in their appetites that they will grow anywhere, but some, the more beautiful races of bulbous and other early flowers, will only thrive and stay with us where they like the soil. It should be clearly seen therefore that what may be done with any good result in the wild garden cannot be determined beforehand, but must depend on the nature of the soil and other circumstances which can be known only to those who study the ground.

Flowers beneath Trees—Where the branches of trees, both evergreen and summer-leafing, sweep the turf in pleasure-grounds many pretty spring-flowering bulbs may be naturalised beneath the branches, and will thrive without attention. It is chiefly in the case of deciduous trees that this can be done ; but even in the case of Conifers and Evergreens some graceful objects may be dotted beneath the outermost points of their lower branches. We know that a great number of our spring flowers and hardy bulbs mature their foliage and go to rest early in the year. In spring they require light and sun, which they obtain abundantly under the summer-leafing tree ; they have time to flower and grow under it before the foliage of the tree appears ; then, as the summer heats approach, they are overshadowed, and go to rest ; but the leaves of the tree once fallen, they soon begin to reappear and cover the ground with beauty.

Some Plants for the Wild Garden.

The following are the chief families of plants that may be used in the wild garden. Where families are named which are British as well as natives of the Continent of Europe, as in the case of, say, Scilla, the foreign kinds are meant. In considering what may be done in naturalising plants in a given position, it may be well to cast the eye over the families available. Success will depend on how the plants are chosen to go in any one position, but about country seats soils are so much varied that it is not easy to generalise.

Acanthus	Crane's-bill	Honesty	Narcissus	Snapdragon
Aconite, Winter	Crocus	Honeysuckle	Omphalodes	Snowdrop
Asphodel	Cyclamen	Houseleek	Ox-eye Daisy	Snowflake
Aubrietia	Daffodil	Iris	Pæony	Solomon's Seal
Barrenwort	Day Lily	Knotwort	Pea, Everlasting	Star of Bethlehem
Bee Balm	Dog's tooth Violet	Lavender	Periwinkle	Starwort
Bellflower	Ferns, Hardy	Leopard's-bane	Phlox	Stonecrop
Bindweed	Forget-me-not	Lily	Plantain Lily	Sun Rose
Blood Root	Foxglove	Lily-of-the-valley	Pond-flower	Sun flower (Peren-
Borage	French Willow	Loosestrife	Poppy	nial)
Broom	Giant Fennel	Lungwort	Primrose, Evening	Thyme
Christmas Rose	Giant Scabious	Lupine	Rest Harrow	Tulip
Clematis	Globe Flower	Mallow	Rocket	Viola
Columbine	Globe Thistle	Meadow Rue	Rose, wild kinds	Virginian Creeper
Comfrey	Golden Rod	Meadow Saffron	St. Bruno's Lily	Virginian Poke
Compass Plant	Grape Hyacinth	Meadow Sweet	St. John's Wort	Wallflower
Cornflower	Heath	Mimulus	Sandwort	Water Lily
Coronilla	Heliotrope, Winter	Monk's hood	Scabious	Windflower
Cotton Thistle	Hepatica	Mountain Avens	Scilla	Wistaria
Cow Parsnip	Holly, Sea	Mullein	Snake's head	Wood Lily

Wreath of old Wistaria, Efford Manor.

CHAPTER XII.

SPRING GARDENS.

I have seen foreign flowers in hothouses of the most beautiful nature, but I
do not care a straw for them. The simple flowers of our spring are what
I want to see again."—JOHN KEATS (Letter to James Rice).

IN our islands, swept by the winds of iceless seas, spring wakes early
in the year, when the plains of the north and the mountains of the
south and centre are cold in snow. In our green springs the flowers
of northern and alpine countries open long before they do in their
native homes; hence the artistic error of any system of flower-
gardening which leaves out the myriad flowers of spring. It is no
longer a question of gardens being bare of the right plants; nurseries
and gardens where there are many good plants are not rare, but
to make effective use of these much thought is seldom given.
Gardens are often rich in plants but poor in beauty, many being
stuffed with things, but in ugly effect.

If we are to make good use of our spring garden flora we should
avoid much annual culture, though it is not well to get rid of it
altogether, as many plants depend for their beauty on rich ground
and frequent cultivation. But many grow well without these, and
the most delightful spring gardens can only be where we grow
many spring blooming things that demand no annual care, from
Globe-flowers to Hawthorns.

A common kind of "spring gardening" consists of "bedding
out" Forget-me-nots, Pansies, Daisies, Catchflies, and Hyacinths;
but this way is only one of many, and the meanest, most costly, and
inartistic It began when we had few good spring flowers, now we

have many ; and hence this chapter must deal with other and better ways

The fashion of leaving beds of Roses and choice shrubs bare of all but one subject should be given up. The half-bare Rose and choice shrub beds should be a home for the prettiest spring flowers— Pansies, Violets, early Irises, Daffodils, Scillas, and many other dwarf plants in colonies between the Roses or shrubs. Double Primroses are happy and flower well in such beds. The slight shade such plants receive in summer from the other tenants of the bed assists them. Where Rhododendrons are planted in an " open way (and these precious bushes never ought to be jammed together), a spring garden of another kind may be made, as the peat-loving plants (and there are many fair ones among them) will be quite at home there. The White Wood Lily of the American woods (Trillium), the Virginian Lungwort, the Canadian Bloodroot (Sanguinaria), the various Dog's-tooth Violets, double Primroses, and many early-flowering bulbous plants enjoy the partial shade and shelter and the soil of the beds for " American " shrubs.

In the kitchen garden, in its usual free and rich soil, simple beds of favourite spring flowers, such as Polyanthuses, Bunch Primroses in their coloured forms, self-coloured Auriculas, and Pansies of various kinds, are a good way of enjoying such plants, and more easily managed than the " bedding out " of spring flowers That may follow the fashion of the hour, and with such plants as Forget-me-nots, Daisies, Silene, Pansy, Violet, Hyacinth, Anemone, and Tulip showy effects may be formed ; but without any of these pattern beds under the windows, fair gardens of spring flowers may be made in every place, and the problem of the design for the few set beds of the " spring parterre " will not be so serious a matter as in the past, there being so many aids in other ways, as we shall see.

ROCK AND ALPINE PLANTS.—There are so many hardy plants among these that flower in spring (many alpine plants blooming as soon as the snow goes), that there is not room to name them all in an essay devoted to the more effective groups and their best garden use We must omit any detailed notice of plants like Adonis, Cyclamen, Draba, Erodium, and the smaller Rockfoils and Stonecrops, Dicentra, Fumaria, Orobus, Ramondia, Silene, and many other flowers of the rocks and hills, which though beautiful individually do not tell so well in the picture as many here named

ROCK CRESSES AND WALLFLOWERS —Among rock plants the first place belongs to certain mountain plants of the northern world, which, in our country, come into bloom before the early shrubs and trees, and among the first bold plants to cheer us in spring are those of the Wallflower order—the yellow Alyssum, effective and easy to grow, the white Arabis, even more grown in northern France than in England (it well deserves to be spread about in sheets and effective groups), and the beautiful purple Rock Cresses (Aubrietia), lovely plants of the mountains of Greece and the countries near, which have developed a number of varieties even more beautiful in colour than the wild kinds. Nothing for gardens can be more precious than these plants, the long spring bloom being effective in almost every kind of flower gardening—banks, walls, edgings, borders of evergreen, rock plants, or carpets beneath sparsely set shrubs The white evergreen Candytufts are also effective plants in clear sheets for borders, edgings to beds, tops of walls, and the rougher flanks of the rock garden These are among the plants that have been set out in hard lines in flower gardens, but it is easy to have better effects from them in groups, and even in broken lines and masses, or as carpets beneath bushes, thus giving softer and more beautiful, if less definite, effects. Happy always on castle wall and rocks, the Wallflower is most welcome in the garden, where, on warm soils and in genial climates, it does well, but hard winters injure it often in cold and inland districts, and it is almost like a tender plant in such conditions. Yet it must ever be one of the flowers best worth growing in sheltered and warm · gardens ; and even in cold places one may have a few under the eaves of cottages and on dry south borders It is where large masses of it are grouped in the open and are stricken—as the greens of the garden are stricken—in cold winters, that we have to regret having given it labour and a place which might have been better devoted to things hardy everywhere. The various old double Wallflowers are somewhat tender too and rarely seen in good character, save in favoured soils, which is all the more reason for making the most of them where the soil and air favour them Certain allies of the Wallflower, mountain plants for the most part, such as the alpine Wallflower, also give good effects where well done and grouped on dry banks or warm borders

THE WINDFLOWERS are a noble group among the most beautiful of the northern and eastern flowers, some being easily naturalised (like the blue Italian and Greek Anemones), while the showy Poppy Anemones are easily grown where the soils are light and warm, and in genial warm districts ; but they require some care on certain soils, and are among the plants we must cultivate and even protect on cold soils in hard winters. The same is true of the brilliant Asiatic Ranunculus and all its varied forms—Persian, Turkish, and French, as they may be called, all forms of one wild North African buttercup, unhappily too tender to endure our winters in the open air, but they should be abundantly grown on the warm limestone and other soils which suit them, as about our coasts

Lilies, and Rhododendrons. Warley Place.

and in Ireland. There is no more effective way of growing these than in simple 4-foot beds in the kitchen or reserve garden. The Wood Anemone is so often seen in the woods that there is rarely need to grow it, but some of its varieties are essential, most beautiful being A. Robinsoniana, a flower of lovely blue colour, and a distinct gain in the spring garden grown in almost any way. The Hepatica is a lovely little Anemone where the soil is free, though slow in some soils, and where it grows well all its varieties should be encouraged, in borders and margins of beds of American bushes as well as in the rock garden The Snowdrop Windflower (A. sylvestris) is most graceful in bud and bloom, but a little capricious, and not blooming well on all soils, unlike in this way our Wood Windflowers, which are as constant as the Kingcups The Pasque-flower is lovely on the chalk downs and fields of Normandy and parts of England in spring, but never quite so pretty in a garden. It would be worth naturalising in chalky fields and woods or banks.

COLUMBINE, MARSH MARIGOLD, CLEMATIS, LENTEN ROSE, AND GLOBE-FLOWER.—Columbines are very beautiful in the early part of the year, and if we had nothing but the common kind (Aquilegia vulgaris) and its forms, they would be precious; but there are many others which thrive in free soils, some of which are very graceful in form and charming in colour The Kingcup or Marsh Marigold, so fine in wet meadows and by the riverside, should be brought into gardens wherever there is water, as it is a most effective plant when well grown, and there are several forms, double and single. The Clematis, the larger kinds, are mostly for the summer, but some (C. montana, C alpina, C cirrhosa) are at their best in the spring; they should be made abundant use of on house walls and over banks, trees and shrubs. The Winter Aconite (earliest of spring flowers) naturalises itself in some soils, but on others dwindles and dies out, and it should not be grown in the garden, but in shrubberies, copses, or woods where the soil suits it. Some kinds of hardy Ranunculus, the herbaceous double kinds, are good in colour, and in bold groups pretty; but taller and bolder and finer in effect are the Globe-flowers, easily naturalised in moist, grassy places or by water, and also free and telling among stout herbaceous plants The most distinct addition to the spring garden of recent years is the Oriental Hellebore in its many beautiful varieties, of which some have been raised in gardens. They are handsome and stately plants, with large flowers, often delicately marked. With the usual amount of garden shelter and fairly good soil they grow bold and free, and have a stately habit and fine foliage, as well as beautiful flowers excellent for cutting. They are most effective, sturdy, impressive plants for opening the flower year with, often blooming abundantly at the dawn of spring, and have the essential merit of not requiring annual culture, tufts remaining in vigour in the same spot for many years

DOG'S-TOOTH VIOLETS, SNOWDROP, SNOWFLAKE, CROCUS, SCILLA, FRITILLARY, AND HYACINTH.—The European Dog's-tooth Violet is pretty in the budding grass, where it is free in growth and bloom. The Fritillary is one of the most welcome flowers for grass, and is best in moist meadows; the rarer kinds do well in good garden soil, those with pale yellow bells being beautiful Every plant such as these, which we can so easily grow at home in grassy places, makes our cares about the spring garden so much the less, and allows of keeping all the precious beds of the flower garden itself for the plants that require some care and rich soil always

The Hyacinth, which is often set in such stiff masses in our public gardens, gives prettier effects more naturally grouped, but it is not nearly so important for the open air as many flowers more easy to grow and better in effect, though some of the more slender wild species, like H. amethystinus, are beautiful and deserve a good place The Snowdrop is of even greater value of late years, owing to new forms of it, some of which have been brought from Asia Minor and others raised in gardens. In some soils it is quite free and becomes easily naturalised, in others it dwindles away, and the same is true of the vernal Snowflake (Leucojum vernum), a beautiful plant The larger Snowflakes are more free in ordinary soils, and easily naturalised in river bank soil. The Crocus, the most brilliant of spring flowers, does not always lend itself to growing naturally in every soil, but on some it is quite at home, especially those of a chalky nature, and will naturalise itself under trees, while in many garden soils it is delightful for edgings and in many ways

To the Scilla we owe much, from the wild plant of our woods to the vivid Siberian kind, some kinds are essential in the garden, and some, like the Spanish Scilla (S. campanulata), may be naturalised in free soils Allies of these lovely early flowers have come of recent years to our gardens—the beautiful Chionodoxa from Asia Minor, of about the same stature and effect as the prettiest of the Scillas, and some of them even more precious for colour These are among the plants which may be planted with best results in bold groups on the surface of beds planted with permanent flowers, such as Roses—where Rose beds are not surfaced with manure, as all Rose-growers unwisely advise.

IRIS, GRAPE HYACINTH, NARCISSUS, AND TULIP.—In warm soils some of the more beautiful of the flowers of spring are the early Irises, but in gardens generally the most beautiful of Irises come in late spring with the German Iris, which is so free and hardy throughout our country. Orchid-houses themselves cannot give any such array as these when in bloom, and they are often deserving of a little garden to themselves, where there is room for it, while they are useful in many ways in borders and as groups. About the same time come the precious Spanish Iris in many colours, lovely as Orchids, and very easily grown, and the English Iris. The Grape Hyacinths are pretty and early plants of Southern Europe, beautiful in colour. They increase rapidly, and some kinds do very well in the grass in free and peaty soils , but the rarer ones are best on warm borders and groups in the rock garden. The Narcissus is worth growing in every way—the rarer kinds in prepared borders or beds and the many that are plentiful in almost any cool soil in the grass. In our country, where there are so many cool and rich soils allowing of the Narcissus being naturalised and grown admirably in many ways, it is, perhaps, on the whole, the most precious of all our spring flowers. But the Tulip is the most gorgeous in colour of all the flowers of spring, and for its effectiveness is better worthy of special culture than most—indeed, the florists' kinds and the various rare garden Tulips must be well grown to show their full size and beauty Replanting now and then is almost essential with a Tulip garden if we are to keep the bulbs free from disease ; the wood Tulip and certain wild species may be naturalised, and in that state are as beautiful, if not so large, as the cultivated bulbs. The Tulip deserves a far better place among spring flowers than it has ever had, as, apart from the two great groups of early and late Tulips hitherto cultivated in European gardens, a number of handsome wild kinds are being introduced from Central Asia and other countries, many of them having early flowers of great beauty and fine colour, and if they will only take kindly to our climate the Tulip garden will soon leave all hot-house brilliancy a long way in the rear

PÆONY, POPPY AND LUPIN.—Pæonies are nobly effective in many ways Where single or other kinds are plentiful they may be well used as broad groups in new plantations, among shrubs and low trees, and as to the choice double kinds, no plants better deserve a little garden or border to themselves, while the tree kinds make superb groups on the lawn and are safer from frost on high ground. The great scarlet Poppies are showy in spring, and best grown among trees and in the wild garden, and with them may be named the Welsh Poppy, a very effective plant in spring as well as summer, and often sowing itself in all sorts of places. The various garden forms of the opium Poppy and of the field Poppy, both double and single, are very showy where any space is given to annual flowers

The common perennial Lupin is a very showy, pretty plant grown in a free way in groups and masses, and may sometimes be naturalised, and, associated with Poppies and free-growing Columbines in the wild garden, it is very effective.

PRIMROSE, TULIP, COWSLIP, POLYANTHUS AND AURICULA.—

The Yulan (Magnolia conspicua) at Gunnersbury House.

Primroses are a lovely host for the garden, especially the garden varieties of the common Primrose, Cowslip, and Oxlip. Few things deserve a better place, or are more worthy of good culture in visible groups and colonies or rich garden borders. Apart from the lovely races of garden forms raised from the Primrose, the Cowslip, and the Oxlip, and also the Alpine Auriculas, double Primroses should not be forgotten, as in all moist districts and in peaty and free soil they give such tender and beautiful colour in groups, borders, or slightly shaded among dwarf shrubs Primroses and Polyanthus of native origin, are well backed up by the beautiful Indian Primrose (Primula rosea), which thrives apace in cool soils in the north of England and in Scotland, and which, when grown in bold groups, is very good in effect, as are the purplish Indian Primroses under like conditions.

ROCKFOIL, GENTIAN, AND ALPINE PHLOX. — The large-leaved Indian Rockfoils (Saxifraga) are in many soils very easily grown, and they are showy spring flowers in bold groups, especially some of the improved varieties Although it is only in places where there is rocky ground or large rock gardens that one can get the beauty of the smaller Mountain Rockfoils (Saxifraga), we cannot omit to notice their beauty—both the white, yellow, and crimson-flowered kind—when seen in masses. The same may be said of Gentians , beautiful as they are in the mountains, few gardens have positions where we can get their fine effect, always excepting the old Gentianella (G. acaulis), which in old Scotch and English gardens used to make such handsome broad edgings, and which is easily grown in a cool soil, and gives, perhaps, the noblest effect of blue flowers that one can enjoy in our latitudes in spring. The tall Phloxes are plants of the summer, but there is a group of American dwarf alpine Phloxes of the mountains which are among the hardiest and most cheery flowers of spring, thriving on any dry banks and in the drier parts of rock gardens, forming mossy edgings in the flower garden, and breaking into a foam of flowers early in spring.

PANSIES.—The Viola family is most precious, not only in the many forms of the sweet Violet, which will always deserve garden cultivation, but in the numerous varieties of the Pansy, which flower so effectively in the spring The best of all, perhaps, for artistic use are the Tufted Pansies, which are delightfully simple in colour—white, pale blue, or lavender, and various other delicate shades. Almost perennial in character, they can be increased and kept true, and they give us distinct and delicate colour in masses as wide as we wish, instead of the old " variegated " effect of Pansies Though the separate flowers of these were often handsome, the effect of the Tufted Pansies with their pure and delicate colours is more valuable, and these also, while pretty in groups and patches, will, where there is space, often be worth growing in little nursery beds

FORGET-ME-NOTS are among the most welcome flowers of spring.

Before the common and most beautiful of all—the marsh Forget-me-not—comes, there are the wood Forget-me-not (M. sylvatica) and M. dissitiflora and M. alpestris, all precious early flowers. Allied to the ever-welcome Forget-me-not is the common Omphalodes, or creeping Forget-me-not, valuable for its freedom in growth in half shady or

Rhododendron garden, Bidston, Cheshire.

rough places in almost any soil—one of the most precious of the early flowers which take care of themselves if we take a little trouble to put them in likely places. Among

ANNUAL FLOWERS that bloom in spring where the soil is favourable, excellent results are often obtained by sowing Sweet Peas in Autumn. Where this is done, and they escape the winter, they give welcome hedges of flowers in the early year   So, too, the Cornflower, a lovely spring flower, and perhaps the finest blue we have among annual plants ; but to have it good and early it should be always sown in Autumn, and for effect it should be in broad masses, sometimes among shrubs or in recently broken ground which we desire to cover.   Some of the Californian annuals are handsome and vigorous when sown in autumn, always provided they escape the winter   The White Godetia is very fine in this way.   In all chalky, sandy, and warm soils the Stocks for spring bloom are handsome and fragrant, but it is a waste of time to attempt to grow them on cold soils.   It would be taking too narrow a view to omit from our thoughts of spring gardens the many beautiful flowering.

SHRUBS AND TREES THAT BLOOM IN SPRING, as some of the finest effects come from the early trees and shrubs   Among the most stately are the Chestnuts, particularly the red kinds, fine in all stages, but especially when old.   The snowy Mespilus is a hardy, low-sized tree, blooming regularly, and well deserves a place in the pleasure garden or the fringes of shrubberies.   The Almonds, more than any shrubs, perhaps, in our country and in France, light up the earliest days of Spring, and, like most southern trees, are best in warm valley soils, growing more slowly in cool heavy soils   They should be in groups to tell in the home landscape   The double Peaches are lovely in France, but as yet rarely so with us, owing, perhaps, to some defect of the stock used   Perhaps of all the hardy shrubs ever brought to our country the Azaleas are the most precious for effect   They are mostly wild on the mountains of America, and many forms have been raised in gardens which are of the highest value.   Many places do not as yet show the great beauty of the different groups of hardy Azalea, particularly the late kinds raised of recent years.   A neglected tree with us is the Judas-tree, which is very handsome in groups, as it ought always to be grown, and not as a starved single tree.   The various double Cherries are noble flowering trees, being showy as well as delicate in bloom, and the Japanese kinds do quite as well as the old French and English double Cherries, though the trees are apt to perish from grafting.   The American Fringe-tree (Chionanthus) is pretty, but some American flowering trees do not ripen their wood well enough in England generally to give us the handsome effects seen in their own country   Hawthorns are a host in themselves ; those of our own country make natural spring gardens of hills and rocky places, and should teach us to give a place to the many other species to be found in the mountains of Europe and America, which vary the bloom and prolong the season of early-flowering trees   There are many varieties of our native hawthorn—red, pink, double, and weeping   The old Laburnum has for many years been a joy with its golden rain, and of late we are doubly well off with improved forms, with long chains of golden flowers These will become noble flowering trees as they get old , hence the importance of grouping Laburnum trees to get the varieties together.

Among the early charms in the spring garden are the slender wands of the Forsythia, hardy Chinese bushes, pale yellow, delightful in effect when grown in picturesque ways , effective also on walls or grouped in the open air on banks Another plant of refined beauty, but too little planted, is the Snowdrop-tree (Halesia) Unlike other American trees, it ripens its wood in our country, and often flowers well. The Mountain Laurel of America (Kalmia) is one of the most beautiful things ever brought to our country, and as a late spring flower is precious, thriving both in the open and in half shady places

BROOM AND FURZE.—There is no more showy plant or one more beautiful in effect in masses than the common Broom and all its allies that are hardy enough, even the little Spanish Furze giving fine colour. The common Broom should be encouraged on bluffs and sandy or gravelly places, so as to save us the trouble of growing it in gardens, for in effect there is nothing better. The same may be said of the Furze, which is such a beautiful plant in England and the coast regions of France, and the double Furze deserves to be massed in the garden in picturesque groups In country seats, especially those commanding views, its value in the foreground is very great, and it is so easily raised from seed that fine effects are very easily secured, though it may be cut down now and then in hard winters.

RHODODENDRON AND MAGNOLIA —The glory of spring in our pleasure grounds is the Rhododendrons , but they are so over-mastering in their effect on people's minds that very often they lead to neglect of other things It would be difficult to overrate their charms , but even amongst them we require to discriminate, and avoid the too early and tender kinds Many of the kinds raised from R ponticum and the Indian Rhododendron, while they thrive in mild districts in the south of England and West of France, near the sea, are not hardy in the country generally Some of these tender hybrids certainly flower early, but we get little good from that The essential thing, when we give space to a hardy shrub, is that we should get its bloom in perfection, and therefore we should choose the broad-leaved hardy kinds, which are mostly raised from the very hardy North American R catawbiense, and be a little particular in grouping the prettiest colours, never using a grafted plant. For many years the Yulan Magnolia has, when well grown, been one of the finest trees in English southern gardens, and nothing is more effective than the Lily-tree in gardens like Syon and others in the Thames valley, while of late years we have seen precious additions to this, the noblest family of flowering trees. Some of these, like M. stellata, have proved to be valuable; all are worth a trial, and, as to the kinds we are sure of, the great thing is to group them. Even in the case of the common Lily-tree (M Yulan) it makes a great difference whether there are four or five trees or one.

Amongst the most beautiful of the smaller alpine bushes ever brought to our country is the alpine forest Heath, which is cheery and bright for weeks in spring. It is one of the plants that never fails us, and only requires to be grown in bold ways to be effective—in groups and masses fully exposed to the sun. Other Heaths, like the Mediterranean Heath, are also beautiful in some favoured parts of the country, but not so hardy generally as the little alpine forest Heath, which has the greatest endurance and most perfect hardiness, as becomes a native of the Alps of Europe

Pyrus japonica, a handsome old shrub often planted on cottage garden walls, may in many soils be used with good effect in groups and hedges. The evergreen Barberries in various forms are beautiful early shrubs, with soft yellow flowers, and excellent when grouped in some quantity. Two very important families are the Deutzias and Syringas which are varied and beautiful, mostly in white masses. They should never be buried in the common shrubbery, but grouped in good masses of each family. The flowering Currant (Ribes) of the mountains of N.W. America is in all its forms a very cheery and early bush, which tells well in the home landscape if rightly placed; but perhaps the most welcome and important of all early trees and shrubs is the Lilac which in Britain is often grown in a few kinds only, when there are many in France. Beautiful in almost any position, Lilacs are most effective when planted together, so as to enjoy the full sun to ripen their wood, the danger of thick planting can be avoided by putting Irises or other hardy flowers over the ground between the shrubs, which should never be crowded.

CRAB BLOOM —Apart from the many orchard trees grown for their fruit, we have in our own day to welcome some of their allies— lovely in flower, if often poor in fruit. Our country has never been without some of this kind of beauty, as the Crab itself is as handsome a flowering tree as are many of the Apples which are descended from it in all the countries in Europe, from Russia to Spain, and in our gardens there were for many years the old Chinese double Pyrus, a handsome tree which became popular, and the American Crab, which never became so But of late years we have been enriched by the Japan Crab, a lovely tree for some weeks in spring and other handsome kinds including Parkman's Crab, which comes to us under more than one name, and a red form of the Japanese flowering Crab before mentioned. All these trees are as hardy as our native Crab, and differ much in colour and sometimes also in form. It is difficult to describe how much beauty they give where well grown and well placed ; they are not the kind of things we lose owing to change of fashion, and in planting them it is well to put them in groups where they will tell Apart from these more or less wild species there are numbers of hybrid Crabs—raised between the Siberian and some common Apples in America and in our country—that are beautiful also in flower, and remarkable too for beauty of fruit, so that a beautiful grove of flowering trees might be formed of Crabs alone With these many fine things, and the various Honeysuckles, we are carried bravely down to the time of Rose and Lily—summer flowers, though Roses often come on warm walls in spring.

SPRING FLOWERS IN SUN AND SHADE AND NORTH AND SOUTH ASPECTS —It is worth while thinking of the difference in the blooming of spring flowers in various aspects, as differences in that way will often give us a longer season of bloom of some of our most precious things Daffodils do better in half shade than in full sunshine, and Scillas and other bulbs are like the Daffodils in liking half shady spots , so also Crown Imperials, which, like the Scillas, bleach badly if fully exposed to the sun. We may see the Wood Hyacinth pass out of bloom on the southern slopes of a hill, and in fresh and fair bloom on its northern slopes Flowering shrubs, creepers on walls, and all early plants are influenced in the same way Such facts may be taken advantage of in many ways, especially with the nobler flowers that we make much use of. If different aspects are worth securing for hardy flowers generally, they are doubly so for those of the spring, when we often have storms of snow and sleet that may destroy an early bloom. If fortunate enough to have the same plant on the north side of the hill or wall, we have still a chance of a second bloom, and a difference of two or three weeks in the blooming of a plant

Let all who love the early flowers look at this list, not of the kinds of spring flowers (which are innumerable), but of the families , some of these, such as Narcissus and Rockfoil, comprise many species of lovely flowers, and the story of these, too, is the story of the spring .—

N

Some Spring and Early Summer Flowers Hardy in English Gardens.

Adonis	Convallaria	Fritillaria	Muscari	Sanguinaria
Alyssum	Crocus	Fumaria	Myosotis	Saponaria
Androsace	Cyclamen	Galanthus	Narcissus	Saxifraga
Anemone	Dentaria	Geum	Omphalodes	Scilla
Aquilegia	Dianthus	Gypsophila	Ornithogalum	Sedum
Arabis	Dicentra	Helleborus	Orobus	Silene
Arenaria	Dodecatheon	Hepatica	Pæonia	Trillium
Armeria	Doronicum	Hesperis	Papaver	Triteleia
Asperula	Draba	Hyacinthus	Phlox	Trollius
Asphodelus	Epimedium	Iberis	Polemonium	Tulipa
Aubrietia	Eranthis	Iris	Potentilla	Uvularia
Bellis	Erinus	Leucojum	Primula	Veronica
Caltha	Erodium	Linum	Pulmonaria	Vinca
Centauræ	Erythronium	Lychnis	Ramondia	Viola
Clematis	Ficaria	Meconopsis	Ranunculus	

Spring-flowering Trees and Shrubs.

Æsculus	Cratægus	Genista	Mespilus	Styrax
Amelanchier	Cydonia	Halesia	Philadelphus	Syringa
Amygdalus	Cytisus	Kerria	Prunus	Tamarix
Andromeda	Daphne	Laburnum	Pyrus	Ulex
Azalea	Deutzia	Lonicera	Rhododendron	Viburnum
Berberis	Erica	Magnolia	Ribes	Weigela
Cerasus	Exochorda	Mahonia	Spartium	Wistaria
Cercis	Forsythia	Malus	Spiræa	

Climbing Rose on cottage porch, Surrey.

THE SUMMER GARDEN BEAUTIFUL.

CHAPTER XIII.

THE NEW ROSE GARDEN.

WHATEVER may be thought of the reasoning in this chapter, of one fact there can be no doubt, namely, that the nobler flowers have been rejected as unfit for the flower garden in our own day, and first among them the Rose. Since the time when people went in for patterned colour many flowers were set aside, like the Rose, the Carnation, and the Lily, that did not lend themselves to flat colour ; and thus we see ugly, bare, and at the same time costly gardens round country houses ; and therefore I begin the summer garden with the Rose, too long left out of her right place, and put in the background.

There is great loss to the flower-garden from the usual way of growing the Rose as a thing apart, and its absence at present from the majority of flower gardens. It is surprising to see how poor and hard many places are to which the beauty of the Rose might add delight, and the only compensation for all this blank is what is called the rosery, which in large places is often an ugly thing with plants that usually only blossom for a few weeks in summer. This idea of the Rose garden arose when we had a much smaller number of Roses, and a greater number of these were kinds that flowered in summer mainly. The old standard Rose had something to do with this separate growth of Roses, it being laid down in the books that the standards did not "associate" with other shrubs, and so it came about that all the standards grafted were placed in the rosery and there held up their buds to the frost! The nomenclature, too, in use among Rose-growers—by which Roses that flower the shortest time were given the name of Hybrid Perpetuals—has had something to do with the absence of the Rose from the flower garden Shows, too, have had a bad effect on the Rose in the garden, where it is many times more important than as a show flower. The whole aim of the man who shows Roses, and who is too often followed as a leader, was to get a certain number of large flowers grown on the Dog Rose, Manetti, or any stock which enabled him to get this at the least cost, so, if we go to any Rose-showing friend, we shall probably find his plants for show grown in the kitchen garden with a deep bed of manure on the surface of the beds, and as pretty as so many broomsticks. This idea of the Rose as a show flower leads to the cultivation of Roses that have not a high value as garden flowers, and Roses that do not open their flowers well in our country in the open air, and are not really worth growing, are grown because they happen to produce flowers now and then that look well on a show bench. So altogether the influence of the shows has been against the Rose as a garden flower, and a cause why large gardens are, in the flower garden, quite bare of the grace of the queen of flowers.

THE ROSE NOT A "DECORATIVE" PLANT!—It is instructive to study the influence of rose books upon the Rose as well as that of the Rose exhibitions, as they brought about an idea that the Rose was not a "decorative" plant in the language of recent days. In these books it was laid down that the Rose did not associate properly with other flowers, and it was therefore better to put it in a place by itself, and, though this false idea had less influence in the cottage garden, it did harm in all large gardens. In a recent book on the Rose, by Mr Foster-Melliar, we read

I look upon the plant in most cases only as a means whereby I may obtain glorious Roses I do not consider the Rose pre-eminent as a decorative plant, several simpler flowers, much less beautiful in themselves, have, to my mind, greater value for general effect in the garden, and even the blooms are, I imagine, more difficult to arrange in water for artistic decoration than lighter, simpler, and less noble flowers.

It must be remembered that the Rose is not like a bedding plant, which will keep up continual masses of colour throughout the summer, but that the flush of flowers is not for more than a month at most, after which many sorts, even of the Teas will be off bloom for a while, and the general effect will be spoiled.

This is not a statement peculiar to the author as he is only embodying here the practice and views of the Rose exhibitors which most unfortunately ruled the practice of gardeners, and it is very natural many should take the prize-takers as a guide.

There was some reason in the older practice, because until recent years the roses most grown were summer flowering, that is to say, like our wild roses, they had a fixed and short time of bloom, which usually did not last more than a few weeks; but in our days, and within the last fifty years, there have been raised mainly by crossing with the Bengal Rose and some others a number of beautiful Roses, which flower for much longer periods There are, for example, the monthly Roses and the lovely Tea Roses, which also come in some way from the Indian Rose, and which, when well grown, will flower throughout the whole summer and autumn; not every kind, perhaps, but in a collection of the best there is scarcely a week in which we have not a variety of beautiful flowers So that, while our forefathers might have been excused for taking the view that Roses are only fit to plant in a place apart, there is no need for the modern grower to do so, who is not tied to the show bench as his one ideal and aim, and nothing could be more untrue and harmful than this ideal from a garden point of view.

THE ROSE TO COME BACK TO THE FLOWER GARDEN.—The Rose is not only "decorative" but is the queen of all decorative plants, not in one sort of position or garden, but in many—not in one race or sort, but in many, from Anna Olivier, Edith Gifford, and Tea Roses of that noble type in the heart of the choicest flower-garden, to the wild Rose that tosses its long arms from the hedgerows in the rich soils of midland England, and the climbing Roses in their many forms, from the somewhat tender Banksian Rose to climbing Roses of British origin And fine as the old climbing Roses were, we have now a far nobler race—finer indeed than one ever expected to see—of climbing teas which, in addition to the highest beauty, have the great quality of flowering, like Bouquet d'Or, throughout the fine summer and late into the autumn. Of these there are various climbing Roses that open well on walls, and give meadows of beauty, the like of which no other plant whatever gives in our country. See, too, the monthly Roses in cottage gardens in the west and cool coast country, beautiful through the summer and far into the cool autumn, and consider the fine China Roses, such as Laurette Messimy, raised in our own day, all decorative in the highest sense of that poor word.

The outcome of it all is that the Rose must go back to the flower garden—its true place, not only for its own sake, but to save the garden from ugliness and hardness, and give it fragrance and dignity of leaf and flower. The idea that we cannot have prolonged bloom from Roses is not true, because the finer monthly and Tea Roses

flower longer than any bedding plants, even without the advantage
of fresh soil every year which bedding plants enjoy. I have Roses
growing in the same places for seven years, which have the fine
quality of blooming in autumn, and even into winter. And they
must come back not only in beds, but in the old ways—over bower
and trellis and as bushes where they are hardy enough to stand
our winters, so as to break up flat surfaces, and give us light and
shade where all is usually so level and hard. But the Rose must
not come back in ugly ways, in Roses stuck—and mostly starving
—on the tops of sticks or standards, or set in raw beds of manure,
and pruned hard and set thin so as to develop large blooms; but,
as the bloom is beautiful in all stages and sizes, Roses should be
seen closely massed, feathering to the ground, the queen of the
flower garden in all ways

The Rose is not only a "decorative" plant of the highest order,
but no other plant grown in European gardens in any way approaches it in this quality. The practice of exhibitors of any kind
is of slight value from the point of view of beauty of the garden, and
not always of the very flower itself, as we see in the case of the Dahlia
Thirty years ago the florists, like the late Mr. Glenny, who had the
law in their own hands as regards the Dahlia, would have knocked
a man on the head who had the audacity to dissent from their lumpy
standard of beauty. It was really a standard of ugliness as so many
of these "florists' ' rules are. Then came the Cactus Dahlias, of free
and distinct form, and the single Dahlias, and now we see proof
in cottage gardens even that the Dahlia is a nobler thing by a long
way than the old florist's idea of it. And so we shall find with
the Rose, that, brought back to its true place in the flower garden,
it will be a lovelier thing than ever it has been on the show bench,
seen set in the finely coloured and graceful foliage of the "Teas,"
and with their many buds and charming variations as to flower and
bud, from week to week, until the first days of winter.

THE STANDARD ROSE.—A taking novelty at first, few things
have had a worse influence on gardening than the Standard Rose
in all forms. Grown throughout Europe and Britain by millions,
it is seen usually in a wretched state, and yet there is something
about it which prevents us seeing its bad effect in the garden, and
its evil influence on the cultivation of the Rose, for we now and then
see a fine and even a picturesque Standard, when the Rose suits the
stock it is grafted on, and the soil suits each, but this does not
happen often   The term grafting is used here to describe any modes
of growing a Rose on any stock or kind, as the English use of the
term budding, as distinct from grafting, is needless, budding being
only one of the many forms of grafting. There is no reason why

those who like the form of the Standard should not have them if they can but get them healthy and long-lived ; but in that case they should train hardy and vigorous Roses to form their own stems.

While of the evil effect of the Standard Rose any one may judge in the suburbs of every town, its other defects are not so clear to all, such as the exposure high in the air to winter's cold of varieties

Climbing cluster Rose at Belmont.

more or less delicate. On the tops of their ugly stick supports they perish by thousands even in nurseries in the south of England (as in Kent). If these same varieties were on their own roots, even if the severest winter killed the shoots, the root would be quite safe, and the shoots come up again as fresh as ever; so that the frost would only prune our Rose bushes instead of killing them and leaving us a few dead sticks from the Dog Rose. Even if "worked" low on the "collar" of the stock, grafted Roses have a chance of rooting and keeping out of the way of frost, which they never have when stuck high in the air. Then there is the fact of certain Roses disliking stocks, or certainly some stocks, as all buyers of Roses may see certain varieties always "growing backwards" so to say, and soon dying. This happens even where the first year's growth and flower are all we could desire. The question for the seller is how his stocks look the year of sale no doubt, but the buyer should see whether his Roses improve or not after the first year, and it is certain that many varieties do go back when "worked" as the term is.

Another element of uncertainty is the kind of stock used. Even if the propagator knows the right stock for the sort he may not for some reason use it, as many have found to their cost who have bought Tea Roses grafted on the Manetti stock—a stock that in any case has no merit beyond giving a few large blooms for a show the first year. And in many cases it paralyses all growth in the kind grafted on it.

There is a way to solve the question as to any kinds we are really interested in—say Gloire Lyonnaise, Princess Marie d'Orleans and Bouquet d'Or, or any other hardy and good Roses we fancy, old or new. It is easy to try a few of each kind in the same soil in the natural way on own roots, and also grafted on the wild Dog Rose or any other stock that may be recommended for a given variety, using the "worked" kinds both as Standards and half Standards or dwarfs as may be preferred. The first care should be to get plants on own roots about as strong as those worked, and it is not difficult to do this with a little patience, as some gardeners and even cottagers strike Roses from cuttings very successfully. But no trial would be of any use which did not go over the first year or two, because of the dread phase of the grafting humbug above alluded to, that the things are grown to sell, and although they look well when they come to us, after a year or two they perish, and we are as much in want of Roses as ever. This may look very "good for trade," but any practice which leads to the vexation and disappointment of the grower is not good for trade, as many people give the Rose up as hopeless on their soil when they get a poor result.

If we go into the Rose garden of the Luxembourg at Paris or any of the regular roseries in England, we shall find more than half the plants in a sickly, flowerless state. So sickly are the bushes, or what remains of them, that it is common to see a rosery without any Roses worth picking after the first flush of bloom is past, and this is a great waste of time and temper. When we think of the number of beautiful things which this has to do with to their harm :—the flowers fairest of all in form, colour, and odour, from the more beautiful tea-scented Roses raised in our own days to the oldest Roses—the Moss and Provence Roses—these, too, being often seen in a

Rose La Marque on south wall, July, 1899.

miserable state in the rosery, though by nature vigorous and quite hardy, there is surely some reason for looking into ways of Rose growing that have led to this end.

Even where the Rose thrives as a Standard, on deep, good loamy soils, there would be other things of interest to determine—length of bloom and endurance of the grafted plant, as compared with plants on their own roots—my own view being that own root plants generally would give the most continuous and finest bloom in the end, good cultivation and soil being understood in each case, and that in hot seasons, of which we have had severe examples of late years, the own root plants are far the best.

THE MANETTI STOCK.—Often I have reason to wish that Signor Manetti of Naples had never been born or given his name to the wretched Rose stock that bears it, as among my blighted hopes is a wall of Maréchal Niel Rose, the plants on which have remained "as they were" at first for the last five years; but this year beside one of them is in bloom the poor Manetti Rose, on which the Maréchal was grafted, and, as the Tea Rose will not grow, the Manetti begins to take its place. In some soils and conditions, the Manetti may give some apparent advantages for the first year in making the plant grow rapidly, and perhaps giving one or two flowers to be cut off for a show, but afterwards it is all the other way; the Rose fails on it, and Tea Roses do not grow on it at all. It is quite distinct in nature from them, and nurserymen who use the Manetti for Tea Roses do no good to their own art or to gardens. People ordering Tea Roses should be careful to order them never to be sent on Manetti stock. But even if they do so they may be disappointed, as the large growers have often to buy from others and so send out Tea Roses on the Manetti stock, an absolutely sure way to prevent the Roses growing or ever showing their extraordinary beauty.

Why do trade-growers do this sort of thing to the injury of their own art and the loss to the buyer who supports them? Unfortunately routine takes hold of every business and has taken deep hold of this to its real injury. Roses are not only propagated by the trade for the garden, but also for forcing, for sale, and for showing; and it is the quickest way to make a presentable growth that is taken. In various cases the plant is only wanted for one year, as when florists want to get strong blooms and throw the plants away afterwards In this case the life of the plant does not matter, but to the private grower the result could not be worse.

ROSES AND MANURE.—In most gardens where people pay any attention to Roses the ground in which they grow is in winter densely coated with manure, often raw and ugly to see in a flower-garden— perhaps under the windows of the best rooms of the house. This is the regulation way of catalogues and books, but it is needless and impossible in a beautiful Rose garden. Most of our garden Roses being grafted on the Dog Rose of our hedgerows, which does best in the heavy, cool loams of the midlands, if we want the

Climbing and Bush Tea Roses in Rose Garden, July.

ordinary grafted garden Rose to do well we must give it not less than 30 inches in depth of like soil.   This is often of a rich nature, and it is very easy to add, in putting the soil in, all the manure which the Rose may want for some years, so that the surface of the bed might be planted with light-rooting rock and like plants, one of the prettiest ways being to surface it with Pansies and Violets   I have beds of Tea Roses over which the Irish mossy Rockfoil has been growing for years without the roses suffering   Beautiful groups of mossy plants of all sorts, or pretty little evergreen alpine plants associated with the earliest flowers, show that the surface of the Rose garden itself might be a charming garden of another kind, and not a manure heap.   In the old way of having what is called a " rosery " it did not matter so much about covering the surface with manure, but where we put our Rose beds in the centre of the very choicest flower garden or under the windows of the house it is a very ugly practice   The Rose can be nourished for six or eight years without adding any manure to the surface, and after six, eight, or ten years most beds will probably require some change, or we may change our view as regards them.

If we free our minds from the incubus of these usual teachings and practices, many beautiful things may be done with Roses for garden adornment.   What is wanted mainly is that the very finest Roses, and above all long-blooming ones like Monthly Roses and such Tea Roses as George Nabonnand, Marie Van Houtte, and Anna Olivier, should be brought into the flower garden in bold masses and groups to give variety and prolonged bloom, using the choicest Tea Roses in the flower beds, with wreaths of yellow climbing Roses swinging in the air, and on walls, especially the climbing Tea Roses   Perhaps it may be worth while, to encourage others, to tell the story of

My Rose Garden, as a record of a trial that succeeded may be of more use to the beginner   My idea was to get the best of the Roses into the flower garden instead of bedding plants or coarse perennials, to show at the same time the error of the common ways of growing Roses, and also the stupidity of the current idea that you cannot near the house (and in what in the needless verbiage of the day is called the " formal " garden) set flowers out in picturesque and beautiful ways   Another point was to help to get the flower garden more permanently planted instead of the eternal ups and downs of the beds in spring and autumn and the ugly bareness of the earth at these seasons, and to see if one could not make a step towards the beautiful permanent planting of beds near the house and always in view.   Tea Roses only were used for the sake of their great freedom of bloom, and these were all planted in large groups, so that one might judge of their effect and character much better than by the usual way

·of mixed ineffective planting of one kind in a place The success of the plan was remarkable both for length of bloom and beauty of flower and foliage, variety of kind and charming range of colour, and also curious and unlooked for variety in each kind. That is to say, each Tea Rose varied as the weather varied, and the days passed on . the buds of Anna Olivier in June were not the same as the buds of the same rose in September, and all kinds showing ceaseless changes in the beauty of bud or bloom from week to week

NO STANDARDS.—It was easy to abolish the standard as hopeless and diseased in many cases and ugly in effect, but not so easy to get out of the way of grafting on something else, which is the routine in nurseries, and here I had to follow the usual way of getting all the Tea Roses grafted on the common Dog Rose, but always getting the plants " worked " low either on the base of the stock or on the root, so that it is easy in planting to cover the union of the stock with the more precious thing which is grafted on to it, and so protect the often somewhat delicate kind from intense cold   There is also a chance in this way of letting the plant so grafted free itself by rooting above the union If we plant firmly in the earth, slightly inclining it to one side, and scrape a little off the lower part of the stems of the Rose, we may encourage the rose to root itself above the stock, and in any case we escape the ravages of frost. Certainly it is so in my garden in a cool and upland district. For ten years or so, of the many kinds we have planted we have had no losses from cold. The Tea Roses were often cut down by the frost, but they came up again, often vigorously , some kinds undoubtedly go back or fail, but not, I think, because of cold, but rather through not liking the stock. Making all our beautiful and often tender roses grow on one wild stock only may have bad effects, just as grafting all the precious Rhododendrons on the wretched R. ponticum has bad effects. Some kinds flower, do well for a year or two, and then rapidly diminish in size and beauty ; some are very vigorous the first year but die off wholly in the second The Wild Rose stock has the power to push the Rose into great growth the first year, and then, owing to the stock and graft being of a wholly different origin and nature, there is a conflict in the flows of the sap, and death quickly ensues There has been such a number of beautiful Tea Roses raised and lost that it is worth while inquiring if we have not lost many of them from this cause Some Roses that grew freely did not open their buds in our country, and others broke away into small heads and· buds which made them useless. However, out of the thousands planted some kinds did admirably, and quite enough of them to make a true garden of Roses, lasting in beauty throughout the summer and autumn.

PREPARATION OF THE ROSE BEDS.—Knowing that we had to face the fact of all the Roses being grafted on the Dog Rose it was important to give them a deep, cool loam, and the beds in most cases were dug out to a depth of thirty inches below the surface. Although a somewhat rocky and impervious bottom no drainage was used, no liquid manure was ever given, and no water even in the hot summers. The beds were filled with the cool heavy loam of our best fields, mixed with the old dark soil of the beds and raised gently above the surface, say, to an average height of not less than 6 inches, so that there was about 3 feet of good rich soil. And this

Summer Roses on cottage wall (Surrey).

preparation was sufficient for years, the beds being in some cases quite vigorous after six and seven years' growth.

ROSE BEDS AND ALPINE FLOWERS.—Instead of mulching the beds in the usual way, and always vexing the surface with attentions I thought dirty and needless, we covered them with Pansies, Violets, Stonecrops, Rockfoils, Thymes, and any little rock-plants to spare. Carpeting these rose beds with life and beauty was half the battle. Every one asks us how we mulch. Well, we do not mulch except with these living plants, many of which are so fragile in their roots that they cannot have much effect in a bed of 3 feet of moist,

good soil   So that instead of the bare earth in hot days, the flower
shadows are thrown on to soft carpets of green Rockfoil and Thyme,
or any other fragile rock or mountain plant that we think worth
growing for its own sake also   It may even be that these "mossy"
plants prevent the great drying out of the soil in hot summers and
autumns, such as we have had of recent years

SHELTER.—The position was not at all protected in the direction
of the prevailing winds, or by walls in any way, so that little was
owing to the natural advantages of site   The first thing that occurred
to people on seeing the Roses was that they were due to some
peculiar merit of the climate or the soil ; but the same things were
carried out in several gardens formed by me in quite different soils
and districts—Shrubland Park, and Hawley, in Hants, for instance—
and the results were equally good in every case, in some cases better
than in my own garden   It is very likely that working in the same
way all should be able to grow Tea Roses—that is, the best of all
Roses—on many warm soils which are supposed to be useless to
grow Roses now.   There is a limit no doubt as to how far north one
would get these Roses to open, but over a large area of the country
now roseless for half the summer, and in some dry soils with few
or no roses at all, we could make a change towards a real Rose-
garden.   All who have hot and warm soils should enrich them as
much as possible, but in view of the failure of the Rose in the brier
they should never try any Standard Tea Roses, but grow these on
their own roots or grafted low, and the point of the graft buried in
the soil so as to allow of the plant rooting itself in a soil which it
may be able to enjoy perfectly well without the aid of a horrid and
corrupting "middle man" in the shape of a Dog Rose, longing all
the time for its home in the clay.

CLIMBING ROSES —In the sketch of Rose pillars taken by Miss
Willmott in her garden at Warley Place, we see some of the grace
of the Rose treated as a climber, in the flower garden   There are a
great number of Roses that lend themselves to this, the old climbing
Roses being now backed up by a splendid series of long-blooming
climbing Tea Roses which are more valuable still, and much in want
of planting in simple ways to break up the level of gardens and
the chessboard appearance they usually have   Wreaths and garlands of this sort were very much more frequent before everything
was cleared away for the flatness and hardness of bedding out, and
this way of treating Roses ought to be practised more than ever.
They should be trained abundantly over well-formed pergolas, covered
ways, trellises, and fences   In countries a little warmer than ours we
see what can be done with Roses as noble climbers , in Algeria, and in
Madeira, the climbing Tea Roses running up trees in the loveliest

bloom, all of the finest sorts, seeming as free as the Monthly Rose is in the West of England   In our country we have to face hard winters, but we have many Roses which will stand the test of our hardest, and there is little difficulty in getting good effects from the Rose as a bold climber, and better than anything else able to break up the hardness and monotony too visible in flower-gardens

"OVER PRUNING CLIMBING ROSES —The way the unpruned Rose behaves is this   the plant, as soon as fairly established in a good soil, throws up plenty of strong shoots, and the following year these shoots break their buds freely along the stem, and each branch produces a mass of bloom, which, after a shower, weighs the branch almost down to the ground   They are often best let alone when among shrubs or in groups on the lawn, and it is the climbing Roses that show what the Rose is capable of when cultivated in this free and natural manner   One of my best rose bushes is an old double white Ayrshire Rose growing in a shrubbery for more than thirty years—sending out a shoot of white flowers sometimes on this side, and sometimes on that side of the clump of bushes, and sometimes scrambling up to the tops of the tallest branches, and draping them with blossoms throughout June and July.   Some time ago I measured the ground covered by the plant and found it rather over 70 feet in circumference. It is growing in a deep dry loam, and this, together with head room, seems to be all it requires   There are far too few examples of this kind, for our efforts have not been in the direction of showing what could be done with the Rose as a tree or bush.   The common Dog Rose teaches us a lesson in pruning and climbing   It forms a mighty mound of branches, the older stems dying down as the young ones grow till a large bush is formed, covered with flowers, and they are never the less for the absence of all pruning !

"Climbing and strong-growing Roses make handsome bushes in a few years on pleasure-ground lawns   I have seen bushes of this kind twenty years old in which the wood had accumulated about 2 feet or more deep, and yet nowhere was any dead wood to be seen, owing to the plants throwing out annually fresh shoots which covered the old ones   The plants, in fact, grow exactly in the same manner as the wild Brier, which keeps sending up from its centre long shoots, increasing its size every year.   Except against walls and in similar situations, there is no occasion to prune climbing Roses. They make the finest display when left to themselves, and it is only necessary to provide them with a deep, strong soil, and to let them have light on all sides.   Whether planting be carried out with the object above described, or for the purpose of covering naked tree-stumps or branches, or for draping any unsightly object whatever, good soil in the first instance is the main thing "—J S

WILD AND SINGLE ROSES —Another way of attacking the monotony and barrenness of the "rosery" of the books, is to plant many of the wild roses, from which all the garden roses come. They do not, however, appear to advantage in shows; but on cool grass in the hot summer days there is nothing more delightful, whether they be those of our own country like the Sweet Brier, Dog and Field Roses, or those of other countries, such as the beautiful Altai Rose, the Rosa gallica and many others. As to growing wild Roses, the best way is not to put them in the flower-garden, but rather by grass walks or rough banks, or in newly made hedgerows. If their beautiful bloom does not last long, the fruit is pretty, and though they are not of the things that repay us well for garden cultivation, as the best garden Roses do, the wild Roses may often be used with good effect.

Among the wild Roses, not natives of Britain, that give us most pleasure there may be named the Needle Rose of Japan (R acicularis); the Carolina Rose, charming for its distinct clusters and late bloom, the alpine Rose and its Pyrenean variety, excellent for rocky banks, the glossy Rose (R. Lucida), one of the most excellent in marshy or almost any ground, pretty in colour too in winter, the Austrian Brier, a native of Central Europe, and thriving even among wild Roses, R macrantha, R. brunonis and the Musk Rose and all its forms, the many-flowered Rose R. multiflora, and the Japanese Roses (R. rugosa). The creeping Rose of China and Japan (R. Wichuriana) is quite distinct from any, and excellent for running about rocky banks and as a climber. These are but a small number of the Roses with which the northern and mountain world is clothed, and of which many have yet to come to our gardens

Apart from the wild Roses of which there are so many, there are also the single and other roses of garden origin which were thrown away by raisers so long as the show standard was the only one thought of, but a few of which are now coming into use, such as the Paul's Carmine, Bardou Job, the hybrid sweet Briers and Japanese and other hybrids, and to such roses we may hope for many additions.

AN ESSEX ROSE GARDEN

What causes the difference between the burnt up gardens of Sussex and Surrey and this Essex garden land? It can surely only be the open, dark, friable soil, that gives the trees their deep verdure, the hardy plants their handsome growth, the turf its fine texture and

O

good colour. In the fashionable flight to the country south of London garden lovers do not always know that they are turning

An Essex Garden, with border of Tea and Monthly Roses in the foreground.

their backs on the good soil ; chalky hills and sandy heaths and poor clays can never give anything like the same results, no matter how we labour. The difference in soil values is very great, and a vital question for those who expect to get good results in flowers or fruit, and the worst of it is that on many poor soils no money or no manurial or any other additions can ever make them as good as a naturally good soil.

So here, on a good soil, we have a beautiful garden showing how Roses love the soil and air, especially the Tea and Monthly Roses, which have the precious quality of coming out again with ever so little encouragement—an hour or two of sun, or even without this in gentle rains It may be noticed in the engraving that the border below the house at the bottom of a terraced-lawn is planted with Tea Roses of the best sorts, so that it comes into the garden-picture, and is convenient for cutting or seeing the flowers, and not thrust away into a separate corner out of the flower garden as Roses so often are. And well the Tea Roses repay for the good place, from the ever-constant Princess de Sagan to the rain-and-storm proof G Nabonnand To these ever-welcome Roses, as good for the house as the open garden, the best of the wild Roses are a great aid, all the more so when we come to the adornment of walls, pergola, or the house-walls, and here in August the Macartney, Prairie, and Japanese creeping Rose (Wichuriana) come in so well after the early wild Roses are past. Drooping from a pergola the Japanese creeping Rose is graceful in the toss of its branches and the purity of its flowers And these late wild Roses go so well with the Clematis, Vine, Passion-flower, Jasmine, and the best climbers we have for house-walls, the good use of which does so much to grace the house

And as we have seen that in this garden near the house the garden Rose occupies its true place (although a modest one compared with what it deserves), here, round the water-lilies the wild Roses are grouped Now that the taste for these beautiful wild Roses from various countries is reviving, it is well to know what should be done with them. Their season is too short to entitle them to a place in the flower garden and a very good one is the margin of pools and small lakes which are now very rightly given up to precious water-lilies The Roses for the flower garden are the long blooming Tea and Monthly Roses, which reward us by months of changeful flower.

The wild Rose is much better placed in the more picturesque parts of grounds where we neither expect nor look for continuous bloom, and all the more so because these wild Roses are hardy shrubs that want no attention for years at a time.

THE SUMMER GARDEN BEAUTIFUL

(continued)

CHAPTER XIV.

CARNATION, LILY, IRIS, AND THE NOBLER SUMMER FLOWERS

THE flowers of our own latitudes, when they are beautiful, are entitled to the first place in our gardens, and among these flowers, after the Rose, should come the Carnation, in all its brilliancy of colour, where the soil and climate are fitted for it, as is the case over a large area of our sea-girt land.

Our flower-gardens have to a great extent been void of beautiful flowers and plants; but instead, acres of mean little sub-tropical weeds that happen to possess a coloured leaf—Coleus, Alternanthera, Perilla, &c.—occupy much of the ground which ought to be true flower-gardens, but which is too often set out with plants without fragrance, beauty of form, or good colour

It is not enough that the laced, flaked, and other varieties of *D Caryophyllus* should be grown in frames or otherwise; we should show the flower in all its force of colour in our flower-gardens, and this is an entirely distinct question from the growth of kinds hitherto known as "florists' flowers" Many who have not the skill, or the time, for the growth of the "florists'" flowers, would yet find the brilliant "self" Carnations delightful in their gardens in summer and autumn, and even in winter, for the Carnation, where it does well, has a fine colour-value of foliage in winter, which makes it most useful to all who care for colour in their gardens, adorning the garden throughout the winter and spring, and full of promise for the summer and autumn

What Carnations are the best for the open air? The kinds of Carnations popular up to the present day are well known by what is seen at the Carnation shows, and in the florists' periodicals, like the *Floral Magazine, Harrison's Cabinet,* and, indeed, all similar periodicals up to our own day, when I began to insist that all flowers should be drawn as they are. The artist should never be influenced by any " rules " or " ideals " whatever, but be allowed to draw what he sees. This all conscientious artists expect, and it is the barest justice. If we raise new forms, or what we consider " perfect " flowers, let the artist see them as they are, and draw them as he sees them, without the confusion of drawing impossible hybrids between what he sees and what he is told is perfection in a flower. It was the want of this artistic honesty which has left us so worthless a record in illustrated journals of the century, where the artist was always told to keep to the florist's " ideal " as to what the flower should be, and hence the number of plates of flowers of many kinds, all " drawn " with the compass. Behind the florists' plates of this century we have the pictures of the Dutch flower-painters containing fine Carnations, well grown and admirably drawn after nature. These artists were not confused by any false ideal to which they were to make the flower approach, and so we have a true record of what the Carnation was 200 years ago In these pictures we generally see the finer striped and flaked kinds given the first place, which is natural, as such varieties are apt to strike people the most , and in those days little consideration had yet been given to the question of *effect* in open gardens, but in our own day this question has been forced upon us in very unpleasant ways by masses of crudely arranged, and not always pretty flowers One of the aids in effect is the Carnation in its pure and lovely colours—colours which no other flowers possess It would be a pity to use these lovely colours only for " button-holes ' and for the house, when they may afford us such welcome colour in our summer and autumn gardens, in the days when people see and enjoy their gardens most

Hitherto the effect of the Carnation in masses has been mostly judged or from the Clove Carnation, but fine as this is, it is not so good as other varieties which are better, stronger, flower longer, and are finer in form, such as " Murillo," " Carolus Duran," ' Comte de Melbourne," " François Lacharme," " Madame Roland," " Paix d'Amiens," " Marquis de Dampierre," " Mdlle Rouselle," " Alice, Aline Newmann," "Countess of Paris," and "George Maquay " These represent the Carnation of our own day in its finest form, perfectly hardy, if layered in the summer, and planted early. Rooting well before winter in easy and bold groups, they afford pretty effects of colour from foliage alone, and even in winter time adorn the garden. Some varieties are very continuous in bloom, like the " Countess of Paris," and these should be added to as time goes on

Over a very large area of the United Kingdom Carnation culture may be carried out well, and perhaps most successfully near the sea.

The gentler warmth of the shore in some way influences this, and in any case the best results I have seen from out-door culture have been in places like Scarborough, Edinburgh, Anglesea, the shores of Dublin Bay, and in sea-shore gardens generally where the soil is warm and good. It is wonderful what one may do in such places as compared with what is possible, say, in the Weald of Kent. At Scarborough we may see Carnations almost forming a bush; near Edinburgh I have seen tufts of the Clove Carnation 5 feet in diameter, whereas in Sussex and Kent we have to plant annually. In our island the area for shore gardens being very large, we may see how important the flower in gardens in sea-shore districts may be, valuable as it is in any place where it happens to do well; but some sandy and warm soils, like that of the Bagshot sands for example, are singularly adverse to the Carnation.

In advocating an extension of ways of growing this noble flower, I may perhaps be permitted to state the results obtained in my own garden in Sussex, and in a garden in Suffolk, two districts widely different as regards soil and climate. In my own garden I collected all the kinds of Carnations of the self, or one colour, that could be got in France or England, and grew them in lines in a very exposed and quite unprotected situation, about five hundred feet above the sea; and also in groups and masses in the flower-garden, generally with very happy and distinct results both as to colour and beauty of bloom, the failures being mostly from late planting

So far as hardiness is concerned, we had no trouble in proving the absolute hardiness of the plants—the harder the winter, the happier the flowers An "open," changeable winter is more against them, by exciting growth, than a hard winter. They were planted in large and simple flower-beds near the house, between groups of Tea Roses, occasionally running into the more open groups. In mixed beds where there are many Tufted Pansies and other hardy and half-hardy flowers, it is easy to get places for groups of Carnations in early autumn, and it is best to get enough of each kind to give a fair expression of its colour

On the margins of mixed borders the same Carnations may be used with excellent effect, especially for those who frequent their gardens late in the summer and autumn. Beautiful effects of colour may occasionally be had in such borders by associating with the Carnations other grey-hued plants, such as Lavender and Rosemary, also planted in bold informal groups. The soil of my own garden was a deep unctuous loam, the rainfall of the district being rather higher than that of the surrounding country, and though successful, the experiment could not be said to have been made under the best conditions.

The next made was at Shrubland Park, in Suffolk, under conditions totally different, where Lord de Saumarez entrusted me with
the remodelling of this garden, which was for long perhaps the most
famous " bedding-out " garden in England. I had to consider the
question of its embellishment with beautiful hardy flowers, the carpet
and bedding systems, white gravel and broken coloured brick, having
been given up. The soil here is a light warm friable loam, delightful
for gardening ; and so I determined to plant to a great extent with
the Carnation, Tea Rose, Tufted Pansy, Lavender, Rosemary, and all

Carnations and Roses in front of Tudor House.

the beautiful and hardy plants obtainable. Many of the self Carnations were used, and with excellent effect. The beds were simple
and bold, and we had large masses, in groups, of the finest self
Carnations known.

The climate, like that of the eastern counties generally, is colder
than that of Sussex in winter, but brighter in summer, and a better
result was obtained than in my own garden ; so that between these
two very different districts we have evidence that the Carnation can

be used (not merely the Cloves, but many other handsome forms ranging through the best colours) with in every way satisfactory effects in the flower garden.

The hardiness of the flower is proved by the natural habitats of the plant, which is found in rocky upland places in many countries of Europe, and finds a substitute for its native rocks on Rochester Castle, and at Château Gaillard, in Normandy. It never suffers from cold, though alternations of mild and hard weather will often affect it on cold soils by starting the plants into growth at a time when on the mountains they are at rest under snow.

LILY AND IRIS AND THE NOBLER SUMMER FLOWERS —The Lily had to go too from the flower-garden of our own day ; it was too tall, and no doubt had other faults, but like the Rose it must come back, and one of the gains of a free way of flower-gardening is that we are able to put Lilies or any other flowers in it at any season that suits their planting, and that their bloom is welcome whenever it comes, and leaves us content with brown stems when it goes. If in the large flower-garden we get some diversity of surface through groups of the rarer flowering evergreen shrubs, we have for these the very soil that our Lilies thrive in, and we break up in pretty ways these groups by planting Lilies among them, gaining thereby two seasons of bloom, light and shade in the masses, and diversity of form

The Iris too, with its Orchid-like beauty and flower, and with a higher value of leaf than either Lily or Orchid, is in summer flowering kinds fit to grace the flower-garden with some permanent beds Some will tell us that we may not do these things in the set flower-garden under the windows, but from an artistic point of view this is not true and very harmful There is no flower-garden, however arid or formal in its plan, which may not be planted in picturesque ways and without robbing it of fine colour either. But to do that in the face of ugly plans we must be free to choose among all beautiful things of the open air, not forgetting the best of the half-hardy plants that enjoy our summer—Heliotrope, great Blue Salvia, not forgetting Scarlet Geranium—no more than Cardinal Flower ; annual summer flowers, too, from Sweet Pea to Stocks, Mignonette, and Pansy. A true flower-garden is one which has a place for every flower its owner cares for.

There is no reason for excluding the best of the summer flowers from Hollyhocks to Sea Hollies, choosing always the best and those that give the most pleasure, and never coarse or weedy plants For these the true place is the shrubbery and wild garden It was the use of these coarse and weedy plants that did much harm in old mixed borders when they were allowed to eat up everything. In those days they had not the choice of fine plants we now have, many

of the finest we have coming in our day, like the Lilies of Japan and
of Western America, and also the new Water Lilies. These last
are above all flowers of the summer, and whenever there is any
garden water, they add a distinct and enduring charm to the summer
garden. We should not only represent them, but also the other
water plants of the summer; and as shown in the chapter on the
water garden, many handsome plants can be grown in rich soil that
often occurs near water, massed in picturesque groups, like Loosestrife, Meadow Sweets, and Japanese Iris.

Basket of fine leaved plants in the Gardens, Regent's Park.

THE SUMMER GARDEN

(continued)

"Another thing also much too commonly seen, is an aberration of the human mind, which otherwise I should have been ashamed to warn you of It is technically called carpet-gardening. Need I explain it further? I had rather not, for when I think of it, even when I am quite alone, I blush with shame at the thought."—W. MORRIS, HOPES AND FEARS FOR ART

CHAPTER XV.

SUMMER-BEDDING [1]

WHEN the bedding system first came into vogue, it was no doubt its extreme brightness, or what we should now call its "gaudiness," that caused it to hold the position it did ; but it was soon done to death. Only scarlet Geraniums, yellow Calceolarias, blue Lobelias, or purple Verbenas were used ; and the following year, by way of a change, there were Verbenas, Calceolarias, and Geraniums,—the constant repetition of this scarlet, yellow, and blue nauseating even those with little taste in gardening matters, whilst those with finer perceptions began to inquire for the Parsley bed, by way of relief. Such a state of things could not continue ; but yet the system could not be given up for several reasons—a very good one being that the great bulk of hardy flowers had been ruthlessly swept out of the garden to make room for bedding plants, and so—gardeners being, as it were, in desperate straits—the development of the bedding system began, and foliage plants of various colours were mixed with the flowers. Then followed standard graceful foliage plants and hardy carpeting plants ; and now dwarf-growing shrubs are freely associated with the

---

[1] As the aim of this book is to show in how many ways we can make a garden beautiful apart from the bedding system, that system is described by one who carries it out with great success

commoner types of bedding plants. Indeed, the system improved so rapidly that its most relentless opponents admitted that it had some redeeming qualities. I think, however, that the strongest reason of all for its retention is its suitability to formal or geometrical parterres

Most people have their own notions as to what constitutes perfection of colour in bedding arrangements This perfection I have not attained to, nor have I, perhaps, any decided preference for one colour over another ; but I have very decided notions that the various colours should be so completely commingled that one would be puzzled to determine what tint predominates in the entire arrangement This rule I have followed for years, and have had a fair amount of success in working it out I am even still learning, my latest lesson being that, if any colour at all may predominate, it is "glaucous," that is, a light gray or whitish green. Of this colour the eye never tires, perhaps because it is in harmony with the tints of the landscape, and particularly of the lawn To carry out my rule as to colour successfully, there are other rules which must be studied The first is that high colours, such as scarlet and yellow, must be used in much less proportion than colours of a softer tint, for high colours overweigh all others ; the second is that there must be no violent transition from one colour to another—the contrast of colours must as far as possible be avoided in favour of their gradual intermingling or harmonising ; the third, that the most decided or high colours, being the heaviest, ought to occupy the most central part of the beds, or be distributed in due proportion over the entire garden, so as to ensure an even balance throughout. Further, when dealing with such colours, use them in necessary proportion, and no more, and, if you err at all, err on the side of niggardliness By close adherence to these rules, I have for years had no difficulty in producing a harmony of colour that has worn so well as to be as welcome at the end of the season as at the beginning , for the quieter the colouring the more lasting is the enjoyment of it And it is pleasant to observe the great advance yearly made in favour of the quieter tints—gaudiness, in bedding-out, having become the exception rather than the rule To fully carry out the ideal of colour here advocated, a great variety of plants is needed, though not more than is generally grown where bedding-out is practised to any extent. But there is *colour* and *colour ;* and those who cannot have elaborate designs and variety in colour, may have an equivalent in graceful foliage and beautiful tinted shrubs of hues varying from deep green to bright yellow, and in habit tapering, weeping, or feathery. Cypresses, Yews, Yuccas, and many others, not only associate well with all kinds of bedding plants, but with the various kinds of hardy Sedums

Saxifrages, and Veronicas. These are all within the means of most owners of small gardens, and may be arranged in bedding-out form, the shrubs for centres and panels, and the dwarf hardy plants for massing and carpeting.

SOIL AND CULTIVATION.—Next to position, soil is the most important element in the formation of a garden. In selecting a soil, two things should be kept in view—first, that an open or well-drained soi¹ assists climate (that is, the more porous a soil is the warmer is the ground, and the better able to withstand extreme cold are the plants); and secondly, that the soil should be deep Unless there is depth, permanent things will not flourish satisfactorily. And for less permanent things, depth of soil is just as important, as it renders unnecessary frequent dressings of fresh soil to maintain, fertility. Wherever these conditions of soil exist, flower-gardening is easy, but in many cases opposite conditions have to be dealt with, and though it is hopeless to attempt to rival a naturally suitable soil, a very near approach can be made to doing so The best soil is good loam, that is, soil of a clayey nature, but sufficiently sandy not to be sticky. Of the two states, light and heavy, the light is the better, because it is the warmer, and the more easily cultivated. In dealing with heavy soil, we must have drainage, deep tilth, and the working-in of material rendering it more porous, such as half-decayed leaves, mortar or brick rubble, charcoal, and ashes If manure be needed, it should be used in the long straw state as it comes from the stables. One mistake frequently made with regard to soil is, that sufficient attention is not paid to the kind of plants that the soil of a given district is best suited for Were this always remembered, we should see fewer garden failures, and the gardening in different districts would possess an interest from variety If each possessor of a garden were to strike out a line for himself, the question of suitability of soil would soon be settled, for a man would be too observant to plant a Rhododendron in chalky soil because he had admired a friend's Rhododendrons in peaty or vegetable soil A healthy Yew or Box is infinitely preferable to a sickly Rhododendron. The annual dressing of flower-beds is needed to get the best effects; and by all means continue it, but not to the entire neglect of hardy flowers and shrubs. These though they will do a long time without fresh food, enjoy rich top-dressings of good soil or manure, it is only by so treating them that their best effects are developed.

Flower-beds occasionally require to be deeply dug Trenching is perhaps the proper term, but it scarcely expresses what I mean The time to do it is when the beds are empty. I trench up my flower-beds once in two years—in autumn, after the summer bedders are removed, and before the spring-flowering plants are put in. Stirring flower-beds creates a wider field of action for the roots, and gives them an opportunity of getting out of the reach of drought in a dry season.

COLOURED FOLIAGE.—The use of coloured and fine-leaved plants in the flower garden has increased, the causes being, the introduction of a number of suitable plants ; and the weather, which has often been so wet that, no sooner have ordinary bedding plants got into full flower, than they have been dashed to pieces by the rain. Hence the desire for plants that would withstand such washings, and yet give bright effects As regards coloured-foliaged bedding plants in particular, I do not think that if half of the bedding plants used were what are termed foliage plants, it would be out of proportion , in such coloured foliage I would include the variegated Pelargoniums, together with hardy variegated plants, such as Japanese Honey-suckles, variegated Periwinkles, Ivies, and the hardy Sedums and Saxifrages The effects to be had from this class of plants combined with variegated and coloured-leaved plants of the tender section, and with graceful-leaved plants, are better than any to be had from flowering plants alone, as they stand all weathers without injury One of the brightest coloured beds I have ever seen planted in geometrical form for summer effect was composed of the following plants—viz Sedum acre elegans, creamy white ; Sedum glaucum, gray , Herniaria glabra, green ; Mesembryanthemum cordifolium variegatum, light yellow ; and the bright orange and scarlet Alternantheras, all dwarf plants ; the standard or central plants being Grevillea robusta and variegated Abutilons.

BEDDING AND FINE-LEAVED PLANTS.—There can be no doubt that the use of the freer-growing green and graceful fine-leaved plants has done a great deal of good. In the South of England one may grow a great variety of plants of this kind. A number of greenhouse and even of stove plants may be placed in the open air without injury, and even with benefit to themselves But some plants put out look sickly all the summer and make no good growth Others always look well, even in the face of damaging storms. Where the climate is against the tenderer plants, a very good selection may be made from hardy things—from shrubs, plants like the Yucca, or young trees cut down and kept in a single-stemmed state. But there are errors in the system from which these things cannot save us A geometrical bed is little the less geometrical because we place green-leaved or graceful plants in the middle of it A more radical alteration is required, and that is the abolition of geometry itself, of formalism and straight lines, and of all the hateful gyrations which place the art of gardening on a level so much lower than it deserves to occupy. We can have all the variety, all the grace, all the beauty of form, all the glory of colour of the world of flowers and plants, without any of the pattern business which is now the rule. But we cannot make much progress in this direction except by suppressing the elaborate pattern beds as much as convenient, and by letting the vegetation tell its own story. The plants we must feed and the soil we must enrich; but finicking beds, reminding one of the art on fire-shovels and such productions, are not necessary. Let us then begin by adopting a bold, large, and simple type of bed, from which the flowers will spring and make us think more of them than of the pattern. By way of variety, succu-

Stone basket of flowers and fine-leaved plants (Heckfield Place).

lents are desirable plants for dry positions and under the shade of trees, where other bedding plants do not flourish satisfactorily. From their power of withstanding storms of wind and rain, and even drought and cold, they are always in good form; and they should have a place in summer flower-garden arrangements of any extent. They harmonise well with many hardy plants that may serve as cushions for them to display their quaintness on. The term "succulent" includes all plants of a fleshy character, the more common types being the Echeverias, Cotyledons, and Kleinias. Agaves and Aloes are more rare, but are none the less valuable for bedding.

VASES —In their proper place, and in due proportion, vases and baskets are useful in flower gardens, but they are frequently to a great extent out of all harmony with the style of the garden and its surroundings. Perhaps the tendency to over-decorate in this way is due to the geometrical plan of many gardens, when vases are placed on every pedestal and at every corner to square with many meaningless angles Happily, this style of gardening is giving place to one in which vases and baskets can be used or not, according to the taste of the owner. When vases are used in large numbers, much may be done by planting plants of a drooping character in them, indeed, vases look most natural when trailers or climbers droop over the sides. Basket-formed beds are well suited to almost any position in pleasure-grounds; but the best of all spots is in an isolated recess on the turf, and next, in the central bed of a flower garden, where the surrounding beds are circles or ovals. I have one, the extreme length of which is 16 feet; it is 8 feet wide in the middle, stands 2 feet 6 inches above the turf, and is made of Portland cement The principal plants in it are Marguerites, Pelargoniums, Heliotropes, Fuchsias, Marvel of Peru, Abutilons, Castor-oils, Cannas, Japanese Honeysuckles, and Tropæolums. More rustic-looking baskets would be better suited for isolation on the turf and for distant parts of the pleasure-grounds; and very good ones can be formed of wirework, lined inside with zinc, or made of barked Oak boughs instead of wirework. In baskets and vases of this kind permanent plants should be used, such as the variegated Ivies, Periwinkles, Japanese Honeysuckles, Clematises, and climbing Roses —space being reserved for flowering plants in summer and for small shrubs in winter.

SUB-TROPICAL BEDDING —There are four types of summer flower-gardening · 1, the massing (the oldest); 2, the carpet; 3, the neutral—quiet and low in colour, mainly through use of succulents; and 4, the sub-tropical, in which plants of noble growth and graceful foliage play the chief part. To my mind, a mixture of the four classes is the very ideal of flower-gardening It is possible to plant a formal garden in such a manner that the severest critic could not complain of excessive formality; for, after all, it is the abuse of carpet bedding that has brought it into disrepute. And justly so, for when one sees bed after bed and arrangement after arrangement repeated without end, with no plants to relieve the monotony of flat surfaces, one has good reason to protest. I have charge of a terrace garden which has to be planted with a view to obtaining the best display from June to November, and I am therefore compelled to adopt the carpet-bedding system, but

I supplement it by dotting over the surface, of necessarily formal arrangements, plants of noble or graceful aspect, such as Acacia,

Flower-garden at Madresfield Court.

Dracæna, and Yucca. In such arrangements a judicious blending of beds of flowering plants, principally Pelargoniums, adds brightness to the whole ; but, save under exceptional circumstances, flowers, and even fine-foliaged and flowering plants, should never be put in the same bed as succulents. The colour-massing or grouping style of summer-gardening is best adapted to a terrace or parterre that is well backed up or surrounded by evergreens, as these afford relief from the glare of brilliant colours, and at the same time set them off to advantage. A few plants of fine form distributed apart over the garden, and especially in beds of glaring colours, will be found to enhance the beauty of the whole. My view of sub-tropical gardening is, that it is only suitable for positions where it can be associated with water, or for sheltered nooks and dells, where the force of the wind is broken before it comes in contact with the plants. Where such positions are not at command, it is best to choose the hardier class of noble or handsome foliaged plants, many of which may be permanently planted, such as Ailantus, Rhus, Arundo, Salisburia, Yuccas, and the hardy Palm (Chamærops humilis) Of half-hardy plants that will withstand wind there are numbers, such as Araucaria, Acacia, Ficus, Cycas, Dracæna, Aralia In planting sub-tropical plants, care should be taken that the beds when fully furnished do not have a " bunchy " appearance To avoid this, plant thinly, and use as undergrowth dwarfer plants, of which there are many suitable kinds.

SUMMER AND WINTER BEDDING —Now that there is such a wealth of plants suited for furnishing the flower-beds in winter, there can be no excuse for their remaining empty after the summer-bedding plants are cleared away. Much labour is required to carry out both summer and winter bedding; but I strongly recommend this kind of decoration. There are reasons why winter bedding should be encouraged. First, winter is the season when all around us is bleak, dull and bare—leaden skies, leafless trees, flowerless meadows, and silent woods, all of which have a depressing effect on most temperaments. It therefore behoves us to endeavour to neutralise this prevailing dulness by making our gardens as cheerful as possible. Another reason— which to those fond of summer bedding should be the great reason for adopting winter bedding—is the short period during which summer bedding continues in perfection. The thought is continually haunting one that it will fade all too soon. The adoption of winter bedding, however, in my own case obliterates such thoughts, and one looks forward to real pleasure from both systems. Nor has this been the only result It being necessary that summer and winter bedding should meet, ingenuity had to devise means to this end This led to my using as summer bedders many hardy plants which otherwise I should not have thought of using, but which are just as effective as

P

tender exotics ; nay, in some cases, more so ; and which, when planted in the spring, serve till the following spring, when they are taken up, divided, and replanted for another year.

Principal Plants used for Bedding-out.

Abutilon	Cerastium	Gladiolus	Œnothera	Santolina
Agathæa	Cheiranthus	Gnaphalium	Oxalis	Saponaria
Ageratum	Chrysanthemum	Heliotropium	Pachyphytum	Sempervivum
Ajuga	Cineraria	Hollyhock	Pansies	Senecio
Alternanthera	Coleus	Iberis	Pelargonium	Silene
Alyssum	Convolvulus	Iresine	Pentstemon	Solanum
Amaranthus	Cotyledon	Lantana	Petunia	Stachys
Anagallis	Cuphea	Leucophyton	Phlox	Stocks
Anthemis	Dahlia	Lobelia	Plantain Lily	Tropæolum
Begonia	Daisies	Matricaria	Plumbago	Tussilago
Blue Marguerite	Dianthus	Mesembryanthemum	Polemonium	Verbena
Brugmansia	Echeveria	Mimulus	Pulmonaria	Veronica
Calceolaria	Erigeron	Myosotis	Pyrethrum	Viola
Canna	Fuchsias	Nertera	Salvia	Vittadena
Centaurea	Gazania	Nierembergia		

Garden near Loch Kishorn, Ross. From a water-colour drawing by F. Stainton.

Orange-trees in tubs, Tuileries.

THE SUMMER GARDEN BEAUTIFUL
(continued).

CHAPTER XVI.

PLANTS IN VASES AND TUBS IN THE OPEN AIR.

In old days and for ages it was not easy—not always possible to many—to have a garden in the open air. The need of mutual aid against the enemy threw people into closely-packed cities, and even small towns in what might seem to us now the open country. In our own country, free for many years from external enemies, we have spread our gardens over the land more than others ; but in France farmers still go home to a town at night from the open, and often homeless and barnless plain, where they work. And so it came that the land of Europe was strewn with towns and cities, often fortified, and many of those most able to enjoy gardens had to do the best they could with little terraces, walls, tubs by the door, and even windows. And often in Italy and other countries of the south of Europe and north Africa we see beautiful plants in tubs, on balconies, on flat roofs, and every imaginable spot where plants can be grown in a house in a street. Happily, in our country, there is less need nowadays for the garden in tubs ; but the custom is bound up with ways of growing plants which are still essential to us in some cases.

In many gardens plants in tubs are often used without good reason, for example, when hardy evergreen trees are grown in tubs, and in front of the Royal Exchange in London there are hardy Poplars in tubs ! But some may pursue this sort of gardening with advantage

P 2

—first, those who have no gardens, and, secondly, those who have and who may desire to put half-hardy bushes in the open air, for example Myrtle or Oleander or Orange, which may not be grown out-of-doors throughout the year, and which yet may have fragrance or other charms for us. Many plants can be grown in the open air in summer which will not endure our winters, but which placed in a cellar, dry room, or cool greenhouse would be quite safe, and might then be put out-of-doors in summer. This way is commonly the case abroad with large Datura, Pomegranate, and Myrtles, and a great variety

Vase plants at Turvey Abbey.

of plants such as we see put out in tubs in certain old palace gardens, like those of Versailles. What was called the orangery, which has almost disappeared from English gardens, was for keeping such plants alive and well through the winter, and in old times, if not now, had a very good reason to be.

There are many charming plants too tender for the open altogether that are happy in tubs, and may be sheltered in an outhouse or greenhouse through the winter—such as the Pomegranate, the Myrtle, and Romneya (the White Bush Poppy). The blue African Lily is often happy in tubs, its blue flowers when seen on a terrace walk having a distinct charm, but in England, generally, it must be kept indoors in winter

Excellent use may be made of the great handsome oil-jars, which are used to bring olive oil from Italy to London, and the best things to put in them are half-hardy plants, which can be taken intact into the cool greenhouse or conservatory at the approach of frost.   Even Seakale-pots can be filled with half-hardy plants, as scarlet Pelargoniums, which have a good effect in them.   In some rich and moist soils the Pelargonium all grows to leaves and does not flower, and in such cases we can humour it into good bloom by growing it in pots or vases in the light soil that suits the plants.

ORANGE TREES IN TUBS.—One of the most curious examples of routine and waste I saw in the Tuileries gardens on the last day of September, 1896, when the Paris people were preparing for the Czar, and among their labours was the refurbishing of the old Orange trees in these gardens.   There were a regiment of them set all along the gardens at regular intervals in immense and costly tubs, involving herculean labour to move in and out of the orangery.   One might suppose this labour to be given for some beautiful end in perfecting the flower or fruit of the plant, but nothing of the kind ; the trees being trained into mop heads, and when the plants make any attempt to take a natural growth they are cut sharply back, and often have an uglier shape than any mop.   The ground was strewn with shoots of the orange trees which had been cut back hard   When the tree was in poor health, as it was often, the dark stems were the most visible things seen against the blue sky.   This costly and ugly work is a survival of the time when the "golden apples" were a novelty, and it was not so easy to go and see them growing in the open air as it now is, and so what was worth doing as a curiosity hundreds of years ago is carried out still.   Since the idea of growing these trees in such an ugly fashion arose we have had a noble garden flora brought to us from all parts of the earth, and it would be easy to take our choice of different ways of adorning this garden in more artistic ways with things in the open ground, and of far greater beauty.   If this thing at its best and done with great cost has such a result, what are we to think of the English imitations of it, such as those at Panshanger, in which hardy shrubs are used, like Portugal laurels, and sham tubs placed around them ?

I saw the vast orangerie terrace at Sans Souci in July 1897, and was deeply struck by its "ornaments" in tubs , the branches of the poor distorted trees like black skeletons against the summer sky showing that even with all the aids of artifice, no good result with tubbed oranges is got in northern Germany no more than in northern France   In the warmer south a little better result may be had from trees in tubs, but a few days' journey brings us to orange trees growing as freely and gracefully as willows in Tunis and Algeria and the countries round the Mediterranean.

THE POET'S LAUREL IN TUBS.—The Laurel is a winter-garden

The Blue African Lily (*Agapanthus umbellatus*) in its summer quarters.

plant over a large area of northern and central Europe, where the true Laurel (our gardeners and nurserymen erroneously give the name to the vigorous evergreen Cherry, of which we have too much in England) is a tender evergreen, requiring the protection of a house in winter, it is grown to a vast extent in tubs to place in the open garden, on terrace, or in courtyard during the summer. The cultivation of the Laurel for this purpose is carried on to such an extent that miles of handsome trees in various forms may be seen in one nursery. There is no plant more worthy of it than the true Laurel, which we usually call the Sweet Bay, and those who cannot enjoy the plant out of doors, as we may in many of the warmer districts of the British Isles, would do well to grow it in tubs, in which state they may enjoy it both in winter and summer. It would be worth while growing it in the same way in cold and northern districts, where it is killed or much hurt in winter, and this sometimes occurs in parts of southern England. Near the sea it may flourish, and twenty miles inland be cut down to the ground, or so badly hurt that it gives no pleasure to see. In gardens where one may have fine groups of the tree on sunny slopes, we should never think of it in any other way, and no evergreen tree gives us more beauty when old and untrained and unclipped. Growing in tubs, the need of storing away in winter, often in a small space, and keeping the plant in health in boxes not too heavy make some training necessary, and the shapes common in Continental gardens are as good as could be obtained under the circumstances, while the health of the bush in these artificial conditions is singularly good. It is often surprising to see what fine heads arise in good health from small tubs, the soil being helped now and then by a little weak liquid manure water not oftener than once a week. Once the plants are stored for the winter, sometimes in sheds with little light, it is best to give no water during the winter months In the same way we may also enjoy the Laurustinus in districts where it is killed by frost out of doors which in hard winters happens, even in the southern countries which is all the more unfortunate as this shrub and its varieties flower so prettily. If grown well in tubs, we may flower them in the cool house and place them out of doors in summer.

CULTIVATION OF PLANTS IN ORANGERIES—The old way of growing plants in the orangery is still much more practised in France than with us, and a few words as to the mode of culture in use may be useful Though the orange from which the structure gets its name is not often happy in it, other plants like the Myrtle, Pomegranate, African Lily, and Hydrangea may often be kept with safety through the winter in such a house

Among shrubs we have the Pomegranate, Oleander, Orange, Fuchsia, Myrtle, Camellia—in fact, all those that are commonly placed for shelter in greenhouses during winter. For shrubs like these the year has two seasons· (1) that during which they are placed for shelter in the orangery or the cool house, or, in the absence of these, some place where the conditions of temperature, air, light, and construction are similar; and (2) the summer season, when they are taken out into the open air and set in variously exposed situations in order that they may mature, grow, and bloom.

WINTER CULTIVATION.—In October the shrubs are removed to warm corners. The shedding of the leaf in some plants gets rid of one difficulty in their cultivation, that of their preservation during the winter, as the summer-leafing kinds are so easy to store away if the frost be kept out. Half-hardy evergreen shrubs require to be kept in a well-lighted house, but shrubs, which, like Fuchsias and Pomegranates, shed their leaves in autumn, can during winter be conveniently kept in any dark place, such as a cellar or warm shed,

Orangery, Holm Lacey, Hereford.

and in their case watering will scarcely be required. As a general rule, for orangery shrubs, the temperature may be such as will exclude frost; some kinds, however, will be found to withstand a hard frost like the Oleander. Although the summer-leafing shrubs scarcely need water at all during the winter, it is needed for evergreen shrubs. Yet even here we shall have to make a distinction. For instance, the Orange-tree requires more water than the Myrtle, and the Myrtle more than the Proteads. In the majority of orangeries the plants are watered every two or three weeks during winter, and daily after the month of April, and those who cultivate Orange-trees are able to tell us that want of water, which is always prejudicial to this tree, may even result in a complete loss of leaf. There are two plans for avoiding the ill effects of too-abundant watering, the former of which is to plant in soils which allow the water to run away freely ; the second is to use boxes with sides that can be opened from time to time to enable the roots to be seen.

SUMMER CULTIVATION.—In May, and, if possible, during cloudy weather, all plants in the orangery are transferred to sunny and sheltered places outside. The pots, if small, will have to be plunged, as this keeps the roots in good condition. In this, as in other cases, where the plants are in pots or boxes, we shall have occasionally to give some manure, and weak liquid-manure gives good results. This is the Belgian method, and one of its effects is that it enables us to postpone the repotting of the plants and permits of the employment of smaller boxes and vases as compared with the size of the trees. So in the nurseries of Ghent and France, too, we often see Sweet Bays with heads more than a yard in width, whilst the tubs they are in scarcely measure twenty inches in diameter, and under such conditions the plants thrive for years without enlargement of the tubs or change of soil, thanks to feeding with liquid-manure.

The same things may be said of the plants in the cool house, or any house in which we store almost half-hardy Palms, Cycads, Tree-Ferns, or other plants which may with advantage pass a few months in the open air in summer All of these, in fact, may be treated much as the Blue African Lily is treated, allowing always for the differences between evergreen shrubs, like the Orange, Eugenia, and Myrtle , herbaceous plants, like the sweet-scented Plantain Lily, grown in pots and in courtyards in France, and summer-leaving shrubs like Fuchsia, Justicia, and Pomegranate.

AN AMATEUR ON PLANTS IN TUBS FOR THE FLOWER GARDEN. —The need of the orangery strictly so-called, is now lessened by two causes ; (1) our rich, hardy garden-flora with many things as lovely as any that grow in the tropics ; (2) the nearly universal adoption of the greenhouse, in which many plants find shelter in winter that in old times would have been housed in the orangery But notwithstanding these changes there are still some plants worth while to keep over the winter in any convenient way, and the following extract from *The Garden* shows how a good amateur gardener manages them as an aid to her flower-gardening.

" A great deal of real gardening pleasure is to be had from growing plants in pots and tubs or in vases and vessels of various kinds both in small and big gardens. I use large Seakale pots, when they are no longer wanted for the Seakale, by turning them over, putting two bits of slate in the bottom of the pot, some drainage, and a few lumps of turf, and then filling up with good garden mould. Another useful pot is one called a Rhubarb pot. If you live near a pottery they will turn you out almost any shaped pot you fancy. Flat ones like those used by house painters, make a pleasant change, especially for small bulbs. Petroleum casks cut in two, burnt inside, then tarred and painted, are invaluable tubs. I use butter-casks treated in the same way, and have some little Oak tubs in which bullion came from America. These are very strong, and some water-loving plants do much better in wood, since the evaporation in summer is not nearly so rapid as from the earthenware. That is an important thing to remember both as regards sun and wind. If the plants are at all

Plants in Italian oil-jars, Woodlands, Surrey.

delicate and brought out of a greenhouse, the pots, when standing out, ought to be either quite sunk into the earth or shaded. This cannot be done in the case of pots placed on a wall or terrace or on a stand, and so they must not be put out in the open till the end of May. Constant care about watering is also essential. Even in wet weather they often want more water if the sun comes out, as the rain wets the leaves, but hardly affects the soil at all. On the Continent, where all kinds of pot cultivation have been longer practised than in England, flower-pots are often glazed outside, which keeps the plants much moister because of less evaporation, and makes less necessity for frequent watering. The large red jars in which oil is still conveyed from Italy, covered with their delightful· coarse wicker-work, are useful ornaments in some gardens. They are glazed inside, and boring a hole in the bottom of them is not very easy work. They have to be more than half filled with drainage, and plants do not do well in them for more than one season, as the surface of the earth exposed at the top is so small In old days the oil merchants in the suburbs of London used to cut them in two vertically, and stick them against their houses, above their shops, as an advertisement or ornament. The enthusiastic amateurs will find that they get two very nice pots by sawing them in half horizontally just below the sham handles. The top part when reversed requires the same treatment as was recommended for the Seakale pots."

WHAT TO GROW.—The first rule, I think, is to grow in them those plants which do not grow well in your own local soil To put into a pot what is flourishing much better in a bed a few yards off is, to my mind, a mistake. I grow large old plants of Geraniums in the open ground, and they are kept on in the greenhouse from year to year, their roots tied up in Moss, and crowded into a pot or box with no earth and very little water through the winter; they can be kept in a cellar or spare room. Early in April they are potted up and protected by mats in a pit, as I have no room for them in the greenhouse This causes them to be somewhat pot-bound, and they flower splendidly during the latter part of the summer Marguerites, the yellow and the white with large leaves, are good pot plants early in the year, far prettier than the narrow-leaved kinds. A double Pomegranate I have had for many years in a pot, and if thinned out in the summer it flowers well; also two small Orange trees. The large old-fashioned Oak leaved, sticky Cape Sweet Geranium, which has a handsomer flower than the other kinds, makes a very good outdoor pot plant. Fuchsias, especially the old-fashioned fulgens, are satisfactory. Carnations Raby Castle, Countess of Paris, and Mrs Reynolds Hole I grow in pots, and they do well; they must be layered early in July, and answer best if potted up in September and just protected from severe frosts. In fine summers, Myrtles and Oleanders flower well with me in tubs, not in the open ground. I treat Oleanders as they do in Germany—cut them back moderately in October and dry them off, keep them in a coach-house, warm shed, or wherever severe frosts will not reach them. When quite dry they stand a moderate amount of frost. Then in March they are brought out, the surface is stirred and mulched, they are taken into a greenhouse and brought on a bit. In May they are thickly covered with good, strong horse manure and copiously watered At the end of the month they are stood out in the open on a low wall During May, June and July they cannot have too much water; after that they want much less, or the leaves turn yellow and drop off. Some years I grow Solanum jasminoides over bent wires in pots; grown thus it is pretty. The

American Aloe. Example of greenhouse plants set in open air in summer. Engraved from a photograph taken in Knightwick Rectory Garden, Worcestershire.

variety of plants which can be tried for growing in pots out of doors in summer is almost endless. Love-lies-bleeding (Amaranthus caudatus) is an annual, but if sown in January and very well grown on as a fine single specimen plant, it looks handsome and uncommon in a green glazed pot or small tub. Nothing I grow in pots is more satisfactory than the old-fashioned Calceolaria amplexicaulis ; it does not grow to any perfection with me in the beds, the soil being too dry, but potted, it makes a splendid show through the late summer and autumn months. The shrubby Veronica speciosa rubra, and V. imperialis, I grow in pots because they flower beautifully in the autumn, and the drowsy bumble-bees love to lie on them in the sunshine when Sedum spectabile is passing away. They are not quite hardy with me, as they cannot withstand the long, dry, cold springs. This in itself justifies the growing them in pots ; in mild, damp districts they are large shrubs. The blue Agapanthus everybody grows in tubs. The plants have to be rather pot-bound and kept dry in the winter to flower well, and as the flower-buds form they want well watering and a weekly dose of liquid manure. Hydrangeas I find difficult to grow when planted out ; the common kinds do exceedingly well in tubs in half shady places if they get a good deal of water. Large standard Myrtles I have had covered with bloom in August in tubs. My large old plant, which I had had many years, was killed last spring by being turned out of the room it had wintered in too early, because I came from London sooner than usual. The great difficulty in small places is housing these large plants in winter. They do not want much protection, but they must have some, and the death of large old plants is grievous.

Woodlands, Surrey.   M. T. E.

Spray of Myrtle.

Sheltered dell, with tree ferns and stove plants placed out for the summer (Battersea).

CHAPTER XVII.

BEAUTY OF FORM IN THE FLOWER GARDEN, AND HEREIN ALSO OF THE SUB-TROPICAL GARDEN.

THE use in gardens of plants of fine form has taught us the value of grace and verdure amid masses of flowers, and how far we have diverged from artistic ways. In a wild state brilliant blossoms are often usually relieved by a setting of abundant green, and where mountain or meadow plants of one kind produce a sea of colour at one season, there is intermingled a spray of pointed grass and leaves which tone down the colour masses.

We may be pleased by the wide spread of colour on a heath or mountain, but when we go near we find that it is best where the long moss cushions itself beside the ling, and the fronds of the Polypody come up around masses of heather. If this be so on the hills, a like state of things is more evident still in the marsh or wood. We cannot attempt to reproduce such conditions, but the more we keep them before our eyes the nearer shall we be to success, and we may have in our gardens (without making wildernesses of them either) all the light and shade, the relief, the grace, and the beauty of natural colour and form too.

A recent demand for £2,000 for the building of a glass house for Palms for the subtropical garden of Battersea Park here throws light on the costly system of flower gardening in this and other

Hardy Palm in the open, Cornwall.

public gardens. It may be noted that this is only a small part of the cost of keeping the tender and half-hardy plants in a glass nursery and not a demand of money for a Palm-house which the public might enjoy; but was to be part of the expenditure on some glass-sheds which they never see, and which were merely to grow the plants to be put out for a few months in summer.

In our flower gardens Palms can only be seen in a small state, nor can they, as shown in pots and tubs in Battersea, give one any idea of the true beauty of the Palm on the banks of the Nile or the Ganges But, worse than this, the system leads to the neglect of the many shrubs and trees of the northern world, which are quite as beautiful as any Palm. The sum mentioned as the cost of the house for young Palms would go far to plant Battersea Park with the finest hardy shrubs and trees. The number of these public gardens that are being opened in all directions makes it all the more important that the false ideal they so often set out should be made clear. I do not say we should have none but hardy plants in public gardens, but the concentration of so much attention, and of the greater part of the cost on such feeble examples of tropical plants as can be grown in this country set out for a few months in the summer has a very bad effect. The lesson all connected with gardening in any way want most to learn is that the things which may be grown to perfection in the open air in any country are always the most beautiful, and should always have the first place in their thoughts.

It would be much better in all ways to place a like artistic value on everything that stands in the open air in a garden, and regard all parts of the garden as of equal importance without wholly doing away with tropical plants, at least with those that can be grown with advantage in our country

Looking round the London parks we see much waste in trying to get effects of form from Palms and various tender plants, strewn in all directions in Hyde Park, often dotted about without good judgment, and marring the foreground of scenes that might be pretty. Where this is done there is rarely any attempt to get effects of fine form from hardy trees, shrubs, and plants, which is a much simpler and easier process than building costly glasshouses to get them.

For our gardens, the first thing is to look for plants that are happy in our climate, and to accustom ourselves to the idea that form may be as beautiful from hardy as from tender things. Many tropical plants, which we see in houses cut down close and kept small, would, if freely grown in the open air in their own country, be no more striking in leaf than the hardy Plane or Aliantus. Many plants that are quite hardy give fine effects, such as the Aralias, herbaceous and shrubby. Aristolochia among climbers, Arundo,

Pampas Grass in a Sussex garden (Chichester).

hardy and very pretty beside water; Astilbes, rough herbaceous plants which can be put anywhere almost; the hardy Bamboos of Japan and India, which are increasing in number, and are very distinct and charming, and often rapid growers in genial parts of the country, especially near the sea. A considerable number will probably be found hardy everywhere. The large leaved evergreen Barberries are beautiful in peat soils, and, grouped in picturesque ways, effective for their noble leaves as well as flowers

The Plume Poppy (Bocconia) is handsome for its foliage and flowers, even in ordinary soil. A great number of the larger hardy Compositæ (Helianthus Silphium, Senecio, Telekia, Rudbeckia) are fine in leaf, as are some of the Cotton Thistles and plants of that family. The common Artichoke of our gardens and its allies are fine in form of leaf and flower, but apt to be cut off in hard winters in some soils. The Giant Fennels are most graceful early leafing things, thriving admirably in sandy and free soils. Plantain Lilies (Funkia) are important, and in groups their foliage is excellent. The Pampas Grass is precious where it grows well, but in many districts is gradually killed by hard winters Where it has the least chance, it should be planted in bold masses.

The great leaved Gunneras are superb near water and in rich soil. The giant cow parsnips are effective, but apt to take possession of the country side, and are not easily exterminated, and, therefore, should be put in with a sparing hand in islands and rough places only. The large Indian evergreen Rockfoils are fine in form, and in their glossy foliage are easily grown and grouped in picturesque ways, and they are very hardy In sandy and free soils a handsome group of beautiful leaved things may be formed of Acanthus. The new water lilies will help us much to fine foliage, especially in association with the many graceful plants that grow in and near water, as are also certain hardy ferns which may be grown near water, like the Royal Fern, which in rich soil and shade makes leaves as fine as any tropical Fern. In southern districts the New Zealand Flax is effective in gardens, and the great Japan Knotworts (Polygonum) are handsome in rough places in the wild garden, and better kept out of the flower garden. Some of the Rhubarbs, too, are distinct and handsome, and very vigorous by the waterside, where the great water dock often comes of itself. It is a stately genus, and though we may not find room for many in the garden, it may be easy to do so by the water side or in rich ground anywhere.

With our many fine-leaved plants from temperate and cool climes it is possible to have beautiful groups of hardy fine-leaved plants, for trees like the Ailantus and Paulownia make almost tropical growth if cut down close to the ground every year. We have also the hardy Palm (Chamærops), the Yuccas, and graceful Bamboos, and Siebold's

Plantain Lily (Funkia), and plants of a similar character. Amongst those annually raised from seeds, and requiring only the protection of glass to start them, we have much variety from the stately Castor-oil-plant to the silver Centaurea. Although tender plants in pots are effective in summer in special positions, plants that cannot stand out-of-doors from the beginning of June until the end of September can hardly be called fit for summer gardening. Among the most suitable are several kinds of Palm, such as Seaforthia elegans, Chamærops excelsa, and C. humilis; Aralias, various; Dracænas, do.;

Group of house plants placed out for summer. Harrow Lodge, Dorking.

Phormium tenax and its variegated form; Yucca aloifolia variegata Ficus elastica, and some Eucalyptus. Erythrinas make fine autumn groups and are brilliant in colour, and useful for lighting up masses of foliage.

The hardiest Tree Fern, Dicksonia antarctica, looks well when plunged in shady dells with overhanging foliage for shelter; and several varieties of dwarf Ferns, such as the Bird's-nest Fern, are admirable for undergrowth to this Fern. Plants raised from seed will, however, usually form the majority, owing to the lack of room under glass for many large plants. Of plants raised from seed the most useful are Cannas, which may be taken up and wintered under glass, or securely protected in the soil   Most of the tall light green-foliaged varieties flower freely and make excellent centres for groups, while the dwarf bronze-foliaged sorts are•good for vases. Solanums have also been effective in the south. The spiny-leaved S. robustum, the elegant cut-leaved S. laciniatum, and S. Warscewiczi make good single specimens, or edgings to groups of taller plants. Wigandias, Ferdinanda eminens, and Melianthus major are all useful , and Acacia lophantha, Amaranthus, Cineraria maritima   Bocconias, with their tall spikes of graceful flowers and noble foliage, are very effective and permanent plants and several varieties of Rhus or Sumach have good foliage, Rhus glabra laciniata among them.

As to arrangement, the best beds or sets of beds are those of the simplest design   Shelter is a great aid, and recesses in shrubberies or in banks clothed with foliage form the most fitting background for beds or groups to nestle in. Avoid Musas or Caladiums, the leaves of which tear to shreds if winds cannot be shut out, and also plants that look unhappy after a cold night or two. Make the most of plants that grow under nearly all conditions, and use any dell overhung by trees for half hardy fine-leaved plants. A garden where each plant spreads forth its delicate foliage will form a pleasant change from brilliant bedding plants, or severely geometric carpet beds.—J. G.

Better effects may be obtained from hardy plants only than from tender ones.   There are the Yuccas, hardy, and unsurpassed by anything of like habit grown in a hothouse ; the Arundos, con-spicua and donax ; fine hardy plants like Crambe cordifolia, Rheum in variety, Ferula and umbelliferous plants, as graceful as tenderest exotics.   Then we have a hardy Palm that through all our recent hard winters has preserved its health and greenness wherever its leaves could not be torn to shreds by storms.

As an example of fine form from hardy plants, I cannot do better than give the New Zealand Reed (Arundo conspicua). This handsome Grass produces its blossom-spikes earlier than the Pampas, and is more elegant in habit, the silky white tufts bending like ostrich plumes at the end of slender stalks   It is best adapted to a sheltered corner, where it is protected from rough winds, and does admirably in the cold and warmer districts, but, like the Pampas Grass, not very hardy in cool and inland districts.

As to tender plants in the open air, it would be difficult to give a better illustration than the stately Musa Ensete in Berkshire. In sheltered nooks in the southern counties this plant makes a very fair growth in the summer.   In 1877 I was struck with its health and vigour at Park Place, Henley-on-Thames. Mr. Stanton, the gardener, raised a batch from seed, and it was surprising what fine plants they became in fifteen months. The plant is quite as effective in a conservatory in winter as out-of-doors in summer.

In the illustration of a bold mass of fine leaved plants near Hyde Park Corner, we see some of the best features of recent fine-leaved gardening. It had a great Abyssinian Plantain in the middle, and was fringed by a few sub-tropical plants, and edged by an extra-

Fine-leaved herbaceous plant (Plantain Lily).

ordinary fringe of the fine hardy Siebold's Plantain Lily, long-enduring in beauty. The reason of the success of this bed is clear; it was not a finicking angle or a wormy scrawl, but a bold circle, and presented no confusion to the observer, who simply saw the plants rising in a well-defined group from the turf. It was by itself, could be seen unopposed, and was not hedged in by a lot of other beds. Lastly, the plant forms were strong and well selected, and contrasted well with the ordinary tree vegetation near. The way in which the Plantain Lilies began early in the year to adorn the spot, and continued

to do so throughout the whole summer and autumn, was a pleasure
to see   The drawing was made about the end of September, shortly
after some heavy storms which tore the Musa a little, but the effect
remained excellent till October.

YUCCAS IN GROUPS.—Wherever space can be afforded, hardy
Yuccas should be grown, for few hardy plants are so distinct in
foliage and manner of growth, but they appear to best advantage
arranged in bold groups, near trees and shrubs, and forming a harmonious contrast to them.   Perhaps the best situation is a sloping
ground fully exposed to the mid-day sun, and backed by evergreens.
If allowed space for development, they will every year add beauty
to the place.   The handsome spikes of their large cream-coloured
flowers are extremely effective, especially when relieved by a background of verdure.   Yuccas like a well-drained soil, and thrive on a
subsoil of pure chalk, and they delight in full exposure to the sun,
and enjoy shelter from rough winds.   Hence the advisability of planting them near trees or shrubs

In grouping Yuccas, a better effect is obtained if some of the
specimens have the head of their foliage from 3 feet to 6 feet
above the soil.   These tall plants should not, however, be placed in
a back line, but some should be allowed here and there to advance
into the foreground, some of the smaller specimens nestling at
their feet.   The effect of a group thus arranged charms by its
irregularity and quaint beauty.

Among the more tender plants, we must choose such as grow
healthily in sheltered places in the warmer parts of England.   The
kinds with stout evergreen foliage, such as the New Zealand Flax
and the hardier Dracænas, will be as effective here as they are
around London and Paris, and to them the northern gardener should
direct his attention   Even if it were possible in all parts to cultivate
the softer-growing kinds to the same perfection as in the south of
England, it would not be always desirable, as they cannot be used
indoors in winter.   The best are the many evergreen plants that stand
out in summer without injury, and may be transferred to the conservatory in autumn, to produce through the cold months as fine an
effect as in the flower garden in summer.   One kind of arrangement
in particular must be guarded against   I mean the geometro-pictur-
esque one, which is seen in some parts of the London parks devoted
to sub-tropical gardening.   The plants are often of the finest kinds
and in the most robust health, and all the materials for the best
results are abundant; yet the result is not artistic, owing to the
needless formality of the beds and the heaping together of many
specimens of one kind in long masses straight or twisting, with
high raised edges of hard-beaten soil

The first and the last word to say about form is, that we should

.try and see beauty of form everywhere among plants that suit our climate. The willows of Britain are as beautiful as the olives of Italy, or the gum trees as seen in Algeria and the South of France, so that, although the sub-tropical as a system of flower gardening has failed throughout our country generally, and can only be carried out well in the south of England and the warmer countries of Europe, nevertheless we need not deprive ourselves of the enjoyment of the finest forms near and in our gardens. The new Water Lilies take us to the waterside, and there are many good forms even among our native flowers and weeds. The new hardy Bamboos are also very graceful and most distinct, of which several of the highest value promise to be

Gunnera and Bamboo (Fota, co. Cork).

hardy in our country. What can be done with them, and a few other things, we can now see in the Bamboo garden at Kew, at Batsford Park, and other places. The common hardy Japan Bamboo has thriven even in London, and it is not only waterside or herbaceous plants of all kinds we have to think of but the foliage of trees, which in many cases is quite as beautiful as that of the dwarfer plants. The hardy trees of North America are many of them beautiful in foliage, from the Silver Maple to the Scarlet Oak, and Acacias from the same country have broken into a number of beautiful forms; some are as graceful as ferns. These trees, if obtained on their own roots, will afford us fine aid as backgrounds. The Aralias of Japan and China are quite hardy and almost tropical in foliage, while the beauty that may be got from ferns is very remarkable indeed, our native Royal Fern being·of noble proportions when well-grown in half-shady and sheltered places in deep soils, as at Newick Park, and the same is true of all the bold American ferns, plants too often hidden away in obscure corners, whereas the boldest of them should be brought out in our cool British climate to form groups on the lawn and turf. This applies also to our larger native ferns, which, massed and grouped away from the old-fashioned fernery, often tell ,better. In this way they are used in some German gardens. We do not illustrate them in this chapter, because the reader has simply to turn to the chapter on the Fern garden to see some of their fine forms.

If any one objects that some of the plants mentioned in this chapter are coarse, such as the great leaved composite, the answer is that, on the other hand, many of them are refined and delicate, such as the Acacias, Acanthus, Asparagus, Bamboos, and Ferns. Great Reed, Pampas and Bulrush evergreen, Barberry, and graceful Cypress, Cedar and Fir. Plaintain-Lily and Adams needle—not forgetting the fine foliage of the Tea Rose.

During recent years the most graceful things and of permanent value in our gardens are Bamboos.

THE BAMBOO GARDEN AT KEW.—" The Bamboo garden formed a few years ago at Kew has proved so well adapted for the plants, that a few notes as to its position and soil may be of value to the numerous readers who intend to grow the Bamboos. A position was selected in the middle of a wood near the Rhododendron dell, and taking advantage of a hollow already existing there, the ground was lowered some 5 feet or 6 feet below the surrounding level. A belt of shrubs on the north and east sides, between the trees and the Bamboos together with the low level, affords them a shelter almost as perfect as can be furnished out of doors. Even the bitterest north-easter loses a good deal of its sting before it reaches .these Bamboos. What the cultivator of Bamboos has most to fear is not a low temperature merely—most of the Bamboos will stand 20° or 25° of frost in a still atmosphere—but the' dry winds of spring

Bamboos like best a free, open, sandy loam, and the greater part of the soil at Kew is poor and sandy ; but there is, in one part, a belt of good stiff loam extending for a few hundred yards, and it is on' the border of this that the Bamboo garden is situated. At the com-mencement the ground was trenched to a depth of 3 feet, and enriched with leaf-soil, and where necessary lightened with sandier soil These plants can scarcely be over-fed, and in well-drained soil can scarcely be over-watered, and an annual mulching with rich manure is of the greatest advantage. -

In regard to transplanting, the best time to plant is in spring, when growth begins. The renewal of growth is indicated by the unrolling of the young leaves, which may be in April or May, according to the winter. Bamboos are very difficult to kill outright, but treated improperly they are apt to get into a stunted condition, which it takes them a long time to recover from. I would advise those who wish to try these plants to obtain them from the nurserymen in autumn or winter, if they have been grown in pots, and to give them greenhouse treatment till the end of May, when they can be planted out in a growing state; but, on the other hand, if they have been planted out in the nursery ground, not to have them sent off till the end of April or later, when they can be set out at once. A yearly clearing out of the older, worn-out stems, dead leaves, &c., prevents that choked-up appearance one

In Bamboo garden, Kew.

sees so often in ill-tended Bamboos, and whilst giving a lighter and more graceful aspect to the plants allows freer play to the young growths.

Such, briefly, has been the system of cultivation pursued at Kew, and that it is the right one is shown by the luxuriant growth of almost all the kinds—so luxuriant, indeed, as to be rather embarrassing in the somewhat restricted space occupied by the collection. The Bamboo garden was made in 1892, and the following are the lengths of a few of this year's growths, exceeded, of course, by specimens in older collections and in warmer parts of the country, but of some interest, perhaps, as showing the rate of growth of Bamboos in a district which has not proved particularly favourable to the growth of tender shrubs

as a rule : Arundinaria Simoni, 17 feet ; Phyllostachys viridi-glauces-
cens, 17 feet ; P. Henonis 15 feet ; Arundinaria nitida, 13 feet ; A.
japonica, 12 feet ; Phyllostachys aurea, 12 feet ; P. nigra, 12 feet ;
P. fastuosa, 11 feet 6 inches ; Arundinaria Hindsi, 11 feet 6 inches ;
Phyllostachys Boryana, 9 feet ; P Castillonis, 8 feet 6 inches ;
Arundinaria anceps, 7 feet 3 inches   A. tessellata 4 feet 6 inches ;
A. Fortunei (variegated), 4 feet.

Bamboos are not all of equal merit, but some of them are the
most beautiful of evergreens. Just now when Christmas is at hand,
and the days are at their shortest and darkest, there is nothing out of
doors that equals the best Bamboos in the fresh greenness and beauty
of their foliage.—W. J. B."

*Plants hardy or half-hardy, with fine Foliage or Form, for use in
British Gardens.*

Acacia	Cannabis	Dracæna	Ligularia	Ricinus
Acanthus	Carduus	Equisetum	Megasea	Rumex
Agave	Carex	Eryngium	Melia	Sagittaria
Ailanthus	Carlina	Eucalyptus	Melianthus	Scirpus
Alsophila	Carludovica	Farfugium	Molospermum	Seaforthia
Amaranthus	Caryota	Ferdinanda	Montagnæa	Senecio
Andropogon	Centaurea	Ferula	Morina	Silphium
Aralia	Chamædorea	Ficus	Mulgedium	Silybum
Aristolochia	Chamæpeuce	Funkia	Musa	Solanum
Artemisia	Chamærops	Gourds	Nicotiana	Sorghum
Arum	Cordyline	Gunnera	Nuphar	Struthiopteris
Arundo	Corypha	Gynerium	Onopordon	Thalictrum
Asparagus	Crambe	Gymnocladus	Osmunda	Tupidanthus
Asplenium	Cucurbita	Hedychium	Paulownia	Typha
Astilbe	Cyathea	Helianthus	Petasites	Uhdea
Bambusa	Cycas	Heracleum	Phœnix	Veratrum
Berberis	Cynara	Inula	Phormium	Verbascum
Bocconia	Cyperus	Jubæa	Polygonum	Wigandia
Bupthalmum	Datisca	Kochia	Polymnia	Woodwardia
Caladium	Dicksonia	Kœlreuteria	Rheum	Yucca
Calla	Dimorphanthus	Latania	Rhus	Zea
Canna	Dipsacus			

Bed of fine-leaved plants in Hyde Park. From a sketch by H. G. Moon.

Torch lilies (Longleat).

CHAPTER XVIII.

THE FLOWER GARDEN IN AUTUMN.

Now who hath entered my loved woods,
  And touched their green with sudden change?
Who blanched my Thistle's rosy face,
  And gave the winds her silver hair?
Set Golden-rod within her place,
  And scattered Asters everywhere?
Lo ! the change reaches high and wide,
  Hath toned the sky to softer blue ;
Hath crept along the river side,
  And trod the valleys through and through !

RECENT additions to our garden flora have made such a difference that the flower garden in th. autumn may be even more beautiful than that of the spring, rich as that is in flowering trees and shrubs.

The use of half hardy, or bedding plants, which are often showy in autumn, gives a certain amount of colour which is very precious ; and the introduction of many beautiful hardy flowers gives us the means of making the autumnal garden very fine in colour effects. It would be easy to give the names of many things that are to be found in flower in gardens in autumn, but that is not nearly so important as getting an idea of many of the nobler class of plants which may be effectively used at that time, no matter almost what the season may be. Half hardy plants for the garden depend very much on the weather of the summer, and certain seasons are so much against them that they make no show; but this cannot be said of the hardy flowers of nobler stature and beauty, which are so well fitted for our climate, like the many Sunflowers. Certain plants may depend for success on soil and situation, or even climate, even when they are hardy as the Fuchsia, which is so much better in the coast and west country gardens; but, when everything is left out that wants any extra culture or advantages of climate and soil, there remain for every garden many beautiful things for the garden in the fall.

Of those that can generally be trusted for our country, I should say that, of all the gains of the past generation, the brilliant groups of plants of the Sunflower order were the finest, handsomest, and most generally useful for their disregard of any weather likely to occur. The masses of fine form and colour one may have with these when grouped in picturesque ways are remarkable With the Sunflowers are included not only the Helianthus strictly, of which there are so many good kinds now, but also other showy prairie flowers of the same natural order, which approach them in character, such as Rudbeckia, Silphium, Helenium, and other vigorous families of this numerous tribe of plants The best character of many of these is that they thrive in any soil, and make their way in rough places and among shrubs, or in parts of gardens less precious than those we keep for our best flowers.

For delicate and fine colour, however, the first place belongs to Tea and monthly Roses, of which the best kinds should always be grown in the open air Of the kinds which open best in England, a delightful garden may be made in autumn, in fine seasons enduring right to the end. Until quite recently no one trusted the Tea Rose out in bold masses in the flower garden, and hence the ordinary red Rose, not generally flowering late, was kept by itself. A greater mistake could not be, because these most precious of all Roses (the Teas) go on blooming throughout the summer and autumn, and very often they vary in bloom; that is to say, the flowers of September will not be the same as the flowers of June, the buds also varying. So we have not only lovely Roses throughout the fine season, but also variety every week, every shower seeming to influence the bloom. There is such great variety among them that every week seems to give us a new aspect of beauty. In my own garden were planted several thousands of Tea Roses in this way, not only for their beauty, but also with a view of testing the kinds best for our country. Some kinds which are fine abroad do not open well with us, but a number of beautiful kinds do, and we have never seen any picture of garden beauty equal to theirs in such a fine autumn as that of 1895. We had thousands of blooms open until the end of September, almost as showy as bedding plants, but far more refined in colour, fragrance,

and everything that makes a plant precious   Almost the same thing
may be said of the neglected monthly Roses, which have this charm
of late flowering, in many cases even in cold northern districts
  But the most precious, perhaps, of all flowers of autumn for all
parts of the country, grouped in an artistic way, are the hardy Asters
of the American woods, which lived for ages in our gardens in mean
bundles tied up in mixed borders like besoms   The best of these
massed and grouped among shrubs or young plantations of trees,
covering the ground, give an effect new and delightful, the colour
refined and charming, and the mass of bloom impressive in autumn.
Some kinds come in flower in summer, but nearly all the loveliest
Asters in colour flower in September and October, and no such good
colours of the same shades have ever been seen in the flower garden
  It is not only the Asters of America we have to consider, but the
still more precious Asters of Europe, which, by their extraordinary
beauty, make up for their rarity   Professor Green, of California, who
knows the American Aster well, on seeing here a plant of Aster
acris, said, „ We have none so beautiful as that." This is the Aster
with the beautiful blue purple flower which is so effective when
massed   Under different names this plant is grown in nearly allied
forms, some having specific names, enabling us to enjoy plants of
different stature but the same high beauty, flowering at slightly
different times, but always at their best in autumn.   With these
should be grouped the handsome large Italian Aster, which also has
its half-a-dozen forms, not differing much, but precious for their
variety, and among the prettiest plants ever seen in our gardens.   It
is none the less valuable because as easily cultivated as the common
Balm of the kitchen garden.   For the last two years I have had
several thousand plants of these European Asters beneath a group of
half-grown Fir, just as they might be in their wild state, but rather
thicker, as the spot is a cultivated one, and have never had the
same return of beauty from anything else.   Be the weather what it
may, the lovely blue and purple was a picture, and landscape
painters came to paint the scene.
  The Sunflowers and Starworts we give the first place to because
they are almost independent of soil or cool climates   Hardy as the
Chrysanthemum is, the same cannot be said for it, because, as an
outdoor flower, it must have a sandy soil and warm positions, and
cool soils, even in southern England, are against it ; whereas in warm
and free soils, like that at Hazlemere, one may see delightful results
from the cottage Chrysanthemums, which are very pretty where they
can be grown against low walls or palings   Other plants which are of
the highest value in endurance and freedom of bloom are the Heaths
of our own islands.   Their effect is good, summer and winter ; but in

autumn some of them flower in a pretty way, particularly the Cornish
and the little Dorset Heath, and the Irish Heath in its purple and
white forms.

Among the half hardy plants of the garden perhaps the first place
belongs to the Dahlia, which was always a showy autumn flower, but
of late has become more precious through the beauty of what are called

Border of Michaelmas Daisies (Munstead), Surrey.

Cactus Dahlias, which are so much better in form and colour than the
roundheaded Dahlias.

The hardy Fuchsia is in the warmer and milder districts often
very pretty in autumn, especially where it is free enough to make
hedges and form large bushes ; but in cold and midland places the
growth is often hindered by hard winters. Gladiolus is a splendid
flower of the south, but coming more into a class of flowers requiring
care, and if they do not get it soon disappearing, liable also to disease,
and, on the whole, not so precious as showy. Nurserymen are raising

kinds of a hardier nature, but we have more precious flowers. The last few years have brought us magnificent varieties of the Cannas through the crossing of some wild species with the old hybrid kinds. Unfortunately, although in warm valleys and under special care here and there they do well, our country is not generally warm enough to show their fine form and colour as in France and Italy. Their use in pots is another matter

The addition of Lilies to our garden flora within the past generation has had a good effect on the autumn garden. Where the finer kinds are well grown, the varieties of the Japanese Lilies, with their delicate and varied colours, are splendid autumn flowers for the open air. The Anemones, usually flowers of the spring, come in some forms for the autumn garden, particularly the white and pink kinds. The handsome Bignonia, or trumpet creeper, is precious on all warm soils, but generally it has not done so well with us as in France. Several kinds of Clematis come in well in autumn, particularly the yellow and the fragrant kinds. The Pentstemons are handsome and very valuable in warm soils and districts where they may live out of doors in winter, but in London districts they are not so good. A splendid autumn flower is the Cardinal Flower, and happy should be those who can grow it well. It fails in many gardens in loamy soil, and where there is insufficiency of water, being a native of the bogs, and thriving best in moist and peaty soil. A number of fine varieties have been raised, and are brilliant in suitable soils ; but without these they are best left alone.

The Torch Lilies are extremely effective in autumn, and in warm soils they are often among the handsomest things, but, not being northern plants, are unable to face a northern winter. Happily this is not so with the beautiful new Water Lilies raised by M Latour Marliac, which are hardy in the open air, even with such weather as that of the early part of 1895. Though perhaps the best bloom comes in summer, they flower through the autumn, varying, like the Tea Rose, according to the weather, but interesting always up to the end of September. We should also name the Hollyhock which is, however, so liable to accident from disease, and those who care for it will do well to use seedling plants. Seedsmen are now saving seed of different colours which come fairly true.

A handsome group of vigorous perennials for the autumn are the Polygonums. Some of the large kinds, such as the Japanese and Indian, are not showy, but massed picturesquely on margins of a wide lawn, and on pieces of stiff soil which are useless in any garden sense, are effective for many weeks in autumn, as the flower is pretty, and the foliage of one kind is often fine in colour. I have three kinds of them massed together, growing like great weeds, namely, P.

cuspidatum, sachalinense, and complexum, and a very soft and good effect they gave together in a rough hollow where no garden plants less vigorous than these would have grown.

Thus we have a noble array before coming to some old flowers of autumn, the Meadow Saffrons or "autumn Crocuses," many of the common kind of which fleck the meadows in autumn There are other kinds, too, which of recent years have been added in greater numbers to our gardens, some of them pretty, and the double kinds prettier than most double flowers As they grow naturally in meadows, in turf is a delightful way to have them in gardens, though new and rare kinds should be grown in nursery beds until they are plentiful They are not difficult to grow, and should often be placed in moist grassy places.

Then there are the true autumn Crocuses, which are very little seen in gardens, but are most delicate and lovely in colour. Coming for the most part from sunny lands, they do best in light soils , but some, like C. speciosus, grow in any soil, and all are worth growing. Among the best is C. nudiflorus, naturalised in Britain, in colour one of the most lovely flowers. To get little pictures from such plants we must have them happy in grass or among dwarf plants, and on sunny banks and grassy corners of the lawn or pleasure ground.

In mid-October they have often taken away large areas of bedding plants in the London parks ; while, at the same time, there are many lovely hardy flowers in perfect bloom. No doubt severe frosts may destroy any kind of flower soon, but for those who live in the country in the autumn it is something to have bright colours and beautiful plants about them late, and these are afforded as well by the Starworts and other hardy plants in October, as the fairest flowers that come in June. When we have a severe September about London, many gardens of tender plants are shorn of their beauty, whereas, the hardy flowers go on quite untouched for a month or six weeks later, and not merely bloom as do heliotrope and geranium, in a fine autumn, but as the meadow flowers in summer, with vigour and perfect health Therefore, it is clear that, whatever the charms of tender plants may be for the summer, those who live in the country in autumn are unwise to trust to anything but the finer hardy plants.

Thus, without touching on rarities or things difficult to grow, we have a handsome array of beauty for the autumn garden, even leaving out of the question the many shrubs and trees which are beautiful in foliage or fruit in autumn, and there are many of these in any well-stored garden.

Some Hardy and Half-hardy Plants blooming in British gardens.
September—October.

Abutilon	Crocus	Hyacinthus	Œnothera	Snapdragon
Aconitum	Cuphea	Hypericum .	Pampas Grass	Solanum
Agapanthus	Cyclamen	Iberis	Pansy	Solidago
Ageratum	Dahlia	Impatiens	Papaver	Statice
Amaryllis	Delphinium	Lantana	Pentstemon	Strawberry
Anagallis	Desmodium	Lauristinus	Petunia	Sweet Peas
Anemone	Dianthus	Lavender	Phlox	Sweet William
Arnebia	Diplacus	Liatris	Phygelius	Telekia
Aster	Diplopappus	Lilium	Physalis	Trachelium
Berberidopsis	Eccremocarpus	Linaria	Physostegia	Tradescantia
Bignonia	Erica	Linum	Plumbago	Tritoma
Brugmansia	Escallonia	Lobelia	Polygonum	Tritonia
Calceolaria	Fuchsia	Lonicera	Prince's-feather	Tropæolum
Campanula	Gaillardia	Lupin	Pyrethrum	Tuberose
Canna	Geum	Lychnis	Rose .	Valerian
Cassia	Gladioli	Lythrum	Rudbeckia	Venidium
Ceanothus	Godetia	Magnolia	Salpiglossis	Verbascum
Celsia	Gypsophila	Marigold	Salvia	Verbena
Centaurea	Helenium	Matthiola	Scabious	Veronica
Chrysanthemum	Helianthus	Mignonette	Sedum	Viola
Clematis	Heliotrope	Mimulus	Senecio	Yucca
Colchicum	Hieracium	Montbretia	Silene	Zephyranthes
Convolvulus	Hollyhock	Nicotiana	Silphium	Zinnia
Coreopsis	Honeysuckle	Nigella		

Belladonna Lily and Zephyranthes, Kew. Engraved from photograph by G. Champion.

Winter Jasmine.

CHAPTER XIX.

THE FLOWER GARDEN IN WINTER.

THE idea that winter is a doleful time for gardens must not be taken seriously even by those who only grow hardy things out of doors ; because between the colour of the stems and leaves of trees, or shrubs, there is much beauty left, even in winter, and in mild winters good things venture to flower. Mr. Moore, of Dublin, wrote to me in midwinter :

After a very open winter we have had a sharp snap of cold, and to-day (Jan. 20) it is blowing a bitterly cold storm from the east. To-day has opened Winter Sweet and Winter Honeysuckle ; Iris Stylosa, blue and white, Christmas Roses and Winter Heliotrope are beautiful ; in fact, I never saw them so good.

But even where, owing to hard winters, we cannot enjoy our flowers in this way, there is much beauty to be had from trees and shrubs, evergreen and summer-leafing. Hitherto we have been all so busy in planting evergreens in heavy masses, that the beauty one may realise by using a far greater number of summer-leafing shrubs and fine herbaceous plants among the evergreens is not often seen.

But gardens are too often bare of interest in winter, and some of the evil arises from the common error that plants are not worth seeing in winter. The old poet's wail about the dismal winter is a false one to those who have eyes for beauty. Woods are no less beautiful in winter than in summer—to some, more beautiful from the refined colour, tree form and the fine contrast of evergreen and summer-leafing trees. In any real garden in winter there is much beauty of form and colour, and there are many shrubs and trees which are beautiful in the depth of winter, like the Red and Yellow Willow and Dogwoods, and even the stems of hardy flowers (Polygonum); the foliage of many alpine plants (Epimedium) are not only good in colour, but some of these plants have their freshest hues in winter, as the mossy Rockfoils of many kinds In the country garden, where there are healthy evergreens as well as flowering shrubs and hardy plants, how much beauty we see in winter, from the foliage of the Christmas Roses (Helleborus) to the evergreen Barberries ! The flower gardener should be the first to take notice of this beauty, and show that his domain as well as the wild wood, might be interesting at this season

For the dismal state of flower-gardens in winter the extravagant practice of our public gardens is partly to blame A walk by the flower beds in Hyde Park on Christmas Day, 1895, was not a very enlivening thing One by the bent-bound dunes of the foam-dashed northern shore, on the same stormy day, might be more instructive— for here is a large garden carried out with the very extravagance of opulence, and not one leaf, or shoot or plant, or bush in it from end to end ; giants' graves and earth puddings—these and iron rails and the line of planes behind. The bare beds follow each other with irritating monotony—only five feet of grass between those in line The southern division of this garden is nearly 500 paces long, and so even that those not in the habit of seeing this costly garden may imagine its ill effect in winter. Nearly 500 yards of a garden sacrificed for its kaleidoscopic effects in summer, and barer and uglier in winter than words can tell of. A more inartistic arrangement would be impossible and there is no chance of variety, breadth, or repose even in summer

How are we to break up such an arid space as this in winter ? One of the best ways would be to group families of the choicest flowering shrubs, which would be worth having for their own sakes, and at the same time would give relief to the wintry waste of desolation. At present any relief is only to be obtained by carrying out, in early summer, Palms and Bamboos from the hot-house, which is a very expensive and poor way in a country like ours. In forming groups of the more beautiful flowering shrubs, I do not mean anything like the present brutal treatment of shrubs in the London squares, where the surface is dug, and the shrubs are trimmed like besoms, ending in frightful ugliness ; but each group of plants grown well by itself and let almost alone when once established They would give relief in the summer , they often flower beautifully , and here and there

R 2

they might form dividing masses, so as to throw the unwieldy space into parts, which would help to secure variety and contrast

The result of planting and placing rightly well chosen hardy shrubs would be a good background here and there, a smaller area to plant with summer things ; less dependence on such feeble examples of tropical plants as one can grow in Britain ; light and shade, and a variety of surface as well as more variety of plants and bushes ; in short, all the life of the garden, instead of a dead waste. And not only would the winter effect be improved, but the summer also. The objection that some shrubs do not flower long enough is not serious, as we have their beauty of form and leaf, and delicate green and other fine colour of foliage. Moreover, the tropical plants put out to relieve the flowering plants do not, many of them, flower at all, and do not give such good relief as hardy shrubs and choice trees.

This is not a question of town or public gardens only, as it arises in many private places, and especially in large gardens, where much of the surface is given to half-hardy summer flowers. As to the common plan for getting rid of the winter bareness of such beds by evergreens and conifers in pots, it is impossible on a large scale, and sticking potted conifers in a flower-garden to drag them away in spring, is at best a very inartistic and very costly business Some permanent way of breaking up the flatness is the best way , and this way would enable us to limit the excessive area of ground to be planted with tender things, the real root of evil.

KEEP THE STEMS OF HARDY PLANTS —The stems of all herbaceous plants, reeds, and tall grasses in winter, are very good in colour, and should always be allowed to stand through the winter and not be cut down in the fidgety tidy way that is so common, sweeping away the stems in autumn and leaving the surface as bare and ugly as that round a besieged city. The same applies to the stems of all waterside and herbaceous plants, stems of plants in groups often giving beautiful brown colours in many fine shades Those who know the plants can in this way identify them in winter as well as in summer—a great gain in changing one's plantings and in increasing or giving away plants. Moreover, the change to all these lovely browns and greys is a distinct gain as a lesson in colour to all who care for refined colour, and also in enabling us to get light and shade, contrasts and harmonies in colour. If these plants are grouped in a bold and at the same time picturesque way, the good of letting the stems remain will be far more evident than in the weak "dotty" way generally practised, the seed pods and dead flowers of many plants helping the picture. There is no need to remove any stem of an herbaceous plant until the spring comes and the growing shoots are ready to take the place of the brown and dead ones, which then may be cleared away.

EVERGREEN PLANTS.—Apart from our evergreen shrubs, so happy as these are in many parts of the British Isles, there are the oft-neglected evergreen rock and herbaceous plants, such as Christmas Roses, Barrenworts, Heuchera, Alexandrian Laurel, the bolder evergreen ferns, and the large Indian Rockfoils, Saxifraga or Megasea. In early winter these fine evergreen plants become a deeper green, some forms getting red They have been in our gardens for years, but are seldom made a right use of; thrown into borders without thought as to their habits, and soon forgotten or overshadowed by other things ; so that we never get any expression of their beauty or effect in masses or groups. Yet, if grouped in effective ways, they would go on for years, giving us fine evergreen foliage in winter. In addition to the wild kinds, a number of fine forms have been raised in gardens of late years. Some thought should be given to the placing of the large Rockfoils, their mountain character telling us that they ought to be on open banks, borders, or banky places exposed to the sun, and not buried among heaps of tall herbaceous and miscellaneous vegetation. They are so easily grown and increased that a little thought in placing them in visible masses is the only thing they call for ; and the fact that they will endure and thrive under almost any conditions should not prevent us from show-ing how fine they are in effect when held together in any bold way, either as carpets, bold edgings, or large picturesque groups on banks or rocks

The Alexandrian Laurel (Ruscus racemosus) is a most graceful plant, somewhat shrubby in character, with glossy dark green leaves and Willow-like shoots. It is most free and happy on peaty and friable soils, growing 3 feet or 4 feet high; in winter the effect is very good, and it is valuable for the house, to give a graceful and distinct foliage to accompany various flowers at this season. It grows very well in Ireland on the limestone. In clay soils it may want a little encouragement, and it thrives well in partial shade.

The Christmas Rose is a noble winter flower where well grown, and is lovely in its wild state in the foot-hills of the Alps, in Italy and countries near ; and, happily, it flowers in our gardens very well also, varying a little in its ways The stout kind (H. maximus) flowers in the early winter in front of walls and in sheltered spots, and is hardy and free in ordinary soil. The true Christmas Rose (H. niger) is a little more particular ; it thrives much better on chalky and warm soils, and grows best on a northern aspect or shaded place ; and even in its own country the finest plants are found in places where it escapes the sun. These are true winter flowers , but hardly less so are the Lenten Roses, or forms of the Oriental Hellebores. In the southern counties, five seasons out of six, no weather stops them from being fine in flower before the winter is past ; they often bloom in January and make a handsome show in February, and they are the finest of all flowers to end the winter The Winter Heliotrope (Tussilago fragrans) is not to be despised, although it is a bad weed, and hard to get rid of The way to deal with it is to put it on some rubbish heap, or gravel bank, right away from the garden, where a handful of it may be gathered when wanted

The Algerian Iris flowers in warm sandy borders in the country around London, and in mild winters is a great treasure, not merely for its beauty in warm sheltered corners, but also its precious qualities for the house, in which the flowers, if cut in the bud state, open gracefully if placed in basins in moss In warm and sheltered gardens, on warm soils, others of the winter blooming Iris of the East may be grown, while in such gardens, in the south at least, the good culture of the sweet Violet will often be rewarded with many flowers in winter

A beautiful Italian Crocus (Imperati) often flowers in winter in the southern counties at least, as, where people take the trouble to get them, do C. Sieberi, Dalmaticus Etruscus, Suaveoleus and others. This habit of some of the winter flowers of the south of Italy and Mediterranean region to open in our green and open winters should be taken advantage of. The fate of these Crocuses is interfered with by the common field vole, and the common rat is also a great destroyer of the Crocus Where these enemies do not prevail, and the soil favours these charming winter and early flowers, we can grow them, not only in the garden, but on the turf of sunny meadows and lawns in which these beautiful Crocuses will come up year after year in winter and early dawn of spring.

SHRUBS AND TREES IN THE WINTER GARDEN —The Wintersweet (Chimonanthus fragrans) is in bloom often before Christmas in the country around London, and every shoot full of fragrant buds opening on the trees against south and west walls. It is invaluble both for the open garden and the house. The many bright berries which adorn our country, both in the wild land and in well-stored gardens, are rather things of the autumn ; and by mid-winter the birds are apt to clear them off Wild Roses, Briers, Barberry, and Thorns, American as well as British The Pyracantha, however, stays with us late ; and Hollies, Aucuba, Cotoneaster, Snowberry, and the pretty little hardy Pernettya, from the Straits of Magellan, which has broken into such variety of colour in our country, are among those that stay late. But, however the cheery berries may fail us in hard winters, the colour of the trees and bushes that bear them never does ; and the red and yellow Willow, Dogwood, Thorns, Alders, Birch, and many Aspens and Maples, give fine colour when massed or grouped in any visible way. Still more constant are the flowering shrubs of winter, where in sheltered gardens and warm valleys any attention is given to them— Winter Jasmine, Winter Sweet, Winter Honeysuckles, Wych-Hazel, Japan Quince in many forms, Laurustinus, several Heaths, Arbutus, at least one variety of Daphne Mezereon, the pale Southern Clematis (Calycina) happy in our warmer gardens, Eleagnus, the Nepal Barberry, a Chinese Plum (P. Davidiana), and the catkin bearing Garrya and Hazel. The Winter Honeysuckles are a bit slow in some districts, and a better result is got from them on free soils, and from walls in sheltered corners, an immense difference resulting if we can have them near the sea, with its always genial influence in favour of things from climates a little warmer than our own. In heavy soils in the inland country and around London the Laurustinus often comes to grief or fails to flower well, but has great beauty in seashore districts, and often on sandy and gravel soils is charming, even in inland places.

The hardy and beautiful Winter Jasmine, which is so free on cottage walls and wherever it gets a chance, is most precious, owing to the way it opens in the house especially if gathered in the bud state. If we have it in various aspects, such a contingency as the sun scorching the shoots after a frost and killing

Winter Sweet, drawn by H. G. Moon from shoots gathered at Gravetye New Year's Day, 1895.

the flowers may be avoided, and the flowers will come later. The plant is so free that, if the shoots are allowed to hang down, they root in the ground like twitch, and therefore it can be increased very easily, and should be seen in visible groups and lines, and not only on the house or on walls, as in the milder districts it forms pretty garlands and bushes in the open. I have a little oak fence covered with it, which is usually very pretty about Christmas. In mild winters its beauty is extraordinary out of doors, and in the hardest winters the buds will open in the house.

And when the Dogwood has lost all its leaves and is a deep red by the lake, and the Cardinal Willow has nearly taken its winter colour, the dwarf autumn blooming Furze flowers far into winter, and is in perfect bloom on the drier ground, telling us of its high value where dwarf vegetation not over a yard high is desired. It is seen in abundance on many hills and moors, but is hardly ever planted by design. A good plant for all who care for low foreground vegetation, it may be planted like common furze, but by far the best way is to sow it in spring in any bare or recently broken ground The Common Furze, too, of which the season of bloom is spring and mild winters, often flowers at Christmas ; odd plants here and there in the colonies of the plant bearing quite fresh flowers, and if from the nature of these native shrubs they do not find a place in the flower garden, there are few country places where they may not be worth growing not far from the house, in covert, or by drives or rough walks, as no plants do more to adorn the late autumn and winter

The hardy Heaths are excellent for the winter garden in their brown and grey tuftiness. The forms of the common Heather and the Cornish Heath are best for rough places outside the flower-garden but some kinds of Heath are among the best plants for the choicest winter garden of the open air, particularly the Portuguese Heath (E. Codonodes), which in mild winters is of great beauty ; also a hybrid between the Alpine forest Heath (E. carnea) and the Mediterranean Heath, with the port and dense flowering habit of the Alpine Heath and the earlier bloom of the Mediterranean Heath. The Alpine forest Heath, the most precious of all hardy Heaths, often flowers in mild winters, and in all winters is full of its buds ready to open

So far we are speaking of districts where there are few advantages of climate ; if we include others there might be more flowers in the winter-garden, and many varied flowers are seen in gardens in the Isle of Wight, Isle of Man and many other favoured gardens—not always confined to the southern parts of England and Ireland : the Cornish, Devon, South Wales or Cork Coasts being far more favourable. From these places Roses, Indian Daphne, and many other flowers, have often been sent to me in perfect bloom in January.

And if the snow shrouds the land, all's well, as the leaves of ever-green plants, like Carnations, are at rest in it, and some plants are all the better for the peace of the snow for a time. And even if our eyes are not open to the beauty of the winter let us make the flower-garden a real one for spring, summer and fall, as if it were true that in winter

> The year
> On the earth her deathbed, in a shroud of leaves dead,
> Is lying.

But it is not true: there is in winter no death, every root works and every bud is active with life; the wooded land is tender with colour:—Alders by the busy wintry stream and Birch on the airy hill, Reeds fine in colour round the lake or marsh, and if even our wild marsh or rough woodland be beautiful in winter, our gardens, with the flora of three continents to gather from, should not then be poor in beauty. No! Winter is not a time of death, but of happy strife for plants and men.

> Until her
> Azure sister of the spring shall blow
> Her clarion o'er the dreaming earth, and fill
> (Driving sweet buds like flocks to feed in air)
> With living hues and odours plain and hill:

Hazel catkins. From a drawing by H. G. Moon.

Upper part of my Water Garden   From a photograph by Sir Henry Thompson, August, 1896.

CHAPTER XX

WATER GARDENS BY VARIOUS WATER GARDENERS

IT is not only from the mountain's breast, dyed with Violet and Gentian, the Sunflower-strewn prairie of the north, or the sunny fields where Proserpine gathered flowers, that our garden flora comes River and stream are often fringed with handsome plants, and little fleets of Water Lily—silvery fleets they look as one sees them from the bank—sail on the lakelets far away in North America and Asia, even where the water is solid ice in winter. One need not go so far to see beautiful plants, as our own country rivers and back-waters of rivers possess many. Our gardens are often made about towns where there are few chances of seeing our native water plants, but by the back-waters of rivers and by streams in many situations, and by lakes like the Norfolk Broads one may often see as handsome plants in these places, and also in the open marsh land, as in any garden, and some that we do not often see happy in gardens, such as the Frogbit, the Bladderwort, and Water Soldier.

Where, as often is the case in artificially made ponds, the margin of the water is not the rich deep soil that we have by the Broads and by the sides of rivers, which themselves carry down deep beds of rich soil, a good way is to put the mud which we take out of the pond around its sides a little above and below the water line. This will encourage a rich growth of such Reeds as are found beside natural waters Water with a hard, naked, beaten edge and little or no vegetation is not good to look at, and a margin of rich living plants is better for fish and game as well as for effect. The waterside plants one may establish in that way are worth having and give good cover for duck

Perhaps the most beautiful of all water gardens are the river and stream gardens, as their form is so much better than anything we can make and the vegetation is often good even without care. With a little thought we can make it much more so, and in our river-seamed land there are so many charming opportunities for water-garden pictures.

WATERSIDE PLANTS. — The water-margin offers to lovers of hardy flowers a site easily made into a fair garden. Hitherto we have used in such places aquatic plants only, and of these usually a very meagre selection , while the improvement of the waterside may be most readily effected by planting the banks near with vigorous hardy flowers, as many of the finest plants, from Irises to Globe Flowers, thrive in moist soil. Bank plants have this advantage over water plants that we can fix their position, whereas water plants spread so much that some kinds over-run others. The repeating of a favourite plant at intervals would mar all ; groups of free hardy things would be best : Day Lilies, Meadow Sweets, tall Irises, which love wet places ; Gunnera, American swamp Lilies in peaty soil, the rosy Loosestrife Golden Rods, Starworts, the Compass plants, Monkshoods, giant Knotworts, Moon Daisies, the Cardinal Flower, the common Lupine—these are some of many types of hardy flowers which would grow freely near the waterside. With these hardy plants, too, a variety of the nobler hardy Ferns, such as the Royal Ferns and Feather Ferns, would associate well.

WATER PLANTS of northern and temperate regions associated with our native water plants, add much beauty to a garden. If the soil be rich, we usually see the same monotonous vegetation all round the margin of the water, and where the bottom is of gravel there is often little vegetation, only an unbroken, ugly line of washed earth A group of Water Lily is beautiful, but Water Lilies lose their charm when they spread over the whole of a piece of water, and even waterfowl cannot make their way through them. The Yellow Water Lily (Nuphar lutea), though less beautiful, is well worthy of a place, and so is the large N. advena (a native of America), which pushes its leaves above the water. The American White Water Lilies (Nymphæa odorata and N tuberosa) are hardy and beautiful, and of recent years much beauty has been given our water plants in the hybrid hardy Water Lilies raised by M Latour-Marliac, who has added the large and noble forms and the lovely colour of the Eastern Water Lilies to the garden waters of northern countries. The splendid beauty of these plants should lead people to think of artistic ways of planting garden waters. Our native Water Lily was always neglected and rarely effective, except in a wild state ; but when people see that they may have in Britain the soft yellow and rose and red flowers of the tropical Water Lilies throughout summer and autumn, they may take interest in water gardens, and even the wretched duck ponds which disfigure so many country seats will begin at last to have a reason to be. The change should be the means of leading us to think more of the many noble flowers and fine leaved plants of the water-side, apart from Water Lilies. The new hybrid kinds continue blooming long after our native kind has ceased, and from the middle of May to nearly the end of October flowers are abundant.

For many years, pond, streamlet, and lake to a very considerable extent were left very much to themselves, with scarce a thought bestowed upon them or the plants for beautifying their surface or margin. In a large London nursery nearly twenty-five years ago, where a very large and, perhaps, complete collection of water plants existed, I was surprised to find that so very few aquatic plants should be required year after year ; so few, indeed, that the cost of maintaining the whole was barely met. This was most discouraging, because even water plants, where a representative collection is grown, cannot

Pond at Enys, Cornwall. From a photograph sent by Mr. F. W. Meyer, Exeter.

receive the necessary space for their free growth in a nursery. This was even so in the case of that lovely and fragrant Cape Pond Flower (Aponogeton), that, seeding in such abundance, was floated hither and thither in thousands, and in consequence had to be kept in check. The rapid increase of this plant, however, is by no means common ; indeed, many instances are known where it cannot be induced to flourish in the open. But in the nursery referred to, by reason of the quantity and size of the plants, flowers of this Aponogeton were gathered the greater part of the year, in the wintry season even its flowers floating on the surface by hundreds. The water in this instance, supplied from an artesian spring, contributed to the success of the plant, as also its freedom of flowering. Gradually, however, the aquatics are coming to the front, and an altogether fresh impetus, as well as a great one, has resulted from the introduction of the many charming new hybrid Nymphæas which are fast making their appearance in some of the best-known gardens. As yet many of these hybrids are scarce, and care will be needed, and possibly protection required, on the larger pieces of ornamental water where water-fowl are encouraged.

In planting these choicer kinds, some precaution is necessary when sinking them into their places. Very deep water is not essential, but if the pond be an artificial one, it will be found a good plan to take a few bags of heavy loamy soil to the spot by means of a punt and empty the soil over the side. Then the plant itself, well fixed by wire to the side of a basket already filled with similar soil, should be gradually lowered on to the mound of soil already deposited. In the natural lake no soil will be needed before sinking the plant in position, though similar means may be used to lower the plant, which will quickly take to the accumulation of earth and leaves that years have deposited. Many of the most lovely of aquatics may be grown with considerable success even where neither pond, lake, rivulet, nor ornamental water is found, some very good results having been derived by growing them in tanks 2 feet or 3 feet deep into which a depth of some 12 inches of clay earth has been placed   The recent hybrids are well worthy of attention in this way, and if a fair-sized tank be made and so placed that it will catch the rain water, so much the better for the plants. In this way also fountain basins on the terrace garden may be made to do some service. Besides the hybrid Nymphæas, such places are well suited if the water be fairly deep for such things as Orontium aquaticum, the Pontederias, and Arrowheads, all of which are perfectly hardy with their crowns 8 inches or 10 inches below the surface of the water, while Thalia dealbata, a rarely seen plant from Carolina, is quite safe with similar treatment Indeed, it is to be regretted that this handsome plant is not more frequently seen in the water where its handsome leaves and heads of purple blossoms are very showy, but our country is too cool to show its fine form and stature.

FORMING THE WATER GARDEN.—Fortunate indeed are those through whose grounds runs a brook or streamlet. As a great many of our most effective and most graceful hardy plants can be grown either in the water itself or in the moisture-laden margin of a pond or brook, it is surprising that more advantage is not taken of this fact when the opportunity occurs   Even where natural ponds exist it frequently happens that the banks of the pond, as well as the water itself, are either perfectly bare, or are covered only by the rankest weeds. The ponds chiefly considered here are those mostly formed without cement, by natural flooding from a brook, streamlet or river. If the water supply is abundant and continuous, it matters little whether a portion of the water is wasted by percolating the sides of the pond, but when only a small supply can be had, the bottom and sides of the pond must be either concreted or puddled with clay. It often happens that when the excavations for a pond are completed, the bottom is found to consist of impervious clay, but the sides consist of ordinary soil, which would allow a large portion of the water to waste. In such cases the best way out of the difficulty is the cutting of a narrow trench, say 18 inches wide, to a depth a little beyond the surface of the natural clay subsoil. This trench, which should skirt the whole pond at some little distance from the actual

Riverside plants in front of an old manor—Levens.

edge of the water, is then filled with clay "puddle" till just above the water-line and forms an effective remedy against waste, while the water-soaked soil between the trench and the actual outline of the pond forms an excellent home for all kinds of marsh plants of the bolder type. The outline of a pond is of the utmost importance. Regular curves of circles or ovals are utterly out of place and look ridiculous in a landscape with irregular and naturally undulating ground. In order to be effective, the outline of the pond must not only be irregular, but it must be also in accordance with the laws of Nature, and as in most cases the natural pond or lake is merely an expanded stream or river, we must look to the shore-lines of the latter for guidance in the forming of artificial ponds. In a natural stream the curves are mostly due to the water meeting with some obstacle which caused a deviation in its course. We find invariably that where a promontory, a projecting rock, or some other obstacle caused an alteration in the course of the water, the latter is thrown against the opposite bank with greater force, and unless the ground be very hard a good portion of it is washed away by the force, and an extended recess is the natural result In the same way an irregular pond to look natural should have the largest and boldest recesses opposite or nearly opposite the largest promontory on the' other side. The shore-line should not terminate abruptly, but should form a slope continued below the water level.

In planting the shore of a pond or lake it is the ground which projects into the water which should be furnished with the largest and boldest plants. This is not only perfectly natural, but has also the effect of partially concealing some of the recesses of the water. A pond thus treated will appear larger than it really is, and a walk around the shore-line will reveal fresh surprises with every step

AQUATICS —Of all plants suitable for the water garden, none can surpass the Nymphæas now that we have a variety of shades of colour undreamt of a few years ago. The delicate pink Nymphæa Marliacea carnea and the yellow N. M. Chromatella seem to make the most rapid progress in English water gardens, while the white Nymphæa pygmæa alba and the yellow N p. Helvola are the Liliputians of the race. Perhaps the most exquisite of the newer kinds are N. M. Seignoretti (which is red, shaded with orange). N M. Robinsoni and the deep carmine N. M. ignea A little less expensive is the large deep red N. Laydekeri lilacea, while the following are now to be got · N. Laydekeri rosea, deep rose, changing to carmine ; N. odorata exquisita, rosy carmine ; N. o. rosacea, tender rose shade ; N. o. rubra, deep rose, and N. odorata sulphurea, deep yellow. Nuphar advena should not be used except in places where there is plenty of room, when, as shown in the picture, even the leaves alone produce a bold effect. The same might be said of our native Water Lilies, Nymphæa alba and Nuphar lutea. Stratiotes aloides (popularly known as the Water Soldier) is attractive, not so much for its flowers as for its long leaves, which form a striking contrast to other aquatics. Villarsia Humboldtiana and the native Villarsia nymhpæoides, with its small round leaves and yellow flowers, form a good contrast to plants of a bolder type. Another interesting aquatic is Vallisneria spiralis, with very long, narrow leaves and small white flowers floating on the surface of the water.

AQUATICS FOR SHALLOW WATER.—The common Sweet Flag (Acorus Calamus), the Flowering Rush (Butomus umbellatus), and the Bulrush or Reed Mace (Typha latifolia) are bold as well as graceful objects in shallow water, especially in a large lake, but in ponds

of only moderate size they should be used with caution, or they
would soon shut out Nymphæas and other aquatics whose leaves and
flowers float on the water. Much less robust in their growth are
Typha angustifolia and T. minima. Very striking, too, are the
arrow-shaped leaves and white spikes of blossom of Sagittaria
sagittæfolia and the Buckbean (Menyanthes trifoliata). The flowers
of the latter are very sweet-scented and arranged in racemes ; they
are beautifully fringed, pure white, slightly tinged with pink outside.
This also must be kept in check to prevent injury to other aquatics.
A handsome American aquatic, quite hardy in shallow water, is
Pontederia cordata, with handsome spikes of blue flowers and almost
erect leaves on long stalks about 18 inches or more in height. The

Natural grouping of waterside plants. From a photograph sent by M. Louis Kropatsch, Imperial
Gardens, Vienna.

Bog Arum (Calla palustris), though only about 9 inches high, when
planted in groups is most effective. The well-known Arum Lily
(Calla æthiopica) may—in the west and south of England at all
events—also be used as an aquatic for shallow water. Though a
severe winter will cut it down, the roots below the surface of the
water will push forth new leaves and flowers in great profusion. At
Trelissick, near Truro, the pond was skated on for several weeks,
and 16° and 18° of frost were registered during the severe winter two
years ago, but in the following spring many thousands of Arum
Lilies were cut from the very same pond.

MARGINS OF WATER.—The water-soaked margins of our ponds
and brooks would furnish a home for many graceful fine-foliaged and

S

flowering plants. One of the noblest of our plants with large leaves delighting in such a position is Gunnera manicata. Gunnera scabra also likes a similar position, but its leaves seldom attain a diameter of more than 5 feet, while Gunnera magellanica is quite a pigmy. Rheum Emodi from the Himalayas, Rheum palmatum from Northern Asia, and the Siberian Rheum undulatum are also effective plants for the waterside. Of an entirely different type are the noble Arundo donax and its variegated variety. In the south-west of England they are, as a rule, hardy without protection, and their elegant grace is most striking. The Pampas Grass (Gynerium argenteum) and its early-flowering companion, Arundo conspicua, from New Zealand, may also be mentioned as graceful plants for the waterside. Much dwarfer, but also effective, is the deciduous grass, Elymus glauco-phyllus, with broad glaucous foliage contrasting well with the fine deep green foliage of Carex pendula or the still finer Carex riparia and its variegated form. Cyperus longus is another suitable companion from the same family. Juncus effusus spiralis, with its stems twisted like corkscrews, is perhaps more curious than pretty, but Acorus gramineus variegatus and Juncus zebrinus have an uncommon as well as a pretty effect in consequence of their variegated leaves.

The plants just mentioned as suitable for the waterside are valued mostly on account of their foliage. But among flowering plants also handsome varieties may be found that might with great advantage be used for decoration at the waterside much oftener than is at present the case. Few things are brighter than the brilliant purple flowers of Lythrum salicaria var. roseum superbum, or the large yellow flowers of Inula Helenium and Telekia speciosissima. Groups of Iris Kæmpferi and the well-known Iris germanica, also look exceedingly well on the margin of a pond, and the "flowering" Fern (Osmunda regalis) delights in that position. Senecio japonica grows really well only when its roots can find abundance of moisture; its large deeply-cut leaves are as handsome as its deep yellow flowers, 4 inches across, and borne on a stem 3 feet to 4 feet high. A similar position is required by Spiræa gigantea, which bears its flowers on stems 5 feet to 6 feet above the ground. Spiræa Aruncus, though not so tall, is, nevertheless, most suitable, as are also its smaller, but still more handsome companions, Spiræa palmata, S alba, S astilboides, and Astilbe rivularis. Very bright and effective, too, in such a position are Chelone barbata and Lyoni, and the Globe Flowers (Trollius) show by the waterside a vigour they do not develop elsewhere. This might also be said of the double Marsh Marigold (Caltha palustris fl.-pl) and of several varieties of Hemerocallis.

FOR A SHADY NOOK by the waterside we are by no means

limited to Ferns. It is in such a position Primula japonica and sikkimensis delight   Here also the blue Himalayan Poppy (Meconopsis Wallichi), the tall yellow Gentian (Gentiana lutea), and the bright blue Mertensia virginica will flourish as well as Saxifraga peltata, Sanguinaria canadensis, Podophyllum Emodi, the handsome P. peltatum, and Rodgersia podophylla, while Trillium grandiflorum and Solomon's Seal will be at their best.   There is, no doubt, a number of other suitable plants for the water garden, especially if we include the plants generally known as bog plants, which, however, are perhaps more suitable for the bog bed of a rock garden than the bolder margins of ponds or lakes, but enough plants have been enumerated to show that we have a great variety to pick from, and that certainly there is a great future for the water garden —F W MEYER, *Elmside Exeter.*

It is now some fifteen or sixteen years since I planted the common white Water Lily in the pond here   Noting how well it grew, I was induced to try the pink or rose-coloured form of it which had been introduced from Norway—*i e*, Nymphæa alba var rosea   Finding, too, that this was thriving, I further extended the Lily culture by the addition of a dozen more varieties and species.   Of these I have only lost N flava, and that occurred during the severe frost of 1894-95 All that I gave in the way of protection then was laying a few mats upon the ice when it was sufficiently strong to bear one's weight, and that small amount of protection was more in the form of a preventive against any skaters running over them where the ice was none too strong, and possibly cause injury should it have given way   During that winter the ice was unusually thick , so much so here must it have been as to almost, if not quite, reach the Lily roots, the depth of water over them then being only about 12 inches   No better test of their hardiness is, I think, needed than this, save in the case of N flava.   Last spring I added N. Robinsoni, the present winter being of course its first test, but of its hardiness I have not the slightest doubt In addition to the foregoing I have three of the pigmy varieties, which, with a distinct form of the common white from Norway, make in all eighteen kinds or varieties

In the spring, when I added the twelve varieties (chiefly those of M Latour-Marliac's raising), these being small tubers, I commenced by putting them carefully into soil in large-sized punnets, the entire dozen coming to hand in one parcel by post   I mention this so that some idea may be formed of the then size of the tubers compared with the present time   During the summer of 1894 they grew well, making steady progress, and towards the autumn a few flowers appeared on the strongest plants.   The following summer (*i.e*, 1895) a most marked progress was made the stronger-growing kinds beginning to give some indications of their true character, whilst the flowering period was well prolonged and a considerable number of flowers produced   Seeing that more room was essential for their perfect development, I decided to provide for this by carefully lifting the plants last spring when the first indications of growth were visible.   This operation was performed about two years from the time of first planting them, but so well had they rooted in the case of the strong growing kinds, that it took three men to lift them with digging forks, several of the roots being as large as one's fingers and of considerable length   These came up with good balls, and were immediately transferred to large circular baskets which had been half-filled with good loam and leaf-soil, a few handfuls of bone-meal being allotted to each basket according to its size   When the roots were carefully spread out more soil was added to fill each basket, which was at once sunk again into the water, but at a greater distance apart than in the first instance.   This time the strongest were placed at some 10 feet or so from each other, but I can see already, after only one more year's growth that they will require more room even than this   These plants were sunk in about 18 inches of water this time in order to be more in accord with their growth.   The more moderate growers were arranged in front of these and in about 12 inches of water.   No apparent check ensued even at the first, for they grew away most vigorously, and in most cases have flowered as profusely. By the autumn the strongest clumps were fully 6 feet across, and this season I shall not be surprised if they touch each other.   The lake has a fair quantity of mud in it, about 6 inches perhaps where the plants are at present, the bottom being puddled with clay   The supply of water is from a spring which continuously discharges into the lake.

These fine water plants as grown and bloomed here are singularly beautiful and effective ; either one or another is always producing the distinct and pleasing flowers   The flowers remain open, too, for a prolonged period each day, either one or another being in good condition from 9 a.m to nearly dusk when the weather is bright. On more than one occasion I have also noted how beautiful they have been during showery weather , the water then being clear added to their beauty, the flowers glistening and sparkling like diamonds when under a brilliant light   When seen in this state, scarcely anything in the way of flowers could be more beautiful.—JAS HUDSON, *Gunnersbury House, Acton.*

ARUM LILIES AS AQUATICS IN BRITAIN —Whether or not the common Arum (Richardia æthiopica) is naturally an aquatic it may be taken as proved that it is at least amphibious, as a friend of mine has for years past grown Arum Lilies in a fresh water lake by the banks of the river Fàl within 20 feet of salt water, and his success has been great, as may be imagined when I say that the plants now form a broad margin to a portion of the lake about 300 yards in length and varying in width from 1 yard to 3 yards. The flowers on this belt open, at one time in June last, were estimated at 10,000, and the annual number is not less than 50,000 After a mild winter, such as that of 1895-96, cutting commences in February; by Easter the number of flowers is immense, and their production is continued to the end of September. The hardiness of the plants was well tested in the winter of 1894-95, when ice sufficiently thick to be skated on was formed on the lake, but this only served to check and not to destroy any of the plants, the check on those plants with crowns near the surface being sufficiently severe to prove that a good depth of water over the crowns is safest.

The method adopted for planting is simple enough and involves but little labour. Plants which have been forced are taken direct to the water, carried in a boat to the position selected, and then simply dropped overboard, after which they soon commence to root freely in the pond mud A large waggon-load was treated in this way last year, and this represents about the usual rate of annual increase by new plantings The position chosen for the Arums by the lake-side is a sunny, but well-sheltered one, and here the plants revel to such a degree as to have induced owners of other estates in Cornwall to plant largely on the same lines, with, of course, greater climatic advantages than can be found in the country at large. But does not the proved well-doing of the plants in water 2 feet deep open up possibilities for their cultivation in colder climes?—J C TALLACK, *Livermere*

ENEMIES.—Many water plants will grow almost anywhere and bid defiance to game or rats, but the newer and rarer Water Lilies are worth looking after, as they will not show half their beauty if they are subjected to the attacks of certain water animals They may, indeed, when young be easily exterminated by them, and even when old and established the common water rat destroys the flowers and, taking them to the bank, eats them at its leisure, and I have often found the remains of half a dozen fine flowers in one spot. When the plants are small, the attacks of the common moorhen and other water-fowl may mean all the difference between life and death to a Water Lily. Perhaps, therefore, the first thing to be done in establishing these plants is to put them in some small pond apart from the rougher water-side plants, and especially where they will be safe from the attacks of the water rat and other creatures which cannot be kept out of ponds fed by streamlets. By these and river banks or back-waters water rats are hard to destroy, and guns, traps, ferrets, or any other means must be used   The common brown rat is not so fond of these flowers as the true water rat, but it is so destructive to everything else, that it is essential to destroy it at the same time, as it often abounds near water   The water or moorhen is continuously destructive to all the Water Lilies, pecking at the flowers until mere shreds are left, and no one can fairly judge of the rare beauty of these plants where these birds are not kept down.

PLANTING THE WATERSIDE —People are so much led by showy descriptions in catalogues, and also by their own love for ugly things, that we often see misuse by the waterside of variegated shrubs—a bold lake margin almost covered with variegated bushes, like the yellow elder, the purple beech, and even down to the very margin of the water with variegated shrubs, absolutely the worst kind of vegetation which could be chosen for such a place

Of all places that one has to deal with in gardening or planting, islands and the margins of water—lake or river—we have the clearest guidance as to the trees and shrubs that inhabit and belong to such places, and that always thrive and look best in them.   The vegetation best fitted for those places is mostly of an elegant and spiry character , willows in many forms often beautiful in colour, in summer or winter, dogwoods and aspen poplars   There is no scarcity of such trees and shrubs at all , even the willows of Europe and Britain furnish a fine series of trees, and some form tall timber trees like the white willow, and low feathery willows like the rosemary-leaved one   There is also a superb group of weeping trees among these willows, some of them more precious and hardy even than the Babylonian willow   As regards reeds and herbaceous plants, our country and the northern world are very rich indeed, so that we need never use any grossly unsuitable plant for the waterside

These facts are worth bearing in mind in seeking true and artistic effects, as the side water properly or improperly planted is strangely different from an artistic point of view.   Take for example a piece of water, good in form of margin, and right in every way as to its relation to the landscape ; it is quite easy to spoil the effect of it all by the use of shrubs which have not the form or colour characteristic of the trees and shrubs of the water side.   By the right use of the trees or shrubs—true to the soil, so to say—we may, on the other hand. make the scene beautiful in delicate colour and fine form, at all seasons, right, in a word, either as a picture, as a covert, and even for timber, for some of the willows have a high value as timber.

The best materials for waterside planting are distinctly those of our own country, or of Europe and the northern world generally , but we need not despise things that are very suitable and which come to us from other countries, and among them some of the bamboos promise very well, having, to some extent, the same character of graceful, pointed leaf of the willow and the reed.

WILLOWS AND THEIR COLOUR.—Some say that to enjoy the colour of willows we should cut them down once a year and that the young shoots so grown are more showy. In that case they are thicker together and more level in colour ; but it is a very stupid practice to carry out, because some of the finest willows are trees, and by cutting them down we lose the form, which is very beautiful throughout the year. Colour also is bound up with form and light and shade, and we cannot see the most beautiful effects of colour without these ; so that it is wrong in every way to cut down our willows for the sake of enjoying their colour. A small patch may be treated in that way, especially if we follow the good old plan of using the twigs. If we cut these every year we have a useful aid in packing, tying the branches of trees, and for other purposes. Even in the wild willows of our own country we can notice the great error of this practice of cutting down—in such places, for instance, as Brandon in Norfolk, and other eastern county places, where we see the far greater beauty of the naturally grown tree, even from the point of view of colour.

Pool with Calla Lilies, Trelissick, Truro.

CHAPTER XXI.

THE BOG GARDEN.

THE bog garden is a home for the numerous children of the wild that will not thrive on our harsh, bare, and dry garden borders, but thrive cushioned on moss or in moist peat soil. Many beautiful plants, like the Wind Gentian and Creeping Harebell, grow on our own bogs and marshes, much as these are now encroached upon. But even those who know our own bogs have, as a rule, little notion of the multitude of charming plants, natives of northern and temperate countries, whose home is the open marsh or bog In our own country we have been so long encroaching upon the bogs and wastes that some of us come to regard bogs and wastes as exceptional tracts all over the world, but when we travel in new countries in northern climes we soon learn what a vast extent of the world's surface was once covered with bogs In North America, even by the margins of the railways, one sees, day after day, the vivid blooms of the Cardinal-flower springing erect from the wet peaty hollows , and far under the shady woods stretch the black bog pools, the ground between being so shaky that you move a few steps with difficulty.   And where the woody vegetation disappears the Pitcher-plant (Sarracenia), Golden Club (Orontium), Water Arum (Calla palustris), and a host of other handsome bog plants cover the ground for hundreds of acres, with perhaps an occasional slender bush of Laurel Magnolia (Magnolia glauca) among them In some parts of Canada, where the painfully long and straight roads are often made through woody swamps, and where the few scattered and poor habitations offer little to cheer the traveller, a lover of plants will find beside the road conservatories of beauty in the ditches and pools of black water fringed with a profusion of stately ferns, and bog and water bushes.

Southwards and seawards, the bog flowers, like the splendid kinds of herbaceous Hibiscus, become tropical in size and brilliancy, while far north and west and south along the mountains grows the queen of the peat bog—the beautiful and showy Mocassin-flower (Cypripedium spectabile). Then in California, all along the Sierras, a number of delicate little annual plants continue to grow in small mountain bogs long after the plains are quite parched, and annual vegetation has quite disappeared from them. But who shall record the beauty and interest of the flowers of the wide-spreading marsh-lands of this globe of ours, from those in the vast wet woods of America, dark and brown, hidden from the sunbeams, to the little bogs of the high Alps, far above the woods, where the ground often teems with Nature's most brilliant flowers? No one worthily; for many mountain-swamp regions are as yet little known to us. One thing, however, we may gather from our small experience—that many plants commonly termed "alpine," and found on high

Mocassin-flower in rocky bog.

mountains, are true bog plants. This must be clear to any one who has seen our pretty Bird's-eye Primrose in the wet mountain-side bogs of Westmoreland, or the Bavarian Gentian in the spongy soil by alpine rivulets.

In many country seats there are spots that with a little care can be made into pretty bog gardens. Where there are no natural sites a bog garden may be made by forming a basin of brickwork and Portland cement, about one foot in depth; the bottom may be either concreted or paved with tiles laid in cement, and the whole must be made water-tight; an orifice should be made in the side, at the height of 6 inches, to carry off the surplus water, and another in the bottom at the lowest point, with a cork, or, better still, with a brass plug valve to close it. Five or six inches of stones and bricks are to be first laid in, and the whole must be filled with good peat soil, the surface being raised into uneven banks and hillocks, with large pieces of sandstone imbedded in it, so as to afford drier and wetter spots. The size and form of this garden may be varied at discretion; it should be in an exposed situation; the back may be raised with a rocky bank of stones imbedded in peat, and the moisture, ascending by capillary action, will make the position a charming one for Ferns and numberless other peat-loving plants. It is in every way desirable that a small trickle of water should constantly flow through the bog, ten or twelve gallons daily will be sufficient, but if this cannot be arranged it may be kept filled by hand. Such a bog may be bordered by a very low wall of flints or stones, built with mortar, diluted with half its bulk of road-sand and leaf-mould, and having a little earth on the top, the moisture will soon cause this to be covered with moss, and Ferns and all kinds of wall-plants will thrive on it

Where space will permit, a much larger area may be converted into bog and rockwork intermingled, the surface being raised or depressed at various parts, so as to afford stations for more or less moisture-loving plants. Large stones should be freely used on the surface, so as to form mossy stepping-stones; and many plants will thrive better in the chinks between the stones than on the surface of the peat. It is not necessary to render water-tight the whole of such a large area. A channel of water about 6 inches deep, with drain-pipes and bricks at the bottom, may be led to and fro or branched over the surface, the bends or branches being about 3 feet apart The whole, when covered with peat, will form an admirable bog, the spaces between the channels forming drier portions, in which various plants will thrive vigorously.

Perhaps the best place for an artificial bog is on sloping ground. The water flows in at the top, and the surface must be rendered water-tight with Portland cement or concrete. Contour or level lines should then be traced on the whole surface at distances of about 3 feet apart, and a ridge, two bricks in height, should be cemented along each of the horizontal lines. These ridges, which must be perfectly level, serve to hold the water, and the surplus escapes over the top to the next lower level. Two-inch drain tiles, covered with coarse stones, should be laid along each ridge to keep the channel open, and a foot of peat should be thrown over the whole. Before adding the peat, ridges may be built on the surface, the stones being built together with peat in the interstices These ridges need not follow the horizontal lines. The positions thus formed are adapted both to grow and to display Ferns and alpine bog plants to advantage

Perhaps the most charming plants to commence with are our own native bog plants—Pinguicula, Drosera, Parnassia, Menyanthes, Viola palustris, Anagallis tenella, Narthecium, Osmunda, Lastrea Oreopteris, Thelypteris spinulosa, and other Ferns ; Sibthorpia europæa, Linnæa borealis, Primula farinosa, Campanula hederacea, Chrysosplenium alternifolium and oppositifolium ; Saxifraga Hirculus, aizoides, stellaris, Caltha, and Marsh Orchises.   These, and a host of plants from our marshes and the summits of our higher mountains, will flourish as freely as in their native habitats, and may all be grown in a few

| *Cypripedium.* | *Trillium.* | *Sarracenia.* | *Helonias.* | *Pinguicula.* |

A bog garden.

square feet of bog ; while Rhododendrons, Kalmias, dwarf Ferns, and Sedges will serve for the bolder features.

One of the great charms of the bog garden is that everything thrives and multiplies in it, and nothing droops or dies, but the real difficulty is to prevent the stronger plants from overgrowing, and eventually destroying, the weaker. A small pool of water filled with water plants is a charming addition to the bog garden. The only precaution needed is to destroy the weeds before they gain strength—a single plant of Sheep Rot (Hydrocotyle), for example, would smother and ruin the entire bog in a season.— LATIMER CLARK.

In the bog garden many of our most beautiful plants, which in a summer like that of 1895 have been languishing for moisture in the borders, may be grown to perfection surpassing in beauty all our former impressions of them. Of primary importance, of course, is the position, and where this is naturally of a moist, boggy or swampy character, matters will be much simplified. We will assume there is such a spot at disposal, a swampy, treacherous, and, as we are wont to regard it, useless piece of land, under water the greater part of the year Such a spot will be sure of its crop of naturally water-loving plants, such as Rushes, Sedges, or the like, and the first care must be to root them out one and all In doing so, be careful that 12 inches or so of the margin be overhauled, as in all probability there will be here roots and seeds of all these wildlings. According to the nature of the boggy piece and also the depth of the water, it may be necessary for cleansing the ground to cut a deep trench and allow the water to pass away, as, without the moisture, the whole is much more convenient for preparation, and roots are more readily eradicated The ground thoroughly cleansed at the outset, attention should next be directed to the soil This may be variable, according to the variety of plants it is intended to introduce. For instance, strong growing subjects like the Astilbes and Meadow Sweets are all at home in a fairly stiff and moist soil On the other hand, Iris Kæmpferi, Trilliums, Cypripediums, Lilium pardalinum, L superbum, and other such things have a decided preference for soil of a vegetable character, such as peat, leaves, and the like. These latter, again, have a preference for the drier parts of the bed, while such as the Calthas and Menyanthes trifoliata revel in wet mud. To meet the varied degrees of moisture which the plants prefer will be quite an easy matter in an artificially constructed bog by the adoption of an undulating surface throughout Slightly raised mounds are by far the most convenient, and certainly the most economical, way of providing for the greatest number of plants

FORMATION —The shape, of course, should be irregular, and, unless a depression of the whole exists, let this receive the next attention, and in such a way that the highest part will be 9 inches below the average surrounding soil The paths should next be dealt with, excavating these nearly a foot deep in the central parts and gradually rising at the entrances The soil taken from the paths may, if good, be used to form the raised beds for the planting of moisture-loving plants, such as are content if their roots only reach water. The sides of these beds may need rough support, such as rude sandstone blocks, to keep the soil in its place These, or similar things, may also form stepping-stones in the wetter parts, as by this means the plants may be viewed without inconvenience Beds of various sizes will be needed in proportion to the kind of plants that shall hereafter occupy them For instance, the sloping banks at the edge, which may also take the form of a slightly projecting mound, would constitute excellent positions for some of the hardy Bamboos. Similar opportunities may occur at intervals throughout the margin for planting with such things as Acanthus, Yuccas, Eulalias, Astilbe rivularis, Spiræa Aruncus, Bocconia cordata, and others of similar proportions, while the lower slopes and depressions between these would make excellent places for Osmunda regalis, Lilium giganteum, L. pardalinum, L. canadense, and L. superbum in peaty beds The latter three of these are really swamp-loving by nature, and it is scarcely possible to see them in anything approaching perfection elsewhere In the moisture so close at hand such things simply revel, and the owner of them may for years see them towering far above his head in their day of flowering—a picture of health and beauty With such things it should always be borne in mind that constant saturation is not absolutely essential, though, indeed, they receive it more or less in their native habitats

Where space for bog gardens is limited, a very charming carpet to the Lilies just named would be the Wood Lily of North America (Trillium grandiflorum)   The two things may be planted or replanted at the same season when necessity arises   The Trillium, moreover, would come in spring-time and would protect the growth of the Lilium against our late spring frosts   For the Liliums a foot deep of peat, leaf-soil, and turf, with sharp river grit, would form a good bed, and with a mulch each year of leaf-soil and a little very rotten manure would serve them for many years   It may surprise many to know that under such conditions these Trilliums would in a few years, if left alone, attain to nearly 2 feet and be lovely in the size and purity of their flowers   In another of these depressions Cypripedium spectabile could easily be established, or a bed may be devoted to the more showy hardy species, giving 6 inches of peat or more, with leaf-soil added   The species named is rather late in sending up its growth, and affords plenty of time for a carpet of Trillium to flower before much headway is made   Other beautiful carpeting plants for these would be found in the American Mayflower (Epigæa repens or Pratia angulata), and if the position be shaded, as it should be for the Cypripediums, a charming, yet delicate, fringe may be found in Adiantum pedatum   Besides C. spectabile, C. pubescens and C parviflorum are well deserving attention, together with Orchis foliosa, the beautiful " Madeira Orchis," and the Habenarias, especially H ciliaris and fimbriata , all delight in moisture and require but little root room   Then if a glow of rich colour was needed in such places it could be supplied in Spiræa venusta or S palmata, both delighting in moist soil   Another fine effect may be had by grouping Lobelia fulgens, or indeed any of the scarlet Lobelias   In wet parts may be planted Osmunda regalis, Onoclea sensibilis, Struthiopteris germanica, and Astilbe rivularis, allowing room for each   Groups of the herbaceous Phloxes in their best and most distinct shades, particularly of salmon scarlet and the purest white, would find their natural wants completely satisfied in the bog garden and give fine colour   In English gardens it is only in a moist season that we see the Phlox in even fair condition, for the reason that the original species is a native of wet meadows   This condition we can best imitate by deep digging and heavy manuring, and so much the better if the beds of these be saturated with water   Only in the constant cooling moisture of the bog can Primula japonica be seen in perfection, for here will it produce rosettes of leaves 2½ feet across, and giant whorls of its crimson flowers, attaining to nearly the same height.   Another charming Primrose is that from the swampy mountain meadows of the Himalayas, P. sikkimensis, essentially moisture-loving ; but to get the best results this must be treated as a biennial, grown on quickly, and planted in the bog as soon as large enough to handle.   Other species of Primula suited to the higher and drier parts of the bog would be found in P cashmeriana, capitata, denticulata, rosea, farinosa, involucrata, viscosa, and others, all alike beautiful in their way, and attaining greater vigour with the abundant moisture   Some of the smaller kinds of the viscosa type are better for slight shade, such as may be provided by Dielytra spectabilis (a really delightful plant in boggy ground) and various Spiræas   It should be noted that many shade-loving plants delight in full sun when given abundant moisture at the root.   Particularly noticeable is this with the Liliums   have noted previously   In the early part of the year the bog garden should be aglow with such things as Marsh Marigolds, in single and double forms.   In the wet mud in the lower parts and about the stepping stones these would appear quite natural, and in like places Ficaria grandiflora, a plant too rarely seen, with its blossoms of shining gold ; then Senecio Doronicum, with golden orange flowers, Dielytra eximia, Trollius   any of the Dentarias and Dodecatheons likewise are all well suited for the raised parts where the roots will touch the moisture. The Dodecatheons in peat, loam, and leaf soil in equal parts, particularly D. Jeffreyanum, grow to a large size : Hepaticas, too, are greatly improved in company with these last, while the charming effects that may be produced are almost without end. Corydalis nobilis in peat and loam, C. lutea, together with the Water Mimulus (M. luteus), all provide rich masses of yellow. Gentiana asclepiadea, G. Andrewsi, as well as G. verna, grow charmingly in the bog. Nor is the list of plants exhausted ; indeed, they are far too numerous to give in detail, but yet to be mentioned as among the grandest are many Irises, I. Kæmpferi in particular. Meconopsis Wallichiana (the blue Poppy of the Himalayas) produces quite a unique effect in the moister parts. Saxifraga peltata, S. Fortunei, S. Hirculus, S. granulata plena, Soldanellas, Senecio pulcher, Sisyrinchium grandiflorum, and many more are all benefited by the varying degrees of moisture to be found in the bog garden.

In gardens where no moist piece of ground exists, such as those with gravel or sandy subsoils, it will be necessary to select a low part and mark out an irregular outline. Next dig out the soil 18 inches or 2 feet in depth, so as to allow of at least 6 inches of clay being puddled in the bottom to retain the moisture. For bog plants clay is far better than concrete, because it supplies food for many moisture-loving plants. To keep the clay in position, sloping sides will be best, and for the soils named it will scarcely be necessary to have more than a small outlet for excessive moisture, and this at about 12 inches high from the deepest part. For this a narrow clinker or rough brick drain will suffice, so placed that the outlet may be blocked, if necessary, for affording greater moisture. By digging a shallow trench around the upper margin of the bog-bed, and using Bamboos, such as Metake or glaucescens, or Bocconia cordata— the last two valuable for their rapid annual growth—such things would give the needful shade in summer.

In large gardens and cool, hilly districts the bog garden should always be found. Some years ago I had charge of just such a garden : in the flower garden was a fountain basin wherein water plants were grown ; the overflow from this went tumbling in many ways over a series of rocks into the rock garden pond containing Orontium aquaticum, Nymphæas, and Sagittarias. In turn the overflow from the rock garden was conducted to the bog garden proper, where many masses of Cypripedium spectabile, with fully a score of spikes of its beautiful flowers to each tuft, grew in luxuriance in peat and leaves under a welcome shade. In the swampy watercourse, before the bog was entered, the Marsh Marigold in variety abounded, being very conspicuous. Here, too, Osmundas were rampant, together with Primula japonica and a variety of plants already mentioned, and Ourisia coccinea, tightly pressing the surface of a stone, flowered splendidly.—E. J.

CHAPTER XXII

THE HARDY FERN GARDEN

THE marriage of the fern and flower garden is worth effecting, our many hardy evergreen Ferns being so good for association with hardy flowers. There are many varieties of our native Ferns which would be excellent companions to evergreen herbaceous plants suited for sheltered, half-shady nooks, and there are hardy and vigorous exotic kinds. Graceful effects may be had in fore-grounds, in drives through glades, through the bold use of the larger hardy Ferns, whether evergreen or not The Bracken is everywhere, but there are Ferns of graceful form which delight in the partial shade of open woods and drives, and succeed even in the sun Ferns have, as a rule, been stowed away in obscure corners, and have rarely come into the garden landscape, though they may give us beautiful aspects of vegetation not only in the garden, but by grassy glades, paths, and drives. In countries where hardy Ferns abound, they are often seen near water and in hollow and wet places, and it will often be best to group them in such localities, but without any of the ugly aspects of "rockwork" too often supposed to be the right thing in a hardy fernery.

In the home counties there is probably not a better fernery than that at Danesbury It is on a sloping bank in a rather deep dell, overhung with trees and Ivy, in the shade of which the Ferns delight. As regards the planting, the various families are arranged in distinct groups, and each group has a position and a soil favourable to its requirements. The best way to grow Ferns, however, is with flowers, as in Nature, and a hardy fernery may be very beautiful. As a rule, Ferns have in their natural state both soil and locality exactly suited to their requirements, and the soil is yearly enriched by the decaying foliage of surrounding trees, which protects them in winter. In arranging a fernery, study the habits and requirements of each species, and allot to it the position most likely to give the best results. At Danesbury the most

Effect of native Ferns in foreground   From a photograph by Miss Willmott.

sheltered, moist spot is given to the evergreen Blechnums, which delight in a damp atmosphere, and to the delicate forms of Asplenium Osmunda, which thrives amazingly, is in a low swamp   The soil used for these Royal Ferns is a mixture of good loam and fibrous peat.   The better deciduous kinds of Polypodium, such as P. Phegopteris and P. Dryopteris, have sheltered positions ; and in quiet nooks may be found charming groups of the Parsley Fern, and Cystopteris fragilis, a most delicate and graceful Fern.   Lastrea Filix-mas and its varieties occupy the more exposed positions in company with fine colonies of the evergreen kinds, comprising some unique varieties of the Polystichums, Scolopendriums, Polypodiums, etc.   A plentiful supply of water is available.

The Fern-lover will remember that not only have we our own beautiful native Ferns for adorning our gardens, but also the hardy Ferns of America, Asia, and the continent of Europe   As to the hardiness of exotic Ferns, Mr. Milne-Redhead writes from Clitheroe :—

Is it not strange that we so seldom see, even in good gardens, any well-grown plants of exotic Osmundas, Struthiopteris, &c ? Here, after a long spell of hot, dry weather, we had on May 20, 1896, a sharp snap of frost which completely cut off the more than usually beautiful flowers of Azalea mollis, and seriously injured the young growths of some Japanese Pines, such as Abies firma, A. sachalinensis, and others. This frost turned the young fronds of our English Filix-mas and Filix-fœmina quite black   Close by these plants, and under similar conditions of soil and exposure, the American Adiantum pedatum, 1 foot high, and the tender-looking Onoclea sensibilis were quite unhurt, and Osmunda interrupta and O cinnamomea entirely escaped and are now very fine. Our English O regalis was slightly touched, but the Brazilian O. spectabilis brought by myself from dry banks in the Organ Mountains was not even browned in its early and delicate fronds. All the Ferns I have named are great ornaments to any moist and rather shady place in the shrubbery. In a sheltered nook in the rock garden I find, to my surprise, that Gymnogramma triangularis has survived the perils not only of a frosty spring, but the still greater ones of a wet autumn and winter, and is now throwing up healthily its pretty triangular fronds, whose under surface is quite white with the powder peculiar to the genus—in fact a hardy silver Fern

A visit to Mr Sclater's Fern garden at Newick shows us the good effects that may be had by using the nobler hardy Ferns—both native and foreign—in a bolder way, and often in the open sun.   The idea that a fernery is best in a dark corner has had unfortunate results in keeping the grace of such plants out of the garden picture.   Hardy Ferns are being used in bold and simple ways at Kew, where at one time they were in an obscure fernery, and even if some Ferns require shade, many do not in our cool climate   Shade is, moreover, an elastic term , the bold hardy Ferns one sees in the American wood-

T

lands would not have too much sun in the open in Britain, provided they were in the right soil.

Many hardy Ferns are excellent for association with hardy flowers, and many may be grouped with evergreen rock and hill plants in

Native Ferns massed by shady walk (Devon). From a photograph by S. W. Fitzherbert.

forming borders and groups of evergreen plants. Though we have enough native Ferns in these islands to give us very fine effects, as we see at Penrhyn, or wherever Ferns are boldly grouped, some of the finest Ferns we see at Newick, and also at Rhianva and other gardens, are natives of North America. Foremost among the strong-growing hardy exotic kinds, there are the handsome North American Osmunda cinnamomea, and O. Claytoniana, O. gracilis, a very pretty species of particularly slender habit, the Sensitive Fern (Onoclea), Dicksonia punctiloba, the beautiful Canadian Maiden-hair, the American Ostrich Feather Fern, Lastrea Goldiana, Woodwardia virginica, all of North American origin and attaining between 2 feet and 3 feet in height Among the smaller ferns are Aspidium nevadense, novaboracense and thelypteroides, Asplenium angustifolium, Athyrium Michauxi and Woodwardia angustifolia, all of which grow from 18 inches to 24 inches. Allosorus acrostichoides, the handsome Polypodium hexagonopterum, Woodsia obtusa, oregana and scopulina, and also two pretty Selaginellas, viz, oregana and Douglasi. All these are of small dimensions, varying as they do from 6 in. to 12 in in height The pretty Hypolepis anthriscifolia of South Africa; the robust Lastrea atrata, from India, the Japanese Lastrea decurrens, the massive Struthiopteris orientalis, also a native of Japan, and the pretty Davallia Mariesi are all equal in hardiness to any of our British deciduous Ferns.

EVERGREEN HARDY FERNS —Some of the evergreen Ferns, whether British or exotic, which stand the severity of our climate, are as hardy as those which lose their leaves in winter, and no Fern could be hardier than the various small-growing Aspleniums, which grow in old walls exposed to severe frosts, such as the black-stemmed Spleenwort (several), and its pretty crested and notched forms, the little Wall Rue or Rue Fern, the forked and other native Spleenworts. All these are small, seldom exceeding 8 in in height, while the black Maiden-hair Spleenwort Blechnum and its several beautiful forms usually average from 9 in. to 12 in. in height. Polypodium also contains some handsome evergreen plants; even the common Polypody is a fine plant in its way, and is seen at its best when growing on a wall, on the branches of a tree, or on the roof of a low house. But by far the handsomest of its numerous forms are the Welsh Polypody, the Irish and the Cornish, and its handsome, finely-cut varieties in which the fronds are of a light and feathery nature Then there are the more or less heavily crested forms, all of larger dimensions than the species from which they are issue The common Hart's-tongue, also perfectly hardy, supplies us with many forms giving fine effect and free growth

As regards strong-growing evergreen hardy Ferns, however, none can compare with the Prickly Shield Fern and the soft Prickly Shield Fern and its beautiful varieties which produce massive fronds 18 ins. to 24 ins. long Then there is an extensive section of varieties in which the fronds in many instances are as finely cut as those of the Lace Fern, and infinitely finer in effect.   The soft Prickly Shield Fern has also produced some remarkably crested forms, all of which are equal in vigour and in dimensions to the typical species.   The Holly Fern is also perfectly hardy, and is one of those plants which are usually killed with kindness, through being grown in a temperature higher than is required.   As regards

EXOTIC EVERGREEN KINDS, North America supplies the greatest part of those hardy in England   The larger-growing kinds from that country are Aspidium cristatum Clintonianum, A floridanum, Asplenium angustifolium, Lastrea marginalis, Polystichum munitum and P. acrostichoides, all of which sorts attain from 18 ins to 24 ins. in height.

Not less effective and quite as interesting as the above, though of smaller dimensions, are the North American Asplenium ebenum, Phegopteris alpestris, Pellæa atropurpurea, Woodsia alpina and W. glabella varying in height from 6 ins to 12 ins.   There are also some remarkably handsome strong-growing sorts, native of Japan, the most decorative as also the most distinct among these being Lastrea Standishi, with fronds 24 ins. to 30 ins. long, and of a lovely and cheerful green colour ; Lastrea erythrosora, with fronds 18 ins to 24 ins long, of a beautiful bronzy red colour when young, and of a deep dark green hue when mature.   Lastrea opaca is another handsome Japanese form, broad and massive, of a fine metallic colour when young, and of a deep velvety green when mature.   In Lastrea Sieboldi we have a totally distinct plant, having the general aspect of a somewhat dwarf Polypodium aureum and of the same bluish colour. This and Dictyogramma japonica, which have somewhat bold and broad fronds, are also quite hardy, and so are the Japanese Lastrea prolifica, a species with finely-cut fronds, bearing numerous small plants ; the handsome Polystichum setosum, with beautiful dark green, shining foliage ; Polystichum Tsus-simense, Lastrea corusca and L aristata   Lomaria chilensis is a large-growing Fern with fronds 24 ins to 30 ins long and of a particularly deep green colour.   Niphobolus lingua is a very distinct Fern with entire fronds of a very leathery nature, dark green above and silvery beneath, having somewhat the general appearance of our common Hart's-tongue, but in this case the fronds, instead of starting from a single crown, are produced along a slender rhizome of a wiry nature.   Perhaps one of the prettiest of the hardy evergreen Ferns is the violet-scented Lastrea fragrans   This charming little plant, seldom more than 4 ins in height, succeeds well when planted outside, as it is on the outside rockery in

Ferns and flower border.

Kew Gardens, where its crown is simply protected by a handful of dry leaves during the winter.

ROCK AND SUN-LOVING FERNS —It is a mistake to consider all Ferns as plants requiring shade and moisture. There are, on the contrary, ferns which like full sunshine and bright light. Without counting Cystopteris alpina and fragilis, which grow in our walls as well in sun as in shade, there is one class of Ferns which actually requires sunshine. Cheilanthes from the Old World, as well as those from the New, only do well in a sunny aspect. I could not succeed at Geneva in cultivating Cheilanthes odora, lanuginosa and vestita. In spite of every care given to them, they suffered from general weakness, ending in decay. At last I one day saw Woodsia hyperborea, that delicate and fragile plant, in full sun along an alpine road in Italy, and on returning I planted all my Cheilanthes in sunshine on a south wall. The result was good, and I recommend the plan to Fern growers. But it was necessary also to change the soil in which these plants were cultivated, and I set them in soft porous mould composed of Sphagnum Moss, peat and sand ; good drainage and frequent watering ensured an immediate and excellent result. That which proved satisfactory for Cheilanthes I then tried for Woodsia hyperborea and ilvensis (the treatment did not do for W. obtusa) ; then for Scolopendrium Hemionitis, that pretty and curious Fern from the south so rarely met with in gardens, where it is considered difficult to grow. Then I gave the same treatment to Nothochlena Marantæ ; and this lovely Fern, which formerly did not do with me, turned out marvellously well. It is, then, certain that many species of Ferns require sun and plenty of air —H. CORREVON, in *Gardeners' Chronicle*.

The following exotic Ferns may be grown in the open air if the more tender ones are protected in winter by a covering of old fronds or soft hay pegged down over the crowns. These would be better in sheltered nooks in the rock garden in good peaty earth. Those kinds marked with an asterisk should receive protection in this form. Unless otherwise mentioned, the Ferns are natives of North America, and this list is contributed by Mr. Birkenhead, Sale, an experienced cultivator of these plants.

Exotic hardy Ferns.

Adiantum peadtum
Allosorous acrosti-
  choides
Aspidium cristatum
  Clintonianum
  fragrans
  nevadense
  novaboracense
  rigidum argutum
  spinulosum
  thelypteroides
Asplenium angustifo-
  lium
  ebenum
  *fontanum (Europe)
  thelypteroides
Athyrium Filix-
  foemina ameri-
  canum
  Michauxi

Botrychium virgini-
  cum
*Cyrtomium caryoti-
  deum (E. Indies)
  *falcatum (Japan)
  *Fortunei (Japan)
Cystopteris bulbifera
  fragilis (American
  var).
Dennstædtia puncti-
  lobula
Hypolepis mille-
  folium (N. Zea-
  land)
  anthriscifolia (S.
  Africa)
Lastrea (Nephro-
  dium)
  *atrata India)
  *decurrens (Japan)
  fragrans

Lastrea (Nephro-
  dium)—continued.
  Goldiana
  intermedia
  marginalis
  *opaca (China)
  prolifica (Jamaica)
  Sieboldi (Japan)
  *varia (China)
Lomaria alpina (New
  Zealand)
  chilensis (Chili)
  crenulata (Chili)
Onoclea sensibilis
Osmunda cinna-
  momea
Osmunda Claytoni-
  ana
  gracilis
  japonica

*Pellæa atro-
  purpurea
  *gracilis
Phegopteris alpestris
  Dryopteris
  hexagonoptera
  polypodioides
Polystichum acros-
  tichoides
  a. grandiceps
  a. incisum
  Brauni
  concavum (Japan)
  munitum (Califor-
  nia)
  m. imbricans
  polyblepharum (Ja-
  pan)
  *proliferum (Austra-
  lia)
  *setosum (Japan)

Selaginella Douglasi-
  denticulata (hel.
  vetica)
Struthiopteris ger-
  manica (Europe)
  *orientalis (Japan)
  pennsylvanica
  p. recurva
Woodsia
  glabella
  obtusa
  oregana
  scopulina
Woodwardia angusti-
  folia
  *japonica (Japan)
  orientalis (Japan)
  radicans S.
  Europe)
  r. americana
  virginica

A hardy fernery at Broomfield, Caterham.

CHAPTER XXIII

COLOUR IN THE FLOWER GARDEN

ONE of the first things which all who care for gardens should learn, is the difference between true and delicate and ugly colour— between the showy dyes and much glaring colour seen in gardens and the beauties and harmonies of natural colour There are, apart from beautiful flowers, many lessons and no fees ·—Oak woods in winter, even the roads and paths and rocks and hedgerows ; leaves in many hues of life and death, the stems of trees · many birds are lovely studies in harmony and delicate gradation of colour , the clouds (eternal mine of divinest colour) in many aspects of light, and the varied and infinite beauty of colour of the air itself as it comes between us and the distant view.

Nature is a good colourist, and if we trust to her guidance we never find wrong colour in wood, meadow, or on mountain. "Laws" have been laid down by chemists and decorators about colours which artists laugh at, and to consider them is a waste of time. If we have to make coloured cottons, or to "garden" in coloured gravels, then it is well to think what ugly things will shock us least , but dealing with living plants in their infinitely varied hues, and with their beautiful flowers, is a different thing ! If we grow well plants of good colour, all will be right in the end, but often raisers of flowers work against us by the raising of flowers of bad colour. The complicated pattern beds so often seen in flower gardens should be given up in favour of simpler beds, of the shapes best suiting the ground, and among various reasons for this is to get true colour. When we have little pincushion-beds where the whole "pattern" is seen at once through the use of dwarf plants, the desire comes to bring in colour in patterns and in ugly ways For this purpose the wretched Alternanthera and other pinched plant rubbish are grown—plants not worth growing at all

When dwarf flowers are associated with bushes like Roses, and with plants like Carnations and tall Irises, having pointed and graceful foliage, the colours are relieved against the delicate foliage of the plants and by having the beds large enough we relieve the dwarfer flowers with taller plants behind.   In a shrubbery, too, groups of flowers are nearly always right, and we can follow our desire in flowers without much thought of arranging for colour.   But as the roots of the shrubs rob the flowers ; the best way is to put near and around shrubberies free-running plants that do not want much cultivation, like Solomon's Seal and Woodruff, and other plants that grow naturally in woods and copses, while with flowers like Pansies, Carnations, Roses, that depend for their beauty on good soil, the best way is to keep them in the open garden, away from hungry tree-roots.

By having large simple beds we relieve the flowers, and enjoy their beauty of colour and the forms of the plants without " pattern " of any kind.   Instead of " dotting " the plants, it is better to group them naturally, letting the groups run into each other, and varying them here and there with taller plants.   A flower garden of any size could be planted in this way, without the geometry of the ordinary flower garden, and the poor effect of the " botanical " " dotty " mixed border   As, however, all may not be ready to follow this plan, the following notes on colour, by a flower gardener who has given much thought to the subject, will be useful —

" One of the most important points in the arrangement of a garden is the placing of the flowers with regard to their colour-effect. Too often a garden is an assemblage of plants placed together hap-hazard, or if any intention be perceptible as is commonly the case in the bedding system, it is to obtain as great a number as possible of the most violent contrasts ; and the result is a hard, garish vulgarity. Then, in mixed borders, one usually sees lines or evenly distributed spots of colour, wearying and annoying to the eye, and proving how poor an effect can be got by the misuse of the best materials   Should it not be remembered that in setting a garden we are painting a picture,—a picture of hundreds of feet or yards instead of so many inches, painted with living flowers and seen by open daylight—so that to paint it rightly is a debt we owe to the beauty of the flowers and to the light of the sun ; that the colours should be placed with careful forethought and deliberation, as a painter employs them on his picture, and not dropped down in lifeless dabs

" HARMONY RATHER THAN CONTRAST —Splendid harmonies of rich and brilliant colour, and proper sequences of such har-monies, should be the rule , there should be large effects, each well studied and well placed, varying in different portions of the garden scheme   One very common fault is a want of simplicity of in-tention , another, an absence of any definite plan of colouring.   Many people have not given any attention to colour-harmony, or have not by nature the gift of perceiving it Let them learn it by observing some natural examples of happily related colouring, taking separate families of plants whose members are variously coloured. Some of the best to study would be American Azaleas, Wallflowers, German and Spanish Iris, Alpine Auriculas, Polyanthus, and Alstrœmerias.

"BREADTH OF MASS AND INTERGROUPING.—It is important to notice that the mass of each colour should be large enough to have a certain dignity, but never so large as to be wearisome , a certain breadth in the masses is also wanted to counteract the effect of fore-shortening when the border is seen from end to end. When a definite plan of colouring is decided on, it will save trouble if the plants whose flowers are approximately the same in colour are grouped together to follow each other in season of blooming. Thus, in a part of the border assigned to red, Oriental Poppies might be planted among or next to Tritomas, with scarlet Gladioli between both, so that there should be a succession of scarlet flowers, the places occupied by the Gladioli being filled previously with red Wallflowers.

"WARM COLOURS are not difficult to place . scarlet, crimson, pink, orange, yellow, and warm white are easily arranged so as to pass agreeably from one to the other.

"PURPLE and LILAC group well together, but are best kept well away from red and pink ; they do well with the colder whites, and are seen at their best when surrounded and carpeted with gray-white foliage, like that of Cerastium tomentosum or Cineraria maritima ; but if it be desired to pass from a group of warm colour to purple and lilac, a good breadth of pale yellow or warm white may be interposed

"WHITE FLOWERS.—Care must be taken in placing very cold white flowers such as Iberis correæfolia, which are best used as quite a high light, led up to by whites of a softer character. Frequent repetitions of white patches catch the eye unpleasantly , it will generally be found that one mass or group of white will be enough in any piece of border or garden arrangement that can be seen from any one point of view.

"BLUE requires rather special treatment, and is best approached by delicate contrasts of warm whites and pale yellows, such as the colours of double Meadow Sweet, and Œnothera Lamarckiana, but rather avoiding the direct opposition of strong blue and full yellow. Blue flowers are also very beautiful when completely isolated and seen alone among rich dark foliage

"A PROGRESSION OF COLOUR in a mixed border might begin with strong blues, light and dark, grouped with white and pale yellow, passing on to pink , then to rose colour, crimson, and the strongest scarlet, leading to orange and bright yellow. A paler yellow followed by white would distantly connect the warm colours with the lilacs and purples, and a colder white would combine them pleasantly with low-growing plants with cool-coloured leaves.

"SILVERY-LEAVED PLANTS are valuable as edgings and carpets to purple flowers, and bear the same kind of relation to them as the warm-coloured foliage of some plants does to their strong red flowers, as in the case of the Cardinal Flower and double crimson Sweet William. The bright clear blue of Forget-me-not goes best with fresh pale green, and pink flowers are beautiful with pale foliage striped with creamy white, such as the variegated forms of Jacob's-ladder or Iris pseudacorus. A useful carpeting plant, Acæna pulchella, assumes in spring a rich bronze between brown and green which is valuable with Wallflowers of the brown and orange colours These few examples, out of many that will come under the notice of any careful observer, are enough to indicate what should be looked for in the way of accompanying foliage—such foliage, if well chosen and well placed, may have the same value to the flowering plant that a worthy and appropriate setting has to a jewel

"IN SUNNY PLACES warm colours should preponderate ; the yellow colour of sunlight brings them together and adds to their glowing effect

"A SHADY BORDER, on the other hand, seems best suited for the cooler and more delicate colours. A beautiful scheme of cool colouring might be arranged for a retired spot, out of sight of other brightly coloured flowers, such as a border near the shady side of any shrubbery or wood that would afford a good background of dark foliage Here would be the best opportunity for using blue, cool white, palest yellow, and fresh green. A few typical plants are the great Larkspurs, Monkshoods, and Columbines, Anemones (such as japonica, sylvestris, apennina, Hepatica, and the single and double forms of nemorosa), white Lilies, Trilliums, Pyrolas, Habenarias, Primroses, white and yellow, double and single, Daffodils, white Cyclamen, Ferns and mossy Saxifrages, Lily-of-the-Valley, and Woodruff The most appropriate background to such flowers would be shrubs and trees, giving an effect of rich sombre masses of dusky shadow rather than a positive green colour, such as Bay Phillyrea, Box, Yew, and Evergreen Oak. Such a harmony of cool colouring, in a quiet shady place, would present a delightful piece of gardening

"BEDDED-OUT PLANTS, in such parts of a garden as may require them, may be arranged on the same general principle of related, rather than of violently opposed, masses of colour. As an example, a fine effect was obtained with half-hardy annuals, mostly kinds of Marigold Chrysanthemum, and Nasturtium, of all shades of yellow, orange, and brown This was in a finely designed formal garden before the principal front of one of the stateliest of the great houses of England. It was a fine lesson in temperance, this employment of a simple scheme

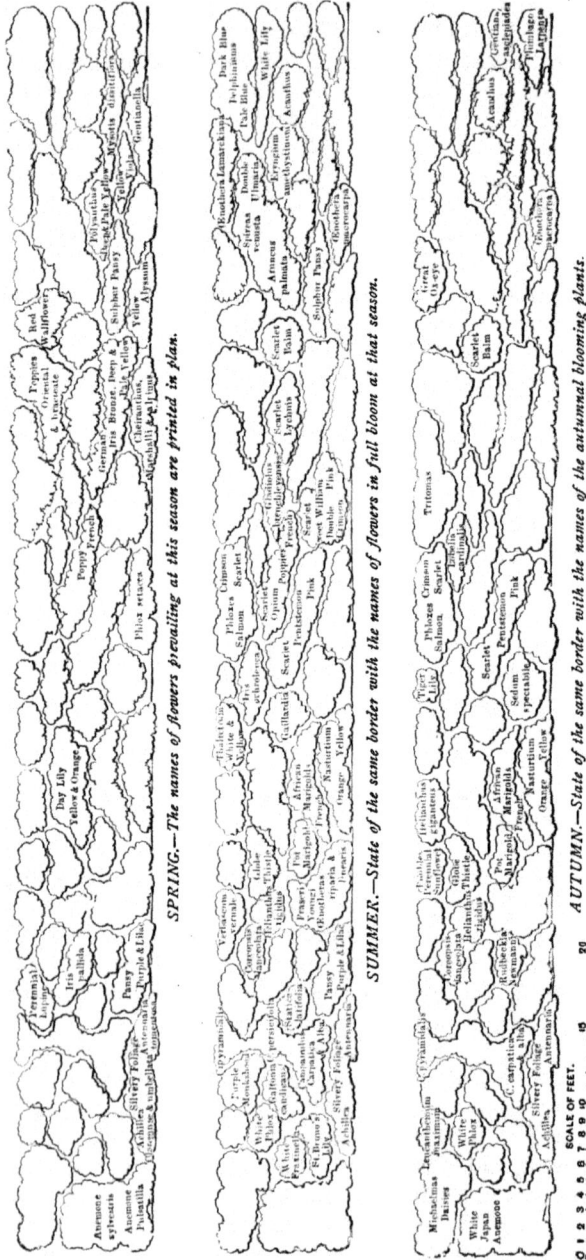

SPRING.—The names of flowers prevailing at this season are printed in plan.

SUMMER.—State of the same border with the names of flowers in full bloom at that season.

AUTUMN.—State of the same border with the names of the autumnal blooming plants.

SCALE OF FEET.

0 1 2 3 4 5 6 7 8 9 10　　　15　　　20

Plan showing the principal groups in a border of hardy flowers; the plants placed to form masses of harmonious colouring, and their progression simply, but carefully, arranged to produce a fine colour-effect. Many groups of small plants and bulbs, that could not be shown on the plan, are planted between and among the larger masses, their colour always agreeing with that of the surrounding flowers.

of restricted colouring, yet it left nothing to be desired in the way of richness and brilliancy, and well served its purpose as a dignified ornament, and worthy accompaniment to the fine old house

"CONTRASTS—HOW TO BE USED.—The greater effects being secured, some carefully arranged contrasts may be used to strike the eye when passing ; for opposite colours in close companionship are not telling at a distance, and are still less so if interspersed, their tendency then being to neutralize each other. Here and there a charming effect may be produced by a bold contrast, such as a mass of orange Lilies against Delphiniums or Gentians against alpine Wallflowers, but these violent contrasts should be used sparingly and as brilliant accessories rather than trustworthy principals.

"CLIMBERS ON WALLS—There is often a question about the suitability of variously coloured creepers on house or garden walls. The same principle of harmonious colouring is the best guide   A warm-coloured wall, one of Bath stone or buff bricks, for instance, is easily dealt with. On this all the red-flowered, leaved, or berried plants look well—Japan Quince, red and pink Roses, Virginian Creeper, Cratægus Pyracantha, and the more delicate harmonies of Honeysuckle, Banksian Roses, and Clematis montana, and Flammula, while C. Jackmanni and other purple and lilac kinds are suitable as occasional contrasts   The large purple and white Clematises harmonise perfectly with the cool gray of Portland stone, and so do dark-leaved climbers, such as White Jasmine, Passion Flower, and green Ivy. Red brickwork, especially when new, is not a happy ground colour, perhaps it is best treated with large-leaved climbers—Magnolias, Vines, Aristolochia—to counteract the fidgety look of the bricks and white joints   When brickwork is old and overgrown with gray Lichens, there can be no more beautiful ground for all colours of flowers from the brightest to the tenderest—none seems to come amiss.

"COLOUR IN BEDDING-OUT—We must here put out of mind nearly all the higher sense of the enjoyment of flowers ; the delight in their beauty individually or in natural masses, the pleasure derived from a personal knowledge of their varied characters, appearances, and ways, which gives them so much of human interest and lovableness ; and must regard them merely as so much colouring matter, to fill such and such spaces for a few months   We are restricted to a kind of gardening not far removed from that in which the spaces of the design are filled in with pounded brick, slate, or shells   The best rule in the arrangement of a bedded garden is to keep the scheme of colouring as simple as possible. The truth of this is easily perceived by an ordinary observer when shown a good example, and is obvious without any showing to one who has studied colour effects ; and yet the very opposite intention is most commonly seen, to wit, a garish display of the greatest number of crudely contrasting colours. How often do we see combinations of scarlet Geranium, Calceolaria, and blue Lobelia— three subjects that have excellent qualities as bedding plants if used in separate colour schemes, but which in combination can hardly fail to look bad? In this kind of gardening, as in any other, let us by all means have our colours in a brilliant blaze, but never in a discordant glare One or two colours, used temperately and with careful judgment, will produce nobler and richer results than many colours purposely contrasted, or wantonly jumbled. The formal garden that is an architectural adjunct to an imposing building demands a dignified unity of colouring instead of the petty and frivolous effects so commonly obtained by the misuse of many colours. As practical examples of simple harmonies, let us take a scheme of red for summer bedding. It may range from palest pink to nearly black, the flowers being Pelargoniums in many shades of pink, rose, salmon, and scarlet ; Verbenas, red and pink ; and judicious mixtures of Iresine, Alternanthera, Amaranthus, the dark Ajuga, and red-foliaged Oxalis Still finer is a colour scheme of yellow and orange, worked out with some eight varieties of Marigold, Zinnias, Calceolarias, and Nasturtiums—a long range of bright rich colour, from the palest buff and primrose to the deepest mahogany Such examples of strong warm colouring are admirably suited for large spaces of bedded garden. Where a small space has to be dealt with it is better to have arrangements of blue, with white and the palest yellow, or of purple and lilac, with gray foliage. A satisfactory example of the latter could be worked out with beds of purple and lilac Clematis, trained over a carpet of Cineraria maritima, or one of the white-foliaged Centaureas, and Heliotropes and purple Verbenas, with silvery foliage of Cerastium, Antennaria, or Stachys lanata These are some simple examples easily carried out The principle once seen and understood (and the operator having a perception of colour), modifications will suggest themselves, and a correct working with two or more colours will be practicable , but the simpler ways are the best, and will always give the noblest results. There is a peculiar form of harmony to be got even in varied colours by putting together those of nearly the same strength or depth. As an example in spring bedding, Myosotis dissitiflora, Silene pendula (not the deepest shade), and double yellow Primrose or yellow Polyanthus, though distinctly red, blue, and yellow, yet are of such tender and equal depth of colouring, that they work together charmingly, especially if they are further connected with the gray-white foliage of Cerastium —G J "

The Poet's Laurel.

CHAPTER XXIV.

FRAGRANCE.

A MAN who makes a garden should have a heart for plants that have the gift of sweetness as well as beauty of form or colour. And what a mystery as well as charm—wild Roses sweet as the breath of heaven, and wild Roses of repulsive odour all born of the earth-mother, and it may be springing from the same spot. Flowers sweet at night and scentless in the day; flowers of evil odour at one hour and fragrant at another; plants sweet in breath of blossom, but deadly in leaf and sap; Lilies sweet as they are fair, and Lilies that must not be let into the house; with bushes in which all that is delightful in odour permeates to every March-daring bud. The Grant Allens of the day, who tell us how the Dandelion sprang from the Primrose some millions of years ago, would no doubt explain all these things to us, or put long names to them—what Sir Richard Owen used to call "conjectural biology,"—but we need not care where they leave the question, for to us is given this precious fragrance, happily almost without effort, and as free as the clouds from man's power to spoil.

Every fertile country has its fragrant flowers and trees; alpine meadows with Orchids and mountain Violets; the Primrose-scented woods, Honeysuckle-wreathed and May-frosted hedgerows of Britain; the Cedars of India and of the mountains of Asia Minor, with Lebanon; trees of the same stately order, perhaps still more fragrant in the warmer Pacific breezes of the Rocky Mountains and Oregon, where the many great Pines often spring from a carpet of fragrant Evergreens, and a thousand flowers which fade away after their early bloom, and stand withered in the heat, while the tall Pines overhead distil for ever their grateful odour in the sunny air. Myrtle, Rosemary, and Lavender, and all the aromatic bushes and herbs clothing the little capes that jut into the great sea which washes the shores of Greece,

Italy, Sicily, and Corsica; garden islands scattered through vast Pacific seas, as stars are scattered in the heavens; enormous tropical forests, little entered by man, but from which he gathers on the out-skirts treasures for stove and greenhouse; great island gardens like Java and Ceylon and Borneo, rich in spices and lovely plant life; Australian bush, with plants strange as if from another world, but often most delicate in odour even in the distorted fragments of them we see in our gardens.

It is not only from the fragile flower-vases these sweet odours flow; they breathe through leaf and stem, and the whole being of many trees and bushes, from the stately Gum trees of Australia to the sweet Verbena of Chili. Many must have felt the charm of the strange scent of the Box bush before Oliver Wendell Holmes told us of its "breathing the fragrance of eternity." The scent of flowers is often cloying, as of the Tuberose, while that of leaves is often delicate and refreshing, as in the budding Larch, and in the leaves of Balm and Rosemary, while fragrance is often stored in the wood, as in the Cedar of Lebanon and many other trees, and even down through the roots.

It is given to few to see many of these sweet plants in their native lands, but we who love our gardens may enjoy many of them about us, not merely in drawings or descriptions, but the living, breathing things themselves. The Geraniums in the cottage window bring us the spicy fragrance of the South African hills; the Lavender bush of the sunny hills of Provence, where it is at home; the Roses in the garden bring near us the breath of the wild Roses on a thousand hills; the sweet or pot herbs of our gardens are a gift of the shore-lands of France and Italy and Greece. The Sweet Bay bush in the farmer's or cottage garden comes with its story from the streams of Greece, where it seeks moisture in a thirsty land along with the wild Olive and the Arbutus. And this Sweet Bay is the Laurel of the poets, of the first and greatest of all poet and artist nations of the earth—the Laurel sacred to Apollo, and used in many ways in his worship, as we may see on coins, and in many other things that remain to us of the great peoples of the past. The Myrtle, of less fame, but also a sacred plant beloved for its leaves and blossoms, was, like the Laurel, seen near the temples of the race who built their temples as the Lily is built, whose song is deathless, and the fragments of whose art is Despair to the artist of our time. And thus the fragrant bushes of our gardens may entwine for us, apart from their gift of beauty, living associations and beautiful thoughts for ever famous in human story.

It is not only odours of trees and flowers known to all we have to think of, but also many delicate ones, less known, perhaps, by reason of the blossoms that give them being without showy colour, as the wild Vine, the Sweet Vernal, Lemon, and other Grasses. And among these modest flowers there are none more delicate in odour than the blossoms of the common white Willow, the yellow-twigged and the other Willows of Britain and Northern Europe, which are all the more grateful in air coming to us

O'er the northern moorland, o'er the northern oam.

What is the lesson these sweet flowers have for us? They tell us —if there were no other flowers to tell us—that a garden should be a living thing, its life not only fair in form and lovely in colour, but in its breath and essence coming from the Divine. They tell us that the very common attempt to conform their fair lives into tile or other patterns, to clip or set them out as so much mere colour of the paper-stainer or carpet-maker, is to degrade them and make our gardens ugly and ridiculous, from the point of view of Nature and of true art Yet many of these treasures for the open garden have been shut out of our thoughts owing to the exclusion of almost everything that did not make showy colour and lend itself to crude ways of setting out flowers

Of the many things that should be thought of in the making of a garden to live in, this of fragrance is one of the first. And, happily, among every class of flowers which may adorn our open-air gardens there are fragrant things to be found. Apart from the groups of plants in which all, or nearly all, are fragrant, as in Roses, the annual and biennial flowers of our gardens are rich in fragrance—Stocks, Mignon-ette, Sweet Peas,. Sweet Sultan, Wallflowers, double Rockets, Sweet Scabious, and many others These, among the most easily raised of plants, may be enjoyed by the poorest cottage gardeners The garden borders of hardy flowers bear for us odours as precious as any breath of tropical Orchid, from the Lily-of-the-Valley to the Carnation, this last yielding, perhaps, the most grateful fragrance of all the flowering host in our garden land. In these borders are things sweeter than words may tell of—Woodruff, Balm, Pinks, Violets, garden Primroses, Poly-anthuses, Day and other Lilies, early Iris, Narcissus, Evening Prim-roses, Mezereon, and Pansies delicate in their sweetness.

No one may be richer in fragrance than the wise man who plants hardy shrubs and flowering trees—Magnolia, May, Daphne, Lilac, Wild Rose, Azalea, Honeysuckle—names each telling of whole families of fragrant things From the same regions whence come the Laurel and the Myrtle we have the Laurustinus, beautiful in our sea-coast and warmer districts, and many other lovely bushes happy in our climate; one, the Wintersweet, pouring out delicious frag-rance in mid-winter; Sweet Gale, Allspice, and the delightful little Mayflower that creeps about in the woodland shade in North America So, though we cannot boast of Lemon or Orange groves, our climate is kind to many lovely and fragrant shrubs.

Even our ugly walls may be sweet gardens with Magnolia, Honey-suckle Clematis, Sweet Verbena, and the delightful old Jasmine, still

U

clothing many a house in London. Most precious of all, however,
are the noble climbing Tea Roses raised in our own time. Among
the abortions of this century these are a real gain—the loveliest flowers
ever raised by man. Noble in form and colour, and scented as
delicately as a June morn in alpine pastures, with these most precious
of garden Roses we could cover all the ugly walls in England and
Ireland, and Heaven knows many of them are in want of a veil.

Some Fragrant Plants for British Gardens.

Abelia	Crinum	Lupins	Pondflower	Sweet Scabious
Abronia	Cyclamen	Magnolias	Plantain Lily	Sweet Sultan
Allspice	Datura	Marvel of Peru	Primroses	Sweet Verbena
Almond	Day Lily	May-flower	Rhododendrons	Sweet William
Alyssum	Deutzia	Meadow Sweet	Rock Rose	Thyme
Apples	Evening Primrose	Mexican Orange	Rockets	Tuberose
Auricula	Forsythia	Flower	Rose	Tulip Tree
Azalea	Grape Hyacinth	Mezereon	Rosemary	Tulips
Balm	Hawthorns	Mignonette	Scilla	Twinflower
Balm of Gilead	Heartsease	Mock Orange	Stocks	Vine
Bee Balm	Heliotrope	Musk	St. Bruno's Lily	Violets
Belladonna Lily	Honeysuckles	Myrtle	Snowflake	Wallflower
Blue Bells	Horse Chestnut	Narcissus	Southernwood	Water Lilies
Brugmansia	Hyacinths	Night-scented Stock	Styrax	Willows
Burning Bush	Iris	Pæony (some)	Sweet Bay	Winter Green
Carnation	Jasmine	Pancratium	Sweet Cicely	Winter Heliotrope
Clematis	Lavender	Pansy	Sweet Fern Bush	Winter Sweet
Clethra	Lilac	Pelargonium	Sweet Flag	Wistaria
Columbine	Lily	Phlox	Sweet Gale	Woodruff
Cowslips	Lily-of-the-Valley	Polyanthus	Sweet Pea	Yarrow

Honeysuckle (Baeres, Henley-on-Thames). From a photograph
by Miss Maud Grenfell.

CHAPTER XXV.

SIMPLER FLOWER GARDEN
PLANS AND THE RELA-
TION OF THE FLOWER
GARDEN TO THE HOUSE.

A GREAT waste is owing to
frivolous and thoughtless "design" as to plan and shapes of
the beds in the flower-garden.
What a vision opens out to any
one who considers the design of
the flower garden when he
thinks of the curiosities and
vexations in the forms of beds
in almost every land where a
flower garden exists! The
gardener is the heir—to his
great misfortune—of much useless complexity and frivolous
design, born of applying conventional designs to the ground.
These designs come to us from
a remote epoch, and the designing of gardens being from very
early times in the hands of the
decorative "artist," the garden
was subjected to their will,
and in our own days we even
see gardens laid without the
slightest relation to garden use,
difficult to plant, and costly to
form and to keep in order. At South Kensington the elaborate
tracery of sand and gravel was attractive to some when first set out,

Type of complex parterre, copied out of books for all
sorts of situations.

but it soon turned to dust and ashes. It was, indeed, to a great
extent formed of broken brickdust, in a vain attempt to get rid of
the gardener and his flowers   The colours were supplied from the
building sheds, where boys were seen pounding up bricks and slates,
and beds were made of silver sand, so that no gardener could disfigure them.   The Box edgings of beds a foot wide or smaller soon
got out of order, and after a few years the whole thing was painful to
see, while good gardeners were wasting precious time trying to plant
paltry beds in almost every frivolous device known to the art of conventional design.

Even where such extravagances were never attempted we see the
evil of the same order of ideas, and in many gardens the idea of
adapting the beds to the ground never occurs to the designer, but a
design has been taken out of some old book.   If the ground does not
suit the plan, so much the worse for the ground and all who have to
work on it.   The results of this style of forming beds the cottage
gardens escaped from, the space being small and the cottage gardener
content with the paths about his door.   To some people this objection
on my part to intricate design is mistaken for an objection to formality
altogether.   Now there are bold spirits who do not mind setting
their houses among rocks and heather, but we must cultivate a flower
garden, and simplicity as to form of the beds should be the rule in it.
There are many ways of growing flowers and all sorts of situations fit
for them, but the flower garden itself near the house must be laid
out with formal beds, or else we cannot cultivate the flowers or get
about the ground with ease.   It is a question of right and wrong
formality.   The beds in my own work are, as will be seen by the
plans here given, as formal as any, but simpler, and are made on
the ground and to the ground.   Our object should be to see the
flowers and not the beds, so that while we have all the advantage
of mass and depth of soil, and all the good a bed can give for convenience of working or excellence of growth, we should take little
pride in its form, and plant it so that we may see the picturesque
effects of the plants and flowers, and forget the form of the bed in
the picture

The relation of the beds to each other is often much too complex
and there is little freedom.   Designs that were well enough for
furniture or walls or panels when applied to the garden gave us a
new set of difficulties   Carried out in wood or in the carpet they
answer their purpose, if we like them , but a flower bed is a thing
for much work in cultivating, arranging and keeping it, and it is
best to see that we are not hindered by needless complexities in dealing with the beds   In good plans there is no difficulty of access,
no small points to be cut in Grass or other material, no vexatious

obstruction to work, but beds as airy and simple as possible and giving us much more room for flowers than beds of the ordinary type. The plans given are those of wholly different kinds of gardens.

GOLDER'S HILL.—This at Hampstead, is, perhaps, the best and most interesting example of a London garden one could find for its beauty, airiness, repose, and fine distant view, in which one can scarcely see a house, although near London   This plan is also instructive in various other ways, as showing that where it is desirable to keep a lawn open and quiet for view, play, or any other like reason, it is often easy to do this without interfering with the flower-gardening or any other charm of the place   The lawn is so open and airy, that any number of people may assemble on it without inconvenience or injury to anything. The lawn falls gently from the house, so that any walled terracing is needless, and, excepting a few steps for the convenience of level, little has been done in that direction. The plan also disproves the thoughtless assertion of certain writers that landscape gardening means twisting the walks about   It is seen here that nothing of the kind is done in this most picturesque garden The flower beds are rather few and bold, and made large for the sake of ease of cultivation and breadth of effect.

The next plan is that of the gardener's house at Uffington, near Stamford ; it is an example of the older-fashioned garden not uncommon before nearly all old gardens were altered for the sake of the Perilla and its few companions.   At one end of the little garden is the gardener's house, and high walls surround the rest of the garden, so that there is shelter and every comfort for the plants.   The garden is simply laid out to suit the ground, the plants—Roses and hardy flowers in great variety, a plan which admits of delightful effect in such walled gardens.   Picturesque masses of Wistaria covered one side of the wall and part of the house—the whole was a picture in the best sense , and it would be difficult to find in garden enclosures anything more delightful during more than half the year.

The main drawback in gardens of this sort in the old days was the absence of grouping or any attempt to hold " things together " —a fault which is easily got over.   It is easy to avoid scattering things one likes all over the beds at equal distances, and, without " squaring " them in any stupid way, to keep them rather more together in natural groups, in which they are more effective, and in winter it is much easier to remember where they are. In this way, too, it is easy to give a somewhat distinct look to each part of the garden.   Box edgings may be used in such a garden, and where they thrive and are well kept they are very pretty in effect, but always distinctly inferior to a stone edging because

Garden at Golder's Hill, showing fine view over distant country. Flowers to left of house and on margins of lawn.

more troublesome, and also because dwarf plants cannot grow over them here and there as they can over a rough edging of natural stone, the best of all edgings.

FLOWER GARDEN OF TUDOR HOUSE.—This shows two flower gardens close to a Tudor house, with a garden door from the house into each. One being small (that on the south), it was thought better to devote it all to flowers and the necessary walks, all being done with a view to simplicity of culture and good effect of the plants. In the other garden, there being more space, the lawn is left open in the centre, while all round and convenient to the walk are simple, bold beds easy to deal with, and also spaced in a free and open way for people to get among them or about the lawn. The little south garden being much frequented in all weathers, and the paths among the beds rather small, it was thought best to pave them with old flagstones, and that has proved very satisfactory, because rolling and much weeding are thereby avoided and the walks are pleasant to walk or work on at all seasons.

South of the house and of these gardens there is an open, airy meadow lawn, the Grass of which is studded with many bulbs that flower in the spring. The vigorous kinds of spring bulbs are grown in great quantities in this field, and only the choicer and rarer early bulbs are put among the Roses and other flowers in the flower garden proper, which is mainly devoted to the finest hardy flowers of summer and to Tea Roses.

HAWLEY.—This garden shows two essential things in the art of garden-design : First, the general idea of this book that it is by well studying the ground itself, rather than bringing in any conventional plans, we arrive at the best results. Gardening is so pleasant in many ways that almost any plan may pass for pretty and yet be far from being the most artistic result that could be got among a given set of conditions, or difficulties it may be of ground. If in such a case we adopt such plans as are sent out from offices both in France and England, it is possible that (with considerable cost) we may adapt them to the situation, but assuredly that way cannot give us the most artistic result.

The second point is, that where the vegetation of a place has distinct characters of its own, these should be made the most of. If this were the case generally we should see much less of the stereotyped in garden-design. This garden is in the charming Pine district of Hampshire—the Pine, beautiful in groups and in distant effects and this was taken advantage of, and the Pine look of the place preserved in all ways, and even heightened where it could be done with good effect. These Pine groups and masses were naturally more of the framework of the garden—the woods and trees surrounding it.

The next thing done was to take advantage of the natural vegetation of the ground apart from the trees, *e.g.*, the heathy vegetation of the country, and instead of destroying it for turf or any of the usual

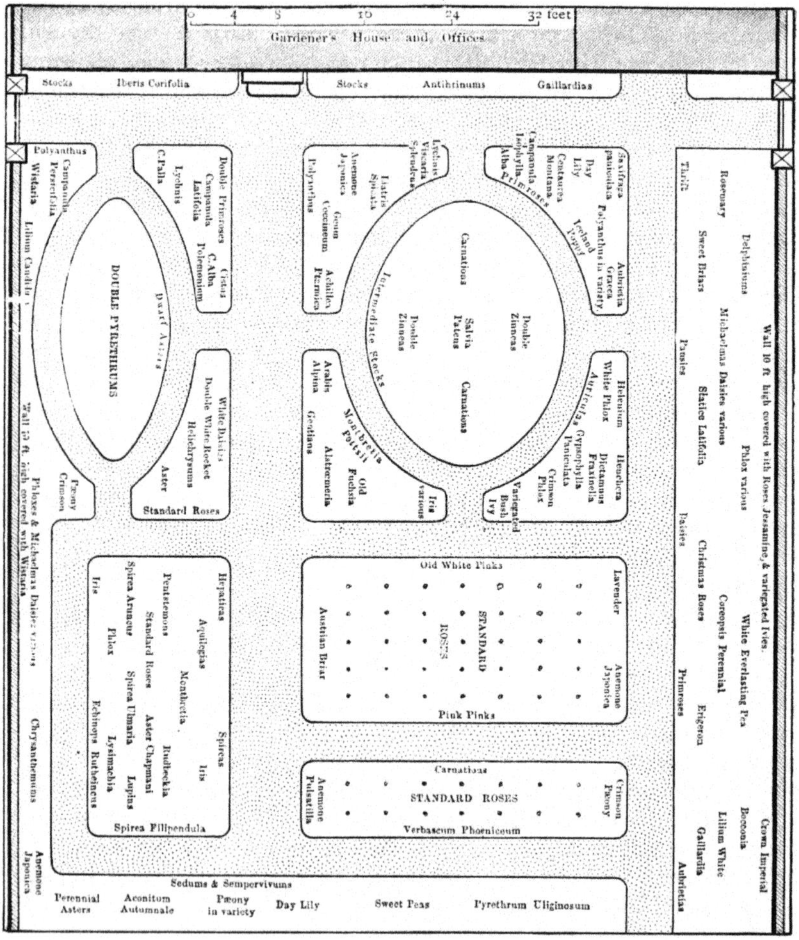

4 5 10 24 32 feet

Gardener's House and Offices

Stocks | Iberis Corifolia | Stocks | Antirrhinums | Gaillardias

Wistaria — Lilium Candidum — Tall 13 ft. high covered with Wistaria — Phloxes & Michelmas Daisies various — Chrysanthemums — Anemone Japonica

Polyanthus — Campanula Persicifolia — C. Pelia — Lychnis — Campanula Latifolia — Double Primroses — Cistus — C. Alba — Polemonium — spard Azure pt — White Daisies — Double White Rocket — Heliedryanna — Aster — Peony Crimson — Standard Roses

DOUBLE PYRETHRUMS

Lychnis Viscaria Splendens — Latris Spicata — Polyanthus — Anemone Japonica — Geum Coccineum — Achillea Ptrmica — Carnations — Arabis Alpina — Gentians — Aralis Grediana — Alstramcria

Intermediate Stocks — Double Zinnias — Salvia Patens — Carnations — Double Zinnias — Maidenhair Spleenwort — Old Fuchsia — Iris various — Variegated Busht Ivy

Campanula lactiflora Alba — Lilium Poppy — Campanula Montana — Day Lily — Saxifraga pasciculata — Polyanthus in variety — Aubrietia Graeca — Centaurea Montana — Helenium — White Phlox — Auricula — Gypsophila Paniculata — Dictamnus Fraxinella — Crimson Phlox

Tulips — Rosemary — Sweet Briar — Pansies — Michelmas Daisies various — Statice Latifolia — Christmas Roses — Daisies

Wall 10 ft. high covered with Roses, Jessamine, & variegated Ivies.

Delphiniums — Phlox various — White Everlasting Pea — Coreopsis Perennial — Erigena — Primroses — Lavender — Anemone Japonica

Crown Imperial — Bocconia — Lilium White — Gaillardia — Anthericus

Old White Pinks — STANDARD ROSES — Pink Pinks — Austrian Briar — Hepaticas — Aquilegias — Montbretia — Penstemons — Standard Roses — Iris — Lavender — Anemone Japonica

Iris — Spirea Aruncus — Spirea Armena — Phlox — Lysimachia — Echinops Ruthenicus — Spirea Ulmaria — Lupins — Aster Chapmani — Rudbeckia — Montbretia — Iris — Spirea — Spirea Filipendula

Carnations — STANDARD ROSES — Verbascum Phoeniceum — Anemone Pulsatilla — Crimson Peony

Perennial Asters — Aconitum Autumnale — Sedums & Sempervivums — Paeony in variety — Day Lily — Sweet Peas — Pyrethrum Uliginosum

Anemone Japonica

Sheltered little garden in front of gardener's house at Uffington, Stamford, with simple beds of Roses and hardy flowers. The space enclosed in walls.

features of a garden, preserving all its prettiest effects, its groups of Heath, wild Fern, and some Birch and Broom. Enough mown grass being left to walk upon outside the garden, it was thought the prettiest thing instead of a shaven lawn would be to leave the wild Heaths and bushes and grass of the country, here and there scattering a few bulbs on the grass, but generally leaving things as nature had left them. The walks, instead of following the French sections of eggs pattern or the conventional serpentine walks of some landscape work were made in the line of easiest grade and where they were most wanted—and are not more in number or area than were necessary. There was no attempt made to make the walks conform to any preconceived idea. The grass walk under the Oaks was suggested by the Oaks themselves, and it is very pretty in effect. Originally several terraces had been run up at all sorts of awkward angles, and the ground was consequently more difficult to deal with than can well be imagined ; these were thrown into one simple terrace round the house planned in due relation to its needs and the taste of the owner. The flower garden was laid out in simple beds as shown on the plan, and below these the necessary grass walks lead out towards the open country. Once free of the flower garden and the walk leading to it the ground took its natural disposition again. The kitchen garden had been in its present place originally ; its position could not be changed, and was therefore accepted and walled round with Oak. The whole garden is quite distinct from any other, which in itself is a great point. This garden was, as I think all gardens ought to be, marked out on the ground itself without the intervention of any plan A plan is always a feeble substitute for the ground, and even if made with the greatest care and cost has still to be adapted to the ground. The plan shown in the engraving was made after my work was done.

SHRUBLAND PARK —The plan here given is that of the new flower garden at Shrubland Park, which is situated exactly in front of the house, and tells its own story. It shows the simple form of beds adopted, planned to suit their places, in lieu of the complex pattern beds for carpet bedding, sand, coloured brick, and also the change from such gardening to true flower-gardening. The names of the plants used are printed in position, but the actual way of grouping cannot well be shown in such a plan—the plants are not in little dots, but in easy, bold groups here and there running together. The flower gardening adopted is permanent, *i e.*, there is no moving of things in the usual wholesale way in spring and autumn. The beds are planted to stay, and that excludes spring gardening of the ordinary kind. But many early spring flowers are used in the garden, the mainstay of which is summer and autumn flowers, the period chosen for beauty being that when the house is occupied and all beautiful hardy flowers from Roses to Pansies that flower from May to November are those preferred. There is no formality or repetition in the flower planting but picturesque groups, here and there running

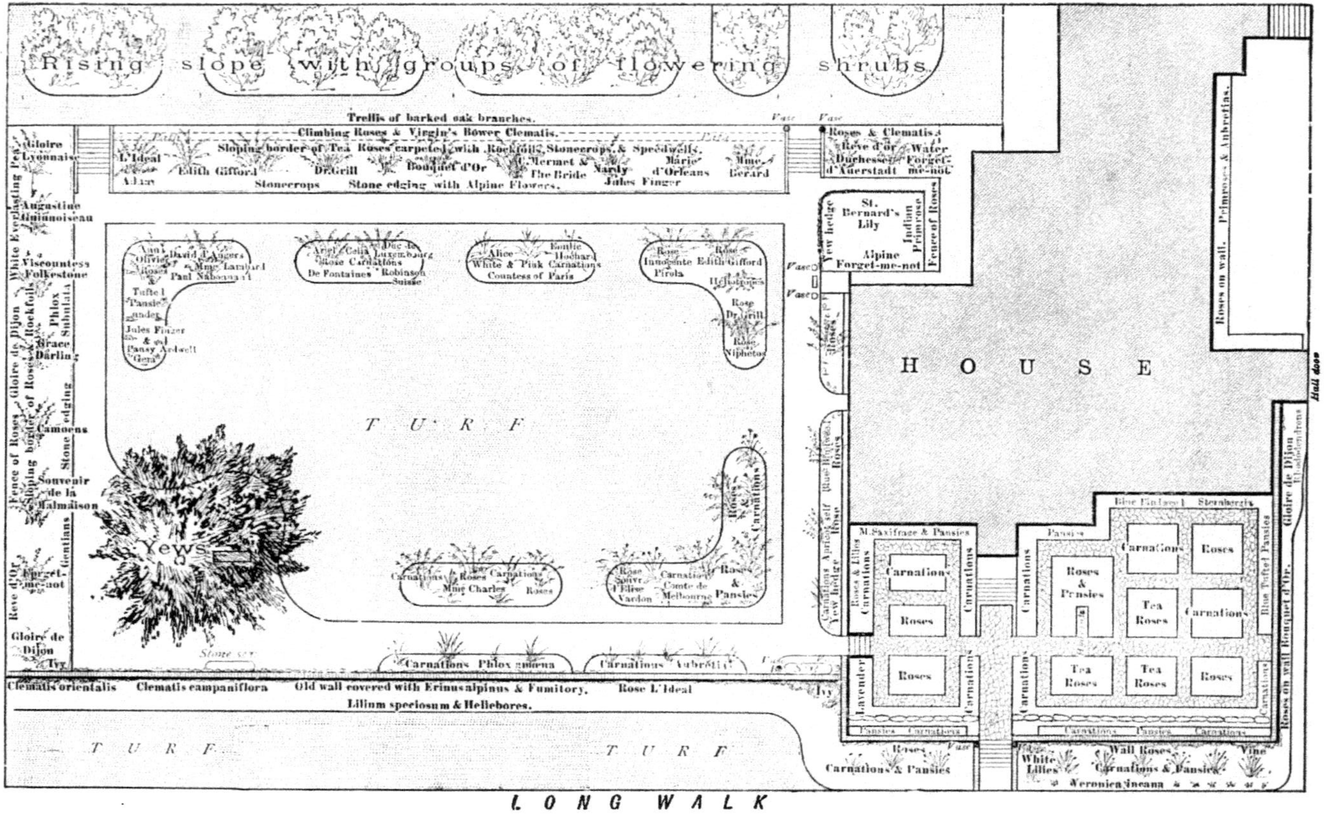

HOUSE

Garden of Tudor house designed to secure easy cultivation and good effect, and planted with choicest hardy flowers, as one alternative to "bedding out."

L O N G   W A L K

T U R F

together, and sometimes softened by dwarf plants running below the taller ones   The beds are set in a pleasant lawn, and there is easy access to them in all directions from the grass   The area of gravel was much greater in the old plan than in the present one, in which what is essential only for free access to the garden is given.

EVERGREEN FLOWER GARDEN IN SURREY VILLA —Bearing in mind the conventional bareness and hardness of the common garden of our own day, there is no improvement greater than results from breaking into this by permanent planting of things of a bushy kind. The plan of this garden shows a choice evergreen garden instead of the usual summer planting and autumnal death   The beds are simple and planted with choice shrubs, not crowded, but leaving room for different kinds of hardy flowers so as to get the relief of flower and shrub, and the charm of beds alive and filled at all times   Most of the evergreens (like Kalmia, Japanese Andromeda, and Rhododendrons of beautiful colour) are choice flowering ones, so that we have bloom in spring and summer , and after, or with the shrubs, the flowers between.   Such a garden in pure air well begun might be almost permanent, because in such soils as these light peaty Surrey soils, the shrubs would thrive for many years , and the same may be said of the Lilies and choice bulbs between, only slight changes and additions being required from time to time   Many large gardens, which in similar soils are bare even in early summer, might thus be made charming and graceful gardens throughout the year, and, if this way is not so loud in colour as other ways of flower-gardening, it suits certain positions well.   This way of planting need not exclude some summer planting of the usual character, in fact would give zest and relief to it· it is the one evanescent system carried out everywhere that steals the varied beauty from the garden

BITTON VICARAGE GARDEN.—This is one of the oldest and most richly stored with good hardy flowers of all English gardens, and, unlike many gardens where much variety is sought, it is pretty in effect and quite by itself as all gardens should be, and an example of a small garden of the highest interest, and withal of simple and sensible plan.

The garden is not a large one, being about an acre and a half in area, and in shape a parallelogram, or double square   As its owner, Mr. Ellacombe, tells us

" It lies on the west side of the Cotswolds, which rise, about half a mile away, to the height of 750 feet, and about 15 miles to the south are the Mendips.   These two ranges of hills do much to shelter us from the winds, both from the cold north and easterly winds, and from the south-west winds, which in this part of England are sometimes

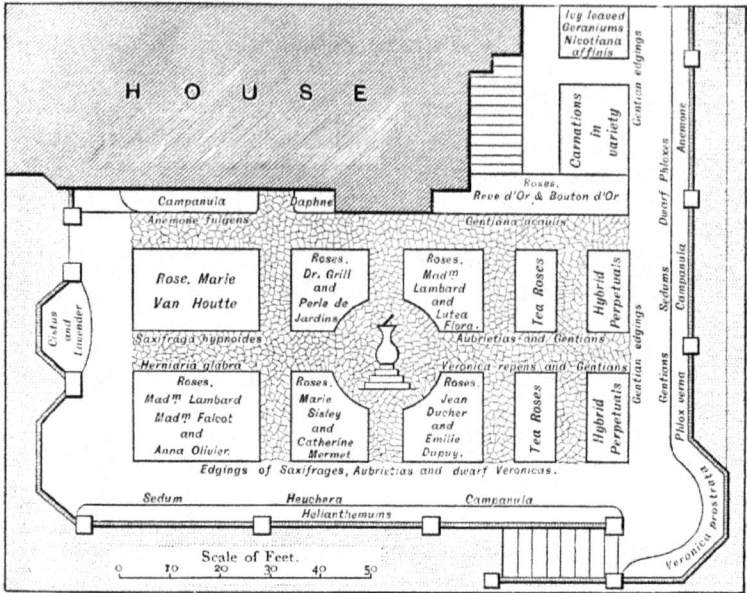

H O U S E

Ivy leaved Geraniums Nicotiana affinis

Carnations in variety

Roses. Reve d'Or & Bouton d'Or

Gentian edgings

Dwarf Phloxes

Anemone

Campanula   Daphne

Anemone fulgens

Gentiana acaulis

Sedums

Campanula

Rose. Marie Van Houtte

Roses. Dr. Grill and Perla de Jardins

Roses. Mad.m Lambard and Lutea Flora.

Tea Roses

Hybrid Perpetuals

Gentian edgings

Gentians

Phlox verna

Cistus and Lavender

Saxifraga hypnoides

Aubrietias and Gentians

Herniaria glabra

Veronica repens and Gentians

Roses. Mad.m Lambard Mad.m Falcot and Anna Olivier.

Roses. Marie Sisley and Catherine Mermet

Roses. Jean Ducher and Emilie Dupuy.

Tea Roses

Hybrid Perpetuals

Veronica prostrata

Edgings of Saxifrages, Aubrietias and dwarf Veronicas.

Sedum   Heuchera   Campanula

Helianthemums

Scale of Feet.

0   10   20   30   40   50

Hawley flower garden.

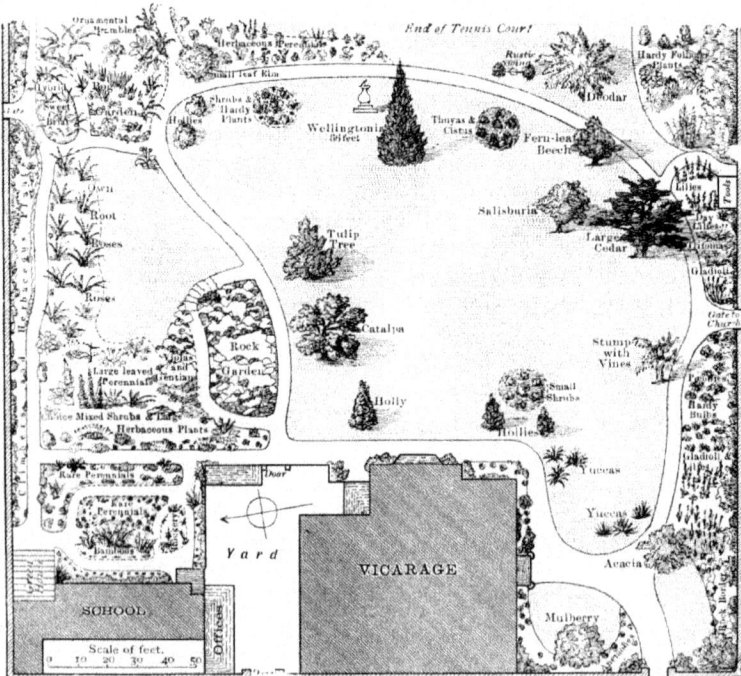

End of Tennis Court

Ornamental Brambles

Herbaceous Perennials

Rustic

Hardy Foliage Plants

Small leaf Elm

Shrubs & Hardy Plants

Deodar

Holly Garden

Hollies

Wellingtonia 50 feet

Thuyas & Cistus

Fern-leaf Beech

Own Root Roses

Salisburia

Lilies

Tulip Tree

Large Cedar

Lilies

Roses

Catalpa

Stump with Vines

Rock Garden

Large leaved Perennials

Holly

Small Shrubs

Mixed Shrubs & Trees

Herbaceous Plants

Hollies

Yuccas

Rose Perennials

Yuccas

Perennial

Hardy Bulbs

Door

Gladioli

Yard

Acacia

VICARAGE

SCHOOL

Offices

Mulberry

Scale of feet.

0   10   20   30   40   50

Bitton : part of the plan of the garden near house for flowers and shrubs.

very violent   I attach great importance to this kindly shelter from
the great strength of the winds, for plants are like ourselves in many
respects, and certainly in this, that they can bear a very great amount
of frost, if only the air is still, far better than they can bear a less
cold if accompanied by a high wind."

The garden then has the advantage of shelter ; it has also the
advantage of a good aspect, for though the undulations are very slight
the general slope faces south ; and it has the further advantage of a
rich and deep alluvial soil, which, however, is so impregnated with
lime and magnesia that it is hopeless to attempt Rhododendrons,
Azaleas, Kalmias, and many other things, and it has the further disadvantage of being only about 70 feet above the sea level, which makes
an insuperable difficulty in the growth of the higher alpines.   On the
whole, the garden is favourable for the cultivation of flowers, and especially for the cultivation of shrubs, except those which dislike the lime

The garden is in many ways an ideal one, lying deep down in a
happy valley and forming with the fine old church the centre of an
old world village   It is a quiet, peaceful garden of grass and trees
and simple borders, and every nook and corner has its appropriate
flower , in a word, it is just such a garden as one would expect a
scholar to possess who has sympathy for all that lives or breathes and
who has given us such a book as " The Plant Lore and Garden Craft
of Shakespeare "   The garden at Bitton Vicarage is no new garden,
for it was famous more than half a century ago, when Haworth and
Herbert, Anderson, Falconer, Sweet, Baxter and others took such an
interest in bulbs and hardy flowers.   By the same token it is by no
means a new-fangled garden , there is all due and proper keeping, but
it is patent to any plant-lover that its owner thinks more of seeing
his plants happy and healthy than he does of any unnecessary
trimness —F. W. B

RESERVE GARDEN —We have an example in this plan of what
is meant by a reserve garden.   An oblong piece of ground having
the walls of the kitchen garden for two of its boundaries, and a Yew
hedge sheltering it from the east winds, while the other is screened
by evergreen trees, with which are intermingled hardy plants of tall
growth.   The plants are set in beds without reference to the general
effect, and all the borders, being edged with stone dug on the place,
give no trouble after the stones are properly set , when old and moss-
grown the stones look better than anything else that could be used—
the dwarfer plants being allowed to run over them and break the
lines.   Every year the plan of such a garden may be varied as our
tastes vary and as the flowers want change.   A similar garden ought
to be in every place where there are borders to be stocked and
maintained in good condition, and particularly where there is a
demand for cut flowers.

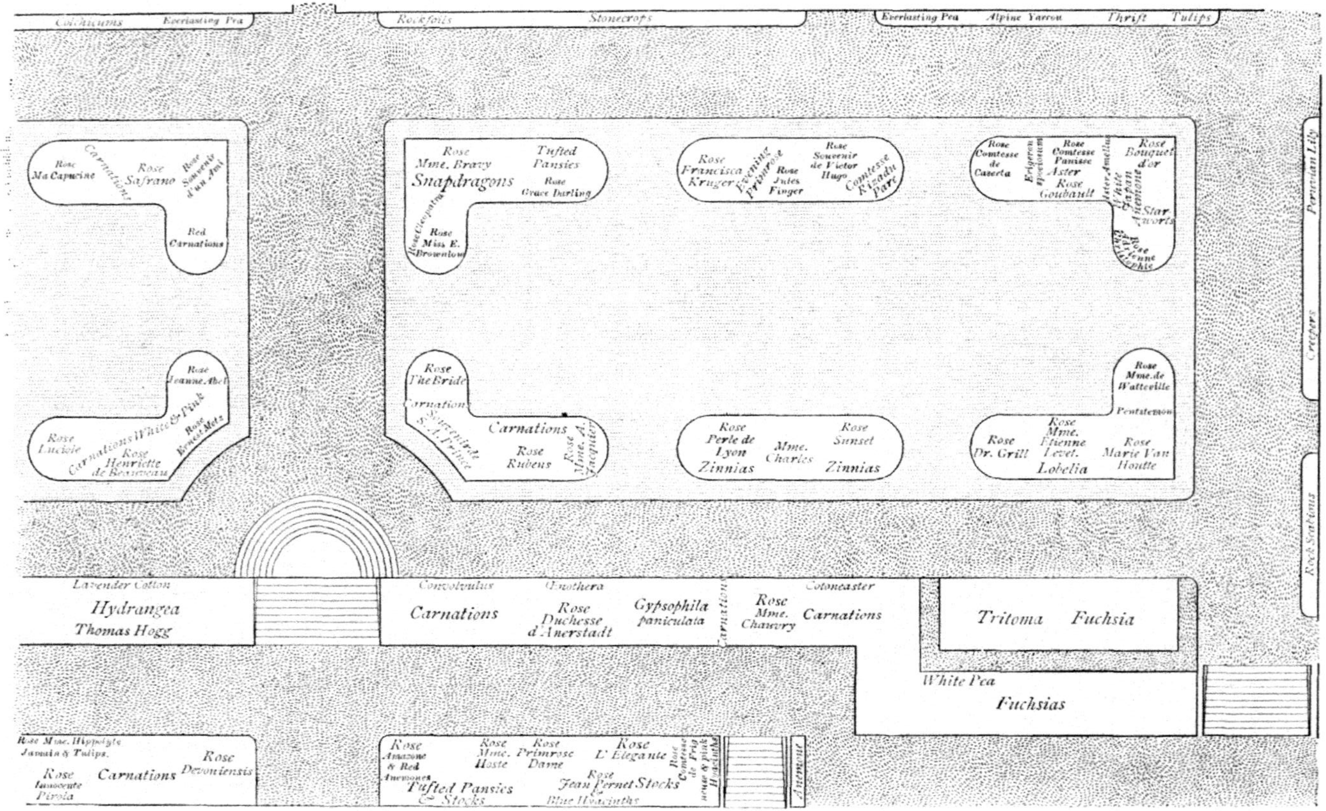

Peruvian Lily   Crocuses   Rock Scabious

Tulips
Thrift
Alpine Veronica
Everlasting Pea
Snowcrops
Rockets
Candytufts
Everlasting Pea
Candytufts

Rose Bouquet d'or
Rose Comtesse Fontaine
Japan Anemone
Star Glory
Rose Comtesse de Camondo
Rose Mme de Watteville
Penstemon
Rose Mme Gustave...
Rose Dr Grill
Rose Pierre Tevel
Lobelia
Rose Marie Van Houtte

Rose Souvenir de Victor Hugo
Rose Jules Finger
Rose Francisca Kruger
Rose Mme Eugene Resal
Rose Perle de Lyon
Rose Mme Charles
Zinnias
Rose Sunset
Zinnias

Tufted Pansies
Rose Gruss Teplitz
Rose Mme Berry
Snapdragons
Rose Miss E...
Carnation A. Alegatiere
Rose Mlle A. Prince
Carnations
Rose Ruben
Rose Duchesse d'Auerstadt
Rose Viscountess...

Cotoneaster
Rose Mme Chauvry   Carnations
Gypsophila paniculata
Godetia   Rose Duchesse d'Auerstadt
Carnations
Lavender Cotton
Hydrangea Thomas Hogg

Tritoma   Fuchsia
White Pea   Fuchsias

Rose Francisca
Rose Mme Primrose Dame
Rose L'Elegante
Rose Comtesse de Prat
Tufted Pansies   Ten-Week Stocks
Stocks

Rose McCarpenter
Rose Carnation Sulphur
Red Carnations

Rose Uncle John
Rose Mlle Henriette de Beauveau
Rose Marechal Niel

Rose Mme Hoste   Jannaks & Tulips
Carnations Peoniensis
Rose Innocente   Paria

Such a garden may be made in any shape which is convenient for cultivation, for access and for cutting ; but some general throwing of the ground into easily worked beds is desirable.   The more free and less hampered with gravel, permanent edgings, and the like, the better it will be for future work.   The gardener is often hindered by need-less impedimenta in the flower garden, but in the reserve garden, where only the cultivation of flowers has to be thought of, he should be able to get to work at any time with the least possible difficulty,

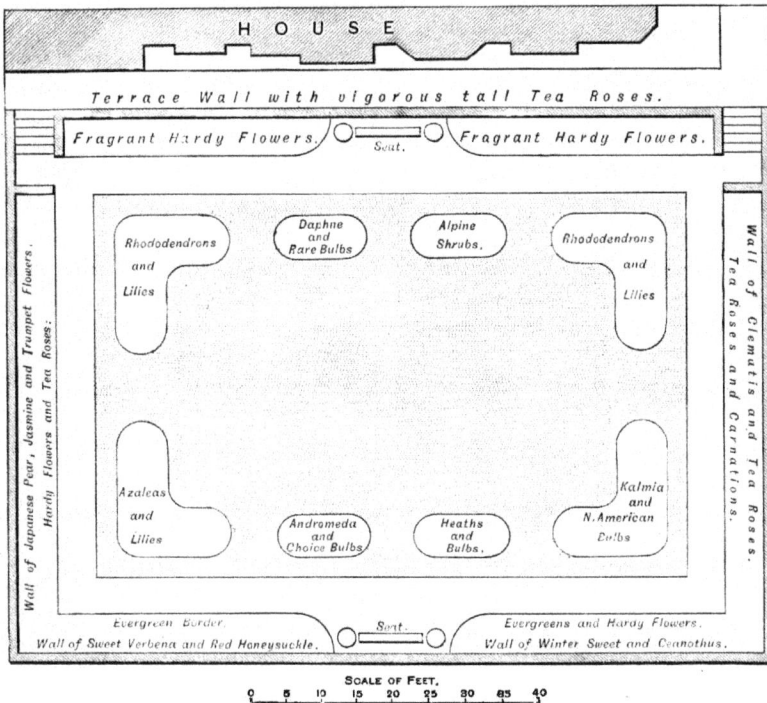

Flower garden of Surrey villa on peaty soil for choice evergreen shrubs with hardy flowers between.

and in dry and good soils it would not be necessary to have much more than a beaten walk for the foot.   It would be possible to do without edgings ; but where edgings are used they should be of a kind that might be removed at any time, the best for this end being of natural stone.   The drainage should be good, and if possible the place should be not too far to the manure heap, while the soil should in all cases be good, as very often it has to give two crops a year ; in the case of bulbs that perish early it is easy to get after crops of annuals or ornamental grasses.

YEW HEDGE

Seat

PÆONIES AND DAHLIAS
The Dahlias preceded by Wallflowers.

PERENNIALS
IN GROUPS

| SCILLAS | { HYACINTHS
{ MIGNONETTE | { RANUNCULUS
{ ZINNIA | { MUSCARI
{ TIGRIDIA |

{ DAFFODILS
{ PHLOX
{ DRUMMONDI

SNAPDRAGON

FLOWERING SHRUBS AND TREES

PINKS	IRIS	LILIES
SWEET WILLIAMS	EARLY GLADIOLUS	DOUBLE ROCKET	PHLOX
SWEET SULTAN	CARNATIONS	ALSTROMERIA	BLUE CORNFLOWER

{ SPRING
{ CROCUS
{ STOCKS

SCHIZOSTYLIS	SALVIA PATENS	PYRETHRUM	PENTSTEMON
AMERICAN COWSLIPS	LATE GLADIOLUS	COLUMBINES	DELPHINIUM
{ TULIPS { CHINA { ASTERS	DOUBLE WALLFLOWERS	LILIES	SCARLET LOBELIA

{ ANEMONES
{ GRASSES

PANSY

| { FRITILLARIES
{ CYCLAMENS | { DOUBLE PRIMROSES
{ COLCHICUMS | { POLYANTHUS
{ AUTUMN CROCUS | { DOGS TOOTH
{ VIOLET |

{ HEPATICA
{ CHRISTMAS ROSE
{ ALEXANDRIAN LAUREL

VIOLETS   Seat   ALPINE AURICULAS

JAPAN
ANEMONES

SHRUBS AND TREES

Wall of Tea Roses with border in front for Gladioli, Belladonna Lilies, Vallota, Agapanthus, Lilies and other Bulbs.

E
N   S
W

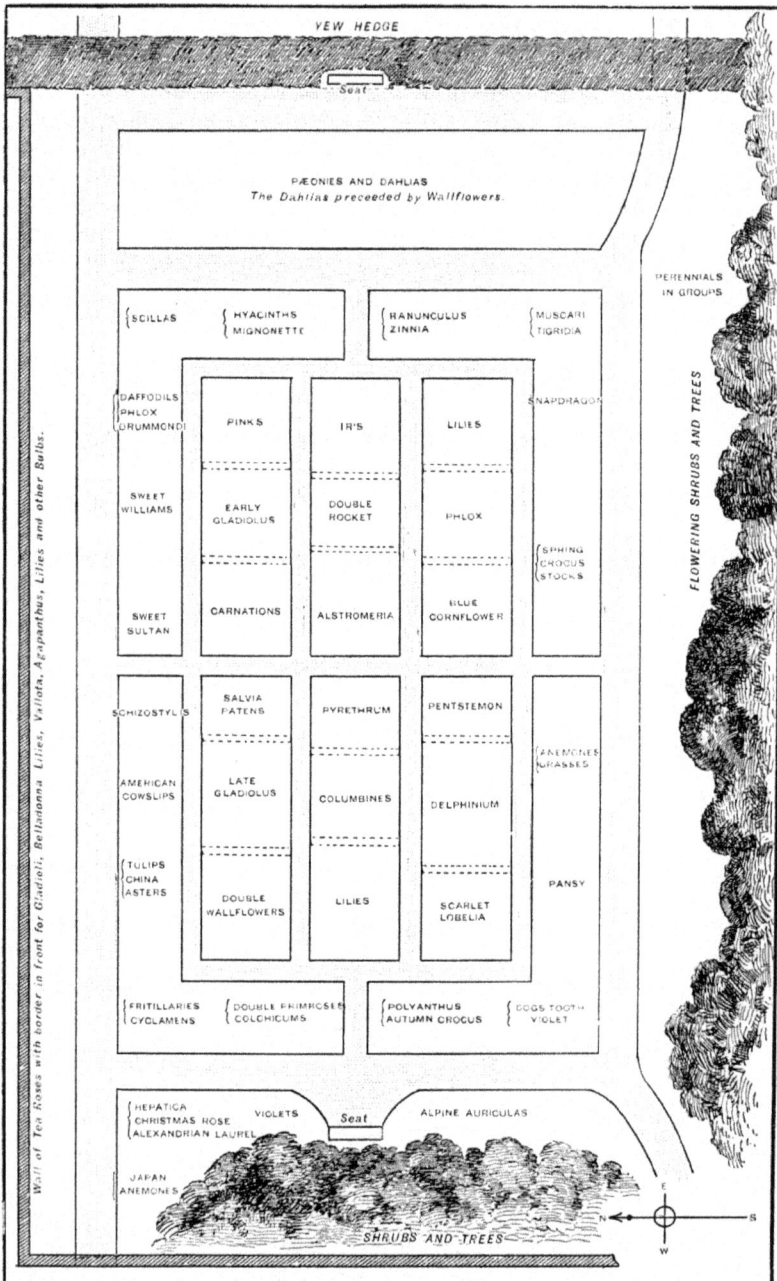

Reserve garden for the choicer families of hardy plants, grown in beds without reference to general
effect, and serving also as a garden for cut flowers and a nursery.

CHAPTER XXVI.

WALKS AND EDGINGS.

OUR gardens are often laid out in a complex way : with so many needless walks, edgings, and impediments of many kinds that work cannot be done in a simple way, and half the time is lost in taking care of or avoiding useless or frivolous things. Efforts thus wasted should be turned to account in the growth of flowers In many large places there is no true flower-gardening , wretched plants are stuck out in the parterre every year, and a few stunted things are scratched in round the choke-muddle shrubbery, but little labour or love is bestowed on the growth of flowers In others there are miles of walks bordered by bare stretches of earth, as cheerful as Woking Cemetery in its early years The gardener is impotent to turn such a waste into a paradise , his time and his thoughts are often eaten up by keeping in order needless and often ugly walks The gardeners, owing to the trouble of this wasteful system, have little time for true flower-gardening—forming a real garden of Roses, or groups of choice shrubs, or beds of Lilies, or of other noble hardy plants, so that the beds may fairly nourish their tenants for a dozen years Instead of the never-ending and wearisome hen-scratchings of autumn and spring, we ought to prepare one portion of the flower garden or pleasure ground each year, so that it will yield beauty for many years. But this cannot be done while half the gardener's time is taken up with barber's work

Our own landscape gardeners are a little more sparing of these hideous walks than the French ; but we very often have twice too many walks, which torment the poor gardener by needless and stupid labour The planning of these walks in various elaborate ways has been supposed to have some relation to landscape gardening ; but one needless walk often bars all good effect in its vicinity. Flower-beds are often best set in Grass, and those who care to see them will approach them quite as readily on Grass as on hard walks. For the three or four months of our winter season there is little need of frequent resort to flower-beds, and for much of the rest of the year the turf is better than any walk. I do not mean that there should be no walk to the flower-garden, but that every walk not necessary for use should be turfed over. Few have any idea how much they would gain, not merely in labour, but in the beauty and repose of their gardens, by doing away with needless walks

GRAVEL WALKS —For hard work and general use the gravel walk is the most important of all for garden and pleasure grounds The colour of walks is important ; that of the yellow gravels being by far the best. Of this we have examples in the country around London, in the gravels of Croydon, Farnham, and also those of Middlesex. These walks are not only good in colour but also excellent in texture, consolidating thoroughly It is a relief to see these brownish-yellow walks after the purple pebble walks of the neighbourhoods of Dublin and Edinburgh After the sound formation of these walks the main point is to keep them to the essential needs of the place, and when this is done their effect is usually right. Even this excellent gravel is sometimes improved about London by the addition of sea shells, cockle shells mostly gathered from the coasts of Kent , and, after the walk is formed and hardened, this is lightly scattered over the surface and rapidly breaks down and gives to the walk a clean smooth surface.

In public gardens and parks large areas of gravel are sometimes necessary, and in some ways of " laying out," such as those round French châteaux, wide arid areas of gravel are supposed to have a *raison d'être* , but in English gardens they are better avoided English roads, lanes, and pathways are often pictures, because consecrated by use and often beautiful in line, following as they often do the line of easiest grade or gentle curves round hills , but in gardens, roads and paths are often ugly because overdone, and nothing can be worse than hot areas of gravel, not only without any relation to the needs of the place, but wasting precious ground that might be made grateful to the eye with turf, or of some human interest with plants

STONE WALKS IN SMALL FLOWER GARDENS —A walk which is much liked is the stone walk, suggested by the little stone paths to cottages. In large open gardens such walks would not be so good, but in small inclosed spaces and flower gardens, where we have to plant very closely in beds, stone walks are a gain. In some districts a pretty rough, flat stone is found, of which there is a good example at Sedgwick Park. In cities, when renewing the side-walks, it is sometimes easy to get old flagstones, which are excellent for the purpose. . I use such old stones and mostly set them at random, or in any way they come best. The advantages are that we get rid of the sticky surface of gravel in wet weather or after frost, avoid rolling and weeding for the most part, the stones are pleasant to walk on at all times, and we can work at the beds or borders freely in all weathers without fear of soiling gravel. The colour of the stones is good and in sunny gardens in hot summers they help to keep the ground moist, while the broken and varied incidents of the surface get rid of the hard unyielding lines of the gravel walk and help the picture. They should never be set in mortar or cement of any kind, but carefully in sand or fine sandy soil, and the work can be done by a careful man with a little practice. If in newly-formed ground there is a little sinking of the stone, it can be corrected afterwards Small rock plants, like Thyme, the fairy Mint, and little Harebells, may be grown between the divisions of the stone, and, indeed, they often come of themselves, and their effect is very pretty in a small garden Another point in favour of the stone walk is that it forms its own edging, and we do not need any living edging , and if for any purpose, in a wet country or otherwise, we wish to somewhat raise the flower beds, we can use the same kind of stone for edging the beds.

GRASS, HEATH, AND MOSS WALKS —Once free of all necessary walks about the house of gravel or stone, which constant work and use make essential, it is often easy in country gardens to soon break into grass walks which are pleasantest of all ways of getting about the country garden or pleasure ground Not only can we take them into the wild garden and rough places, but they lead us to flowering shrubs and beds of hardy plants and to the rock garden, or through the pleasure ground anywhere, as easily and more pleasantly than any regularly set out walks There is much saving of labour in their formation because given sound drained ground which is to be found around most country houses, we have little to do except mark out and keep the walks regularly mown , when this work is compared with the labour of carting, the knowledge and the annual care which are necessary to form and keep hard walks in order, the gain in favour of the grass walk is enormous It is perhaps only in our country that the climate enables us to have the privilege of these verdant walks, which are impossible in warmer lands owing to the great heat destroying the herbage, and, therefore, in Britain we should make good use of what our climate aids us so much in doing.

We have, of course, to think of the fall of the grass walk for the sake of ease in mowing and in walking too, as very much of their comfort will depend, at least in hilly ground, on the careful way these walks are studied as regards their gradation. There is really not much difference in the degree of moisture in such walks and gravel walks, and, besides, so little use is made of walks of any kind in wet weather, that generally, taking them all the year round, they serve as well as any other where there is but gentle wear.

Apart from the grass walks which can be formed in so large an area of Britain we may have walks through heath and the short vegetation that grows in heathy districts, and these walks will be no less pleasant than the grass walks The short turf of the heath, and often the mown heather itself forms an excellent springy walk, as in parts of Surrey. Such walks want little making, only some care in laying down their lines so as to take them into the prettiest spots and letting them edge themselves with heather, ferns and Whortleberry. But no more than any other should such walks be multiplied beyond what is necessary, and they ought to be broad enough and airy enough to take us in the pleasantest way to the most interesting parts of the garden or pleasure ground or woods. In woody or half shady places we may enjoy the mossy walk as in very sandy or light soils we may have a turf almost of Thyme.

TAR WALKS.—Among the curious mixture of good and bad, ugliness and beauty, we see often in country seats are tar walks, and they are a main " factor " in making many a garden ugly. They have almost every fault that a walk could have, being hideous in colour, hot in summer, and sticky, hard and unpleasant to the feet, wearing into ugly holes and an uneven and unpleasant surface. The only excuse that could ever be made for them was that they offered an escape from continual hoeing, a great labour, but now needless, owing to the weed-killers If walks are simply made, and not one yard more is made than is required for use, the labour of cleaning is immensely reduced, and one dressing a year of an effective weed-killer often keeps them right If there were no other objection than the colour of the tar walk, it should be sufficient to condemn it, and gravel in the home counties and about London is so good in colour, that one is surprised that anybody can tolerate a tar walk. In small, close courtyard gardens, where gravel is objected to, we may have a well-made stone walk of good colour

CONCRETE AND ASPHALT WALKS.—Apart from tar walks, which on hot days may give us the idea that we are stuck in a bog, there are also well-made walks to be had from concrete and true asphalt. These walks have distinct advantages for courtyards and small spaces, or even small gardens in certain places ; they are better in colour than the tar walk, and more enduring if well made. They are clean, but they have certain disadvantages as compared with stone walks. They require a much more expensive and careful setting, and they are certainly not more enduring Also, they do not allow us the privilege of putting plants between the joints, one of the great charms of the stone walk, which can be easily set to allow Thyme and dwarf rock-plants to come up between them ; and therefore in all districts in which a warm-coloured stone is procurable, or rough flagstone from quarries, it is very much better to use it, as we can always have gravel for any roads that have to be traversed by carriages or carts ; the space for concrete, asphalt, or stone walks is not considerable, and the natural material should be used wherever it be possible.

FLOWER GARDEN EDGINGS, LIVE AND DEAD.

Even small things may mar the effect of a flower garden, however rich in its plants, and among the things that do so are cast edgings of tiles or iron, often very ugly, and as costly as ugly, some of the earthenware edgings perishing rapidly in frost. But if they never perished, and were as cheap as pebbles by the shore, they would be none the less offensive from the point of view of effect, with their hard patterned shapes, often bad colour, and the necessity of setting them with precision in cement or mortar ; whereas the enduring and beautiful edging wants none of these costly attentions. The seeming advantage of these patterned and beaded tile edgings is that they appear

Stone edging. From a photograph by Mr. A. Emblin, Worksop, Notts.

permanent, and get rid of the labour of clipping and keeping box edgings in good order ; but these ends are met quite as well by perfectly inoffensive edgings. Edgings may, for convenience sake, be divided into dead and permanent ones and living ones formed of plants or dwarf bushes, which involve a certain amount of care to keep in order, and which will some day wear out and require a change or replanting.

The true way in all gardens of any good and simple design is to get edgings which, while quite unobtrusive in form or colour, may remain for many years without attention. In all good gardens there is so much to be done and thought of every day in the year, that it is important to get rid of all mere routine work with edgings of Box and other things that want frequent trimming or remaking, in which work much of the labour of gardeners has been wasted in the past.

NATURAL STONE is the best of all materials for permanent edgings for the flower garden, or any garden where an edging is required, and no effort should be spared to get it. In many districts it is quite easy to do so, as in some of the home counties the refuse of quarries (in Surrey Bargate stone, and in Oxfordshire and Gloucestershire the flaky stone used for the roofs of old time) is excellent for edgings. Much difference will occur in stone in various districts, and some will not be so good in colour and shape as the stone just mentioned, but the advantage of natural stone in various ways is so great that even inferior forms of it should be chosen before any other material. In undressed, or very roughly dressed natural stone, it does not matter in the least if the stones vary in size, as we have not to set them rigidly like the cast tiles ; sunk half-way firmly in the earth, after a little time they soon assume a good colour ; green mosses stain them in the winter, and if we wish to grace them with rock flowers they are very friendly to them, and Rockfoil, or Stonecrop, or Thyme may creep over them, and make them prettier than any edging made wholly of plants, like Box or Thrift, or Ivy. Unlike the tile, stones are none the worse if they fall a little out of line, as they are easily reset, and also easily removed by handy garden men without expensive workmen, or any aid from mortar or trowel. In large and stately gardens dressed stone may be used to frame a grass plot or handsome straight border, but in most cases this expense would be thrown away, as we get so good a result with the undressed stone. But in a flower garden like that at Shrubland Park, the dressed stone of good and simple form, and properly set as it should be in such a position quite near the house, is quite rightly used. Near cities and towns the removal of old or half-worn stone pavements, like the York stone used in London, often gives us opportunities of securing it for forming edging ; and being often got in large pieces, it requires rough dressing to allow of its being firmly and evenly set in the ground. I have used this largely for edgings, which will last as long as they are allowed to remain. The beautiful green stone of Cumberland would

Edging of Foam Flower.

make as good an edging as one could desire, and many kinds of stone may be used.

In districts where there is no stone to be had, and we have to use any kind of artificial stone or terra cotta, these should never have any pattern or beading, but be cast in quite simple forms, never following the patterns usually adopted by the makers of garden tiles. Certain inferior forms of dead edgings should be avoided, such as boards, that soon rot, and are wholly unfit in all ways as edgings. Iron, too, as used in continental gardens or in any shape, should never be used as an edging, ordinary bricks half set in the ground being far better than any of these.

GRASS EDGINGS sometimes are used to flower borders, but are always full of labour and trouble. And they have various drawbacks, apart from the mowing and edge-cutting, chief among these being that the border flowers within cannot ramble over them as they do over the stone edgings in such pretty ways. These narrow grass margins are often used as edgings to flower borders in the kitchen garden in places where very little labour is to spare for the garden, but, little as it is, it has to be given throughout the season to these grass edgings, which are worse than useless as a finish to a flower border. By these I do not mean the grass margins to the garden lawns, or a carpet of turf, as these are easily attended to when the lawn is being mown, but the foot wide grass edgings which require attention when

Bold evergreen edging to rough border.

time can be badly spared for them, and are often so narrow that it is not easy to use a machine for mowing them.

BOX.—Of all the living things used as edgings in gardens, the first place belongs to Box, used for ages and deservedly liked from its neat habit and good colour. When there were many fewer plants to look after than we have now, to tend some miles of box edging was often the pride of the gardener, and even now we see it sometimes done, though the hand often fails with the ceaseless care the edging requires if it is to be kept in good order, and it gets spotty and in some soils worn out and diseased. Where cared for it must be clipped with much care and regularity every May after the danger of hard frosts is past, as these sometimes touch the young growth. By cutting in May the young growth soon hides the hard mark of the shears. Pretty as it is in certain gardens, the drawbacks to Box as a flower-garden edging are serious ; it requires much labour to keep it in order, and not every garden workman can clip Box well ; it is a harbour for slugs and weeds, drying and starving the soil near ; whereas the stone edging keeps the soil moist and comforts the rock flowers that crawl over it. We cannot allow dwarf and creeping plants to crawl over the Box, or they will scald and injure it, but with the stone, we are free in all ways, and get a pretty effect when Pinks and other dwarf plants, crossing the stone edging here and there, push out into the walk itself. I like Box best as a tall, stout edging or low hedge, used in a bold way as high Rosemary edgings are used in southern gardens, about 18 in. high, or even a little higher, to enclose playgrounds or separate gardens or to mark an interesting site as that of the old house at Castlewellan. Sometimes old and neglected Box edgings grown into

Ivy edging.

low hedges are pretty in a garden, as in George Washington's old home at Mount Vernon in Virginia. And low hedges of Box are now and then a good aid near the flower garden as at Panshanger.

YEW, IVY, HEATH AND VARIOUS EDGINGS.—Among other edgings made of woody or shrubby things, we have the Yew, which bears clipping into edgings a foot high, and which might be worth using in some positions, though much clipping of this sort causes much labour and to me sorrow. Ivy is more precious for its shoots, which garland the earth as well as wall or tree. It is more used abroad than in Britain, the freshness of its green being more valued where good turf is less common, and Ivy is of the highest value as an edging in various ways, but better as a garland round a plot or belt of shrubs than near flower beds, and it enables us to make graceful edgings near and under trees. Like the Box, it may also be used as a bold hedge-like garland to frame a little garden or other spot which we wish to separate from the surrounding ground. The Tree Ivy is best for this, but the common Ivy, if planted as an edging in any open place, will in time assume the shrubby or tree form, and make a handsome and bold garland Where, for any reason, we desire Ivy edgings, it is better not to slavishly follow the French way of always using the Irish Ivy for edgings. The dark masses of this in the public gardens of London, Paris, and also in the German cities are very wearisome, and help to obscure rather than demonstrate the value of the Ivy as the best of all climbers of the northern world The common Ivy, of which the Irish form is a variety, is a plant of wide distribution throughout Europe, North Africa, and Asia, and varies very much in form There being in Britain over fifty cultivated forms of it, it is in England that it is best known. The Irish variety seems to have taken the fancy of continental European gardeners, and is much more cultivated than any other but many of the other varieties less known are more graceful and varied in form, and even colour, some of them having in winter a bronzy hue, instead of the dark look of the Irish Ivy. Some, too, are fine in form, from the great Amoor and Algerian Ivies to the little cutleaved Ivy. Even the common Ivy of our woods is prettier than the one so much used.

Among the bold edgings one sees enclosing the " careless " and broad borders of Spanish or Algerian or other southern gardens, overshaded by orange or other fruit trees, is the Rosemary, clipped into square topped bushy edges, about 15 ins high. Though tender in many parts with us, it may be used in the same way on warm soils and in mild districts, and the Lavender may be used in the same way, though in its case it is best not to clip it, and there is a dwarf form, which is best for edgings to bold borders.

DWARF EVERGREEN EDGINGS —Among various dwarf evergreen shrubs which may be used as edgings are the dwarf Cotoneasters, Periwinkles, smaller Vacciniums, Partridge Berry, the alpine forest Heath and some of the smaller kinds of our native Heaths, varying them after the nature of the soil and the kind of plants or shrubs we are arranging ; heaths and shrubs of a like nature being best for association with peat-loving evergreen shrubs, though they need not all be confined to these or to such soils. Such evergreen edgings of low shrubs are often very useful where we plant masses of select evergreen flowering shrubs, and they may be used in free belts or groups as well as in hard set lines, the last being in many cases a sure way to mar the effect of otherwise good planting in pleasure grounds

Where we are dealing with nursery or cut flower beds, borders

in the kitchen garden or elsewhere, no such objection to the continuous edging holds.   And in such cases those who use plants have
a great variety to choose from : Strawberries, wild, Quatre-saison, and
any favourite larger sort ; Rockfoils—of this rich and varied family
the Mossy Rockfoils make soft and excellent green margins to beds
of hardy flowers ; Houseleeks, Stonecrops, Gentianella, which forms
such a fine evergreen edging in cool soils ; Tufted Pansies, Thrift,
purple Rock-Cresses which are among the most precious of rock flowers
for evergreen edgings, and bloom often throughout the spring ; dwarf
Speedwells, Edelweiss in open country gardens where it thrives ;
alpine Phloxes, Sun Roses, Arabis, evergreen Candytuft, excellent as

White Pink edging.

a permanent margin to bold mixed groups of spring flowers and
shrubs ; Pinks, both white and coloured, pretty on warm and free soils,
but useless where they are hurt in winter ; Daisies and Polyanthuses
and garden Primroses: in Scotland and cool places, the rosy and
some of the Indian Primroses make beautiful edgings.   Dwarf Harebells, and some of the silvery or striped Grasses and Moneyworts may
also be used.   There is, in fact, scarcely a limit to the choice one may
make from the more free and vigorous rock and alpine flowers, the
choice being governed by the nature of the soil, rainfall, and elevation,
or closeness to the sea, which is so often kind to plants slow or tender
in inland situations, like some of the grey Rock Scabious which form
such pretty marginal plants where they thrive.

PLASTERED MARGINS TO FLOWER BEDS.—Here is an illustration showing a wretched mud edging. These miniature ramparts, though less common than formerly, are a blot in London gardens and parks. They are made of muddy compounds, and in addition to the offensive aspect of the little walls when first plastered up, there are the cracks which come after—well shown in the cut. In a hot year, or any year, it is madness to cock the beds upon a little wall like this. The proper way to make a flower bed is to let the earth slope gently down to the margin, as was the practice for ages before this ugly notion came about.

Example of ugly cracked mud edging (London Park.)

Rocky border with edging of dwarf plants in groups.

Tufted Pansies.

CHAPTER XXVII.

THE FLOWER GARDEN IN THE HOUSE

ONE of the real gains in any flower garden worthy of the name is that we have in it lovely forms and delicate colours for the house, from the dawn of spring, with its noble Lenten Roses on sheltered borders, until autumn goes into winter in a mantle of Starworts. Many English and all German and French flower gardens in parterres offer us only Lobelias, and various plant rubbish of purplish or variegated hues, very few of them worth cutting, whereas our real flower garden is a store of Narcissus, Azalea, Rose, Lily, Tulip, and Carnation, and all the fairest things of earth. All we have to care about is placing them in simple ways to show their form as well as colour. Apart from the good plan of having a plot for the culture of any flowers we wish to cut for the house, a true flower garden will yield many flowers worthy of a place on an artist's or any other table, and worthy of it for their forms, colour, or fragrance. Many of these, from the Narcissus to the Tea Rose, give flowers so freely that we need not be afraid to cut; indeed, in many cases, careful cutting prolongs the bloom (as of Roses). Many shrubs we may improve as we cut their branches for the house, for example Winter Sweet, Forsythia, and Lilac.

It is not merely the first impression of flowers, good as it may be, that we have to think of, but the charms which intimacy gives to many of the nobler flowers—some opening and closing before our eyes, and showing beauties of form in doing so that we never suspected when

passing them in the open air.   In the changing and varied lights of a
house we have many opportunities of showing flowers in a more
interesting way, particularly to those who do not see them much out
of doors, and now we have in gardens many new flowers of great
beauty of form—Californian, Central Asiatic, Japanese, even the
mountains of China and India giving precious things, as well as the
rich flora of North America, as yet not as much seen in our gardens
as it deserves to be.   So that it will be seen how good is the reason
why care should be given to show the flowers in the house when we
have them to spare out of doors.

At first sight there may not seem much against our doing justice to
flowers in the house, but our flower vases have shared the fate of most

Rose in a Japanese bronze basin.

manufactured things within the past generation, *i.e.*, they suffer from
the mania for overdoing with designs, called "decorative," which
at the South Kensington schools is supposed to have some connection with "art."   Every article in many houses, being overcharged
with these wearisome patterns, it was not to be expected that the
opportunity of "adorning" our flower pots would be lost, and so we
may have ugly forms and glaring patterns, where all should be simple
in form, and modest and good in colour.   The coalscuttle, with its
"decoration," does not stand in our way so much as the flower vase,
as in this we have to put living things in their delicate natural colours
and shapes, and to look at these, stuck in vases with hard colours and
designs, is impossible to the artistic mind.

And when we have seen the ugliness of much of this work, what is to be done in the way of remedy as the shops are so much against us? The first need is a great variety of pots, basins, and jars or vases ; so that no flower that garden, wood, or hedgerow can give us, need be without a fitting vessel the moment it is brought into the house. What are known as the Munstead glasses are a great help, because their shapes are carefully made to suit various flowers, and they are very useful and good in form—made, too, of plain glass. But, however good this series is, it is well to use a variety of other things in any simple ware that comes in our way, very often things on the way to the rubbish heap, such as Devonshire cream jars in brown ware. Nassau seltzer bottles, in the brown ware too, may well take a single flower or branch, while old ginger pots, quite simple shallow basins in yellow ware, and other articles made for use in trade, come in very well.

Pæonies in Munstead glass.

There is no need to exclude finer or more costly things than these if good in shape and not outrageous in colour, but various reasons lead us to prefer the simpler wares, in which the flowers look often quite as well as in any others, though a mass of Edith Gifford Rose looks very well in a good old silver bowl, and good china, silver, or bronze vases or basins may be used for choice positions or occasions, though it will generally be best not to submit fine or fragile vessels of this kind to the risks of constant use. Among the finest things ever made in the shape of vases for cut flowers is the old Japanese work, which is often as lovely in form and as beautiful with true ornament as anything made by the old Greeks ; but the Japanese, like others, have taken to "potboiling" in bronze, and many of the things now seen at sales in London are coarse in workmanship. It might be worth while to have good and avowed reproductions of some of the more useful old forms—the slender, uprising ones are so good for many tall flowers ; Italian bronze bowls are often useful too ; and the darkness within the bronze vessels tends to keep the flowers longer than when they are in glass vessels exposed to the light.

Japanese ways of arranging flowers are extremely interesting, and may sometimes be practised with advantage; but, with a great variety and good shape of vessels, the Japanese way is not so necessary as a system, for the reason that, given a variety of good shapes and different materials, we can place any single flower, branch, or bunch in a way that it will look well with very slight effort and in very little time. Any way involving much labour over the arrangement of flowers is not the best for us or for the result—far from it.

Lenten Roses, February.

Having got a good and constant supply of flowers, and variety of vessels, the question of arrangement is the only serious one that remains to be thought of, and it is not nearly so difficult if we seek unity, harmony, and simplicity of effect, rather than the complexities which we have all seen at flower shows and in "table decorations," many of them involving much wearisome labour, while a shoot of a wild rose growing out of a hedge or a wreath of honeysuckle would put the whole thing to shame from the point of view of beauty. In all such matters laying down rules leads to monotony, and yet there is much to be said for ways distinctly apart from the old nosegay masses and the

modern jumble, and generally it is best to show one flower
at a time, especially if a noble one like the Carnation, which
varies finely in colour.   The baskets and basins of Carnations
arranged by the late Lady Henry Grosvenor, at Bulwick, were
lovely to see, and the best of them were of one Carnation of good
colour.   These were the flowers from her fine collection of outdoor
Carnations, so useful for cutting in summer and autumn, when
people are enjoying their gardens.   But the improved culture of
the Carnation as a plant for winter and spring bloom under glass
gives us quantities of this precious flower for six months more,

Mexican Orange-flower.

when the outdoor supply is over.   These are among the best
flowers for the dinner table as well as the house generally, and on
the dinner table the effect, by artificial or by natural light, of one or
two flowers of the season, is often better than that given by a
variety of flowers.   What is just said of the Carnation applies to
various noble groups of hardy flowers, such as the Tulip, Narcissus
and Lily.

It is not only in vases we see the good of showing one flower or
group at a time ; a good result will often come through a single
spray or branch of a shrub.   The Japanese have taught us to see

the beauty of form and line in a single twig or branch, with its
natural habit shown, apart from any beauty and form or colour
its flowers may have. This is important, in view of the many
shrubs that flower in our climate in spring, and of which, if flowering shoots are cut when in bud, the flowers open slowly and
well in the house. They are best placed in Japanese bronze or
other opaque jars. The taller Japanese bronze jars with narrow

Foliage of Evergreen hardy plant (Epimedium.)

necks are very useful for these, and it is an excellent practice to
cut the bud-laden shoots of Sloe, Plum, Apple, Crab, and like plants,
and put them in jars to bloom in the house. By this means we advance their blooming time; and, in the case of severe weather
the beauty of early shrubs may be lost to us unless we adopt this
plan. We see how well the French practice of growing Lilac in
the dwelling house prolongs the beauty of this shrub, and it is not
difficult to do something of the kind for the hardy shrubs and early

Y

trees that come with the Daffodils, but are not so well able to brave the climate   These shoots of early shrubs are also usually best arranged each by itself, though some go well together, and graceful leaves of evergreens may be used with them   One advantage of dealing with one flower at a time is that we show and do not conceal the variety of beauty we have   For, all thrown together, that variety will be much less evident than if we make clear the colour and form of each kind   Some proof of this may be seen in the work of the best flower painters.   In the work of M Fantin-Latour, for example, his nosegays of many flowers, evidently bought at some country market stand, are painted as well as his simple subjects but these last are far the best pictures.   However, there is such a wide range of plants, shrubs, and woodland and hedgerow flowers, that we must not hesitate to depart from any general idea if it tends to keep us from making the best of things in simple and ready ways

WATER LILIES AND WATER-SIDE PLANTS FOR THE HOUSE — Often the water and the water-side will give us fine things for house decoration, and the new Water Lilies of rare distinction help very much, as cut in the freshly expanded state they keep very well for some days and give us quite a new order of beauty.   For this purpose we want bold and simple basins, as if we can put some of their handsome leaves in with them the effect is all the better.   Although very fine in the open water, where they do admirably, the effect of the flower near at hand in the house is quite different and very beautiful, and as these plants increase their value as cut flowers for the house will be found to be great.   There are also plants of the water-side which may help with foliage or flower , one of the best being the Forget-me-not, which flowers so well in the house, and the great Buttercup.

LEAVES —Many as are the flowers of the open air excellent for house, the leaves of the open air tree or shrub or plant are hardly of less use for the same end : notably the foliage of evergreen shrubs in warm and sea coast districts, from evergreen Magnolia, Poet's Laurel, Cypress, Juniper and Thuja, Cherry Laurel, and Bamboo , even in the coldest districts we have the evergreen Barberry, and more than fifty forms of the best of all evergreen climbers, the Ivy, and the Holly with its scarlet, yellow or orange berries.   The trees in autumn give us leaves rich in colour—Maple, Medlar, Mespilus, Parrottia, Tulip-tree and many others.   The shrubs and climbers, too, help—Bramble, Wild Roses, Water Elder (Viburnum), Common Barberry, with its graceful rain of red berries , Vines in many forms ; hardy flowers, too, help with Acanthus, Alexandrian Laurel, Solomon's Seal, Iris, Plantain Lily, Rock plants are rich in good leaves : Cyclamen, Heuchera, Christmas and Lenten Roses, the large Indian Rockfoils and the Barrenworts; and then there are the hardy ferns of our own country and Europe, and also those of North America as hardy as our own.

A great help in a house is ready access to a handy water supply in a little room, near the flower garden or usual entrance for flowers, where vessels may be stored and flowers quickly arranged, used water and flowers got rid of and so planned that the mistress of the house, or whoever arranges the flowers, may use it at all times without other aid. This greatly helps in every way, and makes the arrangement of flowers for the house more than ever a pleasure.

The Chimney Campanula, Staunton Court.

CHAPTER XXVIII

EVERGREEN TREES AND SHRUBS.

"Oh the oak and the ash and the bonny ivy tree,
They flourish at home in my own country "—*Old Ballad*

THE above lines might be worth thinking of by those bent on planting evergreens for any of these uses, as if it were borne in mind that the evergreens we plant have to face winters in an Oak and Ash land, we should have less of the frightful waste owing to the planting of rampant but not hardy evergreens which perish in numbers after hard winters

There are no background hues prettier than afforded by some evergreens like the Yew, Box, and Ilex ; but their use requires care , we may have too many of them, and they should not take the place of flowering shrubs and flowers of many kinds It is outside the flower garden that evergreens are most useful generally, and in a cold country like ours, especially on the eastern coasts and in wind-swept districts, Holly banks and hedges of other hardy evergreens are often a necessity In our country we have the privilege of growing more evergreen shrubs and trees than continental countries, species resisting winter here which have not the slightest chance of doing so in Central Europe

NOBLE NATIVE EVERGREENS—Into our brown and frozen northern woods come a few adventurers from southern lands that do not lose their green in winter, but take then a deeper verdure—Ivy, Holly, and Yew enduring all but the very hardest frosts that visit our isles, some bright with berries as well as verdure ; giving welcome shelter to northern and wind-swept gardens, and in our own time each varying into many noble varieties These native evergreens and their varieties are, and for ever must be, the most precious of all for the British Isles

When after a very hard winter we see the evergreen trees of the garden in mourning, and many of them dead, as happens to Laurels, Laurustinuses, and often even the Bay, it is a good time to consider the hardiness and other good qualities of our British evergreens and the many forms raised from them. If we are fortunate

Old clipped evergreens, Berkeley Castle.

enough to have old Yew trees near us, we do not find that a hard winter makes much difference to them, even winters that brown the

evergreen Oak. We have collected within the past 200 years evergreen trees from all parts of the northern world, but it is doubtful if
any of them are better than the common Yew, which when old is
often picturesque, and which lives for over a thousand years   Of this
great tree we have many varieties, but none of them quite so good as
the wild kind when old   In the garden little thought is given to it
and it is crowded among shrubs, or in graveyards, where the roots are
cut by digging, so that one seldom sees it in its true character when old,
which is very beautiful.   The Golden Yew is a variety of it, and there
are other forms one of which, the Irish form, is well known, and too
much used

After the Yew, the best of our evergreen shrubs is the Holly,
which in no country attains the beauty it does in our own, certainly
no evergreen brought over the sea is so valuable not only in its
native form, often attaining 40 ft. even on the hills, but in the
varieties raised from it, many of them being the best of all
variegated shrubs in their silver and gold variegation, in fruit, too,
it is the most beautiful of evergreens.   Not merely as a garden tree is
it precious, but as a most delightful shelter around fields for stock in
paddocks and places which want shelter   A big wreath of old Holly
unclipped on the cold sides of fields is the best protection, and a
grove of Holly north of any garden ground we want to shelter is the
best evergreen we can plant ; the only thing we have to fear being
rabbits, which when numerous make Holly difficult to establish by
barking the newly-planted trees, and in hard winters even barking
and killing many old trees   As to the garden, we may make
beautiful evergreen gardens of the forms of Holly alone

Notwithstanding the many conifers brought from other countries
within the past few generations, as regards beauty it is very doubtful
if more than one or two equal our native Fir.   In any case few things
in our country are more picturesque than old groups and groves of the
Scotch Fir, few indeed of the conifers we treasure from other
countries will ever give us anything so good as its ruddy stems and
frost-proof crests

Again, the best of evergreen climbers is our native Ivy, and the
many beautiful forms that have arisen from it   This in our woods
arranges its own beautiful effects, but in gardens it might be made
more use of, and no other evergreen climber comes near it in value.
The form most commonly planted in gardens—the Irish Ivy—is
not so graceful as some others, and there are many forms varying
even in colour.   These for edgings, banks, screens, covering old trees,
and summer-houses, might be made far more use of   In many
northern countries our Ivy will not live in the open air, and we rarely
take enough advantage in such a possession in making both shelters,

wreaths, and screens of it. It requires care to keep it close on our houses and on cottage roofs or it will damage them ; but there are

Evergreen trees in natural forms (Cedars : Gunnersbury).

many pretty things to make of it away from buildings, and among them Ivy clad and Ivy-covered wigwams, summer-houses, and covered ways, the Ivy supported on a strong open frame-work.

Box, which is a true native in certain dry hills in the south of England, is so crowded in gardens, that one seldom sees its beauty as one may on the hills full in the sun, where the branches take a charming plumy toss   To wander among natural groves of Box is pleasant, and we should plant it in colonies by itself full in the sun, so that it might show the same grace of form that it shows wild on the chalk hills   It is, I think, the best of our native evergreens for garden use, making pretty low hedges as at Panshanger, for that purpose for dividing lines near the flower-garden it is better than Yew or Holly

Also among our native evergreens is the common Juniper, a scrubby thing in some places, but on heaths in Surrey, and favoured heaths elsewhere, often growing over twenty feet high and very picturesque, especially where mingled with Holly. The upright form, called the Irish Juniper, in gardens is not nearly so good as the wild Juniper though more often grown.

The Arbutus, which borders nearly all the streams in Greece, ventures into Ireland, and is abundant there in certain parts in the south   This beautiful shrub, though tender in midland counties, is very precious for the seashore and mild districts not only as an evergreen, but for the beauty of its flowers and fruit   Still, it is the one British evergreen which must not be planted where the winters are severe in inland districts, and usually perishes on the London clay

It is the best of our native evergreens that deserve the preference instead of the heavy Laurels, and various evergreens not even hardy, so that after a hard frost we often see the suburbs of country towns black with their dead

UGLY EVERGREEN TREES AND SHRUBS —One of the most baneful things in our gardens has been the introduction of distorted and ugly conifers which often disfigure the fore-grounds of beautiful houses   These are often sports and variations raised in modern days, as is the case with the too common Irish Yew   It is not only that we have to deplore the tender trees of California, which in their own country are beautiful, though, unhappily, not so in ours, but it is the mass of distorted, unnatural, and ugly forms—the names of which disfigure even the best catalogues—that is most confusing and dangerous   In one foreign catalogue there are no less than twenty-eight varieties of the Norway Spruce, in all sorts of dwarf and monstrous shapes—some of them, indeed, dignified with the name monstrosa—not one of which should ever be seen in a garden   The true beauty of the pine comes from its form and dignity, as we see it in old Firs that clothe the hills of Scotland, California, or Switzerland   It is not in distortion or in little green pincushions we must look for the charm of the Pine, but rather in storm-tossed head and often naked stems; and hence all these ridiculous forms should be excluded from gardens of any pretence to beauty

Another most unfortunate tree in this way, as helping to fill out gardens with graceless things, is the western Arbor vitæ (Thuja occidentalis) This, which is a very hardy tree but never a dignified one, even where it grows in the north about Lake Superior and through the Canadas, is, unhappily, also hardy in our gardens, and we may see in one catalogue no less than twenty-three forms of this tree all dignified with Latin names There are plenty of beautiful things, new and old, worthy of the name, without filling our gardens with such monstrosities, many of which are variegated Of all ugly things, nothing is worse than the variegated Conifer, which usually perishes as soon as its variegated parts die, the half dead tree often seeming a bush full of wisps of hay.

EVERGREEN WEEDS—In many once well-planted pleasure grounds the Pontic Rhododendron almost runs over and destroys every other shrub, and hides out the most beautiful tree effects, growing often a little above the line of sight. Even where people have taken the greatest trouble to plant a good collection of trees, the monotony of it is depressing, always the same in colour, winter or summer, except when dashed by its ill-coloured flowers. The walk from the ruins at Cowdray to the new house is an example that might be mentioned amongst a thousand others of a noble bank of trees, varied and full of beauty, but, in consequence of this shrub spreading beneath them all along the walk, showing nothing but a dank wall of evergreen. How this ugliness and monotony come about is through the use of the Pontic kind as a covert plant, and also owing to its facility of growth, the beautiful sorts of Rhododendron are usually grafted on it In a garden where there are men to look after plants so grafted and pull away the suckers, this plan may do, but when planting is done in a bold way about woods, or even pleasure grounds, this is not attended to, nor can it always be, so that the suckers come up and in time destroy the valuable sorts! The final result is never half so pretty as in the most ill-kept natural wood, with Bracken and Brier in fine colour and some little variety of form below the trees; therefore everybody who cares for the beauty of undergrowth should cease this covering of the ground with this poor shrub, not so hardy as the splendid kinds of American origin often grafted on it to die With the Cherry Laurel and the Portugal Laurel it is the main cause of the monotony and cheerless air of so many pleasure grounds.

The nurseryman who grows rare trees or shrubs very often finds them left on his hands, so that many nurseries only grow a few

stereotyped things, mainly those that grow freely, and, owing
to the over-use of weed-evergreens like Privet, which are without
beauty, and offensive in odour when in flower   The presence
of such things is one of the causes of the miserable aspect of the
shrubberies in many gardens, which might be very beautiful and
interesting with a varied life.   Many shrubs of little or no beauty
in themselves very often destroy by their vigour the rare and
beautiful garden vegetation, so that we have not only the ugliness
of a brake of Laurel, or half-evergreen Privet, or Pontic Rhododendron to survey, but often the fact that these shrubs have overrun and
killed far more precious things.   And this nursery rubbish having
killed every good thing begins to eat up itself, and hence we see so
many shrubberies worn out

THE NOBLER EVERGREEN FLOWERING SHRUBS.—It is not only
the ill-effect of these all-devouring evergreens we have to consider,
but what they shut out ·—the evergreen flowering shrubs and
trees of the highest beauty of colour as well as of foliage, and
the many hardy Rhododendrons of finest colour   If we would only
cease to graft them, and instead get them from layers on their own
roots, we should not be overcrowded with the R ponticum of the
present system   They are not only hardy in the sense that many of
our popular evergreens are hardy, i e in favoured districts or by the
sea, so kind as it is to evergreens, but everywhere in England   I
mean the many broad-leaved Rhododendrons which have mostly
come to us from the wild American species, and are hardy in North
and Eastern America.   Apart from the use of such things, by carefully selecting their colours we may have not merely an evergreen
background of fine and varied green, but also the most precious
flowering shrubs ever raised by man and in their natural forms, often
varying in fine colour and form too, if we will only cease to compel
them to live on one mean and too vigorous shrub

As to the kinds of Rhododendron that are raised from the Pontic
kind or even from the Indian Rhododendrons, so far as tried they are
not in any way so good as the varieties raised from the North
American kinds, and which have the fine constitution of R Catawbiense
in them, and of which many are hardy not merely in Old England
but in the much more severe winters of New England   Apart from
plants of these kinds from layers we may also have them as seedlings, though the named kinds from layers give us the means of grouping a finely coloured kind which may often be desirable   It is also
very probable that we shall, as various regions of the northern world
are opened up, introduce to cultivation other fine wild species, and get
precious races from them, so for many reasons the sooner we get out
of the common routine of the nurseries in grafting every fine kind we

already have on, R. ponticum, the better. And if this plan be wrong with the varieties, what are we to say to grafting any of the fine wild species that come to us on the same Pontic kind kept in every nursery for the purpose? For however vigorous the growth at first, the stock is sure to get its head in the end, and then good-bye to the precious natural species it has borne—for no sound reason

THE NOBLER EVERGREEN TREES —Apart from trees of poor forms, there are others which are stately in their own country but a doubtful gain to ours, like the Wellingtonia and other Californian trees, and the Chili Pine Sometimes the foregrounds of even fine old houses are marred by such trees, and unfortunately people use them in the idea that they are by their use doing something old-fashioned and "Elizabethan," whereas they are marring the beauty of the landscape and of our native trees, often so fine beyond the bounds of the garden We ought not to spoil the beauty of our home landscapes by using such things, which are so abundant in many places that the Nobler Exotic Evergreen Trees like the evergreen Oak are forgotten This European tree from Holkham in Norfolk to the west of England and in many gardens round the coasts of our islands, is a noble evergreen tree and a fine background and shelter

Then there is the Cedar of Lebanon, which is perhaps the finest evergreen tree ever brought to our country and as hardy as our own trees If we use evergreen trees they ought to be the noblest and hardiest The loss of this tree by storms could not happen to anything like the same extent if people went on planting young trees The many catalogues issued, help towards the neglect of the really precious trees by "bringing out" novelties from all parts of the world—absolutely unproved trees, whilst the planting of such grand trees as the Cedar of Lebanon and the Ilex of Europe are often forgotten A mistake in Cedar planting is the fashion of only planting isolated trees with great branches on all sides on enormous surface exposed to strong wind In their own country, where Cedars are naturally massed together, although the gales are severe, the trees are not destroyed by wind in anything like the same degree The Cedar of Lebanon is beautiful in the "specimen" way, but it is at least equally beautiful massed in groups In their own countries, in addition to being massed and grouped together, the soil is often stony and rocky, the growth is slower, and the trees take a firmer hold, whereas in our river valleys, where the Lebanon Cedar is often planted in an isolated way, the growth is softer and the resistance to wind less, and a more artistic and natural way of planting would lessen the accidents to which this noblest of evergreen trees is exposed.

SHELTER AND WIND SCREENS IN AND NEAR THE FLOWER GARDEN —Few countries are so rich in the means of shelter as our own, owing to the evergreens that grow freely with us and thrive in seashore and wind-swept districts Shelter may be near flower beds and distant or wind-breaks, across the line of prevailing winds, and the north and east winds, and may be of Yew, Holly, Cedar of Lebanon (never Deodar) native Fir, and a few other hardy Firs, and the Ilex.

In old times shelter was often obtained from clipped hedges of Yews and Limes, but the fine evergreen shrubs we now possess make it more easy and effective, as naturally grown shrubs soften the wind better than clipped lines, while often themselves beautiful in leaf and bloom.   There is, indeed, in gardens the danger of planting too densely at first, so that after some years the place becomes dank and the very house itself is made cheerless.   The pretty young conifers planted are not thought of as forest trees, and parts which should be in the sun are gradually overshadowed—a great mistake in a climate like ours

Among the kinds of shelter, walls, thickly clad with climbers, evergreens and others, are often the best for close garden work, because they do not rob the ground, as almost any evergreen tree will, and in doing their work, they themselves may bear many of our most beautiful flowers.   Half-hardy evergreens, like the common Cherry, Laurel and Portugal Laurel, should never be planted to shelter the garden, because they may get cut down in hard winters. But happily, even in the most exposed places, a good many hardy flowers may be grown with success, such as Carnations, Pinks, and many rock plants which lie close to the ground, and are therefore little exposed to wind, and thrive in exposed places where soil and cultivation are not against them.   English gardens are often well sheltered by the house itself and by old walls and enclosures, so that in old gardens it is easy to secure shelter for plants.

PLANTING NEAR THE SEA —Some are doubtful of planting near the sea, considering the bleak look of things and the cutting winds Yet even in places where the few trees that are planted are cut sharp off by the sea wind above the walls, as in Anglesea, we may see how soon good planting will get over difficulties that seem insurmountable By the use near the sea of small-leaved trees like the Tamarisks, Sea Buckthorn, and small Willows, we very soon get a bit of shelter, and by backing these with the close-growing conifers like our common Juniper and some of the sea-loving Pines like Pinaster, and in mild southern and western districts the Californian Cypress and the Monterey Pine, we soon get shelter and companionship, so to say, for our trees, and fifty yards away we may soon walk in woods as stately as in any part of the country.   Having got our shelter in this way the growth of the hardy Pines of the northern world seems as easy by the sea as anywhere ; indeed, more so, because if there is any one place where the rather tender Pines are grown well it is near the sea in places around our coast, where if the soil is good, one has not to be so careful about the hardiness of trees we select as we have to be in inland places

THE ILEX —The evergreen Oak takes a lead among the trees near the sea, and it ought to be largely used , but as it is not very easily transplanted from nursery-bought plants, it is just as well to raise it on the place and plant it young   Seed may be scattered with some advantage in places we wish it to grow in, as it grows freely from seed.

This evergreen oak withstood the great gales of 1897 in the south and west of England better than any other   At Killerton and Knightshayes, and many other places where the destruction was greatest I was glad to see that the evergreen oak was not among the many victims   It is a precious tree for the south and west, and all sea shore districts, and should never be forgotten among the crowd of novelties among trees , not one out of fifty is worth naming beside it Like many other trees, it suffers from indiscriminate planting with other and sometimes coarser things, and is rarely grouped in any effective way, although here and there, as at Ham House, Killerton, and St Anns we may see the effect of holding this tree together in groups or masses

In addition to the common evergreen trees of Europe, the Scotch, Spruce and Silver Firs, we have the noble Corsican Pine, which, from its habitat in Calabria and in Corsica, can have no objection to the sea   The Pines of the Pacific coast, too, are well used to its influences, and hence we see in our country good results from planting them near the sea, as, for example, Menzies' Spruce at Hunstanton, the Monterey Pine at Bicton, the Redwood in many places near the sea   One good result of planting in such places is that we may use so many evergreen trees, from the Holly to the Cedar, and so get a certain amount of warmth as well as shelter.

Though our country generally is not perhaps fitted for the growth of the Cork Oak, a fine evergreen tree, it is here and there seen in southern and sheltered parts on warm soils, as in certain parts of Devonshire and on the warm side of the Sussex Downs, even in good condition   Of this fact we have an example in the Cork Oaks at Goodwood, all that could be desired in health and beauty   This Oak naturally inhabits the southern parts of Europe and the northern parts of Africa, and it is interesting to see that it can attain the size of a stately tree in our own country in some favoured places, but the evergreen oak for our islands is the Ilex and its various forms

Some Genera of Evergreen Trees and Shrubs Hardy in the British Isles.[1]

Abies	Choisya	Euonymus	Magnolia	Rhododendron
Aralia	*Cistus	*Fabiana	Myrica	Rosmarinus
Araucaria	Cotoneaster	Garrya	Olearia	Ruscus
*Arbutus	Cratœgus	Gaultheria	Osmanthus	Sequoia
Arundinaria	Cupressus	Hedera	Pernettya	Skimmia
Aucuba	Daphne	Ilex	Phillyrea	Smilax
Azara	Daphniphyllum	Juniperus	Phlomis	Taxus
Bambusa	*Desfontainea	Kalmia	Phyllostachys	Thuja
*Benthamia	Diplopappus	Laurus	Pieris	Thujopsis
Berberis	Elœagnus	Ledum	Pinus	Ulex
Buxus	*Embothrium	Leiophyllum	Quercus	Veronica
Camellia	Ephedra	Leucothœ	Rhamnus	Viburnum
Cedrus	Erica	Libocedrus	Raphiolepis	Vinca
Cryptomeria	*Escallonia	Ligustrum	Retinospora	Yucca
Chamœrops				

[1] Some of those marked * are hardy only in seashore districts or warm soils, and in some genera named few species are evergreen.

Juniper showing natural growth.

CHAPTER XXIX.

" Vous travaillez pour ainsi dire à côté de Dieu, vous n'êtes que les collaborateurs de la loi divine de la végétation. Dieu, dans ses œuvres immuable, ne se prête pas à nos chimères ; la nature n'a pas de complaisance pour nos faux systèmes. Elle est souveraine, absolue comme son Auteur. Elle résiste à nos tentatives folles ; elle déjoue, et quelquefois rudement, nos illusions. Elle nous seconde, elle nous aide, elle nous récompense, si nous touchons juste et si nous travaillons dans son sens vrai ; mais si nous nous trompons, si nous voulons la violenter, la contraindre, la fausser, elle nous donne à l'instant même des dementis éclatants en faits par la stérilité, par le dépérissement, par la mort de tout ce que nous avons voulu créer en dépit d'elle et à l'inverse de ses lois."—LAMARTINE, DISCOURS AUX JARDINIERS.

CLIPPING EVERGREEN AND OTHER TREES.

THE Yew in its natural form is the most beautiful evergreen of our western world—finer than the Cedar in its feathery branching, and more beautiful than any Cedar in the colour of its stem. In our own day we see trees of the same great order as the Yew gathered from a thousand hills—from British Columbia, through North America and Europe to the Atlas Mountains, and not one of them has yet proved to be so beautiful as our native Yew when unclipped root or branch. But in gardens the quest for the exotic is so active that few give a fair chance to the Yew as a tree, while in graveyards, where it is so often seen in a very old state, the cutting of the roots hurts the growth, though there are Yews in our churchyards that have seen a thousand winters. It is not my own idea only that I urge here, but that of all who have ever thought of the beauty of trees, foremost among whom we must place artists who have the happiness of always drawing natural forms Let any one stand near the Cedar-like Yews by the Pilgrim's Way on the North Downs, and, comparing them with trees cut into fantastic shapes, consider what the difference means to the artist who seeks beauty of tree form !

What right have we to deform things so lovely in form ? No cramming of Chinese feet into impossible shoes is half so foolish as the wilful and brutal distortion of the beautiful forms of trees The cost of this mutilation alone is one reason against it, as we see where miles of trees cut into walls have to be clipped, as at Versailles and Schonbrunn, and this shearing is a mere "survival" of the day when we had very few trees, and they were clipped to fit the crude notion of "garden design" of the day. The fact that men when they had few trees made them into walls to make them serve their ways of "design" is no reason why we, rich in the trees of all the hills of the north, should go on mutilating them too

Thus, while it may be right to clip a tree to form a dividing-line or hedge, it is never so to clip trees grown for their own sakes, as by clipping such we only get ugly, unnatural forms Men who trim with shears or knife so fine a *tree* as the Holly are dead to beauty of form and cannot surely have seen how fine in form old Holly trees are To give us such ugly forms in gardens is to show one's self callous to beauty of tree form, and to prove that one cannot even see ugliness For consider, too, the clipped Laurels by which many gardens are disfigured. Laurel in its natural shape in the woods is often fine in form , but it is planted everywhere in gardens without thought of its fitness for each place, and as it grows apace, the shears are called in, and its fine leaves and shoots are cut into ugly banks and formless masses, spoiling many gardens. There is no place in which Laurel is clipped for which we could not get shrubs of the desired size that would not need the shears.

In the old gardens, where from other motives trees were clipped when people had very few evergreens, or where they wanted an object of a certain height, they had to clip. It is well to preserve such gardens, but never to imitate them If we want shelter, we can get it in various pleasant ways without clipping, and, while getting it, we can enjoy the natural forms of the evergreens Hedges and wall-like lines of green living things are useful, and even may be artistically used. Occasionally we find clipped arches and bowers pretty, and these, when very old, are worth keeping. Besides, there is much difference between evergreen archways or bowers, hedges, and shelters, and the fantastic clipping of living trees into the shapes of bird or beast or coffee-pot, and while it may be well to keep any old specimens of the sort when we find them, clipping is better not carried out with our lovely evergreens on a large scale.

Now and then we see attempts on the part of those having more knowledge of some half-mechanical grade of decorative "design" to galvanise the corpse of the topiary art. Such an idea would not occur to any one knowing the many beautiful things now within our reach, or by any one like a landscape painter who studies beautiful forms of earth or trees or flowers, or by any lover of Nature in tree or flower. Sometimes these puerilities are set into book form. For one author there is no art in gardening, but cutting a tree into the shape of a cocked hat is "art," and he says :—

I have no more scruple in using the scissors upon tree or shrub, where trimness is desirable, than I have in mowing the turf of the lawn that once represented a virgin world . . . and in the formal part of the garden my Yews should take the shape of pyramids, or peacocks, or cocked hats, or ramping lions in Lincoln green, or any other conceit I had a mind to, which vegetable sculpture can take.

After reading this I thought of some of the true "vegetable sculpture" that I had seen ; Reed and Lily, models in stem and leaf ; the Grey Willows of Britain as lovely against our British skies as Olives are in the south ; many-columned Oak groves set in seas of Primroses, Cuckoo flowers and Violets ; Silver Birch woods of Northern Europe beyond all grace possible in stone ; the eternal Garland of beauty that one kind of Palm waves for hundreds of miles throughout the land of Egypt—a vein of summer in a lifeless world ; the noble Pine woods of California and Oregon, like fleets of colossal masts on mountain waves—thought of these and many other lovely forms in garden and wood, and then wondered that any one could be so blind to the beauty of the natural forms of plants and trees as to write as this author does.

From the days of the Greeks to our own time, the delight of all great artists has been to get as near this divine beauty as what they work in permits. But this deplorable *vegetable sculptor's* delight is in distorting beautiful forms ; and this in the one art in which we have the happiness of possessing the living things themselves, and not merely representations of them. The old people from whom he takes his ideas were not so foolish, as when the Yew was used as a hedge or was put at a garden gate it was necessary to clip it to keep it in bounds. Apart from the ugliness of the cocked-hat tree or other pantomimic trees, the want of life and change in a garden made up of such trees, one would think, should open the eyes of any one to its drawbacks, as in it there is none of the joy of spring's life, or summer's crown of flowers, or winter's rest.

The plea that such work gives variety does not hold, because

z

English cottage garden with protecting fence. Showing right use of clipped Yew. Great Tew, Oxfordshire.

wherever labour and time are wasted upon such things the true work of the garden does not, and very often cannot, get the attention it needs. In few of the places where such work is done, is seen much of beauty in the garden—that is, beauty of flower and form and fine colour such as an artist would put in a picture, and which is a picture in itself to begin with.

THE ABUSE OF YEW HEDGES IN FLOWER GARDENS —In old days, whether in a manor house or castle garden, the use of Yew hedges had some clear motive of shelter or division, or clothing against massive walls as at Berkeley, or at a cottage door, as a living shelter   But when we use Yew hedges from the mere desire for them, and without much thought of the ground or other reasons, we may find ourselves in trouble. At a place where Roses were earnestly sought, the Rose borders were backed up close by Yew hedges ; the Yews were not very troublesome the first year or two, but, as they grew, they became merciless robbers   There are many ways of growing Roses, but it would be difficult to invent any worse way than this, which leaves the gardener always " between the devil and the deep sea," trying to keep back the hungry Yew roots all the while, it being quite easy to secure a background which, instead of eating up the Roses, would support and shelter them beautifully ; such as walls of solid or of open work, Oak palings, Bamboo and other trellises, or espaliers of bushy climbers, like Honeysuckle and Clematis. It is surely easy to enjoy the Yew without letting it eat up the very things we wish to cherish.

Another bad way is to place lines of Yew hedges so close together that the sun can hardly sweeten the ground between them, this being generally the result of carrying out some book plan, without thought of the ground or its use.   More stupid still is cutting up level lawns with Yew hedges across them, or sometimes projected into them a little way, with flower beds in between, within a couple of feet of the all-devouring Yew ·—and all this very costly Yew planting working for ugliness, and against the health, and even life, of all the flowers near   For ugliness distinctly, as while such broad and impressive Yew hedges as we see at Holme Lacy and in the older gardens are good in effect, it is quite different with small, hard Yew hedges, set one against the other and repeated *ad nauseam*

It is not only the needs of our own greatly increased garden flora —new races of plants never known to the old people, such as our tea Roses and the rich collections of shrubs from Japan and other countries, that will not bear mutilation or robbing at the root—that should make us pause, as, even in such evidence that remains to us of old flower gardens on ancient tapestries and pictures, we may see some evidence that the lady had room in her flower garden to look around and work among her flowers, unencumbered by a maze of robbing hedges. Some, perhaps, of these close lines of yews, set with such little thought, owe their origin to the maze idea ; but the maze was for a wholly different end, and in it we have only to grow its trees and the paths are free for the roots ; while in the rose and flower garden our costs and cares to get an artistic and beautiful result are too heavy to have them eaten up before our eyes by the hungriest of tree roots. If there were no other way to enjoy these evergreen trees, clipped or otherwise, one would not, perhaps, have so much to say against them ; but we have only to step out of the flower garden to indulge in the love of many evergreens to our heart's content.

CLIPPED EVERGREEN SHRUBS IN THE BEDS OF THE FLOWER GARDEN.—A gardener with shears in his hand is generally doing fool's work, but there is much difference between his clipping old or sheltering

Example of old topiary work.

lines of Yews, or even the Peacock in box, and the clipping which goes on in some gardens where beds are filled with small evergreen bushes instead of flowers. We may see it practised in gardens laid out by Paxton and his followers, their object being no doubt to get rid of the trouble of real flower-gardening, and also to have evergreen beds in winter. This effect may be obtained in a way, but the bushes usually get far too thick, and then the shears are used to keep them in bounds, and what ought to be graceful groups of flowers or shrubs of good form becomes flat, hard, and ugly. The clipping may be designed at first, but oftener it is done to repress overgrowth. A more stupid way of filling the beds of a flower garden could hardly be imagined, because we lose all the grace and form of the shrubs, and also the chance of seeing flowers growing among them, which is one of the prettiest phases of flower gardening when Lilies, Gladioli, and other graceful plants spring from groups of choice evergreens. The end of all this laborious mutilation is to cause disease and overcrowding, and the best thing is to clear the deformed things away and plant in more natural ways. If we want flower beds, .et us have them ; by doing so we can have varied life for more than half the year If we want beds of choice evergreens we can have them without destroying their forms by the shears There is a wide choice of beautiful things like Rhododendrons and Azaleas, and if we set these in open ways we can have flowers among them, thus doubling the variety of bloom obtainable from the surface, getting light and shade and the true forms of shrub or flower

THE DISFIGUREMENT OF FOREST TREES BY CLIPPING — Recently magazines and illustrated journals, in the great chase after subjects have dealt with the clipped gardens of England, and some of the most ridiculous work ever perpetrated in this way has been chosen for illustration Of English counties, Derbyshire is the most notorious for examples of disfigured trees. The Dutch, who painted like nature, and built like sane men, left their plantations to the shears, but they always cut to lines or had some kind of plan, judging from their old engraved books. British clipping, however, has one phase which has no relation to any plan, and so far it exceeds in extravagance the methods of the Dutch, Austrian, and French, and that is the clipping single, and often forest, trees into the shape of green bolsters The late Mr. McNab, of the Edinburgh garden, excellent planter though he was, had an idea that he kept his conifers in shape by clipping A false idea runs through all growers of trees of the pine tribe, the most frequent victims of the practice, that these' trees should be kept in a conical shape, the truth being that all the pine trees in the world in their state of highest beauty lose their lower branches, and show the beauty of their stem and form when growing in their natural way With a few exceptions, it is the way of these trees to shed their lower branches as other trees shed their leaves Even in countries where pines often stand alone, as on the foothills of California, I have often seen them with 100 feet or more of clean stem

Articles on this subject are usually of the see-saw sort, the writer praising and blaming alternately, and wabbling about like a blind man in a fair We are told that Elvaston, in Derbyshire, is not remarkable for natural beauty, and that the grounds there are so flat that landscape gardeners, in despair of any other planting, are compelled to have recourse to topiary work ; that "even that man of fame, 'Capability' Brown, seems to have shrunk from the work of laying out the grounds. Whereupon the earl demanded his reason, and Brown replied, 'Because the place is so flat,' &c "

Instead of there being any truth in the assertion that we cannot

make level ground beautiful by planting in natural ways, level ground
has a great deal in it that is favourable to artistic ways of planting
That is to say, with such ground we may more easily secure breadth,
simplicity, and dignity, get dividing lines in the easiest way, richer
soil and finer and more stately growth and nobler shelter   Many of
the most beautiful gardens of Europe are on perfectly level ground,
as Laxenberg in Vienna, the English garden in Munich, not to speak
of many in our own river valleys and in counties like Lincolnshire
What would be said of planting in all the flat countries of Northern
Europe if this assertion were true, to say nothing of the absurdity of
assuming that the only way out of the difficulty is in the stupid
disfigurement of trees?   I shall not imitate the example of these
writers in leaving the matter in doubt, but give some reasons against
the wasting of precious labour in order to rob trees of their natural
charm.   The old poets and satirists, who laughed at it, did not go
into the reasons against clipping big trees, which are serious nevertheless.

LOSS OF FORM.—First of all is the loss of tree form—a wonderful
and beautiful gift, so wonderful and beautiful, indeed, that the marvel
is that we should have to allude to it at all, as in nearly every parish
in England one has only to walk one hundred yards or so to come
face to face with fine examples of good tree form   There is more
strength and beauty of line in many an ash tree by a farmhouse yard
than in all the clipped forest trees in Britain   Some protest against
the cropping and docking of animals' ears and tails, but, when the
worst is done in that way, the dog or the horse remains in full beauty
of form in all essential parts, but if we clip a noble tree, which in
natural conditions is a lesson in lovely form in all its parts, we reduce
it at once to a shapeless absurdity.

LIGHT AND SHADE.—The second great loss is that of light and
shade, which are very important elements of beauty.   These are
entirely neutralised by shaving trees to a level surface, whether the
trees take the form of a line, or we clip them singly, as in the British
phase of tree clipping   If we see old examples of the natural yew,
a forest tree, and the commonest victim of the shears among evergreen
forest trees, and if we look at them in almost any light, we may soon
see how much we lose by destroying light and shade, as the play of
these enhances the force and beauty of all the rest.

COLOUR.—The third objection is the loss of refined colour.   In
gardens we are so much concerned with garish colour that we often
fail to consider the more delicate colours of nature, and such fine tone
as we see in a grove of old Yews, bronzed by the winter, or in Ilex
with the beautiful silver of the leaf, or a grove of coral-bearing Hollies
Even the smallest things clipped, such as juniper, have in a natural

way much beauty of colour if left alone. All the favourite trees for clipping are far more beautiful in colour in a natural state ; the loss of the stem colour alone is a great one, as we may see wherever old Yews show their finely-coloured stems

MOTION —In the movement of these trees stirred by the wind, and the gentle sighing of their branches, we have some most welcome aspects of tree life. In groves of Ilex, as at Ham House, and masses of the same tree, as at St Ann's, the effect of the motion of the branches is to many a beautiful one. This movement is also of great beauty in groves of old Yew trees, and is seen in every cedar and Pine that pillars the hills The voice of the wind in these trees is one of the most grateful sounds in nature, and has often inspired the poet.

> " I see the branches downward bent,
> Like keys of some great instrument "

And even when the storm is past we hear delicate music in the free pine tips

> " What voice is this ? what low and solemn tone,
> Which, though all wings of all the winds seem furled,
> Nor even the zephyr's fairy flute is blown,
> Makes thus for ever its mysterious moan
>   From out the whispering Pine-tops' shadowy world ?
>
> Ah, can it be the antique tales are true ?
> Doth some lone Dryad haunt the breezeless air,
> Fronting yon bright immitigable blue,
> And wildly breathing all her wild soul through
>   That strange unearthly music of despair?
>
> Or, can it be that ages since, storm-tossed,
> And driven far inland from the roaring lea,
> Some baffled ocean-spirit, worn and lost,
> Here, through dry summer's dearth and winter's frost,
>   Yearns for the sharp sweet kisses of the sea ? "

DEATH AND DISEASE OF THE TREES.—The fifth objection is that the constant mutilation of trees leads to death and disease not unfrequently, as may be seen constantly at Versailles. In the Derbyshire examples, recently so much illustrated, the stems of dead Pines are shown in the pictures ! It is simply an end one might expect from the annual mutilation of a forest tree, which the Yew certainly is, as we see it among the cedars on the mountains of North Africa, as well as in our own country and in Western Europe Other trees of the same great Pine order are yet more impatient of the shears, and some of them, like the cedar, escape solely because of their dignity. However, we distort the Yew, which is in nature sometimes as fine as a Cedar.

ANNUAL COST.—The sixth objection is that of cost Few

begrudge it if it gives a good result, but merely to use the labour of
scores of men with shears is to miserably waste both time and money
where there is so much of the country to be planted with beautiful
trees. Where, as often in the French towns, there is much clipping,
the waste of labour is as appalling as the result is hideous.

THE MAZE is an inheritance from a past time, but not a precious
one, being one of the notions about gardening which arose when
people had very little idea of the dignity and infinite beauty of the
garden flora as we now know it. Some people may be wealthy
enough to show us all the beauty of a garden and at the same time
such ugly frivolities as this, but they must be few. The maze is not
pretty as part of a home landscape or garden, and should be left
for the most part to places of the public tea-garden kind. One of its
drawbacks is the death and distortion of the evergreens that go to
form its close lines, owing to the frequent clipping ; if clipping be
neglected the end is still worse, and the whole thing is soon ready
for the fire.

Plan of Maze

CHAPTER XXX

AIR AND SHADE.

THE glorious sun of heaven, giver of life and joy to the earth, gives, too, the green fountains of life we call trees to shade her, and this beautiful provision might often be borne in mind in thinking of our often hard and bare gardens! Air and shade, as we cannot, near houses in hot weather, enjoy the shade without free air, and shade may be often misused to cultivate mouldiness and keep the breeze away from a house, though it is very easy to have air and shade in a healthy way To overshade the house itself with trees is always a mistake, and sometimes a danger, though even against a house, by the use of climbers, like Vines, pretty creeper-clad pergola, and by the wise use of rooms open to the air, creeper-shaded, flat spots on roofs, so often seen in Italy and France, it is easy to have welcome shade even forming part, as it were, of the house. We have the gain, too, of the grace and bloom of the climbers, from climbing Tea Roses to Wistaria, and we get rid of the bald effect of such houses as Syon and the excruciating effect of the newer French châteaux, often on the warm side without gardens or shade of any kind, and hard as a new bandbox

A little away from the house, shade of a bolder kind is always worth planning for. In planting for shade it is well to select with some care and avoid things that have a bad odour when in flower, like the Ailantus and the Manna Ash and ill-smelling undergrowth like Privet In many places there is a fine field for cutting groups of pleasant shade trees out of the crammed shrubbery, neglected as that so often is, with dark barriers of Laurel, Privet, and Portugal Laurel. Nothing is easier than sweeping off and burning much of this evergreen rubbish, and getting instead shade over cool walks, or over paths leading through Ferns and Foxgloves, such woodland plants allow us to get light and shade and do not weaken the trees.

Vain attempts are often made in our gardens, public and private, to get grass to grow under certain trees which it would be much better to frankly accept as they are and gravel the spaces beneath

them for use as playground or for seats.   In dealing with such trees we
must be unsparing in cutting off the lower boughs, which are rarely
of much use to the tree and often impede the air and movement
underneath ; they should be cut carefully to an airy but not hard
line.

Wych Elm on Lawn at Oak Lodge, Kensington.

Where the flower garden is small we may rightly object to much
shade in it, and must get as much as we can outside it.   In many
cases in open lawn gardens, where we may pass easily from the flower
beds into grassy, open ground near, we may have delightful groups of
shade trees not far from the flowers, and this sort of garden, of which

there are so many in the level country, is that which is perhaps the most easy of all to keep cool, airy and sunny too

But in large open flower gardens, which are often bare and hard, it is better to have some light shade   Great areas of gravel and flat beds everywhere are most tiresome to the eye, and in many large flower gardens, it would be an improvement to have covered ways of Rose and Jasmine or wreaths of Clematis and alleys of graceful trees such as the Mimosa-leaved Acacia, or other light and graceful trees   In that way we should get some of the light and shade which are so much wanted in these large chessboard gardens, and in getting the shade we might also get trees beautiful in themselves, or carrying wreaths of Wistaria or other climbers.

Among the most beautiful shade-giving trees are the weeping ones, which in our own day are many and beautiful, among them, the Weeping Ash, of which we see many trees even in the London squares   We are all so busy with exotics from many parts of the world, that the native tree does not always get a fair chance, and yet no deciduous tree ever brought to our country is for form and dignity finer than the mountain or Wych Elm.   Trees over twenty feet round are not rare, and, being a native of the mountains of Northern England, its hardiness need never be in doubt.   This tree is the parent of the large-leaved Weeping Elm (of which there are so many good trees to be seen), and the wild tree itself in its old age has also a weeping habit.   But the weeping garden form is quite distinct and a tree of remarkable character and value, and like other weeping trees, it increases in beauty with age, like the grand old Weeping Beeches at Knaphill.   The various Weeping Willows afford a welcome shade, and the White Willow and any of its forms give a pleasant light shade'

A fine kind of shade is that given by a group of Yews on a lawn near the house on a hot day—a living tent without cost, and this is almost true of any spreading tree giving noble shade, as the great Oak in the pleasure ground at Shrubland   There are many noble Horse Chestnuts which give great shade, as at Busbridge, and the Plane tree in Southern England gives noble shade.

There is no more beautiful lawn tree than the Tulip tree, and nothing happier in our country on an English lawn, in which its delightful shade and dignity are very welcome in hot weather, as at Esher Place and Woolbeding   Petworth also has a fine tree, but rather closed in by others.   Owing partly to the attractive catalogues of conifers and other trees not of half the value of this from any point of view, young trees of these fine deciduous things are not so often planted as they used to be ; and why should not a tree like this be grouped now and then, instead of being left in solitary state ?

Trees with light shade might be welcome in certain districts, among the last being various Acacias, of which the common old American is good, while several beautiful varieties have been raised in France, light, elegant trees, especially the Mimosa-leaved one   In warm soils this would grow well and give very light shade   There are so many rapid-growing trees that in places devoid of shade trees it would not be difficult to establish some soon.

Those who have small gardens, and cannot have them robbed by the roots of trees, may get shade from climbers and often great beauty of flower from the climbers that give the shade   It is curious how little use is made of the Vine, with its beauty of leaf and form, for covered ways, loggias, and garden houses, not only in the country, but in town also   It is one of the best of plants for covering the fronts of houses, and good Vines spring out of London areas far below the level of the street, where it would be difficult to imagine worse conditions for the aeration of the soil or its fertility.   These remarks apply not only to the common Vine, valuable though it is with all its innumerable varieties, but to the wild Vines of America and Japan, some of which are fine in foliage and colour

The last few years we have seen so many hot seasons that one turns to the Continental idea of shade in the garden with more interest ; and why should we not have outdoor loggia and Vine-covered garden rooms ?   We do not only neglect the outdoor shaded structures, but the even more essential loggia forming part of the house   A garden room entered from the house, and part of it, is a great comfort, and may be made in a variety of pretty ways, though never without provision for a few light graceful climbers.

After all is said about shade, the most essential thing about it in British gardens is not to have too much of it.   Most of us plant too thickly to begin with , the trees get too close and we neglect to thin them, the result being mouldy, close avenues, dripping, sunless groves, and dismal shrubberies, more depressing than usual in a wet season   It is only when we get the change from sun to shade with plenty of movement for air that we enjoy shade.   We cannot feel the air move in an over-planted place, and there are in such no broad breadths of sunlight to give the airy look that is so welcome.   Over-planting is the rule ; the regular shrubbery is a mixture fatal to the play of light and shade and air, and not only the sun is shut out, but often many beautiful views also

Very harmful in its effect on the home landscape is the common objection to cutting down, or ill-placed trees crowded to the detriment of the landscape and often to the air and light about a house   The majority of the trees that are planted in and near gardens are planted in ignorance of their mature effects, the landscape beauty of half the

Air and shade : Type of weeping native lawn tree.

country seats in England being marred by unmeaning trees and trees out of place I have known people who wanted to remove a solid Georgian house rather than take down a tree of modeiate dimensions which made the house dark and mouldy and obscured the view of far finer trees beyond it, and it is not long since a man wrote to the *Times* after a storm to say that one of his Elm trees had fallen through the dining-room ceiling when he was at luncheon, and that Elms were not good trees to put over the house !

Where without the limits of the garden there are drives through old mixed or evergreen woods, like the Long Cover at· Shrubland or the drive at Eastnor, it is important not to let the undergrowth close in on each side, as trees are very apt to do. It is difficult to give an idea of the difference in the effect of such a drive when " light and shade " are let into it, and when, as is commonly the case, the Yew, Box, and other things are clipped back to hard walls, good views, fine trees, and groups being all shut out by this neglect. It is better never to clip in such cases, but always to work back to a good tree or group, cutting encroachers clean out of the way, and so getting room for the air to move, the shade of the trees above being sufficient in each case The pleasure of driving or walking is much greater when the air is moving, and when one can see here and there into the wood on each side, with perhaps groups of wild flowers and beautiful views into the country beyond.

The old fashion of having plashed alleys near· the garden, of which there are good examples at Hatfield, Drayton, and other old gardens, was a pretty one, but as done with vigorous Lime trees it was troublesome and laborious work to keep down the vigour of such forest trees which, in point of looks, were not in any way the best to use for the purpose. However charming those old covered walks are it is well to remember that we have much nobler things for forming them now, that do not want cutting back, and that are beautiful in foliage and bloom. It is also well in planting such things to see that the shaded alley is sufficiently high and airy There is no reason why it should not be made reasonably big, especi- ally as we have noble climbers to cover it that do not keep rushing up in the air like the Lime and other forest trees which were used for this purpose in old times, when there were few trees to select from, and when probably the quick growth of the Lime was the cause of its selection Its shade in this cut-down form is not so pleasant as the nobler climbers, which will cause no trouble in springing above the surfaces we wish them to cover.

PLANTING IN LIGHT AND SHADE.—This helps to get us out of the hard ways in which flowers are set in gardens There is too sharp a line between the open parterre and the shady grove

There are no gardens surrounded by more pleasant groves than English gardens generally, even small gardens having their belt of

Air and shade : Shaded walk, Belvoir.

trees, with opportunities for flower grouping in light and shade, but now for the most part occupied bye heavy vergreens, massed together and preventing all chance of light and shade, and even shutting out air and beauty.

We cannot do much good, in such cases, unless we first destroy the Privet and facile evergreens, like Laurels, which overrun everything, and then comes the question of the plants which will grow best in such places, as shade in gardens varies whether it comes from light-leaved or heavy-leaved trees, and there are so many different degrees of shade. We should think of the plants that grow in woody places naturally, as in our woods we may see handsome tall Grasses, Foxgloves, large Ferns, herbaceous plants like the French Willow and the Ragwort, tall Harebells, and many ground plants like Primroses and Bluebells There is not any hard and fast line between plants that grow in shady places and other herbaceous plants, although some difference exists, and there are so many varieties of climate, elevation, and conditions of soil that the plants often vary in their ways. Foxgloves and Bracken, which are seen happy in the woods of the south, thrive on sunny rocky places in the north, so that there is an interplay among these things which helps us in making our gardens more varied. Not only we have to consider wood plants, but the fact that a great many plants of the northern world grow in partial shade, and we could arrange our borders, if we get out of stiff ways, so as to let the plants often run from the light into the shade

In making borders through groves or shrubberies, it would be easy to have no hard line at the back of the border, but simply let the plants run in and enjoy the shade here and there. Where there might be some doubt of choice herbaceous plants thriving in shade there need be no doubt as to the larger woodland ferns and such plants as Solomon's Seal

Among the interesting plants that thrive in shade are alpine and mountain plants. Many of these, being shrouded in clouds and enduring much rain in cool gorges, very often rejoice in shady places, as the varieties of the Irish Rockfoil (Saxifraga Geum), which carpet the ground in places that the sun never touches. Other Rockfoils have the same habit, including the large Indian kinds and their varieties. The Irises are often very beautiful in half-shady places, German Irises especially. By planting, too, in various aspects, shade and open, we get a succession of favourite flowers, that under a hot sun last but a short time. In the cooler light their colours have a greater charm—the blues more tender, the deeper colours still richer.

Pæonies are never handsomer than in subdued light, their colours richer and longer lasting than when bleached by the sun. This is true especially of the frailer single forms, which open out quickly under a hot sun and are gone all too soon. Many beautiful plants are happiest in the shade—not too dense—but where the sun's rays filter through the tree-leaves. Gardens of great beauty may be made in the shade—gardens of greater charm than those who know not the store of plants for this purpose little dream of, and not confined to the hardy plant alone, but including also shrubs as well—as the hardy Azaleas. These are never so fine as when seen in shady or half shady places in a wood, as at Dropmore and Coolhurst, their colours more intense from the subdued light, and the flowers more lasting in the shade. Air, shade, and light are a trinity essential about a country house, and we cannot enjoy any one of them unless some thought is given to all.

Sun and Shade. (The Hoo, Welwyn).

A A

CHAPTER XXXI

LAWNS AND PLAYGROUNDS.

THE lawn is the heart of the true British garden, and of all forms of garden the freest and, may be, the most varied and charming, adapted as it is to all sorts of areas from that around the smallest house. It is above all things the English form of garden made best in the rich level valley land, and, with the least amount of trouble and labour to make or keep it, certainly gives the best result in effect. The terrace garden we have seen, in its origin and best meaning, arises from wholly different sort of ground from that on which we make a lawn. If the Italians and others who built on hills to avoid malaria had had healthy and level ground they would have been very glad of it, and thought it beautiful. With the lawn there is little or no trouble in securing fine background effects, variety, pretty dividing lines, recesses for any favourites we may have in the way of flowers, freedom, relief, air and breadth. There is room on the lawn for every flower and tree, from the cedar, and the group of fruit trees planted for the beauty of their flowers and fruit, down to rich beds of lilies or smaller flowers.

One of the most foolish dogmas ever laid down about a garden is that made in a recent book by an architect, in which we are told emphatically that there is no such thing as a garden to be made except within four walls. Many of the most beautiful gardens in the British Isles are without any aid but a background of trees and evergreens, and no trace of walls, which are absolutely needless in many situations to get the most artistic results in a garden. And lovely gardens may be made around lawns without marring the breadth and airiness which is the charm of a lawn, or in the least interfering with the use of its open parts as a playground.

CLIMBER-COVERED ALLEYS AROUND PLAY LAWNS.—Where there is space enough there are reasons in country places for

cutting off by a hedge a playground from the garden or pleasure
ground, as is done at Madresfield and Campsey Ash and many of the
older gardens; and what is used generally is the yew or holly, but
clipped hedges give little shade and no flowers. Now, in the like
position, if we adopt the pergola, we get shade, and many graceful
flowers. Clematis, tall roses, wistaria, and almost every beautiful
climber could be grown thereon, some better than on walls, because we
can allow more *abandon* than on walls, and it is not at all so easy to
crucify vine or climber on a pergola. We can have evergreens too if
we wish, with garlands of handsome ivies among them, and players

Chambers Court, Tewkesbury. From a photograph sent by Mrs. Ward, Tewkesbury.

might rest in the shade and lookers on sit there to see the play.
Various bold openings should be made on the play lawn side, and the
whole so arranged as to be a sort of living cloister. Well done,
the structure might be, apart from its shade and coolness and use as
a dividing line, a garden of a very graceful kind, while the recent
hot seasons lead one to think that the Italian way of putting a roof of
vine leaves between one's self and the sun is worth carrying out in our
own country.

Pergolas have various uses in covering paths which are too much
exposed to the sun, and are a great aid in the garden, and there is no
better way of growing beautiful climbing plants than a green covered

way, whether supported by oak posts, or brick or stone pillars as in Italy.

The ordinary covered ways made in England of plants are often too narrow and "pokey" In forming all such things a certain amount of freedom is essential; and we cannot enjoy the air in the usual narrow covered way, which, apart from its own error as to size, is also soon narrowed by growth. It should always be made at least wide enough for two people to be able to walk abreast. Where oak is not distinctly preferred, 14 in brick pillars are best, and the plants take to them very soon   Common brown or rough stock bricks are far better for this use than showy red bricks the last being often too the most costly. In stone districts stone would do as well or better, and it needs no fine dressing or designing after any pattern. It is better in fact done in the free way the Italians do it; but then in Italy every man is a mason, or knows what to do with stone, and also the stone there comes out in long posts or flakes, which serve as posts   This is also the case in the north of England, where beautiful posts of the green stone may be seen in use on the farms. In Cornwall, too, it would be easy to have stone pillars   We are in the iron age and many resort to iron, ugliest of all materials; but if simply done and not disfigured with galvanised wire, even iron may help our purpose if painted carnation green or some other quiet colour. If we use iron, we may take from its hardness by tying wooden trellis work over it, which is better for tying the climbers to than iron or wire, using the most enduring wood we have for this purpose   For this an excellent aid will be found in the bamboo stakes which now come in quantities to our ports as underpacking for sugar cargoes. These are sold in quantity at a reasonable rate, and are an excellent aid in making the iron pergola wired across and along the iron supports. Thus we get an enduring material, good in colour and excellent to tie the shoots of rose, clematis, or vine to.

The beautiful climbing shrubs and other plants that would find a good congenial home on such a pergola are a good reason for its use. Among them various graceful forms of our grape vine, as well as the Japanese and American wild vines, a group which now includes the Virginian creepers of our gardens, which are also useful, but not so good as the true vines , the lovely Wistaria, and not only the old Chinese kind, the best of all, but the beautiful Japanese long-racemed kind (*W. multijuga*), and various others too, though we think none come near to these in beauty , the brilliant flame Nasturtium in cool districts, and where light shade is desired , the green briar (Smilax) of America, and also the South of Europe, for warm soils; handsome double and white-stemmed brambles; wild and single roses; box thorn, with its brilliant showers of berries; European, American and Japanese honeysuckles, jasmines; over fifty kinds of ivy, the noblest of northern and evergreen climbers; evergreen thorn, with its bright berries, cotoneasters of graceful habit; clematises, especially the graceful wild kinds of America, Europe, and North Africa. In mild districts particularly, the winter blooming clematis of North Africa and the Mediterranean Islands, which flowers in winter or early spring, would be very pretty and give light shade. The showy trumpet flowers (*Bignonia*), quite hardy in southern and midland counties; and the Dutchman's pipe (*Aristolochia*), with its large leaves, would also be useful. The fine-leaved Lardizabala of Chili, the brilliant coral barberry of the same country (*Berberidopsis*); the graceful, if not showy silk vine (*Periploca*) of Southern Europe; the Chinese Akebia, the use of the rarer climbers depending much on the climate, elevation, soil, and nearness to the sea.

THE PLASHED ALLEY is an alternative to the yew hedge and the covered way, but in some Elizabethan gardens it was often planted with trees of too vigorous growth, such as the lime, which led to excessive mutilation and eventual distortion of the tree. Now, with our present great variety of trees—some of them very graceful and light in foliage—it is by no means necessary to resort to such ugly mutilation, and it would be easy, as an alternative to the pergola, the clipped hedge or the plashed alley, to have a shaded walk of medium-sized or low trees only. These might even be fruit trees, but the best would be such elegant-leaved trees as the acacias, which preserve their leaves for a long time in summer. One drawback of the lime, in addition to its excessive vigour, is the fact that it sheds its leaves very early in the autumn, and, indeed, we have often seen the leaves tumble off in St. James's Park at the end of July, and in Paris also. It is most unpleasant to have in an alley a tree which is liable to such an early loss of its leaves. The common lime is a tree of the mountains and cool hills of Europe, and it cannot endure great heats and hot autumns; whereas some of the trees of North America and other countries are quite fresh in the hottest days. Among these none is better than the acacia, of which, in France especially, a number of elegant varieties have been raised, as hardy as the parent species which charmed William Cobett, but more graceful in foliage. Among the best of these is the mimosa-leaved acacia, an elegant tree, which gives us a pleasantly shaded walk, and yet is not likely ever to become too coarse in habit.

FINE TURF IN AND NEAR THE FLOWER GARDEN.—Fine turf is essential in and near the house and garden—turf wholly apart from the open park or playground. Flower beds are often set in turf, or there are small grassy spaces near the house or the garden, on the good effect of which depends very much the beauty of the home landscape, as coming so much into the foreground of what should be pictures One reason why we should take care to get the best turf which the conditions of soil or climate allow is that no other country but ours can have such good turf. In many countries, even in Europe, they cannot have it at all, but grass seed has to be sown every year to get some semblance of turf. Where, however, our natural advantages are so great, our care should be to get the full benefit of them ; and though in many places the turf, through the goodness of the soil, is all that could be desired even in Britain, in others a very poor turf is often seen, and much effort is often given in vain attempts to get a turf worthy of a flower garden.

Many people think that any rough preparation will secure them a good sward, and merely trench and turf the ground , even experienced ground workmen fail to get a fine turf for the flower garden, though they may lay turf well enough for a cricket ground. Others think that turf will come of itself, but are often rudely disappointed , and therefore some instructions as to the best way of laying down turf, where the work has to be done from the beginning, and also for repairing it when out of order, may be useful to some readers The following is written by Mr. James Burnham, who has made for me some of the most beautiful garden lawns I have seen, some of them laid in hot spring weather

"FORMATION OF GOOD TURF —Should the spot chosen be on heavy soil, such as clay, take the levels and fix them 16 feet apart around the outside of the piece intended for a lawn Take some levels across the piece, then take 12 inches of earth out below the levels. Should any of these 12 inches contain good soil, wheel that on to the outside of the piece, removing all the clay to a place near and burning it into ballast, using slack coal Find the natural fall of the ground, and place pegs 16 feet apart in lines from top to bottom the way it falls, then dig out the soil in line of pegs with a draining tool, 12 inches deep at top end, bottom end 18 inches deep This will give a fall of 6 inches. Then lay in 2-inch drain pipes, with a 3-inch pipe at the bottom end for a main to take the water that drains from the sub-soil See that this main is taken to some outlet Cover the pipes with 3 inches of burnt ballast, and spread 3 inches of burnt ballast all over the piece of ground. Dig the ground over 12 inches deep, at the same time mixing the 3 inches of burnt ballast with the clay, taking care not to disturb the pipes or dig below them. After treading all over firmly, place on the surface 2 inches of burnt ballast, filling to the level with loam mixed with the good soil you have laid on one side from the surface   If you have no good soil, fill up with loam mixed with coarse gravel, brick rubbish, and burnt ballast.   Tread all over again as before, making it level with a spade, pressing in any lump or stone that appears level with the ground.   No rake should be used.   You have now 2 feet of trenched earth.   Do not dig down deeper in one place than another   A stick cut 2 feet long by the worker's side is the best   He can, with the stick, test his depth from time to time.

In laying the turf keep the joints of each piece half-an-inch apart. When it is all laid down pat it gently all over with a turf-beater.   It is better to take up the turf that is a little higher than the rest and take out a little of the soil than to beat it down to the level.   Then spread some burnt ballast, ashes from the burnt refuse of the garden, and the top 2 inches of soil from the wood, sifted through a half-inch mesh sieve, mixed well together, all over the grass   Move it about until all the joints in the turf are level.   Wait for rain, then go over the lawn and take out all weeds   Give another dressing of the soil as before, adding to this a little road grit and old mortar   If no old mortar is available, slaked lime will answer.   Move this about until all is level again   In the month of March or the first week in April, if the weather is fine, sow all over the lawn some of the best lawn grass seed.   Get some fine Thorn bushes and lace them together in the shape of a fan heavy enough for two men to drag about the lawn in various ways.   Roll with a light roller, and keep off the lawn until the grass has grown 3 inches, then cut it with a scythe.   Roll with a light roller the first season, and when mowing with the machine is commenced, see that the knives are not set too close to the ground.

Should the ground selected for turf not contain clay, so much the better   Dig holes here and there 2 feet deep in the winter months   If no water lies at the bottom of the holes, this shows it will not want artificial draining ; if there is water drain as on heavy soil.   In trenching the ground, if the subsoil be bad, take 3 inches of this away, filling up to the level with good soil, to which have been added half-inch crushed bones in the proportion of four tons to the acre, fine brick rubbish and burnt ballast in the same proportions as for the heavy soil   Turf and treat as on heavy soil.   If you have a good grass field, take the turf for your lawn, also top spit away, replace with rough soil, and place 3 inches of the loam that has been dug out upon the rough soil you have put in, then sow, bush harrow, and lightly roll

TREATMENT OF OLD LAWNS —Weeds, moss, and bare places on lawns show that they are worn out   To remedy this, take off the turf in rolls 3 feet long, 1 foot wide, and 1 inch thick.   If the turf cannot be rolled, take 6 inches of the surface away, then trench 2 feet deep, keeping the good soil on the top as you proceed. Tread firmly all over and fill up to the level with good soil ; mix with the loam, burnt ballast, old brick rubbish, half-inch crushed bones, and road sidings or sweepings. Then turf and treat as in the case of new lawns. On old lawns there are very often handsome deciduous trees too close to which it would be dangerous to trench   To get grass to grow under these, take away 2 inches of the exhausted soil, replace with good, and sow thereon grass seed thickly. Rake the seed in gently, roll it lightly, and water when necessary. This may be repeated in the same way as often as the soil under the trees becomes bare

In some cases where turf is scarce, a roll of turf 3 feet long and 1 foot wide may be taken and cut in half lengthways. With this form the outlines of the beds, which have been staked out previously, beat down to the level required, and bring up the intervening spaces to the level of the turf with good soil   Make this firm, rake it level, and on this sow some good grass seed. Bush harrow it over, roll lightly, and protect from birds where these are troublesome. Cut the grass when 6 inches high with a scythe, and keep it well watered during the summer if the weather is dry.   In this way a beautiful lawn may be had at little expense as compared with turfing it completely over

LAWNS ON PEATY AND SANDY SOILS —In some parts of Hampshire and Surrey, where peat and sand abound, seeds are by far the best to use to form a good turf   Remove all peat from the site you wish for a lawn, pile it on the outside of the work and cast plenty of water upon it.   Then take out 2 or 3 inches of the dark sand that lies under the peat, and cast this also over the pile of peat. Take out 12 inches of the sand, dig all over 12 inches deep and tread it firmly. Get all the road scrapings and road trimmings to be had with a little clay and stiff loam, and cast upon the peat pile. Having got together the quantity you think will fill up to your level, cut up small the peat you have in the pile and mix all well together with this, fill up to the level, tread firmly all over, then give everywhere a good coating of cow manure, turned 3 inches under the surface, and tread firmly all over   In the month of March sow thickly.   Do not let the surface get dry the first summer, and cut the grass when 6 inches high with a scythe.

Attention should be paid to keeping all lawns free from weeds. Dress lawns once a year with one bushel of salt mixed with fourteen bushels of wood ashes not too much burnt, using for this purpose refuse, underwood, waste faggots, old laurels or other condemned shrubs. When you see the wood is consumed spread the ashes abroad and cover them with good soil. Break the charred wood small, mix all well together, do not sift, spread upon the lawn, and roll it in."

Lawn Garden, Herts. Engraved from a photograph by Mr. Newman, Berkhampstead.

Stone bench (Dropmore).

CHAPTER XXXII.

FLOWER GARDEN AND PLEASURE GROUND HOUSES, BRIDGES, SEATS AND FENCES.

THE first thing to be thought of in all building, apart from the house itself, is the absolute need of the structure, as there has been much effort lost in useless garden buildings, and no way of garden over-doing is so full of waste and ugliness. Recently we have seen attempts to revive the old garden houses, but the result has not often been happy. In old houses like Hatfield and Montacute, the little houses near the gate often had a true use at the entrance side, but now we see such things revived for the mere sake of carrying out a drawing, and as soon as built we see the aimlessness of the work, and then comes the difficult question of "planting it out" from different points of view. Isolated building in a garden is difficult to do with any good result, though at one period the building of temples was very common in pleasure gardens, and many of them are still to be seen. It is best, when these are of good form and structure, to keep them with care and make some simple use of them, by removing at once all suggestion of the grotto and having simple oak benches or other good seats. The interior also should be made simple in colour and free from covert for woodlice or earwigs. It is in connection with the house, or part of its lower storeys, that garden shelters, loggias and the like may be most effectively made ; of this we see examples at North Mymms and Bramshill, and where they give shade or a "garden room' as part of the house they are a real gain.

BRIDGES.—Few things about country houses and gardens are worse in effect and construction than the so-called "rustic work." It is complex and ugly as a rule, its only merit being that it rots away in a few years. It is probably at its worst in garden chairs, "summer" houses, and rustic bridges. An important rule for bridges is *never* to make them where they are not really needed, though the opposite course is followed almost in every place of any size where there is water. On rustic bridges over streams, natural or otherwise, there is much wasted labour. A really pretty bridge of a wholly different sort I saw once with the late James Backhouse near Cader Idris on a

Tree bridge over streamlet. From a photograph by M. Philippe de Vilmorin.

farm which had a swift stream running through it, to cross which some one had cut down a tree that grew near, and had chopped the upper side flat and put a handrail along it. Time had helped it with Fern, Lichen, and Moss, and the result was far more beautiful than is ever seen in more pretentiously "designed" rustic bridges. It is not, however, the far prettier effects we have to note, but the advantage which comes from strength and endurance. It looked very old and Moss-grown, and no doubt it is there now, as the heart-wood of stout trees does not perish like the sap-wood of the "rustic"- work maker. The sound oak tree bridge was the earliest footway across a stream, and it will always be one of the best if the sap wood is carefully adzed off. It would not please those, perhaps, for whom there is nothing good unless it has a pattern upon it, but it is a strong and beautiful way. Foot-bridges these should be called, as they are, of course, too narrow for any other

purpose, but with a good oak rail at one side the tree bridge is
distinctly better than a bridge of planks. Where stones are plentiful, stone put up in a strong, simple way is the best to make a
lasting bridge, and a simple structure in brick or stone is better
in effect than any rustic bridge. Where stream beds are rocky
and shallow, stepping stones are often better than a bridge, though
they cannot be used where the streams cut through alluvial soils
and the banks are high.

Some of the worst work ever done in gardens has been in the
construction of needless bridges, often over wretched duck-ponds

A garden room, by Harold Peto, Bridge House, Weybridge.

of small extent. Even people who have some knowledge of
country life, and who ought to possess taste, come to grief over
bridge building, and pretty sheets of water are disfigured by bridges
ugly in form and material. For the most frivolous reasons these
ugly things are constructed, though often by going ten yards further
one could have crept round the head of the pond by a pretty path,
aided, perhaps, by a few stepping stones.

EARTH-BANK BRIDGES.—But there are many cases where some
kind of bridge is necessary in pleasure grounds or woodlands where
there might be more excuse for the rustic worker's bridge. The difficulty
of the light woodwork bridge is that it begins to rot as soon as it is put

up, and we find that, even when done in the best way, with larch or oak, and by old-fashioned workmen, who get as much simplicity of form and endurance out of it as they can, the years pass so rapidly and British rain is so constant, that rot and decay are all we get out of it, and very often such bridges fall into such a dangerous state before we have time to repair them, that animals often get into danger from them.

A much better way is the earth bank, with a drain pipe through, and this suffices where there is a slight, steady, or an occasional flow of water, and also to cross gorges or depressions. We can find the earth to make it on the spot, and by punning, and in the case of larger work of this kind, carting over it, we can get it to settle down in one winter to the level we want it, and soon have an excellent and permanent way across. Such banks will support any weight, and are as free from decay as the best stone bridge. One of their best points

Oak-pale fencing, Surrey.

is that the sides and approaches and slope of the earth bank can be made pretty at once by planting with Honeysuckle, Broom, Sweetbrier, or any other hardy things. Another advantage of the bank is, that the simplest willing workman can form it. The materials being on the spot, it is foolish to cart things a long way. Even when we have stone or brick at hand the labour has to be considered. By making a culvert of bricks and cement, the earth-bank is equally good to cross constantly running streamlets.

THE SUMMER-HOUSE is generally a failure and often a heap of decay. To make such a structure of wood that soon decays is labour wasted. It may be possible, by using the best woods and good oak slabs, to make a summer-house which will be picturesque and enduring, but it is better to build it of stone or some lasting material and cover it with vines and quick-growing climbers.

One can make an enduring and charming summer-house out of living trees. An old Yew or a group of old Yews, or a low-spreading Oak
(there is a fine example of this kind of living summer-house at Shrubland), an old Beech or a group of evergreen Oaks will make a pleasant
summer-house, and with a little care for effect, and by pruning away
old and worn-out branches, so as to get air and room without injuring
the beauty of the trees, it is easy to form cool tents for hot days.

FENCES AND DIVIDING LINES.—The iron fence destroys the
beauty of half the country seats in England, and the evil is growing
every day. There are various serious objections to iron fencing,
but we will only deal here with its effect on the landscape. Any
picture is out of the question with an iron fence in the foreground.
Where an open fence is wanted, nothing is so fine in form and colour
as a split Oak fence and rails made of heart of Oak with stout posts.
A sawn wood fence is not so good. As Oak is so plentiful on many
estates, good examples of split Oak post and rail fences should be

Simple form of garden seat, Warley Place.

more often seen. Oak palings are often used, and sometimes where a
good live fence of Holly, Quick and wild Rose on a good bank would
be far better ; but Oak paling is often a precious aid in a garden as a
dividing line where the colour of brick or other walls would be against
their use, or where for various reasons walls would not be desirable or
a live fence suitable.

SUNK FENCES AND RETAINING WALLS.—Sunk fences of stone
or brick are often of the highest value in the pleasure ground, and
sometimes near the flower garden, as they help us to avoid the
hideous mechanical fences of our day, and they are often the best
way of keeping open views, especially if planted with a garland of creeping plants or wild roses above. They should be strongly
if roughly built, without mortar, and they may be a home for beautiful plants. They should be made on a "batter" or slightly sloping
back, the stones packed close together, *i.e.* without much earth and
layers of alpine plants should be put between them. Retain-

ing walls or sunk fences could be made admirably in this way, and where they permit of it may be made into beautiful alpine gardens. Apart from the sunk fence, there is often need for low retaining walls, especially in places of diversified surface. These walls also may be made the home of delightful plant beauty in the simplest way. Particulars of these things will be found in fuller detail in the chapter on Rock Gardens.

SEATS.—It is rare to see a garden seat that is not an eyesore. Few make them well and simply in wood, and there is always decay to be considered. Of our own woods, Oak is the best. Stout heart of Oak laths screwed into a simple iron frame without ornament make a good seat. They are best without paint and in the natural colour of the

Log seat, Tresserve.

Oak wood. No seat is so good as one of good stone simply designed and strongly made, and in our country one objection to stone is met by the use of a mat or a light trellis of Bamboo or split laths of Oak held together by cross pieces and placed on top of the stone. In Italy and France one often sees good stone seats, and there they are not expensive. I have made good stone seats out of steps and other stones which had been displaced in buildings. Stone seats should always be set on stone supports bedded in concrete. A good oak seat is one with strong stone supports, the top being a slab of Oak laid with two bars across its lower side to keep it in place. The top in this form being so easily removed, may be stored away for the winter, as wooden seats should always be. Tree stems of some size and little value may also be cut into the form of seats, and make very good ones for a time, but they soon decay. The common iron seats with cast patterns on them are ugly, but iron seats need not be so, and some old iron seats quite simply made of lath or rod iron were fairly good, and it is not difficult to cover the seat with bamboo trellis-work or matting for the summer season. Some of the French wooden seats are simple and good in form, and, painted a nice carnation-leaf green, they look very well. Bamboos, which come in such quantities now in the sugar ships, might be more used for making pretty garden seats. Sometimes old tree stumps help to make useful seats, and the bole of the tree, if cut, makes a very good rustic seat. Where stone is plentiful, as in many hill and other parts, it is often easy to make useful seats out of blocks of stone in rocky places. Of this sort I saw some pretty examples at Castlewellan and the rocky district around.

THE COVERED WAY may be a charming thing in a garden and make a home for climbers, as well as a shady way, and also form a

Marble slab seat with Oak lattice cover.

valuable screen. Shade is more essential in other countries than in ours, and the Italian covered way is often a very picturesque object. The best material to make the supports of is rough stone or brick. On an enduring support like this the woodwork is more easily constructed afterwards. Simple rough stone posts may be had in certain quarries in the north of England, in the lake country, but in the absence of these it will be better to build columns of brick or stone than to trust to any wood. In all open-air work the enduring way is true economy, and though we cannot all readily get the hard green stone gate posts stained with yellow Lichen of the farms about Keswick, or the everlasting granite fence posts that one sees in Italy, we should make a stand against work which has to be done over and over again. Of woods, Oak free of sapwood makes the best supports; Larch is good, but best of all, perhaps, is the common Locust tree, which, however, is seldom plentiful in a mature state. For all the other parts of covered ways nothing is better than old

Oak branches or the stems of stunted Oaks, or of old stub Oaks that are often found about a country place, and are of very little value as timber. Larch lasts well in the absence of Oak, but is not nearly so good in effect. By using Oak with stone or brick supports, a covered way may be made which will last for years without falling into decay, as is the case with this kind of work when done with more perishable woods and without lasting supports. It would be far better to employ strong iron wire than wood of this sort. An advantage which woodwork has over iron lies in its good effect. Carefully done, a covered way made as above described may be picturesque even before there is a plant on it.

LIVING SUPPORTS.—A pretty way of supporting plants and forming covered ways is to use certain trees of a light and graceful

Bower with stone table at end of garden. From a photo sent by the Marquis de Fontreira.

character for supporting climbers, just as the Italians often support their Vines on living trees kept within bounds. Such trees as the weeping Aspen, weeping Birch, and fruit trees of graceful, drooping forms, like some Apples, would do well, and would be worth having for their own sakes, while through the trees hardy climbers could freely run.

BOATHOUSES.—Among the things which are least beautiful in many gardens and pleasure grounds is the boathouse. Our builders are not simple in their ways, and are seldom satisfied with any one good colour or material to make a house with, or even a boathouse, but every kind of ugly variegation is tried, so that harshness in effect is the usual result, where all should be simple and quiet in colour, as it is in boathouses on the Norfolk Broads made of reeds and rough posts. The simpler the better in all such work, using local material like Oak,

B B

which comes in so well for the posts, and reeds for the roof; but the simplest brickwork and brown tiles would be far better than the contrast of ugly colours which the modern builder both in France and England delights in. The place, too, should be carefully chosen and the building not conspicuous. It is well to avoid the cost of railway carriage in the making of simple structures like boat-houses, and also carting, which is such a costly matter in many districts. It is best to use materials of the estate or country. Ivy and living creepers may help to protect the sides of airy sheds. Larch comes in well where Oak is not to be spared, and Larch shingling for the roof might be used,

A thatched summer-house.

as is commonly done in farm-houses in Northern Europe and America. Little shelters for mowing machines, tools and the like can be made with wood covered with Larch bark, as at Coolhurst, and a very pretty effect they have, besides being less troublesome to make than the heather or thatched roofs, especially in districts where the good thatcher is getting rare. The chip roof, also, of the wooded country around London is an excellent one, lasting for half a century or so if well made, but the men who made it so well are now less and less easy to meet with. And on the whole the best roof for any structure that has to last is of tiles of good colour : tiles made and tested in the locality being often the best.

. FOUNTAINS IN GARDENS.—In this moist climate of ours water needs to be used with great discretion. Above all things it must flow and not stagnate. Bacon, who said so many things about gardens well, summed up the case with his usual felicity :—"For fountains, they are a great beauty and refreshment ; but pools mar all." No doubt we can all of us recall some pool of great beauty, some moat with little broken reflections that made almost all the charm of the garden wherein it lay, but as a general rule Bacon is right.

As nothing is drearier than a dry fountain except the exasperating trickle of one that refuses to be drowned out by the continuous drip of the eaves, it is better to place your fountain in a part of the garden which you are only likely to visit on a fine day, and if possible it should be set where its tossing spray will catch the sunbeams while you repose in the cool shade ; then the supply of water may be as it should—unfailing. Fountains on such an extensive scale as those of Versailles or Chatsworth are only to be excused, when, as at Caserta, they run day and night from one year's end to the other. It is only in such great places too that large and monumental fountains, basin above basin, adorned with sculpture and connected by cascades, have any fitness, and even where they are fit they are apt, here in England, to cease very soon to be fine. Lead is the best material for such foun-

Entrance to Bishop's Garden (Chichester).

tain sculpture in our damp-laden atmosphere, as it discolours more becomingly than stone or marble. This tendency to discolour in blotches and afford a foothold for mosses and lichens, though a blemish on statues, is an added charm to the necessary basins and copings which should confine the waters of our fountain. A fountain is a work of art and as such should always be placed in the more formal portions of the grounds. The feathery spray of a jet is always a beautiful thing but can be ill-placed—as for instance, in the centre of a large and informal " piece of ornamental water."

The fountain in the Temple is one of the most charming examples of the single jet, rising from the centre of a circular basin and falling back with a melodious splash. It has lost some of its charm since

B B 2

it was surrounded by a clinker-built rockery in which nothing will grow. This sort of fountain should be set in a grass plot, and a few moisture-loving plants allowed to break the severity of its outline. I remember one such, only about 5 feet in diameter, in a lawn near London ; a simple brick and concrete basin with a jet in the centre, which threw its spray up to the overhanging boughs of a stately elm, and nourished one of the most splendid clumps of Osmunda regalis I ever saw ; Flowering Rush too throve in its friendly neighbourhood. There is a very attractive little fountain against the wall of the fruit garden at Penshurst. If the fountain be on a larger

Vine-shaded bower.

scale than these the basin may be made lovely in the summer with many varieties of aquatic plants, which being planted in boxes or pots can be removed to the greenhouse before the frosts set in.

One of the great merits of a fountain in a garden to the true lover of nature is the attraction it forms for the birds ; they will haunt its neighbourhood with delightful persistency, bathing and drinking at all hours of the day.

A fountain for the exclusive benefit of the birds was made in a garden in New England by sinking a saucer-shaped hollow, about 6 inches deep, in the lawn, which was allowed to become grass-grown like the rest of the turf; in the centre stood up a jet which threw up a very fine spray. For an hour or two every morning and evening this was turned on, soon filling the hollow to the brim; the effect was very pretty with the grass at the bottom of the water, and the birds soon learned to know the hours of the bath and came in flocks to enjoy it.—G. H. B.

Loggia Dropmore.
Engraved from a photograph by Mr. J. James.

CHAPTER XXXIII.

THE ORCHARD BEAUTIFUL.

THE spirit of beauty must have been at the birth of the trees that give us the hardy fruits of the northern world—Crab, wild Plum, Pear and Cherry—yielding back for us in their bloom the delicate colours of the clouds, and lovelier far in their flowers than Fig or Vine of the south   The old way of having an orchard near the house was a good one.   Planted for use, it was precious for its beauty, and not only when the spring winds bore the breath of the blossoms of Cherry, Plum, Apple, and Pear, as there were the fruit odours, too, and the early Daffodils and Snowdrops, and overhead the lovely trees that bear our orchard fruits—Apples, Pears, Cherries, Plums, Medlars, Damsons, Bullaces, and Quinces.   To make pictures to last round the year, I should ask for many of these orchard trees on a few acres of fair ground, none the worse if too hilly for the plough; a belt of Hollies, Yew, and Scotch Fir on the cold sides to comfort trees and men, with careless garlands of Honeysuckle, Rose, and fragrant Clematis among them here and there, and in the fence bank plenty of Sweet Brier and Hawthorn.   If we see fine effects where orchards are poorly planted with one kind of tree, as the Apple (in many country places in our islands there are no orchards worthy the name), what might not be looked for of an orchard in which the beauty of all our hardy fruit trees would be visible?   If we consider the number of distinct species of fruit trees and the many varieties of each, we may get some idea of the pictures one might have in an orchard, beginning with the bloom of the Sloe and Bullace in the fence   The various Plums and Damsons are beautiful in bloom, as in the Thames valley and about Evesham   The Apple varies much in bloom, as may be seen in Kentish and Normandy orchards, where the flowers of some are of extraordinary beauty.   The Pear, less showy in colour, the Medlar, so beautiful in flower and in foliage, and the Quince, so pretty in bloom in Tulip time, must not be forgotten   The Cherry is often a beautiful tree in its cultivated as well as wild forms, and the Cherry

Orchard bloom. Engraved from a picture by Mark Fisher.

orchards in parts of Kent, as near Sittingbourne, are pictures when in bloom. There is no better work in a country place than choosing a piece of good ground to form an orchard; and, considering the number of trees that are worth a place for their beauty as well as their fruit, a dozen acres are not too much in a country place where there is land to spare.

POOR SOIL SHOULD NOT HINDER.—In planting some may be deterred by the fear that their soil is too poor, and no doubt it is a much simpler matter on the good fruit tree soils of Devon, Hereford, and Kent than in other districts; but the difference in soils is no reason why some counties and districts should be bare of orchards, and in many the soil is as good as need be. Indeed, in the country south of London, as in Kent, where much of the land is taken up with orchards, we may notice the trees suffering much more from drought in dry years than they do in the good sandstone soil of Cheshire or in Ireland and Scotland, where there is a heavier rainfall. Few of our orchard trees require a very special soil, and where chalky or very warm soil occurs, the best way is to keep to the kinds of fruit it favours most. But though the orchard beautiful must be of trees in all their natural vigour, and of forms lovely in winter as in spring and summer, the trees must not be neglected, allowed to perish from drought, or become decayed from bug, scale or other pests, and it should be the care of those who enjoy their beauty to protect them from all such dangers. The idea that certain counties only are suited for fruit growing is erroneous, and even if it were true, the fact need not deter us from planting orchards of the hardier trees and of good local kinds. Much of Ireland is as bare of orchards as the back of a stranded whale, but who could say this was the fault of the country?

THE TREES TO TAKE THEIR NATURAL FORMS —Where we plant for beauty we can have no choice for any but the natural form of the tree. Owing to the use of what are called dwarfing stocks and like contrivances, fruit gardens and orchards are now beginning to show shapes of trees that are not beautiful compared with the grand old orchard tree. However much these dwarf and pinched shapes may appeal to the gardener in his own domain, in the orchard beautiful they have no place. For the form of all our fruit trees is very good indeed, winter or summer, and that is a great point if we seek beauty. We know what the effect in flower-time is in the orchard pictures of such painters as Mark Fisher and Alfred Parsons, if we have not taken the trouble to see the finer pictures of the orchards themselves, seen best, perhaps, on dark and wet days in flower-time. Lastly, the effect of finely-coloured fruit on high trees is one of the best in our gardens. Therefore, in every case, whatever pruning we do, let the tree take its natural form, not only for its own sake or the greater beauty of natural form generally, but also for the variety of form we get even among the varieties sprung from the same species.

Clearly if we prune to any one ideal type of tree we can never see the interesting variety of form shown by the varieties of one species, as the Apple and Pear Keeping to the natural form of each tree, moreover does not in the least prevent thinning of the branches where overcrowded—the best way of pruning.

ROOT PRUNING IN THE ORCHARD—We have not only to avoid ugly and constrained forms of training and pruning, but never in the orchard where the true way is to let the tree take its natural free and mature form, should the practice of root pruning be allowed

Our orchard trees—especially the trees native of Britain like the Apple and the Pear—are almost forest trees in nature and take some years first of all to make their growth and then mature it, which in gardens for various reasons make men try to get in artificial ways the fruit that nature gives best at the time of maturity : so root pruning was invented in our own day, and it may have some use in certain soils and in limited gardens, but we may well doubt its value taken all in all, and we have to pay too dearly for it. One would hardly think it would enter into people's heads to practice root pruning in the orchard , but the word is a catching one and leads people astray I have several times had the question seriously put to me as to how to root prune forest trees—a case where all pruning is absurd in any proper sense save in the way effected by the forest itself The trees in the orchard should be allowed to come freely to maturity, and in the way the years fly this is not a long wait. By planting a few well chosen young trees every year the whole gradually comes into noble bearing, and the difference between the naturally grown and laden tree and one of the pinched root-pruned ones is great in beauty

CIDER ORCHARDS are often picturesque in the west of England and in Normandy, and so long as men think any kind of fermented stuff good enough for their blood, cider has on northern men the first claim from the beauty of the trees in flower and fruit, and indeed throughout the year. The cider orchard also will allow us to grow naturally-grown trees and those raised from seed. These cider orchards are extremely beautiful, and the trees in them often take fine natural forms They have a charm, too, in the brightness of the fruit, and also a peculiar one in the lateness of the blooms of some, many of the cider Apples flowering later than the orchard Apples In some cider orchards near Rouen (Lyons-la-Forêt) I saw the finest, tallest, and cleanest trees were raised from seed. The owner, a far-famed cider grower, told me they were his best trees, and raised from seed of good cider Apples. If he found on their fruiting that they were what he wanted as cider Apples he kept them and was glad of them ;

if not, he cut their heads off and regrafted them with sorts he wanted. These were free and handsome trees with good grass below them, just like the Cherry orchards in the best parts of Kent, where the lambs pick the early grass   But however beautiful such an orchard, clearly it will not give us the variety of form and beauty found in the mixed orchard, in which Cherry, Apple, Plum, Pear, Medlar, Quince, Walnut, and Mulberry take a place ; there also the various interesting trees allied to our fruit trees might come in, such as the true and common Service tree, Almond, Cornelian Cherry, Hickory, and Crab

GRAFTING —Where we make use of grafted trees—and generally there is no choice in the matter—we should always in the orchard use the most natural stock that can be obtained.   It is much better, for instance, to graft Pear trees on the wild Pear than on the Quince, a union harmful to the Pear on many soils   If we could get the trees on their own roots without any grafting it would often be much better, but we are slaves to the routine of the trade, and in our day he who asks for a fruit tree on its natural roots is regarded as a wandering lunatic The history of grafting is as old as the oldest civilisations—its best reason, the rapid increase of a given variety.   In every country one or two fruit trees predominate, and are usually natives of the country, like the Apple in Northern Europe and the Olive in the South. When men found a good variety of a native fruit they sought to increase it in the quickest way, and so having learned the art of grafting, they put the best varieties on wild stems in hedgerows, or dug up young trees and grafted them in their gardens.   The practice eventually became stereotyped into the production of the nursery practice of grafting many varieties of fruit trees on the same stock, often without the least regard to the lasting health and duration of the trees so grafted   In some cases when we use the wild form of the tree as a stock for the orchard tree we succeed ; but grafting is the cause of a great deal of the disease and barrenness of our orchards.   It is now possible to get some Apple trees on their own roots, and in France, and here and there in England also, some kinds of Plums in that way.   Where we graft, it is well to graft low , that is to say, in the case of Cider Apples, for example, it is much safer and better to take a tree grafted close to the ground than grafted standard high, as the high graft is more liable to accident and does not make so fine a tree   In the orchard the good old practice of sowing the stone or pip of a fine fruit now and then may also be followed with interest.

STARVED ORCHARDS.—Even in the good fruit counties like Kent one may see in dry years orchards starved from want of water, and the turf beneath almost brown as the desert   Where manure is plentiful it is well to use it as a mulch for such trees, but where it is not, we may employ various other materials for keeping the roots safe from the effects of drought. Not only the tree roots want the water, but the roots of the competing grass suck the moisture out of the soil. The competition of the grass could be put an end to at once, and the trees very much nourished, by the use of any easily found mulching from materials which are often abundant in a country place. Among the best of these, where plentiful, is the common Furze, if cut down in spring and placed over the ground round the base of young or poor orchard trees   It prevents the grass from robbing the trees and lets the water fall through to the ground, helping to keep it there, too, by pre-venting direct evaporation ; moreover, the small leaves falling off nourish the ground   So again the sweepings of drives and of farm or garden yards are useful, and also any small faggots—often allowed to rot in the woods after the underwood is cleared. They fetch such a low price that they are not worth selling, but if placed round the roots of fruit trees they often do good. Then also there are the weeds and refuse of gardens of all kinds which form detestable rubbish heaps that would be much better abolished, and all cleanings from the garden placed directly over the roots of young poor orchard trees

Even rank weeds, which swarm about yards and shrubberies, would help, and one of the best ways to weaken them and help towards their destruction is by mowing them down in the pride of their growth in the middle of summer—nettles and docks, as the case may be—and instead of burning them or taking them to the rubbish heap, use them over the tree roots. Even the weeds and long grass grow-ing round the base of the trees, if mown and left on the ground, will make a difference in the growth and health of fruit trees   Such care is all the more needed if our orchard is upon poor or shaly soils in the southern or home counties, where the rainfall is less than in the western counties or in Ireland or Scotland · in naturally rich and deep soil we do not need it

FENCING THE ORCHARD BEAUTIFUL.—All fences should be of living things at once the most enduring, effective, and in the end the best. We see the hideous result of the ironmonger's fence in marring the foregrounds of many landscape pictures   Holly, Quick, or Cock-spur Thorn, with a sprinkling of Sloe or Bullace here and there, give us the best orchard fence ; once well made, far easier to keep up than the iron fence. Yew is a danger, and a Yew hedge should never be planted where animals come near as they usually do, the orchard, and if the Yew comes by itself, as it often will, it should be cut clean out and burnt as soon as cut down   Holly is the best evergreen orchard fence for our country, and we should be careful about getting the plants direct from a good nursery—clean seedling plants not much over a yard high. The best time to plant Hollies is in May if growing in the place, but on light soil plant in autumn , all the more need to do this if we bring the plants by rail. Unless the soil is very light I should make the fence on a bank, because a turf bank is itself such a good fence to begin with, and a free Holly hedge on a good bank, with, perhaps, a Sloe here and there through it, is one of the prettiest sights of the land, and forms the best of shelters for an orchard in our country. Where shelter is much sought the hedge should not be clipped, and is much handsomer free grown. The orchard fence should not be cut in every year to a hard line, but Sloe, and May, and Sweet Brier, and wild Rose left to bloom and berry, the hedge to be a shelter as well as a fence, and not trimmed oftener than every ten years or so. Then it should be cut down and woven together in the strong way seen in parts of Kent on the hills

KINDS TO PLANT—The English fruit garden is often a museum of varieties, many of them worthless and not even known to its owner. This is wrong in the garden, and doubly so in the orchard, where the fruit trees should be trees in stature and none of poor quality. Too many varieties is partly the result of the seeking after new kinds in the nurseries. In orchard culture we should be chary of planting any new kind, and with the immense number of Apples grown in our own country already, it is always possible to select kinds of enduring fame, and it is the more necessary to do this now when good Apples are coming from various countries, where people do not plant a collection when they want a crop of a few first-rate kinds which they know will be precious in the market. So we should in our orchards never plant single trees, but always, if possible, having chosen a good kind, plant enough to make it worth gathering. It would be better here not to mention any particular kinds, because local kinds and local circumstances often deserve the first attention, and some local kinds of fruit are among the best When in doubt always end it by choosing kinds of proved quality like Blenheim, Wellington, and Kentish Filbasket to any novelties that may be offered. Any fruit requiring the protection of walls or in the least tender should never be put in the orchard. It is probable that some of the fruit trees of Northern and Central Europe, and particularly Russia, would be well suited for our climate, but as yet little is known of these except that they are interesting and many of them distinct. The vigour of the tree should be considered and its fertility. Kinds rarely fertile are not worth having, always bearing in mind, however, that a good kind is often spoiled by a bad stock or by conditions unsuited to it

The beauty of flower of certain varieties may well influence in their choice. Once when talking with Mr. Ruskin of the beauty of the fruit as compared with the flower of our northern fruit trees, he said in reply to my praise of the fruit "Give me the flower and spare me the stomach-ache!"

In view of the confusion brought about by fat catalogues, new varieties of doubtful value, the number of early kinds worthless for winter and spring use, and the planting of untried kinds, a good rule would be to put any kind we propose to plant under separate study as to its merits in all ways, and only plant one kind a year. The kind chosen for orchard culture should be of undoubted merit and distinction, and of high quality when cooked, without which apples to keep are worthless, so many which quickly fall into a mawkish state being without table or market value if there be any crisp-fleshed apples to be had In fixing but one kind a year, the first consideration should be its quality, and the second its constancy in bearing, as to which there is a great difference in apples Perfect hardiness and vigour are essential, and the judgment as regards orchard planting should never be based on the produce of bush trees or trees grafted on the paradise or other stocks which limit the natural growth of the tree

Apples known for many years, such as the *Blenheim, Kentish Filbasket, Wellington, French Crab, Keswick* and *Alfriston* should never be left out of our consideration n this respect, as, however they may be affected by local situation or soil, their character and value has been long proved, and that is a great point, as in the case of new varieties chosen for some one minor quality, such as colour, it is only after they have been grown for years we begin to find out their bad qualities

STAKING ORCHARD TREES.—Fruit trees grown in any way are fair to see in the time of flower and fruit, but our beautiful orchard must be in turf if we are to have the best expression of its beauty In fruit gardens where the whole surface is cultivated with small fruits below and taller trees overhead we may get as good, or, it may be, better fruit, but we miss the finer light and shade and verdure of the orchard in turf, the pretty incidents of the ground, and the animal life among the trees in spring, as sheep in Kent, and the interest of the wild gardening in the grass. Also the orchard turf, by its shade or shelter, or in some way, becomes most welcome nibbling for lambs and calves in the spring. A gain of the orchard in turf is that we can plant it on any ground, however broken or steep, and in many parts of the country there is much ground of this sort to be planted. Now, while we may in the garden or the fruit garden plant trees without stakes, we cannot do so in the grass orchard, because of the incursions of animals , therefore staking is needed, not only to support the tall and strong young trees which we ought to plant, but also to guard against various injuries The best way is to use very strong stakes and make them protect and support the trees, and also carry the wire netting which is essential wherever rabbits, hares, goats, or other browsing animals exist. The best way to do this is to have a very stout stake—Larch or old Oak. Sometimes in the *débris* of old sheds a number of rafters are turned out which are of no use for building, and are excellent for staking strong young trees in orchards, first digging the hole and putting the stake firmly in to a depth of 3 feet below the surface   Cradles of Oak and iron are much in use ; the first is very well in an Oak country where labour is plentiful , iron is costly and ugly, and not so good as the single stout stake, which is easy to get of Larch or stub Oak in many country places.   The common way of tying a faggot of Quicks or any thorny shrub is often good when done by a good fencer.   The trees should be tied with care with soft ropes of straw or other material, and when planted be loosely but carefully wired with netting well out of the reach of browsing animals   This wiring is supported well by the strong stake, and, well done, it keeps rabbits and hares, as well as cattle, at bay, and, worse than all for trees, young horses   A usual way in Kent is to drive in three stout stakes, 6 feet or more in height, round the tree, and fasten cross-bars to them   This can be done at a total cost of about 10*d* a tree, and should last twelve to fifteen years

THE ORCHARD WILD GARDEN —One of the reasons for a good orchard, from the point of view of all who care for beauty, is its value for wild gardening.   It is so well fitted for this, that many times Narcissi and other bulbs from the garden have even established themselves in its turf, so that long years after the culture of flowers has been given up in the garden, owing to changes of fashion, people have been able in old orchards to find naturalised some of the most beautiful kinds of Narcissi.   Where the soil is cool and deep, these flowers are easily grown, and in warm soils many of our hardiest and most beautiful spring flowers might easily be naturalised.   Those who care for beauty as much as fruit may throw careless garlands of the hardier Clematis over the trees here and there.   They do not rob the ground much and add a careless grace which is always welcome.   On the cool side of the orchard bank, Primrose and Oxlip would bloom long and well, and on all sides of it Daffodils, Snowflakes, Snowdrops, wild Tulips, or any like bulbs to spare from the garden ; and from the garden trimmings, too, tufts of Balm and Myrrh to live for ever among the grass of the bank.   The robin would build in the moss of the bank, the goldfinch in the silvery lichen of the trees, and the thrush, near the winter's end, herald the buds with noble song.

CHAPTER XXXIV

LABOURS FOR GOOD OR EVIL · SOILS : WATER DRAINING : EVAPORA-
TION ROTATION WEEDS AND RUBBISH HEAPS · MONOTONY
STAKING GLASS. WASTED LABOUR IN MOVING EARTH ·
WOODEN TRELLISING BEST

THE cost of the making and keeping of the gardens and pleasure
grounds of the British Isles is too vast to realise ; no other people in
the world spending so generously on their gardens and plantations—
not a selfish end either, as all noble planting and gardening add to the
beauty of the land. In every case it is therefore worth asking, does
the labour so freely given work for good ends .— for ugliness or beauty ,
waste in stereotyped monotony ; or days well spent in adding to the
treasures of our gardens and plantings, both in enduring variety and in
picturesque effects ; pictures, in fact, all round the year?   In any case
there is immense and hideous waste in misapplied labour and bad art,
and therefore some of these enemies of good work deserve a little
thought

SOILS GOOD AND BAD —Most garden lovers strive for an ideal soil,
but this does not always lead to happy results, and, even if we could have
it, would only lead to monotony in vegetation   No doubt many will seek
at all costs for the soil called the best, but the wisest way is rather to
rejoice in and improve the soil fate has planted us on   A good deep
and free loam is best for many things, and from the view of high
cultivation or market work, deep valley soils are almost essential, but
we often see poor peats giving excellent results, from a flower
gardening point of view, in enabling us to grow with ease many
more kinds of plants than could be grown on heavy soil   How fertile
sand may become with good cultivation is shown by the fact that
some of the very best soils for hardy plants are those that have been
poor sea sand, but improved by cultivation, and sometimes such soils
are drought-resisting, as on reclaimed seashore lands.   Yet now and
then we see certain sandy soils absolutely refuse to grow Roses and
Carnations, and in such cases it is often better to give up the struggle
Chalky hills are wretched for trees and some shrubs, but there are few
soils more congenial to garden vegetation than some chalky soils, and
chalk tumbling into a valley soil is often excellent.   In limestone

soils people often take much trouble to get peat, in the vain hope of growing a few Rhododendrons, labour which would be better bestowed on improving the staple of the natural soil of the place.

The most hopeless soils are the true clays, but the word "clay" is used in a loose way by many who have never seen a real clay. In the east of England and in Ireland, for example, the term is often used for dark free soil. The true clay which occurs in the northern suburbs of London and near Horsham, Sussex, is not a soil on which a man could get a living, or if he does so he will get one anywhere! With such a soil our only hope is to cart good earth on to the ground. Whatever the nature of the soil in a given garden, it should to a large extent govern what we grow. If happy enough to have a sandy peat, how easy it is to grow all the lovely evergreens of the northern mountains, which rejoice in such soil—things which, if they live on loamy and heavy soils, are never really happy thereon. On such soil, too, all the most beautiful kinds of hardy shrubs may be grown without trouble, and planted among these shrubs the Lilies and hardy bulbous flowers of Japan and America. If a deep and at the same time poor sea sand comes in our way, we can make perfect bulb gardens on it, and also grow trees and flowering shrubs very well after a time.

LOCAL AND NATURAL SOILS.—Soil must not always be blamed for failure with certain plants, because rainfall, elevation, and, very often, nearness to the sea will affect plants very much. Thus shrubs that do well near the sea will, on the same kind of soil, perish far inland. It is essential to study the secret of the soil and find out the plants that thrive best on it. Once free from the limits and needs of the flower garden proper, the best way will often be to use any local peculiarities of soil instead of doing away with them: A bog? Instead of draining it keep it and adorn it with some of the often beautiful things that grow in bogs; A sandy knoll? Plant with Rosemary or Rock Roses; A peaty, sheltered hollow? Make it into a beautiful Rhododendron glade, and so get variety of plant life in various conditions.

Then, as regards the soil and the natural habitats of plants, there is no doubt that it is useful to know where they come from, whether plains, valleys, or rocks, and what soil they grow on, but it is a knowledge that may sometimes mislead, because rainfall and elevation and other causes may lead us to suppose results due to soil which are really owing to accident of position. Many of the beautiful plants of the mountains of the East, such as Aubrietia, and a number of rock plants which grow in any soil, would do no better if we tried to imitate their actual conditions of life in their native habitats, which are often absolutely different from the soils of our lowland gardens in which many rock plants thrive and endure for years.

CULTIVATION AND WATER —Many think that heavy watering is necessary in seasons of drought, and it may be worth while showing how such heavy labour may be avoided. There are soils which are so thirsty, like the hot sandy soils of Surrey, that watering is essential, and some chalky soils, too, are almost hopeless without heavy watering, while water is often extremely difficult to get enough of on dry hills But under general conditions there is not much trouble in getting rid of this labour and its attendant ugliness The essential thing is to make the beds deep enough Even with the best intentions, many people fail to do this, and workmen in forming gardens are sometimes misled as to the depth of soil in beds, made when gardens are being laid out, the soil when it settles being really much less than it seems in the making The best way for those who care for their flowers is to dig the beds right out to a depth of 30 inches below the surface before any of the good soil is put in. Then, if for general garden use such beds are filled in with good, rich, loamy soil and are gently raised, as all beds should be in wet countries, 4 inches or 6 inches above the surface, they will rarely be found to fail in any drought Much depends on the size of the bed , the little, angular, frivolous beds which have too often been the rule in gardens cannot resist drought so long as broad simple beds With these precautions, and also autumn and winter planting, we ought, in the British Isles, to free ourselves from much of the heavy labour and cost of watering, and it would be better to have half the space we give to flowers well prepared, than always be at work with the water barrel

To be busy planting in autumn and early winter is a great gain too, because the plants get rooted before the hot time comes, and the kind of plants we grow is important as regards the water question If it is merely the mass of bedding plants with which many places are adorned in summer, these being all put out in early June, in the event of a hot summer there is nothing else to do but water all the time, or we lose them, as of course the roots are all at the surface in June But where we have deep beds of Roses, Lilies, Carnations, Irises, Delphiniums, and all the noble flowers that can be planted in autumn or winter, we may save ourselves the labour of watering often Well prepared beds of choice evergreen or other flowering shrubs, with Lilies and the choicest hardy flowers among them, also resist drought well. Thus it will be seen how much we gain in this way alone by the use of right open-air gardening.

What is here said, although true of the south of England and dry soils generally, is not so as to soil on cool hills, and in the west country where the rainfall is heavier. In such cases it is not nearly so important to have the soil so deep, and a good fertile soil half the depth, with copious rain, may do But, taking the country generally, there is no doubt that such deep culture well repays the doing. The farmer is often unable to alter the staple of his ground owing to its extent, but the flower gardener, dealing with a much smaller area, should never rest until he has got a deep as well as a good soil This is given to many by Nature in rich valley lands, and on such happy soil the flower gardener's main work as regards the labours of the soil is changing the crop now and then, with some modification of the soil to suit certain plants

SOFT WATER BEST.—Where, however, owing to the dryness of the soil or subsoil or to shortness of the rainfall, we have to resort to much artificial watering, it is a great point to save the rain water as the best of all water not only for household uses, but for plants. Next to it comes river water, but to the gardens that want most water, rivers, unfortunately, do not come, so that for garden use it would often be very wise to do what people do more in other countries than ours, and that is, save all the rain water we can instead of letting it run to waste, as it does so often.

DRAINAGE.—In our country too much thought and labour are given to drainage in the flower garden, to the neglect of change of plants and deep cultivation, and during our hot summers some way to keep water in the beds is more important than getting rid of it Some soils, too, are in little need of artificial drainage, such as free sands, sandy loams, chalky and limestone soils, and much ground lying high, and much alluvial land. Houses are not usually built on bogs or marshy land, and in the course of years the ground round most houses has been made dry enough for use, and hence elaborate work in drains, bottoming with brick-rubbish or concrete, is often wasted labour. In some years even in the west country we may see plants lying half-dead on the ground for want of water, and the same plants in deep soil, and where no thought was given to drainage, in perfect health at the same time. There are places where, owing to excessive rainfall and the wet nature of the soil, we may have to drain, but it is often overdone.

Apart from the over-draining for ordinary garden things, it may be well to remember that flower garden plants in our country are often half starved through drainage, like Phlox and scarlet Lobelia, which in their own country are marsh plants, or inhabit the edges of pools In the southern country they simply refuse to show their true character where the ground is drained in the usual way. The men who began the crusade about draining land in this century found its effects so good on sour, peaty clay and saturated land, and talked so well and so much about it, that some harm has been done—draining where it does more harm than good not being uncommon.

Gardeners' land and farmers' land are usually wholly different.

Drainage is often the simplest and best way for the farmer to alter the tilth and texture of saturated and cold or sour land, whereas the flower gardener, dealing with a small space for his beds, has the power of altering the tilth and texture of his land in a thorough way, and so making it open to the influence of rain and air. The position of the flower garden also is usually wholly different from that of agricultural land. The flower garden itself is frequently raised, and in a terraced or at all events often dry position, where the main drainage is long settled, and gently raising the surfaces of flower beds, to a height say of 4 inches to 6 inches, enables us to get rid in our flower beds of the surface water, which very often troubles the farmer, and which he can best get rid of by drainage By raising our beds slightly—not in the ugly way practised in the London parks—we free the surface of any water lying on it, and this is a good plan to follow, except in hot and shallow soils, where it would be better not to raise the surface above the level.

ROTATION IN THE FLOWER GARDEN.—Flower gardeners do not think enough of change of crop, or what in farming is called rotation. A farmer soon comes to grief if he does not change his crops, but in gardens one may see the same plants grown in the same beds for many years A cause of the poor growth of hardy flowers is want of change of soil, and in addition the soils in which they grow are often robbed by a network of hungry tree roots. There are botanic gardens in Europe where the same wretched plants have been starving in the same soil for fifty years, and little ever done to help them So, again, there are favourite borders in gardens which are almost as much in want of a change, but, owing to their position sometimes being a favourite one, people hesitate to give it to them. In such cases we should prepare a new border for the plants and remove them, and trench, renew and improve the soil of the old beds or borders, afterwards taking a crop as different as possible for a year or two. If we take a crop of annual flowers, the annuals rejoice in the fresh ground, and they might be followed by a year of Carnations, after which a return might be made to a good mixed border When, however, we do change a border or bed, the staple of the soil ought to be made deep enough—changed if need be. In dealing with a soil which is too rich in humus, an addition of lime will improve it, but generally the soils are too poor, and require renewing and deepening Bedding plants have the advantage of fresh soil and often a total change every year, and hence the bright vigour they often show when the seasons are fair. A little of the same generous change would help Roses, Lilies, and all the finer things in an equal degree, though many of these will be quite happy in the same soil for years if it be well prepared at first

WEEDS AND RUBBISH HEAPS.—Upon suggesting once in a beautiful garden in Essex that an opening should be made from a pleasure ground into a picturesque grove of old Oak trees, we were met with the objection that the rubbish heap was there, and, on making our way in, this was found to cover half an acre almost picturesque in its wild up and down heaps of rubbish, earth, leaves, branches and broken crockery, &c. A fire was kept alight for six months in the year to get rid of some of this rubbish, and this being very near the house, was a frequent nuisance in certain states of wind and air. This is a common state of things, but as wrong in practice as it is unnecessary. We gain nothing by destroying organic matter by fire, but lose a good deal and get only the ash. The garden weeds, the good soil scraped up with them, and the many other things that go to make up these rubbish heaps would be of far more use put directly over young trees to protect and nourish them. Refuse of hard materials, such as iron or delf, should be buried separately ; and if any roots of bad weeds occur, they may be burned at once where they are. Yet there is no practice more firmly established than the ancient one of the garden rubbish heap, often disfiguring spots which might be pretty with ferns or shrubs, encouraging vermin, filth, and vile odours, all things that we do not want in or near the flower garden or pleasure ground. We may see these heaps made even where labour is scarce and the gardener is over-weighted with work, he adding to his toil by barrowing or carting away weeds and earth. This means moving the costly product two or more times   (1) to the rubbish heap , (2) turning over and burning , and (3), finally, again removing the result in ash , whereas we may easily, as in the above and many other cases in a garden or pleasure ground, get rid of it at once by one move, and find it acts in a more useful way, even as a fertiliser, than when we go through the ugly labours, pains, and penalties of forming the regulation rubbish heap. Nor does this plan in the least prevent us burning where burning is a prompt aid in getting rid of the roots and bad weeds or any worn-out branches or roots that incommode us , but in such a case we burn on the spot and scatter the refuse there or thereabouts. Here are a few instances of other ways of getting rid of what usually is carried or carted to a rubbish heap, that were carried out during one summer in my own garden.

Protecting Hollies—A very fine group of Hollies was planted on a slope facing south. Seedling trees of the largest size that could be planted with safety were brought from a distance by rail. These were planted in May, and afterwards any grass mowings, prunings, weeds, clearings, reeds, dead roots of shrubs, &c, that happened to be near, were placed at the base of each Holly for about 3 feet all round ; also, where any ground near was cleared of summer weeds, these were also put over the roots, even branchlets of evergreens being used, as preventing the direct action of the sun   Not one of these Hollies was lost in spite of the drought, though the turf near, on the same slope, was like dust, but the covering of waste material given kept the earth about the trees moist during the drought

A Bamboo Plantation.—A plantation of hardy bamboos was made in quite a different situation in mid June—a hollow slightly shaded with trees, and therefore not nearly so much exposed to danger as the southern slope above mentioned.   It is known, however, that bamboos are the better for mulching in any situation, and as there was no manure at hand, and even if there had been it would have needed a good deal of carting, the waste and weeds near were placed over the surface of the ground   In this case, mowings, dead flower-stems, scum of a pond (which was very bad this year, coming off in masses of most indestructible stuff), were laid over the surface of the bamboo plantation, in which the plants did remarkably well, and never turned a leaf.   On taking up some plants of the Japan bamboo, which had been put in too thickly and were wanted for another place, we found the roots and suckers growing finely after only five months' growth

Protecting Young Orchards.— An orchard of fine young standard trees was planted in 1897 on a rather steep slope to the south, where the soil was not good.   Faggots of little value, the sweepings of roads, and any vegetable refuse about the yards were put over these 4 feet all round.   It would be impossible to see trees healthier or less affected by the starving drought of the hot year. Such aid would not be so precious in good valley land, but in many soils it is of the greatest help

Using Weeds Where They Grow — Very often weeds are removed from the surface of garden ground which would be much more useful if left where they grew—buried, if there be room, or allowed to dry up if cut off very small, as they always, if possible, should be   The upper surface of garden ground is the best of it, owing to mulching and manuring, and to take away the best of the ground is bad gardening.   What would become of the farmer who systematically removed an inch of the surface of his best fields ?   It would be folly, and it is no less so in the garden   The winter being a very mild one, encouraged the growth of weeds very much, and, where there was other work going on, they got too big   A planta-tion of barberries, evergreen and others, was in this state in early summer, the weeds nearly as high as the bushes   They were cut down with much labour, and I just came upon the scene when the carter was beginning to take away the surface of rich weeds and soil, and I left the weeds and soil where they were, spreading them equally over the surface As it happened, this was followed by many dry weeks, and the dead weeds formed a protection for the bed itself, which did not suffer in the least during the heats. To remove this mass of stuff would have been a costly labour, the surface would have been exposed to direct evaporation, and the plants starved by the drought.

Fallen Leaves —Sometimes leaves are massed in these rubbish yards, and the leaf question is bound up with it. Many people fidget at the sight of beautiful leaves in autumn, instead of enjoying them, as Shelley did, and gardeners are often sweeping them up when they would be much better employed planting good plants or shrubs. What are we to do with the garden leaves? We cannot, it is true, have them in drifts in the flower garden, but it is better to let them all fall before we take much trouble in removing them. In gathering them up, we may best add them to a place set apart for leaf mould. But in every case where they may be let alone, it is much better to let them stay on the surface of wood, grove, shrubbery, or group of shrubs, for protection and nourishment for the ground If any one during the hot years that we have recently had—such as 1893— stood on a height in a woody country, he would see that, while the fields were brown and bare, and cattle and crops distressed for want of water, the wood retained its verdure, and the growth of the year was as good as usual. Why is this? It is explained by the beautiful function of the leaf, which not only does the vital work of the tree, but also shields the ground from the direct action of the sun, and when the leaf has fallen its work is not half done, as it protects and nourishes the roots throughout the year, so that in the hottest years the fibres of the trees find nourishment in decaying leaves. This surely is a reason that leaves should not be scraped out from beneath every shrub or tree, and there is no reason whatever why they should form part of the rubbish heap

And let it be noted that it is not only the better use of the waste as a fertiliser that is a gain, it is the saving of very troublesome labour, often occurring in the warmest part of the year, when every hour is precious over the really important work of the garden—getting in crops of all kinds at the right time and in the best way Also we save the disfigurement of the rubbish yard itself, and get rid of the smoke of the fires kept going to consume it—another nuisance about a country house or garden The ash, the one result of all the waste of labour and filth of the rubbish heap is certainly of some use, but not one-sixth the good of the stuff used in the direct way And it is not only the summer aid we gain, but all we put on in this way settles down in winter to a nice little coat of humus, which nourishes the roots and protects them from frost as well as heat.

WEEDS AND THEIR SEEDS.—The destruction of the seeds of
weeds is the only shadow of reason for the rubbish heap, but it is
bad gardening to let weeds go to seed   And though certain areas of
town gardens have no neighbours from which seeds can be blown, this
is not so in the country, where weed seeds from woods and fields and
young plantations abound in the air.   There is no good remedy for
weeds except early and regular hoeing and cleaning.   Moreover, there
are many conditions in which even if we do allow weeds to go to seed,
they can be used as a mulch ; as, for example, in young orchard and
turf and other planting in or near turf where weed seeds can do no
harm   Burning therefore should be kept to a few essential uses
The source of success in flower gardening is to be always busy
sowing or planting ; there is scarcely a day or a week when some
things have not to be planted or attended to if we want a succession
of beauty ; but when the men are from morn to night busy hoeing
and watering and with other routine work, it is difficult to get time
for securing the successions of plants of various kinds on which the
lasting beauty of a garden at all seasons, depends.

The old labour of grubbing up walks, which was so constant and
dreadful in the very heat of summer, is got rid of by weed-killers, of
which one dressing a year will sometimes suffice to keep the walks
clean, and, better still, prevent us from having to rip up the surfaces
of the walks, which was common in every garden until quite recently,
and is carried on still in many places.   The great gain of abolishing
ignoble routine work, in this and all ways we can, is that we have
time for the real work of the garden, in adding to its beauty with new
or beautiful things and improved ways of growing and arranging them

FIRE AS A CLEANSER.—A fire on the spot is a great aid in the
garden when active changes have to be made, and foul borders or
shrubberies renovated or replanted   Where, in stiff soils, Twitch and
other bad weeds take possession, with perhaps a number of worn-out
shrubs, the simplest way is often to burn all, not trying to disentangle
weeds from the soil in the usual way, but simply skinning the surface
2 inches, or more if need be, and burning it and the vital parts of the
weeds, first removing any plants that are worth saving.   In light
soils the labour of cleaning foul ground is less than in heavy, adhesive soils, but fire is a great aid in all such cases.   If we are removing ugly and heavy masses of Laurels or other evergreens, which have
never given grace or flower to the scene, we should burn them root
and branch at the same time, the result being that we get rid of our
worst weeds, and turn enemies like Goutweed into ashes   This weedy
surface of garden ground is often some of the best of the soil, and it is
much better to keep it where it is, but purified.   Regular cleaning
will keep down all young weeds, but it is a struggle to get the old and

bad weeds out of the soil, owing to the broken roots of Bindweed, Twitch, and Goutweed which escape the closest forking and sharpest eyes. Next there is barrowing or carting to take the weeds to some rotting heap, while, on the other hand, the friendly fire eats up and kills at once the whole of the weeds, and converts them and the burnt surface they infested into good earth, and all this is gained at once without barrow or horse labour.   So that, whatever we may think of cremation for ourselves, it is a good friend in fighting weeds and in helping us to thoroughly cleanse foul garden ground   We have not even the trouble that they had with Don Quixote's books—to carry them into the yard to burn them—as we can so often burn the weeds on the spot, insects and grubs included

EVAPORATION.—Mulching or covering the surface with various kinds of light materials, such as leaf mould, cocoa fibre, manure, and sand, or anything, in fact, which gives an inch or two of loose surface to the earth and prevents evaporation, is a great aid on many soils, but not so important where the beds have been thoroughly prepared, at least not for Roses, Carnations, and many of the best flowers, because, if the roots can go down and find good soil as far as they go, they really do not want mulching, save on very hot soils   Mulching of various kinds or loosening the surface of the ground is, moreover, much easier to carry out in the kitchen and fruit gardens or orchard than in the flower garden, all the surface of which should be covered with living things during the fine season   This is the prettiest way and is not difficult to carry out, as we often see it in cottage gardens and in Nature itself, where the health of the forest and other fertile lands depends to a certain extent on the ground being covered with vegetation, which of itself prevents direct evaporation.   Taking a hint from this, I am very fond of covering the surface with dwarf living plants of fragile nature, which do not much exhaust the soil, and which in very hot weather may help to keep it moist   This is done in the case of Roses and other plants which, being rather small and bare at first, want some help to cover the ground, and a number of very pretty plants may be used for this purpose, which will give us bloom in spring and good colour on the ground.   This, of course, prevents the use of manure, hitherto common on the surface of flower beds, Roses especially.   It is much better that the aid of manure should be given at the root instead of the surface, and if we have plenty of manure and rich soil, there is no need for surface mulching it. Covering the surface with living plants is worth doing, for the sake of the effect alone, even if we have to pay for it in other ways. One result of it is that we may have a beautiful spring garden in addition to the summer garden—that is to say, if our garden is planted for summer and autumn with Roses and the like, by the use of Tufted Pansies and other dwarf plants in the beds we get pretty effects early in the year, and through this living carpet may come up many pretty bulbs. Thus we may have in the same beds, with a little care and thought, two or three different types of flower life.

The plants that may be used in this way are numerous, and mostly rock and mountain plants of Europe and cold countries, evergreen, often bearing pretty flowers and good in colour at all seasons, spreading into pretty carpets easily, and quite hardy, taking often a deeper green in winter, so that used over permanent beds they help to adorn the flower beds in winter, and through them in the dawn of spring the early Crocus, Scilla and Windflower come up to find themselves in green turf of Thyme; Rockfoil; Stonecrop; or varying these according to soil, altitude or position, the cooler north favouring many mountain plants, though some face the ardours of the warmer sun.

THE WASTE OF MONOTONY —A grievous source of wasted effort in gardens is monotony arising from everybody growing what his neighbour grows   Thus it comes that the poor nurseryman who attempts to grow new or rare trees or shrubs very often finds them left on his hands, so that many country nurseries only grow a few stereotyped things, and we see public gardens and squares in London given over to the common Privet, the common Lilac let to run as a weed, and the common Elder, as in Lincoln's Inn Fields

Every lover of the garden could do something to check this fatal monotony by taking up some plant, or family of plants, for himself, which perhaps he is unable to find in the nursery gardens near at hand.   There are not only many beautiful species of plant which are excluded from the ordinary nurseries, but even special nurseries, as for Roses, often exclude good kinds from their collections.   It is not only the introduction of new plants or species we have to think of, but the raising of new forms (hybrids or varieties), the fine cultivation of neglected groups, as the beautiful forms of our native Primrose by Miss Jekyll, the making more artistic use of old and well-known plants, the skilful adaptation of plants and trees to the soil so as to get the highest beauty of which it is capable without excessive care, and without the deaths visible in many places after hard winters   Those who seek to vary the monotony of gardens must be prepared to face some trouble, and they must not take the least notice of what is thought right in the neighbourhood, or of what can be obtained from the nearest nursery garden   The further afield they look, probably the better in the end it will be for them if they would escape from the trammels of monotony

ATTACHING CLIMBERS AND FRUIT TREES TO WALLS —Perhaps the most miserable of all garden-work is that of nailing the shoots of trees to walls, on cold days, and the value of climbing plants now in our gardens is so great, that the best mode of attaching them to walls is a question which, though it may seem a small one from some points of view, is important, and by no means settled for the best. In our self-styled scientific age—the age also of the galvanised iron church and the ironmonger's fence, which is no fence—our gardens have been invaded by galvanised wire, which is put up at great expense on garden and house walls, and is thought to be an essential improvement in all new work. The question does not merely concern walls for climbers round the house, but also the fruit garden In our cold country we cannot ripen the Peach or the choicer fruits without the aid of walls, galvanised wire is used in many gardens, but many growers discover that its effect on the trees is not good. There is a foundation of fact in these complaints, and they are common to French and English gardeners In France, where the cultivation of wall fruit to supply the market with Peaches and fine winter Pears is carried out well, the best growers are against the use of galvanised wire, and think it much better to have the wooden lattice only against the wall, so they keep to the older and prettier way of trellising the wall. For those who care about effect this is well, for whatever harm the wire may do to the tree, of its ugliness there can be no doubt The old French and English way of fixing branches to walls—having trellis-work made of Oak in about 1 inch strips—was a very good one. Chestnut, too, was used, and was thought to be the best, and is often used now in France One advantage of such woodwork is that it looks well on the walls even before we get our plants up, and there is the great facility of being able to tie where we wish, thus avoiding the use of nails and the other miseries of training against walls.

I use Bamboos in forming trellises, with very good results. Trellis-work made of Oak or Chestnut lasted for many years, and was efficient, and a well-made trellis of this sort saves us all the trouble and injury to the wall of pock-marking it with nail holes, forming nests for destructive vermin

There remains the question of fixing our lattice-work of Oak, Chestnut, Pine or Bamboo. In old walls, holdfasts must be driven ; in new ones, pieces of iron with strong eyes should be laid along here and there in the courses of brick or stone as the work goes on

It is a great thing to be relieved from the ugliness and injury of the galvanised wire. We would like to go a little further and keep to old ways of tying things on walls. Those who look through their bills may perhaps come upon items, and not small ones, for tarred twine and other bought means of tying In old times people would have used the shoots of the yellow Willow, which did the work of tying fruit trees to walls better than any tarred twine as far as the main branches were concerned. To say that it is impracticable now is nonsense, as in some great nurseries where millions of plants are

sent out every year, every lot is tied with Willow. Also, the French
way of using a Rush for tying, instead of twine or matting, is an
excellent one. It is a Rush which is harvested and dried carefully,
and it is the simplest thing in the world to tie with so as to allow for
the free growth of the branch, and yet keep the shoot quite secure

THE STAKING OF TREES AND SHRUBS.—Whether staking trees
and shrubs or wind-waving is the worst evil is doubtful, but much
harm is done by staking, and it is costly and troublesome, especially
so for those large trees that are seen in pleasure grounds, surrounded
by a kind of crinoline of galvanised wire. The evil of staking arises
largely from planting trees too big as " specimens " To plant these is
tempting to many, but generally we get a much better result from
small trees that want no staking ; but planting ornamental trees of
considerable size is so common that staking is frequently done, and
very often the trees are injured by the stakes, not only at the root,
but also much in the stem, which sometimes leads to canker It is
known that canker (as in the Larch) enters the trees more readily
where the wounds are ready to receive the spores, and we often see
fruit-trees badly cankered through staking

The wire-roping business for trees is a nuisance, as the ropes
cut in if neglected in the least, and the tree often snaps there,
and when the ropes are finally removed the trees often go down in
gales The best cure for the waste and dangers of staking is to plant
small trees, but often where this is not done for any reason (and sometimes there may be good ones, as in planting vigorous-growing Poplars
to shut out things we do not care to see) we may do good by cutting
in the side shoots close to the stem This leaves the tree with little
for the wind to act upon, and we escape the need of staking without
injury to the tree. Transplanting trees involves so much injury to
the roots that somewhat reducing the tops does good in all ways.

At Kew, when a large tree is transplanted, it is guyed up with
three lengths of soft cord (commonly called " gaskin ") if it appears
likely to become loose. This is better than a stake, cheaper, and less
likely to injure the stem by abrasion. A tree with branches low
enough can be stayed by driving into the ground three stout stakes
at equal distances round the tree, nearly at the circumference of the
branches, and tying a branch to each of the stakes

The picturesque grouping of trees and shrubs is a gain in the
avoidance of the trouble and danger of staking For example, the
pinetum, as seen in many country seats, is a scheme in which trees are
isolated and dotted so as to encourage them as " specimens," which
is the wrong way and the ugly way. In Nature these trees are
almost always massed and grouped in close ways, so that they shelter
each other, and if in planting them we plant as a wood, closely, thin-

ning them very carefully, we find them make trees and give better effects than in the common way they are generally placed, as the trees protect and comfort each other, and shade the ground   I have planted true pinetums in this way, the trees in which have stood violent gales without giving way, and which were never staked, any more than they are on their wild mountain homes   But in this case, as with sailors, we must begin young

WASTED LABOUR IN GLASS-HOUSES —Among the evils of the "bedding" and "carpet system" is the need of costly glass-houses in which to keep the plants all the winter, not one in ten of these plants being as pretty as flowers that are as hardy as the Grass in the field,— like Roses, Carnations, and Delphiniums   It is absurd to grow Alternantheras in costly hothouses, and not to give a place to flowers that endure cold as well as Lilies-of-the-Valley.   Glass-houses are useful helps for many purposes, but we may have noble flower gardens without them   To bloom the Rose and Carnation in mid-winter, to ripen fruits that will not mature in our climate, to enable us to see many fair flowers of the tropics—for these purposes glass-houses are a precious gain ; but for a beautiful flower garden they are almost needless, and the numerous glass-houses in our gardens may be turned to better use   It would not be true to say that good hardy flower-gardening is cheaper than growing the half-hardy plants that often disgrace our gardens, as the splendid variety of beautiful hardy plants tempts one to buy, and it is therefore all the more necessary not to waste money in stupid ways, apart from the heavy initial cost and ceaseless costly labour of the glass-house system of flower garden decoration

For those who think of beauty in our gardens and home landscapes, the placing of a glass-house in the flower garden or pleasure ground is a serious matter, and some of the most interesting places in the country are defaced in that way   In the various dividing lines about a country house there can be no difficulty in finding a site for glass-houses where they cannot injure the views   There is no reason for placing the glass-house in front of a beautiful old house, where its colour mars the prospect, though often, in looking across the land towards an old house, we see first the glare of an ugly glass shed   If this were the case only in the gardens of people lately emerged from the towns to the suburbs of our great cities, it would not be so notable ; but many large country places are disfigured in this way   And, apart from fine old houses and the landscape being defaced by the hard lines and colour of the glass-house, there is the result on the flower garden itself ; efforts to get plants into harmonious and beautiful relations are much increased if we have a horror in the way of glass sheds staring at us   Apart from the heavy cost of coal or coke, the smoke-defilement of many a pretty garden by the ugly vomit of these needless chimneys ; the effect on young gardeners in leading them to despise the far more healthy and profitable labours of the open garden , all these have to be considered in relation to the cost, care and ugliness of the glass nursery as an annual preparation for plants for the flower garden, these plants being with few exceptions far less precious in every way for flower garden or for room than those that are quite hardy.

A few years ago, before the true flower garden began to get a place in men's minds, many of the young gardeners refused to work in places where there was no glass A horrid race this pot and kettle idea of a garden would have led to men to get chills if their gloves were not aired. I met the difficulty myself by abolishing glass altogether. Only where we do this we must show better things in the open-air garden, than ever flourished in a glass house.

WASTED LABOUR IN MOVING EARTH.—Next to moving heaven, the heaviest undertaking is that of moving earth, and there are no labours of gardening men that lead to more wasted effort, where care and experience are not brought to bear on the work Labour in many parts of the country has become dearer, and the question of moving earth without needless waste of energy is a serious one for all who have much groundwork to do We may often see instances of misuse of labour , the soil from foundations carted far, and then put deep over the roots of old trees, to their death or injury. A man of resource in dealing with ground would place this soil in some well-chosen spot near, having first removed the surface soil, and, resurfacing with it, planted it with a handsome group of beautiful shrubs or trees, so that the surface would in no ugly way differ from the general lie of the ground near. The presence of carts and horses seems very often to lead to waste of labour in carting earth when barrows and a few planks would do the work better

In necessary groundwork there is inevitably much moving of earth in getting levels, carrying roads and paths across hollows, and for various other reasons We should make a rule of getting the soil in all such cases as near at hand as possible Mistakes in levelling ground are frequent, and often lead to twice moving of soil. The best man for groundwork is often one with a good navvy's experience, and many such men know how to make heavy groundwork changes without putting a barrowful of soil in the wrong place Very often spare soil has to be removed, and in this necessary work ugly mounds are made, when, by a little care in choosing the place well and never leaving any ugly angles, but making the ground take the natural gradation of the adjacent earth, it could be well planted Hardy trees take well to such banks if the good soil is kept on the top, as it should always be.

The same remarks may serve for the moving of turf, gravel, stones and soil, save that to get good soil for the formation of beds, we must go where the good soil is ; whereas for the bottoms of roads and paths, the support of banks, base of terraces or mounds, much saving may be effected by getting what we want in the nearest possible place, never fearing to make a hollow if need be, as that can be so easily planted with some free-growing tree or shrub ; the hardy Pines, like Scotch, Corsican, and Silver Firs, being excellent for this, as they thrive in almost any earth, and often on surfaces from which the whole bed of fertile soil has been removed

Apart from essential groundwork, there is the diversifying of ground artificially, as may be seen in our parks, owing to the false idea that you cannot make level ground picturesque with planting. Proof that this is not impossible may be seen in many a level country planted by Nature, as in the forest plain and in many a park and pleasure ground both in Germany, France, and Britain. Trees are given to us to get this very variety of broken surface, and the idea that to make a place picturesque we must imitate—and usually badly imitate—naturally diversified ground is most inartistic. No doubt broken ground has many charms, but so has the fertile plain, and the best way is to accept and enhance the beauty of each variety of surface To do so is the planter's true work. In cities and suburbs there is often occasion to conceal ugly objects, and earth, if to spare, may be used well and wisely in raising at once the base of a plantation of young trees, but an enormous amount of labour given to making artificial mounds might be saved without any loss, and with much gain to garden design

There are yet certain landscape gardeners who make mounds or earth-pimples everywhere, regardless of the growth of the plants. If people would only spend more on good planting and less on trying to "diversify," as they call it, the surface, it would be better for our gardens. In many cases when planting time comes, so much effort has been spent on needless groundwork, that there are no means to spare for the best work of all in garden making, namely, good planting. But any one can make earth dumplings of the sort we see too many of, while planting to give enduring and beautiful effects requires a knowledge of trees and shrubs.

In our public parks the mania for foolish groundwork may be often seen, one of its results being the burial of the tree base, surrounded, perhaps, with a brick-lined pit-hole, as in St. James's Park. Shooting earth and rubbish to fill up the hollows on such a precious space as Hampstead Heath is common, and as the surrounding district is busy in building, these attempts are, we fear, often the result of finding a shoot for earth and rubbish Therefore the bringing in of such rubbish should be absolutely forbidden, as the only effect of this filling up of hollow places is to destroy the incidents of the ground, usually far prettier in form than the results of smug levelling up, or, worse still, the formation of such artificial mounds as we see examples of in the parks. Even the squares in our level Thames valley are not exempt from outrage of this kind, of which, perhaps, the most hideous example is that of Euston Square, in which a high and ugly earth-bank has been put all around the Square, so steep that even the cheap nursery rubbish of the London squares—Privet and Elder—refuses to grow upon it, and so in the summer days, instead of the grass and tree-stems and cool shadows, a bank of dusty rubbish meets the eye!

Another serious source of waste of the inexperienced in ground-work is burying the top surface, the most precious, and in many cases the result of ages of decay of turf and plants. In alluvial land and light friable hill soils this mistake does not so much matter, but in heavy land where there is a clay subsoil it is fatal The first thing in all groundwork is to save the top soil with the greatest care, for the sake of using it again in its proper place , and how to save it, so that it may be available at the end of the work, is one of the most essential things the good ground-worker has to think of.

Trenches for the reception of pipes, drains, and foundations should not be opened until the materials are at hand, as in wet weather, doing so often leads to the sides falling in and much needless labour The direction of walks, roads, or designs for beds, borders, or gardens, should be carefully marked out and looked at from every point of view before carrying them out, having regard to their use and their relation to all things about them, and not merely to any plan on paper. Attention to this will often save much labour in groundwork

A cause of much waste of labour in moving soil is the usual way of treating mud after the cleansing of artificial ponds—often a poor inheritance to leave to one's children. The silting up with mud goes on for ever, and while the mere expense of getting this out of the pond bed in any way is usually great, the cost is often increased through the idea that the stuff is of manurial value This leads people frequently to heap it up on the banks to dry, then to liming it, and eventually to moving it on to the land, these various labours adding to the disfigurement of the foreground of beautiful ground often for a long time Pond mud has very little manurial value generally, though it will differ to some extent according to the sort of soil the supply comes from Usually, however, it has very slight value, and any labour bestowed upon it from that point of view is nearly always wasted. The best and simplest way is to put it direct on to some poor pasture near, or on to any ground where it may be got rid of with least labour to man or horse Where the pond is ugly in outline and not essential either for its beauty in the home landscape or for its uses for fish or water store, it may often be worth considering whether the best way would not be to let the water off and turn the mud bed into a handsome grove of Willows and Dogwoods, and an excellent covert at the same time. I know nothing among trees quite so good in effect in the landscape, winter and summer, as the white, red, and yellow Willows, with an undergrowth of the red Dogwoods.

LABELS.—Where possible it is best to do without labels, except where we grow many kinds of things that differ by slight shades, as Carnations and Roses. The contents of a garden are usually in a state of change ; we are continually adding to and taking from them ; new plants are introduced ; a severe winter kills a number of shrubs, which we determine not to replant. Fashion changes the garden vegetation too, and then the permanent labels, cast and burnt into hardware and cemented in cast iron, are thrown aside. I prefer a label which can be used again, such as a cast-iron label of " T shape " or, in other words, a slip of cast iron with an oblong head slightly thrown back. These are cast very cheaply in the iron districts. We have to paint them and write the names of the trees on them when they come to hand ; but that can be readily done by a handy painter in winter. In a large garden, where much naming is required, the best way is to train a youth who is likely to remain in the place, by placing a copy of the desired kind of letters before him. It is an advantage to give the label a coat of copal varnish when the letters are dry, and generally to use white letters on a black or dark ground, and give three coats of black over one of red lead. These are the best labels for the shrubs and choice young trees of a pleasure ground or flower garden. The painting will last for twenty years, and if we cease to cultivate the plants to which they belong, the labels may be repainted.

Simplest label for trees.

Position for tree label.

With big trees it is always a mistake to use a ground label. The best labels for large trees are made of pieces of tin about 4½ inches by 3½ inches. About half an inch of the upper edge should be bent at a right angle so as to form a little coping for the label, two holes should be made just beneath the little angle, through which a strong copper wire should be put and firmly nailed to the tree. Place it so as to be easily read, at about 5½ feet from the ground. Paint it dark brown or black with white letters and it will last for many years. All labels inserted in the grass in pleasure grounds are liable to be pulled up by mowers or others, and in this way to get lost, while the labels on the stems are safe from such mishaps.

For low trees and bushes to which copper wire may be fixed with ease, the simplest and most enduring labels are those that are made of cast metal galvanised, and as they are very enduring they are best for hardy trees and shrubs. The words on them should be as few as may be, and all needless ones omitted. Thus in fruit-tree labels it is needless to use the word Pear or Apple, but simply the variety, as " Ribstone. " This plan makes these labels more legible than when they are crowded with letters. For half-hardy plants, annuals, and plants of a season only, wooden labels are often the most convenient. In most gardens it is the practice to write the name at the part that goes in the ground, and to go on from thence to the top— a bad way, for the label always begins to decay at the base, and thus the beginning of the name is lost, while the end of it may be quite legible. After a little practice it becomes as easy to write from the top as from the other end, and, in writing the names, always begin as near the top as possible.

Cast-iron labels; the simplest, neatest, and best form for shrubs, bold herbaceous plants, and for all cases where the label has to be fixed in the ground

The use of the wooden label should be given up in favour of labels with raised or incised letters. The main reason is that the endurance of the wooden label is too slight ; moreover, some kinds of good stamped-metal label are less conspicuous in the garden than the wooden label, and any kind of conspicuous label is bad. As regards labels for large gardens and trees, at Kew they now use a lead label of their own stamping, so that should many labels get out of use, as is the case in large collections, it is easy to melt them down and use the metal again for trees and enduring plants of all kinds.

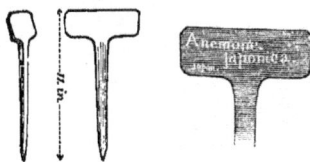

THE

ENGLISH FLOWER GARDEN
AND HOME GROUNDS

PART II

CONTAINING THE FLOWERS, FLOWERING SHRUBS AND
TREES, EVERGREENS, AND HARDY FERNS FOR
THE OPEN-AIR FLOWER GARDEN IN THE
BRITISH ISLES, WITH THEIR CUL-
TIVATION AND THE POSITIONS
MOST SUITABLE FOR THEM
IN GARDENS

"A garden is a beautiful book, writ by the finger of God every flower and every leaf is a letter You have only to learn them—and he is a poor dunce that cannot, if he will, do that—to learn them and join them, and then to go on reading and reading. And you will find yourself carried away from the earth by the beautiful story you are going through . . And then there are some flowers that seem to me like overdutiful children tend them but ever so little, and they come up and flourish, and show, as I may say, their bright and happy faces to you "—DOUGLAS JERROLD

THE

ENGLISH FLOWER GARDEN

AND HOME GROUNDS

ABELIA. — Beautiful shrubs, of the Honeysuckle order, little grown in our country, and best in warm districts. The best known is the Rock Abelia (*A. rupestris*), a Chinese shrub, delicate pale pink in autumn, is always best planted in a raised bank in light soils, as it is then less liable to injury during winter. *A. uniflora,* also from China, is of like habit. The Three-flowered Abelia (*A. triflora*) coming from N. India, is less hardy than the Chinese kinds, but will clothe a wall in a few years. It bears fragrant pink flowers in clusters at the end of summer. *A. floribunda* is rather too tender for the open air, except in the mildest parts of the country ; it is evergreen, with clusters of rose-purple flowers, and makes a good wall shrub. In mild districts in the southern parts of England and Ireland Abelias sometimes do well in the open air.

ABIES (*Silver Fir*).—Beautiful evergreen trees of northern and mountainous regions, many hardy in our country, and valuable timber trees in their own. Some of the Indian and Japanese Silver Firs suffer in our country by starting too early in our open winters and harsh springs ; in their own frost-bound mountain lands the young shoots only start when all danger is past, but with us they often start owing to the mild weather and are injured afterwards. One remedy for this is the selection, where possible, of exposed and elevated positions which will not encourage early growth, and also, perhaps, not making the soil so rich and deep as is the rule. In our country, as with many of the conifers, the usual way is to put them apart as "specimens," but that, from an artistic point of view, and that of their own health, is not always the best. Where there is room these trees should be grouped together so as to shelter each other, in which state they are more effective and protect the ground from the sun. Grafting of rare kinds, is very often resorted to, which should, in all cases where we hope to secure their long life and health, be on their own roots.

There is still much confusion of names owing to the American trees having originally been sent over under various names, and from different localities. The following selection includes the best and most distinct so far as the trees are known. In this, as in many other families, there are a variety of variegated and other sorts which are given fine names, these are generally useless to those who think of the natural dignity and beauty of the tree. We do not refer by this to natural geographical varieties which may be valuable as coming from diverse climates.

A. AMABILIS (Cascade Mountains Fir).—A tall, massive tree with deep bluish-green foliage, and dark purple cones thriving in Britain. It is not easy to get it true to name and on own roots. Owing to propagating by grafting from side shoots the trees do not make a good leader. British Columbia.

A. BALSAMEA (Balsam Fir).—A slender northern forest fir rarely attaining a height of more than 80 feet, and much smaller in high Arctic regions. Hardy in our country but somewhat uncertain as to soil, owing to the great difference in our climate to its own. Northern America, and the mountains in N. E. America.

A. BRACHYPHYLLA (Jesso Silver Fir).—A handsome and hardy tree, over 100 feet high, with bright green foliage and short leaves. The densely crowded leaves are very silvery underneath, and the general effect of a healthy specimen very pleasing. Japan.

A. BRACTEATA (Santa Lucia Fir).—A stately tree, often 150 feet high in its native country. The foliage is long and rather scattered, sharply pointed. It is injured in some districts by starting early in the spring. There are very few good specimens of it in Britain, the best being at Tortworth Court and Eastnor. N. W. America.

A. CEPHALONICA (Cephalonian Fir).—A vigorous Fir of about 60 ft. high, hardy in this country in a variety of soils, but is best planted in an exposed position to prevent it starting into growth too early. In Britain, is handsome till it reaches a height of about 30 ft., when

Abies magnifica. From a photograph by the Earl of Annesley, Castlewellan.

the leaders give way and the side branches grow vigorously. Even in old specimens with several heads it forms a picturesque tree. Greece.

A. CILICICA (Mount Taurus Fir).—A graceful tree, 40 ft. to 60 ft. high, with slender branches. It grows freely, but is apt to be injured by spring frosts; the leaves are soft, and of a peculiar shade of green where it thrives. Cilicia.

A. CONCOLOR (Hoary White Fir). — A whitish tree of medium height, with thick, grey bark. The flat leaves are about 2 ins. long, and it has small, pale yellow cones. It is hardy in Britain, and a rapid grower. Colorado.

A. FIRMA (Japanese Silver Fir).—A tree of sometimes 150 feet in height, with light brown bark and foliage of a glossy green. Hardy in Britain, and grows freely when established, although it is late in starting. It is a handsome tree with short branches and stiff habit. Japan.

A. FRASERI (Allegheny Fir).—A forest tree, reaching 90 feet high in its own country, with smooth bark having resinous blisters. It is allied to the Balsam Fir, but has shorter and more oval cones, and leaves with silvery undersides. Mountains of Virginia, N. Carolina, and Tenessee.

A. GRANDIS (Puget Sound Fir).—A beautiful and stately tree of over 200 feet, with dark green cones 2 to 3 inches long, and dark shining leaves, white below. Hardy and free in various parts of Britain; best in moist soils, trees in Scotland at Ochertyre being over 60 feet high in 1899. N. W. America.

A. LASIOCARPA (Alpine Fir).—A beautiful spire-like tree 150 feet high with white bark, and very small cones, purple, 2 to 3 inches long, and red male flowers, the foliage luxuriant and gracefully curved. Alaska, B. Columbia.

A. LOWIANA (California White Fir).—A lovely tree, often 150 feet high, long leaves and light green cones, turning yellow at maturity. Oregon to Southern California.

A. MAGNIFICA (California Red Fir).—A stately mountain tree of 200 to 250 feet, with brown bark (red within), and very large light purple cones 6 to 8 inches long. The foliage is dense on the lower branches, but thinner towards the top, of olive-green. Grows rapidly in Britain. N. California.

A. MARIESI (Maries' Silver Fir) is a tall, pyramidal tree with robust spreading branches and dark purple cones 4 to 5 inches long. Japan.

A. NOBILIS (Columbia Fir).—A mountain tree, 200 to 300 feet high, with deep glaucous foliage and brown cones 5 to 7 inches long. Hardy and rapid grower in Britain. Oregon.

A. NORDMANNIANA (Crimean Fir). — A beautiful dark green tree, with rigid branches and dense dark green foliage and large cones. Hardy and good grower in Britain. Caucasus and Crimea.

A. NUMIDICA (Mount Babor Fir).—A tree of medium height with bright green foliage. Hardy in this country, but may fail from starting too early. Mountains of N. Africa, growing with Cedars and Yew.

A. PECTINATA (Silver Fir).—A noble tree of the mountains of Central Europe, often planted in Britain, and growing well over 100 feet high at Longleat, Burton Park, and many other places. It was the first of the Silver Firs planted in Britain, and one of the best. When young it grows well in the shade of other trees, and it is an excellent tree to plant for shelter, as it will grow in the most exposed situations, and in peaty as well as ordinary soils.

A. PINSAPO (Spanish Silver Fir).—A large Fir, with bright green prickly foliage, and thriving in almost any soil and in chalky districts. Often suffers from too early a start in spring, and the usual method of isolation by which the grass exhausts the moisture. Spain.

A. SACHALINENSIS (Saghalien Silver Fir).— A tall tree with greyish-brown bark, narrow leaves and small cones. It is hardy, and of distinct and graceful habit, a native of Japan and Saghalien.

A. SIBIRICA (Siberian Silver Fir).—A slow-growing tree of medium size, injured by spring frosts.

A. VEITCHI (Veitch's Silver Fir).—A tall tree of over 100 feet. The bark is light grey and the leaves a bright glossy green with silvery streaks, the cones being a purplish-brown, thriving in Britain. Japan.

A. WEBBIANA (Webb's Fir).—An Indian Fir, sometimes nearly 100 feet high, and one of the most distinct. The leaves are deep glossy green with silvery undersides, and the cones are large. A variety Pindrow is without the silver markings. Both suffer much from spring frosts. Himalayas.   F. M.

ABRONIA (*Sand Verbena.*) — Small Californian annuals or perennials of a trailing habit, with showy blossoms in dense Verbena-like clusters. *A. arenaria* (*A. latifolia*), a honey-scented perennial, has trailing stems and dense clusters of lemon-yellow flowers; *A. umbellata*, also an annual with succulent trailing stems and clusters of rosy-purple, slightly fragrant flowers; *A. fragrans*, forming large branching tufts from 1¼ to 2 ft., and white flowers which expand late in the afternoon, and then emit a delicate vanilla-like perfume; *A. villosa* is a fine species with violet flowers, and *A. Crux Mastæ* a pretty species with white scented flowers. *A. arenaria* and *A. umbellata* should be planted in rather poor, light, and dry soil, on an open, well-drained border or rockwork. The seeds often remain dormant some time before vegetating; those of *A. umbellata* germinate more readily. *A. fragrans*, which does not ripen seed in this country, is best in friable soil, and is larger than the others. Abronias flower in summer and autumn, and are pretty and effective when well planted. *Nyctagineæ.*

ABUTILON—Plants mostly requiring greenhouse temperature in winter, but growing freely out-of-doors in summer, and a graceful aid in the flower garden,

Abutilon, Boule de Neige.

at least in the southern counties. *A. Darwini* and its forms, as well as the varieties related to *A. striatum*, under favourable conditions, grow from 4 ft. to 8 ft. in height. They can be made bushy by stopping, and they flower better than they do in pots. They are useful among the taller and more graceful plants for the flower garden, and are easily raised from seed and cuttings. *A. vitifolium* is a very handsome wall-plant in mild districts, and several sorts may be grown in the open air in gardens in warm sea-shore districts. *A. Sellowianum marmoratum* is a fine variety. Among the best in cultivation are the following, and new varieties are often raised: Admiration, Anna Crozy, Buisson d'Or, Darwini majus, Elegantissimum, Grandiflorum, Lemoinei, Lady of the Lake, Leo, Orange Perfection, Boule de Neige Delicatum, Pactole, Darwini tesselatum, Thompsoni variegatum, vexillarium variegatum, Brilliant, King of Roses, Canarybird, Golden Queen, and Scarlet Gem.

ACACIA (*Tassel Tree*).— Beautiful shrubs and trees, mostly thriving in warmer countries than ours, but some few are grown out of doors in the warmer parts of our country. *A. Julibrissin.*—By confining this to a single stem and using young plants, or those cut down every year, one gets an erect stem covered with leaves as graceful as a Fern, and pretty amidst low-growing flowers. The leaves are slightly sensitive : on fine sunny days they spread out fully and afford a pleasant shade ; on dull ones the leaflets fall down. It is better raised from seed. *A. lophantha*, though not hardy, grows freely in the open air in summer, and gives graceful verdure

among flowers. It may easily be raised from seed sown early in the year to give plants fit for putting out in early summer. Plants a year old or so, strong and well hardened off for planting out at the end of May, are best. *A. dealbata* may be grown in gardens in the south, and against walls. And other kinds, such as *armata* and *verticilata* are hardier, and being closer in habit, better fitted for open air culture away from walls in southern sheltered gardens.

ACÆNA.—Alpine and rock plants belonging to the Rose family. Though not pretty in their flowers, if we except the crimson spines that give a charm to the little New Zealand *A. microphylla*, these plants have a neat habit of growth that fits them for very dwarf carpets in the rock garden, and now and then, to cover dry parts of borders and tufts on the margins of borders, they are very useful ; among the most useful being argentea, millefolia, pulchella, ovalifolia, and sarmentosa, all of free growth and increase.

ACANTHOLIMON (*Prickly Thrift*). —Dwarf mountain herb plants of the Sea Lavender order, extending from the east of Greece to Thibet, and having their headquarters in Persia. The flowers resemble those of Statice and Armeria, but the plants form branching, cushion-like tufts ; the leaves are rigid and spiny. They are dwarf evergreen rock-garden

Acæna microphylla.

and choice border plants. We have had the following species for years, but have not been very successful in propagating any except *A. glumaceum*, which is the freest in growth, the others being very slow. Cuttings taken off in late summer and kept in a cold frame during winter make good plants in two years, but by layering one gets larger plants sooner. All are hardy, and prefer warm, sunny situations in sandy loam. There are only a few kinds in cultivation, such as *A. glumaceum, venustum,* and *androsaceum. A. Kotschyi* is handsome, with long spikes rising well above the leaves and white flowers ; *A. melananthum* has short, dense spikes, the limb of the calyx being

Acantholimon glumaceum.

bordered with dark violet or black ; and other pretty species, not all in cultivation perhaps, are *cephalotes, acerosum, laxiflorum, libanoticum,* and *Pinardi,* and so far as we know them, thriving best on the sunny rock-garden, in light deep soil. Where large plants of the rare kinds exist, it is a good plan to work some cocoa-nut fibre and sand, in equal parts, into the tufts in early autumn, but before doing this some of the shoots should be gently torn so as to half sever them at a heel ; water to settle the soil. Many of the growths thus treated will root by spring. Cuttings made in the ordinary way are uncertain, but August or September is the best time to try them.—E. J.

ACANTHOPANAX.—*A. ricinifolium* is the most striking of the shrubby Araliads, hardy and grows freely at Kew. Professor Rein, of the University of Bonn, mentions trees 90 feet high, with stem 9 feet to 12 feet in circumference in the forests of Yezo, the great northern island of Japan. *A. sessiliflorum* is a new species, a native of China, Manchuria, and Japan. It has rugose, dark green leaves, consisting of three to five leaflets, the midribs having a few scattered bristles. *A. isspinosum.*—A small shrub with leaves divided into five segments (sometimes only three).

The stem is armed with a few sharp prickles. This plant is more frequently grown in a greenhouse than out of doors, more especially the variegated form. They are both hardy in sheltered positions, although they do not grow so freely as indoors. *A. palmatum atro-sanguineum, p. sanquineum,* which have very rich crimson foliage, and *pinnatifidum,* in which the leaves are much divided, are the finest of the Japanese kinds. The plants should not be grafted.—W. J. B.

ACANTHUS (*Bear's-breech*).—Stately perennials with fine foliage, mostly coming from the countries round the Mediterranean, and are hardy, though the foliage may suffer now and then. On rocky banks, borders of the bolder sort, and in almost any position among the more vigorous hardy plants they look well, and will live in shade, yet to flower well should have full sun. Acanthuses succeed best on warm, deep soil, though they will grow in almost any garden soil. They are easy of increase by division of the roots in winter, and may be raised from seed. *Acanthaceæ.*

Acanthus.

There are several hardy kinds.—*A. hispanicus, A. longifolius, A. mollis, A. m. latifolius* (*A. lusitanicus*), *A niger,* and *A. spinosissimus.*

ACER (*Maple*). — Trees, mostly of

northern regions, often of the highest value in pleasure-ground planting, some of the species breaking into a great number of varieties. Among the best are the Silver Maple (A. eriocarpum), naturally a very beautiful tree, though we get from it variegated and other forms which are not of much value, except the cut-leaved one. The Norway Maple (A. platanoides), a beautiful tree, has many varieties, the purple ones being effective. The common Sycamore Maple (A. Pseudo-platanus) has also a number of variegated and other varieties, though none of them better than the natural tree; it is doubtful if there is any finer tree than this when old. The sycamore walk in the Bishop's Garden, at Chichester, and the trees near Knole House, remind us of its fine qualities for avenues or groups ; and it is the best of forest trees to face the sea, as it

Acer circinatum.

does in Anglesey and many other places. Our Native Maple (A. campestre), is also a pretty tree, seldom planted in gardens, but of which fine trees may be seen at Mereworth in Kent and many other places. The variegated forms are usually tree rubbish. The Virginian or Red Maple (A. rubrum) is a beautiful tree, as is also the Sugar Maple (A. saccharinum) and the Colchic Maple (A. lætum). The Japanese Maples are interesting and beautiful, but not quite hardy and robust, except in the most favoured districts. Moreover, the fine varieties are often grafted, which makes them still less able to endure severe weather. A. Negundo is the kind which has given us the much overplanted variegated Maple so common in gardens. A. Ginnala is worth mentioning as a low tree—almost a shrub—whose leaves die off a rich red in colour. The North American and European species are hardy as forest trees and thrive in almost any soil, but the Southern

American kinds and Japanese Maples want warmer soils and positions to thrive in our climate. The variegated varieties in this family are too many, and our nurserymen insist upon sending out many forms which, however attractive they may appear to them in the hand, planted out soon give a poor and even harmful effect.

The known and cultivated species are the following : *Acer campestre*, Europe ; *caudatum*, N. India ; *circinatum*, California ; *cissifolium*, Japan ; *carpinifolium*, Japan ; *cratægifolium*, Japan ; *creticum*, Asia Minor ; *diabolicum*, Japan ; *distylum*, Japan ; *eriocarpum*, N. America ; *glabrum*, N. America ; *grandidentatum*, N. America ; *Heldreichi*, E. Europe ; *heterophyllum*, E. Europe ; *hyrcanum*, Caucasus ; *insigne*, Persia ; *japonicum*, Japan ; *Lobeli*, S. Italy ; *macrophyllum*, California ; *micranthum*, Japan ; *monspessulanum*, S. Europe ; *Negundo*, N. America ; *nikoense*, Japan ; *opulifolium*, Europe ; *palmatum*, Japan ; *pectinatum*, N. India ; *pennsylvanicum*, N. America ; *pictum*, Japan ; *platanoides*, Europe ; *Pseudoplatanus*, Europe, Asia ; *rubrum*, N. America ; *rufinerve*, Japan ; *saccharinum*, N. America ; *Sieboldianum*, Japan ; *sikkimense*, N. India ; *spicatum*, N. America ; *tataricum*, E. Europe ; *Volxemi*, Caucasus.

ACHILLEA (*Milfoil, Yarrow*). — Hardy herbaceous and Alpine plants spread through Northern Asia, S. Europe, and Asia Minor, varying in height from 2 in. to 4 ft., their flowers being pale lemon, yellow, and white, but rarely pink or rose. They grow freely in most garden soils, and, with the exception of the dwarfer mountain species, increase rapidly. Some of the large kinds are fine plants for groups, as *A. Eupatorium*. The alpine kinds, such as *A. tomentosa*, are for the rock-garden, or margins of choice borders.

The best of the larger kinds are excellent for large groups in mixed borders and also in shrubberies ; among the best being *A. Eupatorium*, *A. Fili-pendula*, *A. millefolium roseum* (a rose-coloured variety of a native plant), and *A. Ptarmica* (the Sneezewort), the double variety being one of the best perennials. The variety known as the "Pearl" is a larger improved form. *A. Ægeratum* (Sweet Maudlin) is a distinct old kind, about 2 feet high.

The dwarfer species come in for groups for the rock garden or the margins of rock borders, and, occasionally, as edging plants, most of them growing freely and being easy of increase ; but some of the higher Alpine kinds are not very enduring in our open winters. Among the best are *A. aurea*, *A. rupestris*, *A. tomentosa*, and *A. Clavennæ*.

ACIPHYLLA.—A small and not important group of New Zealand plants, suitable for the rock-garden in sandy soil. They may be raised from seeds or by division. *A. Colensoi* is quite a bush with bayonet-like spines, and *A. squarrosa* is called the Bayonet plant for this reason.

ACONITUM (*Monkshood*).—Tall and handsome herbaceous plants, of the Buttercup order, dangerous from their poisonous roots. There are many names—not so many species,—of value for our gardens. They should not be planted where the roots could be by any chance dug up by mistake for edible roots, as they are so deadly : almost all the kinds may be easily

Aconitum Napellus (Monkshood).

naturalised in copses or shrubberies away from the garden proper, or beside streamlets or in openings in rich bottoms.

The best kinds are *A. Napellus* and its forms, *versicolor* and others ; *A. chinense*, *A. autumnale*, *A. japonicum*, and *A. tauricum* ; *A. Lycoctonum* is a yellow-flowered and vigorous species. They are from 3 ft. to 5 ft. high and flower from July to September. *A. Fortunei*, the old *A. chinense* of gardens, is the best for late blooming.

ACORUS (*Sweet Flag*).—Waterside or marsh plants of the arum order, easily cultivated, and of wide distribution. *A. Calamus* (Sweet Flag) is a marsh or waterside plant, now naturalised in most parts of Europe. A variety has gold-striped leaves. *A. gramineus* (Grass-leaved Acorus) has a slender creeping rhizome covered with numerous Grass-like leaves, from 4 in. to 6 in. in length, and

there is a variety with white-streaked leaves. This plant is often seen in the little bronze trays of water-plants in Japanese gardens and houses. China.

ACROCLINIUM.—*A. roseum*, the only species, is a pretty half-hardy annual from Western Australia, growing over 1 foot high with rosy-pink flowers, which, owing to their chaffiness, are used as "everlasting" flowers. Seeds should be sown in frames in March, and the seedlings planted at the end of April or early in May in a warm border ; or the seeds may be sown in the open ground in fine rich soil at the end of April. If the flowers are to be dried as everlastings, it will be well to gather them when fresh and young—some when scarcely out of the bud state. This annual might be made graceful use of in mixed beds. There is a white variety. *Compositæ.*

ACTÆA (*Baneberry*). — Vigorous perennials of the Buttercup order, 3 ft. to 6 ft. high, thriving in free soil ; flower spikes, white and long, with showy berries. The white Baneberry has white berries with red footstalks. The var. *rubra* of *A. spicata* has showy fruit ; the plants are best suited for rich bottoms in the wild garden, as though the foliage and habit are good, the flowers are short-lived in the ordinary border, and somewhat coarse in habit. *A. spicata* (common Baneberry or Herb Christopher), *A. racemosa* (Black Snakeroot), *A. alba* (white Baneberry), having white berries with red stalks, and one or two American forms of the common Baneberry are in cultivation. The flowers have often a very unpleasant smell.

ACTINELLA.—North American composites of which there are three kinds in gardens, dwarf-growing plants with yellow flowers. The finest is *A. grandiflora* (Pigmy Sunflower), a native of Colorado, an alpine plant with flower-heads 3 in. in diameter, growing from 6 in. to 9 in. high. The other species, *A. acaulis*, *A. Brandegei*, and *A. scaposa*, are somewhat similar. They are all perennial, and thrive in a light soil.

ACTINIDIA.—Climbing summer-leafing shrubs of the Camellia order from Japan and China, thriving in warm rich soil. They all have climbing or twining stems and bear waxy white flowers. *A. Kolomikta* should be grown against a wall or against a buttress or tree trunk placed against the wall, on which the stems support themselves. The leaves are brightly tinted in autumn, and the flowers of *A. polygama* are fragrant. *A. volubilis* is free-growing and has small white flowers.

ADENOPHORA (*Gland Bellflower*).— Hardy perennials of the Bellflower family, 18 in. to over 3 ft. high. . They are mostly from Siberia and Dahuria, with, flowers generally blue in colour. Some of the most distinct species are *A. corono-pifolia*, *A. denticulata*, *A. Lamarckii*, *A. liliiflora*, *A. polymorpha*, *A. stylosa*, and *A. pereskiæfolia*. In these occur slight variations in colour and size of flower. Their thick fleshy roots revel in a rich loam, and like a damp subsoil; they are impatient of removal, and should not be increased by division. Unlike the Platy-codons, they seed freely, and are easily increased.

ADIANTUM (*Maidenhair Fern*).— Elegant ferns, few of which are hardy, growing best in a rough fibry peat, mixed with sand and lumps of broken stone or brick. *A. pedatum*, the hardy N. American kind, is charming among shade-loving plants in the wild garden with the more beautiful wood-flowers, such as Trillium, Hepatica, and blue Anemone, in moist soil. *A. Capillus veneris*, the British Maidenhair Fern, is best in a sheltered nook at the foot of a shady wall, and in the southern warmer countries might be found near fountain basins and moist corners of the rock garden and hardy fernery. There are several varie-ties or forms of this Maidenhair.

ADLUMIA (*Climbing Fumitory*).— Climbing biennial plants. One species only (*A. cirrhosa*) is known, a rapid grower. Its Maidenhair-Fern-like leaves are borne on slender twining stems with abundant white blossoms, about ½ in. long. There is

Adlumia cirrhosa.

a variety with purple flowers. It thrives in a warm soil, and its place is trailing over a shrub or twiggy branch, placed either against a wall or in the open.

ADONIS (*Pheasant's Eye*).—Beautiful perennial or biennial plants, belonging to the Buttercup order, chiefly natives of cornfields in Europe and Western Asia, dwarf, with finely divided leaves, and red, yellow, or straw-coloured flowers. *A. vernalis* (*Ox-Eye*) is a handsome Alpine herb, forming dense tufts 8 in. to 15 in.

Adonis pyrenaica.

high of finely divided leaves in whorls along the stems. Blooming in spring, with large, yellow, Anemone-like flowers 3 in. in diameter. Of *A. vernalis* there are several varieties, the chief being *A. v. sibirica*, which differs in having larger flowers. *A. apennina* is a later-blooming form, and is a good plant for moist spots on the rock-garden. *A. pyrenaica* is from the Eastern Pyrenees, but with broader petals. *A. amurensis* is a new kind from Manchuria, with finely cut leaves, bloom-ing with the snowdrop, and seems to be of easy culture. *A. autumnalis* is a pretty bright-coloured annual.

The rock-garden or borders of sandy loam suits the perennial kinds well. Division, or by seed sown as soon as gathered.

ÆSCULUS (*Horse Chestnut, Buckeye*). —The Horse Chestnuts are mostly me-dium-sized trees, hardy in nearly every soil, and excellent for park and garden.

The common variety is an exception as to size, and one of the most beautiful of flowering trees There is at least one handsome variety of it with very long spikes The red Buckeye (*Æ Pavia*) is a handsome small tree, with dense and large foliage, together with bright red flowers in large loose clusters in early summer Sometimes it rises from 15 to 20 ft high, but some of its varieties are only low-spreading or trailing shrubs *Æ. humilis, pendula, arguta,* and *lacimata* are forms of *Æ Pavia,* and the plants are useful for grouping with taller trees *Æ flava* (the yellow Buckeye) is common, and sometimes 40 ft high It has something of the habit of the red Horse Chestnut (*Æ rubicunda*), but smoother leaves. A variety called *purpurascens* (sometimes *Æ discolor*) has much showier flowers, larger, and of a reddish tint The Æsculi, named in gardens and nurseries as *Æ neglecta, hybrida, pubescens, Lyoni, rosea,* and *pallida,* may be included in one of the foregoing species, and some differ but slightly from them. They are all low trees or large shrubs, coming into leaf early and losing their foliage in early autumn, especially in light or dry soils One of the best of all the forms is the brightly-coloured *Æ. Brioti* A distinct species is the Californian Buckeye (*Æ californica*), which in this country does not usually rise above shrub height It has slender-stalked leaves, broad leaflets, and in early summer dense erect clusters of white or pinkish fragrant flowers ; a valuable hardy tree. Quite different from the rest is the North American *Æ. parviflora* (dwarf Horse Chestnut), a handsome shrub, 6 ft to 10 ft high, flowering in late summer Its foliage is much like that of other Æsculi, and its small white fragrant flowers are in long, erect, plume-flowers A variety of the preceding, *Æ. macrostachya,* is an August-blooming North American shrub of great beauty The growth is spreading and bushy, with creamy white flowers in dense plumy spikes A specimen on the outskirts of the lawn is effective. We have grouped the Pavias with the Æsculus

ÆTHIONEMA —A beautiful group of Alpine and rock plants found on the sunny mountains near the Mediterranean They grow freely in borders of well-drained sandy loam, but their true home is the rock-garden. The tall *Æ grandiflorum* forms a spreading bush about 1 ft. high, from which spring numerous racemes of pink and lilac flowers It also grows well in borders in ordinary soil, and, when in flower

in summer, is among the loveliest of alpine half-shrubby plants As the stems are prostrate, a good effect will come from planting them where the roots may descend into deep earth, and the shoots fall over the face of rocks at about the level of the eye Easily raised from seed, and thrive in sandy loam. There are many species, but few are in gardens All the cultivated kinds are dwarf, and may be grouped with alpine plants The other best kinds are *A cordifolium, A. pulchellum, A persicum*

AGAPANTHUS(*African Lily*) —Beautiful bulbous plants from the Cape, with blue or white flowers in umbels on stems 18 in to 4 ft high. *A umbellatus,* the old kind, is hardy in some mild seashore districts, and a fine plant in rich warm soil, but better for the protection of leaves or cocoa fibre round the root in winter It is worth growing for the flower garden and vases in summer, but should be protected in winter by storing under stages, in sheds or cellars The fleshy roots may be so stored without potting Enjoys plenty of water during out-of-door growth, and is easily increased by division Various new kinds have been introduced, but their out-of-door value has not been so well tested as the favourite old African Lily Of the best-known kind, *A. umbellatus,* there are several varieties , *major* and *maximus* are both larger than the type, and of *maximus* there is a white-flowered variety There is a smaller one with white flowers, one with double flowers, and variegated-leaved kinds. *A. Saunder sonianus* is a distinct variety with deeper-coloured flowers than the type

The largest is *A umbellatus giganteus,* the flower-spikes of which attain a height of from 3 ft to 4 ft , with umbels bearing from 150 to 200 flowers The colour is a gentian blue, while the buds are of a deeper hue *A. u pallidus* is a pale porcelain blue, a short-leaved variety *A u minor* is a dwarf variety Of *A umbellatus* there is a double-flowered variety, a distinct plant There is, moreover, *A u atrocœruleus,* a dark violet variety *A u maximus* has flower-stalks 4 ft. long, and full heads of flowers, one set opening while a second is rising to fill up the truss as the first crop fades *A. u Mooreanus* deciduous and hardy ; it grows from 12 in to 18 in. high, has narrow leaves, and comes true from seed *A u albiflorus,* a pure white kind, also is deciduous, the leaves turning yellow in autumn and dying off It forms a stout root-crown

AGATHÆA (*Blue Daisy*) *A. cœlestis* is a tender spreading Daisy-like plant, with blue flowers, useful for the margins of beds. There is also a pretty golden variegated form. It is among the prettiest of the half-hardy bedding plants, but is not so effective or good on heavy soils. Cuttings or seed.

AGAVE. — Tropical-looking succulent plants of the Amaryllis order, of which the common kind, *A. americana* and its variegated varieties are useful for placing out-of-doors in summer in vases or pots plunged in the ground, and also for the conservatory in winter. When the plant flowers, which it does only once, and after several years' growth, it sends up a flowering stem, from 26 ft. to nearly 40 ft. high. The flowers are a yellowish-green, and are very numerous on the ends of the chandelier-like branches. It may be placed out-of-doors at the end of May, and should be brought in in October. Easily increased from suckers. *A. Deserti, utahensis, cærulescens,* and *Shawi* have lately come into cultivation, and are supposed to be hardy, in which case they will be interesting for the rock-garden. North America.

AGERATUM (*Floss Flower*).—Half-hardy herbaceous plants, varying in height from 6 in. to 24 in., with pale-blue, lavender, or white blossoms. The dwarf Ageratums are among the best, but all are greatly overvalued, though they are among the most lasting of summer bedding plants, and as they will withstand a few degrees of frost they may be planted out earlier than most of the bedding plants. The flowers are not readily injured by rain, and do not fade in colour, but continue the same throughout the long flowering season. There are numerous varieties of varying merit, some in good soil attaining a height of 2 ft., and others not more than 6 in. The very dwarf kinds are disappointing; they flower so freely, and the growth of the plants is so sparse, that they always appear stunted. For back lines in borders, or for grouping in mixed flower borders, there is no variety better than the oldest kind, *A. mexicanum.* They strike best when placed on a gentle bottom-heat, and will winter in any position where there is plenty of light, and the temperature does not go below 40°. Cuttings.—W. W.

AGROSTEMMA (*Rose Campion*).—*A. coronaria* is a beautiful old flower, of the Pink family, hardy and free, most at home in chalky and dry soils. It is a woolly plant, 2 ft. to 3 ft. high, bearing many rosy-crimson flowers, in summer and autumn, easily raised from seed, excellent for borders, beds, and naturalisation on dry banks. It is biennial or often perishes on

some soils. There is a white variety and a double red one; the last is a good plant. The name is sometimes given to the annual Viscarias. *A. Githago* is a large annual, occasionally grown in botanic gardens. *A. Walkeri* is a hybrid between *A. coronaria* and *A. Flos-Jovis,* very compact, free flowering, and rich in colour.

AGROSTIS (*Cloud Grass*).—A large family of Grasses, the best of which in the garden are the annual kinds so useful when dried. There are some half-a-dozen annual kinds grown, the

Young Ailantus tree with Cannas.

best *A. nebulosa,* which forms delicate tufts about 15 in. high, and is useful for rooms. If cut shortly before the seed ripens and dried in the shade, it will keep for a long time. The seed may be sown either in September or in April or May, and lightly covered. *A. Steveni, multiflora,* and *plumosa* require the same treatment. *A. Spicaventi* is very graceful, especially if grown from self-sown seeds. *A. pulchella* is also useful for the same purpose, dwarfer and stiffer than *A nebulosa.*

AILANTUS (*Tree of Heaven*).—? Chinese hardy tree, young plants of which cut down every year give a good effect. It should be kept when young with a single stem clothed with its fine leaves. This can be done by cutting down annually, taking care to prevent it from breaking into an irregular head. Vigorous young plants and suckers in good soil will produce handsome arching leaves 5 ft. or more long, not surpassed by those of any stove plant. Cuttings of the roots.

AIRA (*Hair Grass*).—Graceful grasses, of which one of the prettiest is *A. pulchella*, with many hair-like stems, growing in light tufts 6in. high. It is useful for forming graceful edgings, amongst plants in borders, or for pots for rooms. Its delicate panicles give a charm to the finest bouquets. Seed may be sown either in September or in April. This comes from South Europe, and the British *A. cæspitosa* is handsome. *A. c. vivipara*, with its innumerable panicles of graceful viviparous awns, resembles a miniature Pampas Grass. *A. flexuosa* (the Waved Hair grass) is a pretty and graceful perennial. Of easy culture in ordinary garden soil.

AJUGA (*Bugle*).—A small family of dwarf herbs of the sage order, flowering in spring and early summer, and having blue flowers. They grow on mountain

Ajuga genevensis.

or lowland pastures, are easily cultivated and increased by division. *A. genevensis* is among the best, and is distinguished from the Common native Bugle (*A. reptans*) by the absence of creeping shoots. The flower-stems are erect, from 6 in. to

9 in. high ; the flowers deep blue, and in a close spike. It is suitable for the front of mixed borders or for the margin of shrubberies, and also for naturalising. There is a white variety of *A. reptans*, also a form with variegated leaves, and another with purplish ones, this being finer than the type.

AKEBIA.—Of these climbing or twining shrubs of the Barberry order, *A. quinata* is best known. It comes from China, often grown in greenhouses, but hardy. It is a good plant for a trellis, pergola, wall, or any such place in cold districts, growing 12 ft. or more high. In southern localities it does not need this, but rambles like a Clematis. It is best to let it run over an Evergreen, being then better protected against cold winds, which may injur e its flowers. It has long slender shoots, and fragrant claret purple flowers of two kinds—large and small, which are produced in drooping spikes. The Japanese *A. lobata* is a climber of elegant growth, and, although the flowers are small and dull, they are very fragrant.

ALISMA (*Water Plantain*). — Water plants, of which two are fitted for growing with hardy aquatic plants. *A. Plantago*, is rather stately in habit, having tall panicles of pretty pink flowers. When once planted it sows itself freely. The other kind is *A. ranunculoides*, a few inches high, in summer bearing many rosy blossoms. Both are adapted for wet ditches, margins of pools, and lakes. *A. natans* is a small floating pretty British plant. There are one or two Chinese kinds, single and double.

ALLIUM (*Garlic, Chive, Onion*).— Liliaceous bulbs. Not often important for the garden, and frequently with an unpleasant odour when crushed ; but to growers of collections there are some interesting kinds, of which a few are worth growing. They thrive in ordinary soil, the bulbs increasing rapidly. Some kinds give off little bulblets, which in certain situations make them too numerous. The following are among the kinds worthy of culture : *A. neapolitanum, paradoxum, ciliatum, subhirsutum, Clusianum pulchellum, triquetrum* (all with white flowers), *azureum* and *cæruleum* (blue), *pedemontanum* (mauve), *Moly* and *flavum* (yellow), *fragrans* (sweet scented), *oreophyllum* (crimson), *descendens* (deep crimson), *narcissiflorum* (purplish), *Murrayanum, acuminatum,* and *Macnabianum* (deep rose). These mostly grow from 1 ft. to 18 in. high, some 2 ft. or 3 ft.

ALLOSORUS (*Parsley Fern*).—*A.*

crispus is a beautiful little British Fern found in mountainous districts. It requires abundance of air and light, but should be shaded from the hot sun. In the rock-garden it does well between large stones, with broken stones about its roots, and its fronds just peeping out of the crevice.

ALNUS (*Alder*). — A somewhat neglected group of trees which have some value in moist places and to help to bind the banks of streams. Of the native kind *A. glutinosa* there are several varieties, and of the cut-leaved one there are fine specimens at Wynnstay and many other places. *A. incana* has also several varieties seldom of more value than the wild tree. Among other cultivated kinds are *japonica, cordifolia, barbata, occidentalis, Oregona,* and

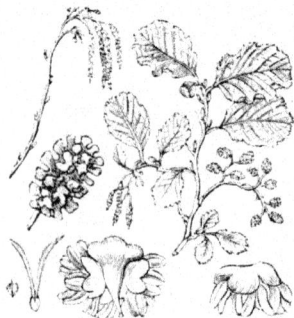

Alnus glutinosa

serrulata : all of easy culture. None are of greater value as to effect than our own native kind.

The common Alder does not seem to have been regarded with much favour by many writers, but Gilpin places it, after the Weeping Willow, as the most picturesque of all. With Gilpin Sir Thomas Dick Lauder fully agrees. He says :—

It is always associated in our minds with river scenery, both of that tranquil description which is most frequently to be met with in the vales of England, and with that of a wilder and more stirring character which is to be found among the glens and ravines of Scotland. In very many instances we have seen it put on so much of the bold, resolute character of the Oak, that it might have been mistaken for that tree but for the depth of its green hue. The river Mole may doubtless furnish the traveller with very beautiful specimens of the Alder, as it may also furnish an example of quiet English scenery, but this is too high a value to place on the tree, but nowhere will the tree be found in greater perfection than on the banks of the river Findhorn and its tributary streams.

An advantage the tree possesses is its tendency to retain its foliage. There is, however, a great deal of difference in this respect among the species and varieties. Although in a state of Nature most of the Alders are found where their roots have an abundant supply of moisture, they will grow well in Britain in all but the lightest soils.

ALONSOA (*Mask-flower*). — Mostly Peruvian annual plants, of the Snapdragon order, of which the best species are *A. Warscewiczi,* having small bright orange-red flowers ; *A. linifolia,* and *A. acutifolia,* —a slender-growing herb ; *A. incisifolia,* also a pretty kind ; similar to this is *A. myrtifolia* of vigorous habit with flowers larger than any other kind, and of a more intense scarlet than those of *A. linifolia* ; *A. albiflora* has pure white flowers, yellow in the centre, and *A. linearis* has a profusion of light scarlet flowers. All the species are easily grown, both in pots and the open ground : from seed in spring and also by cuttings in the spring.

ALOYSIA (*Sweet Verbena*).— *A. citriodora* is a fragrant-leaved bush with small and not showy flowers. Its pale green foliage goes well with any flower, and it may be grown against a sunny wall, where, if protected by a heap of ashes over its roots and a warm straw mat over its branches, it will pass through the winter safely. If uncovered too soon in spring, the young growths get nipped by late frosts. It is increased from cuttings and is a hardy wall plant in mild seashore districts, but not so common, owing to the cold, in inland districts. Verbena order, Chili. Syn. *Lippia.*

ALSTRÖMERIA (*Peruvian Lily*).— Handsome tuberous plants of the Amaryllis order, which require a richly manured and thoroughly warm and well-drained soil, the best place being a south border, or along the front of a wall having a warm aspect, where, if the soil is not light and dry, it should be made so. Dig out the ground to the depth of 3 ft., and spread 6 in. or so of brick rubbish over the bottom of the border. Shake over the drainage a coating of half-rotten leaves or short littery manure, to prevent the soil from running through the interstices of the bricks, and stopping up the drainage. If the natural soil be stiff, a portion should be exchanged for an equal quantity of leaf soil, or other light vegetable mould, and a barrow-load of sand. The plants should be procured in pots, as they rarely succeed from divisions, and, once planted, should never be interfered with. Place them in rows about 18 in.

apart, and with 1 ft. from plant to plant. If planted during the winter, they should be placed from 6 in. to 9 in. deep, so as to keep them from frost; and a few inches of half-rotten leaves shaken over the soil. Should there be any difficulty in obtaining established plants in pots to start with, seed may be had; and this sow in pots or beds where the plants are to remain. The seeds should be sown 2 or 3 in. deep, with three or four in a patch. If well treated, they will begin to bloom at a year old, and if not disturbed will in-

varying much in their colour markings. While growing and blooming they should have occasional watering, otherwise they get too dry, and ripen off prematurely. A good mulching of old Mushroom dung or of leaf soil is a great assistance while in bloom. When going out of flower carefully remove the seed-heads, otherwise the plants are apt to become exhausted, as almost every flower sets. In removing the pods, do not shorten the stems or reduce the leaves in any way, as all are needed to ripen the tubers and

Alströmeria (Peruvian Lily).

crease in strength and beauty every season. If one takes the seed of Alströmerias as soon as it is ripe and sows it, every seed will germinate the first season. It is also much better to sow three to five seeds in each pot and let the seedlings remain in the same pot the first year. The young plants of Alströmerias are very difficult to handle, being as brittle as glass, and a very great percentage will die if replanted when still young.

When grown in masses in this way they are very beautiful, as every stem furnishes a large number of flowers,

form fresh crowns for the following year. Any one having deep light sandy soil resting on a dry bottom may grow these beautiful flowering plants without preparation; all that is necessary being to pick out a well-sheltered spot, and to give the surface a slight mulching on the approach of severe weather. No trouble is involved in staking and tying, for the stems are strong enough to support themselves, unless in very exposed situations. They last long when cut.

The species in cultivation are

A. aurantiaca (*A. aurea*).—A vigorous

E E

growing Chilian kind, 2 ft. to 4 ft. high, flowering in summer and autumn. The flowers are large, orange yellow, streaked with red, and umbels of from 10 to 15 blooms terminating the stems.

A. brasiliensis.—A distinct kind with red and green flowers, and dwarfer than the preceding. Known also as *A. psittacina.*

A. chilensis.—A quite hardy kind from Chili, with many varieties that give a wide range of colours from almost white to deep orange and red.

A. Pelegrina.—Not so tall or robust as the last ; but the flowers are larger, whitish, and beautifully streaked and veined with purple. There are several varieties, including a white one, (*A. p. alba*) which requires protection. When well grown it is a fine pot plant, compact, and crowned with almost pure white flowers. It is called the Lily of the Incas. *A. peregrina* is synonymous.

Other good kinds are the hardy variable-coloured *A. versicolor* (*A. peruviana*) and St. Martin's flower (*A. pulchra*), this, however, requiring protection.

ALTERNANTHERA (*Joy-Weed*).— Little tropical weeds of the Amaranthus order, which, owing to their colour, have been used in our gardens far beyond their merits. These tender plants are natives of Brazil, and can be used only in the more favoured parts of the country. The varieties range in colour of foliage from dull purple to bad yellow, and why they are used in flower gardens is a question to which no good answer can be given.

ALTHÆA (*Hollyhock*).—Biennial or perennial plants of the Mallow family consisting chiefly of coarse-growing plants. Some, such as *A. rosea*, from which the Hollyhock has sprung, are showy garden flowers. The other wild species are generally characterised by great vigour, and hence are not very suitable for the choice flower garden. They thrive in almost any situation or soil. Among them *A. armeniaca, officinalis, narbonensis, cannabina, ficifolia, Hildebrandti hirsuta, caribœa, Froloviana syriacus,lavaterœfolia* are the best—mostly natives of S. Europe and the East, flowering in summer and autumn.

A. rosea (*Hollyhock*).—One of the noblest of hardy plants, and there are many positions in almost all gardens where it would add to the general effect. For breaking up ugly lines of shrubs or walls, and for forming back-grounds, its tall column-like growth is well fitted. So, too,

it is valuable for bold and stately effects among or near flower beds. Cottage bee-keepers would do well to grow a few Hollyhocks, for bees are fond of their flowers.

CULTURE. — Deep cultivation, much manure, frequent waterings in dry weather, with occasional soakings of liquid manure,

Althæa rosea (Double-flowered Hollyhock).

will secure fine spikes and flowers. Hollyhocks require good garden soil, trenched to the depth of 2 ft. A wet soil is good in summer, but injurious in winter, and to prevent surface wet from injuring old plants left in the open ground remove the mould round their necks, filling up with about 6 in. of white sand. This will preserve the crowns of the plants. It is best, however, if fine flowers are desired, to plant young plants every year, as one would Dahlias, putting them 3 ft apart in rows at least 4 ft apart , or if grouped in beds, not less than 3 ft. apart In May or June, when the spikes have grown 1 ft high, thin them out according to the strength of the plant, if well established and strong, leaving four spikes, and if weak two or three. When for exhibition, leave only one spike, and to get fine blooms cut off the side shoots, thin the flower buds if crowded together, and remove the top of the spike, according to the height desired, taking into consideration the usual height and habit of the plant. By topping you increase the size of the flower, but at the same time shorten its duration, and perhaps disfigure its appearance. Stake them before they get too high, tying them securely, so as to induce them to grow erect. The most robust will not require a stake higher than 4 ft. If the weather is dry, they may be watered with a solution of guano or any other liquid manure poured carefully round the roots, but not too near the stem But it is in the garden, not the exhibition, one wants the Hollyhock

PROPAGATION is effected from eyes, cuttings, seeds, or careful division Hollyhocks may be propagated by single eyes, put in in July and August, and also by cuttings put in in spring, on a slight hotbed. Plants raised in summer are best preserved by putting them in October into 4-in. or 5-in pots in light, rich, sandy earth, and then placing them in a cold frame or greenhouse, giving them plenty of air on all favourable occasions Thus treated they will grow a little in winter In March or April turn them out into the open ground, and they will bloom as finely and as early as if planted in autumn Plants put out even in May will flower the same year. If seeds are sown in autumn in a box or pan in heat, as soon as they are ripe, potted off and grown on in a pot through the winter, and planted out the following April, they will flower in the same summer and autumn If allowed to remain in the beds or borders where they have flowered, choice Hollyhocks often perish from damp, or from snow settling round their collars, or penetrating the cavity left by the too close removal of the flowerstems. At the approach of winter, say in October, carefully lift all it is desired to save, and lay them close together in a slanting direction, at an angle of about 45°, in a warm mellow soil at the foot of a wall or hedge, where, in hard weather, shelter can easily be given. The ground

that is to receive them can then be thoroughly worked in winter, and if a little rotten turf is put in with them when replanted in March or April, good spikes and large flowers may be expected Choice and scarce varieties may be either potted up or planted out in a frame Potting them is the better way, because they can be placed in a greenhouse or vinery, on shelves near the glass Some of the stools will have numerous growths starting from them, and unless the plants have a little heat early in the year, many of the cuttings cannot be propagated soon enough to flower the same season Growers in the south of England have an advantage with these springstruck cuttings as there is quite three weeks' difference between the time of flowering in the south and in the northern districts of England and in Scotland Root-grafting gives the propagator a little advantage, and early in the year the plants are propagated more readily in a light frame fixed in a heated propagating house A hotbed is uncertain, as there is sometimes too much heat, and then not enough Although the young side shoots of old stocks will root in a gentle bottom-heat in spring, they may also be increased in July, just before the plants come into flower The side shoots from the flower-spikes, or the smaller flower-spikes, if they can be spared, should be cut up into single joints, and dibbled in thickly in a prepared bed in a frame or pit, where they can be kept close and cared for by shading from bright sunshine, and sprinkling occasionally with water that has been warmed by standing in the sun Nearly every cutting will then develop a bud from the axil of the leaf, rapidly strike root, and make a good strong plant by the following spring ; as a rule, young plants propagated at this season give the best spikes When cutting down the flowering stems of Hollyhocks after blooming, they should be left a good length, as they are impatient of damp about their crowns ; in spring the old stems may be removed altogether Owing to the Hollyhock disease it is often a better plan to abandon the named kinds increased from cuttings and resort to seedlings only for stock This way is all the more sure, as seed growers of late years have fixed and separated the colours so that a fine variety of good ones may be secured in this way, while the plants are more vigorous, and in any case will often start free from the disease

INSECT PESTS AND DISEASES — Red spider and thrips are both very troublesome, but the first does most injury. It appears on the under sides of the leaves as soon as the hot weather·sets in, and is difficult to dislodge. If there is any trace of red spider before planting out, the whole plant, except the roots, should be dipped in a pail of soft soapy water, to which a pint or so of tobacco liquid has been added. It will be well to syringe the under sides of the leaves with the mixture if the plants have been planted out before the pest is perceived. Thrips may be destroyed in the same way, and it is well to syringe the plants every day in hot weather.

THE HOLLYHOCK FUNGUS (*Puccinia malvacearum*) is very destructive to the Hollyhock. When once it seizes a collection, probably the best way is to destroy all the plants affected. Those that do not appear to be attacked should be washed with soapy water in which flowers of sulphur has been dissolved. The sulphur will settle at the bottom of the vessel, and must be frequently stirred up when the mixture is being used. Sulphur seems to destroy almost any fungus ; and may destroy this in its very earliest stages, but will not when established.

ALYSSUM (*Madwort*). — Rock and alpine plants, the species much resembling each other. *A. saxatile* (the Rock Madwort or Gold Dust) is one of the most valuable of yellow spring flowers, hardy in all parts of these islands. The colour of its masses of bloom and its vigour have made it one of the best-known plants. It is often grown in half-shady places ; but like most rock-plants it should be fully exposed. It is well fitted for the spring garden, and the mixed border, and for association with evergreen Candytufts and Aubrietias. In winter it perishes in heavy rich clays when on the level ground. A native of Southern Russia, it flowers with us in April or May. There is a dwarfer variety, distinguished by the name of *A. saxatile compactum*, but it differs very little from the old plant. *A. Gemonense* has the habit of *A. saxatile*, but larger flowers. *A. montanum* is a dwarf plant, spreading into compact tufts, 3 in. high. *A. podolicum*, is a small hardy alpine from South Russia. It has in early summer, a profusion of small white blossoms, and is suited for the rock-garden or the margins of borders. *A. pyrenaicum* is a neat rock-plant with white flowers. *A. spinosum* is a silvery little bush with white flowers. *A. serpyllifolium* is a grey-green leaved form, with yellow flowers. Small plants quickly become Liliputian bushes, 3 in. to 6 in.

high ; and when fully exposed, are almost as compact as Moss.

Among other kinds sometimes grown are *A. Wiersbecki*, and *A. olympicum*, but they are not quite so good as the common kind. The alpine and rock kinds are

Alyssum montanum.

of easy culture in light or dry soil, as indeed are all the species. *A. maritimum* is the Sweet Alyssum, a small annual with white flowers, useful as a carpet plant. It grows on the tops of walls in the west country, and in sandy places. In these situations it is perennial, but in gardens is grown as an annual, sowing itself freely. There is a variegated form.

AMARANTHUS (*Prince's Feather, Love-lies-bleeding*).—Annual plants, some of distinct habit and striking colour. The old Love-lies-bleeding (*A. caudatus*) with its dark red pendent racemes, is a fine plant when well grown, but *A. speciosus* and some other varieties are finer. The more vigorous species grow from 2 to 5 ft. high. It is best to give them room to spread, otherwise much of their picturesque effect will be lost ; and to use them in positions where their peculiar habit may be seen to advantage, as, for example, in large vases and edges of bold beds. Easily raised as any annual, they deserve to be well thinned out and put in rich ground, so that they may attain full size. The foliage of some varieties is very rich in its hues, and planted with Canna, Wigandia, Ricinus, Solanum, their effect is good. The varieties of *A. tricolor* require a light soil and a warmer place. They do well in gardens by the seaside, and sow the seed in April in a hot bed, pricking out the seedlings in a hot bed, and plant out about the end of May. The cultivated kinds embrace *bicolor, tricolor, atro-purpureus. A. melancholicus ruber*, a useful bedding plant with bright crimson leaves, *A. Henderi, A. salicifolius*, and *A. s.* Princess of Wales may be used in the summer garden with good effect. *Amaranthus* order. Old and new world.

Amaranthus (Prince's Feather).

AMARYLLIS.—Showy bulbous tropical plants few of the species of which are hardy, though the beautiful Belladonna Lily (*A. Belladonna*) may be grown well in the open air, and is, in fact, almost too free in some soils in Cornwall. It is a noble bulbous plant from the Cape of Good Hope, from 1½ ft. to 3 ft. high, blooming late in summer, the flowers, as large as the white Lily, and of delicate silvery rose in clusters on stout leafless stems, arising from the large pear-shaped bulbs. To grow it in inland and less favoured districts choose a place on the south side of a house or wall, take out the whole of the soil to the depth of 3 ft.

and place about 6 in. of broken brick in the bottom. Over this put some half-rotten manure to keep the drainage open, and feed the plant. If the natural soil is not good, add some sandy mellow loam, or if stiff, a few barrow-loads of leaf mould, and one or two of sharp sand mixed with it. Having trod this firm, plant the bulbs in small groups. Each clump should be about 1 foot apart, and if the border is of such a width as to take a double row, the plants in the second should be alternate with those in the first. In planting, place a handful or so of sharp sand round the bulbs to keep them from rotting. If planted in autumn, or at any time during the winter, it will be well to protect them from severe weather by half-rotten leaves, cocoa-nut fibre, or fern. The plants begin to push forth their new leaves early in spring, and upon the freedom ·with which they send forth these during summer the bloom in the autumn depends. During dry weather give an occasional soaking of water, and with liquid manure once or twice. As soon as the foliage ripens off remove it, and clean the border before the blooms begin to come through the soil. *A. B. blanda* is a variety with larger bulbs, bearing noble umbels of white flowers, turning to pale rose in summer, and there are other varieties.

Amberboa. *See* CENTAUREA.

AMELANCHIER (*Snowy Mespilus, June Berry*).—Pretty hardy shrubs and low trees, or medium sized, associating well with the Almond, Laburnum, the Cherry, Plum, and such things. *A. canadensis* is one of the most precious of our flowering trees, nothing giving better general effect or more distinct, and long before it comes into flower it is pretty with its soft brown-grey masses. It has also the advantage of being perfectly hardy in our country, thriving as well on sands as on stiff soils; and being a Canadian tree, no cold ever touches it. It is more slender in habit than many of our flowering trees, and often weakened in the crowded masses of the shrubbery, where everything is so often sacrificed to hungry evergreens. In its own country it varies very much in size, some forms being mere shrubs, whilst others make trees 40ft. and even more in height. In botanic gardens and nursery catalogues we find the names of several other trees of this genus, but there seems to be little distinction among them, and none quite so good as this, though the one which grows in the Maritime Alps (*A. vulgaris*) should be worth a place. The Americans have selected some forms of the shad bush, which bear better fruit than the common form; if they would bear it in our own country it would make the bush more valuable, but whether this prove so or not, there is no prettier thing than a group of this tree, which will grow anywhere we choose to put it, on a rocky bluff or bank, or even fight its way in a copse. It has also the advantage of being raised very easily from seed, and increases rapidly by suckers, so that the grafting nuisance is easily avoided in its case.

AMELLUS—*A. annuus* is a pretty dwarf hardy annual, with Daisy-like flowers, of a deep purple, but with white,

take it up and pot it in winter. With me it has stood the cold, rain, and gales far better than the variegated Maize and big Solanums. The flower, though bright, is not large enough to be effective."

AMMOBIUM (*Winged Everlasting*). —*A. alatum* is a handsome Composite from New Holland 1½ to 3 ft. high, bearing white chaffy flowers with yellow discs from May till September. In sandy soil it is perennial, but on heavy and damp soils must be grown as annual or biennial. Seed.

AMORPHA (*Bastard Indigo*).—Hardy shrubs of the Pea order, thriving in ordin-

A group of the Belladonna Lily.

rose, scarlet, and violet varieties, which are named in catalogues *alba, rosea, kermesina,* and *atro-violacea.* It forms a compact tuft, suitable for groups or masses, if sown in the open in April, flowering in June. It makes a pretty ground or "carpet" plant with taller plants here and there through it. Cape of Good Hope. Compositæ. Syn. *Kaulfussia amelloides.*

AMICIA—*A. zygomeris* is a quaint plant from Mexico, occasionally used in the sheltered flower garden. Mr. E. H. Woodall praises it : " for those who like a bold and distinct plant in a warm situation in summer, and have means to protect or

ary garden soil but requiring a sheltered situation in bleak localities. Increased by layers or cuttings in autumn, or from suckers. *A. canescens* (the Lead Plant) is a native of Missouri. It has clusters of blue flowers and hoary leaves. *A. fruticosa* (The False Indigo) comes from California, and there are many forms of it, differing but slightly, all having bluish or dark purple flowers.

Ampelopsis. *See* VITIS.

ANAGALLIS (*Pimpernel*).— Usually rather pretty and half-hardy annuals of the Primrose family. The best-known is the Italian Pimpernel (*A. Monelli*), with large blossoms, deep blue, shaded with rose. There are several varieties—*rubra grandiflora*, *Wilmoreana*, bright blue purple, yellow eye ; *Phillipsi*, deep blue, rose-coloured centre ; *Breweri*, intense blue ; *linifolia*, fine blue, very dwarf ; Napoleon III., maroon ; and *sanguinea*, bright ruby, all flowering from July to September. The Indian Pimpernel

Bastard Indigo.

(*A. indica*) has small bright blue flowers. It is a hardy annual, but the Italian Pimpernel should be grown as a half-hardy annual. The seed may be sown any time from March till July, the later sowings to be made in pots and put into a greenhouse or window in autumn. Pimpernels grow well in ordinary garden soil, and are used with good effect in broad masses in borders, or edgings to beds, and make good pot plants. The pretty little bog Pimpernel (*A. tenella*) is a native creeping plant, with slender stems and myriads of tiny pink flowers. It is pretty in suspended pots or pans, and may be grown in the bog or a moist corner in the rock-garden.

ANCHUSA (*Alkanet*).—Stout herbaceous and biennial plants of the Forget-me-Not family ; some worth growing, amongst the best being *A. italica*, which is vigorous, 3 to 4 ft. high, with beautiful blue blossoms. *A. hybrida* is similar, about 2 ft. high with flowers of rich violet. *A. capensis* is a pretty plant with large bright blue flowers, rather tender ; it should be planted in a sheltered well-drained border. *A. sempervirens* is a British perennial, 1½ to 2 ft. high, with blue flowers, worth a place in the wild garden. Seeds or division.

ANDROMEDA. — Handsome dwarf hardy shrubs of the Heath Family, thriving in peaty soil. Various shrubs usually called Andromedas in gardens, belong in reality to several other genera, and there is only one true species of Andromeda known,

viz. :—*A. polifolia* (Moorwort), a native of Britain and N. Europe growing from about 6 to 18 inches high, and bearing purplish-red flowers from May to September. It is best grouped in peat beds or in the bog garden. For allied plants usually known as Andromeda see *Cassandra*, *Cassiope*, *Leucothoë*, *Lyonia*, *Oxydendrum*, *Pieris*, and *Zenobia*.

ANDROSACE.—Alpine plants, of very small stature and great beauty, belonging to the Primrose order. Other families, like Primroses and Hairbells, do come down to the hill-pastures, the sea-rocks, or the sunny heaths, but these do not. They are more alpine than even the Gentians, which are as handsome in a hill-meadow as on the highest slopes ; and as Androsaces are, among flowering plants, the most confined to the snowy region, so they are the dwarfest of this class. Growing at elevations where the snow falls very early in autumn, they flower

Amelanchier canadensis.

as soon as it melts. Sometimes, like some other alpine flowers, they frequent high cliffs with a vertical face, or with portions of the face receding here and there into shallow recesses. Here they must endure intense cold—cold which would destroy all shrub or tree life exposed to it. And here in spring they flower. Their small evergreen leaves, often downy, retain much more dust and soot than smoother and larger-leaved evergreen alpine plants do, making them more difficult of culture near cities than most alpine plants. The Androsaces enjoy in cultivation small fissures between rocks or stones, firmly packed with pure sandy peat, or very sandy or gritty loam, not less than 15 in. deep. They should be so placed that no wet can gather or lie about them, and they should be so planted in between stones that, once well rooted into the deep earth—all the better if mingled with pieces of broken sand-stone—they could never suffer from drought. It is easy to arrange rocks and soils so that,

Androsace sarmentosa.

once the mass below is thoroughly moistened, an ordinary drought can have little effect in drying it.

The names of the species here given mainly require the treatment above described, excepting the spreading Himalayan, *A. lanuginosa*, which thrives on walls and sandy borders—*A. alpina, carnea, chamæjasme, helvetica, imbricata, Laggeri, obtusifolia, pubescens, pyrenaica, sarmentosa, Vitaliana* and *Wulfeniana*. They are mostly from the Alps and Pyrenees, a few from the mountains of India.

ANDRYALA.—Small plants of the Dandelion order; some with woolly leaves. The shrubby *A. mogadorensis,* forms snowy masses on a little islet on the Morocco coast, and has not been found elsewhere. It bears flowers as large as a half-crown, of a bright yellow, the disc being bright orange. Little is known of its culture and hardiness. *A. lanata* has woolly silvery leaves, and grows well in any soil not too damp.

ANEMONE (*Windflower*).—A noble family of tuberous alpine meadow and herbaceous plants, of the Buttercup family, to which is due much of the beauty of spring and early summer of northern and temperate countries. In early spring, or what is winter to us in Northern Europe, when the valleys of Southern Europe and sunny sheltered spots all round the great rocky basin of the Mediterranean are beginning to glow with colour, we see the earliest Windflowers in all their loveliness. Those arid mountains that look so barren have on their sunny sides carpets of Anemones in countless variety. These belong to old favourites in our gardens—the garland Windflower and the Peacock Anemone. Later on the Star Anemone begins, and troops in thousands over the terraces, meadows, and fields of the same regions. Climbing the mountains in April, the Hepatica nestles in nooks all over the bushy parts of the hills. Farther east, while the common Anemones are aflame along the Riviera valleys and terraces, the blue Greek Anemone is open on the hills of Greece ; a little later the blue Apennine Anemone blossoms. Meanwhile our Wood Anemone adorns the woods throughout the northern world, and here and there through the brown Grass on the chalk hills comes the purple of the Pasque-flower. The Grass has grown tall before the graceful Alpine Windflower flowers in all the natural meadows of the Alps ; while later on bloom the high alpine Windflowers, which soon flower and fruit, and are ready to sleep for nine months in the snow. These are but few examples of what is done for the northern and temperate world by these Windflowers, so precious for our gardens also.

A. alpina (*Alpine Windflower*). — On nearly every great mountain range in northern climes this is one of the handsomest plants, growing 15 in. to 2 ft. high. It grows more slowly in gardens than most of the other kinds, and should have deep soil. *A. sulphurea* is a fine variety. Many fail with it through transplanting in autumn and winter. Seed is the best way to increase it. Sow this in November in a rather moist peaty bed out-of-doors and allow the seedlings to remain for two years. When growth commences in spring transplant to where they are to flower. Full exposure, good drainage, and moisture in summer are essential.

A. angulosa (*Great Hepatica*). — Larger than the Hepatica, with sky-blue flowers as large as a crown-piece, and five-lobed leaves. In rock-gardens, or near them, it will succeed in spaces between choice dwarf shrubs in beds. Seed and division. Transylvania.

A. apennina (*Apennine Windflower*). —A free blue and hardy kind scattered among the native Anemones in our woods, or making pictures with Daffodils, adds a new charm to our spring. It is readily increased by division, and grows about 4 in. to 9 in. in height. There is a white form and others not so important, however, as the wild one. Italy.

The Blue Apennine Windflower.

A. blanda (*Blue Winter Windflower*).—A lovely plant from the hills of Greece, of a fine blue, and blooming in winter, mild years. It should be grown in every rock-garden, planted on banks that catch the early sun, whilst it may be naturalised in Grassy places in warm soil. It is distinguished by round and bulb-like roots; increased by division and seed, and varies in size and colour. Greece, Asia Minor.

A. coronaria (*Poppy Anemone*).—One of the most admired flowers of our gardens from earliest times. There are many varieties, single and double. The single sorts may be readily grown from seed sown in the open air in April, and, being varied in fine colour, they deserve to be cultivated, even more than many of the doubles. The planting of the double varieties may be made in autumn or in spring, or at intervals all through the winter, to secure a continuity

of flowers; but the best bloom is secured by October planting. The Poppy Anemone thrives in warm deep loam, and the roots of the more select kinds may be taken up when the leaves die down. They are, however, seldom worth this trouble, as many fine varieties may be grown from seed sown in June. Prick out the plants in autumn : they will flower well in the following spring, so that the plant is as easily raised as an annual. Apart from the old florists' or double Anemones and the single ones, there are certain races of French origin of much value — the Anemones de Caen, for example. These are raised from the same species, but are more vigorous and have larger flowers than the older Dutch kinds. Of the Caen Anemones there are both single and double kinds, and the Chrysanthemum-flowered is another fine double race, whilst one may also note the deep scarlet double form—Chapeau de Cardinal, and the double Nice Anemones. The fine variety of the Poppy Anemones leads to mixed collections being grown. While it is well to plant mixtures now and then, it is better to select and keep true some of the finer forms in any desired colour. A fine scarlet, purple, or violet should be grown by itself and for itself, as in that way the Poppy Anemone will be a greater aid to the garden artist. All kinds thrive in light ·garden soils of fair quality, and, in many districts there is no trouble in their culture ; in others this plant never does well and is often killed in winter. By resorting to spring planting we avoid this last. The plan is not worth following out, especially as we have so many really hardy species introduced of recent years. The St. Bridgid Anemones, like those of Caen and Nice, are simply selections from the Poppy Anemone, depending for their value on care in selection, and also on good culture in the warm limestone soil the plants enjoy so well.

The following method will enable any one to raise anemones from seed in a moist loam. To save time, I sow as soon as the seed is ripe, selecting it from the brightest flowers only. Separate the seed thoroughly. Spread a newspaper on the table, pour over it a quart of sand, dry ashes, or fine earth, and sprinkle the seed over this, rubbing it together till its separation is complete. The seed bed need not be larger than 3 ft. by 9 ft., and choose the sunniest part of the garden. Make the surface fine, tread it down, and give it a good watering. Wait until it is dry enough to scratch with a fine rake ; then sow broadcast, covering the seed with a very thin coat of fine earth, about the thickness of a shilling ; beat flat with a spade, and give a light sprinkling of water. Never let a ray of sunshine reach the bed ; cover it with newspapers, spreading a few Pea sticks or something to retain the covering in its place. Keep the surface of the bed moist. In about twenty days the young plants will begin to appear, and when all seem up, remove the covering ; they will need no further care except watering. If the bed once gets thoroughly dry, the plants are apt, after forming small bulbs about the size of Peas, to stop growing, the foliage to die, and the bulbs to lie dormant for months. If kept, however, well watered through the summer, they will go on growing through the winter, and begin to blossom the following spring. The seedlings may be left to blossom where they are sown, or be transplanted in September or October.—J.

What are termed French Anemones are thought an improvement on the Dutch, with large flowers of brilliant and varied colour; the plants vigorous, the climate of Normandy in some parts suiting the plant ; but in our country, away from the sea, the Poppy Anemone may perish in cold weather.

Poppy Anemones, double and single, are useful for edgings and for borders either singly or in tufts. They are cultivated alone in beds or in clumps in borders, and answer well for planting under standard Rose Trees or other light and thinly planted shrubs. Cut the flowers when just open.

A. fulgens (*The Scarlet Windflower*).— A native of the south of France, over a limited area, for the most part in vineyards. It withstands severe frosts in the open border, but stagnant moisture injures it. In good well-drained soils it will thrive, but is best in a rich manured loam in a northern aspect and in a shaded situation. Division is the surest way of increasing it, as it is liable to sport if raised from seeds. Roots may be transplanted almost all the year round, though the resting time extends only from June to August, and to insure early and good flowers plant the roots as early as possible in the autumn. A large bed of well-grown plants in bloom is a brilliant sight. The flowers last indoors for a week or more if cut when just coming into bloom and kept in water in a moderately warm room.—H. V.

The Greek form of *A. fulgens* is larger, and very intense in colour. A fine strain was raised by the late Rev. J. G. Nelson,

and called by him *A. fulgens major.* The peacock Anemone (*A. Pavonina*) is double form of this.

A. Hepatica (*Common Hepatica*).—A beautiful early hardy flower. In sheltered spots on porous soil the foliage will remain through the winter. The Hepatica is a deep rooter—hence it thrives so well upon made banks, and it will do as well as Primroses or Violets in any good garden soil. Where let alone, and not often pulled to pieces, it makes strong tufts. Clumps of the rich-coloured blues and reds when a mass of bloom in March are very beautiful. The best-known kinds are

Anemone japonica alba.

the double red and single blue, both amongst the hardiest of the section. Then there are the single white ; single red ; double blue, rich in colour ; *Barlowi*, a rich-coloured sport from the single blue ; *splendens*, a single red ; *lilacina*, a pretty mauve kind ; and some others— every variety being worthy of culture.

A. japonica (*Japan Anemone*).—A tall autumn-blooming kind, 2 ft. to 4 ft. high, with fine foliage and large rose-coloured flowers. The variety named Honorine Jobert, with pure white flowers, is a beautiful plant ; and all good forms of the plant should be cultivated where cut flowers are required in autumn. By having some on a north border, and some on a warm one, the bloom may be prolonged. The secret of success seems to be to prepare at first a deep bed of rich soil and to leave the plants alone.

The various forms of the Japan Anemone are useful for borders, groups, fringes of shrubbery in rich soil, and here and there in half-shady places by wood walks.

A. nemorosa (*Wood Anemone*).—In spring this native plant adorns our woods, and also those of nearly all Europe and Asia, but it is so abundant in the British Isles that there is little need to plead for its culture. There are double varieties, and the colour of the flower is occasionally lilac, or reddish, or purplish.

A sky-blue variety of the Wood Anemone, *A. Robinsoniana*, has of recent years been much grown. It is of easy culture and much beauty, especially if seen when the noon-day sun is on the flowers. It is useful for the rock-garden in wide-spreading tufts ; or for the margins of borders, or as a ground plant beneath shrubs, or for the wild garden or for dotting through the Grass in the pleasure-ground in spots not mown early.

A. palmata (*Cyclamen-leaved Anemone*).—A distinct kind, with leathery leaves and large handsome flowers in May and June, glossy, yellow, only opening to the sun. A native of N. Africa and other places on the shores of the Mediterranean, this charming flower should be planted in deep turfy peat, or light fibrous loam with leaf-mould, but not placed on the face of rocks, but rather on level spots, where it can root deeply and grow into strong tufts. There is a double variety. This Anemone may be increased by either division or seeds.

A. Pulsatilla (*Pasque-flower*).—There are few sights more pleasant to the lover of spring flowers than the Pasque-flower just showing through the dry Grass of a bleak down on an early spring day. It is smaller in a wild than in a cultivated state, forming in the garden strong healthy tufts, but it is one of the plants more beautiful in a wild state than in a garden. In Normandy with Mr. Burbidge I came upon plants of it on the grassy hill about Château Gaillard and also in the woods and by the roads near, and we thought we had never seen so fair a wild flower. There are several varieties, including red, lilac, and white kinds, but they are not common, and there is also a double variety. It prefers well-drained and light but deep soil, and is increased by division or seeds.

A. ranunculoides (*Yellow Wood Anemone*).—Not unlike the Apennine and the Wood Anemone in habit, this is distinct in its yellow flowers in March and April. It is S. European, and less free on common soils than the Apennine A., but is happier on chalky soil.

A. stellata (*Star Windflower*).—The star-like flowers, this ruby, rosy purple, rosy, or whitish, vary in a charming way, and usually have a large white eye at the base, contrasting with the delicate colouring of the rest of the petals, and the brown violet of the stamens and styles of the flower. It is not so vigorous as the Poppy A., and requires a sheltered warm position, a light, sandy, well-drained soil. Division and seeds. *Syn. A. hortensis* : S. Europe.

A. sylvestris (*Snowdrop Windflower*). —A handsome plant, about 15 in. high with large white flowers in spring and

Pasque-flower (Anemone pulsatilla).

beautiful buds. Hardy and free on all soils, but fails to bloom. The aspect of the drooping unopened buds suggested its English name — the Snowdrop Anemone. Division.

A. thalictroides (*Thalictrum anemonoides*).

The previously named Anemones are the most beautiful of the family, which, however, contains many other interesting plants, but many of the higher Alpine kinds are grown and increased with difficulty and only in carefully chosen situations. Some again, however distinct as species, are not strikingly so in gardens, and for the flower-gardener the best way is to make good use of the proved species. The lovers of alpine flowers will no doubt look with a longing eye over the following names of the species, while no doubt many unknown species adorn the vast solitudes of Asia and Arctic America and probably other countries too.

Known species.—*A. acanthifolia*, Hab? *acutiloba*, N. America; *æquinoctialis*, Peru; *albana*, N. Asia; *alchemillæfolia*, S. Africa; *alpina*, Europe, N.America; *altaica*, Siberia; *angulosa*, E. Europe; *anomala*, N. America; *antucensis*, Chili; *appennina*, S. Europe; *armena*, Asia Minor; *baicalensis*, Asia; *baldensis*, Switzerland; *barbulata*, China; *Bauhini*, Europe; *biflora*, Himalayas; *blanda*, E. Europe; *Bogenhardiana*, Europe; *Bonngeana*, Siberia; *cælestina*, China; *cærulea*, Siberia; *caffra*, S. Africa; *capensis*, S. Africa; *cernua*, Japan; *chinensis*, China; *coronaria*, S.Europe; *crassifolia*, Tasmania; *cylindrica*, N. America; *dahurica*, Temp. Asia; *debilis*, Siberia; *decapetala*, N. W. America; *deltoidea*, N. W America; *demissa*, Himalayas; *dichotoma*, N. Asia and N. America; *Drummondii*, California; *elongata*, Himalayas; *eranthoides*, Temp. Asia; *exigua*, China; *Falconeri*, Himalayas; *Fannini*, Natal; *Fischeriana*, Siberia; *flaccida*, China; *formosa*, Asia Minor; *fulgens*, S. Europe; *Glazioviana*, Brazil; *Gmeliniana*, Siberia; **gracilis**, Japan; **Grayi**, California; **Griffithi**, Himalayas; **Halleri**, Switzerland; **helleborifolia**, S. America; **Hepatica**, Europe, N. America; **hepaticifolia**, Chili; **heterophylla**, N. America; **integrifolia**, Cent. America; **isopyroides**, Sibirica; **Jamesoni**, Ecuador; **Jankæ**, Transylvania; **japonica**, Japan; **lineariloba**, Kamtschatka; **mexicana**, Mexico; **minuta**, Siberia; **montana**, S. E. Europe; **multifida**, N. and S. America; **narcissiflora**, Europe. N.Asia, N.America; **nemorosa**, Europe, N. Asia, N. America; **nikoënsis**, Japan; **obtusiloba**, Himalayas; **ochroleuca**, Switzerland; **octopetala**, Hab? **palmata**, S. Europe; **parviflora**, N. America; **patens**, Europe, N. America; **Pavoniana**, Iberia; **Pittoni**, Europe; **polyanthes**, Himalayas; **pratensis**, N.Europe; **Pulsatilla**, Europe; **Raddeana**, Amur; **ranunculoides**, S. Europe; **reflexa**, Siberia; **Richardsoni**, Arctic America; **rigida**, Chili; **rivularis**, E. Indies; **Rossii**, China; **rupestris**, Himalayas; **rupicola**, Himalayas; **Sellowi**, Brazil; **sibirica**, Siberia; **slavica**, Europe; **speciosa**, Caucasus; **sphenophylla**, Chili; **stolonifera**, Japan; **sumatrana**, Sumatra; **sylvestris**, S. Europe; **tenuifolia**, S. Africa; **tetrasepala**, Himalayas; **thalictroides**, N. America; **Thomsoni**, Trop. Africa; **transylvanica**, Europe; **trifolia**, Europe, N. America; **triternata**, S. America; **trullifolia**, Himalayas; **Tschernaewi**, Temp. Asia; **udensis**, Manchuria; **umbrosa**, Siberia; **vernalis**, Europe; **virginiana**, N. America; **vitifolia**, Himalayas; **Wahlenbergii**, Europe; **Walteri**, N. America; **Wightiana**, E. Indies; **Wolfgangiana**, Europe.

ANOMATHECA (*Flowering grass*).— *A. cruenta* is a pretty little South African bulb of the Iris order, from 6 to 12 in. high, flowers ½ in. across, carmine crimson, three of the lower segments marked with a dark spot; in loose clusters on slender stems and Grass-like leaves. Hardy on warm soils, but in others it should be planted on slopes, in very sandy dry soil or on warm borders; the bulbs planted rather deep. In many soils it increases rapidly. *Syn. Lapeyrousia.*

ANTENNARIA (*Cat's-ear*).—Mostly hardy alpine or border flowers. *A. margaritacea* is a North American plant, 2 ft. high, with flowers in clusters, white and chaffy, hence are kept in a dry state, and dyed in various colours. The pretty but rare *A. triplinervis* from Nepal is closely allied to this plant. The Mountain Cat's-ears, *A. dioica* and *A. alpina*, and such forms as *A. minima*, are neat little plants with whitish foliage, used as carpeting. All are of simple culture

in ordinary soil in exposed positions. These are good rock garden plants and the pretty little rosy heads of one form of the Mountain Everlasting may often be seen in the cottage gardens of Warwickshire. *A. tomentosa* has been much used as a dwarf silvery plant in the flower garden.

ANTHEMIS (*Rock Camomile*).—Vigorous perennials and rock plants, Of the kinds in cultivation *A. Aizoon* is a dwarf silvery rock-plant, 2 to 4 in. high, with Daisy-like flowers. *A. Kitaibeli* is pretty in the mixed border, with large, pale, lemon-coloured, Marguerite-like flowers. *A. tinctoria* is similar and both are

Anthemis Macedonica.

excellent for cutting, growing very freely in ordinary soil. The double-flowered form of the Corn Camomile (*A. arvensis*) is sometimes cultivated among annual plants. *A. Biebersteini* forms dense carpets of silvery leaves with large and handsome yellow blossoms one on a stem. *A. Macedonica* is a neat species with white flowers, excellent as a rock-garden plant. There is also a variety called *A. nobilis*.

ANTHERICUM (*St. Bruno's Lily*).— Bulbous plants of the Lily family, containing a few species hardy in this country. These are the European kinds, among the most beautiful of hardy flowers. *A. Hookeri* (*syn. Chrysobactron*) is a distinct New Zealand plant, 15 to 20 in. high, with bright yellow flowers, in long spikes in early summer. It grows best in moist deep soils. *A. Liliago* (St. Bernard's Lily) is about 2 ft. high, with white flowers in early summer. *A. ramosum* has flower stems about 2 ft. high, much branched, and small white flowers. *A. Liliastrum* (St. Bruno's Lily) is a graceful alpine meadow plant in deep free sandy soil, in early summer throwing up spikes of snowy-white Lily-like blossoms. In dry soils a covering with rotten manure helps it, and in early spring the plants should be protected from slugs and cater-pillars. Division of the roots in autumn, or it may be raised from seed. The major variety of the St. Bruno's Lily has much larger flowers (2 in. across) coming up from the root, these opening before the flowers on the spike. It grows 3 ft. high in good soil, and is a fine border plant.

ANTIRRHINUM *(Snapdragon).* — A numerous family of rock plants and peren-nial herbs, mostly hardy and many of them from mountainous regions, but none so popular in gardens as the handsome Snapdragon (*A. majus*) which like the wallflowers often grows on walls and stony places. There are many species, but they do not take a large place in gar-dens, among the best being *A. Asarina* and *A. rupestre.* Of the common Snap-dragon, the garden varieties are now numerous, and often showy in effect, the best being the pure colours (*i.e.*, not striped).

CULTIVATION.—Snapdragons are easy of cultivation, sandy and free soils suiting them. They are sown : (1) In August in the place where they are to grow, or preferably in seed-beds, in which latter case plant close to a south wall, sheltering from continued frosts with dry leaves or straw, planting out in spring 16 in. to 24 in. apart. (2) In June or July in seed-beds in a well-exposed posi-tion, planting out the seedlings in the spring. (3) In seed-beds (March to April) at the foot of a south wall. Transplant when the plants are sufficiently developed, and they may also be transplanted to seed-beds and planted out when the flowers commence to show themselves. By means of successive sowings it is possible to obtain an almost uninterrupted bloom from June until frost comes. Snap-dragons are also propagated by cuttings made in the spring or summer, and even during the whole of flowering time. As with a great number of plants, the colour of the stems and leaves of the young plants may to a certain point indicate to us what the colour of the flowers will be. Thus, kinds with green or light-coloured stems and leaves will have in nearly all cases white, or mainly white flowers, or of which the colour is undecided ; whilst of the plants which produce flowers of a decided colour the stems and the leaves are of a pronounced green tint, more or less purple or ruddy also.

APONOGETON *(Cape Pond-flower).—A. distachyon* is a beautiful and fragrant water-plant from the Cape of Good Hope, hardy in many parts of these islands.

About London during the late severe winters there has been no more interest-ing sight than the profuse bloom of this plant in springs, and in cold districts it is necessary, for the perfect culture of this plant in the open air, to grow it in spring or other water that does not freeze ; but in mild districts this is not needed. It may be flowered in an inverted bell-glass in a room. In Devonshire it is grown to greater perfection than in the home counties. Failures often result from put-

Aponogeton (Cape Pond-flower.)

ting it in too shallow water. There is a variety (*roseus*) with rosy tinted blossoms. *A. spathaceum* is a poor form with flowers tinged with rose. *Naiada-ceæ.*

AQUILEGIA *(Columbine).* — Alpine rock and meadow perennials of the But-tercup order, often beautiful and widely distributed over the northern and moun-tain regions of Europe, Asia, and America. They are of great variety in colour—white, rose, buff, blue, and purple, and also stripes and intermediate shades, the American kinds having yellow, scarlet, and most delicate shades of blue flowers. The Columbines are frequently taller than most of the plants strictly termed alpine, but are nevertheless true alpine plants, and among the most singularly beautiful of the class. Climbing the sunny hills of the sierras in California, one meets with a large scarlet Columbine, that has almost the vigour of a lily, and in the mountains of Utah, and on many others in the Rocky Mountain region, there is the Rocky Mountain Columbine (*A. cærulea*), with its long and slender spurs and lovely cool tints, and there is no family that has a wider share in adorning the mountains. Although our cottage gardens are alive with Columbines in much beauty of colour in early summer, there is some difficulty in cultivating the rarer alpine kinds. They require to be carefully planted in sandy or gritty though moist ground, and in well-drained ledges in the rock-garden, in half-shady positions or northern ex-

A white Aquilegia.

posures. Most rare Columbines, however, fail to form enduring tufts in our gardens, and they must be raised from seed as frequently as good seed can be got. It is the alpine character of the

home of many of the Columbines which makes the culture of some of the lovely kinds so uncertain, and which causes them to thrive so well in the north of Scotland while they fail in our ordinary dry garden borders. No plants are more capricious; take, for instance, the charming *A. glandulosa*, grown like a weed at Forres, in Scotland, and so short-lived in most gardens. Nor is this an exception; it is characteristic of all the mountain kinds. The best soil for them is deep, well-drained, rich alluvial loam. It is probable many of the species are biennial, and that it is necessary to raise them from seed frequently; and to avoid the results of crossing it is better to get the seed, if we can, from the wild home of the species. The seeds should be sown early in spring, and the young plants pricked out into pans or into an old garden frame as soon as they are fit to handle, removing them early in August to the borders; select a cloudy day for the work, and give them a little shading for a few days.

A. alpina (*Alpine Columbine*).—A beautiful high mountain plant 1 ft. to 2 ft. high, with showy blue flowers, and there is a lovely variety with a white centre to the flower. In the rock-garden in a rather moist and sheltered, but not shady, spot in deep sandy loam or peat. Seed or division.

A. Bertoloni.—A pretty little alpine, about 1 ft. high, with violet-blue flowers having short knobby spurs.

A. californica (*Californian Columbine*). —One of the finest of the American species, with one bold woody stem, 3 ft. high, and handsome, bright orange flowers. The seeds should be carefully looked after, as having once blossomed the old plant may perish. This plant thrives best on a deep sandy loam and moist.

A. canadensis (*Canadian Columbine*). —The flowers are smaller than the Western American kinds; but this is compensated for by the brilliancy of the scarlet colour of the sepals and of the erect spurs, and by the bright yellow of the petals. The true plant is a slender grower, 1 ft. in height. It is a plant for borders, or placing here and there among dwarf shrubs and plants in the rougher parts of the rock-garden.

A. chrysantha (*Golden Columbine*).— This tall and beautiful species endures as a perennial on many soils where the other kinds perish, thriving even on the stiff clay soils north of London, though it is no less free in more happy situations.

It comes true from seed, which is most safely raised under glass, and the plant grows 4 ft. in height in good soil.

A. cœrulea (*Rocky Mountain Columbine*).—This is very beautiful, the green-tipped spurs of the flower being as slender as a thread, and having a tendency to twist round each other. It is hardy, flowering early in summer, from 12 in. to 15 in. high, worthy of the best position on the rock-garden, and in choice mixed borders, where the soil is free and deep. Unlike the Golden Columbine, it is not perennial on many soils, though longer-lived in cool hill-gardens. To get healthy plants that will flower freely, seeds should be sown annually.

A. glandulosa (*Altaian Columbine*).— A beautiful plant of tufted habit, flowering in early summer—a fine blue, with tips of petals creamy-white, the spur curved backwards towards the stalk, the sepals dark blue, large, with a long footstalk. It is a native of the Altai Mountains, and one of the most precious flowers for the rock-garden, in deep sandy soil. Seed and division.

A. Skinneri (*Skinner's Columbine*).— A distinct plant, the flowers produced later on slender pedicels, the sepals greenish, the petals small and yellow; the spurs are 2 in. long and bright orange-red. Though from Guatemala, it comes from mountain districts, and is nearly hardy. While the name is often seen, the true plant is rare.

A. viridiflora.—A charming Siberian Columbine, the sage-green of the flower and the delicate tint of the leaf offering a delicate harmony. In the border it may not be noticed, but if a spray or two are put in a glass its beauty is seen. It has a delicate fragrance, and is raised from seed.

A. vulgaris (*Common Columbine*).— There are many forms of this, and double kinds, flowering from May till towards the end of summer. One may often see a variety of the common Columbine nearly as handsome as any of the finest alpine species. Its varieties, and some hybrid forms, may well be used in the wilder and more picturesque parts of large pleasure-grounds, by streams, in copses, or among Foxgloves, Geraniums, or long Grasses. The ground should be well dug if the vegetation is dense, and the seed sown on the spot. Where bare places occur, and seedlings have a chance of coming up without being strangled by other plants, seed may be scattered as soon as ripe.

Known species.—*A. advena*, Hab? *alpina*, Siberia; *Amaliæ*, Thessaly; *aragonensis*, Spain; *arbascensis*, Europe; *Bertoloni*, Europe; *Brauni*, Europe; *brevistyla*, N. America; *Buergeriana*, Japan; *californica*, N. W. America; *campylocentra*, Europe; *canadensis*, N. America; *chrysantha*, N. Mexico; *cærulea*, N. W. America; *dichroa*, Europe; *dioica*, Europe; *discolor*, Spain; *Einseleana*, Europe; *eximia*, Europe; *flabellata*, Japan; *flavescens*, California; *formosa*, Kamtschatka; *fragrans*, Himalayas; *Gaertneri*, Europe; *Gebleri*, Europe; *glandulosa*, Siberia; *glauca*, Himalayas; *grata*, Europe; *Haynaldi*, Europe; *Huteri*, Europe; *Jonesi*, N. America; *Kareliniana*, Hab? *Kitaibeli*, Armenia; *lactiflora*, Siberia; *leptoceras*, Siberia; *longisepala*, Europe; *longissima*, N. America; *lutea*, Hab? *lutescens*, Europe; *macrocentra*, Europe; *mollis*, France; *Moorcroftiana*, Himalayas; *nemoralis*, France; *nevadensis*, Spain; *olympica*, E. Europe; *orthantha*, Europe; *Ottonis*, Greece; *oxysepala*, E. Asia; *parviflora*, Siberia; *pubiflora*, E. Indies; *pycnotricha*, Europe; *pyrenaica*, S. Europe; *ruscinonensis*, France; *Schotti*, Europe; *sibirica*, Siberia; *sinensis*, China; *Skinneri*, Mexico; **stenopetala**, Europe; **sulphurea**, Europe; **Szaboi**, Europe; *viridiflora*, Siberia; *volubilis*, Manchuria; *vulgaris*, Europe.

Siberian Columbine.

ARABIS (*Rock Cress*).—A large family of hill-plants, few of which are grown, though some are worth a place. *A. albida* (White Rock Cress) is a popular plant in gardens, and in the barrows of every London flower-hawker in spring. It will grow in any soil, where its sheets of snowy bloom may open in early spring. It is easily increased by seed, or cuttings, and is useful for the mixed border the spring garden, and for naturalising in bare or rocky spots. It is closely allied to the alpine Rock Cress or Bee Flower (*A. alpina*) so widely distributed on the Alps, but is distinct, and by far the best kind. A variegated form is the dwarfest and whitest of the Rock Cresses. *A. blepharophylla* (Rosy Rock Cress) is not unlike the white Arabis, but the flowers are rosy purple. It varies a good deal, but there is no difficulty in selecting a strain of the deepest rose, its healthy tufts being effective in April. There are variegated forms of the commoner species, the prettiest of them being *A. lucida variegata*, but none have much value. *A. arenosa*, from the south of Europe, is a pretty annual in the spring garden or naturalised on old ruins or dry bare banks. *A. petræa* is a neat sturdy little plant, with pure white flowers; it is a native of some of the higher Scottish mountains, rare, but very pretty when well grown on a moist well-exposed spot on the rock-garden. *A. Stelleri*, a Chinese species, is a much freer flowering plant than *A. blepharophylla*, ripening seed freely, and easily grown in the rock-garden. *Cruciferæ.*

ARALIA.—Shrubs, or stout herbaceous plants of the Ivy order, of diverse

Aralia chinensis.

aspects, few fitted for open air, except *A. canescens* and *A. spinosa*, which thrive in our gardens, and which in size and beauty of leaf are far before many " fine-foliaged plants" carefully grown in hothouses. The Aralias described are now placed under Fatsia, but we retain the older name

as better known in gardens. *A. papyrifera* (Chinese Rice-paper plant), though a native of the hot island of Formosa, is useful for the greenhouse in winter and the flower garden in summer. It is handsome in leaf, but is only suited for southern or very warm gardens.

A. chinensis. — A handsome hardy shrub, with very large much-divided spiny leaves, resembling those of the Angelica tree of North America. In this country it attains the height of from 6 to 12 ft. In a well-drained deep loam it thrives vigorously. May be useful in a flower-garden where tender fine-leaved plants will not thrive.—*Syn. Dimorphanthus mandschuricus.*

A. Sieboldi.—A shrubby species, with fine green leaves, nearly hardy, and a handsome bush on dry soils and near the sea. It may be used in the flower garden or the pleasure-ground, for isolated specimens on the turf, or for association with fine-leaved plants; but it soon turns yellow and unhappy-looking if exposed to much sunshine. It is also hardier in the shade, its foliage browning badly if caught too suddenly by the sun after hard frosts. Syn. *Fatsia Japonica.*

A. spinosa (*Angelica Tree*) is the oldest species in our gardens. Its small white flowers appear in autumn in great panicles. This fine shrub has often been put in exposed places, but is better where its great leaves will not be torn, and in every size may be used in the flower garden or pleasure ground. Cuttings of the roots. N. America.

ARAUCARIA (*Monkey-Puzzle*).—A noble group of Cone-bearing trees, most of which, unfortunately, are too tender for our winters. *A. imbricata* (the Monkey-Puzzle Tree) is a native of Chili, and the only species which does at all well in favourable situations. As a rule it soon presents an unhappy appearance, and is therefore not to be recommended for planting. It was killed by thousands in the nurseries and gardens in the severe winter of 1860, and it is no way worthy of its popularity in the garden, being really a forest tree of a climate very different to ours.

ARBUTUS (*Strawberry Tree*).—Evergreen shrubs of much beauty, both of flower and form of leaf or bush, but coming from warmer countries thrive only on our sea shore or warmer districts and on warm soils. The beautiful *A. Unedo* grows 20 ft. high or more in the coast districts, but inland it is cut down in severe winters. There are varieties of it, one of the best being *A.*

Croomei, which has longer and broader leaves than the common kind. The variety *rubra* has almost bright scarlet flowers in autumn. One variety has double

Aralia spinosa. From a photograph sent by Mr.
C. L. Mayor, Paignton, Devon.

flowers, and there are a number of so-called varieties differing only a little in the form of the leaf. S. Europe, and also wild in the south of Ireland. The other species are not so important as flowering trees, though good evergreens where they will face the climate. *A. Andrachne*, with smooth ruddy-tinged bark, is hardy in the south and coast districts ; about London it reaches a height of over 15 ft. It grows wild in Greece, and is a very old tree in gardens. The fine Californian *Arbutus* are not hardy with us. These shrubs succeed best in a deep light loam, and will thrive on chalky soils much better than many other evergreen shrubs. In planting them, a warm sheltered

position is best. In the south and west of England, and in Ireland, the fruits are freely borne, and a large specimen is very handsome in fruit.

ARCTOSTAPHYLOS (*Bear-berry*).—Mostly trailing Alpine evergreens of the Heath order, of which few are in cultivation. Of this group *A. alpina* is useful for rocky banks, edging bog-beds, or even in bogs. *A. Uva-ursi* (Bear-berry) is a dwarf evergreen mountain shrub, 1 ft. high—often less—sometimes grown with rock-plants. It has small rose flowers in early summer and red berries in autumn. *A. alpina.*—The Black Bear-berry has trailing stems and white or flesh coloured flowers. It is abundant in hilly places in Europe and N. America. Grows in any soil, but prefers a moist border or ledge. Division. *A. nitida* is a Mexican half-hardy evergreen with shining green leaves and white flowers. The dwarf, much branched, *A. pungens*, is also a native of Mexico ; while the shrubby, hardy *A. tomentosa* comes from N. W. America.

ARCTOTIS.—Showy half hardy composites from the Cape, numbering between forty and fifty species, for the most part little known. The bright colours of many of the species are more intense in the open air than when the plants are cramped in pots in a greenhouse. Dry sunny banks often devoid of plant life might be beautifully clothed with them. Although true sun-loving plants, they may be used as a groundwork in spots where, unmindful of the shade if not too dense, they flower almost as freely as when fully exposed to

Arctotis arborescens.

F F

the sun. They require warm greenhouse treatment in winter.

A. acaulis is a very variable dwarf species. The flowers are large, attractive, and of a deep rich orange. It does not ripen seed freely, but is easily propagated from side shoots.

A. aspera is a half-shrubby species, with deeply cut and wrinkled leaves and creamy flowers, purplish outside. It may be used in vases and hanging baskets, the pink buds being pretty. Cuttings strike readily in heat.

A. aureola is of shrubby habit, 1 to 2 ft. in height, with handsome orange flowers towards the end of the branches. Cuttings. Syn. *A. grandiflora.*

A. leptorhiza is one of the most showy annuals we grow, with abundance of rich orange flowers, as is also *A. breviscapa,* which likes a sunny position. The seeds may be sown in the open air, the plant being treated as a hardy annual. A sunny spot should be chosen, and the seedlings well thinned.—K.

ARENARIA (*Sandwort*).—A numerous family of rock and mountain plants, of vast distribution over northern and alpine ranges, and in temperate countries. Few kinds are in gardens, and these are dwarf plants, easy to grow.

A. balearica (*Creeping Sandwort*).—A pretty little plant, which coats rocks and stones with verdure, and scatters over the green mantle countless white starry flowers. Plant firmly in any common soil near the stones or rocks it is to cover, and it will soon begin to clothe them. Flowers in spring. Division. I first used it for carpets beneath tea roses at Gravetye, and also for low rough stone walls, over which it spreads in myriads. Corsica.

A. montana (*Mountain Sandwort*).—A pretty rock-plant, having the habit of a

Mountain Sandwort (Arenaria montana).

Cerastium, and fine large white flowers. It is the best of the large Sandworts, and should be in every collection of rock-plants, being hardy and free. France. Seed or division.

A. norwegica is one of the best kinds, forming dense cushions about 6 in. in diameter, and covered with large white flowers throughout the summer. A fine alpine plant. Norway.

A. purpurescens (*Purplish Sandwort*). —An interesting kind with purplish flowers, on a dwarf tufted mass of smooth pointed leaves. It is plentiful over the Pyrenean mountains, hardy, and, like the other kinds, increased by seed or division. It should be associated in the rock-garden with the smallest plants.

There are a great number of other species, but it is not easy to find among them plants of such garden value as those named above.

ARETHUSA.—*A. bulbosa* is a beautiful American hardy Orchid, which grows in wet meadows or bog-land, blossoming in May and June. Each plant bears a bright rose-purple flower that shows well on its bed of Sphagnum, Cranberry, and Sedge. The little bulbs grow in a mossy mat formed by the roots and decaying herbage of plants and moss. In cultivation it requires the same soil, and get the leaf as well matured as possible. A shady moist spot with a northern exposure is best, and the soil should be a mixture of well-rotted manure and Sphagnum. During winter, protect the bed with some cover, for it is not so hardy in gardens as in its bog home.

ARGEMONE (*Prickly Poppy*).—Handsome Poppy-like plants, said to be perennial, but perishing on moist soils after the first year. As they come from the warmer parts of California and Mexico, and even there grow on dry hill-sides and in warm valleys, their perishing here may be understood. Usually about 2 ft. high, they have large white flowers 4 in. across with a bunch of yellow stamens in the centre. They require a warm loam, and go with the choicest annual flowers. The kinds mostly grown are *A. mexicana, A. grandiflora,* and *A. hispida,* which are so much alike in habit as not to need separate description. Seed in a warm frame.

ARISTOTELIA.—*A. macqui* is a hardy Chilian shrub of the Lime tree family, chiefly esteemed for its handsome evergreen foliage. The pea-like berries are at first dark purple but eventually black. There is a variegated form, but not quite so hardy as the species. Commoner in southern Ireland than in England.

ARISTOLOCHIA (*Dutchman's Pipe*).
—Climbing Birthworts of curious form of
flower, and effective in foliage. *A. Sipho*
is generally used as a wall-plant, but is
finer for covering bowers, or for clambering up trees or over stumps. *A.
tomentosa* is smaller, distinct in its tone
of green, and useful in like ways ; both
plants are N. American, growing with
freedom in ordinary garden soil. The
family is a large one, mainly tropical, but
some of the forms go into northern countries. Propagated by cuttings.

ARMERIA (*Thrift, Sea Pink*).—Rock
and shore plants of the Statice Order,
of which the best known is the common
A. vulgaris (Thrift). This native of our
shores, and of the tops of the Scottish
mountains, is very pretty, with its flowers
of soft lilac or white springing from

The Tufted Thrift (Armeria cæspitosa.)

cushions of grass-like leaves ; but the
deep rosy form, rarely seen wild, best
deserves cultivation. It is useful for the
spring garden, for banks or borders in
shrubberies, for edgings, and for the rock-
garden, and is easily increased by division.
As old plants do not bloom so long
as young ones, occasional replanting is
desirable. In addition to the white
variety and the old dark red one, there
are *Crimson Gem* and *Laucheana*, the
flowers intense pink. *A. cæspitosa* is a
rose-coloured kind from the south of
Europe, 5000 to 8000 ft. above the sea-level.
Its flower-heads, each from ¾ in. to 1 in. in
diameter, are borne on slender stems 1 to
2 in. high, from June to September. The
leaves are in dense tufts, with a branching
woody root-stock. A rock-garden plant,
thriving in any well-drained, rather poor,

sandy loam, in wet weather it is apt to damp
off at the neck in rich soil. Seed. *A.
cephalotes* (Great Thrift) is one of the
best hardy flowers from South Europe and
South Africa, and should be in every good
border and rock-garden among the taller
plants. Hardy on free and well-drained
soils, it now and then perishes in hard
winters, especially on cold soils. It varies
a little from seed which is easily raised,
but all the forms are worth growing. It
is not, however, so readily got from
division. This species and its forms have
flowers much larger than the common
Thrift. *A. setacea* is an alpine species,
with little globose heads of pink flowers so
numerous as almost to conceal the plant
on flower-stems from 1 to 3 in. high.
This and *A. juncea* are found in the S.
of France on barren stony mounds and
on elevated tablelands.

ARNEBIA (*Prophet-flower*).—A handsome and distinct perennial herb, 1 ft. to
18 in. high. *A. echioides* has flowers of a
bright primrose-yellow, with five black
spots on the corolla, which gradually fade
and finally disappear. It is hardy either
on the rock-garden or in a well-drained
border, and prefers partial shade. It is a
native of the Caucasus and Northern
Persia, and though long introduced is
still among the rarest of hardy flowers.
Young plants bloom long, which adds to
their charms. Cuttings. *A. Griffithi* is
a tender annual, and though pretty not so
valuable as *A. echioides*.

ARTEMISIA (*Wormwood*). — Herbs
and low bushes covering a large part of
the surface of northern and arid regions.
Though often poor weeds, some have a
use in gardens, though rarely for their
flowers. *A. anethifolia* is one of the most
elegant herbaceous perennials, 5 ft. in
height. *A. annua* is a graceful plant
with tall stems 5 or 6 ft. high, the foliage
fine, and the flowers not showy in elegant
panicles. The hue is a fresh and pleasing green, and the plant is a graceful
centre of a flower-bed or group. Other
kinds, like *A. alpina* and *A. frigida*, belong to an alpine group which is at home
in the rock-garden, while there are many
taller herbaceous and half-woody plants
of a silvery hue, such as *A. Stelleriana*,
A. cana, *A. maritima*, and some with
handsome Fern-like foliage like *A. tanacetifolia*.

ARUM (*Cuckoo Pint*). — Tuberous
rooted herbaceous plants of distinct form,
of which some from South Europe are
hardy, and of interest in our gardens.
They thrive best in warm borders and
about the sunny side of garden walls.

F F 2

Some nine or ten kinds are found in South Europe, two coming as far north as our own country. They have, when in bloom, a very offensive odour of carrion.

A. crinitum (*Dragon's Mouth*).—This plant when in flower is very grotesque, from the singular shape of its broad speckled spathe. The leaves are cut into deep segments, and the leaf-stalks,

mottled with black. It loves best a corner to itself in sandy loam at the foot of a south wall. Many would not care for a plant having such an odour. Division.

A. italicum (*Italian Arum*) is larger than our native Arum ; the veins blotched with yellow. As the leaves come very early in the season, they are attractive. In the autumn, when they have died

Arum crinitum (Dragon's Mouth).

overlapping each other, form a sort of spurious stem 1 ft. or 14 in. high, marbled and spotted with purplish-black. Warm borders, fringes of shrubberies, or beds of the smaller sub-tropical plants suit it best. Division of tubers.

A. Dracunculus (*Dragons, Snake Plant*), from South Europe, attains a height of 2 to 3 ft. ; the leaves large ; the stalks and stem of a fleshy colour, deeply

away, the clusters of scarlet berries, on foot-stalks 10 in. or 12 in. long, are showy. The true use for it is as a naturalised plant, or in the shrubbery.

Arundinaria. *See* BAMBUSA.

ARUNDO (*Great Reed*).—Important Grasses of fine form sometimes of great height. *A. conspicua* (*New Zealand Reed*) is a Grass of noble form—a companion for the Pampas Grass, especially in the western and southern counties and on light soils. In fine deep loams it reaches a height of nearly 12 ft., but perishes from cold or other causes on many soils. It flowers before the Pampas Grass. It likes plenty of water nearly all the year round, and may be increased by seeds or division. *A. Donax* (*Great Reed*) is the great Reed of the south of Europe, a noble plant on good soils, in the south of England making canes 10 ft. high, in rich soil, but in our country it has suffered much in recent severe winters. Its variegated variety is of some value for the flower garden, and is nearly hardy in the southern counties. *A. Phragmites* (*Common Reed*) is the native marsh plant, 6 ft. or more high, bearing when in flower a large, handsome, spreading, purplish panicle. It is an excellent cover for water birds. There is a good variegated form which has more claims as a plant for the water side.

ASARUM(*Asarabacca*).—Curious little plants resembling Cyclamens in their leaves, but of little value except as curiosities, or as wood plants in ordinary garden soil. *A. canadense* is the Canadian Snakeroot, which bears in spring curious brownish-purple flowers, the roots being strongly aromatic, like Ginger. *A. virginicum* is the Heart Snake-root, its leaves thick and leathery, with the upper surface mottled with white. *A. caudatum* is from Oregon, and much like the others in habit, but the divisions of the flower have long tail-like appendages. *A. europæum* is the Asarabacca, the flowers greenish, about ½ in. long, and close to the ground.

ASCLEPIAS (*Milk-weed, Silk-weed*). —A large genus of strong growing herbaceous perennials, few of which are adapted for the flower garden, as they require a good deal of room, and are not attractive. They thrive in a light or peaty soil and may be increased by division. *A. acuminata* has red and white flowers. *A. amœna*, purple ; *A. Cornuti* (the common Milk-weed)—also known as *A. syriaca*—grows vigorously to a height of 4 ft., and bears umbels of deep purple fragrant flowers, of which bees seem to be fond. *A. incarnata* (the Swamp Milk-weed) is a good waterside plant with rose-purple flowers. *A. quadrifolia* (Four-leaved Milk-weed) bears fragrant terminal heads of lilac-white flowers early in the summer. *A. purpurascens* is also a waterside plant with purple flowers. *A. rubra* (the Red Milk-weed) is a distinct tall-growing plant with long bright green foliage, and large umbels of purple-red flowers. *A. tuberosa* (the

Butterfly Silk-weed) is the prettiest species, with its clusters of showy bright orange-red flowers in the autumn. Good flowering plants may be obtained from seed in three years, but it is mostly increased by dividing the tubers. This species likes sandy soil and a warm situation. *A. variegata* (Variegated Milk-weed) has dense umbels of handsome white flowers with a reddish centre. The downy stems reach a height of 2 to 4 ft., and are mottled with purple.

ASIMINA (*Virginian Papaw*). — A North American shrub, or low tree of the Custard Apple family. *A. triloba* forms a small tree, with dull purple flowers, about

A climbing Asparagus.

2 in. across. It bears fruits eaten by the inhabitants of the Southern States ; hence the name. Sometimes grown against a wall in this country, but is hardy as a standard, at least about London.

ASPARAGUS.—Herbaceous plants or climbers of the Lily Order, of fine habit with elegant leaves. The vigorous and tall *A. Broussoneti* is quite hardy in warm sandy soil, and so are *A. tenuifolius* and others. The common Asparagus is as good as any, and a tuft or group of it is graceful in a border of flowers or a bed of fine-leaved plants.

ASPERULA (*Sweet Woodruff*).—*A. odorata*, which belongs to the same family as the Coffee Plant, is abundant in many parts of Britain, and worthy of the garden or shrubbery, especially in districts where it does not occur wild. Its stems and leaves give off a fragrant hay-like odour when dried ; and in May the small white flowers, dotted over the tufts of whorled leaves, are pretty. It is sometimes used as an edging to beds in cottage gardens, and it goes prettily with some of the smaller ivies, in forming edgings about rocky banks and borders. *A. azurea setosa* (*A. orientalis*) is a pretty hardy blue annual, flowering in April and May. Sow seed in the previous autumn. *A. cynanchica* is a rosy-red perennial, and a good bank or rough rock-plant. *A. hexaphylla* is a tall slender white-flowered species.

ASPHODELINE.—Plants nearly allied to the following, but the stems of Asphodelus are leafless, while in Asphodeline the leaves are produced on erect stems. About six kinds are in cultivation, the best-known being *A. lutea*, which grows about 3 ft. high, with yellow flowers in dense clustered spikes. *A. taurica* has white flowers, on stems 1 to 2 ft. high. *A. liburnica* (*A. cretica*) and *A. tenuior* have yellow flowers in loose racemes. *A. damascena* has white blossoms in dense racemes, and *A. brevicaulis* has yellow flowers in loose racemes. These all thrive in any common garden soil, and may be used in bold masses with good effect among other tall plants.

ASPHODELUS (*Asphodel*).—Tuberous plants of the Lily Order, with spiked flowers and not of a high order of beauty, thriving in any free garden soil. The best-known is the bold *A. ramosus*, a South European species, familiar in most old herbaceous plant borders, but better fitted for the shrubbery. Other kinds are *A. fistulosus* and *tenuifolius*, with white flowers, the plant growing from 1½ to 3 ft. high. The last-named kind has delicate feathery foliage. *A. creticus*, the Cretan Asphodel, has yellow flowers, and is an easily cultivated border plant.

ASPIDIUM (*Shield or Wood Fern*).—This family now embraces the Polystichum and some species of Lastrea. There are numerous hardy kinds, among them the Male Fern (*A. Filix-mas*) and the Prickly Shield Fern. These thrive even in small town gardens and places similarly confined if given plenty of water in hot dry weather. Either alone or in groups they have a fine effect, as an under-growth to trees in the pleasure-ground or in the shadier parts of the garden, and are evergreen. Their varieties are endless, no fewer than a hundred named sorts of *A. aculeatum* and fifty of *A. Filix-mas* being enumerated in trade lists. The smaller and more delicate kinds require some care. *A. aculeatum* succeeds best in rich loam, with sand and leaf-mould, well drained, and so does the Male Fern. The bolder Ferns of this group give fine cool effects in rightly chosen spots in and near the flower garden.

ASPLENIUM (*Spleenwort*).—The fine dark green colour and free-growing character of most of the Spleenwort Ferns give them distinct value. The best soil for them is a well-drained mixture of peat, sand, and loam, in which the finer kinds of flowering shrubs, such as Kalmias and Andromedas, thrive. *A. Adiantum nigrum* (the black Spleenwort) would be at home amongst hardy Azaleas, as they lose their foliage in winter, and the Spleenwort would then carpet the surface. The shade of Azaleas in the summer, if not planted too thickly, would suit this Spleenwort, which, when wild, fringes copses or is found on hedge-banks, where it gets a little protection from the summer sun. The various smaller species of this genus belong more to the choice fernery than to the flower garden, unless when we are happy in having old walls near or around it, often so congenial a home for the smaller rock-ferns.

ASTER (*Starwort, Michaelmas Daisy*).—Hardy perennial plants of much beauty

Aster Stracheyi.

and variety. There is a quiet beauty about the more select Starworts, which is charming in the autumn days, and their variety of colour, of form, and of bud and blossom is delightful.

For the most part Starworts are regardless of cold or rain. Less showy than the Chrysanthemum, they are more refined in colour and form. Even where not introduced into the flower garden, they should always be grown for cutting ; and they are excellent for forming bold groups to cover the bare ground among newly-planted shrubs. Nothing can be more easy to cultivate. The essential point is to get the distinct kinds, of which the following are among the best that flower in early October — *Aster amellus, acris, cassubicus, turbinellus, Chapmani, versicolor, pulchellus, cordifolius, elegans, Reevesi, discolor, laxus, horizontalis, ericoides, Shorti, multiflorus, dumosus, Curtisi, lævis, longifolius, coccineus, sericeus, Nova-Angla, Nova-Belgii, puniceus,* and *vimineus.* Every year adds to our

bundling may be wholly got rid of, if the plants were supported and relieved by the bushes, and their flowers massed above them here and there. Asters, dwarfer than the shrubs among which we place them, are not less valuable, as they help to give light and shade, and to avoid the common way of setting plants to a face as if they were so many bricks. This is not the only way of growing these hardiest of northern flowers, but it is a charming one, and it lights up the garden with a new loveliness of refined colour.

Of recent years many seedling forms have been raised and named, but in no case are these so good as the best of the wild species, such as *amellus, acris* and *cordifolius.*

ASTILBE (*Goat's Beard*).—A vigorous group of chiefly tall-branching herbaceous

Aster elegans (Lilac Starwort).

autumn-blooming hardy plants, and a choice of Starworts may be made by autumn visits to collections. As yet gardeners seldom look at general effects—at the whole of things. The flowers are so dear to them that the garden, as a picture, is left to chance, and hence there is so much ugliness and formality in gardens, to those at least who regard the robe as more than the buttons. Some years ago Starworts were rarely seen except in bundles in botanic gardens. Since the hardy flower revival, they have become more frequent in collections, but as yet they have no important place in gardens generally, and we may often still see them tied in bundles, though the effective way of grouping is so clear and simply carried out. The bad effect of staking and

perennials. The robust kinds resemble the Spiræas of the Aruncus group, but are bolder, and perhaps better suited for the margin of water. There are eight kinds in cultivation, the best known of which are *A. japonica* and *A. rivularis.* Moist places in the wild garden are most suitable for *A. decandra, A. rivularis, A. rubra, A. Lemoinei,* and *A. Thunbergi,* the last being also known as Spiræa. These plants group well, and the handsome foliage makes healthy undergrowth, over which the tall plumes of white or red flowers tower with good effect. Division of the roots, and some by the runners.

ASTRAGALUS (*Milk Vetch*).—A large family of alpine and perennial leguminous plants, not many of which are valuable for the garden. The best are rock-plants, but they grow freely on the level ground in borders. *A. monspessulanus* is useful for the front of borders and for the rock garden. The vigorous shoots are prostrate, so that it is seen to greater advantage when its long heads of crimson and rosy flowers droop over rocks. It grows well in any soil. There are several varieties. *A. Onobrychis* (Saintfoin Milk Vetch) is a handsome species from South Europe and Siberia (in some varieties spreading, and in others about 18 in. high), with racemes of purplish-crimson flowers in June. It thrives well on any good loam. *A. dasyglottis* is well suited for the rock-garden. Its numerous showy flower-

pleasantly of sour milk. A third species is *A. Biebersteini* ; in some of its characters it is intermediate between the other two. Its habit is good and compact, and it flowers freely. There are two or three smaller species, the commonest of which is *A. minor*, often brought from the Alps by collectors. The Astrantias have a quaint beauty of their own ; they are not showy, nor particular about soil or aspect. They are easily established in woodland walks where the growth of weeds is not too rank.— C. W. D.

ATHYRIUM (*Lady Fern*).—Beautiful hardy Ferns, which *A. Filix-fœmina* may

Purple Rock Cress (Aubrietia).

heads, of a clear bright purple, are set off by the fresh green foliage. *A. adsurgens* is dwarf, with numbers of violet-carmine flowers. *A. vaginatus* succeeds in an exposed position in any ordinary border. The showy deep violet-purple flowers are borne in dense erect clusters for a long time.

ASTRANTIA (*Master-wort*).—These herbs are amongst umbelliferous plants, and consist of not more than four or five true species, all natives of the mountains of Southern Europe. The two most distinct are *A. major* and *A. helleborifolia*. *A. helleborifolia* is from the Caucasus, with the largest flower of any, the colour clear pink ; but the habit of the plant is straggling, and the flowers smell un-

be taken to represent. They like a compost of loam, leaf-mould, and peat, mixed in about equal proportions, with the addition of some sharp sand. They require abundance of water during their growing period, but not in winter, because all the varieties are deciduous, the ground at that period being wet enough naturally. Among many fine hardy evergreen and herbaceous plants Lady Ferns might be planted with advantage ; they will thrive in a little shade where protected from drying winds. There are many beautiful forms.

Atragene. *See* CLEMATIS.

AUBRIETIA (*Purple Rock Cress*).— charming group of rock plants from the mountains of South Europe. There are many varieties in gardens, but probably all may be reduced to some half-dozen species, whilst all are beautiful. The oldest is called *A. purpurea*. Then there is what is called *deltoidea*, and the free-branching variety of it known as *Eyrei*, which has large violet-purple flowers. We have also *grandiflora*, with a lax habit, a pretty rock-plant. Then we have *Leichtlini*, *Mooreana*, *Columnæ*, and *Campbelli*; but the names of the species are too numerous in this family, and are often only varieties from different localities. Some, like Dr. Mules, Beauty of Baden and W. Ingram, are of higher value as garden plants.

The Aubrietia is excellent as a wall-plant. We need only sow the seed in any mossy or earthy chinks in autumn or spring, indeed they will sow themselves on walls, and often bloom on the sunny sides in February. Rock-gardens, stony places, and sloping banks suit Aubrietias perfectly. They make neat edgings, and may be used as such with good effect. There are one or two variegated varieties. Aubrietias are easy to naturalise in rocky places, and may be easily got from seeds, cuttings, or by division.

AUCUBA.—Evergreen berry-bearing shrubs of the Dogwood order, which brighten gardens in winter. It is one of the best shrubs for planting under trees, as its strong fleshy roots enable it to live where other shrubs would starve. It may be safely removed at midsummer or midwinter, but requires shelter and shade. To get a good crop of berries, plant males about 30 ft. apart among the ordinary forms. Smoke and dust seem to have slight effect upon Aucubas, making them valuable for town gardens. The variegated form is more vigorous and rapid in growth than the green or plain-leaved variety, though we have now many fine green forms extremely handsome when in good berry.

AZALEA (*Swamp Honeysuckle*).— These are beautiful upland and bog shrubs from North America, and, if only as a relief from the heaviness of Rhododendrons, their graceful growth is precious. There is nothing in the open garden so charming as old Azalea bushes in flower, with their branches in table-like tiers; but the brilliant tints always seem most effective in the subdued light of a shady wood, and happily few shrubs flower better in partial shade than Azaleas. They like shelter, even from southerly winds, and peaty soil suits them best, though they grow well in loam.

The hardy Azaleas, called Ghent Azaleas, have sprung chiefly from the wild kinds of North America — *A. nudiflora*, *A. calendulacea*, and *A. viscosa*. These and *A. pontica* have been so hybridised with the wild Azalea of South Europe that we have a race in which the colours of the various species are blended and diversified in a great variety of tints, and they all intercross so freely that it is difficult to single out a variety identical with any of the wild species. Fifty years ago, Latin names were given to every fine variety, but they could soon be numbered by the hundred from Belgian gardens alone. Now very few sorts are named. Every variation of tint, from the most fiery scarlets to delicate pinks, whites, and dark and pale yellows, is to

Flowers of Azalea mollis.

be had in Ghent Azaleas, a very beautiful one being the pure white Mrs. Anthony Waterer. Of late years there has sprung up a new race with double Hose-in-hose flowers, collectively called the Narcissiflora group, the chief sorts of which number about a score—Graf von Meran, one of the first, being still among the best yellows. A Californian species, named *A. occidentalis*, is distinct from the deciduous Azaleas, as it flowers after the others are past. It has bunches of fragrant white flowers and broad foliage. *A. mollis*, a dwarf deciduous shrub from Japan and China, has given rise to a variety of kinds, yellow, salmon-red, and orange scarlet being the prevailing colours. It is hardy, and being dwarf may be grouped as a foreground to a mass of the tall kinds. The Chinese *A. amœna*, with small magenta flowers, common enough in greenhouses, is quite hardy in mild localities and rich in bold masses. The Chinese *A. indica*, the ordinary Azalea of greenhouses, is hardy in many places, especially the white variety, which, even in mid-Sussex, thrives in the open air. The Ledum-leaved Azalea (*A. ledifolia*) is a hardy evergreen shrub, also from China, with white flowers, large and open, like A. indica. It grows from 5 ft. to 6 ft. high, and Loudon states that in Cornwall, on Sir Charles Lemon's estate at Carclew, it was planted in hedges, which flowered magnificently without the slightest protection.

Azalea nudiflorum.

AZARA.—Distinct and graceful Chilian shrubs, nearly hardy in favourable soils. On east or west walls they flower freely ; while in the southern counties, at least, they do well in the open. Well-drained loam and the partial shade of taller shrubs suit them. *A. Gillesi* is probably the most handsome, its toothed leaves resembling in colour and texture those of the Holly, with the branches tinged with red. Both in the open air and under glass it blooms in late autumn and winter, the flowers small, and resembling golden catkins. *A. celastrina* has rather smaller leaves, and yellow blossoms. *A. integrifolia* has drooping spikes of fragrant yellow blossoms, which form a dense bush a few feet in height. *A. microphylla* is a graceful evergreen shrub, with many small flowers, succeeded in autumn by small orange-red berries. The best place for it is a sheltered position, not too low. Among other kinds are *A. dentata*, a quick grower ; and *A. serrata*, with prettily serrated leaves, and umbels of yellow blossoms. Order, Bixineæ.

AZOLLA.—*A. Caroliniana* is a very small and curious water-plant, which floats on water quite free of soil, the tufts of delicate green leaves like tiny emeralds. During summer it will grow out-of-doors, and then becomes bronzed, and perhaps it is prettier when light green, as it is in the greenhouses or window. Syn., *A. rubra*. *A. pinnata* is a distinct species.

BABIANA (*Baboon-root*).—Charming

bulbs of the Iris order, from South Africa, allied to Sparaxis and Tritonia, but having broader foliage, often hairy and plaited ; they grow from 6 to 12 in. high, with spikes of sometimes sweetly scented brilliant flowers ranging in colour from blue to crimson-magenta. The bulbs should be planted from September to January, about 4 in. deep and 2 to 4 in. apart, in light loamy soil thoroughly drained, with a due south aspect. The early plantings make foliage in autumn, and require protection of mats against frost. Those planted later will only require a covering of Fern, which should be removed as the foliage appears. In wet soils surround the bulbs with sand, and raise the beds above the level. Many varieties are in cultivation, but in the open air their growth is only worth attempting in very favoured spots.

BAMBUSA (*Bamboo*).—There are some forty or more varieties of these graceful woody grasses, which are hardy in all but the coldest parts of our Islands, though best in sheltered places. Grace and elegance are the characteristics of the Bamboo, and in no species more conspicuous than in the lovely group of Phyllostachys, while some of the Arundinarias will, if planted in suitable places, grow into dense thickets of almost tropical aspect. There are few gardens in which some sheltered nook, backed by evergreens, might not be beautified by a feathering group of *Phyllostachys Henonis* or *nigra* ; while in the wilderness fine effects may be produced by the grand foliage of *Arundinaria Métaké* or the stately plumes of *A. Simoni*. Background is the great secret of getting the best effect out of plants in which beauty of form is the dominant feature ; and above all let the Bamboos be sheltered from our biting easterly and north-easterly winds, as they are more deadly than frost. The softer and moister westerly winds, blow they never so hard, will do but little damage to plants which come from such storm-vexed regions as the coasts of China and the islands of Japan. It is important that every autumn the plants should be well mulched with cow manure, and this again should be covered with dead leaves. To prevent the latter from blowing away it is expedient to surround the plant or group with wire netting. This has the additional advantage of keeping out rabbits and hares. The mulching protects the roots from frost in the winter, and prevents evaporation in summer. When the plants are thoroughly established these precautions become unnecessary.

The plants should only travel during the period when they are at rest. They will be received therefore during the late autumn or winter. If they have come from abroad, the balls of earth round the roots should be thoroughly soaked ; they should then be potted and placed in a cool house for the winter ; the leaves syringed with rainwater twice a day, but the roots should not be kept too wet. In this way many species will keep their leaves as green and fresh as if they had never been disturbed ; but even those that lose their leaves will early in February begin to show little fat buds that will soon develop into branchlets. Early in May begin to harden off the plants, as you would Geraniums for bedding out, and, at the end of May, place them in their permanent homes.

When you take the plants out of the pots be careful not to disturb the roots in any way. You must not attempt to comb them out as you would the roots of trees, for they are as brittle as glass : place them in the earth as they are, and they will soon find their way about. If possible the newly planted Bamboos should be well watered during growth. It must be remembered that Bamboos will not show their true characteristics for several years. But by taking the above precautions much time will be saved, and many disappointments avoided. For transplanting Bamboos (from one part of the same garden to another, not for sending them on a journey), May and June are perhaps the best months, though I have moved them without any ill effects during the whole summer up to the end of September. The worst time is from November to March ; for the plants need to have made some roots in their new homes before they can resist our cold winters and biting winds. As regards propagation, very little need be said here, for I doubt whether the propagation of hardy Bamboos, except by division, is likely to become a successful industry in this country.

PROPAGATION BY DIVISION. — The best moment for this operation is, in our climate, the latter end of April or May. The process is very simple. The plants should be divided into clumps of two or three culms with their rhizome, in order to insure a new growth from the buds on the internodes of the root-stock. If the tufts can be lifted with a ball of earth, so much the better. They should be planted in beds at distances of 2 ft., carefully watered, and protected by a top-dressing of well-rotted cow manure and dead leaves. With the same care they may be planted at once in their permanent homes.

NATIVES OF THE HIMALAYAS.

Arundinaria racemosa.—This grows about 15 feet high in its own country. Stem smooth and round. Internodes about 2 in. apart, leaves 2 to 4 in. in length and narrow, cross veins well defined. After the trying winter of 1895, quite green and fresh at Kew Gardens ; found at an elevation of 12,000 ft. in the N.E. Himalayas.

A. aristata. — A pretty variety of moderate size, with purplish stems and tessellated leaves. This latter quality, also the great altitude at which it is found in the North Eastern Himalayas —as high as 11,000 feet above the sealevel—indicates it as a hardy Bamboo.

A. spathiflora.--Another hardy Bamboo with tessellated leaves, from the Himalayas, where it is found at an altitude of 9,000 feet. Most of the specimens which I have seen grown under this name in English gardens are not the true *A. spathiflora.* *A. falcata* and *A. Falconeri,* though fine kinds in their native country, are not quite hardy in ours.

NATIVES OF CHINA AND JAPAN.

A. Fortunei.—Three plants of no relationship to one another are at present the bearers of this name, respectively green, silver variegated, and golden variegated. As there is absolutely no similarity between them, I have re-named two of them *humilis* and *auricoma,* leaving the name *Fortunei* to the silver-striped species which has the prior claim to the title.

A. humilis.—A green species, about 2 ft. to 3 ft. high, with round and green stem, bright evergreen leaves smooth on both sides, 4½ in. long, three-quarters of an inch broad, and tapering to a point. A very pretty plant to form a carpet, or isolated group near rocks. Syn. *Bambusa gracilis.*

A. Fortunei fol. var. — A silvery-variegated dwarf Bamboo about 3 ft. high. Leaves about 5 in. long, by half or at most three-quarters of an inch wide ; a bright colour beautifully striated with white in a young state, but the variegation is apt to fade in the older leaves, which become rather spotty. A strong runner at the roots.

A. auricoma. — A golden variegated dwarf Bamboo, taller than the two preceding sorts. Leaves striped with bright yellow, from 5 in. to 7 in. long, by 1 in. to 1¼ in. broad. Not a strong runner, but a beautiful and conspicuous evergreen plant.

Bambusa pumila (? *Arundinaria*).—A very pretty dwarf Bamboo somewhat like *Arundinaria humilis*, but smaller in habit, the leaves are less broad, shorter, and do not taper so gradually to a point. The teeth of the serrated edges are less conspicuous; the lower sheaths are hardly so hairy, and the nodes are less well defined and far less downy. The stem is more slender.

Arundinaria Hindsii.—A distinct and beautiful species. In its first year with me it has grown to a height of 6 ft. 3 in., but will evidently attain a greater stature. The young dark-green stems have a lovely white wax on them like the bloom on a Grape. The leaves are 6 in. long by about five-eighths of an inch across; they are thicker than in most Bamboos. The colour is a beautiful dark green, fairer underneath; the veins are conspicuously and beautifully tessellated.

A. Hindsii var. graminea.—A smaller plant than the above, with leaves 9 in. long by five-eighths of an inch broad, and yellow stems; considered by the authorities at Kew to be another form of the same species. The tessellation of the veins of the leaves is not quite so strongly marked as in the type.

A. japonica. — A fine and valuable plant, generally grown in gardens under the name of *Bambusa Métaké*. The leaves are from 8 in. to 1 ft. in length by about 1½ in., sometimes more, broad. The upper surface is smooth and shining, the lower side paler, rather glaucous and wrinkled; the edges are finely serrated. The creeping root-stock in well-established plants is very active, so that care must be taken to give the plant plenty of room.

A. Simoni.—Of this fine species, at Kew, old-established plants have reached a height of 18 ft. The leaves are from 10 in. to 1 ft. long, slightly hairy, lanceolate, longitudinally ribbed, ending in a long narrow point. So far as experience at present goes, this is the greatest runner of all the hardy Bamboos. Its young shoots will appear at a great distance from the parent plant. It should be planted apart in the wild garden, where it may wander at pleasure without injury to any neighbour.

Bambusa palmata (? *Arundinaria*).— A beautiful species, about 5 ft. high, conspicuous from the size of its leaves, which are often used by Japanese peasants to wrap up the bit of salt fish or other condiment which they eat with their rice.

These are the chief beauty of the plant, each from 1 ft. to 13 in. long and 3 in. to 3½ in. broad, tapering rather suddenly to a very fine point; the colour a vivid green on the upper surface, glaucous on the lower. Both edges are serrated. The rhizomes are exceedingly active, and travel far.

Bambusa palmata (from a photograph by Lord Annesley).

Arundinaria Veitchi much resembles *Bambusa palmata* in its habit, though on a far humbler scale, the plant being only about 2 ft. high and the leaves smaller and more rounded at the point. The leaves are about 7 in. long by about 2¼ in. broad, green above, glaucous below, glabrous and much ribbed. The edges wither in winter, giving the plant a variegated but shabby appearance; but the thick new foliage of spring is very beautiful, and the plant runs fiercely, soon making a thick carpet and ousting all weeds.

A. metallica.—A species closely resembling *A. Veitchi*, but lacking the ugly withering of the leaf edges in winter. A native of the north of Japan and the island of Yezo, and hardy.

Bambusa tessellata.—A very beautiful species having the largest leaves of any of the hardy Bamboos. The stem is about 2½ ft. high, round, slightly flattened at the top, the colour a purplish-green, much hidden by persistent withered sheaths. The slender new culms spring gracefully from the carpet of arching foliage. Syn., *Bambusa Ragamowski.*

Arundinaria nitida.—A very lovely species from North Western Szêchuan. The culms are purple-black, very slender and round. The leaves are small, lancet-shaped, and tessellated. Quite the hardiest of all our Bamboos.

A. angustifolia.—A lovely little Bamboo, about 9 in. to 1 ft. in height. The stems are round, very slender, and when young of a purplish colour. It is much branched ; the leaves are about 4½ in. in length by three-eighths of an inch in width ; they are serrated on both sides, and somewhat capriciously striped with silver variegation.

A. marmorea. — A pretty and distinct little Bamboo, for which I have chosen the name *marmorea* on account of the very peculiar appearance of the young stems, which are folded in purple sheaths, delicately marbled with a pinkish silver-gray, through which, near the knots, peep glimmers of the bright emerald-green or dark purple of the stem itself. The leaves, which are bright green, are about 4½ in. long by three-eighths to five-eighths of an inch broad ; they are serrated on both edges, and have a marked constriction at about half an inch from the very sharp end. The rhizome is very active, new shoots appearing at some distance from the parent plant.

A. pygmæa.—The best and the smallest of the dwarf Bamboos, invaluable for making a carpet of soft brilliant green. It grows with extraordinary rapidity, the root-stock travelling great distances and at a considerable depth. Stem about 6 in. to 16 in. high ; leaves about 4 in. long by half an inch to three-quarters of an inch broad. It grows so thick and close that no weed has a chance against it, but it should have plenty of room.

A. Laydekeri.—Apparently a semi-dwarf Bamboo, not, so far as my experience of it goes, particularly attractive, though it should have a place in a collection. The stems in the third summer are about 3 ft. high, but will probably grow higher ; round, much branched ; apparently, therefore, it is an *Arundinaria.* The leaves are about 6 in. long, dark green, but rather shabbily mottled on both surfaces, serrated on one edge and slightly so on the other ; leaf-sheaths hairy at top.

The branches, which are long in proportion to the length of the stems, from which they stand out rather markedly, give the plant a conspicuous habit.

Phyllostachys heterocycla.—This is called by the Japanese Kiko-chiku, or the " tortoise-shell Bamboo," from the curious arrangement of the alternately and partially suppressed internodes at the base of the stem, which sheathe it in plate armour like the scales on a tortoise's back. At about 2 ft. or 3 ft. from the ground the nodes are regularly defined, as in other Bamboos. The other characteristics of this Bamboo do not differ from those of the *Phyllostachys* of the *mitis* and *aurea* group. The leaves are from 3 in. to 4 in. long and about half an inch wide, very minutely serrated on one edge and almost imperceptibly so on the other, bright green on the upper surface, bluer underneath. The imported stems are about 5 in. round, and the plant has the appearance of growing into a large and important Bamboo.

P. Marliacea. — A rare, handsome species. The only plant of it I possess has in its third year grown to a height of 8 ft., and promises to become very tall and vigorous. The stem is a dark green, shining like enamel ; the internodes at the base are very close together, not more than 1½ in. to 2 in. Its habit is very graceful, the culms forming the most elegant arches, beautiful both in form and colour.

P. fastuosa.—This very stately and beautiful plant stands out quite conspicuously among its fellows. The leaves are from 5 in. to 7 in. long by three-quarters of an inch to 1 in. in width, tapering to a sharp point, and markedly constricted at about an inch from the end, which has the appearance of a little tongue. Their colour is bright green on the upper surface and very glaucous underneath. This Bamboo will probably prove to be one of the most valuable of the group. Tall, spreading, gracefully plumed with foliage which for richness and beauty of colour is without a rival, it cannot fail to make a striking feature in the wild garden.

P. aurea.—The distinctive name *aurea* is not very happily chosen, for there is nothing golden about the plant unless it be the yellow stems, and these are not peculiar to the variety named. At Shrubland Park, *Phyllostachys aurea* is 14 ft. 6 in. high, the canes being 2¾ in. round.

P. mitis.—This is the tallest, and in that respect the noblest, of all the Bamboos capable of being cultivated in this country. At Shrubland the culms of plants imported seven years ago are 19 ft 5 in high and 4¼ in in circumference. In China and Japan it grows to 60 ft high. The stems, some of which spring out of the ground like spears, are, when fully developed, beautifully arched The young shoots, when once they start, are very rapid, growing in this country as much as 6 in in the twenty-four hours

P sulphurea.—A handsome golden-stemmed Bamboo, which in appearance has great affinity with *P mitis* It is perfectly hardy and well worth cultivating, but difficult to obtain At Shrubland it is growing to a height of 13 ft, with a circumference of 2¾ in round the stem

P. Quilioi.—A very distinct Bamboo, introduced from the north of Japan To me it appears to have a character altogether its own, and the many botanists and gardeners to whom I have shown it have without exception come round to my opinion Altogether a notable Bamboo, growing at Shrubland to a height of 18 ft 6 in, the canes having a circumference of 3¾ in Syn, *Phyllostachys Mazeli*

P. viridi-glaucescens —A most elegant and graceful Bamboo, growing to a great height—nearly 18 ft at Shrubland The root-stock is very active, the plant being a great runner, while many of the culms come almost horizontally out of the ground, giving the plant a very wide spread The leaves are generally about 3 in or 4 in long and about three-quarters of an inch across The stem is much zigzagged This is a perfectly hardy Bamboo, but it should be established in pots before planting out

P. violescens —This is sometimes said to be a variety of *P viridi-glaucescens*, but quite different both in appearance and behaviour. It is somewhat more tender, the leaves being apt to be cut by frost, which gives the plant an ugly appearance in winter, but with the spring the culms are clothed with new foliage, and after all it is only those shoots which come into existence in the late autumn which suffer The foliage is rather darker and larger than in *P viridi-glaucescens* and the plant more straggling, the rhizomes running rampantly But the most distinctive feature is the deep purple colour of the young stems during their first year This is lost in the two-year-old stems, which change to a greenish yellow or brown The plants at Shrubland are 15 ft. high, and the culms 2¾ in in circumference.

P. Henonis — To my taste this is the loveliest of all our Bamboos, and it is

perfectly hardy, bearing up bravely against our coldest weather. Of all the plants that I imported not one has gone amiss, though they were subjected to hardships which proved fatal to a good many of their travelling companions The slender tall stems are green at first, growing yellower with age, slightly zigzagged. The root-stock runs rather freely, but it is to its habit that this Bamboo owes its surpassing loveliness The two-year-old culms, borne down by the weight of their own foliage, bend almost to the earth in graceful curves, forming a pretty groundwork from which the stems of the year spring up, arching and waving their feathery fronds, the delicate green leaves seeming to float in the air

P. nigra.—This is perhaps the best known, and from its black stems the most easily recognised of the hardy Bamboos. Varieties of this said to be more free than the species are *P nigro-punctata* and *P Boryana* With me the plant has been a little capricious and difficult to establish, but once it has taken hold of the ground no Bamboo seems hardier The stems are of an olive-green colour during their first year of growth, changing to shining black the following year. They are slightly zigzagged The leaves, which are from 3 in to 4½ in. long by three-quarters of an inch broad, are green on the upper surface and glaucous underneath

P. Boryana.—One of the handsomest and most vigorous of the hardy Bamboos, very graceful in its habit. Like *P nigra*, the stems are green during their first year, but change colour the second year to a dull brown splashed with large deep purple or black blotches

P. Castillonis.—A most lovely plant The foliage is larger than it is in most of the Bamboos, some of the leaves being as much as between 8 in. and 9 in long by nearly 2 in broad. When they first appear they are striped with bright orange-yellow, which in time fades to a creamy white As the sheaths of the branchlets are of a very pretty pink, the plant has a tricoloured effect, which is most pleasing ; the branches come in twos and threes Twenty-four degrees of frost January, 1894, did them no harm.

P. ruscifolia.—A pretty little Bamboo, described by Munro as *P. kumasaca*, though the Japanese name is *bungozasa* The stems are about 18 in high, purplish green in colour, with brown sheaths, much zigzagged and very slender, distinctly channelled from the pressure of the branches, which spring in twos and threes, sometimes in fours, from the nodes The leaves are from 2 in. to 4 in in length, and an inch, more or less, in width , ovate , soft hairs very conspicuous on the lower surface, but none on the upper surface or on the insertion of the leaves, which are serrated on both edges

Arundinaria anceps.—A very beautiful Bamboo discovered by Mr. Jordan, superintendent of Regent's Park, in the stock of a dead nursery gardener, whose books being destroyed or lost, it was impossible to trace its origin It is probably a Chinese species. The culms are brown when ripe , the leaf-sheaths are hairy, and the petiole of the leaf is yellow

A. nobilis.—A grand Bamboo, probably of Chinese origin, growing to a height of 24 ft at Menabilly, in Cornwall It is quite hardy, only losing its leaves in early summer when the new ones are ready to appear. The tall stems are yellowish in colour with very dark purplish nodes, of which the lower rim is broadly marked with grey

Bambusa disticha—A pretty little dwarf Bamboo Stem about 2 ft high, round, very slightly zigzagged , branches and leaves distichous ; leaves hairy, especially at the base, and serrated at the edges, about 1½ in. long by three-quarters of an inch broad, tapering to a point , leaf-sheaths hairy ; rhizome inclined to run A very distinct little plant, most useful for a choice corner in a rock garden.   A B F -M

BAPTISIA (*False Indigo*) —A hardy and vigorous Lupine-like group of perennials from North America, forming strong bushy tufts 3 to 5 ft high, with sea-green leaves , the flowers, mostly of a delicate blue, in long spikes *B australis, exaltata,* and *alba* are the best-known kinds, and should be placed in the mixed border in any garden soil

BARBAREA.—Mountain and marsh cruciferous herbs of the Old World, few of much garden value, only two varieties being worth growing. The finest is the double yellow Rocket (*B vulgaris fl -pl.*), which is a beautiful and curious plant It is about 18 in high, flowers bright yellow, from June till late summer, and often till autumn. It succeeds in almost any soil, preferring a rich light loam Division

Barkhausia. *See* CREPIS.

Bartonia aurea *See* MENTZELIA

BEGONIA (*Elephant's Ear*) —A large tropical and sub-tropical family of plants, many of them of much value in our hot-houses, and, of recent years, in our open gardens. The Tuberous Begonia is the most familiar to flower gardeners, and now plays a large part in summer bedding Grouped together in beds a fine effect is produced, and the colours vary from the darkest scarlets and crimsons to the various shades of rose and pink ; also white and blush-coloured kinds

The cultivation of the Begonia is not difficult. Seedlings raised in March will make good plants for planting early in June One can just prick them off into pans , from these, when large enough, they are put in shallow boxes, and not disturbed again until planted out, unless getting overcrowded. The beds should be well prepared for them, if the soil is heavy, using plenty of well-decomposed leaf-mould, and failing this old Mushroom manure During the first year those of inferior quality should be discarded when lifted, marking the finest for another year For the second and after seasons' display start the tubers in a gentle heat in boxes in March, transferring them to a cold frame or pit in May. A north frame is best, as the plants make very free growth, and get a good size for planting out the first week in June The beds should be surfaced with either a dwarf kind of plant or with Cocoa-nut fibre When, however, they are planted thickly together, use the fibre, which will soon be covered by the foliage. Begonias planted in dry positions should always be kept moist at the root Damping the beds overhead as the sun leaves them in the after part of the day when the weather is dry and warm will greatly refresh them When lifted, the tuberous varieties require careful attention so as to prevent the decaying stems from imparting any ill effects to the tubers Remove these stems as soon as they can be twisted out without any trouble Some growers expose the tubers in a light, dry, and airy house until the stems are quite dried up. Later on the bulbs when quite at rest should be kept in a cool place, neither too dry nor too moist, but where frost cannot reach them, being stored in either Cocoa-nut fibre or silver sand in shallow boxes until again required for starting It is better to have single than double flowers for bedding out, and there is no want of good colours

A class getting more popular each year is that called the shrubby set, these being known as forms of *B semperflorens*. They are neat and shrubby in growth, with an abundance of rather small leaves, varying in shade. Conspicuous is Vernon's variety, the leaves deep crimson to light green, and pinky blossoms. There are many varieties, and as easily and similarly raised as the tuberous kinds. The plants are, when in beauty, a mass of bloom, the small flowers almost hiding the leaves. But many of the kinds are very dull in colour, and get shabby towards the end of summer. There are many uses for them in gardens—as distinct groups, or as a groundwork to beds filled with taller plants.

Bellevallia. *See* HYACINTHUS.

BELLIS (*Daisy*).—*B. perennis*, daisies raised from our Wild Daisy are among the most popular of garden flowers, although not used so much as formerly. They need only simple culture, increase rapidly, and in the spring garden are of great service in large clumps or masses. Though we have numerous kinds, growers have adhered most closely to the old flat-petalled white and the old quilled red, both of which are grown by millions as market plants. Besides these are the flat-petalled Pink Beauty, a charming pink of the quilled class ; a deep rich red or crimson quilled kind, called Rob Roy ; White Globe, with large white quilled petals ; and many others. The yellow-blotched or Aucuba-leaved kinds have originated by sporting, and one named *aucubæfolia* is a pretty kind, but rather tender, though it will do well in winter on a free porous soil, and in summer in a cool shady border, if transplanted there. The giant or crown-flowered Daisies almost form a distinct section, and, though vigorous, are much less free of bloom than the better-known kinds. These have large and usually mottled red flowers upon long stalks, and are best suited for mixed borders. A very old favourite is the Hen-and-Chickens Daisy. It differs in no respect of habit or foliage from the double kinds, except that when the flowers are at their best they send out small ones from the axils of the scales—hence the name.

Propagation is simple, and may be done in spring and autumn. Well-dug soil suits well, and pull the plants to pieces, dibbling them in six inches apart, or a little closer. Where the soil is good the Daisy increases so rapidly that it may be transplanted twice in the year.

BELLIUM.—Plants belonging to the same order as the Daisy (Compositæ), of which some three or four forms are in cultivation. Although from the south of Europe, they are hardy on the rock-garden, but are apt to exhaust themselves in flowering. *B. bellidioides*, *B. crassifolium*, and *B. minutum*, are much alike and are easily grown in light soil. *B. rotundifolium cærulescens* (Blue Daisy)

is a native of Morocco, and a pretty rock-plant. Division or by seed.

BERBERIDOPSIS (*Coral Barberry*). —*B. corallina* is a beautiful evergreen climbing shrub from Chili, hardy enough for open walls in the southern counties. It has large spiny leaves very much like some Barberries, the flowers bright coral-red, hanging in clusters on slender stalks, and borne for several weeks in summer. It is charming for a wall, preferring partial shade, such as that of a wall facing east or west, and does best in peaty or sandy soil. Seed or layers.

BERBERIS (*Barberry*).—A valuable group of hardy shrubs, among the most beautiful of which is Darwin's Barberry

Berberis nepalensis.

(*B. Darwini*). *B. stenophylla* is a hybrid between *B. Darwini* and the small *B. empetrifolia*. *B. dulcis* is a pretty Barberry, whose slender shoots are hung with tiny yellow flowers. The common Barberry (*B. vulgaris*) is brilliant when in fruit in autumn, and it has several varieties, some of which differ considerably in habit of growth and colour of the berries. A beautiful shrub-group could be formed of the fruiting Barberries alone, using *B. vulgaris*, *B aristata* (which has berries covered with white powder, like Plums), and the small-growing *B Thunbergi*, also remarkable for its scarlet berries, which remain on the bush throughout the autumn *B Wallichiana* has handsome flowers and foliage, and is worthy of cultivation in the best collections

The Mahonias are now merged in the genus Berberis As flowering shrubs they are of much value, as is shown by the beauty of flower and fruit of the common evergreen Barberry *B. aquifolium* and its varieties *M fascicularis*, though not hardy everywhere, is fine when in bloom, its stems being wreathed with golden clusters for some weeks, while *M hybrida* is scarcely less ornamental and certainly hardier. *M repens*, *M glumacea* and *M trifoliata* are all good dwarf Evergreens In mild districts there is not a finer flowering shrub in spring than *M. nepalensis*, with large clusters of yellow bloom and massive foliage *M japonica* is a good Evergreen in sheltered places, and a fine flowering shrub Most of the evergreen kinds thrive best in leafy or peaty soils, the ordinary hardy kinds in any garden soil

Berkheya. *See Stobæa*

BETA. *(Chilian Beet)* — *B cicla variegata* is a variety of common Beet, the leaves being more than 3 ft long, vivid in colour, their midribs varying from dark waxy orange to vivid crimson The plant should be sown in a gently heated frame, and afterwards planted out in rich ground It varies much from seed, and the most striking individuals should be selected before the plants are put out Used sparingly, its effect is often perhaps more telling than if in quantity, but it is a mistake to use this or any such vegetables in the flower-garden Other varieties of the common Beet are used in the flower-garden for the sake of their dark colours, but no artistic flower-gardening is possible where such vegetables out of place are used

BETULA *(Birch)* — Trees of cold and arctic regions, often forming vast forests Sometimes, in the extreme north, even the tall and graceful Birches of more temperate lands take a bushy form, and there are also arctic and northern species which are small and give us little effect or interest except for botanic gardens The Birches, generally, are easy to grow, and should be raised from seed, in which way they come very easily, excepting what are called the garden or nursery varieties These are grafted, and might be propagated by layers, if anybody would take the trouble, and in this way might be

longer lived and useful in some ways Owing to the beauty of our native species in all sorts of positions north and south, we have not lost so much by neglecting the American species, and it would be difficult to expect, however, any of them to show anything finer in effect than such woods as we see in northern and central Europe, of Birch alone, the silvery stems rising out of heath or ferns Among the greater, or tree, Birches after our own (including its varieties or allies, *verrucosa* and *pubescens*) are the Canoe Birch (*B papyrifera*) or paper Birch, a forest tree of Northern America, which is hardy in Britain, the River Birch (*B nigra*) also a tall tree of Northern America, the Cherry or Sweet Birch (*B lenta*) which is sometimes 80 ft. high and also of northern distribution (Canada, Newfoundland), the Yellow Birch (*B lutea*) sometimes 100 ft high, the Western Birch (*B occidentalis*), a medium-sized tree of Western America and British Columbia, and the White Birch (*B populifolia*) also a slender tree of Canada and the Northern States with tremulous leaves like some of the Aspens Among the dwarf or shrubby kinds are *B nana*, *pumila*, *humilis* and *fruticosa*, but the Birches of any real value for our home landscapes are the tree kinds From a garden point of view, perhaps the most important trees of the genus are the varieties of our common Birch and its allies, such as the weeping and cut-leaved forms, also those with purple leaves, and the nettle-leaved Birch *B maximowiczi* is a distinct and fine Japanese kind which grows very high and with a trunk 2 to 3 ft in diameter, the bark orange-coloured, the leaves very large *B ermani* is also a common kind in Japan

An incident in my own planting of birches may be worth recording here Having got a collection from America, I planted them by some ponds where I thought they might have a better chance, as they often grow well near water in their native country. I lost a good many of them, not knowing the cause until I happened to pull up some of the dead young trees, when I found the main roots were all barked round by the common waterrat, working below the line of the snow during a hard winter

As regards the positions of Birches in a pleasure-ground, there is is not a more graceful lawn tree than the cut-leaved and weeping kinds, the more so where trees of light shade are desired

The American tree kinds might take their places in the mixed woodlands of a country place, or by streams or pools   W. R

G G

Bignonia. *See* TECOMA.
Blechnum. *See* LOMARIA.
BLETIA.—*B. hyacintha* is a beautiful
Chinese Orchid, having ribbed leaves, and
slender flower-stems 1 ft. or more high,
bearing about half a dozen showy flowers
of a deep rosy pink. It is hardy, and

an interesting annual flower, showy, the
foliage elegant, and the growth dwarf,
the structure of the flowers singular. Its
culture is that of a hardy annual, but it is
better sown in spring than in autumn. It
flowers from July to September in warm
light soils. The other species in cultiva-

Weeping Birch.

thrives in sheltered and shaded situations
in peat borders in winter. In cold districts
it would be well to cover the roots. It is
very interesting for the bog garden or a
bed of hardy Orchids.
Blitum. *See* CHENOPODIUM.
BLUMENBACHIA.—*B. coronata* is

tion are *B. insignis* and *B. multifida.*
South America. (Loasa Order.)
BOCCONIA (*Plume Poppy*).—*B. cordata* is a handsome and vigorous perennial
of the Poppy Order, growing in erect tufts
5 to over 8 ft. high, with numerous flowers
in very large panicles, not showy, but the

inflorescence, when the plant is well grown, has a fine effect. It is best in the shrubbery in ordinary garden soil, and is excellent in bold groups, the leaves, too, being fine in form. Division. China. Syn. *B. japonica. B. frutescens.* -- A vigorous Mexican shrub, 3½ to nearly 6 ft. high, with few and very brittle branches, large, seagreen, handsome leaves, and greenish flowers. Very effective on Grass plats,

The Plume Poppy (*Bocconia cordata*).

in groups or as isolated specimens. It requires a somewhat warmer climate than ours, but may be placed out from June to the end of September. It is difficult to propagate by cuttings, easier from seed.

Boltonia. *See* Aster.

BOMAREA.—Curious and handsome plants of the Amaryllis order allied to Alstrœmeria, requiring greenhouse temperature so far as now known. Mr. Archer Hind, of Newton Abbot, has *B. edulis* out-of-doors, and it has flowered well after surviving a temperature of 25° below freezing. If any of the other species should prove hardy in the southern counties, their fine bold twining habit and handsome flowers would be a gain. Best in free sandy or peaty soil.

BONGARDIA.—*B. rauwolfi* is a plant of the Barberry Order, though remarkably unlike one, as it has a Cyclamen-like rootstem, from the apex of which spring the flower stems 6 in. high, bearing roundish golden blossoms from ¾ to 1 in. across, which droop gracefully from slender stalks. Though now rare, this beautiful plant was among our earliest garden plants. Found from the Greek Archipelago to Afghanistan, and hardy on dry soils. Seed. Syn., *Leontice.*

BORAGO (*The Cretan Borage*).—*B. orientalis* is a vigorous perennial, bearing pale-blue flowers early in spring, having very large leaves through the summer. Easily naturalised in any rough place, but not worth a place in the garden proper, being coarse and taking up much space. The common Borage is very pretty, naturalised in dry places or banks, where it might often be welcome for use as well as beauty. There is a white variety. *B. laxiflora* is pretty with suspended blue flowers ; it grows very freely on sandy soils.

Borkhausia. *See* CREPIS.
Botryanthus. *See* MUSCARI.
BOUSSINGAULTIA (*Madeira Vine*). —*B. baselloides* is a luxuriant trailing plant of the Spinach Order with shoots 16 to 20 ft. long, flowering late in autumn, the flowers small, white, fragrant, and becoming black as they fade The fine green leaves are shining, fleshy, and slightly wavy ; stems twining, tinged with red, growing with extraordinary rapidity, and bearing many tubercles. Suited only for dry banks and chalk-pits, associated with climbing and trailing plants. Increased by tubercles of the stem ; these break with the least shock, but the smallest fragment will vegetate. South America.

BRACHYCOME (*Swan River Daisy*). —*B. iberidifolia* is a pretty Australian annual of simple culture, about 8 to 12 in. high, the flowers about 1 in. across, in loose terminal clusters, and are bright blue, with a paler centre. There are other sorts, with flowers of various shades of blue and purple, and one of pure white. Sow in cool house in September as soon as ready, prick off four or five in a 4-in. pot, keep in cold pits during winter, and guard against damp. Pot on again in March singly into 4-in. pots, and finally at end of April plant out into open borders ; or sow on slight hotbed in March, prick out into pits for transplanting into open in May ; or sow in open in April and May *B Sinclairi* is a pretty little kind with tiny daisy-like heads which sometimes sows itself in sandy soil

BRASSICA.—Some forms of the Cabbage, particularly the variegated Kales, are used in the flower garden for winter effect, where people are ignorant of what a flower-garden means—in winter even a beautiful thing to those who know how to make it so   So we will forego descriptions of how to grow kail for the flower-garden   The odour of such things about a house after a hard frost should be enough of itself to condemn them And as for beauty, a corner of a labourer's garden with a few snowdrops and hepaticas is worth all the displays of the floral kailyard ever seen

BRAVOA (*Scarlet Twinflower*) —*B geminiflora* is a pretty Mexican bulbous plant of the Amaryllis Order   From 1 to 2 ft high, the flower-stems stout and erect, bearing on the upper part numerous pairs of nodding tubular flowers of a rich scarlet outside, but inclined to yellow within   It succeeds well in warm sheltered situations in borders of light and well-drained soil, but requires some protection over the bulbs in winter It flowers in autumn, and remains a long time in bloom

BREVOORTIA (*Crimson Satinflower*) —*B coccinea* is a beautiful bulbous flower, of the Lily Order, also known as *B Ida-Mai*   It is one of the prettiest Californian plants   The flowers grow on stems, 1½ to 2 ft high, and are tubular and of a deep crimson-red, the lips a vivid green   It succeeds best in friable loam Plant in October, and the roots may remain undisturbed for several years. Not less than three plants should be grouped together, and a dozen will produce a still better effect, an Osier rod in their midst will support the fragile stems   Offsets and seed.

BRIZA (*Quaking Grass*) —A graceful family of Grasses, American and European   *B maxima* is one of the handsomest, growing 12 to 18 in high ; may be sown in the open in March in any garden soil, is quite hardy and graceful while growing, and useful for decoration either green or dried   *B media* (Common Quaking Grass) is smaller, 9 to 15 in high. Borders, Seed

BRODIÆA (*Brodie's Lily or Californian Hyacinth*) —A charming family of North American liliaceous plants

B. congesta has the stems long and wiry, the flowers in a dense umbel , purplish blue in colour, and very lasting   *B*

alba is a pretty white-flowered variety *B. capitata* much resembles this kind

B. grandiflora.—This is an old and pretty plant, about 5 in high, with deep purplish-blue flowers in a loose umbel in July. At the time of flowering the foliage is often withered, and to hide the nakedness of the stems it is sometimes best planted among other low-growing plants

B. Howelli —This pretty species has flowers in a fine umbel, bell-shaped and milky white   A beautiful variety of it (*lilacina*) has delicate bluish flowers, retaining its fine deep-green foliage at the time of flowering, and throwing up sturdy stems about 2 ft high, crowned by large flat umbels of well-shaped flowers

B. laxa is a very old garden plant, of which there are several varieties, not only varying in colour, but in the size of the flowers and the umbels

B. minor, probably a variety of the foregoing, is very pretty , the scape is not more than an inch high, about fifteen flowers in the umbel , the colour purplish blue, with a lighter centre.

B. peduncularis is a pretty white-flowered species, with large umbel of porcelain-white blossoms

These bulbs may be planted from October until December, and in mild localities will pass the winter in the open unprotected   In Holland, where the winters are often very severe, they are covered with reeds or straw at the approach of the cold season   This covering will keep the cold off, the soil open, and ward off the effects of a treacherous winter sun —C G. V. T

BROMUS (*Brome Grass*) --At least one of this large genus of Grasses is very graceful and worthy of culture—that is *B brizæformis*, a hardy biennial about 2 ft high, with large graceful and drooping heads   It is more valuable for cutting and drying than any of the Quaking Grasses   It may be grown as an annual sown out-of-doors in spring, and autumnal-sown plants would be best in warm soils

BROWALLIA.—Annual plants of the Nightshade Order, chiefly Peruvian. *B elata* has usually been regarded only as a beautiful pot-plant, but it does well in the open air, either in a bed by itself or in large patches with other things It supplies a shade of colour difficult to obtain, and is useful to cut from   Sow the seed in March, prick off the young plants when large enough to handle, grow them on till they are strong, and plant out in May   There is a white variety equally useful *B Roezli* is a dense compact bush, 16 to 20 in. high, with shining green leaves. The flowers are of a delicate azure blue, or are white with a yellow tube, and are unusually large for the genus. They come in uninterrupted succession from spring till autumn. Rocky Mountains.

Brugmansia. *See* DATURA.

BRYANTHUS (*Hybrid B.*).—*B. erectus* is a dwarf evergreen Ericaceous bush, from 8 in. to 1 ft. high, bearing pretty pinkish flowers. Said to be a hybrid. In very fine sandy soil or in that usually prepared for American plants, it grows well, and is suitable for the rock-garden or in collections of very dwarf alpine shrubs.

BUDDLEIA (*Orange Ball Tree*).—*B. globosa* is a favourite shrub from Chili, often seen in the southern coast gardens, where it is hardier, and in Ireland ; the flowers, balls of bright yellow, are showy in early summer. It is of rapid growth, and if badly cut down during a severe winter generally grows again in the following summer. *B. Colvillei* is a tender Himalayan kind, with bunches of pale rose-coloured flowers. It is a shrub for mild districts only. Other species less satisfactory for open-air culture are *B. crispa, B. Lindleyana.*

BULBOCODIUM (*Spring Meadow Saffron*).—*B. vernum* is a pretty Liliaceous bulb from 4 to 6 in. high, and one of the earliest of flowers, sending up large rosy purple flower-buds, distinct in colour. The tubular flowers are nearly 4 in. long, and are usually prettiest in the bud state. Associated with very early flowering plants like the Snowflake, Snowdrop, and Greek Anemone, it is welcome in the rock-garden or in warm sunny borders. Easily increased by dividing the bulbs in July or August, and replanting them from 4 in. to 6 in. apart. One other species, *B. trigynum,* is sometimes met with in cultivation. Alps of Europe.

BUPHTHALMUM.—*B. speciosum* is a bold free and showy perennial, hardy, and growing in any soil, with large heart-shaped leaves in great tufts, and, in summer and autumn, handsome heads of showy yellow flowers with dark centres. An excellent plant for shrubberies and covering the ground here and there in bold masses, as it grows so close that it keeps the weeds down and in such ways also gives a better effect than in small tufts in the mixed border. Central Europe. Division. Syn. *Telekia speciosa.*

BUTOMUS (*Flowering Rush*).—*B. umbellatus* is a handsome native water-plant, often very fine in a rich muddy soil and hardy and free to flower. Common by some river banks, and growing with water-side seeds in garden ponds and lakes, flowering in summer rose-red in bold umbels. Division.

BUXUS (*Box*).—This beautiful bush or low tree grows wild on some of our southern chalk hills, and is much cultivated in gardens as an edging and also in shrubberies. The beauty of its habit is seldom seen in gardens, owing to its being grown under other trees or to its being too much crowded, but seen wild its habit is most graceful, and it might be well to secure the same beauty of habit by planting in groups upon exposed knolls. Almost all the species and varieties have variegated forms, which,

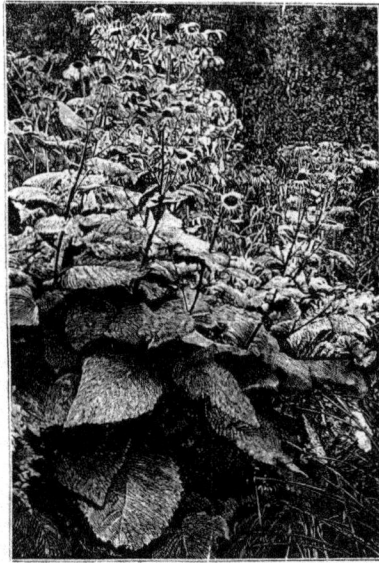

Buphthalmum speciosum.

though pretty, are not so good as the natural forms. *B. sempervirens* (the Common Box) from its close bushy habit is one of the most useful Evergreens for garden hedges. It may be pruned or clipped into any shape ; and when topiary gardening was in fashion, it shared with the Yew in the formation of designs and figures of men and animals. While there are few soils in which it will not thrive, it prefers such as are light, with a warm gravelly subsoil. Among the typical species is *Japonica,* a form of the common Box, but hardier. The Minorca Box (*B. balearica*) is a native of Balearic and other islands in the Mediterranean, as well as Italy and Turkey, where it forms a fine tree of from 60 to 80 ft. in height. The leaves are larger than those of the common Box, and when exposed to the sun are of a lighter green, but it only succeeds well in warm well-sheltered situations with a dry soil and a warm subsoil. Other species are *Harlandi*, *microphylla* and *Wallidiana*, few of these so precious as the common Box. The variegated forms of Box are seldom so good in effect as the green kinds, at least after they have left the nursery stage.

climate, and the best places are, as a rule, on well-drained ledges in the rock-garden. Plants of this family should be planted in the rock-garden in open airy situations, free from dripping water, and where the drainage is perfect. Probably hardy alpine species will be found farther south, and we may yet see, in warmer counties, a good collection of bright-flowered Cactaceous plants on warm rocky borders or banks.

CAESALPINIA. — A graceful and distinct summer-leafing shrub or low tree, even at this early date after its introduction,

Calandrinia oppositifolia.

CACTUS.—Various plants belonging to the Cactus Order of plants have proved hardy in England. Opuntia, Echinocereus, Mammillaria and Echinopsis are among the hardiest. Pretty effects are shown by some Cacti in the open air in Southern England, the plants blooming freely when fully exposed in the sun on a warm rock-garden ; but the want of the sunshine of their native plains is against their being very happy in Britain.

When the foliage of a plant is perennial, as in Cacti it is well to place it so that it may be safe from injuries, apart from

proving a picturesque one. It is one of a genus usually tropical, and the interest lies in finding a species which is hardy in the country around London. *C. japonica* is a loose or free growing shrub with hard prickles, leaves a foot long and very graceful, and handsome yellow flowers in racemes. It grows well with me in very poor soil and seems quite happy as a wall or bank bush. R.

Calampelis. *See* ECCREMOCARPUS.

CALANDRINIA. (*Rock Purslane*).— Dwarf annual or perennial plants of the Purslane Order. This genus is large, and many species have been introduced, though few are very effective for gardens, but if well grown and placed they are pretty, and sometimes brilliant border or rock plants, thriving in warm and dry soils. *C. discolor* is a beautiful S American plant, from 1 to 1½ ft. high, with fleshy leaves, pale green above and purple beneath, and bright-rose flowers in a long raceme, 1½ in across *C. grandiflora* is a handsome annual with showy blossoms It thrives in a warm and good loam, and blooms throughout the autumn *C oppositifolia* is a distinct plant, and is well marked by its larger, very thick, succulent leaves and delicate white flowers *C speciosa* has flowers from ½ to 1 in across, purple-crimson ; on sunny mornings they open fully, closing early in the afternoon *C. umbellata* is a distinct and pretty plant, the flower dazzling magenta-crimson It does well in fine sandy peat or in other light earth, and is perennial on dry soils and in chinks in a well-drained rock-garden, readily raised from seed sown in pots or in the open air in fine sandy soil It may also be treated as an annual sown in frames very early in spring Chili

There are other kinds, such as *C Lindleyana*, *C. procumbens*, *C compressa*, and *C micrantha*, but not so good as the kinds just mentioned

CALCEOLARIA (*Slipper Flower*) — Handsome and distinct herbs or low shrubs of the Foxglove Order, mostly from South America Many of them are of high garden value, but few are hardy In the London district they are employed very much less than they were some years ago, as many of the varieties die from disease, or are short-lived as regards bloom, but the handsome *C. amplexicaulis*, with its bold habit and lemon-yellow flowers, is always a favourite.

PROPAGATION —The best time for propagating the shrubby varieties is the end of September and October, in a cold wooden or turf frame on a dry bottom , fill it to within 6 in of the top with sandy loam, and over that spread some clean silver sand Then select stubby firm side shoots, pick out any flower-spikes that are visible, remove one or two of the base leaves, cut horizontally below a joint with a sharp knife, and dibble them thickly, regularly and firmly into the frames, giving a sprinkling of water through a fine rose to settle the soil and to prevent their flagging Keep the frames close and shaded for a day or two, but afterwards remove the shading, and only use it during the succeeding month to counteract the effects of bright sunshine

WINTERING —These frames require no further care beyond protection from frost, by covering the sashes, and banking up the sides, if of wood, with soil Wooden boxes, seed-pans, or pots might also be used for striking Calceolarias in , and in them the plants might be wintered in any pit, greenhouse, or conservatory Whether propagated in frames or boxes, they should be transplanted farther apart than previously, into other frames filled with rich open soil, where they will become fit for planting out by the middle of May

SPRING PROPAGATION —Spring cuttings are mostly rooted in hotbeds, in boxes, or in pans, and often as many damp off as survive to become plants , nevertheless, where the stock is deficient, this mode must be resorted to It is best to strike them after the middle of March in pure sand in a hotbed or propagating pit where there is no stagnant moisture, and, when well rooted, to pot them, or put them in boxes in light sandy soil, still keeping them in warm quarters for a few days. After that, gradually shift them into places in which there is less heat Powdered charcoal or wood ashes strewed on the soil among the cuttings prevents damp, and the watering-pot should be used judiciously

Species of Calceolaria —Apart from the varieties, a number of species are of some merit for the flower garden, and some are neglected and unknown The greater number of them inhabit mountain valleys, and ascend to an elevation of from 13,000 to 14,000 ft within the tropics in South America, where they enjoy a temperate climate

C. alba.—A lovely sub-shrubby species from Chili growing 3 to 4 ft high, with clusters of snowy white flowers A native of Chili

C amplexicaulis —A fine bold kind with soft green leaves clasping the stem and many lemon-yellow flowers Owing to its tall habit it groups well with bold plants, and it is usually handsomer in autumn than any of the other kinds Ecuador

C hyssopifolia is one of the best of the small-growing kinds, bearing loose clusters of lemon-yellow blossoms from early summer till autumn, the foliage resembling that of Hyssop Ecuador

C. Kellyana—A curious hardy hybrid, with short downy stems, 6 to 9 in high, flowers about an inch across, of a deep yellow with numerous small brown dots, and two or three grow together on the top of the stems. Its foliage resembles that of one of the Mimulus, creeping along the ground, and it is a very interesting dwarf rock-garden plant.

C. Pavonii is a noble species, the largest in cultivation It is from 2 to 4 ft. high, has large light-green, much-wrinkled foliage, from June to September bearing large, pale-yellow, slipper-shaped blossoms It is a fine object against a warm south wall, but at the approach of winter it should either be lifted or protected Peru.

C. violacea is a pretty species, with small helmet-shaped flowers, which are rich purple and spotted ; succeeds well on warm borders or the rock-garden, and, if slightly protected, withstands mild winters in the south Chili

Calendula officinalis (*Pot Marigold*) — An interesting old hardy biennial , one of the best for autumn and winter flowering in almost every garden ; the petals were formerly used to flavour dishes in old English cookery, hence its name A variety of kinds is now offered by the seed houses The plants are among the best biennials for autumn and even winter flowering For late blooming, seed should be sown in July The plants usually sow themselves freely, and may be sown in the open ground either in spring or autumn The pretty variety called meteor and other forms are improvements on the old showy form

CALLA (*Bog Arum*) — *C palustris* is a small hardy trailing Arum, which has pretty little white spathes Though often grown in water, in a bog or muddy place it will grow larger For moist spongy spots near the rock-garden, or by the side of a rill, it is one of the best plants, but its beauty is best seen when it is allowed to ramble over rich muddy soil N America and N Europe Flowering in summer, and increasing rapidly by its running stems

Callichroa. *See* LAYIA
Calliopsis. *See* COREOPSIS
Calliprora. *See* BRODIÆA

CALLIRHOË (*Poppy Mallow*) — A small and handsome genus of North American plants, of the Mallow order, of which some half-dozen kinds are known in our gardens They are hardy herbaceous perennials, and succeed well in the open border in rich light soil

C alcæoides is an erect herbaceous perennial, with the habit and general appearance of *Malva moschata*, the flowers from 1 inch to 1½ inches in diameter Barren Oak lands, Kentucky and Tennessee

C. digitata. — A distinct-looking glau-

cous perennial herb, 2 or 3 ft. high, with reddish-purple flowers in summer ; it is not so showy as the other kinds

C. involucrata is a charming dwarf prostrate perennial, with large violet-crimson flowers 2 in in diameter It is excellent for the rock-garden, as it bears a continuous crop of showy blossoms from early in summer till late in autumn It has the best effect when allowed to fall over the ledge of a rock California

C macrorhiza alba is a pure white form of a kind with purplish-carmine flowers, and erect stems, from 1½ to 2½ ft high, with a corymbose raceme of flowers It occurs in several shades of colour, from rosy-purple to pale rose and white, and sown early it will bloom the first year South-western States of N America

C. Papaver, figured in *The Garden*, has a trailing habit, and flowers incessantly from early summer until late autumn The flowers are of a bright purple-red, as large and somewhat resembling those of our common field Poppy, hence the name

C pedata is one of the prettiest species A perennial, with trailing stems bearing lobed foliage, and handsome crimson flowers, fully 2 in in diameter When sown early the plants bloom the first season, and continue in flower until late in autumn In dry soils the roots survive our average winters It succeeds best in dry soils The varieties *nana* and *compacta* are pretty dwarfer varieties.

CALLISTEPHUS (*China Aster*) — Among the many annuals now in cultivation China Asters (*C chinensis*) are among the best, and when well grown and cared for they do as much to render a garden gay during summer and autumn as any annual plant To see them in their beauty, however, they must be grown in masses, and well cultivated—not at any stage left to haphazard or poor culture

VARIETIES —China Asters may be classed according to height, habit, character of flower Tall Asters comprise the fine Pæony-flowered, the tall Chrysanthemum, the Emperor, the tall Victoria, the Quilled, and a few others Kinds of medium height are the dwarfer forms of the Victoria, the fine Cocardeau, the Rose, and the Porcupine The dwarf forms comprise the short Chrysanthemum, the dwarf pyramidal, and specially the dwarf bouquet, which is one of the most beautiful for pot culture The best bedding kinds are the medium-growing Victoria, the Rose, and the dwarf Chrysanthemum, as these vary from 9 to 12 in in height, and form good bunches of bloom on each plant, and fine masses of colour collectively. The dwarf bouquet kinds, whilst specially good for pot culture, are valuable as edgings to beds of taller kinds For pot culture for exhibition the best are the medium-growing Victorias, as these, if of a good strain, possess quality, and handsome even heads of bloom

CULTURE —Mr J. Betteridge writes —" For several years after I commenced the culture of quilled Asters I always sowed the seed in bottom-heat ; but during the last decade I have sowed it, between 26th March and 26th April, in a cold frame, under glass, in drills 6 in apart, and not too thick in the drills A few days suffice to bring the plants above the soil, when a liberal supply of air must be given, or they will be weak. When large enough, prick them out into another cold frame, slightly shaded, where they will soon be established, and after they are strong enough to handle plant them out in well-manured soil, and be careful not to break the tender fibres of the roots Let the rows be 1 ft apart, and plant the strongest plants 1 ft from each other, in showery weather, and they will soon get established If the weather be hot and drying, give them a little watering till rooted afterwards keep them clear of weeds by hoeing among them About the first week in August top-dress with rotten manure from an old hotbed, giving a good soaking all over if the weather continues dry

" SOIL.—China Asters like a deep rich soil, and, should dry weather set in, it is only in such soil that really fine flowers can be obtained and the plants induced to hold out Planted in the ordinary way, they are weeds in comparison with those that are well nourished and watered Confined to the top shallow crust of earth. they soon dry up and starve The best way to manage them is to dig and cast off the top spit to one side, handy to be returned to its place again, and then to trench and break up the soil below, working in with it plenty of short manure In very light soils a few barrow-loads of clay, chopped fine and mixed well in, will do more than any other to grow fine China Asters The thing to aim at is to keep the bottom cool and moist , then, if the weather be favourable, the plants will take care of themselves But considering this work has all to be done for one year's bloom only, the question is whether the same labour would not be better given to hardy plants or choice

shrubs which thrive for many years in the same spot after such preparation as is here spoken of to secure one year's bloom, and that perhaps a short one "

Calluna *See* ERICA VULGARIS

CALOCHORTUS (*Mariposa Lily*) —A lovely family of bulbous plants from Western North America, belonging to the Lily Order Forming one of the most charming groups of hardy bulbous plants, the colours being so varied and delicate Excepting the Mexican species, which are, fortunately, few, Calochorti are hardy , but my experience is that unless on very warm soils their culture is precarious in our country, and no wonder, considering they come from one of the most genial and sunny of climates

They are so singularly beautiful, however, that many will attempt their cultivation, and the advice of Mr Carl Purdy, who has studied the wild species in their native wilds, and cultivated them, is the best we can have

THE CULTURE OF CALOCHORTI — Calochorti are natives of a vast region in North America, stretching from far east of the Rocky Mountains to the Pacific Ocean, and from Northern Mexico to British America From the sea-coast and islands they grow from 6000 feet to 9000 feet altitude on the peaks Some are natives of the intensely hot deserts of Southern California and Arizona, and some grow in the moist meadows of Oregon in a climate differing but little from that of England In Montana and other States of the inland region the species indigenous there have to bear as low a temperature as 40° below zero In the soils in which they naturally grow there is as much diversity Clay, sand, loam and rocky *débris* are respectively the chosen homes of certain species, and several choose the blackest and stickiest of clays One is found in salt meadows and many in grassy meadows

I have at different times tried nearly every known species in many soils and situations The winter climate of Ukiah is quite wet, with the thermometer often at 20° to 24°, and sometimes as low as 15° above zero Often the Calochorti leaves are frozen till they crackle, but I have never known any injury to result In spring there is abundant rain until their flowering time, while our summer is perfectly dry Perfect drainage is the first essential to success for all sorts I have gradually come to the use of three mixtures Along our river banks there is a winter deposit of sandy silt This is excellent Calochortus soil, but not so good as the next. I find the best results follow from the use of about one half half-rotten spent tan bark with one half sandy or clay loam. The tan bark rots slowly and gives a loose, well-drained soil, which will not pack. This suits all Calochorti and gives a splendid bloom and firm, well-ripened bulbs. For English growers many substitutes will occur. I know of but one disease to which Calochorti are subject. This is a mildew, the "Lily leaf ash." It attacks them in the spring, just before the flowering stalk appears. It attacks the leaf tissue, and in a week entirely destroys the leaf and injures the bulb. In their susceptibility to the attacks of the fungus Calochorti vary greatly. All of the species having a single glossy radical leaf are free from its attacks. This includes all of the Star Tulips and the *C. nitidus* group. While all of the desert species, such as *C. splendens, C. Kennedyi, C. Palmeri, C. Gunnisoni, C. Nuttalli, C. macrocarpus,* and *C. flexuosus* are subject to it to such an extent as to make their successful culture very near hopeless unless some cure can be found for this mildew.

While the amateur may prefer to try all sorts and get his experience for himself, I believe that many growers will appreciate a list of the best growers among the Calochorti. For such I would recommend the following :—

In the globular-flowered Star Tulips, *C. albus,* white, *C. pulchellus,* yellow, and *C. amœnus,* rose-coloured, are all thrifty and beautiful. Among the open-cupped Star Tulips, *C. Benthami,* in yellow, and *C. Maweanus* var. *major* are the best. There is, however, a race of giant Star Tulips, sturdy plants 9 in. to 16 in. high, with large flowers of the same delicate style as *Maweanus,* which, although rare now, will soon quite displace the smaller ones. These are *C. apiculatus,* straw-coloured, *C. Greeni,* blue, and *C. Howelli,* yellow. *C. lilacinus,* a lavender-coloured sort, is a splendid grower and very desirable. In the next section, *C. nitidus* is a fine hardy and very beautiful plant, combining the attributes of Star Tulip and Mariposa. In the *C. Weedi* set, *C. Plummeræ* is best. Of the true Butterfly Tulips, *C. Vesta* is by far the best grower. It is a sort which has great vitality, can be propagated very rapidly by offsets (three or four a year), and grows well in any well-drained soil. *C. venustus* var. *purpurescens* is almost as good a grower, and the two are by all odds the easiest Calochorti to grow. *C. venustus* var. *citrinus* in lemon is very

thrifty. That grand plant *C. clavatus* is a fine grower.

I have found that by very late planting I can bring sorts to flower which planted early invariably succumb. I had the same experience a year ago. It would seem that when planted early they reach a standstill period in late winter and cannot resist disease, while planted late they are in full growth at the critical period.

Clearly if so much care is needed in their own lovely climate, in ours it will require all our care to secure them perfect drainage, porous soil and warmth, though no doubt some of naturally warm soils may suit them.

Calochortus flavus.

C. albus.—This is a charming species and more easily grown than most. This may be planted in the open border without much fear of failure, unless the soil be very stiff. It increases rapidly by offsets and seeds, which ripen and produce good flowering bulbs in three years. These require rich soil during the first two years, after which they may be planted in the general collection.

C. apiculatus is a tall stout-stemmed species 9 to 18 in. high, with large straw-coloured flowers. The variety *minor* has creamy flowers with a fringe of yellow hairs in the centre.

C. Benthami.—A pretty dwarf species

from 4 in. to 8 in. high, the leaves long and narrow ; the flowers, of a rich citron-yellow, often deep brown at the base, and densely covered with yellow hairs, are erect, from three to six in an umbel, and produced in June and July. California.

C. clavatus has strong much-branched flower stems, bearing very large widely expanded blossoms of golden-yellow.

C. cœruleus.—A dwarf species, rarely exceeding 6 in. in height, with umbels of three to five large flowers of a bright lilac, dotted and lined with dark blue, the gland at the base being covered with a pretty fringed scale. California.

C. elegans.—A fine dwarf species, variable, bearing in June three to five drooping flowers, white or greenish-white with a purplish base, bearded, but not ciliate. The gland is covered by a fringed scale. The narrow leaf is longer than the flower-stem, smooth, and nerved.

C. flavus.—It represents a form in which the flowers are upright, and the petals have an outward curve instead of an inward curve. It is, perhaps, not quite so hardy as most kinds, but it will be found to do well at the base of a south wall. It is also known as *C. pallidus* and *C. luteus.* Mexico.

C. Greeni.—A fine bold species, growing a foot or more in height, and blooming in early June, three to five large, clear, lilac flowers, barred below with yellow and purple, and often loosely covered with long hairs. The leaves are broad, glaucous green, and pointed. California.

C. Gunnisoni has larger flowers of a bright lilac, yellowish-green below the middle, where they are banded and lined with purple. A native of the Rocky Mountains from Wyoming to New Mexico, flowering with us in July.

C. Howelli is a strong growing species with long glossy leaves and large creamy white flowers.

C. Kennedyi.—This is the most brilliant of the Mariposa Lilies known to us, and the flowers are dazzling scarlet in colour. It has proved perfectly hardy, and grows about 18 in. high. California.

C. lilacinus.—This is of very distinct habit, and has curious, hairy flowers, which are borne from four to ten on a stem, from 6 in. to 8 in. high, and they are pale lilac in colour. California.

C. longibarbatus.—A curious species from Oregon and Washington Territory. It grows about a foot in height, the stem bearing one to three pale purple-lilac flowers each 1 to 1½ in. in diameter, with a dark purple stripe across the base of

each petal, and a long beard just above it. Flowers in July.

C. luteus.—A handsome and variable species, from 1 ft. to 2 ft. in height ; the flowers vary from one to six to a stem, the colour varying from yellow to deep, rich orange, and lined with brownish-yellow below the middle. In the variety *citrinus* the whole flower is rich lemon-yellow, with a central circular brown or purple blotch ; and in the variety *oculatus* it varies from white and lilac to yellow, with a dark-brown spot.

Calochortus fuscus

C. Lyoni.—One of the earliest Mariposa Lilies, with numerous large blossoms varying from pure white to rose with a large black spot at the base of each petal.

C. macrocarpus.—A tall handsome species, found on the undulating barren grounds around the great falls of the Columbia River. It grows from 1½ ft. to 2 ft. in height, the flowers, 3 in. to 4 in. in diameter, purplish-lilac, somewhat paler at the base and with greenish mid-vein.

C. madrensis.—A pretty little species with bright orange-yellow flowers in

August and September, and a tuft of deep-orange hairs at the base of each segment. It rarely exceeds a span in height, the stems bearing several flowers in a loose head. Mexico.

C. Maweanus is a low plant, from 5 in. to 9 in. in height, and bearing from four to six bell-shaped flowers in July, each 1½ in. to 2 in. in diameter. The petals are white, tinged with bright purple at the base, and densely clothed with purple hairs. California.

C. nitidus is a lovely strong growing species with five to ten large white flowers in an umbel, each petal having a large indigo blotch in the centre, and covered with long hairs.

C. Nuttalli has large white flowers with a blackish purple blotch at the base of the broader segments, the narrow segments being green striped with red. The rare variety *Leichtlini* has white flowers also, but is more beautifully marked.

C. Plummeræ throws up a broad leaf about 2 ft. long, and a strong branching spike with numerous soft lilac flowers of a satiny lustre and about 4 in. across, the base of each petal being clothed with golden hairs.

C. pulchellus.—A hardy plant, the bulbs, left in the open border, flower regularly. It grows about a foot high, much-branched, each branch terminating in an umbel of three to four fragrant, bright orange-yellow pendulous flowers.

C. splendens.—A pretty species, the flowers of a pale lilac, with a dark blotch at the base of each of the petals. California.

C. Tolmiei.—This very scarce Star Tulip is a vigorous grower, with tubular flowers covered with bluish hairs.

C. venustus.—One of the prettiest of the Mariposa Lilies, from 1 ft. to 2 ft. high, the flowers very large, white or pale lilac, with a prominent red blotch at the top of each petal, the centre brownish-yellow, the base brown. California from Alameda County southwards.

C. Weedi.—A handsome and remarkable species in having the bulbs fibrous-coated. The stem grows about a foot in height, one to three flowered, large, deep yellow, dotted and frequently margined with purple.

CALOPOGON.—*C. pulchellus* is a beautiful hardy Orchid suitable for boggy ground, the flowers pink, 1 in. in diameter, in clusters of two to six upon a stem, beautifully bearded with white, yellow, and purple hairs. Plant in the rock-

garden, bog, or in an open spot in the hardy fernery in moist peaty soil, as it is a native of wet spots at the edges of Pine woods in the Moss in Cranberry swamps, and in wet Grassy marshes, and occasionally seen on solid ground, in low, wet, woody situations in N. America.

CALTHA (*Marsh Marigold*).—The Marsh Marigold (*C. palustris*), that in early spring " shines like fire in swamps and hollows gray," and is one of our good hardy plants, though it is so frequent in a wild state that there is little need to give it a place, except on the margin of water. Its double varieties, however, are worth a place in a moist rich border, or, like the single form, by the water-side. There is a double variety of the smaller creeping *C. radicans*, about half the size of the common plant. There are double-flowered forms, bearing beautiful golden rosettes. There are also *C. leptosepala*, a Californian kind, and *C. purpurascens*, distinct and handsome, about 1 ft. high, with purplish stems, and bright-orange flowers, the outside of the petals flushed with a purplish tinge. The various forms of the Marsh Marigold are handsome in their golden blossoms, and in groups or bold masses are effective ; they are easily grown, and increase freely.

CALYCANTHUS (*Allspice Tree*).— North American shrubs with handsome flowers of pleasant fragrance. *C. occidentalis* is from 6 to 8 ft. high, with large maroon-crimson flowers of fine fragrance, and is worthy of cultivation. *C. floridus* is smaller and not so dense, with purplish-red flowers, strongly scented. The names in catalogues, such as *C. glaucus, lævigatus, oblongifolius, macrophyllus,* represent forms or varieties of either the eastern or the western species. The two described are hardy, the Carolina species

Calycanthus lævigatus.

having been grown since 1757, while the Californian has been cultivated over fifty years. They flourish best when somewhat shaded by other trees and where the ground is damp. They grow wild near streams and wet places. The Winter-Sweet, Chimonanthus, is sometimes included among these shrubs in Continental lists. Calycantheæ.

CALYPSO.—*C. borealis* is a pretty little hardy Orchid, with rosy-purple sepals and petals, and a white lip, heavily blotched with cinnamon brown, from the cold regions of N. America. It succeeds in half-shady spots on the margin of the rock-garden or bog, or in a select spot among choice shrubs in light, moist vegetable soil, covered with Coco fibre or like material to keep the surface open.

Calystegia. *See* CONVOLVULUS.

CAMASSIA (*Quamash*).—North American plants of the Lily Order, hardy and valuable for cutting.

C. esculenta (*Quamash*) is a native of meadows and marshes in N. W. America from 1 to 3 ft. high, its stalks bearing a loose raceme of from ten to twenty flowers about 2 in. across, the colour from deep to pale blue. There is also a pure white, and various other forms thriving in moist situations in a deep light soil. A bold group in flower has a fine effect in July, and it is excellent in the cut state, as the buds of the spike open in the house.

C. Cusicki is a new species discovered a few years ago in the Blue Mountains of Oregon, and it was described in *Garden and Forest* as the most vigorous species yet found with large broad leaves, a stout flower-stem growing 3 ft. high, and flowers of a pale delicate blue, large and spreading.

C. Fraseri (*Eastern Quamash*). — A native of the States east of the Mississippi, its flowers are rather smaller than those of the western species ; about 1½ ft. high, the scape bearing a raceme of ten to thirty pale-blue flowers, each about 1 in. across. It is, however, later in flowering than other Camassias, thriving in a light rich soil. All Camassias may be propagated by dividing the bulbs or by seeds.

C. Leichtlini (*White Camassia*).—This often grows on sandy ridge-tops, and is found in dry spots in ravines ; its bulbs are generally deep in some stiff soil. The flower-spike is large, being 9 in. long by 4 in diameter, while in rich deep soils it is sometimes compound, and contains several hundred florets, creamy white and about 1 in. in diameter, the stem often 3 or 4 ft. high. It is vigorous, but not so handsome as the Quamash. British Columbia.

CAMELLIA.—Handsome shrubs of the Tea Order, mostly grown under glass in our country, and those who live in northern districts may well be surprised to see this shrub healthy out-of-doors, even if it does not flower well ; but

in the Isle of Wight and the southern coasts of England and Ireland it is often laden with as many flowers, as it is in Madeira. Most people who have Camellias in the open air find that they flower well five out of every six years, and that the plants are hardy—indeed, hardier than many shrubs that make their new growth early in the year. Their greatest enemy is fierce winds, which beat them about. Any one planting them out for the first time will do well to plant first some of the commoner kinds, and in

Alpine Hairbell in rock garden. Engraved from photograph by Ellen Willmott.

sheltered spots ; then, when these thrive, to continue with more valuable ones. The best aspect for Camellias is a south or south-west one, sheltered by a bank or wall, but in some districts they do best on a north wall. Planting from pots may take place at any period, but about July is the best time, as the wood is then well ripened. Duke of Devonshire, Halfida, Chandleri, Florida, imbricata, elegans, Alberti, Double White, Donckelaari, Countess of Orkney, Mathotiana, and Lady Hume's Blush are good varieties for outdoor culture. The late Robert

Marnock, the landscape gardener, wrote as follows to *The Garden* about Camellias out-of-doors : " Permit me to remind those who, like myself, have an affection for the great beauty of the Camellia, when in vigorous health in the open air, that although it is true that the plant will bear a greater degree of cold than the Common Laurel, and other evergreen shrubs which by common consent have long been regarded as hardy, yet the main stems and stouter branches of the Camellia are, nevertheless, liable to injury from severe frost. Now, all that is necessary to protect the plant at this weak point is to closely wrap the stem with straw or hay bands ; and if a little Fern or other loose material be laid over the roots, so much the better. The portions of the stems near the ground are the most liable to suffer, while the leaves and branches, if not exposed to fierce gales, will bear much frost, provided the stems are protected."

In Cornwall, the Camellia grows in a most beautiful way at Tregothnan, Menabilly and many other places, flowering in this county better than I have seen it in warmer countries even. It is also grown out of doors in home counties, though not quite successfully ; still the plant is hardy in many districts, even more hardy than the common laurel and it will grow even on the north side of walls.

At Scorrier House, Tremough, and Pengreep, among the varieties that do best are *Mathotiana*, the largest, *anemonæflora*, very profuse flowering, *Countess of Orkney, Donkelaari*, which comes very early, and the old *japonica*. *C. reticulata* is the handsomest of the Camellias, but needs a warmer and more sheltered place than the varieties of the Japan Camellia.

CAMPANULA (*Hairbell, Bellflower*). —A large, beautiful, and most important family for the flower garden. The alpine species are charming for rock-gardens, being as a rule not difficult to cultivate. Some are very easy and free. A group of kinds somewhat larger than the high alpines adorn rocks and old walls on the mountains, and may be used for these in our gardens. Some are pretty window-plants, thriving in dry rooms ; numbers are good border and edging plants of easy culture ; the tall and straggling kinds admirable for the wild garden, or rough woody places or hedgerows, but these tall species must not be used much in the flower garden or mixed borders, as their time of bloom is short and they are very apt to overrun rarer plants. Some of the annual kinds, if well grown, are showy. The Canterbury Bell is one of the finest of biennials, the tall chimney Campanula a very handsome and precious plant.

C. Allioni, an alpine kind forming an underground network of succulent roots, surmounted by stemless rosettes of leaves, about an inch long, from which arise stalkless erect flowers. Succeeds in exposed positions in the rock-garden in a moist, free, and sandy loam, but dislikes limestone. Division. Alps.

C. alpina (*Alpine Hairbell*).—Covered with stiff down, giving it a slightly gray appearance, 5 to 10 in. high ; flowers of fine dark blue, scattered in a pyramidal manner along the stems. Valuable for front margins of mixed border, as well as the rock-garden. Division or seeds. Carpathians.

C. Barrelieri has prostrate one-flowered stems and roundish heart-shaped leaves and blue large flowers. On rocks by the seaside about Naples ; a good trailing rock-plant, which thrives also in baskets or pots in windows.

C. cæspitosa (*Tufted Hairbell*).—A charming and vigorous little plant, its roots ramble very much, and it soon forms large patches in any garden soil. Excellent for edgings and rocks, the angles of steps in rock-gardens, and where flagstones are used to form paths it is one of the plants that run about among the stones with very pretty effect.

C. carpatica (*Carpathian Hairbell*).— A dwarf plant of free-flowering habit, the light-blue flowers large and cup-shaped, borne on foot-stalks 12 to 15 in. high in July and August in succession. There are pale and white forms of this plant and the hybrid forms, none of them better than the species though giving variety.

C. cenisia (*Mont Cenis Hairbell*).—A high alpine plant growing among Saxifraga biflora on the sides of glaciers, making little show above ground but vigorous below, sending a great number of runners under the soil, and here and there it sends up a compact rosette of light-green leaves, with blue flowers. It should have a sandy or gritty and moist soil on the rock-garden. Division.

C. fragilis (*Brittle Hairbell*) is a glabrous plant, except that the young branches are coated with soft down ; the flowering branches prostrate, 12 or 15 in. long ; the flowers 1 in. or more in diameter, delicate blue. If planted in the rock-garden, a watchful eye must be kept'against snails. A variety *C. hirsuta* is covered with stiff down, and looks almost woolly. Division, cuttings, and seeds.

C. garganica (*Gargano Hairbell*).—A compact and tufty plant. The flowers in branching racemes, pale blue, towards the centre shading off to white in summer,

Campanula carpatica.

thriving in a rock garden or a border ; but, owing to its pendent flowering branches, a good place for it is against a rocky ledge, over which its masses of flowers may hang. Division or by cuttings taken in early spring.

C. glomerata (*Clustered Bellflower*).— A handsome plant about 2 ft. high, the stems terminated by dense clusters of pretty flowers, intense purple. The pure-white form is somewhat rare, and there are various forms and allies. One of the finest of all the Bellflowers.

C. grandiflora. *See* PLATYCODON.

C. isophylla (*Ligurian Hairbell*).—A very pretty Italian species ; the leaves are roundish or heart-shaped, the flowers of a pale but very bright blue, and with whitish centre. A charming ornament for the rock-garden, in sunny positions in well-drained, rather dry fissures, in sandy loam. The variety *alba* is a beautiful form with white flowers. Seed and cuttings.

C. macrantha.—The stems of this handsome plant rise to a height of 5 ft., terminated by clusters of large deep-blue flowers almost as large as Canterbury Bells, but less contracted at the mouth of the tube. It is a free vigorous perennial from Russia, best fitted for naturalisation in woody places.

C. macrostyla (*Candelabra Bellflower*).

—A singular plant, having large flowers, with blue netted veins on a white ground which gets purple at the edges, and with a huge stigma, wholly distinct from any of the Campanulas in our gardens, and well deserves culture. It is readily recognised by its candelabra habit of growth. A native of Asia Minor, and a fine annual of easy culture.

C. Medium (*Canterbury Bell*).—A familiar old plant having now varieties of various colours bearing single flowers, doubles, in which two, three, and even four bells seem to be compressed into the outer one ; and duplex flowers, in which one bell grows in the other, the two combined resembling a cup standing in a saucer. There are many colours, such as white, lavender, mauve, several shades of purple, pink, rose, salmon, and blue. The duplex strains have hitherto been confined chiefly to white and blue, but other colours are now being introduced. The habit of the plants as a rule is compact, when in bloom, ranging from 18 to 24 in. in height, and forming perfect pyramids of flowers. The Calycanthema section usually exhibits a taller and a looser growth, and should be planted in borders behind the double and single kinds.

March or April is the best time to sow seed in a warm spot in the open ground, but it is much safer to sow some also in shallow pans or boxes placed in a frame

Campanula hirsuta.

or on a shelf in the greenhouse. When the seedlings are large enough to handle, prick them out into some shady spot, and keep them watered until well rooted. From that time they may be safely left to take care of themselves until

September, when they should be transplanted into their permanent places in the flower borders, where they will get well established before the winter and develop blooming crowns for the next year.

Campanula pyramidalis.

C. persicifolia (*Peach - leaved Bellflower*).—A beautiful species, the cupshaped flowers of which are fully 2 in. across. The plant is 1½ to 3 ft. high, flowering in July and August.

Besides the double blue and white forms there is an interesting variety named coronata, in which the corolla is doubled. All the varieties well repay good culture, and there is a new and very large form, *maxime*. Plants occasionally divided and grown in rich beds give very fine crops of flowers.

C. Portenschlagiana (*Wall Hairbell*).—A dense tufted-evergreen species, with small bright-green leaves, irregularly notched, so dense as to obscure the foot-stalks, 1 in. or more in length, by which they are supported. The flowers pale blue in August or September. It spreads slowly by underground stems, and succeeds in crevices of the rock-garden. Dalmatia.

C. pulla (*Austrian Hairbell*).—This,

when well grown, is one of the most charming of Hairbells. It is a native of the Austrian Alps, on high mountain pastures ; if planted in the rock-garden, therefore, it should have to itself a shelf of soil in which a little peat and sand have been mixed. After blooming the foliage disappears and the plant goes to rest. An excellent rock-garden plant. Division.

C. pusilla.—Smaller than *C. cæspitosa*, rarely exceeding 4 in. in height, the shining green leaves heart-shaped and toothed, the flowers pale blue, in racemes, in June and July. Switzerland. Very gritty moist loam in the rock-garden is best for it. Syn. *C. modesta.*

C. pyramidalis (*Steeple Bellflower*).—A vigorous plant, with thick and fleshy flower-stems, rising to a height of 4 to 6 ft., with numerous broad ovate leaves ; the flowers, close to the stem, giving the inflorescence a steeple-like form. The flowers are blue or white ; coming in succession, over a considerable time, in July, August, and September. Though not quite a biennial, it is better in general cultivation to treat it as such, as from seedling plants, well grown on during the first year, the finest stems arise. A border flower of the highest merit in favourable soils ; so important, indeed, that occasional batches of seed should be sown to keep up a

Campanula turbinata var.

vigorous supply. It is often grown in pots for the house both in England and France.

C. Raineri (*Rainer's Bellflower*). —A dwarf, compact, sturdy plant, varying in height from 3 to 6 in., each branch bearing a large dark-blue flower. It thrives best in sunny positions in loam freely inter-mingled with pieces of stone, and well watered in dry weather, and is a gem for the rock-garden. Alps of N. Italy.

C. rotundifolia (*English Hairbell*).— In this pretty wild plant we have a true type of the Hairbell. There is a white variety, generally dwarfer, and there are several forms all beautiful, and of easy culture in any soil. These are all ex-cellent border flowers, and also good for the rougher parts of the rock-garden, and I love to see the wild plant growing in Grass on rough slopes or places not mown till autumn.

C. turbinata (*Tur-ban Bellflower*) is a dwarf plant with grayish-green leaves, the flowers borne singly on stems about 6 in. long, deep blue, and 1½ in. across. Mountains of Transylvania ; a charming plant for border or rock cul-ture.

CAMPTOSORUS (*Walking Leaf*).—*C. rhizophyllus* is a cu-rious N. American Fern, remarkable for its narrow fronds, which taper into slender prolonga-tions, and take root at the tips like run-ners, giving rise to young plants. Thrives in gritty loamy soil in a some-what shaded position in the rock-garden or hardy fernery.

CANNA (*Indian Shot*). — Handsome tropical plants of the Ginger Order with fine foliage. The tendency of most half-hardy flower-garden plants is to flatness, and the grace of the Cannas makes them valuable, though our country in many parts is too cool for their fair development ; in the warmer south and in sheltered gardens they may be grown with profit. Another good quality is their power of withstanding the storms of autumn. Sheltered situations, places near warm walls, and sheltered dells are the best places for them. As to cul-ture and propagation, nothing can be

more simple ; they may be stored in winter under shelves in the houses, in the root-room—in fact, anywhere, if covered up to protect them from frost, in spring pulling the roots in pieces and potting them separately. Afterwards it is usual to bring them on in heat, and finally to harden them off previous to planting out in the middle of May. The soil should be deep, rich, and light. Cannas, pro-tected by a coating of litter, have been left out in Battersea Park through severe winters, and attained a height of nearly

Canna iridiflora Ehemanni.

12 ft. ; but this was on raised beds in a very warm and sheltered place. Wherever they are grown as isolated tufts, in small groups, or in small beds, it will be best not to take them up oftener than every second or third year, if the ground be warm and well drained. These noble plants would also adorn the conservatory, which is often as devoid of graceful vegetation as the un-happy flower gardens all over the country. Few subjects would be more effective, and none more easily obtained.

Cannas are pretty in pots when grown

H H

with a few corms of gladiolus. The flowers of the Gladioli nestle among the foliage of the Cannas, and lend a charm to groups.

LARGE-FLOWERED CANNAS.—This is a race of Cannas for which we are mainly indebted to M. Crozy, of Lyons, France, who crossed the Iris-flowered

Cannabis sativa (Hemp Plant).

Canna with the older kind. Here, however, they are more valuable for the greenhouse than the open air. The plants as a rule are dwarfer than the old type of Canna, the newer French varieties ranging between 1½ ft. to 4 ft. in height, the leaves of many shades of colour.

In commencing the cultivation of these Cannas, by far the best time to get them is during the winter (say soon after Christmas), when the rhizomes, then in a dormant and well-ripened state, can be sent by post. The list of varieties is now a considerable one, so that a careful selection is absolutely necessary, otherwise some of them will be found to greatly resemble each other. A few of the finer ones are Paul Bert, Louise Chretien, Geoffrey Saint-Hilaire, Capricieux, Revol Massot, Lutea splendens, Ulrich Brunner, François Crozy, Antonin Crozy, Admiral Courbet, Félix Crousse, Francisque Morel, and Antoine Chantin, and there are many others.

CANNABIS (*Hemp Plant*).—A well-known annual of the Nettle Order, *C. sativa* being largely cultivated for its fibre. In our country it is 4 to 10 ft. high, but in Italy sometimes 20 ft. high. In plants growing singly, the stem is much branched, but in masses it is generally simple. It is useful where the tender sub-tropical plants cannot be easily grown, well-grown plants looking graceful, and are useful at the backs of borders; and a few look well as a separate group. It should be sown in the open ground early in April, and to get larger plants it would be best to raise it in frames. It loves a warm sandy loam, and is one of the few plants that thrive in small London gardens.

CARAGANA (*Siberian Pea-tree*).— A curious group of wiry bushes of the Pea order which, as seen in gardens generally, are not pretty enough to justify their getting a place in this book, but as the name occurs so often, and the wretched appearance they usually present may be in part owing to their being grafted, I give them a place. They are mostly rock or desert shrubs of arid regions in Central Asia, and the species are *C. arborescens* and its varieties, *C. aurantiaca* which is the prettiest, and would, perhaps, be a graceful rock shrub, *C. chamlagu*, *C. jubata*, *C. microphylla*, *C. pygmæa*, and *C. spinosa*. If we could get these curious shrubs on their own roots the best place for them would be the rock garden or dry banks.

CARBENIA (*Blessed Thistle*).—*C. benedicta* is a handsome biennial, having bold, deep-green leaves, blotched and marbled with silvery white. It is useful for associating with plants of fine foliage, but must have good deep soil and plenty of space. It grows freely and luxuriantly in a thin shrubbery, or on any bank of rubbish. S. Europe. Syn. *Cnicus benedictus*

CARDAMINE (*Cuckoo-flower or Lady's Smock*).—Plants of the Wallflower Order, few of which are cultivated, the best being the native Cuckoo-flower in its double form. This will grow well almost any-

Caragana Chamlagu.

where, although, like the wild plant, that colours the meadows with its soft-hued flowers, it delights in swampy ground. The single kind is too common to need cultivation ; the double kind is a pretty subject for the spring garden and for borders. Division. *C. trifolia* is a pretty species, with white flowers, from Switzerland ; 9 to 12 in. high ; a border or rough rock-plant. *C. latifolia, C. asarifolia,* and *C. rotundifolia* are pretty dwarf plants when in flower, but not popular in gardens.

The Toothworts (syn. Dentarias) are interesting spring-flowering plants. They grow best in a light sandy or peaty soil enriched by decayed leaf-mould. Their flowers are welcome in early spring, and remain some time in beauty, and they are easily increased from the small tuber-like roots. Some, like *C. bulbifera* (Coral Root), bear bulblets on the stem, and from these the plant may be increased. *C. digitata,* a handsome dwarf kind, about 12 in. high, flowers in April ; rich purple, in flat racemes at the top of the stem. *C. maxima* is the largest of the species, being 2 ft. high, with many pale-purple flowers, and is a native of N. America. *C. pinnata* is a stout species at once distinguished by its pinnate leaves ; it is from 14 to 20 in. high, flowering from April to June, bearing large pale-purple, lilac, or white flowers, in a cluster. It is a native of mountain and sub-alpine woods in Switzerland.

CAREX (*Sedge*).—Waterside grass-like herbs well known in all northern and temperate countries, but few have a place in the garden.

C. paniculata is a very large Sedge, something like a dwarf Tree Fern, with strong thick stems and luxuriant masses of drooping leaves, the roots forming dense tufts, 1 to 3 ft. high, flowers in a large and spreading panicle. A few tufts are very effective in wet places. The finer specimens are of great age, and are found in the bogs where the plant is wild.

C. pendula.—A graceful British sedge, growing in large tufts, with numerous flowering stems and shoots from 3 to 6 ft. high, the leaves 2 ft. or more in length. When in flower the graceful pendent spikes, from 4 to 7 in. long, are pretty, and the plant is very suitable for the margin of water or for shady or moist spots. Common in Britain in evergreen patches in cool or marshy woods.

CARPENTERIA.—A lovely and distinct shrub of the Saxifrage Family *C. californica* living out-of-doors against walls in favoured situations. It is 6 to 10 ft. high, having long narrow pale-green leaves, and great clusters of large white fragrant flowers. The first account of it in England was from Mr. Saul, of Wash-

Carpenteria californica in a Sussex garden.

ington, who sent specimens of it to *The Garden* in 1880. It is nearly related to the Mock Oranges, which it somewhat resembles, but is handsomer : thrives in light warm soil, and increased from

H H 2

suckers, cuttings, or seeds. In cool districts will require the protection of a greenhouse.

CARPINUS (*Hornbeam*).—*C. betulus* is a native tree, especially of the south, sometimes attaining a height of 70 feet, frequent in some woodlands, and in Epping

Hornbeam.

Forest. There are several varieties of this tree, such as the fern-leaved, cut-leaved and purple kinds, and also the never-failing variegated kind. The common kind is often used as a fence plant, and also, in many continental gardens, to form green walls and hedges. It is one of the best of all woods to burn, and if we ever go back to the best of all ways of firing for a dwelling-house in the country, a wood fire, it should not be forgotten. It is easily lighted, burns cheerfully and equably, and gives a good heat. Other species are *C. caroliniana, cordata, japonica, orientalis* and *Turczaninovii.*

CARYA(*Hickory*).—A very interesting and distinct group of forest trees, little planted in England in our own day, but so valuable in their own country for their wood, and some for bearing delicious fruit, that they deserve a place in our choice plantations. Mostly trees of North Eastern America and usually hardy, they are sometimes well over 100 ft. high; in their own country inhabiting moist woods and swampy grounds, and therefore likely to be useful in ours in soil not thought good enough for many trees. Among them are :—*C. olivæformis Pecán,* a tree which sometimes attains to a height of over 150 feet with a trunk diameter of 6 ft., and which bears a delicious nut. It has rather a southern distribution, and therefore would be best, no doubt, in good warm soils in our country. *C. amara,* (the bitter nut), a tree of about 100 feet in

moist woods, from Canada downwards, ascending high on the mountains. *C. aquatica* (*Water Hickory*), a swamp tree sometimes nearly 100 ft. high in wet woods and swamps from Virginia south and westwards. *C. alba* (Shell-bark Hickory) also often over 100 feet high ; a native of Canada and of the Western and Southern States. *C. sulcata* (King-nut), a tall forest tree over 100 feet high in the New England States and westward. *C. tomentosa* (Fragrant Hickory) growing nearly 100 feet high and inhabiting the cold regions of the West and New England. *C. microcarpa* (Small-fruited Hickory). A tall tree of nearly 90 ft. high. New England and westwards. *C. porcina* (Pig-nut Hickory).—A very tall tree of over 100 ft. bearing very bitter seeds, also a tree of cold northern regions. They are trees of fine growth with walnut-like leaves and the wood of some kinds in its own country is most valuable.

Carya aquatica.

CARYOPTERIS.—*C. mastacanthus* is a small shrub with grayish foliage, distinct in habit, and with purple flowers, not quite hardy, perhaps, in all soils, but pretty on warm banks and in warm gardens. There is a white variety. It would group well with the dwarfer shrubs, and in cool districts and on cool soils it will grow against warm walls. On good soils it would come in well with borders of grayish plants such as Lavenders, Carnations, and the like.

CASSIOPE (*Himalayan Heather*). —Tiny alpine bushes, thriving in peaty soil well drained, as they are all impatient of stagnant moisture about their roots, whilst absolute shade from the midday sun is also necessary. The best plan is to raise small banks of peat, and plant them on the top, taking care that they do not want for water both at the roots and overhead. They are increased by division, rooting freely when pegged down. *C. fastigiata* is one of the most fragile and beautiful of alpine woody plants; it may be grown without much trouble with the more common *C. tetragona*. Both are pretty for the rock or bog garden.

Cassiope fastigiata.

CASTANEA(*SweetChestnut*).—A noble tree, native of eastern and southern Europe. There are fine old trees in many of our country seats in all parts of the south of the country, though excepting in the warmer counties, such as Devonshire, the fruit is not as good as on the continent of Europe. The Chestnut thrives best in airy and warm situations, and upon stony or free soils, not caring much for chalk or heavy soils. There are various garden forms of the Chestnut which are all increased by grafting, but none of them are

so important as the common tree. As regards its uses, it is common in our underwoods and most effective, perhaps, in all the instances we know of, grouped on turf and occasionally as an avenue tree, but in that case it ought to be planted wide apart. It is easily raised from seed planted directly where it is wanted to grow. There are on the Continent, where the tree is much more grown than here, a good many varieties distinguished by the value of their fruits. Variegated varieties as usual are useless for the garden. There are a few other species such as *C. crenata* (Japan), *dentata* (N. America), and the dwarf *C. pumila* of the Southern states of N. America, but these are of slight value

Castanea pumila.

compared to that of *C. Vesca*, the beauty of old trees of which is very great, as seen at Shrubland, Tortworth, Cowdray, and many other places.

CATALPA. — Handsome flowering trees of the Bignonia order, one of them forming quite a beautiful tree even in London gardens. The Catalpas thrive best in warm ground and in sheltered positions, the common kind often thriving by the margin of water, though it is more liable to be injured in severe winters in such places.

C. bignonoides (*Indian Bean*). — A handsome tree, native of the Gulf States of Eastern America, but hardy in southern Britain and the kind which flowers so well in London. There is no more precious lawn tree giving good shade and flowering at a season when all the early trees are out of flower. It is best propagated by seed and is not difficult about soil. This tree has a number of synonyms, the best known being *C. syringæfolia*.

C. speciosa (*Catawba Tree*).—This is a forest tree in its own country in America, rather westwards in Illinois and Missouri, and is little known in our country yet, though promising to be a handsome tree as it reaches 120 ft. high in its own country. It deserves a very good position among the best flowering trees for lawn or for a group. Syn. *C. cordifolia.*

C. Bungei and *C. Kaempferi* are two other kinds known in gardens, both much so pretty that they are often planted by those who are fond of flowering shrubs. Some, however, are hardy enough on light soils in sunny places to withstand our climate, even if fully exposed as bush plants. The majority form beautiful wall shrubs. In all the species the flowers are small, but this is compensated for by their abundance, as they come out in succession during the greater part of the summer. As wall shrubs it is neces-

Catalpa bignonioides.

inferior in size to the foregoing trees, and less attractive unless where collections are desired.

CATANANCHE (*Blue Cupidone*).—*C. sœrulea* is an old border plant, about 2 ft. high, flowering in summer ; fine blue, and growing freely in borders and margins of shrubberies. There is a white variety as common as the blue and a bicolor one. It is easily grown in any soil, and quickly raised from seed. Compositæ. Italy and S. France.

CEANOTHUS (*Mountain Sweet*).— Though these beautiful shrubs of the Buckthorn Family are not quite hardy, they are sary to prune them in April, or as soon as danger from frost is over ; and as all the sorts flower on the shoots of the current year's growth, from one to three eyes of the preceding year's wood should be left, reserving, or at most only topping, such shoots as are required for filling up the open spaces on the wall. All the species are of free growth in warm garden soil, if it is dry, and they will ripen their wood best and flower most freely in sunny exposures. As they are often natives of a charming climate — the Pacific slope of N. America—no one should attempt their culture except in warm soil. The following are distinct and pretty :—

C. AMERICANUS (*New Jersey Tea*). — Though one of the hardiest, this thrives best against a wall, and in a dry porous soil ; the flowers, which come in succession from about the middle of June till August, are white, and numerous. E. America.

C. AZUREUS.—From the temperate regions of Mexico, where it grows as a straggling bush about 10 ft. high. It is one of our prettiest wall shrubs, flowering abundantly in dry sunny situations, the flowers bright blue, from June till September. C. pallidus is a handsome variety, with pale-blue flowers. The result of crossing with this species may be seen in such lovely shrubs as C. Gloire des Versailles, Arnoldii, Lucie Simon, Theodore Froebel, Bertinii, President Reveil, Lucie Moser, and others, all of which have flowers in large plumy clusters, some white, others rose, but mostly of some shade of blue.

Ceanothus azureus.

C. DENTATUS is an elegant little evergreen shrub, rarely higher than about 3 ft. The flowers, which appear in May or June, are deep blue, and continue the greater part of the season.

C. DIVARICATUS grows as a dense broad evergreen bush of about 10 ft. high. It is a free-growing handsome wall plant, flowering from May to autumn, the flowers a bright blue.

C. PAPILLOSUS is a pretty species from the mountains of California, where it is a densely branched straggling bush 6 to 10 ft. high. The panicles of pale-blue flowers are borne on long foot-stalks from the sides of the young shoots. Like the other kinds, it loves the protection of a wall, on which it blooms in summer.

C. RIGIDUS is a sub-evergreen, or in sheltered places an evergreen, rarely exceeding 6 ft. in height, the branches stiff and wiry ; the flowers, in clusters on the sides of the young shoots, are deep purple, in April and May.

C. VEITCHIANUS is one of the best kinds, the flowers of a rich deep blue, in dense clusters at the ends of leafy branches.—G.

C. VERRUCOSUS forms a thickly branched evergreen bush about 6 ft. high. As a wall plant it is of free growth, and has a good effect, the flowers coming in May and during the summer months, borne in corymbs along the whole length of the young branches, often so profusely as to hide the foliage.

CEDRELA.—*C. sinensis* is somewhat similar to the "Tree of Heaven" (*Ailanthus glandulosa*), but this Chinese tree is much more uncommon in gardens. In some places, however, it might be a more suitable tree, for whilst it has much the same character of foliage and habit, it is not so rampant a grower. The Ailanthus is often somewhat of a nuisance through its habit of sending up root-suckers at long distances from the stem. The Cedrela has not this habit, although it can, like the Ailanthus, be increased by root-cuttings. The largest specimens I have seen are about 30 ft. high. The tree is chiefly noteworthy for the large pinnate leaves it bears, these being, indeed, amongst the most striking to be met with in the large or medium-sized trees hardy in this country. *C. sinensis*, which is the

Catananche cœrulea.

only one hardy in Britain, was for a long time known as *Ailanthus flavescens*. It has small yellowish flowers arranged in great numbers in pendent clusters said to be agreeably scented. Among the trees of the genus there are some remarkable for their uses, but they are tropical, and we have no object in giving any particulars of them in this book. As far as we know *C. sinensis* it promises to be a graceful lawn tree, but has not been long enough in the country yet to speak with certainty of its hardiness, although we see it flourishing in unlikely places. W. J. B.

CEDRONELLA (*Balm of Gilead*) is a distinct half-bushy herb of the Sage order, *C. triphylla* having leaves with a pungent but grateful odour, in our country 2½ to 4 ft. high, varying much according to soil, and not quite hardy, but living out-of-doors most winters if in dry free soil and planted against walls.

A few plants against a wall are worth having where curious plants are cared for, but the flowers are not showy Easily raised from seed.

CEDRUS (*Cedar*).—Noble trees of the mountains of Asia Minor and India, some hardy, and often planted on lawns and within sight of the flowers. The India Cedar (Deodar) is really a tender tree, and though it may seem to promise well in sea-shore and favoured districts, planters

seen the trees on their native mountains, I think the Atlas Cedar is the same species as the Lebanon Cedar (*C. Lebani*). There are varieties of each in catalogues, rarely so valuable as the wild tree, except the glaucous or silvery forms, which are worth planting. The Deodar (*C. Deodari*) is distinct from the N. African Cedars, and differs so also in its tenderness and unfitness for our country generally.

The Cedars though hardy in our country are nevertheless the victims of storm and snow to an often painful but partly needless extent owing to the nearly universal "specimen" way of planting these trees. The pinetum is not only a mistake from an artistic point of view, with its stuck-about trees, but it also is so in the exposure of the trees to all the storms and accidents of weather, including heavy snowfalls. Naturally, pines often grow together and shelter each other, and where this is so, great falls of snow do not harm them to the same degree. The lower boughs fall off in due time, as is their nature, the tree often showing a bare, mast-like stem beneath its crown of leaves. Clearly, when we isolate any tree in the open, and induce a tree which

Cedrela sinensis.

should not forget that it is to the Cedars of the northern mountains they must look —the Lebanon and Atlas Cedars, which have been proved so hardy, and so well fitted for our country. No finer things can be within view of the flower garden, but they should never be planted near the house, or their great branches will darken it, and in small flower gardens they are sure to be in the way.

In books and catalogues a form called *C. Atlantica* is considered distinct enough to merit a separate name, but having

naturally grows upright in a great mountain forest to throw its limbs out in all directions, we expose it to an unfair test; hence the Cedars of which we in England are so proud are often swept down ·in numbers by heavy gales and snowfalls. The idea that every choice tree in our pleasure grounds should be set out by itself like an electric lamp-post is deeply impressed in the gardening mind, and we have to pay dearly for it. Even where the Cedars are naturally grown and grouped very exceptional falls may do some injury, but nothing like what happens to the specimen trees. Think of the weight that a Cedar of Lebanon, with its great spreading arms, would have to carry in a snowstorm, and how much more able to bear it or to meet such a test are the Cedars planted in woods and allowed to group and grow mast-like shafts !

The cure for much of this loss and waste of valuable trees lies in planting in more natural ways and in grouping and keeping the trees together.

With regard to soil and situation, each planter seeks the best possible development for his Cedars, and so selects the best soil and position he has, and, probably, digs a big hole for each tree and puts many loads of earth in. The result of this is not good, in more ways than one, first in creating a too rapid growth in the young tree, and soft unresisting wood in the old, and, secondly, any proof that the natural soil and other conditions of the

Cedar of Lebanon.

place suit the tree is withheld from us by the deep preparation of soil made, entirely altering the natural conditions. Any one who has seen the trees in their native countries will know that the Cedar usually inhabits high mountains, often on bare, shaly slopes, in which they are happy enough, though never so well developed as when growing where a little soil collects. That soil is always of a poor rocky or pervious nature. Surely this points out that in pleasure grounds and country seats, instead of taking the very best soil, we should plant on rocky or sandy places where the tree will, though growing at first slowly, eventually get a safer and harder growth than it ever would on rich deep soil. This would not preclude us from putting a group in the pleasure grounds for the sake of shade, but holding the trees together. Also, it would be well to plant it in the ordinary woodland, in which the trees would be drawn up with a tall stem, very effective near drives or in woods. The difficulty of dealing with the Cedar is increased by its being made a

kind of fetish in our nurseries, always being offered in the "specimen" state, so that nowadays it is not easy to get a nice healthy stock of young plants of it, and those offered are generally highly priced as if they were some rare novelty instead of a tree known for some centuries. The seed of the tree is plentiful in Asia Minor and North Africa, and it really ought to be grown in forest nurseries and offered among the other forest trees. The seed being as easy to raise as that of any other conifer, people should not buy the tree in the " specimen " state but in the smaller state, a much safer and better way, especially where we group and hold our trees together and where they can shade the ground. This plan by no means precludes us from sufficient thinning in good time, so as to secure great trees, always, however, holding to the principle of letting the trees shade the ground and shelter each other. W. R.

CELASTRUS (*Staff Vine*). — *C. scandens* is a shrubby climber from North America, flourishing in any ordinary garden soil, and valuable for its rapid twining growth, which is excellent for trailing over trellis-work and arbours, or on a bank, or to run over other shrubs and trees to a height of 12 or 15 ft. The flowers are inconspicuous, and the fruits orange-red, like those of the Spindle Tree, to which order it belongs.

CELOSIA (*Cocks-comb*).—Indian annuals of the Amaranth family. They are generally too tender for the open air, though we have occasionally seen them used with effect in bold groups. For this purpose they should be sown in pans in March, and kept near the glass to prevent the seedlings being drawn, and as soon as they are large enough to handle they should be pricked off into small pots, grown on fast in gentle heat until the crowns are formed. Planted out in June in rich soil, and liberally watered, they continue in good condition for a long time.

CELSIA (*Cretan Mullein*).—*C. cretica* is a pretty plant, allied to the mulleins, with rich yellow flowers and polished buds, may be treated as an annual. Well grown in good soil, it is distinct and effective. Candia, N. Africa.

CELTIS (*Nettle tree*).—Trees of the Elm order, natives of temperate countries, much mentioned in books, and introduced to Britain many years, but which have never made much way with us, and are less attractive to planters than other trees of the same order. Among a cloud of synonyms, the following are the names :—

C australis, caucasica, glabrata, japonica, mississipiensis, occidentalis, and *Tournefortii* Some of the kinds are tropical, and not hardy in our country.

CENTAUREA (*Knapweed*) —Perennial or annual herbs inhabiting Southern and Middle Europe, some being good garden plants, most of them hardy Some of the southern species require the greenhouse in winter, but, making free growth out-of-doors in summer, are freely used for their silvery foliage.

C. argentea has elegant silvery Fernlike leaves, and when planted out or plunged in pots has a good effect , for bedding it must be plunged and partly starved to bring out its whiteness

C. babylonica.—A distinct perennial, tall and with silvery leaves, hardy, and when in good ground its strong shoots with yellow flowers reach a height of 10 or 12 ft The bloom, which continues from July to September, is less attractive than the leaves, but the plant is at all times picturesque A free sandy loam suits it best Seed Levant

C. Clementei. — A silver-gray-leaved plant of fine form Small plants from seed are useful for edging bold beds, and when too large for that purpose they may be transferred to borders, or planted out singly on Grass The blossoms are best picked off, as they detract from the beauty of the plant

C Cyanus (*Blue Cornflower*) — A beautiful native flower, an annual of easy culture, often sowing itself The young plants stand our hardest winters, and flower better grown thus than if sown in spring It is best sown in September, either where it is to flower, or in beds to be transplanted Self-sown plants too may be transplanted, or allowed to remain where they come up, as they are often the finest plants The many garden varieties range through white, rose, sky-blue, striped, to dark purple, the delicate tints of which are most attractive They are favourites in the flower market, but by far the most beautiful is the true wild kind There are also a number of double kinds The Cornflower will flourish in almost any soil or position, but best, perhaps, in strong soil

C dealbata.—A hardy perennial, with graceful and somewhat silvery leaves, 15 to 18 in high, flowering in summer , rose-coloured Borders. Division Caucasus

C. gymnocarpa.—A half-shrubby plant from the south of Europe, nearly 2 ft high, with hard, branching, bushy stems, and elegantly cut leaves, covered with short whitish-satiny down Useful as it is for edging or bedding, it is when grown in fine single specimens that its beauty is most seen

C. macrocephala (*Great Golden Knapweed*) —A strong plant from 4 to 5 ft high, with a great golden head of bloom In the back part of a herbaceous border, or where herbaceous plants must compete with the roots of trees and shrubs, this robust plant deserves a place Armenia

C. montana (*Mountain Knapweed*) — A handsome border plant, 1 to 2½ ft high, with slightly cottony leaves, and flowers resembling those of the Cornflower There is a white and a red variety, all thriving in borders, margins of shrubberies, or the wild garden in any soil This kind is somewhat coarse in borders, and scarcely worth a place therein, but when cut, its flowers are pretty, and larger than those of the Blue Cornflower Division

C. moschata (*Sweet Sultan*) —A fragrant annual, of which there are two shades—delicate purple and creamy white, the first giving the finest flowers , but both are valuable Aphides are very partial to the young seedlings, and unless the pests are quickly cleared off the plants soon dwindle away The first essential is a calcareous soil, and any soil deficient in lime should have lime rubble worked into it The best time to sow is about the middle of April, in an open and sunny place, sowing the seed where the plants are to remain, as they do not move well Syn, *Amberboa moschata* —J R

C. ragusina.—A showy silvery-leaved plant, tender, but of rapid growth out-of-doors in summer, and valued much for summer-bedding It thrives in the coldest situation throughout the summer When taking cuttings, they should not be cut away, but pulled off with a "heel" so as to have a firm base , small firm shoots should be preferred , in taking them the knife should be used very little, and each cutting put singly into a small 2½-in pot filled with a mixture of loam, leaf-mould, A cold frame from which frost can be excluded is their best winter quarters , the leaves should be kept dry, as they are rather liable to damp during the short days, and every opportunity should be taken for giving them air They also winter well in an airy vinery or greenhouse Old plants are sometimes lifted and kept over the winter , where very large plants are required this is a sure means of obtaining them ; but for ordinary use autumn-struck cuttings are the best.—J. M.

C. suaveolens (*Yellow Sweet Sultan*). —A pretty citron-yellow hardy annual and favourite border flower, thriving best in light dry soil. Sow in beds in April, raising one batch in frames, and sowing another in the open air in light rich earth where it is to remain. *Syn.,* Amberboa odorata.

CENTAURIDIUM.—A showy half-hardy annual from Texas, *C. Drummondi* being from 2½ to 3 ft. high, and flowering from July to September. It should be sown in a frame on slight heat in April, and planted out in May. It has large citron-yellow flowers, much resembling those of Centaurea. Compositæ.

CENTRANTHUS.—*C. macrosiphon* is a hardy Spanish annual of the Valerian order with pretty rose-coloured flowers, is useful for the rock-garden or flower border. It may be sown in September and pricked off into pots for winter for transplanting in spring, or again in the open ground in March and April, the seedlings being thinned out about 1 ft. apart. There are several varieties— white, red, and two-coloured, and a dwarf form.

C. ruber (*Red Valerian*).—A handsome hardy border plant from the Mediterranean, and an old inhabitant of gardens, often also naturalised. There are two or three varieties—white, purple, and red or crimson. It has stout stems, woody at the base, and bold clusters of flowers, blooming in June and through the summer. It is often naturalised on walls, ruins, and on rocky or stony banks. Seeds, division, and cuttings.

CERASTIUM (*Mouse-ear Chickweed*). —Dwarf herbaceous or alpine plants of the Pink order, containing few garden plants of value, and these mostly used as edgings, among the best being *Biebersteini, tomentosum,* and *grandiflorum,* all hardy plants of easy culture, and increase in ordinary soil.

Cerasus. *See* PRUNUS CERASUS.

CERCIDYPHYLLUM.—A very beautiful tree, so far hardy in Britain, and always pretty for its graceful and distinct leaves. It is a forest tree abundant in certain parts of Japan on the slopes of hills and mountains, reaching a height of between 80 and 100 feet, and forming a stately and beautiful tree. We read that it cannot be grafted, which is a blessing, as the natural way of producing it is much better. It is likely to make a beautiful lawn tree, though the flowers are not conspicuous.

CERCIS (*Judas Tree*).— Flowering trees of much beauty of bloom and form of tree. Of the three different kinds of Judas Tree in gardens, the most beautiful is *C. Siliquastrum* from South Europe, which for nearly 300 years has been a favourite in English gardens. It is from

Celsia cretica (Cretan Mullein).

15 ft. to 30 ft. in height, and thrives in a light deep loam soil. There are several varieties, differing chiefly in the colour of the flowers. It is of slow growth, and though young specimens flower profusely, only very old ones show the picturesque growth of the tree. Other kinds are *C. Chinensis,* and the better known *canadensis,*

or Red Bud, a handsome tree of the American forests. Pea order.

CERINTHE (*Honeywort*).—Annual or biennial herbs of the Borage family, of which there are two or three interesting plants. *C. aspera* bears many yellow flowers, the tube of which is black at the base. In *C. minor* the flower-stems arch over considerably, so that at the apex of the stem the delicate yellow tube-shaped bloom is hidden by the imbricated pale-green leaves with which the stem is furnished. *C. retorta* is a beautiful kind, the floral leaves of a rich purple tint, and from among them peep the yellow-purple-tipped flowers in charming contrast. There are various other species, but the above are the best. Cerinthes are half-

Mountain Knapweed.

hardy annuals, requiring to be sown in early spring on warm borders or in frames, and afterwards to be planted out in good soil. They are, however, not likely to be much in favour, owing to their quiet colours. Greece and Southern Europe.

CETERACH (*Stone Fern*).—This is now placed with the Aspleniums, but is known so well under its present name that we retain it. *C. officinarum* is a distinct and beautiful little native Fern, admirably suited for rock or alpine gardens, as it thrives best when planted between the chinks of rocks or of stone walls. The chinks and crevices should be filled with a mixture of sandy peat and pounded limestone.

CHÆNOSTOMA.—A small group of the Figwort family, natives of the Cape. They are naturally perennial, but in open air must be treated as half-hardy annuals. *C. fastigiatum* is the prettiest. It grows 6 to 9 in. high, forming a dense compact tuft, with many small pinkish, and sometimes white, flowers. The seeds should be sown in warm frames in spring or in August, when the seedlings require to be wintered in a pit, and flowers are borne from June to November. Other species in cultivation are *C. cordatum*, *C. hispidum*, *C. linifolium*, and *C. polyanthum*.

CHAMÆBATIA (*Tarweed*).—*C. foliolosa* is a little shrubby plant of the Rose family, remarkable for the Fern-like beauty of its leaves. The flowers are white and something like those of a Bramble. It grows about 1 ft. high, forming a dense spreading tuft, and covering the ground in California, its native country. I have seen it growing in mountain districts often covered with snow, and believe it to be worth trial in our rock-gardens. W. R.

CHAMÆPEUCE (*Fish-bone Thistle*).— Spiny-leaved plants allied to the Thistle, often used in the flower garden, as their foliage is handsome. *C. diacantha* has foliage of shining green, marking with silvery lines, and the spines are ivory white. *C. Casabonæ* has deep-green white-veined leaves with brown spines. Both kinds grow in compact rosette-like masses about 9 in. high, till the second year, when the flower-stems grow 2 to 3 ft. high. They require light well-drained soil and a warm position, and should seldom be watered. Seed sown in February will furnish good plants by May; but the best for immediate effect are those sown in a border in the open ground in September, potted up carefully, and given greenhouse treatment during winter. Syn. *Cnicus*.

CHAMÆROPS.—Handsome palms, hardy, and some giving distinct effects in the garden.

C. Fortunei (*The Chusan Palm*).—A most valuable Palm, often confounded with *C. excelsa*. It is stouter and has a more profuse matted network of fibres round the bases of the leaves; the segments of the leaves are much broader, and the leaf-stalks shorter and stouter, being from 1 to 2 ft. long, and quite unarmed. It grows 12 ft. or more high, and has a handsome spreading head of fan-like leaves, slit into segments about half-way down, and is perfectly hardy. A plant in the garden at Osborne has stood out for many winters, also at Kew, though protected in winter. On the water side of the high mound in the Botanic Gardens, Regent's Park, it is in even better health than at Kew, though it has had no protection ; and severe frosts have not hurt it. If small plants are procured, grow them on freely for a year or two in the greenhouse, and then turn them out in April, spreading the roots a little and giving them a deep

grown in gardens. The Wallflower is a native of Southern Europe, but naturalised on old walls, in quarries, and on sea-cliffs. It loves a wall better than any garden ; it grows coarsely in garden soil, but forms a dwarf enduring bush on an old wall if planted in mortar, and grows even on walls quite new. No variety is unworthy of cultivation ; but the choice old garden

Chamærops Fortunei in a Surrey garden.

loamy soil. Plant in a sheltered place, so that the leaves may not be injured by winds when they get large. A gentle hollow, or among shrubs on the sides of some sheltered glade, is the best place. *C. humilis* is also hardy—at least on sandy soil.

CHEIRANTHUS (*Wallflower*). — Beautiful cruciferous plants made familiar by the favourite Wallflower (*C. Cheiri*), which [is almost the only species much

kinds—the double yellow, double purple, double orange, dark, &c.—are worthy of a place among the finest border plants. These are the varieties most worthy of a place on dry stony banks near the rock-garden, and also on old ruins, on which the common kind is likely to find a home for itself.

The superb dark crimson-marked kinds grown around London need no description, and can be bought in the seed trade under the designations of Harbinger and Covent Garden Blood-red and Golden Yellow, all good strains. The Belvoir Castle Yellow is a close compact kind, with bright yellow flowers, and suitable for spring bedding. The Golden Yellow is as robust and tall as the crimson kinds, and bears masses of rich orange-yellow bloom.

The double perennials familiar to us are the yellow, dark crimson, red, and dwarf yellow. The yellow is most common, and a beautiful clear-coloured kind it is, a great favourite with cottagers, who propagate it by putting in slips about the time the plants are in flower. It can be propagated freely by means of slips put in under hand-lights in sharp sandy soil, and the plants will flower the next spring. The old dark crimson is now almost extinct ; in colour the flowers are almost black, and very striking ; the dwarf yellow has flowers of a dull, almost buff tint ; the Raby Castle variety is valuable and sturdy.

INCREASE AND CULTURE. — Many persons sow seed too late—in June and July, instead of April and May. If dry weather follows close on the sowing, or after the plants have grown 2 or 3 in., they receive a check, and, instead of being dwarf, vigorous, and bushy, they are thin and poor. The winter will sometimes injure the Wallflower severely, especially when very severe frost follows close on heavy rains, and the stronger and better rooted the plants are, the more likely are they to stand the weather. The plants used for filling beds should have been once transplanted at least, because the moving induces them to throw out fibry roots near the surface, and they can be lifted with soil adhering to them. When the Wallflower is allowed to grow where it is sown, a strong tap-root is formed, which strikes deep into the soil, and but few surface roots are put forth. In transplanting from the seed-beds, it is well to pinch off the tap-root, and thereby induce fibry roots.

In London market-gardens, where the Wallflower is well cultivated, seed is sown in the open ground early in February ; the young plants are put out into their permanent quarters in May, and by Christmas, if the winter be mild, they bloom, and are so large that they could not be covered by a bushel basket. Some market-growers sow seed late in summer, allow the young plants to remain in the seed-bed all the winter, plant out in March, and, if the season be favourable, reap a good crop of flowers all through the next winter.

Save seeds from plants with the best branching habit and the darkest blossoms. When the plants are in flower, place a stake by each possessing those qualities, so as to mark it. Allow the plants to remain undisturbed until the seed is ripe ; they may then be pulled up, roots and all, and housed in a dry place until a convenient season for threshing out the seed. Cuttings of the double kinds may be put in as soon as they can be got after the plants go out of bloom. Put them in firm sandy soil under a hand-light, and, when struck, plant them out. Cuttings put in in August, September, or October strike freely without any protection, in a shady border, or in pots or boxes of sandy soil.

Besides the Wallflower there are several perennial species of doubtful hardiness, such as *C. arbuscula* and *mutabilis*, natives of the Canary Islands, which therefore, though pretty pot plants, cannot be recommended for general open-air culture. Besides these there are various hybrids, such as *Marshalli*, the finest of the hybrid kinds, from 9 in. to 1 ft. high, with many bright orange-scented blossoms, and is a brilliant border plant, and good for groups in spring.

All these perennials prefer dry soil during winter, or a place on rough stone walls. Propagation is by cuttings, and top dressing with fine soil often induces the summer wood to root freely, and by autumn a good stock can be had.

CHELONE (*Turtle - head*). — North American plants nearly allied to Pentstemon, the species in cultivation are handsome border plants, flowering in late summer and in autumn. *C. Lyoni* grows from 2 to 3 ft. high, forms a dense mass of stems, with deep-green foliage, from July to September bearing dense clusters of showy pink blossoms. *C. obliqua* is taller and more slender, but the colour of the typical form is a richer pink, and there is a white-flowered variety. Both are of easy culture, thriving in open borders of good deep soil, and increased by seeds, cuttings, or division of the roots. These plants, though bearing pretty flowers, and free in growth, are not of high garden value.

CHENOPODIUM (*Goosefoot*).—Few of these plants of the Spinach order are of much garden value, except *C. Atriplicis*, a vigorous Chinese annual, with erect reddish stem, slightly branched, over 3 ft. in height, and with its young shoots and leaves covered with a rosy-violet powder, pretty in foliage, in any soil. *C. scoparium* (Belvedere) is a curious and graceful annual plant, like a miniature

Cypress in form, and worth a place among curious annual plants. *C. Blitum capitatum* (*Strawberry-blite*) is a hardy annual, growing from 1½ to 2 ft. high, the flowers small, followed by high-coloured fruit calyxes resembling small Strawberries. Sow in April in the open air.

CHIMAPHILA (*Pipsissewa*).—Small shrubby plants of the Heather order, natives of the dry woods of N. America. *C. maculata* (Spotted Wintergreen) has small leathery leaves variegated with white, 3 to 6 in. high, and is pretty for a half-shady and mossy, but not wet, place in the rock-garden, with such plants as the dwarf Andromeda and the Pyrola, and succeeds best in very sandy leaf-soil. *C. umbellata*, with glossy unspotted leaves and somewhat larger reddish flowers, is also suited for like positions.

CHIMONANTHUS (*Winter-Sweet*). —*C. fragrans* is a lovely shrub, which in our country enjoys a wall, flowering in December and January; beautiful, and of delicious fragrance, the flowers coming upon young wood after the leaves have fallen, brownish-yellow, marked with purple inside ; and precious for gathering for the house. The best variety is *grandiflora*, its flowers being longer and more open, but the shrub varies a little from seed, in which way it is often raised in nurseries. This shrub does best on a wall with a southern or western aspect. A few shoots with blooms upon them placed in a room last a long time, and diffuse their pleasant fragrance, and little harm need be done by cutting these twigs, as in the ordinary course they would be pruned away after their flowers have faded. In fact we may in cutting with some care the precious shoots for the house prune the bush. Layers and seed. Japan. *Calycanthaceæ*.

Chionanthus virginica.

CHIONANTHUS (*Fringe Tree*).—A beautiful small hardy tree of the Olive family ; in some old English gardens there are fine specimens, but it is rarely met with in modern gardens. Fully grown in this country, in sandy loam or warm soil, it is a dense bush about 12 ft. high, but in its native country it is a tree. In early summer it bears long clusters of white flowers, with petals long and narrow like a fringe. N. America. A newer species is the Chinese *C. retusus*, which is not so pretty, though its flowers are white and fringed.

CHIONODOXA (*Glory of the Snow*). —Among the most beautiful of our early spring-flowering bulbs, and a precious addition to our garden flora. Their great hardiness, beauty, and the rapidity with which they increase in ordinary soils make them great favourites.

C. Luciliæ.—A plant variable in size as well as in the form and colour of its flowers, but of usually a pretty blue and white. Newly imported bulbs as a rule give small and few flowers, but when well established size and number are almost doubled. It is one of the hardiest bulbs we possess, flowering during March and April. There is a white-flowered form, but it is rare. *C. grandiflora* is more robust, the flowers larger and more numerous and of a distinct soft violet-blue with a small white centre. *C. Sardensis* is a charming kind, the flowers, fine Gentian blue. The bulbs were found close to the ruins of the ancient town of Sardis, at 4000 to 5000 ft. above sea level. There are various other names, but the above are distinct and the best of the family.

CHOISYA (*Mexican Orange-flower*). —A handsome shrub, of the Rue order, *C. ternata* in the south and west often thrives with the shelter of a wall and a southern or western aspect, and often in high ground, at least, thriving as a bush. It is fast-growing, the flowers a lovely contrast to the deep rich green foliage.

CHRYSANTHEMUM. — Perennial and annual plants, some of which are valuable for the garden.

C. arcticum.—A good plant for the rock-garden about a foot high, flowering all the summer, white tinged with lilac or rose.

C. carinatum (*Tricolor Chrysanthemum*).—A showy annual from N. Africa, which varies much in cultivation, and is valuable if only for its yield of flowers for cutting. There are double white and yellow forms ; and the showy ones known as C. Burridgeanum. Dunnett's varieties of the same plant are also good. They are propagated from seeds sown in April in open beds or borders where the plants are to flower ; or they may be sown earlier in pans or boxes of light rich earth in a pit or frame, from which they can be transplanted after all danger from frost is over. Plant singly in rich soil in an open and sunny position.

C. coronarium (*Crown Daisy*).—A bold and handsome annual 2 to 3 ft. high in its wild form in S. Europe and N. Africa, and, in cultivation, breaking into a number of forms, few of them so pretty as the single wild flower, pale yellow or buff, treated as a half-hardy annual, and sown in good ground in April or early in May.

C. frutescens (*Paris Daisy, Mar-*

trying to secure them where the soil and climate are not unfavourable.

The following varieties will make a capital display out of doors : Lady Fitz-wygram, Mdme. C. Desgrange, G. Wermig, Comtesse Fouchier de Careil, La Vierge, Gustave Grunerwald, Roi des Précocés, Ryecroft Glory, Vicomtesse d'Avene, Maria, Mrs. Gifford, Montague, Mdme. Eulalie Morel, Florrie Parsons, Strathmeath, Arthur Crepey, Carrie Denny, Mdlle. Rénée Cohn, October Yellow.

In many well-kept gardens there are open spaces on the walls, and the question is often asked, What can be done to hide them? The answer is,

Chionodoxa sardensis.

guerite).—A vigorous half-hardy plant from the Canary Isles ; the foliage glaucous ; the flowers large, pure white, with a yellow centre, and appearing from June until cut down by frost. It is a fine Daisy-like plant, and several forms or allies are also valuable, such as the yellow Etoile d'Or and Comtesse de Chambord. These are of easy culture and propagation, being for the outdoor garden, treated as half-hardy plants and put out in May.

C. indicum.—This is a native of China and Japan, and from it has originated the numerous varieties of the Chrysanthemum. Although in our country, generally, open air culture will often be impracticable, nevertheless, the outdoor kinds are so pretty that it is worth while

train Chrysanthemums upon them ; if well nailed in they take up but little room, and afford a pleasing background to the other occupants of the borders. Strong cuttings or suckers, or, what is better still, the old roots or stools that flowered in pots the previous season, planted at the foot of the wall 3 ft. apart early in March, in soil similar to that just recommended, will make remarkably rapid growth, and, if kept neatly nailed in and all the side-shoots removed as they appear, will soon cover a wall of ordinary height. Should it be desirable to protect the blossoms from wind and weather it can be effectually done by nailing a 12-in. board on the top of the wall, so as to form a coping. This, supported by a few poles in front, is all that is required, and, if practicable, a canvas covering fastened in front when the nights are cold will generally prove sufficient protection ; with these simple precautions the duration of the flowers will be greatly prolonged. The varieties named below are best for wall culture. Many early-flowering Japanese and reflexed kinds are included, as they are more suitable than the incurved section, the natural form of the petals being less likely to hold water from night dews and rains.

White.—Eynsford White, Lady Selborne, Mdlle. Lacroix, Elaine, Fair Maid of Guernsey, Mrs. Forsyth, Felicity, Avalanche. *Yellow and Orange.*—G. Glenny, Jardin des Plantes, Sunflower, Buttercup, Mrs. Horril, President Hyde,

'Paris Daisy (C. frutescens).

Phœbus. *Blush and Rose.*—Bouquet Fait, Princess of Teck, Venus, Maiden's Blush, Peach Christine, Christine, Etoile de Lyon, Annie Clibran, Viviand Morel. *Crimson.*—E. Molyneux, Cullingfordi, W. Holmes, King of Crimsons, M. Mousillac, M. Henri Jacotot, and Progne. *Red and Brown.*—Triomphe du Nord, Gloire du Rocher, Val d'Andorre, Félix Cassagneau, Wm. Robinson, Julie Lagravère, and Source d'Or. *Purple and Amaranth.*—Dr. Sharpe, M. Bernard, Alberic Lunden, and Mrs. Nisbet.

Pompons.—These are useful for wall covering ; they grow compact and flower freely. The following is a good selection : *White.*—Sœur Mélanie, Mdlle. Marthe, La Pureté, White Perfection, Snowdrop. *Yellow.*—Golden Circle, St. Michael, Primrose League, William Westlake,

Nelly Dainford. *Red and Brown.*—Black Douglas, Prince of Orange, Tiber, Vulcan, Victorine, Prince Victor, James Forsyth, Fremy, Eleonore. *Purple.* — President, Comte de Morny, and Pygmalion.

Single-flowered Varieties are very useful for covering walls. The best are— *White.*—White Perfection, The Virgin, Exquisite. *Yellow.*—Yellow Jane, Golden Star, Prince of Yellows, Canariense, and Charming. *Blush and Pink.*—Florence, Mary Anderson, America, and Crushed Strawberry. *Red.*—Lady Churchill, Souv. de Londres, Scarlet Gem, David Windsor, and Effie.

Summer and Early Autumn Flowering Kinds.—This is an important class, furnishing a number of varieties that are valuable for cutting from, and they enliven the borders when other hardy flowers are on the wane. But there are many good early autumn flowers, and setting chrysanthemums much before their natural season is a practice of doubtful value in the flower-garden. Some are very dwarf and of various shades of colour, and for the open air are of much value.—A. S.

C. latifolium is the largest of the Ox-eye Daisies, with fleshy, coarsely serrated, broad leaves. The seeds have large flower-heads, 3 in. to 4 in. across ; a strong growing species requiring plenty of room. Division and seeds. A number of varieties of this and the following species have been raised which have some value as border plants and for cutting.

C. maximum is nearly allied to *C. pallens*, from which it is distinguished chiefly by its involucre and larger flowers. The leaves of *C. maximum* are bluntly serrated, stems more or less branched, each carrying a single white flower, leafless towards the flower-heads, the involucre flattish, composed of numerous narrow bracts. Maritime Alps.

C. Zawadskii, of tufted habit, bears numerous rose-tinted flowers all through the summer months.—D.K.

C. segetum (*Corn Marigold*).—A showy yellow native plant, as worthy of cultivation as many an exotic, and in certain cases worth growing for cutting. Treat as a hardy annual, preferring autumn sowing.

Chrysobactron Hookeri. *See* ANTHERICUM.

Chrysurus. *See* LAMARCKIA.

CICHORIUM (*Chicory*).—A pretty native plant, from 2 to 5 ft. high, *C. Intybus*, bearing in summer and autumn handsome blue flowers. It is worth introducing as a wild plant into localities where it is not common. It is a rampant grower, and will take care of itself under almost any con-

I I

ditions. The seed may be sown on rubbish heaps and in stony places, old quarries, and by roadsides.

Baneberry. They are tall herbaceous plants ; one at least is handsome—*C. racemosa* (Black Snakeroot), 3 to 8 ft. high,

Chrysanthemum Mdme. Desgrange, grown in the open air.

CIMICIFUGA (*Bugbane*).—Plants of the Crowfoot Order, nearly allied to the

with feathery racemes of white blossoms 1 to 3 ft. long, which, being slender, droop gracefully ; but the plants generally are not of much garden value. They are of easy culture in rich soil, and may be used as groups in the wild garden. The flowers have an offensive odour. Division. N. America and Asia.

Cineraria maritima. See SENECIO.

Cissus. See VITIS.

CISTUS (*Rock Rose*).—The Rock Roses are amongst the most beautiful of flowering shrubs, but in our country it is only on the lightest and warmest soils and on walls that they may be trusted to survive our winters. Most of the species have

Chicory.

been at one time or another in cultivation in this country, but their value is greatly lessened by the recurring severe winters which kill unprotected plants of so many of the kinds. All the species are Old World plants, most of them being natives of South-western Europe ; some extend to North Africa and Asia Minor, and one to the Canary Islands. Many of the species vary a good deal in colour, size of leaves, and not a few appear to hybridise freely. In spite of the fugacious character of the flowers (they do not last more than one day), their bright colours and the profusion in which a succession is kept up for a considerable time render the Cistuses amongst the

most welcome of garden shrubs during the summer months. They prefer a dry sandy soil, and, although some grow freely enough in almost any garden soil, they are much more likely to suffer during winter in rich ground. The positions best for them are sunny banks on warm sandy soil, and something may be done by protection and frequently raising and propagating the plant ; but the question as to whether such labour would not be better bestowed on some family of shrubs quite hardy in our climate, may be worth considering save by those who seek collections in face of all difficulties. There are many natural hybrids, some confusion of names, and many more names than distinct plants, this, and the fact that these sun-loving bushes from the south are tender over a large area of our islands makes us limit the species named here to the more distinct and hardier kinds.

Among the more distinct species are :— *albidus, corbariensis, crispus, cyprius hirsutus, ladaniferus, laurifolius, longifolius, lusitanicus, monspeliensis, parviflorus, purpureus, salvifolius, Thureti, villosus,* with many hybrid forms, one of the best of these being *C. Florentinus.*

CLADIUM.—*C. Mariscus* is a vigorous native fen plant, 2 to 6 ft. high, in flower crowned with dense, close chestnut-coloured panicles, sometimes 3 ft. in length, the leaves glaucous, rigid, and often 4 ft. long. Worthy of a place on the margin of water.

CLADRASTIS, the Yellow-wood of N. America. *C. tinctoria* is a pretty lawn tree of medium size and symmetrical growth, but not a good flowering tree. Its leaves, in autumn, turn to a rich yellow, and remain bright for weeks until cut off by frosts. The white pea-shaped flowers are borne in loose clusters. Syn. *Virgilia lutea. C. amurensis* is a shrub introduced a few years ago from the Amoor Valley. Its leaves resemble those of the Yellowwood, but are of thicker texture, not so large, and of a duller green. In late summer it produces a plentiful crop of flowers, even when only a few feet high. The spikes are dense, the blossoms white, and inclined to yellow, and endure a long time. Small bushes flower freely. It is hardy in sandy loams. *Leguminosæ.*

CLARKIA.—These Californian plants of the Evening Primrose and Fuchsia Order are among the prettiest of hardy annuals, robust, of easy culture, and flower for a long time. There are two species from which the numerous varieties now in cultivation have been obtained. *C. elegans* grows 2 ft. high, erect, much branched, and bears long leafy racemes of flowers with undivided petals, varying from purple to pale red or a salmon colour. The principal varieties of this normally, but there is every variation between deep purple and pure white, and there are also several double-flowered forms. Many varieties are mentioned in seed lists, most of which are distinct from each other, and well worth

Chrysanthemum "Cottage Pink."

species have double flowers, and two—Purple King (deep purple) and Salmon Queen (salmon-pink)—have flowers produced freely on strong branching plants, and are very effective border flowers. The other species, *C. pulchella*, varies in height from about 1 ft. in the Tom Thumb sorts to 2 ft. It has magenta flowers growing where annuals are much grown.

CULTURE.—Their growth is much affected by the nature of the soil. Like all other hardy annuals, they may be sown either in autumn or spring, and by sowing in the beginning of September the seedlings gain strength before the winter, and flower well in early spring, but these autumn sowings are liable to accident, and should only be tried on warm soils. The first spring sowing should take place in the middle of March, when the plants would flower in July. Until about the middle of June other sowings may be made for flowering later. The best soil is ordinary garden mould, not too rich or dry.—G.

CLAYTONIA.—A small group of the Purslane Order, of which three species are pretty garden plants. *C. caroliniana* is a spreading dwarf species bearing in spring loose racemes of pretty rose flowers, and *C. virginica* (Spring Beauty) is a slender erect plant, with pink blossoms. Both are suitable for warm spots in the rock-garden in loamy soil, but *C. sibirica*, also a dwarf species with pink flowers, requires a damp peaty soil like an artificial bog.

CLEMATIS (*Virgin's Bower.*)—Beautiful climbing shrubs and herbs from northern and temperate regions and of the highest value for gardens. Among hardy climbers there is no group of plants that equals the Clematis in variety and number, or perhaps in beauty.

The Clematis vary in habit from herbaceous plants little more than 1 ft. high to woody climbers with stems 50 ft. or more in length. Most of the climbing species support themselves by means of the leaf-stalks, which curl round twigs or other slender objects near. The Clematis flower possesses no true petals, but in their place a coloured calyx consisting of usually four, but sometimes as many as eight sepals.

The Clematis like an open loamy soil, which should always be fairly rich, and in the case of the largest-flowered kinds even very rich in vegetable humus and fertilising material. All of them appear to succeed best in a chalky soil, and in gardens naturally devoid of chalk or lime it is well to supply it. An annual mulching with rotted manure given about November is of benefit, especially on poor soil. Such pruning as may be necessary for these wild types should be done in February. The stronger growers stand pruning well, and if they grow up their supports too high and form a thick heavy tangle at the top, they may safely be cut hard back. The weaker ones rarely need pruning at all. The Clematises may be used to cover walls, mounds, arbours, pergolas and fences, and in the open, where no other support is available, rough Oak branches may be used for them, either singly or several set together

to form a pyramid, while the more vigorous species will run over trees.

C. æthusifolia.—A graceful climber, with slender stems and branches. The flowers have not bright colour, but are gracefully borne and pendulous, from half an inch to three-quarters of an inch long, bell-shaped or tubular, the sepals yellowish white. Like most of the Clematis, this varies a good deal in shape of leaf, and one form has been considered distinct enough to receive the name of *latisecta.*

C. alpina (*Alpine Clematis*).—A very pretty plant flowering in spring. The flowers are nodding, the four large sepals being soft blue with a whitish margin, or sometimes almost entirely white. The

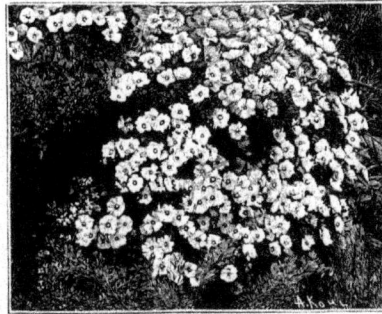

Cistus florentinus.

flower is 2 ins. or more across. Syn., *Atragene austriaca.*

C. apiifolia.—A vigorous climber with ternate leaves, growing 10 ft. high, flowering in August and September in panicles dull white. Japan and China. Closely allied to this is *C. brevicaudata.*

C. aromatica is closely allied to *C. Viticella*, and if it be a hybrid, as it is supposed to be, that species must be one of the parents. It is a slender plant, 6 or 7 ft. high. The solitary flowers are about 2 ins. in diameter, and of a rich purplish blue, and have a sweet, delicate, and slightly aromatic odour.

C. campaniflora (*Bell-flowered C.*)—This has rather small bell-shaped flowers each about 1 in. in diameter, with the pointed tips of the sepals recurved. Pale violet or almost white. The plant 10 to 15 ft. high. The flowers are very freely borne, and against the deep green, often finely-divided foliage they are very effective.

C. calycina (*Winter flowering C.*) (*C. balearica* of Richard).—A native of

Minorca and Corsica, evergreen with dark brown angled stems, and during the winter the foliage acquires a fine bronzy hue. The flower is about 2 in. across, yellowish white, stained inside with oblong, irregular, reddish-purple spots. December to April. In the London district it ought to have the shelter of a wall to flower well. From its near ally, the following species, it differs in its narrower and more divided foliage.

C. cirrhosa (*Evergreen C.*) (*C. balearica* of Persoon). This evergreen species has been much confused with. *C. calycina* *C. cirrhosa* however, if it comes from the Balearic Islands at all, is not confined to them, but is a native also of various

somewhat leathery and over an inch long. A larger-flowered variety is known as major, and various hybrids have been raised by crossing this and other species.

C. connata.—This species is found on the Himalayas. It is a climber with stout woody stems with leaflets 3 to 5 in. long, coarsely toothed, or sometimes more or less three-lobed. The bell-shaped flowers appear during autumn and are of a clear light yellow, pointed tips recurved.

C. crispa (*Frilled C.*)—This name applies to a number of plants alike in all essential characters, but differing in the shape of the leaves and in the size and

Cistus formosus.

parts of Spain, and is found also in Algiers and on the mountains of N. Africa. The flowers are dull white or cream coloured, downy outside, smooth within, and about 1½ in. in diameter. In South Europe it climbs over big trees, but it grows only some 8 or 10 ft. high in these colder latitudes.

C. coccinea (*Scarlet C.*)—A distinct and beautiful species. Its stems grow some 6 to 10 ft. high, and as a rule in this country die back to the ground in winter. It is a native of Texas, the flowers vary in colour from rosy carmine to scarlet ; they are swollen at the base, but narrow towards the top, where, however, the tips of the four sepals are recurved. These sepals are very thick and

colour of the flower. The leaf consists of three, five, or more leaflets, which vary in outline. The calyx is cylindrical or bell-shaped, and from 1 to 2 in. long, the upper part of each sepal spreading. The colour is purple margined with white, or in some forms pale lilac. The flowers are fragrant and appear in June, continuing up to autumn. Some of the forms are bright in colour and pretty, but others are amongst the least effective of the shrubby Clematis, the thick, heavy sepals being of a dull purple (N. America).

C. Douglasi (*Douglas's C.*)—A Rocky Mountain species discovered by David Douglas, and at present scarcely known in English gardens. The flower is bell-shaped, 1 inch long, the sepals being recurved at the tips and of an intense purple inside, paler without.

C. flammula(*Fragrant Virgin's Bower*). —A vigorous grower, its leaves are of a rich dark green and remain fresh till well into the winter. The flowers are small (half-inch to three-quarters of an inch across) and appear in late summer

creamy white and the tuft of stamens purple. There is a double-flowered variety and others with violet or blush-tinted flowers (Japan).

C. Fremonti.—This has herbaceous stems 1 to 2 ft. high, rarely branched, and carrying numerous leathery leaves, 3 or 4 in. long, without stalks ; the purple flowers

Cistus ladaniferus.

and autumn fragrant, creamy-white, the fruit white and feathery. This is a variable species, in the size and shape of the leaflets and in the flower panicles, some of which are large and with numerous blossoms, whilst in other forms the panicles are few-flowered and scarcely branched.

C. florida.—A distinct species, grows 9 to 12 ft. high, the flowers 2 to 4 in. across, flat when fully expanded, sepals of a

drooping with recurved tips. The tails of the fruits are downy when young rather than feathery (N. America).

C. fusca.—A sub-shrubby or nearly herbaceous species, with prostrate rather than climbing stems. When given support, however, it grows 6 to 8 ft. high. The bell-shaped flowers are covered with a short, very thick, brown wool, the sepals being a reddish brown colour. The fruit forms a thick globular head, 1 in. across, of plumose tails (N. Asia).

C. Hendersoni (*Henderson's Virgin's Bower*).—This is considered to be a hybrid between *C. Viticella* and *C. integrifolia*, and was raised in 1835 by Mr. Henderson, at Pine-apple Place, St. John's Wood. The plant grows to a height of 8 or 10 ft. The flowers, which have a faint sweet perfume, are over 2 in. across and of a deep bluish purple, appearing from June to September.

C. Heracleæfolia (*David's Virgin's Bower*).— A dwarf, sturdy plant under 2 ft. high, with large leaves and short-stalked corymbs of flowers of a Hyacinth-like shape and of a purplish blue colour. Much superior to it as a garden plant is the variety *Davidiana*, which often ranks as a species. Its stems are about 4 ft. long, but are rarely strong enough to stand erect without support. The largest leaflets often measure 6 in. in length by nearly as much in width, and are thus the largest of any of the cultivated Clematises. The bright lavender blue flowers are in dense heads, borne on long stalks in early autumn, but they also frequently appear in short, closely packed clusters right in the axils of the leaves. Each flower is three-quarters of an inch long, the points of the sepals reflexed and resembling a Hyacinth blossom (N. China).

C. integrifolia.—Herbaceous, 2 to 3 ft. high, its erect stems furnished with leaves 2 to 4 in. long and stalkless, or nearly so. The blue, drooping flowers are on the top of the stem and from the axils of the uppermost leaves from June to August. (Europe).

C. lanuginosa (*Great flowered Virgin's Bower*).—A noble Chinese species 5 or 6 ft. high, the leaves covered beneath with greyish wool, the flowers the largest of any of the wild kinds, 6 in. across and the sepals flat and overlapping and of a pale lavender colour. It is to this species more than to any other that the beauty of the garden hybrids of Clematis are due. Its flowers vary in colour from pure white to deep rich purple, and appear from July to October.

C. ligusticifolia.—The flowers of this (male and female ones of which are borne on separate plants) appear in panicles white, three-quarters of an inch across. The variety *californica* is distinguished by its smaller, tomentose leaves. It is one of many examples that occur in the North American flora, where a widely-spread species is found to be glabrous on the eastern side of the continent, but tomentose or even woolly on the drier

and hotter western side. This plant will climb to a height of 30 ft.

C. montana (*White Indian Virgin's Bower*).—This is one of the most beautiful of all the Clematis, and when covered with its white flowers during May, which bear a strong resemblance to a white Anemone, is one of the loveliest of all hardy climbers. It is quite hardy and vigorous and may frequently be seen covering walls to a great height.

C. ochroleuca.—A herbaceous species confined to the eastern side of North

Clematis lanuginosa alba growing through Azara.

America, whilst the other is purely western. Its stems are 1 to 2 ft. high, its leaves silky beneath, especially when young. The flowers are yellow outside, cream-coloured within.

C. orientalis (*Yellow Indian Virgin's Bower*).—A vigorous climber growing 12 to 30 ft. high, flowering abundantly in August and September, the four sepals being of a yellow colour, tinged with green, and having a sweet but not very strong fragrance. The fruit heads are handsome with the silky tail attached to each seed vessel (Mountains of India and N. Asia).

C. paniculata. (*Japanese Virgin's Bower*).—A vigorous climber, growing to a height of 30 ft. or more. The flowers have a hawthorn-like fragrance, the four sepals being of a rather dull white. It is hardy in Britain and flowers during September, but with nothing like the profusion that makes it so beautiful a climber in America. By planting it against a sunny wall its best qualities would perhaps be brought out.

C. patens.—Next to *C. lanuginosa*, this is perhaps the most important of the wild types of Clematis. It is a native of Japan (having been found on the isle of Nippon), and possibly of China also. It was introduced about sixty years ago by Siebold, who obtained it in the gardens near Yokohama, where it had, no doubt, been long in cultivation. The sepals are from six to eight in number, narrow in the form originally introduced, and of a delicate mauve colour, but the varieties subsequently obtained from it under cultivation have flowers much larger, the colours varying from white to deep violet and blue. Its value as one of the parent species of the garden Clematis is due not only to its beauty, but more especially to its flowering as early as May and June.

C. Pitcheri.—The flowers of this are pitcher-shaped, being broad and swollen at the base, narrow at the centre where the sepals press closely round the bunch of stamens, but have the tips expanded and recurved. They are 1 in. long and three-quarters of an in. wide at the swollen base, of a purplish blue outside, and in the typical form the recurved tips of the sepals are yellowish. The fruits are of a reddish purple colour (Colorado and Western America).

In the variety *lasiostylis* the sepals have but little of the yellow colour seen in the type, the recurved portion of the sepals being of a deep purplish blue. The fruits, too, are larger and of a richer red colour.

C. recta (*White Herbaceous Virgin's Bower*). — This is one of the best herbaceous species, its tufted stems growing about 3 ft. high and producing from June to August numerous white flowers sweetly scented, and each about 1 in. across. A handsome double-flowered variety, and in its own country the plant varies much (S. Europe).

C. Robertsiana (*Robert's Virgin's Bower*).—The nodding flowers of this are of a pale lemon-yellow, and are 3 to 5 ins. in diameter. The flowers have none of the petals or antherless staminodes of the Atragene group, but otherwise,

both in flower and foliage, the species bears a resemblance to the Alpine Clematis.

C. stans.—An herbaceous plant, growing 4 or 5 ft. high, with dark green leaves; the flowers are not borne in such dense heads as in L'Abbé David's Clematis, but often in a large terminal panicle,

Clematis Lady Caroline Nevill.

frequently also in clusters close in the leaf axils. In early autumn each flower is about three-quarters of an inch long, pale blue, and of the hyacinth-like form common to this group of Clematis (Japan).

C. verticillaris (*Atragene americana*).—A climber with woody stems 8 to 10 ft. high or more. The flowers bluish purple and from 2 to 3 ins. in diameter (N. America).

C. Viorna (*the Leather Flower*).—Although this is one of the oldest of the American Clematises in cultivation (having been introduced in 1730), it is not a common plant, being, indeed, one of the least attractive in the genus. It is not very vigorous in habit, growing 8 or 10 ft. high. The flower is pitcher shaped and very thick and leathery with sepals of a dull reddish purple colour appearing in summer (Eastern United States).

C. virginiana (*American Virgin's Bower*).—The common Virgin's Bower of the United States and Canada. The

Clematis Davidiana.

flowers are borne in flat panicles, the sepals thin, and dull white, and although hardy enough, is not in Britain so strong and woody a grower as our native Traveller's Joy.

C. Vitalba (*Traveller's Joy*).—There is no climber native to Britain that gives so near an approach to tropical luxuriance of vegetation as this. Even in winter when destitute of foliage its naked stems are ornamental. The numerous dull white flowers are each three-quarters of an inch or so across, with a faint odour resembling that of Almonds. It is, perhaps, most beautiful when covered with its white fruits, the seeds having long feathery tails.

C. Viticella (*Purple Virgin's Bower*).— A graceful climber, from 8 to 12 feet high ; its flowers in summer 1½ inches to 2 inches in diameter, the sepals blue, purple, or rosy purple, and the fruits have only short tails, which are devoid of the plumose covering so often seen in this genus. There are now numerous varieties of the species superior to it in size of flower, and offering also a variety of shades, some very pretty. —W. J. B.

Hybrid Clematis.—Among the best

of the many hybrids raised both abroad or in England are Alba magna, Ascotensis, Beauty of Worcester, Belle of Woking, Blue Gem, Countess of Lovelace, Countess of Onslow, Duchess of Albany, Duchess of Edinburgh, Duchess of York, Fair Rosamond, Fairy Queen, Gem, Gipsy Queen, Henryi, Jackmani, Jackmani superba, Jackmani alba, John Gould Veitch, Lady Bovill, Lady Caroline Neville, Lucie Lemoine, Mme. Grange, Mme. Edouard André, Mme. Van Houtte, Miss Bateman, Miss Crawshay, Mrs. Geo. Jackman, Mrs. Hope, Otto Froebel, Princess of Wales, Purpurea elegans, Rubella, Sir Garnet Wolseley, Star of India, Stella, The Queen, William Kennett. It has been usual in treating of these and other Clematis to throw them into groups, a misleading and useless plan from a garden point of view ; the best way is to regard the species each separately, as they differ so much in vigour and in their use : the hybrids also are better to look at as a class apart, fitted more for flower-garden use than some of the species. The hybrid kinds are all grafted, and this is no doubt the reason why they die off like flies, and why these fine plants, of which hundreds have been raised, are so rarely seen well grown in gardens. The stock used is C. Viticella, very different in its nature from the fine species from China and Japan, and though a vigorous growth is obtained at first an early death too often follows.

CLERODENDRON.—Tropical or subtropical trees or shrubs, only two species of which have any claim to hardiness, C. *trichotomum*, a Japanese plant, and C. *fœtidum*, a native of China, an old garden plant usually seen in greenhouses, but hardy enough for open-air culture in all southern and warm parts. In southern gardens, especially near the sea, it grows 5 ft. high and is handsome for the several weeks it is in bloom. The other species is less common, and is a freegrowing shrub, 6 ft. high or more, bearing large loose clusters of flowers, the corollas white, the calyces a

Clethra alnifolia.

deep brownish-red, blooming in September.

CLETHRA (*Sweet Pepper Bush*).— Shrubs and small trees of the Heath Order, the hardy species natives of North America. The Alder-leaved Clethra (*C. alnifolia*) in the wet copses of Virginia reaches a height of 10 ft. or more. With us it grows from 3 to 5 ft., makes a dense bush, bearing in summer white sweet-scented flowers in feathery spikes. *C. acuminata* has more pointed leaves, and it also has spikes of white scented flowers; it is quite a small tree in the woods of the Alleghanies. Both are valuable shrubs for moist peaty places.

CLIANTHUS (*Glory Pea*).—Brilliant plants seldom seen out-of-doors in the London district or home counties, but one

Clianthus puniceus.

kind is quite free as a wall plant in Irish and west-country gardens, and should be more frequently planted in sea-shore and warm places. It is *C. puniceus* a native of New Zealand, and as handsome a shrub when in bloom as one could wish to see, its splendid crimson blooms borne in large bunches during summer. Cuttings.

Clintonia. See DOWINGIA.

Cnicus benedictus. See CARBENIA.

COBÆA (*Cups and Saucers*).— In favourable localities in the southern and western counties *C. scandens*, a well-known greenhouse plant, thrives against an outside wall, and will cover a considerable space of trellis-work during summer. It should be planted in light rich soil, and if watered liberally during the growing season will soon cover a large space and flower freely. With some protection it will survive an ordinary winter.

CODONOPSIS.—Interesting and sometimes pretty plants of the Bellflower Order, easy to cultivate in light and warm soils, *C. ovata* being a fine bushy plant. They are suited for warm borders. Some

are annuals, but most are hardy perennial flowers from the mountains of India.

COLCHICUM (*Meadow Saffron*). — Hardy bulbs, some handsome in autumn. The individual flowers do not, as a rule, last long, but, as they come in succession, there is a long season of bloom. The flowers are often destroyed through being grown in bare beds of soil, where the splashing of the soil in heavy rains impairs their beauty. In the rock-garden among dwarf plants Colchicums thrive, and make a pretty show in autumn, when rock-gardens are often flowerless. They look better in grassy places or in the wild garden than in any formal bed or border. Their naked flowers want the relief and grace of Grass and foliage. There are about thirty kinds, though only about half of them are in cultivation, and among these the differences are often slight. Though there are so many names to be found in catalogues, the distinct kinds are few, and there is such a striking similarity among these that they may be conveniently classed in groups. The best known is

C. autumnale, commonly called the autumn Crocus. The flowers appear before the leaves, rosy purple, in clusters of about six, 2 or 3 in. above the surface, flowering from September to November. There are several varieties, the chief being the double purple, white and

Colchicum in Grass.

striped; rose-lilac; rose-lilac, striped with white; pale rose; and pure white.

C. Parkinsoni.—A distinct and beautiful

plant, readily distinguished from any of the foregoing by the peculiar chequered markings of its violet-purple flowers. Its flowers come in autumn and its leaves in spring. Similar kinds are *Bivonæ, variegatum, agrippinum, chionense, tessellatum,* all of which have the flowers chequered with dark purple on a white ground.

C. speciosum, from the Caucasus, is large and beautiful, and valuable for the garden in autumn, when its large rosy-purple flowers appear nearly 1 ft. above the ground. Like the rest of the Meadow Saffrons, this is as well suited for the rock-garden as the border, thriving in any soil; but to have it in perfection, choose a situation exposed to the sun, with sandy soil—in fact, a spot likely to dry up during summer.

COLEUS.—A few kinds of these pretty-leaved plants, of the Sage Order, succeed in the open air in summer, and, when used judiciously, give a fine effect. In some of the London parks

Colletia cruciata (*C. bictoniensis*).

they are arranged by themselves in large masses, generally of one kind only. Though there is a host of varieties, few succeed in the open air. Mr. Wildsmith, of Heckfield, wrote : " We have tried at least a score of varieties for bedding-out, with the result that the first kind recommended (*Verschaffelti*) is still the only one that succeeds well. The culture of all the varieties is of the simplest nature ; cuttings strike freely in any sandy soil, in a moist heat of 70°.

COLLETIA.—Curious shrubs of the Buckthorn Order from Chili, some species

of which are hardy enough for the open air in all but the coldest parts of the country, in free sandy soils. They have spiny branches with a few minute leaves. *C. cruciata* is the commonest ; its stems are armed with stout flattened spines, its flowers white and small, making a bush about 4 ft. high. *C. spinosa* has its spines round or awl-shaped, the white flowers, though small, are very numerous in summer. Under favourable conditions it makes a formidable hedge in the southern counties, where it flourishes.

COLLINSIA.—Pretty N. American annuals. If sown in autumn, they will, on some soils, survive the winter, and flower much better than spring-sown plants, the flowers coming early. They are of the easiest culture. Plants from seed sown in spring flower in twelve weeks. There are from nine to a dozen species or varieties in cultivation and enumerated in the catalogues, the only one requiring special treatment being *C. verna,* which must be sown in autumn. The prettiest use for these plants is for the spring-garden in beds, or occasionally as a broad edging.

COLLOMIA.—*C. coccinea* is a bright annual, 1 ft. to 18 in. high, flowering in summer and autumn. Sow it in April in open ground ; or else in a frame in autumn and protect it during winter, if good plants are desired either for pots or planting out. On warm soils it grows best and sows itself every year, surviving the winter, and growing much stronger.

COLUTEA(*Bladder Senna*).—The Bladder Sennas cannot be called choice flowering shrubs, but they are very useful for poor hungry soils, particularly for dry sunny banks where few other plants can exist. Like the Gorse and a few other shrubs of the Pea family, they delight in a dry sandy soil, and when in flower, which is during several weeks in late summer and in autumn, they have a pretty appearance, their foliage being light and elegant. They have numerous names, but there are only one or two distinct kinds. The commonest is *C. arborescens,* which, under favourable conditions, grows 6 or 8 ft. high, has large flowers, varying in different varieties from

Colutea arborescens.

yellow to a deep reddish-yellow. *C. cruenta,*
C. halepica and *C. media*—all natives of
Europe—are smaller, and have bright
yellow flowers ; but all have much the
same aspect.

COMMELINA *(Blue Spiderwort)*.—A
charming old garden plant with flowers
of a fine blue, *C. Cœlestis* delights in
light, warm soils. The roots are fleshy,
and in some districts it is well to cover
them with coal-ashes on the approach of
winter. In cold wet districts the roots
may be lifted, and stored in dry leaf-mould.
On some warm or stony soils, and in
districts near the sea where light soil
prevails, it grows like a weed. It is so
fine in colour that a group or small bed is
always welcome. There is a white form
(Mexico).

Comptonia. See MYRICA.

CONANDRON.—*C. ramondioides* is a
small Japanese plant allied to Ramondia,
having thick wrinkled leaves, in flat tufts,
from which arise erect flower-stems some
6 in. high, bearing numerous lilac-purple
and white blossoms. Though said to be
quite hardy, it requires a sheltered position, such as is afforded by a snug nook in
the rock-garden. Plants placed between
blocks of stone thrive if there is a good
depth of soil in the chink and the soil is
moist.

CONVALLARIA *(Lily-of-the-Valley)*.
—*C. majalis* is a beautiful plant found in
mountain copses sheltered by shrubs,
and in the forest, and the best situation
for it is partial shelter and shade from
wall, fence, or trees. It is well to have a
plantation of Lilies-of-the-Valley upon a
south aspect, for the sake of earliness and
of producing them in succession, for by
this means flowers may be gathered a
fortnight or three weeks earlier than
otherwise. The best places are those
under shady walls. Give liberal surface-
dressings of rotten manure, and an
abundant supply of moisture throughout
active growth. Frost is destructive to
the blooms, which appear with the leaves.
A few Spruce or other evergreen branches
placed sparsely over the beds are a
protection, and encourage growth. Preference should be given to a soft loamy
soil well enriched with rotten manure
and with plenty of sand, though fine Lilies
may be grown in rather heavy loam.
Whatever the soil, it should be moderately firm before planting.

The best time to plant is early in
autumn, immediately after the foliage
decays, selecting the crowns singly and
dividing them. For beds likely to remain
undisturbed for several years, the crowns

may be planted 2 or even 3 in. apart, as they
do not become crowded so soon as to require thinning out. Cover the surface after
planting with 1 or 2 in. of rotten manure,
thorough maturity being only insured by
repeated applications of water—weak
manure-water being the most effective.
Treated thus, with annual surface-
dressings of manure, the beds will keep
in good condition for years, and bear fine
blossoms in abundance. When the plants
become crowded with shoots they should
be thinned out, or, better still, lifted and
replanted. It is now largely forced into
flower early, the roots being usually im-

(Lily-of-the-Valley).

ported from the Continent, where they are
grown and prepared for the purpose. It may
be naturalised, too, on any place sufficiently
moist and shaded, and soon spreads into
broad masses. There is a variety with
gold-striped foliage, and another with
double flowers, but this is not pretty. The
finest form is called Fortin's, which is
more robust than the common kind,
having larger flowers.

CONVOLVULUS *(Bindweed)*.—Handsome climbing herbs ; very hardy, and
where properly used effective.

C. dahuricus *(Dahurian C.)*—A showy
twining perennial, bearing in summer
rosy-purple flowers. Excellent for covering bowers, railings, stumps, cottages,
&c., and also for naturalisation in hedge-

rows and copses. It grows in almost any soil, and, like its relation the Bindweed, is readily increased by division of the roots, which creep. Syn. *Calystegia* (Caucasus).

C. major. See IPOMŒA.

C. mauritanicus (*Blue Rock Bindweed*).—A beautiful prostrate twining plant from N. Africa, with slender stems. The flowers blue, 1 in. across, with a white throat and yellow anthers. The rock-garden, and raised borders ; supposed to require sunny positions, in sandy, well-drained soil, but I find it fine on stiffish cool soils, and even hardy on them. Division or cuttings.

C. pubescens fl.-pl. (*Double Bindweed*). —Handsome and useful for clothing trellises, stumps, porches, and rustic-work. It grows rapidly to the height of 6 ft. The flowers are large, double, and of a pale rose, appearing in June and onward. The Double Bindweed likes a light rich soil and a warm aspect. It may be grown in large pots, tubs, or boxes, and prettily used for forming small bowers on balconies, to hide low fences, or to climb round posts. Division. (China).

C. Soldanella (*Sea Bindweed*).—A distinct trailing species with fleshy leaves ; flowering in summer, pale-red, and handsome in the rock-garden, if planted so that its shoots droop over stones. Also suited for borders, in ordinary soil. Division. Europe and Britain.

C. sylvaticus.—No plant forms more beautiful and delicate curtains of foliage and flowers than this, which grows vigorously in any soil. The wild garden is the place where it is most at home, and where its vigorous roots may ramble without doing injury to other plants. Among bushes or hedges, over railings, or on rough banks, it is charming, and takes care of itself. The rosy pink form *incarnata* is supposed to be a native of N. America, but is naturalised in some parts of Ireland. Native of S. Europe and N. Africa.

C. tricolor.—One of the most beautiful of hardy annuals, too well known to need description. There are numerous varieties, varying more or less in colour of flowers or in habit of growth. The flowers of the type are blue, yellow, and white, but there are varieties entirely white, and almost every variety is worth growing. The plant being perfectly hardy, may be sown in the open ground in September for flowering in spring, or sown in February, in a heated frame, for transplanting in May for midsummer flowering, and in the open ground from April to the end of May for flowering in late summer and autumn. Syn., C. minor.

COPTIS (*Gold Thread*).—*C. trifolia* is a little evergreen bog plant 3 or 4 in. high with trifoliate shining leaves, deriving its common name from its long bright yellow roots. Northern parts of America, Asia, and Europe, flowering in summer ; white. Easily grown in moist peat or very moist sandy soil. Division.

CORDYLINE (*Club Palm*).—Although these fine-leaved shrub plants are common in greenhouses, it is only in the mildest parts of England and Ireland that they can be grown well in the open air. In the Isle of Wight, and from thence along the shores of Devonshire and Cornwall to the Scilly Isles, they succeed well, forming a fine feature even in cottage

Convolvulus sylvaticus.

gardens, whilst in some larger gardens whole avenues are planted. But, in far less favoured places, it is often seen thriving for years in the open air, though it is not worth trying in cold, high, and inland places, especially on clay soils.

The true *C. indivisa* is distinct, and a large number of plants have at different times been in cultivation ; owing, however, to their being treated as tropical plants, they usually proved short-lived. One of the finest specimens in the country is in Mr. Rashleigh's garden at Menabilly, Cornwall. *C. i. lineata* is a fine variety, with leaves much broader than those of the type, and sometimes 4 in. across, coloured with reddish pink at the sheathing base. There are many forms. At Knockmaroon Lodge, near Dublin, a plant, 16 ft. high, with a stem some 6 in. in diameter, annually flowered and bore an abundance of seeds, from which seedlings.

were easily raised in a cold frame. In the Scilly Islands the plant becomes a great tree, in the warmth and moisture from the Gulf Stream. The fact that in Dublin young plants annually flower and ripen seed is sufficient proof of its hardiness and of its prospects of success in many districts. It is readily increased also from pieces of the stem and offsets. If a plant is cut down close to the ground, there soon spring up a number of young shoots, which can be taken off as cuttings, and which strike soil. *C. tenuifolia* is a pretty plant, with elegant feathery foliage and rich golden-yellow blossoms from summer till autumn. *C. verticillata* is similar to it, and is also a showy border plant. Neither of these is so robust as the taller kinds, and they therefore require more select spots, such as the front rows of a mixed border in the rougher parts of the rock-garden. The annuals are among the showiest summer flowers; being hardy, they make a fine display in

Cordyline australis, Bosachan, Cornwall.

with freedom. Recent severe winters may have hurt it in many places; but after so many years' success no one in a likely district will give up its culture.—B.

COREOPSIS (*Tickseed*).—Showy North American herbs, perennial or annual; the annuals being pretty summer flowers, and the perennials valuable late-blooming plants. One of the best of the perennials is *C. auriculata*, about 2 ft. high, with a spreading growth, and bearing, in autumn, abundance of rich yellow blossoms on slender stalks. Nearly allied and similar to it is *C. lanceolata*, an equally showy plant, also delighting in a rich damp spring from seeds sown in September; while an almost continuous bloom may be had from July to October by sowing successively from early March till the middle of June in ordinary garden soil—that of a moist description being preferable for the spring sowings. The following are the principal annuals: *C. aristosa*, 2 to 3 ft. high, with large golden-yellow blossoms; *C. Atkinsoniana*, 1 to 3 ft. high, flowers orange-yellow spotted with brown in centre; *C. coronata*, orange-yellow, with a circle of brownish crimson in centre; *C. Drummondi*, 1 to 1½ ft. high, golden-yellow; *C. tinctoria*, 1 to 3 ft. high, flowers crimson-brown tipped with orange-yellow.

C. grandiflora is a very fine showy plant. It fully deserves its name, as its flowers are very much larger than those of any other Coreopsis grown in gardens.

Even if we eventually come to treat it entirely as an annual, this will not detract from its value, for it is a graceful flower and worthy of special care. Raising a batch of seedlings once a year is easily done. The seed may be sown at any time in spring, and strong plants be ready to put out into their flowering quarters in autumn. Its handsome flowers are borne on strong stems 12 to 18 in. in length. In the garden the flowers are brilliant and long-lasting, and they are also valuable for cutting.—A. H.

CORIS (*Montpelier C.*)—*C. monspeliensis* is a pretty dwarf plant of the Primrose order, about 6 in. high, usually biennial in our gardens, thriving on dry sunny parts of the rock-garden, in sandy soil, and among dwarf plants. South of France. Seed.

CORNUS (*Dogwood : Cornel*).—Most of the Dogwoods known in cultivation are shrubs or small trees. Many of the Cornels are pretty shrubs, and useful in the park and pleasure-garden, or along watercourses, and in wild unkept spots, the shoots of some giving fine colour in winter ; and there are two very dwarf species pretty for the bog.

C. alba, the white-fruited Dogwood, is a native of Asia, growing to a height of from 5 to 10 ft., with slender branches clothed with bright-red bark, giving a charming effect all through the year, either in a mass or as a specimen plant on a lawn or in the shrubbery. The flowers, white or cream-coloured, are in crowded cymes, followed by white fruits. The variety *Spathi* is one of the finest —in our climate, at any rate—of shrubs with coloured leaves. In

Cornus alba.

spring the leaves are bronzy, in summer deeply and irregularly margined with gold. The habit of the plant is vigorous, the variegation constant, and the foliage does not scorch in bright sunlight, as is the case

in not a few plants with golden variegated leaves.

C. alba sibirica is dwarfer in habit than typical C. alba, but has still brighter-coloured bark. Nothing is definitely known of the origin of this charming shrub. Apparently the first mention of it is in Loddiges' catalogue for 1836. There is a form of this variety with variegated leaves, but it is not so desirable as the type.

C. canadensis (the dwarf Cornel or Bunchberry) is a pretty little herbaceous plant with creeping underground rhizomes and upright simple stems from 4 to 8 in. high, the leaves in a whorl of four or six near the summit of the stems ; the true flowers are minute, but the four rather large white or cream-coloured bracts conspicuous. The berries are red and show well above the short stems : in taste they are sweet and palatable. This species grows in Japan and Manchuria, and across the continent of N. America, and is one of the prettiest plants for the bog garden or the cool parts of the rock-garden.

C. capitata (*Strawberry-tree*).—This plant is more widely known under the name of *Benthamia fragifera*. It is a sub-evergreen tree, a native of N. India and China. Unfortunately, it is not hardy in this country, except in Devon and Cornwall, where some remarkably fine specimens exist. In the gardens of Mr. R. G. Lake, Trevarrick, St. Austell, some trees are about 40 ft. high, and the trunk of one is 5 ft. in diameter at 5 ft. from the ground ; these are believed to be the largest in this country. There are numbers of fine specimens at Trelissick, and also in the gardens of Mr. J. Rashleigh. The large bracts, white tinged with pink or rose, make this one of the most beautiful trees when in flower, and the large clear red fleshy fruits, somewhat resembling a Strawberry in appearance, make it equally attractive when in fruit.

C. circinata.—This is conspicuous by reason of its large round leaves, which are 4 or 5 in. long and 3 in. or more wide, and its clusters of bright-blue fruits, each being about the size of a Pea. It is 3 ft. or more—rarely reaching 10 ft.—in height, and has rather rigid erect stems covered with warted bark, which is at first pale green, and later becomes light brown or purple. The flowers are small, yellowish white in colour. A native of the Eastern United States.

C. florida (the *Flowering Dogwood*) is very showy in flower, scarcely less so in fruit, and very beautiful in autumn when the leaves change colour before falling. Unfortunately, we do not obtain sufficient summer heat to thoroughly ripen the wood, and so the flowering of this species in Britain is a rare occurrence, although it was one of the earliest amongst North American shrubs to find its way to British gardens.

C. Kousa is a native of Japan, and a new species, quite hardy, but needs to be thoroughly well established and several years old before it really shows to advantage. The white flowers appear in May and June. Syn. *Benthamia japonica.*

C. Mas (*Cornelian Cherry* or *Jew's Cherry*).—Although the individual flowers of this species are small, they are borne so freely by old trees that, perhaps with the exception of the Witch Hazels, there are no large shrubs flowering in February or March which can vie with it, the clusters of bright-yellow flowers being very conspicuous on the leafless twigs. Old trees fruit freely, and bear fruit half an inch long or more, bright red and individually as handsome as a Cherry. On the Continent in many places selected varieties are grown for the sake of the fruit, which is excellent for preserving. Amongst the forms are some with yellow, bright blood-red, and violet-coloured fruits, and another with fruit much larger than that of the wild plant. The Cornelian Cherry is a native of Central and Southern Europe, and sometimes attains 20 ft. in height. There are many fine-leaved varieties ; the best are *C. Mas variegata*, a pretty shrub with white variegated leaves, and *C. Mas elegantissima*, with gold and green leaves often suffused with red.

C. Nuttalli is the western representative of the eastern *C. florida*, and is even a more beautiful tree, in its native habitats 50 or 60 ft. high. Generally it has six large, broad white bracts 2 in. or 3 in. long, so that the so-called flower measures 4 in. or 6 in. across. It is one of the most beautiful trees in the forests in many parts of California and Oregon, and has been recently introduced to European gardens, and no difficulty is experienced in its cultivation.

C. stolonifera (*Red Osier Dogwood*) is widely distributed throughout the Northern United States. It spreads and multiplies freely by prostrate or subterranean shoots, and grows 6 or 8 ft. high ; the leaves light green above and paler beneath ; fruit varying from white to lead colour. In winter the growths, especially those of the previous season, are of a bright red-purple colour. In its native habitats it affects wet places, but in Britain I have seen it do well in dry ground.

C. suecica is a native of Northern and Arctic Europe, Asia, and America, in Britain occurring on high moorlands from Yorkshire northwards, and ascends to 3000 ft. It is a charming little plant, flowering in July and August, with conspicuous, rather large white bracts, followed by red drupes. It should be grown in light soil or in peat in partial shade in the bog garden.—N.

CORONILLA. — Flowering shrubs of the Pea family, consisting chiefly of shrubs, but containing at least two really good herbaceous plants, which are valuable for the rock-garden and the mixed border. They are *C. iberica* and *C. varia.*

C. Emerus (*Scorpion Senna*).—An elegant loose bush, 3 to 6 ft. high, with small pinnate leaves, which, in mild seasons, remain green through the winter. The flowers are reddish when first expanded, but become quite yellow. It blooms freely in early summer, and flowers again in autumn. This is the only bushy Coronilla that can be well grown in the open air generally, but in mild districts *C. glauca*, a beautiful shrub with glaucous foliage and yellow flowers, usually grown in greenhouses, may be grown out-of-doors. S. Europe.

Coronilla.

C. iberica is about 1 ft. high, and has a dense tuft of slender stems that trail on the ground or fall gracefully over the ledge of a rock. It makes a pretty show in early summer with its bright-yellow blossoms, resting on deep-green foliage. Its place is the rock-garden, where it delights to send its roots down the side of a big stone, to plenty of good soil, not less than 18 in. deep. It also does well on the margins of borders, but not so well as on a bank or in the rock-garden. Cuttings, inserted in early spring. Asia Minor.

C. varia. — A handsome plant, with pretty rose-coloured flowers ; found in stony places and on many railway banks in France and Northern Italy, forming low dense tufts, sheeted with rosy pink, their beauty marking them among the weeds. Seeds.

CORYDALIS (*Fumitory*).—A numerous family, of the Poppy order, not many of the species worth cultivation, though some are important.

C. bulbosa (*Bulbous Fumitory*).—A compact tuberous-rooted kind, 4 in. to 6 or 7 in. high, with dull purplish flowers in April, and a solid bulbous root, quite hardy, and of easy culture in almost any soil. A pretty little plant for borders, for naturalising in open spots in woods, and also for the spring garden. It is naturalised in several parts of England, but its home is in the warmer parts of Europe. Syns., *C. solida* and *Fumaria solida*.

C. Ledebouriana (*Ledebour's Fumitory*).—Distinct on account of its peculiar glaucous leaves, arranged in a whorl about half-way up the stem, 9 to 12 in. high. Flowers are a deep vinous purple, with pinkish spurs. It is early and hardy. Siberia.

C. lutea (*Yellow Fumitory*).—This well-known plant has graceful masses of delicate pale-green leaves dotted with spurred yellow flowers. It is pretty in borders, and grows to perfection on walls, and the tufts, when emerging from some chink in a fortress wall where rain never falls upon them, are often as full of flower as when planted in fertile soil. A naturalised plant in England. Seeds.

C. nobilis (*Noble Fumitory*).—A distinct and handsome plant, 10 in. or 1 ft. high; the flower-stems are stout and leafy to the top, and in summer bear a massive head of rich golden-yellow flowers with a small reddish-chocolate protuberance in the centre of each. It is easy of culture in light borders, but is rather slow of increase. Division. Siberia.

CORYLOPSIS. — A small and little-known group of hardy shrubs, allied to the Witch Hazel (Hamamelis), from China, Japan, and N. India. They are thin and dwarf, have ribbed leaves resembling the Hazel, and bear flowers in drooping racemes. The oldest and best known is the Japanese *C. spicata*, 3 or 4 ft. high, with cowslip-coloured and cowslip-scented flowers, in spikes produced before the leaves in spring, like those of the Witch Hazel. As these are early spring-flowering shrubs, they should be planted in spots sheltered from cold winds.

CORYLUS (*Hazel-nut*). — A small group of European and Asiatic trees, represented in our country by the Hazel, *C. avellana*, which is precious in its nut-bearing forms for our gardens. There are varieties, including a weeping one, *pendula*, and cut-leaved and nettle-leaved forms. Other species worth growing are *C. americana, heterophylla, mandshurica*, and *maxima*, with its very fine variety *atropurpurea*, and other forms, among them the varieties of cobs and filbert nuts grown for their fruits. It is a very pleasant way to plant a group of the best fruiting Hazel in the pleasure ground, or to form what is called a Hazel walk. This used to be done in old times, and where there

is sufficient room is often worth doing, for the sake of the fruit as well as the associations of the trees.

COSMOS. — Mexican plants of the Composite family. One species, *C. bipinnatus*, is a handsome annual, 3 ft. to 5 ft. high, having finely divided feathery foliage, and large Dahlia-like bright-red-purple blossoms, with yellow centres. It requires to be treated as a tender annual, sowing the seeds in February or March in a heated frame, and the seedlings transplanted in May in good, rich, moist soil with a warm exposure. It flowers from August to October is good for grouping with bold and graceful annuals, and

Corylus avellana.

better than many more popular ones. *C. atropurpurea*, called the " Black Dahlia," is a handsome plant with nearly black Dahlia-like flowers and does well in ordinary soil.

COTONEASTER (*Rockspray*).—Valuable rosaceous rock-shrubs and low trees of much variety. Some of the rock-trailing kinds are common, but the bright-berried low trees from the mountains of India are little used. These might give good effects if grouped here and there on rough banks, and they are very hardy and easy to grow. The trailing kinds are excellent rock and wall plants of very easy culture and propagation.

C. buxifolia.—A free-growing bush that at times attains the height of 6 ft., forming a rather wide-spreading bush, the branches clothed with deep-green box-like leaves ; the crimson berries, nestling in profusion among the leaves, are pretty in autumn.

C. frigida.—A low tree reaching 20 ft. or more. During mild winters some of the leaves will be retained throughout the year, while if the weather is very sharp it will become quite bare, the showy fruits being of a bright crimson. If untouched by birds, the berries retain their beauty a long time ; but, if the weather be severe, they soon disappear. Mountains of India. The berries of this Cotoneaster are when ripe of an orange-scarlet tint, and the long shoots are in many cases crowded with them for some distance. It is useful for grouping here and there, its main value, however, being from the beauty of its berries. Himalayas.

C. horizontalis (*Plumed C.*).—In this the branches are frond-like and almost horizontal, while the small leaves are regularly disposed along the thick sturdy branches. A charm of this species is the manner in which the leaves die off in the autumn : frequently the leaves will be of a glowing red colour, with the exception of those on the tips of the shoots. The berries are very showy, bright vermilion, and the flowers large and pretty. China.

C. microphylla (*Wall C.*).—An evergreen clothed with tiny deep-green leaves, in spring crowded with whitish blossoms, the berries crimson, and, if untouched, remaining on the plants for a long time. There are some well-marked varieties of *C. microphylla*, one of which—*thymifolia* —is smaller in all its parts, while *congesta* is even more of a procumbent habit. *C. microphylla* is useful for sloping banks or like positions, while it will cover a wall with such a dense mass that nothing else can be seen. Again, in the larger parts of the rock-garden a place may be found for it ; and its variety, *congesta*, is more at home when draping a large stone than in any other way. On the lawn the spreading shoots dispose themselves in a very pretty way when planted as a small group. Himalayas.

C. rotundifolia is like the preceding, but with thicker branches and rounder leaves. The berries are of a brighter tint. Both these species may, where a group of the larger Cotoneasters is planted, be used for the outskirts of the clump.

CRAMBE. — One of the finest of hardy and large-leaved herbaceous plants, as easily grown as the common Seakale, and in rich ground having many stout leaves and dense sprays of small white flowers. C. cordifolia may be planted wherever a bold type of vegetation is desired. C. juncea, a dwarf kind, has white flowers and much-branched stems, the ramifications of which are elegant, but it is not so valuable as C. cordifolia.

CRATÆGUS (*Thorns*). — Beautiful hardy flowering trees, of which some of the most beautiful kinds are seldom seen outside botanical gardens : many are charming for their flowers, others for their pretty fruits, while in a few the habit is picturesque. Perhaps the most beautiful of all is C. Oxyacantha, the Hawthorn or Whitethorn, and its varieties have every

gradation of tint from deep crimson, through pinks, to the snowy whiteness of the double sort. Paul's Double Scarlet, the double pink, double white, the single scarlet (Punicea), rose (Carminata or Rosea), and various others are precious for the garden. Some varieties, like the graceful Pendula, are remarkable for their habit, others have distinct foliage, and a few differ as regards fruit, there being white and yellow-berried varieties.

Other species deserving of a place in gardens are many. A selection of the best includes : The Cockspur Thorn (C. Crus-galli), from North America, usually about 10 ft. high, is remarkable for peculiar growth, especially the variety pyracanthi-folia. In this the branches spread out like a table, and the older the tree becomes the more pronounced the table-like growth. Other distinct sorts of the Cock-

Cratægus parvifolia.

spur Thorn are nana, linearis, ovalifolia, and prunifolia. The Scarlet-fruited Thorn, also North American, is beautiful both when covered with white bloom in early summer or with scarlet fruits in autumn. The Tansy-leaved Thorn (C. tanaceti-folia) is distinct in foliage, with cut leaves of a whitish hue, and it is one of the latest Thorns to flower. C. Azarolus, Aronia, and orientalis are all natives of the Levant, and they are so beautiful in autumn, with fine-coloured fruits as big as Hazel nuts, that they deserve a place. One specimen of any of these on a lawn would be sufficient in a small garden, as they are spreading, and in good soils 15 or 20 ft. high. The Washington Thorn (C. cordata) flowers when all the others are past ; hence its value. C. glandulosa, also known as C. flava, has yellow fruits. C. Douglasi has dark-purple haws, and C. melanocarpa and C. nigra have black haws. The Pyracantha (C. Pyracantha), so common as a wall climber, is a favourite because of its orange-scarlet berries and evergreen foliage. It is suitable for planting in the open, and some beautiful effects may be made by making its spreading and trailing growth serve as a margin to groups of taller Thorns, or other small trees. The variety Lælandi fruits more freely than the common Pyracantha when planted as a bush, and another variety, Pausiflora, is dwarfer and closer in habit, and, in France, where these shrubs are much grown, is found to be the hardiest.

CREPIS (*Hawk's-beard*). — Of this genus of Compositæ few, save B. rubra, the Red Hawk's-beard, are worthy of culture. It is a hardy Italian annual, bearing pretty pink flowers about the size and form of the Dandelion, and should be sown in spring or autumn like other hardy annuals in any ordinary garden soil. It flowers from June to September, and is suitable for borders or beds of annual flowers. There is also a variety with white flowers. C. aurea is a perennial, 6 to 12 in. high, with small orange blossoms, but seldom more than one to each slender stem. C. incisa is a good species for border, owing to its compact habit and large showy light-purple flowers, as is also indica, a dwarf species, free-flowering and pretty. Division and seed.

CRINUM.—A few South African species of these are hardy, and very beautiful. One of the best-known and the hardiest is C. capense, a handsome bulbous plant, 2 to 3 ft. high, flowering late in summer, the large funnel-shaped pink blossoms in umbels of ten or fifteen blooms on a stout stem. There are several varieties— album, pure white; riparium, deep purple; fortuitum, white; and striatum, striped pink and white; and fine hybrids have also been raised—all good in borders or small beds, with groups of hardy plants, especially those that flower in late summer and early autumn; or for grouping and massing near the margin of water. Few plants repay better for a sheltered and warm position, and deep rich soil, with abundance of water in summer, and in very cold situations a little pile of leaves may be placed over the roots in winter; by planting the top of the bulbs 6 in. deep there need be no fear of the weather. Division and seed.

C. campanulatum is also hardy, but as it scarcely ever flowers it is not worth growing in the open. C. Moorei and ornatum are in warm districts hardy, and certain hybrids of recent origin may prove hardy.

CROCUS.— Of a genus of nearly seventy species, it is surprising that only three or four are generally used for garden decoration; and these—C. aureus and C. vernus and their varieties, and perhaps one or two other species—have been in cultivation at least three hundred years. Crocuses flower at a time when every flower is of value; and we do not doubt that ere long species recently introduced will add largely to our means of garden decoration during the dull months from late autumn to early spring.

CULTURAL DIRECTIONS seem almost superfluous; but there are a few points to which it may be convenient to refer. The genus must be viewed as in succession, from the beginning of August till April; but of these only the earlier autumnal, or the distinctly vernal, species can be relied upon for open-air decoration. Although all are hardy, those that flower in November, December, and January are

Crinum Moorei album.

so liable to injury by frost and rain that they are practically worthless.

Crocuses are easily multiplied by seed, which should be sown in July as soon as ripe, though germination will not take place till the natural growing period of the species. Seedlings take from two to three years to arrive at maturity, and should be left for the first two years undisturbed in the seed-bed, and then taken up and replanted. Holland, with its rich light alluvial soil, and Lincolnshire, with its "Trent warp," have for many generations been the sources from which the English market has been supplied with the varieties of the three or four species grown in English gardens. The last five or six years have put us in possession of nearly the whole of the known species, and we must commend them to the Dutch and Lincolnshire bulb-growers.

For the less robust and less floriferous

species a brick pit is necessary The bottom of this should be well below the level of the ground, and it should be filled up with about 1 ft in depth of fine river silt or sandy loam, the surface of which should be a little below the level of the adjacent ground Proper drainage is essential, but Crocuses delight in a uniformly moist subsoil during their period of growth It is convenient to separate the different species by strips of slate or tiles, buried below the surface, the corms being planted about 3 in deep. A mulching of rotted Cocoa-nut fibre or finely sifted peat keeps the surface moist, and prevents the loam from clogging or caking on the surface At the time of the maturity of the foliage, generally about the end of May, water should be withheld and the bed covered up and allowed to get quite dry till the end of July, when a copious watering may be given, or the pit may be exposed to rain

Of the earlier autumnal species suitable for the open border the following may be enumerated for successional flowering —

C Scharojani, orange , early in August
  ,, vallicola, straw-coloured , late in August and early in September
  ,, nudiflorus, blue , September
  ,, pulchellus, lilac ; Sept. and Oct
  ,, speciosus, blue , Sept and Oct
  ,, iridiflorus, blue , Sept and Oct
  ,, Salzmanni ⎫ lilac or blue ; October
  ,, Clusi   ⎭ and November
  ,, cancellatus ⎫
  ,, Cambessidesi ⎬in the early autumn
  ,, hadriaticus ⎭

These are succeeded by a long series of late autumnal, winter, and early vernal species, which are grown to best advantage in a brick pit

Of the vernal species suitable for the border, the earliest is C Imperati, flowering in February, followed by

C. susianus, or Cloth of Gold, in February
  biflorus
  ,, etruscus
  ,, suaveolens
  ,, versicolor
  ,, vernus
  ,, Tommasinianus   Flowering from
  ,, dalmaticus   the end
  ,, banaticus   of February to
  ,, Sieberi and var versicolor   the first
  ,, chrysanthus   week in
  ,, aureus   April
  ,, sulphureus
  ,, vars pallidus and striatus
  ,, stellaris
  ,, Olivieri
  ,, minimus

Of the Crocuses recently introduced, many vernal species will probably be suitable for the spring garden, but, as they are rare and scarcely procurable, we give those more generally known and easy to obtain

C. alatavicus —The flowers of this new Asiatic species are white, yellow towards the throat, the outer surface of the outer segments being freckled with rich purple It is a free-flowering species, but from its early-flowering time, January and February, it can only be grown to advantage under a cold frame A white variety without external purple freckling is not uncommon. The leaves are produced at the flowering time in early spring

C. aureus.—A handsome plant from the Banat, Transylvania, European Turkey, Greece, and Western Bithynia, generally at low elevations, flowering in February It was one of the first introduced to cultivation, and is the parent of our yellow garden or Dutch yellow Crocus, and of a number of old varieties—lacteus, sulphureus, pallidus, striatus, &c , the history of which is unknown , they are not found wild, and are sterile The wild plant varies considerably, from unstriped orange to varieties striped with gray lines, like those in the Dutch yellow Crocus The stigmata are short, unbranched, pale yellow, and much shorter than the anthers , in the Transylvanian plant the stigmata are occasionally orange The anthers are wedge-shaped, tapering towards the point, and notably divergent The unstriped form readily produces seed when in cultivation, but the striped Dutch yellow is sterile, though effete capsules are occasionally formed C Olivieri resembles C aureus but is smaller

C. banaticus —Common in the Banat, Hungary, and Transylvania, where it takes the place of C vernus, to which it is allied It is highly ornamental , the flowers are a deep rich purple, occasionally varied with white, with a darker purple blotch near the end of the segments The throat is glabrous, which easily distinguishes it from C. vernus It is cultivated in several Continental and English gardens under the name of C. veluchensis—a distinct species Flowers in February and March

C. biflorus.—-The Scotch, or Cloth of Silver, Crocus is a large variety of the typical form, and is abundant throughout a large portion of Italy. The segments vary from white to a pale lavender, the outer surface of the outer segments being distinctly feathered with purple markings In var estriatus, from Florence, the flowers are a uniform pale lavender,

Crocus etruscus

Crocus biflorus pusillus

Crocus balansae

Crocus leucorhynchus

Crocus reticulatus

orange towards the base In var Weldeni, from Trieste and Dalmatia, the outer segments are externally freckled with bright purple In C nubigenus, a very small variety from Asia Minor, the outer segments are suffused and freckled with brown , C Pestalozzæ is an albino of this variety In C Adami, from the Caucasus, the segments are pale purple, either self-coloured or externally feathered with dark purple C biflorus is an early-flowering spring species, and is highly ornamental for border decoration

C. Boryi.—Flowers white, but bright orange at the throat Abundant at Corfu and in the neighbourhood of Patras, flowers in October, but it does not bloom freely in cultivation, and requires the protection of glass for the development of its flowers

C. byzantinus *See* C iridiflorus.

C. cancellatus.—A beautiful autumnal species, varying from white to pale bluish-purple The flowers are generally veined or feathered towards the base of the segments They appear without the leaves, which come in spring The flowering time is from the end of October to December A robust species, easy of culture, but, like many late autumnal species, is seen to best advantage under a cold frame It is known as C. Schimperi, C Spruneri, C cilicicus, and C damascenus The western forms are nearly white, and the eastern are either blue or purple , but the differences of colour are not sufficient to distinguish them as species

C. chrysanthus.—A vernal Crocus, flowering from January to March according to elevation, which varies from a little above the sea-level to a height of three or four thousand feet The flowers are smaller than those of C aureus, and are usually of bright orange, but occasionally bronzed and feathered externally. A white variety is also found in Bithynia and on Mount Olympus above Broussa , this species also varies with pale sulphur-coloured flowers, occasionally suffused with blue towards the ends of the segments dying out towards the orange throat There are four varieties of this Crocus, distinct in colouring , they are fusco-tinctus, fusco-lineatus, albidus, and cœrulescens.

C. Imperati.—One of the earliest vernal species, abundant south of Naples, and said to extend to Calabria. Lilac Very variable in colour and markings Two varieties occur near Ravello—a self-coloured white and a clear rose The outer surface of the outer segments is coated with rich buff, suffused with

purple featherings Its robust habit and early flowering make it one of the most valuable species for spring gardening It flowers a fortnight and three weeks before C vernus Similar to it is C minimus, abundant on the west coast of Corsica, the neighbouring islets, and in parts of Sardinia , it flowers from the end of January to March The flowers resemble those of C Imperati in miniature, but are of a darker purple and heavily suffused with external brown featherings Although perfectly hardy, it is not robust enough for gardens C suaveolens is also closely allied to C Imperati, and flowers in February The flowers are somewhat smaller than the segments more acute than in C Imperati It is hardy and free-flowering, and under bright sunshine is a good ornament to the early spring garden

C iridiflorus.—The Banat and Transylvania Bears in September and October bright-purple flowers before the leaves Remarkable for purple stigmata and the marked difference between the size of the inner and the outer segments of the perianth This beautiful plant should be secured if possible It is often sold as C byzantinus

C. lævigatus.—A pretty species from the mountains of Greece and the Cyclades The flowers vary from white to lilac, being distinctly feathered with purple markings Its usual flowering time is from the end of October to Christmas, but through the winter to March under cultivation It does not flower freely in cultivation, and, like the allied species, it is seen to best advantage under a cold frame

C. longiflorus.—Abundant in the south of Italy, Sicily, and Malta , flowers in October The flowers are light purple, yellow at the throat In general aspect it somewhat resembles C sativus, especially in the stigmata, which are usually bright scarlet and entire, but occasionally broken up into fine capillary divisions In Sicily the stigmata are collected from the wild plant for saffron It is free-flowering, and very ornamental

C. medius.—A beautiful purple autumn-flowering species, limited to the Riviera and the adjacent spurs of the Maritime Alps The flowers are produced in October before the leaves, which appear in the following spring, and rarely exceed two or three to a corm , the blossoms are bright purple, veined at the base , the stigmata bright scarlet and much branched

C. nudiflorus.—A pretty and well-known species Pyrenees and North of

Spain Naturalised at Nottingham and elsewhere in the midland counties Its large bluish-purple flowers are produced in September and October before the leaves Where established it is difficult to eradicate, the corms produce long stolon-like shoots, which form independent corms on the death of the parent, and the plant soon spreads to considerable distances

C. ochroleucus bears many creamy-white flowers, with orange throat, from the end of October to the end of December It well deserves a cold frame, to preserve its showy flowers from frost and rain

C. pulchellus.—An autumnal species, invaluable for the garden The pale lavender flowers, with bright yellow throat, are freely produced from the middle of September to early in December. Seed

C. serotinus.—S of Spain Flowers in November The blossoms are more or less distinctly feathered with darker purple C Salzmanni is closely allied to C serotinus, but is of larger stature, flowering with the leaves in October and November It is robust and readily multiplied As the flowers are liable to injury by frost and snow, it is seen to best advantage under a cold frame C Clusi closely resembles C serotinus, and flowers with the leaves in October

C. Sieberi.—A vernal species common in the Greek Archipelago and the mountains of Greece The flower is usually bright lilac, orange at the base, but the form found in Crete and the Cyclades presents a great variety of colour, from white to purple, and these colours are mottled, intermixed, and striped in endless variety, contrasting with the bright orange throat The Cretan variety is of exceptional beauty It flowers in cultivation from the end of February to the middle of March

C. speciosus.—Among the handsomest autumn Crocuses, flowering at the end of September and early in October Ranges from North Persia, through Georgia, the Caucasus, and the Crimea, to Hungary The perianth segments, 2 in high, are rich bluish-purple, suffused with darker purple veins, with which the bright orange much-divided stigmata form a beautiful contrast It has been long in cultivation, and readily multiplies by small bulbels at the base of the corm

C. susianus.—The well-known Cloth of Gold Crocus, an early importation from the Crimea Both the orange and bronzed susianus are among the earliest vernal Crocuses, flowering in the open

border in February C. stellaris is an old garden plant somewhat resembling C susianus The flower is orange, distinctly feathered with bronze on the outer coat of the outer segments It is sterile, and never produces seed It flowers early in March

C. vernus (*Spring Crocus*)—One of the earliest cultivated species Alps, Pyrenees, Tyrol, Carpathians, Italy, and Dalmatia Naturalised in several parts of England Remarkable for its range of colour, from pure white to deep purple, endless varieties being generally intermixed in its native habitats, and corresponding with the horticultural varieties of our gardens Flowers early in March at low elevations, and as late as June and July in the higher Alps The parent of nearly all the purple, white, and striped Crocuses grown in Holland

C. versicolor.—This well-known species has long been in cultivation The flowers present a great variety of colouring, from purple to white, and are variously striped and feathered It differs from the two preceding species in having the whole of the perianth segments similarly coloured, and the external buff coating of C. Imperati and C suaveolens is absent Its flowering time is March

C. zonatus.—Mountains of Cilicia Bright vinous-lilac flowers, golden at the base, abundant about the middle of September It is highly ornamental and free-flowering, and easy of culture The flowers come before the leaves, which do not appear till spring It has been in cultivation about fourteen years

This account of the genus is condensed from an article in *The Garden* of 28th January 1882, by Mr Geo Maw, of Benthall Hall, near Broseley The article contains a full account of the family with descriptions of species not in cultivation, giving botanical authorities, and fuller technical descriptions

CRYPTOMERIA—*C japonica* is a graceful and famous Japanese and Chinese tree much planted in Britain, but rarely thriving except under the genial influence of the sea, and even there never attaining to the noble dimensions which it does in Japan It has a number of synonyms and some varieties, *elegans* being the most popular This, which looks well in the nursery state, is not a hardy or a good tree, suffering much in cold and snow, and is really a "sport" rather than a true form, such sports rarely or never forming good trees

CUCURBITA (*Gourd*)—There is no Order more wonderful in the variety and shape of its fruit than that to which the Melon and Cucumber belong From the writhing Snake Cucumber, which hangs down 4 or 5 ft long from its stem, to the enormous round Giant Pumpkin or Gourd, the variation in colour, shape, and size is marvellous There are some pretty little Gourds which do not weigh more than ½ oz , while, on the other hand, there are kinds as large as a barrel Eggs, bottles, gooseberries, clubs, caskets, folded umbrellas, balls, vases, urns, balloons. all have their likenesses in the family Those who have seen a good collection will understand Nathaniel Hawthorne's enthusiasm when he says "A hundred Gourds in my garden were worthy, in my eyes at least, of being rendered indestructible in marble If ever Providence (but I know it never will) should assign me a superfluity of gold, part of it should be expended for a service of plate, or most delicate porcelain, to be wrought into the shape of Gourds gathered in my garden As dishes for containing vegetables they would be peculiarly appropriate Gazing at them, I felt that by my agency something worth living for had been done A new substance was born into the world They were real and tangible existences which the mind could seize hold of and rejoice in " They may be readily grown in this country, and there are many ways in which they may be grown with great advantage—on low trellises , depending from the edges of raised beds , the smaller and medium-sized trained over arches or arched trellis-work, covering banks, or growing on the level earth Isolated, too, some kinds would look very effective , in fact, there is hardly any limit to their use They cover arches, and the large leaves make a perfect summer roof A cool tent might be made with free-growing Gourds, and it would have the additional merit of suspending some of the most singular, graceful, and gigantic of fruits from the roof A bold and effective use may now and then be made of them on walls and on the roofs of sheds or outhouses, as the roofs "carry" the large leaves and showy fruit so well

A SELECTION OF GOURDS --Amongst the most beautiful are the Turk's-cap varieties, such as Grand Mogul, Pasha of Egypt, Viceroy, Empress, Bishop's Hat, &c , the Serpent Gourd, Gooseberry Gourd, Hercules' Club, Gorilla, St Aignan, M Fould, Siphon, Half-moon, Giant's Punchbowl, and the Mammoth, weighing from 170 lbs to upwards of 200 lbs , while amongst the miniature varieties the Fig, Cricket-ball, Thumb, Cherry, Striped Custard, Hen's-egg, Pear, Bottle, Orange, Plover's-egg, &c , are very pretty examples, and very serviceable for ornament All these are well suited to our climate, and there are many others equally suitable Mr. W. Young, indeed, exhibited a collection of 500 varieties, all English-grown, the greater number of which had been sown where grown, and had come to maturity without protection. The ground being manured and dug one spit deep, the seed was sown the second week in May. Many of the plants had no water through the season, but others had it in various quantities, and the more the water the larger, freer, and better the produce. Sowing in a frame at the end of April, and exposing the plants to the air during the day to prevent their being drawn, and then removing the frame altogether to harden them off before planting out, is the best way to secure an early growth Sowing in the open ground under hand-lights would do, but not so well Where there are waste heaps of rubbish or manure it is a good plan to cover them with Gourds. Although they grow under the conditions described above, they do best with plenty of manure, and should be mulched or well watered if the soil be not deep and rich

CUPHEA.—Pretty plants, of which C. platycentra (Cigar-plant) is useful in the summer flower garden It is a dwarf plant, about 12 in. high, with vermilion tube-shaped blossoms. Easily propagated by cuttings taken in September or April, and put in slight heat, and also raised from seed sown in heat in spring C strigulosa is a pretty variety, useful for planting out as single plants in the mixed border for cutting from, but chiefly used as a pot plant for the autumn greenhouse C Zimapani is a most useful annual, growing about 1½ ft high, with flowers of a rich deep purple bordered with a lighter hue, resembling those of a Sweet Pea, and of about the same size They are well fitted for cutting, as the branches lengthen and the flowers expand a long time in water Other kinds are C eminens, Galeottiana, miniata, ocymoides, purpurea, Roezli, and silenoides, all of less importance for the flower garden than those before named

CUPRESSUS (*Cypress*) — Graceful evergreen trees, forming charming backgrounds, but not many really hardy, save in seashore and in warm southern districts, and even there they often perish in hard winters The Monterey Cypress is beautiful in Ireland and in the western coast gardens, but there it even perishes in hard winters

The beautiful Eastern Cypress, so fine in the Italian and Eastern landscape, is worth planting under the best conditions ; so distinct a tree would, if hardy, have been everywhere planted long ago. I have seen very fine specimens of it here and there, as at White Knights.

Many know the beauty of a few of these trees in the small state, but few realise their dignity and beauty as forest trees, such as the great Japanese Cypress, and if we take the trouble to grow and group them well there are no more effective trees in their perennial verdure. But the system of increasing them adopted in nurseries by which these trees, being very free in growth, lend themselves to increase from cuttings like verbenas and geraniums, does not help to the possession of the trees in all their dignity. *Trees* we should raise always in the natural way, *i.e.* from seed, and I find some of these cypresses and their allies break into a number of stems and lose the tree form, the result of this cutting propagation, so entirely needless in the case of forest trees of the highest beauty which some of these are. In the case of the numerous variegated and other garden varieties, cuttings or grafting must be followed in order that one particular variety may be preserved. In the tree this is quite needless and wrong ; but once started on the path of disease and novelty-hunting, and artificially increasing what are often mere " states " of the conifer, it is not so easy to return to more natural ways unless the planter protects himself by raising the tree from seed, or by insisting upon seedling plants. In the case of the Lawson Cypress there are, without end, variegated (*i.e.* merely diseased) forms, and many others with pompous Latin names, nòt only worthless themselves, but filling the catalogues with a pretence of sham science, chaotic lists of long and absurd names, the laughing stock of the learned. Unhappily the public is likely to think one name as good as another, and the really good points of a noble tree are obscured by the system of giving a name to every trifling " form " that happens to occur in a nursery.

C. FUNEBRIS (*Chinese Funeral Cypress*).— A hardy picturesque tree in its own country, and sometimes reaching a height of nearly 50 feet. Robert Fortune described it as having a beautiful effect in the Chinese landscape ; but, unhappily, it is not hardy in our country, though here and there it may be seen in sheltered and warm places.

C. GOWENIANA (*Gowen Cypress*).—A low growing tree from the neighbourhood of Mon-

terey, in California, and of doubtful hardiness in our country. It may be classed with a group, unhappily, many of them tender in this country. It is known from the Monterey Cypress by its spreading, slender, and pendulous habit and small cones.

C. LAWSONIANA (*Lawson Cypress*).—A tall and beautiful tree of the Pacific coast of N. America, 100 feet high and very free in our climate. Unfortunately, I think, owing to propagation from cuttings instead of in the natural way from seed, the tree often breaks into a number of stems which interferes with its natural habit and beauty. It varies very much into what is called " sports," and which is really often a manifestation of disease, especially when they take the variegated form. There are a number of fastigiate forms of which, perhaps, the best is Waterer's ; but they are mere malformations, and as they get old the branches are pressed so closely together that they die, unless we take the trouble to tie or wire them up in some way to prevent them falling about. The spreading varieties are not so liable to this, but many of them go back, as they get older, towards the natural form of tree of which they are mere states. For the pendulous ones there is perhaps a little excuse—for the globular ones none at all ; and the multiplicity of Latin names for these things in catalogues does harm in weakening the interest in the natural tree.

C. LUSITANICA (*Cedar of Goa*).—A name well known through books and lists, and a graceful tree of uncertain origin, but not succeeding in our country, save in seashore gardens and very mild districts. It is naturalised in temperate countries like Spain and Portugal.

Cupressus sempervirens.

C. MACNABIANA (*Macnab's Cypress*).—A Californian tree, rather dwarf and without much of the grace of the Cypress generally. Compact, glaucous, not more than 10 feet high ; coming from a cold country the true plant is quite hardy.

C. MACROCARPA (*Monterey Cypress*).—A very graceful and often stately tree, much planted and succeeding well near the sea coast. It is described in catalogues and even in books on Forestry as hardy, but it is not so, perishing in severe winters, even near the coast. Like many other conifers, it has varieties of little value.

C. NOOTKATENSIS (*Yellow Cypress*).— Really a most distinct tree, and I think the most precious of the whole family for our country, being quite hardy. It is a native of the Northern Pacific coast and British Columbia, and has various synonyms and several variegated varieties of no value compared with the wild tree. I have found it to thrive in cold ordinary soils, and it is a pleasure to see

it at all seasons. The English name of Yellow Cypress was given by the colonists of Vancouver's Island from the fresh wood being yellow in colour. Syn : *Thuiopsis borealis.*

C. OBTUSA (*Great Japanese Cypress*).—A very beautiful evergreen tree of the mountains of Japan, better known in our gardens under the wrong name of *Retinispera.* It has many forms and so-called varieties which are really states of growth only, and which are nearly always grown in nurseries under the name of " *Retinospera.*" The confusion of names in this plant and its varieties has caused its great value as a tree to be overlooked. It grows nearly 100 feet high, and is very handsome. In its own country it is much used to form avenues. It has many varieties with Latin names, but few of them of real value as they grow old.

C. PISIFERA (*Peafruited Cypress*).—Here, as with *C. obtusa*, there is much confusion of names and giving of Latin ones to mere

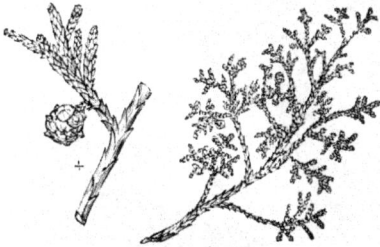

Cupressus thyoides.

varieties and states of growth. It is a much smaller tree than the great Japanese Cypress, but a hardy and useful one. Syn., *Retinospora.*

C. SEMPERVIRENS (*Eastern Cypress*).—One of the most graceful of all evergreen trees, giving distinct and good effects in many parts of the East and Northern Africa, spreading into Northern India also. In some North Italian gardens it grows well over 100 feet, as in the Giusti Garden at Verona, and there are very old trees in Rome and many other parts of Italy. In Algeria and Tunis I have seen it forming noble shelters for the orange gardens, far better than any clipped tree could do. Unhappily, it is not generally hardy in England, though it has some chance near the sea in mild districts.

C. THYOIDES (*Southern White Cedar*).—This is a tree of the North American woods, sometimes reaching nearly 100 feet high in its best state, inhabiting wet places and swamps in New England, westward and southward, rather near the coast, and forming very dark woods. Coming from a very cold country it is hardy, and may be planted in wet and marshy places. There are several varieties, one variegated and of no value. .W. R.

CYANANTHUS (*Lobed C.*).—A pretty Himalayan rock-plant, about 4 in. high,

flowering in August and September ; *C. lobatus* has purplish-blue flower, with a whitish centre, and thriving in sunny chinks in the rock-garden. It grows best in a mixture of sandy peat and leaf-mould, with plenty of moisture during growth, and is increased by cuttings. The seed requires a dry season ; in wet weather the large, erect calyx becomes filled with water, which rots the seed-vessel. Campanulaceæ.

C. incanus.—This flowers more freely than C. lobatus ; like that species, it should be planted in a dry, sunny, well-drained position, as, if the situation be too damp, the fleshy root-stock is liable to rot. It is even a good plan to place something over the plant during the resting season. The flowers are not so large as those of the other species, but are more charming in colour, their beauty enhanced by the white tuft of silky hairs in the throat of the corolla. Campanulaceæ.

CYATHEA (*Silver Tree-fern*).—This very handsome Fern, C. dealbata, known in N. Zealand as the Silver Tree-fern, has a slender, almost black stem, 4 to 8 ft. high, ending in a fine crown of fronds, dark-green above and milk-white below. It may be placed in the open air, in the southern and milder districts, from the end of May till the end of September.

CYCAS. — *C. revoluta* is a tropical plant, with a stout stem, sometimes 6 to 10 ft. high, from the top of which issues a beautiful crown of superb dark-green leaves 2 to 6 ft. long. It is one of the most valuable greenhouse plants, that may be placed out from the end of May till October, and is particularly graceful in the centre of a bed of flowering plants, or isolated with the pot or tub plunged to the rim in the turf, always in a warm position. It is increased by seeds, or separation of suckers, which are occasionally thrown up.

CYCLAMEN (*Sowbread*). — Except the Persian, Cyclamens are as hardy as Primroses ; but they love the shelter and shade of low bushes or hill copses, where they may nestle and bloom in security. In the places they naturally inhabit there is usually the friendly shelter of Grasses or branchlets about them, so that their large leaves are not torn to pieces by wind or hail. The Ivy-leaved Cyclamen is in full leaf through winter and early spring, and for the sake of the beauty of the leaves alone it is desirable to place it so that it may be safe from injury. It is easy to naturalise the hardier Cyclamens in many parts of the country. Good drainage is necessary to their open-air culture, as they grow naturally among broken rocks and stones mixed with vegetable soil, grit, &c., where they are not surrounded by stagnant water. Mr. Atkins, of Painswick, who paid much attention to their culture, thought that the tuber should be buried, and not exposed like the Persian Cyclamen in pots. His chief reason was that in some species the roots issue from the upper surface of the tuber only. They enjoy plenty of moisture at the root at all seasons, and thrive best in a rich, friable, open soil,

of-doors. As soon as they begin to appear, which may be in a month or six weeks, gradually remove the Moss. When the first leaf is fairly developed, they should be transplanted about 1 in. apart in seed pans of rich light earth, and encouraged to grow as long as possible, being sheltered in a cold frame, but always allowed abundance of air. When the leaves have perished in the following summer, the tubers may be planted out or potted, according to their strength.

There appears to have always been great difficulty in defining the species of

Head of Cycas revoluta.

with plenty of well-decayed vegetable matter in it. They are well suited for the rock-garden, and enjoy warm nooks, partial shade, and shelter from dry, cutting winds. They may be grown on any aspect if the conditions above mentioned be secured, but an eastern or south-eastern one is best. We have seen them under trees among Grass, where they flowered profusely every year without attention.

They are best propagated by seed sown, as soon as it is ripe, in well-drained pots of light soil. Cover the soil after sowing with a little Moss, to insure uniform dampness, and place them in shelter out-

Cyclamen, from the great variation in shape and colour of the leaves both above and below. Too much dependence on these characteristics has caused confusion and an undue multiplication of species. Some of the varieties become so fixed, and reproduce themselves so truly from seed, as to be regarded as species by some cultivators. The following are the more important species and varieties.

C. Atkinsi.—A hybrid variety of the Coum section. The flowers are larger than in the type, varying in colour from deep red to pure white, and are plentiful in winter.

C. Coum (*Round-leaved Cyclamen*).—

This, like the others of the same section, is perfectly hardy, and frequently in bloom in the open ground before the Snowdrop ; yet, to preserve the flowers from unfavourable weather, the plants will be better for slight protection, or a pit or frame in which to plant them out. Grown in this way during the early spring, from January to the middle of March, they are one sheet of bloom. When so cultivated, take out the soil, say 1½ to 2 ft. deep, place at the bottom a layer of rough stones 9 to 12 in. deep, and cover them with inverted turf to keep the soil from washing down and injuring the drainage ; then fill up with soil composed of about one-third of good free loam, one-third of well-decayed leaf-mould, and one-third of thoroughly decomposed cow manure. Plant 1½ to 2 in. deep ; and, every year, soon after the leaves die down, take off the surface as far as the tops of the tubers, and fresh surface them with the same compost, or in alternate years give them only a surface

.Cyclamen Coum.

dressing of well-decayed leaves or cow manure. During summer, or indeed after April, the glass should be removed, and they ought to be slightly shaded with Larch Fir boughs (cut before the leaves expand) laid over them, to shelter from the extreme heat of the sun. As soon as they begin to appear in the autumn, gradually take these off. Do not use the glass until severe weather sets in—at all times, both day and night, admitting air at back and front—and in fine weather draw the lights off, remembering that the plants are hardy, and are soon injured if kept too close. They do not like frequent removal. There is a pretty white variety of C. Coum. Syn. C. hyemale.

C. cyprium.—This well-defined species has rather small heart-shaped leaves of dark green, marbled on the upper surface with bluish gray and of a deep purple beneath. The flowers, which are pure white, tinted with soft lilac (the restricted mouth being spotted with carmine-purple), are well elevated above the foliage. This distinguishes it from most of its allies, except C. persicum, and its foliage distin-

guishes it from that at a glance. It is one of the most chaste and beautiful of the hardy kinds. Cyprus and other places in South Europe. It is found on shaded rocks in mountainous districts. Syn. C. neapolitanum.

C. europæum (*European Cyclamen*).— The leaves of this species appear before and with the flowers, and remain during the greater part of the year. Flowers from June to November, or, with slight protection, until the end of the year. The flowers are a reddish purple. Some of the southern varieties, by attention to cultivation under glass, may even assume a perpetual flowering character. C. Clusi, littorale, and Peakeanum are varieties of this section. The flowers are much longer, and of a more delicate colour, often approaching peach colour, and are almost the size of those of C. persicum ; pure white are rare, but pale ones are not uncommon : they are very fragrant. C. europæum thrives freely in various parts of the country in light, loamy, well-drained soil, as a choice border and rock-garden plant. Where it does badly in ordinary soil it should be tried in a deep bed of light loam, mingled with pieces of broken stone. In all cases it is best to cover the ground with Cocoa fibre. It is very desirable on account of its fragrance and long succession of flowers. It luxuriates in the *débris* of old walls and on the mountain side, with a very sparing quantity of vegetable earth to grow in. The bulb varies considerably in size and shape ; sometimes it is elongated and irregular, and the plant is then the C. anemonoides of old authors. Syn. C. odoratum, C. æstivum.

C. hederæfolium (*Ivy-leaved Cyclamen*).—Switzerland, South Europe, and the north coast of Africa. Tuber not unfrequently 1 ft. in diameter, and covered with a brownish rough rind, which cracks irregularly so as to form little scales. The root-fibres emerge from the whole of the upper surface of the tuber, but principally from the rim ; few or none issue from the lower surface. The leaves and flowers generally spring direct from the tuber without any stem (there is sometimes, however, a small stem, especially if the tuber be planted deep) ; at first they spread horizontally, but ultimately become erect. The leaves are variously marked ; the greater portion appear after the flowers, and continue in great beauty the whole winter and early spring, when, if well grown, they are one of the greatest ornaments of borders and rock-gardens. Often these leaves are 6 in. long, 5½ in diameter, and 100 to 150 spring from one tuber. They are admirable for table decoration during winter. The flowers continue from the end of August until October, and are purplish red, frequently with a stripe of lighter colour. There is a pure-white variety, and also a white one with pink base or mouth of corolla ; these reproduce themselves tolerably true from seed. Strong tubers will produce 200 to 300 flowers. Some are delightfully fragrant. They are quite hardy, but are worthy of a little protection to preserve the late blooms, which often continue to spring up till the end of the year. This species is so perfectly hardy as to make it very desirable for the rock-garden and the open borders. It will grow in almost any soil and situation, though best in a well-drained rich border or rock-garden, which it well deserves. It does not like frequent removal. It has been naturalised on the mossy floor of a thin wood, on very sandy poor soil, and may be naturalised almost everywhere. It would be peculi-arly attractive in a semi-wild state in pleasure-grounds and by wood walks. C. græcum is a very near ally, if more than a variety, and requires the same treatment. The foliage is more like C. persicum, or the southern form of C. europæum. C. afri-canum (algeriense macrophyllum) is hardy in warm sheltered situations. It is much larger in all parts than C. hederæfolium, but otherwise is very nearly allied.

C. ibericum (*Iberian Cyclamen*).— Belongs to the Coum section. There is some obscurity respecting the authority for the species and its native country. The leaves are very various. It flowers in spring, the flowers varying from deep red-purple to rose, lilac, and white, with intensely dark mouth ; and are more abundant than those of C. Coum.

C. vernum (*Spring Cyclamen*).—The leaves rise before the flowers in spring ; they are generally more or less white on the upper surface, and are often purplish beneath. Though one of the most interesting species, and perfectly hardy, it is seldom cultivated successfully in the open border or rock-garden ; it is impatient of excessive wet about the tubers, and likes a light soil, in a rather shady nook sheltered from winds, its fleshy leaves being soon injured. The tubers should be planted deep, say not less than 2 to 2½ in. below the surface. C. vernum of Sweet is considered by many as only a variety of Coum, and it is known as C. Coum var. zonale. It is also known as C. repandum. There is a white-flowered variety.

Cyclobothra. *See* CALOCHORTUS.

Cydonia. *See* PYRUS.

CYNARA (*French Artichoke*).—This plant, C. Scolymus, much grown for cook-ing, has as a foliage-plant much beauty ; its long silvery deeply divided leaves, height (4 to 5 ft.), purplish flower-heads, and habit render it very suitable for the rougher parts of pleasure grounds, grass, &c.,which are often occupied by fine plants far less handsome.

CYPERUS (*Galingale*).—A water plant of fine form from 2 to 3 ft. high, C. longus is crowned by a handsome, loose, umbellate panicle of chestnut-coloured flower-spikes, at the base of which there are three or more leaves, often 1 or 2 ft. long, the lower ones of a bright shining green arching gracefully. The root-stock is thick and aromatic, and was formerly much used as a tonic. A rare native plant, suitable for the margin of water.

CYPRIPEDIUM (*Lady's Slipper*).— Handsome Orchids, embracing several beautiful perfectly hardy species, of which the Mocassin-flower (C. spectabile) is the finest cultivated hardy kind. The follow-ing are a few of the cultivated kinds.

C. acaule (*Stemless Lady's Slipper*).— A dwarf species with a naked downy flower-stalk, 8 to 12 in. high, bearing a green bract at the top, flowers early in summer, large, solitary purplish with a rosy-purple (rarely white) lip, nearly 2 in. long, which has a singular closed fissure down its whole length in front. Northern States of North America in woods and bogs. Thriving in moist peaty or sandy soil or leaf-mould.

C. Calceolus (*English Lady's Slipper*). —The only British species and the largest flowered of our native Orchids, 1 to 1½ ft. high, flowers in summer, solitary (some-times two) large flowers of a dark-brown colour, with an inflated clear yellow lip netted with darker veins, and about 1 in. in length. North Europe, and occasion-ally in the northern counties of England, where, however, it is now almost exter-minated. Very ornamental for the rock-garden, where it should be planted in sunny sheltered nooks of calcareous soil, or in narrow fissures of limestone rock, in well-drained, rich, fibrous loam, in an east aspect.

C. guttatum (*Spotted Lady's Slipper*). —A handsome kind, seldom seen in gar-dens, 6 to 9 in. high, flowers in summer, solitary, rather small, beautiful, white, heavily blotched, or spotted with deep rosy purple. Found in Canada, N. Europe (near Moscow), and N. Asia, in dense forests amongst the roots of trees in moist, black vegetable mould. Requires a half-shady position in leaf-mould, moss, and sand, and should be kept rather dry in winter.

C. japonicum (*Japanese Lady's Slipper*).—About 1 ft. high, and its hairy stems, which are as thick as one's little finger, bear two plicate fan-shaped leaves of bright green, rather jagged round the margins. The flowers are solitary, the sepals being of an apple-green tint; the

present rare plant grows best in pure loam of a heavy nature. Siberia.

C. pubescens.—A dwarf species with a pubescent stem, seldom more than 2 ft. high, flowers early in summer, on each stem one to three flowers; scentless, greenish yellow, spotted with brown, with a pale-yellow lip from $1\frac{1}{2}$ to 2 in. long, and flattened at the sides. America, found in bogs and low woods, from Pennsylvania to Carolina. Does well on dry

Mocassin-flower (Cypripedium spectabile).

petals, too, are of the same colour, but are dotted with purplish crimson at the base; the lip large, and curiously folded in front, as in the better-known C. acaule, to which it seems most nearly allied; the colour of the lip is a soft creamy yellow, with bold purple dots and lines.

C. macranthum (*Large Lady's Slipper*).—This bears a considerable resemblance to C. ventricosum, but has lighter-coloured flowers, large, of a uniform purplish rose with deeper-coloured veins; early in June. Lip globose, inflated, and finely marked with deep purple reticulations. This handsome and at

sunny banks, among loam, stones, and grit.

C. spectabile (*Mocassin-flower*).—The most beautiful of this group; 15 in. to $2\frac{1}{2}$ ft. high, flowers in summer, one or two on each stem (rarely three), large, with inflated, rounded lip, about $1\frac{1}{2}$ in. long, white, with a large blotch of bright rosy carmine in front. A variety (C. s. album) has the lip entirely white. In America it grows in open boggy woods, moist meadows, and also in peaty bogs in the Northern States. Good native specimens produce from fifty to seventy flowers on a single tuft, 3 ft. across, formed on a thick mat of fleshy roots. The plant is hardy, and succeeds if planted out in a deep, rich peaty soil, with a few nodules of sandstone or rough sandstone grit mixed with the soil. It also thrives in turfy loam on a moist bottom; in any case, however, deep planting is necessary, as the roots are then cool and moist during the hot weather, and do not suffer from frost in the winter.

CYSTOPTERIS (*Bladder Fern*).—The cultivated kinds of this native group are small elegant Ferns of delicate fragile texture. They grow on rocks and walls, chiefly in mountainous districts. The best-known are : C. fragilis, which has finely cut fronds about 6 in. high. It is of easy culture, succeeding in an ordinary border, though seen to best advantage on shady parts of the rock-garden in a well-drained soil. There are two or three varieties, Dickieana being the best. C. alpina is much smaller, and when once established not difficult to cultivate or increase, but more affected by excessive moisture than C. fragilis. A sheltered situation in a well-drained part of the rock-garden suits it. C. montana is another elegant plant requiring the same treatment as C. fragilis.

CYTISUS (*Broom*).—The few kinds of hardy Cytisus are all valuable ornamental shrubs. Common as the British Broom (C. Scoparius) is, it should certainly be in gardens in places where it does not grow wild ; and in company with Heath and Furze it is most useful for dry sandy banks where other shrubs would fail. It is easily raised from seed. C. Andreanus is a handsome form of the common Broom well worth growing, and coming fairly true from seed. The White Portuguese Broom (C. albus) is well known as one of the finest of all early-flowering shrubs. A strong bush, particularly in light soils, and frequently 10 ft. high. Towards the end of May every slender twig is wreathed with small white flowers. The Spanish Broom is a handsome and distinct shrub, often flowering a long time on dry banks. C. nigricans is also a beautiful shrub. The purple Broom is naturally a long

Cytisus nigricans.

trailing shrub with purplish flowers, but is generally seen grafted mop fashion on Laburnum stems. It is really an alpine shrub, and its place is among rocks and boulders, where its wiry branches can fall over and make dense cushion-like tufts. The foregoing are the most important kinds. Others, suitable for a fuller collection, are C. austriacus, biflorus, sessilifolius, capitatus, monspessulanus, purgans, and C. Ardoini. The last is a pretty alpine shrub a few inches high, and suitable for the rock-garden ; its tufted growth is covered in summer with yellow flowers. There is a great number of names and synonyms, but the above are the most generally accepted and embrace the best varieties.

Dabœcia. See ERICA.

DACRYDIUM (*Huon Pine*).—A tree of the Pine order of exquisite grace, but not hardy in Britain except in the Cornish and Devon gardens, and others of the south of England and Ireland, where it is occasionally very beautiful. In other parts of the country if people want them they must be grown in the cool greenhouse or winter garden, but in the face of the number of beautiful hardy Pines we have that is a doubtful practice except in botanic gardens. There are two species, *D. Franklini* (*Huon Pine*) and *D. cupressinum* (*New Zealand Cypress*), a common New Zealand tree attaining nearly 100 feet in height, like the other kind.

DACTYLIS (*Cocksfoot*). — The variegated forms of this native Grass are attractive to those concerned much with bedding out, D. glomerata variegata being one of the most useful of edging plants, and easily increased by division in autumn or spring, thriving in almost any soil, but if the soil be too poor the plant is apt to look rusty in dry autumns. There are several other variegated forms graceful as edgings to beds, as carpets or mixtures, or as tufts in borders. The graceful leaves should not be clipped.

DAHLIA.—The Dahlia group is not a large one, so far as wild plants go, and every species is a native of Mexico. It is valued chiefly for the many beautiful varieties that have been raised from seed, the garden varieties being separated in various classes. When well placed in the garden the Dahlia is superb, its profusion of bloom creating fine masses of colour in the late summer and autumn months, especially when the best forms of the Cactus section are used. Distinct beds of Dahlias present a fine aspect, if the colours are well contrasted, and many otherwise good effects are spoilt by mixing up tall and dwarf bushy kinds indiscriminately. A mass of one colour looks well, especially if backed by dark-leaved shrubs, whilst distinct beds are a welcome feature in the flower garden, being gay far into the autumn when the weather is not frosty.

CLASSES.—The recognised classification of Dahlias is convenient, but not very distinct. A few years ago the two leading classes were the Show and Fancy Dahlias—distinctions confusing to some, as a White or Yellow Dahlia, edged or tipped with a dark colour, was classed as an edged, tipped, or laced Dahlia, and included among the show flowers ; but if the disposition of colour was reversed, and dark-coloured flowerets were tipped with a light colour, the plant was classed as a Fancy Dahlia. All the kinds with Carnation-like stripe were Fancy Dahlias. The catalogues abound with names of varieties, and the grower can make his own selection, especially as new forms are often raised. Varieties that do not conform to the stiff ideal of the hard-shell florist sometimes please the artist or the gardener best.

SHOW AND FANCY DAHLIAS.—These are not so much grown in gardens as formerly, but are still seen at the exhibition, Dahlias being shown in a far freer way than was usual a generation ago, and the Cactus and Single classes have, to some extent, overshadowed the formal Show and Fancy varieties. The reason why these are less valuable than many other kinds of Dahlia in the garden is because of the weight of the flowers. There is little graceful beauty about them, the stems being bent with the burden of a too heavy blossom, hence the greater popularity of the many lovely Cactus varieties.

Show Dahlias.—Agnes, Alexander Cramond, Bendigo, Colonist, Crimson Globe, Canary, Eclipse, Ethel Britton, George Gordon, George Rawlings, Glowworm, J. T. West, John Walker, Harry Keith, John Wyatt, Mr. Harris, Mrs. W. E. Gladstone, Mrs. S. Hibberd, Nellie Cramond, Queen of the Belgians, Richard Dean, R. T. Rawlings, Shirley Hibberd, J. T. Saltmarsh, W. H. Williams, W. Garratt, Wm. Keith, Wm. Rawlings.

Fancy Dahlias.—Buffalo Bill, Charles Wyatt, Comedian, Duchess of Albany, Frank Pearce, Gaiety, General Gordon, H. Eckford, H. Glasscock, Fanny Sturt, Mrs. Ocock, Mrs. Saunders, Peacock, Rebecca, Rev. J. B. M. Camm, Sunset, T. W. Girdlestone.

POMPON OR BOUQUET DAHLIAS are not so popular as either the Cactus or single forms. They seem to have gone out of cultivation to some extent, though they are useful for cutting. The tendency of recent raisers has been to increase the size of the flowers, but they should be quite small, as the name Pompon suggests, not like a Show or Fancy Dahlia. Although many additions have been made to this section, the pure-white variety White Aster, still retains its popularity, and it is grown largely for cutting, and also for its effect. The Pompon Dahlias are very free-blooming, throwing their charming flowers well above the leaves.

Pompon Dahlias.—Admiration, Arthur West, Countess von Sternberg, Coquette, Crimson Beauty, Cupid, Darkness, Dove, E. F. Jungker, Eurydice, Eva, Fairy Tales, Gem, German Favourite, Glowworm, Golden Gem, Hedwig Pollwig, Juno, Lilian, Little Bobby, Little Ethel, Marion, Midget, Pure Love, Tommy Keith, Vivid, White Aster.

SINGLE DAHLIAS.—D. coccinea (D. Mercki), D. variabilis, and others formed the foundation, so to say, of this group. The value of Single Dahlias as beautiful garden flowers was not considered until a reaction set in against the show blooms, and then the elegant single kinds became popular. It is so easy to cross them and raise seedlings that the earlier varieties were quickly improved upon in colour and habit of growth, until we have now a delightful group of garden plants, free, and making a continuous display through the late summer and early autumn months. In the best kinds the flowers are carried erect above the foliage, the growth bushy, and the flowers abundant. No summer flower gives a greater variety of brilliant colours, rich selfs and delicate hues of mauve and rose to pure white. With all this choice, one, unfortunately, sees much of the striped kinds, too often praised, for the reason perhaps that they are well shown at some exhibition, but a new Dahlia should be seen in the garden to judge of its merits. The striped kinds are also sportive, like striped Carnations, and depend in a large measure for their peculiar colour upon the weather. This class must not be confounded with those that have flowers boldly margined with colour. As the round-flowered form of Single Dahlia is declining in popularity one sees less of the big saucer-shaped blooms, so large that it was necessary to support them when gathered. These flabby varieties won few friends, and the more recent kinds are far smaller and better.

Single Dahlias.—Annie Hughes, Butterfly, Chilwell Beauty, Conspicua, Duke of York, Duchess of Westminster, Eclipse, Evelyn, Gulielma, Jack, James Scobie, Miss Glasscock, Midget Improved, Mikado, Magpie, Nellie Ware, Paragon, Rose Queen, Yellow Boy, Yellow Satin.

"CACTUS" DAHLIAS.—These originated from D. Juarezi, which was introduced from Mexico about 1879, and they retain the characteristic shape of that species, the petals twisted, so to say, and reminding one of those of some of the Cacti. The earlier Cactus Dahlias had one fault—hiding the flowers amongst the leaves; but this is to a large extent changed, so that we have now a beautiful race of garden plants for summer and autumn, with flowers of bold form and charming and varied colours. A new group is formed by the single Cactus kinds. The flowers are quite single, about as large as those of a good single Dahlia of the ordinary type, and with twisted petals.

Cactus Dahlias.—Beauty of Eynsford, Bertha Mawley, Cannell's Own, Countess of Gosford, Countess of Radnor, Delicata, Ernest Cannell, Juarezi, Kentish Invicta, Kynerith, Lady Penzance, Matchless, Mrs. Francis Fell, May Pictor, Professor Baldwin, Robert Cannell.

TOM THUMB DAHLIAS.—This is a very dwarf race, the plants forming little bushes, but they are not satisfactory, as they appear not to bloom with great freedom, whilst the growth does not retain its true dwarf character. When true, the habit is compact, dense, and the single flowers borne well above the mass of leaves. Fortunately the colours of the flowers are for the most part simple, and raisers should steer clear of the ugly striped kinds. Dwarfing any flower naturally tall and graceful is a doubtful practice.

BEDDING DAHLIAS.—This is the name given to a small list of dwarf varieties, which are used for massing, blooming profusely. One kind named Rising Sun has the flowers brilliant scarlet, and used with good effect in the London parks.

SPECIES.— Amongst these we may note the following :—

D. coccinea, a tall plant with bright-scarlet flowers that rarely vary. Nearly related to it, and differing only in some slight points, is D. Cervantesi, also with showy scarlet flowers.

D. glabrata is a beautiful plant of dwarf spreading growth, more slender than any of the other species. The flowers are smaller than those of other kinds, and vary from pure white to deep purple. It is hardier than any other Dahlia, and plants left in the ground are generally uninjured throughout the winter. Its dwarf growth adapts it for positions unsuitable for the latter kinds, and it has a good effect in masses, its colour being unlike that of any other Dahlia. It is known also as D. Mercki, repens, and Decaisneana.

D. gracilis is a distinct and graceful plant, with slender stems and finely divided foliage, which gives it a freer habit than any other Dahlia. The bright-scarlet flowers are of the ordinary size.

D. imperialis has large and graceful much-divided leaves, and flowers of a beautiful French white, thrown up in a great cone-like mass. It rarely flowers in the open air, but it is of service both in the flower garden and conservatory. Planted in rich soil, and placed in a warm, sheltered position in the open air at the end of May, it grows well in summer, and its large and graceful leaves make it an ornament worthy of being used as a "fine-foliaged" plant. Similar to this, but not so fine, is D. Maximiliana.

D. Juarezi is now well known. It is the more desirable because of its easy culture, as it requires no different treatment from ordinary Dahlias. It is not quite double, but is very fine in form and brilliant in colour, though it flowers somewhat sparsely.

D. variabilis is the supposed parent of all the garden varieties. The wild plant has scarlet flowers like coccinea, and is of similar growth. A packet of seed, however, will yield plants with flowers of all shades, from crimson to white and yellow.

CULTURE.—To get a good result it is essential to have rich, deep, and moist soil, and to put out strong plants as early as may be safe, so as to secure a good growth or autumn bloom. Where weak plants are put a little too late they may only give a few poor blooms before the frost comes. If planted in May and frost is feared, protect the young plants at night by turning a garden pot over them. If the soil is not deep, rich, and moist, manure-water should be used. Watering is usually necessary in early growth, afterwards it is not so in moist districts where the plant is well treated as regards depth and quality of soil. In dry places water is essential in most seasons. Staking and tying out the shoots must be attended to, as the stems are brittle and break under little wind-pressure. Earwigs are great enemies to Dahlias, but can be trapped in small round troughs which may be got from any pottery. They may also be caught on pieces of Hemlock stem, 6 in. long, by leaving a joint at one end, and sticking the pieces here and there through

cuttings every two or three days. These may be taken off even as early as March, close to the crown, without however injuring it, as others will come up at the base of those removed. The cuttings must not be too long before they are taken from the tubers, as then they flag. When the crowns have supplied all the cuttings that can be got from them they may be divided, and therefore

Cactus Dahlia " Juarezi.

the Dahlias. Small pots, with a little bit of dry Sphagnum Moss inside, inverted on the tops of stakes, also form good traps.

INCREASE.—The usual practice is to take up the roots and store them in a dry frost-proof cellar in winter. Dahlias may be propagated by cuttings, root-division, and seed, the last way being used only where new kinds are sought. Cuttings are the best means of propagating Dahlias, though division of the roots is usually practised. If started in February or March in a temperature of 60° to 70° F., each crown will produce three or four

nothing is lost. Cuttings may be successfully struck during the summer months ; but this is unusual except in the case of choice varieties. Three-inch pots are best for putting the cuttings into, six cuttings being put in each pot. They should be plunged in a brisk bottom-heat, covered with hand-glasses, and shaded from bright sunshine. In less than a fortnight they will be all rooted, and may be potted off singly into large 3-in. pots. Harden them off gradually until planted out in May

To raise seedlings sow the seed in heat in February, and treat the young plants in the same way as cuttings. To propagate from layers the lowest branches of the plant should be pegged down. If the soil be sandy they will root freely, but in the absence of sandy soil a quantity of leaf-mould with a mixture of sand may be laid down for them to root into. Pure white sand alone is best suited for striking them in, and a mixture of leaf-mould and sand is very good to start the crowns in.

WINTERING.—As long as the weather keeps mild Dahlia roots are best in the soil, and need not be taken up till the end of November; but should sharp frosts be followed by heavy rain they should be promptly removed from the ground. Lift the roots on a dry day, and cut off the stems to within 2 or 3 in. of the crown. Remove the greater portion of the soil from the tubers and lay the latter out in the sun to dry before storing. The floor of a greenhouse where frost can be excluded, or a dry cellar, is a good place to store the roots in. A little ventilation is necessary to keep them from getting mouldy; but a hot dry atmosphere must also be avoided, as the tubers might shrivel in it. By lifting the roots with some soil adhering to them, they are kept plump during the winter, which is best when they are required for early forcing. They will generally keep well on the floor of a greenhouse, as it is light and airy, and during mid-winter much water should not, as a rule, be given. The tubers of some sorts are more difficult of preservation than others, and choice varieties are frequently bad keepers.

The species of Dahlia are natives of Mexico and adjacent regions: 1, arborea; 2, astrantiæflora; 3, coccinea; 4, excelsa; 5, gracilis; 6, imperialis; 7, Maximiliana; 8, Mercki; 9, platylepis; 10, pubescens; 11, scapigera; 12, variabilis; 13, Juarezi.

DAPHNE (*Garland-flower*).—Beautiful dwarf flowering shrubs. There is a group of small-growing species among them that claims a place in the rock-garden. The best-known and the most popular Daphne is the old Mezereon (D. Mezereum), whose leafless branches are often wreathed with fragrant blossoms before winter is past. The common sort has reddish-purple blooms, but there are pink and white, single and double-flowered forms. It is indispensable for every garden, and should always be planted where its beauty can be enjoyed in early spring, and it does best in an open sunny place in almost any soil. In some seasons it flowers from the end of January until

April. The pretty D. Cneorum (the Garland-flower) is a favourite little shrub, 6 to 12 in. high, more suited for the rock-garden than the shrubbery. The deep-pink flowers are deliciously fragrant, and appear in dense clusters at the tips of the shoots, the unopened buds being crimson. It flowers in April and September, often twice a year, the fragrant flowers being borne in dense terminal umbels. It is a native of most of the great mountain chains of Europe, and is suitable for the rock-garden, for the front margin of the mixed border, or as an edging to beds of choice low shrubs, being of trailing growth, and forming dense cushion-like masses of evergreen leaves a few inches high, thriving best in an open situation in sandy peaty soil. Increased by layers. D. rupestris (Rock Daphne) is a neat little shrub, with erect shoots forming dense, compact tufts, 2 in. high and 1 ft. or more

Garland-flower (Daphne Cneorum).

across, which are covered with bloom which sometimes almost eclipses the plant. Its colour is a soft-shaded pink or rose, and its flowers are larger and more waxy than those of D. Cneorum, but form clustered heads in the same way. It is essentially a rock-plant, growing wild in fissures of limestone in peaty loam. In cultivation it is of slow growth, and it takes some years to form a moderate-sized tuft, but the plant is a gem worth waiting for. It seems to thrive in very stony and peaty earth with abundance of white sand, and should be planted in a well-drained but not in a dry position. D. Blagayana is a beautiful dwarf alpine shrub, 3 to 6 in. high, also suitable for the rock-garden. It is of straggling growth, the leaves forming rosette-like tufts at the tips of the branches, and encircling dense clusters of fragrant white flowers   It blooms in spring for several weeks, and is of easy culture, thriving in the rock-garden in well-drained spots surrounded by stones for its wiry roots to ramble among. It is hardy, and in open spots thrives in any good soil, increased by layers pegged down in spring and separated from the plants as soon as roots are emitted Another Daphne is the Japanese D Genkwa, introduced about twenty years ago, but still uncommon   In spring, before the leaves appear, it bears freely large lilac fragrant flowers   D. Fortunei, from China, is similar to it   The foregoing are the best hardy Daphnes, others in cultivation are   D alpina, a dwarf deciduous shrub, about 2 ft high, with clusters of fragrant white flowers, D collina, from South Europe, a dwarf evergreen form, 2 or 3 ft high, bearing clusters of fragrant pink blossoms during the first half of the year, D neapolitana, from Italy, similar to this, and probably only a variety of it ; D altaica, with neat growth, like that of D Mezereum, has white scentless flowers, D. pontica and Laureola are good Evergreens, although not remarkable for blossom, while the pretty D odora and its variety Mazeli are scarcely hardy enough for open-air culture Such a beautiful family deserves the best attention   The following is a list of the species, to which some beautiful things, it is hoped, will be added from the often little-known lands some of the species inhabit

Species — *D alpina*, S Europe and Himalayas *altaica*, Siberia. *aurea*, Orient *Blagayana*, Carniolia *cannabina*, Himal *caucasica*, Caucas *Championi*, China *Cneorum*, S Europe *decandra*, Java *Genkwa*, China *glomerata*, Caucasus *gnidioides*, Asia Minor *Gnidium*, S Europe *involucrata*, India. *jasminea*, Greece *jezoensis*, Japan *Kiusiana*, Japan *Laureola*, Europe *linearifolia*, Syria *Mazeli*, Japan *Mezereum*, Europe and N Asia *odora*, Japan *oleoides*, S Eur Asia Minor *pendula*, Burma *petraea*, Tyrol *pontica*, Asia Minor *pseudomezereum*, Japan *Rodriguezi*, Minorca *Roumea*, China. *sericea*, S Eur and Asia Minor *Sophia*, Asia *striata*, S Europe *tangutica*, China *tenuiflora*, Ins Timor *triflora*, China

DAPHNIPHYLLUM. — Evergreen shrubs of fine effect of foliage and little beauty of flower. *D Glaucescens* grows well in the home counties so far as tried, especially at Lydhurst in Sussex, the leaves over 6in long, and glaucous underneath, the flowers small, in the autumn, but the habit is so fine wherever evergreens are cared for that this will be worth growing at least in the southern and warmer counties The other species known is *D josoenses.* It is a much dwarfer plant, and is an under shrub in the forests of Yezo   These plants seem to be hardy enough in the Southern districts of Britain, but may require a little care to establish   Rich as we are in ever-

green plants in Britain, these are distinct enough to take a good place

DARLINGTONIA (*Californian Pitcher-plant*) —A most singular plant, resembling the Sarracenias, but very distinct   the leaves of *D californica* rise to a height of 2 ft or more, are hollow, and form a curiously shaped hood, from which hang two ribbon-like appendages, the hood often a crimson-red, and the flowers are almost as curious   This remarkable plant is found to grow in our climate if care be taken with it, and it would be difficult to name a more interesting plant for a sheltered bog garden   It is less trouble out-of-doors than under glass, indeed, it only requires a moderately wet bog in a light spongy soil of fibrous peat and chopped Sphagnum Moss   A place should be selected by the side of a stream, in an artificial bog or in any moist place, and the plants should be fully exposed to direct sunlight, but sheltered from the cold winds of early spring when they are throwing up their young leaves.   They require frequent watering in dry seasons, unless they are in a naturally wet spot When they become large they develop side shoots, which, if taken off and potted, soon make good plants   The plant is also raised from seed, but this requires several years

DATISCA —*D cannabina* is a tall and graceful herbaceous perennial from 4 to 7 ft high, the long stems clothed with large pinnate leaves, yellowish-green flowers appearing towards the end of summer The male plant is very strong and graceful in habit   the female remains green much longer than the male, when it is laden with fruit, each shoot droops gracefully, and the plant should be included in any selection of hardy plants of good form Seed will be found the best way to increase it, and would secure plants of both sexes The border is not its place, it is, above most other plants, suited for the grassy margin of an irregular shrubbery, and will be all the more effective if planted on a grassy slope, where its deep-seeking roots will soon defy the most protracted drought

DATURA (*Thorn Apple*) —Plants of the Nightshade family, including several handsome garden plants that well deserve cultivation   Being natives of Mexico and similar countries, none are hardy, but owing to rapid growth some succeed well if treated as half-hardy annuals, and make effective plants in a short season   The best are   D ceratocaula, from 2 to 3 ft high, with large, scented, trumpet-like flowers, often 6 in in length, and 4 or 5 in across, white, tinged with violet-purple, expanding in the afternoon and closing on the following morning. D. fastuosa is a handsome species, having white blossoms smaller than the preceding; there is a fine variety of it with the tube of the flower violet and the inside white. The most striking forms of this species

humilis flava of the gardens ; but although they offer a greater variety of colour, they are less hardy than the older forms just described, and appear to require a warmer climate for their complete development. D. meteloides is a handsome Mexican plant, called in gardens Wright's Datura. Isolated specimens of it have a

D. cornigera (Brugmansia Knighti) in the flower garden.

bear "double" flowers, the primary corolla having a second and sometimes a third corolla arising from its tube, all being perfectly regular in form, and often being particoloured, as in the single variety with violet flowers. D. fastuosa Huberiana of the seed catalogues, and several varieties of it that are offered, are reputed to be hybrids of this species with the dwarf D. chlorantha flore-pleno or D.

fine aspect in sunny but sheltered nooks. It is from 3 to 4 ft. high, has widespreading branches, and blooms from the middle of July till frost sets in, the flowers white, tinged with mauve ; from 4 to 6 in. across, showy and sweet, but the leaves emit a disagreeable odour. Besides these there are other kinds in cultivation, such as D. ferox and quercifolia, but those described are the finest. Fresh seeds are readily raised, in an ordinary hot-bed ; the young plants while small should be pricked out singly in pots, and finally planted out where they are to stand. They need ample space for their full growth, and should be grown in light warm soils.

The plants hitherto known as Brugmansia are now considered to belong to Datura.

They are of easy cultivation, and soon make large plants. The best way of growing is as standards, so that their long drooping flowers may be better seen. In the flower-garden a sheltered but sunny position should be chosen. The plants may be safely put out about the end of May in good warm soil. It would be best to pot them into large pots or tubs, and turn them out of these, as thus treated they would not die back so far in the winter, and when planting time again came round the growth would be stronger. When in a house either in tubs or in the border, an annual pruning should be given early in the spring, and they should be kept within bounds. Under glass the chief enemy is green-fly, but fumigation soon disposes of this. For the open border of a large house a few standards with stems 8 ft. or so in height make a grand show. Their propagation is simple, the young shoots being merely taken off in spring and struck in a gentle heat, one cutting in a small pot. Grow them on as fast as possible, keeping them to the one stem until of good height. They will yield a few flowers the first autumn when planted out, but as they get older they flower more profusely, the growth being less luxuriant. When planted out in the open ground, they are best as centre plants to fairly large beds, with a carpet of dwarf things under them. They should not be smothered up, the example of D. cornigera (Brugmansia Knighti) in the illustration being an instance of good effect when not overcrowded. This is one of the best varieties, with many large handsome double flowers. It is more robust and compact in growth than other kinds, its leaves too of a darker green. D. suaveolens, another good white variety, is a profuse bloomer, its flowers being perhaps larger than those of D. cornigera, but single. D. sanguinea has flowers of a deep orange-yellow tinged with green towards the base ; it does not flower quite so freely as the white kinds, but should be grown for its distinct character. There is also a double yellow variety of D. chlorantha, which is free-flowering and well worth growing, being pleasing in pots.

Some years ago, at Nuneham Park, Oxford, D. suaveolens was used with good effect in the flower garden during summer and autumn. Mr. Stewart, the gardener, used to raise plants annually by striking cuttings in autumn in bottom heat. They were potted as soon as rooted, and kept growing gently in a warm greenhouse all through the winter. About the end of February they were placed in an atmosphere of about 55°, when they were encouraged to grow freely. As soon as the roots appeared above the surface, liquid manure and sometimes a top-dressing of old cow manure were given. They were kept growing on in this way until the middle of May, when they were 2½ ft. high, after which they were gradually hardened off, and during a dull time taken out-of-doors, placed in a sheltered corner, and screened from the sun before being planted out. Out-of-doors the plants flowered freely, and gave off a sweet perfume during the evenings in July and August.

Species.—*D. arborea*, S. America. *ceratocaula*, tropical America. *chlorantha. cornigera*, Mexico. *discolor*, Mexico. *dubia. erinacea*, Brazil. *fastuosa ferox*, China. *floribunda*, S. America. *inermis*, Abyssinia. *Leichhardti*, Australia. *Metel*, tropical countries. *meteloides*, W. America. *microcarpa. nigra*, Malaya. *præcox. quercifolia*, Mexico. *sanguinea*, S. America. *scandens*, Brazil. *Stramonium*, common everywhere. *suaveolens*, Mexico. *trapezia*, India.

DECUMARIA.—Two species of this interesting genus are in cultivation ; both are hardy, and useful climbers for walls and buildings. D. barbara, a native of Carolina, where it is found in shady places along the margins of swamps, is a very elegant plant. The branches cling to the wall by small rootlets, as in the Ivy, and when allowed to ramble at will are very grotesque, ascending trees or walls to a considerable height, and requiring no nailing and little attention. The flowers are in large bunches in May and June, pure white and fragrant, resembling Hydrangea. D. sinensis is a native of Central China, and a beautiful hardy species. It is a climber, and was found by Dr. Henry covering the cliffs of the Ichang Gorge with clusters of fragrant white flowers.

DELPHINIUM (*Larkspur*). — Few plants contribute so much to the beauty of the garden as these fine plants of the Crowfoot Order. There are in cultivation many species, both annual and perennial, but the most important are the tall hybrid perennials, of which there are many varieties with a wonderful range of lovely colour. They are very valuable for their great variety in height, from 1 to 10 ft. ; for their greater variety in shades of colour, which range from almost scarlet to pure white, from the palest and most chaste lavender up through every conceivable shade of blue to deep indigo ; and for the variety of size and form of their individual blooms, some of which are single, some semi-double, and some

Delphinium.

perfectly double, and all set on spikes ranging from 1 to 6 ft. in length. About a dozen species have given rise to the cultivated varieties, the chief species being D. grandiflorum, formosum, lasiostachyum, cheilanthum, elatum, and peregrinum.

CULTURE AND POSITION.—The combinations in which they can be placed are numerous. They are splendid objects in various positions, and may be used in various ways—in the mixed border, in

masses or groups in one or several colours, or associated with other flowering plants or with shrubs. Perennial Larkspurs thrive in almost any situation or soil ; they are easily increased, and are quite hardy. A deep friable loam, enriched with rotten manure, is a good soil for them, but they will grow well in a hot sandy soil if it be heavily manured and watered. Every three or four years they should be replanted and divided, and this is best done in spring, just as they are starting into growth, or in summer ; if it is done in summer, cut down the plants intended for division, and let them remain for a week or ten days until they start afresh ; then carefully divide and replant them, shading and watering until they are established. Late autumn division is not advisable. Delphiniums can be made to bloom for several months by continually cutting off the spikes immediately after they have done flowering. If the central spike be removed, the side shoots will flower, and by thus cutting off the old flowers before they form seeds we cause fresh shoots to issue from the base, and to keep up a succession of bloom. Another plan is to let the shoots remain intact until all have nearly done flowering, and then to cut the entire plant to the ground, when in about three weeks there will be a fresh bloom. In this case, however, to keep the plants from becoming exhausted, they must have a heavy dressing of manure or manure-water. Top-dressings keep the soil cool and moist, give the plants a healthier growth, increase the number and improve the quality of the flowers.

The following is a selection of the good kinds : *Single Varieties.*—Belladonna, Hendersoni, Cambridge, Granville, Gloire de St. Mande, Barlowi, versicolor, Coronet, magnificum, Lavender, pulchrum, formosum, lilacinum, Celestial, Madame Hock, mesoleucum superbum, Defiance, and Attraction. The grower should consult his own taste, and raise seedlings of his own, taking care to have a good stock of the standard varieties he likes best. *Double Varieties.*—Madame E. Geny, Madame Henri Jacotot, Madame Richalet, Pompon Brilliant, Roi Léopold, Hermann Stenger, Claire Courant, George Taylor, Roncevaux, Le XIXe. Siècle, Keteleeri, Prince of Wales, General Ulrich, Arc en Ciel, Sphere, Michael Angelo, Delight, Glynn, Barlowi vittatum, Star, Perfectum novum, Triomphe de Pontoise, Pompon de Tirlemont, Victor Lemoine, Trophée, Madame Henri Galotat, Louis Figuier, Azureum plenum, and Madame Ravillana. The beautiful old D. grandiflorum fl.-pl., another double variety, is one of the most charming of border plants.

The best of the numerous perennial species distinct from the hybrids are—D. cashmerianum, with flowers nearly as large as those of D. formosum, and with stems about 15 in. in height. The flowers are 1 in. in diameter, and are usually of a light blue-purple, but they vary in shade to mauve and dark blue, and are produced in terminal corymbs of six or more. D. cashmerianum is well suited for the border or for a large rockery; in either case perfect drainage is essential, and

spurs, and is neat and rather dwarf in growth, having finely cut feathery foliage, and freely producing spikes of large blossoms, usually of a rich blue-purple, but sometimes white. It is a good perennial, is easily raised from seed, and continues to flower throughout the summer till late in autumn. It is suited for borders and beds. D. nudicaule has scarlet blossoms, a dwarf, compact, branching growth, a hardy constitution, and a free blooming habit, 1 to 3 ft, high. The flowers are in loose spikes, each blossom being about 1 in. in length; the colour

Delphinium grandiflorum.

this is best attained in rock-garden culture. Its branches have a prostrate habit, apparently adapting it to such conditions. It is best increased from seed. D. cardinale is a beautiful species of tall growth, having bright-scarlet flowers, like those of D. nudicaule. It blossoms later in summer, and continues longer in flower than D. nudicaule, owing in part to its slower development. It is a most desirable plant, and as hardy as D. nudicaule. Seedlings will probably not flower till the second season. In very damp soil it would be prudent in winter to protect the root with a hand-light or inverted pot. D. chinense is distinct from other Lark-

varies from light scarlet to a shade verging closely on crimson, and when seen in the open air, especially in sunshine, dazzles the eye by its brilliancy. D. nudicaule is perfectly hardy, and commences growth so early that it may almost be termed a spring flower, but it may be had in bloom during several of the summer months, and is handsome for warm borders. Although somewhat apt to damp off on level ground, it is a perennial on raised ground, and keeps up a succession of bloom. It is as easy to raise from seed as other Larkspurs. A tall variety of nudicaule is called elatius.

THE ANNUAL LARKSPURS.—In these

hardy annuals there is also a wealth of beauty for the summer garden, and we have a host of beautiful sorts with a wide

Portion of a group of Delphiniums in the garden at The Grange, Knutsford, Cheshire.

range of colour. There is great diversity too in the habit of growth, some being as dwarf as a Hyacinth, others 3 or 4½ ft. high, others with a branching habit re-

sembling a candelabrum. The species which have given rise to these varieties are D. Ajacis (Rocket Larkspur) and D. Consolida. D. Ajacis has the flowers in long loose spikes forming an erect and spreading panicle, the stem vigorous with open spreading branches. All the varieties of the Rocket Larkspur may be arranged in three great groups : 1. D. Ajacis majus (large Larkspur).—The stem of this is single, and varies in height, from 3 to 4 ft. 6 in. ; the flowers double, in a long, single, and compact spike, generally rounded off at the extremity. This kind has given the following varieties—white, flesh-coloured, rose, mauve or puce-coloured, pale violet, violet, ash-coloured, claret, and brown. 2. D. Ajacis minus (dwarf Larkspur).—The stem of this is from 20 to 24 in. in height, and is even shorter when the plant is sown thickly or in dry or poor soils. The flowers are very double, and in a single well-furnished spike, usually cylindrical, and rounded off at the extremity, but rarely tapering. The principal varieties are—white, mother-of-pearl, flesh colour, rose, mauve, pale mauve, peach blossom, light violet, violet, blue-violet, pale blue, ash-gray, brown, light brown, white striped with rose, white striped with gray, rose and white, and flax-coloured and white. 3. D. Ajacis hyacinthiflorum (dwarf Hyacinth-flowered Larkspur).—The varieties of this group have been raised in Belgium and Germany. They do not differ from other kinds in form of flower, but only in the spike on which the flowers are set, being more tapering, and the flowers farther apart than those of the two previously mentioned groups. There is a strain called the tall Hyacinth Larkspur. Other strains mentioned in catalogues are the Ranunculus-flowered (ranunculiflorum) and the Stock-flowered, both of which are worth cultivating.

D. Consolida (Branched Larkspur).— This species has branching stems and beautiful violet-blue flowers hung on slender stalks, and coming later than those of D. Ajacis. It embraces several varieties, both single and double, all of which may be reproduced from seed. The principal sorts are white, flesh colour, red, lilac, violet, flaxen, and variegated. The varieties especially worthy of cultivation are candelabrum, bearing pyramidal spikes of flowers of various colours ; and the Emperor varieties, of symmetrical bushy habit, which form compact and well-proportioned specimens, 1½ ft. high by 3½ ft. in circumference, doubleness of flowers possessing great constancy. There are three colours—viz dark blue, tri-coloured, and red-striped In D tricolor elegans the flowers are rose-coloured, streaked with blue or purple, and about 3 ft high

CULTURE —Annual Larkspurs should be sown where they are to remain at any time after February when the weather permits—usually in March and April They may also be sown in September and October, and even later when the ground is not frozen, but the produce of winter sowing is liable to be devoured by slugs and grubs The sowing may be made either broadcast or in rows 4 in to 8 in apart, and the plants should stand 4 in or 5 in asunder. The branching varieties may be sown in reserve beds, and in March when about 12 in or 16 in. high should be transferred to the flower beds, lifted carefully with balls of earth round the roots, so that they may not suffer These branching varieties are well suited for the garden, either in masses of one colour or of various colours They may be planted in borders or among shrubs thinly planted One great advantage of this class is that it flowers earlier and longer than the dwarf Larkspur—that is to say, it flowers throughout the summer, and, according to the period of sowing, from the end of June or July to September, and even to October if the flower-stems that have shed their blossoms be cut off. They succeed, moreover, in the driest calcareous soils, and even upon the declivities of hills By pinching, dwarf plants useful under certain circumstances may be obtained. Seed should be taken only from flowers perfectly double ; and for this purpose single-flowered plants should be carefully weeded out Larkspurs are at their best in June and July, they bloom almost anywhere, especially in dry localities, and do not require much attention They look well whether they are all of one colour, or of all the colours mixed, and, by separately using varieties possessing different colours, striking contrasts may be produced.

DENTARIA (*Toothwort*) —Interesting spring-flowering plants of the Crucifer Order, of which there are in cultivation some half a dozen species all worth growing in half-shaded positions in peat beds, among shrubs, on the margins of borders, or in the cool shrubbery. They grow best in a light sandy or peaty soil enriched by decayed leaf-mould. Their flowers are welcome in early spring, and remain some time in beauty, and they are easily increased from the small tuber-like

roots Some, like D. bulbifera, bear bulblets on the stem, and from these the plant may be increased None of them ripen seed freely. The species are—D. bulbifera, 1 to 2 ft high, flowering in spring , purple, sometimes nearly white, rather large, and borne in a raceme at the top of the stem. D digitata, a handsome dwarf kind, about 12 in high, flowers in April , rich purple, in flat racemes at the top of the stem A native of Europe D diphylla is a pretty plant, from 6 to 12 in high, bearing but two leaves, the flowers purple (sometimes white) and yellowish N America D. enneaphylla is about 1 ft. high , has in April and June clusters of creamy-white flowers, and is a pretty plant for a shady border Mountain woods in Central Europe D maxima is the largest of the species, being 2 ft high, with many pale-purple flowers, and is a native of N America. D pinnata is a stout species at once distinguished by its pinnate leaves , it is from 14 to 20 in high, flowering from April to June, bearing large pale-purple, lilac, or white flowers, in a cluster It is a native of mountain and sub-alpine woods in Switzerland D polyphylla, similar to D. enneaphylla, is about 1 ft high, with cream-coloured flowers in clusters. It is a handsome plant , from woods in Hungary *Syn* Cardamine

DESFONTAINEA.—In favoured gardens along the southern coast and in other mild parts *D spinosa*, a very beautiful evergreen shrub from Chili, can be grown and flowered out-of-doors It is of moderate growth, having foliage very much like the Holly, and handsome flowers in the form of a tube of bright scarlet tipped with yellow It usually flowers about the end of summer, and in some parts of Devonshire it blooms profusely, thriving in a light loamy soil, and even round the coasts as far as the north of Ireland, but once a few miles from the protection of the sea air it ceases to thrive and perishes, and is therefore only of value in very favoured places

DESMODIUM (*Tick Trefoil*) — A few of the North American species are cultivated, but their weedy appearance prevents their general culture These are D canadense, marilandicum, and Dilleni, all from 2 to 4 ft. high, with slender stems, terminated by dense racemes of small purplish flowers. D. penduliflorum is a really pretty shrub, and hardy if the stems are annually cut down, with graceful shoots, bearing along their upper portions numerous rich violet-purple blossoms in September. It is the name by which the beautiful Lespedeza bicolor is generally known. It is a slender shrub, graceful when in flower, 6 ft. or more in height, bearing drooping racemes of small Pea-shaped flowers of a carmine-purple colour. It is a native of China and Japan, and hardy enough for open-air culture except in cold districts. It makes a good wall shrub.

DEUTZIA. — The best of the few species in cultivation are D. gracilis and crenata, both common and well-known

abundance of double snow-white flowers. This is one of the finest hardy flowering shrubs, and is called the Pride of Rochester. Deutzias grow in any good soil, best in slight shade ; if too much exposed they are liable to suffer during drought. They should be pruned annually, the old wood being cut away, and the young growths thinned.

The species are *D. gracilis*, Japan. *grandiflora*, China. *macrantha*, Himal. *mexicana*, Mexico. *parviflora*, China.

Deutzia parviflora.

shrubs, the first generally seen in greenhouses, the second in almost every shrubbery. D. gracilis, so often grown in pots, is quite hardy, and, under good conditions, makes a dense bush about 2 ft. high, in a free soil flowering as freely as when in pots. D. crenata (commonly called D. scabra) is a much larger bush 6 to 8 ft. high, its leaves large and rough, and, when in flower, its slender stems are wreathed with racemes and panicles of pure-white blossoms. There are two distinct and beautiful varieties of it—viz. flore-pleno, with double flowers, tinged with purple, and candidissima, with an

scabra, Japan. *Sieboldiana*, Japan. *staminea*, Mountains of India.

DIANTHUS (*Pink*). — Plants of the highest garden value, containing several of our finest families of hardy flowers—the Carnation, Pink, and Sweet William—besides numerous alpine and rock plants that are among the most charming of mountain plants. Many of the species are plants of the heath, dry meadow, or maritime Alps ; or shore plants, such as the Fringed Pink (D. superbus) ; and, so far as our climate is concerned, they are almost at home in lowland gardens. On the other hand, some are among the very highest alpine plants, like the Glacier Pink and the Alpine Pink.

The following is a selection of the best species for gardens.

D. alpinus (*Alpine Pink*).—A beautiful and distinct plant, distinguished at a glance from any other cultivated Pink by blunt-pointed shining green leaves. The stems bear in summer solitary circular flowers, of deep rose spotted with crimson, and when the plant is in good health they are so numerous as to hide the leaves. In poor, moist, and very sandy loam this Pink thrives and forms a dwarf carpet, though the flower-stems are little more than 1 in. in height ; but both leaves and stems are much more vigorous and tall in deep, moist peaty soil. Wire-worms cause its death more frequently than unsuitable soil. It should be placed in a fully exposed spot, and carefully guarded against drought, especially when recently planted. It is not difficult to increase from seed, and it comes true ; and it may be also increased by division.   Alps of Austria.

D. barbatus (*Sweet William*).—One of the most admired of garden flowers, hardy and vigorous ; bearing a profusion of bright flowers which form sheets of bloom, the colours being vivid and pretty, and the flowers often finely and distinctly marked. What makes the Sweet William of such high value for small gardens is that its culture is so easy, and it may be raised from seed without the aid of glass.

The Sweet William has been greatly improved of late years, and the old varieties are surpassed. The points the "florist" improver aims at are a circular flower, with no indentation where the petals meet, thick in petal, and with all the petals marked alike, the colours meeting each other in clearly defined lines without any feathering or flushing into each other ; but in this, as in other flowers, the more variety the better. In the Sweet William colours vary, and they may be classed under two heads—dark and light kinds. Of the latter there is a strain known as the Auricula-eyed, the blooms of which have a clear white eye in a setting of red or purple or some other rich dark colour. Smooth-edged flowers, such as Hunt's strain, have their admirers. Fine, evenly rounded trusses are always present in a good strain, but size is generally allied to high culture. Except for shows, however, very large trusses are not the best, as they usually need support. The finest strain is usually found where year after year care has been exercised in selecting only the finest flowers, with the largest trusses and most varied mark-

ings. The only self-coloured flowers are those of pure white, pink, or crimson ; all the others are parti-coloured or variously marked, some very prettily mottled, others more or less edged with white or pale pink.

CULTURE.—This is very simple ; sow the seed in April, in a well-prepared bed in a sunny spot, thinning out the young plants when they are large enough, or, if a large stock is required, planting them out about 6 in. apart in good soil. About the end of September transplant them to their permanent quarters, and in the following summer they will bloom. When, however, any particular strain is to be rapidly increased the following plan is a

Dianthus alpinus (Alpine Pink).

good one : Sow in pots, and allow the seedlings to become a little drawn and lanky before planting out. Plant out in light loam, dressed only with a little leaf-mould or loam from rotted turfs, placing the seedlings so that a few of the lower joints are under the soil. When the blooming stems are well above the foliage, prick in a dressing of guano all round the plants, give plenty of water in dry weather, and a further slight dressing of guano just before the flowers begin to open. The result will be vigorous stocky shoots from the buried joints, all rooted and ready to plant out as soon as the bloom is over. Sweet Williams may also be propagated by cuttings taken off in early summer ; for the main stems, which should rise for bloom, creep along the ground, and throw up from every joint shoots suitable for cuttings ; and a little sheaf of cuttings may be taken from the tips of the main stems, so that each plant would furnish over a hundred cuttings.

Double-flowered kinds, as a rule, are not desirable except the double dwarf magnificus, the deep velvety crimson flowers of which are the finest among the double kinds : the large heads of flower are numerous, the colour is rich and effective, it is a dwarf, vigorous grower, and soon forms a strong tuft.

D. Caryophyllus (*Carnation*).—This beautiful flower, so much loved in all countries where it can be grown both under glass and in the open air, in all its forms, is derived from a wild Dianthus of Western Europe and the Alps, which as regards our own country is wild on Norman castles such as Rochester. From very early days it seems to have been a favourite flower, as in Dutch pictures nearly 200 years old the Carnation, mostly in its striped forms, is shown in perfection. Clearly at this early date the tendency of the flowers to vary in colour and markings was greatly admired. At a very early date the Carnation was divided into four classes—viz. Flakes, Bizarres, Picotees, and Painted Ladies. The Flakes had two colours only, the stripes going the whole length of the petals. Bizarres (from the French, meaning odd or irregular) were spotted or striped with three distinct colours. Picotees (from the French, *piquotée*) had a white ground with additional colours in spots, giving the flowers the appearance of being dusted with colour. Painted Ladies had the under side of the petals white and the upper side red or purple, so laid on as to appear as if really painted. Unfortunately this class has so entirely disappeared that many growers are not aware that it ever existed. The first two classes still remain unchanged ; but the Picotee, instead of being spotted, has the colours confined to the edge of the petals, and any spot on the ground colour (which may be either white or yellow) would detract from the merits of the flower as an exhibition flower.

Another class, too long neglected, consists of self-coloured kinds. A familiar type is the old crimson Clove, a sweet and lovely thing, which may be had also in several different shades of self-colour. The florists of the old school did not pay much attention to self-coloured Carnations, and till recently there was a scarcity of fine varieties. We may now have them in all shades of colour. They combine hardiness and vigour with free blooming and great effect. For the flower garden they are the most important. They should be grown in bold groups or simple masses associated with Roses or choice hardy flowers.

The Tree Carnation is very valuable as a pot plant ; or, if planted out in a greenhouse border, it produces flowers in winter and spring, when none can be had out-of-doors. The most popular of this class is Souvenir de la Malmaison, with large cream-coloured blossoms and delightful fragrance, and from this have been obtained sports of different colours ; so that, with these and other varieties, there is now no difficulty in obtaining all colours, from pure white to bright scarlet.

As a rule, the choice-named varieties of Picotees and Carnations for show are grown in pots, but we confine our remarks to their culture in the garden, also treating of it, shortly, from the exhibiting florist's point of view.

A great number of people still think Carnations are tender, and they coddle them up in frames throughout the winter. The florists, too, continue much in their old ways, which do not tend to the advancement of Carnation culture in gardens where we should see and grow fine selfs of brilliancy and beauty. As garden flowers Carnations have been badly treated, and yet there is no brighter and sweeter flower for the garden throughout summer and autumn. This fact is dawning on English raisers, but we have had the greatest success with fine French-raised selfs that combine hardiness with good form and colour, and, what is more precious, a perpetual blooming habit. Nothing could be better than Countess of Paris, Carolus Duran, Colin de Harville, Mad Roland, Murillo, Madame Lafausse, Mdlle. Rouselle, Veronica, Jenny Lind, Comte de Melbourne, and Flora. Of English kinds the only one we have had to equal the preceding is Alice, a white self of perfect form and a perpetual bloomer. Some standard kinds of the present are : Ketton Rose, Purple Emperor, Mrs. Muir, Germania, Rose Celestial, Emma Lakin, Hebe, Mary Morris, Mrs. Reynolds Hole, Aline Newman, Celia, and Joe Willett.

SOILS.--The soil has a marked influence upon Carnations. In very light hot soils as in Surrey they cannot be grown well at all. They want a loamy soil, but as this varies in texture and richness so the plants vary in growth. In very rich soils they are so luxuriant that it is necessary to make new plantations, annually destroying the old plants. In some soils however they make a harder growth, and stand two or more years, spreading into great tufts and bushes.

CULTURE FOR BORDERS AND BEDS.—First, then, of the wants of the general grower, who rightly esteems a good crimson or white Clove as it grows in the open garden as much as the most exact staged flower. And rightly so, because, in the opinion of those who have thought and studied most about it, the superiority in form is wholly with the bold, free, undressed flower. What applies to the individual flower applies with greater force to its culture in the garden. It does not appear at its best in lines, or

surpassed. Layering has to be performed when the plants are in full flower, and as it is undesirable to interfere with the groups in flower, the best plan is to have a few plants of each kind grown in nursery quarters solely for layering. We can then enjoy all that is gained from planting groups thickly, and suffer no inconvenience. We shall also have plenty of flowers, and can cut great numbers without missing them. Varied colour is the distinctive charm of the florist varieties. Few of them are likely to produce bold effects like the selfs, but they may be grown in special beds and borders in a less prominent spot. Some nurserymen are beginning to see the mistake of neglecting a noble

Bed of Carnations at Bulwick.

circles, or dotted here and there as in pattern gardening ; but good kinds planted in groups of from twelve to fifty, according to room, will give us when in flower the truest idea of the value of fine Carnations for ornamenting the garden. These groups should be renewed annually, or fresh ones should be made elsewhere, a stock of plants having been raised from layers. Only in a few cases are Carnations likely to spread and make healthy tufts, able to stand for two or three years. It is generally advisable to destroy the old plants after flowering, and, if we do not, the frost often does. Young strong layers, planted during September about 9 in. apart, will produce an effect hardly to be

flower like this, and are trying to raise bold, free, and varied border flowers easily grown in every garden. They will succeed, and our gardens will be all the better for it. In specially cultivating the better kinds in beds, it is usual to cover the surface with 1 in. or more of fine rotten manure passed through a sieve, and in dry weather to give plenty of water ; but as many will not pay more attention than is necessary, it may be stated that neither water nor top-dressing is usually required in good garden soil, and, without either, the result will be quite as valuable from an ornamental point of view. But when a good collection is grown in special little beds in a warm border of the kitchen garden, a top-dressing of one barrow of mould to three of decayed manure could be given in a very short time, and if the weather or soil were very dry an occasional heavy watering would improve matters. Varieties are endless ; and as English, Continental, and American florists are busy raising seedlings, these varieties are likely to be much added to, though enough attention has not as yet been paid to the raising of vigorous border and flower garden kinds with a great range of colour, form, continuity of bloom, and fragrance. It would be well for raisers to discard the kinds which burst their flowers. This is a great defect, an unnatural habit too long condoned, and its evils are most manifest in the flower garden. In ordering, the public should distinctly make known their wishes as to colour, form, and fragrance. The Carnation

Carnation.

does not depend for its beauty on elaborate instructions, which only the special grower for exhibition cares to master.

CARNATIONS IN POTS AND VASES.—It is a common practice to have pots and vases of flowers in the garden, but the Carnation is rarely seen in them. It is a grand flower for the purpose if naturally grown, allowing its flower spikes to droop where they will. The flowers on these last longer in bad weather, as they protect themselves from wet. Wherever pots can be stood they look admirable, but are seen to special advantage if above the line of sight. In window boxes they would make a pretty picture. The essential thing to do them well is to pot up some good strong layers in autumn and keep in a frame all the winter. In spring they should be potted into their flowering pots or vases. There should be no tying or training.

PERPETUAL CARNATIONS IN THE OPEN AIR.—These, if from a good strain of French seed, are very satisfactory plants, and useful for cutting. Their drawback is the habit of flowering in winter, but this can be obviated by sowing early, so as to get them to a good

size by autumn, when they will flower in the spring and continue to bloom all the summer. Pipings struck in the spring and planted out in the autumn will behave in the same way. Old plants are difficult to manage in the open air, but survive the winter if well thinned out ; the only danger is damp cold, which rots them at the surface of the ground. They grow very well in light rich soil on chalk. Their free-rooting habit makes them unsuitable for pots. Many of my plants filled almost 3 ft. of soil with their roots ; it is manifest waste to cram such free-growing plants in pots.—J. D.

GARDEN CULTURE FOR EXHIBITION. —About the end of July cover the bed intended to be devoted to Carnations, &c., about 2 in. with good rotten manure, and if the soil be sandy add to this 2 in. of good mellow loam, or, if it be stiff, add the same quantity of sand. Then, whenever time can be spared, fork in the dressing well and dig it over. Then put the plants in firmly, putting all of the same sort in a row with a good legible label at the end. Being perfectly hardy, they will need no attention till next spring. At the same time take up and put in in the same way any seedlings sown in the spring, which will now be fine strong plants. The next spring, when the severe cold has ceased (about March or April), hoe the beds over carefully between the rows, and in fine weather water them if they are dry. When the flower-stems begin to rise, place a stick about 30 in. long to each plant. These sticks should be painted a light whitish green. The flower-stems must be kept well tied up as they grow, but they must be tied quite loosely, for if they are tied tightly they will knee and bend, and finally break. About 20th June (or later), when the buds appear, take off all but three on each shoot, so as to leave each bud a little footstalk to itself when it grows (what is lost by this in quantity will be regained twenty-fold in quality). From this time until the buds are near showing colour, give occasionally a little weak manure-water—a handful of well-rotted stable manure to a large pot of water. As soon as they show colour at the top, tie them round with a little strip of bass about half-way down. This should be done every morning in July, as it saves much trouble as well as the unsightly peculiarity termed a "split pod." If in spite of this the pods split on one side, carefully open the bud all round at the other segments, using the flat wedge handle of a knife used for layering. Unless it is intended to save seed, cut off dead blooms as soon as they wither, and the flower-stems as soon as all the buds have come out, which will be about the end of August or beginning of September. Not later than the last week in July see to layering. As soon as the layers are rooted, which will be early in September, take them off and lay them in by the heels for a time, while taking up and throwing away the old stools, top-dress and fork over the bed with 2 in. of well-rotted stable litter or cow-house

very lightly with finely sifted compost, and put them in a cold frame or house out of danger of frost. When they show three pairs of leaves, prick them out about 2 in. apart round the edges of 5-in. pots filled with the same compost, and keep them still in the cool house till there is no fear of frost. When they are about 3 in. high, prick them out into beds, keeping them about 4 in. apart. The beds may be enriched with a little sand and manure. In the autumn they will be

Redbraes Picotee.

sweepings, replace the layers, and they will be in the same condition as at the beginning.

PROPAGATION BY SEED.—The proper time to sow is about April or May. Prepare a compost of equal parts of loam, leaf-mould, and silver sand, sift it fine, and fill a number of 3-in. pots (as many as you have sorts of seed) to within 1 in. of the rim. Sprinkle each pot with a fine rose, flatten the surface, and with the point of a knife put down the seeds separately about $\frac{1}{2}$ in. apart. Cover them

nice little plants, and may be planted where they are to flower, which will be the next year. Keep and name any really good kind, discarding all singles, and using the rest for borders or beds for cutting from.

BY PIPINGS.—When the plants throw up shoots too numerous to layer, or when the root is attacked by disease, the shoots may be taken off as follows : Take the shoot just above the fourth or fifth joint from the top, and with a sharp pull draw it out from the socket formed by the next

M M

joint, which it will pull away with it. Just through the joint make a little upward slit in the cutting, and thrust it firmly into a pot filled to within 1 in. of the top with the compost described, and the rest with silver sand. Water the pot and plunge it in fibre under a hand-light for three or four weeks, when the pipings will be rooted. They may then be potted off singly or bedded like layers, and will flower the next year. Plants thus struck are never so good as those propagated by layers, but this method is a useful expedient to save a good sort or to get up a good stock.

BY LAYERS.—This is the best and most generally accepted method of propagating Carnations and Picotees. It should be commenced at latest the last week in July, and finished by the second week in August. It is performed as follows : Scrape away the earth round the plant to the depth of 2 in., and substitute for the earth removed the compost prescribed. Strip each shoot up to the top three or four joints, going all round the plant before proceeding farther. Then with a fine sharp knife cut half through a shoot, just below a joint, make a slanting cut up through the joint, and bring the knife out just above it ; take a peg with a hook in it, and thrust it into the fresh compost just above the tongue, so that as the peg comes down it will catch the tongue and peg it into the earth. Cover it with a little more compost placed firmly. Proceed thus all round the plant, finally watering carefully with a fine rose waterpot to settle the soil around the layers. In about a month the layers will be rooted, and by the second week in October all the young plants ought to be in their winter quarters.

SEVERAL DISEASES affect Carnations. Two of the worst are fungoid growths. One of these is a fungus which grows between the membranes of the leaf, and the only method of destroying it is to pick off and burn every infected leaf. It appears at first as a small blister which bursts, scattering its spores and leaving a dark-brown scar. A more familiar disease is that known as spot; a damp atmosphere or overcrowding of the plants being the causes. It spreads rapidly, but some kinds enjoy a complete immunity from it. Dusting the plants two or three times with a mixture of soot and sulphur has been found effectual. The gout is a swelling of the stem close to the surface of the ground, which eventually bursts, supposed to be caused by little worms which eat their way into the collar of the plant and lay eggs there which hatch worms that feed upon and eventually kill the plant. The Maggot is a small insect with great powers for mischief. It comes in the spring from an egg laid no doubt in the skin or tissues of the leaf, and, eating its way down under the skin of the leaf, it makes a home in the main stem of the plant, eating out the centre and killing it. The only remedy appears to be diligently searching for and hunting it out before it has traversed the leaf. Wire-worm is a pest to be reckoned with, but usually only gives trouble in fresh soil. Spittle fly, which appears when the flower-spikes are growing, must be destroyed, or it will do serious harm. An open situation and a well-drained soil are conditions unfavourable to the spot diseases, whilst rotation in planting keeps the stock free from the worm pests and maggots.

D. cæsius (*Cheddar Pink*).—One of the neatest and prettiest of the dwarf Pinks, the fragrant and rosy flowers appearing in spring, on stems 6 in. high, and in good soil sometimes taller. This Pink requires peculiar treatment, as in winter it perishes in the ordinary border, while quite happy on an old wall. It is a native of Europe and Britain (the rocks at Cheddar, in Somersetshire). To establish it on the top or any part of an old wall sow the seeds on the wall in a little cushion of Moss, if such exists, or, if not, place a little earth in a chink with the seed, and it may also be grown upon the rock-garden, in firm, calcareous, or gritty earth, placed in a chink between two small rocks.

D. deltoides (*Maiden Pink*).—A pretty native plant, with bright pink-spotted or white flowers, on stems from 6 to 12 in. long. It grows almost anywhere, in borders or on rockwork, does not appear to suffer from wire-worm, like most other Pinks, and often flowers several times during the summer. It may be readily raised from seed, and is easily increased by division. The variety glauca has white flowers with a pink eye. It is abundant on Arthur's Seat, near Edinburgh, and forms a charming contrast to the crimson kind.

D. dentosus (*Amoor Pink*).—A distinct and pretty dwarf Pink, with violet-lilac flowers, more than 1 in. across, the margins toothed, and the base of each petal having a regular dark-violet spot, which forms a dark "eye" nearly ½ in. across in the centre of the flower. The plant flowers from May or June till autumn, and thrives in sandy soil, in borders, or on rockwork ; seed. South Russia.

D. neglectus (*Glacier Pink*). — A

brilliant alpine plant, forming, very close to the ground, tufts like short wiry grass, from which spring many flowers, 1 in. across, and of bright rose. It grows freely in very sandy loam, either in pots or on the rock-garden, rooting into the sand through the bottom of the pots as freely as any weed, is hardy, easily grown, increased by division and seed. Alps and Pyrenees. *Syn.*, D. glacialis.

D. petræus (*Rock Pink*).—A charming Pink, forming hard tufts, 1 or 2 in. high, from which spring numerous flower-stems,

plants, as they live longer and thrive better when raised above the general level of the ground, though they grow well in ordinary soil. They have for many years been amongst the favourite "florists'" flowers in European countries, and are hardier and dwarfer than the Carnation. In August, Pinks should be planted 9 in. apart, the ground being rich and well prepared. If the winter be very severe, a little litter should be put over them, and in spring the surface of the beds should be stirred a little, and given a top-dressing of fine old manure and a

Dianthus neglectus (Glacier Pink)

each bearing a fine rose-coloured flower. It seems to escape the attacks of wire-worm. It flowers in summer, and should be planted on the rock-garden in sandy and rather poor moist loam. Hungary; seed or division.

D. plumarius (*The Common Pink*).— This is the parent of our numerous varieties of Pinks, and has single purple flowers, rather deeply cut at the margin, and is naturalised on old walls in various parts of England. The wild plant is rather handsome when grown in healthy tufts, but on the level ground it is apt to perish. The many fragrant double varieties are welcome everywhere, and should be cultivated as rock or bank

slight dusting of guano. As they push up their flower-spikes these should be staked, and if they are for exhibition the buds should be thinned, as many varieties produce buds too freely. The culture of Pinks, however, either for exhibition or for the garden, is simple, and the outlay small. Get newly struck pipings in August and September—the best months to plant them in a sunny place. In a smoky town a cold frame will be needed; but if the air be clear, an open bed will do. When the pipings are once planted in the open garden, they require little care till they begin to push up their flower-stems. Spring planting should be commenced as early as the weather permits, and, as soon as the plants begin to grow, the bed should be mulched about 1 in. deep with equal quantities of well-rotted horse manure and leaf-mould   The plants will then fast push on their new growth

INCREASING STOCK — If the plants have made good growth in July, cut the strongest shoots with a sharp knife, cut off the ends of the grass, and cut the shoot two or three joints below the grass or leaves   Prepare some ground as follows   Scatter a little salt on the surface, then riddle on 2 in deep of fresh soil, prick in the pipings, and put a light or hand-glass over them , and they will be rooted in a few weeks

Where seed is wanted, protect the flowers from wet, and as they decay remove the withered petals, which encourage damp and form a harbour for insects   Seed should be saved only from the finest and most constant varieties of vigorous and hardy growth, and may be sown early in June in pots, or in the open ground

GARDEN OR BORDER PINKS —The show Pinks may be left to the exhibitor. There are certain kinds both old and new which must be taken care of by the "general lover" of flowers   These are the hardier border kinds, grown for their beauty and fragrance   As in the case of the hardier Carnations, we must encourage these   Some of the best of the hardier kinds are—Anne Boleyn, Ascot (soft pink), Fimbriatus major, Fragrans (pure), George White, Hercules, Lady Blanche, Mrs Moore, Mrs Pettifer, Mrs Sinkins (Mule Pink), Marie Paré (Mule Pink), Napoleon III , Multiflorus, Newmarket, Pluto, Purity, Robustus, Rubens, Thalia, White Queen, Wm Bruce, High Clére, Multiflorus flore-pleno, Multiflorus roseus, Striatiflorus, Speciosus fl -pl , Coccineus, Early Blush, Fimbriatus albus (old white), Lord Lyons, Miss Joliffe, Nellie, White Perpetual, the Clove Pink, Her Majesty

DWARF SINGLE AND DOUBLE PINKS —Messrs Dicksons, of Edinburgh, have raised some dwarf profuse - blooming Pinks so compact in habit and stiff in stem that they do without stakes   Most Pinks are better without stakes, especially when their foliage is healthy, and is in such wide tufts as to shield the flowers from splashed earth , but these new dwarf sorts may be compact enough for the rock-garden   Mr. J Grieve, who raised them, says   " Both the single and the dwarf double varieties will prove quite a boon to the flower-gardener and for bouquets   To the ordinary eye all florists'

Pinks consist of but one variety , whereas amongst the single and dwarf sorts there are endless colours, and many of the flowers are so varied in colour as to render them easily mistaken for other plants   Numbers of the single sorts look like miniature Petunias "   Carnea Beauty, Delicata, Rosea, Spicata, and Odorata are among the best of these new dwarf Pinks, and the class will no doubt be added to

D. sinensis (*Chinese Pink*) —This has given rise to a race of beautiful garden flowers   It is an annual, or biennial, according to the way it is sown and grown   If sown early, the plants will flower the first year , if late, the second.   On dry soils, and if the winters be mild, they will live for two or three years   The varieties, both single and double, are now very numerous and beautiful, and may be classed under D. Heddewigi and D laciniatus   The forms of Heddewigi, the Japanese variety, are dwarf and handsome, while there are double-flowered forms, particularly diadematus, the flowers of which are large and very double   The petals of the laciniated section are very deeply cut into a fine fringe   Of this class there are also double-flowered forms   The colours of both are much varied, and there are striped crimson and white sorts   There is a pretty dwarf class (nanus), about 6 in high, but it is less useful than the taller varieties for cutting from   Two beautiful and distinct selected sorts, Crimson Belle and Eastern Queen, are among the best varieties   Sow D sinensis under glass in February, with very little or no bottom-heat , give air freely during open weather, and in April plant out in well-cultivated soil, which need not be rich.   Place the plants 9 in to 12 in apart each way, and they will form compact tufts   Encourage the laterals by pinching off decayed flowers, and the result will be a mass of blossom throughout the summer, and probably till November   Some sow in autumn, and winter the young plants in frames or under hand-glasses, — hardening them off by degrees in spring, until they have become fully established   These Pinks are admirable for the flower garden, either in beds by themselves, or mixed , they may be well used with taller plants of a different character dotted sparsely among them

D superbus (*Fringed Pink*) —A fragrant wild pink, easily known by its petals being cut into strips for more than half their length   It inhabits many parts of Europe from Norway to the Pyrenees, and is a true perennial, though it perishes so often in gardens that many regard it as a biennial. It is more likely to perish in winter on rich and moist soil than on poor and light soil, and, when it is desired to establish it as a perennial, it should be planted in fibry loam, well mixed with sand or grit. It grows, however, on nearly any soil; and, by raising it every year from seed, an abundant stock may be kept up even where the plant perishes in winter. It comes true from seed, and is often more than 1 ft. high; flowering in summer or in early autumn, and is better suited for mixed beds and borders than for the rock-garden.

DIAPENSIA (*D. lapponica*) is a sturdy and dwarf evergreen alpine shrub, often under 2 in. in height, growing in dense rounded tufts, having narrow closely packed leaves, and bearing in summer solitary white flowers, about half an inch across. It may be grown well on fully exposed spots on the rock-garden, in deep sandy and stony peat which is kept well moistened during the warm season. It is a native of N. Europe and N. America, being found on high mountains or in arctic latitudes.

DICENTRA (*Bleeding Heart*).—Graceful plants of the Fumitory Order, including about half a dozen cultivated species, of which the finest are—

D. chrysantha.—This handsome plant forms a spreading tuft of rigid glaucous foliage, from which arises a stiff leafy stem, 3 to 4 ft. high, with long branching panicles of bright golden-yellow blossoms, about 1 in. long in August and September; it seems hardy in light rich soil if warm and sheltered. Seed. California.

D. Cucullaria (*Dutchman's-breeches*) and D. thalictrifolia are less important, and rather belong to the curious garden.

D. eximia combines a Fern-like grace with the flowering qualities of a good hardy perennial. From 1 to 1½ ft. high, with numerous reddish-purple blossoms in long drooping racemes. It is useful for the rock-garden and the mixed border, or for naturalising by woodland walks; thriving in rich sandy soil. Division. N. America.

D. formosa is similar to the preceding, having also Fern-like foliage, but is dwarfer in growth, its racemes shorter and more crowded, and its flowers lighter. Suitable for same positions as D. eximia. California.

D. spectabilis.—A beautiful plant, too well known to need description, as nearly every garden is adorned with its singular flowers, which resemble rosy hearts, and, in strings of a dozen or more, are gracefully borne on slender stalks. It succeeds best in warm, light, rich soils, if in sheltered positions, being liable to be cut down by late spring frosts. It is moreover suited for the mixed border, but is of such remarkable beauty and grace that it may be used with the best effect near the lower flanks of rockwork, in bushy places near it, or on low parts where the stone or "rock" is suggested rather than shown. It is worthy of naturalisation on light rich soils by wood walks. It is also excellent for mixed borders, and for snug corners on the fringes of choice shrubs in peat, as such soil suits it well. There is a "white" variety, which is by no means

Dictamnus Fraxinella.

so ornamental, though worth growing for variety's sake. Propagated by division in autumn.

The species are *D. canadensis*, N. Amer. *chrysantha*, Calif. *Cucullaria*, N. Amer. *eximia*, do. *formosa*, do. *lachenaliæflora*, Siberia. *ochroleuca*, Calif. *pauciflora*, Calif. *pusilla*, Japan. *Roylei*, Mts. of India. *scandens*, do. *spectabilis*, Japan. *thalictrifolia*, Mts. of India, *torulosa*, do. *uniflora*, N. America.

DICKSONIA. — A noble evergreen Tree Fern, *D. antarctica* having a stout trunk, 30 ft. high or more, the fronds forming a magnificent crown, often 20 to 30 ft. across. They are from 6 to 20 ft. long, becoming pendulous with age. It is the hardiest of Tree Ferns, and the most suitable for the open air, in sheltered shady dells. From the end of May to October. In favourable localities it may even be left out all the winter.

DICTAMNUS (*Fraxinella*). — *D. Fraxinella* is a favourite old plant, about 2 ft. high, forming dense tufts, flowers pale purple, and with darker lines (there is a white form) borne in racemes in June and July. This plant does best in a light soil. It is propagated by seeds sown as soon as they are ripe, or by its fleshy roots, which, if cut into pieces, in spring, will form good plants much quicker than seedlings. It is a slow-growing plant in most gardens, though it is freer in some warm soils, and a very long-lived plant where it likes the soil. It is at home in the sunny mixed border among medium-sized plants. Caucasian Mountains.

DIDISCUS.—A native of New Holland, and from 1 to 2 ft. high. In *D. cœruleus* the stems are erect and much branched, each branch terminating in a flat umbel of small flowers, of a pleasing clear blue colour, which are borne freely from August to October. It is a half-hardy annual, and requires rather careful treatment, as it is impatient of excessive moisture, especially in the early stages of its growth. It requires to be raised in a gentle hotbed, and the seedlings should be transplanted in May to a warm friable soil, in which they will flower freely. Those who seek distinct and novel effects might use this plant, as its pretty blue flowers are uncommon in the Parsley Order, which usually has pale flowers. A little bed or groundwork would be charming if only as a change. *Syn.*, Trachymene cœrulea.

Dielytra. See DICENTRA.

Diervilla. See WEIGELA.

DIGITALIS (*Foxglove*).—The most important plant of this genus is our native Foxglove, and the handsomest of the several species in cultivation. The best of the exotics is D. grandiflora, a tall slender plant, bearing large bell-shaped yellow blossoms in long racemes. The other kinds are D. ferruginea, aurea, eriostachys, fulva, lævigata, lanata, lutea, ochroleuca, parviflora, Thapsi, tomentosa, but these are suited mainly for botanical collections.

D. purpurea (*Foxglove*).—Wild Foxgloves seldom differ in colour, but cultivated ones assume a variety of colours, including white, cream, rose, red, deep red, and other shades. The charm of these varieties, however, lies in their pretty throat-markings--spots and blotchings of

deep purple and maroon, which make large flowers resemble those of a Gloxinia ; hence the name gloxiniæflora is applied to some finely-spotted kinds. The garden plants make grand border flowers ; they are more robust than the wild plant, and have stouter stems and larger flowers. If associated with other tall plants, they look well as a background to mixed borders ; and the improved varieties have a fine effect in the wild garden if planted or sown in bold masses. They are good, too, among Rhododendrons, where these bushes are not too thick, and they charmingly break the masses of foliage. The seed is small, and is best sown in pans or boxes, under glass, early in May. When the young plants are well up they should be placed out of doors to get thoroughly hardened before being finally planted out. In shrubbery borders several plants produce a finer effect than when set singly. The Foxglove frequently blooms two years in succession ; but it is always well to sow a little seed annually ; and if there be any to spare, it may be scattered in woods or copses where it is desired to establish the plants. Those who do not require seed should cut out the centre spike as soon as it gets shabby, and the side shoots will be considerably benefited, especially if a good supply of water be given in dry weather. In a good variety a side shoot will supply an abundance of seed.—D.

The species are :—*D. ambigua*, W. Asia. *atlantica*, Algeria. *ciliata*, Caucas. *cochinchinensis*, Cochinch. *dubia*, Balearics. *eriostachya*. *ferruginea*, S. Europe. *Fontanesii*. *gloxinioides*. *laciniata*, Spain. *lævigata*, Danube and Greece. *lanata*, do. *leucophœa*, Greece. *longibracteata*, Austria. *lutea*, S. Europe. *lutescens*, France. *mariana*, Spain. *minor*, Spain. *nervosa*, Persia. *obscura*, Spain. *orientalis*, As. Min. *parviflora*, S. Europe. *purpurascens*, Europe. *purpurea*, do. *sibirica*, Siberia. *Thapsi*, Spain. *viridiflora*, Greece.

DIGRAPHIS(*Ribbon Grass*).—Grasses, of which the Ribbon Grass (D. arundinacea variegata) is the most familiar. Being hardy and perennial, it is valuable for good effect in the flower garden. It should be treated liberally, and renewed by young plants every other year. If it be not desired in the flower garden proper, a few tufts by a back shrubbery will suffice. It grows anywhere.

Dimorphanthus. See ARALIA.

DIMORPHOTHECA (*Cape Marigold*). —A hardy annual from the Cape, 18 in. to 2 ft. high ; the flowers of *D. pluvialis* are white and purplish-violet beneath, expanding in fine weather. Plants from spring-sown seed flower from July to September. It is a bold free annual thriving in any good soil and an effective ground plant with the larger flower-garden subjects; alone, however, it is well worth growing Compositæ.

DIOTIS (*Sea Cotton-weed*) —*D mari-tima* is a dwarf cottony herb suitable for the rock-garden, and sometimes employed in the flower-garden as an edging plant. It is apt to grow rather straggling, and to prevent this it is kept neatly pegged down and cut in well It should have deep sandy soil. Increased by cuttings, as it seldoms seeds in gardens. Native of our southern shores.

Diplopappus See ASTER

DIPSACUS (*Teasel*) —Coarse-growing plants, annual or biennial, striking in form, in woods and hedgerows, where their fine foliage and habit have a good effect. There are three native species, D Fullonum, pilosus, and sylvestris, the boldest kind is D laciniatus, a European species growing 5 to 8 ft high, with large deeply-cut foliage. The seed may be sown in woody places and by freshly broken hedge-banks, where the plants will often perpetuate themselves

DODECATHEON (*American Cowslip*) —Beautiful plants, of the Primrose family, perennials from N. America, where they are called Shooting Stars. They are all hardy, requiring a cool situation and light loamy soil. The nature of the soil is, however, of small importance, as they grow almost as freely in peat or leaf-mould as in loam, situation is the principal point In borders where Primulas and Soldanellas thrive, Dodecatheons will soon establish themselves. All the kinds grow freely in sandy loam, and soon form large tufts, which should be divided every third or fourth year The best time for transplanting them is the end of January or the beginning of February, when the roots are becoming active, but care must be taken not to divide them into pieces too small, for fear of losing the plants while they are in a weakly condition All may be easily raised from seed.

D. integrifolium --A lovely flower, the petals have a white base, and spring from a yellow and dark orange cup, the flowers deep rosy crimson, on stems from 4 to 6 in high, in March It is a native of the Rocky Mountains, and a choice plant for the rock-garden, if planted in sandy peat or sandy loam with leaf-mould It is easily grown in pots placed in the open air in some sheltered and half-shady spot during summer, and kept in shallow cold frames during winter Strong well-established plants produce abundance of seed, which

should be sown soon after it is gathered. Careful division.

D. Jeffreyanum.—A stout kind, more than 2 ft high in good soil, with larger and thicker leaves than D Meadia, reddish midribs strong and conspicuous, and the flower somewhat larger and darker. D. Jeffreyanum is a hardy and distinct plant, thriving in light, rich, and deep loam, in a warm and sheltered spot, where its great leaves are not broken by high winds.

D. Meadia (*American Cowslip*), a graceful plant and a favourite among old border flowers, its slender stems from 10 to 16 in. high, bearing umbels of elegantly drooping flowers, the purplish petals springing up vertically from the pointed centre of the flowers, something like those of the greenhouse Cyclamen. It loves a rich light loam, and is one of the most suitable plants for the rock-garden, for choice mixed borders, or for the fringes of beds of American plants. In many deep light loams it thrives without any preparation, but where a place is prepared for it, it is best to add plenty of leaf-mould and plant in a somewhat shaded and sheltered position, though it often thrives in exposed borders. It is best increased by division when the plants die down in autumn, but if seed is sown, it should be sown soon after it is gathered. There are numbers of pretty and distinct varieties, differing more or less in height of plant and size and colour of flower. Among the best are D giganteum, elegans, albiflorum, and violaceum D californicum, though sometimes thought a species, is probably only a variety of D Meadia It is, however, a distinct and pretty plant, and worth growing.

DONDIA (*D Epipactis*) is a singular and pretty little herb, 3 to 6 in high, having small heads of greenish-yellow flowers in spring, and suitable for the rock-garden, margins of borders, or banks, increased by division after flowering A model rock plant, a native of Carinthia and Carniola. *Syn*, Hacquetia Epipactis

DORONICUM (*Leopard's Bane*) — Showy plants of the order Compositæ, of which half-a-dozen species are in gardens, all of vigorous growth, flowering in spring, and thrive in any soil, they are therefore excellent for rough places, for naturalising, or for dry banks, where little else will thrive All are readily increased by division of the roots They range in height from 9 to 12 in, and have large, bright yellow Daisy-like flowers. The best species are D. austriacum and caucasicum, both of which are neater than the rest and produce in early spring a profusion of blossoms that enliven the borders besides being useful for cutting. The other kinds are D. Clusi, carpetanum, Columnæ, Pardalianches, and

Doronicum plantagineum excelsum.

plantagineum, all natives of Europe. D. plantagineum var. excelsum (*syn.*, Harpur Crewe) is by far the best.—D.

The species are: *D. altaicum*, Siberia. *austriacum*, Europe. *Bourgaei*, Canaries. *cacaliæfolium*, As. Minor. *carpetanum*, Spain. *caucasicum*, As. Minor. *Clusii*, Pyrenees. *Columnae*, S. Europe and As. Min. *corsicum*, Corsica. *croaticum*, S. Europe. *dentatum*. *Falconeri*, Spain. *glaciale*, do. *grandiflorum*, Europe. *hirsutum*, do. *hungaricum*, S.E. Europe. *macrophyllum*, Caucas., Persia. *maximum*, Armenia. *oblongifolium*, Caucas. *Orphanidis*, Greece. *Pardalianches*, Europe. *plantagineum*, Europe. *Roylei*, Mts. of India. *scorpioides*, Europe. *stenoglossum*, China. *Thirkei*, Bithynia.

DOWNINGIA.—Charming little Californian half-hardy annuals, generally known as Clintonia. There are two species, D. pulchella and elegans, similar to each other, resembling the dwarf annual Lobelias in habit, but more brilliant in colour. D. pulchella is of dwarf habit, rarely exceeding 6 in. in height, and is suitable for edging small beds or borders, as when covered with its bright blue flowers it is very pretty. In March and April the seed should be sown in the open ground in a free soil and an open situation, but, if the plants are intended for pot culture, the sowing should be two months earlier. Each plant should be allowed

quite 8 in. for development, and in hot weather those from the latest sowing should be well watered. The flowers of the several varieties of D. pulchella differ in colour, the best variety being alba (white), rubra (red), and atropurpurea (dark purple).

DRABA (*Whitlow Grass*).—Minute alpine plants, most of them having bright yellow or white flowers, and leaves often in neat rosettes. They are too dwarf to take care of themselves among plants much bigger than Mosses, and therefore there are few positions suitable for them ; but it would be very interesting to try them on mossy walls, ruins, or bits of mountain ground with sparse vegetation. The best-known and showiest is D. aizoides, found on old walls and rocks in the west of England. It forms a dwarf, spreading, cushion-like tuft, which, in spring, is covered with bright yellow blossoms. D. Aizoon, alpina, ciliaris, cuspidata, lapponica, rupestris, frigida, and helvetica are very dwarf, compact-growing plants. In each the small flowers, white or yellow, are produced abundantly. Rarer kinds are D. Mawi, glacialis, and bruniæfolia, all worth growing in a full collection of alpine flowers for a choice rock-garden.

Dracæna. See CORDYLINE.

DRACOCEPHALUM (*Dragon's-head*).—Plants of the Sage family, among them a few choice perennials suitable for the rock-garden or the mixed border, succeeding in light garden soil and increased by division or seed. D. altaiense has bright green leaves, and axillary clusters of large tubular flowers of a dense Gentian-like blue, spotted with red in the throat. D. austriacum has flower-stems nearly 1 ft. in height, densely covered with rich purple blossoms ; D. Ruyschianum, a handsome species, has narrow Hyssop-like leaves and purplish-blue flowers, but its variety japonicum, a new introduction from Japan, is even more showy. D. peregrinum, with pretty blue flowers always produced in pairs, is desirable, and so is D. argunense, which is a variety of D. Ruyschianum. The most beautiful of all is D. grandiflorum, a rock-garden plant, which is the earliest in flower. It is very dwarf, and has large clusters of intensely blue flowers, which scarcely overtop the foliage. In D. speciosum, a Himalayan species, the small deep purple flowers are nearly smothered by the large green bracts. The hardy annual kinds, such as Moldavicum and D. canescens, are ornamental, and worth a place in a full collection.

DROSERA (*Sundew*).—Most interesting little bog-plants, of which all the hardy species but one are natives of Britain. All are characterised by tufts of leaves which have their surfaces covered with dense glandular hairs. When the native kinds are grown artificially the condition of their natural home should be imitated as far as possible. In a bog on a very small scale it is not easy to secure the humid atmosphere they have at home, but they will grow wherever Sphagnum grows. The native kinds are intermedia, longifolia, obovata, and rotundifolia. The North American Thread-leaved Sundew (D. filiformis) is a beautiful bog-plant, with very long slender leaves covered with glandular hairs, the flowers purplerose colour, half an inch wide, and opening only in the sunshine. It is quite hardy, but appears difficult to cultivate.

DRYAS(*Mountain Avens*).—Mountain plants of the Rose family, containing two or three dwarf alpine plants of spreading growth and neat evergreen foliage. They thrive in borders in light soil, though they are seen to best advantage in the rockgarden, where they can spread over the brows and surfaces of limestone rocks, best on an exposed spot, not too dry, though when well established they will flourish under almost any conditions. Division in spring. The kinds are *D. Drummondi*, a dwarf, hardy, evergreen trailer, with flower-stems 3 to 8 in. high ; its yellow flowers, 1 in. across, appear in summer. A native of N. America. *D. octopetala*, a creeping evergreen, forming dense tufts, with pretty white flowers. It is a British plant and there are two others, *D. lanata*, a native of Europe, and *D. integrifolia*, American.

ECCREMOCARPUS.—*E. Scaber* is a delightful old climber for walls, trellises, and pillars, its orange-red flowers are beautiful, and its rambling shoots graceful. If the roots are protected during winter, they are uninjured and the plant annually increases in size. Increased freely by seed, and should be raised in this way occasionally. Syn., Calampelis.

ECHEVERIA. — Dwarf succulent plants, much used in the flower garden, especially the half-hardy species like secunda. Other species are tenderer and need a greenhouse to keep them through the winter, and a warm house or frame to propagate them in the spring. E. secunda is well known by its pale green rosette, leaves tipped with red. E. s. major is but a mealy form of the same. E. s. glauca differs only in having leaves rather more pointed and glaucous. E. s. pumila is a smaller form, with narrow leaves of the same colour as E. s. major. E. glauca

metallica is intermediate between the well-known E. metallica and E. secunda glauca. Dwarf and massive, the leaves are very solid and fleshy. E. metallica is a noble species, and distinct in the size of its leaves and in their rich metallic hue. The dwarfer kinds are used mostly as edgings or panels. The fine E. metallica is very effective on the margins of beds and groups of the dwarfer foliage plants, or here and there among hardy succulents. It should be planted out about the middle of May.

INCREASE.—As soon as the seed is ripe prepare to sow it. Fill some 4-in. pots to within ¼ in. of the rim with equal proportions of leaf-mould and well-sanded loam. Make the surface very firm, and water the soil so that the whole body of it becomes thoroughly moistened. Having allowed the moisture to drain away, scatter the seed lightly and cover it thinly with silver sand. Place the pot in a hand-light or in a close frame ; cover with a pane of glass and shade. The seed will germinate before the soil can dry, and if it is sown as soon as it is ripe every seed will come up. As soon as the seedlings are large enough to handle, prick them out thinly into pans or 6-in. pots ; keep them close until they are fairly established, and then allow them the full benefit of sun and air. After the middle of September give no water, and take care to remove all decay as soon as it is perceived. If planted early in April in well-worked and fairly-enriched soil, these little plants will be strong by the autumn. There is another method of increasing them. With a sharp knife cut out the heart of the plant, so as to induce offshoots. These taken off will speedily make good specimens. E. metallica may be increased in the following manner : Take off the flower-stems which come early in the season ; cut off the embryo flowers and place the stems in pots of sandy soil. These stems will strike and will produce little offsets from the axils of the flower-stem leaves. If these are taken off they will readily strike. E. metallica may also be raised from seed in the manner above described.

Echinacea. See RUDBECKIA.

ECHINOCACTUS.—*E. Simpsoni* is a beautiful little Cactaceous plant, a native of Colorado, occurring at great elevations, and believed to be hardy. It grows in a globular mass, 3 or 4 in. across, which is covered with white spines. It flowers early in March, bearing large pale purple blossoms which are very beautiful. No one appears to have had any lengthened experience in cultivating it, but, so far, it seems to thrive. Its natural conditions should be imitated as far as may be. In its native habitat it enjoys a dry climate, and, in some seasons at least, is more or less protected from frost by a covering of snow. In this country, however, it has withstood 32° of frost, and therefore in a dry spot may escape and flourish.

ECHINOCEREUS. — Plants of the Cactus family (from arid regions in N. America), some of which have been said to be hardy. Mr. E. G. Loder, of Weedon, Northamptonshire, grows and flowers them successfully. He thus writes to *The Garden*: " I have a wall here where the Ivy hangs over in such a way that it keeps a large portion of the winter's snow and rain off the plants growing underneath. In this position I have grown several species of Echinocereus and Opuntia, an Echinocactus, and a Mammillaria. Only small plants were tried, yet several flowered in spite of our very severe winters and not favourable summers. We had 41° of frost one winter, but none of these Cacti were injured by it. No species of Cactus which I have tried does well in a level border. A narrow rock border, raised about 1 ft. high, against a south wall, would be a capital position, but it is much improved if the wall has a good wide coping. The most attractive is a natural one of Ivy. What success I have in the culture of these plants has amply repaid me for all the trouble and care spent upon them ; but much greater success may reasonably be expected by any one who will undertake their cultivation in a more sunny part of England. All of them are beautiful, and some quite splendid when in flower. E. Fendleri bears some of the brightest coloured flowers that I have ever seen—a rich purple." The species of Echinocereus that Mr. Loder grows are E. nœphiceus, gonacanthus, Fendleri, viridiflorus, and paucispinus. We have no doubt that various hardy Cacti of N. America would flower well on raised stony borders and sunny banks in rock-gardens. Give them soil which is well drained and sunny, but exposed, away from all coping or artificial protection, but take great care so to place them in relation to surrounding objects that their stems cannot easily be hurt in clearing or passing. A few protecting stones and low evergreens can be grouped so as to keep off the digger and also dangerous animals. A close turf of some dwarf clean alpine will prevent earth-splashings and will improve the effect.

Echinochloa. See PANICUM.

ECHINOPS (*Globe Thistle*).—A fine hardy plant from S. Russia, 3 to 5 ft. high, covered with a silvery down, *E. ruthenicus* having the flowers blue, in round heads. Thrives in ordinary soil. Easily multiplied by division of the tufts, or by cuttings of the roots in spring. It is the most ornamental of its distinct family, and is highly suitable for grouping with the bolder herbaceous plants. It would also look well when isolated on the turf. There are other species, mostly from S. Europe and the Levant, among which are E. Ritro and E. banaticus ; but we have never seen any so good as E. ruthenicus, and, as the species are very much alike, it is enough to grow the best. E. sphærocephalus is

Echinops ruthenicus (Globe Thistle).

a fine species tall and handsome ; giganteus is a garden variety of the above, more robust, and with larger heads.

ECHIUM (*Viper's Bugloss*).—Handsome plants of the Forget-me-not Order, the finer kinds of which, though superb in the open gardens of S. Europe, are too tender for flower gardens. E. plantagineum is one of the handsomest of the annual or biennial species. Its showy flowers, of rich purplish-violet, are in long slender wreaths that rise erect from a tuft of broad leaves. It is handsomer than our indigenous species, E. pustulatum and E. vulgare. E. rubrum is a scarce and handsome species, its habit is similar to those above mentioned, but its colour is a reddish-violet, similar to the attractive E. creticum. The Salamanca Viper's Bugloss (E. salmanticum) is another fine kind, but difficult to obtain, except from its native locality. These five species are now in cultivation, and are representative of the annual and biennial Echiums. They are all showy and of the simplest culture. The seeds should be sown in ordinary garden soil, either in spring for the current year's flowering, or late in autumn for flowering in early summer. Our native E. vulgare is good in certain positions ; its long racemes of blue flowers are handsomer than those of the Italian Anchusa. Against a hot wall, where nothing else would grow, Dr. Acland, of the Grammar School, Colchester, planted some, and they gave a beautiful bloom. It is valuable for such positions, particularly on hot gravelly or chalky soils.

Edraianthus. See WAHLENBERGIA.

Edwardsia. See SOPHORA.

ELÆAGNUS (*Oleaster*). — Several of the Oleasters are beautiful shrubs, and deserve to be much more widely cultivated than they are now.

E. angustifolia, the form which grows wild in South-eastern Europe, is the wild Olive of the old Greek authors, and in some modern books is called Jerusalem Willow. The long silvery-gray fruit is constantly sold in the Constantinople markets under the name of Ighidé agâghi, and is sweet and pleasant to the taste, abounding as it does in a dry, mealy, saccharine substance ; it possesses the property of retaining, for a considerable time after being gathered, its usual size and form. The general aspect of this form is much more that of a Willow than an Olive, the long lanceolate leaves being grayish above and silvery-white beneath. Under cultivation I have seen this thrive in a dry, hungry, sandy soil, and attain tree-like proportions with a stem as much as a foot in diameter. This deciduous species is capable of being turned to good account by the landscape gardener; the yellow tubular flowers are produced in profusion.

E. argentea, or **E. canadensis** (the *Silver Berry,* or *Missouri Silver Tree*), has very fragrant tubular yellow flowers, followed by an abundance of nearly globular, dry, mealy, edible fruit. This species gives a characteristic feature to the vegetation of the Upper Missouri valley, and in a wild state grows 8 or 10 ft. in height, and throws up an abundance of suckers, a habit which, at any rate in a young state, does not appear to occur so much under cultivation. The oval leaves are silvery-white. In nearly all British and foreign nurseries this species is confused with the Buffalo Berry (Shepherdia argentea), a genus belonging to the same natural order as the Elæagnus, but altogether different from it.

E. hortensis, a somewhat variable plant with a wide geographical distribution, is cultivated in many countries for the sake of its fruit. In Dr. Aitchison's *Botany of the Afghan Delimitation Commission* it is described as a shrub or tree occurring at an elevation of 3,000 ft. and upwards, near running streams, and cultivated largely in orchards for its fruit.

E. longipes, a thoroughly deciduous Japanese species, is one of the most desirable members of the genus. Prof. Sargent thus writes of it in *Garden and Forest* : "The plant may well be grown for the beauty of its fruit alone, which, moreover, is juicy and edible with a sharp, rather pungent, agreeable flavour. Both the size and the flavour can doubtless be improved by careful selection, and it is quite within the range of possibility that it may become a highly esteemed and popular dessert and culinary fruit. To some persons, even in its present state, the flavour is far preferable to that of the Currant or the Gooseberry." The fruit, as implied by the specific name, is borne on long stalks ; it is bright red in colour and covered with minute white dots. The branches are covered with rusty brown scales, and the somewhat leathery leaves are dark-green above and silvery-white beneath. Pheasants are said to be very fond of the fruit, and I can vouch for the fact that blackbirds and other fruit-eating birds will soon strip a bush unless it be netted. Some French growers make a preserve of the fruit, and this is said to be very similar to that made from the fruit of the Cornelian Cherry (Cornus mas) ; a spirit, too, with a taste like kirsch, has also been made from the fruit. E. longipes, known in some gardens under the names of E. edulis, E. odorata edulis, and E. rotundifolia, is apparently as hardy as the first-named species.

E. macrophylla, an evergreen species from China and Japan, has large roundish leaves, grayish above and silvery beneath. Old plants are said to produce suckers freely, but the species is a somewhat recent introduction to British gardens, and all the specimens which I have seen up to the present have not shown any tendency to sucker. It is quite distinct in appearance from any other hardy cultivated shrub, and is worthy of much more general employment in the ornamental shrubbery. In its native habitats it is said to sometimes attain tree-like dimensions ; under cultivation I have only seen it as a dense bush.

E. pungens, E. glabra, and **E. reflexa** are beautiful evergreens, which are not very dissimilar in general aspect, and which without long dry scientific descriptions it would be impossible to distinguish. Variegated forms exist of all three, and any of them, as well as the types, are thoroughly well worthy of a place in the garden or pleasure-ground. They are all natives of Japan, &c., but do not appear to be quite as hardy as the species previously mentioned ; all could be tried, however, with every prospect of success in the southern counties. Some of them in the south of Europe assume a somewhat climbing habit, and round the North Italian lakes, for example,

the upper surface ; in a young state earlier in the season they are silvery-gray, and silvery-white beneath. The creamy-white flowers are produced in the greatest profusion in June. In some localities the plant is practically evergreen; in the neighbourhood of London, however, it is—at any rate during such winters as the two last—to all intents and purposes deciduous. It is probably perfectly hardy throughout Britain, as it withstands the

Lyme Grass (Elymus arenarius).

grow up to the tops of high Fir and Pine trees.

E. Simoni, said to be a native of China, seems quite hardy, but is the least ornamental of those which have been mentioned in these notes. A variegated form of this, with leaves margined with dark green and with the centres constantly variegated with golden-yellow and yellowish-green, originated in the Belgian nurseries a few years ago ; it is highly spoken of in some of the Belgian periodicals.

E. umbellata is a beautiful bush. . The leaves are deep green and glabrous on

much severer winters of Northern Germany without protection. In a wild state it occurs from the Himalayas to China and Japan. Elæagnus parvifolia is a name under which this species occurs in some gardens.—G. N.

ELYMUS (*Lyme Grass*).—*E. arenarius* is a wild British Grass, vigorous and distinct, which if planted in deep soil near the margin of a shrubbery, or on a bank on the Grass, makes an effective plant, growing 4 ft. high, and as we should cultivate it for the leaves, there would be no loss if the flowers were removed. It is frequent on our shores, but more abundant in the north than in the south. E. condensatus (Bunch Grass) is a vigorous perennial Grass from British Columbia, forming a dense, compact, column-like growth, and more than 8 ft. high. It is covered from the base almost to the top with long arching leaves, and in the flowering season is crowned with erect rigid spikes 6½ in. long, so that it resembles an elongated ear of wheat. It is very ornamental, and may be grown in the same way as the Lyme Grass. Other kinds might be mentioned, but one or two give us the best effect of the race.

EMBOTHRIUM (*Fire Bush*).—*E. coccineum* is a very beautiful S. American evergreen shrub of the Protea family, hardy in warm parts of Britain, even without the protection of a wall. At Coombe Royal, in South Devon, it grows quite 20 ft. high, and is a spectacle of wondrous beauty about the end of April or the beginning of May, when every twig carries a cluster of fiery flowers. Even on the favoured Devonshire coast a sharp late frost will sometimes injure the flowers. It thrives near the coast in southern Ireland and in Wicklow at Mr. Acton's, but soon perishes in less favoured places.

EMPETRUM (*Crowberry*). — *E. nigrum* is a small evergreen Heath-like bush, of the easiest culture, which may be associated with the dwarfer rock shrubs. It is a native plant, and the badge of the Scotch clan McLean.

ENKIANTHUS.—*E. campanulatus* is a pretty shrub, native of Northern Japan. It has slender branches covered with a light brown bark, and campanulate flowers produced in a pendulous cluster, and of a pale rosy-red colour, with three darker lines on each of the five sections of the corolla.

E. cernuus.—A little-known species only recently introduced from Japan, where it is said to be a bush 6 ft. to 8 ft. high. The reddish flowers are campanulate, and slightly five-lobed. Syn., *Meisteria cernua*.

E. japonicus.—A rare and desirable shrub, first discovered by Sir Rutherford Alcock near Nagasaki, Japan, in 1859, and afterwards introduced by Messrs. Standish. The leaves turn to a beautiful deep orange colour before falling in autumn. The pendent flowers are pure white, globose, and contracted to a much narrower mouth than in *E. campanulatus*. Ericaceæ.

EOMECON (*Cyclamen Poppy*).—*E. chionanthus* is a very charming hardy perennial Poppy intermediate between Stylophorum and Sanguinaria. The rootstocks are usually as thick as the finger ; they run freely underground, and increase rapidly ; leaves all from the base, long-stalked, and resembling those of the hardy Cyclamen. The flowers, 2 to 3 in. in diameter, are pure white, with a bunch of yellow anthers in the centre ; several borne on stems about 1 ft. high. It is a native of China, and will be found perfectly hardy out-of-doors ; it has stood the winters of 1890 and 1891 without injury. This Poppy will be found a delightful plant in moist situations in free soil, and fully exposed to the sun. The pure pearly-white Poppy flowers, in a setting of bold yellow-green foliage, make

Epigæa repens (Mayflower).

an elegant picture, and as it continues in flower all through the summer, it is a good plant for the rock-garden. It can be increased to any extent by division.

EPHEDRA. — (*Shrubby Horsetail*). Curious greyish, wiry trailing bushes of Southern Europe and Northern Africa, rare in our gardens, but hardy here and there, as in the Cambridge Botanic Gardens, where there is light warm soil.

All these plants resemble to a certain extent the Equisetums, and though they are leafless, or nearly so, the bright green colour of the bark makes them conspicuous at all seasons. *E. distachya* is a native of the southern part of France and Spain, in sandy soils on the seashore, a yard or more high, forming a spreading mass of bright green cylindrical branches distinct from our hardy shrubs ; the berries, which do not always appear in this country, are red. In the front of the shrubbery, where the slender branches can grow at will, this Ephedra is seen to advantage, breaking up the outline, and it is a good plant for bold arrangements in the rock garden as it will succeed in dry spots. It is also known as *E. nebrodensis. E. vulgaris* is a smaller plant and one that will resist more cold as it is a native of Siberia, also some of the more southern districts of Asia. Other species are found in different parts of the world, but the nomenclature of the entire genus is confused, and it is probable that the list of names would be reduced if they were grown together, as slight geographical variations would no doubt disappear under cultivation.—T.

Ephedra.

EPIGÆA (*Mayflower*).—A small Evergreen found in sandy soil in the shade of Pines in many parts of N. America, *E. repens* having pretty rose-tinted flowers in small clusters, which exhale a rich odour, and appear in spring. Its natural home is under trees, and it would be well to plant some of it in the shade of Pines or shrubs. It was at one time lost to our nurseries and gardens, owing to the habit of planting all things in the same kind of exposed situation. It is a charming plant for the wild garden, in sandy or peaty soil under trees, growing only a few inches high. Ericaceæ.

EPILOBIUM (*French Willow*).—Few of these plants are worthy of cultivation, but some are important, and the best perhaps is the showy crimson native E. angustifolium, of which there is a pure white variety. This plant runs in a border so quickly as to soon become a troublesome weed, but is fine when allowed to run wild in a rough shrubbery or copse, where it may bloom with the Foxglove. It is a native of Europe and many parts of Britain. Division. Other kinds somewhat less vigorous are E. angustissimum, E. Dodonæi, and E. rosmarinifolium. The common native E. hirsutum is stouter than the French Willow, and is only useful by the margins of streams and ponds, associated with the Loosestrife and such plants. There is a variegated form. The Rocky Mountain Willow Herb (E. obcordatum) is a beautiful rockplant. The Willow Herbs of our own latitudes are very tall and vigorous, but

on the dreary summits of the Rocky Mountains and the Californian Sierras one species has succeeded in contending against the elements by reason of its very dwarf stature ; it has imitated the Phloxes and Pentstemons of the same region ; though not more than 3 in. high, it has retained the size and beauty of flower of the finest species, the colour being rosy-crimson. It is hardy, and thrives in ordinary sandy soil in the rock-garden. Some of the small New Zealand species, such as glabellum nummulariæfolium, and longipes, are very useful for draping stones on rock-gardens.—D.

EPIMEDIUM (*Barren-wort*).—Interesting and, when well grown, elegant plants of the Barberry Order, but not shrubby. E. pinnatum is a hardy dwarf perennial from Asia Minor, 8 in. to 2½ ft. high, with handsome tufts, and bearing long clusters of yellow flowers. The old leaves remain fine until the new ones appear in the ensuing spring. It is not well to remove them, as they shelter the buds of the new leaves during the winter, and the plants flower better when they are allowed to remain. Cool peaty soil and a slightly shaded position are most suitable. Other species are alpinum, macranthum, Musschianum, purpureum, rubrum, niveum, and violaceum, all loving half-shady spots in peat, or in moist sandy soil. None are so valuable for general culture as the first-mentioned.

Known species.—*E. alpinum*, Europe. *concinnum*, Japan. *elatum*, Himal. *macranthum*, Japan. *Musschianum*, do. *Perralderianum*, Algeria. *pinnatum*, Persia. *pteroceras*, Caucas. *pubescens*, China. *pubigerum*, Caucas. *rubrum*, Japan. *sagittatum*, do.

EPIPACTIS (*Marsh E.*)—*E. palustris* is a somewhat showy hardy Orchid, 1 to 1½ ft. high, flowering late in summer, and bearing rather handsome purplish flowers. A native of moist grassy places in all parts of temperate and southern Europe. A good plant for the bog-garden, or for moist spots near a rivulet, in soft peat. In moist districts it thrives very well in ordinary moist soil.

EQUISETUM (*Giant Horse-tail*).—*E. Telmateia* is a tall British plant, of much grace of habit when well developed, and from 3 to 6 ft. high in moist peaty or clay hollows in woods. The stem is furnished from top to bottom with spreading whorls of slender branches, slightly drooping, the whole forming a graceful pyramid. It is fit for the hardy fernery, shady peat borders, near cascades, or among shrubs, and grows best in deep vegetable soil. Division. E. sylvaticum is another native Horse-tail, much dwarfer, but graceful when well grown, the stem standing 8 to 15 in. high, and being covered with slender branches.

ERAGROSTIS(*Love Grass*).—Grasses, some of which are worth cultivating for their elegant feathery panicles. E. ægyptiaca, with silvery-white plumes, maxima, elegans, pilosa, amabilis, pellucida, capillaris, plumosa, are all elegant annuals. They are useful for cutting for the house during summer. Seed may be sown in autumn or spring in the open air, on or in a slightly heated frame. For preserving, the stems should be gathered before the seeds are too ripe.

ERANTHIS (*Winter Aconite*). — *E. hyemalis* is a pretty early plant with yellow flowers surrounded by a whorl of shining green. It is 3 to 8 in. high, and flowers from January to March. It is seen best in a half-wild state, under trees or on banks in woody places, though it is occasionally worthy of a place among the earliest border flowers. It often naturalises itself freely in Grass, and is very beautiful when the little yellow flowers peep out in early spring. *E. cilicicus* is a recent introduction of like stature and character, though distinct as a species, and seems to be of like value and hardiness. We may therefore enjoy it without giving it positions suited for more delicate plants, or taking any trouble about it, but it is more vigorous on chalky or warm soils. and dwindles on some cold soils.

EREMURUS.—Noble bulbous plants from Northern India, Persia, and Central Asia, as yet little seen in our gardens. Of their culture or fitness for our climate generally little can be said with certainty. Most of the forms are handsome, and well suited for the warm sheltered glades of gardens where hardy flowers and plants are grown in a natural and informal way. In such a home they can be associated in bold groups with some of the finest hardy plants, with a background of fine-foliaged subjects and choice shrubs. In planting, however, care should be taken to place the roots where they would not be overgrown or shaded by other plants, so that the crowns should receive the greatest amount of sunshine during the ripening period previous to going to rest. They thrive admirably in deep, rich, sandy loam, such as would suit Lilium auratum, with the addition of some thoroughly decayed cow manure. My own plants were grown in a bed filled in 3 ft. deep with a compost of good fibrous loam, sharp river-sand, peat, decayed cow manure, and charcoal, with a well-drained sheltered situation facing due south. Once well planted,

they should never be disturbed, as the roots are extremely brittle and very liable to injury. The surface soil above the roots should be kept clean by hand weeding and enriched by occasional surfacings of old manure, leaf-soil, and a little grit, thoroughly broken up and mixed together. Autumn is the best period for planting, which should take place as soon as the young plants have ripened their growth, the sites being well and deeply prepared some little time beforehand, so as to allow the soil to thoroughly settle before the plants are placed in it. As the whole family dislike stagnant moisture, care should be taken to avoid this at the time of planting, and in any favourable situation this can be managed by spreading out the roots of the young plants upon the prepared surface of the bed and covering them with soil so as to form a mound. This can be afterwards surfaced with Cocoa-nut fibre refuse to exclude frost. In any case it is a great advantage to keep the crown of the plant slightly above the soil. I found a plan adopted by Mr. Gumbleton, who is a most successful cultivator of these plants, to be an excellent protection during winter and early spring, especially at the latter period, when the young growth is liable to be injured by frost and the plants to be disfigured for the whole season, if not permanently injured. The shelter, in fact, is very simple and is easily managed — being merely the placing over each plant of a hand-light upon supports. As it takes some of the forms several years to flower, old plants are valuable, but are difficult to move. It is better, therefore, to begin with three year-old plants if possible, and care should be taken to obtain the plants from a trustworthy source, or, after waiting patiently, cultivators may find that instead of the beautiful E. robustus or E. himalaicus, they have the uninteresting E. spectabilis, or some other species that they do not care for.

Owing to losing my garden, I had, unfortunately, to break up my collection in the finest condition, before all the forms I had collected had flowered. I, however, flowered E. robustus, Olgæ, himalaicus, and Bungei, all of which are very beautiful, and amenable to cultivation.

These four forms all flowered finely, and throve admirably in a Herefordshire garden. A most interesting account of this family, with a list of the species and varieties known to cultivation, may be found in vol. xxix. (p. 96) of *The Garden*, which cannot fail to assist those who contemplate the introduction of these beautiful plants into their gardens.—W. J. G.

The Rev. F. Page-Roberts writes from Scole Rectory :—

Eremurus robustus.

" With a little trouble Eremuri may be grown successfully by every lover of beautiful flowers. All that is necessary for their well-being is protection from slugs, which soon scent them from afar.

I keep a perforated zinc collar round the crown and protect from spring frosts. The plant early forces its way up even through the frost-bound earth, but the tender flower-spike, tender only in infancy, is nipped in the bud if rain fall on it and freeze. Protection also from cutting winds which destroy the foliage is needed. With such precautions and planted in loam, deep, but not too stiff, in a well-drained sunny border, and with an occasional dose of weak liquid manure, they will repay one for all the care given to them."

E. Aitchisonii.—This is a very fine species, nearly allied to E. robustus. It was introduced a few years ago from Karshátal, Afghanistan, where it grows on ridges of the hills nearly 12,000 ft. above sea-level, flowering in June. It is a rather fine species, producing dense spikes of pale reddish flowers. The robust and very striking stems vary from 3 to 5 ft. high.

E. aurantiacus. — A charming dwarf plant somewhat resembling E. Bungei, and perfectly hardy in gardens. It flowers in April, the numerous spikes of bright citron-yellow flowers giving quite a character to part of the Hariab district, where it is one of the commonest plants on rough stony ground. It is very interesting as the vegetable proper of the Hariab district, and is said to be the sole vegetable upon which the inhabitants depend for at least two months of the year. The leaves are simply cut from the root-stock, as close to the ground as possible, and cooked. It is extremely palatable, and Dr. Aitchison recommends its growth as an early spring vegetable.

E. Bungei.—A pretty dwarf species now plentiful in nurseries. The leaves, contemporary with the flowers, are narrow, linear, and about 1 ft. long. Flower-stem somewhat slender, 1 to 3 ft. long. Flowers bright yellow, the segments reflexing from above the base, and having a distinct green keel. The stamens are about twice as long as the perianth. Native of Persia, flowering in July.

E. himalaicus is a beautiful white-flowered species, introduced to cultivation by Mr. Gumbleton, and is one of the most lovely hardy plants in cultivation. In form and height it reminds one of E. robustus, but it starts into growth later, escaping spring frosts. The flower-stems are 4 to 8 ft. high, the dense raceme taking up quite 2 ft. of the upper portion, with flowers as large as a florin It is one of the hardiest and best of the known species. It flowers in May and June, and is a native of the temperate Himalayas

E. Olgæ is a comparatively dwarf form, received with E Bungei from Herr Max Leichtlin, and one of the latest to flower The flower-stem is nearly 4 ft high, and is densely set with handsome lilac flowers as large as a five-shilling piece It is certainly one of the handsomest and most conspicuous flowered species It was introduced about eight years ago by Dr. Regel A native of Turkestan, flowering in June and July

E. robustus, a lovely species, and one of the best known in gardens It produces a huge flower-stem 6 to 10 ft. high, bearing on its summit a dense raceme of peach-shaded lilac flowers nearly 2 in in diameter It is perfectly hardy, and may often be seen forcing its shoots through frozen ground It is one of the easiest to manage Native of Turkestan, flowering in June —D

Known species.—They are Asiatic plants coming chiefly from Asia Minor, Persia, Afghanistan, India, and Turkestan. E. Aitchisoni, Afghan Alberti, albo-citrinus, altaicus, angustifolius, anisopterus, Aucherianus, bachtiaricus, buchancus, Bungei, cappadocicus, Capusi, Griffithii, himalaicus, inderiensis, Kaufmanni, Korolkowi, luteus, Olgæ, persicus, robustus, spectabilis, stenophyllus, Stocksii, Suworowi, tauricus, turkestanicus.

ERIANTHUS —A fine Grass from S. Europe, *E Ravennæ* is somewhat like the Pampas Grass in habit, but smaller in size, having violet-tinged leaves The flowering stems grow from 5 to 6½ ft high, but as it only flowers with us in a very warm season, it must be valued for its foliage alone. Its dense tufts are strongest with us in light or warm soil, in positions with a south aspect It is poor on cold soils, and will probably not grow well north of London It is fitted for association with such Grasses as Arundo conspicua Division of the tufts in spring or autumn E strictus is another species, but is not so good as E Ravennæ

ERICA (*Heath*) —Beautiful shrubs, of which the kinds that are wild in Europe are very precious for gardens We should take more hints from our own wild plants and bring the hardy Heaths of Britain into the garden Why should we have such things as the Alternanthera grown with care and cost in hothouses, and then put out in summer to make our flower gardens ridiculous, while neglecting such lovely hardy things as our own Heaths and their many pretty varieties? But very many

people do not know how happy these Heaths are as garden plants, and how well they mark the seasons, and for the most part at a time when people go into the country A pretty Heath garden is that of Sir P Currie at Hawley, where, near his house he has kept, instead of a lawn, a piece of the Heath land of the district almost in its natural state, save for a little levelling of old pits In such places the native Heaths of Surrey and Hampshire sow themselves, and nothing can be better in the situation Where, as in many country places, the Heaths abound, there is less need to cultivate them, although we cultivate nothing prettier In places large enough for bold Heath gardens it would be well to plant them, but a small place is often large enough for a few beds of hardy Heaths Once established, they need very little attention To some it may be necessary to state that most of our Heaths break into white and various coloured, the common Heather having many pretty varieties, also the Scotch Heath These forms are quite as free as the wild sorts, and give delightful variety in a Heath garden, which need not by any means be a pretentious affair, but quite simple, for Heaths are best on the nearly level ground Though they grow best, perhaps, in northern and upland peat bogs and wastes, we see them in the southern counties in ordinary soils, though on heaths they seem to form their own soil by decay of the stems and leaves for many years Choice Heaths form often the very best adornment of rocky banks, but these are by no means necessary, and some of the best groups I have seen were on the level ground, as in the late Sir William Beaumont's garden in Surrey This group of plants has as yet had but scant care, and, if grown at all, is grown in a poor way and more for its "botanical interest" than from any just sense of its great beauty. That can only be fairly judged of by those who see Heaths on mountains and moors, where they are among the most beautiful of plants in effect in broad masses This can hardly ever be shown in small gardens, but why should it not be in large ones? We need not even have a garden to cultivate Heaths in a picturesque way, as almost any rough open ground will do, and some kinds will do among bushes and in woody places The larger Heaths, where grown, should be massed in visible groups, and the dwarf ones seen in masses also, and not treated as mere "specks" on rockeries They are all of easy culture and all the dwarf kind of easy increase by pulling in pieces and replanting 'at once any time from October to April.

E. ARBOREA (*Tree Heath*).—A tall and graceful shrub of Southern Europe, N. Africa and the Canary islands; white flowered, and covering vast areas in the upland woods of Oak or other trees, attaining a height of 12 feet or more in N. Africa, and in the Canaries becoming a tree. This Heath is tender in Britain generally, but may be grown in southern and warm districts and on warm soil in sheltered valleys near the sea with its friendly warmth.

E. AUSTRALIS (*Southern Heath*).—A pretty bush Heath of the sandy hills and wastes of Spain and Portugal, 2 feet to 3 feet high, flowering in spring in Britain. The flowers are rosy purple and fragrant. It deserves a place in heathy soils and sheltered places near the coast.

E. CARNEA (*Alpine Forest Heath*).—A jewel among mountain Heaths and hardy as the rock Lichen. On many ranges of Central Europe at rest in winter, in our mild winters it flowers in January in the south, and in all districts is in bloom in the dawn of spring—deep rosy flowers, carpeting the ground, the leaves and all good in colour. There are one or two varieties, one white. This Heath is not averse to loamy soils, and often thrives on them as well as on peat soil. Syn., *E. herbacea.*

E. CINEREA (*Scotch Heath*).—A dwarf and pretty Heath common in many parts of Britain, and particularly Scotland, very easily grown, and has pretty varieties of white and various colours. Its flowers of reddish purple begin to expand early in June. Among its varieties are alba, bicolor, coccinea, pallida, purpurea, and rosea.

E. CILIARIS (*Dorset Heath*). — A lovely dwarf Heath, and as pretty as any Heath of Europe. A native of Western France and Spain in heaths and sandy woods it also comes into Southern England, and is hardy further north than the districts it inhabits naturally. The flowers are of a purple-crimson, and fade away into a pretty brown. It is neat in habit and excellent in every way, thriving also in loamy as well as in peaty soils, and flowering from June to October.

E. HYBRIDA (*Hybrid Heath*).—A cross between *E. carnea* and *E. mediterranea.* It is a remarkable plant and flowers through the winter and far into the spring, thriving in loamy soil almost as well as in peat, and is excellent as a ground work below Azaleas.

E. HIBERNICA (*Irish Heath*).—Mr. Boswell Syme, whose knowledge of British plants was most profound, considered this Irish plant distinct from the Mediterranean Heath, "the flowering not taking place in the Irish plant till three or four months after the Mediterranean Heath;" a fine shrub in Mayo and Galway, growing from 2 to 5 feet high.

E. LUSITANICA (*Portuguese Heath*).—This is for Britain the most precious of the taller Heaths, 2 to 4 feet high, and, hardier than

the Tree Heath, it may be grown over a larger area. Even in a cool district I have had it in a loamy soil ten years, and almost every year it bears lovely wreaths of flowers in mid-winter, white flowers with a little touch of pink, in fine long Foxbrush-like shoots. In about one year in five it is cut down by frost, but usually recovers. This would probably perish in the north, but is a shrub of rare beauty for sea coast and mild districts. Syn. *E. codonodes.*

E. MEDITERRANEA (*Mediterranean Heath*).—A bushy kind, 3 to 5 feet high, best in peat, and flowering prettily in spring. Although

Erigeron speciosus.

a native of Southern Europe, it is hardier in our country than the Tree Heaths of Southern Europe. Of this species there are several varieties.

E. STRICTA (*Corsican Heath*).—A wiry-looking shrub, compact in habit, about 4 feet high, and a handsome plant. A native of the mountains of Corsica, flowering in summer.

E. SCOPARIA (*Broom Heath*).—A tall and wiry-looking Heath, reaching 8 feet or more in our country, flowering in summer, not showy. I have seen this in cold parts of France (Sologne), and it is hardier than most of the larger Heaths; it is often naked at the bottom and bushy and close at the top.

E. TETRALIX (*Marsh or Bell Heather*).— This beautiful Heath is frequent throughout the northern, as well as western, regions, thriving in moist or boggy places but also in ordinary soil in gardens. This Heath has several varieties, differing in colour mainly. *E. Mackaiana* is thought to be a variety of the Bell Heather. There is also a supposed hybrid between this and the Dorset Heath. *E. Watsoni* is a hybrid between the Bell Heather and Dorset Heath. Flowering summer and early autumn.

E. VAGANS (*Cornish Heath*) is a vigorous bush Heath thriving in almost any soil, 3 to 4 feet high. A native of Southern Britain and Ireland, and better fitted for bold groups in the pleasure ground or covert than the garden. There are several varieties, but they do not differ much from the wild plant.

E. VULGARIS (*Heather: Ling*).—As precious as any Heath is the common Heather and its many varieties, none of them prettier than the common form, but worth having, excluding only the very dwarf and monstrous ones, which are useless except in the rock garden, and not of much good there. Heathers are excellent for forming low covert, and, of all the plants, none so quickly clothes a bare slope of shaly soil, not taking any notice of the hottest summer in such situations. Among the best varieties are *alba, Alporti, coccinea, decumbens, Hammondi, pumila, rigida, Searlei,* and *tomentosa.* Syn., *Calluna.*

E. DABŒCII (*Dabœcs Heath*).—The name of this fine plant has been so often changed by botanists that it is difficult to find it by name in books, and I give it by the Linnean name here. It is a beautiful shrub 18 inches to 30 inches high, bearing crimson-purple blooms in drooping racemes. There is a white variety even more beautiful, and one with pruple and white flowers, called *bicolor.* I have had the white form in flower throughout the summer and autumn on a slope fully exposed to the sun, and in very hot years, too. Syn. *Menziesia polifolia,* also *Dabœcia* and *Boretta.* West of Ireland.

E. MAWEANA (*Maw's Heath*).—Of this Heath, Mr. Robert Lindsay writes as follows: "This is one of the handsomest of all the hardy Heaths and was discovered by Mr. George Maw in Portugal in 1872. It may be best described as a very vigorous-growing *Erica ciliaris,* which it resembles, but is more robust in all its parts; the flowers also besides being larger than those of *E. ciliaris,* are darker in colour. It flowers from July to December."

E. MULTIFLORA (*many flowered Heath*).— Somewhat like a white Cornish Heath but dwarf and close-set; flowers in the form usually grown white; many in close racemes. Southern Europe and North Africa on calcareous soil thriving in ordinary soil in gardens. W. R.

ERIGERON (*Fleabane*).—Michaelmas

Daisy-like plants of dwarf growth, somewhat alike in general appearance, and having pink or purple flowers with yellow centres. They flourish in any garden soil, but one or two are best suited for the rock-garden. Of these, E. alpinum grandiflorum is the finest. It is similar to the alpine Aster, having large heads of purplish flowers in late summer, and remaining in beauty a long time. Suitable for the rock-garden and well-drained borders Division or seed. E. Roylei, a Himalayan plant, is another good alpine, of very dwarf, tufted growth, having large blossoms of a bluish-purple,

Erigeron multiradiatus.

with yellow eye. By far the best of the taller kinds is E. (Stenactis) speciosus, a vigorous species, with erect stems, that grow about 2½ ft. high, and bear during June and July many large purplish-lilac Aster-like flowers, with conspicuous orange centres. E. macranthus, another showy species, is of a neat habit, and about 1 ft. high. It bears an abundance of large, purple, yellow-eyed blossoms in summer, and, like E. speciosus, will grow in any soil. E. mucronatus, known also as Vittadenia triloba, is a valuable border flower, neat and compact, and for several weeks in summer is a dense rounded mass of bloom about 9 in. high. The flowers are pink when first expanded, and afterwards change to white, and the plant therefore presents every intermediate shade Other kinds in gardens are E multiradiatus, glabellus, glaucus, bellidifolius, strigosus, and philadelphicus—the last two being the prettiest All are easily increased by division in autumn or spring. The most effective and useful of the genus is E speciosus, which is excellent for groups or borders

ERINUS (*Wall E*)—*E. alpinus* is a pretty alpine plant, with racemes of violet-purple flowers, abundant on dwarf tufts of leaves in early summer In winter it perishes on the level ground in most gardens, but it is permanent when allowed to run wild on old walls or ruins, and it is easily established on old ruins by sowing seeds in mossy or earthy chinks It is well suited for the rock-garden, where it grows in any position, and often flowers bravely on earthless mossy rocks and stones E. hirsutus is a variety covered with down There is a white variety Pyrenees.

ERIOBOTRYA (*Loquat*). — A large-leaved shrub from Japan, *E. japonica* being in our country tender, and only suitable for walls. Its large evergreen leaves are handsome at all seasons, and in warm districts it flowers freely, the blossoms being white, but it does not fruit in the open air in England.

ERIOGONUM. — North American alpine plants which, in the mountain regions of California, are of much beauty, but are rarely good in cultivation, with the exception perhaps of E umbellatum. From a dense tuft of leaves E umbellatum throws up numerous stems, 6 to 8 in high, on which golden-yellow blooms, in umbels 4 in or more across, form a neat and conspicuous tuft In light sandy soil of the rock-garden it has never failed to bloom profusely. The variety Sileri is much better than the type Other species are E compositum, flavum, racemosum, ursinum

ERIOPHORUM (*Cotton Grass*) — Sedge-like plants, whose heads of white cottony seeds make them interesting in the bog-garden or in wet places in grass E polystachyon is the best for a garden , it is plentiful in some marshy districts

ERITRICHIUM (*Fairy Forget-me-not*) —*E. nanum* is an alpine gem, closely allied to the Forget-me-nots, which, however, it far excels in the intensity of the azure-blue of its blossoms Though reputed to be difficult to cultivate, a fair amount of success may be ensured by planting it in broken limestone or sand-

stone, mixed with a small quantity of rich fibry loam and peat, in a spot in the rock-garden where it will be fully exposed and where the roots will be near masses of half-buried rock, to the sides of which they delight to cling The chief enemy of this little plant, and indeed of all alpine plants with silky or cottony foliage, is moisture in winter, which soon causes it to damp off. In its native habitat it is covered with dry snow during that period Some, therefore recommend an overhanging ledge, but if such protection be not removed during summer, it causes too much shade and dryness A better plan is to place two pieces of glass in a ridge over the plant, thus keeping it dry and allowing a free access of air, but these should be removed early in spring Alps, at high elevations —G

ERODIUM (*Stork's-bill*).—Like hardy Geraniums, but usually smaller and more southern in origin Suited for chalky banks or the rock-garden, and some are suited for borders, while others may be naturalised in the Grass in warm soil Among the best species are—

E. macradenium.—A charming dwarf Pyrenean plant, 6 to 10 in high, with the blooms of French white delicately tinged with purple, and veined with purplish-rose , the lower petals are larger than the others ; the two upper ones have each a dark spot, which at once distinguishes them from other Erodiums This plant should be exposed to the hottest sun The best position for it is a crevice where it is tightly placed between two rocks, and where the roots can penetrate dry, sandy, or stony soil to the depth of 3 ft When grown in this way, it is extremely pretty ; the dryness of the situation keeps the leaves dwarf, they nestle to the rock, and the flowers come in great abundance during the summer months. The plant has an aromatic fragrance

E. Manescavi is a vigorous herbaceous plant, and the most showy of the Erodiums. It grows 1 to 1½ ft high, and throws up strong flower-stalks above the foliage, each with seven to fifteen showy purplish flowers, 1 to 1½ in across It is not fastidious as to soil or situation, but its best place is in dry, hard soil, fully exposed to the sun If the soil be too rich, the plant bears so many leaves that the flowers are hidden Seed, or careful division

E. petræum (now **Moltkia petræa**) —This has three to five purplish-rose flowers on each stalk, which are 4 to 6 in high. The leaves and flower-stalks

are densely clothed with minute hairs
It thrives best among the dwarfer alpine
plants, in warm positions, in deep sandy
or gravelly soil

E. Reichardi.—A miniature species 2
to 3 in high when in flower   The small
heart-shaped leaves lie close to the ground,
and form little tufts from which arise
slender stalks, each bearing a solitary
white flower, marked with delicate pink
veins   It often continues in flower for
many weeks   It should be grown in
gritty peat mixed with a small portion of
loam, like the Androsaces and Gentians

To the foregoing may be added   E.
caruifolium, 6 to 10 in high , flowers,
red, about ½ in in diameter, and in
umbels of nine or ten blossoms   E
alpinum, which resembles E Manescavi,
but is much dwarfer, growing 6 to 8 in
high, and flowering continuously from
spring to autumn   E strictum is a fine
annual with deep azure-blue flowers from
India   E romanum, allied to the British
E cicutarium, but with larger flowers,
growing 6 to 9 in high , flowers, purplish,
appearing in spring and early summer
E trichomanefolium, a very pretty dwarf
kind, 4 to 6 in high, with leaves so deeply
cut as to resemble a Fern , flowers, flesh-
coloured, marked with darker veins   All
the preceding, with the exception of E
Manescavi and E hymenodes, are suited
for the rock-garden or borders, in light
sandy or calcareous loam   E. Manescavi
should, perhaps, be confined to the border,
as it is somewhat too tall and spreading for
the rock-garden

Erpetion   See VIOLA

ERYNGIUM (*Sea Holly*)—Handsome
perennials or biennials of the Parsley
order, but so unlike that class of plants in
general appearance as to be often mistaken for Thistles.   For the garden,
whether the decoration of the border, or
rock-garden, or the lawn, few plants
yield a greater charm from the size and
colour of involucres and stems   The stems
are so singularly beautiful with their vivid
steel-blue tints, surmounted with an involucre even more brilliant, that the effect
of good large groups is hardly excelled by
that of any plants that live in our climate
The great diversity in the form of the
leaves is very interesting, ranging from
the great Pandanus-like foliage of E.
pandanifolium to the very small thistle-
like leaves of E dichotomum   Those belonging to the Pandanus set, such as
E Lasseauxi, eburneum, bromeliæfolium,
and others, are useful among fine-leaved
plants , their leaves being mostly of a
thick succulent nature, are not liable to

be damaged by the cold nights in early
autumn , indeed, in all but very damp
places or heavy soils they continue effective as regards foliage all through the
winter season   E alpinum, Oliverianum,
giganteum, and the finer herbaceous species
are very useful for borders, and all are the
more valuable for this purpose owing to
the length of time they continue in bloom,
and for the long time they retain their handsome blue tints   A good rich and well-
drained soil suits most of the species ,
damp carries off more of the tender species
during winter than cold   Protection is not
needed, as the Sea Hollies will stand any
exposure so long as the drainage is perfect.
E alpinum may be made an exception to
the above directions, as in the south of
England at any rate it prefers a shady
spot in a good stiff soil   Much the same
treatment will also answer in the case of
E Oliverianum.

The only really safe way to increase
these Sea Hollies is by means of seed.
Some few sorts may be increased by
division or root cuttings, but they take
such a long time to recover strength, that
a vigorous batch may be raised from seed
in about the same time   Sow the seed in
pans as soon as gathered, and place in a
cold frame. The seeds will germinate in the
spring, and if properly managed will be
ready to plant out the following year
These plants often "sow themselves,"
and seedlings come up in all sorts of
places

The under-mentioned are a few of the
best kinds —

E. alpinum (*Alpine Sea Holly*).—This
is found in the alpine pastures of Switzerland, and, when well grown, is certainly
not surpassed in beauty by any plant in
the genus   It does well in shady borders,
developing a tint almost equal to that
when the plant is fully exposed to sunshine   The involucres, as well as the
stems, are of a beautiful blue, and its
flower-stems averaging about 2 ft high,
appear during July and August   There
is said to be a white variety

E. amethystinum (*Amethyst Sea
Holly*)—This has been confounded with
the much more robust E Oliverianum,
although they have little in common   E
amethystinum rarely exceeds 1 ft to 1½
ft in height, is of a somewhat straggling
habit, and has flower heads and stems
of the finest amethyst-blue. Apart from
the great beauty of its flower-heads and
stems, this plant is chiefly welcome on
account of its pretty dwarf habit   It
answers well for a first or second row in
the border, and makes on the rock-garden

charming little groups. It can be in-creased by division, and easily raised from seed. It flowers during July and August, and is a native of Dalmatia and Croatia.

E. giganteum (*Giant Sea Holly*).—This does well in almost all positions and varieties of soil. The large flower-heads are excellent for winter decoration ; and although not highly coloured like those of many of the others, they make pretty bouquets arranged with Grasses. It is an excellent plant for grouping, and in

The Amethyst Sea Holly (E. amethystinum).

large masses it forms a very picturesque object, growing from 3 ft. to 4 ft. high, with stout stems and deeply-lobed, spiny, glaucous leaves. The involucre, of eight to nine large, oval, spiny leaves, pale grey or glaucous, is very effective. Caucasian Alps and Armenia.

E. maritimum (*Common Sea Holly*).—This plant is found growing along the coast in company with the Oyster plant (Mertensia maritima) and is a very pretty kind, requiring no special culture, and does well in a stiff, loamy soil. It is one of the most glaucous of the species, flower-ing from July to October, and grows from 6 inches to 1½ feet high.

E. Oliverianum (*Oliver's Sea Holly*).—This is of easy cultivation, and the abun-dance of its highly coloured flower-heads renders it very attractive in the flower border. It has often been, and is even yet, confounded with the Amethyst Sea Holly. E. Oliverianum grows 2 feet to 3 feet and often 4 feet in height. The ten to twelve bracts composing the involucre are longer than the head of flowers and have about half a dozen teeth on each side. In habit and general appearance it is more nearly allied to E. alpinum than to any of the other kinds. It ripens seed freely and in this way it may be readily increased, and is a native of the Levant.

Other attractive kinds are E. Bourgati, campestre, cœruleum, planum, of which there is a very beautiful variety, dicho-tomum, triquetrum, creticum, glaciale spina-album.

THE PANDANUS GROUP.—To this group, chiefly natives of Mexico and Brazil, belongs some of the extraordinary forms in this highly ornamental genus. Beginning with Serra, we have a large broad-leaved species with curious double spines ; Carrierei, said to be the finest of all, having a compact habit combined with large, beautiful leaves. E. bromeliæ-folium is a charming plant, striking and distinct in habit and forming elegant Yucca-like tufts, with its graceful leaves surmounted with whitish flower-heads. E. pandanifolium is a noble plant, very effective when grown as an isolated plant on a lawn. E. Lasseauxi is nearly allied and quite hardy in the open air. E. eburneum, aquaticum, virginianum, Leavenworthi, and others are all worthy of attention for their fine foliage.—D. D.

ERYSIMUM.—Wall-flower-like peren-nials, biennials, and annuals, mostly of dwarf growth. Of the perennials the following are the finest :—

E. ochroleucum (*Alpine Wallflower*).—This handsome plant forms, under cultivation, neat rich green tufts, 6 to 12 in. high, and in spring is covered with beautiful sulphur-coloured flowers. The rock-garden is most congenial to it ; but it does very well on good level ground, though it is apt to get naked about the base, and may perish on heavy soils during an unusually severe winter. It thrives best when rather frequently divided. Division and cuttings. A capital dwarf border plant on light soils. Alps and Pyrenees. Flowers in spring.

There are several varieties. Syn., Cheiranthus alpinus.

E. pumilum (*Fairy Wallflower*).—A very small plant, rare in cultivation, resembling the alpine Wallflower in the size and colour of its flowers, but lacking its vigorous and rich green foliage. It is often only 1 in. high, and it bears very large flowers for its size. They appear above a few narrow sparsely toothed leaves which barely rise from the ground. High bare places in the Alps and Pyrenees. It requires an exposed spot of very sandy or gritty loam in the rock-garden, where it must be surrounded by a few small stones to guard it from excessive drought and

The common Sea Holly (E. maritimum).

from accident, and must be associated with the most minute alpine plants. It is nearly related to the alpine Wallflower, E. ochroleucum, but is separated from it by its minuteness, and by its greyish-green leaves.

E. rhæticum. — A pretty mountain flower which, though rare in cultivation, is a common alpine in Rhætia and the neighbouring districts, where in early summer its broad dense-tufted masses are aglow with pretty clear yellow blossoms.   E. canescens, a South European species with scentless yellow flowers, is also a neat alpine, and so is E. rupestre, which is desirable for the rock-garden. All of them are easy to grow, and delight in gritty soil and a well-drained and sunny position on the rock-garden. Among the biennial and annual kinds the best is E. Perofskianum, 1 to 1½ ft. high, with dense racemes of orange-yellow flowers. For early flowering it should be sown in autumn, and again in March and April for later bloom. E. arkansanum and pachycarpum are similar to E Perofskianum.

ERYTHRÆA (*Centaury*). — A small genus of rather pretty dwarf biennials belonging to the Gentian family. The native species, E. littoralis, common in some shore districts, is worth cultivating. It is 4 to 6 in. high, and bears an abundance of rich pink flowers, which last a considerable time in beauty, and will withstand full exposure to the sun, though partial shade is beneficial. The very beautiful E. diffusa is a similar species. It is a rapid grower, with a profusion of pink blossoms in summer.

E. Muhlenbergi is another beautiful plant. It is neat and about 8 in. high, putting out many slender branches. It bears many flowers, and the blossoms are 3½ in. across. They are of a deep pink, with a greenish-white star in the centre. Seeds should be sown in autumn, and grown under liberal treatment till the spring; the plants will then flower much earlier and produce finer flowers than spring-sown plants. They are excellent for the rock-garden and the margins of a loamy border, but the soil must be moist.

ERYTHRINA (*Coral Tree*).—These beautiful trees are pretty general through the tropics. Some attain great dimensions, while others are dwarf bushes with woody root-stocks. Many produce beautiful large Pea flowers, usually of a blood-red or scarlet colour, in terminal racemes. The varieties have proved very hardy and useful in the summer garden, flowering freely and showing considerable beauty of foliage. E. ornata, Marie Belanger, laurifolia, Crista-galli, profusa, Madame Belanger, ruberrima, and Hendersoni, have stood out with slight protection. The common old E. Crista-galli will thrive for years against a warm south wall in a light soil, if protected about the roots in winter, and when so grown, it is often very handsome in the warmer countries. How far E. herbacea will prove an efficient substitute for the older and better known species remains to be seen, but, having resisted a New York winter, it may be assumed to be hardy enough for England, and it deserves a trial. It is rather dwarfer than the old species, and has a woody root-stock, which under favourable conditions throws up in summer stems 2 to 4 ft. high. These stems are of two kinds, one bearing leaves only, the other bearing flowers with few leaves. The flowering stems have a raceme, 1 to 2 ft. long, of narrow flowers about 2 in. in length, the deep scarlet standard, erect in so many genera, being horizontal and folded over the wings and keel. The seeds are bright scarlet, and should be sown in heat as early as practicable, the seedlings being kept in a frame for the first winter. This species is a native of Texas, and is found as far north as Carolina, and as far west as Sonora.

ERYTHRONIUM (*Dog's-tooth Violet*). —Lilaceous bulbs, among the loveliest of our hardy flowers, though the old favourite Dens-canis is the only one commonly cultivated. The genus contains only about a dozen species and varieties. These belong to N. America, with the exception of

E. Dens-canis, a beautiful plant found in various parts of Europe. It has hand-

Eryngium Oliverianum.

some oval leaves, with patches of reddish-brown. The rosy-purple or lilac flowers are borne singly on stems 4 to 6 in. high, and droop gracefully. One variety has white flowers, one rose-coloured, and one flesh-coloured. E. longifolium has longer and narrower leaves and larger flowers, and the sorts enumerated in catalogues under the name of majus are apparently derived from this variety. E. Dens-canis thrives in moist sandy or peaty soil, when fully exposed to the sun. It is most valuable for the spring or rock-garden, or for a border of choice hardy bulbs, and, where it is sufficiently plentiful, for edgings to American plants in peat soil. The bulbs are white and oblong, resembling a dog's tooth, hence its name.

It is increased by dividing the bulbs every two or three years, and replanting rather deeply. Central Europe. The varieties sibiricum, a robust plant from the Altaian Mountains, and japonicum, with violet-purple flowers, are not, so far as we are aware, yet in cultivation.

E. americanum (*Yellow Adder's-tongue*) is common in the woods and low copses of the Eastern States of N. America, where it flowers in May. Its pale green leaves are mottled, and commonly dotted with purple and white. Flowers 1 in. across, pale yellow, and spotted near the base; they appear on slender stalks 6 to 9 in. high. A variety (E. bracteatum) differs in having a bract developed, as E. grandiflorum sometimes has. It is very pretty, but, being a somewhat shy flowerer, is seldom seen in cultivation. The late Mr. M'Nab was very successful with it in the Edinburgh Botanic Garden, and writes in an early volume of *The Garden :* "This interesting plant formerly grew in the open border here, but its flowers were rarely seen. Some years ago I put a tuft of the bulbs in one of the stone compartments of the rock-garden, with a southern aspect, the soil being a mixture of peat and loam. As soon as the space became filled with roots, flowers were freely produced, and on the 20th of April it was covered with yellow blooms. In these confined spaces the bulbs are better matured than in open borders, where the ground is generally covered with small green leaves growing from unmatured bulbs, and there are few of the larger spotted leaves which generally accompany the flowers." The rich soil of our gardens probably develops growth at the expense of flower. In poor sandy soil, in copses, or in the wild garden, this little plant may bloom better.

E. giganteum.—This, the noblest of the genus, is considered a variety of E. grandiflorum. Its showy flowers of pure white have a ring of bright orange-red, and measure 3 in. in diameter. It is found in California at an elevation of six to ten thousand feet, and also in Vancouver's Island. It was called E. maximum by Douglas, and E. speciosum by Nuttall.

E. grandiflorum.—The only cultivated kind with more than one flower on a stem. It is extremely handsome when well grown. In a peat bed, with Lilies and other peat-loving plants, it is very fine, and produces as many as five flowers on a stem. The late Mr. M'Nab used to grow the larger American kinds as well as the European Dens-canis very successfully in grass Writing of them in spring, he says, "Many Dog's-tooth Violets are in bloom on the northern grassy slopes of the rock-garden , they were thickly dibbled in, here and there, when the turf was first laid, and, being placed in all exposures, a longer flowering season has been obtained In such places they do not multiply fast, as only single flowers proceeding from the two or three spotted leaves are produced On grass banks with a southern aspect the leaves are all ripened off before the first grass cutting, which is not the case on grass slopes with a northern aspect '

I have planted them largely in grass, and find they thrive in every soil in that way, and are very early and pretty both in leaf and flower, scattered in groups and colonies in turf

Little known or rarer kinds are E revolutum, albidum, purpurascens, propullans, and Hartwegi

Known species —*E albidum*, N. Amer *americanum*, do *Dens-canis*, Europe, N Asia *grandiflorum*, N W Amer *Hartwegi*, N W Amer *propullans*, do *purpurascens*, Calif

ESCALLONIA.—The Escallonias in cultivation are often beautiful shrubs, unfortunately sometimes perishing in hard winters save in favoured districts In mild places the common E macrantha succeeds in the open. but, as a rule, it must be regarded as a wall shrub Even in the mild districts it is cut down during severe winters, but it usually shoots up again strongly in the returning spring There is a variety called sanguinea with deeper-coloured flowers Somewhat similar to E macrantha is E rubra, but the foliage is less handsome and the flowers are paler E Philippiana is very beautiful and hardy, as it may be grown as a bush in the neighbourhood of London It is an Evergreen with small leaves, and bears a profusion of large panicles of small white flowers It is a first-rate shrub, and one of the best of the Escallonias E pterocladon is very free-flowering, the small flowers being white and pink, while E punctata has dark red flowers, somewhat similar to those of E. rubra Another species, E montevidensis, also known as E floribunda, bears large loose clusters of white flowers, and there are varieties—usually seedling forms—known under different names, especially in seaside gardens Among these, that called E Ingrami is one of the best, being hardier than E macrantha, though not so hand-

some Escallonias are mostly natives of S America, chiefly Chili, Brazil, and Peru

ESCHSCHOLTZIA (*Californian Poppy*) — Brilliant annuals, long and favourably known The beautiful new forms recently seen are acquisitions , the rich reddish-orange of Mandarin and the unique form of double crocea are of real value, and they make, with crocea alba, and the orange aurantiaca, most attractive plants To have these showy flowers in all their beauty, they should be sown in August and September for early summer bloom They may be sown even later—and should then be allowed to bloom where they are sown They get deeply and firmly rooted, and flower much longer than if sown in spring They are very hardy, and snails and slugs do not molest them There are some half a dozen kinds, well worth growing, viz E californica, orange, very strong , E crocea, saffron colour , E c alba, white , E.c Mandarin, orange and crimson, very fine , E c fl -pl , double ; E c. rosea, and E tenuifolia , and new forms are raised from time to time

Known species —Nearly all natives of California E Austinæ, californica, elegans, glyptosperma, mexicana, minutiflora, Parishii, peninsularis, rhombipetala.

EUCALYPTUS (*Gum Tree*) —Large and handsome Australian trees and shrubs, of which a number of species grow to a great height The leaves are thick and leathery, and vary much in shape In the south of England and Ireland a few of the species live in the open air About London some grow them for their aspect in the open air after a single year's growth, and in that case they should be put out about the middle of May Some letters in the *Times*, by persons unaware of the results of planting the tree in this country, induced many to plant the common Gum tree, which perished with the first severe frost Only in the more favoured districts have these trees any chance, and they never present the graceful and stately port which they show in countries that really suit them, such as parts of Italy and California What the higher mountain species may do remains to be seen, and the common Gum tree is sometimes made fair use of in the London parks among the larger plants put out for summer I think these trees are unfitted for our climate, and even in Algeria, where many species were planted by the French Government, the result, as I saw it some years ago, was anything but good

EUCHARIDIUM —Pretty hardy annuals of the Evening Primrose family, thriving under the same treatment as all annuals from California They may be sown in autumn for early summer-flowering, or from March to June for late summer and autumn bloom. They flower about eight weeks after sowing, and remain in bloom a long time. Three species are cultivated —E concinnum, about 9 in high, with many rosy purple blooms, E. grandiflorum, larger rosy-purple flowers, streaked with white, which has a white variety (album), and a variety with pink flowers (roseum), and E Breweri, an elegant new annual, more robust, and with red flowers of a deeper, richer colour than E grandiflorum These species are of secondary importance in the flower garden, but may occasionally be used as surface plants or in bold masses Like many other annuals, they suffer in general estimation through being judged by spring-sown plants, with poor and short-lived bloom

EUCNIDE.—*E bartonioides* is a half-hardy annual of the Loasa family, from Mexico The stems are about 1 ft high, and bear sulphur-yellow flowers, 1½ in across, showy in August and September when several are expanded Seeds should be sown in heated frames in early spring, but the seedlings should be very carefully transplanted to the open border in May, as they are then very liable to injury. Syn Microsperma

EUCOMIS. — Cape bulbs, not very showy, though deserving of cultivation in the out-door garden, on account of their broad handsome foliage, more or less spotted with purple at the base, from which rise tall cylindrical spikes of blossoms surmounted by a crown of leaves Like many Cape plants, they are hardy on light and dry soils There are four species, all of which are in cultivation E undulata has leaves 18 in long, wavy at the margins, and profusely marked on the under surface with dark purple blotches which, in the variety striata, assume the form of stripes The flower spike is 2 to 4 ft high On the upper half are densely arranged, in a cylindrical manner, numerous greenish-white blossoms, with purplish centre, crowned by a tuft of narrow green leaves E punctata is the largest kind, having leaves about 3 ft long E regia is dwarfer than either of the preceding The raceme of flowers is about 1 ft high, and the tuft of leaves at the top is larger than in other kinds E. nana is the smallest The spreading leaves lie horizontally, while in the others they are more

erect They thrive best in light sandy soil, with the roots protected by a covering during winter. The foot of a south wall suits them if they are associated with the larger hardy bulbs, but they are not the most effective or graceful of the Lily family.

EUCRYPHIA (*The Brush Bush*) — A distinct shrub, *E. Pinnatifolia* being hardy, though a native of South America It belongs to the Rose family, but the flowers remind one in size and form of those of St John's Wort, except that they are white, and the central tuft of stamens is very conspicuous. The flowers, borne plentifully, are very pretty, among foliage resembling that of some of the Roses.

It is one of the most beautiful shrubs of recent introduction, and valuable on account of producing its flowers about the end of the summer, when blooming shrubs are getting scarce. It is deciduous, somewhat upright, and has pinnate leaves, and large white flowers about 3 in in diameter. It is of rather slow growth, but has withstood severe winters in the neighbourhood of London, and may therefore fairly be classed as hardy It can only be satisfactorily propagated by layers, which will, to a certain extent, account for its scarcity. Till more plentiful, it should be placed in warm positions and in good free soil. Chili. There is another species in cultivation, E cordifolia, but it is rarer

EULALIA.—This Japanese Grass, *E. gracillima*, is less vigorous in growth than either of the better known kinds, the leaves being more narrow and more gracefully recurved They are bright green in colour, with a comparatively broad stripe of white down the centre of each. So pronounced is this white stripe, that this form is sometimes called E. gracillima univittata Plants of it in pots are pretty.

E. japonica.—A hardy and ornamental perennial Grass of robust growth, 6 to 7 ft high Established plants form clumps 17 to 18 ft in circumference. The brownish-violet flower-panicles have at first erect branches, but as the flowers open, these branches curve over gracefully, and resemble a Prince of Wales' Feather Each of the numerous flowers has at its base a tuft of long silky hairs, which contribute greatly to the feathery lightness of the whole. For isolated positions on lawns it is excellent, or it might be used in groups, or on the margin of the shrubbery Even more valuable than the type are the two variegated forms, variegata, with leaves longitudinally striped with white and green; and zebrina, with distinct cross bars of yellow on the green, which render it singularly attractive. These variegated forms, particularly zebrina, are not quite so

vegetable matter, and, as a rule, they prefer open sunny situations, particularly the evergreen sorts, and all thrive near the sea. The following are among the most distinct of the kinds at present in cultivation :—

Eulalia japonica.

hardy as the type. Division or seed. Japan.

EUONYMUS (*Spindle Tree*).—Low trees with little beauty of flower, but this defect is compensated for by their foliage, habit, and bright fruit which some of the sorts bear. They grow well in almost every variety of soil, but are most luxuriant in such as are rich in

E. europæus (*Common Spindle Tree*). —This is a native of England, and is a bushy tree, from 10 to 25 ft. high; the leaves are of a warm green colour, changing as they decay to a reddish tint. Its small greenish-white flowers expand in May, and are followed almost always by an abundant crop of fruit, in bright pink capsules, which, opening up in the autumn, reveal the orange-coloured sac which envelops the seeds, producing a beautiful effect. Of several varieties, the most interesting are the white fruited kind, which differs from the species in producing white instead of pink capsules; the variety with scarlet leaves; and nanus or pumilus, a neat little plant, very bushy, and one which never grows higher than about 2 ft. and is admirably suited for the rock-garden, or any situation where a dwarf plant is desirable.

E. latifolius (*Broad-leaved Spindle Tree*).—A species wild in the south of France and in some parts of Germany, and a tree of from 10 to 20 ft. high, the leaves shining green, larger than those of the common Euonymus; the flowers, which expand in June, are of a purplish-white; the capsules large, and deep red, contrasting, as they open, most effectively with the bright orange sacs with which the seed is enveloped. It is quite hardy, and forms an ornamental tree, well fitted for a lawn.

E. americanus (*American Spindle Tree*).—This is a small deciduous, or, in mild winters and sheltered situations, sub-evergreen shrub, of about 6 ft. in height, found wild over a wide area in Canada and the United States. It has an erect habit of growth, with numerous long slender branches covered with a smooth light green bark; the flowers open in June, succeeded by rough warted brilliant crimson capsules, which in its native habitats are so showy and abundant that it is named the Burning Bush. In this country it is generally cultivated as a wall plant, and as such it is ornamental. It succeeds best on the shady side, and prefers a moist rather than a dry porous soil.

E. angustifolius (*Narrow-leaved Spindle Tree*).—A twiggy or sub-evergreen shrub about 4 ft. in height, with long wiry branches, abundantly clothed with remarkably narrow oblong leaves, of a deep green colour in summer, changing in autumn to a dull red tint. The flowers are very small, of a greenish-white colour, followed by red fruit capsules. It is a very distinct and interesting shrub for a low wall, and has a pretty effect on raised banks, growing freely in shady sheltered aspects, and in damp heavy soils.

E. japonicus (*Japan Spindle Tree*).—An evergreen species 4 to 6 ft. in height, of bushy habit, the branches clothed with numerous leaves of a dark glossy green colour. Though hardy in sheltered districts, it seldom flowers in this country. Few evergreens thrive better near the sea;

and either it or some of its varieties are frequently met with on the west and south coasts of England, and west coast of Scotland, forming handsome specimen shrubs on lawns and shrubberies. In the inland districts it suffers from frosts, and can only be depended upon on walls or in favoured situations. During recent years a number of varieties have been sent home from Japan; several of these, and particularly the variegated forms, are favourites.

All the varieties thrive best in warm sunny exposure, and in well-drained soils. The kind called argenteus variegatus has leaves clothed with silver; aureus variegatus, leaves margined with deep yellow; latifolius argenteus and latifolius aureus, leaves with white and yellow variegations respectively. E. radicans variegatus is a dwarf creeping variety, its leaves are variegated with white; it is hardy, and useful for planting as an edging. On rockeries or low walls it has a pretty effect; and as it forms roots similar to those of the Ivy, it requires little care to keep it to the wall or other support.—*The Garden.*

EUPATORIUM (*Thorough-wort*). — Coarse Composite perennials, most of which are better suited for the wild garden than for borders, though two or three kinds are worth a place for supplying cut flowers in autumn. The most suitable are E. ageratoides, altissimum, and aromaticum, which are 3 to 5 ft. high, and bear a profusion of white blossoms in dense flat heads, E. cannabinum (Hemp Agrimony), E. perfoliatum, and E. purpureum (Trumpet-weed), which is a fine object in the rougher parts of a garden, being 12 ft. high, with stems terminated by huge clusters of purple flowers. All grow in any kind of soil.

EUPHORBIA (*Spurge*).—Perennials and dwarf bushy plants, including few hardy species of value for the flower garden. The foliage of some, such as E. Cyparissia (Cypress Spurge) is elegant. In spring E. pilosa and amygdaloides are attractive by their yellow flowers when little else is in bloom, but they are scarcely worth growing in a general way. Some of the dwarf kinds, such as E. Myrsinites, portlandica, capitata, and triflora, are neat and distinct in habit and grow in any soil. There are a few variegated forms. The well-known Caper Spurge (E. Lathyris) is often seen in cottage gardens, and in habit is a distinct plant, with a certain beauty of foliage and habit. A few plants of it on a bank or rough place are not amiss.

Eurybia See OLEARIA.
Eutoca. See PHACELIA
EXOCHORDA (*Pearl Bush*) — *E grandiflora* is one of the loveliest of hardy shrubs allied to the Spiræas, but with larger flowers It is a graceful shrub, making when full grown a rounded bush of about 10 ft high and as much through It flowers about the middle of May, just after the foliage unfolds, and affords a charming contrast between tender green leaves and snow-white flowers as large as florins It likes shelter, and grows best in warm loam *Syn.*, Spiræa.

EXOGONIUM (*Jalap Plant*) — A graceful perennial trailing plant, none more beautiful among climbing plants than *E Purga*, and of its hardiness there can be little doubt. It has lived for years at Bitton, Gloucestershire, without any protection, and each year it has flowered well It has also grown well at Kew, Fulham, and in the Edinburgh Botanic Gardens Mr Ellacombe grows it in a sheltered corner, and provides a tall wire trellis with a spreading top for it to grow up It does not flower in the lower parts, but the entire top and the pendent shoots become a mass of lovely bloom. If not checked by late spring frosts at Bitton, it comes into blossom early in September, and continues, to flower till cut down by frost It has roundish tubers of variable size, those of mature growth being about as large as an orange and of a dark colour. These are the true Jalap tubers The plant gets its name from Xalapa, in Mexico, its native region, and is increased by division of tubers

FABIANA (*False Heath*) — *F imbricata* is a pretty shrub of the Potato family, but so much resembling a Heath, that it might well be mistaken for one. It is slender, with evergreen leaves, and in early summer every shoot is wreathed with small white trumpet-shaped flowers A native of Chili, it is not perfectly hardy as a bush except in the southern and western counties, in which it is often a very distinct and beautiful shrub

FAGUS (*Beech*) — Not a very large family of trees, but including one of the noblest of all our native beech. It is a great tree in all the countries of Europe, from Northern Greece to Denmark, thriving admirably in soils useless for the oak and other trees, and a beautiful object in many of our poor chalky and limestone soils It is so often seen in our woodlands that there is no need to advocate its use elsewhere, a wild tree common in the woodlands and

forests in Europe everywhere can have little place in gardens, although it is one of the trees which used to be clipped and mutilated to conform to the architect's notion of a garden, but wrong, and ugly so treated The varieties of the beech, however, are of the highest garden value as lawn trees Some of the most beautiful weeping trees in England are those of the weeping form of the beech, as in the Knaphill nurseries, and at Lough nurseries, Cork (in Ireland) and elsewhere The fine character of the pendant beech is that it is not only graceful in a young state, but improves remarkably every year of its life, very old trees being picturesque in a high degree It is needless to enumerate all the varieties, which are almost without end Every state or chance variegation is given a Latin name and sent out from nurseries, though many of them are worthless Merely curious and variegated varieties are not worth getting The fern-leaved variety is one of the best, and the purple beech is the most striking of all our coloured trees, and very popular The purple form will often come truly from seed, which is a gain Even if all the seeds do not come true it does not matter in the least as long as we get some plants of the colour we seek, and in raising trees from seed we always obtain some slight variation The copper beech is a little paler and more coppery than the old purple beech, and there is a weeping form as well as a dark purple form If anything the danger is using these dark coloured forms too freely Our proportion would be one to three purple beeches in each parish, but a weeping one in many gardens Among the best varieties of the European beech are the following *Millonensis, pendula, heterophylla, macrophylla, purpurea, purpurea pendula, purpurea tricolor*, and a new variety *Zlatia*

Fagus Americana (the American beech) is in its own country a forest tree well above 100 ft. high, inhabiting the northern regions, Canada, and Nova Scotia, as well as westwards and southwards, but the European beech is a so much greater tree, for our climate at least, that little importance is attached to the American variety As to other species of which there are birch-like evergreen ones as well as summer leafing kinds, such as those inhabiting the antarctic regions and Terra del Fuego, little is known of them in this country *F Betuloides*, an evergreen one, is a very graceful, low tree, and so is *F Cunninghami*, and others probably will be found in antarctic regions

If they will only thrive in our climate their distinct habit will be a great gain to us.

FARFUGIUM.—A vigorous perennial, *F. grande* having fleshy stems 1 to 2 ft. high, and with broad leaves of light green variously streaked, spotted with yellow in one variety, and having white and rose in another. It does best in a half-shady position in free moist soil. During the heats of summer it requires frequent watering, and at the approach of winter it should be moved to the greenhouse, except in mild districts. In colder parts it is scarcely worth planting out, as it grows slowly; but where it thrives it is handsome in borders, or on the margins of beds. Multiplied by division in spring; the offsets being potted and kept in a frame until they are well rooted.

FERULA (*Giant Fennel*).—Among the finest umbelliferous plants that have so long remained unnoticed in our botanic gardens, their charm consisting in large tufts of the freshest green leaves in early spring. The leaf is apt to fade early in autumn, but this may be retarded by cutting out the flower-shoots the moment they appear, though these are not ugly, but on the contrary the plants are striking when in flower. Ferulas should be well planted at first, and it is only when established that their good effect is seen. Where bold spring flowers are naturalised or planted in colonies, a group of these fine-leaved plants will be valuable, with their fine plumes rising in early spring. They are among the true hardy plants of the northern world, never suffering from cold. Their fine forms in summer or autumn, when they throw up flowering-shoots to a height of 10 ft. or so, are remarkable enough; but their appearance when breaking up in spring charms us most. A good way is to place them singly or in small groups, just outside a shrubbery, or isolated on the Grass, so that their verdure may be seen in early spring. Deep free soil should be supplied before planting, if the soil be not good and deep. Ferulas are readily raised from seed, which as soon as gathered should be sown in a nursery bed in the open air. The plants, even when well established, do not bear division well, though with care they may be transplanted. One of the best known and most valuable is F. tingitana, which is elegant and vigorous. It takes several years to form strong plants, and the plants look like massive plumes of large filmy Ferns. F. communis is also a good species, and others, including F. glauca, neapolitana, Feru-

lago, and persica, may be added where variety is sought, but the first two are not surpassed. The flower-stems developed the second or third year from seed are 6 to 10 ft. high, are branched, and bear numbers of small inconspicuous flowers. S. Europe and N. Africa.

FESTUCA (*Fescue Grass*). — Annual and perennial Grasses, containing few species for the garden. A variety of Sheep's Fescue (F. ovina), named glauca, is a pretty dwarf hardy Grass, forming dense tufts of leaves of a glaucous hue or soft blue, and on this account sometimes called "blue" Grass. It makes good edgings, and when it is used for this purpose the flower-spikes should be cut away. F. ovina viridis is also a pretty edging plant, and, being of slow growth, does not require renewal for years.

FICARIA (*Pilewort*).—Plants of the Crowfoot family, much resembling some kinds of Buttercup: F. ranunculoides (Lesser Celandine) is a common British plant, 3 to 6 in. high, producing golden-yellow flowers in early spring. It is so common that it would not be mentioned but for its pretty double and white varieties. Moist borders, in any soil. A good plant for growing under trees. Division.

F. grandiflora.—A large-flowered kind, about twice the size of our own, the flowers being nearly 2 in. across. It is easily grown and showy, and could be naturalised. Southern Europe and Northern Africa.

FICUS (*India-rubber Plant*).—F. elastica is not only in fair health in the open air in summer, but sometimes makes a good growth under our northern sun. It is best suited for select mixed groups, and in small gardens, for isolating among low-bedding plants. It will best enjoy stove treatment in winter. It should be put out at the end of May. In all cases it is best to use plants with single stems. The trailing F. repens and F. stipulata also thrive in the open air in summer, and have a pretty effect, trailing up stems of trees in the sub-tropical garden. In mild districts they are hardy against walls or rocks. Cuttings.

FORSYTHIA (*Golden Bell*). — Very beautiful spring-flowering shrubs, especially F. suspensa, whose long, slender, wand-like shoots are studded for a considerable distance with bright golden blossoms. F. suspensa is certainly one of our finest shrubs, and should be found in any garden however small. It is at home under various conditions. Being of a rather loose rambling habit, it is well suited for training on a wall; indeed, few subjects are superior to it for a sunny spot, where the wood will thoroughly ripen, and a good display of spring bloom will be ensured. F. suspensa should not be employed as a wall plant in a shady position, as the yield of flowers will be meagre; nor where a close-fitting subject is required, as it is seen to the greatest advantage when the principal branches are secured to the wall till the allotted space is covered, and the shoots are afterwards allowed to grow at will, since by this mode of treatment the long slender branchlets dispose themselves in a very graceful manner, and the upper ones hang down for a long distance. A wall treated in this way is quite a mass of gold. If any pruning is required, it should be done as soon as the flowers are over, so that the young shoots may have as long a growing and ripening season as possible. As a rule, however, they need little pruning beyond the removal of weak or exhausted shoots. When rambling about in a semi-wild state, or when hanging over a bank or a cutting, this Forsythia is seen to very great advantage. It also forms a most ornamental specimen in the open if it is secured to a good stout stick when planted, and is afterwards allowed to grow at will; for the long slender shoots, which are produced in considerable numbers, will dispose themselves in a graceful manner, and in favourable situations many of them will root at the points, and will soon form quite a colony around the central plant. A large mass of Forsythia grown in this way is most striking. F. viridissima, another species, is quite a shrub. It needs a spot fully exposed to the sun, so that a good display of bloom may be ensured. A certain Forsythia was sent here from the Continent two or three years since under the name of F. intermedia, and was announced as a hybrid between F. suspensa and F. viridissima. Though at first very little disposed in its favour, I have recently seen it in a better light. Its general appearance is about midway between its alleged parents. Forsythias may be flowered under glass in the greenhouse or the conservatory during the early months of the year, and, if so treated, they will bloom in a very satisfactory manner. Owing to the time the blossoms expand when in the open ground, very little forcing is necessary to have them in bloom quite early. Fortunei and Sieboldi are names often used; but these represent only vigorous forms of F.

suspensa. As the shoots of the rambling kinds root from the points almost as readily as a bramble, and cuttings strike freely, there are no obstacles in the way of their rapid propagation. The shrubby F. viridissima also strikes without difficulty from cuttings, though scarcely to the same extent as the others.

FOTHERGILLA.—*F. alnifolia* is a North American dwarf shrub, desirable on account of its flowering early in spring, its feathery tufts of fragrant white flowers appearing before the leaves, which resemble those of the common Alder. Suitable for a moist peat border or the low part of the rock-garden.

FRAGARIA (*Strawberry*). — The Strawberry is much more useful in the fruit garden than in the flower garden, yet some kinds are pretty in the rock-garden. The common English Strawberry is very pretty on banks, and occasionally most useful on old mossy garden walls where it establishes itself. One kind, F. mono-phylla, is a beautiful rock-garden plant, with large white flowers. The Indian strawberry, F. indica, is a pretty little trailer, bearing many red berries and flowering late. All are of the easiest culture in any not too wet soil, and of facile increase by division.

FRANCOA (*Maiden's Wreath*). — Chilian plants of the Saxifrage family, somewhat tender, and suitable for dry sheltered positions on warm borders or banks, preferring a light loam. They are good for cutting, as the long branching stems 18 in. to 2 ft. high, bear numerous white or pink blossoms on stalks. The plants are raised from seed, and in spring furnish flowers for a long time. F. ramosa, bearing white or pink flowers, and having a short stem, differs from F. appendiculata, which is stemless, and has flowers deeper in colour than the others. F. sonchifolia has also a short stem, but its leaves are sessile and not stalked, and its flowers are rose-coloured. They are often grown as window plants, and are best as such where they do not thrive in the open air.

FRAXINUS (*Ash*). Trees of some distinction and value for their timber; natives of cold and northern regions, and one of them our precious native Ash, of great beauty of form, often in places quite away from gardens. Important as the foreign trees of this race are our native kind is so much better known to us, and so remarkable, that we cannot be surprised at the neglect of the other kinds. The British Ash is a variable tree, and its varieties are more valuable than those of many other trees, the best of them not depending on mere variegation, which mostly means disease, but sometimes on habit, such as in the pendulous variety, so well known, much used as it is for bowers and on lawns. There is a form of this with golden shoots, and certain kinds with singular leaves, and here again we come upon mere monstrosities, for this

as much as good oak trees, as at Ochtertyre, Drummond and Lawes. America is rich in species, and in old times, before the conifers mania arose, they were planted, but of late very little attention has been given to them, and few of these reach the size and fine form of our native ash, at least as we know them.

Francoa ramosa (Maiden's Wreath).

fine tree has not escaped the attention of the variegation hunter, these varieties being without value. There is a variety of *F. Lentiscifolia,* a native of Asia Minor, which is pendulous in habit.

The Ash is never more beautiful than when we see it fully exposed in the cool and northern parts of the country and in Ireland, sometimes in Scotland, girthing

Occasionally very picturesque effects arise from grafting the weeping ash on a very tall stem of the ordinary kind, of which there is a good example at Elvaston.

F. ornus is the celebrated Manna Ash, a native of the East and Mediterranean regions, (sometimes called *Ornus*) which has several varieties. It is an effective and hardy tree in England, and even in London gardens is vigorous and handsome. It is grafted on the Common Ash, so what it would be if on its own roots we have no knowledge. Its place is among the larger flowering trees. *Syn. Ornus.*

FREMONTIA (*F. californica*). — A handsome Californian shrub, but scarcely hardy enough for the open air without protection. There are few more beautiful wall shrubs. It has large yellow bowl-shaped flowers, 2 in. across, the deep green leaves being lobed. In favourable

Fraxinus.

spots it reaches 10 or 12 ft. in height, and flowers in early summer. It succeeds best against a north, west, or east wall, a southern exposure being usually too hot and dry.

FRITILLARIA (*Fritillary*).—Bulbs of the Lily family, several of which are valuable, some, such as the Crown Imperial, being stately, others such as F. recurva, being delicate and pretty, but most have dull-tinted curiously interesting flowers. They may be put to many uses : the Crown Imperial is a fine plant for the mixed border or the shrubbery, and, being vigorous, is able to take care of itself in the wild garden. Its early spring growth makes it valuable. The Snake's-head (F. Meleagris) and others, such as F. latifolia, pyrenaica, together with the choicer kinds, are fitted for the bulb border and for grassy places. Only one or two require special treatment ; all the others thrive in ordinary garden soil. They may all be readily increased by offsets from the old bulbs, which should be lifted every three or four years and planted in fresh soil—a process very

beneficial to the plants. The lifting should be done in autumn, and the bulbs replanted without delay. The following are among the most desirable for general cultivation :—

F. aurea, one of the prettiest of the genus, is quite hardy, is about 5 in. high, and has a stem of four to six in. thick, fleshy, deep green leaves, with a nodding flower, which is pale yellow spotted, or chequered with brown. Silesia.

F. Burneti, a handsome hardy plant about 9 in. high, with solitary drooping blossoms, 2 in. long, which are of a plum colour chequered with yellowish-green. Alps. Flowers with the Snowdrop, and is as easy to grow.

F. imperialis (*Crown Imperial*).—A showy and stately plant, from 3 to 4 ft. high, with stout bright green shoots, crested by large dense whorls of drooping bell-like flowers and a crown of foliage. There are several varieties, differing chiefly in the colour of the flowers. The principal are—lutea (yellow), rubra (red), double red and double yellow, rubra maxima (very large red flowers), Aurora (bronzy orange), sulphurine (large sulphur-yellow), Orange Crown (orange-red), Stagzwaard (a fasciated stem form, with very large deep red blossoms), and aurea marginata (gold-striped foliage) ; every lead being margined with a broad golden-yellow band, blending with the rest of the foliage. This plant thrives best in a rich deep loam, especially if the bulbs remain undisturbed for years. Its best place, perhaps, is in a group on the fringe of the shrubbery or a group of American plants. For artistic effects it is not so valuable as the common Snake's-head ; and its odour is against it when gathered.

F. Karelini.—An interesting kind, 4 to 5 in. high, with two or three broad leaves clasping its stem, and having a terminal raceme of slightly-drooping bell-like flowers. These flowers, about 1 in. across, are of a pale purple, with darker veins, a few darker spots, and a distinct yellowish-green pit at the base of each reflexed segment. It is a native of Central Asia, and, flowering in late autumn or early winter, is valuable for a collection of winter-flowering outdoor plants. According to Dr. Regel it must be kept in dry sand till November, and should not grow or show bloom before spring. If planted in November, growth is retarded, and it does not bloom in spring, which it ought to do ; while those flowering in autumn invariably dwindle away, and do not produce any new bulbs. It should be planted in light soil in well-drained borders with a warm exposure.

F. latifolia.—A most variable species as regards the colour of the flowers, which are larger than those of our native F. Meleagris. They are borne on stems about 1 ft. high, are pendulous, and vary in colour through various shades of purple, black, lilac, and yellow. The principal named varieties are—Black Knight, Captain Marryat, Caroline Chisholm, Cooper, Dandy, Jerome, Maria Goldsmith, Marianne, Mellina, Pharaoh, Rembrandt, Shakespeare, Van Speyk, each representing a different shade of colour. They

White Fritillary.

grow freely in an open situation in any soil, and are excellent for naturalising. Caucasus.

F. Meleagris (*Snake's-head*) is an elegant native species, of which there are numerous varieties. It is 9 to 18 in. high, and in early summer bears a solitary drooping flower, beautifully tesselated with purple or purplish-maroon on a pale ground. The chief varieties are — the white (alba), which has scarcely any dark markings; nigra, a deep purplish-black; pallida, light purple; angustifolia, with long narrow leaves; major, with flowers larger than the type; praecox, which flowers about a week earlier than the other forms; flavida yellowish; and the

rare double variety. All forms of this beautiful plant may be used with excellent effect. It grows freely in grass not mown early, and is therefore admirable for the wild garden; its various forms are among the most beautiful inhabitants of the hardy bulb garden, and tufts of the chequered or white-flowered variety are among the most graceful plants in cottage gardens.

F. Moggridgei (*Golden Snake's-head*). —A beautiful plant with pendulous blossoms, 2 in. long, which are of fine golden-yellow, chequered with brownish-crimson on the inner surface of the bell. It may be seen on its native Alps, at an elevation of five to seven thousand feet, among the short stunted Grass, accompanied by alpine plants, and giving the slopes the appearance of a sheet of golden bloom. It is hardy, and flowers early in spring. It is a lovely flower for planting in the choice bulb portions of the rock-garden, and, when plentiful, for dotting in groups in Grass where it may escape the mower.

F. pudica is one of the most charming of hardy bulbs, and takes a place among yellow flowers similar to that of the Snow-drop among white ones. It is a native of the Rocky Mountains and the Sierra Nevada of California, where it grows in a dry barren soil. It is one of the principal spring ornaments of the flora, being nearly 6 in. high, and having bright golden-yellow flowers, graceful in form and drooping like a Snowflake. It thrives in warm sunny borders of loamy soil.

F. recurva.—The showiest of the Fritillaries, its red colour being as bright as some Lilies, and mixed with bright yellow especially on the inside of the flower. It flowers early in May or towards the end of April. The bulbs consist of a slightly flattened tuberous stock, covered by articulated scales, somewhat widely placed, which at first sight resemble those of Lilium philadelphicum. A tuft of bright green linear leaves appears above the soil, and from this rises a slender purplish stem, 6 in. to 2½ ft. high, with several pendent Lily-like flowers. It is not robust, and has succeeded only under careful cultivation, growing best in fibry loam, on a warm sunny border, near a wall. In winter it is advisable to cover the bulbs with some protective material or with a hand-light. California.

F. Sewerzowi.—A singular-looking plant, growing from 1 to 1½ ft. high, having broad glaucous leaves and nodding flowers that are greenish outside and vinous-purple within. A native of the mountains of Turcomania, quite hardy in our climate. Propagated by bulblets or seed.

Many others are in cultivation, but the majority are unattractive, though some are useful for naturalising among Grass in the wild garden; the most suitable are—F. delphinensis, a robust plant with stems 1 ft. or more high, bearing brownish-purple flowers, more or less chequered with greenish-yellow; F. pyrenaica, a similar species, but more robust; F. liliacea, liliorhiza, lanceolata, lusitanica, pallidiflora, tulipifolia, ruthenica, and tristis, all with dull brownish-purple or greenish flowers.

Fritillaria species.—*F. acmopetala,* Syria. *alba,* N. Amer. *armena,* Armenia. *assyriaca,* Mesopotamia. *atropurpurea,* N.W. Amer. *biflora,* Calif. *bithynica,* Bithyn. *Boissieri,* Spain. *bucharica,* Bokhara. *camschatcensis,* E. Asia. *cirrhosa,* Himal. *conica,* Greece. *cornuta. Cornuti. crassifolia,* As. Min. *cuprea,* Mexico. *dagana,* Siberia. *dasyphylla,* Lycea. *Eduardi,* Bokhara. *Ehrharti,* Greece. *Elwesii,* Lycea. *Fleischeriana,* Asia Min. *Forbesii,* Lycea. *Gardneriana,* Himal. *gibbosa,* Persia, Afghan. *græca,* Greece. *imperialis,* Persia, Himal. *involucrata,* Italy. *japonica,* Japan. *kurdica,* Kurdistan. *lanceolata,* N. W. Amer. *latifolia,* Caucas. *libanotica,* Syria. *liliacea,* Calif. *lusitanica,* Portugal. *lutea,* Caucas. *Meleagris,* Europe, Caucas. *meleagroides,* Siberia. *messanensis,* Mediterr. region. *minuta,* Kurdistan. *Munbyi,* Algeria. *obliqua,* Greece. *Olivieri,* Persia. *oranensis,* Algeria. *oxypetala,* India. *pallidiflora,* Siberia. *parviflora,* Calif. *persica,* Armenia. *Pinardi,* As. Min. *plantaginifolia,* East. *pluriflora,* Calif. *pontica,* Greece. *præcox,* S. Europe. *Przewalskii,* E. Asia. *pudica,* N. W. Amer. *pyrenaica,* Pyrenees. *racemosa,* do. *recurva,* N. W. Amer. *Reuteri,* Persia. *rhodocanakis,* Grec. Archip. *Roylei,* Himal. *ruthenica,* Caucas. *Schliemanni,* Asia Min. *Sewerzowi,* Cent. Asia. *Sibthorpiana,* Greece. *tenella,* Europe, Caucas. *tubæformis,* S. Europe. *tulipifolia,* Caucas. *usuriensis,* Amoor. *verticillata,* Siberia. *Walujewi,* Turkestan.

FUCHSIA. — Graceful and distinct shrubs, too seldom seen in our flower gardens. All round our coasts, and especially in the southern and western parts, several species are hardy, and are perhaps the most beautiful objects in gardens. In other districts Fuchsias are cut down by frost, but spring up again vigorously and, in fact, live the life of herbaceous plants; but in mild districts, and near the coast, they frequently escape being cut down for years, and become large and handsome bushes. No plants are more likely to improve the garden. Not showy, in mass of flower

they are of the highest beauty; the drooping shoots of most kinds afford a grace that no garden should be without. Even in dwarf kinds, where this drooping tendency is not seen to such advantage, or, it may be, is seen to a disadvantage, the Fuchsia is very valuable; but its full beauty is seen when we use plants with rather tall stems or pyramids. In the milder districts, where it is a shrub, we see it to perfection; in others, the tall-stemmed or pyramidal plants have to be placed out in summer. The right way to manage Fuchsias put out for the summer only is to induce them, as far as possible,

Crown Imperial (Fritillaria imperialis).

to produce all their growth in the open air; for if you start them, nurture them, and make them full of leaves and strong young growth in the spring, they will be disappointing; but if you keep them back and do not let them burst into leaf until put in the open air in May, they will go on and retain all the strength they gather, suspending graceful blossoms until the leaves desert the trees. They should then be taken up and put in a dry cave, cellar, or shed for the winter, and it would not be difficult to "keep them back" in spring. And even if they seem inclined to push forth before the time to put them in the flower garden there should be no difficulty in placing them in some quiet sheltered nook, where they may receive more

O O 2

protection than in the flower garden proper, and yet have full opportunity to make growth in the open air—the great point to be attained In many places refuse plants may be turned to good account in this way Nothing is simpler than to make of these standards for the flower garden by cutting away the lower and middle side-shoots and leaving the head All may be freely propagated from cuttings in spring or autumn There are about a dozen more or less hardy kinds that succeed in the open air in the south and midland counties, and many more in warm seaside localities , in fact, there is not a Fuchsia in cultivation that will not thrive in the open air in summer , if used judiciously they give an air of grace afforded by no other plants The following are among the hardiest kinds —

F. coccinea — A well-known bushy plant, graceful and beautiful in growth and bloom, readily adapting itself to any locality, unless the soil be of the wettest and coldest description, and even then a slight covering of coal ashes after the stems are cut down in autumn will protect the roots in winter In favourable situations it is often 6 ft. high. From the axils of the leaves, which are a fine green, beautifully tinged or veined with red, the flowers, which before they fully open are not unlike crimson drops, are produced in profusion during the greater part of the summer Chili

F. conica.—A vigorous compact species 3 to 6 ft. high, but not such a free flowerer as some of the others The flowers have scarlet sepals, and dark purple petals Chili

F. corallina.—A beautiful plant, taller and more slender than the others, and therefore specially suited for walls and houses The flowers are large and of a showy red colour, and the plant is a vigorous grower and free bloomer

F. discolor is a dwarf variety with numerous small scarlet flowers It is the hardiest of all, not being injured by the winters in the milder parts of Scotland if treated as a herbaceous plant F pumila is similar, but more slender, and equally desirable

F. globosa.—One of the best of the hardy Fuchsias The flowers are globose in bud, and retain their shape for some time after they begin to expand, on account of the petals continuing to adhere at the tips It is a profuse bloomer, and the flowers are richly coloured. It forms a sturdy and often a large shrub in seashore districts There is no reason why it should not be grown in drier districts,

even if cut down by frost every year, as it is always handsome.

F. gracilis.--A very distinct slender plant, with flowers on remarkably long slender stalks The young shoots are a purplish - red, the calyx is a brighter scarlet, and the corolla has a greater infusion of red than other hardy kinds In mild and moist districts it is nearly 7 ft. high, from 12 to 15 ft in circumference, and is of rapid growth In some winters it is not cut down by frost There is a variety called multiflora, which is very free - flowering, and which has shorter flowers and of darker crimson. F tenella is a seedling variety of F gracilis Chili.

F. Riccartoni —One of the prettiest and hardiest sorts, growing well without protection even in parts of Scotland It is compact and twiggy, and in summer bears many bright red blossoms A garden hybrid.

Besides these, other kinds are in cultivation, such as procumbens—a curious little New Zealand species—seriatifolia, magellanica, thymifolia, and microphylla, and nearly all the hybrid kinds do out-of-doors in summer, and bloom well, though they may be cut down in winter Among the most distinct and pretty are the dwarf and fragile kinds, such as F microphylla, F pumila, and several hardy hybrids of the globosa section, all of which seem to flourish unusually well near the sea, and to grow almost anywhere

Fuchsias are mostly S American plants, chiefly from Brazil, Bolivia, Chili, Ecuador, Peru, New Grenada, and Venezuela, but some from Mexico, some—viz Colensoi, Euchandra, Kirkii, procumbens—from N Zealand, and one, racemosa, from the Island of San Domingo The known species are —

F alpestris, ampliata, apetala, arborescens, ayaovacensis, bacillaris, boliviana, canescens, caracasana, chonotica, coccinea, Colensoi, confertifolia, cordifolia, corymbiflora, curviflora, decussata, denticulata, dependens, Euchandra, excorticata, fulgens, globosa, Hartwegii, hirsuta, hirtella, insignis, integrifolia intermedia, Kirkii, Lenneana, longiflora, loxensis, macrantha, macropetala, macrostemma, macrostigma, membranacea, microphylla, miniata, minimiflora, minutiflora, mixta, montana, nigricans, Notarisii, ovalis, parviflora, petiolaris, procumbens, pubescens, quinduensis, racemosa, rosea, salicifolia, scabriuscula, serratifolia, sessilifolia, simplicicaulis, spectabilis, spinosa, splendent, sylvatica, thymifolia, triphylla, umbrosa, venusta, verrucosa, virgata

FUNKIA (*Plantain Lily*)—Valuable Japanese plants of the Lily Order, of which there are about half-a-dozen species and numerous varieties The different species are free-flowering herbaceous plants, with spikes of bell-shaped flowers, but the chief value is in the foliage. They are noble plants, most useful for many positions in the garden, while few lend such a fine effect as F. Sieboldi when finely developed. They are highly suitable for grouping, and few plants thrive better in open places in shrubberies. The bold striking foliage of some of the strongest plain-leaved section renders them very effective for edging large beds, while the kinds with variegated foliage, such as F. undulata variegata, make good groups, or are suitable for edgings.

as a flower-garden plant, but with us it does not flower regularly unless in sunny spots and warm, well-drained, and very sandy loam. The young leaves are a favourite prey of slugs and snails. It is also known as F. subcordata.

F. lancifolia is a small species, with tufts of lance-shaped leaves, narrowing from the middle towards both ends. There are some interesting varieties, chief among which are the white-flowered variety (alba or speciosa as it is more commonly called), a beautiful plant,

Plantain Lily (Funkia Sieboldi).

They are best seen in well-drained deep soil. All are easily multiplied by division in spring or autumn. The best are—

F. Fortunei.—This strong species has smaller and more leathery leaves than F. Sieboldi, and they are of a much more bluish or glaucous tint. The flowers are pure white or pale mauve.

F. grandiflora is 12 to 18 in. high, producing in August and September numerous large, handsome, pure white, sweet-scented flowers. In some places it is used for edging, but is best seen in tufts, in beds or borders, in a well-drained sandy loam. About Paris it is grown

spathulata, and plantaginifolia, with long narrow leaves. There are some very pretty varieties with leaves of different variegation, all well worth growing; notably albo-marginata, with a narrow white line along the margin of the leaf; undulata variegata, in which the leaves are undulated on the margin and variegated on the greater part of the surface; and umvittata, with a broad white midrib to the leaf.

F. ovata has large tufts of broad, deep, shining green leaves. Flower-stems 12 or 18 in. high, terminating in a short raceme of lilac-blue flowers, which appear in late summer and autumn. One of the strongest species, and when in flower is very handsome. There is a variegated-leaved form.

F. Sieboldi is the most ornamental of the species. It is 18 in. to 3 ft. high, and has large glaucous leaves, somewhat heart-shaped, often over 1 ft. across. The flowers are in tall one-sided racemes well above the foliage, and are a creamy-lilac. There is an interesting variety with yellow-margined foliage. Admirable in tasteful hands for picturesque groups or massive edgings.

GAILLARDIA (*Blanket Flower*).— Handsome perennial and biennial herbs including some of the showiest flowers, valuable for their long duration both on the plants and in a cut state. The genus numbers some half-a-dozen species from N. America, and many garden varieties. The numerous kinds now in gardens appear to fall under three species, but there is a strong family likeness throughout the series. The kinds are

G. aristata, a perennial, 1 to 1½ ft. high, with narrow leaves, sometimes deeply cut. The flowers are 1½ to 4 in. across, the ray florets having an outer zone of orange-yellow and an inner one of brownish-red, while the centre is deep bluish-purple. It is the commonest kind, and having been raised largely from seed, has many varieties, differing more or less widely from the type, with various names. G. picta somewhat resembles G. aristata, but has smaller flowers, and is a biennial. It is dwarfer, and its flowers are brighter. G. amblyodon is a beautiful Texan annual, introduced a few years ago. Its flowers are even smaller than those of G. picta, and are of a deep cinnabar red. On strong plants they are borne plentifully towards the close of the summer for several weeks. G. pulchella is the oldest form cultivated, and was introduced about a century ago. It is 1 to 1½ ft. high, and bears bright yellow and purplish-red flowers, 2 in. across. An annual. G. bicolor and pinnatifida are seldom seen in gardens, probably owing to their being somewhat tender. The garden varieties, as has been stated, are numerous, but the most distinct of those named are—

G. grandiflora, said to be a hybrid, presumably between G. picta and G. aristata. It is a beautiful and vigorous plant with large brightly-coloured flowers, which are only surpassed by its variety maxima. It is by far the finest of all.

G. hybrida is another garden cross, much resembling G. grandiflora; the variety splendens has brighter flowers.

G. Telemachi, Drummondi, Loiselli, and Bosselari appear to be synonymous with some of the preceding, and G. Richardsoni scarcely differs from them.

All thrive in good friable garden soil but not on a cold stiff soil or on one that is too light or dry. Where possible they should be grown in bold groups, for they thrive better if so placed than as solitary plants in a parched border, and no plants have a finer effect in a bed by themselves. Where apt to die in winter, they may be used in mixed borders, if treated as half-hardy annuals; for if sown in a mild hotbed at the end of February or the beginning of March, they may be grown into good plants, and give a full display of their fine flower-heads as early as those that have withstood the winter in the borders. It is well to note that these in many soils are not nearly so hardy or enduring as many of the perennials we have from N. America, and therefore cannot in cold soils be depended on.

The culture of the perennial Gaillardia is not beset with difficulties, and the plant is seen best in bold groups, rather than small clumps here and there in the border. If established plants in pots are obtained in April and put out in the places they are to occupy about 2 ft. apart each way, a good bloom may be expected the same season if the soil is well dug and mixed with well-decayed manure. Mr. W. Kelway, of Langport, Somerset, in a note to *The Garden* on January 27, 1887, mentions that a collection planted in this manner bore the drought of the last five years better than any other herbaceous perennial grown at Langport, and stood the winter so well that not 3 per cent. suffered. Some commend the Gaillardia for bedding, though it is seldom grown in this way, but a pretty effect is obtained when plants of one distinct variety, or shades of the same colour, are put about 1 ft. apart with the stems pegged down. The situation, however, where the Gaillardias remain out winter after winter must be warm, the soil not too heavy, but light and dry. In very cold and wet seasons in Midland counties the plants often succumb; but it is very easy in the autumn to strike cuttings, which may be taken off and treated similarly to the Pelargonium, or seeds raised in March, and the plants hardened off before putting out, will also give a quick return in the shape of flowers. Increased by cuttings in autumn or spring, and division in spring.

Species of Gaillardia—*acaulis*, N. Amer. *amblyodon*, Texas. *aristata*, N. Amer. *arizonica*, Arizona. *comosa*, Mexico. *lanceolata*, N.

Amer. *megapotamica*, Braz. *mexicana*, Mex. *odorata*, N. West Amer. *pinnatifida*, N. W. Amer. *pulchella*, N. Amer. *Roezli*, Calif. *simplex*, N. W. Amer. *spathulata*, N. W. Amer. *tontalensis*, Argent.

GALANTHUS (*Snowdrop*). — Always loved in English gardens, the old Snowdrop is now known to be only one member of a large family most of which have bud is, however, essential, as they can be carried better and open fresher in water than if cut when fully open. Buds so gathered will remain beautiful for ten days or longer, while flowers cut after expansion will fade in about a week.

The present growing state of our knowledge of Snowdrops may best be gleaned

Gaillardia.

merits for garden culture. The Snowdrop never looks better than when naturalised amid tender herbage in old orchards and paddocks, on the margins of lawns, or beside woodland walks. Almost any soil suits the Snowdrop, but rich open soils are best. All the Snowdrops are hardy, and may be naturalised in Grass, or on the rock-garden, or in the wild garden, where they may be associated with Anemone, early Crocuses, Winter Aconites. As cut flowers, Snowdrops are most attractive, but to cull the flowers in from a paper read by Mr. Jas. Allen before the Royal Horticultural Society, of which the following is an abstract :—

In speaking of Snowdrops we must not forget that, besides the division into species and sub-species, we have the arrangements into classes, according to colours and other peculiarities. Consequently we hear of white Snowdrops and yellow Snowdrops, and also green Snowdrops.

G. IMPERATI.—I think no botanist would be able to say where nivalis ended and Imperati commenced In the section to which G nivalis and G Imperati belong there are some most lovely Snowdrops, amongst which I would mention first Mr Melville's Dunrobin form G n Atkinsi is second to none in size, form, quality, and freedom in growth It is the plant known to some as Imperati of Atkins

G PLICATUS is very distinct and its best forms possess great beauty The foremost place in this section belongs to G p maximus G. plicatus usually flowers late, but I have a selected form, G p præcox, which flowers with the early varieties of G nivalis Another selected form, G p Omega, flowers with the very latest

G ELWESI —The best forms of this are large and handsome, but it wants the most sheltered spots in the garden to thrive Many find G Elwesi difficult to manage, but with me it grows very freely, especially in one bed of very light soil, where the seedlings are almost a nuisance

G LATIFOLIUS —This is the most distinct of all Snowdrops, with its broad grass-green foliage and small pure white flowers, and it has a delicate beauty all its own, more especially just before the bud expands, when the two leaves curve so lovingly round the flower-stem

G FOSTERI —The markings on the inner petals are very similar to those of G Elwesi, but the foliage is quite different, being broad and somewhat blunt, and in shape and colour much like the leaves of Scilla sibirica M Max Leichtlin thinks very highly of G Fosteri, and considers it to be the "king of Snowdrops"

G ALLENI —Mr Barker thinks this is probably a hybrid between G latifolius and G caucasicus, as it has some of the features of each species The flower is of much the same character as that of G latifolius, but nearly twice as large, and the foliage corresponds in size with the blossoms

AUTUMNAL SNOWDROPS —In Greece and the adjacent countries several Snowdrops have been found which flower in the autumn or early winter. They seem to belong to the nivalis section One peculiarity I have noticed in them is that they have a glaucous line running down the centre of each leaf, and by this they can be at once distinguished from the spring-flowering forms of nivalis So far as I can learn, all these Snowdrops grow on high ground, mostly on mountains I understand that the Snowdrops on the lower grounds do not flower until early in the year.

G OLGÆ —From the descriptions given of it, G Olgæ must be a fine variety, and it is very unfortunate that it is lost to cultivation. M Tanka, the Hungarian botanist, asserts that this and G octobrensis are identical, but I do not think so, and the difference between G octobrensis and G Rachelæ confirms my opinion

G OCTOBRENSIS —Lord Walsingham, when travelling in Albania about the year 1875, collected some bulbs on one of the mountains and sent them to the late Rev H Harpur-Crewe Amongst these was a bulb which proved to be a Snowdrop flowering in the autumn, usually in October I am sorry to say that it is somewhat delicate and increases very slowly with me

G RACHELÆ —This is of the same type as G octobrensis, but the flower is a little larger, and the leaves are quite a third broader, and it seems to have a stronger constitution than that variety It also differs in being a week or ten days later in flowering

THE YELLOW SNOWDROPS form but a small class, two varieties only being known at present, G lutescens, and G flavescens It must not be supposed that the petals of the flower are yellow, the name is given because of the rich yellow colour of the ovary, and the markings on the inner petals are also of that colour, instead of the usual green, and even the flower-stalks are more yellow than green

THE WHITE SNOWDROPS also consist, at present, of two varieties only G poculiformis was first brought into notice by Mr D Melville, who found it in the grounds at Dunrobin Castle It has since been found in Wales by Mr A D Webster, and I have also received bulbs of a very similar form from a lady near Ayr, in whose garden it grew with several other peculiar forms

GREEN SNOWDROPS. form quite a large class, but none of the blossoms are entirely, or even mostly, green in colour They come into this class in consequence of having more or less green on the outer petals G Scharloki was so named in 1868 by Professor Caspary in honour of its discoverer, Herr Julius Scharlok, who found it in the valley of the Nahe, a tributary of the Rhine This variety, in addition to large pale-green spots towards the tips of the outer petals, has the peculiarity of a twin or divided spathe, which curves down on the two sides much like a pair of wings This variety grows and increases very freely G virescens is a very singular-looking Snowdrop, reminding one somewhat of an Ornitho-galum. The outer petals are pale green, shading off to pure white at the edges, and especially at the tips ; the inner petals are entirely green. G. Fosteri Leopard is a great curiosity, having flowers of quite unusual shape, and at the tip of each outer petal a large dark-green spot. M. Max Leichtlin kindly sent me ten collected bulbs of G. Fosteri in January 1890, and one of these flowered as described, and has kept true this season. G. Fosteri Spot is quite distinct from Leopard. It has long outer petals, some-what pearshaped, and at the tip of each is a small pale-green spot. The spots are not sufficiently prominent to give a decided character to the flower, but it is valuable as a variety.

SOIL FOR SNOWDROPS.—With me G. nivalis grows freely in all soils and situations. G. plicatus is not very particular, but still some of its varieties require extra care, as they have an un-pleasant way of disappearing. G. Elwesi does not do well in close retentive soil. G. latifolius and G. caucasicus, I believe, prefer gritty loam, and I should say that G. Fosteri would also like it. Mr. A. D. Webster tells me that peat has quite a magical effect on Snowdrops, but I have not tried it. My ideal soil for Snow-drops in general would be half good sweet yellow loam and almost half unsifted river-grit and a little leaf-mould. The situa-tion I should choose would be a gently sloping bank, more or less shaded by trees whose roots were allowed to wander freely among the Snowdrops. I believe that all bulbs are healthier when planted amongst active roots than in ordinary beds. When the bulbs are at rest it is very essential that the soil should be kept sweet by the activity of other roots. We too often lose sight of this fact. I think the autumnal-flowering Snowdrops should be treated as alpine plants. All my best Snowdrops are grown under trees, the soil being quite full of their roots. I do not use manure for them. The only drawback to my situation for these spring gems is the soiling of the flowers from the drippings of the trees. I should mention that the climate is so trying that I cannot grow such hardy plants as Primroses, Pinks, Daisies, etc. All these disappear after a season or two. I move most of my Snowdrops when in full flower, and do not find they are injured by it. I have noticed that the more green colour there is in any Snowdrop the more freely it grows and the more rapidly it increases, while the

absence of green, or the substitution of yellow for the green, makes the plant delicate and slow of increase.

Galatella. See *Aster.*

GALAX (*Wand Plant*).—*G. aphylla* is one of the neatest little plants for the rock-garden ; its white wand-like flowers must have suggested its common name ; its round evergreen leaves are beautifully toothed and tinted, on slender stems 6 or 8 in. high. Of easy culture in moist peat or leaf-soil, in the bog-garden, or on the margins of beds of dwarf shrubs in peat. America.

GALEGA (*Goat's Rue*). — Graceful perennials of the Pea family flourishing

Garrya elliptica.

in any soil. On account of their growth they are useful for the wild garden, free and are very effective in groups. They are herbaceous perennials, growing from 2 to 5 ft. in height, according to position and soil. The kinds are—G. officinalis, or Common Goat's Rue, a native of Southern Europe, and 3 to 5 ft. high, in summer bearing dense clusters of Pea-shaped blossoms of a pretty pink. There is a white variety (alba) useful for cutting. A variety called africana has longer racemes and blossoms of a purple tinge. G. orientalis is from the Caucasus, 3 to 4 ft. high, with bluish-purple flowers. G. persica is a later-flowering kind, from 2 to 4 ft. high, with white flowers in dense racemes on slender stalks. G. biloba has pretty bluish-lilac flowers.

GALTONIA (*Cape Hyacinth*).—A noble bulb from the Cape, *G. candicans* having spires of waxy, white bell-like blossoms, 1½ in. long, on stems 4 to 6 ft. high, in late summer and autumn. It is of easy culture, hardy in light soils, and valuable for bold groups in the mixed border, in the flower garden, or between choice shrubs and among hardy Fuchsias. Increased by offsets from the bulbs, or from seeds, which flower about the fourth year. The distinct habit of this plant makes it one of the most valuable. Syn. Hyacinthus candicans.

GARRYA.—*G. Elliptica* is a fine Californian Evergreen, and beautiful winter-flowering shrub. In mild winters it begins to flower as early as December, and bears among handsome deep-green leaves gracefully - drooping tufts of pale-green catkins, which if cut with the twigs endure a long time in vases, and are welcome in winter. Though often grown on walls, it is hardy and makes a dense bush, 5 to 8 ft. high. In cold districts it is well to give it shelter, but in the south and west it does not require this. Other varieties are *G. Fadyenii, Fremonti, Thureti* and *macrophylla,* but *G. elliptica* is the best. There are male and female forms, the most elegant being the pollen-bearing or male plant.

Garrya elliptica.

GAULTHERIA (*Partridge Berry*).—Dwarf evergreen shrubs, *G. procumbens* having berries which give it a charm in winter, when it is one of the brightest plants on the rock-garden. Its drooping white flowers are also pretty. A native of sandy places and cool damp woods from Canada to Virginia, and often found in the shade of evergreens, it does best in moist peat, and forms edgings to beds where the soil is of that nature, but it will also grow in loam. Easily increased by division or seeds. Suitable for the rock-garden, for the front margins of borders, and for edgings to beds of dwarf American plants, and it is best where well exposed. G. Shallon is too large for all but the rougher flanks of the rock-garden, being a vigorous shrub.

GAURA.—*G. Lindheimeri* is a graceful perennial, 3 to 4½ ft. high, flowering in summer and autumn, on long slender spikes bearing numerous white and rose flowers. It thrives in borders, in sandy loam, and plants for the flower garden may be used with the larger bedding plants. Increased by division and seed. N. America.

Gaultheria procumbens.

GAZANIA (*Treasure Flower*).—Handsome and distinct dwarf plants ; of much value, though only hardy enough for our summers. They are most useful on warm soils, and should always be placed in open sunny spots and among dwarf plants. They strike freely in a cold frame in August, but later require bottom-heat. Unless struck very early, spring-struck plants are almost worthless, so that it is best to put in the stock in August and let them stand in cutting-pots till potting-off time in spring. They will then come well into flower when put out in May ; whereas, if they are topped for spring cuttings, both lots will be small and late. Short young tops should be used for cuttings, and may be inserted pretty thickly in the cutting-pots. When established, they must be just protected from frost, and kept in dry airy quarters. If kept warm, they grow too much, and are in spring poor lanky plants that can hardly be handled ; but cool airy treatment keeps them short and sturdy. G. rigens is the best known. It has long deep-green leaves, silvery beneath, and bears flowers 2 in. across, which are of bright orange-yellow, with a dark

Gaultheria shallon.

centre. G. splendens is a fine variety, and there is also one with variegated leaves.

The known species (from S. Africa) are :—
G. arctotoides, arminioides, Burchellii, caespitosa, canescens, coronopifolia, heterochaeta, Jurineaefolia, Kraussii, Krebsiana, Lichtensteinii, lineariloba, longifolia, longiscapa, mucronata, multijuga, nivea, othonnites, oxyloba, Pavonia, pinnata, pygmaea, rigens, serrulata,

subbipinnata, subulata, tenuifolia, uniflora, varians.

GENISTA (*Rock Broom*).—Some of these are good garden and rock-garden shrubs, thriving in almost any soil which is not too wet, and readily raised from seeds.

G. ætnensis, a native of Sicily, is one of the best kinds. In a young state the twigs are sparsely clothed with linear silky leaves, but when old no leaves are developed, and the green slender twigs perform the functions of leaves. An old tree—for this species attains a height of 12 ft. or more—is a beautiful sight in July or August when in full flower.

G. anglica (*Needle Furze*) is a prostrate spiny shrub, sometimes growing to a

Gazania nivea.

height of 2 ft., widely distributed throughout Western Europe, and in Britain occurring on moist moors from Ross southwards. The short leafy racemes of yellow flowers appear in May and June.

G. aspalathoides, a native of South-western Europe, makes a densely-branched, compact, spiny bush from 1 ft. to 2 ft. in height. It flowers in July and August (the yellow blossoms are somewhat smaller than those of G. anglica), and is a good shrub for the rock-garden. Other names for it are Spartium aspalathoides and S. erinaceoides.

G. anxantica, found wild in the neighbourhood of Naples, is very nearly allied to our native Dyer's Greenweed (G. tinctoria). It is very dwarf in habit, and its racemes of golden-yellow flowers are produced in great profusion in late summer. A beautiful rock-garden plant.

G. ephedroides, a native of Sardinia, is a much-branched shrub, 2 ft. in height, bearing yellow flowers from June to August. The aspect of the plant much resembles that of Ephedra distachya.

G. germanica, a species widely distributed throughout Europe, makes a

Genista pilosa.

bright rock-garden shrub not more than a couple of feet in height. It flowers very freely during the summer and autumn months, and the stems are inclined to arch when 1 ft. or more high. Sometimes met with under the name of Scorpius spinosus.

G. hispanica, a native of South-western Europe, is a compact undershrub, evergreen from the colour of its shoots. It scarcely attains more than 1 ft. or 18 in. in height, and the crowded racemes of yellow flowers are borne at the tips of the spiny twigs from May onwards.

G. pilosa, a widely distributed European species, is a dense, prostrate bush and a delightful rock-garden plant. In Britain it is rare and local, being confined to gravelly heaths in the south and south-west of England. It grows freely and flowers abundantly in May and June. Like the rest of the British species of the genus, it has bright yellow blossoms.

G. radiata is a native of Central and Southern Europe, 3 ft. or 4 ft. in height, evergreen from the colour of its much-branched spiny twigs. The terminal heads of bright yellow flowers are produced throughout the summer months. It is quite hardy at any rate in the South of England.

G. ramosissima.—A native of Southern Spain, and one of the best garden plants in the genus,

Genista radiata.

growing about 3 ft. high, the slender twigs laden in July with bright yellow flowers. This also passes under the name of G. cinerea.

G. sagittalis is widely distributed throughout Europe. In habit it differs widely from any of the other species here mentioned, the leaves being replaced by a winged-jointed stem. It scarcely grows a foot high, and forms a mass of branches bearing racemes of yellow flowers in May and June.

G. tinctoria (*The Dyer's Greenweed*). Occurring in a wild state in Britain, it rarely exceeds 18 in. in height, and is a spineless shrub bearing a profusion of bright yellow flowers from July until September. A double-flowered variety of this makes a pretty rock-plant.

G. tinctoria var. elatior is a tall-growing form from the Caucasus, which under cultivation frequently grows from 4 ft. to 5 ft. high, and bears huge paniculate inflorescences.

G. virgata.—A native of Madeira and one of the most beautiful species of the genus. At Kew there are many old plants from 6 ft. to 10 ft. high, and as much through, which in July are one mass of colour, every one of the slender branchlets terminating in a raceme of golden-yellow blossoms.

G E N T I A N A (*Gentian*). — Dwarf evergreen alpine plants, some of them difficult to cultivate, but others easily grown (on the rock-garden and in borders). The most precious are the perennial alpine kinds, which are such a beautiful feature on the mountains of Europe, and with care in our gardens spread into healthy tufts and flower as well as on the mountains. Of these plants there are two sections—the first, strong easily-grown kinds, suitable for borders ; and the second, dwarfer kinds, which should be grown in the rock-garden, or in borders or beds of choice dwarf plants. The Willow Gentian, some of the American perennials, and those with herbaceous shoots generally grow freely in borders, in good moist soil. So does the Gentianella (G. acaulis). The dwarfer Gentians are represented most familiarly by the Vernal Gentian (G. verna).

G. acaulis (*Gentianella*).—An old inhabitant of English gardens, among the most beautiful of the Gentians, and easily cultivated, except on very dry soils. In some places edgings are made of it, and where it does well it should be used in every garden, as, when in flower, edgings of it are of great beauty, and, when not in flower, the masses of little leaves gathered into compact rosettes, form a good edging. It is at home on the rock-garden, where there are good masses of moist loam in which it can root. It is also good for forming carpets in the rock-garden or on raised borders. With us the flowers open in spring and in early summer, but on its native hills they open according to position, like the Vernal Gentian. G. alpina is a marked variety with small broad leaves, and there are several other varieties. Their colours vary from the deepest blue to white, and in one white flower the tips of the corolla are a rich blue. In all the forms except the white the throat of the corolla is spotted with blue on a greenish ground, and all have greenish marks on the outside. Alps and Pyrenees.

G. asclepiadea (*Willow Gentian*).— A good herbaceous kind ; this gives no trouble, but dies down out of harm's way in winter. Well grown, it will spring up

Gentiana affinis.

to 2 ft. and freely produce good-sized flowers of a purple-blue along nearly the whole stem in late summer and autumn. This Gentian will grow in open woods. It may therefore be naturalised, and its effect among the Grass in a wood is charming. There is a white form. Division. Europe.

G. bavarica (*Bavarian Gentian*).—In size this resembles the Vernal Gentian, but it has smaller Box-like leaves of yellowish-green, and its tiny stems are thickly clothed with dense little tufts of foliage, from which arise flowers of lovely iridescent blue. While G. verna is found on dry ground, or on ground not overflowed by water, G. bavarica is in perfection in boggy spots, by some little rill. We must imitate these conditions if we desire to succeed, and a moist peat or bog bed, and with no coarse plants near, will enable us to grow this lovely plant. Alps.

G. septemfida (*Crested Gentian*).—A lovely plant, bearing on stems 6 to 12 in. high clusters of cylindrical flowers widening towards the mouth, and a beautiful blue-white inside, and greenish-brown outside, having between each of the larger segments one smaller and finely cut. In the variety cordifolia leaves are more cordate, but it grows about only half the height of the type, with a much neater habit. The dwarf form, again, seems to subdivide itself when raised from seed, and I have got plenty of plants with very small leaves flowering at a height of only 3 in.—J. W. One of the most desirable species for the rock-garden, and thriving best in moist sandy peat. Division. Caucasus.

G. verna (*Vernal Gentian*).—One of the most beautiful of alpine flowers, thriving in deep sandy loam, with abundance of water during the warm and dry months, and perfect exposure to the sun. The absence of these conditions is a frequent cause of failure. It thrives wild in cool pastures and uplands, where it is rarely subjected to such drought as it is in a parched border. Grit or broken limestone may be mingled with the soil ; if there be plenty of sand this is not essential ; a few pieces half buried in the ground will tend to prevent evaporation and guard the plant till it has taken root. It is so dwarf, that if weeds be allowed to grow round it they soon injure it, and tall plants overshadow or overrun it. In moist districts

Gentiana verna.

it may be grown in a deep sandy loam, on the front edge of a border carefully surrounded by half-plunged stones. Well-rooted plants should be secured to begin

with, as failure often occurs from imperfectly-rooted, half-dead plants. It is abundant in mountain pastures on the Alps, in Asia, and also in Britain.

There are other Gentians in cultivation, such as G. caucasica, adscendens pneumonanthe, cruciata, affinis, algida, arvernensis, crinita, and Andrewsi. Most Gentians may be raised from seed, but it is slow work.

GERANIUM (*Cranesbill*).—The hardy Geraniums are usually stout perennials and natives of the fields and woods of Europe and Britain, though some are

A group of hardy Geraniums.

dainty alpine flowers. The handsomest of them is probably G. armenum. It is sometimes 3 ft. in height, flowering in midsummer abundantly, and sometimes till late in autumn to a less degree. Its flowers are large and handsome. It requires only ordinary garden soil, and is well suited for the mixed border, or for grouping with the finer perennials in beds or on the margins of shrubberies. Some other kinds are showy, and the best of these are : the dwarf G. sanguineum ; its beautiful Lancashire variety, with rose-coloured blossoms finely marked with dark lines ; G. pratense, a tall kind, with large purple flowers ; and its pure white variety. There is also an intermediate form with white and purple flowers. The Caucasian species, G. gymnocaulon and ibericum, are beautiful, with their rich purple blossoms, 2 in. across, delicately pencilled with black. G. platypetalum, striatum, ibericum, and Lamberti are suited for shrubbery borders, and most of them are free and vigorous enough for naturalisation. G. Endressi, with light rose-coloured blossoms, is also very attractive. All the above-mentioned

Geraniums are hardy, easily cultivated, and grow in ordinary soil The pretty rock-garden kinds, G cinereum and G argenteum, are charming alpine plants, and, unlike stout perennials, they must be associated with very dwarf rock-plants All the Geraniums are increased by seed, and with the exception perhaps of the G. cinereum, and G. argenteum, all are freely multiplied by division

GERARDIA—I have never, either in gardens or in the wild land or in the Alpine mountains, where beauty of plant life is at its highest, seen anything that struck me more than a Gerardia I once met with in the roadside in New Jersey, growing abundantly here and there, like a little tree in habit, 15 in to 18 in high, bearing most graceful miniature Pentstemon-like flowers, but far more refined in colour and distinct in form than any Pentstemon Naturally I asked why such a plant was not in cultivation, and learnt that the Gerardias are mostly parasites on the roots of other plants In spite of this, I brought home some seed of one or two kinds and sowed it where I thought it would have some chance, but nothing ever came of it. There are a number of kinds in America, and some of the plants are pretty, but hitherto they seemed to have resisted all attempts at cultivation Gerardia is a genus called after John Gerard, who wrote the famous Herbal in the time of Queen Elizabeth, and is as a group of the highest interest I hope that some of them may be introduced G tenuifolia is a species long known, which thrives in the open, and forms charming tufts covered with pretty flowers in summer It is dwarf and bushy in habit, light and graceful effect with its numerous pale blue flowers

GERBERA.—G Jamesoni is a curious perennial, hardy in southern counties, but too tender for northerly places Its leathery dark-green leaves are arranged in a rosette, and the flower head glowing scarlet. Where it cannot be grown in the border, it should be placed in pots in the greenhouse, in which it succeeds well At Kew the plant is grown in a mixture of loam, peat, and sand, and is watered as one would water a Cineraria It is kept in a sunny, airy greenhouse all the year round   S. Africa

GEUM—Dwarf handsome perennial herbs, G montanum being one of the best of the dwarf kinds for the rock-garden, and very beautiful when well established in early spring It has a compact habit, the leaves lying close on the ground, the erect stems of solitary clear yellow flowers being abundant It likes plenty of moisture G. reptans is also a pretty rock-plant, differing from G. montanum in its finely cut leaves, large flowers, and in producing stolons, which are absent in G montanum There is a variety, however, of the latter, which is by far the most ornamental plant of the European kinds It is of a very vigorous habit, with large, fine leaves, and bears freely deep yellow flowers on each stem This form was cultivated in the Liverpool Botanic Garden over twenty years, and is said to be of garden origin

G. chiloense.—A double-flowered form of this was figured in *The Garden*, December 21st, 1878, under the name of G coccineum fl -pl, an erroneous name, under which it is known in many gardens A very large-flowered variety, under the name of G chiloense grandiflorum, was figured in the *Botanical Register*, vol xvi, t 1348 This I think is one of the best single-flowered forms in the genus, and does not seem to have altered much since the above-mentioned plate was drawn At t 1088 of the same work another plant is figured as G coccineum, but this does not at all agree with the original figure in Sibthorp's *Flora Græca*, t 485, and may be taken to represent as nearly as possible the typical G chiloense A native of Chiloe, introduced to cultivation somewhere about 1826.

G. chiloense var. grandiflorum (syn, coccineum grandiflorum) is a magnificent border plant, its dazzling scarlet flowers and bold habit making it a favourite with all who love brilliant patches in their mixed borders. The double-flowered form of this, however, seems to be a more general favourite, the blooms lasting longer, though I think they lack the elegance of those of the simpler form They begin to expand soon after May and continue until October

G. chiloense var. miniatum.—This plant, figured in *The Garden* in 1890, is said to have originated in the nursery of Robert Parker at Tooting, and was named by him G miniatum Another plant known as the Altrincham variety, or G hybridum, was raised about the same time, but unless in the flowers being brighter, I see no difference But there can be no question as to the value of this plant, its robust constitution standing it in good stead in almost every kind of soil, and enabling it to be propagated with the greatest facility by cutting the tufts in pieces It flowers from April until the end of July, and when doing well often attains a height of from 2 ft to 3 ft.

G. coccineum is a rare and entirely different plant   A native of Mount Olympus —D K

GILIA —Hardy annuals, 1 to 2 ft high, and bearing for a long time a succession of blossoms either blue, white, lavender, or rose-coloured   Seed may be sown in autumn for spring-blooming, and in April for summer and autumn blooming   Gilias should be grown in masses and the soil should be light and enriched with decomposed manure , they are useful for small bouquets or vases, and last for a long time in water   The best are G achilleæfolia major (blue), G a. alba (white), G capitata (lavender), G tricolor (white and purple), G rosea splendens (rose), G nivalis (white), G liniflora, G dianthoides, and G. laciniata   A mixed packet of seed will give a fine variety of colours   They may occasionally be made graceful use of as carpet plants, or used effectively among annuals

GILLENIA.—*G trifoliata* is a Spiræa-like plant with numerous erect slender stems, about 2 ft high, and branching in the upper part into a loose panicle of white flowers   Distinct and graceful, is of value for the garden growing in peat or free loamy soil, and may be given a place in the shrubbery, or in the wild garden   North America   Division

G stipulacea.—This is a rather taller plant and not quite so compact in habit, but it is graceful, and no more charming plant could be introduced to parts of the garden where there chances to be an extra amount of moisture and a little shade from mid-day sun

Mr J Wood says   " It makes more distinct offsets, so that in the case of plants a few years old you may take the rooted offsets with a fair amount of fibre, and they make good plants the first year   The Gillenias have a distinct and delicate beauty all their own, and are pre-eminently suited for growing in semi-boggy places interspersed with such subjects as the Bog Lilies, Irises, Bamboos, and other similar strong growers "

GLADIOLUS(*Sword Lily*) —Beautiful bulbs, for the most part natives of S Africa   Every species introduced is of ornamental value, is easily grown, and is suitable for many garden uses   The chief charm of the Gladiolus is derived from the beautiful hybrid varieties now in cultivation   G gandavensis and brenchleyensis are the principal kinds from which these hybrids come, and are by far the most important class, though the earlier-flowering kinds (descendants of G ramosus, Colvillei, trimaculatus, and others) are valuable for early summer-flowering. The gandavensis section suffers from cold autumn rains, and the bulbs must be lifted in autumn

In growing Gladioli it is necessary to prepare soil where they will be most effective.   They are happy in clumps between Dahlias, Phloxes, Roses, and subjects of a somewhat similar character, and are very effective in clumps alternating with Tritomas, and also when associated with masses of Cannas , while they are suitable for intermixing with American plants, whose dark foliage shows off rich flowers to good advantage   The position should be marked out in the autumn or winter, and a few spadefuls of manure should be dug in   As a rule, the space of each clump should be 18 in in diameter, and the soil should be turned up to a depth of 18 to 24 in   March and April are the best months for planting, as Gladioli planted then are at their best during August and the early part of September   A succession of planting is desirable to secure a late bloom   Those who desire their gardens to be beautiful late in the autumn should not fail to employ the Gladiolus largely, as it is the handsomest of late-blooming garden plants, and its spikes are seen to great advantage about the time of heavy autumn rains   When spikes of extra fine bloom are required it is necessary to give special treatment, and an open situation is of the utmost importance   A deep loamy soil, not too heavy, is the most suitable for spikes for exhibition, but very satisfactory results even may be obtained by deep digging and liberal manuring in soils of an uncongenial character   Early in autumn the soil should be liberally dressed with manure from an old hotbed   After it is spread regularly over the surface, trench the soil up to a depth of 2 ft , and leave the surface as rough as possible, so as to expose a large body of it to winter frost and rain , this is of special importance in the case of heavy soils, which should be thoroughly pulverised by the weather   If this is done, the soil will be fit for working in spring, and a pricking over with the fork will reduce it to a fine tilth, and will admit of the bulbs being planted, even in wet seasons, without unnecessary delay   Planting should commence in March, and be continued until June, at intervals of a fortnight   By this means will be obtained a succession of bloom, from the earliest moment at which the show varieties may be had in flower until the end of the season   The beds should be 4 ft in width, with rows 18 in apart   They will then admit of a row down the centre, and one on each side, these outside rows being 6 in. from the edge of the bed. As soon as the plants have made sufficient progress to require support, stout stakes should be put to them. The top of the stake must not be higher than the first bloom, and the stem should have one tie only, a strong one of bast. After staking, the bed should be covered with partly-decayed manure, to a uniform depth of 2 to 3 in. This dressing materially assists during hot weather in keeping the soil cool and moist about the roots. As soon as the plants show bloom, liquid manure promotes full development of the flowers. For exhibition the spikes should be cut when about two thirds of the blooms are expanded, as the lower flowers are generally finer than those towards the top.

To ensure a given number of spikes at a particular date, a number of different sorts should be planted. For example, instead of six to twelve bulbs of a sort, it is preferable to plant one to three, and to increase the number of sorts ; and, in purchasing a hundred bulbs, to select fifty to seventy varieties. For decoration it is also better to have a large number of sorts, because of the greater variety of colour they afford. The improvements of the last few years have been so rapid, that many sorts which a few years ago occupied a foremost position are now surpassed, and for exhibition purposes are comparatively worthless. Most large nurseries and seed houses supply the finest exhibition bulbs, as well as bulbs for ordinary planting.

EARLY-FLOWERING KINDS.—During the past few years these beautiful flowers have rapidly become popular on account of their great value for cutting. They have been obtained by hybridising several South African species, particularly G. ramosus (the branching kinds which are a distinct group), G. trimaculatus, G. blandus, G. venustus, and G. Colvillei forming what is known as the nanus section. Of G. ramosus a great number of varieties are dwarfer in habit, more graceful in appearance, earlier in flower, than those of G. gandavensis, and almost as variable in colour ; they are, moreover, much hardier, and beds of them may be left unprotected during winter, so as to afford early flowers for cutting, for, unless the weather is very severe, these beds never require any covering. This remark applies only to bulbs established in the ground, for fresh bulbs are as tender as other Gladioli, and must be protected from frost. Amateurs often make a

mistake in this matter. Many plants are hardy only after they are well established. The nanus section has a great many varieties of almost every shade of colour, 1 to 2 ft. high, and invariably having the three characteristic blotches of G. trimaculatus on the lower segments of the flower. G. Colvillei is one of the prettiest and hardiest of all, and is most valuable for cutting, particularly the white variety, which has many beautiful white flowers in early summer. The time of flowering depends upon the time of planting, but the dwarf sections are the earliest. If the varieties of G. ramosus are planted at the same time as the dwarfs, the dwarfs are in flower a fortnight before the others.

Gladiolus the Bride.

These early-flowering kinds are of simple culture, and succeed best in well-drained raised beds of good loamy soil, in a sunny position. Some varieties, such as Colvillei are safe if undisturbed, but some persons prefer to take the bulbs up and thoroughly dry them, and then to plant them again about November ; in which case they will flower early in June. If the bulbs remain in the ground through the winter, care must be taken to protect them in severe cold. Propagation may be effected rapidly by seeds and offsets. By seeds, flowering bulbs are produced the second season, and can be left in the ground during the winter, provided the soil is light and dry and the bulbs are protected from frost. These Gladioli are extremely useful for pot culture, and, by gentle forcing, can be had in flower at mid-winter, and, for securing bloom between the flowering of the forced plants and of the plants in the open beds, they may be grown in cold frames. For this purpose a bed of loam, leaf-mould, and sand in nearly equal proportions should be made up in October. It should be about 1 ft. deep and well drained, and in it the bulbs may be planted thickly 4 in. in depth. The lights should then be replaced, and air left on always, except during severe frosts. No water should be given until the leaves appear (which will be about February, or earlier if the season be mild), and then only enough to keep the soil moist. The lights should be removed during mild weather, and altogether in April. During the latter part of May and in June plenty of bloom may be cut for decoration. Besides those named, the following are some of the best kinds : The Bride, Grootvoorst, Rubens, Maori Chief, The Fairy, Elvira, Rembrandt, Philip Miller, Beatrice, Baron von Humboldt, Sir Walter Raleigh, and Rose Distinctive.

Another interesting race of hybrids has lately been obtained between G. gandavensis and G. purpureo-auratus, a Cape species, with yellow and purple flowers. These hybrids have large flowers of a creamy-white and a deep purplish-crimson. The named kinds are G. hybridus Frœbeli, G. h. Lemoinei, and Marie Lemoine. Although by no means so showy as many others, they are most graceful and distinct in port, and in the shape and colour of their flowers. In deep sandy soil they attain a height of nearly 5 ft., and the gradual development of the flowers renders them effective for at least five weeks after the first and lowermost blossom. As graceful plants they well deserve culture, being hardier than many home-raised hybrids ; but a warm deep soil and a sheltered position near the foot of a south or west wall are the most congenial to their strong growth.

A few of the true species almost equal the hybrids in beauty. One of the finest is G. Saundersi, about 2 ft. high, with large flowers of a brilliant scarlet and a conspicuous pure white centre. It is not often grown, though hardy and of very easy culture, and only requiring a sunny position in a light rich soil.

The European Gladioli are pretty plants for the mixed border. There is a strong similarity among them, all of them being from 1 to 1½ ft. high, and bearing rather small rosy-purple flowers. The best-known are G. byzantinus, communis, segetus, illyricus, neglectus, serotinus. They like warm dry soil and a sunny situation. They are of particular interest from their free and hardy habit, which makes them as easy to grow as native plants. They are admirable for

Hybrid Gladiolus (Lemoine's).

the wild garden as they thrive in copses, open warm woods, in snug spots in broken hedgerow banks, and on fringes of shrubbery in the garden.

DISEASE.—This is frequently, if not always, accompanied by some condition of the fungus known as Copper-web, the Rhizoctonia crocorum of De Candolle, which is known in France under the name of Tacon. The fungus attacks also the Narcissus, the Crocus, Asparagus, Potatoes, and other bulbs, roots, etc. A good deal of attention was paid to it in

1876, when Mr. G. W. Smith detected in abundance the curious fungus named by him Urocystis Gladioli. The Urocystis and Rhizoctonia are probably two conditions of the same thing, the Rhizoctonia being possibly the spawn and the Urocystis the fruit. The latter Urocystis is capable of remaining in a resting state for a year or more, and is frequently found in the decayed red-brown portions of the diseased corm. No attempts have been made in the direction of a cure, as far as we know. The disease is confined to certain localities and to certain gardens, and is unknown in some districts.

GLAUCIUM (*Horned Poppy*).—Plants of the Poppy family, mostly biennials. G. luteum is quite hardy and has handsome silver foliage, almost as white as the silvery Centaurea. The leaves are much more deeply cut, and, planted close, are effective either in masses or lines. To ensure strong plants for winter borders or beds, seed should be sown about May, as the plant is a biennial. When in bloom it makes a striking border plant, the flowers being large and orange-red. G. Fischeri is a handsome plant; its snow-white woolly foliage is very telling, and its blossom is an unusual flame colour. G. corniculatum is similar, but not so handsome. Both require the same treatment as G. luteum.

GLOBULARIA (*Globe Daisy*).—Interesting and dwarf alpine plants, good on the rock-garden in light and peaty soils. G. Alypum is among the best; it inhabits dry rocks. Other kinds are G. cordifolia, G. nana, G. nudicaulis, and G. trichosantha.

GOODYERA (*Rattlesnake Plantain*).— A beautiful little Orchid, G. pubescens having leaves close to the ground, delicately veined with silver; hardy, distinct, and charming, though its flowers are not showy. It has long been grown in botanic and choice collections, thriving in a shady position, such as may be found in a good rock-garden, in moist peaty soil, with here and there a soft sandstone for its roots to run among. Eastern United States. G. repens and Menziesi are less desirable and much rarer.

GRAMMANTHES. — A pretty half-hardy annual, G. gentianoides being a capital plant for the dry parts of a rock-garden, about 2 in. high, forming a dense tuft, with fleshy leaves about ⅓ in. long, with many flowers, about ⅔ in. across: orange when first expanded, with a distinct V-shaped mark at the base of each petal, but finally assuming a deep red. G. gentianoides is sometimes used with good effect in the flower-garden, and succeeds in dry warm soil. Seeds should be sown in heat in February and March, and the seedlings planted out in May. Stonecrop family. Cape of Good Hope.

GREVILLEA. — Australian shrubs, generally grown in the greenhouse, but a few are quite hardy enough for wall culture; and G. sulphurea, the hardiest in cultivation, lives against walls about London. Its pale yellow flowers, of curious shape, as in all Grevilleas, come throughout the summer. G. rosmarinifolia is another hardy kind with Rosemary-like leaves and clusters of red flowers. The Grevilleas do best against a warm wall in a sheltered situation.

GUNNERA (*Prickly Rhubarb*).—South American plants remarkable for large and handsome foliage, somewhat resembling that of gigantic Rhubarb. They are hardy if slightly protected during the severest cold, for instance by a layer of dry leaves placed among the stems, and having their own leaves bent down upon them. In spring these dry leaves should be removed, and the tender growth slightly protected by a piece of canvas-shading or by an ordinary mat. In mild winters this precaution is scarcely necessary, especially in the south and other favoured localities. Where there is any diversity of surface it will be easy to select a spot well open to the sun and yet sheltered by shrubs. A large hole, about 6 by 4 ft. deep, should be dug out, a good layer of drainage material put at the bottom, and the hole filled with a rich compost of loam and manure. In summer the plants ought to have plenty of water, and a ridge of turf should be placed round them, to compel the water to sink down about their roots. They should also have a mulching of well-rotted manure early in every spring. They thrive on the margins of ponds or lakes where their roots can penetrate the moist soil, and if judiciously placed in such a position, they have a fine effect. Though the two kinds G. scabra and G. manicata greatly resemble each other, they have well-marked characteristics. The leaves of G. manicata are more kidney-shaped and attain a much larger size, often measuring 4 to 6 ft. across. The spikes of fruit are also much longer, and the secondary spikes are long and flexuose, whereas in G. scabra they are short and stiff. Propagated by seed or division of established plants.

G. manicata.—Writing from Trelissick

Truro, Mr. W. Sangwin says : " It never attains the extraordinary dimensions it is capable of, unless planted in deep rich soil with its roots in the water by the side of a pond or stream. Our plant covers a space fully 30 ft. across, and consists of from twenty-five to thirty leaves, some of them over 9 ft. in diameter, upon clear stems 8 ft. high. The crowns are as large as a man's body, of a delicate pink colour. Flower-spikes are produced freely, which should be cut as soon as seen, or they will check the growth of the leaves. When they die down in autumn, the leaves should be placed loosely over the crowns, with their stems on top to prevent them being blown away by the wind. Protected in this way the plants have

noble Grass, *G. argenteum*, 6 to 14 ft. high, according to soil or district, is most precious for our gardens, but in many districts suffers from our severe winters, and we seldom now see the fine plants of it that were not uncommon soon after its introduction. Some varieties are better in habit than others, and flower earlier, and it would be better to patiently divide such than to trust to seedlings. There are a number of varieties, some of a delicate rosy colour, and one variegated. The soils of many gardens are insufficient to give it the highest vigour, and no plant better repays a thorough preparation, and we rarely see such fine specimens as in quiet nooks where it is sheltered by the surrounding vegetation. It should be

Gunnera manicata at Narrow Water Park. Engraved from a photograph sent by Mr. F. W. Burbidge.

stood the winter with a thermometer ranging on several occasions below zero. It grows freely from seed, but it can be divided as easily as Rhubarb. The individual flowers are very minute, more curious than beautiful, the chief attraction being in the truly magnificent leaves."

The known species of Gunnera are : *G. Berteroi*, Chili. *bracteata*, do. *brephogea*, N. Granada. *chilensis*, Chili. *commutata*, do. *cordifolia*, Tasman. *densiflora*, N. Zeal. *scabra*, J. Fernand. *Hamiltoni*, N. Zeal. *insignis*, Chili. *lobata*, Magellans. *macrophylla*, Java. *magellanica*, Magellans. *manicata*, Brazil. *monoica*, N. Zeal. *teltata*, J. Fernand. *perpensa*, E. Africa. *petaloides*, Sandwich Isles. *broretens*, N. Zeal. *strigosa*, do.

GYNERIUM (*Pampas Grass*).—This

planted about the beginning of April in deep open soil mulched with rotten manure, and watered copiously in hot dry weather. G. jubatum is very well spoken of, but as yet has not been tried much except in favoured spots. The leaves resemble those of G. argenteum, but are of deeper green, and droop elegantly at the extremities. From the centre of the tuft, and exceeding it by 2 or 3 ft., arise numerous stems, each bearing an immense loose panicle of long filamentous silvery flowers, of a rosy tint with silvery sheen. It is a native of Ecuador, and is earlier in bloom than G. argenteum. The sexes are borne on separate plants in all the species, and the plumes of male flowers are neither so handsome nor so durable as the plumes of female flowers.

GYPSOPHILA.—Plants of the Stitchwort family, the larger kinds usually very elegant, and bearing myriads of tiny white blossoms on slender spreading panicles. Of these the best is G. paniculata, which forms a dense compact bush, 3 ft. or more high, the numerous flowers small white, on thread-like stalks on much-branched stems, with the light, airy effect of certain Grasses, and very useful for cutting. G. paniculata thrives in any soil, and is suitable for borders and for naturalisation in woods or banks. G. fastigiata, perfoliata, altissima Steveni, are very similar. G. prostrata is a pretty species for the rock-garden or the mixed border. It grows in spreading masses, and from midsummer to September has loose graceful panicles of small white or pink flowers, on slender stems. G. cerastioides is about 2 in. high, and has a

Gypsophila cerastioides.

spreading habit ; the leaves are about 1½ in. long, and small clusters of blossoms, ½ in. across, white with violet streaks. It is from Northern India, and quite unlike any of the group now in our gardens, being dwarfer and having larger flowers. It is a rapid grower, and in good soil and an open position on the rock-garden soon spreads into a broad tuft. Division, seeds, or cuttings in spring. G. elegans is a graceful feathery annual much used for bouquets.

HABENARIA *(Rein Orchis).*—Terrestrial Orchids from N. America, 1 to 2 ft. high, some of which are pretty. For outdoor culture, a partially-shaded spot should be prepared with about equal parts of leaf-mould or peat and sand, and well mulched with leaves, grass, or other material, to keep it moist. H. blephariglottis bears in July spikes of white flowers beautifully fringed. H. ciliaris has bright orange-

yellow flowers with a conspicuous fringe, and appear from July to September. H. fimbriata has a long spike of lilac-purple flowers beautifully fringed. H. psycodes bears spikes 4 to 10 in. long of handsome and fragrant purple flowers. They are charming plants for the bog-garden.

HABERLEA.—*H. rhodopensis* is a pretty little rock-plant resembling a Gloxinia in miniature, forming dense tufts of small rosettes of leaves, which somewhat resemble those of the Pyrenean Ramondia (R. pyrenaica), every rosette bearing in spring one to five slender flower-stalks, each with two to four blossoms nearly 1 in. long, of a bluish-lilac colour with a yellowish throat. Messrs. Frœbel of Zurich, who grow it well, write of it : " We have treated this plant in the same manner as the Pyrenean Ramondia, *i.e.* we have planted it on the north side of the rock-garden ; so that the sun never directly reaches it. We grow it in fibrous peat, and fix the plants, if possible, in the fissures of the rock-garden, so that its rosettes hang in an oblique position, just as they do in their native country. It succeeds well in this way ; but if no rock-garden be at hand, it may be grown equally well on the north side of a Rhododendron bed. We have it thus situated quite close to a stone edging—a way in which we also grow the Ramondia, —and the Haberlea flowers profusely every year in May and June. The plant is very hardy, having withstood our often very hard winters, without any protection." It is a native of the Balkan Mountains, where it is found among moss and leaves on damp, shady, steep declivities at high elevations.

HABRANTHUS.—A brilliant bulb of the Amaryllis family, hardy, at least in the southern and eastern parts of the country. *H. pratensis* has stout and erect flower-stems, about 1 ft. high, and the brightest scarlet flowers, feathered here and there at the base with yellow. The variety fulgens is the finest form. It blooms freely in the open border of the Rev. Mr. Nelson's garden at Aldborough, in Norfolk, flowering at the end of May or beginning of June. It grows very freely in strong loam improved by the addition of a little leaf-mould and sand. Its propagation is too easy, for in many soils it is said to split up into offsets instead of growing to a flowering size. At Aldborough it made numerous offsets. A choice plant for the select bulb-garden or rock-garden. Chili. H. Andersoni is much inferior.

HALESIA (*Snowdrop Tree*).—Beautiful North American trees, hardy in this country. The commonest is H. tetraptera, one of the prettiest of flowering trees. It grows in England from 20 to 30 ft. high, has a rounded head, with sharply-toothed leaves, in May bearing many pure white blossoms, in form like the Snowdrop, hence its popular name. It is of moderately rapid growth, and flourishes in any good garden soil, and as it grows naturally by river banks, it enjoys a moist, but not waterlogged soil. In some parts it ripens its seed in abundance. A similar species, distinguished in having but two wings to the seed-vessel (tetraptera having four), is H. diptera, of smaller growth, and not such a suitable tree for this climate; neither is H. parviflora, which, like the others, has small bell-like flowers. As a lawn tree, or planted near the margin of a lake or stream, H. tetraptera is very beautiful.

Halesia tetraptera.

HALIMONDENDRON (*Salt-tree*).— H. argenteum is a small shrub belonging to the Pea family, with elegant leaves, silky and whitish, the flowers purplish in early summer: a native of Asiatic Russia, it is hardy, and grows from 5 to 6 ft. high, and sometimes is grafted on to the tall stems of the Laburnum.

HAMAMELIS (*Witch Hazel*).—Hardy shrubs with singular blossoms flowering in winter. They have a peculiar value as ornamental shrubs, and one species at least is worth planting in all good gardens. This is H. arborea, or Tree Witch Hazel, though in this country it does not rise generally above 8 ft. high. In January, and sometimes before, its leafless branches are covered with flowers, which have twisted, bright yellow petals and crimson calyces, so that a well-flowered plant is very pretty. It is a hardy Japanese shrub, and thrives in most kinds of soil, but must have an open situation. Another Japanese species is H. japonica, a smaller and dwarfer plant than H. arborea, and bearing flowers of a lighter yellow colour, while that called H. Zuccariniana is very similar to it. Of less value perhaps is the American Witch

Hazel, which has small yellowish flowers in winter, and sometimes in autumn. Though not so showy when in flower as the Japanese species, it is a pretty shrub, and, like the others, thrives in any soil.

HEDERA (*Ivy*).—*H. Helix* is the most beautiful evergreen climber of our northern and temperate world, and is a noble garden plant that may be used in many ways. The common Ivy of the woods is familiar to all, but its many beautiful varieties are not so common as this. All are not of the same vigorous habit, as will easily be seen by cultivating a collection; but the rich self green-leaved kinds are usually as free and as hardy as the wild plant. Although there are many varieties, there are only two accepted species—the Australian, that is confined to the continent of Australia; and Hedera Helix, which is found wild in the British Isles, and spreads over Europe, reaching into N. Africa and Central Asia. It is under our English Ivy that the large number of forms in cultivation are classed. Although there are only two species, we can classify the Ivies in several groups, after the variation in the leaves. If we want Ivies in their fullest beauty, it is necessary to pay some attention to position, soil, and training. This applies to all kinds, but especially to the more delicate varieties. Ordinary garden soil will grow the Ivy well, and the strong growers, as Emerald Gem, Rægneriana algeriensis, canariensis or the Irish Ivy, sagittæfolia, lucida, palmata, gracilis, dentata, digitata, pedata, and angularis, will need no special position; but in the case of kinds like madeirensis variegata, a showy form, some little care is needed. It is better to plant these kinds as edgings to a bed of shrubs or permit them to clamber over a root-stump, arbour, or form a pyramid of them, where they will be less exposed to the full force of wind than if they were stiffly trained on walls. Cuttings may be struck in the latter part of the summer, and quickly root if put in a shady border where the soil is fairly good. It is sometimes well to cut the plants down to the ground after the first year, as often the shoots are very weak; but this severe pruning induces a stronger growth later on. As regards the best time to plant, the spring months are the most suitable; but the Ivy may be planted any time if it is in a pot, and during the first summer, if the weather is hot, give plenty of water. In the case of variegated sorts, it is advisable to plant in a poor soil, so as to bring out the variegation. A word should be said for Tree Ivies, which make fine bushes in the garden, and may be associated with other shrubs in beds. Healthy plants make dense rounded heads of foliage, relieved during the blooming season with many flowers. By far the most important Ivies, however, are the green-leaved forms, — many, various, and nearly all beautiful in form. Whatever kinds among these we may prefer, a fuller and more graceful use of the Ivy in or near the flower-garden and its surroundings is desirable.

HEDYCHIUM. — *H. Gardnerianum*, though usually grown in the greenhouse, will flower out-of-doors, and live through an ordinary winter with a little protection. It should be planted out in May, in a loose sandy loam, enriched with manure. While the plant is making its growth a mulching should be given, and in dry weather an occasional watering of liquid manure. It is excellent for choice groups in the sub-tropical garden, in warm sheltered spots. A heap of cinders or half-rotten leaves laid over the crowns in winter will ensure their safety ; or the roots may be lifted in autumn and wintered in any dry place with Dahlias and Cannas. It is increased by dividing the roots in spring, but each piece must have a young crown attached.

HEDYSARUM (*French Honeysuckle*). — Plants of the Pea order, mostly weedy, only a few perennials being ornamental. H. coronarium is a showy plant, 3 or 4 ft. high, bearing in summer dense spikes of red flowers. It grows in any ordinary soil, but is not a perennial, though it usually sows itself where it is established. There is a white variety. Among the dwarfer kinds the two following are desirable : H. obscurum, a brilliant and compact perennial ; 6 to 12 in. high, with racemes of showy purple flowers. It is suitable for the rock-garden, for borders, and for naturalisation amongst vegetation not more than 1 ft. high, chiefly on banks

and slopes in sandy loam, and is increased by division or seed. H. Mackenzii is said to be the handsomest of the genus. It grows about 2 ft. high, and has long racemes of from seven to thirty rather large rosy-purple Pea-like flowers. It is perfectly hardy in any situation, and flowers in June and July. It is rather too tall for the rock-garden, and is more suited for the mixed border.

HELENIUM (*Sneeze-weed*).—Vigorous

Pyramid of large-leaved Ivy, 7 ft. high.

Composites from North America, flowering in autumn, and thriving in any soil, and, where rightly used, excellent plants. There are two or three species, the most useful being H. autumnale, about 6 ft. high, bearing yellow flower-heads. The varieties grandiceps and pumilum are very distinct : grandiceps being of gigantic growth with a fasciated head of bloom, which makes it very showy ; pumilum being much dwarfer and better than the type. H. atropurpureum grows 3 or 4 ft.

high, and has reddish-brown flower-heads. H. Hoopesi is desirable, as it flowers in early summer, but is a rather coarse grower, with large yellow flowers. The first-mentioned species and its varieties are excellent border plants, and, though vigorous, remain long in bloom. They are very useful for cutting, as they remain a long time fresh.

HELIANTHEMUM (_Sun Rose_). — Though strictly shrubby plants for the most part, these dwarf evergreens possess so much the aspect of rock-plants, that they cannot well be separated from them.

Helianthemum lignosum.

There are few more brilliant sights than masses of them when in full beauty, and they are of the easiest possible culture, dwarf and compact, bearing in great profusion flowers with fine diversity of colour. The common Sun Rose. (H. vulgare) is variable in colour, and from it have sprung the many varieties enumerated in trade lists ; indeed, we need only this species to represent, for garden purposes, the variation in all the dwarf shrubby species of the family. The colours range from white and yellow to deep crimson. There are also double-flowered kinds and one with variegated foliage. Other pretty, dwarf, shrubby species, similar to H. vulgare, are H. rosmarinifolium, pilosum, and croceum. There is also a herbaceous perennial species, H. Tuberaria (Truffle Sun Rose), which in aspect differs completely from the shrubby species, and is second to none in beauty. It grows 6 to 12 in. high, with flowers 2 in. across resembling a single yellow Rose, with dark centre, and drooping when in bud. It is suited for warm ledges on the rock-garden in well-drained sandy or calcareous soil. When sufficiently plentiful it should be used in the mixed border. It is propagated by either seed or division. When a full collection is required there are other species introduced, but the above fairly represent the beauty of the family.

HELIANTHUS (_Sunflower_)—PEREN-NIAL SUNFLOWERS. — Usually stout, vigorous, and showy plants, typical of the coarse yellow Composites abounding in North America, of which not a few have found their way into English gardens. All the perennials are vigorous growers, and generally attain a great height, being most precious for the autumnal garden when well placed. Sunflowers may be cultivated with the greatest ease ; they are gross feeders, and the richer the soil the better the result. It is true that not a few of this genus are coarse and weedy, unfitted for the flower-garden, but a good many, some of which are not yet in general cultivation, could be utilised with striking effect in the best-kept flower-garden ; and for mixed borders, etc., they are valuable. The Sunflowers, like the Michaelmas Daisies, could ill be spared from the autumn garden, where, when most other hardy perennials are beginning to show the sere and yellow leaf, they are generally at their best and in their greatest numbers. Although the flowers are somewhat restricted in their range of colouring, the plants vary considerably in their seasons of blooming, in habit, and also in the positions in which the most may be made of them. From their robust growth, the majority of them are essentially suitable for borders where plenty of scope may be had, and where attention may be given to the proper grouping of the different species and varieties. Some few of the species which may not be considered showy enough for the flower border proper could be planted in the woods, in isolated beds or among shrubs, where their particular and characteristic habits could be seen to advantage.

Helianthemum sabrosum.

It would hardly be policy to grow the whole genus in any one garden unless shrubberies abound on a large scale. H. multiflorus and its varieties, H. rigidus and its varieties, H. decapetalus, and a few others are essentially border plants, where, when doing well and in full flower, they form a feature of no mean beauty. H. lætiflorus, H. orgyalis, H. lævigatus, and H. divaricatus would make handsome groups in open shrubberies, and giganteus, doronicoides, grosse-serratus and others might with advantage be relegated to the wood, where, in open exposed positions, they would form interesting groups. They increase so rapidly as a whole that it will be needless to say anything about propagation, which may be done in autumn or spring with good results. Other species not mentioned, but which may be of interest to many, are H. angustifolius, Maximiliani, mollis, and occidentalis, the two last being early-flowering species rare in gardens.

H. DECAPETALUS is one of the most charming species in the whole genus as a background to mixed borders or as a feature in open shrubberies. It forms large, bushy, well-balanced plants 4 to 6 ft. in height, with strong, much-branched stems, rough on the upper half

Double Perennial Sunflower.

and usually quite smooth on the lower. The leaves are broadly oval, pointed and thin in texture ; flowers 2 to 3 in. in diameter, of a rich sulphur-yellow, produced in great abundance, and very showy. It is found plentifully on the banks of streams in Canada and Georgia.

H. GIGANTEUS is a very tall, elegant plant. The stems often exceed 10 to 12 ft. high, the leaves narrow, tapering to both ends ; the flowers deep yellow, 2 to 3 in. in diameter. It is one of the latest to flower, and has been found variable under cultivation, giving rise to several garden names. Moist ground, Canada and Louisiana.

H. LÆTIFLORUS is a handsome species, very little known in gardens, although the

name was freely used for forms of H. rigidus. It is, as a rule, rather later in flowering than the H. rigidus forms, and unfortunately in cold wet seasons or early winters does not bear good flowers. It is a much taller and stronger plant than H. rigidus, the flowers, 4 to 5 in. across, of a bright yellow with yellow disc. The leaves are thin, entire, or coarsely toothed, and the bracts of the involucre always acute, a very distinctive character in this genus. The roots are somewhat similar to those of H. rigidus, perhaps larger, and they certainly travel further. It is a native of prairies and barrens, Illinois, Wisconsin.

H. MULTIFLORUS.—The late Dr. Asa Gray always considered this plant a garden variety of H. decapetalus. There is strong evidence, however, of its being a hybrid, the parents of which it would be difficult now to ascertain with accuracy. It is so very distinct from all the other species so well known in gardens under its present name, and such a good all-round plant, that it well deserves specific rank. It rarely exceeds 3 to 5 ft. in height, producing numerous large fine rich yellow flowers, remaining a considerable time in good form. The var. maximus has larger flowers with more pointed rays, and the varieties plenus and Soleil d'Or are both very desirable double-flowered forms. All the varieties of H. multiflorus should find a place in collections, however small.

H. ORGYALIS, though a small-flowered plant, is yet one of the best of the genus for the picturesque garden in southern counties. It is one of the late-flowering species, and is often damaged by early frosts. It grows from 6 to 10 ft. high, having numerous linear leaves and bunches of deep golden yellow flowers. It should be grown in sheltered spots, otherwise it requires a great deal of staking. It is a native of dry plains of Nebraska and Texas.

H. RIGIDUS.—This distinct, though variable species is perhaps the best known of all the perennial Sunflowers. It is still found labelled Harpalium rigidum in some gardens, and is often confounded with H. missuricus and H. atro-rubens, the latter of which, so far as I know, is not now in cultivation. Typical H. rigidus is figured in the *Botanical Register*, t. 508, and *Botanical Magazine*, t. 2668, as H. atro-rubens. H. rigidus grows from 4 to 5 ft. in height, with a rough hispid stem, the upper leaves always alternate, distinctly three-nerved and veined. The lower ones are opposite, broader, thinner, often serrated, and rarely pointed. All the leaves narrow to a winged petiole, and are easily distinguished from those of any other species. The flowers, bright yellow and very showy, are produced very freely. It is a native of the plains and prairies of Georgia and Texas. The varieties of this species, most of which have undoubtedly originated in gardens, are superior to the type as garden plants.

H. grandiflorus, semi-plenus, elegans, and æstivus are all worth a place in the flower border. All should, however, be grouped by themselves, as they form underground tubers, which spread a considerable distance from the parent plant in the course of a year. Some of these varieties have been tried at Kew and elsewhere grouped singly in beds, and are always much admired in the autumn months when the members of this genus are so much in evidence.—D. D.

ANNUAL SUNFLOWERS.—All the larger kinds are noble plants, requiring plenty of space, a sheltered position, and a good background. They are all easily raised from seed, which may be sown in pans in early March or in the open air in April where they are intended to flower, and thinned out to from a foot to a yard apart according to the vigour of the plant. The regulation row of Sunflowers along a choice mixed border often ruins its effect, but there are various ways of arranging the annual Sunflowers with excellent effect —among large beds of fine-leaved plants being one of them.

H. ANNUUS (*Common Sunflower*).— Although often regarded only as a cottagers' flower, the annual Sunflower is one of the noblest plants we have, and one of the most effective for various positions. In order to dispense with support, it should be planted in a sheltered place, as among tall shrubs. Here it assumes a dense branching tree-like habit, and often produces flowers each over a foot in diameter. It requires a strong rich soil, to which may be added a quantity of old cow manure just before planting. There are many varieties in gardens, the most notable being one called californicus, a more robust and darker-flowered form. Macrocarpus, lenticularis, and ovatus, are synonyms or slight varieties of the cultivated annual Sunflower; sulphureus, multiflorus, globosus, grandiflorus, and fistulosus are garden variations. The sulphur-coloured variety is charming, and less strong in growth than the richer yellow forms. North America. H. argophyllus, little more than a variety of H. annuus, is a charming plant from Texas, for the back of mixed borders, open

borders, and in thin shrubberies. The whole plant is white, being covered with soft and silky wool, the flowers large with very broad ray florets. H. Dammanni and H. D. var. sulphureus are said to be garden hybrids between H. argophyllus and H. annuus. H. cucumerifolius, the miniature Sunflower, is a good annual, growing from 2 to 3 ft. high, usually with purple mottling on the stems, the leaves thin, and bright apple-green. The stems are much branched, and when allowed plenty of room the plants form perfect symmetrical specimens. The flowers are yellow, about 3 in. in diameter, nicely set off with the almost black disc. Sandy soil in woods from Texas westwards.

H. EXILIS.—A very slender species, rarely more than a couple of feet in height,

Annual Sunflowers.

with lance-shaped leaves and yellow flowers about 2 in. in diameter. N. California. H.

H. PETIOLARIS.—A fine kind rarely seen in gardens, though from its neat habit and profusion of flowers it should be a welcome addition to the mixed border. It grows about a yard high, loosely branched, the stem as well as the leaves being covered with stiff hairs; flowers yellow, 3 to 4 in. in diameter. The variety canescens is covered with white pubescence. Texas.

H. SCABERRIMUS.—A very distinct plant with large deep yellow flowers, stout branching stems, and broad, oval, coarsely-toothed leaves. California.—D.

HELICHRYSUM (*Everlasting Flower*).—Composites, mostly natives of the Cape of Good Hope, of which a few are cultivated   The most important garden plants are H macranthum and H. bracteatum   They are generally treated as annuals, and, unless exceptionally well managed by being sown early under glass, they commence flowering so late that the best period for laying on the brightest colours is lost, and early frosts find them just approaching their best   They are particularly suited for background plants on dry borders   If they are sown in pans or boxes where they can be slightly protected during winter, and are planted out early in April, they have a chance of producing a good crop of flowers for drying.   The colours vary from deep crimson to yellow and white   The hardy perennials are not important, and seldom succeed   H orientale, which furnishes the Immortelle of the French, flowers poorly except in very hot seasons   None of the other hardy kinds are worth growing, except perhaps H. arenarium, which has bright golden-yellow flowers

HELIOPHILA — Small and pretty Cruciferous annuals   H araboides is a pretty blue annual, of which occasional use might be made, being dwarf, and free in growth and flower   Another kind is H. pilosa

HELIOTROPIUM (*Cherry Pie*) —A great favourite for flower gardens on account of its delicate fragrance.   For the flower garden spring-struck plants are the best   It is a good plan to lift a few plants from the beds in September, winter them in a warm greenhouse, and in spring to put them in a warm place, where they will soon produce plenty of cuttings   These cuttings may be struck on slight heat like Verbenas, potted on, made to grow rapidly, so as to be fit to plant out at the end of May when danger of frost is past   Heliotropes may be raised from seed and flowered the same year—in fact, treated as annuals   Sown early—in February or the beginning of March—they become sturdy little plants before planting time   When bedded out they should be placed in good dry soil   The following are good varieties, and new varieties are raised from time to time   Anna Turrell, General Garfield, Roi des Noirs, Triomphe de Liége, and the old H peruvianum, which many like from its associations if for no other reason   Heliotropes, though quiet in colour, are charming flower-garden plants, either when grown for their own sakes as simple masses or when associated with tall plants which grow above them

HELLEBORUS (*Christmas Rose*) — One of the most valuable classes of hardy

perennials we have, as they flower in the open air when there is little else in bloom   They appear in succession from October till April, beginning with the Christmas Rose (H niger), and ending with the handsome crimson kinds.   The old white Christmas Rose is well known and much admired, but the handsome kinds with coloured flowers have, hitherto, not been much known   Recently too there have appeared some really beautiful hybrids, which add a great deal of beauty to our winter and spring garden, for their flowers withstand the winter, and their verdure and the vigorous growth of their leaves distinguish them throughout the year

The Hellebores, besides being excellent border flowers, are suited for naturalising   There are a few kinds—those with inconspicuous flowers, but handsome foliage—whose only place is the wild garden, such as the native H fœtidus, H lividus, viridus, and H Bocconi, which have elegant foliage when well developed in a shady place in rich soil, like that usually found in woods   The Hellebores may be classed in three groups, according to the colour of the flowers—those with white flowers, those with red, and those with green, which last will get little place in the garden   The white-flowered group is the most important, as it contains the beautiful old Christmas Rose

H niger is a well-known kind, scarcely needing description   It may be recognised at once by its pale green smooth leathery leaves, divided into seven or nine segments, 3 to 6 in long and 1 to 2 in broad   The flowers, which are usually borne singly on stems 6 in long, are about 3 in across, and vary from a waxy-white to a delicate blush tint   The variety minor is smaller in every part, and is also known as H angustifolius. H altifolius, though sometimes considered a variety of H niger, is a distinct kind, and much larger than H niger   It has leaf-stalks over 1 ft long, and blossoms 3 to 5 in across which are borne on branching stems, each stem bearing from two to seven flowers, which have a stronger tendency to assume a rosy hue than the ordinary kind   Another characteristic is that the leaf and flower stems are beautifully mottled with purple and green, while in H. niger they are of a pale green   H. altifolius also flowers much earlier—in some seasons in the beginning of October   It has been known a long time under the names of H. niger var. major, maximus, giganteus, and grandiflorus

Other white kinds are H. olympicus—a tall slender species with cup-shaped blossoms that appear in early spring and vary from pure white to greenish-white. H. guttatus is like it, but has the inside of the blossoms spotted with purple. There are several forms ; in some the markings assume the form of small dots, in others of thin streaks. It is one of the parents of the many beautiful hybrids.

The finest of the red or crimson kinds is H. colchicus, which is larger than any produced from the end of January to the end of March. A fine hybrid has been obtained by crossing it with H. guttatus, the result being a form with large spreading flowers lighter than in H. colchicus, and profusely marked with dark carmine streaks. Another hybrid between this and H. altifolius resulted in a form with larger flowers of a lighter purple. H. atro-rubens has leaves much thinner and

Christmas Rose.

other, and may be readily recognised by thick dark green leaves, with five to seven broad and coarsely-toothed divisions, the veins of which are raised on the under sides, and are of a dark purple when young. The blossoms, borne on forked stems rising considerably above the foliage, are dark purple. Under good cultivation the leaves attain the length of $1\frac{1}{2}$ and 2 ft., forming fine specimens, and flowers are flowers much smaller than H. colchicus, the latter dull purple on the outside and greenish-purple within. It is a native of Hungary, and is common in gardens, but is often confused with H. abchasicus, a taller and more slender plant, the flower-stems of which are longer, and the blossoms nodding and smaller. H. abchasicus is much superior to atro-rubens, the colour of the blossoms—a deep ruby-crimson—

making them very attractive   Other fine varieties of the red-flowered group are Gretchen Heinemann, James Atkins, and Apotheker Bogren, all worthy of culture   Other reddish kinds, such as H. purpurascens and H cupreus, are not worth growing

All the kinds will thrive in ordinary garden soil, but for the choicer kinds a prepared soil is preferable   This should consist of equal parts of good fibry loam and well-decomposed manure, half fibry peat and half coarse sand   Thorough drainage should always be given, as stagnant moisture is very injurious   A moist and sheltered situation, where they will obtain partial shade, such as the margins of shrubberies, is best, but care should be taken to keep the roots of shrubs from exhausting the border   In the flowering season a thin mulching of moss or similar material should be placed on the soil round the plants, as this prevents the blossoms from being spattered by heavy rains, etc   Any one beginning to grow these useful plants should give the soil a good preparation.   If well trenched and manured, they will not require replanting for at least seven years, but a top-dressing of well-decayed manure and a little liquid manure might be given during the growing season when the plants are making their foliage, as upon the size and substance of the leaves will depend the size of the flowers   The common white Christmas Rose is a favourite pot-plant, and if required for potting its foliage should be protected from injury, when the blooming season is over it should be protected by a frame until genial weather permits it to be plunged in the open air   Hardy subjects like the Christmas Rose frequently suffer when removed from under glass, for although hardy enough to withstand our severest winters when continuously exposed, their growth, when made under more exciting circumstances, will not withstand sudden variations of temperature   For this reason it is advisable to keep them in as cool a position as possible when in flower, so that the growth of young foliage may not be excited before its natural season

Propagation may be effected by division or by seeds, which, in favourable seasons, are plentiful, as soon as thoroughly ripened they should be sown in pans under glass, for they soon lose their vitality   As soon as the seedlings are large enough they should be pricked off thickly into a shady border, in a light rich soil, the second year they should be transplanted to their permanent place,

and in the third season most of them will bloom   In division the clumps must be well-established, with root-stocks large enough to cut up   The divided plants, if placed in a bed of good light soil, and undisturbed, will be good flowering plants in a couple of years, but four years are required to bring a Christmas Rose to perfection.   By July the Hellebore is in its strongest vigour, and lifting and dividing the plants should then be carried out

HELONIAS (*Stud Flower*).—A distinct and handsome bog perennial, *H bullata* being 12 to 16 in high, with handsome purplish-rose flowers in an oval spike   It is suitable for the bog-garden or for moist ground near a rivulet   In fine sandy and very moist soil it thrives as a border plant   N America   *Syn*, H latifolia

HEMEROCALLIS (*Day Lily*)—The Day Lilies, though not numbering many distinct species, are varied both in habit and flower, and are very useful in the mixed border and in groups by the water-side   Few plants surpass a strong well-flowered clump of Hemerocallis fulva, as we have seen it mixed with a group of male Fern near a brook   The leaves of this Day Lily were overhanging the banks of the stream, intermingled with the Fern fronds, while the flower-heads, tall and straight, were towering upwards   If the ground is well broken up and some lasting manure supplied at planting time, they may be left undisturbed for years   The forms of H disticha, both single and double, are also useful for clumps by water, or intermixed with other robust or bold-foliaged plants, indeed, there seems no reason why all the Day Lilies could not be treated in this picturesque way, the trouble entailed being small, and that chiefly at planting time only.   For cutting, H flava, minor, and Dumortieri are useful, the flowers lasting a few days and the buds opening well in water   The fragrance of these flowers is delightful, they are readily increased by division, and grow with such rapidity that in the course of a few years they may be increased to almost any extent

The following are the species as they are now recognised, with the principal varieties —

H DUMORTIERI (Dumortier's Day Lily)—This valuable kind is the first to flower of all the Day Lilies   Coming as it does from Japan and W Siberia, it proves hardy in the open air   It does not require protection during winter, and we have never known it fail to bear freely its charming and fragrant flowers.   The blooms are short-lived, but the reserves are so numerous as to keep up the succession for a long time. This Day Lily dwindles in vigour of the plants and size of the flowers if allowed to remain too long in one place. If the plants are examined, the centres will be found to be matted together, the stronger shoots appearing on the outside. If the whole plant is divided and replanted it will amply repay the trouble by increased vigour and flowers. It is closely allied to H. minor, also known as H. graminea, but it is a much stronger plant, however, with leaves twice as broad, the flower-stems short, and the divisions of the perianth divided almost or entirely to their base. The leaves are about five or six to a growth, about 18 in. long and half an inch broad, bright green above and pale but not glaucous on the under surface; flower-stem 1 to 2 ft. in height, bearing a corymb of large orange-yellow flowers. H. rutilans and Sieboldi of gardens belong to the same species.

H. FLAVA (the yellow Day Lily).—Few plants can be grown with so little trouble in the border, and give such a valuable return as this one. The flowers large and in such quantities, emitting such an agreeable fragrance, as to earn the name of *yellow* Tuberose. The length of time the flowers last enhances its value as a border plant. It is hardy, and though not so robust in habit as H. fulva, it increases rapidly, and where the soil is good might be naturalised. On banks the beautiful light green curving leaves hang gracefully, surmounted by bunches of large yellow heads of flower in June and July. Europe and N. Asia. H. Thunbergi and japonica are forms of this species.

H. FULVA (copper-coloured Day Lily) is a much larger plant than H. flava, and more suitable for extensive planting in semi-wild or rough parts of the garden. It is variable under cultivation, and the numerous forms now grown, many without names, are all worthy of attention. H. disticha is a well-known garden variety of this species, notable for the fan-like form of its growths. The flower-stem is forked near the summit, and carries two or three heads of flowers, six to eight blooms on each, of a brown-orange colour. There is also a double-flowered variety of this. H. Kwanso is a variety with variegated or striated leaves. It is a handsome plant for edgings or for the rock-garden. Of this there is also a double-flowered form. H. f. var. angustifolia, narrow-leaved; longituba, crocea, natives of

China, flowering in July and August, belong to this section.

H. MIDDENDORFIANA is from Amur-land, in appearance resembling H. Dumortieri; the leaves are, however, broader, the flowers about the same size, closer, and paler in colour, and with a distinct cylindrical tube half an inch or so long. It is of easy cultivation.

H. MINOR, also known in many gardens under the highly characteristic name of H. graminea, from its Grass-like foliage, was formerly classed by the older botanists

Yellow Day Lily (Hemerocallis flava).

as a variety of H. flava, though now considered distinct. It is the smallest, though not the least showy, and, like flava, sweetly scented, the flowers lasting two or three days. It makes a handsome plant for a rocky bank, and even when flowers are absent the pretty Grass-like leaves are welcome. It flowers during June and July. It is also known under the names graminifolia and pumila. Siberia.

H. AURANTIACA MAJOR.—This is the name given by Mr. Baker of Kew to a new and handsome kind from Japan, and of which a coloured plate was given in *The Garden*, November 23, 1895. It is certainly one of the finest new hardy plants of recent years, and reminds one of H. fulva (*syn.*, H. disticha). The new kind has bold leafage, a glaucous tinge overlying the deep green body colour; the flowers are rich apricot in colour, open out widely, and of great substance.

HERACLEUM (*Giant Parsnip*). — Umbelliferous perennials, mostly of gigantic growth, having huge spreading leaves and tall flower-stems, with umbelled clusters of small white flowers 1 ft. or more across. Though well-developed plants of the large kinds have a fine effect when isolated in a position not too obstructive, they are generally suitable only for the rougher parts of pleasure-grounds, the banks of rivers or lakes, and

1 to 3 ft. high, and has pinkish flowers, but the double kinds are much more valued. There are two distinct forms of the double white Rocket, as well as of the double purple Rocket in cultivation. One is a tall white, turning to a pale flesh colour with age; the other is the old white variety, of dwarfer growth, with smaller and more compact flowers. It is met with in the north, but is little known in the south, where it does not flourish so well as the common variety. There is the old purple double Rocket and a free-growing dwarf form known as Compactness, which has also larger and darker flowers. Rockets require care in cultivating, and will soon be lost if left to themselves. They should be divided at least every second year and transplanted, for they seem to tire of the soil and to require more change than most perennials. If

Double White Rocket.

other places where they can grow freely and well, and can show their stately growth to advantage. The finest are H. giganteum, lanatum, sibiricum, eminens, Wilhelmsi, and pubescens, all of which, when in flower, are 5 to 10 ft. high. All are increased by seed.

HERNIARIA. — Dwarf perennial trailers, forming a dense turfy mass, green throughout the year. There are two or three species, but the most important is H. glabra, which has been largely used as a carpeting plant on account of its dwarf growth. Always a deep green, even in a hot and dry season.

HESPERIS (*Rocket*).—H. matronalis is a popular old garden plant, and among the most desirable of hardy flowers. It bears showy varied, and fragrant flower-spikes. The original single-flowered kind grows

the young shoots are formed into cuttings when they are about 3 in. long, they strike very freely in the open ground, and the spikes of bloom on the remaining stems are all the finer when some of the others have been removed. When shaded from the sun for about three weeks with a few Laurel branches, the cuttings do better than when covered with a pot or box, as has been advised. They like a rich soil, rather moist, and are all the better for repeated applications of liquid manure if the soil is not as deep and good as it should be. Double Rockets really belong to the garden plants requiring annual attention, and they therefore cannot well be used as true perennials. It is always worth while having a bed of them in the reserve garden in case the plants should be lost or neglected in the borders. We have seen them best grown where there was a yearly transfer of plants from the reserve garden to the mixed border, and the groups look very well. The single Rocket is easily naturalised, and is a showy·plant in woods or shrubberies.

H. tristis (*Night-scented Stock*).—A quaint plant with dull-coloured flowers, sweet - scented at night. It is rather tender, and requires a light warm soil and a sheltered position.

HEUCHERA (*Alum Root*). — Dwarf, tufted, perennial herbs, with distinct and sometimes finely-coloured leaves and modest but inconspicuous flowers. Of little value for their flowers, one or two kinds give pretty effects of foliage either as edgings to or beneath groups of shrubs ; the best are also worth growing for their leaves for cutting for the house in winter, lasting as they do fresh for weeks in winter, the foliage being good in form as well as colour. Among the best are *H. hispida* (*Richardsoni*), *americana*, *pubescens*, and *sanguinea*, the last the only one with any showy bloom. They are North American plants, of the easiest cultivation in ordinary soil. Division. Saxifrage order.

HIBISCUS (*Rose Mallow*).—Shrubby and herbaceous perennials and annuals. They are numerous in hothouses, but few are suited for the flower-garden. The splendid hardy Rose Mallows of the woods and swamps of N. America will live with us, but our climate is not warm enough for them, though it would be well to try tufts of them in warm sunny places in the southern parts of England, in deep, moist soil. They have splendid crimson or rosy flowers, as large as saucers, and are from 4 to 7 ft. high. The finest are H. Moscheutos, H. palustris, H. grandiflorus, and H. coccineus. They seldom bloom in the open air in England, as they flower late in the season. There are two or three annual kinds, the finest being H. Manihot, which forms handsome pyramids 4 to 6 ft. high, the flowers being 3 or 4 in. across, and pale yellow with a dark centre. H. Manihot should be treated as a half-hardy annual, sown in heat in February, and in May planted out in good deep soil. H. africanus is a hardy annual with showy pale yellow flowers that only open in fine weather. In light soil it usually sows itself. H. Trionum appears to be extremely variable, and has long been cultivated in gardens. It is widely scattered over all the warm regions of the Old World, and is usually described as a common sub-tropical weed, found plentifully in

cultivated fields in Afghanistan. It is found in several places in China, and is a very common weed in waste garden ground and rich damp soil throughout the Cape Colony, and has given rise to almost innumerable varieties, a few of which are so distinct as to have at one time been considered species. The great objection to the type is the short-lived flowers, which Gerard says open at eight in the morning and close at nine, and which supposed fact gave rise to the curious appellations, " Flower of an hour," " Good night at noon," or " Good night at nine."

In a fine form, figured in *The Garden*, this objection is quite done away with, the flowers opening in the morning, and, on bright days, remaining so until late in the afternoon. Individual flowers do not last very long, but there is a succession on a well-grown plant, and these are large and beautiful. It is quite as hardy as the

Venice Mallow (Hibiscus Trionum).

one usually grown, seeds as freely, and much more striking, especially in bold clumps. Simply scatter the seeds in the open on the spots where they are intended to grow, thinning, where too close together, to 6 in. or 1 ft. apart, and leaving the sun, etc., to do the rest. It will even sow itself, the seeds coming up in plenty the following spring if the winter has not been too severe, but sowings should be made at different times to ensure bloom all through the summer and autumn.

H. Syriacus (*Syrian Mallow, Rose of Sharon*). — A beautiful shrub, bearing showy blossoms in late summer and in autumn. It is a very old favourite, and in good moist 'soils it rises 8 and even 10 ft. high. The wild form has bluish-purple flowers with crimson centres, but now there are forms representing every tint from white (*totus albus*) to crimson and purple, while the blooms of one sort (*Celeste*) are almost blue. There are also double flowers of varied colours. The best kinds, single and double, are *Totus albus, Celeste, Violet Clair, Leopoldi, bicolor, roseus plenus, Pompon Rouge, carneoplenus, Du. de Brabant, albus plenus, puniceus plenus*, and *anemonæflorus.*

In the South German gardens this shrub assumes a larger growth, and bears much larger flowers than in England. The usual form has flowers not so attractive in colour as some of the newer forms raised from seed mainly in France, and there are some double kinds poor in colour and effect. The pure white kind (*totus albus*) and a few others lead to the hope that it is a plant capable of real improvement through raising seedling forms, and perpetuating the best of them. Our experience of this shrub in our own islands is that it is best on free and warm soils ; not too dry. Where it thrives it is well worth more attention than is usually the fate of flowering trees in the British shrubbery ; all the more so now that we are getting varieties of good colour—like the pure white one named above, and Celeste.

Hibiscus syriacus.

HIERACIUM (*Hawkweed*). — Perennial herbs with yellow flowers, very numerous, and often beautiful in nature, but not much grown in gardens. Among the best are *aurantiacum* with orange flowers, a good plant, but apt to spread too much in the garden ; and *villosum*, the Shaggy Hawkweed, a handsome plant with silvery leaves and large yellow flowers. Free in ordinary soil. Borders. Division. Daisy order.

HIPPOPHÆ (*Sea Buckthorn*).—*H. rhamnoides* is a beautiful seashore native shrub, developing its full beauty in the rich soils of inland gardens, though it is happy in any soil but hungry clay and peat. The best position for it is a rather damp spot near a running stream, where the subsoil is always moist. It forms, when wild, a straggling bush, which, when the shrub is sheltered, rises 8 or 10 ft. high. In gardens it grows taller. The Sea Buckthorn has silvery-looking Willow-like leaves and bears a profusion of orange berries.

HOLBŒLLIA.—*H. latifolia* is a beautiful evergreen climbing shrub from the Himalayas, hardy against walls in the southern and the warm districts. The foliage is thick with three or five leaflets of a deep shining green. The flowers are a deliciously fragrant dull purplish green, but it does not bloom so freely out of doors as in a cool conservatory. As it is of tall growth, it must be planted against a high wall, such as that of a house or stable. It is known also as Stauntonia latifolia. The variety angustifolia has smaller and more numerous leaflets.

HORDEUM.—Grasses, of which the Barley is the most familiar type, few of ornamental value except H. jubatum (Squirrel-tail Grass), which has long feathery spikes. It grows in any soil in open places, is easily raised as an annual, and is one of the most distinct dwarfer Grasses. Sow in autumn or spring.

HOTEIA.—*H. japonica* is a fine tufted herbaceous plant 1 ft. to 16 in. high, with

Hippophæ rhamnoides.

silvery-white flowers early in summer in a panicled cluster. In a rich soil it is excellent for a shady border. Strong clumps planted in autumn will flower in the following spring. Where there are forced plants to spare they may be planted out when they have done blooming, but will not make much show in the following season. Much used indoors, is seldom good in the open garden, partly because it does badly in heavy and poor soils. Where it thrives and flowers well it would be a graceful aid in the varied flower-garden. Increased by division in autumn. Japan. *Syns.*, Spiræa japonica, Astilbe barbata.

HOTTONIA (*Water Violet*).—*H. palustris* is a pretty British water-plant, which, however,.thrives better on soft mud-banks than when submerged. The deep-cut leaves form a dwarf deep-green tuft over the mud, and from this tuft arise stems bearing at intervals whorls of handsome pale lilac or pink flowers. As water and bog may be associated with the rock-garden, this plant may with advantage be grown at its margin in the water or on a bank of wet soil. It grows from 9 in. to 2 ft. high, flowers in early summer, and is abundant in many parts of England.

HOUSTONIA (*Bluets*).—A very pretty little American plant, *H. cœrulea* forming small, dense cushion-like tufts, and from late spring to autumn bearing crowds of

Houstonia cœrulea.

tiny slender stems, about 3 in. high. The flowers are pale blue, changing to white. There is also a white variety. It succeeds best in peaty or sandy soil, in sheltered shady nooks on well-drained parts of the rock-garden. As it sometimes perishes in winter, it is advisable to keep reserve plants in pots. Propagated by careful division in spring, or by seed. H. serpyllifolia and H. purpurea are allied species and alike in stature and wants.

HUMEA.—A very graceful half-hardy biennial, 3 to 8 ft. high, *H. elegans* having large leaves with a strong balsamic odour, and forming, when in flower, an elegant feathery pyramid of reddish-brown blossoms. It is highly ornamental as a back line to a long border, as a single

specimen to let into the lawn, as the centre of a bed or vase, or in masses with other elegant foliage plants. Excellent effects may be obtained by combining it in masses or groups with other good plants. For cutting, its light feathery sprays are useful. The proper time to sow seed is July or August, as plants do not bloom the first year, and, if raised before those months, get too large to winter conveniently, often becoming leafless below, and the nakedness of stem detracts from their beauty. To .prevent this, they should be well fed during winter with weak liquid manure, and be shifted into larger pots early in spring. Rich soil should be used, as they can only be kept healthy by good feeding. When planting them out in beds, which may be done by the first week in June, put under each a spadeful of rotten manure and mix it up with the soil. As the plants, when large, hold a good deal of wind, they must be securely staked to prevent their being damaged. Compositæ. Australia.

HUMULUS (*Common Hop*). — *H. Lupulus*, a well-known vigorous twining perennial is admirable for bowers, especially when vegetation that disappears in winter is desired ; and will soon run wild in almost any soil, among shrubs or hedgerows. A slender plant climbing up an Apple or other fruit tree, near the mixed border, looks well. Division.

HUNNEMANNIA.—*H. fumariæfolia* is an erect perennial, 2 to 3 ft. high, with glaucous foliage, like some of the Fumitories. Its flowers are large and showy, of a rich orange, and in form are like Eschscholtzia californica. They continue long in perfection. Being a native of Mexico, it is rather tender, and not satisfactory for open-air culture. Poppy family.

HUTCHINSIA.—A neat little alpine plant, *H. alpina* having shining leaves and white flowers, in clusters about 1 in. high, quite free in sandy soil, and easily increased by division or seeds. In an open spot,.either in the rock-garden or in good free border soil, it becomes a mass of white flowers. Its proper home is the rock-garden, though in borders of dwarf and choice hardy plants it may be grown with success. Central and S. Europe. Cruciferæ.

HYACINTHUS (*Hyacinth*). — The familiar garden Hyacinth is not generally included among hardy plants, though it is perfectly hardy, and, when treated as it should be, is most important. The parent of all the varieties is H. orientalis ; this is as hardy as a Daffodil, and its varieties are scarcely less hardy. Hyacinths in the open air are generally the refuse, as it were, of the forced bulbs of preceding years, but even these create a good display in suitable positions. To have a fine bloom of Hyacinths in the open air, however, it is essential that the bulbs should be good and sound, and due regard paid to assortment of colour, as tints massed by themselves are far more effective than a confusion of various colours. Now that bulbs may be obtained cheap there is no difficulty. The hyacinth will grow well in any good garden soil, but a light rich soil suits it best, and the bed should be effectually drained, for though the plant loves moisture, it cannot stand in a bog

flowering, if there is fully 6 in. of earth over the crowns. No protection is better than dry litter, but a thin coat of half-rotten manure spread over the bed is safer if severe frosts are likely to come at any time before the growth has fairly pushed through. The bulbs need no further attention until the flower-stems are much advanced, unless very severe weather intervenes, when a mat or some oiled calico should be thrown over them. Waterproof calico is also useful in very wet weather, as too much water, especially when iced by February frosts and March winds, is by no means good for Hyacinths, which will thrive all the better for a waterproof covering. Hyacinths in the open

Hyacinths.

during the winter. It is advisable to plant early and deep. If a rich effect is required, the bulbs should be 6 in. apart, but a good effect may be produced by planting them 9 in. or even more apart. The time of blooming may to some extent be influenced by the time and manner of planting, but no rules can be given to suit particular cases. Late planting and deep planting both tend to defer the bloom, but make no great difference, and as a rule late bloom is to be preferred, being less liable to injury from frost. The shallowest planting should ensure a depth of 3 in. of earth above the crown of the bulb, but, generally speaking, they will flower better, be a few days later, and form stronger bulbs after

air seldom require artificial watering, the natural moisture of the soil and the strength of the manure mixed with it being sufficient. When grown in beds they do not require sticks or ties; simply proper planting. After blooming, the bulbs, if intended to flower again, must be left undisturbed until the leaves wither or die. The bulbs should then be taken up, dried in a stack for a week or two, and finally placed in the sun for a few hours, the dry leaves being pulled off. Offsets should also be removed from the bulbs, and stored in dry sand or earth till the next planting time. Some take up the bulbs every year, but we have seen handsome beds that were not disturbed for several years. Offsets, carefully cultivated in rich light soil for two or three years, will produce many flowering bulbs, but, as a rule, imported ones are stronger. However carefully cultivated in England, they seldom flower again so well as in the first season, but it is a mistake to throw them away, as many people do. Selections for bedding in distinct colours of red, yellow, white, blue, or mixed are to be bought cheap.

H. azureus.—One of the earliest as well as the most charming of our early spring flowers. Indeed, one of its chief charms lies in the fact of its producing its numerous dense heads of pretty azure blooms long before we have ceased to expect falls of snow. Many a time have I gone in quest of flowers when the ground was white with its winter covering and have only been able to obtain flowers of this and some Snowdrops and Crocuses. In the case of a dwarf bulb of this kind flowering so early a handlight or bell-glass is simply placed over the clump on the approach of a storm, taking the cover off when all danger is past. The flowers stand any amount of frost without injury, and it is only the chance of their being broken with snow that renders a covering necessary. H. azureus is one of those half-way types that one finds so often in the Lily order. It has the habit, appearance, and many of the characters of a Muscari, with the campanulate flowers of a Hyacinth. It was first brought to the Vienna Botanic Garden by Kotschy in 1856, and it was some years after before it was in cultivation in England. The bulb is whitish, round, an inch or so in diameter, producing in great abundance stolons or bulbils from the base; the leaves, in number from six to eight to a bulb, are broad, strapshaped, glaucous, and deeply channelled; the flower-heads dense, conical, upper flowers sky-blue, campanulate, the lower deep azure blue, and larger than those of the ordinary Grape Hyacinth. It is an excellent plant for the rock-garden, and even in situations where it gets densely shaded by overhanging plants.

H. amethystinus, though nearly related to H. azureus, is quite different, and flowers a month later and at a time when there is a dearth of flowers of this description in the hardy bulb-garden. It is one of the very old plants, and although cultivated by Miller as early as 1759, it was until recently a scarce plant. The great mistake with a bulb like this is to have two or three or even a dozen in a clump. Instead of the dozen it should be grown by the hundred, and no prettier sight can well be imagined than a large

sheet of this graceful Hyacinth, with its loose racemes of vivid amethyst flowers. Its pleasing flowers are produced in May and June, when there is little chance of their being disfigured by frosts. Spain and Italy.—D. K.

H. candicans. See GALTONIA.

HYDRANGEA.—Handsome flowering shrubs, some well known in gardens, others neglected. In warm districts and on good warm soils it would be well worth while to grow many of the rarer and finer forms of the common Hydrangea, which always flowers best in seashore districts where its shoots are not cut down by frost or by the knife every winter.

H. Hortensia.—The common Hydrangea (H. Hortensia), from China, may be grown well out-of-doors, but is not always satisfactory in the midlands and the north, being liable to injury in winter. It likes a sheltered yet sunny spot and

Hyacinthus amethystinus.

good soil. In order to get good heads of bloom, the Hydrangea must be pruned so as to induce the growth of strong shoots. In favoured spots it reaches a height of 6 ft., and as much through, making a beautiful object on a lawn or in the shrubbery margin. From time to time, and especially in recent years, other forms have been introduced and described, some of them as distinct species. Dr. Maximowicz, who has had opportunities of studying them in European and Japanese gardens, and also in a wild state, arranges the following forms under H. Hortensia :—

(*a*) **H. Hortensia acuminata.** — A much-branched shrub, 2 to 5 ft. high; flowers blue. It sports according to locality, and Maximowicz enumerates four such sports, viz.: In open places and in a rich soil it is stouter, with erect thick branches, large, broad, firm leaves, and larger flowers with somewhat fleshy sepals ; under cultivation it becomes more showy, passing into H. Belzonii. In woods and on the shady banks of rivers it grows taller with slender stems, pointed leaves, and much smaller flowers. In a very fertile soil, a stout plant with toothed sepals in the barren flowers, which are commonly of a blue colour. This is the true H. Buergeri of Siebold and Zuccarini's *Flora Japonica*, and the H. japonica cœrulescens of Regel. Sometimes it produces white or rose-coloured flowers, and then it is the H. roseo-alba, as figured in the *Flore des Serres*. These variations are all beautiful, but perhaps not constant.

(*b*) **H. Hortensia japonica.**—This is the H. japonica of Siebold and Zuccarini's *Flora Japonica*, and the H. japonica

Hydrangea quercifolia.

macrosepala of Regel's *Gartenflora*. It is exactly like acuminata, save that the flowers are tinged with red, and the sepals of the barren flowers are elegantly toothed.

(*c*) **H. Hortensia Belzonii.** — A short stout plant, with beautiful flowers, the inner sterile ones being of an indigo-blue, and the enlarged sterile ones white, or only slightly tinged with blue, and having entire sepals. There is a sport of this in which the leaves are elegantly variegated with white. This was raised by Messrs. Rovelli, of Pallanza.

(*d*) **H. Hortensia Otaksa.** — This has all the flowers sterile and enlarged. A very handsome variety with rich dark green leaves nearly as broad as long, and large hemispherical heads of pale pink or flesh-coloured flowers, very fine when well grown.

(*e*) **H. Hortensia communis.** — This is the old variety with rose-pink flowers,

commonly cultivated in European gardens. It differs from the last in being perfectly glabrous in its longer, less-rounded leaves, and in its deeper-coloured flowers.

(*f*) **H. Hortensia Azisia.** — This is not in cultivation, but it differs remarkably from all of the preceding varieties in the sterile flowers, which have a very long, slender calyx tube.

(*g*) **H. Hortensia stellata.** — The chief character of this variety is in the flowers, which are all sterile and double. The variety in cultivation has pink flowers, but they are described as being either pale blue or rose, finally changing to a greenish colour, and distinctly net-veined.

The white variety Thomas Hogg is a very fine one, now widely cultivated. Most of the above-named deserve the attention of all who have soil and climate suited to these shrubs.

H. paniculata (*Plumed Hydrangea*). —A shrub or small tree. According to Maximowicz, the only Japanese Hydrangea which becomes a tree. It grows as much as 25 ft. high, with a

The Plumed Hydrangea.

dense rounded head and a straight trunk 6 in. in diameter. But it more commonly forms a shrub a few feet high, bearing enormous panicles of flower. With the exception of H. Hortensia, it is the commonest species in Japan, growing throughout that country both in the mountains and the plains, being more abundant in the northern parts, and it is said to vary very much It is commonly cultivated by the Japanese The massive clusters of pure white blossoms, terminating every shoot in autumn, are very beautiful, and there are few finer autumn effects than a well-flowered mass of this shrub It must have a good soil, and be well mulched with manure in winter To encourage the new growth the old and useless shoots must be cut away. It is from 3 to 4 ft high, and spreads its branches gracefully and widely on all sides The clusters are often 1 ft. long and half as much in diameter, but to get such flowers we must cultivate well and prune the shrubs hard down in winter

H. hirta (*Nettle-leaved H.*)—A dwarf shrub, 3 or 4 ft. high, with slender hairy branches and Nettle-like leaves The leaves and branches become nearly or quite glabrous with age. This, although not a showy species, seems to be a pretty, compact dwarf shrub, with numerous clusters of white flowers. A native of the mountains of Japan.

H virens (*Changing H*)—This is a remarkable and elegant shrub, varying in height from 2 to 6 ft The branches, straight, slender, and polished, bearing small, thin, deeply-toothed leaves, 2 to 3 in long, yellowish-green above, and pale beneath, with small clusters of flowers, some of which are sterile Altogether this is a pretty little shrub, and it is somewhat surprising that it has not been introduced, as it is common in the neighbourhood of Nagasaki in Japan

H chinensis (*Fortune's H*) — Near the last, but of more robust habit, with leaves 3 to 5 in long, and with cymes of flowers much larger. It differs from H. virens in the leaves being green on both sides, and in the enlarged sepals being nearly equal in size, much thicker, in fact almost fleshy in substance, and remaining on the branches until the fruit of the fertile flowers is ripe. This species was collected by Mr Fortune in N. China

H. Thunbergi.—A small shrub with slender branches, small leaves, and small cymes of flowers A few only of the outermost ones are sterile, and these are not more than ½ in in diameter According to the *Gardeners' Chronicle*, Messrs Cripps, of Tunbridge Wells, flowered this species in June 1870 They describe it as

hardy, though not so showy as some of the varieties of H paniculata and H Hortensia The sterile flowers are of a delicate Peach-blossom colour It is a native of the mountains of Sikok and Nippon, Japan

H. quercifolia (*Oak-leaved H*)—This is a fine distinct kind, and though not showy like the popular kinds, it is an excellent shrub, and one I have noticed growing with fine vigour in sea-shore gardens The leaves have a good deep colour in the autumn, and the flowers are beautiful, while old plants have a picturesque habit

The whole family is in want of looking up by some enthusiastic admirers who have good soil and other favourable conditions Although there is a large range of land in Great Britain in which Hydrangeas seem happy, there are other inland and cold districts in which they make poor growth, or are cut down so frequently that experiments come to little I made a trial myself on a cool hill-side in Sussex without getting any bloom or a healthy growth ; but on the other hand we see, especially in the South of England and Ireland, beautiful results in warm valleys and on sandy and alluvial soils even from the use of one kind, so that I have often thought that any one who should take up the Hydrangeas in earnest, and grow them and group them well, might have some very interesting results.

HYDROCHARIS (*Frog-bit*) — *H Morsus-ranæ* is a pretty native water-plant, having floating leaves and attractive white flowers, and well worth introducing in artificial water It may often be gathered from ponds or streams in spring, when it floats after being submerged in winter

HYPERICUM (*St John's Wort*) — Often handsome plants, for the most part shrubs and under-shrubs, but including a few herbaceous perennials and annuals. The Rose of Sharon (H calycinum) is probably the most familiar, but there are other shrubby species of some beauty Some of the perennials are good border and rock-garden plants, and the best of these is H olympicum, one of the largest flowered kinds, though not more than 1 ft high It is known by its very glaucous foliage and erect single stems, with bright yellow flowers about 2 in. across It forms handsome specimens that flower early, and its value as a choice border plant can scarcely be over-rated It may be propagated easily by cuttings, which should be put in when the shoots are fully ripened, so that the young plants may become well established before winter. H. elodes is a pretty native plant suitable for the banks of pools and lakes. H. nummularium and humifusum, both dwarf trailers, are also desirable for the rock-garden. Owing to their dwarf compact growth, several of the shrubby species are well suited for the rock-garden. Of these, the best are H. ægyptiacum, balearicum, empetrifolium, Coris, patulum, uralum, and oblongifolium. The last three are larger than the others, but as they droop they have a good effect among the boulders of a large rock-garden, or on banks. H. Hookerianum, triflorum, aureum, orientale are among the kinds having some beauty, but the species from warmer countries than ours are apt to disappear after hard winters. H. Moserianum is a handsome hybrid kind raised in France and well worth a place.

Hypericum uralum.

HYPOLEPIS (*New Zealand Bracken*). —*H. millefolium* is a very elegant New Zealand Fern, with a stout and wide-spreading rhizome, from which arise erect light green fronds, 1 to 1½ ft. high, very finely cut. There can be no doubt about its hardiness, as it has flourished for two or three years in a Surrey garden, and was also quite hardy and vigorous in Mr. F. Lubbock's garden in Kent. It requires a sheltered nook and peaty soil.

IBERIS (*Candytuft*). —Valuable hardy perennials and annuals, the perennials somewhat shrubby and evergreen, and precious as rock-garden, border, and margining plants :—
I. corifolia.—A dwarf kind 3 or 4 in. high, and covered with small white blooms early in May. Few alpine plants are more worthy of general culture either in the rock-garden or the mixed border—for the front of which it is well suited. It is probably a small variety of I. sempervirens, but is distinct and true to its character. Easily propagated by seeds or cuttings, and thriving in any soil. Sicily.
I. correæfolia is known by its large leaves, its compact heads of large white flowers, by flowering later than other common white kinds, and both the flowers and the corymb are larger and denser than in the other species. It is an invaluable hardy plant, and useful in coming

into beauty about the end of May when the other kinds are fading. It is excellent for the rock-garden, the mixed border, and the spring-garden, and is well suited for the margins of choice shrubberies, and may be used as an edging to beds. Said to be a hybrid. Increased by cuttings, not coming true from seed.
I. gibraltarica, a beautiful plant, larger in all its parts than the other kinds, with flowers of delicate lilac in low close heads, in spring and early summer. It is a pretty species, but does not rival the best white

Iberis gibraltarica.

border kinds. Its hardiness is doubtful, and it should, therefore, be planted on sunny spots in the rock-garden or on banks in light soil, and wintered in frames. Increased by cuttings, as it rarely produces seeds in our climate. Spain.
I. jucunda, distinct, growing about 2½ in. high, the leaves small, the flowers, in small clusters, of a pleasing flesh colour and prettily veined with rose in early summer. It does not possess the vigour of the common evergreen Iberises, but it is valuable as a rock-plant, and is fitted for association with dwarf alpine flowers on warm and sunny parts of the rock-garden in well-drained sandy loam. *Syn.* I. Æthionema.
I. petræa, a pretty alpine species, 3 in. high, with a flat cluster of pure white flowers, relieved in the centre by a tinge of red, thriving among the rock-plants. Many cultivators cannot succeed with it, but it thrives in a well-drained position, with plenty of moisture.

I. semperflorens.—A shrubby plant, with large dense corymbs of white flowers, and not suited for border culture, but hardy enough to stand our winters when grown at the foot of a south wall or in a very sunny corner of the rock-garden. Under those favourable conditions it forms a pretty evergreen bush in bloom nearly all the year. Sicily and other Mediterranean islands.

I. sempervirens.—The common rock or perennial Candytuft, and as often seen as the yellow Alyssum and the white Arabis. Half-shrubby, dwarf, spreading, evergreen, and perfectly hardy, it escapes

Iberis jucunda.

where many plants are destroyed by cold; and in April and May its neat tufts of dark green change into masses of snowy white. Where a very dwarf evergreen edging is required for a shrubbery, or for beds of shrubs, it is one of the best plants known, as on any soil it quickly forms a spreading mass almost as low as the lawn-grass. Like all its relatives, it should be exposed to the full sun rather than shaded. Readily increased by seeds or cuttings. Its common garden name is I. saxatilis. I. Garrexiana is not sufficiently distinct to be worthy of cultivation; in fact, it and several other Iberises prove, when grown side by side, to be very slight varieties of I. sempervirens; it, however, seeds more abundantly, and is less spreading. I. superba, another variety, is of good bushy habit, and bears many large dense heads of pure white flowers.

I. Tenoreana is a dwarf species, with white flowers, changing to purple. As the commonly-cultivated kinds are pure

white, I. Tenoreana will be more valuable from its purplish tone as well as its neat habit. It has not, however, the perfect hardiness of the white kinds, being very apt to perish on heavy soils in winter; but on light sandy soils and in well-drained positions on the rock-garden it is pretty. Where no rock-garden exists it should be placed on raised beds or banks, and is easily raised from seed; it should be treated as a biennial. S. Italy.

I. umbellata (*Annual Candytuft*).—This and its ally (I. coronaria) are the hardy annual Candytufts. They are varied in colour, and are among the most beautiful of annual flowers. They may be sown at all seasons, but, as in the case of most other hardy annuals, the finest flowers are from autumn-sown plants, which flower from May to July. They like a rich soil and plenty of room to flower freely. There are a great number of varieties, differing both in growth and colour. What are known as the dwarf or nana strain are neat and dwarf in growth, are abundant bloomers and showy. I. umbellata nana rosea and alba are two of the most distinct, being about 9 in. high; the dark crimson, carmine, lilac, and purple sorts, about 1 ft. high, are also fine. The Rocket Candytuft (I. coronaria) in good soil grows 12 to 16 in. high, with pure white flowers in long dense heads, and there is a dwarf variety of it (pumila), 4 to 6 in. high, forming spreading tufts 1 ft. or more across. The Giant Snowflake is also an excellent variety. These Rocket Candytufts require the same treatment as the common varieties.

IDESIA I. polycarpa is a Japanese tree of recent introduction, growing out of doors in mild districts; but we have no proof of its hardiness for our country generally. It has large leaves, bright green above, and whitish beneath. The flowers form long, drooping branched racemes and are fragrant. The colour is not brilliant, but their effect, combined with the red leaf stalks, the varying green of the leaves, and their drooping habit is good. There are male and female forms, and, although the tree may be increased by cuttings, it is better raised from seed. There is a crisp-leaved form. *Syn. flacourtia.*

ILEX (*Holly*). — Beautiful evergreen shrubs of northern temperate countries, of which the most precious is our own native Holly, *Ilex Aquifolium*. It would be difficult to exaggerate the value of this plant, whether as an evergreen tree, as the best of all fence-shelters for our fields, or as a lovely ornament of our gardens; whether grown naturally or clipped as it must be to form fences; embracing also in its numerous varieties the most enduring of variegated shrubs known,—variegation in most other things being mere disease, whereas in the Holly it is quite consistent with health and beauty. No other shrub known to us may be so often used with good effect near the house and garden, and it will be clear, therefore, how much one should consider the common Holly in all its forms and ways. Valuable as many varieties are, probably none are quite so good as seedlings of the common kind. Good seedling plants are the easiest to transplant and establish. The art of grafting—most delusive as well as most curious of arts — should be carefully guarded against as regards Hollies. Hitherto the way has been to graft the many variegated kinds on the common Holly, and although we often see good results in that way, it is by far the safer plan to insist on the variegated and curious kinds being raised from layers or cuttings. Nurserymen are very apt, having large quantities of stocks of common things, to graft indiscriminately; and though time seems at first to be gained by it, it is dead against the cultivator in the end in almost every case. It will perhaps take a long time to recognise the immense superiority of own-root plants, but if purchasers inquire for and insist upon getting them, it will very much hasten progress. My own experience is that old plants grafted are extremely difficult to move with safety, and, generally, Hollies and other trees are best not moved when old. It is an expensive and troublesome business, and often a failure. Young healthy bushes, seedling or layer, will in a few years beat old grafted trees,—that at least is my experience. Very often old specimens from the nursery live for a number of years, but their appearance is deplorable, whereas healthy well-grown young plants, from 3 to 5 ft. high, when transplanted in May, are often beautiful from the first. No doubt healthy seedling plants might be transplanted at various times, but experience has proved that there is a distinct gain in transplanting Hollies in May; and if we transplant them carefully at that time we shall probably see good healthy growth the same year.

As regards the uses of the Holly, they are so many in the garden that it is difficult even to generalise them. As shelter in bold groups, dividing lines, hedges, beautiful effects of fruit in autumn, masses of evergreen foliage, bright glistening colour from variegated kinds; elegant groups of the most beautiful varieties,—every kind of delightful use may be found for them in gardens.

According to the late Mr. Shirley Hibberd, who was a very keen observer of the Holly, the following is a good selection of varieties. In the selection of Hollies it will be well to bear in mind that the variety known as Scotica answers best of any plant near the sea. The variety known as Hodgins's is the most free in growth in a town garden, being less affected by smoke than most others. The most fruitful varieties are catalogued as fœmina, glabra, madeirensis, balearica, lutea, and flava. The most distinct and beautiful of the variegated kinds are Golden Queen, Silver Queen, Painted Lady, Broad-leaved Silver, Gold Milkmaid, Watereriana, and Argentea marginata. The following classification of Hollies in relation to their several characters will be useful :—

"MALE-FLOWERING HOLLIES.—Ciliata, Heterophylla, Latispina, Laurifolia, Tortuosa, Gold Tortuosa, Bœtii, Cookii, Gold Cookii, Cornuta, Doningtonensis, Ferox, Ferox fol. arg., Ferox aurea, Foxii, Furcata, Ovata, Picta marginata, Golden Queen, Longifolia aurea, Longifolia argentea, Watereriana, Gold Few-spined, Silver Queen, Shepherdii.

"FEMALE - FLOWERING HOLLIES.— Angustifolia, Angustifolia aurea pendula, Angustifolia medio picta pendula, Balearica, Broad leaf, Dark shoot, Fisherii, Flavo fructo aurea, Fœmina, Golden Milkmaid, Glabra, Handsworthiana, Silver Handsworthiana, Heterophylla, Hodginsii, Latifolia argentea, Latifolia aurea, Lutea, Madame Briot, Madeirensis, Madeirensis nigrescens, Madeirensis variegata, Myrtifolia, Milkmaid, red berry; Milkmaid, yellow berry; Moonlight, Perry's weeping, Picta aurea, Platyphylla, Scotica, Watereriana, Weeping.

"HERMAPHRODITE-FLOWERING HOLLIES. — Shepherdii, Smithiana, Silver Queen, Heterophylla, Hodginsii, Laurifolia, Handsworthiana, Lutea, Flava, Scotica, Balearica, Rotundifolia."

By far the best of all known Hollies is our native Holly, but there are other Japanese and American kinds worth growing, such as Ilex crenata, and the fine I. latifolia. This, however requires our most temperate districts to thrive.

ILLICIUM.—An interesting half-hardy evergreen shrub from the Southern States of N. America, *I. floridanum* bearing fragrant flowers of a deep red, like those of the Carolina Allspice. I. religiosum, also known as I. anisatum, from China and Japan, with pale yellow flowers, is also interesting, if not worthy of general culture. It may be grown against walls in warm localities.

IMPATIENS (*Balsam*).—The species of Impatiens that thrive in the open air are all annual and hardy, and sow themselves freely where they get a chance. The best are—the common I. glandulifera, which attains a height of 4 to 6 ft., and bears numerous flowers, varying in colour from white to rose. It will soon take possession of the shrubbery if not checked ; and it is seen to advantage in cottage gardens. I. longicornu is beautiful, and has the same habit as glandulifera, but the lower part of its helmet-shaped flowers is bright yellow, marked by tranverse lines of dark brown ; while the upper part is rose colour. I. Roylei is much dwarfer than the preceding, and has blossoms of a deep rose. I. cristata has light rose-coloured blossoms.

I. balsamina (*Garden Balsam*) may be grown in the open air, and makes a pretty display in warm places. The plants should be raised in a frame and transplanted. Soil which is too rich should be avoided ; but soil manured for a previous crop, and which has been well pulverised by forking, gives the finest flowers and a less sappy growth. Colours and markings in any good and valued strain include the following, and probably a few others, as some sorts sport continually : Pure white, buff-white, rosy-white, lavender-white, pale mauve, peach, pink, carmine, scarlet-cerise, crimson, violet, purple, purple-white blotch, scarlet-white blotch and others.

INCARVILLEA.—Interesting shrubby plants, hardy only in southern counties. There are few kinds. I. Delavayi has lately come from China, and has proved hardy, Mr. Thompson, of Ipswich, writing that it has been a year or more in the open border, having stood the full brunt of a zero temperature. The flowers are in corymbs, lengthening into racemes, and like those of Bignonia grandiflora, twelve or thirteen to a raceme, and delicate rose or rose-pink in colour, the throat yellow streaked with purple. Where it is not happy out-of-doors it is worth growing in the greenhouse. I. Olgæ was introduced earlier from Turkestan and has purple flowers ; it grows from 3 to 4½ ft. high.

INDIGOFERA. — *I. Gerardiana* is a pretty plant which may be grown as a bush or against a wall, which it clothes gracefully with feathery leaves, towards the close of summer, bearing small Pea-like bright pink blooms. In cold districts it may be well to give it protection in cold winters if not against a wall, and the only attention it requires is close pruning in early winter. The kinds known as I. floribunda, I. coronillæfolia, and by other names, are either synonymous with I. Gerardiana or varieties of it. I. decora, from China, is sometimes grown against a wall in warm parts, but is much less hardy than I. Gerardiana, which comes from the Himalayas.

INULA.—Perennial Composites, few of which are important for the garden. I. Helenium (Elecampane), a vigorous British plant, 3 or 4 ft. high, with a stout

Inula glandulosa

stem, large leaves, and yellow flowers, is well suited for planting with other large-leaved plants, or in isolated specimens on rough slopes or wild places, in good soil. I. Oculus Christi grows 1½ to 2 ft. high, and bears orange flowers in summer. I. salicina, montana, and glandulosa are similar, the last being the finest. Easily propagated by division or seed.

IONOPSIDIUM (*Violet Cress*). — *I. acaule* is a charming little Portuguese annual about 2 in. high, whose dense tufts of violet flowers spring up freely where plants of it have existed the previous season. Its peculiar beauty makes it useful for various purposes. On the rock-garden, associated with even the choicest of alpine plants, it holds its own as regards beauty, and never overruns its neighbours, and it is particularly suitable for sowing near pathways or rugged steps, growing freely in such places ; indeed it would even flourish on a hard gravel walk. It flowers a couple of months after sowing, and often produces a second crop of blossoms in the autumn. Portugal and Morocco. Cruciferæ.

IPOMÆA (*Morning Glory*).—Beautiful, slender, twining plants of the Convolvulus family, for the most part tropical. A few succeed in the open air when treated as half-hardy annuals. The most popular of these is—

I. purpurea, or Convolvulus major as it is called, which is too well known to need description, as it is one of the oldest cultivated plants. Its varieties are numerous ; there are white, rose, and deep violet varieties, while the Burridgei is crimson, Dicksoni deep blue, and tricolor striped with red, white and blue. A mixed packet of seed would contain most of these. This beautiful though common plant deserves much attention, as its uses are various. It may be used for the open border, for festooning branches, for covering arbours, trellises, and the like, or for rambling over shrubs, growing freely in any good ordinary garden soil. Seeds should be sown in heat in early spring, and the seedlings transplanted in May as soon as large enough. In some localities seed may be sown at once in the open border, but as a rule plants raised under glass succeed best. It is known also as Pharbitis hispida. Tropical America and Asia.

I. hederacea (*Ivy-leaved Morning Glory*) is somewhat similar to the common Morning Glory (I. purpurea), but has lobed leaves like Ivy. Its flowers, too, are smaller, of a deep blue striped with red. The varieties grandiflora (light-blue), superba (light-blue, bordered with white), and atroviolacea (dark-violet and white) are all worth cultivating, and so are the Japanese variety, Huberi, and its variegated-leaved form. The Ivy-leaved Morning Glory is somewhat hardier than I. purpurea, and seeds may be sown in the open border in April, in light rich soil, where it will flower from July to September. It is also known as I. Nil.—North America. Other kinds of Ipomæas for open-air culture are I. rubrocœrulea, a half-hardy annual, and I. leptophylla, a hardy perennial from North America, but neither is so pretty as those mentioned above.

IPOMOPSIS.—Graceful biennials from California, thriving in light, dry, and warm soils in the milder districts. There are three kinds ; each forms a tuft of finely-cut feathery foliage, and has slender flower spikes from 2 to 3 ft. high thickly set with flowers that open in succession. In I. elegans the flowers are scarlet and thickly spotted, and in I. superba they are much the same, while in the rosea variety they are a deep pink. The seeds should be sown in spring in pots in the open border in ordinary soil. During the first year the plants make growth, and early the following summer they flower. If planted out to stand the winter it is advisable to give a little protection. Other kinds mentioned in catalogues belong to Gilia, of which Ipomopsis is really a synonym. On light soils early autumn-sowing should be tried. These plants are very seldom well grown.

IRESINE.—Dwarf half-hardy plants, remarkable for their foliage, and much used in the flower garden with other tender plants in summer. There are two types, from which have sprung several varieties. I. Herbsti grows from 1 to 2 ft. high, and has crimson stems and rich carmine-veined foliage, the brilliancy of which continues until late in autumn, and is more effective in wet than in hot dry seasons. It requires a moist rich soil, and is readily increased by cuttings taken in September and wintered in a green-house. In early spring the plants should be repotted, and grown on in heat, and fresh cuttings taken in March and April will make them fit to put out in May. I. brilliantissima and Wallisi are two varieties possessing more brightness of colour in their foliage. Lindeni is quite distinct from the foregoing, having more pointed leaves, which are of a deep blood-red. It is compact and graceful, and bears pinching back and pegging down to any height. It makes a good edging plant, and requires the same treatment as I. Herbsti. Amarantaceæ.

IRIS (*Flag*). — Beautiful bulbous or tuberous plants numerous in kind and wonderfully varied in beauty, more than most flowers. By some, Irises have been compared to Orchids, and those who delight in singular and beautiful colour, and to whom greenhouses and hothouses are denied, may find a substitute for Orchids in Irises. The plants are for the most part hardy and have much diversity of habit and colour, varying in height from a few inches to 6 ft. They may be conveniently divided into two classes—those with bulbous roots, which are now called Xiphions, and those (the greatest number) with creeping stems. In treating of culture it is well to consider these separately. The bulbous kinds should have a warm and sheltered situation, such as the protection of a south wall, and succeed in almost any light garden soil, but prefer one that is friable, and sandy, not too poor, but enriched with rotten leaf-mould and manure. Sun they must have, and the shelter must be without shade. They need an autumn drought to ripen, and a dry soil in winter to preserve the bulbs and keep them at rest, but in spring, when the leaves are pushing up, they love moderate rain. These observations apply to the Spanish and English Irises as well as the rarer bulbous kinds. The great point is not to meddle with the bulbs as long as the plants are doing well, and, when the soil is exhausted and it is necessary to transplant, the bulbs should not be allowed to become dry or shrivelled. It is advisable to place a thin layer of Cocoa-nut fibre refuse or some similar material for protection during severe weather, and to prevent the flowers from being bespattered by mud during heavy rain. Some kinds produce seeds very freely in some seasons, which should be carefully collected, and when well ripened sown at once. This will be found a ready way of increasing the stock, as they will make strong flowering bulbs in about three years.

Most of the non-bulbous Irises like rich soil, the coarser and stronger forms relishing even rank manure, but to the more delicate ones this is almost poison ; and all indeed thrive the better if the manure is given in a decayed state. If it is well rotted they can hardly have too much of it. As regards moisture, they vary a good deal. The condition that suits most is comparative dryness in winter and an abundance of water in summer. Unfortunately, this is the reverse of what they generally get, and they also vary a good deal as to the nature of the soil they like best, some preferring a deep, somewhat stiff, but rich loam, and their long thong-like roots reach down an amazing distance, while others prefer a lighter, looser soil, richer in vegetable matter. The more vigorous kinds are suited for planting among large shrubs, which ought to be wider apart than they generally are in shrubberies ; and may be enjoyed in tufts near water, in isolated groups on the Grass, and also on mixed borders and beds. In the smallest gardens, where there is not space to plant them in these various ways, one of the best ways would be to establish healthy tufts in the fringes of the shrubbery. Another good way is to place them here and there in carpets of low evergreens, above which their flowers would be seen in early summer. Tufts of the finest kinds look very beautiful here

and there among dwarf Roses. The flowering season of the Iris extends over the greater part of the year. The following selection of the more important kinds for our gardens is arranged in alphabetical order for convenience of reference.

I. alata (*Scorpion Iris*).—A beautiful bulbous kind with fine large blossoms, the ground colour delicate lilac-blue, with showy blotches of bright yellow, copiously

Iris asiatica.

spotted with a darker hue. The foliage, which appears with the flowers, much resembles that of a Leek. I. alata generally commences to bloom in October, and, if the weather is not too severe, flowers also about Christmas time. It is easy to grow, requiring a warm, dry, sunny border ; the bulbs should be planted in autumn in ordinary garden soil.

I. asiatica (*Asiatic Flag*).—Allied to the German Iris, but the handsome flowers are much larger, the lip especially being very long and broad ; its colour is a very fine pale purplish-blue, the standards a little paler than the falls. A good border kind.

I. atro-purpurea. — This Iris may be

considered as coming within the iberica group, as the foliage is not unlike that kind, and the stem, though always of some length, never rises very high. The flower is somewhat small, and for the most part of deep purple colouring. The plant varies somewhat, one variety being called "Odysseus."

I. aurea (*Golden Flag*).—This is a fine Iris, a native of the Himalayas, with golden-yellow flowers of great beauty, is a tall stately kind, hardy in the coldest soils. It does well among shrubs or in borders of the best perennials, and groups of it so placed are very handsome. Division and seed.

I. Bakeriana.—This is one of the most beautiful of the bulbous early spring flower-

Iris cristata.

ing Irises. It comes from Armenia, and the flowers, which smell like violets, remind one strongly of those of the netted Iris (I. reticulata). The colouring varies, the yellow streak on the fall, which is conspicuous in some of the forms, being almost entirely absent in others; the size and number of the violet spots and the breadth of the rich violet edging as well as the size and brilliancy of their tints vary in individual flowers. It blooms quite early in the year, and is delightful in pots.

I. Barnumæ. This Iris, a native of the hills of Kurdistan, belongs to the iberica group. The flower is smaller than

that of that Flag, and both falls and standards are vinous red-purple marked with darker veins, the standard being lighter in colour than the fall and its veins more conspicuous. There is a yellow variety described by Prof. Foster as "an exceedingly charming plant," and fragrant, the odour not being unlike the Lily of the Valley.

I. biflora.—A handsome Flag, 9 to 15 in. high, bearing large violet flowers on stout stems. Similar to it are I. sub-biflora and I. nudicaulis, which is one of the best of the dwarf Flags, from 4 to 10 in. high; its flowers large, of a rich violet-blue, four to seven on a stem in early summer. It has the vigour of the German Iris and the dwarfness of the Crimean Iris, but is much sturdier, and is suited for the margin of the herbaceous border and for the rock-garden.

I. Bismarckiana.—This "Cushion" Iris, found in Lebanon, is little known as yet, but it is described as having a flower as large as I. susiana, with gray falls and sky-blue standards.

I. cristata (*Dwarf-crested Iris*) is a charming dwarf Flag, flowering in spring and also in autumn, delicate blue and richly marked. It is a fragile plant, 4 to 6 in. high, with broad leaves, and throws out long slender rhizomes, wholly above ground, thriving in sandy earth in beds, borders, or on the rock garden.

I. florentina (*Florentine Flag*).—Its large delicate flowers are nearly 6 in. deep, faintly tinged with blue, the falls veined with yellow, and green at the base, with an orange-yellow beard, whilst the broad leaves are rich dark-green. A native of Southern Europe, flowering during May and June. The variety albicans is almost pure white.

I. fœtidissima (*Gladwin*).—A British plant, 1½ to 2 ft. high, with bluish flowers. There is a variety with variegated leaves. The common green form is worth growing in semi-wild places for its brilliant coral-red seeds.

I. Gatesi.—This is a remarkably handsome Flag from Armenia, and very near to susiana, but the rhizome is more compact, and the foliage smaller, shorter, and narrower, and of a darker green than in susiana. The stem is taller, 1½ ft. or even 2 ft., and the flower when well grown larger. The prevailing colour of the specimens so far cultivated is, when the flower is seen at a distance, a soft delicate gray, brought about by very thin clear veins and minute dots or points of purple on a creamy-white ground, the dots being predominant on the fall and the veins on the standard. The ripe capsule is as much as 5 in. in length.

I. germanica (*Common German Flag*). —This is common in gardens, and is one of the few plants that succeed well in London. I. nepalensis is a charming form from India, with flowers from 5 in. to 6 in. long, the standards rich dark violet-purple, the falls intense violet, striped white and purple at the base, with yellow and reddish markings. It flowers during May and June, and may be increased quickly. The German Flags flourish in ordinary garden, dry gravelly soil, or sandy banks, for which they are well suited. A good selection of varieties of the German Iris, all good garden flowers, would be composed of Atro-purpurea, Aurea, Bridesmaid, Calypso, Celeste, Gracchus, Mme. Chereau, Queen of May, Rigolette, Victorine, and George Thorbeck.

I. Histrio.—This beautiful bulbous Iris, when peeping through the ground in winter or early spring, reminds one of I. reticulata, but it is rather taller, and its sweetly-scented flowers are broader and more conspicuously spotted or blotched, the colour being rich bluish-purple, flushed towards the base of the petals with rose-pink, whilst the markings are of the deepest purple, relieved by a crest of gold. Syria.

I. histrioides.—One of the most charming of the spring flowering bulbous Irises. So far, though it has only been in cultivation a few years, it has proved of easy culture. The flowers are larger than those of any of the group, the falls mottled with white and rich lilac both on the claw and on the broad rounded blade. It is a native of Eastern Anatolia, and blooms in early March.

I. iberica (*Iberian Flag*).—One of the most singular and handsome of Irises. The flowers are large, the standards white, pencilled and spotted with purple or violet, while the falls are veined with dark purple or purple-black on a yellowish ground, with a conspicuous dark blotch in the centre. This is the colour of the commonest form, but there are several, and one, ochracea, is very distinct, is hardy and thrives best in a rich fibrous loam, where it can send its long roots deep into the soil. The rhizome should not be planted deep, but only just below the surface as in most cases the roots perish when planted deeply. Coarse river sand should be used, the rhizome being planted completely in it, and by this means it is kept rather dry during the winter. Dry borders or warm spots on the rock-garden.

I. juncea (*Rush-leaved Flag*) is a lovely bulbous Iris, graceful in habit and with bright yellow flowers of a delightful fragrance, whilst it can be grown almost as easily as the English Irises. It requires a light, rich deep soil, and will be all the better if planted where it can be kept fairly dry during winter. Spain.

I. Kæmpferi (*Japanese Flag*).—The many varieties in cultivation under this name have sprung from I. lævigata and I. setosa, and form a fine race of garden plants, whilst every year many beautiful sorts are added, chiefly from Japan, though many seedlings have been raised in this country. The flowers are variable in size and colour, some measuring as much as 9 and 10 in. across. The varieties of I. setosa differ from those of I. lævigata

Iris fœtidissima (Gladwin).

in having broader and less-drooping petals, and the three inner petals are often of the same size as the outer, so that the flower is symmetrical. I. Kæmpferi will grow in almost any soil, but is best in a good loam, with peat added to it, though this is not so much for nourishment as to retain moisture during the hot and dry summer months, for this Flag likes moisture, and its numerous roots will often go 2 ft. deep in search of it. It dislikes shade, preferring a warm sunny position, being especially happy when planted by the margin of a lake, pond, or stream. Two-year-old seedling plants of it bloom in June and July, and amongst them will be found an endless variety of colours from white to the richest plum, the deep blues being very rich. The mottled flowers are objectionable, and unfortunately these are common, but they are poor in effect, nothing like so handsome as the self-coloured kinds, nor do we care about the more double varieties. In these the natural grace and fine outline of the flower are lost. When transplanted this moisture-loving Flag does not bloom well until the second season after planting. Propagated by division or seeds, which should be sown as soon as gathered either in pots or in the open ground; they will vegetate in the following spring.

I. Kolpakowskiana.— An ally of I. reticulata and introduced from Turkestan, it is perfectly hardy in the open air, flowering about the same time, and effective in groups. The chief difference from the netted Iris is in the bulb and leaves, which are narrow, linear, deeply channelled

Iris iberica.

on the inner face, with a central band or rib like a Crocus leaf, and pale-green without the glaucous tint usual to this group. The falls are deep violet-purple, with a beardless bright yellow keel from which are purplish branchings, whilst the standards are pale self-lilac with creamy anthers.

I. Korolkowi.—Of this the leaves are tall, narrow, and upright, the scape, which is about 1 ft. or so high, bearing two large flowers of delicate shades of gray and brown, and beautifully veined. Warm and dry spots on the rock garden.

I. lacustris (*Dwarf Lake Iris*).—A dainty, quite hardy Iris, with beautiful sky-blue flowers in spring and again in the autumn. It belongs to the rhizomatose group, is free both in growth and bloom, and succeeds in full sun and in sandy soil. North America.

I. Lorteti.—This Iris comes from South Lebanon. In general features it is

near to I. Sari, but its wonderful colouring makes it, perhaps, the most beautiful Iris in the world. "In a plant flowered by myself this summer (1893)," writes Prof. Foster, "the falls showed a creamy-yellow ground marked with crimson spots, concentrated at the centre into a dark crimson signal, while the standards were nearly pure white, marked with very thin violet veins, hardly visible at a distance.

I. lupina (*Wolf's Ear Iris*).—This is from Armenia and Central Asia Minor, and resembles both I. susiana and I. iberica. The rhizome is compact and the foliage, though somewhat variable, is dwarf like that of I. iberica, and 3 in. or so in length. The flower, borne on a stem varying from 1 in. to 6 in. or even more in length, differs in form from both I. susiana and I. iberica in that the fall is distinctly lance-shaped, whilst the colouring consists of irregular brownish-red veins on a yellow or greenish-yellow ground, the red of the veins often merging into purple. The claw of the standard is furnished with quite numerous hairs.

I. Mariæ, which belongs to the iberica group, was discovered on the confines of Egypt and Palestine. The rhizome is compact, rather slender, the foliage being not unlike that of iberica, but narrower. The flowers, on a stem of about 6 in. high, are somewhat smaller than I. iberica, of a uniform lilac colour, though marked with veins, but the uniformity is broken by a conspicuous "signal" patch of deep purple on the fall. The standard is larger and more rounded than the fall, whilst the claw of the latter is beset by numerous deep purple hairs, which, scattered at the sides, are crowded together along the middle line more after the fashion of the beard of an ordinary bearded Flag.

I. Meda is a native of Persia, and has a small, slender, and compact rhizome. The leaves are narrower than I. iberica, and for the most part erect, the stem being about 6 in. in length, more or less, but seems to vary a good deal. The fall, which spreads horizontally, is narrow and pointed, the blade being sharply curled back on itself. The standard is rather larger than the fall, and the style, which lies close down on the claw of the fall, is narrow, ending in two small triangular crests.

I. missouriensis (*Missouri Flag*).— This was found in the Rocky Mountains, and is a good kind, graceful, and with delicate purplish-blue flowers, which are valuable to cut in the month of May. It grows well in a border of good soil, and is not seen as often as one might expect in gardens.

I. Monnieri.—A noble Flag, distinct from any other in cultivation, the leaves being dark-green, and the flower-stem nearly 4 ft. high, whilst the outer divisions of the flowers, which are very fragrant, are recurved, and of a rich golden-yellow, margined with white. It is by no means common, and blooms later than most of the other species, in most seasons even after the varieties of Kæmpfer's Flag. It is a native of Crete, and succeeds best in rather moist soil, whilst increased easily by division or seed.

I. Monspur is a seedling, raised by Prof. Foster, between I. Monnieri and I. spuria, and is a very beautiful plant. The variety Notha differs from I. spuria in being altogether larger, considerably more rigid both in stem and leaves, and with a much longer spathe valve. This plant is said to be found in the salt marshes of Siberia. When grown well, by no means difficult in ordinary garden soil, it is most effective in full flower. Some of the varieties, such as stenogyna, sub-barbata, &c., have been bandied about between I. spuria and the nearly allied I. Guldenstaedtiana, but the simpler way is to call them all varieties of I. spuria.

I. neglecta is amongst the commonest Flags in cultivation, and one of the tallest growing species, having given rise to numerous garden varieties. Its flowers rarely measure more than 2½ in. across, the standards being of a pale blue, with darker shading, and the much reflexed falls are of a deep blue, veined with purplish-red; the crest or beard is bright yellow, and very striking.

I. ochroleuca (*Yellow-banded Flag*).— There are few handsomer or more stately Flags than this. It is an old plant in our gardens, but never seems to have become common. The foliage is slender, about 4 ft. long, and comes up in a most graceful twist. The spikes usually bear four or five flowers, white or nearly so, with large yellow blotch on the fall, and some reach nearly 6 ft. in height, strong clumps producing four or five. It does not seem particular as to moisture in the soil, and few Flags will thrive better or give more satisfactory results in the ordinary mixed border, where its large flowers and luxuriant foliage present a fine appearance. There is a variety called gigantea which has larger and finer flowers, but differs in no other way. I. Kerneriana differs only in its smaller flowers and much narrower leaves.

I. orchioides.—There are a great beauty

and distinctness in the rich, dark yellow blossoms of this lovely species that are not found in any other Iris of spring, while the black spots on the lower petals only tend to make the flowers still more effective. Added to this distinct beauty is the vigor-

Iris ochroleuca.

ous leafy growth so characteristic of this kind. Coupled with this is the fact of its being also a profuse flowering species, often bearing as many as six blossoms on a single spike. It is a tuberous-rooted species and a handsome plant when thoroughly established. It seems hardy and free at least on warm soils.

I. pallida (*Great Purple Flag*).—This is a variety of the common German Flag and one of the stateliest and most beautiful

Iris pallida.

of the genus. When in full vigour, the spikes will reach 4 ft. in height, with a succession of from eight to twelve of its large pale-mauve or purple flowers, scented like the elder. It is known also as the Turkey Flag, and there are forms of it, such as the Dalmatian and also Man-draliscæ, which have deep blue flowers. It is a fine border-plant, and charming in large groups.

I. paradoxa. — This is a singular Cushion Iris, a native of West Persia and the Caucasus, and fitly called "paradoxi-cal." The fall is reduced to a narrow strap half an inch or less in width, but the standard is large, erect, and while the small fall is stout and firm, almost leathery, is delicate and flimsy in texture. The ground colour of the claw is a rich crimson or deep pink, but beneath the claw and for some little distance in front of it the crimson hue is all but entirely hid by numerous short dark-purple, almost black, hairs, so thickly set as to imitate velvet very closely indeed. This velvet area, at

some distance in front of the end of the style, comes abruptly and squarely to an end, being marked off by a cross bar of rich crimson devoid of hairs. The small portion of the fall in front of this bar is of a creamy-white, traversed by radiating thick dark-purple veins, which are so closely set as to leave little of the ground visible. The plant varies much in size and colour, and the total effect of the flower is very striking and beautiful.

I. persica (*Persian Iris*).—This is one of the most charming of the early kinds, and deserves a place wherever the soil is warm and dry. Its flowers, produced from a tuft of bright green leaves that just peep over the soil, are white, suffused with pale Prussian blue, and blotched with velvety purple. It comes from Persia, and is therefore somewhat tender, but in warm sheltered spots, in light sandy soil, suc-ceeds well enough, and flowers in winter and spring, according to the weather.

I. Pseudo-acorus (*Common Water Flag*).—Common as is this Flag, everyone who has grown it fairly will admit its beauty. Whoever has in his garden a pond or a ditch, or even a thoroughly damp spot, ought to plant this Flag.

Iris paradoxa.

I. pumila (*Dwarf Flag*).—The best of the dwarf Flags, for to it we owe the many lovely varieties that create such a rich dis-play of bloom in spring. It grows from 4 to 8 in. high, and has deep violet flowers, unusually large for its size. There are several named varieties, the most attractive being the sky-blue (cœrulea), which in early spring forms sheets of bright colour edgings in free soil.

I. reticulata (*Netted Iris*).—One of the most beautiful of hardy flowers. While the snow is still on the ground—in January,

Iris persica.

or even earlier—its leaves begin to shoot, and while these are only a few inches high, the bud opens to the pale wintry sun a beauty of violet and gold. After the flower has faded, the erect narrow leaves grow apace, attaining a height of 1 ft. or more, and, as in the Crocus, the ripened ovary is in due time thrust upwards from the soil. This little treasure is indeed the Iris companion of the Crocus, and those who have seen large clumps of it growing in some sheltered but sunny spot in the bright and gusty days of February or March, may well wish that its netted bulbs were as plentiful as Crocus corms. The plant comes from some parts of the Caucasus and from Palestine, and there are several varieties. Krelagei may be recognised by flowers of a purple or plum colour, with the yellow marking less vivid, and the whole flower is smaller, also less fragrant, in fact is almost wholly without scent, and it flowers ten or fourteen days earlier. An exquisite gem is I. r. cyanea which is very bright in colour, a slaty blue, and dwarf. Sophonensis, with red-purple flowers and a bold crest, is a native of Asia Minor, and blooms in early February. I. r. purpurea, a small variety with deep purple flowers, is pleasing. A sunny sheltered spot is, however, advisable, that its tall narrow leaves may, after flowering, be protected from the wind. Sandy soil will do, but it is not particular

in this respect. Sometimes, however, it refuses to grow, and in damp places the bulbs rot in summer. Since the flowers come before the leaves grow tall it makes a good pot plant, and a well-grown clump is a charming addition to the Christmas table. Unfortunately I. reticulata refuses to grow at all in some localities through disease. Although this disease may be somewhat retarded by lifting and careful storing it is very difficult to eradicate, and in wet seasons carries the bulbs off by the thousand.

I. Rosenbachiana.—This is a charming bulbous Iris, and found on the mountains of East Buchara, Turkestan, at an elevation of 6,000 ft. to 7,000 ft., we are told, in two varieties, both growing together, the flowers of one form being blue, those of the other of a fine violet, whilst the bulbs of both the varieties are small, with thin tunics, never reticulated, as in the netted Iris.

I. Sari. This derives its name from the river Sar, in Cilicia, in the neighbourhood of which it was found. It comes near to I. susiana, having a compact rhizome, relatively large foliage, a fairly tall (a foot or less in height) stem and large flowers; indeed the var. lurida, which Prof. Foster

Iris reticulata

mentions as the only one he has seen in cultivation, is often mistaken by a casual observer for I. susiana.

I. sibirica (*Siberian Flag*).—A slender plant, 2 to 3 ft. high, with narrow grassy leaves and in summer somewhat small showy blue flowers, beautifully veined with white and violet. There are several varieties, the white variety, also called I. flexuosa, being pretty, and so is I. acuta, but the double-flowered form is not. The finest variety is I. orientalis, having larger flowers of a deeper colour, with a different veining, and the falls especially broad and expanding. The Siberian Iris is very

flowers hidden in grassy foliage. When mixed with even the most delicate flowers of the stove or Orchid-house, its silky sky-blue fragrant flowers possess a charm and softness equalled by scarcely any other flower of the same colour. Although the plant is hardy, its flowers are so delicate that it should have protection from heavy rains unless the position

Iris susiana.

hardy and spare plants are easily established in ditches or damp spots.

I. sindjarensis.—This is an interesting species with the habit and general character of I. caucasica, but has bluish flowers and a distinct crest. It flowers however at a time when no other Iris except I. reticulata is in bloom, and possesses a certain distinctive charm.

I. stylosa (*Algerian Iris*).—A beautiful plant, flowering in mid-winter, its

is well sheltered. It is perhaps best known as I. stylosa. There are several varieties in catalogues, speciosa being one of the best, this having larger flowers of a deep blue colour. Alba has white flowers. They all require very light warm soil on well-drained or raised borders in sheltered gardens. Division.

I. susiana (*Mourning Iris*).—One of the most singular of all flowers, from 1½ to 2½ ft. high; the flowers very large and densely spotted and striped with dark purple on a gray ground. It should be grown in sunny nooks in the rock-garden, or on sheltered banks or borders, but always in light, warm, or chalky soils. We have seen it flowering well in a border in the Archbishop of Canterbury's garden near Broadstairs, where it is hardy. Asia Minor. Division.

I. tuberosa (*Snake's-head*).—This is an interesting if quiet-coloured kind, 12 or 13 in. high, the flowers small, brownish-green marked with yellow, and a purplish-brown tinge on the upper part. There are usually two tubers. It is not showy enough for every garden, but where admired it may be naturalised in light soil. S. Europe.

I. variegata is a handsome Flag of the Germanica group, 1 to 2 ft. high, with large, slightly fragrant flowers, having bright yellow standards and claret-red falls beautifully veined. Similar in aspect is I. aphylla, with deep lilac falls and white standards veined with purple, whilst there are numerous varieties, the colours of which are varied and beautiful. I. lurida and its varieties also come under this group.

I. xiphioides (*English Iris*).—This is a beautiful flower, and the many garden varieties are amongst the finest things we have in early summer.

The English Iris got its popular name in a rather curious way, being sent from its Pyrenean home, where its distribution is limited, to Bristol traders, thence to Holland. The Dutch, supposing it to be a native of our shores, called it the English Iris. The flowers are quite distinct in aspect from those of the Spanish Iris and appear a fortnight or so later. They are broad and display a delightful diversity of colour, from deepest purple to pure white. Among the good varieties are Leon Tolstoi, Mont Blanc, Grande Celeste, King of the Blues, La Charmante, and Vainqueur. There are, of course, many other varieties in which one gets flowers splashed and mottled with various colours. These are not so fine as the bold self kinds, and raisers should think less of them, rather giving us self colours, which are always more effective both in the garden and when gathered for the house. There is a curious variety called Thunderbolt, which is of a dusky dull colour.

Dr. Wallace, of Colchester, writes as follows :—" The English Irises are easily cultivated and well worthy of a place in all gardens. Flowering at the end of June and during July, they come in when most of the other Irises are over, and a bed of their large flowers is beautiful for

several weeks, their strong spikes mostly carrying two or more flowers, in all shades of white, blue, and reddish-purple, some splashed and streaked, others with clear decided colours, formidable rivals to the Iris Kæmpferi, which they closely resemble in shape and pose of flower, but of dwarfer habit. I find them quite hardy here at Colchester planted out in light soil, with plenty of sand round the bulbs. They increase rapidly, and are

"The English Iris."

best taken up and divided about every two years, at the beginning of August when the bulbs are at rest. Starting again into growth early, they should not be planted after the middle of November, otherwise success will be less certain."

I. Xiphium (*Spanish Iris*).—A very beautiful flower, and an old inhabitant of gardens. The prevailing colours are blue, with various shades of purple or violet, yellow, and white. The blue tints of the cultivated seedlings seem to be derived from the typical Spanish plant; the yellow hues may be traced to the Portuguese variety, sometimes known as I. lusitanica.

The Spanish Iris must not be waterlogged in autumn and winter, preferring a loose, friable, sandy soil, which, however, should not be too poor, for it repays feeding with thoroughly rotten leaf-mould or manure. Sun it must have, but as its slender stalks suffer from winds it should have shelter without shade. The golden rule of not meddling over-much applies distinctly to the Spanish Iris, as the new roots begin to shoot out almost before the old stalk has withered, and the bulb must not be kept out of the ground. Plant, then, the Spanish Iris in clumps on some rich, loose, friable plot, where their bright colour may be shown to advantage, and let them stay there year after year until

compact, the flowers $\frac{1}{2}$ in. across, star-shaped, and of a pale blue, continuing a long time, even till cut off by frosts. If preserved in a frame during winter, after the manner of bedding Lobelias, it is perennial, and may be propagated in spring by cuttings. New Holland.

IXIA.—Charming South African bulbs, slender and elegant in growth, and brilliant in flower. They are not grown much because some are tender and require glass protection. For culture outdoors, choose a light loamy soil, thoroughly drained, and with a due south aspect ; if backed by a wall or a green-

Spanish Iris (I. xiphium).

the dwindling foliage tells you that they have exhausted their soil. The beautiful varieties of Spanish Iris are well worth a place in the reserve garden for supplying cut flowers.

ISOPYRUM.—A graceful little plant allied to the Meadow Rues, but *I. thalictroides* has prettier white flowers, and is valuable for its Maiden-hair Fern-like foliage. It is well suited for the rock-garden, and for the front edge of the mixed border, is hardy, and easy to grow on any soil. Division or seed. Europe. Ranunculaceæ.

ISOTOMA.—*I. axillaris* is a showy half-hardy plant, resembling some of the dwarfer Lobelias, its growth dense and

house so much the better. Plant from September to January, 3 to 4 in. deep, and 1 to 3 in. apart. As the early plantings make foliage during the autumn, it is necessary to give protection during severe frost, and this may be best accomplished by hooping the beds over and covering when necessary with mats ; or if tiffany is used it may be allowed to remain till the danger of severe frosts has ceased. The December and January plantings require no protection in winter, but as they will flower later in the summer than the early plantings, an aspect where the sun's rays are somewhat broken will prolong the blooming period. On stiff soil, or on soils that lie rather wet in winter, the beds should be raised, and the bulbs should be surrounded with sand, care being taken that they are planted 1 or 2 in. above the level of the path ; and, where protection cannot conveniently be given, planting should not take place till December or January. A large number of varieties are in cultivation, and the chief species from which they appear to be derived are I. crateroides, patens, maculata, fusco-citrina, ochroleuca, columellaris, speciosa, and viridiflora, which last is of a beautiful sea-green, a colour quite unique among cultivated plants, and in no case to be omitted. A collection of varieties might include the following : Achievement, Amanda, aurantiaca, Cleopatra, Conqueror, Duchess of Edinburgh, Gracchus, Hercules, Hypatia, Isabelle, Lady of the Lake, Lesbia, Loela, Miralba, Nosegay, Pallas, Pearl, Princess Alexandra, Sunbeam, Surprise, Titian, and Vulcan.

IXIOLIRION (*Ixia Lily*).—Beautiful plants of the Amaryllis Order somewhat resembling each other, and about 1 to 1½ ft. high, with grassy foliage, and bearing large trumpet-shaped flowers in a loose elegant manner. I. Pallasi has flowers of the deepest shade, and I. tataricum of the palest, the intermediate shades being I. montanum and I. Ledebouri. Such beautiful hardy plants are deserving of a place in the most select collection, and the flowers last long on the plants. They should be treated like the rarer bulbs, such as Calochorti, Habranthi, and Zephyranthes, for though they may be hardy, it is not advisable to plant out such rare bulbs in ordinary borders. They should be grown in an open and dry position—in a sunny border, for example, which is all the better with a wall at the back, so as to catch all the sun-heat possible in early spring, when the bulbs are pushing up their young leaves. The border should be well drained, and a bed of light, rich loamy soil, about 1 ft. in depth, placed upon the drainage. When the young growth appears, place a common handlight over the plants—even two panes of glass will be beneficial—and if similar protection is afforded at the latter part of summer, it will tend to keep the soil dry and warm, and so ripen the bulbs. A handful of dry sharp sand placed in a layer under and around the bulbs is conducive to the formation of roots. Western Asia.

JAMESIA.—*J. americana* is a dwarf shrub from the Rocky Mountains, 2 to 3 ft. high, with deciduous leaves, and in summer many clusters of white flowers, which, with the whitish foliage, give the plant a pretty appearance. It is hardy, of easy culture in ordinary soil, and fitted for association with flowering shrubs of a medium size.

JANKÆA.—*J. Heldreichi* is one of the prettiest of the Ramondia family, a native of the mountains of Macedonia, growing in ravines. It has been considered a miffy plant, dying away in our gardens in spite of the most careful handling, but it is likely to grow as well as other Ramondias

Jankæa Heldreichi.

if its special wants are attended to. It likes to be moderately moist at the roots and have shade and moisture in the air. Some place on a well-constructed rock-garden should be chosen, where it will thrive in peat. The blooms are of a deep blue, nodding, and shaped like those of a Soldanella, and it has silver grey leaves.—M. L.

JASIONE (*Sheep's Scabious*).—Dwarf perennials and annuals of the Bell-flower family. J. humilis is a creeping tufted plant, about 6 in. high, bearing small heads of pretty blue flowers in July and August. Though a native of the high Pyrenees, it often succumbs to the damp and frosts of our climate, and it therefore requires a dry well-drained part of the rock-garden, and should have a little protection in winter during severe cold and wet. J. perennis is taller, often above 1 ft. high, with dense heads of bright blue flowers, from June to August ; it is a rock-garden plant, stronger than the preceding, thriving in good light loam, and a native of the mountains of Central and South Europe. These perennial kinds may be propagated best from seed as they do not divide well. J. montana is a neat, hardy annual with small, pretty bright blue flower-heads in summer.

Seed in autumn or spring. A native plant.

JASMINUM (*Jasmine*). — Beautiful shrubs, the hardy ones among the best introduced to our country, and of very wide and precious use.

J. fruticans (*Shrubby Jasmine*).—This is a wiry-looking shrub from Southern Europe and the Mediterranean region; hardy in England, and though not so important as some of the free-growing kinds, is worth a place on dry banks. It has numerous small yellow flowers.

J. humile (*Indian Yellow Jasmine*).—A handsome kind, being quite hardy for wall culture in all parts ; with evergreen foliage, which adds to its value. It flowers freely, and its yellow bloom amidst the deep green foliage is welcome in summer and autumn. Being an Indian plant it should have a warm aspect and good warm soil. (*Syn. J. revolutum* and *J. wallichianum.*)

Jasminum fruticans.

J. nudiflorum (*Winter Jasmine*).—A lovely Chinese bush which is happy enough in our northern climate to flower very often in the depth of winter, clustering round cottage walls and shelters, and often very lovely when not too tightly trained. In wet

Jasminum humile.

years it will be noticed increasing as freely as twitch at the points of the shoots. It should be planted in different aspects so as to prolong the bloom, planting each side of a house or cottage, for example. The sun coming out after hard frost may destroy the bloom on one side, and it may escape on the other.

J. officinale (*White Jasmine*).—The old white Jasmine of our gardens, one of the most charming shrubs ever introduced for walls and warm banks ; it is best on warm and sandy soils and often thrives in the heart of our cities.

The white Jasmine should be planted in every garden against a wall, or used for trailing over arbours. It is one of the best of all climbing shrubs on account of its hardiness and rapid growth in almost any soil. There are several varieties of it, the best being *J. affine*, with flowers larger than those of the ordinary kind. There is a variegated-leaved kind, not of much value, and one with golden foliage, and there is a rare double-flowered form. It is almost evergreen, except in exposed places.

Jasminum officinale.

It is a native of Persia and the north western mountains of India, but naturalised here and there in Southern Europe.

JEFFERSONIA (*Twin-leaf*).—An interesting dwarf plant, allied to the Blood-root, *J. diphylla* being from 6 to 10 in. high, the flowers white, about 1 in. across, in early spring. It is a good plant for peaty and somewhat shady spots on the rock-garden, and for the margins of beds of dwarf American plants. Seed should be sown in sandy soil as soon as gathered, but careful division of the root in winter is the best way to increase the plant. A native of rich shady woods in N. America.

JUGLANS (*Walnut*).—Stately trees of northern and eastern regions, among them being our noble European Walnut. A tree as well known to the ancients as to ourselves, and useful and beautiful in all ways.

Our Walnut (*J. regia*), like many other fruit trees, is cultivated so long that no one is clear as to its origin, but it is a tree of wide distribution in the east, and in countries where it is much cultivated has many varieties, differing very much in size and in the tenderness of their shells and even in earliness. Though the Walnut is not so much grown in Britain as in countries of Southern Europe, it is very happy in some of our southern, western and eastern

counties, occasionally attaining fine proportions, especially on warm and chalky
soil ; but as we go further north it becomes
less and less likely to ripen its fruit, and
in Scotland it has to be grown against
walls. In parts of Central and Southern
Europe it is so much cultivated that the
wood and fruit and oil produced by it form
a principal source of commerce. There
is very much of interest as regards the
uses of the various products of the
Walnut in countries where it is at home,
but here we are concerned with its culture
and beauty as a lawn, pleasure ground or
orchard tree, and in this way with us it
thrives best in good and rather dry soils
on calcareous base though thriving in
other soils.

The form of single trees is often very fine,
as indeed it is as a group, and sometimes
as a short avenue. It may also be grown
as an orchard tree where the soil is favourable and there is plenty of room. The
finest specimens are occasionally nearly
100 feet in diameter in spread of branch.
The cut-leaved form will appeal to some.
Among the other species there are remarkable trees, but our common Walnut has in
Europe so many good qualities that it is
the best to plant, although some of the other
species are good for collections of hardy
trees, such as *J. cineria*, the butternut, *J.
nigra*, the black Walnut, both of America ;
a very hardy, fine tree which would thrive
in situations where our common Walnut
might not be so free ; *J. mandshurica*, of
the Amoor region ; *J. rupestris*, of the
Western United States ; and *J. Sieboldi*,
of Japan ; besides several hybrids between the common Walnut and other
species.

JUNCUS (*Rush*).—Water or marsh
plants, generally with long round leaves.
J. effusus spiralis is a very singular plant,
whose spreading tufts of leaves, instead of
growing straight, are twisted in a cork-
screw form. It is worth cultivating on the
margins of water. It is easily multiplied
by division of the tufts. J. zebrinus is
apparently a form of the common Rush
(J. communis). The long round leaves
are barred with bands of yellow and
green, and it is a striking plant, as its
rigid habit and singular markings stand
out in bold relief.

JUNIPERUS.—Evergreen shrubs and
medium sized trees, natives of northern
and temperate countries. The wood of
some kinds is fragrant and the foliage
containing an acrid principle as in the
Savin. The Junipers vary much in size
and habit in their native countries owing
to their usually wide geographical range,

and growing in all sorts and conditions
of soil and climate, probably mere forms
of varieties have been considered species.
Some are too tender for our climate,
although of much value in their own,
while others are quite hardy and vigorous

with us. Such beauty as the hardy kinds
possess is very much diminished by the
common way of planting among shrubs,
or, in the case of the pinetum, isolating in
grass, both ways being against their good
effect and even good cultivation. Where
possible the really effective way is to
group them. The good effect of this is
well seen in the case of the common
Savin, as indeed it would be in most of
the others, and where there is no room to
do this, and do them justice, it would be
better to leave them out altogether, as,
starving in the embraces of the common
British shrubbery, they soon come to a
bad end. The following embrace, so far
as we know, the most distinct of the hardy
kinds only :—

J. CHINENSIS (*The Winter-flowering
Juniper*).—A low tree or bush, hardy and
useful in gardens as during winter or in
early spring, when covered with its yellow

Juniperus chinensis.

male flowers, it is beautiful, and of the easiest
culture, succeeding well on loamy soil ; several

varieties are in cultivation. *J. Japonica* is thought to be an Alpine form of this.

J. COMMUNIS (*The British Juniper*) is chiefly found growing in England on sandy or chalky soils or on open downs, while in Scotland, its native home is amongst the granite or trap on hill and mountain sides. The Irish Juniper is a close erect form, not confined to Ireland but occurring also wherever the Juniper is plentiful. *J. communis* varies much in gardens, and we often see forms of it where the wild plant is never cultivated, though we doubt if any of the varieties are better, if as good. The Swedish and Canadian Junipers are supposed to be varieties of this. *J. oxycedrus* is the Mediterranean representative of our common Juniper, but in our climate it does not generally thrive.

Juniperus communis.

J. DRUPACEA (*Plum-fruited Juniper*) is a native of Syria and Asia Minor, on the mountains there attaining a height of some 15 ft. Thrives in gardens best on good well-drained soil. It has a close, conical habit of growth with branches of a light grassy-green colour. This Juniper makes a good tree for a lawn. The fruit is a fleshy one, enclosing a hard kernel, about the size of the Sloe, and of a plum-like purple.

Juniperus oxycedrus.

J. EXCELSA (*Tree Juniper*).—A graceful tree native of many countries in Northern India, Persia, Arabia and Asia Minor, in some of the most favourable conditions forming large forests at very high elevations. A close tapering form was sent out from Messrs. Rollisson's nurseries as *J. e. stricta*, and is a very glaucous and attractive shrub.

Juniperus drupacea.

J. PHŒNICEA (*Phœnicea Juniper*).—A shrub of conical form from the Mediterranean region, the male and female flowers on the same plant but on different branches. Although long introduced to our country it is as yet far from common.

J. RECURVA (*Weeping Juniper*).—A distinct kind with graceful drooping branches, from the mountains of India and Cashmere, varying in size from a low bush to a medium sized tree according to climate and soil. The male form is more close in habit than the seed-bearing one. A graceful kind for banks or the outer flanks of the rock-garden. At Brynmeirig, near the Penrhyn slate quarries, there is a number of these graceful junipers, which for size are perhaps not excelled in Britain. The soil is loam and peat resting on shaly slate rock—the situation is shady and with a northern aspect, which seems to suit this species.

Juniperus phœnicea.

J. RIGIDA (*Mount Hakone Juniper*).—A graceful and picturesque kind with free and often drooping habit, and in southern England at least vigorous and hardy, assuming in autumn and winter a pleasant bronzy hue of green. It is not long enough in cultivation to judge of its stature or permanent habit and value in Britain, but promises well. Japan.

J. SABINA (*Savin*).—A hardy and plumy bush of the mountains of Europe, few evergreen shrubs being more beautiful. In the garden at Goddendene, near Bromley, a dwarf form is very prettily used as a lawn plant. Among the varieties of the Savin the most

Juniperus virginiana.

useful forms are *J. prostrata* and *J. tamariscifolia*—variegated ones as usual being ugly and useless.

J. THURIFERA (*Frankincense Juniper*).—A small distinct tree, in its native country attaining a height of 40 ft. As a lawn tree it is attractive, and from its dense conical shape associates well with trees of the same race, and is very hardy. Spain and Portugal.

J. VIRGINIANA (*Red Cedar*).—It is of the easiest culture and succeeds in almost any situation. A graceful, hardy tree on the hills and mountains of N. E. America, giving somewhat of the effect of the Eastern Cypress in Italy. This tree, like many Conifers that have been much grown and observed, has had its forms and varieties propagated a good deal, few of them being better than, if as good as, the common kind, the exception, perhaps, being the glaucous or silvery forms, which sometimes occur among plants raised from seed, as they should always be. Garden or curious varieties must, of course, be grafted, as if raised from seed most of these would revert to the wild form.

KALMIA (*Mountain Laurel*).—The Kalmias are among the most beautiful of North American shrubs, evergreen in foliage and charming in flower. The broad-leaved Kalmia latifolia is the finest, as it is also the commonest in gardens. Like the Rhododendron and Azalea, it must be grown in a moist peaty soil, or one light or sandy. It will not thrive in stiff or chalky soils. Its lovely clusters of pink wax-like flowers open about the end of June, when the bloom of the Rhododendron and Azalea is on the wane, and last for a fortnight or longer. The broad foliage makes it almost as valuable an evergreen shrub as the Rhododendron. There are varieties of the common kind having, in some cases, larger flowers, and in others, flowers of a deeper colour, the finest being maxima, which is much superior in size of flower and richness of tint. The Myrtle-leaved Kalmia (K. myrtifolia) seems to be only a variety of K. latifolia, with smaller Myrtle-like foliage. The growth is dwarf and compact, and the flowers are almost as large as those of K. latifolia. The other species of Kalmia, though very beautiful, are of less value, because they are smaller, more delicate, and less showy, but in peat-soil gardens they should be grown. K. angustifolia grows about 1½ ft. high, and bears in early June dense clusters of rosy-pink flowers. K. glauca and K. hirsuta are also pretty shrubs, K. glauca flower-

Kalmia angustifolia.

ing in early summer, and K. hirsuta in August.

Kaulfussia. See AMELLUS.

KERRIA (*Jew's Mallow*). — The double variety of this Japanese shrub, *K. japonica*, is an old favourite in cottage gardens, where it is most commonly seen. The large bright yellow rosette flowers are much more showy than those of the single

Kerria japonica.

kind, which is rarer. Though usually planted against walls, the Kerria is hardy, and may be grown as a bush except in the coldest parts. The variegated-leaved form of the single variety is more delicate than the double form, or the green-leaved single form.

Knautia. See SCABIOSA.

KNIPHOFIA (*Torch Lily or Flame Flower*).—Handsome and very distinct perennials which are prevented by severe winters from becoming very popular. The genus, as understood by botanists, is restricted to the mountains of Abyssinia and the Cape, with the exception of one species found by Speke and Grant near the Equator, and one or two kinds indigenous to the mountains of Madagascar. There are twenty or thirty species, and none of the six found in Abyssinia is identical with any sort found at the Cape. The Kniphofias, and especially the forms of K. Uvaria, are among the most striking of autumn flowers. Large irregular groups in open spots give a brilliant effect in autumn, and they require no attention beyond an occasional top-dressing of rich soil or well-rotted manure. During the late winters many kinds have perished from frost, but these dangers may be averted by a covering of dry leaves or ashes in late autumn. The stemless kinds are easily propagated by division and by seed when produced in favourable seasons ; but not the stemmed or caulescent kinds. However, those who wish to increase their stock of the stemmed kinds need not fear to behead them ; in fact, this is the only way in which K. caulescens can be propagated, as, otherwise, it seldom develops offshoots. When so treated it will throw up a large number of shoots, which, if allowed to remain until a few roots are produced, may be taken off and kept in a close frame for a time, and then potted in a sandy compost. K. sarmentosa is the easiest to increase, as it throws out underground shoots, which may be taken off at any time. K. Quartiniana develops small shoots almost at right angles with the base of the stem, and if these be taken off and treated as cuttings they will strike freely. The following are amongst the best of the kinds in cultivation :—

Kniphofia grandis.

K. aloides (*Flame Flower or Torch Lily*), or Tritoma Uvaria as it is still called in many gardens, is perhaps the oldest, and is certainly one of the very best of its family. It is the Flame Flower of cottage gardens, and is one of the noblest and most brilliant of Lily-worts : an excellent border-plant, it is suitable for all soils, and while few plants are better for picturesque grouping in the pleasure-ground, in the shrubbery, with a fairly open space and with deep rich soil, it forms handsome groups. It begins to flower in late summer and lasts for many weeks in perfection,

and nearly 70 per cent. of the garden varieties are traceable to it. K. pumila is a pretty dwarf form. The variety præcox flowers much earlier than K. aloides, from the middle to the end of May; its leaves are broader than those of the type, and are not glaucous, while the raceme is shorter, the stem being about half as long as the leaves. The variety nobilis, which very much resembles grandis, if indeed it is not the same kind, is a robust and noble plant, its leaves more distinctly serrated than those of grandis, its flowering stem 5 to 8 ft. in height, with flowers varying from scarlet to orange-scarlet ; the anthers are prominent. It blooms throughout August. The variety serotina is interesting from blooming a month or so after all the other Kniphofias are over ; its flowers are greenish-yellow, occasionally tinged with red. The variety Saundersi has bright green leaves and very rich orange-scarlet flowers ; the variety longiscapa has very long flower-heads, and is a most desirable form ; the variety maxima globosa has globose heads of yellow and red flowers ; and the variety glaucescens has large flower-spikes, the flowers being vermilion-scarlet shading to orange. It is a free-flowering plant, and is one of the best for heavy rich soil.

K. Burchelli, introduced by Mr. Burchell from the Cape, is a distinct and beautiful plant with a purple-spotted stem and bright green leaves, firm in texture, 2 to 3 ft. long, which taper gradually to the apex. It flowers soon after midsummer, and just between præcox and the other forms of K. aloides. The flower-heads are moderately dense, and the flowers are bright red, excepting those at the lower end of the head, which are bright yellow, the style protruding, the stamens being included in the tube. A useful and distinct plant, suited for dry banks and borders.

K. carnosa is a beautiful plant, forming low spreading leaf-rosettes, from the midst of which a number of flower-stalks rise to the height of 1 ft., with cylindrical flower, spikes about 3 by 1½ in. ; the smallness of the flowers is compensated for by their glowing apricot colour, enhanced by bright yellow anthers. The flowers open first on the top side in September. Abyssinia.

K. caulescens and K. Northiæ differ from all other cultivated kinds in their caulescent habit. K. caulescens differs from all the forms of aloides in being smaller, and in having very glaucous leaves, short heads, and smaller and less curved flowers. The stem, at 5 or 6 in. from the ground, can just be spanned by both hands ; the scape is about 4½ ft. high with a dense head of flower 6 in. in length of a reddish-salmon colour in its earlier stages, but in the fully-expanded flower it gradually becomes white, faintly tinged with greenish-yellow, producing an effective contrast. The glaucous blue-gray foliage is pretty Though less brilliant than most of the species, it is one of the hardiest, and is distinct and robust It is a very striking plant for the bold rock-garden, and it does well and flowers freely on dry slopes in light warm soils, and in open sunny positions It should have a little protection in severe cold Suckers or offsets taken off in early autumn root freely in sand in a cold frame

K. comosa seems to be closely allied to K pumila, and has a peculiar appearance with its long protruding style and anthers It is much dwarfer than K aloides, its leaves are much narrower, while its flowers are smaller and its bright green leaves are in dense rosettes, narrow, very pointed, and almost three-cornered The bright yellow flowers droop in a dense oblong head, the stamen and style being about twice the length of the flower tube K. comosa is a showy plant, flowering in September, but is rather tender

K. foliosa may be said to be the counterpart of K caulescens, but it has distinct stems, being also one of the most robust of all the Kniphofias, and easily distinguished by its broadish leaves and its protruding stamens The leaves form a dense tuft on the top of a stem 1 to 3 ft high and are 3 or 4 in broad at the base, tapering to a long point flowers in a dense oblong head nearly 1 ft long, bright yellow or tinged red, appearing in late autumn Cape *Syn* K Quartiniana

K Leichtlini is a native of Abyssinia, and requires winter protection even in the South of England. Its spreading bright green leaves form a dense tuft , they are 2 to 4 ft long, three-cornered, with entire margins, the flower-stems 2 to 4 ft high, the flower-head about 6 in long, the drooping flowers of a dull vermilion-red and yellow The variety disticha, which is quite distinct from the type, is more robust, its leaves broader, and flower-tube shorter, two or three heads of bright deep yellow flowers are borne on the same stem in August Some have suggested that it is a hybrid between K Leichtlini and K comosa.

K. Macowani —This differs from most Kniphofias in having the segments of its corolla reflexed, and in being of dwarf habit, 12 to 18 in high, the narrow grassy leaves 1 to 2 ft long, the flower-heads small, the flowers of a bright orange-red It is hardy, and is suitable for rock-gardens

Rigidissima and maroccana are garden synonyms The variety longiflora has much longer flowers K corallina is a robust hybrid. It is exactly intermediate between K Macowani and K aloides, and is a very pretty plant

K. Northiæ.—This is most nearly allied to K caulescens, but its leaves are much broader, are not keeled, and are serrulate on the margins The dense flower-heads are about 1 ft long, the flowers being pale yellow, but the upper ones are tinged with red towards the tips S Africa

K. Rooperi is nearly allied to K aloides, but is an early, or summer, flowering plant, while the stamens are included in the tube; the flowers are paler and less curved, and the leaves are broad and very glaucous K Rooperi is a native of Caffraria, and requires a little protection during severe winters It has a fine bold effect when in full flower, the flower-heads, 6 in to 1 ft long, being crowded with bright orange-red flowers, which get yellowish with age The plant usually but wrongly called Rooperi flowers in November and December, and is a variety of K aloides

K. sarmentosa is distinguished from K aloides by its smaller glaucous leaves, the cylindrical flower-heads from 6 in to 1 ft long, the flowers red in the upper half, and yellow, or yellow tinged red in the lower It is perfectly hardy There is a good hybrid between K sarmentosa and K aloides Cape

K. triangularis, at first sight, reminds one of K Macowani, especially as regards the flower-spike, which is about the same size and of a similar tint The foliage, however, is broader and longer, and in this respect it resembles K Uvaria It is desirable because it is earlier in flower than most varieties, and also because it is a free grower

K. Uvaria *Syn K aloides*

Other species not noticed in detail are K pumila, pallidiflora, pauciflora, natalensis, Kirki, Tysoni, modesta, Granti — D K

HYBRIDS AND VARIETIES —As we are getting to know the value of the Flame Flowers, many beautiful hybrids have been raised. We are indebted to Mr Max Leichtlin for quite a group of them Others have given us beautiful forms, such as the varieties John Waterer, Otto Mann, Max Leichtlin, and others, but all these owe their origin to red-flowered species, and do not much depart from the typical forms Since the introduction, however, of yellow-flowered species, a new field was opened to the hybridiser

The predominating colour in these new hybrids is yellow, in all shades varying through orange to a crimson-scarlet. In habit the plants vary quite as much as in the colour and form of the flower-spikes. Of some, whose parentage to K. Leichtlini must be very near, the foliage is narrow and deciduous, and the spikes not more than 3 ft. high. Other varieties have massive foliage some 3 in. or 4 in. broad,

Kniphofia Obelisk.

the spikes attaining a height of 7 ft. The variety Obelisk is robust, with broad leafage and spikes some 5 ft. in height. The colour of the spikes is a pure golden-yellow, and strong spikes often produce two or three additional spikelets.

Other beautiful forms are Triumph, a very fine hybrid; Star of Baden-Baden, straw-yellow, the spikes more than 7 ft. high; Ophir, orange-yellow, very free-flowering; Lachesis, very hardy and rapid in growth, the flower deep yellow,

turning to straw colour. Turning from the yellow varieties we have Leda, a beautiful and early-flowering form, about 4 ft. high, the flowers coral-red with an orange tinge. Matador seems to have nobilis for one of its parents; the spikes are large, broad, and the colour a deep red. Van Tubergen, jun., of Haarlem, finds that in his deeply dug, rich sandy soil where water can never be stagnant, all the above Kniphofias safely pass the winter outside if superfluous water is warded off. This gathers in the central parts of the plants, and may prove disastrous when suddenly sharp frosts occur.

There are now fifty or sixty varieties of these brilliant Torch Lilies, in place of the few known, say twenty years ago, but had we only the old Kniphofia (Tritoma) Uvaria, it is a plant capable of yielding very fine effects as planted in quantity either alone or grouped along with other suitable vegetation. All the hardy kinds grow well in deep well-drained loam and are readily increased by division or by seeds, which some varieties bear freely in mild localities. Once well planted in bold groups, Kniphofias form the most effective masses of colour, and their effect is visible at long distances, so that they are plants of much value to the landscape gardener who may use them on lawns, or wood margins, on banks, and near water, either alone or along with other vigorous plants, such as Spiræas, Pampas Grass, Arundo, or the Giant Polygonum sachalinense and P. Sieboldi. A bold group of these flowers backed or partly surrounded by hardy Bamboos, is a sight in October not readily to be forgotten. K. Obelisk is the splendid Kniphofia, of which an illustration is given in the accompanying woodcut.

KOCHIA (*Belvedere*).—*K. scoparia* is a curious and seldom-grown annual of the Goosefoot family, forming a neat pointed bush from 3 to 5 ft. high, the flowers insignificant. The graceful habit of the plant makes it valuable, placed either singly or in groups, especially from July to September, the time of its full development. It should be sown in April, in a hot-bed, and afterwards planted out in beds or borders. S. Europe.

KŒLREUTERIA.—*K. paniculata* is a small tree, beautiful when in flower; the long-divided leaves elegant throughout summer, in autumn die off a rich yellow, and the yellow flowers form large clusters over the spreading mass of foliage. It is picturesque, valuable for groups, is a native of China, hardy, and thrives in any good soil.

A new variety, *K. bipinnata*, has

recently been introduced from China, but it has not yet been established sufficiently long in this country to enable us to judge of its value.

Koniga. See ALYSSUM.

LABURNUM (*Golden Rain*).—Flowering trees of Europe of singular beauty and quite hardy and vigorous in our islands, and giving fine effects, all the more so if placed with some care as to position and surroundings.

L. alpinum (*Scotch or Alpine L.*).—A very beautiful hardy tree, a native of the hill forests of France, Central Europe, reaching a height of nearly 40 ft. The natural form is a very beautiful tree, and from it varieties of the highest value have been raised and increased from time to time, among the best *Parkesi, Watereri,*

Laburnum.

autumnalis, biferum, grandiflorum; *hirsutum, pendulum, Vossi.* The Alpine Laburnum and its best varieties may be known from the other European species by its longer raceme, broader and deeper green leaves and later bloom. *Syn.: Cytisus alpinus.*

L. vulgare (*Common L.*).—Also a beautiful flowering tree of mountain woods on calcareous soil, but growing freely in any soil in our gardens, flowering densely and earlier than the Alpine Laburnum, and like it reaching almost tree-like stature—30 to 40 ft.—in the best conditions. It has several varieties, among them *Carlieri intermedium, pendulum, semperflorens,* and *quercifolium,* and the inevitable worthless variegated variety.

L. Adami is a curiosity, a graft-hybrid. The same tree, and even the same branch,

bearing racemes of both yellow and purple flowers, and sometimes flowers of a dull purple. Old trees of these are quaint and not without beauty, though it is far from having the effect of the natural species and their varieties.

LAGURUS (*Hare's-tail Grass*).—A pretty annual Grass, about 1 ft. high, *L. ovatus* having hare's-tail-like plumes, useful for bouquets. It should be sown in pots in August, wintered in frames, and divided and transplanted in spring, or sown in open ground in April. It flowers from July to September, and it is pretty in the flower garden in large patches as a relief to showy-flowering things.

LAMARCKIA.—*L. aurea* is a small hardy annual Grass, with silky plumes, becoming golden as they mature. It is suitable for bouquets, and may be dried for winter use. Seeds should be sown in spring or autumn, in the open border in light soil. *Syn.: Chrysurus cynosuroides.* S. Europe, N. Africa.

LAMIUM (*Dead Nettle*).—Perennial herbs of which there are a few plants occasionally worth a place in poor dry soils, where little else will grow—such as are found on dry banks or beneath trees. L. garganicum, from 1 to 1½ ft. high, has in summer whorls of purplish blossoms. L. Orvala is taller and has deep red flowers in early summer. L. maculatum, a native plant, has leaves blotched with silvery-white. Of this species the variety aureum is one of the best golden-leaved plants for edgings. It does not withstand the full exposure that suits the yellow Feverfew, but in sandy or moist soils its peculiar tint is unequalled by any other hardy plant, and its blooms are pretty. It does not require to be constantly trimmed like the Feverfew.

LANTANA.—S. American plants, usually grown in greenhouses, and also in the summer garden. The Verbena-like heads of bloom are rich and varied in colour, and range from crimson, through scarlet, orange, and yellow, to white, the colours varying in the same head. They flower freely for about nine months, and are easy to grow, requiring the protection of the greenhouse during winter after being lifted in autumn. Propagated in spring by cuttings or seeds, the plants being grown in rich light soil till planted out in a warm position. There are many sorts grown, and a selection should include Phosphore, Don Calmet, Distinction, Eclat, Victoire, La Neige, Feu Follet, Pluie d'Or, Ver Luisant, Ne Plus Ultra, Eldorado, and Heroine. Like many dwarf half-hardy plants, they have various uses in the flower garden, and may be trained as standards. The pretty L. Sellowi is a good dwarf plant ; but the odour of these plants is unpleasant, and they are not worthy of much use. West Indies. Verbenaceæ.

LAPAGERIA (*Napoleon's Bell*).—A beautiful climber usually grown in the greenhouse, but hardy and flowering well in the open air in Cornwall and the south of Ireland ; with care it would be found to do over a larger area round the coast. It forms a lovely picture at Caerhays, trained on a north-west wall, and flowers quite freely. Often at Christmas and onwards through the winter and spring it comes out beautifully ; the rose and white and other forms have been tried, as

Lapageria in a Cornish garden.

well as the original form. Soil should be peaty with plenty of sand and leaf-mould. The great enemy of the plant is the slug, which is fond of browsing about cool north walls, and must be well watched day and night. The plant may be nailed direct to a wall, or planted among choice shrubs to take its own way as a climber, and it might be well to try it in various aspects, as the conditions that suit it in the extreme south of England may not do so in all parts.

Sometimes, where there is the least doubt in less favoured places, success may be obtained by letting a plant growing in a greenhouse get through the glass and make its way along any wall surface near. This has been several times done with success in various gardens about London and elsewhere. Chili and Patagonia.

LARDIZABALA.—*L. biternata* is a handsome evergreen climber from Chili,

hardy enough for walls in the south and coast districts ; the foliage a deep green, the leaflets thick. Along the south coast it makes a beautiful wall-covering, reaching a height of 20 ft. or more, but its inconspicuous purple flowers are seldom borne in the open air. It should be planted in light or well-drained soil.

LARIX (*Larch*).—One of the most beautiful trees of the north, and though much cultivated in our woodlands for its value as a timber tree is none the less precious for the lawn and home grounds. Belonging to the great Pine family it has the summer-leafing habit of our ordinary trees, which enhances its charms, not only showing the form better in winter, but the fine colour of the budding leaves in spring, and the ripening leaves in autumn. A true child of the northern mountains, the Larch is hardy everywhere in our country, perhaps thriving better in the north, as in the case of the lovely old trees at Dunkeld, its only enemy being a dreadful parasitic fungus which eats into the tree and mars its beauty and vigour. Other kinds of Larch are known, and some coming into cultivation, but it is not always easy to obtain them in a good state, and we have yet but little evidence as to their value. All are worth a trial, though it is probable that none will ever rival the charms of the European Larch.

L. europæa (*European Larch*).—A tall and lovely tree with pendant branches emitting a delicate fragrance in the spring when budding. It is a native of the northern and central European Alps, and also the mountains of Northern Asia. The weeping variety is picturesque, but *L. dahurica* is considered to be a form of this, and is likely to be of distinct value for gardens.

L. Griffithii (*Sikkim Larch*) is a Himalayan Larch, attaining in its own country to the height of a stately tree, but often dwarfed into an alpine bush. It bears large cones, and in our country has not yet been proved to be of great value.

L. Kæmpferi (*Chinese Golden Larch*). —A beautiful tree of Western China, attaining in its own country a height of over 100 ft. and of good growth and habit in our country, though not so rapid as other species. A choice lawn tree, and also, when it can be got in any quantity in the form of healthy seedling plants, as a group in park or woodland.

L. leptolepis (*Japan Larch*).—In its own country this is described as a medium-sized tree resembling our European Larch, to which it is said to be inferior, but from experience gained by planters this is

Larix.

thought doubtful, as it promises very well indeed as a woodland tree, and is said to escape the Larch fungus canker which is so deadly to the European Larch.

L. americana (*Tamarack*).—A slender tree, in its own country reaching a height of nearly 100 ft., but not thriving so well in England, and not so remarkable for beauty as our European Larch. It grows naturally in low-lying ground or swamps, and has not been fairly tried in our gardens, in which such ground does not often occur. *Syn., Microcarpa* and *Pendula.*

L. occidentalis(*Western Larch*).—Said to be the noblest of all the Larches, from the mountains of North-west America. It is of great height, but as yet little tried in our country, though promising well.

LASTHENIA.—A pretty hardy annual, *L. glabrata* being from 9 in. to 1½ ft. high, with many rich orange-yellow blossoms. It should be sown in autumn or early summer, or in spring for later bloom. Like other annuals, it looks best in broad tufts, but care must be taken that the plants are properly thinned. The autumn-sown plants come in with the Iberis, Wallflowers, and early Phloxes. L. californica is a variety. California. Compositæ.

Lastrea. *Syn., Aspidium* and *Nephrodium.*

LATHYRUS (*Everlasting Pea*). — Hardy annual and perennial plants, several of them very beautiful for the garden. The perennial kinds of Peas are valuable, as they are of such free growth and last long in bloom. The kinds worth growing are not numerous, yet sufficient to keep up an unbroken display from May till October. They have long fleshy roots, which, when once established, will go on for years without giving further trouble or needing attention. Near a low wall or trellis they succeed admirably, and climbing gracefully drape such surfaces with veils of foliage and blossom. Upon banks, raised borders, or on the bold rock-garden few things are prettier, and they never look better than when scram-

The White Everlasting Pea (Lathyrus latifolius albus).

bling over the face of a rock, flowering as they go. The way to spoil them is to attempt to tie and train them in a stiff or formal way. They may be used with good effect in mixed borders, and they are valuable for cutting from. The best varieties are pretty if allowed to grow through beds of medium-sized shrubs, and there are few effects in gardens prettier than that of the best white varieties when allowed to trail and bloom on a grassy place untrained in any way, a few tufts so placed are charming and live for many years Most of the species ripen seed freely, and all may be divided either in autumn or spring

L. latifolius (*Everlasting Pea*) —One of the hardiest and most easily cultivated of plants, thriving almost anywhere, even in courtyards amongst flags. There are good white varieties and some striped with deeper coloured flowers than the old kind All are peculiarly suited for rough places, and will scramble over bushes Staking, tying, and training only spoil them An old tree-stump, or the side of a trellis or summer-house, is where they delight to grow undisturbed, but there are many uses for this fine plant and its forms in the flower-garden, and in rich hedge-banks it would be easy to naturalise In warm seasons these Peas ripen seed in the south and on warm soil, and advantage should be taken of increasing the stock in this way. Generally, however, little if any seed is borne

L. grandiflorus (*Two-flowered Everlasting Pea*) is a very handsome plant for the early summer garden, succeeding anywhere, and, as the name implies, is the largest-flowered species, the blooms being as large as those of a Sweet Pea. It is at its best in June and early July, the flowers usually borne in pairs, of a rosy-purple colour, the stems in good soil reaching 6 ft It is one of the hardiest of the genus, and from its neat and free-flowering habit a very useful border-plant, common in cottage gardens. It has not so far varied in colour as the Everlasting Pea, but it may do so yet, and varieties of it would be welcome

L. rotundifolius (*Persian Everlasting Pea*).—This pretty Everlasting Pea is also known under the name of L Drummondi, but there is no necessity for this name, as it only leads to confusion. This is a very old species, but it is not so common as the larger kinds, though good from its earliness and freedom of flowering It grows about 5 ft high, the leaves are nearly round, the flowers in large clusters, bright rose-pink, about an inch in diameter, and open in early June It is of easy culture, and increased by division Asia Minor and Persia

L. Sibthorpi (*Early Everlasting Pea*) —This is valuable because it is so early, being at its best in May and June It

does not grow very tall, rarely more than 2 or 3 ft, but it bears many fine spikes of delicate flowers of a beautiful purplish-red colour In Mr Thompson's garden at Ipswich there is a fine bed of this pretty and somewhat rare species The plants are all in a large nursery bed, and are supported with a few branched stakes, upon which the flowers cluster in rich masses It has been in cultivation at Oxford Botanic Garden for many years, and is said to have been introduced by Sibthorp It flowers a month earlier than L rotundifolius, and may be increased by division or seed, but is not so vigorous in ordinary conditions as the commoner Everlasting Peas, and should be until plentiful be planted in warm borders

L. tuberosus (*Tuber Pea*) is a pretty low-growing kind, with flowers of a bright dark pink It is found in many of our cornfields, and is cultivated in Holland for the tuberous roots, which are said to be edible The tubers are about 2 in long, broadest at the root end and tapering to the apex It will be found a useful plant for the flower border, it being a true perennial, of neat habit, and very free-flowering It climbs like other Peas, but also grows in little tendril-bound heaps without any further effort at going higher, and then the matted herbage soon becomes densely studded over with the rose-coloured flowers in small clusters of five to seven each It will thus be seen that this free and long-flowering Pea is suited for draping bold rocks Europe and W Asia, naturalised in England

L. magellanicus (*Lord Anson's Pea*) is the most beautiful of blue-flowered Peas In many gardens a particularly bright form of L sativus will be found under the name of Lord Anson's Pea, which is a true perennial, almost evergreen, the stem and leaves being covered with a bluish bloom It grows from 3 to 5 ft high, the flowers, many in a bunch, are of medium size, violet-blue with darker veins, opening in June and continuing until the end of July This species is said to have been originally introduced by the cook of H M ship *Centurion*, commanded by Lord Anson, in 1744, and was cultivated by Philip Miller in the Botanic Garden at Chelsea In the Fulham Nurseries it stood the winter against a wall It is a maritime species, and a little salt may help its growth under cultivation It ripens seed freely, and may also be increased by division Straits of Magellan, and probably not quite hardy unless planted near a wall or house

L. maritimus (*Beach Pea*) —This is a

very interesting native plant, inhabiting the sea-shore, and not so vigorous as the preceding kinds It is, however, pretty and worth a place on open parts of the rock-garden, in gravelly or gritty soil The stems are prostrate, 18 in to 3 ft long, sea-green in colour, flowers in summer, purple fading to blue   N Europe, America, and Asia

L. odoratus (*Sweet Pea*) —Perhaps the most precious annual plant grown There are many ways in which it may be prettily used in a garden A common method is to sow little patches in borders, the seed being generally that of mixed varieties, and, by placing some stakes against them, to secure pillars of flower Where it can be done, a hedge of Sweet Peas is an attractive sight, and sometimes Sweet Peas can be used to hide an unsightly place during the summer Many people grow a hedge of Sweet Peas in order to yield a supply of cut flowers, but it is useless to grow the Sweet Pea except in good soil Some sow in late autumn, this is not always satisfactory, though, when it succeeds, the result is good By sowing indoors in pots or boxes about the middle of February, and gradually hardening off the young plants when they are 1 in high, Sweet Peas may be made to acquire a sturdiness and toughness which, when they are planted out in good well-manured soil in April, conduces to rapid growth and to immunity from birds and slugs, which would otherwise attack the tender shoots the moment they appeared above the ground The soil should be well trenched, and plenty of good stable manure should be worked in, and after the plants have been rather thickly dibbled in, supports of hazel stakes or netting should be placed round them Then, with a little attention during dry weather and the regular removal of incipient pods, they yield abundance of beautiful and fragrant flowers all through the summer and autumn When getting past their best, they should be cut down level with the tops of the sticks, and the result will be that from the bottom to the top a new growth will spring up, and there will be an abundance of bloom until the end of October There are now many fine varieties of the Sweet Pea, varying chiefly in colour

Mr Eckford, of Wem, Salop, now so well known for the many varieties of Sweet Peas he has raised, in writing to me as to their good cultivation, says " I do not like the Celery-trench fashion. If the ground is in a tolerably good state of cultivation, that is, has been fairly

well dug, simply put on a fair coat of stable manure and dig deep, leaving it rough In the beginning of March when the soil is in good condition, thoroughly break with a fork, which will be sufficient preparation for the seed. To obtain the best results, clumps of two or three plants at 1 yard or 2 yards apart are better than continuous rows In staking put three or four bushy stakes thus   round the clump, but well away from the plants, which should have a few smaller sticks to lead them up to the taller ones Round the whole put a string or bit of wire to keep them together, so that when the plants have grown up a sort of cone may be formed The sticks should be if possible 8 or 10 ft high, as planted in this way the Peas will, if mulched with half-spent manure or any kind of refuse to protect the roots from hot sun, grow very strong and tall, and if the flowers are cut close every morning, so that no seed can form, they will continue to bloom till the frost puts an end to them. Should the weather prove dry, a soaking of weak manure water two or three times during the season would be beneficial Should they from excessive growth get untidy, take the hedge-shears and clip them over neatly, they will in a few days throw out fresh growths and a profusion of flowers. If this way of growing Sweet Peas is adopted, it is a good plan to put the seed singly into small pots, and when the seedlings are strong enough to plant them out, in doing so make the ground very firm about them—they delight in firm ground If the weather be dry tread well in "

Sweet Peas do admirably in Scotland Mr Brotherston thus writes concerning his mode of treatment at Tynninghame Mr Eckford (the raiser of many charming varieties of Sweet Peas) was here a few weeks ago, and he confessed to be unable to grow them so fine He said that he had never previously seen the flowers of his own Peas grown to so large a size or so fine in colour Grow the plants singly, allowing each plenty of room If you are able to get plenty of good loam, allow each plant one and a half barrowfuls, and of leaf-soil half a barrowful, incorporating these with the top spit of the garden soil Heavy dressings of manure produce rank growth when the plants are young I prefer to add manure as a surface dressing, my favourite manures for this purpose being soot, pigeon manure, superphosphate of lime and sulphate of ammonia Peat litter, which has passed through a

S S

stable, is also good. Manure water will of course be also beneficial. For training on, nothing is more satisfactory than a dead Spruce Fir for each plant. Pinching is important, as it not only keeps the plant within bounds, but all through the season it causes the formation of young flowering growths. Seeding is so fatal to the production of bloom, and exhausts the energies of the plant so rapidly and immediately, that in hot weather I should not hesitate to remove every flower and opening bud rather than risk leaving them to form seed-pods. A position little exposed to continuous sunshine will be advantageous. I would make a late sowing about the middle of June, or perhaps even later, always, however, allowing each plant plenty of room. Some sorts are less given to form seed-pods than others. Captain of the Blues and Cardinal produce seed the most freely here. Orange Prince, Countess of Radnor, Mrs. Sankey, and Blanche Burpee are shy to set.

OTHER ANNUAL PEAS.—Though none of the other annual kinds of Lathyrus rival the Sweet Pea, there are several pretty ones. Of these the Tangier Pea (L. tingitanus) grows about 3 ft. high, and has small dark red-purple flowers; the Chickling Vetch (L. sativus) has flowers varying from pure white to deep purple. The variety azureus is a remarkably elegant dwarf kind with many clear blue flowers; L. s. coloratus has flowers, white, purple, and blue; L. Gorgoni, about 2 ft. high, pale salmon-coloured flowers; L. articulatus, Clymenum, and calcaratus are other pretty kinds for borders.

LAURUS (*Poet's Laurel*).—*L. nobilis* is generally known as Sweet Bay, but its true name Laurel should be kept, for it is the true Poet's Laurel, the vigorous Cherry Laurel having wrongly taken the name. Perhaps there is no evergreen shrub we oftener see in cottage and other little gardens. In England it is hardy over large areas, if it suffers occasionally, especially on cold soils, where the ripening of the shoots is not completed. Gardeners in the larger places rather neglect it, and seldom plant it in groups and colonies, as they might well do on dry banks. The plant is interesting in every way for its associations as well as for its beauty. There are several slight varieties, in addition to the common form. It requires some care in transplanting or it will be a long time rooting well. Warm and sheltered places are best for it, if possible on sandy or free soil; and it might be planted in different aspects with advantage.

In northern and central Europe it is grown to an enormous extent in tubs, as in these countries it is quite a tender plant, and the same thing may sometimes be worth doing in colder and more inland and northern parts of our islands, where this handsome evergreen is often cut down by frost.

L. sassafras, which used to be included in this genus, is now referred to *Sassafras*.

LAVATERA (*Tree Mallow*).—For the most part vigorous and somewhat coarse annuals, biennials, and perennials, few of great value in the garden. The most useful is L. trimestris, a beautiful South European annual, from 2 to 3 ft. high, bearing in summer large pale rose or white blossoms, thriving in rich and light soil. It may be sown in the open border in autumn or early spring. Among the taller kinds the best is L. arborea, which has the look of a small tree, in the southern counties sometimes 10 ft. high. The stem branches into a broad, compact, roundish, and very leafy head. In rich well-drained beds it would be a worthy companion for the Ricinus and the Cannas. It is most at home on dry soils, but during the summer months it does on all kinds of soil. A biennial, it should be raised from seed annually. L. cashmeriana, unguiculata, thuringiaca, sylvestris, and others of a similar character are not worth growing except in the wild garden, or naturalised.

LAVANDULA (*Lavender*). — Grey, half-shrubby plants, mostly dwarf with greyish leaves and warm and grateful odour; mostly coming from warmer countries than ours, but, happily, one of the most beautiful survives on all our light and warm soils, and may be cultivated almost everywhere, as even if in winter killed in valleys and on cool soils it is easily raised by division or by seeds, and will escape all save the most severe winters. It succeeds best in an open sunny position, in light soil. The white-flowered variety is as sweet as the blue, and flowers at the same time. Though a bush, the Lavender has been for centuries associated with our old garden-flowers. For low hedges, as dividing lines in or around ground devoted to nursery beds of hardy flowers, and many other purposes, it is admirable, and for dry banks and warm slopes. There appear to be two species and a variety in cultivation— L. spica and L. vera; and there is a dwarf variety also, probably of garden origin, which is very pretty where taller forms might be out of place. The known species are :—

L. abrotanoides (Canaries); atriplicifolia (Egypt); burmanni (E. Indies); cariensis (Asia Minor); coronipifolia (Egypt); dentata (Orient regions); Gibsoni (E. Indies); lanata (Spain); minutolii (Canaries); multifida (S. Europe); nimmoi (Socotra); pedunculata (Spain); pinnata (Canaries); pubescens (Arabia); rotundifolia (Cape Verde); setifera (Arabia); spica (Mediterranean regions); stœchas (Ditto); subnuda (Arabia); Tenuisecta (Morocco) vera (S. Europe); viridis (Portugal).

LEDUM (*Labrador Tea*).—Dwarf hardy shrubs, of which the best of the few species grown in gardens is L. latifolium, which represents the genus well. Its usual height is under 2 ft., but sometimes it reaches 3 ft.; it is dense and compact, and has small leaves, of a rusty brown beneath. During the latter part of May it bears clusters of white flowers. It is a very old garden plant, and was brought from North America more than a century ago. The Canadian form of it (canadense) is found

Ledum.

in some gardens, but does not differ materially from the type. A form called globosum is finer, as the flower-clusters are larger and more globular. L. palustre is commoner than L. latifolium, but being smaller in every part is not so good ; it is dwarf and spreading, and its flowers are white. The Ledums thrive best in a peaty soil or sandy loam, and are usually included in a collection of so-called American plants. They are charming grouped in the bog-garden, fully exposed if possible. North Europe and America.

LEIOPHYLLUM (*Sand Myrtle*).—*L. buxifolium* is a neat, pretty, and tiny shrub, forming compact bushes 4 to 6 in. high, with evergreen leaves resembling those of the Box. The small white flowers are borne in dense clusters in early summer, the unopened buds being of a delicate pink hue, and it is suited for grouping with diminutive shrubs, such as the Partridge Berry, Daphne Cneorum, the small Andromedas, and with Willows like S. reticulata and serpyllifolia, that rise little above the ground. It is generally planted on the margins of peat beds with other American peat-loving shrubs, and it is also a good plant for the rock-garden. A native of sandy "pine barrens" in New

Jersey. There is more than one variety in cultivation.

LEONTOPODIUM (*Edelweiss*). — A pretty and hoary-leaved alpine plant, L. alpinum having small yellow flowers surrounded by star-like heads of leaves clothed with a dense white woolly substance. Some people are so pleased at seeing this plant in cultivation that they send letters to the *Times* to announce the fact ; but its culture is not difficult on sandy soils, or even as a border-plant, and it grows too luxuriantly in moist rich soils. To keep a good stock of flowering plants, the old ones should be divided annually or young ones raised from seeds, which in some seasons ripen plentifully. It succeeds either on exposed spots of the rock-garden or in an

Leontopodium alpinum (Edelweiss).

ordinary border, if not placed too near rank-growing things. Syn. Gnaphalium alpinum. Compositæ.

LEONURUS (*Lion's-tail*).—*L. Leonitis* is a distinct and handsome plant of the Salvia Order, allied to Phlomis, about 2 ft. high, and bearing in summer whorls of very showy bright scarlet flowers. It is a Cape plant, and is not hardy enough for our climate during the winter, even when protected by a cold frame, though in warm light soils, in the southern parts of the country, it thrives out-of-doors in summer, and where it will not bloom out-of-doors, it is worthy of a place as a cool greenhouse plant. Near Paris, established plants placed out for the summer flower well. Wherever it can be grown in the open air, it would be valuable for association with the finer bedding and sub-tropical plants. Cuttings strike freely in spring—more freely than in autumn—in a slight bottom-heat.

LEPTOSIPHON.—Pretty Californian annuals. To produce the best results these charming plants must be strongly grown, and robust specimens can only be obtained by thin sowing. In light dry soils early autumn sowing is recommended, sufficiently early to permit the young plants to attain some size before the setting-in of winter. Fair success however may be looked for, especially in good soils, where spring-sowing will

The Lion's-tail (Leonurus Leonitis). Engraved from a photograph by Miss Willmott.

often yield excellent results; while the advantages of autumn-sowing are best seen in light sandy soils. Of the numerous kinds in cultivation the best is L. roseus, which is one of the most charming of hardy annuals, forming dense tufts, studded with rosy-carmine flowers. The very pretty L. luteus and its deeper-coloured variety aureus are scarcely inferior to L. roseus, which they resemble in habit, though with smaller flowers. The hybrid varieties of these are interesting for the singular variety of shades

occurring among them. The larger-flowered species, L. densiflorus and L. androsaceus, should be too well known to need description; both have lilac-purple flowers, and are most attractive annuals, and of both species there are good white varieties deserving of especial recommendation. All natives of California. Polemoniaceæ.

LEPTOSPERMUM (*South Sea Myrtle*).—One of the few Australian shrubs which thrive in our country, often attaining much beauty in seashore gardens, not only in the south but in the west. Among the prettiest effects in flowering shrubs I have seen were from this in the garden of the late W. O. Stanley at Penross. It should have shelter and as warm a soil as we can give it, although it grows well near the sea and sea gales have power to injure it. It would have less chance in cold and inland places, and valleys where the frost is more severe. It may be increased by cuttings, but best by seed.

LEPTOSYNE.—Californian plants of the Composite family, resembling some of the Coreopsis. L. Douglasi is a pretty half-hardy annual, about 1 ft. high, and having large yellow flowers. L. Stillmanni resembles it, but is smaller. L. maritima, a perennial, is somewhat tender, and should be treated as an annual. It is a showy plant, about 6 in. high, and bears large bright yellow flowers. All these plants thrive best in an open sunny position in a light warm soil. The seeds should be sown early in heat, and the seedlings transplanted in May.

LEUCANTHEMUM (*Alpine Feverfew*).—L. alpinum is a very dwarf plant. The leaves are small, and the abundant flowers are supported on hoary little stems 1 to 3 in long, are pure white with yellow centres, and are more than 1 in. across. It is rather quaint and pretty, and well deserves cultivation in bare level places, on poor sandy or gravelly soil in the rock-garden. It is sometimes known as Chrysanthemum arcticum and Pyrethrum alpinum. It is a native of the Alps, and is readily increased by division or seed. For other species of Leucanthemum see Chrysanthemum.

LEUCOJUM (*Snowflake*). — Pretty bulbs allied to the Snowdrop, but bolder and easily naturalised in rich valley soils.

L. æstivum (*Summer Snowflake*).—A vigorous plant, flowers white drooping on stalks 1 to 1½ ft. high and clusters of four to eight on a stem, with leaves shaped like those of Daffodils. It blooms early in summer (in many places before the end of spring), and is pretty in mixed borders or on the margins of shrubberies. It thrives in almost any soil, but is strongest in deep alluvial soil, and is multiplied by separation of the bulbs. It is excellent for the wild garden, and increases as rapidly as the common Daffodil. A form of L. æstivum is L. Hernandezi, a native of Majorca and Minorca, growing to about the same height as L. æstivum, but with narrower leaves, flowers only half the size, and usually not more than three flowers on each stem, appearing nearly a month earlier.

L. vernum (*Spring Snowflake*).—A beautiful early flower about 6 in. high. The fragrant drooping flower resembles a large Snowdrop, the tips of the petals being marked with a greenish spot. It is excellent for the rock-garden or borders, and thrives in a light, rich soil. Imported bulbs make little show for the first year or two, but when established they flower freely.

L. carpaticum is considered a variety, bearing two flowers on the stem, flowering a month later. Other cultivated Snow-flakes are L. hyemale and L. roseum ; but these are very rare, and somewhat difficult to cultivate.

LEUCOTHOE. — Beautiful evergreen shrubs of the Heath family, most of them very old garden plants, and common in collections of American plants. There is a family likeness among the kinds, the best-known being L. acumin-ata, 1½ to 2½ ft. high, with slen-der arching stems, in early summer wreath-ed with white bell-shaped pretty flowers. L. axil-laris is similar, and so are L. Catesbæi and L. racemosa, all of

Leucothoë acuminata.

which are known under the name Andro-meda. They are natives of N. America, hardy, thriving in light soil, preferring peat, and are suitable for the margins of groups of American shrubs, and for low parts of rock-gardens. A newer and very beautiful species is L. Davisiæ, introduced a few years since from California, and not so hardy as the others. It makes a neat little evergreen bush 2 or 3 ft. high, and has small leaves on slender stems, in May bearing clusters of small white flowers.

It is one of the choicest of evergreen hardy shrubs, and thrives with Rhodo-dendrons and Azaleas in peat soil.

LEWISIA (*Spatlum*).—A remarkable and beautiful Rocky Mountain plant, allied to Portulaca, *L. rediviva* being very dwarf, 1 in. or so high, with a small tuft of narrow leaves, from the centre of which the flower-stalks arise. The blossoms are large for the size of the plant, being from 1 to 2½ in. across, and vary from deep rose to white. The roots are succulent, and can retain life a long time even when dry, and as it sometimes fails to develop leaves annu-ally, is wrongly supposed to be dead. It should be grown in sunshine, for it cannot be flowered in shade, and the crown kept high and dry, though the roots should have moisture. A crevice in the rock-garden is the best situation for it. If grown in pots, the plant should be on broken stones, and the roots in light sandy loam with peat. After flowering, it shrivels up and becomes a withered twisted mass, like so many bits of string. Oregon, Utah, and Rocky Mountains.

LEYCESTERIA (*Flowering Nutmeg*).—*L. formosa* is a distinct flowering shrub, a native of the Himalayas, nearly hardy throughout these islands, but much com-

Leycesteria formosa.

moner in Ireland and the west than in the home counties. It is graceful in flower and form, and reaches 6 ft. high in mild districts, with white flowers tinged with purple , the leafy purple bracts, succeeded in autumn by purple berries, are eaten by pheasants, and therefore it is planted in some places for covert. In mild districts it is an evergreen, but generally loses its leaves in late autumn It thrives in various soils, and under trees.

LIATRIS (*Snakeroot*) —North American perennials of some beauty, having the flower-heads arranged in long dense spikes Some are effective border flowers when well grown, and well repay good cultivation L elegans grows about 2 ft high, and has pale-purple spikes 1 ft or more in length L pycnostachya, 2 to 4 ft high, has deep purple flower-spikes from August to October L spicata is one of the handsomest and neatest, growing 1 to 2 ft high, and its violet-purple spikes continue long in beauty. L scariosa, squarrosa, cylindracea, elegans, and pumila much resemble the foregoing, and, like them, succeed in any rich light soil, and are best here and there in among peat-loving shrubs or in good borders Propagated by division in spring or by seed

LIBERTIA —Beautiful plants of the Iris Order, of which some are hardy enough for the open border L formosa is beautiful at all seasons, even in the depth of winter, owing to the colour of its foliage, which is as green as the Holly, and it bears spikes of flowers of snowy whiteness like some delicate Orchid It is neat, dwarf, and compact, and has flowers twice as large as the other kinds They lie close together on the stem, and remind one of the old double white Rocket L ixioides, a New Zealand plant, is also a handsome evergreen species, with narrow grassy foliage and small white blossoms L magellanica is also pretty when in flower All of these thrive in borders of peaty soil, and in the rougher parts of the rock-garden, but they grow slowly on certain loamy soils, living perhaps, but never showing the freedom and grace which they do on free or peaty soils Increased by seed or by careful division in spring.

LIBROCEDRUS (*Incense Cedar*) —*L decurrens* is a handsome evergreen tree of the mountains of Oregon and Northern California, being very distinct in habit and found in the Sierra Nevada as high as 8,000 or 9,000 feet, is likely to prove a tree that will last in our climate It is a beautiful tree for grouping with the choicer

Pines , more columnar in habit than most, it does not therefore require the wide spacing too often given to our trees in the pinetum This tree, more than most other Pines, illustrates the mistake of supposing that conifers should be clothed to the ground with branches, as the natural habit of such trees is often to shed their branches as other trees shed their leaves In its native country the stem of this tree is often quite free and clear of branches to a height of 70 feet, and this instead of taking from the beauty of the tree really adds to it Syn *Thuja gigantea.*

The Chilian Incense Cedar (*L Chilense*) will just live out of doors in the most favoured situations and is therefore not worth attempting in the country generally

LIGULARIA.—Large perennials, remarkable for bold foliage, one or two of great size, and strikingly distinct aspect, though not quite beautiful in flower. L macrophylla is vigorous, with an erect stem nearly 3½ ft. high, and very large glaucous leaves, the yellow flowers borne in a long spike Free, moist, and somewhat peaty soil is the most suitable for this plant, which is multiplied by careful division in autumn or in spring , it is useful for grouping with fine-leaved herbaceous plants, but will seldom find a place in the select flower garden Caucasus. L sibirica, Fischeri, and thyrsoidea are fine-leaved plants, and worth growing with L macrophylla for their foliage. The Japanese species, L Kæmpferi and Hodgsoni, are better grown under glass, except in summer, when they may be used among fine-leaved plants in the sub-tropical garden , but the hardy kinds are most interesting *Syn* , Senecio

LIGUSTRUM (*Privet*) —The meanest of all mean shrubs, I think, but popular beyond all others, its weed-like facility of increase making it dear to those to whom something growing with a fungus-like rapidity is a treasure. It is not only that Privets are poor in themselves, and, as a rule, without beauty of leaf or flower, but it is the number of beautiful shrubs they shut out, millions being annually sold to take the places of better things, and helping to kill the few that are planted near them or among them The commoner sorts have no beauty whatever, and they all have the same vile odour in summer days when they flower, a sickly smell Happy in the possession of the finest hedging and fencing plants of the northern world, quick, holly, box, yew and sweet briar, nurserymen and jobbing gardeners make hedges and fences with these wretched privets, fences which have the one poor quality of rapid growth, but which a man, let alone a beast, could walk through without effort. I have seen whole towns like Leicester with miles of these poor hedges, and they are even to be seen in pretentious show places, where one would expect people to know what a real fence meant.

Rich in native and other covert plants I have seen the privet recommended by Sir Ralph Payne Galway as a covert plant, for which it is useless beside the beautiful covert plants we have—furze, sloe, sweet briar, juniper, and wild briar rose—and above all things recommended as a covert plant near water, for which Nature has given us the most fitting of all in the spiry-leaved trees of the willow and dogwood order of which there are many kinds.

As to beauty, the wildest briars that vex our legs and sometimes our faces, have far more beauty, whether of leaf, form, flower or fruit.

The land which has given us so many beautiful trees and shrubs and flowers, America, has nothing to do with the privets, which are inhabitants of Asia and Europe,

Ligustrum.

including China and Japan. Some of the species are evergreen, some summer leafing, and others in our mild climate hang between the two, and keep their leaves except in very severe winters. They are all too quickly propagated by cuttings, and there are tropical species not hardy in our country.

The gain of the rapidity of growth of the privet is more apparent than real, as it simply leads to equally quick decay if used as a fence plant or in any other way. The true fence plants when fairly treated, and put in the open in good condition as all fence plants should be, are not by any means slow growers. Holly in good soil will grow two feet in a year, Quick is a rapid grower after the first year or two, neither is the Yew by any means of slow growth, but this is a plant which should never be used for a fence where animals could by chance come.

L. coriaceum.—A distinct and curious species from Japan, evergreen, dwarf and bushy, from 2 to 5 ft. high with thick leathery leaves, of stiff habit, and flowers in white panicles with the sickly odour of the tribe. It might have some use among dwarf bushes on banks.

L. Ibota.—A shrub from 5 to 8 ft. high or more, of free habit and form, blooming freely in summer. The white flowers in spikes followed by dark berries. A native of China and Japan. *Syn. L. amurense.*

L. japonicum is a good evergreen kind, rather dwarf and bushy, with pointed leaves 2 to 3 inches long, leathery, and of a deep green with straggling panicles of flowers. *Syn. L. Sieboldi.*

L. lucidum is one of the best for erect and bold growth, growing 10 ft. high or more with firm lustrous leaves, 5 to 6 ins. long by over 2 ins. wide, and bold panicles of flowers 6 ins. long in summer and autumn. It is a native of China, where it forms a tree. A variety, *L. Alivoni*, has longer leaves, and there is a variegated variety. *Syn. L. sinense latifolium.*

L. ovalifolium.—One of the most popular varieties, and much used for forming hedges, as it retains its foliage through the winter better than the commoner privet, but it is without much character as a shrub. There is a yellow variegated variety which is also very popular, but less showy as it gets old.

L. Quihoni.—A Chinese privet of a wiry dwarf character, with small leaves, and the branches covered with a purple down ; flowering freely and rather showily.

L. sinense.—Not quite hardy on cold soils, but one of the best species, preferring a dry soil and flowering freely and rather handsomely on warm soils. It bears many purple berries, and it is a tall species, often attaining a height of 15 ft. China.

L. vulgare.—This is the kind generally used for hedges and arbours, standing all ill-treatment in town and suburban gardens and growing pretty well where nothing else will grow, but not worth having anywhere. It bears dark purple fruit like most of the kinds, and there are several varieties of it, especially variegated ones of little value.

LILIUM (*Lily*).—The Lilies are among the most beautiful bulbous plants, combining as they do stateliness and grace with brilliant and delicately-coloured flowers. The many kinds in cultivation afford a rich choice. All are beautiful, but some are better suited for particular localities than others. The habit and general character of the plants being so varied, their uses are likewise varied. Some are suited for the rock-garden, others for the mixed border, many for the shrubbery—especially for the Rhododendron beds —while not a few are so robust that they are at home in the wild garden, holding their own against native plants. Their true place, however, is the garden proper, and, when their uses are understood and expressed, there will be a total change in the aspect of the flower garden.

Lilies may be grown in various ways :—

1. Under glass you may have Lilies in flower all the year round.

2. In the open border you may enjoy their beauty each in its own season.

3. You may take them up when coming into flower in the border, and plunging them roots and all into a sufficiently large pot with suitable soil, shade them for two or three days, and then transfer them to bloom in a conservatory or balcony, without damage, providing they are kept well-watered.

Culture is important, but arrangement and grouping are even more so. There are Lilies which will grow in any ordinary soil ; a good, rich loamy soil suits the greater number ; others want plenty of sand, so as to keep the soil free ; while others can be easily grown in ordinary soil if it is mixed with leaf-mould or peat. It will thus be seen that there are no great difficulties in the way of growing a large number of kinds. In nearly all cases Lilies are more vigorous and brilliant where partially protected from severe frosts ; and the flowers last longer when sheltered from the scorching rays of the mid-day sun. The shrubbery border, among Rhododendrons (for those requiring peat), and the mixed border between shrubs and herbaceous plants, where the young shoots get a slight protection from the early frosts, are among the best situations. A very safe place is near the edge of a Rhododendron bed ; soil that will grow Rhododendrons will grow most sorts of Lilies, and afford protection from "blight and spot," which in some seasons, notably when cold and wet follow drought, greatly injure the growth and flowering of some species, even though the bulbs be unhurt. It should be remembered that bulbs of nearly all Lilies occasionally lie dormant a whole season, and push out luxuriantly the following summer, especially the Martagon tribe.

[1] Manure should never be dug in with the bulbs, though they accept it gratefully if liberally applied as a top dressing after they have been established a year. The only manure to be dug in at planting is rich peat and sand, in the proportion

of two parts of peat to one of sand.[1] This is advisedly called manure. In light soils L. auratum and some others are all the better for a top-dressing of dry clay broken small. Though to each brief description below we have appended a word or two upon cultivation, it is perhaps advisable to add a few general remarks. It should be borne in mind that, however beautiful nearly all the known Lilies are, some are extremely fastidious ; but there is a rare choice of beauty among those that are easily cultivated. Lilies may be divided into three classes—first, those that are best grown in pots, such as neilgherrense, Wallichianum, philippinense, and nepalense ; also Wallichianum superbum (sulphureum), Lowi primulinum, Bakeri, new Burmese Lilies ; and, in many soils and climates, speciosum, auratum, and longiflorum ; secondly, those that are best grown out-of-doors in loamy soil ; thirdly, those that are best grown out-of-doors in peaty soil. On light soils the following kinds do remarkably well : L. candidum, longiflorum and its varieties, chalcedonicum, excelsum, and the speciosum section ; all of the umbellatum, croceum, and elegans type ; also tigrinum sinense. For deep loamy soil the best kinds are L. auratum, Szovitzianum, Humboldti, the Tiger family, most of the Martagon group ; while in an intermediate soil of leaf-mould, loam, and sand, we advise the planting of Buschianum, philadelphicum, pulchellum, Browni, giganteum, tenuifolium, Krameri, etc. The North American forms require more peat and more moisture than the other groups. Lilies require, so far as their roots are concerned, a cool bottom, abundant moisture, and, for most kinds a free drainage. The slope of a hill facing south-east or south-west, for instance, with water from above percolating through the sub-soil, so as to always afford a supply, without stagnation, would be an admirable site.

PROPAGATION.—This is generally and most readily effected by separating the bulblets or offsets from the parent bulbs, and these, detached and grown in the same way as the parent, in the course of a year or two make good flowering plants. The scales of the bulbs afford a means of propagation ; but this is a slower method. Raising Lilies from seed is somewhat tedious, though many kinds in this country perfect seed in plenty, and in the case of such kinds as L. tenuifolium the seedlings

---

[1] Experience has shown me that manure may be applied, more liberally than I thought, to the Speciosum group ; while Giganteum literally revels in "muck." I have given with much advantage to pot Lilies (Longiflorum, Speciosum, and Henryi) Clay's Fertilizer, Albert's Concentrated and Fish Manure, so that I begin to believe that, given sound healthy bulbs, manure, especially in the liquid forms, may be given to a much greater extent than was originally supposed. I have seen an acre of Speciosum and Longiflorum Lilies in full luxuriant bloom, whose bulbs were planted at the top of farmyard manure dug in to receive them.— ALEXANDER WALLACE.

---

[1] Sea-sand, where it can be procured, is by far the best kind to use ; all bulbs take to it kindly, as it always attracts moisture.

flower in three or four years ; though others will not flower for several years. The finest kinds, such as the Japanese and Californian Lilies, are now so cheap that it is scarcely necessary to propagate from home-grown plants. It will be well, however, if, by rapid increase, or otherwise, they become plentiful enough to adorn the smallest cottage gardens. Several Lilies, chiefly Japanese and Californian, are largely imported every year. As soon as received, all bulbs should be examined, and decaying matter should be removed. They should then be laid in soil, or, better still, Cocoa-nut fibre in a moderate condition of moisture, until the bulbs recover their plumpness and the roots are on the point of starting from the base. Then they should be potted or planted out as required ; but, before this, decaying scales should again be removed, as a few of the outside ones are often bruised in transit, and after they have been in the soil a little time decay sets in, which if not then taken off may contaminate the whole bulb. Of those so imported, L. auratum and Krameri should, when potted, be surrounded with sand, but some do well without it. The most difficult to import among the N. American Lilies are L. Washingtonianum and L. rubescens, since, as a rule, they suffer much more than the large, solid bulbs of L. Humboldti, or than those of pardalinum, canadense, and superbum. These solid bulbs should be treated as above directed, but L. Washingtonianum, rubescens, and Humboldti should not be potted, as they never succeed in that way ; and indeed all the N. American Lilies do much better if planted out. Those grown in Holland, such as the varieties of davuricum, elegans, and speciosum, etc., arrive plump and sound, but it is much better to lay even these in soil a little while before potting.

L. Alexandræ.—A beautiful new dwarf Lily, apparently a hybrid between longiflorum and auratum, bearing a large, well-opened, reflexed flower, broad petalled and pure white, from a southern Japanese Island ; and therefore grows best under glass. Its native name is Uke uri.

L. auratum.—Some forms have flowers nearly 1 ft. across, with broad white petals copiously spotted with reddish-brown and having broad bands of golden-yellow down the centre. The poorest forms have starry flowers and scarcely any markings. Several named varieties are particularly distinct ; and the chief are cruentum and rubro-vittatum, which have deep crimson instead of yellow bands down the petals. Rubro-vittatum is a variety with a very

distinct bulb, the foliage is darker, and it is a hardier, better doer than the type. Platyphyllum is also more easily grown than the type. The white-petalled variety of platyphyllum, generally called virginale, is perhaps one of the most beautiful forms. Wittei and virginale, the flowers of which have no colour but the golden bands ; rubro-pictum, with a red stripe and spots ; platyphyllum, with very large flowers and broad leaves ; and Emperor, a grand flower, with reddish spots and centre. There are also some beautiful hybrids raised between L. auratum and some of the other species ; for example, L. Parkmanni (between L. auratum and L. speciosum), which has large white flowers banded and spotted with carmine-crimson. It grows freely in peat or loam, a mixture of both with a little road-scrapings best fulfilling its requirements. Where the soil is naturally poor, light, and sandy, it should be taken out to a depth of 18 in., and replaced with the compost above mentioned, or some fine, well-enriched mould. The bulbs should be planted in this, and, as soon as growth commences in spring, should be mulched with decomposed manure or short Grass. If the garden soil be fairly good, it need only be well stirred and manured, but the manure should be thoroughly decomposed. A sheltered situation should be chosen, and if possible screened from the midday sun, and protected from westerly and southerly gales and from heavy driving rains ; for this Lily is very susceptible to injury by cold draughts and cutting winds. No better place can be chosen than a snug nook sheltered from the north and east by shrubs, but at the same time open to the sun. The best examples that have been seen were grown in a Rhododendron bed, and planted in a deep, moist, peaty soil, where they have been for years undisturbed. When planted among other things the young and tender uprising shoots are greatly protected in spring. As to propagation, there is scarcely any need to enlarge upon that, as bulbs are imported so plentifully ; and it is only necessary to separate the young bulbs and replant them in good soil. Those who increase this Lily from seed must be prepared to exercise a little patience, as the seed is long germinating and the seedlings are several years before flowering. The seed should be sown, as soon as ripe, in a frame. The seedlings should be planted out as soon as the bulbs are of an appreciable size.

L. Browni is a fine Lily in the way of L. japonicum, but with larger flowers.

It is readily distinguished from any other kind by the rich brownish-purple markings on the exterior of the blossoms, which in well-grown plants are sometimes 9 in. in length. It is hardy and vigorous, and succeeds without giving much trouble.

Lilium candidum (White or Madonna Lily).

In a soil and position which suits L. auratum it flourishes, and need only be lifted every few years and replanted in fresh rich soil. It grows from 2 to 4 ft. high, and has deep green foliage distinct from allied kinds. The variety Colchesteri is handsome. Quite recently, some remarkably fine and strong-growing varieties of this Lily have been obtained from the district whence L. Henryi came; named by Mr. Baker Chloraster and Leucanthum.

L. bulbiferum is one of the handsomest of European Lilies, and is about 2 ft. high. It bears large crimson flowers shading to orange. The variety umbellatum is finer and stronger, and has large umbelled clusters of flowers. This Lily is generally distinguished from its congeners by bulblets on the axils of the leaves. It grows freely in ordinary soil, and flowers in early summer. A capital plant for bold groups, and thriving under partial shade or in the open.

L. canadense (*Canadian Lily*).—This beautiful flower is among the oldest of cultivated Lilies. It is 2 to 4 ft. high, and bears, on slender stems, terminal clusters of drooping blossoms usually orange, and copiously spotted with deep brown. It also occurs with red flowers (rubrum) and with yellow flowers (flavum). L. parvum, L. Bolanderi, L. Grayi and L. maritimum resemble it, and like it require a partially-shaded position and a moist, deep peaty soil enriched by decayed leaf-mould. It flowers late in summer, and is very attractive in bold masses, such as are often seen in nurseries about London. Like its allied forms it makes elegant groups among choice shrubs such as Azaleas and Rhododendrons ; and by such an arrangement we get a second bloom and a variety of form from beds that had only one blossoming season, and were poor and stiff in outline ; we prevent senseless digging when the groups are once in place ; and we keep the shrubs from growing into a solid ugly mass, while they shelter our Lilies.

L. candidum.—One of the best-known and loveliest Lilies, seen in almost every cottage garden, and producing snow-white blooms in summer. It dislikes coddling or being meddled with, and thrives best when undisturbed for years in good garden soil. Any attempt to deal with it like the more delicate ones generally results in failure. The best-flowered plants are in old gardens, where the bulbs are allowed to run as they like with no attention whatever. In bold masses, no plants can compare with the common white Lily when in bloom. It is so fair a flower that there is scarcely a place which a good plant or well-grown group of it will not adorn But the careful growth and the proper placing of such lovely hardy plants give the highest charm to the garden For years it has been difficult to find even a miserable tuft in many "show" gardens, though they displayed nothing there so good as a tall white Lily in a cottage garden Moist loam seems to suit it generally, though, like other Lilies, it will grow in a variety of soils The varieties peregrinum, striatum, and monstrosum are not so fine, but the striped-leaved variety aureo-marginatis is valuable for its foliage in winter

L. chalcedonicum (*Scarlet Martagon*) is a very old and handsome Lily, of tall and graceful growth, and bears several pendulous, vermilion, turban - shaped blossoms about the end of July It is one of the easiest to cultivate, thrives in almost any soil, and is best when well established and left undisturbed. There are a few varieties, majus being the largest and best The others are græcum, rather taller than the type and having smaller flowers, pyrenaicum, with yellow flowers ; Heldreichi, tall and robust, flowering a week or two earlier, and maculatum, a very handsome form Native of Greece and Ionian Isles Similar to the scarlet Martagon is the Japanese L callosum, a pretty Lily, 1½ to 3 ft high, with slender stems, bearing in summer several brilliant scarlet blossoms L carniolicum, of a similar character, is 1 to 3 ft high, and produces in early summer turban-shaped nodding blossoms of bright vermilion or yellow

L concolor.—A pretty little Lily from Japan, 1 to 3 ft high, bearing three to six bright scarlet flowers, which are spotted with black, star-shaped, and erect There are some three or four varieties—pulchellum, or Buschianum, an early variety from Siberia, 1½ to 2 ft high, with crimson blossoms , Coridion, with flowers somewhat larger than the type, and of a rich yellow spotted with brown , sinicum, a Chinese form, with four to six crimson flowers heavily spotted and larger than the type , and Partheneion, with scarlet flowers flushed with yellow This charming Lily and its varieties are quite hardy, though they require some attention in cultivating They succeed in half-shady places in a soil composed of two parts of peat, one of loam, and one of roadscrapings , but seem to require renewing every few years

L croceum (*Orange Lily*) is one of the sturdiest and hardiest, and therefore one of the commonest of Lilies It grows in almost any soil or position, and bears in early summer huge heads of large rich orange flowers In the mixed border it is attractive, but shows best on the margin of a shrubbery, where its stems just overtop the surrounding foliage It is always best after some years' growth A native of the colder mountains of Europe, it is one of the Lilies that may be naturalised, but is never so strong as in rich gardenground Lilies are said not to like manure, but we have never seen this one so fine as when in well-manured ground after several years' growth Indeed, we have planted it over a subsoil, so to say, of solid cow manure, and have had bulbs and flowers of enormous size in two years

L. davuricum is a slender European Lily with moderate - sized red flowers, spotted with black Like L elegans, it has several varieties, the chief being Sappho, incomparable, erectum, multiflorum, Don Juan, and Rubens Being strong growers and flowering freely, they are fine plants for the mixed border, for margins of shrubberies, or for groups or masses, thriving in partial shade as well as in sunny places

L. elegans.—One of the best and most generally grown of the early Lilies It is commonly known by the name of Thunbergianum It is very variable, and there are about a dozen named varieties The type grows about 1 ft high, and has stout erect stems, which bear numerous narrow leaves, and are terminated by a bright orange-red flower, 5 or 6 in across A native of Japan, flowering with us about the beginning of July Most of the varieties are so distinct as to merit a slight description They are—marmoratum and marmoratum aureum, two of the earliest forms , alutaceum, not more than 9 in high, with a large pale apricot-coloured flower, copiously spotted , armenaicum (venustum), about 1½ ft high, with several moderate-sized flowers (in autumn) of a rich glowing orange-red , atrosanguineum, about 1½ ft high, with large flowers of rich deep crimson , Batemanniæ, about 4 ft high, with several moderate-sized flowers, in late summer, of a rich unspotted apricot tint (L Batemanniæ and L Wallacei are put by Mr Baker as allied to L Leichtlini and the Tiger group I do not consider the above two species to be Thunbergianum), bicolor, about 1 ft high, with large flowers orange-red, flamed with a deeper hue , brevifolium, 1½ ft high, with flowers pale red and slightly spotted , citrinum, like armenaicum, but taller; fulgens, 1 to 1½ ft. high, with four to six large flowers of a deep red; sanguineum, 1 to 1½ ft. high, with one or two large blood-red flowers; L. Horsmanni, a dwarf form with richly-coloured flowers of a blood-red mahogany tint, and Splendens, the early form of L. Wilsoni; Alice Wilson, the beautiful, scarce, lemon-yellow, dwarf form; Van Houttei, 1½ ft. high, with very deep crimson-red flowers, spotted with black; Wallacei, 2½ ft high, with rich orange-red flowers, spotted with black; Wilsoni, 2 ft. high, with large apricot-tinted, yellow striped flowers—one of the latest to bloom. All the L. elegans group are perfectly hardy; they grow vigorously in almost any soil, but prefer a deep loamy

Lilium giganteum.

one with an admixture of peat. They like an open position, and are suitable for planting around the margins of shrubberies. Small groups are beautiful in the open spaces that should exist in every shrubbery or Rhododendron bed. They are all excellent border-plants, and the dwarf kinds may be introduced into the rock-garden. In all cases they must be placed in sunny situations.

L. giganteum.—A noble Lily of huge growth and in aspect different from any other. Its bulb is large and conical, and develops spreading tufts of handsome shining heart-shaped foliage. The flower-stems are stout and erect, 6 to 10 ft. high, terminated by a huge raceme, 1 to 2 ft. in length, of about a dozen long nodding

fragrant flowers, which are white and tinged with purple on the inside. It is one of the hardiest Lilies, and gives very little trouble. It flourishes best in a sheltered position, where there is an undergrowth of thin shrubs to protect the growth in spring. The soil must be deep and well drained, and must consist of sandy peat and leaf-mould, strengthened by a little rich loam, and plenty of rich manure. Years sometimes elapse before the tufts of foliage send up bloom. Nepaul. L. cordifolium, a Japanese plant, is a similar, but inferior, species, very rare in cultivation. It requires the same treatment. Cordifolium is said to grow naturally in Japan in shady damp places, cool and moist. A small group of three or four plants will do well in an open spot among shrubs, in a free peaty soil, and when in flower the effect will be all that can be desired.

L. Hansoni.—A handsome Japanese species, about 4 ft. high, having whorls of bright green leaves and a terminal spike of about a dozen bright, orange-yellow, brown-spotted flowers. It flowers about the beginning of June, is quite hardy, and succeeds in sheltered situations in a soil consisting of two parts of peat, one of loam, and one of road-scrapings.

L. Humboldti is very graceful. The singular beauty of the blossoms and the elegant manner in which they droop from their slender stalks, make it most desirable, and its flowers, on account of their great substance, are more lasting than any other Californian Lily. The stout and purplish stems attain a height of 4 to 8 ft. The leaves are in whorls of from ten to twenty each, and are of a bright green. The flowers differ considerably in colour and markings, but are usually bright golden-yellow, richly spotted with crimson-purple. The variety ocellatum or Bloomerianum is dwarf, and has petals tipped with brownish-crimson. It grows best in an open border of rich peaty or leafy soil of a good depth. Columbianum, *syn.* Nitidum, seems to be a smaller variety of this Lily.

L. japonicum, or Krameri as it is more often called, possesses the most delicate beauty of any. The flowers are of the shape and nearly as large as those of L. auratum. They are either pure white or delicate rosy-pink—generally the latter. L. japonicum is 1 to 3 ft. high, and sometimes bears five blooms—but generally only one or two. It is somewhat difficult to grow, owing to its delicate constitution, but the best specimens produced in this country were grown under the same conditions as L. auratum and speciosum. On account of its beauty it deserves the most careful attention. It is a lovely plant for a select spot between choice dwarf shrubs, in free peaty soil or deep sandy loam with vegetable soil in it. When Mr. Kramer first sent me this Lily he wrote that he obtained it from a mountainous slope at a high altitude.

L. longiflorum (*White Trumpet Lily*). — This is among the most beautiful and most valuable of garden Lilies. The typical form is 1 to 3 ft. high, the stems in summer being terminated by reflexed, tubular, waxy-white flowers, which are sweetly scented. There are several varieties, the best being the early variety now called præcox, of rather dwarf habit, with long, pointed, three-nerved, dark-green foliage; the flowers are of great substance, tubular, and but little reflexed at the tip, which flowers a fortnight earlier than the type, bears larger and more numerous flowers, and is in every way superior to it Takesima is recognised by a purplish tint on the exterior of the blossoms and on the stem. Wilsoni, or eximium, the finest variety, has bold dark foliage, and is nearly 4 ft. high, with numerous flowers about 9 in. long. Takesima is the latest to bloom. Madame Von Siebold is also a fine variety. L. longiflorum giganteum is the variety generally obtained from Japan; strong bulbs will send up a head of from 8 to 12 flowers widely opened; the foliage is bright green; under glass this Lily may easily be forced. L. formosanum, the variety from Formosa, has its flowers ribbed and flushed with rosy-brown; they are somewhat smaller in size than the type. L. Harrisi is L. longiflorum altered by growth in a tropical climate, Bermudas, S. Africa, &c. Jama-Jura and Liukiu are native names for the varieties mentioned. The variegated-leaved form (albo-marginatum) is desirable, as the variegation is distinct and constant. L. longiflorum and its varieties sometimes bloom well in borders, but care should be taken that they are not injured by spring frosts. L. longiflorum is so early that, unless protected by the leaves of evergreens, its growth is apt to be checked. A well-drained light loam,

Lilium Humboldti.

well enriched with leaf-mould, suits it admirably. L. Wilsoni is benefited by a lighter soil and by a warmer and more sheltered position. When just pushing the growth in spring it is advisable to encircle the plants with a few dead branches, if unprotected by shrubs.

Where this fine species and its forms fail in the ordinary soil of the garden, success may be ensured by making a special soil of rotten manure, leaf-mould, or cocoa fibre. In such a mixture, so free and open that the hand could be pushed down below the bulb, we have seen them perfectly grown where the natural soil was too stiff and impervious. The hardier varieties are admirable for artistic gardening, their fine forms being very effective when tastefully grouped on the fringe of beds of choice bushes and when touching and seeming to spring out of the Grass. They are also good in beds either specially devoted to

thrive freely in a good loamy soil; they are perfectly hardy and are rather partial to shade, growing freely in grassy places, open woods, or copses. Some of the finer varieties are good garden plants, and should be grouped in the spaces between hardy Azaleas or similar flowering bushes.

Mr. R. A. Jenkins writes as to the white Martagon: "The white Martagon Lily is one of the most distinct of the family, and if given a suitable soil and position there are but few of its relatives that excel it in beauty, hardiness, or freedom of bloom. As to its free-flowering qualities, suffice it to say that three

Lilium longiflorum Harrisi.

them alone or in combination with other plants. Similar to L. longiflorum are L. neilgherrense, philippinense, Wallichianum, and nepalense, but none is hardy and all are poor and unsatisfactory, except, perhaps, for the greenhouse.

L. Martagon (*Turk's-cap Lily*).—This is so common that we need only mention its varieties. These are very fine, especially dalmaticum, which has flowers larger than the type and of a shining blackish-purple, a contrast to the loveliness of the pure white variety (album). Cattaniæ is a form of dalmaticum and scarcely differs from it. Like the type, the varieties

bulbs in my garden after being planted as many years ago gave me no less than 167 blooms, two of the stems carrying forty-two and forty-nine blooms. Even in the summer immediately after planting the Lilies sent up forty blooms. This I attribute to their being moved early in September, for if planted late in the year, most of the Martagon section refuse to bloom in the ensuing summer. I find that this Lily does best in good deep soil enriched with leaf-mould, and without manure or sand. As the above-mentioned soil suits such plants as Anemone sylvestris and Lily of the Valley to perfection,

I have carpeted the ground with them, and they serve to keep the soil cool during the summer, while in May they furnish me with countless flowers."

L. monadelphum is a magnificent Lily of noble growth. The stout flower-stems vary from 3 to 5 ft. in height, and are terminated by a pyramid of six to twenty turban-shaped flowers, ranging in colour from a rich canary-yellow to a pale lemon-yellow. Some forms have spotted flowers, and some are much larger than others. The varieties are known as L. Szovitzi-anum, colchicum, and Loddigesianum. L. monadelphum thrives best in moist deep loamy soil, well enriched with good manure at the time of planting ; but does

White Martagon Lilies.

not show its true character till it has been planted several years. It rarely fails, and is one of the least disappointing of all. It may be readily increased from root-scales, a fact which is taken advantage of by many cultivators, and is the only method of increasing and keeping pure any really good or marked variety. Seed is, however, the readiest way of acquiring a stock of this truly charming plant. The seeds are usually sown in large shallow pans as soon as ripe, and remain there for two years, by which time the bulbs have attained a considerable size ; they are then planted in beds in rows 6 in. apart, with 4 in. between the bulbs, re-

planting when necessary. By this treatment flowers are frequently produced by seedling plants four or five years after sowing.

L. Parryi is a new and distinct species from California. It is of elegant slender growth, and 2 to 4 ft. high, bearing grace-

Lilium monadelphum, var. Szovitzianum.

ful trumpet-shaped flowers of rich yellow, copiously spotted with chocolate-red, and delicately perfumed. The flowers being borne horizontally, render it very distinct. It grows in elevated districts in South California, in boggy ground. Not much is known of its culture, but the finest plants have been produced where the soil was two thirds common peat and one third loam, with plenty of coarse sand. A bed in a shady spot was selected, in which the bulbs were placed at a depth of 4 in., having underneath about 1 ft. of the soil. Here the strongest bulbs threw up stems 4 ft. in height, and the greatest number of blossoms on one stem for the first season was six.

L. pardalinum (*Panther Lily*).—One of the handsomest of the Californian Lilies, and one of the most valuable for English gardens, as it makes itself thoroughly at home in them and grows as vigorously as in its native habitat. It

Lilium Parryi.

is 6 to 8 ft. high, and has large drooping flowers of bright orange, spotted with maroon. There are several varieties, the most distinct being—Bourgæi, one of the finest, having stout stems 6 to 7 ft. high, with twelve to twenty flowers of bright crimson, shading to orange, and freely spotted with maroon, and blooming a fortnight later than any other; pallida, a dwarf variety, scarcely 5 ft. high, bears flowers nearly double the size of the type, and paler in colour; californicum, a more slender variety, 3 to 4 ft. high, and the brightest in colour; pallidifolium (puberulum), a small form, with lighter flowers; and Robinsoni, a robust variety, with stout stems 7 to 8 ft. high, and with massive foliage, large flowers of a bright vermilion shading to yellow, and freely

spotted. This last is the noblest, and should be grown if possible. The Panther Lily is one of the most satisfactory of all Lilies; it has a strong constitution, increases rapidly, soon becomes established, and rarely pines away, as many kinds do. It likes a deep, light, good soil, enriched with plenty of decayed manure and leaf-soil, where the roots can receive ample moisture. It should always be in a sheltered position, like the sunny side of a bold group of shrubs or low trees. In a special bed the near shelter of hedges is desirable, though their roots should be kept away. Bare borders are not the places where this noble Lily does or looks best—there is no shelter or support for plants which in their own country have many shrubs for companions and are sheltered by the finest trees of the northern world.

L. polyphyllum. — A rare and beautiful Lily, 2 to 4 ft. high, and having large turban-shaped flowers of a waxy-white, copiously spotted and lined with purple. North India. Mr. M'Intosh of Duneevan, Weybridge, who has been most successful with it, writes: "Sandy loam, peat or leaf-mould, sand, and charcoal, with a slight admixture of pulverised horse-droppings, and good drainage under the bulbs, are all I have to tell; and I think early staking and tying may have something to do with many growing taller than they otherwise might."

L. pomponium.—This lovely Lily must not be confounded with the L. pomponium usually sold as such, this latter being simply the red variety of L. pyrenaicum. L. pomponium is elegant and vigorous, and blooms earlier than the varieties of chalcedonicum and pyrenaicum, to which it is related. It is about 3 ft. high, is erect, and has long linear leaves. The flowers appear in a lax raceme 1 ft. through, and a well-established plant will bear as many as twenty flowers. In rich loam it grows luxuriantly in sunshine or shade, and no difficulty is experienced with either home-grown or imported roots. Maritime Alps. L. pyrenaicum, a similar but smaller plant, with small yellow flowers, is a variety of L. pomponium, and the red form is much inferior to the true L. pomponium, though generally sold for it. These varieties require the same culture as L. pomponium. L. pomponium has an extremely offensive odour, and is not, therefore, likely to be used for cutting.

L. speciosum, or lancifolium as it is erroneously called, is one of the most popular for pot-culture, and is no less desirable for the open air, though, being somewhat delicate, it is grown to perfection under glass. It is well known, and we need not describe it, but we will mention the chief varieties. There is the true speciosum, which has large deep rosy blossoms, richly spotted ; vestale, pure white ; album, white or faintly tinged with pink ; rubrum, deep red ; roseum, rosy-pink ; punctatum, white spotted with pink ; Krætzeri, very large white flowers with greenish stripe on the exterior ; album novum, a somewhat finer variety with light orange anthers, and broader petals of great substance ; fasciatum album and fasciatum rubrum, two monstrous varieties bearing numerous flowers on flattened stems. Among the more beautiful Japanese forms are roseum, superbum, and formosum, and rubrum macranthum, cruentum, compactum, and, darkest of all, Melpomene (not the American Melpomene). In this group must also be included the fine L. Henryi, an orange-coloured speciosum, first sent to this country by Dr. Henry from Central China, and appropriately named after him. It is a strong grower, perfectly hardy, and from its unique tint and bold growth a grand acquisition to our gardens. Other fine varieties have originated in America, and among these Melpomene is very distinct. The beautiful hybrid, Mrs. A. Waterer, is large, white, and spotted with pink. All the varieties require shelter from winds and draughts, and a rich loamy soil mixed with peat and leaf-manure. They flower for the most part in September, and last longer in bloom than many other Lilies. In good soils, very happy use can be made of these handsome Lilies in warm and sheltered places where their blooms may be fully developed.

L. superbum (*Swamp Lily*).—One of the stateliest of N. American Lilies, bearing late in summer beautiful orange-red flowers, thickly spotted. It may be recognised at once by its purple-tinged stems, which rise 5 to 10 ft. high, and which are very graceful, waving with the slightest breeze. A pyramid of flowers terminates each stem. L. superbum delights in moist deep soil consisting chiefly of

peaty and decayed leaf-manure, and is one of the best Lilies for growing in shady woods when the undergrowth is not too rank. In the garden it should have snug glades and nooks protected by shrubs, and moist rich soil. L. carolinianum is a less showy form.

L. tenuifolium.—A most elegant dwarf Lily, especially valuable for earliness in flowering. It is 1 to 1½ ft. high, and has narrow leaves on slender stems, furnished with a cluster of about a dozen brilliant red turban-shaped flowers, which shine like sealing-wax. It succeeds in open warm borders of light sandy loam, but is all the better for a hand-light or frame, as it flowers very early. Siberia and N. China. L. callosum and its form, stenophyllum, are similar but less showy.

L. testaceum (*Nankeen Lily*).—This is a distinct-coloured Lily, and should always be grown, being of easy culture

Lilium testaceum.

and thriving in any ordinary soil, though preferring one that is peaty. It has the growth of the white L. candidum, but the flowers are a delicate apricot, or nankeen, colour. When well grown it is 6 or 7 ft. high, and bears several flowers in a large head. Other names for this Lily are L. excelsum and isabellinum. It is one of the plants that grow freely in London.

L. tigrinum (*Tiger Lily*).—This is one of the commonest kinds, and is too well known to need description. No garden should be without it, for few plants are so attractive or have such stately growth. The common kind is handsome, but the variety splendens is much finer, having larger flowers with larger spots, is produced later, and grows 7 ft. high. Fortunei is an early form and as desirable as

T T

splendens. The double-flowered variety (flore-pleno) is showy and vigorous. Erectum also is distinct and desirable. L. pseudo-tigrinum and the varieties of Maximowiczi, though referred to other species, much resemble L. tigrinum. The Tiger Lily is very easy of cultivation, thriving best in deep sandy loam with an open, but sheltered position. The earliest varieties begin to flower at the end of August, and the latest last till the end of October. The Tiger Lily may be quickly propagated by the bulblets, which form in the axils of the leaves.

L. Washingtonianum.—A lovely Californian Lily, 2 to 5 ft. high, bearing a cluster of large, white, purple-spotted flowers that become tinged with purple after expansion. Nearly allied to this, and by some considered a variety, is L. rubescens, which has smaller flowers which are of a pale lilac or nearly white. These flowers are erect—not horizontal, as in the Washington Lily. Neither L. Washingtonianum nor L. rubescens is easy to grow, owing, probably, to their being but little understood at present. The best results have been obtained in partially-shaded situations, in loose, peaty, well-drained, but moist soil.

Known species :—*Lilium alpinum*, Hungary ; *auratum*, Japan ; *bolanderi*, California ; *bulbiferum*, S. Europe ; *callosum*, Japan ; *canadense*, N. America ; *candidum*, S. Europe ; *carniolicum*, S. Europe ; *Catesbæi*, N. America ; *chalcedonicum*, Carniola ; *columbianum*, N.W. America ; *concolor*, China ; *cordifolium*, Japan ; *croceum*, S. Europe ; *dauricum*, Dahruria ; *Davidi*, China ; *elegans*, Japan ; *formosissimum* ; *formosum*, Japan ; *Fortunei*, do. ; *Glehni*, do.; *Grayi*, N.W. America ; *Hansoni*, Manchuria ; *Hansoni*, Japan ; *Heldreichii*, Greece ; *Hookeri*, Himalayas; *Humboldtii*, California; *japonicum*, Japan; *Jeffersoni*, *lancifolium*, Japan; *Leichtlinii*, do. ; *liliacinum* ; *longiflorum*, Japan ; *maculatum*, do. ; *maritimum*, California ; *martagon*, S. Europe ; *medeoloides*, Japan ; *monadelphum*, Caucasus ; *neilgherrense*, E. Indies; *nepalense*, Himalayas; *nitidum*, California; *oxypetalum*, Himalayas ; *pardalinum*, California; *Parryi*, do. ; *parvum*, do. ; *persicum*, Persia ; *philadelphicum*, N. America ; *philippinense*, Philippines ; *polyphyllum*, Himalayas ; *pomponium*, Siberia ; *ponticum*, Asia Minor ; *puberulum*, N. America ; *pulchellum*, Dahruria ; *pygmæum* ; *pyrenaicum*, Pyrenees ; *recurvum* ; *roseum*, E. Indies ; *rubescens*, California ; *Sieboldi*, Japan ; *speciosum*, do.; *superbum*, N. Amer.; *tenuifolium*, Dahruria; *testaceum*, Japan ; *tigrinum*, Japan; *Wallichianum*, Himalayas ; *Washingtonianum*, California.

LIMNANTHEMUM (*Fringed Buckbean*).—*L. nymphæoides* is a pretty native water-plant, growing in ponds or slow streams, with floating leaves, and bright yellow flowers 1 in. or more across. One of the prettiest of floating water plants flowering for months in the summer and autumn. Wild in the southern and eastern counties, and naturalised in other districts. Division as soon as gathered. *Syn.*, Villarsia. Gentian order.

LIMNANTHES.—A vigorous though dwarf hardy annual, valuable because so early ; *L. Douglasi* has yellow and white flowers, and there is a pure white variety. Few annuals are hardier, severe winters not injuring it, and it requires neither a deep nor a rich soil, but thrives where the earth is poor as well as in ordinary garden soil. It often sows itself on light soils, and gives no further trouble ; but if wanted for a special purpose in spring, the seed should be sown in autumn in boxes or in the open ground ; for summer-flowering sow in the spring. Plains of California and foothills of the Sierra Nevada.

LIMNOCHARIS.—*L. Humboldti* is an interesting water-plant, in summer covering the surface with heart-shaped leaves and soft yellow flowers, for several months ; it will thrive either in running or still water, if planted 6 to 9 in. below the surface, and may also be grown in tubs sunk in the ground. These tubs should be about 1½ ft. in depth, should be half-filled with loamy soil, and then filled up with water. In fountain-basins and clear, still waters, where the plant is fully exposed to the sun, it flowers freely during summer, but it will not survive out-of-doors in winter, except in the mildest districts, and unless placed at least 18 in. below the surface. Plants put out of a warm aquatic house in May soon begin to grow in the open air in tanks well exposed to the sun. Division. Butomaceæ.

LINARIA (*Toadflax*).—An interesting family, which includes some beautiful garden annuals and perennials, varying from dwarf alpines to tall coarse plants.

L. alpina (*Alpine Toadflax*) forms dense, spreading, dwarf, and silvery tufts, covered with bluish-violet and intense orange flowers. It is usually biennial ; but in favourable spots, both wild and cultivated, becomes perennial. It sows itself freely, being one of the most charming subjects that we can allow to "go wild" in sandy, gritty, and rather moist earth, or in chinks in the rock-garden. In moist districts it will establish itself even in gravel walks, is readily increased from seed, which should be sown in early spring in cold frames, or in the places where it is to remain out-of-doors. It is found on moraines and in the débris of the Alps and Pyrenees.

L. antirrhinifolia.—This elegant little rock plant forms a very neat spreading mass about 2 feet across and about 6 to 8 inches high and has the advantage of not spreading so rapidly as some of its congeners, and its bright purple flowers are produced incessantly during the summer and autumn. The plant is of the easiest possible culture, and can be highly recommended for the rock-garden.

L. cymbalaria (*Ivy-leaved Toadflax*) often drapes walls in a graceful way, and is grown by cottagers as a window plant, a common name for it being "Mother of Thousands." A moist half-shady place best suits it, and the white variety is even prettier than the species.

L. dalmatica is a handsome plant, 3 to 5 ft. high, much branched, and in summer has a profusion of large showy sulphur-yellow blossoms. It thrives best in warm places in light well-drained soil,

Linaria antirrhinifolia.

and when once established can be eradicated with difficulty. L. genistæfolia, which also has yellow flowers, is similar but inferior.

L. macedonica is a new and distinct plant, from 2 to 3 ft. high, and throwing up shoots from the base. It differs from L. dalmatica in its broader leaves, and is quite hardy.

L. purpurea is a pretty kind with spikes of purple flowers, and one occasionally sees it on old walls, as it thrives well in dry spots.

L. triornithophora is a beautiful plant when well grown, 1 to 1½ ft. high, and with large purple long-spurred flowers in whorls of three. It is rather delicate, and, though perennial, should be raised yearly from seed. L. triphylla is similar.

L. vulgaris (*Common Toadflax*).—This

is well known, and is very pretty as one sees it growing in wild or neglected gardens, but is also a good garden plant. The British variety Peloria is a handsome Toadflax, flowering freely after midsummer in a warm sunny border, and is effective in a mass.

A few other perennial Linarias that may be mentioned are L. hepaticæfolia (Hepatica-leaved Toadflax), from Corsica, and is nearly always in flower in summer and autumn ; L. saxatilis, which has dark brown and yellow flowers ; and L. anticaria, a good rock-plant, forming little tufts and sowing itself freely. The finely-veined flowers are dull white tinged with lilac.

ANNUAL TOADFLAXES.—Some of the annual species are among our prettiest border flowers, growing about 1 ft. high, and very effective in broad masses. Seed should be sown in ordinary garden soil in early spring, and the seedlings will flower in July and August. The best are L. reticulata, with small purple flowers ; the variety, aureo-purpurea, being a charming plant, with flowers which vary from rose-purple to dark orange. L. bipartita is also very variable, the colours ranging from deep purple to white. Perezi has small yellow flowers ; whilst the flowers of maroccana vary from violet to pink ; and those of multipunctata, the dwarfest of the group, are black spotted with yellow.

LINNÆA (*Twin Flower*). — A little evergreen creeper, L. borealis having slender upright stalks bearing two flowers each, delicately fragrant white, often tinged with pink, and drooping. It is usually found in moist woods, where it forms a dense carpet and is wrongly supposed to be difficult to cultivate. Little need be done beyond planting healthy young plants in a moist sandy border or rock-garden. I have often seen it thriving, where the air was pure and the soil suitable ; and it is excellent for a moist rock-garden, growing rapidly, and forming a charming fringe to groups of small alpine shrubs, in cool borders or on cool parts of the rock-garden. N. Europe, Asia, and America ; also Scotch mountains.

LINUM (*Flax*).—Plants of marked elegance and lightness of growth, and including some pretty garden plants.

L. campanulatum (*Yellow Herbaceous Flax*).—A perennial with yellow flowers on stems 12 to 18 in. high, distinct and worthy of a place. A native of the south of Europe, it flowers in summer, and flourishes freely in dry soil on the warm sides of banks or rock-gardens. Similar to it is L. flavum, or tauricum, also a handsome and hardy plant with yellow flowers ; but L. arboreum, a shrubby kind, also with yellow flowers, is not hardy in all districts, though where it thrives it is a pretty little evergreen bush for the rock-garden.

L. grandiflorum (*Red Flax*) is a showy hardy annual from Algeria, with deep red blossoms. By successive sowings it may be had in bloom from May till October. Seed sown in autumn will give plants for spring-blooming, and sowings made from March to June will yield a display through the summer and autumn. By sowing seeds in pots in good rich soil in summer, and plunging in a sunny border with plenty of water, plants may be obtained for the greenhouse or window during October and November. If protected from frost the plant is perennial.

L. monogynum (*New Zealand Flax*). —A beautiful kind with large pure white blossoms blooming in summer. It grows about 1½ ft. high in good light soil, and its neat and slender habit renders it particularly pleasing for the borders of the rock-garden or for pot-culture. It may readily be increased by seed or division ; it is hardy in the more temperate parts of England, but in the colder districts is said to require some protection. L. candidissimum is a finer and hardier variety. Both are natives of New Zealand.

L. narbonnense (*Narbonne Flax*).—A beautiful kind, bearing during summer many large light sky-blue flowers, with violet veins, growing best on rich light soils, and is a fine plant for borders, or for the lower flanks of the rock-garden, forming lovely blue masses 15 to 20 in. high. Southern Europe.

Other similar but inferior blue-flowered kinds are the common L. perenne, usitatissimum, alpinum, sibiricum, alpicola, collinum, and austriacum ; all are hardy European species, and make pretty border or rock-garden plants. The white and rose varieties of L. perenne are pretty plants.

L. salsoloides (*White Rock Flax*) is a dwarf half-shrubby species, essentially a rock-garden plant ; its flowers, white with a purplish eye, reminding one of some of our creeping white Phloxes. In the rock-garden, in a well-exposed sunny nook, the plant is hardy, and trails over stones, flowering abundantly. It produces seeds rarely, so that it must be increased by cuttings of the short shoots taken off about midsummer ; these will strike freely, and make vigorous plants when potted off in the following spring. Mountains of Europe. L. viscosum with

pink flowers, is a closely allied plant not so pretty.

The Common Flax, which gives us the linen fibre, is a pretty annual plant worth a place for its beauty among annual flowers.

LIPPIA.—*L. nodiflora* is a dwarf perennial creeper bearing, in summer, heads of pretty pink blooms. It grows in any situation or soil, and is a capital plant for quickly covering bare spaces in the rock-garden where choicer subjects will not thrive.

LIQUIDAMBAR (*Sweet Gum*).—A very beautiful summer-leafing maple-like tree from Florida westward to the prairie States, often reaching 100 feet in height, the leaves turning an intense deep purplish red in autumn, fine in effect. This tree, thriving in wet and marshy places, is more at home in Great Britain than some of the American trees in our clouded country. It would probably attain a greater stature in river side soil

Liquidambar.

in a warmer country than ours, the best trees in its native country growing in rich moist soils. In Northern Britain, and Northern Europe generally it is somewhat slow and tender. Its name comes from a resinous gum found between the bark and wood, exuding from the cracks of the bark, and having an agreeable fragrance. This is produced in the southern and warmer districts of which the tree is native, and not to the same extent in northern countries. It is a beautiful lawn and home-ground tree, but should be sheltered and in rather deep moist soil. The leaves are fragrant in spring. It is best increased from seed, and good seedling plants greatly facilitate its health and good growth. It is a tree which would be better grown as a group instead of depending upon single plants. There are one or two varieties which, however, have not proved so useful for our country as the wild tree.

LIRIODENDRON (*Tulip Tree*).—*L. tulipiferum* is one of the noblest of flowering trees. It is only when the tree has reached maturity that it bears its beauti-

Liriodendron tulipiferum.

ful Tulip-like flowers of pale green and yellow. Young Tulip trees should be planted on lawns in free or ordinary soils, as the flowers are very pretty in a cut state for the house and the tree a beautiful one at all times. N. America.

LITHOSPERMUM (*Gromwell*). — A few of these Borage-worts are pretty and worth growing. One of the finest is L. prostratum, a spreading little evergreen having flowers of a lovely blue, with faint reddish-violet stripes, in great profusion when the plant is well grown. It is hardy, and valuable as a rock-plant from its prostrate habit and the fine blue of its flowers—a blue scarcely surpassed by that of the Gentians. Its shoots may be allowed to fall down the sunny face of a rocky nook, or to spread into flat tufts on level parts of the rock-garden. On dry sandy soils it forms an excellent border-plant, and becomes, if the soil be deep and good, a round spreading mass, 1 ft. or more high. In such soils, it is suited for the margins of beds of choice and dwarf shrubs, either as a single plant or in groups. In heavy or wet soil it should be in the rock-garden, or on banks, and in sandy earth. It is sometimes grown as L. fruticosum, but the true L. fruticosum is a little bush, and not prostrate. Easily propagated by cuttings. S. Europe.

L. petræum (*Rock Gromwell*).—A neat, dressy, dwarf shrub, something like a small Lavender bush, with small grayish leaves like those of the Lavender. Late in May, or early in June, all the little gray shoots bear small oblong purplish heads, and early in July the plant is in full blossom, the full-blown flowers being a beautiful violet-blue. The best position for it is in the rock-garden somewhere near or on a

level with the eye, on a well-drained, deep, rather dry sandy soil on the sunny side. Native of dry rocky places in Dalmatia and Southern Europe. Propagated by cuttings, or seeds if they can be obtained.

L. purpureum-cœruleum, a British plant, L. Gastoni, L. canescens, L. graminifolium, L. tinctorium, and L. rosmarinifolium, are very pretty plants, but coming

Lithospermum prostratum

from sunnier lands than ours are not really at home in our climate, and for the most part they can only be grown well on dry ledges of the rock-garden in the most favourable districts.

LLOYDIA (*Mountain Spider-wort*).— L serotina is a small bulbous Liliaceous plant, suitable for the cool parts of the rock-garden, and not of the showy order of beauty. It is one of the first flowers the early visitor to the Alps sees by the pathway over the high mountains.

LOASA. — Curious prickly annuals with singular flowers and stinging foliage. L. hispida is pretty, growing about 18 in. high, with deeply-cut foliage and short stinging hairs, the flowers 1 in. across, of a bright lemon-yellow, the centre prettily marked with green and white. It blossoms several weeks in succession during August and September. The other kinds in cultivation are the beautiful L. vulcanica, with its pure white flowers and red-and-white striped centres ; L. lateritia, a twining species, with orange-red flowers ; and L. triloba. All are natives of the cool regions of Peru and Brazil, and can be grown in the open air during summer. Treated as half-hardy annuals, and grown in a light fertile soil, they are interesting for open borders ; the climbing species, such as lateritia, require branches to twine among. All may be freely raised from seed.

LOBELIA.—Distinct and much varied perennials and annuals, some of high value for the flower garden. The perennial Lobelias, of which L. splendens and L. syphilitica may be taken as types, are amongst the most useful of autumn flowers. Although fairly hardy, they are impatient of excessive moisture, and in most districts require protection during winter. This may be done by placing ashes in the shape of a cone over the crowns, or lifting and storing in a dry shed or frame. The latter method, though perhaps more troublesome, is safer, as the plants are always under control and easier propagated in spring. By storing the roots in frames they begin to grow earlier, and where large stocks are required it is most convenient. Although impatient of moisture during the resting period they revel in it when in active growth, and where beds can be prepared in the vicinity of lakes or streams, better results will be obtained than in the mixed border or flower beds. In propagating in early spring they can be divided into single crowns, and these potted on soon form sturdy plants ready to plant out on the approach of warm weather. They thrive best in a free vegetable soil and like plenty of sun, unless in the case of L. cardinalis, which I find thrives best in a partially-shaded bed. In some districts with light soils and often near the sea these plants do not require protection in winter.

L. cardinalis (*Cardinal Flower*).—The true plant is one of the rarest and one of the prettiest of the genus. The brilliant effect produced in autumn by tufts of this species well repays any trouble it may give, for though by no means fastidious, the difficulty of growing it well in small gardens in the absence of shade and moisture is great. It is a bog-loving plant, being found in wet ground in Brunswick, Florida, and the borders of Texas, and is not very hardy. It is, however, a true perennial, although maybe a short-lived one, and should be frequently raised from seed to make sure of keeping up the stock. This species is not so liable to disease as L. splendens and its varieties. Grown on an ordinary border, it invariably has a weak, stunted appearance, but in a free rich soil, in a shady position and well supplied with moisture, I have often seen it 3 to 4½ ft. high and flowering profusely. The flowers are of the most vivid scarlet, and as they last a long time in bloom it well deserves care. So far as I know, there are no varieties of this species in cultivation. Dr. Gray mentions its varying to rose colour and even white, but this, it seems, is rare. Parkinson mentions it as " cherished in

our garden in 1629," and gives it as " growing near the river of Canada where the French plantation in America is seated." It is hardier than L. fulgens, living through the winter in open beds and with little or no protection. Its leaves are shorter and greener than

The scarlet Lobelia.

those of L. fulgens ; the flowers, too, are smaller, but more numerous on the spikes, and of a vivid scarlet colour on spikes from 2 to 3 ft. in height.

L. Gerardi is a hybrid raised by Messieurs Chabanne and Goujon from that superb variety of *L. cardinalis* named Queen Victoria, the seed parent being an improved variety of *L. syphilitica*, with taller and more robust flowering stems than those of the typical species. The raisers named the hybrid in compliment to Mons. Gerard, director of the botanical collections in the park of Tête d'Or, under whose supervision the experiments and culture were carried on.

Lobelia Gerardi is a vigorous growing and very continuous flowering plant. Before the flowering stems make their appearance it forms a rosette of leaves of a very pure green colour, and resembling the rosette of the wild Chicory The running roots are abundantly furnished with fibres When fully grown the plant attains a height of 4 to 5 feet , the strongest flowering stems are as thick as one's thumb at the base, and branch with from twelve to fifteen clusters of fine broad flowers, which all bloom together, the whole forming a compact, rigid pyramid needing no stake or prop to support it All parts of the stems and leaves have lost the reddish tint of the Queen Victoria and also the somewhat glaucous hue of *L. syphilitica*, and are of a fine green colour , the calyx, however, is slightly reddish and ciliated on the margin of the sepals

L. splendens.—This species is also called L fulgens, and is a brilliant and precious plant for the flower garden Its leaves are long and narrow, and the flower-stalks taller and thicker than those of L cardinalis, the flowers larger with broad over-lapping petals The best known, and a handsome form of this, bears the name Queen Victoria Its leaves are a deep purple colour, and the flowers a brilliant crimson-red Firefly is the handsomest variety in this section, and was raised in Ireland In good rich soil it attains to a height of 5 ft , whilst in colour the flowers are intensely vivid and rich A merit of this kind is that it bears lateral flower-spikes around the central one much more freely than Queen Victoria, and these keep up a succession of bloom after the leading spike is past its best. Huntsman is another variety, brighter in colour than Firefly Sir R Napier, Rob Roy, and other varieties have been obtained from it These vary in colour and habit very much, and as they are all robust, free-flowering plants, they are valuable in the autumn garden, giving brilliant effects until cut down by frost The variety ignea has broader leaves and larger flowers

This Lobelia suffers from a kind of rust, which fastens on the main fleshy roots when the plants are at rest, and rots them This disease, working as it does at a time when growth is at a standstill, is not perceived in time to be checked, and makes its appearance towards the end of October or the beginning of November, especially if the weather be

cold and wet The plants should then be carefully taken up, reserving as much of the roots as possible, the soil being shaken off, and the roots well washed The disease will be readily discovered by its rusty-looking spots, which must be cut out with a sharp knife, as the least portion will suffice to destroy the plant. After the plants are examined they may be potted or laid in a frame in some free sandy soil, and very fine specimens may be obtained by potting and plunging in a slight bottom-heat, keeping the top quite cool In about a fortnight they will have made fresh fibre, and all danger will be past They may then be kept in a cold frame during the winter, and planted out where desired in spring The bottom-heat, however, is not indispensable , for they will succeed if carefully and sparingly watered after potting All the plants of the fulgens group show their great beauty only on peaty or deep leafy and moist soils , often on loamy soils the growth is short and weak, the flowers poor, and under such conditions they may not be worth growing

L. syphilitica.—A variable species, not very showy, hardy and robust in free moist soils, it stands our winters well, and is prolific in varieties of violet and purple, varying to rose and white L hybrida of gardens appears to be a hybrid between L splendens and L syphilitica, though this is uncertain Its fine rich violet, purple flowers mark it out for special distinction It is valuable for grouping in the flower garden or mixed border, and is one of the hardiest of the hardy Lobelias It may be left out during winter with safety, and can be lifted, divided, and replanted in spring The leaves are almost as broad as those of L cardinalis, glandular, hairy, and with the long sepals and hairs of L syphilitica

L. Tupa —This is also known as Tupa Fuelli, and although a native of Chili, will be found to stand well in the south protected with sifted ashes, gravel, or other loose material in autumn It is best, however, against a south wall or in front of a house, and when doing well often attains a height of 6 to 8 ft , the flowers large, brick-red, in large racemes, from July to September L Cavanilles is said to be amenable to the same treatment as above In deep free soils near the sea L Tupa is sometimes a very distinct and handsome plant, and is best fitted for borders among large plants or for a warm corner among shrubs

L Erinus—The dwarf section of annual Lobelia is one of the most important, being much used among half-hardy bedding plants The chief points to start with are good soil and well-grown established plants The soil should be light and rich, and rest on a dry bottom perfectly drained. On a porous bottom it may be plentifully watered during a dry time in summer without fear of injuring the roots The roots cannot make way, nor can the plants thrive in a strong adhesive soil of clay or heavy loam, and if the soil be heavy, it must be lightened by a plentiful addition of leaf-mould, sand, or peat This Lobelia thrives admirably in equal parts of some sandy loam and leaf-mould with a sand to keep it open Charcoal dust and peat form good additions to loam, as also does spent manure from Mushroom beds A slight mulching of one-year-old sifted hot-bed manure will be found useful for keeping out the drought and nourishing the roots through a dry season One of the difficulties in carrying dwarf Lobelias in full beauty through the season is the freedom with which they seed, and the moment the flowers fade they should be picked off every week throughout the season Dwarf Lobelias may be propagated by seeds or cuttings, or by lifting the plant, potting it, and placing it in a gentle bottom-heat until established ; then setting it on a light airy greenhouse or forcing-house shelf, when it may be increased by cuttings and root-division in the spring Increase by cuttings, and potting a few old plants in autumn, is the best method of preserving and increasing special varieties They strike freely in a brisk heat in a moist pit or frame in spring The cuttings should be potted by the end of May in the same way as seedlings sown in heat in September, October, or February Those who want early Lobelias from seed should sow in the autumn, and prick the seedlings off in boxes or pans, or shift them into 2½-in pots before winter, store them on shelves near the light, and well exposed to air, shift them again in March into 6-in pots of equal parts of leaf-mould and loam, and they will be perfect for planting by the end of May Spring-sown seedlings may go into smaller pots, and be planted rather more closely, but will not flower so early nor so well On the whole, autumnal propagation, by cuttings or seeds, is preferable to sowing in spring

The varieties are numerous, and it is difficult to make a selection to suit every locality L Erinus is divided into five sections—viz compacta, of which there is a white form, speciosa, of which the best are Blue Stone, Ebor, Blue Beauty, Emperor William, Blue King, Lustrous,

Brilliant, ramosoides, pumila, of which grandiflora and magnifica are fine forms, as is also the pure white Mrs Murphy ; and Paxtoniana, which is a lovely blue The double variety is also beautiful where it succeeds but it is hardly to be depended upon Sometimes it forms a sheet of bloom, and at others the shoots run up through it, as it were, and prevent it from blooming, giving it the appearance of tufts of Grass

Other dwarf Lobelias are ramosa, with large light-blue flowers, and coronopifolia, also with large blue flowers Both are half-hardy annuals, requiring the same treatment as L Erinus L ilicifolia is another dwarf trailing species, a native of the Cape, and is best suited for growing in suspended pots in greenhouses, though in some localities it succeeds as a rock-garden plant

LOISELEURIA —A wiry little shrub, *L procumbens,* growing close to the ground, the plants forming tufts with small reddish flowers in spring. Its bloom is never attractive, and the plants transferred to gardens from the mountains usually perish, because perhaps the strongest specimens are selected instead of the younger ones Its true home is the rock-garden, and it prefers deep sandy peat Heath Order. Arctic and alpine Europe and Asia and higher Scottish mountains *Syn* Azalea procumbens

LOMARIA — Ferns, for the most part tropical, and requiring artificial heat ; but in mild parts two or three thrive in the open air L alpina, a native of New Zealand, is dwarf and produces, from a creeping rhizome, abundance of dark shining green fronds, 4 to 6 in in height It is specially adapted for the rock-garden, should receive similar treatment to the Ceterach (to which it forms a charming companion), and should, like it, be associated with Sedums and alpine plants L crenulata is similar, but not quite so hardy, though it succeeds in the mildest localities, as will also the Chili L chilensis, a Tree Fern of noble growth These Ferns should be placed in the snuggest quarters of the hardy fernery, and care should be taken to protect them during severe cold

LONICERA (*Honeysuckle*) —Graceful and fragrant woody climbers and bushes precious for gardens The Twining Honeysuckles form a distinct group of species with whorled clusters of flowers terminating the young shoots. The Erect-growing or Bush Honeysuckles have the flowers axillary and generally in pairs Among the twining species there are a few that have axillary flowers, and of these *Lonicera japonica* is a typical example, while the commonest example of the Bush Honeysuckles is the Tartarian Honeysuckle.

They all flourish best in a light rich soil in a fully-exposed sunny position. It is a mistake to plant Honeysuckles at the base of shady trees and expect them to climb up and produce crops of flowers as they do when in the open. Honeysuckles naturally delight to twine upon other plants, but in shade they do not flower. One often sees a thicket overrun with common Honeysuckle, but until the trees have been cut the Honeysuckle does not flower so well. It loves to ramble over a hedge, as we see it by the wayside, and in the garden one can make various hedge combinations with it and some other hedge plants, such as Sweet Brier and Holly. To cultivate Honeysuckles to perfection, they should not be planted near any other living shrub, but should be supported by a dead tree trunk or trellis, as then the Honeysuckle gets all the food from the soil. This is why one sees plants of Honeysuckle on a wire trellis bearing much finer blooms than is the case when growing over trees or hedges. A good plan is to plant some in good soil against wooden posts at distances of 12 ft. apart, and when they have reached the top of the posts to connect them by a festooning chain from post to post, as Roses and Clematises are often done.

Some attention is required in pruning, especially the European and American deciduous species. The old stems should be cut away so as to encourage new ones, otherwise if allowed to go unpruned the plants die out. The Japanese Honeysuckles are more vigorous, and only require pruning to keep them in check. This is especially the case with *L. japonica* and its variegated form, which soon form an impenetrable mass of shoots, and that is why they should not be grown on an arbour or over a walk, as owing to the dense shade the under side becomes full of dead leaves and shoots. The Dutch and similar growing kinds are best suited for arbours.

L. Caprifolium (*The Goat's-leaf Honeysuckle*) is a common plant, but not a true native, though it occurs occasionally in a naturalised state. The flowers, borne in clusters, have long tubes, yellowish and blush tinted, and very fragrant, coming in May and June, succeeded in autumn by yellowish berries. It is a robust, twiner, and grows wild in chalky districts in

hedges and woods. There are numerous recorded names of varieties of this Honeysuckle, among them being rubella, pallida, verna, villosa, atrosanguinea, and Magnevillei. The last-named is one of the most distinct.

L. confusa of De Candolle is the beautiful Honeysuckle that is grown under the name of L. Halleana. A slender plant with long twining branches, the leaves are ovate and not pinnatifid, as in L. japonica, deep green, with not such a ruddy tinge as in L. japonica, neither is there a variegated form. The flowers are in pairs from the axils of the leaves on the tips of the young shoots, pure white when first expanded, changing to yellow, and this is the character that makes the plant so beautiful apart from its fragrance and free flowering. It flowers throughout the summer, and its lithe, slender stems will soon reach the top of a wall or tree stump.

L. flava (also named L. Fraseri in collections) is a moderate climber, with broad ovate leaves, pale green beneath, and terminal clusters of flowers, bright rich yellow fading to a deeper shade, and delightfully fragrant. It grows most luxuriantly in the more Southern States, and hence is best when planted against a sunny wall in this country.

L. flexuosa.—Out of flower this resembles L. confusa, but the leaves, though ovate and of a ruddy tinge, show no inclination to become pinnatifid or sinuated. The flowers are tubular, reddish outside, whitish inside, and fragrant. At midsummer it produces quite a mass of sweet-scented blossoms and continues for a long time in bloom.

L. grata (*The American Woodbine*).—This is a vigorous grower, having broad glaucous leaves (almost evergreen). The flowers are in clusters, whitish, with a purple tube fading to a yellowish shade, and fragrant. It flowers in May, and grows wild in rocky woodlands in the New England States.

L. japonica (*Japan Honeysuckle*).—This is as hardy as the common Honeysuckle, and retains its foliage during winter.

Lonicera japonica.

It may be distinguished from the other two Japanese species by its slender growth, deep green shining leaves, which have a marked tendency to vary from the normal ovate form to a pinnatifid or Oak-leaved form, and this tendency is most marked in the varieties named hetero-phylla and diversifolia, though at all seasons it is evident in the true plant.

Syns: Brachypoda, chinensis, aureo-reticulata, and many others.

L. Periclymenum (*Honeysuckle: Wood-bine*).—A native of the middle of Europe and northwards, and is a true native in England, where it is generally seen in hedgerows and thickets. Numerous varie-

Lonicera periclymenum (Honeysuckle).

The flowers of L. japonica are in pairs on the tips of the young shoots, tubular, slender, white tinged with red, and frag-rant, from midsummer till the beginning of autumn. Being hardy, there is no need to protect by a wall, but it is generally seen, especially the variegated form *aureo-reticulata*, as a wall-covering.

ties of this species have sprung up either wild or under cultivation. Some differ in regard to colour of flowers, others in time of flowering, and these are the most im-portant. The wild form flowers about midsummer, according to the season, but the variety *serotina* continues to flower till autumn, and is known as the Late

Dutch Honeysuckle, as its flowers are decidedly redder than those of the type. Another variety, *belgica*, is popularly known as the Dutch Honeysuckle, as distinguished from the Late Dutch, and it is a stronger growing plant than the type. Its branches are purplish and its flowers are reddish outside, yellowish within.

L. semperflorens is probably a variety of *Periclymenum*, though Koch places it as a variety of the allied species *L. etrusca.* The Oak-leaved Honeysuckle (*quercifolia*) is a variety of the common form, having leaves sinuated like those of the Oak.

L. sempervirens (*Trumpet Honeysuckle*) the most beautiful Honeysuckle that has come to us from America, both for the greenhouse and the open garden, where it flourishes well in the southern counties, and none of the Honeysuckles have such brilliant flowers. It is a robust-growing climber, quite evergreen when protected. From the beginning of summer till the end it bears loose clusters of long, tubular flowers, which are scarlet outside, yellow within. It is best against a warm wall in the cooler parts of the country. There are several named varieties of this plant but not very distinct.— W. G.

Lonicera sempervirens.

L. fragrantissima (*The Winter Honeysuckle*). — Among the earliest of all hardy shrubs whose flowers greet the new year are this species and its close ally, L. Standishi. Neither of them can be called showy, yet they are both well worth growing, because their flowers, although small, are abundant, and have besides a fine fragrance. L. fragrantissima is one of Fortune's introductions from China. It is a deciduous shrub (not evergreen, as the books so frequently have it), of low spreading growth, with short leaves, which, except when young, are nearly or quite devoid of hairs (L. Standishi, on the other hand, has hairy ciliated leaves). The flowers are in several pairs from the joints of last year's wood, and they are creamy white or pale yellow. This Honeysuckle is useful for early

forcing, a few plants in flower filling the greenhouse with their fragrance. In the open it likes a sunny, sheltered spot, not because it is tender, but because it blooms more freely, and the flowers, appearing as they do in these inclement January days, deserve all the protection that can be conveniently given them.—B.

LOPHOSPERMUM.—*L. scandens* is a tender climber with long slender stems, pale green hairy leaves, and large pink flowers. It thrives in the open air in summer, and is a beautiful plant for festooning old stumps, or for trailing over dead branches placed against a warm south wall. It may be easily raised from seed in heat in early spring or autumn and kept through the winter, but the best plan is to lift the plants in autumn and to winter them in a greenhouse.

LOTUS (*Bird's-foot Trefoil*).—Trailing or half shrubby herbs, the one best worth growing being the native L. corniculatus, which occurs in almost every meadow, or pasture, forming tufts of yellow flowers with the upper part often red on the outside. Though so common, it is worthy of a place in the garden. The double-flowered variety is the best, as the flowers continue longer in perfection. L. creticus, maroccanus, sericeus, are found in botanical gardens, but are not so pretty. L. Jacobæus, a tender species with almost black flowers, succeeds in the open air in summer, and is all the better for planting out. The Lotus is best planted so that its shoots may fall in long and dense tufts over the face of stones.

LUNARIA (*Honesty*). — When well grown this old-fashioned plant *L. biennis* is beautiful, not only on account of its fragrant purple blossoms, but from the silvery flat seed-pods that succeed them. In borders, on the margins of shrubberies, and in half-shady situations, it is effective in April and May, in any ordinary light garden soil. Honesty is charming in a semi-wild state on chalky or dry banks and in open bushy places. Seed should be sown every spring, and the plants should be thinned out during growth in order to make good ones for the next year. L. rediviva is a perennial similar to the Honesty, but with larger and more showy flowers. It is 2 or 3 ft. high, and flowers in early summer, doing best in half-shady borders of good light soil. Division or seed. Mountain woods of Europe. Cruciferæ.

LUPINUS (*Lupine*). — Beautiful annuals, biennials, and perennials, chiefly from N. America. The species in cultivation are few, though the names occurring in catalogues are numerous. The best of the perennials are—

L. arboreus (*Tree Lupine*).—A precious plant for dry soils and rough rocky banks or slopes, the scent of a single bush reminding one of a field of Beans. Its purplish variety is good, though not nearly so valuable, and there are some inferior yellowish varieties. The best variety is the yellow, because while there are good blue perennial Lupines, there is no other good yellow. It forms a roundish bush, 2 to 4 ft. high, and is easily raised

Lunaria biennis (seed vessels of Honesty).

from seed; handsome forms are increased from cuttings. It may be killed in severe winters, but is worth raising from time to time where the soil suits it.

L. polyphyllus, one of the handsomest hardy plants, 3 to 6 ft. high, with tall flower-spikes crowded with blossoms, varying from blue and purple to reddish-purple and white ; in summer thriving in open positions in any kind of garden soil. It is a fine plant for naturalising, as it holds its own against stout weeds. The principal varieties are argenteus, flexuosus, laxiflorus, Lachmanni, rivularis, and grandiflorus. N. America. Division: seeds.

L. nootkatensis is a dwarfer species, and has large spikes of blue and white blossoms. It flowers earlier than L. polyphyllus, and continues in bloom for a long time, but it is not a good perennial, and requires to be frequently raised from seeds. N. W. America.

ANNUAL LUPINES are among the most beautiful of hardy annuals, extremely varied in colour, and of the simplest culture. As they grow quickly, they need not be sown till about the middle of April. They thrive in any common soil. L. sub-carnosus is a beautiful ultramarine blue, and should always be grown. L. hybridus atrococcineus is the finest of all,

Lupinus polyphyllus

having long and graceful spikes of flowers of a bright crimson-scarlet, with white tips. Other excellent sorts are mutabilis, Cruikshanki, Menziesi, luteus, superbus, pubescens, Hartwegi, and the varieties of Dunnetti. Many other sorts are so much alike that they are not worth separating.

The smaller annual Lupines are very pretty, and could be charmingly used to precede late-blooming and taller plants.

LUZURIAGA. —*L. radicans* is a small Liliaceous evergreen from Chili almost hardy in the mildest localities, though even

Lupinus arboreus.

in these it does not hrive so well as in a cool house. It is wortny of a trial in a cool bed of peat, on the north side of the rock-garden, among the larger alpine shrubs.

LYCHNIS (*Campion*).—Plants of the Pink family, among which are a few well suited for the garden. All are perennial.

L. alpina is a diminutive form of L. Viscaria, the tufts being seldom more than a few inches high and not clammy. In cultivation it is pretty and interesting, if not brilliant, and may be grown without difficulty in the rock-garden, or in rather moist, sandy soil. A British plant.

L. chalcedonica.—An old border plant, 1½ to 4 ft. high, with large dense heads of brilliant scarlet flowers, and of easy culture in any good ordinary soil. There is a handsome double scarlet variety. The double white and single white kinds are less desirable. Division.

L. diurna.—The double deep purple-red sort of this common native plant is very desirable, being very hardy and very showy, and never failing in any soil to produce a fine crop of bloom in early summer.

There are two double red varieties of L. Flos-cuculi (Ragged Robin), pretty border plants. Division.

L. grandiflora.—A handsome plant,

typical of the numerous varieties now in cultivation under the names of Bungeana, and others which grow 1 to 2 ft. high, and bear flowers in a cluster of a dozen or so, each flower being 1 to 2 in. across, fringed at the edges, and varying from vivid scarlet to deep crimson, and from pink to white. If exposed to strong sun the colour of the flowers soon fades, but in a partially-shaded place they retain their true colour for a considerable time. They are good border flowers, thriving in warm sheltered situations in light soil, for though quite hardy they are apt to suffer from moisture and cold. They are greatly benefited by frequent transplanting, say every other year. All the varieties may be raised by seeds or from cuttings. L. fulgens, a Siberian plant, is similar to the forms of L. grandiflora.

L. Haageana is a reputed hybrid between L. fulgens and L. coronata or grandiflora. It is one of the best of this valuable group of border plants, in itself extremely variable, affording nearly every shade of colour, from the brightest scarlet to white. The flowers are large, of good substance, and produced in the greatest

Double Ragged Robin.

profusion all through the summer months ; indeed, as a permanent "bedder" we have rarely seen its equal. Where it can be managed, a partially shady spot should be chosen for the most brilliantly coloured forms, as the flowers fade somewhat when exposed to bright sunshine. Apart from this they will be found to grow more strongly, and continue longer in beauty in a cool spot. The plants vary in height considerably, and this should be taken into account when choosing for permanent bedding use. The variety called hybrida is a veritable gem, dwarf, compact, and giving an abundance of prettily fringed, vivid scarlet flowers. The colours seem fixed, and we have now good distinct scarlet, crimson, pink, salmon, and several white forms, all worthy of attention, and suitable as substitutes for Geraniums in summer bedding. They can be increased with the greatest ease either by cuttings, division, or when in quest of new forms by seed, which is best sown as soon as ripe in boxes and placed in a cold frame. The seedlings by the end of May will be ready to plant in their permanent quarters. They may almost be treated as annuals or biennials, especially in heavy soils, where the hopes of their living through severe winter in northern counties will be limited indeed. In the neighbourhood of London they give very little trouble, and are a source of much enjoyment.

L. Lagascæ.--A lovely dwarf alpine plant, with many bright rose-coloured flowers, about ¾ in. across. It is suited for adorning fissures on the exposed faces of rocks, associated with the smallest alpine plants. It is easily cultivated in the rock-garden in any free sandy or gritty soil. An exposed position should be preferred, as the plant is very free in growth. The flowers appear in early summer, and if not weakened by shade, or by being placed in frames, are in fine condition when the plant is about 3 in. high. Readily increased by seed. *Syn.,* Petrocoptis Lagascæ.

L. Viscaria (*German Catchfly*). — A British plant, with long Grass-like leaves, bearing in June many showy panicles of rosy-red flowers, on stems 10 to nearly 18 in. high. The bright-coloured variety called splendens is the most worthy of cultivation. L. V. alba, a charming white variety, is worthy of a place in gardens, as also is the double variety, which has rocket-like blooms. They are excellent for the rougher parts of the rock-garden, and as border plants on dry soils. The double variety is used with good effect as an edging plant about Paris. Easily propagated by seed or division.

LYCIUM (*Box Thorn*). — Rambling shrubs, the best-known being L. europæum, a common climber on cottage walls. Though not a showy flowering shrub, few others are so rapid in growth, so graceful, and so indifferent to the nature of the soil. It is also suited for covering porches, pergolas, and arbours, and in late summer

and autumn, when every long drooping branch is thickly hung with small orange-scarlet berries, it is pretty. The flowers are small, purple and white, and the unripe berries are of the same tints. The description of L. europæum may be taken as applying to the other kinds in gardens, as they are all much alike, though differing more or less in a botanical sense. The commonest kinds are L. chinense, from China ; L. barbarum, from North Asia ; L. afrum, from North Africa ; L. Trewianum, and L. ruthenicum. They are of rapid growth, and therefore suitable for covering high walls, though all are deciduous. Sometimes hedges are made of Box Thorns, for, as they all throw up numerous suckers, the hedge soon becomes thick. There is a species named L. chilense against

Lycium chinense.

one of the walls at Kew, which seems to be more rapid in growth than the rest.

LYCOPODIUM (*Ground Pine*). — L. dendroideum is a very distinct Club Moss, worth a place in the rock-garden, its little stems, 6 to 9 in. high, much branched, and clothed with small, bright, shining green leaves. It flourishes best in a deep bed of moist peat in a low part of the rock-garden, where its distinct habit is attractive at all seasons. Difficult to increase, it is rare in this country. N. America, in moist thin woods.

LYGODIUM(*ClimbingFern*).—L. palmatum is an elegant North American twining fern, hardy in a deep, peaty, moist soil if in a sheltered and partially shady position. The wiry stems are furnished with delicate green fronds. It may be allowed to trail on the ground, but it prefers to twine around the branches of some shrub.

LYONIA. — Plants allied to Andromeda ; indeed the species belonging to it, numbering about three, are sometimes called Andromedas. They are not important, but would add interest to a collection of peat-loving shrubs. The chief are L. ligustrina, frondosa, and rubiginosa, which have evergreen foliage and small white blossoms.

LYSIMACHIA (*Loosestrife*). — Plants of the Primrose family of much diversity of habit. The most familiar example is the common creeping Jenny (L. Nummularia), than which there is no hardy flower more suitable for any position where long-drooping, flower-laden shoots are desired, whether on points of the rock-garden, or rootwork, or in rustic vases, or on steep banks, growing in any soil ; in moist soil the shoots attain a length of nearly 3 ft., flowering throughout their extent ; it is easily increased by division, and flowers in early summer and often throughout the season. There is a yellow-leaved variety (L. N. aurea), which retains its colour well, can be readily increased, is useful for rock-gardens or borders, and merits its name. The other kinds are tall and erect. L. vulgaris, thyrsiflora, lanceolata, ciliata, verticillata, punctata, and davurica are all 2 to 3 ft. high, have spikes of yellow flowers, and, delighting in wet places, are suitable for the sides of ponds, lakes, streams, and similar spots. Indeed, they grow almost anywhere, but in a border they must have a place to themselves, as by their spreading they soon destroy weaker subjects. L. clethroides, a Japanese species, is a graceful plant, 2 to 3 ft. high, with long nodding dense spikes of white blossoms, and the leaves in autumn of brilliant hues. L. Ephemerum is a similar plant, from S. Europe, but is scarcely so fine. There are some beautiful species, such as L. atropurpurea and lupinoides, which are rare.

LYTHRUM (*Purple Loosestrife*).—The common waterside L. Salicaria is the most familiar plant of this genus, and one of the showiest. It is well worthy of culture where it is not plentiful. The beauty of the ordinary wild kind is surpassed by the varieties originated in gardens, of which superbum and roseum are the finest. The colour of these is a much clearer rose than that of the wild kind, and the spikes are larger, particularly those of superbum, which, under good cultivation, are 5 or 6 ft. high. These plants are well worth growing by lakes or in boggy ground, and are easily increased by cuttings, which soon make good flowering specimens. Isolated plants in good soil make well-shaped bushes, 3 or 4 ft. high and as much through, and look better than when planted closely in rows.

L. virgatum, alatum, Græfferi, flexuosum, and diffusum, smaller plants, and not so showy, are not without beauty.

Macleaya. See BOCCONIA.

MADARIA (*Mignonette Vine*).—*M. elegans* is a hardy Californian annual with showy yellow and brown flowers, requiring the treatment of hardy annuals.

MAGNOLIA (*Lily Tree*).—Most beautiful of flowering trees and shrubs, there are about twenty species of Magnolia known, and all but some half-dozen or so are in cultivation in this country. The headquarters of these trees are in China and Japan, a few are peculiar to the Himalayan region, and a few more to North America. A glance at the engraving, representing a very fine specimen of the Yulan, will show what glorious effects may be obtained in spring, in the South of England at any rate, by its use. It is true enough, unfortunately, that frosts sometimes injure the flowers and change their snowy whiteness into an unsightly brown. Perhaps the reason that this Magnolia and its allies are not more often met with in gardens is owing to the fact of their not transplanting readily. The best results are obtained if the plants are planted just as growth begins in spring. The fleshy roots when injured rot rapidly, and when autumn-planting has been practised, many succumb to the ordeal, those that do not do so outright often struggling on in a pitiful plight for years. A little care in transplanting in spring, in sheltering with mats from dry winds or hot sun, and in syringing the wood to prevent shrivelling, until the plants are established, would do much to prove that the Magnolias can be planted with every prospect of success. Some species occasionally ripen seed freely in this country, and it is well worth while to sow this seed at once. If dried and kept like other seeds until the following season, all chance of germination will have passed. All the species of the natural order Magnoliaceæ have seeds which retain their vitality for but a very limited period.

M. acuminata (*Cucumber Tree*) makes a noble specimen when planted singly in the park or pleasure-ground. It is deciduous, the leaves varying from 5 in. to 1 ft. in length, and glaucous green, the flowers yellow-tinged, bell-shaped, and slightly fragrant. There are fine examples of this tree at Kew, in the gardens of Syon House, and Claremont. In its native country it attains a height of from 60 to 90 ft., with a trunk from 2 to 4 ft. in diameter. The yellow Cucumber tree (M. cordata) is regarded by Professor C. S. Sargent as a variety of M. acuminata. It is a rare plant in a wild state, as it does not appear to have been collected since Michaux found it in Georgia.

M. Campbelli, one of the most gorgeous of Indian forest trees, has not fulfilled the expectations of those who took so much trouble in introducing the species to British gardens. In a wild state it attains a height of 150 ft., and the fragrant flowers, varying from deep rose to crimson, come before the leaves. Probably the finest specimen in the British Islands is the one at Lakelands, near Cork, which ten years ago was 35 ft. high. In 1884 it flowered for the first time, and it has also flowered well at Fota in the same district.

M. conspicua.—In its typical form this has snowy-white flowers, which are borne in the greatest profusion in the latter part of April and beginning of May. Splendid specimens of this beautiful Chinese and Japanese tree are to be seen at Gunnersbury House, Syon House, and Kew. M. Yulan and M. precia are names under which this is found in some books and gardens. Several hybrid forms between this species and M. obovata occur in gardens; of two of these, M. Lenné and M. Soulangeana nigra, coloured plates have been published in *The Garden.* M. Soulangeana has flowers similar in shape and size to those of typical M. conspicua, but they are deeply tinged with red; M. Soulangeana nigra has dark plum-coloured flowers. Both these bloom a week or ten days later than the type. Other seedling forms or slight varieties of the Yulan are M. Alexandrina, M. cyathiformis, M. speciosa, M. spectabilis, M. superba, M. triumphans, and M. Yulan grandis.

M. Fraseri, a native of the southern United States, is recognised by its green spathulate leaves, measuring about 8 in. to 1 ft. in length, and about 3 or 4 in. across at the widest part, the flowers, 3 or 4 in. in diameter, are creamy-white in colour, and appear later than those of any other cultivated species. In a wild state the tree attains a height of from 30 to 50 ft.

Magnolia glauca.

M. glauca, the Laurel Magnolia or Sweet Bay of the eastern United States, is a delightful sub-evergreen shrub, with leathery leaves, bluish-green above and silvery below. The flowers are globular in shape, very fragrant, opening of a rich cream colour and gradually acquiring a pale apricot tint with age. In a wild state this species occurs in swamps and attains a height of 20 ft. It is hardy and easily grown in Britain in peat soil.

M. grandiflora, the great Laurel Magnolia of the southern United States, is— in England—best treated as a wall-plant; under these conditions it thrives well and flowers freely. In order to form some idea of the beauty of this species it is necessary to see it in large symmetrical stately trees in the west of France, where climatic conditions obtain which more nearly approach those of its native habitats. A correspondent in the West

Magnolia grandiflora.

of England writes to *The Garden* as to the culture of this plant: "At one time it was thought necessary to protect the trees with mats during the winter, but this practice, which necessitated restricting the growth considerably, has largely ceased, and the trees in some instances have attained a very great height. For instance, there is one under my charge that is now fully 50 ft. high. The bole of the stem is slightly over a yard in circumference. In some seasons several scores of blooms are borne by this tree, but during the winters of 1891 and 1892 many of the more exposed points were badly injured by frosts, and the bloom lessened in quality accordingly. A very exposed position is not suitable for this heavy-foliaged tree, and shelter from cold winds is desirable. Where the evergreen Magnolia does best is in the nooks between bay windows or irregular fronts of dwelling-houses, but-

Magnolia in a Japanese garden.

U U

tresses on extra high walls also affording a good shelter. The best instance of what can be done in the way of clothing extra high yet sheltered walls with evergreen magnolias is to be seen at Canford Manor, Wimborne, Dorset, while there are also several fine specimens against high walls at Ashton Court, near Bristol. It is quite useless to plant them in a tiny hole, but the site should be well prepared by trenching or forking peat and leaf soil freely into common garden soil, or, better still, fresh loam, a space not less than 3 ft. by 30 in. being prepared for each tree. Once the trees have attained a good size, no further trouble need be taken with the roots, as they are quite capable of foraging for themselves. In planting, it is advis-

charcoal made from it is used for polishing lac. In the southern part of Yesso it is abundant in the forests, and forms fine trees 60 ft. or more in height, with a trunk diameter of 2 ft. The leaves are 1 ft. or more long, and 6 or 7 in. wide, dark green and smooth above, and clothed with white hairs beneath. The flowers are creamy-white in colour, deliciously fragrant, and when fully expanded measure 6 or 7 in. across, the brilliant scarlet filaments forming a striking contrast to the petals. There are no large specimens as yet in this country, but as the species thrives well in the north-eastern United States, it is fair to assume that it will do well in Britain.

M. Kobus, a Japanese species, grown

Magnolia stellata.

able to moisten and then slightly loosen the ball of soil, some of the roots being spread out. During the first summer the soil about the roots should be examined occasionally and watered thoroughly when dry. The tops branch naturally, and all that need be done is to spread them out thinly, and to keep the growths secured to the walls or trellis. In after years the strongest branches will require to be kept to the walls by means of strips of leather and strong nails, the side shoots being tied to these with osier twigs. They ought not to be very closely trained, or so much so as to present a painfully neat appearance, but if the branches or shoots are left too long the strong winds may break them off."

M. hypoleuca.—This is the wood commonly used by the Japanese in the manufacture of objects to be lacquered; it is preferred for sword sheaths, and the

in the United States under the name of M. Thurberi. It is hardy in the south of England, having been grown outside for several years at Kew. The leaves are 6 or 7 in. long by about half as much in width, the flowers 4 to 5 in. in diameter, creamy-white. Professor Sargent, who found the species growing in the forests of Hokkaido, in Japan, describes it as a tree 70 to 80 ft. high, with a tall straight trunk 2 ft. in diameter. He says the flowers appear before the leaves, about the middle of May.

M. macrophylla.—This, unfortunately somewhat tender in a young state, is worth growing simply for its beautiful leaves, which are green above and clothed with white hairs beneath, and attain a length of upwards of 3 ft. The open bell-shaped fragrant flowers are white with a purple blotch at the base of the inner petals, and measure 8 or 10 in. across. It is a lovely flowering tree on warm soils in the southern counties of England, as at Claremont.

M. obovata is a native of China; in Japan it only occurs in cultivation. It is a dwarf-growing bush, perfectly hardy in the South of England, and bears freely its purple sweet-scented flowers, though not in the same profusion as are those of the white-flowered M. conspicua. This species has a number of synonyms, amongst which the following are the most

Magnolias to flower, and it should be extensively grown for the beauty of its starry white flowers. A variety with blush-coloured flowers has been sent from Japan by Mr. Maries. Both are dwarf-growing deciduous shrubs.

M. tripetala, a native of the southern United States, has large slightly-scented white flowers, from 5 to 8 in. across, and obovate-lanceolate leaves, from 1 to 3 ft. in length. In a wild state the tree rarely exceeds 40 ft. in height. Philip Miller

Magnolia obovata var.

frequently met with in books and nursery catalogues : M. discolor, M. denudata, M. liliflora, M. purpurea, Talauma Sieboldi, etc. There are several varieties, but these differ so slightly from each other and from the type, that descriptions without good coloured figures would be next to useless. The best are Borreri, angusti-folia, and erubescens.

M. stellata.—An excellent coloured plate of this very beautiful Japanese shrub was published in *The Garden* in June 1878, under the name of M. Halle-ana. This species is the earliest of the

was the first to introduce this fine species to British gardens. Other names for it are M. Umbrella and M. frondosa.

M. Watsoni.—A coloured plate of this beautiful Japanese species was published in *The Garden* in December 1883, under the name of M. parviflora ; at that time it had not flowered in British gardens. It is hardy, has large creamy-white fragrant flowers with petals of great sub-stance and deep red filaments, which add materially to the beauty of the blossoms. The true M. parviflora is probably not in cultivation in Britain.—N.

U U 2

Magnolia acuminata, N. Amer.; *Bailloni*, Cambodia; *Campbelli*, Himalayas; *compressa*, Japan; *cordata* N. Amer.; *dealbata*, Mexico; *Duperreana*, Cambodia; *Figo*, China; *Fraseri*, N. Amer.; *glauca*, N. Amer.; *globosa*, Himalayas; *grandiflora*, N. Amer.; *Griffithii*, Himalayas; *hypoleuca*, Japan; *inodora*, China; *insignis*, E. Indies; *hobus*, Japan; *macrophylla*, N. Amer.; *obovata*, Japan; *parviflora*, *pterocarpa*, Himalaya Japan; *portoricensis*, Porto Rico; *parvifolia*, Japan; *pumila*, Java, China; *punduana*, Himalayas; *salicifolia*, Japan; *Schiedeana*, Mexico; *stellata*, Japan; *Umbrella*, N. Amer.; *Vrieseana*, Celebes; *Yulan*, China.

Mahonia. See BERBERIS.

MAIANTHEMUM (*Twin-leaved Lily of the Valley*).—A plant allied to the Lily of the Valley, *M. bifolium* is a native of our own country. Its habit and relationship make it interesting, and it is easily grown in shady or half-shady spots, and under or near Hollies or other bushes. It is not fitted for the border, and is more suitable for the rock-garden. *Syn.,* Convallaria bifolia.

MALCOLMIA (*Virginian Stock*). — The old M. maritima is a charming dwarf hardy annual, and grows in any soil. The varieties are—the white (alba), alba nana, a dwarfer white than the other, and Crimson King (kermesina), a dwarf deep red sort, and these are all worthy of culture. The Virginian Stock, like many other annuals, does not show its full beauty from spring-sown seedlings, and where it sows itself in the gravel it is often handsome. Being easily raised it is a good surfacing plant in the spring or early summer garden, bolder flowers standing up from its pretty sheets of bloom, and in flakes, or masses, or beds, it is pretty and effective.

MALOPE.— *M. grandiflora* is one of the most showy of hardy annuals, and effective where a bold, crimson flower is desired. It is 18 to 24 in. high, and the better the soil the finer will be its bloom. If the Malope be sown in the open, the ground should be prepared by digging and manuring, the seeds being covered to the depth of ½ in. in light rich soil, gently pressed down. There is a white variety, M. g. alba. The variety M. g. rosea, white flushed with rose, is pretty and distinct. M. trifida is smaller in every part, but showy. These bold annuals are rarely used with good effect. Like all annuals, they lend themselves to rotation in the flower garden. If from any cause the beds or borders get worn out, it is worth while to try the effect of a crop of the best annuals. The Malopes, being vigorous plants, are, as a rule, best in masses or groups. S. Europe.

Malus. See PYRUS.

MALVA (*Mallow*).—Stout and sometimes showy perennial and half-shrubby plants of which there are few pretty garden plants; the majority being coarse and weedy. One of the most beautiful is the white variety of the native Musk Mallow (M. moschata), which is charming when in flower. It is a branching bush, with stems about 2 ft. high, and many flowers 1 to 1½ in. in diameter. It is a hardy perennial, will grow in almost any soil, is useful for cutting, and is slightly Musk-scented. M. campanulata is a beautiful dwarf plant, but rare and not hardy except in very mild districts. It is dwarf and spreading, and bears numerous lilac bell-shaped flowers. M. Alcea, Moreni, and mauritanica are worth growing in a full collection, and so is the annual M. crispa, 3 to 6 ft. high—an erect pyramidal bush of broad leaves, with a crimped margin, pretty in groups, beds, or borders. By sowing in cool frames and planting it out early in May, strong plants may be obtained early in the season.

MARTYNIA.—*M. lutea* is a pretty Brazilian annual, about 1½ ft. high, with large roundish leaves and handsome yellow flowers in clusters, useful for beds, groups, and borders. It requires a light, rich, cool soil, a warm place, and frequent watering in summer. M. fragrans, another species, has sweet-scented flowers, and, under similar conditions, thrives in the open air in summer. It is best in rich borders, or among groups or beds of curious or distinct plants. M. proboscidea and others are less desirable. Seed.

MATRICARIA (*Mayweed*)—Weeds, excepting the double variety of M. inodora, which is a pretty plant with feathery foliage somewhat like Fennel, and with large white flowers, perfectly double. It is creeping, requires much space, and pegged down forms a dense mass which has a pretty effect in autumn. It is hardy, and perennial on most soils, and is easily propagated by cuttings or division in autumn or spring. *Syn.,* Chrysanthemum inodorum fl.-pl.

MATTHIOLA (*Stock*). — Annual or perennial herbs, sometimes inhabiting sea cliffs. From a few wild kinds have been obtained the numerous varieties of the garden Stocks, which have so long been among the best of our open-air flowers. The principal of these species are M. incana, M. annua, and M. sinuata. M. incana grows wild on cliffs in the Isle of Wight, and is the origin of the Biennial, or Brompton and Queen Stocks ; M. annua has yielded the Ten-week Stocks, and M. sinuata the others. These three primary divisions—the Ten-week, Intermediate, and Biennials—require each different treat-

ment, and Stocks are so easily grown, so
fragrant and handsome, that they will ever
deserve care in our gardens

TEN-WEEK STOCKS, if sown in spring,
will flower continuously during the summer and autumn   The finest strain is the
large flowering Pyramidal Ten-week,
vigorous plants, each branching freely,
bearing a huge main spike of double
flowers and numerous branching spikes
in succession   A bed of these Stocks
should be grown if cut flowers are in
request during the summer   The seed
may be sown at any time from the middle
of March onward, but it is always well to
get Stocks from seed early   The seed
can be sown thinly in pans or shallow
boxes, in a gentle heat, and, as soon as
the plants can be handled without injury,
they should be transplanted to other pans
or boxes and grown on quickly, care being
taken not to draw them so as to make
them lanky   There are various places
in most gardens where a bed or patches
of Stocks might be grown with advantage,
and, given good rich soil, they will amply
reward the grower.   The German growers
have a formidable list of kinds, many of
which are more curious than showy
There are, however, sufficient good colours
among them, such as crimson, rose, purple,
violet, and white, to yield distinct hues
There is a strain of English-selected
Stocks, known as Pyramidal, which are
of tall growth, and remarkable for their
large pyramids of flowers, and there is a
very distinct type known as Wallflower-
leaved, which was introduced many years
ago from the Grecian Archipelago, and
which has shining deep-green leaves, not
unlike a Wallflower   In all other respects
the type is like the ordinary German
Stock   One of the finest varieties of this
type, and one of the most beautiful Stocks
in cultivation, is known as Mauve Beauty.
It has huge heads of pale, lustrous, mauve-
coloured flowers   The culture for the
Ten-week Stock will answer for this   The
autumn-flowering strain is very desirable, as
the plants succeed the German varieties,
and so prolong the season

INTERMEDIATE STOCKS may be sown
either in July or August, to stand the
winter and flower early in the spring, or
in March, to flower in the following
autumn   The strain is dwarf and bushy,
and very free-blooming, and the varieties
may be said to be confined to scarlet, purple,
and white   There is a strain grown in
Scotland under the name of the East
Lothian Intermediate Stock, and much
used there for beds and borders, the
climate exactly suiting it for late summer

blooming   It is sown in the usual way
about the end of March, planted out at
the end of May when 3 or 4 in high, and
blooms finely through August and September, and even later, as the numerous
side shoots give spikes of flowers   Thus,
by using the autumn-sown Intermediate
Stocks for early blooming, the ordinary
large flowering German Ten-week Stock
for summer flowering, and the later East
Lothian Intermediate Stock for late summer, Stocks can be had in flower for eight
or nine months of the year without intermission

BIENNIAL STOCKS comprise the Brompton and the Queen, and they should be
sown in June and July to flower in the
following spring or summer   They are
closely allied, and are probably only
varieties of the same kind , but the seed
of the white Brompton is pale in colour
whilst that of the Queen is quite dark
Old growers of the Stock assert that while
the under side of the leaf of the Queen
Stock is rough and woolly, the leaf of the
Brompton Stock is smooth on both sides
Of the Queen Stock there are three colours
—purple, scarlet, and white , and of the
Brompton Stock the same, with the
addition of a selected crimson variety of
great beauty, but somewhat difficult to
perpetuate   Both types are really
biennials   The seed should be sown at
the end of July in beds, and the plants
transplanted to the open ground in the
autumn   The difficulty of wintering the
Brompton Stocks deters many from
attempting their cultivation, and many die,
even in a mild winter   A well-drained
subsoil with a porous surface soil suits
them best, and shelter from hard frost and
nipping winds is of great service   A
second transplantation of the seedlings
about December has been tried with
success

MAURANDIA.—An elegant Mexican
twining plant, *M barclayana* is often grown
in the greenhouse, but hardy enough for
the open air in summer, and admirably
suited for covering trellises   The deep
violet flowers are very showy, and there
are also white (alba), deep purple (atropurpurea), and rosy-purple (rosea) varieties
Easily raised from seed sown in early spring
in heat , they will flower in the following
summer if planted out in May in good soil
and sheltered situations

MAZUS.—*M pumilio* is a distinct New
Zealand plant, vigorous, and creeping
underground so as rapidly to form dense
tufts, rarely more than ½ in high , the
pale violet flowers are borne on very short
stems in early summer, and the leaves lie

flat on the soil. M. Pumilio thrives in pots, cold frames, or the open air, and does best in firm, open, bare spots in the rock-garden, in warm positions in free sandy soil. Though not showy, it is an interesting plant, easily increased by division. Figwort family.

MECONOPSIS (*Indian Poppy*). — Handsome Poppyworts, the most familiar of which is the common Welsh Poppy (M. cambrica); the other kinds are natives of the Himalayas, hardy, but only of biennial duration. They may be easily raised from seed sown in spring; and, indeed, a good stock of strong plants can be ensured only by annual sowings. The following is the most successful mode of cultivating them: A piece of ground is prepared by digging in good loam and well-rotted stable manure; a two-light frame is placed over it, and seedlings are put in about March. As soon as the plants are fairly established the sashes are removed (unless the weather is frosty), and throughout the summer the plants are well supplied with water. In the following April and May they will have become large plants, often 2 to 3 ft. in diameter, and are then removed to where they are wanted to flower. This may be readily done without needlessly checking them, as they form so many fibrous roots that a good ball of soil usually adheres to them. They are thus grown on as quickly as possible, being treated like biennials. They should be planted out in a well-drained rock-garden in good soil, with plenty of water in summer, but they must be kept as dry as possible in the winter, as excessive moisture in cold weather soon kills them. Sandstone broken fine should be placed under the leaves, to prevent contact with the damp soil. A piece of glass placed over the leaves in a slanting position helps to protect them from moisture. Many plants take three or four years to flower, and some may be kept in store pots for five or six years without showing any tendency to flower, but they are never so fine planted out after being cramped in this way. After flowering they all die.

M. aculeata is a singularly beautiful plant, with purple petals, like shot silk, which contrast charmingly with the numerous yellow stamens. The flowers are 2 in. across, on stems about 2 ft. high.

M. cambrica.—For the wild garden or wilderness the Welsh Poppy is one of the most charming of plants. It is a cheerful plant in all seasons, and a determined coloniser, making its home of the wall, rock, and the ruin. In many places it grows freely at the bottom of walls, or even in gravel walks if allowed a chance. A plant so easily naturalised needs no special care in the garden, where it often comes up unbidden.

M. nepalensis has flower-stems 3 to 5

Meconopsis Wallichi.

ft. high, which are not much branched, the nodding blossoms, borne freely, are 2 to 3½ in. across, and of a pale golden-yellow.

M. simplicifolia has a tuft of lance-shaped leaves, 3 to 5 in. long, slightly toothed, and covered with a short, dense, brownish pubescence. The unbranched flower-stalk is about 1 ft. high, and bears at its apex a single violet-purple blossom, 2 to 3 in. in diameter.

M. Wallichi is the finest kind, and a very handsome plant, between 4 and 5 ft. high. It forms an erect pyramid, the upper half of which is covered with pretty pale blue blossoms, drooping gracefully from slender branchlets. It is a most conspicuous plant in the rock-garden, where it withstands the winter without the least injury. Well-grown specimens have leaves 12 to 15 in. long, and a great number of pale blue flowers, opening terminally. Separate flowers do not last long, but a few expand at a time, and it is fully a month before they are all expanded at the base, by which time the seeds of those which opened first are nearly ripe.

Meconopsis species :—*Aculeata,* Himalayas ; *Cambrica,* Europe ; *heterophylla,* California ; *horridula,* Himalayas ; *nepalensis,* do.; *quintuplinervia,* Manchuria ; *racemosa,* China ; *robusta,* Himalaya ; *simplicifolia,* do. ; *Wallichii,* do.

Megasea. See SAXIFRAGA.

MELIANTHUS (*Cape Honey Flower*). —An effective half-hardy plant for the summer ; *M. major* having finely-cut, large, glaucous leaves contrasting effectively with the garden vegetation, and being of the easiest cultivation, it has become a favourite in sub-tropical gardening. Plants raised from seed early in the season make good growth by planting-out time, and by midsummer obtain a height of 3 to 4 ft. When it is desirable to have larger plants by planting-out time, it is best to sow the seeds in autumn and to keep them growing through the winter, for a stronger and earlier development will result. The Melianthus is all but hardy on a well-drained subsoil in sheltered nooks in the southern and western counties, for though the stems may be cut down by frost, the roots survive and push up in spring. S. Africa.

Melianthus major.

MELISSA (*Common Balm*). — *M. officinalis* is a well-known old garden plant, 2 to 3 ft. high, emitting a grateful odour when bruised ; the variegated form is sometimes used for edging, and the common one may be naturalised in any soil

by those who admire fragrant plants. Division. Europe.

MELITTIS (*Bastard Balm*). — *M. Melissophyllum* is a distinct plant of the Salvia Order, with one to three flowers about 1½ in. long in May. The peculiarly handsome purple lip reminds one of some Orchids. M. grandiflora is a slight variety, differing in colour from the normal form. The plant is distinct, and merits a place by shady wood and pleasure-ground walks, as it naturally inhabits woods. Woody spots near a fernery or a rock-garden suit it ; it grows readily among shrubs, and in the mixed border. It is found in a few places in England, and is widely distributed over Europe and Asia. Seed of division.

MENISPERMUM (*Canadian Moonseed*).—*M. canadense* is a hardy climber, of rapid growth, having slender, twining, large roundish leaves, in summer bearing long feathery clusters of yellowish flowers. It is useful for covering a wall quickly for summer effect or for arbours, trellises, and pergolas, and thrives in almost any soil in shade or sun.

MENTHA (*Mint*).—Marsh herbs or rock plants of which

Moonseed (Menispermum).

the variegated form of M. rotundifolia, is common, and useful for edgings or for clothing any dry spots. Another is M. gibraltarica, a variety of the native M. Pulegium, used in summer for flat geometrical beds on account of its compact growth and deep green foliage, which retains its freshness throughout the season. It is one of the easiest plants to grow, and may be increased with wonderful rapidity, as it bears rapid forcing for early spring cuttings. Inasmuch as its growth hugs the soil, and throws out roots at every joint, all that is necessary is to keep cutting off little plants and potting them, or planting them in shallow boxes, and in a very short time they will in their turn bear cutting up in like manner. Being a native of S. Europe, it is somewhat tender, and is generally killed in winter.

M. Requieni is a minute creeping plant with a strong odour of Peppermint, and trails about among the tiniest plants in the

rock-garden I use it often for covering the ground beneath Tea Roses, and it spreads and grows everywhere It is the smallest flowering plant grown in gardens

MENTZELIA. — Lovely Californian plants, mostly of biennial duration, and requiring more care than most half-hardy plants A successful cultivator of them writes to *The Garden* " I find it necessary to sow the seed as early in the season as possible, and to grow the seedlings on in a frame, giving liberal shifts, and using a compost of fibry loam and a small quantity of leaf-mould and sand After the final shift they should be plunged in a sunny border until autumn, and then removed to a frame for wintering In the spring they should again be plunged in the open air, and by occasionally assisting them with weak manure water, strong and healthy flowering specimens will be produced When beginning to show flower they should be removed to a cool greenhouse or frame, as excessive humidity at this stage is injurious to them They may indeed be grown entirely in the open air if the weather be favourable, but in our climate the former mode is by far the most satisfactory " The following is a selection of the prettiest kinds *M. (Bartonia) aurea I* — A showy golden-flowered hardy annual, 1 to 2 ft high Should be sown in April in groups or patches where it is to remain in light soil and warm situations, the plants being thinned to about 1 ft apart As the seed is very small, care should be taken not to bury it too deep When well grown it might be used as a bold group, relieved here and there by tall plants Chili M lævicaulis is a good kind, with whitish stem, 1 to 3 ft high, both stems and leaves covered with short and stout bristles, the rich yellow flowers opening only in bright sunshine M nuda is 2 to 4 ft high, with flowers resembling the last M oligosperma is a perennial, 1 to 3 ft high, with bright yellow flowers 3 in across, opening in sunshine M. ornata is a biennial, 2 to 4 in height, with creamy-white fragrant flowers 2½ to 4 in across It belongs to the vespertine section, that is, to those in which the flowers expand towards evening *Syn* Bartonia

MENYANTHES (*Buckbean*) — *M trifoliata* is a beautiful and fragrant native of Britain, found in shallow streams or pools, in very wet marshy ground, and in bogs, its strong creeping, rooting stems often floating in deeper water The flowers are borne on stout stalks, which vary in length with the depth of the water, and are beautifully fringed and suffused with pink M trifoliata is easy to establish by introducing

pieces of stems, and securing them till, by the emission of roots, they have secured themselves In some moist soils it thrives in the ordinary border

MENZIESIA. — Dwarf shrubs, resembling Heaths, and, like them, admirably suited for large rock-gardens or wherever there is a moist peat soil They are all of neat growth, and bear pretty flowers

M. cœrulea is a tiny alpine shrub, native of Scotch mountains and of northern European mountains A pretty bush for the rock-garden or for choice beds of dwarf plants, 4 to 6 in high, with pinkish-lilac flowers, flowering rather late in summer and in autumn Europe

M. empetriformis. — A dwarf Heath-like bush, seldom more than 6 in. high, with clusters of rosy-purple bells in summer Though not common in gardens, it is one of the brightest gems for the choice rock-garden, and thrives in exposed positions in moist sandy peat soil, and should be associated with the dwarfest rock plants N America. *Syn* Bryanthus

MERENDERA — *M bulbocodium* is very much like Bulbocodium vernum, but flowers in autumn, having large handsome blooms of a pale pinkish-lilac Suitable for the rock-garden and the bulb-garden till plentiful enough for borders Increased by separation of the new bulbs and by seed S Europe

MERTENSIA. — Beautiful Borageworts, formerly known as Pulmonarias. There is something about them more beautiful in form of foliage and stem, and in the graceful way in which they rise in panicles of blue, than in almost any other family There are in cultivation above half-a-dozen species, all of which are pretty plants.

M alpina is a beautiful alpine kind, and should only be associated with the choicest alpine plants. The leaves are bluish-green, the stem is only 6 to 10 in high, and has in spring or early summer one to three drooping terminal clusters of light blue flowers.

M dahurica, although very slender and liable to be broken by high winds, is hardy. It is 6 to 12 in high, has erect branching stems, and bears in June racemose panicles of handsome drooping bright azure-blue flowers It is very pretty, and suited for the rock-garden or borders, and should be planted in a sheltered nook in a mixture of peat and loam Easily propagated by division or seed *Syn*, Pulmonaria dahurica

M maritima (*Oyster Plant*) — Though one of our British sea-coast plants, I find that it is very little known among owners of choice hardy flowers. Another interesting fact, though a seaside plant and usually found growing in sea sand, it is amenable to garden culture. Given a light sandy soil of good depth, and a sunny position where its long and branching succulent flower-stems may spread themselves out, carrying a long succession of hundreds of turquoise-blue tubular flowers, it is a plant that we may expect to see appearing with renewed vigour year after year. It is a coveted morsel of slugs, and is best on an open part of the rock-garden.

M. oblongifolia is another dwarf species. The stems are 6 to 9 in. high, and they bear handsome clustered heads of brilliant blue flowers, and deep green fleshy leaves.

M. sibirica. — This species has the beauty of colour and the grace of habit of the old M. virginica, and grows and flowers for a long period in ordinary garden soil. The small bell-shaped flowers are borne in loose drooping clusters, gracefully terminating in arching stems. The colour varies from a delicate pale purple-blue to a rosy-pink in the young flowers. It is more vigorous than the Virginian Lungwort (M. virginica), an older and better-known kind. A perfectly hardy perennial propagated by division.

M. virginica (*Virginian Cowslip*).— The handsomest of all, bearing in early spring drooping clusters of lovely purple-

Mertensia virginica (Virginian Cowslip).

blue blossoms on stems 1 to 1½ ft. high, the leaves large and of bluish-grey. In many gardens it never makes the slightest progress; but a sheltered, moist, peaty nook is the best place for it. The finest specimens are grown in moist, sandy peat

or rich free soil, with shelter near. It is a charming old garden plant, and one which unfortunately has never become common.

MESEMBRYANTHEMUM(*Fig Marigold*).—Dwarf or trailing succulent plants, of which there are several grown in the open air, though none are hardy. The Common Ice Plant (M. crystallinum) is grown for garnishing in most large gardens and is also used as a pot-plant; but it is most effective when planted out in the rock-garden or on an old wall. In a sunny situation, however, it will grow in any good soil. It will grow from 3 to 4 ft. in a season, and on warm days has a refreshing look. Its flowers, unimportant compared with the stems and foliage, are bespangled with crystal. Seeds should be sown in heat in March, and the seedlings planted out 6 to 8 in. apart. There are two varieties — one red and the other white. M. cordifolium is a perennial, the variegated form of which is used in carpet-gardening. M. Pomeridianum is a strong species with broad foliage and large purple and rose flowers. It is not so common as the last, but it deserves a place on a south border. *M. tricolor* is the most showy of the annual Mesembryanthemums. It is a neat plant with cylindrical foliage, growing in neat tufts 4 to 6 in. in height; its abundant flowers, of purple rose or white, afford good contrast. It should be sown in sandy soil in the open garden about the end of April; it dislikes transplantation, and lasts longer in the ground than in a pot. Those who possess a collection of Ice Plants in pots should turn the whole out on banks or the rock-garden and leave them there, taking cuttings off them yearly. Out-of-doors they attain beauty never seen in pots. Their foliage is singular and diversified, and the brilliant lustre of their flowers — white, orange, rose, pink, crimson—is unequalled. They are children of the sun, and a rock-garden devoted to a collection in an open sunny spot is worth seeing. A soil consisting of little besides sand and gravel suits them perfectly. As the plants have been so little grown in the open we scarcely know which are hardy and which are tender, but experiments would be interesting, for some would probably prove almost hardy in the south.

MESPILUS (*Medlar*).—*M. germanica* is a beautiful small tree or bush with large and handsome flowers, and a wide-spreading head and is beautiful in early summer when studded with great white flowers among its large pale green leaves. The only other species in gardens is M. grandiflora, also called M. Smithi It is a perfect lawn tree, as its great rounded head droops gracefully. It flowers about the middle of May, and is then beautiful, with its numerous white flowers. In some nurseries (especially on the Continent) it is called Cratægus lobata and other names under Cratægus.

MEUM (*Spignel*).—*M. athamanticum* is a graceful fine-leaved perennial, dwarf in habit, 6 to 12 in. high, free in ordinary soils, and hardy. In dry seasons it might wither too soon for association with autumn-flowering plants, but it is pretty for the rock-garden, borders, or for mixed arrangements of any sort. A British mountain plant, very aromatic. Division. Parsley Order.

MICHAUXIA (*Michaux's Bellflower*). —*M. campanuloides* is a remarkable plant of the Bell-flower family, 3 to 8 ft. high, the flowers white, tinged with purple, and arranged in a pyramidal candelabra-like head. Sometimes it flowers in the third or even in the fourth year, but is usually considered a biennial, and should be

Michauxia campanuloides.

treated as a hardy one. Seedlings should be raised annually, so as to always have good flowering plants. It flourishes best in a deep loam. Its stately form and tall stature are effective in the mixed border or in a nook in a bed of evergreen shrubs. Warm sheltered borders and borders on the south side of walls suit it best. Levant.

MICROLEPIA.—*M. anthriscifolia* is an elegant Fern, 6 to 12 in. high, hardy, deciduous, charming in spring and summer, and of easy culture. It thrives in the open as well as in the shade, and may be used with good effect as an edging to a sheltered border.

MIKANIA (*German Ivy*).—*M. scandens* is a slender twining perennial, with Ivy-like foliage and small flesh-coloured flowers. It is hardy in light warm soils

and is used for covering trellises. N. America. Compositæ.

MILIUM (*Millet Grass*). — Grasses, some of them graceful. Our native M. effusum is worth cultivating for its feathery plumes. It is suitable for associating with flowers in summer, and grows in any soil, preferring moist places. There are one or two other kinds worth growing.

MILLA.—The bulbous plants formerly known under this name are now described under the name of Brodiæa. The only true Milla is said to be M. biflora, a beautiful plant with large snow-white blossoms deliciously scented. It is rather difficult to cultivate, but it is well worth any care. Even if it be quite hardy, which is doubtful, it is too choice to risk in the open border.

MIMULUS (*Monkey-flower*). — The cultivated species are valuable showy border flowers, and are for the most part natives of California. They love moisture, and are suitable for damp places, such as bogs, moist borders, and the margins of streams and artificial water. The old M. cardinalis is showy when well grown, and is deserving of a place in any garden. There are several varieties of it. The common Musk (M. moschatus) is hardy and enduring, and is worth a corner in heavy or wet soil. M. luteus and its varieties, variegatus, cupreus, Tilingi, guttatus, and others, are typical of the beautiful hybrids which are now in gardens, and which combine the dwarf habit and hardiness of M. cupreus with the large flowers, richly spotted and blotched, of the other parent, the old M. variegatus. These hybrids, which are known as M. maculosus, bear exposure to the sun better than the parents. There is also a strain with Hose-in-hose flowers, sometimes called double. These sorts should be grown, and a packet of seeds affords a wonderful variety. The seeds of the Mimulus should be merely sprinkled on the soil; if covered by it they may vegetate less quickly and abundantly. A little damp moss may, however, be laid over the surface, but should be removed as soon as the seeds have germinated.

MIRABILIS (*Marvel of Peru*).—Handsome herbaceous plants, the most familiar of which is M. Jalapa, a dense, round bush covered with flowers, nearly 3 ft. high, the flowers about 1 in. across, white, rose, lilac, yellow, crimson (of various shades), and purple—striped, mottled, and selfs. The plants may be treated as half-hardy annuals, raised from seed in a warm frame, potted on, and planted out in May. They are, however, perennial, and when the leaves are killed by frost the tapering black root must be lifted and stored in sand during the winter. The plants should be started in pots in spring and planted out as before ; but after the second year the roots become unwieldy, and should be discarded. They require a warm soil and all the sunshine of our climate. The seeds ripen rapidly and readily; each flower produces one seed only, and as the seeds are large they can be gathered from the ground beneath the plants. M. multiflora is somewhat similar to M. Jalapa, but dwarfer, and the bright crimson-purple flowers are in large clusters, expanding in bright sunshine. It is a hardy perennial in light warm soils, and is a good border plant. M. longiflora, having long tubular flowers with carmine centres, is capital for the foot of a warm south wall. Mexico.

MITCHELLA (*Deer Berry*).—*M. repens* is a neat, trailing, small evergreen herb, 2 or 3 in. high, with white flowers in summer, succeeded by small bright red berries. It thrives in shady spots on the rock-garden or the hardy fernery, in sandy peat. Division. N. America.

MITRARIA (*Mitre-flower*).-*M. coccinea* is a bright charming little shrub from Chili, hardy in mild districts, but generally requiring winter protection. It is a small evergreen shrub, bearing in summer numerous urn-shaped flowers about 1½ in. long and of a brilliant scarlet, thriving in a mixture of sandy peat and loam, in a moist sheltered spot, with perfect drainage.

MOLOPOSPERMUM.—*M. cicutarium* is a hardy umbelliferous plant, 5 ft. or more high, with large handsome leaves which form a dense irregular bush. It loves a deep moist soil, but thrives in good garden soil and is a fine plant for grouping with other hardy and fine leaved plants. Division. Carniola.

MOLUCCELLA.—*M. lævis* is a singular plant of the Dead Nettle family. It is by no means showy and its only recommendation for the garden is the singular form of its calyces, which are bell-shaped and densely arranged on erect stems about 1 ft. in height. It is a fine subject for skeletonising, and the stems, bracts, and calyces may be skeletonised intact. For this purpose they should not be cut before autumn, when the plant is fully matured. Should be treated as a half-hardy annual. Eastern Mediterranean.

MONARDA (*Bee Balm*).—Showy border flowers of the simplest culture, thriving and flowering in any position or soil ; and therefore, besides being admirably suited

for garden borders, they are excellent subjects for naturalisation in woods and shrubberies. All may be readily divided at the root. They have some variety of colour, and the varieties of M. fistulosa alone represent more than half-a-dozen different shades. The red kind scattered through American woods in autumn is very handsome. M. fistulosa (Wild Bergamot) is a robust perennial, 2 to 4 ft. high, the flowers variable ; the usual colour pale red, and every gradation almost to white may be found in it. M. didyma (Oswego Tea) is robust, about 3 ft. high, the deep red flowers, borne in head-like whorls, continuing a long time in summer. M. Kalmiana is a showy plant, taller and more robust than the

Molopospermum cicutarium.

preceding, and is often 4 ft. high, the deep crimson flowers in dense whorls. M. purpurea is somewhat similar in habit to the last, but the deep purplish-crimson flowers are smaller. All are natives of N. America, and may be increased by division in spring or by seed.

Montbretia. See TRITONIA.

MORINA (*Whorl-flower*).—*M. longifolia* is a handsome and singular perennial, with large spiny leaves, resembling those of certain Thistles, and with long spikes of whorled flowers, 2 to 3 ft. high. It grows well in ordinary well-drained soil, but prefers soil which is mellow, deep, and moist ; and it is easily multiplied by sowing the seed as soon as ripe in light sandy soil It is excellent for the mixed border, and for grouping with medium-sized perennials that have fine foliage M Wallichiana is probably the same, or a slight variety Nepaul Seed

MORISIA.—*M hypogæa* is one of the most charming re-introductions of recent years among alpine flowers. It was first introduced by a Mrs Palliser, from the Valentino Botanic Garden, Turin, from seeds presented to her by Professor Moris, who found the plant on the mountains of Sardinia, and in whose honour it is named. It was first flowered by Mrs Marryat in April, 1834, and is figured in Sweet's *British Flower Garden* second series, tab 190 The flowers, as large as a shilling and of a bright clear yellow, are on short stalks rising very little above the tufted foliage, in April and May, and the contrast between them and the dark glossy foliage is effective It seems to do best in a light rich gritty soil, and the seed should be sown directly it is ripe —D K

MORUS(*Mulberry*) — Usually medium-sized trees of the temperate and sub-tropical countries of which the best kind for our country is the Black Mulberry (*M nigra*) a distinct tree of great value and beauty giving showers of fruit in hot days, and having the charm of association with old gardens in southern and western countries where it was often grown The Mulberry often attains great age, and when old gives deep shade, thriving best always in sheltered gardens in deep soils. It is hardy, coming late in leaf and the leaves fall with the first touch of the frost It grows better in the warm southern counties than in the cooler North, where the shelter of walls is needed if we wish for the fruit The Mulberry is often a beautiful lawn tree though it may well take its place in the orchard or enclosed fruit garden, always, if possible, giving it a free, deep and rather moist soil It is one of those trees cultivated from the earliest times, much longer than we have any idea of, and therefore spread all through the East, so that there is little certainty as to its native country—probably Persia and the adjacent regions

It is not difficult to increase from cuttings or even pieces of branches, and by layers, but not by any means common to find good stocks of the trees in nurseries, owing partly to the slight demand, as in gardening waves of fashion often call attention for long periods to things of little value, and people cease to plant the good ones A very much more cultivated species in Europe and other countries is the White Mulberry (*M. alba*) and its varieties, but as our country is too cold for silk cultivation this is of slight importance with us, and the same may be said of the other species, the one exception being, perhaps, the American Red Mulberry (*M rubra*) a native of the northern United States, and this might find a place in tree collections

MUHLENBECKIA.—These graceful free-growing evergreen trailers are useful as coverings for trellis-work or rocks or stumps The kinds in cultivation are natives of New Zealand , the best known M complexa, a very rapid grower, with long wiry and entangled branches, and small leaves The white waxy flowers are rather inconspicuous M adpressa is larger and has heart-shaped leaves, and long racemes of whitish flowers M varia is a small kind, with fiddle-shaped leaves, and is very distinct from either of the above In severe winters it is advisable to give a little protection like dried Fern, but this is not necessary in ordinary seasons. Cuttings

MULGEDIUM (*Blue Thistle*). — *M. Plumieri* is a native of the Pyrenees, where it is 4 or 5 ft high, but in our borders, and in deep strong soils it is frequently as much as 8 or 9 ft high Its foliage is beautifully varied in outline, and it should be planted in the rougher parts of the wild garden, and left to itself, as nothing seems to interfere with its rapid growth As an isolated plant on Grass its remarkable foliage at once arrests observation, while its blue flowers are pretty. M alpinum is a smaller plant. Seed or division

MUSA (*Banana*) —These fine tropical plants are seen in our parks during summer, but less frequently in private gardens. In the London Parks, Musas, especially the smaller ones, are often plunged in the ground in their pots during the summer, but the larger ones are planted out When they are lifted in autumn, those in pots are stored in houses, but the larger ones are lifted with small balls of earth and placed on shelves in houses with a temperature of not less than 45°. Here they are laid on their sides, their leaves being kept close together, and remain throughout the winter, with only a mat thrown over the roots In February the roots are examined, planted in trenches, and subjected to an increased temperature, when new roots soon form and begin to grow afresh In June, after being gradually hardened, the leaves are tied up, the plants are lifted with as good balls as possible, and placed in their summer quarters. M. Ensete is the kind generally used in the open air, and in form is one of the noblest plants. Any one with a warm house may grow it, and when planted out in June, in deep, warm, rich soil, and a sheltered position, it will grow well during summer; such, at least, is our experience in London and the home counties, but such tender plants must ever have a limited use in our country. *M. Basjoo*, a graceful Japanese species that has some pretensions to hardiness, has been tried as a plant for the open, but it is not hardy enough for our

and its beauty is enhanced by its flowering when most other kinds have finished doing so. Its flower-stems are 8 in. high, and are terminated by dense racemes 3 to 4 in. long, of bright dark blue flowers, with small whitish teeth. The foliage is much the same as the ordinary M. racemosum. Another beautiful kind is M. Szovitzianum, which comes into bloom early and continues in blossom till the latest kinds have done flowering. The blooms are a clear blue, the teeth of the corolla white; the spike oval and larger than in other species.

M. botryoides is a favourite bulb, with little white teeth on blue globose clusters, about 9 in. high, and suitable for the fronts

Musa Ensete.

winters except in Cornwall, where I have seen it very fine in the open air at Caerhays.

MUSCARI (*Grape Hyacinth*).—Pretty bulbs of the Lily family, all of the easiest culture and flowering in spring and early summer. Their proper position is either the front row of the choice border or the rock-garden, but they may be advantageously grown as window-plants in pots or boxes. In all cases they thrive best in rich, deep, sandy loam, and are easily multiplied by separating the bulbs every third or fourth year. There are many names, but few really distinct kinds.

M. armeniacum is one of the best,

of borders. The varieties pallidum and album are distinct and beautiful; and pallidum has pale sky-blue clusters. M. Heldreichi resembles M. botryoides, but is larger, and has a longer spike of flowers. It also flowers later.

M. comosum monstrosum (*Feather Hyacinth*) is distinct from any of the foregoing—1 ft. or more in height; its beautiful mauve flowers, cut into clusters of wavy filaments, bear some resemblance to purple feathers. M. moschatum has clusters of dull yellow flowers, inconspicuous, but its delicious fragrance amply atones for this. Another sweet-smelling

Muscari is M. luteum, with flowers fading by degrees from a dull purplish hue to a clear yellow.

M. racemosum is a familiar old kind, with dark purple clusters and a strong smell of Plums, its long and weak leaves almost prostrate, while in M. botryoides and its varieties the leaves stand erect. It will hold its own anywhere, and will wander all over the mixed border, growing like a weed, and in any soil. It has near relatives in M. commutatum (with blue flowers, darkening by degrees into purple) and M. neglectum—also a handsome kind. There are several other varieties mentioned in catalogues, but the best are those mentioned above. Though coming chiefly from the south of Europe, they are all hardy, and grow in any position in ordinary garden soil.

MUTISIA.—Very curious and distinct half-shrubby climbers from Peru, Ecuador, and Brazil, and characterised by a climbing habit and tendril-pointed leaves. Other kinds are natives of

Mutisia.

the Chilian Andes, and have simple leaves, rigid in texture, whilst the habit is, as a rule, bushy and not climbing. Almost every one of about forty species is remarkable for the size and beauty of its flower-heads. Plants which possess such qualities as these ought, one would think, to be well represented in English gardens. They are found at elevations sufficiently high to admit of their being grown out-of-doors in England, or at any rate in the warmer parts of the country, and yet the Mutisias are scarcely known in our gardens. Some few cultivators have been successful with M. decurrens; once or twice M. ilicifolia has been grown and

flowered very well. M. Clematis is the least delicate of the garden Mutisias.

M. ilicifolia is a native of Chili, where it grows over bushes. The plant has thin wiry stems, and every part is covered with a cobweb-like tomentum. The leaves are about 2 in. long, the margins spiny-toothed, the texture leathery, and the midrib extending beyond the blade, branching and forming a strong twining tendril. The flowers are axillary, 3 in. across, with from eight to twelve ray florets coloured pale pink, or sometimes white with pink tips ; the disc is lemon-yellow. It is a distinct, interesting, and beautiful plant.

M. decurrens.—Of this, the most beautiful of the three garden Mutisias, a fine plate will be found in *The Garden* for 1883, p. 553. Mr. Coleman has grown it well amongst Rhododendrons at Eastnor Castle ; Mr. Gumbleton, Mr. Hooke, Mr. Ellacombe, and Kew have also had it in good condition. Most cultivators kill this species by planting it in a hot, sunny, dry position, where it gets baked, and soon becomes sickly-looking, even if it lives. It wants a moist, cool soil, a sunny, airy position, and a few slender Pea sticks to clamber upon. The stems when mature are wiry, the leaves strap-shaped, with the blade extending a long distance down the stem, forming very conspicuous wings. The midrib is prolonged into a stout wiry tendril, which holds on firmly to anything it once clasps. The flower-heads are terminal, $4\frac{1}{2}$ in. across, with fourteen ray-florets, each half an inch across, spreading, and then curving elegantly downwards, their colour being brilliant orange. The disc is yellow, and the large involucre is bluish green tinged with purple.

M. Clematis. — The first coloured picture of this species ever published in any English work was the plate in *The Garden*, July 27th, 1883. It is a tall herbaceous climber, 10 to 20 ft. high, with pinnate leaves, terminating in branched tendrils, the leaflets being covered on the under side with a fine silky down. The plant grows very freely, does not die off suddenly like the others, and when properly treated it flowers freely. It is probable that this species would thrive out-of-doors in Devon, South Wales, and South Ireland. It grows as fast as Cobæa scandens, and is said to be propagated in the same way, viz. by means of cuttings of the young growth. This species is a native of New Grenada, Peru, and Ecuador, at elevations of from 6,000 to 11,000 ft.—W.

MYOSOTIDIUM (*Antarctic Forget-me-Not*).–*M. nobile* is a lovely herbaceous plant about which very little is known. In its native isle it is a seaside plant, in damp sand. It is said not to be difficult to grow, but to be naturally short-lived. It has a thick root-stock, from which arise the large heart-shaped, shining green leaves, the stalks of which are grooved, and from 6 to 9 in. long ; the flowers are borne on an erect stem which springs from the apex of the prostrate stem and rises to the height of 1 or 1½ ft. ; it is leafy all the way up, and is terminated by a loose corymb of flowers in colour exactly like Forget-me-Not, but the shade of blue varies. After flowering, the plants should be kept in a cool and light position in a frame, and be liberally watered in dry weather. It is a native of the Chatham Islands, a small group in the Pacific, lying 400 miles east of New Zealand. It was flowered in several gardens of recent years—by Mr. Watson,· of St. Albans ; the late Mr. Niven, of Hull ; and very finely by Mrs. Rogers in Cornwall in the open air.

MYOSOTIS (*Forget-me-Not*).—Beautiful perennial and biennial marsh and alpine plants, children of the mountain and marsh land from many parts of Europe and our own land, and of high value and charming in all ways for gardens.

M. alpestris (*Alpine Forget-me-Not*) a compact plant, a cushion of the loveliest blue flowers, thriving on the rock-garden, in moist gritty soil. It should be surrounded by half-buried pieces of sandstone. There are various forms, some very dwarf, with white and rose flowers. Princess Maud is a robust variety with rich deep blue flowers.

M. azorica (*Azorean Forget-me-Not*) is a beautiful somewhat tender kind, with dark blue blooms, 6 to 10 in. high, and, coming from the extreme western Azores, will not survive except in warm corners of the rock-garden. It grows freely in light soil, and may be raised from seed or cuttings. The var. Impératrice Elizabeth is a form or hybrid from it.

M. dissitiflora (*Early Forget-me-Not*), a beautiful and early flowering plant, 6 to 12 in. high, with large handsome flowers deep sky-blue, continuing till midsummer. It is best in broad masses in open spots of the rock-garden, or wherever spring flowers are much valued.

M. palustris.—Although common in wet ditches and by streams and canals throughout Britain, M. palustris should be grown in the garden among shrubs in peat beds, or for edgings, or as a carpet to taller subjects, in small beds or borders in moist soil. There are forms of this, one with white flowers, another with larger flowers than the type, whilst one is called

semperflorens, from its long season of flowering.

M. lithospermifolia.—I think this has the largest flowers of any of the true Forget-me-Nots, flowering freely at a height of 8 in. ; the flowers striking for their size, the leaves distinct and small, but otherwise resembling those of our British Lithospermum purpureocœruleum. The plant is gay from its abundance of flowers and their large size.—W.

M. Rehsteineri.—Under this name I have received one of the prettiest Forget-me-Nots, an effective close-to-the-ground creeper, practically forming a dense cushion of blue for several weeks in April and May. The plant thrives and spreads like a mossy Saxifrage, but keeps flat to

Myosotis alpestris.

the ground. This will be a charming surfacing plant, through which the rarer Snowdrops and Crocuses may spear during winter and early spring.—W.

M. sylvatica (*Wood Forget-me-Not*).—A beautiful woodland plant and of great value for the garden and wild garden. It should be abundant in a wild state by wood walks, in copses, etc., and sows itself freely in half-shady places. For the garden sow seeds in beds in August every year. Britain. Seed. There is a white, a rose-coloured, and a striped variety.

MYRICA (*Sweet Gale*).—The Myricas, though not showy flowering shrubs, are desirable on account of their scented foliage. The native Sweet Gale or Dutch Myrtle (M. Gale) should be wherever sweet-smelling plants are cared for. It is a thin bush, 2 or 3 ft. high, having fragrant leaves. In a moist spot, such as a bog, it spreads by underground shoots and makes a large mass. The North American species, M. cerifera (Wax Myrtle), M. pennsylvanica, and M. californica, are less common. The last is a good evergreen of dense growth, with fragrant leaves, green through the winter. It is a vigorous plant, especially in light soils, and is hardy, but is little known outside botanical collections. The Wax Myrtle is met with in old gardens, where it was planted for its spicy foliage. I find our native Sweet Gale free and vigorous in stiff soils where few things grow well. *M. (Comptonia) asplenifolia (Sweet Fern).* —A quaint little shrub 2 to 3 ft. high, Fern-like in leaf, the leaves long and cut into rounded lobes, and aromatic. It spreads freely in sandy soils, and may be increased by layers, suckers, or seeds. A pretty plant in the sandy woods of many other parts of N. America. In gardens its place is among small shrubs and on the margins of peat beds.

MYRICARIA (*German Tamarisk*).— *M. germanica* is an elegant shrub, hardly differing from the common Tamarisk of our sea-coasts, with feathery foliage and

Myrrhis odorata (Sweet Cicely)

many long plume-like clusters of small pink flowers. It grows 6 or 8 ft. high in warm sandy soils, and, like the true Tamarisk, is a good shrub for dry banks where few shrubs would flourish.

MYRRHIS (*Sweet Cicely*).— *M. odorata* is a graceful native plant, with a peculiar but grateful odour and sweet-tasting stems, 2 to 3 ft. high, with white flowers in early summer, in compound umbels. Suitable for naturalising near wood walks and in open shrubberies in any soil, and may be used among fine-leaved perennials. Division.

MYRTUS (*Myrtle*).—In southern and coast counties the Myrtle is hardy enough to be planted as a bush, for if its shoots are killed by frosts it often recovers the following season. But the common Myrtle is most generally grown as a wall-shrub, and house walls could not have a more beautiful covering, especially if some pretty Clematis or other graceful climber be allowed to ramble amongst the Myrtle. There are many varieties of the common Myrtle, every one with sweet-smelling leaves, and all with white flowers. The chief sorts are the Dutch, Italian, Roman, Rosemary or Thyme-leaved, Nutmeg, Box-leaved, and Andalusian. Besides these there are some with variegated leaves, the leaves being striped with gold or silver, or spotted and blotched. In planting a myrtle against a wall, choice should, if possible, be given to a space protected from northerly and easterly winds, which in early spring are injurious to the leaves. In old gardens the Myrtle is often grown in tubs or pots for placing on lawns or terraces in summer, and is put under protection during winter : it is much more worthy of such protection than many of the plants to which our glasshouses are now devoted in winter.

NANDINA (*Heavenly Bamboo*).—*N. domestica* is a distinct and quaint-looking and rather graceful shrub with dark leathery leaves, becoming flushed with red towards autumn. The flowers are small and whitish, in panicles, succeeded by berries about the size of peas, of a fine red. In our climate, it does not produce these freely, and for its perfecting, no doubt, the plant wants a slightly better climate than ours, but it lives in southern and western gardens, and is best grouped with American plants on peaty or free soil.

NARCISSUS (*Daffodil*). — Beautiful bulbous flowers of mountain and alpine pastures, plains, or woods, thriving admirably in most parts of our islands ; if anywhere, better in the cooler northern parts and in Ireland, though excellent in cool soils in the south. They are to the spring what Roses, Irises, and Lilies are to summer, what Sunflowers and Chrysanthemums are to autumn, and what Hellebores and Aconite are to winter. No good garden should be without the best of the lovely varieties now known. Narcissi vary so much in form, size, colour, and in time of flowering, that a most attractive spring garden could be made with them alone; provided one had suitable soil, and a background of fresh turf, shrubs, and trees. The best of the commoner kinds should be planted by the thousand, and, indeed, in many cases this has been done with the best results. On grassy banks, on turfy bosses near the roots of lawn-trees, or in meadows near the house, their effect is delightful. All the best Narcissi, and practically all the forms of the yellow and the bicolor Daffodils, may be planted in June, July, or August, in three ways—in the lawn or meadow, in the beds and borders of the garden, or in 6 or 8 in. pots. Five bulbs should be planted in a pot, and covered over with coal-ashes or sand until January, when they may be placed in a sunny frame, pit, or greenhouse, or even in a sunshiny window, and a crop of flowers can be secured earlier than on the open ground. The main points in beginning the culture of Narcissi are to get sound and healthy bulbs as early as possible after June, and to plant or pot them at once in good fibrous, sandy, or gravelly loam, or in any virgin soil. They like fresh deep-tilled loam, and the strongest of the bicolor and star Narcissi do not object to soils rich in manure; but it is as well to remember that no manure should be used in its raw or crude state, and that wild species and wild-collected varieties suffer and often fail if planted at once in heavily manured soils.

In naturalising the Daffodil on the Grass, the Poet's Narcissus, or the Star Narcissus (N. incomparabilis in all its forms), do not begin as late as November or December by planting the sweepings out of the bulb-stores, since such bulbs are weak and flabby, and are liable to rot in the frozen ground. The time to begin planting is June and July, and it is a good rule to refuse to plant in quantity after August or September.

In grouping border Narcissi it will usually be found advisable to lift and replant the clumps every three or four years, but if any delicate varieties do not flower well, or if they show signs of weakness or of disease, they should be lifted not later than July, and, after being cleaned, at once replanted, in fresh and good soil, and, if possible, in sandy or gravelly loam

free from fresh manures. It is better to dig and replant Daffodils *too soon* than *too late.* The best time is when the leaves turn yellow in June or July. On well-drained loams resting on gravel, the bulbs lose both leaves and roots in June or July, and may be taken up and removed with advantage; and, indeed, where good round presentable sale bulbs are grown, the rule is to dig them every summer as soon as the leaves wither. Whenever an amateur's stock of bulbs is divided, it is wise to replant some in fresh ground, and any surplus may be

Narcissus Horsfieldi.

naturalised in grass. The rate of increase on good soils is surprising, such splendid sorts as N. John Horsfield, N. Empress, N. Grandee, N. Emperor, and N. Sir Watkin actually trebling themselves the second year after planting. The depth at which the bulbs should be planted varies according to the texture and the drainage of the soil. In strong or wet and retentive soils, shallow planting, say 3 to 5 in. beneath the surface, is ample, but on light, sandy, and well-drained soils, or on what are known as warm soils, the depth may vary from 6 to 12 in.—in a word, the bulbs should be as far as possible below the drought and frost line. The best grown private collections of these flowers I have seen are those at Great Warley, Essex, and at Totley Hall, near Sheffield, where the best kinds are grouped boldly by the thousand.

If cut flowers are desired, then bold

groups on borders, in beds, or on Grass sheltered by hedges or shrubs are desirable. The first crop can be obtained from pots or boxes in the greenhouse, and these will be followed by fully formed and bursting buds, in sheltered and sunny places. These buds will open large, fresh, and fair if placed in pots of water in a warm greenhouse or a sunny frame or window. In March and April comes the prolific harvest of golden openair blossoms. In cutting Daffodils or Narcissi for indoor decoration, cut the flowers when the buds are opening, or even just before, and let the stalks be long, as the flowers group better with long stalks. Do not cut the leaves of choice

Narcissus calathinus.

kinds, but use leaves of common sorts with choice flowers. Put each kind in a separate glass, but put together as many of the same kind as you like.

Such delicate southern kinds as N. Bulbocodium, N. triandrus, N. calathinus, N. juncifolius, and most of the varieties of N. Tazetta may be grown in front of sunny walls on prepared peaty or on sandy borders, or else in glasshouses in the garden; but even in such places their flowers often suffer from spring storms, and the surest plan is to adopt pot-culture in a sunny frame. N. viridiflorus, N. serotinus, N. intermedius, N. elegans, N. pachybulbus, N. Broussoneti, etc., are interesting to collectors; but the difficulties of their culture are out of all proportion to their beauty, and those who only wish for large and beautiful flowers

had better ignore them. Practically, we have only six species of Narcissus worth cultivating—N. Bulbocodium, N. pseudonarcissus, N. poeticus, N. Tazetta, N. jonquilla, and N. triandrus. Then for naturalisation, or for ordinary garden culture, these six may be reduced to three groups—N. pseudo-narcissus, or the Ajax Daffodils; N. poeticus, or the Poet's Narcissus; and the natural hybrid between these two species, the ubiquitous Star Narcissus — N. incomparabilis. These kinds are really the only free and hardy open-air Narcissi, and are the best for the meadow or the lawn.

Of the newer seedlings, perhaps the finest are N. "Ellen Willmott" and N. Madame de Graaff, which first flowered at Leyden in 1883. N. Glory of Leyden is a yellow counterpart of it. The two were offered, one bulb of each, for 7 guineas only a year or two ago. They are so vigorous, and they increase so fast in good soil, that buyers were amply repaid, high as these prices appear. N. Weardale Perfection, N. Monarch, and some others are so fine and so rare that they are practically not to be had, anything less than 10 guineas having been refused for a single bulb of N. Weardale Perfection. These are only show flowers, however, and many others not much less handsome may be had by the hundred or the thousand at a moderate price.

Narcissi flower in continuous succession from February until June; and when pot-culture and warm-house treatment is adopted, the double Roman Narcissus and the Italian paper-white Narcissus flower in November, and there are always some Narcissi in flower from that time to June.

HYBRID NARCISSI.—The species which have best lent themselves to the hybridiser's art are N. pseudo-narcissus, N. poeticus, N. montanus, N. triandrus, N. jonquilla, and N. Tazetta. The type hybrids are N. incomparabilis, Bernardi (both found wild), Nelsoni, Barrii, Burbidgei, Humei, Leedsii, Milneri, tridymus, and odorus. There are wild and garden hybrids between N. Bulbocodium and pseudo-narcissus; N. triandrus and N. pseudo-narcissus; N. jonquilla and N. pseudo-narcissus; N. juncifolius and N. pseudo-narcissus; N. Tazetta and N. pseudo-narcissus; N. Tazetta and N. poeticus; N. poeticus and N. pseudo-narcissus; and N. montanus and N. poeticus; and also N. pseudo-narcissus and N. montanus; while derivative hybrids have been obtained between some of these hybrids and some of the parent species. It is remarkable that while wild hybrids and garden seedlings usually enjoy richly manured soils, wild species, and the white varieties of the Daffodil, N. triandrus, and N. Bulbocodium usually die out on deep richly manured borders, but frequently live on poor, stony, or sandy soils, on dry grassy banks, or amongst the roots on the sunny sides of hedges, shrubs, stone walls, and trees.

N. biflorus (*Primrose Peerless*) is similar in habit to N. poeticus, but has creamy-white flowers, two on a scape, and the rim of the primrose corona is scariose but colourless (*i.e.* not purple). N. biflorus is now known to be a natural hybrid between N. poeticus and N. Tazetta, having been found wild with its parents near Montpellier by Mr. Barr; and also raised from its parents in the garden by the Rev. Mr. Engleheart. N. biflorus is naturalised in England and Ireland, but is a native of Europe. It is one of the easiest of all the kinds to naturalise, and spreads rapidly, but is usually supposed not to bear seed. N. Dr. Laumonier (Wilks) is a very fine seedling of this group.

PRINCIPAL SPECIES OF NARCISSI.

N. (Corbularia) Bulbocodium (*The Hooped Petticoat Daffodil*) represents a kind having slender rush-like leaves. In Spain it grows in wet meadows during winter and spring, but is dried up throughout summer and autumn. The types are golden-yellow in Spain and Portugal, sulphur-yellow in S. France, as at Biarritz and Bayonne, one variety in the Pyrenean district (N. Grællsii) is whitish, but in Algeria grows the exquisite snowy-white N. monophyllus. Hybrids between N. Bulbocodium, N. triandrus, and the Daffodil have been obtained in gardens, and are also found wild. The main varieties are conspicuus, a large, rich, golden-yellow kind with green rushy leaves; tenuifolius, a small golden form, having a six-lobed rim to the corona, and very long rush leaves, which lie on the ground; nivalis, abundant in Portugal and near Leon in Spain, a small golden kind with short erect leaves; præcox, a large early-blooming form, found by Mr. Barr in Spain; citrinus, a pale French form, varying much in size; Grællsii, the European white; and monophyllus, the African white. These are dainty bulbs for pots or for choice borders on warm dry soils. They can rarely be naturalised in our country.

N. cyclamineus (*Cyclamen Daffodil*). —A dainty but not showy species, easily grown in a peat-earth rock-garden or in pots of peaty compost. It seldom exists from year to year in the open air. It has

lived on Grass in peat, and, no doubt, could be naturalised easily enough on sandy peat soils which are wet in winter and spring, and dry in summer and autumn. In April, 1892, I saw a most lovely specimen low down in a damp little grassy bay beside a mill-race at Mount Usher in Wicklow. N. cyclamineus likes the side of a stream, and is found by streams in Portugal. Like N. triandrus, it is readily raised from seed, and the seedlings flower the third year. It is 6 to 8 in. high, and the scapes are about the same length, each bearing a bright golden reflexed flower. It has sap-green leaves. There are large and small forms, and a bicolor variety seems to have been known long ago. N. cyclamineus, although but

Narcissus biflorus.

lately re-discovered, was figured in French books early in the seventeenth century. Like N. Johnstoni, it came from Oporto in 1884-85.

N. incomparabilis (*Star Daffodil*).— To this group belong N. incomparabilis, Barrii, Burbidgei, odorus, Backhousei, Nelsoni, Sabinei, tridymus, and the Pyrenean wild hybrid, Bernardi, which is found wherever N. variiformis and N. poeticus occur together. Of N. incomparabilis there are over a hundred named kinds, the best being: Sir Watkin or Welsh Peerless, Gloria Mundi, Queen Sophia, C. J. Backhouse, Princess Mary, Gwyther, splendens, Beauty, Autocrat, Frank Miles, Cynosure, James Bateman, King of the Netherlands, Commander, Figaro, Goliath, Mabel Cowan, Mary Anderson (delicate, but of a splendid colour), Fair Helen, Lulworth, St. Patrick, and Queen Bess. Mr. Engleheart has a large series of shapely seedlings with richly coloured crowns, such as ' Southern Star,' Lettice Harmer, Red Prince, Beacon, and White Queen. There are three or four handsome double forms of N. incomparabilis, long known in gardens. The most abundant of these is incomparabilis fl.-pl. (Butter and Eggs). There is a white variety, with vermilion chalice

good, and are useful for extended culture on Grass or for cut flowers.

The Burbidge hybrids are like the Barrii forms, but have small crowns. Their chief value lies in the freedom and earliness of their bloom, as they open days before even ornatus—the early April form of N. poeticus. The best varieties are Burbidgei (type), Agnes Barr, Beatrice Heseltine, Baroness Heath, Constance, Crown Princess, Ellen Barr, John Bain, Little Dirk, Model, Mrs. Krelage, and Mary.

Narcissus Sir Watkin.

segments, known as Eggs and Bacon or Orange Phœnix ; and a pale sulphur double called Sulphur Kroon, which is exquisite if well grown. Sulphur Kroon is often known as Codlins and Cream.

Of Barr's Peerless (N. Barrii, hybrids), the best are Conspicuus and Sensation, but Golden Star, Crown Prince, Flora Wilson, Miriam, Barton, Orphée, General Murray, Albatros, Sea Gull, Maurice Vilmorin, and Dorothy E. Wemyss are all

Of Leeds' silver star forms the best are exquisite on good sandy soils, and their whiteness and delicate purity and grace render them most acceptable as cut flowers. The best are : N. Leedsii (type), amabilis, Beatrice, Hon. Mrs. Barton, Katherine Spurrell, Duchess of Westminster, Madge Matthew, elegans, Minnie Hume, superbus, Princess of Wales, Magdalina de Graaff, Gem, Grand Duchess, Acis, and Palmerston. Hume's hybrids are deformed Daffodils, the best being Giant and concolor Sabine's hybrid (N Sabinei) is a bold white bicolor, with a shortened trumpet, and so are the so-called Backhouse hybrids— Wolley Dod and William Wilks, a shapely and effective flower of good substance and with vigorous leaves.

More starry, but with smaller cups, are Nelson's hybrids ; tall, free, and distinct habit ; the best, Nelsoni major, minor, pulchellus (perfect shape), Mrs C J Backhouse, aurantius (orange-red cup), and William Backhouse Collected bulbs of N Bernardi are very variable in size and form, and some, like E Buxton, have fine orange-red cups, which resemble Nelson's aurantius N. tridymus is a variable hybrid between the Daffodil and N Tazetta with two to three flowers on a scape

N. jonquilla (*Jonquil*) —Long known in gardens, and imported from Italy and Holland for forcing in pots. Much grown at Grasse, Cannes, etc , for its perfume N stellaris has narrow perianth lobes, and N. jonquilloides is a robust form from Spain. The varieties gracilis and tenuior are now supposed to be hybrids between the Jonquil and some other species, or between N intermedius and juncifolius, N. intermedius itself being a hybrid between some form of N. Tazetta and the Jonquil The Jonquil, when strongly grown on a warm border, is handsome and very sweet, and N. gracilis is the latest of all single Narcissi, as it blooms with N. poeticus fl -pl in May or early June The double Jonquil is rarely seen doing well in open ground, but as a pot plant it is handsome S France and Spain

N. juncifolius (*Rush Jonquil*) — A small plant, suitable only for sheltered borders, for stone edgings, and for pot-culture in a cold frame It is very variable, and rupicola, minutiflorus, and scaberulus are well-known variations Its small Jonquil-scented flowers have very large cups, often widely expanded, which are crenulate at their edges The var rupicola flowers and seeds annually in the rock-garden at Edinburgh Botanical Gardens, and seems hardier than the type

N. odorus (*Great Jonquil*) — This plant, although found wild in S France, Portugal, and N Spain, is now believed to be a hybrid = N. jonquilla × N pseudo-narcissus The leaves are rushy, and two or three yellow starry flowers are borne on each scape The best kinds are N odorus (Campernelle), and rugulosus, a more robust form, with larger flowers A double form, very handsome on warm soils, is known as Queen Anne's Jonquil

N. poeticus (*Poet's* or *Pheasant's-eye Narcissus*) —One of the oldest, sweetest, and most popular of garden flowers, and erroneously supposed to be the Narcissus of the Greek poets It is widely distributed in France and Germany, and extends to the Pyrenees In upland meadows of the Pyrenees it is very abundant in June and July It flowers from the beginning of April until June The older forms of N poeticus are now far surpassed by Mr. Engleheart's new seedlings, such as Dante, Petrarch, and many others. N ornatus is now grown by the million for Easter decoration. N. grandiflorus is a very large floppy variety, N poetarum has a saffron-red crown, and N tripodalis has reflexed segments and a bold crimson-scarlet ring The typical N poeticus is a tall plant, with a small shapely flower, but is not often seen N Marvel has a bladder-like spathe like an Allium, and a pale and shapely flower N patellaris has a broad crown and a saffron rim, and blooms late ; but the form usually met with early in May is N recurvus, the Pheasant's-eye of cottage-gardens N recurvus has a green eye and a crimson-fringed crown. All the forms, especially ornatus and recurvus, naturalise perfectly, and of recent years bulbs have been dug on the Pyrenees by the thousand for naturalisation They are so variable in habit, size, shape, and colour that any number of varieties could be selected from them The June-flowering double form of N patellaris, or Gardenia Narcissus, is very fine. It does well on deep sandy borders It is a shy flowerer, and many of its buds go blind, so that half the stock should be transplanted every year in August N stellaris, the latest single form of N poeticus, flowers in June Some very fine and shapely seedlings of N. poeticus have been raised by Mr Engleheart

N. pseudo-narcissus (*Common Daffodil*) —There are several hundred varieties of the Common Daffodil, either wild or cultivated The only native of Britain is the common English kind, which extends from Cornwall to Fife, and is specially plentiful in the south-eastern counties. In Normandy, Daffodils by millions light up the woods in April, while many fine forms are wild in Spain and in the Pyrenean region, and the richest of golden Daffodils come from Spain and Portugal The Rev. C Wolley Dod found N maximus growing between Dax and Bayonne, probably naturalised Nearly all Daffodils do well on Grass, if the soil be at all suitable ; and as regards our wild English Daffodil,

Narcissus Emperor.

the Grass is the only place in which to grow it permanently. Daffodils are usually divided into three groups : first, golden Daffodils, such as N. maximus, Tenby, and spurius ; secondly, bicolors, such as John Horsfield, Empress, Grandee, &c.; thirdly, sulphur and white kinds, such as Exquisite, and the white Daffodils, such as the wild Pyrenean and N. moschatus. Nearly all the golden kinds are robust and easily grown, and the bicolor group are even more so, but, speaking broadly, the delicate sulphur and the white sorts are tender and unsatisfactory, except on the most favourable soils. The following are the best in each group :—

Golden Daffodil Group—Abscissus (muticus), Ard Righ, Emperor, Countess of Annesley, Bastemil, Captain Nelson, spurius, coronatus (General Gordon), Golden Spur, Distinction, obvallaris, Henry Irving, Glory of Leyden, Golden Prince, Golden Plover, Golden Vase, Her Majesty, John Nelson, spurius, major, maximus, M. J. Berkeley, and Mrs. Elwes. Nanus and minor are dwarf varieties, minimus is the smallest of all the Daffodils. Shakespeare, Hodsock's Pride, Fred. Moore, Wide Awake, Marchioness of Headfort, P. R. Barr, rugilobus, Santa Maria, Samson, Sir W. Harcourt, Townshend, Boscawen, Stanfield, Croom a Boo (Ard Righ with a frilled trumpet), Weardale Perfection, "Ellen Willmott," Monarch, and many others are not as yet much grown.

Bicolor Group—Empress, John Horsfield, Grandee, Dean Herbert, Michael Foster, Alfred Parsons, George C. Barr, Harrison Weir, J. B. M. Camm, John Parkinson, Mrs. Walter Ware, Mad. Plemp, T. A. Dorien Smith, and variiformis. Carrie Plemp, Princess Colibri, Duchess of Teck, and Victoria are new kinds.

White and Sulphur-flowered Group—Moschatus, albicans (Leda), cernuus (very variable), Cecilia de Graaff, Colleen Bawn, cernuus pulcher, C. W. Cowan, Dr. Hogg, Exquisite, J. G. Baker (volutus), F. W. Burbidge, Lady Grosvenor, Galatea, Mme. de Graaff, Mrs. F. W. Burbidge, Mrs. J. B. M. Camm, Mrs. Thompson, Helen Falkiner, pallidus præcox (the variable sulphur Daffodil of Biarritz and Bayonne), pallidus asturicus, Princess Ida, Sarnian Belle, tortuosus, Wm. Goldring, W. P. Milner, Minnie Warren, Countess of Desmond, Robert Boyle, Silver Bar, Mrs. Vincent.

The best of the double Daffodils are— Telamonius plenus (Van Sion), very free and robust, naturalised everywhere ; double English, minor plenus (Rip van Winkle) ; lobularis plenus ; Scoticus

plenus ; plenissimus (Parkinson's great rose double) ; capax plenus (Eystettensis), an exquisitely pretty and pale six-rowed double, but requiring a warm sandy soil, and remarkable as being a distinct double, of which the single type is unknown ; Cernuus, C. bicinctus ; the last do well in warm, stony soils, and, like other delicate kinds, enjoy the company of tree, shrub, or Rose roots.

Johnstoni (Johnston's hybrid Daffodil) was found by Mr. A. W. Tait near Oporto in 1885, and figured in *Bot. Mag.*, 7012 ; it is a natural hybrid, between N. pseudo-narcissus and N. triandrus, and is variable, Mr. Tait having in March 1892, sent me a bicolor form (Garrett × N. triandrus albus). The best forms are N. Johnstoni (type), Queen of Spain, Mrs. Geo. Cammell, Pelayo, and Mr. Tait's new bicolor form to which I have above

Hybrid Narcissus Snowdrop.

alluded. The Rev. G. H. Engleheart has repeated crosses between the parent species, and has produced a pale sulphur or white Johnstoni (Snowdrop) and others.

N. Tazetta (*Polyanthus* or *Bunch Narcissus*).—This is the classical Narcissus of Homer and other poets, Greek and Roman—the flower of a hundred heads that delights all men, and lends a glory to the sea and the sky. Tazetta is focused in the Mediterranean Basin, but extends from the Canary Islands to the north of India and to Japan. It has long been naturalised in the Scilly Isles and in Cornwall ; but its early habit of growth, acquired in more sunny climes, often with us causes the flowers to be injured by frosts and storms. These Narcissi are hardy on warm dry soils, and as pot-plants many of them are handsome, while in deep, warm, sandy borders, which are sheltered by sunny walls or by plant-houses, they frequently do well, but as a rule bulbs must be imported from France, Italy, or Holland every year. The earliest are the double Roman and the paper-white (N. papyraceus) One variety from China may be grown in a sunny window if placed in water, and the bulbs submerged and held in position by gravel or stones The growth of this variety is rapid, and good bulbs produce five to eight spikes Its shop name is "Sacred Narcissus" or Chinese "Joss Lily"

The best varieties are Grand Monarque, States-General, Newton, Scilly White (White Pearl), Soleil d Or, Bathurst, Baselman major (Trewianus), Gloriosus, Sulphurine, Czar de Muscovie, Grand Sultana, Grand Primo Citroniere, Luna, Her Majesty, Queen of the Netherlands, Lord Canning, and Golden Era

N Baselman minor is now proved by Mr Englcheart and others to be a hybrid between N Tazetta and N poeticus, and a similar hybrid has been found wild near Montpellier

N. triandrus (*Ganymede's Cup*) — A distinct and elegant species which is rarely happy out-of-doors except on warm, moist, and sheltered borders, or in nooks of the rock-garden, but which as a pot-bulb has no superior for delicate beauty, its flowers rivalling in texture those of the Cape Freezias The late Mr. Rawson, of Fallbarrow, Windermere, grew it in pots, and his specimens bore fifty to a hundred flowers His plan was to rest it thoroughly after the leaves faded, and then to top-dress the bulbs, and rarely or never to re-pot them As a rule N triandrus is short-lived, but it naturally reproduces itself from seeds, which bloom the second or third year after sowing The principal varieties are N albus (Angel's Tears), N. calathinus (a robust form from the Isle de Glennans), and L'Ile St Nicholas On the coast of Brittany N. calathinus grows among rocks and short sandy sward close to the sea, and within reach of its spray during rough weather N pulchellus has a primrose perianth and a white cup, and is very pretty In the late Mr R Parker's nursery at Lower Tooting, in 1874, it was very strong and healthy in an open-air bed resting on the gravel, and some of its scapes bore seven or nine flowers. No other Narcissus has a cup paler than the perianth segments Pulchellus has recently been found wild in Portugal and Spain

NEW HYBRID AND CROSS-BRED NARCISSI —Every year at the Drill Hall and elsewhere we see new and improved seedlings by the score, and any one may raise seedlings for themselves if they will take

the trouble to cross-fertilise the flowers either as grown in pots in cool greenhouse or cold frame, or in open-air borders In some gardens, as at Chirnside and Kilmacurragh, series of natural cross-bred kinds have appeared spontaneously, and this is doubtless how White Minor, St. Austin, Countess of Desmond, and many other Irish forms appeared.

DISEASES AND INSECTS —As Narcissi may be grown on dry warm soils, or in grassy lawns and meadows, the insects and fungoid diseases that would affect them on deep-dug and highly manured borders are few and far between Neither cattle nor sheep molest them, and game and poultry, and even the most voracious of rabbits and the most impudent of town-sparrows leave the flowers alone. That their leaves and roots are poisonous, or acridly narcotic, may account for this In some gardens and nurseries the larva of the Narcissus Fly (Merodon equestris) infests old bulbs, and whenever bulbs are imported from abroad or are dug for replanting, this larva should be searched for and exterminated The bulbs affected may generally be known by their necks feeling soft when pinched All such bulbs should be cut open and the larvæ extracted and killed Such means are the only cure, as no insecticides will kill the pest without destroying the bulbs The pest checks both root and bulb growth, but after the larvæ are removed the rare bulbs recently infected may be planted for stock, for although the heart be eaten away, the lateral buds at the base of the bulb-scales often produce young bulbs

N. poeticus and its varieties have rarely been infected by a leaf fungus (Puccinia Schrœteri), and so far its ravages have been limited

Bulbs of Narcissus are now and then found to be afflicted with black canker or "black-rot," probably caused by Peziza cibovioides, but so far little serious injury has been done The most insidious disease that affects Narcissi is one to which Mr. C W. Dod some few years ago originally drew attention, under the name of "basal rot" The stunted flowers come up prematurely, while the leaves have a diseased appearance, and are much dwarfed and contorted The base of the bulb rots away, while no roots are formed from the disc, and the wet and flabby bulb-coats are more or less discoloured, as if parboiled This disease is most prevalent among white Daffodils, white single and double , but yellow kinds such as Ard Righ and maximus are affected on wet and cold soils, and even

N. Tazetta, N. Leedsii, and N. jonquilla are also affected. In many cases this disease is checked by annual digging and re-planting in July or August, and sometimes bulbs, affected on deep rich borders, have recovered on being transplanted to Grass or beds of Moss and Briar Roses Cold and wet, or even richly manured soils, seem especially conducive to this disease, and the only remedy is to alter the conditions of growth as soon as the leaves have died away A celebrated northern grower of Narcissi tells me that some sorts that formerly failed on level borders do well on the drier and warmer grassy banks to which he transferred them Facility in altering conditions of growth is often the best way to save plants that show signs of disease or failing in any way It is a great consolation to know that many of the best and most showy kinds, if broadly and naturally grown on the Grass of meadow or of outlying lawn, are rarely, if ever, afflicted seriously with the above pests — F W B

NEILLIA (*Nine Bark*) —*N opulifolia* is a hardy shrub generally known as Spiræa opulifolia It is usually 3 to 5 ft in height, but in good soils and in sheltered places it makes a bush 8 or 10 ft. high, and as much through It blooms about midsummer, the small white flowers being borne in dense feathery clusters. A more important shrub for ornamental planting is the variety aurea, with golden leaves The yellow tinge of the foliage is extremely bright, and, at a distance, looks like a glowing mass of yellow bloom This variety is a hardy and vigorous shrub suitable for planting anywhere

NELUMBIUM (*Yellow Sacred Bean*) —*N luteum* is the hardiest known Sacred Bean, and therefore the one most interesting for northern gardens. Its large blossoms are a pale yellow, and its large round leaves arise boldly out of the water 3 to 4 ft I have seen it flower strongly in the Garden of Plants at Paris it remained out all the winter in a fountain basin in a sheltered and warm nook in the open air It would probably flower out-of-doors in a sunny and sheltered spot in the south of England It is rare, but may be procured from some nurseries, or from America. The beautiful N speciosum is another noble aquatic, and is well worth a trial wherever there is a contrivance for heating the water of a small pond or tank in the open air

NEMESIA.—Pretty hardy annuals of the simplest culture, N floribunda growing about 1 ft high, and bearing in summer fragrant Linaria-like blossoms, white with yellow throats N versicolor has blue, lilac, or yellow and white blossoms, and its variety compacta, blue and white flowers If sown in ordinary soil in masses in early spring and then well thinned, the plants will have a pretty effect for several weeks after June In N strumosa the flowers display a variety of colours, white, pale yellow, and shades between pink to deep crimson It grows 12 to 15 in high, and has five or six stems, each of which bears a head of flowers, blooming from summer until late in autumn Sow in heat in March, and transplant the seedlings in May, or sow in the open ground after the middle of May S Africa

NEMOPHILA (*Californian Bluebell*) —Pretty Californian hardy annuals of much value for our gardens The species from which the cultivated varieties have been derived are N insignis, N atomaria, N. discoidalis, and N. maculata N insignis has sky-blue flowers, and its varieties are grandiflora, alba, purpurea - rubra, and striata N atomaria has white flowers speckled with blue Its varieties are cœlestis (sky-blue margin), oculata (pale blue and black centre), and alba nigra (white and black centre) N discoidalis has dark purple flowers edged with white, and the flowers of its variety elegans are maroon margined with white N maculata has large white flowers blotched with violet and its variety purpurea is of a mauve colour These kinds are all worth growing. They thrive in any soil, and are of the simplest culture In spring some pretty combinations may be effected by arranging the masses in harmonising colours All Nemophilas are well suited for edgings and for filling small beds, as they are compact in growth The insignis section should always be preferred to the others Seeds should be sown early in August for spring - flowering, and in April for summer - blooming To secure a good display of flower, however, the best time to sow is in August, and the soil should be a light one, where the seed can germinate freely, and where the plants will not become too robust before winter sets in If the seed be sown where the plants are to flower, the results will be most satisfactory ; but if transplanting be necessary, it should be done early in the winter. A ball of earth should be attached to each plant, and to secure this thin sowing is indispensable These plants often grow better and give prettier effects in the cooler northern parts of the country and in Scotland. Hydro-phyllaceæ.

NEPETA (*Cat Mint*).—Herbaceous perennials, of which N. macrantha has rather showy purple flowers, but is too tall and coarse for the border. N. Mussini is an old plant, flourishing in ordinary garden soil, and was once used for edgings to borders, a purpose for which its compact growth suits it well ; but none of these plants are among the best for choice borders.

NEPHRODIUM. — North American ferns, some hardy, and very handsome, and these thrive under the same conditions as our native ferns. The chief sorts are N. Goldieanum, N. intermedium, N. mar-ginale, and N. noveberacense. Several Japanese and Chinese species thrive without protection in mild localities, but they cannot be recommended for general culture. N. fragrans is a sweet-scented little form. It is somewhat delicate, but thrives in a sheltered situation.

NERTERA (*Fruiting Duckweed*).—*N. depressa* is a pretty creeping and minute plant, thickly studded with tiny reddish-orange berries, and with minute round leaves which are suggestive of the Duck-weed of our stagnant pools. It forms densely matted tufts in the open air, best perhaps on level spots in the rock-garden. It is also often grown in pans, and out-of-doors in some places may require pro-tection in winter. N. depressa may be propagated by dividing old plants into small portions and placing them in small pots in a gentle heat until they start into growth, and then removing them to a cooler atmosphere. Rubiaceæ. New Zealand.

NICANDRA. — *N. physaloides* is a pretty Peruvian half-hardy annual, about 2 ft. high, of stout growth, bearing in summer numerous showy blue and white bell-like flowers, and thriving in an open position in light soil. Seed should be sown in heat in early spring or in the open air about the end of March, and the seedlings should be transplanted in May. One plant is sufficient for a square yard. Solanaceæ.

NICOTIANA (*Tobacco*).—Stout half-hardy annuals of rapid growth, and good subjects for grouping with other stately plants. The varieties differ chiefly in the stoutness and the height of their stems, and in size of their leaves and flowers, these dif-ferences depending largely on cultivation. The best growth is got in rich ground and sheltered positions. Seed must be sown in February in a warm house or frame. Prick off the plants as soon as

they appear, and pot them in a genial heat of, say, 60°. Then about the end of May fine plants will be ready for putting out from 6 or 8 in. pots. They will start off at once, and not cease growing until frost comes. The most useful of all is N. affinis, used largely in gardens large and small, in distinct groups or with other things. Some of the best effects are got from this kind in association with Heliotropes and tall plants. It is much smaller in leafage and habit than such kinds as N. macrophylla, and there-fore more suitable for small gardens.

N. colossea is a large-leaved kind which has been grown in recent years, but it is eclipsed by its variegated form which is one of the most graceful plants for beds or borders.

N. wigandioides is well adapted for subtropical bedding in positions where it will be surrounded by dwarfer plants.

NIEREMBERGIA.—The only quite hardy Nierembergia is N. rivularis (White Cup), one of the handsomest of all. The stems and foliage trail along the ground like those of the New Holland Violet, while barely pushed above the foliage are open

Nierembergia rivularis.

cup-like creamy-white flowers, usually nearly 2 in. across. They continue during the summer and autumn, and have a pleasing effect in the distance, as they suggest Snowdrops at first, and are quite as pretty when closely viewed. To ensure success with Nierembergias have heavy, firm soil, a level surface, and sunny aspect. The tender Nierembergias are N. frutes-cens, a sub-shrubby plant of erect growth, and N. filicaulis, or gracilis as it is called, which has slender drooping branches. Both have pretty white flowers pencilled with purple, and are suitable for the rock-garden in summer or for drooping over the edges of vases. Propagate by cuttings in spring in heat.

NIGELLA (*Fennel Flower*).—Hardy annuals of the Crowfoot family, all curious and pretty with feathery Fennel-like foliage and bluish or yellowish blossoms. N. sativa, N. orientalis, N. damascena (Devil in a Bush), and N.

Nigella damascena.

hispanica are the kinds cultivated, N. hispanica being the prettiest, growing about 1 ft. high, and with showy blue flowers from July onwards. There is a white variety and a variety with deep purple blossoms. All the Nigellas should be sown in March, in light warm soil in the open border. They should be sown in the place which they are to occupy, as they do not succeed so well if transplanted. If sown in autumn, the seedlings often survive the winter and flower early and well.

NOLANA (*Chilian Bellflower*).—Pretty hardy annuals from S. America—N. para-doxa, N. prostrata, and N. atriplicifolia among the best. They have slender trailing stems, and flowers generally blue. N. atriplicifolia has beautiful and very showy blue flowers with a white centre,

and there is a white variety (N. a. alba). The Nolanas are suitable for borders or for the rock-garden, as they thrive in any warm open situation in good light soil. As seedlings do not transplant well, seed should be sown in the open in March, and the plants well thinned out. Nolanaceæ.

NOTOSPARTIUM (*Pink Broom of New Zealand*).—N. *Carmichaelliæ* is much like some of the Brooms, hence its name, the leafless, graceful shoots studded late in June with small bright rosy flowers in clusters towards the point. Its grace-

Notospartium Carmichaeliæ.

ful growth is well seen in the bolder arrangement of the rock-garden. In New Zealand it grows 20 ft. in height, and seems to be fairly hardy here, though not a shrub for cold climates or exposed places.

NUPHAR (*Yellow Water-Lily*).—Bold water plants nearly allied to the Water Lily, but not so handsome except in the foliage. The most familiar Nuphar is the common Yellow Water-Lily (N. lutea), which inhabits many of our lakes and slow-running rivers, in company with the Water-Lily It has a very interesting little variety called pumila or minima, which is found wild in some of the Highland lakes, and which has the same vinous perfume as the type. N advena is the N American ally of our yellow Water-Lily, and resembling it, but larger and with leaves which stand erect out of the water, and is a much finer plant N Kalmiana, also a N American kind, much resembles the small variety of N lutea, and is an interesting plant to grow in company with it The cultivation is quite simple—placing the rootstocks in water 2 to 3 ft deep, when they will soon root in the mud

NUTTALLIA (*Osoberry*).—*N cerasiformis* is a hardy shrub, and one of the earliest to flower. Hardly before winter is past its abundant drooping racemes of white flowers appear, and they usually do so before the leaves When in bloom it bears a resemblance to the Flowering Currant (Ribes sanguineum), and forms a dense bush, 6 to 12 ft high, growing in any kind of soil, is hardy, but not showy, and scarcely pretty. California

NYCTERINIA.—Pretty half-hardy annuals from the Cape of Good Hope N selaginoides grows about 9 in high, forming dense compact tufts of slender stems, in late autumn, covered with small white, orange-centred blossoms fragrant at night. N capensis is about the same size as N. selaginoides, and is of similar growth, its flowers larger, and not of so pure a white N selaginoides and N. capensis require to be sown early in heat, and to be transplanted in May in light, rich sandy loam in warm borders N. Lychnidea is a small shrubby perennial with yellowish-white blossoms, thriving in warm borders in summer. It should be propagated either by cuttings in autumn, or by seeds in spring. Scrophulariaceæ

NYMPHÆA (*Water-Lily*).—A beautiful family of water-plants distributed over many parts of the world, some of the northern kinds hardy Our own native Water-Lily was always neglected and rarely effective, except in a wild state, but when it is seen that we may have in Britain the soft and beautiful yellows and the delicate rose and red flowers of the tropical Water-Lilies throughout summer and autumn, we will begin to take more interest in our garden water-flowers, and even the wretched formless duckponds which disfigure so many country seats may have a reason to be The new hybrid kinds continue blooming long after our native kind has ceased, and from the

middle of May to nearly the end of October flowers are abundant

CULTURE OF HARDY WATER-LILIES — These lovely water flowers are not difficult to manage A simple way of planting is to put the plants with soil in some shallow baskets and sink these to the bottom, and before the basket has rotted the plant will have fixed itself to the bottom Or in ponds where there is a rich muddy bottom I plant by tying a drain-pipe or a piece of waste iron to a root and throw it in where the water is between 18 in to 2 ft deep The best season for planting is the spring, and plants put in in April or May make sufficient progress to flower before summer is gone They are often grown in brick and cement tanks, sunk in the ground to a depth of from 2½ to 3 ft These, with a foot of soil and the rest water, would grow excellent Water-lilies, and the plants do not want a great depth of water over their crowns It would be well to arrange that at least a foot might cover them in winter, and then they are virtually safe from frost I find, however, they grow better in the mud of ponds and lakes than under the more artificial conditions of the cemented tank. But if neither ponds nor tanks are available, these Water-lilies can still be easily grown, for, as M. Latour-Marliac wittily observed, like Diogenes, they can content themselves in a tub; we may even go further than this and say that they find themselves quite at home in half a cask buried in the ground and half filled with soil and water On lawns the cask or half cask might be sunk level with the surface, thus giving the leaves and flowers of the Water-lilies the appearance of growing out of the ground

"The enemies of Water-lilies are water-rats and swans and other water birds, especially moorhens, which often pull them to pieces, but the plants can be protected with wire-netting Moorhens are very destructive to the flowers, and should be closely watched There is, however, another enemy. We noticed it first by seeing leaves detached and floating On the water becoming clearer one could see what appeared to be small bits of stick an inch or so long attached in numbers to the leaf-stalk. It was the grub of the caddis fly with its house upon its back In the hollow stick it was safe from the fish, and, fastening upon the young and tender leaf-stalk, the grubs fed away until the leaf was eaten asunder. Strong-established plants are not likely to suffer, but a watch should be kept on young plants if rare varieties" The common water rat or vole is an active destroyer of the flowers, and where it inhabits water, as it commonly does all ponds and streams, nearly all the flowers will be destroyed if this animal is not constantly kept down.

N. alba (*White Water-lily*).—Our native Water-lily is often in flower before May is over, and in a wild state is usually finest where there is a depth of from 2 to 3 ft. of water over the crowns. Rosea is a pretty pink form, but does not bloom freely. N. a. candidissima has broad, showy, pure white flowers, blooming early, and is in beauty often till late autumn. The variety plenissima is remarkable for the number of petals composing the flowers, and maxima, as the name suggests, has large flowers. Minor is a small-flowered form; the flowers very double.

creased by division. There are several varieties. N. o. sulphurea has prettily marbled leaves, and the long-pointed buds are quite 4 in. in length, opening into spreading flowers nearly 8 in. across, and of delicious scent. The colour is a good yellow. The variety grandiflora has yellow, sweet-scented flowers. The large leaves are mottled with brown above, but spotted with red on the reverse side. N. o. rosacea has flowers about 4 in. across, bright rose in colour, with yellow centre, of sweet fragrance; the petals narrow, the flower being like a pink star floating amongst the leaves. N. o. exquisita is a very deep-coloured kind, the flower being rich rose-carmine—in fact, almost red at the base of the petals. Superba is a fine form, with flowers larger than those of the type, and minor, as the name suggests, is small, but pretty. This is found in the

Hardy American Water-lily (N. tuberosa).

N. tuberosa.—This is a North American kind, hardy and beautiful. It has not the long, thick, fleshy root-stock peculiar to most Nymphæas, but instead a thick, fleshy tuberous mass of roots; hence its name. Its flowers, opening in the latter half of summer and throughout the autumn, are white, larger, longer, and broader in the petal than those of other wild species; and it can be increased readily by division, and is free in growth even in open unsheltered water.

N. odorata (*Sweet Water-lily*).—This North American species is a near ally of N. alba, but has rather larger flowers, and borne from June till autumn, sweetly scented, and usually white. The species is found in lakes or slow-running streams, and it grows readily, and is easily in-

ponds of New Jersey. N. o. Caroliniana is described by Mr. Gerard, of New Jersey, as the finest of the odorata varieties, and it is supposed to be a cross between N. odorata rosea and N. alba candidissima. N. o. gigantea is a large-flowered variety; but where to get all these fine forms of this hardy Water-lily is a question that many are likely to ask in vain for the present.

N. pygmæa is the smallest of the Water-lilies. It comes from China and Siberia, flowering before all others, and remaining in beauty over a long season. Its leaves are about the size of the palm of a man's hand, and the flowers, which consist of four white petals, besides the inner parts, are, when open, only about 2 in. across. *Helvola* is a dainty little Water-lily raised by M. Latour-Marliac. It is a seedling of this species, and has pale, straw-coloured flowers ; the leaves of somewhat oblong shape, marked with brown above, and spotted with red underneath.

N. sphærocarpa (*Caspary's Lily*).—This is thought by some a distinct species, and others make it a variety of N. alba. It begins to flower earlier, and with the water at a lower temperature, than any other kind ; its flowers in shape like those of N. alba, but rosy-carmine in colour, blooming flush of flowers in May and June, but not blooming late in summer.

enough for these natives of Florida and Mexico.

M. MARLIAC'S HYBRIDS.—These are the gems of the Water-lily family, and there are many of them of the highest beauty, while they are very hardy.

N. M. albida is finer than any other white-flowered Nymphæa ; vigorous ; the leaves bright purple-red when young, lustrous green as they get older ; the flowers fully 7 in. across, rich yellow in the centre, the outer petals very long, broad, but gradually shorten towards the centre.

N. M. carnea and N. M. rosea are

Bud of hybrid Water-lily, N. Marliacea carnea (natural size), gathered from open water at Gravetye, Sussex, at the end of October.

N. flava (*Primrose Water-lily*).—Instead of having a thick rhizome, this has a mass of fibrous roots, and in addition it sends out long runner-like shoots after the manner of a Strawberry, and these form young plants. The flowers are canary-yellow. *N. Mexicana* is apparently botanically the same as *N. flava*, but Mr. J. N. Gerard, of Elizabeth, N.J., says "it is a charming thing and a fine doer, having a cone-like tuber from which runners start out from thong-like shoots and then flower." We fear our climate is not warm

similar to the preceding kind, but distinct in colour, the first-named kind having flowers suffused with pale flesh tint, and in the other the colour deepens into rosy-pink.

The Canary Water-lily (N. M. chromatella) is one of the finest of the hybrids ; the leaves, at first purplish-red, change to deep red, with distinct and beautiful dark brown-red markings, whilst the flowers are large, soft yellow in colour, with deeper centre.

N. M. rubra punctata is a shapely flower,

4 in. in diameter, with twenty-two sepals and petals ; the four sepals dark olive-green behind, and pale rosy-lilac in front, the petals deep rose-purple and delicately marbled.

N. M. ignea is a larger flower, nearly 5 in. in diameter when fully open ; the sepals pale olive-green, edged with rose behind and pale rose, nearly white, in front. There are eighteen shapely petals, closely imbricated, and forming a beautiful cupped whorl around the vivid orange-red based stamens in the middle of the flower. The petals are of a deep, but bright rosy-crimson.

N. M. flammea varies in colour, which consists of innumerable minute red dots on a white ground, the outer petals appearing pink, and the colour deepening to red in the centre of the flower.

The Laydekeri group of varieties embraces many exquisite forms. Fulgens is a charming Water-lily, the flower small and having fine outer dark green sepals, and about fifteen cupped and shapely crimson-magenta petals, glowing like a ruby in the sun.

N. L. fulva has its flowers washed and pencilled with bright red on a creamy-yellow ground, the stamens golden-yellow, and the leaves mottled with brownish colour on the surface, but the reverse side spotted with red.

Liliacea is a dainty flower, only about 2½ in. across when wide open ; the sepals dark sap green, margined behind with pale rose, while the fifteen peach-blossom-tinted petals are in contrast to the small tuft of golden-yellow stamens ; the rosy petals have quite a silvery lustre in the sunlight.

N. L. lucida has very large flowers of a soft vermilion shade, the stamens orange, whilst the large leaves are spotted with chestnut and with bright red on the reverse side.

N. L. purpurata has beautiful flowers, symmetrical in form and rich red in colour, crimson towards the centre ; the stamens are reddish carmine.

Seignoureti has delicate yellow flowers, shaded with soft rose and flushed with carmine ; they rise nearly six inches above the water, the leaves being spotted with chestnut on the limb, and on the reverse side with red. L. rosea is a lovely kind, quite the finest of the small varieties ; the flowers are about 2 inches across, numerous, and of a rose-purple shade, passing to white at the end of the petals.

N. Robinsoni is a beautiful Lily raised by M. Latour-Marliac, star-like in form, somewhat larger than N. Laydekeri, and

generally of a lovely rose colour, deepening towards the centre. It is distinguished by the rose being finely spotted throughout with white, though the impression given is rather that of suffusion than of spotting. This is a most distinct flower. Other fine hybrid forms are Andreana Gloriosa and Ellisi, and as the plants seed freely no doubt numerous varieties will be raised.

Nymphæa species —*acutiloba*, China ; *alba*, northern temperate regions ; *albo rosea, Amazonum*, Brazil ; *ampla*, W. Indies ; *Basniniana*, Siberia ; *bella*, E. Indies ; *blanda*, S. Amer. ; *capensis*, S. Africa ; *elegans*, Texas ; *flava*, Florida ; *flavo-virens ; fragrantissima*, tropical Africa ; *Gardneriana*, Brazil ; *gigantea*, Australia ; *gracilis*, Mexico ; *hirta*, Sumatra ; *Jamesoniana*, Ecuador ; *lasiophylla*, Brazil ; *Lotus*, Asia and trop. Africa ; *Maximiliani*, Brazil ; *Mexicana*, Mexico ; *nitida*, Siberia ; *nubica*, trop. Africa ; *odorata*, N. Amer. ; *oxypetala*, Ecuador ; *Parkeriana*, Guiana ; *pauciradiata*, Siberia ; *punctata*, Central Asia ; *rosea*, E. Indies ; *Rudgeana*, Guiana ; *rufescens ; stellata*, Asia and trop. Africa ; *stenaspidota*, Brazil ; *Sumatrana*, Sumatra ; *terminerva*, Brazil ; *tetragona*, Asia ; *trisepola*, trop. America ; *tuberosa*, N. Amer. ; *tussilagifolia*, Mexico ; *undulata*, Mexico ; *vivipara* ; *Wenzelii*, Amoor ; *Zanzibariensis*, trop. Africa.

NYSSA (*Tupelo tree*).—A small group of trees little planted, but having certain good qualities. One of the most brilliant sights I remember was a Tupelo tree at Strathsfieldsaye in Hampshire in autumn, a tall slender tree, in splendid colour of leaf. The trees are mostly natives of North Eastern America, a very cold country, so that there can be no doubt about their hardiness ; and the fact that they grow in swampy places should make them easy to find a place in this river and estuary veined land.

Nyssa villosa.

N. sylvatica is the Sour Gum or Tupelo, a tree over 100 feet high in deep swampy ground in Maine and Canada, southwards and westwards.

N. biflora (*Water Tupelo*) is a somewhat smaller swamp and waterside tree, of N. Jersey and southwards.

N. aquatica (*Tupelo Gum*) rises sometimes to a height of 100 feet, and is rather of southern and western distribution. The two first-named species are the most important for our country.

ŒNOTHERA (*Evening Primrose*).—These are amongst the prettiest of hardy flowers, and are easily grown in all soils. From June onward they are in their beauty, many varieties becoming more full of flowers in late summer. They have large bright yellow or white flowers, in many kinds so freely and continuously borne as to make them of great value. Their name notwithstanding, many are open by day; as for instance, Œ. linearis, speciosa, taraxacifolia, and trichocalyx. Many of the finest Evening Primroses are natives of States west of Mississippi, such as California, Utah, Missouri, and Texas. They all bloom the first season from early seedlings. Some of the true perennials, and particularly the prostrate ones, are shy seeders, but the tall ones seed freely. The largest kinds are very beautiful in any position, but from their height and boldness they are suited for the wild garden

Œnothera marginata.

and for shrubberies. Sowing themselves freely, they are apt to become too numerous and somewhat "starved," so that they are best when confined to large groups. In any flower garden not confined to flat beds only, an isolated bed of them looks well. Amongst them we have tall erect sorts like Œ. Lamarckiana, prostrate, as in trichocalyx and cæspitosa, and white flowers, as in the last-named two, while coronopifolia and speciosa often change with age to pink or rose. Few plants have finer yellow blooms than missouriensis and Lamarckiana; and, moreover, they are very large—4 to 6 in. across. Nearly all are more or less fragrant, particularly cæspitosa, marginata, fragrans, and eximia.

Œ. biennis is a handsome biennial, 3 to 5 ft. high, with large bright yellow flowers. Its variety grandiflora or Lamarckiana should always be preferred to the ordinary kind, as the flowers are larger and of a finer colour, having a fine effect in large masses, and is well suited for the wild garden.

Œ. fruticosa (*Sundrops*).—This and its varieties are among the finest of hardy perennials, 1 to 3 ft. high, with showy yellow blossoms. There are about half-a-dozen distinct varieties, the best being linearis, or, as it is usually called, riparia, about 1½ ft. high, bearing an abundance of yellow blossoms. It is one of the best of yellow Evening Primroses for small beds, for edgings, or as a groundwork for other plants, and it goes on flowering even after the first frosts. It is always prudent to lift a few or strike a potful of cuttings in case of accident, though in spring the old plants may be divided to any extent. Given sandy loam, these plants thrive in borders or in the margins of shrubberies. N. America.

Œ. glauca is a handsome N. American species similar to fruticosa. It is of sub-shrubby growth, becomes bushy, and bears yellow flowers. The variety Fraseri is a still finer plant, and where an attractive mass of yellow is desired through the summer there are few hardy plants of easy cultivation so effective. In a large rock-garden a few plants here and there give good colour, and the plants bloom long.

Œ. marginata.—A dwarf plant, never more than 12 in. high, with flowers in May, 4 to 5 in. across, from white gradually changing to a delicate rose; as evening approaches, coming well above the jagged leaves, retaining their beauty all night, and emitting a Magnolia-like odour. It is a hardy perennial, and is increased by suckers from the roots, and by cuttings, which root readily. An excellent plant for the rock-garden and for borders. *Syn.*, Œ. cæspitosa. Œ. trichocalyx, a similar species, but probably only an annual, is a beautiful plant well worth growing.

Œ. missouriensis.—A handsome herbaceous plant from N. America, with prostrate downy stems and clear yellow flowers, sometimes 5 in. in diameter, and borne so freely that they may be said to cover the ground with gold. There is no more valuable border flower, and when well placed in the rock-garden it is effective, especially if the luxuriant shoots are allowed to hang down. As seed is rarely perfected, the plant is better increased by careful division, or by cuttings taken in April. As a border plant it does not grow so freely in cold clayey soils as in warm light ones. The blooms open best in the evening. *Syn.*, Œ. macrocarpa.

Œ. speciosa.—A handsome plant, with many large flowers, at first white, changing to a delicate rose. The plant is erect and its stems almost shrubby, 14 to 18 in. high. A true perennial, valuable for borders, or the rougher parts of the rock-garden in good loam. It is a native of

An Evening Primrose (Œnothera Lamarckiana).

North America, and is increased by division, cuttings, or seeds, but does not seed freely in this country.

Œ. taraxacifolia, a Chilian plant, is one of the finest of those Evening Primroses characterised by a low trailing growth and large blossoms, which attain their fullest expansion towards evening. It has a fine effect in rich deep soil in the rock-garden, where its trailing stems can droop over the ledge of a block of stone. The flowers, 2½ to 3½ in. across,

are pure white, changing to a delicate pink.

Œ. triloba is a handsome hardy annual species, of dwarf growth, with large and showy yellow blossoms. It is also called Œ. rhizocarpa. Other showy annuals are Œ. sinuata and its variety maxima, Œ. macrantha, odorata, bistorta, Veitchiana, and Drummondi. These are all worthy of culture, requiring the treatment of half-hardy annuals, and ordinary garden soil.

OLEARIA (*Daisy Trees*).—Pretty evergreen bushes, natives of Australia and New Zealand. The only drawback is their not proving really hardy, except in warm localities in the southern counties. They may exist in other districts, but gardens are the worse not the better for the presence of shrubs not really hardy in them, or perhaps in a half dead or flowerless state, or requiring protection, which has a tendency to make gardens needlessly ugly for half the year.

O. insignis.—The plant is dwarf, branched, the branches as thick as the little finger; the leaves from 3 to 5 in. long, 2 in. broad, rounded at the ends, thick and hard, shining green on the upper surface. With this exception the whole plant is covered with a thick, felt like coating of pale brownish tomentum. The flowers are on erect peduncles, which are as thick as a goose-quill and from 6 to 9 in. long; the flower-heads are a little over 2 in. across; remaining fresh on the plant for about six weeks. This plant is one of the most interesting and prettiest of the composites which are found in New Zealand. It is a native of Middle Island, where it is said to grow on the driest rocks.

O. Haasti.—This is pretty hardy in various parts of England, growing to a large size in the more favoured localities, and if planted in groups it has a good effect when covered with its Aster-like flowers, and even out of bloom it is attractive. In New Zealand, where it is found at altitudes of about 4,000 ft., it forms a small shrubby tree. The flowers are very numerous, in terminal corymbs, the ray florets ¼ in. long, white, the disc yellow. The plants usually bloom in August, and remain in perfection several weeks. Other kinds grown against walls and on warm soils with some success are ramulosa, ilicifolia, myrsinoides, nilida, macrodonta, stellulata, Traversi, Gunniana, dentata, argophylla, insignis.

OMPHALODES (*Navelwort*).—Pretty dwarf rock or mountain plants belonging to the Borage order.

O. linifolia, a beautiful Portuguese hardy annual, 9 to 12 in. high, with glaucous-green leaves and pure white flowers from June to August; it may be grown in ordinary soil, the seeds sown in April or in September and October; the plant often sows itself.

O. Luciliæ, a lovely rock-plant, with flowers a pretty lilac-blue, and glaucous grey foliage. It is hardy, and succeeds in the rock-garden, but the soil must be thoroughly drained, for though the plant requires abundance of water during growth, it suffers from stagnant moisture. To protect it against slugs, which are too fond of it, strips of perforated zinc, about 3 in. wide, bent so as to form rings round the

den: no plant is more worthy of naturalisation ; in cool, thin woods it runs about like a native plant ; it thrives by woodwalks, and also in open places, and in any position is one of the prettiest plants. There is a white variety, not so pretty as the blue kind.

ONOCLEA (*Sensitive Fern*). — *O. sensibilis* belongs to the group known as "flowering Ferns," from the fertile frond

Olearia Haasti.

plants, are used. Division or by seeds. It grows freely in some light soils, as in Wheeler's nursery at Warminster. Asia Minor.

O. verna (*Creeping Forget-me-not*).—A pretty little plant, bearing in early spring handsome flowers of a deep clear blue with white throats. The plant is useful for borders and the rock and spring gar-

being contracted so as to give it the appearance of an unopened spike of flowers. The fronds are a beautiful fresh green, especially in spring. Though not very fastidious as to soil, it succeeds best in a cool and moist situation, such as the base of the rock-garden, or in the American garden, especially if a little sheltered by neighbouring plants. If the fronds are allowed to remain on the plants until they appear to be ripe, it will be found that the spore-cases are open and the spores shed, as they drop while the fronds look quite green, therefore the best way is to cut off the frond as soon as indications of bursting are perceived, and to lay it in a sheet of paper for a few days, when all the spores will drop out. N. America.

ONONIS (*Rest Harrow*). — Hardy plants of the Pea family, of which the wild Liquorice. (O. arvensis) is one of the prettiest of our wild plants, and is worthy of cultivation on banks and in the rough rock-garden, forming dense tufts covered in summer with racemes of pink flowers. The white variety is also good, and is

Omphalodes Luciliæ.

worthy of a better position than the common form, which grows in any soil. No plants are more readily increased from seed or by division. It is distinct from the spiny O. campestris, which has stems nearly 2 ft. high, and sometimes more. O. rotundifolia is a distinct and pretty plant, which is hardy, and easily cultivated, flowering in May and June and through the summer ; it attains a height of 12 to 20 in. according to soil, and is suitable for the mixed border or the rougher parts of the rock-garden. Seeds or division. Pyrenees and Alps. These are the best of about half-a-dozen garden species, which also include O. fruticosa, Natrix, and viscosa.

ONOPORDON(*Cotton Thistle*).— Handsome vigorous thistle-like plants mostly biennial, and valuable for their stately port and showy flowers. They thrive in exposed places and among shrubs in sheltered ones, and may be effectively used in a variety of ways. Moderation in their use, however, is desirable, as in some situations they seed so freely as to require judicious keeping down. O. Acanthium (Down Thistle) is a bold and vigorous native plant, with very large, stout branching stems, often more than 5 ft. high, covered with long, whitish web-like hairs, and bearing large heads of purplish flowers. The habit of O. illyricum is more branching, the leaves and stems are much more spiny, the stems are stiffer and the leaves are greener and more deeply cut. O. arabicum is 8 to 10 ft. high, is erect and very slightly branching, and both sides of the leaves, as well as the stems, are covered with white down. O. græcum is also a handsome plant.

ONOSMA (*Golden Drop*).—O. taurica is an evergreen perennial, 6 to 12 in. high, soon forming dense tufts, and bearing in summer drooping clusters of clear yellow

Onosma taurica (Golden Drop).

almond-scented blossoms. The best place for it is the rock-garden, drained, with a good depth of soil, so that the plants may root strongly between the stones, the soil a good sandy loam, mixed with broken grit. Seeds or cuttings. Greece

ONYCHIUM.—O. japonicum, an elegant Japanese Fern, often grown in the greenhouse, is hardy in the outdoors fernery. In severe winters, however, some common Brake may be thrown over it. The fronds are finely divided, an intensely dark green, from 1 to 2 ft. high, and useful for bouquets, or for placing loosely in vases with cut flowers.

OPHIOGLOSSUM (*Adder's-tongue*) —
O vulgatum is a native Fern not often seen
in gardens ; found in moist meadows , and
the best position for it therefore is in
colonies in the hardy fernery or the moist
stiff soil in the rock-garden O lusitanicum, a dwarf variety, is interesting, but
capricious, and difficult to cultivate

OPHIOPOGON (*Snake's-beard*) —Herbaceous perennials, about 1½ ft. high, the
flowers, usually small, lilac, appearing
late in summer and in autumn in spikes,
2 to 5 in long, rising from grassy tufts of
evergreen foliage. They thrive in borders
or margins of shrubberies in sandy loam,
but are scarcely ornamental O japonicus, Jaburan, spicatus, Muscari, and longifolius are the best known, and usually in
botanical collections In Italy they are
used to form green turf, in lieu of Grass,
which perishes from the heat Division
Japan and India

OPHRYS —Small terrestrial Orchids,
singularly beautiful, and among the most
curious of plants Many have been in
cultivation, but these being tender plants,
chiefly from S Europe, they must have
protection, and require much attention A
few native species, however, can be grown
in gardens, and of these one of the most
singularly beautiful is the Bee Orchis (O
apifera) This varies from 6 in to more
than 1 ft in height ; it has a few glaucous
leaves near the ground , flowers in early
summer, the lip of a rich velvety brown
with yellow markings, bearing a fanciful
resemblance to a bee It is usually considered difficult to grow, but it may be
easily kept on dry banks in the rock-
garden, in a firm bed of calcareous soil, or
of loam mixed with broken limestone It
thrives best if the soil be surfaced with
some very dwarf plant, or with an inch of
Cocoa-fibre and sand, so as to keep it moist
and compact about the plants. Other interesting species for a collection of hardy
Orchids are O muscifera (Fly orchis),
arachnites, aranifera (Spider orchis), and
Trolli

OPUNTIA (*Prickly Fig*) —There are
several of these succulent plants in cultivation, but few are hardy enough for the
open air in our climate The hardiest are
O vulgaris, missouriensis, humilis, brachy-
antha, and Rafinesquei ; the finest being O Rafinesquei, an evergreen well
worthy of culture, bearing in summer
large showy yellow blossoms on fleshy
branches. It thrives in a sunny corner
of the rock-garden in good dry soil,
sheltered from any passing danger to
the stems, for it is rather fragile, and
anything brushing against it would in-

jure it, but by the skilful placing of a few
rough stones, it is easy to prevent injury
without shading the plant To prevent
splashings, the ground might be surfaced
with a dwarf mossy Saxifrage or Sandwort Snails and slugs are fond of this
plant, and in the spring, and even in mild
winters, may destroy it A dressing of
soot will keep away these pests To increase the plant, the cutting, a single joint,
is potted in sandy soil, and the pot placed
in a sunny airy spot under glass and
watered very sparingly, and in a short
time it will form roots, and commence to
push out young shoots The hardier kinds
are from N. W. America, where the
winters are severe

ORCHIS —These terrestrial Orchids are
beautiful, and well worth cultivation among
hardy flowers. Those who do not want a
full collection will find the species mentioned below easily grown if placed under
good conditions at the outset , some of our
native Orchids are worth a place, but few
succeed with them, chiefly because the
plants are transplanted at the wrong
season The usual plan is to transplant
just when the flowers are opening, but at
this period of growth the plant is forming
a tuber for the following year, and, if this
is in any way injured, it dies. If, instead
of this way, the plants are marked when in
flower and allowed to remain until August
or September, when the tubers are matured,
the risk of transplanting is lessened, provided the plant be taken up with a deep
sod The ground where the plants grow
may be surfaced with such plants as the
Balearic Sandwort, Lawn Pearlwort, and
the mossy Saxifrages The situation for
Orchids should be an open one, and the
soil a deep, fibry loam in a drained border
The following are the kinds most worthy
of culture —

O foliosa —A handsome Orchid, one of
the finest of the hardy kinds, 1 to 2 ft. or
more in height, with long spikes of rosy-
purple blossoms in May, lasting long in
bloom It delights in moist nooks at the
base of the rock-garden, or in the bog-
garden in deep light soil Madeira

O. latifolia (*Marsh Orchis*) —A fine
native kind, 1 to 1½ ft high, with long
spikes of purple flowers in early summer
It thrives in damp boggy soil, in peat or
leaf-mould There are several beautiful
varieties, the best being præcox and ses-
quipedalis , the last being one of the
finest of hardy Orchids, about 1½ ft high,
and a third of the stem is covered with
purplish-violet flowers

O laxiflora is a pretty species, 1 ft to
18 in. high, with loose spikes of rich

purplish-red flowers, opening in May and June, and thriving in a moist spot in the rock-garden. Guernsey and Jersey. Division.

O. maculata (*Hand Orchis*).—One of the handsomest of British Orchids, finest in rich soil, and if well grown in moist and rather stiff garden-loam its beauty will

ORIGANUM (*Dittany, Hop Plant*).— O. Dictamnus (*Dittany of Crete*) is a pretty plant, somewhat tender, and best grown under glass rather than in the open air, though during mild winters it may survive. It has mottled foliage, and small purplish flowers, in heads like the Hop, hence the name Hop-plant. O.

Orchis foliosa (Madeira Orchis)

surprise even those who know it well in a wild state. The variety superba is a fine plant, and should be secured.

Other beautiful kinds, but more or less difficult to establish in gardens, are O. papilionacea, purpurea, militaris, mascula, pyramidalis, spectabilis, tephrosanthos, and Robertiana

Sipyleum is similar, and is quite as pretty. In the open air these plants should have a warm spot in the rock-garden.

ORNITHOGALUM (*Star of Bethlehem*).—Bulbous plants, some of them handsome, others not very distinct, but all useful in the Grass and in borders, in any good garden soil—one or two kinds among the hardy species important for choice borders and bulb beds, *i.e.*, pyramidale and latifolium. Among other kinds worth growing are nutans (free in grass), narbennense, sororium, exscapum and umbellatum—natives mostly of S. Europe, N. Africa, and Asia Minor. The fine, O. arabicum is not to be grown out of doors, save in very warm gardens in the south.

Ornus. See FRAXINUS.

OROBUS (*Bitter Vetch*).—Often pretty plants of the Pea Order, flowering usually in spring. They are suitable for the mixed border, for the rougher parts of the rock-garden, or for naturalising. We mention only the distinct kinds.

O. aurantius is a handsome plant, 18 to 24 in. high, with orange-yellow flowers in early summer. O. tauricus is a nearly-allied species, also with orange flowers. Both require to be well established before they bloom freely, and they are useful for borders in ordinary soil.

O. lathyroides is a lovely border plant, 18 to 24 in. high ; its bright blue flowers borne in dense racemes ; increased freely by seeds, and thrives in ordinary soil.

O. vernus (*Spring Bitter Vetch*).—One of the most charming of border flowers. From black roots spring healthy tufts of leaves with two or three pairs of shin-

Spring Bitter Vetch (Orobus vernus).

ing leaflets ; the flower-buds appearing soon afterwards, almost covering the plant with beautiful purple and blue blooms in April.

Besides the type there are varieties :— tenuifolius, with narrow leaflets and flowers similar, though the habit is more lax ; flaccidus, similar to tenuifolius, but brighter and denser, and with broader leaves ; cyaneus, the most attractive, larger and possessing a strange intermixture of colours, some a bright blue, others a greenish-blue. Then there is a double-flowered kind and a pure

white variety, all thriving in deep warm soils.

Some other species useful for borders and the rock-garden are—O. pubescens, O. canescens, O. varius, and O. Fischeri, but O. vernus and its forms are the handsomest. All are of easy culture in ordinary garden soil, and are increased by seeds or division of the root.

ORONTIUM (*Golden Club*).–O. aquaticum is a handsome aquatic perennial of the Arum family, 12 to 18 in. high ; in early summer its narrow spadix is densely covered with yellow flowers, which emit a singular odour. The plant may be grown on the margins of ponds and fountain-basins, or in the wettest part of the bog-garden. North America.

OSMANTHUS. — Handsome evergreen shrubs, few hardy in our islands ; but some of these are of value :

O. aquifolium.—In a hardy botanical sense all the Osmanthus in Britain are forms of this species. They can scarcely be called varieties, for it is not unusual to see a plant with two so-called varieties on one branch. For convenience and brevity's sake, however, and especially as they keep true to character in the majority of instances, the common nursery names are here kept up. O. aquifolium is a native of China and Japan. In some of its forms it is curiously like the Holly, and is frequently mistaken for it. It is, however, of looser growth and less thickly furnished with leaves, and is also of dwarfer, more shrubby habit. What is generally accepted as the typical form of this species is the one with the largest and broadest leaves. In this the leaves are 3 in. to 4 in. long, of oblong or oval shape, pointed or toothed, but not so deeply as the smaller-leaved forms known as ilicifolius. They are of a deep green colour and of very firm texture. This plant is, according to my experience, the least hardy of this set. It flowers in autumn, and the blossoms are fragrant.

O. ilicifolius.—This is by far the most common and useful kind, and is, moreover, a valuable shrub for town planting. The leaves are usually much smaller than those of the plant just described and may be easily recognised by their deep lobing. The largest specimen at Kew is 9 ft. high, with a spreading base and foliage of the deepest and glossiest green. The leaves average 1½ in. to 2 in. in length and are cut half way to the midrib into several sharply pointed lobes. Some of the leaves, however, are quite entire, others lobed on one side only, but most of them have the upper half lobed, the lower half entire. The following have been given varietal names:—AUREO MARGINATUS.— Leaves similar to those of the green plant, but margined with creamy yellow. ARGENTENEO-MARGINATUS. — Leaves like those of the preceding, but edged with white instead of yellow. LATIFOLIUS MARGINATUS.—Leaves larger than those of either of the preceding, the margin creamy white: — PURPURASCENS.—The young leaves of this variety are tinged with purple, especially on the under side. It is undoubtedly the best of all the Osmanthuses for outdoor work, being much hardier than the variegated forms. At Kew there is a group of this purple-leaved variety near the Palm house, amongst which is planted Lilium candidum, and nothing could more happily set off the beauty of this Lily. O. MYRTIFOLIUS. — There is an Osmanthus at Kew the lower part of which is ilicifolious, the upper part myrtifolious. The origin of the latter is therefore conclusively proved. It appears, however, to be itself constant, and when grown on its own roots I have never noticed any reversion. It makes a neat bush, with leaves like those of the Myrtle in shape, but larger and firmer in texture.

O. rotundifolius.—This is the dwarfest and slowest growing of all the Osmanthuses, and is, moreover, one of the most distinct. Its leaves are very stiff and leathery, and distinguish the variety by their more or less obovate outline. The margins are not distinctly serrated, but have a very shallow irregular lobing. The leaves are each from 1 in. to 1¼ in. long and a little more than half as wide.

The Osmanthuses may all be propagated by cuttings, and although it takes longer to obtain plants on their own roots, they are much to be preferred to those grafted on the Privet. Cuttings should be taken in August when the wood has become firm, and they may be struck in a cool propagating frame. An open soil of fair quality and depth is better than a very rich one for all the forms, but more especially for those that are variegated. —W. J. B.

OSMUNDA (*Royal Fern*).—So-called "flowering" Ferns made familiar by our native Royal Fern (O. regalis), which is found in many bogs and marshy woods, and is well worth cultivating, as it is the largest and most striking of our native Ferns, sometimes attaining a height of 8 ft. It should be planted in moist peaty soil, and the most suitable spots are half-shady places on the banks of streams or of pieces of water. It may also be planted in the water. When exposed to the full sun, it does well, with its roots in a constantly moist, porous, moss-covered soil, if sheltered from strong winds. In shady positions and in deep bog soil it attains a great size.

The various North American Osmundas may be associated with it. O. cinnamomea is an elegant N. American Fern, with pale green fronds; the variety angustata is smaller, and the fronds are less inclined to droop. This species, like O. regalis, is deciduous. O. Claytoniana is another deciduous species, and has vivid green fronds, 2 to 3 ft. high. O. interrupta is the same. O. gracilis is a native of Canada, somewhat resembling a dwarf form of our Royal Fern, the fronds about 2 ft. high. O. spectabilis is a slender form of O. regalis; its fronds are smaller, and the young ones come up reddish-purple. North America. These exotic species are of the simplest culture in the hardy fernery, in moist peaty soil.

OSTROWSKYA (*Great Oriental Bellflower*).—*O. magnifica* is a remarkable and handsome hardy plant found by Dr. Regel

Ostrowskya magnifica.

on the higher mountains of Chanat Darwas, in Eastern Bokhara, and is like a huge Platycodon in aspect, but distinct, the flowers being of great beauty, several inches across, of a delicate purple, veined and varying from seed; the leaves are in whorls. The plant likes a deep sandy loam, as the carrot-like roots when of full size go down to a depth of 2 ft. They must be carefully handled as they are very brittle. The Ostrowskya does not apparently thrive equally in all places, and is often disappointing. Seeds germinate readily in a cold frame, but a few years elapse between sowing and flowering.

OTHONNA (*Barbary Ragwort*).—*O. cheirifolia* is a distinct Composite plant, with whitish-green tufts, 8 in. to 1 ft. high, or on rich soils perhaps more. It is a spreading evergreen, flowering sparsely on heavy and cold soil, but on light soils often blooming freely in May; the flowers yellow, about 1½ in. across, but not pretty. It is useful from its distinct aspect on the rough rock-garden or in the mixed border. Cuttings. Perishes in severe winters, at least on clay soils. Barbary.

OURISIA.—*O. coccinea* is a bright dwarf Chilian creeper, bearing in early summer scarlet blossoms in slender clusters, 6 to 9 in. high. Though hardy, it is reputed difficult to grow, and it should be placed against a block of soft porous stone in a moist place, such as the foot of a wall with an east aspect. Its creeping stems will soon run over the stone, and it will flower freely.

OXALIS (*Wood Sorrel*).—Dwarf and often pretty perennial or annual plants, for the most part more happy and free in temperate countries, but some hardy with us on warm borders and on the rock-garden. They all thrive best in a sandy soil in the warmest and driest place in a garden. The following are the best kinds for our gardens :—

O. Bowieana.—A robust species, forming rich masses of leaves, 6 to 9 in. high, and umbels of rose flowers continuously throughout the summer, suitable for warm borders at the foot of a south wall. In cold soils it seldom flowers, but on very sandy, warm, and well-drained soils it flowers abundantly, and when this is the case it may be used with effect as an edging to beds of autumn - blooming plants, and where it does well it is one of the most precious of hardy flowers. Division. Cape of Good Hope.

O. floribunda.—A free-flowering kind, hardy in all soils; for months in succession it bears numbers of dark-veined rose-coloured flowers. The white-flowered variety flowers as freely as the rose-coloured form, and both are very useful for the rock - garden and for margins of borders, and are easily increased by division. O. floribunda appears to be the commonest kind of Oxalis in cultivation. America.

O. lasiandra.—A distinct and beautiful kind, with large dark green leaves, and in early summer umbels of bright rose-coloured flowers, and useful for warm borders and the rock-garden. Mexico.

O. lobata.—A stemless little plant with three deeply-lobed bright green leaflets, and blossoms about ¾ in. across, rich yellow, the centre delicately pencilled with chocolate. A free-flowering bright little plant during sunshine, thriving in warm sandy loam on well - drained borders. It survives mild winters unprotected. Chili.

O. luteola is one of the prettiest, forming a compact tuft; the flower-buds ½ in. in length, and a soft creamy-yellow, but when open they are as large as a half-crown, and pure white, shading to yellow towards the centre; it is not hardy, but in light sandy soil will survive a winter if protected.

O. Acetosella (*Stubwort, Wood Sorrel*). —The prettiest of the kinds known so far for our gardens is our native Wood Sorrel, which bore in old times the better name of "Stubwort"—a name which should be used always. This grows itself in such pretty ways in woody and shady places that in many gardens there will be

Oxalis Acetosella.

no need to cultivate it. Where it must be cultivated it will be happy in the hardy fernery or in shady spots in the rock-garden, or under trees, or the lawn, or in any shady or half-shady places in ground not dug.

There are other species worthy of a place, especially on very dry sandy soils, and among them are O. Smithi, rosea, Deppei, speciosa, arborea, violacea, versicolor, incarnata, tetraphylla, venusta, and corniculata. O. corniculata rubra is sometimes used for bedding, and should always be encouraged where there are old quarries and rough rocky places, especially in a calcareous district, for this handsome plant speedily covers the most unpromising surfaces. In gardens, however, this Wood Sorrel becomes a troublesome weed. If a collection be grown, it should be borne in mind that it is very difficult to preserve the correctness of the names, for the minute bulblets become mixed up with the earth, and the elasticity of the seed-pods permits the seeds to scatter in all directions.

OXYDENDRUM (*Sorrel Tree*).—A handsome flowering tree reaching a height of over 50 ft. in its native country, with rather large fine leaves and many racemes of white flowers ; thriving in our country, at least on peaty soils, and flowering freely in summer. Ohio and Pennsylvania to Florida, both in mountain and coast lands. The tree is as yet far from common, and the best way at first is to group it with the American shrubs in peaty and free soils. I have

a manageable plant in the rock-garden in deep moist loam. O. uralensis, a dwarf species from the Ural Mountains, has rosy-blue flowers in compact heads, about 4 in. high. Other kinds are—O. montana, fœtida, strobilacea, campestris, and its several varieties ; all of these are dwarf, and thrive in sandy loamy soil in open spots in the rock-garden.

OZOTHAMNUS.—*O. rosmarinifolius* is a neat little evergreen shrub from Tasmania, almost hardy in the south and coast districts, with small, Rosemary-like leaves, and about the end of summer bearing dense clusters of small white flowers. It thrives in any light soil, and should be planted in an open sunny spot or on a warm bank. *Syn.*, Helichrysum.

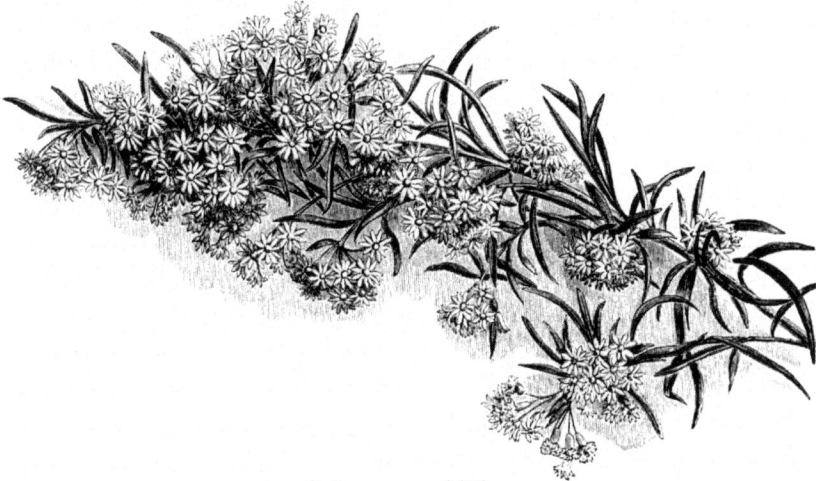

Ozothamnus rosmarinifolius.

planted it in rich leafy soil in most spots in woods, where even small plants so far hold their own among the stoutest sedges of such spots.

OXYTROPIS. — Plants of the Pea family, nearly allied to Astragalus, the best of which is O. pyrenaica, a dwarf species, with pinnate leaves covered with silky down, barely rising above the ground, the flowers a purplish-lilac, barred with white, and borne in heads of from four to fifteen in early summer. It is a native of the Pyrenees, rare in gardens, and increased by seed or division. It should be planted on well-exposed and bare parts of rock-gardens, in firm, sandy, or gravelly soil. O. Halleri has charming, compact flowers, of a decided self colour—as deep a blue as that of the Gentians, and proves

PÆONIA (*Pæony*). — Pæonies are among the most beautiful of hardy flowers, combining good form of growth with beauty of colour and often fragrance. Though there are several typical species in collections, the most important are the hybrids obtained by intercrossing. Pæonies are divided into two groups—the tree or shrubby kinds, comprising the varieties of P. Moutan ; and the herbaceous kinds, of which the common P. officinalis is typical. The hybrid sorts have been obtained chiefly from P. officinalis and other European kinds, together with the Chinese species albiflora, sinensis, and edulis, the forms of the latter class being particularly fine. The European varieties flower early and the Chinese late, so that the flowering season is considerably prolonged.

HYBRIDS.—Among these there is an extensive variety of colours—white, pale yellow, salmon, flesh-colour, and numerous intermediate shades from pale pink to brightest purple. Among the oldest varieties the most remarkable are grandiflora, double white ; Louis Van Houtte, papaveriflora, rubra triumphans, sulphurea plenissima, rosea superba, Zoé, Mme. Calot, Gloria Patriæ, and Prince Troubetskoy The most beautiful of more recent date are : Arthémise, atrosanguinea, Virgo Maria, Mme. Lemoine, L'Espérance, Triomphe de l'Exposition de Lille, Jeanne d'Arc, Eugène Verdier, and Mme. Lemoinier ; and among those most worthy of notice are : Mme. Lebon, Marie Lemoine, Henri Laurent, Mme. Jules Elie, multicolor, Stanley, Charlemagne, Mme. Geissler, Bernard Palissy, and Van Dyck. There are also many commoner varieties—for example, those varieties of P. officinalis (such as anemonæflora, rubra, and Sabini), of P. albiflora, peregrina, paradoxa, and especially of the small P. tenuifolia, with its feathery foliage and large deep red blossoms. There is also a double variety of this species. These as well as the varieties are perfectly hardy, and need no protection against frost, however severe.

CULTURE.—A good moist loam, enriched with cow manure is the soil best suited to them. They can be planted at any time, but from October to April is the best time. Have the ground well prepared by manuring and by trenching to the depth of about 3 ft., and plant them at least 4 ft. apart in each direction. They must not be expected to flower well before the second or third year. An open position renders them robust, and they need not be shaded from the sun until they flower, when some slight shade will prolong and preserve their delicate tints, and enable them to become more thoroughly developed than they otherwise would. As soon as the buds are well formed, water the plants judiciously now and then with liquid manure. When the tufts have become very strong, and have impoverished the soil, separate and transplant them in fresh ground.

POSITION.—Most gardens contain spots so shaded that few plants will thrive in them. In such places Pæonies would grow luxuriantly ; and their colour would often be more intense, while they would last much longer than if fully exposed to the sun. They may therefore be made useful as well as ornamental, even in small pleasure-grounds, although their proper place is undoubtedly the fronts of shrubberies, plantations, and the sides of carriage drives. Where distant effect is required, no plants answer so well, as their size and brilliancy render them striking even at a long distance. When planted on either side of a Grass walk, their effect is admirable, especially in the morning and about sunset ; and when planted in masses, they are invaluable for lighting up sombre nooks. If grown only for their flowers or their buds, or for the purpose of increasing them, they may be placed in nursery lines in some rich part of the kitchen-garden.

Besides being used for the garden proper, there are few plants more fitted for the wild garden ; and the most brilliant and one of the boldest things in wild gardening is a group of scarlet Pæonies in meadow Grass, in early summer. This may be managed so that they come into the garden landscape, so to say, and are seen at a considerable distance from certain points of view. So placed, they could not be an eyesore or in the way when out of flower, as they sometimes are in the mixed border. There is a good deal to be done by the tasteful cultivator in considering the positions suited for some kinds of plants ; in deciding, for example, how to arrange plants which are very handsome in spring and early summer, but which do not continue in perfection very long, so that their effect when out of flower, or even their disappearance, shall not mar any arrangement.

P. Moutan (*Tree Pæony*).—This is another noble plant from which we have beauty, for its varieties, like those of the herbaceous kinds, are very numerous. It is quite hardy, and, when properly planted, requires little care ; precious for borders, and is specially suited for isolation on lawns. Its blossoms are gorgeous in early spring, and its young leaves assume every shade of colour, from violet-crimson to green. Tree Pæonies are not particular as to soil or position ; they grow as well in sand as in strong loam, though they prefer a good strong soil. If the soil is too sandy, decomposed manure and loam, or if too clayey, manure, sand, and similar materials should be added. Moutans are gross feeders, and amply repay occasional top-dressings of half-decomposed cow manure. Of the scarcer and better varieties nurserymen generally send out plants one or two years old, which are grafted on the roots of P. edulis. In a proper place, dig out a pit 1½ ft. deep and 2 ft. in diameter ; put in a few inches of half-decomposed cow manure, and mix it well with the soil, insert the plants with the grafts buried a few inches under the ground, where they will, in time, throw out roots of their own. The plants do not flower well until the third year after planting, but they afterwards blossom freely in profusion. Being of slow growth, they are not propagated by division to any great extent, but are multiplied chiefly by grafting upon the roots of the herbaceous varieties. This grafting is performed in August. The grafts are placed in frames, where they unite, and in the succeeding year are transplanted in rows in the nursery.

September and October are the best months for planting Moutans, but if planted in pots they may be put out in spring, when all danger of frost is over. Good plants set in autumn produce many flowers the second or third year after planting. Each year they increase in size and beauty, and soon become the most attractive features of the garden. They flower the first of any Pæonies, and put forth their blooms early in May. Until the second half of this century only white, rose, salmon, and lilac sorts were known ; and we are indebted to Mr. Fortune for his Chinese varieties, most of which have scarlet, violet, and magenta flowers. Von Siebold, too, introduced a number of Japanese varieties, which, however, form a different race, and are mostly single or semi-double. The following list contains some of the best varieties : Athlète, large, double, lilac ; Bijou de Chusan, pure white ; Carolina, bright salmon ; Colonel Malcolm, violet ; Comte de 'Flandres, very large, rose ; Confucius, deep pink ; Elisabeth, deep scarlet, very double ; Farezzii, large, pale lilac striped with violet ; Fragrans maxima fl.-pl., pale rose ; Lambertiana, blush rose petals, tipped with violet ; Louise Mouchelet, large, double, pink ; Madame de Sainte - Rome, bright lilac - rose ; Madame Stuart Low, bright salmon-red ; Marie Ratier, large, rose ; Odorata Maria, pale rose ; Prince Troubetskoy, very large, double, deep lilac or violet ; purpurea, a deep amaranth, semi - double kind ; Ranieri, bright amaranth ; Rinzii, very large, bright rose ; Rosini, a semi-double, brilliant rose - coloured variety ; Rubra odorata plenissima, very large, double, lilac-rose ; Souvenir de Madame Knorr, large, double blush ; Triomphe de Malines, large, violet, a colour which deepens at the base of the petals ; Triomphe de

Vandermaelen, very large, and double violet-shaded rose ; Vandermaeli, blush, almost white ; Van Houttei, large, double, carmine ; and Zenobia, white. Some of the most strikingly beautiful, such as Gloria Belgarum, Elisabeth, and Souvenir de Gand, are well worthy of glass—that is, having a sash or two put over them in spring to save them from late frosts and rainy weather. Plenty of air must be admitted, and the flowers gain in an astonishing degree, both in size and colour.

Species *P. albiflora*, Siberia ; *anomala*, do. ; *Bieber-steiniana*, Caucasus ; *Brownii*, N.W. Amer. ; *coral-lina*, Europe and Asia Minor ; *coriacea*, Spain ; *decora*, As. Minor ; *fimbriata*, Eastern regions ; *mollis*, Sibe-ria ; *moutan*, China ; *obovata*, Manchuria ; *officinalis*, Europe ; *paradoxa*, S. Europe ; *peregrina*, East ; *sub-ternata*, ; *tenuifolia*, E. Europe, N. Amer. ; *triter-nata*, Russia ; *Wittmanniana*, Caucasus.

PANCRATIUM.—Graceful Lily-like plants of the amaryllis order, the only really hardy kind being the South European P. illyricum, 1 to 2 ft. high, which bears in summer umbels of large white fragrant blossoms. It thrives in a warm exposed border of sandy loam soil, well drained, the bulbs protected by litter in winter. The plants are better for transplantation about every third year in autumn as soon as the leaves are decayed. Increased by offsets from the parent bulbs. The hardiest of the other species are P. parviflorum, maritimum, littorale, and rotatum, but these only succeed on warm soils in mild localities, and are best grown in a frame or a cool greenhouse.

PANICUM.—Grasses, chiefly tropical, though a few are hardy enough for out-door cultivation and easy to grow in ordinary garden soils.

P. altissimum is a very handsome hardy perennial Grass, very much like P. virgatum, forming dense erect tufts, 3 to 6½ ft. high, according to climate and soil, the flowers being a dark chestnut-red.

P. bulbosum.—A strong species, with a free and beautiful inflorescence, about 5 ft. high ; the flowers spread gracefully. It is suited for grouping near the margins of shrubberies.

P. capillare.—A hardy annual, growing in tufts from 16 to 20 in. high, pretty in full flower, the tufts being then covered with large pyramidal panicles, borne at the ends of the stems and in the axils of the stem-leaves. It grows in any soil, often sows itself, and is suited for borders or beds, being one of the most graceful plants in cultivation.

P. virgatum.—A handsome hardy Grass from North America, 3 to 4 ft. high, forming close tufts of leaves, 1 ft. or more long, and with many graceful tall branching panicles. Admirable for borders or for isolation in the picturesque flower garden or pleasure - ground. Its colour, though quiet, is very pretty throughout the autumn, and even the leaves and stems are pretty when left standing through the winter. Division.

PAPAVER (*Poppy*).—Some of the most brilliant of hardy flowers, and of the simplest culture. There are a few good perennials, but the majority are annual a good deal as to colour, there being white, scarlet, and yellow forms in cultivation. The variety albiflorum has white flowers, spotted at the base, while the hairy variety flaviflorum has showy orange flowers. Easily raised from seed. P. pyrenaicum is similar to P. alpinum, but taller: it occurs with white, yellow, and orange-red blossoms, which, however, do not always come true from seed.

P. nudicaule (*Iceland Poppy*).—A dwarf

White Poppies.

and biennial. They range from the tiny alpine Poppy to the stately P. orientale and its varieties. The following is a selection of the best garden kinds :—

P. alpinum (*Alpine Poppy*).—This has beautiful large white flowers, with yellow centres and dissected leaves, cut into fine acute lobes. A native of the higher Alps, it may sometimes be seen in good condition in our gardens, but is liable to perish, unlike a true perennial. It varies kind, with leaves deeply lobed, and large rich yellow flowers on naked stems, 12 to 15 in. high ; it is handsome for borders or the rock-garden, is easily raised from seed, and forms rich masses of cup-like flowers, but is not a true perennial, and should be raised annually. There are several white, yellow, and orange-red varieties, and one large and handsome. Siberia and the northern parts of America.

P. orientale (*Oriental Poppy*) the most

showy of all Poppies, is among the noblest of hardy plants, and the variety bracteatum is larger and handsomer. This variety forms huge masses of handsome foliage; the flowers on stiff stalks, with leafy bracts at intervals, are 6 to 9 in. across, and of brilliant scarlet, each of the four petals marked inside at the base with a purple-black spot, the whole forming a cross, which gives the flower a striking effect. P. orientale has naked flower-stalks, and as a rule the flowers are pure scarlet, but some have a black spot. It seems as if orientale has been crossed by bracteatum, for there are a good many hybrids in gardens. The fault of this Poppy is its weak stalk, owing to which it does not hold its large flowers erect like its rival, and its bloom is sooner past. There are several varieties besides bracteatum; concolor has no spots at the inner base of the petals; triumphans is dwarfer. These are effective for borders, or for isolated masses on Grass, and flourish in almost any well-drained soil. They are most effective in groups in the rougher parts of the pleasure-ground, or in the shrubbery.

P. Rhæas (*Common Corn Poppy*).— The Carnation, Picotee, and Ranunculus Poppies are double forms of the common red field Poppy, possessing almost every colour except blue and yellow; some being self-coloured, others beautifully variegated. They are also known as French and German Poppies. Some are dwarfer than others, but all are between 2 and 3 ft. in height. Of recent years pretty single forms of the Corn Poppy have become popular under the name of "Shirley Poppies." Being hardy annuals, they can be sown where they are to bloom, but should be grown in good soil to bring out fully their size and colour. The seed, being very small, should be sown thinly, and the plants eventually thinned out to 6 or 8 in. apart, so that the lateral shoots may develop and the flowers have sufficient space. Few annuals afford such a brilliant display as the different kinds of Corn Poppy in outlying beds and borders during summer.

P. somniferum (*Opium Poppy*).—This beautiful and variably-coloured Poppy is a valuable hardy annual. It generally grows about 2½ ft. in height, and varies from white to deep crimson. The double scarlet, the double striped, and the double white are all varieties of it, and their great flower-heads have a bold and striking effect planted in masses. By selection, a type called the Pæony-flowered Poppy has been obtained from them; it has large and very double broad-petalled flowers,

which vary in colour from white to dark crimson, and is distinct. P. somniferum and its varieties are treated as hardy annuals in the same way as P. Rhæas.

P. umbrosum is a brilliant hardy annual, about 2 ft. high, in habit like the common field Poppy, the flowers dazzling scarlet, with a jet-black blotch on the inner base of each petal, conspicuous also on the outer face of the petals, making masses of the plant a grand sight early in summer. Its seeds should be sown in autumn, so that strong plants may be ensured for the

Opium Poppies (Papaver somniferum).

following summer. Caucasus. P. arenarium is another showy annual from the Caucasus. Other handsome Poppies, such as P. spicatum, pilosum, and lateritium, are perennial, and all are of the simplest culture.

Paradisia. See ANTHERICUM.

PARNASSIA (*Grass of Parnassus*).— Interesting and pretty plants for the bog-garden or for moist spots in the rock-garden. In our moist heaths and bogs Parnassia palustris is frequent, and a very pretty plant it is—handsome enough to cultivate in moist spots where it will grow as in its native haunts. Three other kinds, natives of North America, are quite as showy. P. fimbriata has large flowers with peculiar fringe-like append-ages, its kidney-shaped leaves resembling those of P. asarifolia, another hardy species, about 9 in. high, which bears similar white flowers without fringes. P.

Parnassia palustris (Grass of Parnassus).

caroliniana differs from P. asarifolia, in having oval or heart-shaped leaves ; it flowers about the same time, usually from the beginning of July till the end of August. These hardy Parnassias thrive best in a moist peaty soil or a spongy bog. Seed, division. Saxifrage order

PAROCHETUS (*Shamrock Pea*).—*P. communis* is a beautiful little creeping per-ennial, with Clover-like leaves, 2 to 3 in. high, bearing in spring Pea-shaped blossoms of a beautiful blue. It is of easy culture in warm positions on the rock-garden and the choice border, and where the climate is too cold to grow it in the open air it may be grown in a cold frame. Division or seed. Nepaul. Le-guminosæ.

PARROTIA (*Iron Tree*).—Low Hazel-like trees, natives of Northern India and Persia, not remarkable for their beauty of flower so much as for fine colour of the leaves in autumn, giving a mixture of crimson, orange, and yellow, unique among colours of leaves of hardy trees.

The best known is the Persian, *P. persica*, which in the London district in warm soils is hardy. In the north it would probably require a wall.

PASSIFLORA (*Passion-flower*).—The hardy blue Passion-flower, *P. cærulea*, so often seen as a wall-climber in southern dis-tricts, from its beauty and distinctness de-serves to be grown wherever the climate permits. It is not so suitable for arbours or trellises as for walls, the heat from the walls aids in ripening the wood, and so enables it to withstand the winter. A southern aspect is best for it, though it grows against west or east walls, only requiring a good soil, and, perhaps, a slight protection during winter. The white variety, Constance Elliot, is as hardy as the older kind. No other variety of P. cærulea is so distinct, and no other Passion-flower is hardy enough for outdoor walls. The blue Passion-flower first came from Brazil two hundred years ago.

PAULOWNIA.—*P. imperialis* is a fine flowering tree from Japan, not suitable for our climate generally though in a few places it succeeds. It comes into flower and leaf so early, that if the winter is mild and the spring late the buds and often the young leaves are injured by late frosts ; otherwise, there may be a lovely bloom. It is fine in leaf as well as in bloom ; the leaves are a foot in length, and have even ex-ceeded 20 in. The flowers are in erect spikes, resembling in form those of a Bignonia ; of a delicate mauve purple, blotched inside with a deeper tint. In countries a little warmer than Britain this tree is very beautiful and much used in public gardens and even in street planting. At maturity the Paulownia assumes a dense rounded head, but rarely exceeds 30 ft. in height, although in some south-coast gardens there are trees nearly 40 ft. in height.

If the young trees are cut back annually, they make strong shoots bearing enormous leaves, of sub-tropical aspect, with the advantage of being much hardier than the house plants used in summer to give such effects. The tree is best on a light deep loam.

Pavia. See ÆSCULUS.

PELARGONIUM (*Stork's Bill*). — Nearly all Pelargoniums are natives of the southern hemisphere, or have origin-ated as hybrid or cross-bred varieties in European countries. They are often erroneously termed Geraniums, but al-though allied to the Geranium family they are distinct from it, Geraniums being chiefly natives of the northern half of the globe, all of them being hardy plants. The genus Pelargonium contains many species, which botanists have divided into several sections, and many kinds will grow and flower in the open air during summer, although unable to withstand our winters.

Of all varieties of the flower garden the "zonals" are the most useful, and they are supposed to be descended from two distinct species, P. zonale and P. inquinans. As bedding-out plants they are of great importance ; and the facility with which they yield improved forms has led to the introduction of numerous beautiful varieties, of nearly all shades of colour, from white to intense scarlet; while the richest purple and violet shades are also to be found, and these would almost appear to foretell the advent of even a blue Zonal Pelargonium. The Zonal Pelargonium, on account of the brilliancy of its bloom, has sometimes been too freely used in the flower garden, but these matters are now better understood. Among the Zonal varieties there are many with variegated and beautiful foliage, this particularly being the case in that section of the Zonals known as Tricolors, which, on account of their not succeeding so well in some soils as might be desired, are less grown out-of-doors than they deserve. Where they succeed, however, they form very attractive beds, when grown for the sake of their foliage, the trusses of bloom being removed from time to time as they appear. The varieties known as the "bronze zonals" are also beautiful outdoor plants, the free exposure intensifying the rich tints of the leaves.

No plants are more easily increased than these : cuttings may be inserted whenever they can be obtained, and will root freely in any ordinary light or sandy soil, in the open air during summer and autumn,

Passiflora Constance Elliot.

and under glass during winter and spring. The principal stock of plants is, however, generally got by cuttings inserted in pots, pans, or boxes in the open air during the early autumn, such cuttings making the best plants. During winter the protection of glass and the exclusion of frost are essential.

ZONAL PELARGONIUMS FROM SEED may also be treated as annuals, and will bloom in less than ten months from the time of sowing ; but the seed should be sown as soon as it is ripe, say during August. Enough seed can always be had by retaining a few plants for the purpose, in front of a greenhouse, in any light, airy spot. If new varieties are sought, recourse must be had to artificial fertilisation ; but this is unnecessary if the plants are merely for planting out in the parterre.

be potted singly into 3-in. pots and placed in a cold pit, or a similar structure where frost is excluded, until the time arrives when they may be safely planted in the flower garden or wherever they are required. During the early part of the season such plants may bloom less profusely than those from cuttings, but their neat habit and healthy foliage will compensate for this.

Many sorts remarkable for the beauty of their blooms, are, nevertheless, by their habit, unsuited for bedding-out ; and few of the many beautiful double varieties of Zonals can be recommended for outdoor culture, unless as standards, with clean stems, 2½ or 3 ft. in length. In this form they are sometimes effective ; for being compelled to draw sustenance through a slender stem, induces a very free-flowering

Pelargonium Dr. André.

If the plants used for seed be all of the same sort, the seedlings may be expected to prove tolerably true—*i.e.* the same variety as the plants. The pots should be of convenient size (say 6 in. in diameter), and filled to within ½ in. of the rims with light turfy soil ; the seed may be sown rather thickly, gently pressed into the soil, and slightly covered with it. Water with a fine rose, cover the pots with a piece of glass, and place them in a temperature of about 65° ; the seeds will soon vegetate, and the piece of glass should then be removed ; the plants when large enough should be pricked off into seed-pans and kept near the glass in a reduced temperature during the winter. Early in the following March they should

habit. Strong stakes are needed to support the heavy heads, and the principal branches should be secured to circular hoops. Single varieties may with equal facility be formed into standards, and in their case seedlings are likely to form specimens sooner than plants from cuttings. Before frost, all standards should be well cut back, taken up, and repotted in pots not larger than may contain the roots ; they should be staked and afterwards placed in a temperature not under 60° until they root. Treated thus annually, such plants are often in perfect health, even when twelve or fourteen years old.

Next in importance to the Zonals for outdoor culture are the Ivy-leaved kinds or the varieties of P. lateripes. More particularly is this the case since their crossing with the Zonal varieties, which has produced many beautiful sorts useful for outdoor culture. As to treatment, it may be said to be in nearly all respects identical with those of the Zonal varieties, with the exception of being somewhat more tender, and requiring a little more warmth in winter.

Among other Pelargoniums few are suitable for outdoor culture, or for bedding, their growth in the open air, in even light or poor soil, being too luxuriant. Each section will now be considered separately, and the varieties that succeed when planted out will be mentioned. There are, however, so many varieties of Zonals, and the older varieties are so often superseded by others that are not always improvements, that it will only be necessary to give a short list of sorts really known to be good. It must, however, be borne in mind that some sorts succeed in certain soils and situations which are by no means successful in others.

The following are a few of the many Zonal varieties suited for outdoor culture or for massing in the flower garden or elsewhere: Anna Pfitzer, Ball of Fire, Corsair, Culford Rose, Distinction, Dr. Orton, Fire King, Harry Hieover, Henry Jacoby, Havelock, Jenny Dodds, John Gibbons, King of the Bedders, Master Christine, Mrs. Lancaster, Mrs. Turner, Mrs. Miles, Mulberry, Newland's Mary, Vanessa, Vesuvius and its salmon-coloured variety, Violet Hill, Nosegay, White Perfection, White Princess, and White Vesuvius.

The bronze Zonal varieties are as well suited for bedding-out as the green-leaved kinds, being in all respects as vigorous. Their flowers vary in colour. The bright golden ground colour and rich leaf zones of some of them, however, show to greater advantage when the blooms are removed. The following are a few of those that may be considered the best bedders: Black Douglas, Bronze Beauty, Bronze Queen, Crown Prince, Gilt with Gold, Golden Harry Hieover.

There are also some useful bedding varieties with yellow zoneless leaves, such as Crystal Palace Gem, Golden Christine, and Robert Fish; while Happy Thought is a singular variety, each leaf having a large disc of a creamy-white colour, while the margins are green, but it is inclined to grow rather too robust in rich soils.

Though the variegated Zonals, or golden Tricolors, do not succeed equally well as bedding plants in all kinds of soil, the following varieties will, with ordinary care, generally give satisfaction: Mrs. Pollock, Sophia Cussack, Sophia Dumaresque, Beautiful Star, Victoria Regina, Edward Richard Benyon, Macbeth, Lady Cullum, Peter Grieve, William Sandy, Prince of Wales, and Howarth Ashton.

The drawback as regards the silver tricolor sorts, when planted out in the open air, is the circumstance of the central or green portion of the leaves expanding faster than the white or coloured margins of the same, so that the centres of the leaves become somewhat puckered. The following are among the best for this purpose: Italia Unita, Lass o' Gowrie,

Pelargonium "Pretty Polly."

Eva Fish, Maxwell Masters, Lady Dorothy Neville, and Miss Farren.

Among silver-margined zoneless sorts, Mangle's Variegated, a very old variety, is still useful, together with Silver Chain, Flower of Spring, Mrs. J. C. Mappin, Princess Alexandra, and Waltham Bride, the three last having pure white flowers.

Of the Ivy-leaved sorts, and their hybrid varieties, the following are useful as bedding plants: Album grandiflorum, Duke of Edinburgh, l'Elégante, Bridal Wreath, Willsi roseum, Dolly Varden, and Emperor.

Comparatively few of the Cape species or of their hybrid varieties are of much use as bedding plants: a few, however, are sometimes used with pretty good effect. Some of these are—Diadematum, Lady Mary Fox, Lady Plymouth, Pretty Polly,

Prince of Orange, Rollison's Unique, Crimson Unique Most of the sweet-scented sorts, when planted out-of-doors during the summer, succeed admirably, and furnish abundance of fragrant flowering shoots for cutting for the house — P G

PENNISETUM. — *P longistylum* is one of the most elegant of Grasses, 1 to 1½ ft high, the flower-spikes are borne on slender stems, they are from 4 to 6 in long, of singular twisted form, and enveloped in a purplish feathery down It is useful for cutting, as it lasts a long time, is perennial and hardy, growing in free garden soil P fimbriatum is a similar species, equally desirable

PENTSTEMON (*Beard Tongue*).— Varied in colour, profuse in flower and of graceful habit, Pentstemons have a value for our flower-beds and rock-gardens, that few other plants possess, especially as their blooming season extends five months, commencing in June with the charming blue P procerus, and finishing with the endless varieties of P Hartwegi, in all shades of rose, scarlet, and crimson, whose beauty holds its own even in November, long after the more fragile plants of the flower garden have perished Within the past few years also much has been done to improve the Pentstemon by selection of varieties of P. Hartwegi and P gentianoides, which, however, with all their wide range of colour, lack the beautiful clear blue of the species, and have a somewhat monotonous effect The garden varieties, or so-called hybrids, resulting from this selection, may be ranged under two series of colours—those from P Hartwegi belonging to the red-flowered set, and those from P gentianoides to the purple-flowered As regards culture, the species have the reputation of being difficult to manage, as some of the shrubby section die when they are apparently in robust health To ensure success, often drainage is essential, as they suffer more from excessive moisture at the roots than from cold The soil best for Pentstemons is friable loam, with a mixture of well-decayed leaf mould and sharp sand It is well to have a few plants in cold frames, to fill any vacancies in the borders They may be propagated either by cuttings or seeds The former mode applies chiefly to the shrubby kinds, which strike freely in spring ; and, in favourable seasons, seeds are borne by those from which it is not practicable to obtain cuttings Any attempt to multiply some kinds by dividing the tufts will result in the loss of the plants, but P barbatus and P procerus

endure this mode of propagation Seed should be sown in February or March on a gentle hot-bed under a frame, in seed-pans well drained with broken plaster and filled with a compost of peat soil and sand In April the seedlings should be pricked out under a frame, and these, planted out in May, will usually come into flower by autumn Another mode is to sow in May or June in the open air, in ground enriched with leaf-mould The seed-beds should be covered with chopped Moss, to preserve a uniform temperature and humidity In August the seedlings should be potted and removed to a greenhouse or conservatory for the winter It is necessary to observe that the seed sown at either of these seasons frequently does not germinate until the following year Foxglove order

The following are some of the best cultivated species. Many are excluded, however, some on account of their rarity, and others, such as P antirrhinoides, cordifolius, and Lobbianus, because they are not sufficiently hardy for border culture, though they succeed well enough against a warm wall

P. azureus is a very pretty dwarf, branching kind, with numerous branches, bearing many blossoms in whorls, clear violet-blue, towards the end of summer, and lasting a long time California.

P. barbatus.—A tall handsome plant, often named Chelone barbata, with underground stems forming tufts, whence rise, to a height of 3 ft or more, several graceful stems, supporting many rosy-scarlet flowers, in long succession There is a white variety The variety Torreyi is a fine robust plant, of greater height and without the beard on the lower lip of the flower which characterises the species Being a native of Colorado and Northern Mexico, it is hardier than the older plants, and is a showy border perennial of easy culture

P. campanulatus is an old inhabitant of our garden borders, a slender plant, about 18 in high, branching freely, and in southern districts having an almost shrubby character, the rose-coloured flowers in one-sided racemes blooming for a long period Mexico P pulchellus is a variety

P. Cobæa —One of the handsomest kinds, bearing late in autumn long leafy racemes of flowers, nearly 2 in long, pale purple, pencilled with red streaks and delicately suffused with yellow, the base of the tube being a creamy-white P Cobæa thrives generally without protection, but it is difficult to increase. The name is used in trade lists for several spurious kinds, but the true plant when in flower can be readily recognised   Texas

P crassifolius —Allied to P Scouleri, but the flowers are of a charming light lavender colour and the plant admirably suited for a dry knoll of the rock-garden , but this knoll must be well exposed to the sun and on a deep mass of bog soil or peat, so that while the situation of the plant is dry, the roots may find what they require   P Menziesi resembles P Scouleri, but has reddish purple flowers

P. cyananthus.—A lovely kind, 3 to 4 ft high, bearing in May and June dense spikes about 1 ft long of bright blue flowers   The new variety Brandegei is an improvement on the type, being more robust, and having brighter flowers Rocky Mountains, and N America

P. diffusus.—A semi-shrubby kind, 2 to 4 ft high, with violet-purple flowers in a large, loose, many-branched head, throughout the greater part of summer and autumn   Its relative P. Richardsoni much resembles it, but is inferior in beauty, and P Mackayanus and P argutus are nearly allied   This plant is liable to succumb to the damp of our winters   Like all the Pentstemons, P. diffusus is readily increased by cuttings, and might come true from seed, but, in this country, seed is rarely matured N W America

P. Digitalis is a large-leaved free-growing kind, of erect habit, not very showy   The same remark applies to P pubescens, lævigatus, perfoliatus, and glandulosus

P. Fendleri.—A distinct glaucous kind, with a long, one-sided raceme of light purple flowers, 12 to 15 in high, hardy in ordinary soils   P. Wrighti is a similar plant with magenta-tinted blossoms, and its variety angustifolius is also pretty

P. Hartwegi, generally known as P gentianoides, is one of our best autumn-flowering plants, its progeny, called into existence by the skill of the florist, including endless variety of colour and increased size of bloom, the narrow tubular flower acquiring almost the dimensions of a Foxglove   About the beginning of this century it was found by Humboldt and Bonpland in Mexico, at an altitude of nearly 11,000 ft, but it was not introduced into cultivation till 1828

THE HYBRID PENTSTEMONS, among the most precious of flowers, are supposed to have descended from P gentianoides, but there is little doubt that most of them have come from the pretty P Hartwegi P Cobæa, too, has probably been em-ployed in hybridising, for some varieties bear a strong resemblance to it   Whatever their parentage, they are beautiful plants, and much use should be made of them, as they are valuable in autumn and carry their beauty into winter, at least in western and seaside gardens

The varieties of Pentstemon succeed in any good soil, and are certain to do well in a good loam enriched with manure and leaf-soil   They can be planted out in groups, in beds or in the mixed border, where their various colours blend charmingly, among them being a wonderful range of colour from white to scarlet, with intermediate shades of pink, rose, purple, carmine, and purplish-lilac   If good plants be put out by the end of April, they will bloom about the middle of June, and yield a succession of flowers until winter   They are increased both by cuttings and by seeds   the cuttings taken in August or early in September from the young growth round the main stem, and they should be put into a prepared sandy bed, on a shady border, under a hand-glass, or into boxes or pots in a cold frame, where they root readily, and those in boxes or pots might be wintered there, and not transplanted till spring   Those in the border should be lifted and potted and planted in a cold frame for the winter, or transplanted to the open ground in a well-prepared bed, and protected during severe weather with a little litter or branches of Evergreens , but the young plants should not usually be planted out till March or April   To increase the stock of any given variety rapidly, the store pots of cuttings rooted in autumn should be put in a gentle bottom-heat in spring, and induced to grow , if the young growths be taken off when they are 2 in in length, and put into pans of sandy soil of the same temperature, they will quickly strike, and by May and June, if properly treated, will be healthy plants

SEEDLINGS —The Pentstemon is a free seeder, and there is no difficulty in obtaining seed   Seed should be taken from only the finest varieties showing distinct or novel character—and such varieties can scarcely fail to yield something worthy of cultivation   The seed should be sown in February or early in March in a gentle heat   it will quickly germinate, and when the plants are large enough to handle, they should be pricked off into shallow boxes, and, after a time, hardened off in a cold frame   Here they can remain till the end of May or later according to size, and they should then be planted out in well-prepared beds   When they flower, which they will do by August and September, any especially good varieties should be marked to propagate from. If the bed of seedlings be allowed to stand for another season (and this is often a good plan), the seed-stalks should be cut away as soon as ripe, and the bed cleaned, top-dressed with leaf-soil and short manure in spring, and there will be a plentiful harvest of flowers the following summer. Seedlings should be protected by a cold frame during winter, and planted out in April in good soil in a sunny spot.

P. heterophyllus. — A dwarf sub-shrubby kind, its showy flowers, singly or in pairs in the axils of the upper leaves, of a pinky lilac ; plants from seed are very liable to vary. Though hardier than many species, it succumbs to severe winters; and plants should be kept in frames. California.

P. humilis.—A very distinct alpine species, rarely exceeding 8 in. in height, forming compact tufts, its large blossoms of a pleasing blue suffused with reddish-purple : it should be planted in the rock-garden in a fully exposed spot in gritty loam and leaf-mould, and during summer the plant should be copiously watered. It blooms in early June, and is a native of the Rocky Mountains, abundant about Pike's Peak.

P. Jeffreyanus.—A showy kind, and the best of the blue-flowered class, its glaucous foliage contrasting finely with its clear blue blossoms borne during the greater part of the summer. It is a handsome dwarf border plant, but not being a good perennial, the stock should be kept up by the aid of seedlings, which will bloom much more vigorously than old plants. North California.

P. lætus is a close ally of P. azureus and P. heterophyllus, and, like them, is of dwarf branching habit, with blue flowers in raceme-like panicles about 1½ ft. high, blooming in July and August. It is a native of California, and is as hardy as most of the species from that region.

P. Murrayanus.—A distinct plant, and one of the most beautiful, 3 to 6 ft. high, with tiers of brilliant scarlet flowers, and broad glaucous leaves. It should be raised from seed annually, and the seedlings should be grown well for flowering the following summer, as few plants are more worthy of care. It is a native of Texas, and loves a warm sunny soil. P. centranthifolius is similar but not so handsome, though easier to grow, and hardier.

P. ovatus, also known as P. glaucus, is a fine vigorous plant, 3 to 4 ft. high, the flowers small, but in dense masses, in colour varying from intense ultramarine to deep rosy-purple ; their brilliant colour, and the handsome form of the plant combine to give it a special value. It should be considered a biennial, as it usually flowers so vigorously in the second year as to exhaust itself. Mountains of Columbia.

P. Palmeri.—A handsome species of robust habit, in good soil 3 to 5 ft. high ; the flowers in a many-flowered panicle 18 to 24 in. long, peach-coloured and streaked with red, corolla with a gaping mouth. The plant is quite hardy, succeeding in almost any well-drained soil, and flowering about midsummer. P. spectabilis is similar.

P. procerus is a beautiful little plant, and about the hardiest of all the species, as it takes care of itself in any soil. It is of a creeping habit, sending up from the tufted base numerous flowering stems 6 to 12 in. high. The small flowers are in dense spikes, and, being of a lovely amethyst-blue, they make it charming for either the border or the rock-garden. It seeds abundantly. It is the earliest to blossom of all the Pentstemons. P. nitidus and P. micranthus are synonymous with P. procerus, and P. confertus is somewhat similar. P. confertus has straggling stems, and is a very distinct species, though by no means showy.

P. Scouleri is a small semi-shrubby plant of twiggy growth. Its large flowers are of a slaty bluish-purple, and are arranged in short terminal racemes : they are not produced in great abundance, but, combined with the dwarf and compact growth of the plant, they have charms sufficiently distinct to render it worthy of cultivation. P. Scouleri may be readily increased in spring by cuttings of the young shoots, since such cuttings strike freely in a little bottom-heat similar to that used for ordinary bedding plants.

P. speciosus, a remarkably handsome kind, has stems 3 to 4 ft. in height, and many-flowered clusters of flowers, which are sky-blue, varying to a reddish hue. P. glaber is nearly related to P. speciosus, but is dwarfer. The flowers are of various shades of purple, and early in summer are borne in crowded spikes about 1 ft. in length. On account of its dwarfness it is better suited for the rock-garden than most of the kinds. P. grandiflorus is very handsome, and allied to P. speciosus and P. glaber. It grows about 3 ft. high, and from July to August produces large flowers of a beautiful pink colour. Another and similar species is P. secundiflorus, which bears in one-sided racemes blossoms of clear blue and violet. It is about 1½ ft. high when well grown. P. acuminatus is a beautiful similar kind. These all require to be raised from seed annually, and to be planted out the second year.

PERILLA.—*P. nankinensis* is a half-hardy annual, with dark vinous-purple foliage. Seed should be sown about the middle of February in pans or boxes in heat ; the seedlings should be transplanted into boxes in soil not over-rich, and after being gradually hardened off, they should be planted out about the end of May. For those without artificial heat in spring it is not a very suitable plant, as it requires heat to get to the requisite size for planting in proper time. It is much used in bedding-out, and often with the worst results as to effect.

PERIPLOCA (*Silk Vine*).—*P. græca* is a rapid-growing shrubby climber of the Stephanotis order, excellent for walls, arbours, trellises, and the like, but on account of the somewhat unpleasant odour of its flowers it is not advisable to plant it against the walls of a dwelling-house. Its long slender stems and branches form a dense mass, and at midsummer are covered with brownish-red velvety flowers ; it is deciduous, and therefore unsuitable for a winter-screen. A native of Southern Europe, it is hardy in garden soil, and has been grown in English gardens for nearly three centuries.

PERNETTYA (*Prickly Heath*).—*P. mucronata* is a little Evergreen of the Heath family from South America, but hardy enough for our gardens, its beauty lying mainly in the berries which it bears in autumn, the size of small Cherries, dull purple, but there are varieties with berries of white, rose, pink, crimson, purple-black, and every intermediate shade. They should be planted where the soil is peaty or sandy, and even a heavy soil may be made suitable by adding decayed leaf-mould and sand. For autumn and winter beds on a lawn near the house they are excellent, as they have a cheerful aspect throughout the winter.

PETASITES (*Winter Heliotrope*).—*P. fragrans* is a rampant weed with fragrant flowers 4 to 12 in. high, in December and January, unless the weather is very severe, bearing flowers, deliciously fragrant, of a pale dingy lilac, in a rather short panicle. It is unfit for garden culture, as it runs very much at the root and becomes a weed, but it may be planted on rough banks, lanes, and in hedgerows, as it is very useful for winter bouquets, and may carpet, so to say, a small clump of shrubbery, where it

can be conveniently gathered. Another species, P. vulgaris (Common Butterbur),

The Winter Heliotrope (Petasites fragrans).

is a native plant, 2 to 2½ ft. high, closely allied to the common Coltsfoot, but having great Rhubarb-like leaves ; the flowers appear in spring before the leaves, and are of a dull pinkish-purple. Exotic plants, with less effective leaves than this have been used in gardens ; but it should not be allowed to come nearer to the garden than the margin of some adjacent stream or moist bottom. Division.

PETROCALLIS (*Rock Beauty*).—*P pyrenaica* is a beautiful little alpine plant

Petrocallis pyrenaica.

forming dense cushions 2 to 3 in. high, when not in flower resembling a mossy Saxifrage ; it flowers pale lilac faintly veined, sweet scented, in April. Though hardy, it is fragile, and is best placed on the well-made rock-garden, in sandy fibry loam, in level sunny spots, where it can root freely in moist soil, mingled with broken stones. It may also be grown in pots plunged in sand in the open air, and in frames in winter, but it becomes "drawn" and delicate under glass. Easily increased by seed or careful division. Alps and Pyrenees.

PETUNIA.—In certain positions, some of these showy half-hardy plants of the Solanum order produce a charming effect in masses ; and all are well suited for large vases, for baskets of mixed plants, for low trellises, and for planting under windows and walls. The spots chosen for Petunias should be open and sunny, and the soil deep and rich, for in low damp situations they mildew and canker as soon as the first cold nights of autumn set in. The best bedding varieties are Spitfire, dark purplish-crimson ; Dr. Hogg, purple, with white throat ; Miss Amy, crimson and white ; Countess of Ellesmere, rosy-crimson, with a lighter throat ; and Delicata, white, striped with purple. If they are sown in heat in February or March, good plants may be had for putting out at the end of May, but it is not safe to plant them out earlier. Seedlings, too, are now so good that they are frequently planted in mixed borders for cutting. The named kinds must be propagated from cuttings. Cuttings should be inserted in August in a bed of leaves or other fermenting material at a temperature of 70° to 75°, and with a top-heat of 65°, since they strike quickly under such conditions. As soon as rooted they should be taken out of the bottom-heat and placed in cold frames till frosty nights set in ; then removed to an intermediate house and placed on shelves near the glass, remaining there in store-pots till spring, then potted off singly and grown sturdily on till planting-out time. The roots are so brittle that, however well they are rooted, the soil does not adhere to them ; and this is why it is necessary to pot singly, for if the plants are put in pans or boxes, and transplanted thence to the beds, they suffer greatly, and are a long time getting re-established.—W. W.

PHACELIA.–Californian hardy annuals of easy culture : none of the cultivated kinds very important. P. congesta is the best, and smaller than either P. tanacetifolia or circinalis. They have dense heads of small blue or violet flowers. Hydrophyllaceæ.

PHILADELPHUS (*Mock Orange*).—Handsome flowering shrubs, with the exception of P.mexicanus, hardy, and many of them from their beauty deserving a good place. They are generally seen struggling for existence in some choked-up shrubbery border, and often in some shady spot where the bloom is sure to be meagre. Where planted in a group or mass, ample space should be allowed for the access of sunshine, as upon this will to a very great extent depend the future display of bloom. The larger kinds are seen to great advantage when isolated on the Grass or disposed thereon in a group of three or four, plenty of room being allowed each for its full development. Some of the smallest, and especially P. microphyllus, look well in a small bed by themselves, or they may be employed as a foreground to the larger kinds. In pruning the Philadelphus, as with most other flowering shrubs, if carried out at all, the main thing should be to remove exhausted and useless wood rather than to interfere with clean recent shoots. The entire genus (and more particularly the larger growing forms) is in a very confused state, and it is no uncommon thing to see two names applied to one plant, or a couple quite distinct bearing one name.

P. microphyllus.—This forms a dense bush, at the most not more than a yard, and frequently less, in height, clothed with small Myrtle-like leaves, disposed in a regular manner on the slender twigs, which in their turn are arranged very regularly. The flowering spray is handsome ; its fragrance is very different from that of any other kind, being more like a combination of ripe Apples and Quince. This little shrub is a native of New Mexico and some of the adjacent States. It was not long in Europe before the hybridist took advantage of such a distinct shrub, and M. Lemoine, of Nancy, raised a variety, Lemoinei, which was announced as the result of a cross between P. microphyllus and the European P. coronarius. It forms a shrub in appearance about midway between its parents, and flowers profusely. The blossoms possess the fragrance of its North American parent, without any of the heavy smell common to the Mock Orange. Since P. Lemoinei was sent out, a second form has made its appearance from the same source, under the name of P. Lemoinei erectus. Though of more erect habit, it is in other respects much like the preceding.

P. grandiflorus. -- While P. microphyllus is the best of the small-growing kinds, this is the best of those with large blossoms, and it is certainly one of the finest flowering shrubs to be met with in gardens. The blooms are a couple of inches in diameter, white, and with little scent, the bush forming a rounded mass

Philadelphus grandiflorus.

from 6 ft. to 12 ft. in height. There is a variety of this (laxus) less in stature and of a more open style of growth than the type. P. speciosus is now regarded as synonymous with P. grandiflorus.

P. Gordonianus is another large-growing kind, native of North America, whose blooms are smaller than those of the last named, but they are very numerous, and later in expanding than most of the others, and on that account this species is especially valuable. It was introduced from North-west America in 1823, and was named in compliment to the late Mr. R. Gordon, of the Horticultural Society's Garden, Chiswick. Other species a good deal in the same way are P. inodorus and P. verrucosus, both North American, while P. mexicanus is too tender to be generally planted.

P. Satzumi is a slender, yet freely branching bush about 6 ft. high, the flowers rather small, borne in little clusters for some distance along the shoots. Slight forms of this are often met with under different names, and it is also very probable that the North American species could be reduced in number if grown under similar conditions.

P. hirsutus.—This derives its name from the hairy undersides of the leaves, while the flowers are, with the exception

of those of P. microphyllus, about the smallest of the genus. They are also generally solitary, but are borne in such profusion that a specimen is wonderfully pretty when in bloom. This, as a rule, grows about 4 ft. or 5 ft. high.

P. coronarius is the common European Mock Orange, which is well known. There are, however, one or two well-marked varieties, viz., nanus, a little bush about 2 ft. high, that rarely flowers ; variegatus, whose leaves are margined with white ; and aureus, of moderate compact growth, whose foliage retains its golden hue throughout the summer. Several varieties with double blossoms are to be met with, among which may be mentioned florepleno, primulæflorus, and rosæflorus.—T.

Known Species *P. affinis*, Mexico ; *asperifolius*, do. ; *coronarius*, S. Europe ; *godokokesii*, N. Amer. ; *Gordonianus*, Calif. ; *grandiflorus*, N. Amer. ; *hirsutus*, W. Amer. ; *inodorus*, N. Amer. ; *insignis* ; *intermedius* ; *Keteleerii* ; *Lewisii*, N. Amer. ; *Mexicanus*, Mexico ; *microphyllus*, N. Mexico ; *myrtoides*, Guatemala ; *parviflorus*, China ; *pendulifolius* ; *rubricaulis*, China ; *serpyllifolius*, N. Mexico ; *stenopetala* ; *trichopetalus*, Costa Rica.

PHILESIA(*Pepino*).—*P. buxifolia* is an exquisite dwarf shrub, with large carmine-red Lapageria-like bells (2 in. long) nestling among and suffusing with their rich colour the sombre evergreen foliage. It is a precious shrub for the cooler parts of the rock-garden in the more favourable coast gardens, in peat or turfy loam. S. America.

PHLOMIS (*Jerusalem Sage*).—Among the finest hardy plants of the Sage family. There are about a dozen kinds in cultivation, showing great diversity of size and habit. Some, like P. fruticosa, are shrubs, others stout herbaceous plants, while others again, as P. armeniaca, are sufficiently alpine for the rock-garden. The most desirable is the South European P. fruticosa, a half-shrubby plant 3 to 4 ft. high, its Sage-like leaves covered with rusty down, while its large rich yellow flowers, attractive in summer, are in dense whorls for about half the length of the branches. It may be grown in the mixed border or associated with shrubs in an open spot. It is hardy in light soils in the southern counties. Of the few other shrubby kinds none is so fine, and though P. ferruginea is similar, it is neither so effective nor so hardy. Of herbaceous kinds the best is P. Herba-venti, a strong plant 1 to 3 ft. high, its rich purplish-violet flowers in dense whorls. P. tuberosa and P. purpurea, with purple flowers, may be naturalised with it, as they flourish in any soil or situation. The best herbaceous kinds with yellow flowers are P. Russelliana and P. Samia, both about 3 ft high, strong growers, and do well for naturalising. The very dwarf P. armeniaca has silvery leaves and reddish-purple flowers. P. cashmeriana somewhat resembles P. Herba-venti, but its flower-heads are denser, and its flowers, besides being larger, have a broad violet-purple lip   All the species are easily propagated—the shrubby kinds by cuttings and seed, the herbaceous sorts by division and seed

PHLOX—For the most part showy garden perennials, but the annual P Drummondi alone has produced distinct varieties enough to furnish a garden with almost every shade of colour. The perennials are numerous, and present such variety in habit, that for the garden they may be divided into three distinct groups One is alpine in habit, of this the beautiful P. subulata, or Moss Pink, is the best known, but there are many others in the Rocky Mountains and westward, some of them more truly alpine. Next to these are several that may be grouped as running or creeping Phloxes, perennial, but with prostrate stems   Lastly, there are the well-known tall garden Phloxes, generally called the perennial Phloxes, though all Phloxes but P Drummondi are perennial Perennial Phloxes have been so hybridised that the types are quite lost sight of in a vast number of garden forms P subulata, for instance, varies so much in the wild state that its forms have been described as species

EARLY OR SUMMER - FLOWERING PHLOXES have chiefly come from P suffruticosa They include many varieties, varying principally in colour, and flowering during June and July They grow in any good border or bed, and if the subsoil be too wet, it must be drained, and about 9 in of good Hazel-loam enriched with good old manure and a small quantity of broken bones laid on the surface   In the herbaceous border a pit can be dug—say, 12 in square and 9 in deep—and filled with this compost   Summer Phloxes are useful in June and July, as they come between the spring and autumn sorts   The following are twenty-four of the finest Beauty, Beauty of Edinburgh, Bridesmaid, Conqueror, Caller O', George Eyles, James Nicholson, Mrs P Guthrie, Mrs Burton, Mrs Gellatly, Philip Pollock, William Mitchell, Allen M'Lean, Dr. Robert Black, Duchess of Athole, Indian Chief, Mary Shaw, Mrs Ritchie, President, Redbraes, Socrates, The Bouquet, The Deacon, and The Shah

AUTUMN OR LATE-FLOWERING PHLOXES have been obtained by hybridising and selecting from various N

American species, principally P paniculata and its varieties acuminata, decussata, and pyramidalis, which are stronger and taller than the early Phloxes, and immediately succeed them in flower, thus prolonging the season at least two months from the end of July   They are bright and varied in colour, including all shades from rich vermilion to pure white, but the many shades of dingy purple and magenta are objectionable. There are endless varieties, more or less distinct, but the following will be found a good selection Coccinea, David Syme, Gavin, Greenshields, Jane Welsh, Jenny Grieve, Lothair, Matthew Miller, Mrs Keynes, Monsieur Rafarin, Rêve d'Or, Robert Paterson, William Blackwood, Andrew Borrowman, Carnation, Henry Cannell, James Alexander, James Cocker, Madame Verlot, Major Molesworth, Miss Wallace, Mrs Tennant, Thos. Chisholm, Triomphe du Parc de Neuilly, and William Veitch For large beds, and to get bold masses of distinct colour, the following are the most effective and can be used according to the shades of colour required, viz   Coccinea, rich vermilion, Carnation, white and spotted with purple, James Alexander, rich crimson; Lothair, bright scarlet, Mrs Keynes, pure white, Robert Paterson, rich crimson, William Blackwood, rosy-salmon, Miss Wallace, pure white, and Major Molesworth, scarlet with a crimson eye   When in beds or borders, the early and late sorts should be planted alternately, and arranged according to height and colour, a mass of bloom, lasting for at least three months, being produced After planting give each plant a good stake, and tie it up when necessary. In spring the number of shoots should be reduced according to the strength of the plant and nature of the variety   Phloxes of this group are also improved by a top-dressing of good rich soil every spring, and in very hot and dry seasons good watering will prolong the bloom

The way to propagate Phloxes is by seed, cuttings of the stems and roots, and division   Seed should be taken from the best sorts, and sown in boxes or pans in good free loam, immediately after being ripe   Keep it in a greenhouse or warm pit close to the glass   The young seedlings will appear in February and March, and when fit to handle prick them into boxes of good soil and keep close and warm for a short time; they can then be grown with the other plants intended for the flower garden   The strongest will be fit to plant out in April and May. They will flower the first season, but will not be strong until the second. In the second year all the best sorts ought to be marked and then grown a third year, to test them with the best named kinds Cuttings can be taken at all seasons, and in propagating from roots cut the oldest into pieces about $\frac{1}{2}$ in in length, sown, so to speak, in boxes, and treated like seedlings

The leaves also strike, but this is a very slow way As regards division, this consists in taking the old plant and cutting it into small pieces The habit of the plant should be strong and erect, with plenty of broad and healthy foliage, and not exceed 3 or 4 ft

P. Carolina is a handsome plant, about 1 ft high, with slender stems terminated by a cluster of large showy deep rose flowers P ovata has broader leaves; while P. nitida is also handsome P glaberrima, is far less important These kinds flower in summer, in ordinary soil and an open spot

P. divaricata.—A handsome plant from North America, larger than either the Creeping Phlox (P reptans) or the Moss Pink (P. subulata), and about 1 ft high with large lilac-purple blossoms in summer, while the leaves are rounded at the base, and are egg-shaped or lance-shaped Rock-garden in good soil Increased by division

P. Drummondi.—One of the most beautiful of half-hardy annuals, varied and brilliant in colour, and not injured by bad weather, like many other flowers It may be used in a variety of ways, such as a carpet to beds of standard Roses, as it does not interfere with the well-being of the Roses, but hides their naked stems It is also suitable for rustic vases and boxes, but it is when in masses that its beauty and diversity of colour are best seen Seed should be sown about the first week in March in shallow pans or boxes, in a light rich soil, and a warm and rather moist temperature Prick off the seedlings when fit to handle in boxes or a bed in a warm house in a temperature of 50° to 60°. Here they will soon grow, and place them out in the shade to harden as the weather gets warm Those growing in a bed should be again transplanted to a prepared bed in a cold frame, kept covered for a few days, and hardened gradually When the plants are 3 to 4 in high, pinch out the main shoot, to induce bushy growth, and prolong the flowering period The bed should be fully exposed to the sun, and if good moist soil, the plants will be uninjured even in the hottest weather Although generally treated as an annual, P Drummondi strikes freely

from cuttings in autumn these are useful for pots and early spring bloom in the conservatory or the greenhouse Varieties are endless, and some very distinct named sorts differ from the type not only in colour but in growth

P. pilosa is a pretty plant 10 or 12 in. high, large flat clusters of purple flowers, $\frac{1}{2}$ to $\frac{3}{4}$ in in diameter, appearing from June to August It is one of the rarest of cultivated Phloxes, though a spurious kind is sometimes sold for it The true plant reminds one of P. Drummondi Another rare species is the true P bifida, an elegant plant, the flowers bluish-purple

P. reptans (*Creeping Phlox*) —This is a beautiful little plant sending up numbers of stems from 4 to 6 in at the end of April or beginning of May, each bearing from five to eight deep-rose flowers It is useful on the rock-garden or border, and makes pretty tufts round beds of hardy plants; thriving in peat or light soils It is known as P verna and P stolonifera as well as P reptans

P. setacea is sometimes considered the same as P subulata, but its leaves are longer and farther apart on its trailing stems, the whole plant being less rigid The flowers are of a charming soft rosy-pink, and have delicate markings at the mouth of the tube P s violacea is a handsome Scotch variety more lax in growth and with deeper coloured flowers, almost crimson Both the variety and the type are lovely plants for the rock-garden, where with roots deeply seated among the fissures and enjoying coolness and moisture, they thrive luxuriantly in any amount of sunshine

P. subulata (*Moss Pink*) —A Moss-like little Evergreen, the flowers pinkish-purple or rose-colour, with a dark centre, and so dense as to completely hide the plant The stems, though 4 in to 1 ft high, are always prostrate, so that the dense matted tufts are seldom more than 6 in high, but in moist, sandy, and well-drained soil, when the plant is fully exposed, the tufts attain a diameter of several feet, and a height of 1 ft or more P frondosa is a vigorous form of P subulata, and in any ordinary light garden soil its trailing branches will soon cover almost a square yard of surface P nivalis is as trailing, but smaller, and with shorter, more densely arranged leaves Its flowers are snow-white P Nelsoni is no doubt a hybrid between P subulata and its forms, as it possesses foliage of an intermediate character, the flowers pure white with a charming pink eye Besides this, the late

Mr. Nelson, of Aldborough, raised a large number of seedlings, as varied in hue as Phlox Drummondi.

The dwarf Phloxes are so closely allied that general cultural remarks will suffice. Well-drained ordinary garden soil and sunny exposure are essential. Though perfectly hardy, the damp atmosphere of mild winters is fatal, and as the plants do not seed freely, they must be increased by cuttings. A sharp knife and a careful hand will soon remove the two or three pairs of leaves with their included buds without damaging either the slender stem or the joint. These should be taken off in July, when the branches are just commencing to harden, and inserted in sandy soil in a frame where they can be shaded from full sunshine, and given the benefit of the night dews by the removal of the lights. They will soon root and become good flowering plants the following season. With large patches, the readiest way is to sprinkle sandy soil over the entire plant and to work the same gently amongst the branches with the hand. If this be done during the summer or the early autumn, the trailing branches will form roots the following season, and may be planted elsewhere. These Phloxes are charming in spring, being hardy and forming gay cushions on the level ground, or pendent sheets from the tops of crags or from chinks in the rock-garden. Rocky hills and sandy wastes in North America.

Known Species *P. adsurgens*, W. Amer.; *amœna*, N. Amer.; *bifida*, do.; *biflora*, Chili; *brevifolia*, N. Amer.; *bryoides*, N.W. Amer.; *cæspitosa*, do.; *canescens*, N.W. Amer; *clarkioides*; *divaricata*, N. Amer.; *Douglassii*, N.W. Amer.; *Drummondii*, Texas; *elata*, N. Amer.; *floridana*, do.; *glaberrima*, do.; *glomerata*, do.; *Hoodii*, N.W. Amer.; *intermedia*, do.; *lineari-folia*; *Listoniana*, N. Amer.; *longifolia*, N.W. Amer.; *maculata*, N. Amer.; *muscoides*, N.W. Amer.; *nana*, do.; *odorata*, N. Amer.; *ovata*, do.; *panicu-lata*, do.; *pilosa*, do.; *reptans*, do.; *Richardsoni*, Arctic Amer.; *Ræmeriana*, Texas; *rosea*, N. Amer.; *siberica*, Arctic regions; *speciosa*, N.W. Amer.; *stel-laria*, N. Amer.; *subulata*, do.; *suffruticosa*, do.; *Thomsoni*, do.; *tigrina*; *virginica*, N. Amer.

PHORMIUM (*New Zealand Flax*).— *P. tenax* reminds one in habit of a large Iris, forming tufts of broad, shining, leathery leaves, 5 to 6½ ft. high, gracefully arched at the top. The lemon-coloured flowers are in erect loose spikes just above the foliage. It will generally enjoy a greenhouse, though in genial places in south and west of England and Ireland it does very well in the open air in a light deep soil. A few specimens well grown and plunged in the Grass or in the centre of a bed have a distinct effect. The variegated variety is also pleasing in the open air in warm situations in the south of England and Ireland, and in any case will do out-of-doors in the

summer. Division of the tufts summer.

·**PHRAGMITES** (*Great Reed*). -- *P. communis* is a common native waterside Grass, suitable for the margins of water, by which it forms excellent covert. There is a good variegated form.

PHYGELIUS (*Cape Figwort*).— *P. capensis*, a Cape plant, is related to the Chelone and the Pentstemon, but distinct in its general effect. It grows some 3 or 4 ft. high, and its many stems are terminated by a long branching raceme of brilliant scarlet flowers, which open in May and June and continue far into autumn. It is hardy near London, though it does not flourish so well in the open as under the shelter of a wall, where it thrives. It prefers a light rich soil, but in warm sea-shore districts is not fastidious. Readily increased by portions of the root-stock, the bases of the stems being furnished with rootlets.

Phyllostachys. See BAMBUSA.

PHYSALIS (*Winter Cherry*).-*P. Alke-kengi* is a handsome and curious South European plant, bearing in autumn bright

Physalis Alkekengi (Winter Cherry).

orange-red bladder-like calyces, enclos-ing Cherry-like fruits. It is a hardy perennial, requiring a warm border; 1

to 1½ ft. high. Division or seed. Solanaceæ.

P. Francheti.—A splendid new hardy plant from Japan, possibly a variety of P. Alkekengi, but so distinct as to merit special attention. It is larger altogether than the old kind both in foliage and calyx which is brilliant coral-red in colour, though varying a little in shade, sometimes touched with orange, and generally 3 in. in length with a circumference of 7 or 8 in. The plant grows 18 in. high and requires a similar position to P. Alkekengi.

PHYSOSTEGIA.—Handsome perennials for associating with the bolder kinds of hardy plants. P. virginiana, 1 to 4 ft. high, has flesh-coloured or purple flowers crowded in terminal racemes. P. imbricata from Texas, has higher and more slender stems, broader leaves, and larger flowers of a deeper colour. P denticulata is similar to P. virginiana, but rarer and less showy. All these kinds flower in summer, thrive in any ordinary soil, and may be naturalised with advantage in moist loam. Division in spring.

PHYTEUMA (*Rampion*).—The Rampions are neat, pretty, and interesting plants of the Bellflower order, with small flowers in profusion. They enjoy a sunny position, and some of them are good rock-plants. P. orbiculare is a rare and desirable native Rampion, 1 to 2 ft. high, and is best among rock-plants, where it would be free from the destructive effects of the

Phyteuma comosum.

hoe and rake. It flourishes in a dry position in a mixture of limestone grit, peat, sand, and loam, and has violet-blue flowers in July. It is extremely impatient of removal or division, and should be raised from seed sown in autumn in a cool frame. P. Sieberi is neat for the rock-garden, requiring a moist sunny situation, and a mixture of leaf-mould, peat, and sand. It forms cushion-like tufts, and in May and June has dark-blue flower-heads, on stems 4 to 6 in. long. Division. P. humile is a neat tufted plant for the rock-garden, where it can get a dry sheltered position in winter, and plenty of water in summer. The flowers are blue, and produced in June on stems 6 in. high. Division. P. comosum is very slow-growing, and must be particularly guarded against slug. It is a genuine rock-plant, suitable for a fissure vertical or sloping to the sun, and does best amongst a mixture of a little loam, peat, sand, or grit, where it can root to the depth of 2 ft. It bears almost stalkless heads of dark purple flowers, has Holly-like leaves in June and July, and comes best from seed. P. Charmeli and P. Scheuchzeri are much alike, P. Scheuchzeri being dwarfer. It bears pretty blue flowers, on stems from 6 to 12 in. in height, and is evergreen. Sow seed in autumn.

PHYTOLACCA (*Virginian Poke*).—This North American perennial, P. decandra, is from 5½ to nearly 10 ft. high, with reddish stems, and flower stalks. The flowers, on cylindrical spikes, are at first white, but afterwards change to a delicate rose. In autumn the colour of the leaves is in rich contrast to the pendent purple berries. It grows in almost any kind of soil, and is raised from seed or division. It is scarcely refined enough in leaf for the flower garden, but is effective near the rougher approaches of a hardy fernery, in open glades near woodland walks, or in any like position. P. icosandra is a bushy plant, 2 to 3 ft. high, the leaves similar to those of a Hydrangea. It has rather long spikes of creamy-white flowers, succeeded by fruit-clusters similar in size and shape to Indian Corn, but composed of ripe Blackberries. Should have the same treatment and position as P. decandra.

PICEA (*Spruce Fir*).—Usually stately evergreen cone bearing trees of the northern world and mountains, including among them the common Norway Spruce, and the Douglas Fir, usually doing best in moist valley soils. Trees that were once included under this head are now placed under *Abies* and also *Pinus*, to which the reader should refer for trees he seeks which are not placed under this heading. As regards grouping and other matters, what has been said of *Pinus* and *Abies* may be considered as applying to a great extent to these trees also.

P. AJANENSIS.—The finest of the Japanese Spruces, distinguished from all others by the bluish silver tint of the young branches on the undersides, but which are upturned so that the whole tree has a silvery appearance. It is very hardy and thrives best in a stiffish soil. It should not be in a too sheltered place or it will commence growth too early and be liable to injury by late frosts. Somewhat similar to this spruce and often confused with it is *P. Alcockiana*, also from Japan, but inferior as an ornamental tree, being of a dull green more like the common Spruce.

P. EXCELSA (*Norway Spruce*).—This is too common to need description, forming as it does beautiful woods in most parts of the country. It is a quick growing tree but too short-lived to be of great value for ornament. It is a mistake to plant it on high exposed places or in very light soil. In most sheltered valleys it is a beautiful tree when seen in masses. There are many forms of it, a good number of which are mere monstrosities not worthy of the garden, especially the so-called golden and silvery varieties. The dwarf forms, such as those named *Clanbrasiliana*, *Gregoryana*, *pygmæa* are suitable for planting in bold rock gardens. The North American white and black Spruces, *P. alba* and *P. nigra*,

Picea Morinda.

are too much like *P. excelsa* to be of any great value here.

P. DOUGLASI (*Douglas Fir*).—Among the noblest trees of the West American forests, this is undoubtedly one of the most valuable trees ever introduced, both for ornament and timber. It is now such a common tree being largely planted, especially in Scotland, for timber, and may be at a glance distinguished from other conifers by its dense soft green foliage on pyramidal trees a hundred or more feet high in the oldest specimens. It should be planted only where the soil and situation are suitable, and not in exposed places, as it thrives best in sheltered valleys or woods, but it will live in all soils ranging from light sands and gravels to moderately stiff clay. There are several varieties of the tree, that known as the Colorado variety being considered the hardiest. The glaucous form is an extremely handsome tree, more rapid in growth than any other silvery conifer. Varieties of this tree, *taxifolia*, *Standishi*, *pendula*, &c., are not remarkable, of far greater importance being the natural variety from the Rocky Mountains.

P. MENZIESI (*Menzies Spruce*).—In places where this Spruce thrives it is a very beautiful tree because of the bluish silvery grey tone of its needle-like leaves. In a damp climate where the soil is deep and moist it grows into a handsome tree, but in dry soils it soon becomes in a wretched condition. This Californian Spruce is also known as *P. sitchensis*.

P. MORINDA.—No other Spruce has such gracefully drooping branches as this Himalayan tree, which is also known well by its other name *P. Smithiana*. It is worthy of a place among the finest ornamental trees, but must have a deep moist soil more heavy than light, and the position not too sheltered. Under these conditions it flourishes in the bleakest parts of the eastern counties, where some of the finest examples of it exist.

P. ORIENTALIS.—This Caucasian Spruce has somewhat the appearance of the Norway Spruce, but it is a smaller growing tree with much shorter leaves and branches, and is more suitable as a garden tree as it is of denser growth and retains its lower branches. It is of a deep glossy green, and on this account, and its dwarfed growth, is especially suitable for grouping with the larger conifers. It is very hardy and thrives best in moist soils.

P. POLITA (*Tiger-tail Spruce*).—This is a comparatively recently introduced Japanese tree, but judging by the largest trees in various parts of the country it is a Spruce that will make a tree of the future in these islands. It is a decidedly handsome tree of very rigid pyramidal outline, and with leaves the stiffest and sharpest-pointed of all, which renders it cattle proof. It stands exposure well and is a tree for high windy places.

P. PUNGENS.—An American Spruce that is proving itself a most valuable tree for this country, as it is very hardy, quick in growth, and withstands exposure in high lying places better than any other. It is most generally known in gardens by the variety *glauca*, which is perhaps the most silvery of all conifers, the whole tree being like a cone of frosted silver. The Spruce is largely raised from seed in order to select from the seedlings these silvery varieties, and it is the green kind which is of less value for gardens that is so useful for exposed plantations and shelter groups. This Spruce is confused with another Californian Spruce called *P. Engelmanni*, *P. commutata* or *P. Parryana*, but which is quite inferior as an ornamental tree to *P. pungens*.

P. OMORICA (*Servian Spruce*).—A recent introduction, which promises to be a good addition to the Spruces notable for ornamental planting. It has somewhat the appearance of *P. orientalis* in its growth, and very dark green foliage, but the leaves are larger, flat and decidedly silvery beneath. It appears to thrive well in light soils, but beyond that not much is known about it in a cultural way.

PIERIS.—Evergreen shrubs of much beauty, natives of Japan, China, and America.

P. FLORABUNDA.—A compact growing free flowering evergreen, hardy in most soils, but thriving best in those of a sandy and leafy nature. Originally figured in the Botanical Magazine as *Andromeda*, it is better known

Flowers of Pieris.

in gardens under that name. It never grows very high, and is best grouped among the medium sized shrubs, and associated with Rhododendrons and other choice evergreens.

P. JAPONICA.—An extremely graceful evergreen bush with long beautiful clusters of flowers giving almost a lace-like effect in the case of well grown bushes. It is quite hardy, but slow and poor on loamy soils, thriving best on good peat, and should be associated with the choicest evergreens.

P. FORMOSA is another beautiful kind, but not quite so hardy as those we have above

described, with pretty clusters of flowers and evergreen leathery leaves ; only likely to thrive in the southern parts of England and Ireland.

Other species of less importance from a garden point of view are *P. mariana*, N. America, *P. nitida*, S. United States, and *P. ovalifolia*, Nepaul, which, among others, are poisonous to animals.

PINGUICULA (*Butterwort*).—These interesting dwarf bog-plants are pretty in the bog-garden or moist spots in the rock-garden. There are about half-a-dozen kinds, all resembling each other and, except P. vallisneriæfolia, natives. P. grandiflora (Irish Butterwort) is the finest. Its flowers are large and blue-purple, the leaves broad, spreading and flat upon the rock or soil. It prefers the shady side of a moist mossy rock, where the face is steep and the narrow chinks are filled with rich loam. If planted in earth alone, where the drainage is imperfect, it usually perishes in winter. P. alpina differs from all other kinds in having white flowers, marked more or less with lemon-yellow on the lip, but sometimes tinted with pale pink. It roots firmly, by means of strong woody fibres, and prefers peaty soil mingled with shale or rough gravel, and shady humid positions, such as are afforded by a high rock-garden with a north aspect, or by the shelter of a north wall. P. vulgaris grows freely in any sunny position in rich moist peat or peaty loam. A small form, with leaves like those of P. alpina, both in form and colour, is found in alpine bogs in the north of England. P. lusitanica, found on the west coast of Scotland and in Ireland, is smaller than any of the preceding, and has pale yellow flowers. It grows in peaty bogs exposed to the sun. P. vallisneriæfolia, from the mountains of Spain differs from others in its clustered habit of growth. Its leaves are pale yellowish-green, and sometimes almost transparent, becoming 4 or 5 in. long, and occasionally even 7 in. towards the end of the season. The flowers are large, soft lilac colour, with conspicuous white or pale centres. Dripping fissures and ledges of calcareous rocks (frequently in tufa) suit the plant perfectly, but it requires very free drainage, continuous moisture, and a humid atmosphere.

PINUS *Pine*). — Noble evergreen, cone-bearing trees of northern and temperate regions, of highest beauty and use, some of them admirably suited for the climate of the British Islands and giving finest evergreen shelter. When the Mexican and Californian Pines were first introduced and much talked of, little care was taken in discriminating between the hardy and tender kinds, so that the Pines of Mexico and Southern California got as good a chance in our pleasure grounds as the most precious of the hardy ones, but if we want to make the best use of the Pines we must plant only the best of the hardy ones, and those likely to endure and be useful and beautiful in our climate The Pines of subtropical countries which live in Devonshire and the west country, and around the coast of Scotland and Ireland in sheltered places, are no proof whatever of their value for the country generally, or even of their surviving hard winters in the places where they thrive when young. Even in many of the places where a show is made of these tender conifers there is nothing so handsome as a group of old Scotch or a grove of the Corsican Pine Nurserymen and others concerned with planting seldom take the trouble to see these trees in their native beauty on their native mountains, and assuming that the nursery or infant state of the tree is the natural form, make ceaseless efforts to keep the trees always in this form, whereas the nature of the Pine is generally to shed its lower branches, and hence we get that wonderful dignity of the Pine as seen on the mountains, both in the new and old worlds, lovely pillars crowding all over the northern mountains I have seen Pines condemned because they began to assume this habit of shedding their lower branches and taking their true character. Like other important families of trees, these have numerous garden and other varieties which are generally best left out if we seek to get the full expression of the natural beauty of the trees ; but, as usual, the practice of professional planters generally is rather against us Ugly, contracted, and monstrous forms are always in catalogues, which should be let alone there While such varieties are often worthless, natural varieties, especially of kinds inhabiting vast regions of the earth, like the Scotch Pine in northern Europe, and the Western Yellow Pine in America, may be important in giving us hardier varieties, or those of special use, like the Russian form of the Scotch Fir Synonyms are numerous, unfortunately, leading to confusion in the nomenclature, but among Pines, if anywhere, what is not worth knowing is not worth growing, and all the great Pines are so distinct in form that those who care about them will soon know them by heart, and the showy labelling method of the "pinetum" is not necessary in any good way of planting

It is this great family of trees which has given the name for the "pinetum" which we see in many country places, and it is not by any means the best way of growing the trees The isolation of specimens in the turf allows the grass in dry seasons to take away all the moisture from the tree, while the effect of this dotting about of trees is very far from artistic The true pinetum is a wood of Pines, the trees all chosen for their perfect hardiness in any given district, sheltering each other, promoting the true growth of the Pine by their close planting, especially in early life, shading the ground and keeping the moisture in it In such a pinetum the trees should be planted in groups and colonies, not necessarily rigidly separated by hard-and-fast lines, but sometimes those of like regions running together, as the European cone-bearing trees do in the mountains of Central Europe.

The advantage of grouping and massing the pines in a natural way is that they not only protect themselves from the sun, but the leaves and dead branches of the trees help to nourish the ground The roots are very near the surface, and they get a source of nourishment which fails them in the ordinary pinetum. In starting woods of Pines I have sown Furze-seed beneath (the little Furze and the common kind), which come very freely whether the ground be fallow at planting or otherwise These give excellent covert, and, in rough districts, I think, prevent rabbits and hares paying too much attention to the little trees. There may be a drawback or two, but on the whole I think there is a gain, because the vigorous young trees soon get their heads above the Furze, which is limited in stature, and eventually destroy it as they do the Grasses

In numerous places where there is not room enough to make a true pinetum, or Pine-wood even, then we should get a better effect in grouping the Pines than by scattering them about as they are often seen even in villa gardens, where there is little room But in many places in every county there is ample room for such beautiful evergreen woods as these precious trees give us, the true and natural way of growing the trees being carried out

In making the ordinary pinetum the richest ground is often taken, and large holes are made and filled with rich soil, whereas I think the better way would be to choose true Pine soil, if we have it— that is, rocky or poor ground of little use for anything else, and, by rightly choosing and planting the trees, doing away with the

Corsican Pine.

need of the costly and special preparation of the regulation pinetum. In this the rich soil and preparation give a rapid growth at first, but no means of testing the value of any Pine in the natural soil of the place. The rapid growth is often followed by weakness of wood, and often by too early destruction from storms, while the timber of such trees is always inferior to that grown in poor or rocky ground. We have the clearest evidence, on the mountains of Europe, California, Scotland, and elsewhere, that very fine Pines may be, and are, grown naturally on very poor rocky soils, and we should take this lesson and make our Pine-wood or pinetum in such a soil, or one as near as we can approach to it.

In some places, on the other hand, we may wish for the effects of a Pine-wood in a given situation, and in that way we must take the soil as it comes.

Not only is it unnecessary to make costly and special preparation of soil for Pines that suit our climate, but they actually seem to do as well in rocky and shaly places where there is almost no soil at all. When in California, I often saw seedling Pines starting vigorously on the bare places where the gold-miners had washed away the surface for many feet, and the little Pines came and sowed themselves on the bare, soilless ground, and, bearing this in mind, I have several times planted Pines in quarries and places where there was literally no soil except the *débris* of the stones that had been turned out, and the result was even better than we got in the natural soil around.

Often in young woods of Pine we find double-headed trees owing to false starts from our exciting mild winters, the attacks of squirrels, and other causes. Where time can be spared it is a good way to go round now and then in spring, and just pinch out the points of the second leader in every case where we see two or more growths where one erect leader should be seen.

The habit of planting "specimen" trees common in our present day pinetums is a costly and not a good way. The best way in all cases is to plant little trees, never over 1 ft high, I have often planted them much smaller with perfect success. They have a struggle at first, but eventually the growth is quicker and cleaner than that of older trees, the specimen trees of the ordinary nursery having a very hard time in dry seasons.

In devoting a piece of ground to the pinetum it is as well to begin by ploughing it and letting it mellow in the frost and air for a year or so, but this is by no means necessary in poor rocky or mountain ground. In some cases it may be quite safe to sow seed of the Pine on the ground where we wish it to grow, instead of the usual nursery system, sowing in lines about 4 ft apart, so as to be able to protect the trees a little in infancy, though that is not always necessary, because Pines that suit the climate will often get over all their early difficulties, except the rabbit and hare. These ought to be excluded by good wiring for at least seven years after forming the plantation, by which time, if the choice of trees has been a good one, they will be too old and vigorous for the teeth of these creatures to kill, and all wire can be taken away and grassy paths and drives may lead freely from the Pine-wood into other woods or plantations near. In the following enumeration of the finer species I have omitted those of doubtful hardiness or fitness for our climate from any cause.

P. AUSTRIACA (*Austrian Pine*).—One of the best and hardiest pines, distinct in form and colour, attaining a maximum height of nearly 100 ft, of close dense growth when young, thriving on calcareous and poor stony or rocky ground and on clay soils (but not on poor sands). Owing to its close "covert" and habit it nourishes the ground beneath it so well with its fallen leaves that it is self-supporting and gives precious shelter. It is often planted in Britain, but generally set out in the usual specimen way so that the tree is slow to take its true form as it does when grouped as trees should be. The final form of the tree, which so far we hardly ever see in our grounds, is very picturesque, with a free open head, but, being a free grower and giving valuable wood, however grouped or massed it should be freely thinned so as to allow of its full development.

In books this Pine is sometimes classed as a variety of the Corsican Pine, but, from a planter's point of view, the trees are as distinct as any other Pines in colour and form. Being a native of the mountains of lower Austria, Styria and Corinthia, sometimes also growing on the low hills and even plains, it would, I think, be distinctly hardier than the Corsican in the case of very severe winters, and their effects in low ground.

P. CEMBRA (*Swiss Pine*).—A hardy northern Pine of distinct, close-growing form, and a very slow grower in our country, as well as in its native land on the mountains of Central Europe or in Siberia, where it attains a maximum height of 100 ft.

P. COULTERI.—A Californian tree, not so large as other kinds from that great country of Pines, but remarkable for the great size of its cones, which are often 20 ins long and weighing 10 lb in its own country. In our country this tree should be planted only under the most favourable conditions, in sheltered valleys and on warm soils.

P. EXCELSA (*Himalayan Pine*).—A handsome tree, much planted in Britain with long, slender, drooping leaves and pendent cones. It is a native of the Himalayas and of very wide distribution in Asia, and also in another form inhabits the mountains of Greece and southeastern Europe on high elevations. In our country it thrives best in warm and well-drained soils.

P. HALEPENSIS (*Jerusalem Pine*).—A distinct and very useful Pine throughout the rocky parts of Greece and its islands, also Crete, Asia Minor, Syria and Palestine. When one travels in those countries the hills seem very bare until you get near their slopes, when the welcome growth of this Pine appears, a frequently graceful and stately tree. Coming from such a hot country it is not likely to be so useful with us, except in warm districts.

P. INSIGNIS (*Monterey Pine*).—A beautiful Pine of the seashore of California, grass green in colour, and often thriving very well in the southern and western parts of our country, but in inland places occasionally suffers in hard winters, and therefore not good for general planting, although on high ground in the home counties I have seen healthy trees. Syn., *P. radiata*.

P. LAMBERTIANA (*Sugar Pine*).—A noble tree of California and Columbia River, reaching a maximum height of 300 ft., and sometimes 60 ft. in girth of stem. We cannot omit such a tree here, but could not expect it to make such progress as in its own genial climate, and where planted with us it is usual to do so in sheltered situations and in free, warm soils. The cones are each sometimes over 2 ft. long.

P. LARICIO (*Corsican Pine*).—The tallest Pine of Europe, reaching 160 ft. high and over in Calabria and its own country, Corsica, and of very rapid growth in our country, as I have raised woods of it in ten years. The tree, if one raises it from seed, as we should in planting, shows a great variety of habit and even foliage, and if one liked to do anything so foolish one could give Latin names to several forms found in one wood. The Calabrian variety has been reckoned as a species by some, as it is a more vigorous tree, especially in poor soils. The variegated or otherwise dwarf, deformed varieties are beneath the notice of anybody who thinks of the dignity and true character of this great tree.

P. MONTANA (*Mountain Pine*).—A dwarf, very hardy Pine, which clothes the mountains of many parts of Central Europe with a low bushy growth not much larger than the Savin or Furze, but under better conditions getting into a larger state, sometimes into a low tree. In our country it is often called *mughus* and *pumilio*, but the best name for the species is the one given here. It is a useful and distinct Pine for clothing banks and giving cover between taller trees.

P. MONTICOLA (*Western White Pine*).

Pine of the higher mountains of California, Oregon and Montana, reaching a maximum height of 80 ft., with a girth of 9 ft. It is considered a western representative of the great White Pine of Canada, and as it is found at elevations of 10,000 ft. is hardy in our country and better worth planting than many of the trees of greater size.

P. PARVIFLORA.—A medium sized and pretty tree, with dense foliage, cultivated much in Japan, and a native of the northern islands, therefore a hardy tree with us, thriving in deep soil.

P. PINASTER (*Cluster Pine*).—A beautiful Pine of pleasant green colour, 70 ft. or more high, native of the Mediterranean region, often by the seashore, and useful in our country near the sea, but often thriving in inland places, best in free and sandy soils. It is also used much in France as a protection against the encroachment of the sea. There are a great many so-called varieties of this Pine, few of any consequence.

P. PINEA (*Stone Pine*).—A distinct and picturesque Pine, old trees attaining a height of 70 ft. to 75 ft. This very characteristic Pine of Italy is not hardy in our country. It has been often planted here, but does not survive hard winters, and should not be planted except in the most favoured parts of the south. It is a native of sandy and rocky places by the seashore in Greece, Syria and Asia Minor.

P. PONDEROSA (*Western Yellow Pine*).—A very noble tree reaching nearly 300 ft. with a trunk girth of over 45 ft., but in the arid regions found much smaller. Sometimes one may see trees branchless for over 100 ft., but in quite healthy condition. It inhabits Montana, British Columbia, Western Nebraska, and Northern California, and is hardy in Britain. There is a form found on the eastern side of the American continent which is hardier. *P. Jeffreyi* (Black Pine) is now supposed to be a variety, also *scopularia*, but it does not grow quite so tall as the others. This *P. Jeffreyi* is found 1,500 ft. high on the eastern side of the Rocky Mountains, this answering for its hardiness.

P. PYRENAICA (*Pyrenean Pine*).—A fine, rapid-growing tree, with bright green foliage. A native of the Pyrenees and Spanish mountains, and also in the south of France; 60 ft. to 80 ft. high. *P. Brutia* is supposed to be a form of this.

P. RESINOSA (*Red Pine*).—A tall Pine, 100 ft. to 150 ft. high, Newfoundland to Manitoba, and southwards through the New England States. From its northern area of habitation this should be a hardy and thriving Pine in Britain.

P. RIGIDA (*Torch Pine*).—A forest Pine reaching a height of 80 ft. on sandy and rocky places in Canada, Kentucky, Virginia, and the Eastern states. This Pine is hardy and a rapid grower in Britain, growing in moist places less likely to suit the greater Pines.

P. SABINIANA (*Grey-leaved Pine*).—A very interesting Californian Pine, inhabiting the dry and warm hills and the coast ranges and foot hills of Sierra Nevada ; not often a very high

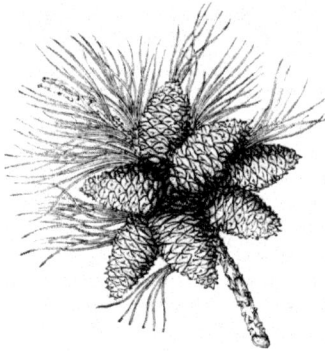

Pinus rigida.

mountain tree. The grey foliage gives the wild trees the appearance of clouds in the distance.

P, STROBUS (*White Pine* : *Weymouth Pine*). — One of the noblest forest trees of the northern world, sometimes reaching a height of over 170 ft., with a girth of trunk of 30 ft., though often found much smaller. Owing to the cutting of the woods in Canada and Northern America, it is seldom seen in its native dignity in the settled parts. It forms dense forests in Newfoundland and Canada, and westwards and

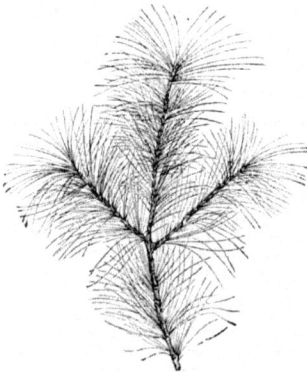

Shoot of White Pine.

southwards along the mountains. Certain varieties are catalogued, but they are of little use beside the parent tree.

P. SYLVESTRIS (*Scotch Pine*).—Our native Pine and, in its old state, one of the most beautiful and useful we can ever have. It is of very wide distribution in Northern, Arctic, and mountain regions, and also on the mountains of Italy and Greece. The Russian

variety is considered a more erect and stronger grower. A great number of varieties is mentioned in books and catalogues, and some hybrids, compact and dwarf varieties, including

Old tree, Scotch Fir.

variegated ones, none of any consequence compared to the wild tree. This Pine sows itself in rough heaths and sandy ground, and thrives there, if allowed to do so under these conditions.

PIPTANTHUS (*Nepaul Laburnum*).— *P. nepalensis* is a Pea-flowered shrub, hardy enough for walls, which it covers with large deep green leaves similar in shape to those of the common Laburnum, and in southern and warm localities withstands our winters without even this protection. But it is only to be recommended for walls, and is not the most desirable of plants even for them. It has evergreen foliage, and in early summer long dense clusters of large bright yellow flowers similar to those of the Laburnum, but larger. It succeeds best in light soils, and in the west and south thrives away from walls and among shrubs as at Madresfield. Himalayan Region.

PITTOSPORUM.—Evergreen shrubs, natives of New Zealand, Australia and China, few of them in cultivation and those usually only seen in southern gardens or those in sheltered places near the sea where they form evergreen bushes and trees of some beauty and distinctness of form. *P. tobara* is a good white flowering shrub in some southern gardens and is among the plants worth growing in tubs or vases for placing out in the summer. *P. undulatum* is a graceful evergreen and *P. Mayi* is also a very pretty evergreen at Castlewellan and other gardens in districts with a climate allowing of the cultivation of the half hardy evergreens.

PLATANUS (*Plane*).—Stately summer-leafing trees of the East and America, of rapid and vigorous growth and high value in the warmer parts of our islands as shade, lawn, or avenue trees ; thriving too in the centre even of smoke polluted cities as in many of the squares in west and central London, and not merely existing, as most trees do in such condition, but attaining much beauty of form and dignity there, as in Berkeley Square and Lincoln's Inn Fields. Here the great trees, getting out of the gardeners' way, or any attack of pruners or self-appointed tree-architects, assume their true and natural form, and are very fine whether in summer or winter. Where the Plane is used in the streets of London, however, as on the Thames Embankment the costly and wasteful labour of pruning the trees to one ugly shape is carried out. The Planes are easily increased by cuttings and layers, but planters should in all cases avoid them, as they cannot expect from such beginnings the fine rapid, natural growth and true form of the tree. The Plane which thrives best in London, or what is often called the London Plane, is not (as it used to be thought) the American or Western Plane, but the Eastern plane or one of its forms of which the accepted name is now *acerifolia*, a name with many synonyms. The true Western Plane, *P. occidentalis*, is rarely seen in Europe outside of botanical gardens, and, when it is, it has little of the beautiful vigour of the Oriental Plane in our country. The name *Orientalis* is still kept up for a deeply cut leaved form of Plane, but it is not really distinct as a species from the London Plane. *P. cuneata* is an Eastern species with deeply cut leaves, but it may be taken for all planting ends that the vigorous London Plane is the Eastern Plane no matter by what name it is called. The Plane, being a tree of vast distribution in the East, accounts for the origin and distribution of the various forms, mainly differing in the shape and lobing of the leaves. While the tree attains its greatest growth in Southern Italy and south-eastern Europe generally, it is a noble tree in the southern parts of England, attaining its best size, height and form in good valley soils, and there are many fine examples of it in the Thamas Valley. There is a peculiarity of the bark in scaling off in large irregular

patches, which leads to rather a striking effect, and is in no way harmful to the tree. The Greeks and Romans used it much as a shade tree near their public buildings, and from all recorded time it has been much planted in Persia. As

Platanus orientalis.

yet this tree has been little used in our woodlands, though it certainly deserves a place in them, especially in those on the alluvial soils.

PLATYCODON (*Broad Bell-flower*).— P. grandiflorum, sometimes called Campanula grandiflora, is a handsome Siberian perennial, hardy in light dry soils, but impatient of damp and undrained situations, where its thick fleshy roots are sure to decay. Sometimes the decay commences below and spreads upward, but it generally begins above and spreads downward, the plant rotting off at the neck. The flowers are 2 to 3 in. across, deep blue with a slight slaty shade, and in clusters at the end of each branch. The branches are 18 in. high, and very slender at the base, so that if unsupported in their early stage of growth, they will fall to the ground, and the plant look untidy. Such neglect will be almost impossible to repair when the flowers are nearly developed, as branch after branch will break away in tying. It is better to leave them alone, merely pegging down the branches to prevent breakage by wind. Perhaps the best position for the plant would be overhanging a ledge in some sunny corner of the rock-garden, where its negligent growth is in keeping with the situation, and its flowers, being on a level with the eye, are shown to advantage. Like most Campanulas it has a tendency to revert from blue to white through various modifications. Equally pretty is the white variety,

3 A 2

though by no means so common as the type. A rich loamy soil, good drainage, and an open situation are best. Propagate by seeds, which can be readily procured. The young shoots, if taken off when about 3 in. long, in spring, and placed in a gentle bottom-heat, will strike, but not freely. The plant is a bad one to divide—division often resulting in failure, and, if attempted, must be carried out in May, when the growth has just commenced. P. autumnale, or chinense, from China and Japan, is taller and more robust than P. grandiflorum, with narrower leaves, but more dense, and its flowers, though smaller, are pretty evenly distributed along the upper half of the stems. Besides a white variety, it has a tendency to become semi-double, by a sort of "hose-in-hose" reduplication of the corolla, similar to what occurs in many of our Campanulas. The dwarf, Mariesi, from Japan, is distinct.

PLATYSTEMON.—*P. californicus* is a pretty Californian hardy annual Poppywort, forming a dense tuft, studded thickly in summer with sulphur-yellow blossoms. It

Platystemon californicus

merely requires to be sown in ordinary soil in the open border either in autumn or spring ; but the seedlings should be well thinned out. P. leiocarpum is a similar kind.

PLUMBAGO (*Leadwort*).—An interesting family of graceful perennials and half shrubby plants, the hardiest being P. Larpentæ the blue-flowered Leadwort, from China. P. capensis usually grown under

glass, may be planted out in summer, bearing its lovely pale-blue flowers continuously throughout the summer. The plants should be specially prepared for out-of-doors, young ones being always the best for edgings, though taller ones may be used in certain positions. P. capensis is used with good effect in German gardens. P. Larpentæ is perfectly hardy, its wiry stems forming neat and full tufts, varying from 6 to 10 in. high, according to soil and position. In September these are nearly covered with flowers, arranged in close trusses at the ends of the shoots, and of a fine cobalt-blue, changing to violet : they usually last till the frosts. A warm sandy loam or other light soil and a sunny warm position should be given, such as above the upper edges of vertical stones or slopes on the rock-garden. It may also be used for borders, banks, or edgings in the flower garden, particularly in the case of slightly-raised beds. Very easily increased by division of the roots during winter or early spring.

POA.—Perennial and annual Grasses, few worth cultivating. P. fertilis has dense tufts of long, soft, smooth, slender leaves, 10 to 18 in. high, and arched gracefully on every side. In the flowering season they bear airy, purplish or violet-tinged panicles, rising to twice the height of the tufts. Isolated on lawns the plant is effective, and if in good soil gives no trouble. P. aquatica is a stout native Grass, 4 to 6 ft. high, usually occurring in wet ditches, by rivers, and in marshes. It is one of the boldest and handsomest of hardy Grasses for the margins of artificial water or streams, associated with such things as the Typhas, Acorus, Bulrush, and Water Dock. It increases rapidly.

PODOPHYLLUM (*Himalayan May-apple*).—*P. Emodi* is similar to P. peltatum, but handsomer. The stem and leaves have a reddish tinge, the fruits 2 in. long, and coral-red. The plant succeeds perfectly in peaty soil if in warm sheltered spots ; and in such positions is useful for the margins of beds of American plants. Seed or division. P. peltatum (May-apple) is interesting with its glossy green, wrinkled leaves, borne umbrella-like, on slender stems, about 1 ft. high. Its waxy-white Christmas Rose-like flowers are produced in May, and succeeded by green Crab-like fruit ; hence the popular name. It is adapted for shady peat borders, or for woods, but requires moist vegetable soil, and shady or half-shady positions. Seed or division.

POINCIANA.—*P. Gilliesii* is a beautiful sub-tropical tree which thrives against walls in the Isle of Wight in the garden of the Rev H Ewbank who writes of it in the *Garden* —"The foliage gives it very much the look of an Acacia at a little distance, and it is often mistaken for one of them But no Acacia that I have ever seen has such splendid blossoms. My great surprise has been in its well doing to such an extent in the open ground that I have now no fear for it at all, and during the worst frost we have had here during the last twenty or thirty years it was entirely uninjured A very great recommendation for it in my eyes is the time of year when it is accustomed to blossom. All spring things have gone by, and the wealth of flowering shrubs and trees has become exhausted when this very beautiful object makes full compensation for any loss that has been sustained Moreover, it goes on for such a very long time—blossoming, it is true, in an intermittent sort of way—but still remaining an attraction in the highest degree in the garden for week after week" Such a handsome and graceful thing deserves trial in warm southern gardens especially where the soil and subsoil is open and warm, and always against south walls

POLEMONIUM (*Greek Valerian*) —A small family of Phloxworts, mostly from North America A few of them are familiar in gardens, and among the best are the following

P **cœruleum** (*Jacob's Ladder*) most people are familiar with Besides the original blue-flowered species, there is a variety with white blossoms, and another handsome form with variegated foliage, which on good garden soil is almost as easily grown as the common one It thrives best in deep, rich, but well-drained loam To propagate it, dig up well-established plants, pulling them to pieces, and planting immediately in early autumn in a bed of good soil. Where merely required for borders and rock-garden, take up, divide, and replant the old stools where desired, in the old-fashioned way of dealing with herbaceous plants As the variegated variety is grown for leaf-beauty alone, the flower-stems should be removed.

P. **confertum.**—This is one of the finest of all, with slender deeply-cut leaves, and dense clusters of deep blue flowers on stoutish stems, about 6 in high It requires a warm spot in the rock-garden and a well-drained, deep, loamy soil, rather stiff than otherwise Though it requires plenty of moisture in summer, excessive dampness about the roots in winter is

hurtful It should be allowed to remain undisturbed for years after it has become established Rocky Mountains

P. **humile** is a truly alpine pretty plant with pale-blue flowers on stems a few inches high In a dry situation and a light sandy soil it is hardy, but on a damp subsoil is sure to die in winter P. mexicanum is similar but larger, and being only of biennial duration is scarcely worth cultivating N America

P. **reptans** is an American alpine plant, and, though far inferior in beauty to P. confertum, is worth growing Its stems are creeping, and its slate-blue flowers form a loose drooping panicle, 6 or 8 in high Snails devour it ravenously, especially the scaly root-stocks during winter, and must be watched for. P sibiricum, grandiflorum and Richardsoni much resemble P. cœruleum, but are more vigorous, with larger flowers There are several other species in cultivation, but not important

POLIANTHES (*Tuberose*) —P. *tuberosa* is a native of the East Indies, but strong imported bulbs from Italy and France of this deliciously fragrant plant, if inserted in warm soil, will flower well in the open air during August In the neighbourhood of London we have seen the Tuberose flowering freely in the open border, the bulbs in a light, sandy, well-drained soil, in which they had remained all the winter, slightly protected during severe weather by ashes or other dry material

POLYGALA (*Milkwort*) —The hardy Milkworts are neat dwarf plants, with flowers much resembling those of the Pea family. P. Chamæbuxus (Box-leaved Milkwort) is a little creeping shrub from the Alps of Austria and Switzerland, where it often forms but very small plants In our gardens, however, on peaty soil and fine sandy loams, it spreads out into compact tufts covered with cream-coloured and yellow flowers The variety purpurea is much prettier, the flowers are a lovely bright magenta-purple, with a clear yellow centre. It succeeds in any sandy, well-drained soil, best in sandy peat, if slightly shaded from the mid-day sun Even when out of flower it is interesting owing to its dwarf compact habit, bright shining evergreen leaves, and olive-purplish stems P paucifolia is a handsome North American perennial, 3 to 4 in high, with slender prostrate shoots, and concealed flowers From these shoots spring stems, bearing in summer one to three handsome flowers about three-quarters of an inch long, generally rosy-purple, but sometimes white. It is suited for the rock-garden, in leaf-mould and sand, and for association in half-shady places with Linnæa borealis, Trientalis, Mitchella. Some of the British Milkworts, especially P. calcarea and vulgaris, are interesting and easily grown in sunny chinks of the rock-garden if in calcareous soil. They form neat dressy tufts of blue, purple-pink, and white flowers, borne profusely in early summer. Seed may be gathered from wild plants and sown in sandy soil. Plants carefully taken up from their native positions have also been established in gardens.

POLYGONATUM *Solomon's Seal*).— Graceful tuberous perennials distributed autumn, germinate in early spring: the creeping root-stocks may also be divided to any extent, and in good soil soon form nice tufts. A few of the species are also in much request for forcing for early spring use in the greenhouse; these are generally imported instead of being grown at home, as they might well be. It simply requires singling out good crowns and growing them in rich loamy soil, lifting and potting when required.

P. biflorum.—A pretty species from the wooded hillsides of Canada, and New Brunswick, of slender graceful growth, the arching stems 1 ft. to 3 ft. in height, the small flower stems jointed near the base of the flowers, which are greenish white, two or three together in the axils of the leaves.

Polygonatum multiflorum (Solomon's Seal).

chiefly in the north temperate regions of the Himalayas, America, Japan, China, and Europe, and with very few, if any, exceptions will be found quite hardy enough to withstand the rigours even of an English winter. There are nine distinct species known to us in cultivation, and perhaps as many varieties, and although there is some similarity amongst them in habit, all are distinct as garden plants. They thrive well in almost any position in good sandy soil, and will be all the better for an occasional liberal dressing of leaf soil. It is in shady nooks, under the shade of deciduous trees, in the wild garden, however, where they do best and are seen to the best advantage. They are increased by seeds or berries, which sown as soon as gathered in

Syns., P. pubescens, P. hirtum, and P. canaliculatum.

P. japonicum. — A distinct species, native of Japan, hardy in this country, flowering in early April, growing about 2 ft. in height, the leaves of a very firm leathery texture, the flowers white, tinged purplish.

P. latifolium, the old Convallaria latifolia or broad-leaved Solomon's Seal, seems to be about intermediate between P. multiflorum and P. officinale. It is a native of Europe, and is said to have been found in Syke's Wood, near Ingleton, Yorkshire. A fine robust species, the stems being from 2½ ft. to 4 ft. high, arching, the leaves bright green; flowers large, two to five in a bunch from the axils of the leaves, greenish-white, in July.

P. latifolium var. commutatum differs from the above in being glabrous throughout, with a flower-stem 2 ft. to 7 ft. in height; large white flowers, three to ten in a bunch. N. America.

P. multiflorum.—This is the common Solomon's Seal, and is the most grown of all the species. It grows from 2 ft to 3 ft. high, glaucous green; the flowers are large, nearly white, one to five in a bunch in the axils of all the leaves. It is a very robust and free-growing species, its arching stems and drooping flowers being very attractive. There are several garden varieties, notably a double-flowered one, and one in which the leaves are distinctly variegated. P. Broteri is a variety with much larger flowers; P. bracteatum, a form in which the bracts at the base of the flowers are well developed, flowering throughout the summer.

P. oppositifolium.—A charming kind confined to temperate regions of the Himalayas and hardy, although usually given as a greenhouse species. It will doubtless do best in a sheltered spot, but even in the open it has given me no trouble, and it is a good plant for shady spots on the rock-garden, the habit graceful, 2 ft. to 3 ft. in height, leaves glossy green; the flowers, white, marked with reddish lines and dots, are borne in bunches of from six to ten in the axils on both sides in late summer. The fruit is red when ripe.

P. punctatum. — Another beautiful species from the temperate Himalayas, where it is found at altitudes of 7,000 ft. to 11,000, ft., and hardy in our gardens; about 2 ft. in height, the stem angular, with hard leathery leaves, flowers white, with lilac dots, two to three in a bunch, in late summer.

P. roseum.—A handsome little plant allied to P. verticillatum. It was first sent to the Royal Gardens, Kew, by Bunge, and is doubtless the plant described in *Flora Rossica.* It appears to vary considerably in the length and breadth of its leaves in their being more or less whorled, and also in the size of its flowers, 2 ft. to 3 ft. in height, the leaves in whorls of three or more; the flowers in pairs in the axils of the leaves, clear rose-coloured, are very pretty amongst the narrow green foliage. N. Asia.

P. verticillatum.—An elegant species distributed over the temperate Himalayas, and pretty general in the northern hemisphere. It was found in Perthshire, Scotland, in 1792, and appears to have been cultivated by John Tradescant,

jun., as early as 1656; 2 ft. to 3 ft. high under cultivation, the leaves four to eight in a whorl; the flowers, two to three in a bunch in the axils of the leaves, are greenish-white, smaller than those of P. multiflorum. The fruits are red when ripe. It flowers in June.—D. K.

POLYGONUM (*Knotweed*).—The vast family of Polygonums, comprising 150 species of world-wide distribution, the majority insignificant weeds, nevertheless includes several noble plants, which are well worth considering for their beauty of form. They thrive in any ordinary garden soil; those of a bushy habit should be allowed plenty of space. Tying in the shoots detracts much from their beauty, which consists in the many flower-spikes rising above a gracefully-developed mass of foliage reaching to the ground. The dwarf perennials, most of which are evergreen, need no support and little attention beyond an occasional trimming; but

Polygonum sachalinense.

the annuals, unless grown as single specimens, and in sheltered situations, require support.

P. affine is a pretty alpine plant of the Himalayas, where it grows on the wet river banks and meadows, and hangs in rosy clumps from moist precipices. In cultivation it is 6 to 8 in. high, with rosy-red flowers in dense spikes borne freely in September and October. P. Brunonis is similar and as desirable; the flowers, of a pale rose or flesh colour, borne in dense erect spikes nearly 18 in. high, and continuing more or less through the summer.

P. compactum is similar to P. cuspidatum, and forming a compact tuft 1 to 2 ft. high. It bears white flowers in great profusion, and its leaves are similar to those of P. cuspidatum, though much smaller. It flowers late in autumn.

P. cuspidatum (*Japan Knotweed*), also known as P. Sieboldi, is of fine and graceful habit, its creamy-white flowers borne in profusion. It should be grown apart on the turf or in some rough part of the wild garden, as, unfortunately, it is weedy, and in light soils springs up everywhere.

P. sachalinense.—A huge perennial with bright green leaves upwards of a foot in length, the flowers greenish-white, in slender drooping racemes. It thrives in a moist soil near water, where it is effective, and it makes a fine feature on the turf or in a spot where it can run about freely. There is no better plant for semi-wild places. Sachalien.

P. vaccinifolium is very distinct in aspect, quite hardy, and thrives in almost

Polygonum vaccinifolium.

any moist soil, but is best seen where its shoots can ramble over stones or tree

stumps. Under favourable conditions it grows rapidly, and produces a profusion of Whortleberry-like leaves and rosy flowers. Himalayas.

POLYPODIUM (*Polypody*). — This large family of Ferns contains several good hardy kinds, the principal being the common P. vulgare, which has about a score of cultivated varieties differing more or less widely from each other. The most distinct and beautiful as well as the freest in growth are cambricum, elegantissimum, omnilacerum, and pulcherrimum. Though preferring shade, they only need a good supply of water at the root during summer, and will thrive even exposed to the full rays of the sun. Plant them in fibry loam and tough and fibry peat, with a liberal

Oak Fern (Polypodium dryopteris).

admixture of leaf-mould and well-decayed woody matter, to which add a thin top-dressing of similar material every autumn. The evergreen Polypodiums associate well with flowering plants that do not require frequent removing, and they may be made to cover bare spaces beneath trees, or to overrun stumps. A beautiful effect, too, is got by their use as a carpet or setting to some of the plants in the rock-garden. Besides P. vulgare and its varieties, there are several deciduous kinds, such as P. Dryopteris (Oak Fern) and P. Phegopteris (Beech Fern), well known to all Fern lovers. They thrive best in peat, loam, and sharp sand, with some broken lumps of sandstone, and prefer a dry situation in the rock-garden ; or any situation which is not fully exposed to the sun. A slightly shaded spot should be selected, where they might be planted among flowering plants suitable for the same treatment, and affording the needed shelter. P. Robertianum (Limestone Polypody) is a beautiful deciduous species, somewhat difficult to manage ; it should have a dry sheltered position, does not mind sunshine, and prefers a mixture of sandy and fibry loam, with a plentiful addition of pounded limestone. P. alpestre resembles the Lady Fern ; the fronds dark green, and sometimes exceed 2 ft. in length. It may with advantage be grouped with Lady Ferns, as it flourishes under similar treatment. P. hexagonopterum, a native of N. America, is hardy in sheltered positions, and has elegant tapering dark green fronds about 1 ft. in height.

Polystichum. See ASPIDIUM.

PONTEDERIA (*Pickerel Weed*).— *P. cordata* is one of the handsomest waterplants, combining grace of habit and leaf with beauty of flower. It forms thick tufts of almost arrow-shaped, long-stalked leaves, from 1½ to over 2 ft. high, crowned with spikes of blue flowers. P. angustifolia has narrower leaves. Both should be planted in shallow pools of water. Division of tufts at any season. North America.

POPULUS (*Poplar*).—Usually forest trees of northern and temperate countries, often of rapid growth, mostly hardy in our country, some giving very fine effects in the landscape, and others of value in woodlands. Generally they are much neglected in country places, and in future they will be worth more attention, not only. because their rapid growth often helps to shut out objectionable things, but some for their timber. Among the best are the white, or the Abele Poplar (*P. alba*), and its variety *Bolleana nivea*, which is whiter in the foliage than the wild tree ; the great *P. monilifera* of North America, grown under various names in our gardens, and the most rapid grower of Poplars ; the Balsam Poplar (*P. balsamifera*) ; Fremont's Poplar (*P. Fremonti*) ; *P. grandidentata* ; *P. heterophylla* of North America, of which there is a pendulous variety ; *P. laurifolia* of Siberia ; the Black Poplar (*P. Nigra*), a native tree which has one or two varieties, one, the Lombardy Poplar ; *P. Sieboldi* of Japan ; *P. Simoni* of China ; *P. suaveolens* of North-West India ; *P. tremuloides* of North America,

and *P. trichocarpa.* Poplars being common in French and Continental gardens generally, their culture has led to what are called improved races and hybrids, among which the variety *Eugenie* is a favourite in the east of France. Few Poplars are ever planted in a fine way in our country, and some of them are not well known yet ; but such as are known are very fine in habit, especially the Abele and its allies, and there is no more beautiful tree than our native Aspen (*P. tremula*), with its cloud of delicate moving leaves. ·

Four kinds of Poplar are considered natives of our country—the White Poplar, sometimes growing 100 ft., the Grey

Populus nigra.

Poplar (*P. canescens*), the Aspen, and lastly, the Black Poplar, though this is not certainly a native. In nature these trees usually inhabit moist ground near streams or lakes, or moist woods, and in cultivation they often do best and look best in such places, as in the Poplar-lined valleys of France. In our moist climate, however, such soil or place is by no means essential to their growth, as we see noble trees of the greater Poplars in good soil away from lake or river ; but where there is water it is often well to group them near it, as, like the Willows, they are rarely so good in effect as when grouped near water. The Lombardy Poplar is often used in that way, and shows its fine form in such situations ; the Grey and White Poplars have claims in the same way, as they, when old, often show very fine form.

Our gardens are so crowded with exotic things—many of them quite unfit for our climate—that it is surprising how little our native Poplars come into the scheme of the planter, and hardly ever into that of the ordinary nursery planters with their conventional trees and pseudo-botanical absurdities in the way of monstrous forms and variegations. The true

Aspen is one of our native trees that is neglected, and rarely ever seen grouped in the pleasure garden in an effective way, though we may see it here and there wild, and in many woodland places, grouping itself very prettily. I know nothing more attractive than a group of the Aspen by the waterside or in almost any position. In Ireland, and on warm limestone soils elsewhere, the leaves become a lovely colour in autumn, but not on stiff soils.

PORTULACA *(Purslane).*—This bright little annual *P. grandiflora* has been introduced many years from its native home in Chili, and few Chilian plants have spread so widely all over the world. It seems as happy under a tropical sun as in an English garden, where no other annual excels it in brilliancy, delicacy, and diversity of colour. It makes itself at home as well on a dry, poor bank as in a rich border

Flowers of Portulaca grandiflora.

among taller things. One can see by its growth that it is a child of the sun, and that is why one finds it so fine in gardens in the parched plains of India and Egypt, as well as throughout North America. The colours vary from crimson and white through every shade to pure yellow. There are single and double-flowered kinds, and it is difficult to say which are the more beautiful. The double flowers last longer, and greater care seems to have been made in selecting the finest of the doubles by crossing the various sorts. Forty years ago M. Lemoine, of Nancy, raised many beautiful double sorts, to which he gave names, but it was soon found useless to keep named sorts, so one buys seed now in mixed colours, as with Cinerarias. Seeds of the Portulaca should be sown thinly during the month of April in pans in a frame, and the seedlings be planted out early in June. They can be also sown in the open ground about the end of May, for succession after the frame-

raised seedlings. The best plants are got when the seedlings, as soon as they are large enough to handle, are pricked out into small pots of rich soil and kept in an airy frame. The seed is best sown in light and rather rich soil, and only just covered. In planting out, choose the sunniest and warmest spots in the garden, and plant in bold masses to get a rich effect. It has proved in India one of the most useful flowering plants for bedding during the cool months. The named varieties of P. grandiflora are Thellusoni, lutea, splendens, and Regeli, while another kind is P. Gilliesi from Mendoza.

POTENTILLA *(Cinquefoil).*—A large family, many hardy herbs and alpine flowers among them. The most important are the fine hybrid varieties got by hybridising showy Himalayan species such as P. insignis and P. atro-sanguinea. These two species are well worth growing. The former has clear yellow and the latter deep velvety crimson flowers. The beautiful rosy-pink P. colorata is also useful ; but these three are about the only typical species of tall growth worth cultivating. The double kinds are most showy, lasting in perfection both on the plants and when cut longer than the single sorts. There are about three dozen distinct named kinds, all to be obtained from any of the large hardy plant nurseries. These varieties represent every shade of size and colour that it is possible to obtain. The culture of Potentillas, like that of most hardy flowers, is simple. They luxuriate in a light deep soil and exposed position.

The following is a good selection of double sorts : M. Rouillard, reddish-crimson ; Belzebuth, dark crimson ; Chromatella, yellow ; Dr. Andry, scarlet, margined with yellow ; Escarboucle, crimson ; Bélisaire, reddish-orange ; Vase d'Or, yellow ; Le Dante, orange shaded with scarlet ; Louis Van Houtte, crimson ; Phœbus, rich yellow ; Le Vésuve, crimson with yellow margin ; Versicolor, yellow suffused with brownish-crimson ; Vulcan, scarlet shaded with yellow ; Variabilis fl.-pl., yellow with scarlet margin ; Eldorado, scarlet-crimson with yellow margin ; Perfecta plena, bright scarlet-crimson slightly tinged with yellow ; Imbricata plena, orange-scarlet ; Etna, reddish-crimson ; Panorama, yellow heavily stained with scarlet ; Nigra plena, dark crimson ; Meteor, yellow suffused and blotched with scarlet ; Meirsschaerti fl.-pl., yellow veined and striped with crimson ; William Rollisson, deep orange-scarlet with yellow centre ; Fénelon, orange and scarlet ;

Purpurea lutea plena, scarlet - crimson slightly tipped with yellow.

Among the dwarf alpine species there are some very beautiful plants for the rock-garden. Of these the following are the best :—

P. alba (*White Cinquefoil*).—The leaves of this pretty plant from the Alps and Pyrenees are quite silvery and have a dense silky down on the lower sides. It is very dwarf, and not rampant; its white Strawberry-like flowers nearly 1 in. across, with a dark orange ring at the base. Easily grown in ordinary soil, and on borders or for the rock-garden. It blooms in early summer, and is increased by division.

P. alpestris (*Alpine Cinquefoil*).—A plant closely allied to the spring Potentilla (P. verna) forming tufts nearly 1 ft. high, with bright yellow flowers about 1 in. across. While enjoying a moist deep soil, it cares little how cold the position is. Though not very common, it is found on rocks and dry banks in several parts of the country.

P. ambigua, from the Himalayas, is a dwarf compact creeper, with in summer large clear yellow blossoms on a dense carpet of foliage ; is perfectly hardy, requiring only a good deep well-drained soil in an open position in the rock-garden.

P. calabra (*Calabrian Cinquefoil*).—A very silvery species from Italy and Southern Europe. It has prostrate shoots, and bears in May and June lemon-yellow flowers nearly 1 in. across. It flourishes freely in sandy soil, in the rock-garden.

P. fruticosa (*Shrubby Cinquefoil*).—A pretty neat bush, 2 to 4 ft. high, and bears in summer clusters of showy golden-yellow flowers. It is suited for the rock-garden or the dry bank.

P. nitida (*Shining Cinquefoil*). — A beautiful little plant from the Alps, a couple of inches high, its silky silvery leaves seldom with more than three leaflets each. The flowers are pretty and delicate rose. It is well worth a good place in the rock-garden, and is of the easiest culture and propagation.

P. pyrenaica (*Pyrenean Cinquefoil*).— This dwarf vigorous and showy kind has fine deep golden-yellow flowers. It will grow in the rock-garden or in the mixed border without particular attention. High valleys in the Central and Southern Pyrenees. Division or seeds. The shrubby kind P. fruticosa and its varieties are worth naturalising and growing among small shrubs in rougher parts of the rock-garden.

PRATIA.—*P. angulata* is a pretty plant for the rock-garden, creeping over the soil like the Fruiting Duckweed ; the flowers white, and like a dwarf Lobelia, numerous

Pratia angulata.

in autumn, giving place to violet-coloured berries about the size of Peas. It is hardy. New Zealand. *Syn.*, Lobelia littoralis.

PRIMULA (*Primrose*).—There is so much charm and beauty among Primroses that no garden is complete without them, and there is scarcely a species not worth cultivating. They have a great diversity of habit and growth. Some are at home on the sunny slopes of the rock-garden, others in shade, many make excellent border flowers, and a few exotic species are at home in the woodland with our common Primrose. The family contains nearly a hundred different sorts ; and we have therefore confined ourselves to the most distinct and desirable kinds. There is so much confusion among certain sections, particularly in the alpine and the Himalayan species, that we have not attempted to deal with these exhaustively ; while others, such as P. nivalis, are too little known in gardens to render it necessary for us to speak of them.

P. amœna (*Caucasian Primrose*) is allied to our common primrose, but is quite distinct. The corolla is purplish lilac in bud or when recently expanded, but turns bluer after a few days. The umbel is many-flowered, and the blooms, which are larger than those of P. denticulata, are borne about 6 or 7 in. high ; the leaves are rather large and are woolly beneath and toothed. The blooms come out before the snow has left the ground. It is so much earlier than the common Primrose, that while that species is in full flower, amœna has quite finished blooming, and has sent up a strong tuft of leaves very much like that sent up by the common Primrose after its own flowers are faded. A sheltered position slightly shaded will be best for the perfect health and development of the plant. It flourishes quite freely in common borders, and is one of the most valuable additions to the early spring garden and mixed border that have been made for many years. It is charming for the rock-garden or for well-arranged borders, and, when plentiful enough, will, no doubt, be used in various ways   There is a stemless variety, which would probably prove a great addition to our gardens   P sibirica is somewhat similar to P amœna, but is rare   Division of the root   Caucasus

P. auricula (*Common Auricula*)—In a wild state this is one of the many charming Primulas that rival Gentians, Pinks, and Forget-me-nots in making the flora of alpine fields so exquisitely beautiful and interesting   Possessing a vigorous constitution, and sporting into a goodly number of varieties when raised from seed, it attracted early attention from lovers of flowers, its more striking variations were perpetuated and classified, and it became a "florists' flower"   Its cultivated varieties may be roughly thrown into two classes · first, self-coloured varieties, or those which have the outer and larger portion of the flower of one colour or shaded, the centre or eye white or yellow, and the flowers and other parts usually smooth, and not powdery, second, those with flowers and stems thickly covered with a white powdery matter or "paste"   The handsomest of the former kinds are known by the name of "alpines," to distinguish them from the florists' varieties, and are the hardiest of all   The florists' favourites are distinguished by the dense mealy matter with which the parts of the flower are covered   They are divided by florists into four sections—green-edged, gray-edged, white-edged, and selfs   In the "green-edged" varieties, the gorge or throat of the flower is usually yellow or yellowish, this is surrounded by a ring, varying in width, of white powdery matter, which is surrounded by another ring of some dark colour, and beyond this a green edge, which is sometimes ½ in in width   The outer portion of the flower is really a monstrous development of the petal into a leaf-like substance, identical in texture with the leaves   The "gray-edged" varieties have the margin of a green leafy texture, but this is so thickly covered with powder that the colour cannot be distinctly seen   The same occurs in the "white-edged" kinds, the difference being in the thickness and hue of the powdery matter   In fact, the terms "green-edged," "gray-edged" and "white-edged," are simply used to indicate slight differences between flowers having an

abnormal development of the petals into leafy substance.   It is a curious fact that between the white and the gray the line of demarcation is imaginary, for both classes occasionally produce green-edged flowers   The "selfs" are really distinct, since the outer portion of the corolla is of the ordinary texture, though a ring of powdery matter surrounds the eye

The classification of such slight differences merely tends to throw obstacles in the way of the general growth and enjoyment of the flower in gardens.   Let the florists maintain these fine distinctions, those who merely want to embellish their gardens with the prettier varieties need not trouble themselves with named sorts at all   It should be borne in mind that the florists' kinds are the most delicate and difficult to cultivate   The curious developments of powdery matter, green margins, &c, tend to enfeeble the plant   They are, in fact, variations that in Nature would have little or no chance of surviving in the struggle for life   The general grower will do well to select the free sorts—alpines, and good varieties of the common border kinds   The special merit of these is that they may be grown in the open air on the rock-garden and in borders, while the florists' kinds must be grown in frames

The free-growing kinds are most likely to be enjoyed in all classes of gardens   Their culture is very simple, light vegetable soil and plenty of moisture during the growing season being the essentials   In many districts the moisture of our climate suits the Auricula to perfection, and great tufts of it are grown in gardens without any attention   In others it must be protected against excessive drought by stones placed round it, and cocoa-fibre and leaf-mould are also useful as a surfacing   However, as none but good varieties of the alpine section are worthy of even this trouble, we would prefer, wherever practicable, that they should be placed in the rock-garden on spots where they would have some shelter and could root freely into rich light soil   They would cause no trouble beyond taking up, dividing, and replanting   This should be done every second or third year, or as often as they become too crowded or lanky.   The very common kinds may be planted as edgings or in beds in the spring garden, but wherever the plant is free, naturally improved varieties should be substituted for the common old border kind

Auriculas are easily propagated by division in spring or autumn, but best in early autumn. They are also easily raised from seed. Seed ripens in July, and is usually sown in a gentle heat in the following January. It should be sown thinly in pans. The plants need not be disturbed till they are big enough to prick into fine rich light soil on a half-shady border. It is most desirable to raise seedlings, as in this way many beautiful varieties may be obtained, and if a desirable variety is noticed, it should be marked, placed under conditions calculated to ensure its health and rapid increase, and propagated by division as fast as possible.

As to the florists' varieties, innumerable and precise descriptions of the culture considered necessary have been given, but the essential points may be summed up in a few words. They require protection in frames or pits during winter and spring, and may be placed in the open air in summer and early autumn. In winter they should be put in pits, and placed as near to the light as may be convenient, the lights being left off in mild weather, and air being given at all times, except in severe frosts. Air by night as well as by day is decidedly beneficial. The pit or frame may be the usual one for the winter months ; but as soon as the plants begin to show flower, they ought to be removed to one with a northern exposure, so as to prolong the bloom. In such a place, with abundance of air, they form objects of much interest and beauty through April and the first weeks of May. After flowering they should be potted in May, and kept shaded till they have recovered. The potting usually consists of carefully shaking away all the soil and putting the plant in fresh compost : and the practice is a good one, for this plant and its wild allies put forth young roots higher up the stem every year, and the encouragement of these young roots is sure to have a good result. The pots generally used (the 4-in. size) are quite large enough where annual dis-rooting is practised, one sucker of a kind being placed in the centre of each pot. The wisdom of potting every plant in this way is doubtful, and it is better to select those that have sound roots, and are set firmly and low in the earth, and while disturbing the ball but little to give them a careful shift into a 5-in. pot. In growing the alpine kinds in pots—and they are as worthy of it as the other kinds—growers should put five or six plants in a 6-in. pot, one in the centre and four or five round the side, so as to form a handsome specimen. The same principle

may be carried out in pans, and applied to the free-growing florists' varieties as well as the alpines. In summer all the plants should be placed in the open air on boards or slates or a bed of coal-ashes, or some substance that will prevent the entrance of worms into the pots. Some careful growers guard the plants from heavy rains, but this is unnecessary if the pots are perfectly drained and everything else is as it ought to be. The florists rarely plunge the pots ; but if plunged in a bed of clean sharp sand, or in any like material on a well-drained bottom, and free from earthworm, they will be safer and less troublesome, because free from the vicissitudes that must attend all plants exposed in a fragile porous shell containing but a few inches of soil. Some pot their plants in August, but the best time is just after the flowering, as if disrooted in the autumn, the plants have not that accumulated strength for flowering which is acquired by a long period of undisturbed growth.

The perfect development of the choicest florists' kinds is secured by mixing one part of good turfy loam and one part of leaf-mould with another of well-decayed cow manure and silver or sharp river sand. Although we have given such full directions in regard to the culture of the florists' varieties, we again earnestly advise all who care for the flower to cultivate the free and hardy forms that thrive in the open air. It is a good plan to select bright or delicate self or other colours that please one. Such kinds should be increased, so that definite effects may be worked out with each colour.

P. capitata.—One of the finest of all Primroses. It is like P. denticulata, but is very distinct as a garden plant. It has a tuft of sharply-toothed pale green leaves, not half the size of that of a fully-developed P. denticulata. In autumn it bears dense heads of flowers of the deepest Tyrian purple, which as regards depth is very variable, and is shown to advantage by the white mealy powder in which the flowers are enveloped. It is not so vigorous as P. denticulata, though hardy, and it cannot be termed a good perennial, as it is apt to go off after flowering well. It is therefore advisable to raise seedlings. This is easy, as the plant seeds freely in most seasons, and the seedlings flower in the second year. An open position with a north aspect in good loamy soil well watered in dry weather suits it best.

P. cortusoides. — A distinct species

bearing clusters of deep rosy flowers on stalks 6 to 10 in. high. In consequence of its tall free habit it is liable to injury if placed in an exposed spot or open border ; and should therefore be put in a sheltered position, such as a sunny nook in the rock-garden, where it is surrounded

Primula capitata.

by low shrubs, etc., or in any place where it is not exposed to cutting winds, and at the same time not shaded to its injury. It forms a charming ornament for the rock-garden, for a sunny sheltered border near a wall or a house, or for the margin of the choice shrubbery. The soil should be light and rich, and a surfacing of Cocoa-fibre or leaf-mould is beneficial in dry positions. It is one of the most beautiful and easily raised of the Primulas, being readily increased from seed, and hardy in any well-drained and suitable position. Siberia.

P. denticulata.—A pretty Himalayan Primrose, of robust growth, 8 to 10 in. high. It has large tufts of broad foliage, and produces in spring, on stout erect stems, large dense clusters of lilac blossoms. It is a most variable plant, and some of its more distinct forms have received garden names, of which the principal are mentioned below. It is paler in colour than any of its varieties, and its foliage and flower-stalks are not mealy. P. pulcherrima is a great improvement on the original. It grows from 10 to 12 in. high, and has a more globular flower-truss, which is of a deep

lilac colour. The stalks are olive-green, and, like the leaves, are slightly mealy. It is very beautiful when in flower, and P. Henryi is a very strong-growing variety but does not otherwise differ from P. pulcherrima. It is a very fine plant, often 2 ft. across, and in Ireland it reaches even larger dimensions. P. cashmeriana is by far the finest variety. The flowers are of a lovely dark lilac, closely set together in almost a perfect globe on stalks over 1 ft. high. They last from March till May. The foliage is beautiful, and, like the stalk, is of a bright pale green, thickly powdered with meal, in which as in many other points the plant strongly resembles P. farinosa.

All the varieties are hardy, though their foliage is liable to be injured by early spring frosts. They may be placed either in the rock-garden or in an ordinary border, and will grow vigorously in a deep moist loamy soil, enriched by manure. They prefer a shady situation, with a clear sky overhead, and delight in an abundance of moisture during warm summers. If grown in masses in beds, the flowers should be protected by a hand-light or frame placed over them to preserve them. P. erosa is similar to P. denticulata, but is smaller and less hardy, it has paler flowers, and altogether it is an inferior plant.

P. farinosa (*Bird's-eye Primrose*).—A charming native species with small rosettes of silvery leaves, and flower-stems generally 3 to 12 in. high, though sometimes more. The flowers, which are borne in a compact umbel in early summer, are lilac-purple with a yellow eye. They vary a little in colour, there being shades of pink, rose, and deep crimson. In our gardens it loves a moist vegetable soil, and in moist and elevated parts of the country it flourishes in the rock-garden and in slightly elevated beds without any attention ; but in most districts a little care is necessary. In the rock-garden it is perfectly at home in a moist, deep, and well-drained crevice, filled with peaty soil or fibry sandy loam. In the drier districts it would be well to cover the soil with Cocoa-fibre, leaf-mould, or broken bits of sandstone to protect the surface from being baked and from excessive evaporation. P. f. acaulis is a very diminutive variety of the preceding. The flowers nestle in the hearts of the leaves, and both flowers and leaves are very small. When a number of plants are grown together, they form a charming little cushion of leaves and flowers not more than ½ in. high. Being so small, the plant should have greater care, whether it is grown in the rock-garden or in pots. P. scotica is a native plant similar to P. farinosa, and requires similar treatment. The flowers, which show in April, are

Primula farinosa (Bird's-eye Primrose).

rich purple with a yellow eye, and are borne on stems a few inches high. Native of damp pastures in the northern counties of Scotland.

P. glutinosa.—A distinct little Primrose, rare in gardens. On mountains near Gastein and Salzburg, in the Tyrol, and in Lower Austria, it flourishes, in peaty soil, at a height of 7,000 to 8,000 ft. It is 3 to 5 in. high, bearing one to five blossoms of a peculiar purplish-mauve, with divisions rather deeply cleft. Suitable for the rock-garden, or for pots in moist peaty soil or very sandy soil. Similar to P. glutinosa are P. tirolensis, Flœrkiana, Allioni, and others, all natives of the Alps.

P. grandis.—A distinct species from the Caucasus, remarkable only for its large foliage and the smallness of its flowers.

P. integrifolia.—A diminutive Primrose, easily recognised by its smooth shining leaves, which lie quite close to the ground, and by its handsome rose flowers, which are borne one to three on a dwarf stem, and are often large

enough to obscure the plant. There is no difficulty in growing this plant on flat exposed parts of the rock-garden, if the soil be firm, but moist and free. The best way is to form a wide tuft, by dotting six to twelve plants over one spot, and in a dry district, scatter between them a few stones or a little Cocoa-fibre mixed with sand, so as to prevent evaporation. P. Candolleana is another name for this plant. P. glaucescens, spectabilis, Clusiana, and Wulfeniana are of a similar character. All are natives of the Alps. Division or seed.

P. intermedia.—A charming hybrid between P. ciliata and P. Auricula. In habit it closely resembles some of the dwarf alpine Auriculas, and its purplish-crimson flowers have a conspicuous yellow eye, and are borne on stout erect scapes. On sheltered portions of the rock-garden its richly-tinted blossoms are seen to advantage. It is delicately fragrant.

P. japonica.—One of the handsomest of Primroses, and now too common to need description. It is a good perennial, and is not in the least tender. It is a first-rate border plant, and in moist shady spots of deep rich loam it grows as vigorously as a Cabbage, throwing up flower-stems 2 ft. or more high, and unfolding tier after tier of its beautiful crimson blossoms for several weeks in succession. It may be grown in the rock-garden as well as in the border, and is an excellent wild-garden plant, thriving almost anywhere and sowing itself freely. It is said to be rabbit-proof. There are several forms differing in colour; there is a white form, a pale pink, and a rose form, but the best is the original rich crimson form. In raising P. japonica from seed it should be borne in mind that the seed remains some time dormant, unless it is sown as soon as it is gathered, and that it must on no account be sown in heat. A cool frame is the proper place for the seed-pan, and till the seed has germinated, care must be taken to prevent or keep down the growth of Moss and Liverwort on the soil.

P. latifolia.—A handsome Primrose, with from two to twenty violet flowers in a head. It is less viscid, but larger and more robust than its alpine congener the better-known P. viscosa. Its leaves sometimes attain a height of 4 in. and a breadth of nearly 2 in., and it grows to a height of 4 to 8 in. Its fragrant flowers appear in early summer, and in pure air it thrives on sunny slopes of the rock-garden, if it has sandy peat, plenty of moisture during the dry season, and perfect drainage in the winter months. Like P. viscosa, it will bear frequent division, and may be easily grown in cold frames or pits. Alps.

P. longiflora is related to P. farinosa, but is distinct from it, being deeper in colour, and is considerably larger than the best varieties of it, the lilac tube of the flower being more than 1 in. long. It is not at all difficult to cultivate either on the rock-garden or in pots, and the treatment recommended for P. farinosa will suit it. Austria.

P. luteola.—One of the handsomest of the yellow Primroses, and a noble plant when well grown. The flower-stems are often 1½ to 2 ft. high, though they are usually under 1 ft. in height. They sometimes become fasciated, and thus carry a huge cluster of flowers 4 to 6 in. across. These flowers are like those of a Polyanthus or an Auricula, but they are borne in more compact heads. P. luteola is hardy. It likes a moist situation in full exposure, and if put out in

Primula nivalis.

rich borders of rather moist soil, or on the lower banks of the rock-garden, or in a copse with a good bed of leaf-soil, it will soon repay the planter. Caucasus. It has been well figured in *The Garden,* from plants that flowered at Chipping Norton, in Oxfordshire.

P. marginata.—One of the most attractive of the family, and readily distinguished by the silvery margin of its grayish leaves, and by its sweet, soft, violet-rose flowers. Even when not in flower it is pleasing from the tone of the margins and surfaces of the leaves. The flowers appear in April or May. Our wet and mild winters are doubtless the cause of its becoming rather lanky in the stems after being more than a year or so in one spot. When the stems become long, and emit roots

above the ground, it is a good plan to divide the plants, and to insert each portion firmly down to the leaves, and this will be all the more beneficial in dry districts, where the little roots issuing from the stems would be the more likely to perish. P. marginata is a charming ornament for the rock-garden, and thrives freely there. In the open ground a few bits of broken rock placed round the plants, or among them if they are grown in groups or tufts, will prevent evaporation, and protect them, as they rarely exceed a few inches in height. Alps.

P. minima (*Fairy Primrose*).—One of the smallest of European Primroses. Usually there is only one flower, which is generally rose-coloured, and sometimes white, and appears in summer. The plant is only an inch or so high, but its single flower is nearly 1 in. across, and almost covers the tiny rosettes of foliage. Bare spots in firm open parts of the rock-garden are the best places for the plant, but the soil should be very sandy peat and loam. It is peculiarly suited for association with the very dwarfest and choicest of alpine plants. Division or seed. Mountains of S. Europe. P. Flœrkiana is much like it, and probably is only a variety, since the sole difference is that it bears two, three, or more flowers, instead of only one. It enjoys the same treatment in the rock-garden. Austria. Of both kinds it is desirable to establish wide-spreading patches on firm bare spots, scattering half an inch of silver sand between the plants to keep the ground cool.

P. Munroi.—This has neither the brilliancy nor the dwarfness of the Primulas of the high Alps, nor the vigour of our own kinds, but it is distinct, and is of the easiest culture in any moist boggy soil. It grows at very high elevations on the mountains of Northern India, in the vicinity of water. Its smooth green leaves have a heart-shaped base, and are 2 in. long, and nearly as much across. From them arise flower-stems 5 to 7 in. high, bearing creamy-white flowers with a yellowish eye, which are more than an inch across. These flowers appear from March to May, and are very sweet. Altogether, P. Munroi highly merits culture in a bog or in a moist spot of the select rock-garden. P. involucrata is a closely-allied kind, also from the mountains of Northern India. It is, however, somewhat smaller, its leaves are not heart-shaped at the base, and it is not quite so ornamental. It thrives under the same conditions as its relative.

P. Palinuri.—This is quite different from other cultivated Primroses, inasmuch as it seems to grow all to leaf and stem ; while many of the other kinds often hide their leaves with flowers. In April its bright yellow flowers appear in a bunch at the top of a powdery stem. They are ornamental, though rarely fulfilling the promise of the vigorous-looking plant, and they emit a Cowslip-like perfume. P. Palinuri flourishes as a border plant in rich light soil in various parts of these islands, and nothing more need be said of its culture. It is well suited for some isolated nook on the rock-garden, where

P. purpurea.—A handsome Primrose, allied to P. denticulata, but far finer, for the exquisite purple flowers are larger. They are borne in heads about 3 in. across. The leaves are entire, and distinguish it from its near relations. Sheltered and warm but not very shady positions either in the rock-garden, or in the open parts of the hardy fernery, will best suit it if the soil is a light, deep, sandy loam, and well enriched with decomposed leaf-mould. It never thrives so well as in nooks at the base of rocks, where it enjoys more heat than it would if exposed. It must not be confused with

Primula rosea.

there is an unusually deep bed of soil. Established plants are easily increased by division. Southern Italy.

P. Parryi.—A pretty Primrose, bearing about a dozen large, bright, purple, yellow-eyed flowers nearly 1 in. across. These flowers are borne on stems about 1 ft. high. Though an undoubted alpine, and growing on the margins of streams near the snow-line, where its roots are constantly bathed in ice-cold water, it has succeeded in the open border in moist, deep, loamy soil mingled with peat ; it is hardy, and requires partial shade from extreme heat rather than protection from cold. N. America.

the variety of P. denticulata commonly called by the same name of P. purpurea.

P. rosea (*Rosy Himalayan Primrose*) is a charming little Primrose, with flowers of the loveliest carmine-pink, produced in heads like the Polyanthus. Its pale green leaves form compact tufts, and the flower-stems, 4 to 9 in. high, are produced in early spring, often as many as half a-dozen from one plant. It is perfectly hardy, and though only recently introduced from the Himalayas, has become quite acclimatised, and grows vigorously in almost any soil, preferring, however, a deep rich loam in a moist shady part of the rock-garden. When plentiful it should be

3 B

tried in various positions and soils, as it has not yet been thoroughly tested.

P. Sieboldi.—Though this handsome Primrose is considered a variety of P. cortusoides, it is very distinct in many important particulars. The size of its flowers, the breadth of its foliage, the creeping character of its root, its exclusively vernal habit, its pseudo-lobed or

marginata, fimbriata oculata, vincæflora, cœrulea-alba, Mauve Beauty, Lavender Queen, laciniata, and maxima. These possess a great diversity of colour, and some have the petals beautifully fringed. One of the chief merits of these Primulas is that they bloom early, flowering about the month of April when other flowering plants are rare; and another is, that they

Primula Sieboldi.

grooved seed-vessel, and the roundish flattened form of its seed, all warrant the belief in its distinctness from P. cortusoides as a garden plant. It is at any rate one of the showiest and most charming of all the Primulas, and is as easy to grow and as hardy as many others. Since its introduction from Japan numerous beautiful varieties have been raised, some of the most distinct being clarkiæflora, lilacina-

are remarkably free bloomers, throwing up successive flower-stems, and lasting a long time in perfection. Their cultivation also is comparatively easy. The best soil for them is light, rich, free material, consisting of fibry loam, leaf-mould, pulverised manure, and some grit to keep it open. They are impatient of excessive moisture, and when put in open ground should be planted in well-drained soil, or

in raised positions in the rock-garden
The roots creep just below the surface,
and form eyes from which any variety can
be easily propagated P Sieboldi is a
hardy herbaceous perennial, which loses its
leaves in autumn and winter, when it goes
to rest, and breaks up again early in spring

P sikkimensis—This is a robust
species, deciduous or herbaceous in our
climate, and quite distinct from all other
sorts It throws up strong flower-stems,
15 to 24 in high, bearing numerous bell-
shaped flowers of a pale yellow, with
mealy pedicels, and having a peculiar but
agreeable perfume Some of the stems
bear a head of more than five dozen buds
and flowers, and each flower is nearly 1
in long and more than $\frac{1}{2}$ in across P
sikkimensis starts into growth in April or
early in May, and should have a shady
position when in bloom, as its delicate
blossoms suffer from cutting winds
and bright sunshine Blossoming in
May, it remains in flower many weeks
It is hardy, and loves deep, well-drained,
and moist ground , but spots in the lower
parts of the rock-garden near water, or
situations in deep boggy places, suit it
best. It is readily increased, either by
seeds sown in summer as soon as they are
ripe, or by careful division in spring
or autumn This Primrose is said to be
the pride of all the Primroses of the
mountains of India, inhabiting wet boggy
localities at elevations of from 12,000 to
17,000 ft , and covering acres of ground
with its yellow flowers

P Stuarti (*Stuart's Primrose*)—A
noble and vigorous yellow Primrose,
about 16 in high. It has leaves nearly 1
ft. long, and many-flowered umbels A
light deep soil, never allowed to get dry
in summer, suits it well , but the most
suitable place for it is some perfectly-
drained and sheltered slightly elevated
spot in the rock-garden It may be
planted against the base of rocks, to
shelter it from cutting winds, though,
when sufficiently plentiful, this precaution
is unnecessary Mountains of India.

P villosa—A lovely little Primrose,
and one of the oldest cultivated It is
known by dark green obovate or sub-
orbicular leaves These leaves have close-
set teeth, and are covered with glandular
hairs, and are viscid on both sides. Its
flower-stems, also viscid, barely elevate
the sweet blooms above the foliage It
is well adapted for the rock-garden, in
which it may be grown in any position,
but it requires light peaty or spongy loam,
about one-half being fine sand, and its
roots should be kept moist during the

dry season It is easily increased by
division, and may be raised from seed
Varieties are sometimes, but rarely, found
with white flowers It is sometimes
grown under the name of P viscosa
The variety nivea or nivalis is a beautiful plant, dwarf and neat in growth,
producing trusses of lovely white flowers,
which are quite distinct from any other
in cultivation It is of very easy culture,
and may be grown either in pots or in
the open ground It deserves a select
position in the rock-garden or in the
border, a light free soil, and plenty of
water during the warm season It flowers
in April and May Alps Similar to P
villosa are P ciliata, Steini, hirsuta,
pubescens, rhætica, pedemontana,
œnensis, and Dinyana, charming little
species from the Alps All thrive under
the same conditions as P. villosa

P. vulgaris (*Common Primrose*)—Of
all the Primula family none excel our
native Primroses in loveliness, and they
are the earliest of all to flower The
Gentians and dwarf Primulas do no more
for the Alps than these charming wild
flowers do for our hedgerows, banks,
groves, open woods, and the borders of
our fields and streams. In some places
the Common Primrose varies a good deal
in colour Some of the prettiest of the
wild varieties are worthy of being introduced into shrubberies and semi-wild
places , and so long as lovely colour and
fragrance are esteemed in the spring
flower garden, some of the more distinctly
toned varieties should be sought after
Varied hues of yellow, red, rose, lilac,
bluish-violet, lilac-rose, and white have
already been raised, and if the good
single varieties become popular, striking
and desirable variations from the
commoner types will be much more
likely to be preserved For shrubberies
and woodland walks, single varieties will
always prove more useful than the old
double kinds, because more vigorous and
more easily increased All the varieties
are readily increased by division of the
offsets, or by seeds, which are produced
in abundance. In woods and shrubberies
the plants will take care of themselves, a
quality which adds to their charms , but
in the flower garden some system of
culture must be pursued The following
very simple one will secure the best
results, both as to the production of
vigorous free-blooming plants and an
abundant stock In autumn, after the
summer occupants of the flower-beds are
faded and removed, the Primroses and
other spring flowers are planted in beds

as the taste of the grower may direct. About the middle or the end of May it will be time to think of preparing the beds for their summer ornaments, and by that time also the Primroses will have begun to fade after yielding a long and abundant bloom. Then take them up, divide the offsets singly, doing this, if the day be sunny, in a shed or in a shady position. New or scarce varieties, or varieties of which a large stock is required, may be divided into the smallest offsets, but where much increase is not desired, the plants should be simply parted sufficiently to allow of their healthy development. As soon as they are parted, plant them in the kitchen-garden or in some by-place. The more rich and moist the soil the better they will grow ; especially if the

be transferred to beds in the flower garden or the pleasure-ground. The varieties of single coloured Primroses are so numerous, that it seems a folly to name them ; but a few of the most distinct of those propagated by division have received names. Among these may be mentioned : Auriculæflora, one of the finest ; Altaica, or grandiflora, also a beautiful sort ; Rosy Morn, deep rosy-red ; Gem of Roses, rosy-pink ; Queen of Violets, deep purplish-violet ; Crimson Banner, deep maroon-crimson ; Violacea, pale purple ; Fairy Queen, pure white with good eye ; Sulphurea, large, sulphur colour ; Virginia, pure white ; Brilliant, rich vermilion-red ; King of Crimsons, rich massive crimson ; Violetta, a very beautiful violet-purple ; Lustrous, very

An Alpine Primrose.

position be a half-shady one. The alleys between Asparagus beds would do admirably if more convenient positions cannot be found. If the weather be very bright, it would be desirable, for a few days after planting, to shade the plants by spreading boughs or old garden mats over them, and they should at this time be thoroughly watered. If the plants are strong and regular in their development, they should be planted in lines, 10 or 12 in. apart each way, but if the offsets are small they should be closer in the lines. By autumn they will make fine plants, and may then be taken up ; as much of the root as will come up with ordinary care, but not necessarily any soil or ball, being preserved, and the plants should

deep crimson, with small perfect lemon eye ; and Scott Wilson, a singular bluish-purple. The propagation of these kinds, as well as of all the perennial Primroses, is slow, unless they can be reproduced true from seed. A seedling may produce two others the first year after blooming ; and these may produce six or eight the next year, so that it takes several years to raise a hundred plants, and some patience must therefore be exercised before the newest forms can be circulated largely.

DOUBLE VARIETIES.—The forms most precious for the garden are the beautiful old double kinds. No sweeter or prettier flowers ever warmed into beauty under a northern sun than their richly and delicately-tinted little rosettes. Once they were in every garden ; but the day came when, like many hardy flowers, they were cast aside to make way for gaudier things ; now, however, people are beginning to grow them again, and are inquiring for old and half-lost kinds which they used to know long ago. The best-known and most distinctly marked are the double lilac, double purple, double sulphur, double white, double crimson, and double red. These and several allied forms are occasionally honoured with Latin names descriptive of their shades of colour. In catalogues will be found the following : Primula vulgaris alba plena, lilacina plena, purpurea plena, rosea plena, rubra plena, sulphurea plena ; but we had better speak of them in plain English and confine the Latin term to the species. The double kinds are slower-growing and more delicate than the single ones, and require more care, and the development of healthy foliage after flowering should be the object of those who wish to succeed with them. In the double kinds the deeper the hue the less robust the plant. The rich crimsons and the deep purples are usually most difficult to cultivate ; but in the extreme north, where the climate is at once moist and temperate, they grow almost with luxuriance. The climate of Ireland also favours them, but in the south and midland districts it is necessary to give them shade and abundant moisture during summer, and in winter the protection of glass against the continued frosts and rains. The white, lilac, and sulphur kinds, on the other hand, are very hardy, and, if established, appear to stand our climate well.

Shelter and partial shade are the conditions chiefly necessary to their successful culture. Open woods, copses, and half-shady places are the favourite haunts of the wild Primrose. In them, in addition to the shade, it enjoys the shelter, not merely of the tall objects around, but also of the long Grass and herbaceous plants growing near. Taking into account the moisture consequent upon such companionship, let these facts guide us in the culture of the double kinds. It will readily be seen that a plant exposed to the full sun on a naked border is under conditions very different from one in a thin wood ; the excessive evaporation and the searing away of the leaves by the wind would be quite sufficient to account for its failure.

It is therefore desirable to plant the beautiful double Primroses, in slightly shaded and sheltered positions, in borders of light rich vegetable soil ; and, to keep the earth from being dried up too rapidly, spreading Cocoa-fibre or leaf-mould on it in summer. It would be better to plant them in some favourite spot permanently than to change them repeatedly from place to place. Indeed, they ought never to be disturbed except for the purpose of division. They may, however, be employed as bedding plants, and treated in the manner recommended for single varieties, but they are not then so useful or so pretty as when in good colonies or large informal groups. Double Primroses well grown, and the same kinds barely existing, are such different objects, that nobody will grudge them the trifling attention necessary to their perfect development. Occasionally they may be seen flourishing by chance in some cottage-garden or some old country garden, where they find a home more congenial than the fashionable prim and bare flower garden. Division of the roots.

The Rev. P. Mules, a most successful grower of the Double Primroses, writes to the *Field* about them. " Unless these flowers have been seen at their best, and that can only be under the favourable conditions of suitable soil, pure air, and great experience in culture, no one can imagine their beauty. I have had a bed of fifty plants of the double white carrying at one time 4,000 fully expanded blooms, averaging $1\frac{3}{8}$ in. in diameter. So also Pompadour, with blooms of still larger size, which has flowered without intermission since October, throwing its rich crimson blossoms well above the succulent green foliage, and presenting a fine picture of form and colour. Then we have double rose, double mauve, double dark lilac, double cerise, double sulphur, double yellow, and double rose white mottled. Besides these are some bright crimsons, making a combination of colours which lend themselves to many varieties of garden and house decoration. Some—the sulphur and the dark lilac— occasionally throw up corymbose heads, polyanthus-wise ; but this is not uncommon with many primroses, and is the result of high cultivation, and occurs towards the end of the flowering period. The reason that the rarer varieties are difficult and expensive to obtain is because their culture is not understood, and stocks once allowed to die out can scarcely be replaced. Their reproduction, as they have no seed, is impossible, and one has to depend on division alone for their increase. Like all perennials, there is a tendency to natural deterioration, and unless they be kept in the highest vigour by change of soil and locality and breaking up, nothing can keep them.

The secret of growing double-primroses differs little, if at all, from that of the more delicate perennials, two points being specially to be observed—protection from cutting and strong winds, and that they be grown together in beds massed, not dotted through the herbaceous border. Beyond this only such knowledge is required as can be obtained by experience in the management of this class of plants.

THE POLYANTHUS.—Though the origin of this beautiful old-fashioned flower is somewhat obscure, it is considered to be a form of the common P. vulgaris with the stems developed. Polyanthuses are not at all sufficiently appreciated, con-

usual, and Maddock, in the following passage, describes a very beautiful variation of the flower: "The ground colour is most to be admired when shaded with dark rich crimson resembling velvet, with one mark or stripe in the centre of each division of the limb, bold and distinct from the edging down to the eye, where it should terminate in a fine point." He further says : "The pips should be large, quite flat, and as round as may be consistent with their peculiarly beautiful figure, which is circular, excepting those small indentures between each division of the limb, which divide it into five or six heart-like segments. The edging should resemble a bright gold lace, bold, clear, and distinct, and so nearly of the

Primrose Munstead Early White.

sidering the wonderful array of beauty they present, and that for rich and charmingly inlaid colouring they surpass all other flowers of our spring gardens. It would require pages to describe even the good varieties. At one time the Polyanthus was highly esteemed as a florists' flower, and none in existence better deserved the attention and regard of amateurs ; but nearly all the choice old kinds are now lost, and very few florists really pay any attention to the flower. In consequence, however, of the great facility with which varieties are raised from seed, nobody need be without handsome kinds, especially as raising them will prove interesting amusement for the amateur. The rules of the florists are in this case of a little more value than

same colour as the eye and stripes as scarcely to be distinguished. In short, the Polyanthus should possess a graceful elegance of form, a richness of colouring, and symmetry of parts not to be found united in any other flower." Here, however, as in most similar cases, the grower will do well to select the most beautiful of his own raising, and not be tied by any conventional rules.

As to the capabilities of the various kinds of Polyanthus, it would be difficult to name any hardy flower which is so generally useful. The finer varieties are worthy of a place in the rock-garden amidst the choicest alpine plants ; while the showier ones are suitable for spring bedding. Numbers of vigorous varieties will form the most appropriate ornaments that can be massed by shady walks in pleasure-grounds, and some may be employed as edgings. Many varieties are worthy of being naturalised abundantly in pleasure-grounds and along wood walks, though the enthusiastic florist grows the finer ones in pots. Polyanthuses are scarcely to be recommended for using in masses in the spring garden as much as the finer varieties of the Primrose, since in order to be admired they require to be seen rather closely; but wherever flowers are placed for their beauty rather than their effect as colour, Polyanthuses are invaluable, and they should be seen in strong colonies in shrubberies and borders.

culture and very vigorous. There are, however, very few, if any, double varieties, but some varieties are curious and interesting from the duplication of the calyx or corolla; these are popularly known as "hose-in-hose" Polyanthus. They grow with the same facility as the others. The beautiful Gold-laced Polyanthuses are much prized. The best are those raised years ago, such as Cheshire Favourite, George the Fourth, Formosa, Duke of Wellington, Black Prince, Lancashire Hero, and others, and they are mentioned in most florists' catalogues of hardy plants. The common Oxlip is a hybrid more or less intermediate between the Cowslip and the Primrose. It differs

" Bunch " Primroses.

Their cultivation is almost as simple as that of meadow Grass. They grow vigorously in almost any garden soil, but best in a soil that is somewhat rich and moist; and though they thrive in the full sun, they best enjoy a partially shaded and sheltered position, and are somewhat impatient of heat and drought. When grown for bedding, they are, like the Primroses, removed in early summer from the flower garden to the kitchen-garden or nursery, and replaced there when the summer bedding plants have passed away.

There have been lately raised some varieties, a good deal larger in their parts than the type, and these are very easy of

from the true or Bardfield Oxlip (P. elatior) in bearing much larger and brighter flowers with longer foot-stalks, and in having in the throat of the flower the five bosses characteristic of the Primrose and the Cowslip. Some of its varieties approach the Cowslip, and some the Primrose in character. The treatment that suits Polyanthuses and Primroses will suit the Oxlip. P. suaveolens is a variety of the Cowslip found in many parts of the Continent, but is not sufficiently distinct or ornamental to merit cultivation. P. elatior, the true Oxlip, is not very ornamental, the flowers being of a pale buff-yellow, and readily distinguished by their funnel-shaped corolla, which is quite destitute of· the bosses present in the Primrose and Cowslip. It is found on clayey soils in woods and meadows in the eastern counties of England, particularly in Essex, Suffolk, and Cambridgeshire. It is of easy culture, and is most suitable for collections of interesting plants, but is neither distinct nor ornamental enough for limited collections of ornamental kinds. It is also known as the Bardfield Oxlip. The blue Polyanthus (P. e. cœruleus) is a singularly handsome variety of it with slaty-blue flowers. It is now rare in gardens, but is well worth growing.

CULTURE.—Where soil is prepared for the choicer varieties, any good loam with a free addition of sand, well-rotted leaf-mould, and decomposed cow-manure will form an admirable compost. The Polyanthus may be raised with great facility from seed, which should be sown immediately after it is gathered, say about the end of June. It will indeed grow with vigour if the seed is not sown till the following spring, but by sowing it immediately nearly a year is gained. The amateur wishing to raise choice kinds had better sow the seed in pans or rough wooden boxes, but for ordinary purposes a bed of finely-pulverised soil in the open air will answer to perfection. Sowings in early spring are better made in pans or rough shallow boxes, placed in cold frames, as time will be gained thereby. The best plan is not to lose time by allowing the seed to lie idle in the drawer all the autumn and winter, but to sow it as soon as it is ripe, and have strong plants in the following spring.

Known species:—*Primula alba*, S. Europe ; *algida*, As. Min. ; *Allionii*, W. Europe ; *amethystina*, China ; *amœna*, Persia ; *angustifolia*, N.W. Amer. ; *aucheri*, Arabia ; *auricula*, Europe ; *auriculata*, As. Minor ; *bella*, China ; *bellidifolia*, N. India ; *bractrata*, China ; *bullata*, do. ; *calliantha*, do. ; *capitata*, Himal. ; *capitellata*, As. Minor, Persia ; *carniolica*, Austria ; *cernua*, China ; *ciliata*, Alps ; *Clarkei*, N. India ; *Clusiana*, Europe ; *cordifolia*, Hungary ; *cortusoides*, Siberia, Japan ; *cuneifolia*, Arctic regions ; *daonensis*, W. Europe ; *darialica*, Caucas. ; *davurica*, Dahurica ; *Delavayi*, China ; *denticulata*, N. India ; *Dickieana*, do.; *dolomitis*, W. Europe ; *dryadifolia*, China ; *egaliksensis*, Arct. Amer.; *elatior*, Himal.; *elliptica*, Himal.; *elongata*, do. ; *Elwesiana*, do.; *erosa*, do. ; *farinifolia*, Caucas. ; *farinosa*, N. Amer. ; *Fedschenkoi*, Turkes.; *filipes*, N. India ; *fimbriata*, N. India ; *flava*, China ; *Floerkeana*, Alp. N. Europe ; *floribunda*, N. India ; *frondosa*,Thracia ; *Gambeliana*, N.India ; *geraniifolia*, do. ; *gigantea*, Siberia ; *glabra*, N. India ; *glacialis*, China; *glaucescens*,W. Europe; *glutinosa*, do.; *grandis*, Caucas. ; *Hampeana*, Europe ; *heterochroma*, Persia ; *Heydei*, Himal.; *hirsuta*, N. India ; *Hookeri*, Himal.; *imperialis*, Java ; *integrifolia*, W. Europe ; *involucrata*, Europe, N. Asia ; *japonica*, Japan ; *Jesoana*, do. ; *Kaufmanniana*, Central Asia ; *Kingii*, N. India ; *Kisoana*, Jap.; *Kitaibeliana*, Europe; *lasiopetala*, do. ; *Listeri*, N. India ; *longiflora*, Europe ; *luteola*, Caucas.; *macrocarpa*, Japan ; *Magellanica*,Magellans ; *marginata*, Europe ; *maxima Maximowiczii*, N. China ; *megasœfolia*, As. Min. ; *minima*, Central Europe ; *minutissima*, N. India ; *mollis*, do.; *moschata*

muscoides, Himal. ; *nivalis*, Asia and N. Amer. ; *obconica*, China;*obtusifolia*, N. India; *officinalis*, Europe and As. Min.; *Olgæ*, Turkest.; *pachyscapa*, Palinuri, Italy ; *Parryi*, N.W. Amer.; *pedemontana*, C. Europe; *petcolaris*, N. India;*pinnatifida*, China ;*prolifera*, N. India ; *pulchra*, do. ; *punilio*, Thibet ; *pusilia*, N. India ; *Reidii*, Jap.; *reptans*, N. India ; *reticulata*, do.; *rosea*, do.; *rotundifolia*, N. India ; *Rusbyi*, N. Mexico; *sapphirina*, N. India ; *secundiflora*,China; *septemloba*, do. ; *serratifolia*, do. ; *sibirica*, Asia and Arct. Amer. ; *Sibthorpi*, Spain and Greece *Sieboldi*. Jap.; *Sikkimensis*, N. India; *simpicissima*, sinensis, China ; *soldanelloides*, N. India ; *sonchifolia*, China ; *spectabilis*, Alps ; *spicata*, China ; *stenocalyx*, do. ; *Stirtoniana*, Himal. ; *stricta*, N. Europe ; *Stuartii*, N. India; *suffrutescens*, Calif. ; *tenella*, N. India ; *tyrolensis*, Alps ; *uniflora*, N. India ; *urticifolia*, China ; *vaginata*, N. India ; *verticillata*, Arabia ; *villosa*, C. Europe ; *viscosa*, Europe ; *vulgaris*, Europe ; *Wattii*, N. India ; *Wulfeniana*, Europe ; *yunnanensis*, China.

PRUNELLA (*Large Self-heal*).—This handsome and vigorous plant *P. grandiflora* is readily distinguished by its large flowers from the common British Self-heal (P. vulgaris), which is unworthy of cultivation. There is a white and a purple variety, both handsome plants, thriving in almost any soil, but preferring one moist and free, and a somewhat shaded position. In winter they are apt to go off on the London clay, at least on the level ground, but are well suited for mixed borders, banks, or copses. The variety laciniata has deeply-cut leaves. Europe. Flowering in summer. P. pyrenaica (Pyrenean Self-heal) is allied to the preceding, and is considered a variety of it. It is about 10 in. high, and its beautiful violet-purple flowers are larger than those of P. grandiflora. It should have the treatment recommended for P. grandiflora. Labiatæ. *Syn.* Brunella.

PRUNUS(*Plum, Almond, Peach, Apricot, Cherry, Bird Cherry, Cherry-Laurel*). —Bentham and Hooker in the "Genera Plantarum" united under Prunus the whole of the species which had at an earlier date been known under one or other of the following names : Amygdalus, Persica, Armeniaca, Prunus, Cerasus, Padus, and Lauro-Cerasus. This arrangement, which was necessary from the fact that no well-defined line could be drawn between them, has resulted in some confusion in garden nomenclature. And we may see in consequence two Apricots, may be growing side by side, the older one called Armeniaca, the newer one Prunus. In the following notes the whole of the species dealt with are considered as Prunus and are arranged alphabetically ; and some, not of much garden value, or those not hardy in Britain, are excluded. But it will be of some value perhaps to first show the section to which each belongs.

THE ALMONDS AND PEACHES.—AMYGDALUS.
P. Amygdalus, P. Davidiana, P. incana, P. nana, P. orientalis, P. Persica, P. Simoni.

THE APRICOTS.—ARMENIACA.
P. Armeniaca, P. brigantiaca, P. dasycarpa, P. Mume, P. tomentosa, P. triloba.

THE PLUMS.—PRUNUS.
P. alleghaniensis, P. americana, P. angustifolia, P. cerasifera, P. cerasifera var. atro-purpurea, P. communis, P. communis var. pruneauliana, P. divaricata, P. insititia, P. spinosa, P. Watsoni.

THE CHERRIES.—CERASUS.
P. acida, P. Avium, P. Cerasus, P. Chamæcerasus, P. humilis, P. Jacquemonti, P. japonica, P. Maximowiczi, P. pendula, P. pennsylvanica, P. prostrata, P. pseudo-Cerasus, P. Puddum, P. pumila, P. serrulata, P. subhirtella.

THE BIRD CHERRIES.—PADUS.
P. Capollin, P. cornuta, P. demissa, P. Mahaleb, P. mollis, P. Padus, P. serotina, P. virginiana.

THE CHERRY-LAURELS.—LAUROCERASUS.
P. ilicifolia, P. Laurocerasus, P. lusitanica.

P. ACIDA.—One of the species from which the Cherries of gardens have been derived, allied to P. Cerasus ; small, dark-green, shining leaves of firm texture and nearly glabrous. A variety is semperflorens, of drooping habit and bearing white flowers (sometimes double) from May to September, and often carrying flowers and fruit. A dwarf tree, usually grafted standard high.

P. ALLEGHANIENSIS.—Usually a shrub from 4 feet to 6 feet high, but sometimes a small tree three or four times that height. The flowers, ½ inch across, at first pure white changing to pink, are followed by handsome fruits, which are blue-purple, nearly globular, and valued for preserving. Pennsylvania.

P. AMERICANA (wild Red Plum).—A handsome tree found in North America to the east of the Rocky Mountains, and one of the hardiest. It is a tree 20 feet or more high, of graceful habit, bearing at the end of April or the beginning of May many pure snowy white blossoms ; fruits red or yellowish-red, the species being cultivated in the United States on their own account.

P. AMYGDALUS (the common Almond).—One of the earliest of trees to bloom, and reaching its best before hardy trees have done more than show signs of reviving life. There are several named varieties in cultivation : amara (Bitter Almond) — flowers slightly larger than those of the common Almond, petals almost white towards the tips, deepening into rose at the base. Dulcis (Sweet Almond)—This has leaves of a grey-green colour, and is one of the earliest to flower. Macrocarpa—This is a strong-growing tree with larger, broader leaves than the type ; the flowers, too which are rose-tinted white, are larger. This tree is hardy and vigorous in our country. There are also double-flowered and pendulous varieties cultivated under names denoting these characters. *Syn.* Amygdalus communis.

P. ANGUSTIFOLIA (Chickasaw Plum).—In Britain this is a shrub 4 to 6 feet high, but in America it is a small tree 15 to 20 feet high ; the leaves 3 inches long ; flowers in clusters of one or two pairs, white, sometimes with a creamy tint, one-third of an inch in diameter. Several excellent varieties of this Plum are grown in the United States for the bright red

Prunus Davidiana.

fruits, and there are variegated forms cultivated in Europe.

P. ARMENIACA (common Apricot).—The wild bush of the cultivated Apricot flowers in February or early March, its blossoms being usually of a pinkish-white, but there are varieties with deeper-coloured flowers, and one in which they are double.   N. China.

P. AVIUM (the Gean).—Wild in the British Isles and is generally a tree 20 feet to 30 feet high, this has long been grown as an ornamental tree, and there are three or four good varieties.   None is more beautiful than the double form, whose pure white flowers are borne in spring.   The var. decumana is a striking tree with large leaves, some of which

Cerasus Watereri.

measure 6 inches to 8 inches in length.   The var. nana is a curious dwarf plant ; var. laciniata has cut leaves ; and var. pendula is of weeping habit.   The fruit is sweet or bitter (not acid).

P. CAPOLLIN.—A native of Mexico and southwards, where it ranks as a fruit tree ; leaves are of a dark glossy green, and hanging loose and pendent, as in some Willows ; flowers in erect racemes, white ; fruits round, dark red and like small Cherries ; a tree 30 feet to 35 feet high.   In France it ripens seed.

P. CERASIFERA (the Myrobalan).—The showiest of all the Plums, flowering whilst the leaf-buds are as yet mere tips of green, the flowers three-quarters of an inch to 1 inch in

diameter, in clusters on the short twigs ; tree round-headed and of spreading habit, 20 feet high.   Prunus Pissardi is a variety of this species (var. atro-purpurea, the purple Myrobalan), a variety of Persian origin.   Its white blossoms are followed by the beautiful red-purple young leaves, which assume their richest tints when just opening and in late summer and autumn.   It fruits in favourable seasons, the fruits being coloured like the leaves, even when young.

P. CERASUS (the wild Cherry).—A native of Britain, and usually a small tree or even a shrub, bearing its pure white flowers in spring. It is the double-flowered varieties, however, that give the species its chief value in gardens. A very old and beautiful Cherry is the variety known as persiciflora, the flowers of which are double and tinged with rose.   One of more recent origin is Rhexi fl.-pl., whose pure white, long-stalked flowers, borne in May, hang from the branches in great abundance.   It is a small tree, and one of the prettiest of all the Cherries. *Syn.* Cerasus vulgaris.

P. CHAMÆCERASUS (Siberian Cherry).—A dwarf cherry, the blossoms white, three-quarters of an inch in diameter, appearing in May.   One form of this species is represented by a tree 10 feet or more high at Kew, but, as a rule, it is only half as high.   It is naturally a small rounded shrub of neat, close habit, but is mostly grown as a standard.   There is a drooping variety (pendula) and another with variegated foliage.

P. COMMUNIS (common Plum).—This species is believed to be the source from which the cultivated Plums have been derived, although in a less degree the Bullace (P. insititia) and the Sloe (P. Spinosa) have each most probably a share in their origin.   It has, however, some value as an ornamental tree, and reaches a height of 15 feet to 20 feet, the flowers white.   Of the varieties cultivated as ornamental trees, var. pruneauliana is perhaps the most beautiful.   It bears in April many white flowers, not large but so thickly borne as to cover the twigs.   There is also a double-flowered form of this variety.

P. CORNUTA (Himalayan Bird Cherry).— This is the Himalayan form of our Bird Cherry. Its leaves are as a rule larger, broader, and of stouter texture than those of our British trees ; they are also distinct in having red stalks.

P. DAVIDIANA.—This is the earliest of all the Peaches to bloom, in mild winters as early as January.   Its branches are of somewhat erect growth, the flowers individually 1 inch across and completely covering the shoots made the preceding year, which are frequently 2 feet along.   The petals in one form (alba) are of a pure white ; in the other (rubra) pink, but not so freely borne.

P. INSITITIA (the Bullace).—A small tree, often wild in hedgerows, which bears its white flowers in pairs during March and April ; its black fruits are ripe in October.   There are several varieties, amongst which may be mentioned that with double flowers, another with yellowish-white fruits, and a third with red fruits.

P. JACQUEMONTI.—A pretty shrub, native of Northern India, where it is found at altitudes from 6,000 to 12,000 ft., with flowers of a bright rosy pink, about half an inch across, but borne in great abundance on the growths of the previous summer. The Chinese P. humilis is nearly related to this.

P. JAPONICA (Double Chinese Plum).—This is one of the most lovely of spring-flowering shrubs. The single form probably not in cultivation ; the double one has white flowers with a more or less rosy tint, some, indeed, of a distinct rose colour. The flowers, each about 1½ in. across, are borne thickly on short stalks from the slender shoots of the previous year.

Prunus Japonica.

It can be struck from cuttings, but it is better to layer the shoots of an old plant. In that way nice flowering plants can be obtained in two years. Grafted plants neither grow nor flower so well, and a constant watch has to be kept for suckers. *Syn.*, P. sinensis.

P. LAURO-CERASUS (Cherry Laurel).—A noble evergreen tree often overplanted and misused, and where this is so Cherry Laurels have to be continually cut back to keep them within bounds, and their hungry roots prevent the cultivation of better things anywhere near. Several varieties are in cultivation, the best of which are colchica, caucasica, and rotundifolia, all with broader, larger leaves than the common Laurel and preferable to it on account of their

hardier constitution. Salicifolia, angustifolia, and parvifolia are narrow-leaved varieties, the last being often grown under the name of Hartoghia capensis. A new variety from the Shipka Pass (shipkaensis) is said to be the hardiest of all.

P. LUSITANICA (Portugal Laurel).—A noble evergreen rarely seen in its full beauty, because it is nearly always choked with other things in the shrubbery. It is as an isolated bush or group, and allowed full freedom of growth, that its value both as a winter and summer shrub is seen. But like the Cherry Laurel it is often over-planted. Var. myrtifolia has smaller leaves than the type and its branches are of more erect growth. Being dwarfer it is also better suited for shrubberies. Var. azorica has much larger leaves and fewer, but larger flowers on the raceme. Spain, Portugal, and the Azores.

P. MAHALEB (the Mahaleb).—None of the European Cherries surpass this in its spring-tide beauty. The Mahaleb is a native of Central and Southern Europe, perfectly hardy in England. Reaching a height of 20 ft. to 30 ft., of free graceful growth ; especially is this the case with the variety pendula, which, although not strictly weeping, is of looser, laxer habit than the type. The leaves are each 2 in. long, and the pure white flowers appear in rather flat racemes in May.

P. MUME.—Under the hands of the Japanese cultivators this has varied into numerous forms, and there are now at Kew varieties with flowers red and white, single and double, as well as one of pendulous habit. The wood resembles that of the common Apricot. The plant is leafless at the time of flowering. It has been in cultivation for some years both here and on the Continent, but disguised under other names, one of which is Prunus Myrobalana fl.-roseis. Corea.

P. NANA (the dwarf Almond).—This, a native of Southern Russia, is one of the dwarfest of the Almonds, being from 2 ft. to 5 ft. high. It flowers during March and April when the leaf-buds are only beginning to burst, the flowers being of a lively rose colour and about three-quarters of an inch across. The leaves are narrow, smooth, dark green, and glossy. It is a charming shrub, and can be easily and quickly propagated by layering. The species will thrive in a dry situation better than most Almonds. There is a pretty double form.

P. PADUS (the Bird Cherry).—This beautiful tree, a native of Britain as well as of North and Central Europe and Asia, is often 40 ft. high, the flowers borne in drooping racemes, in the commonest form being 4 ins. to 6 ins. long. There are varieties, however, finer both in the flowers and racemes. A double-flowered variety (flore-pleno) recently obtained from the Continent is the most striking I have seen. A variety also worth special mention is the Manchurian one, with fine racemes, but chiefly notable for coming into flower early in April, and, therefore, long before our Bird Cherry is showing a bloom   There are other named varieties in cultivation, the most distinct being var stricta, with quite erect racemes   Var aucubæfolia has its foliage mottled with yellow   The common Bird Cherry is a tree rather for the park and woodland than the garden proper, but the Manchurian and double-flowered varieties fully deserve a place among flowering trees

P PENDULA (Cerasus pendula) —A beautiful Japanese Cherry and one of the earliest to come into flower, commencing usually towards the end of March   Its pendent growth has led to its being commonly worked on stocks 5 ft to 6 ft high, but it comes true from seed The leaves are much like those of the common Cherry, the flowers of a lovely shade of soft rose and borne in profusion   In the United States, where the summers are much hotter, it thrives better than in England, and it should, if possible, be planted in a sunny spot sheltered from the north and east.

P PERSICA (the Peach) —Although neither so free-growing nor so hardy as the Almond, the Peach in various forms is beautiful, and in positions sheltered from the north and east ought to be planted freely   There is now a number of varieties at the service of the planter, chiefly single and double forms with white or red flowers   There is one also with purple foliage known as foliis rubris, this colour extending also to the fruit   The many double varieties it is not necessary to specify, they are known by descriptive names, like flore albo pleno   These unfortunately are rarely seen well grown

P PROSTRATA (Mountain Cherry) —A rare species, but one of the most lovely of the dwarf Cherries, a native of the mountains of the Levant, and, although not strictly prostrate (at least in cultivation), is a low spreading bush, the long, slender branches arching outwards and downwards to the ground   The flowers, borne on very short stalks, are of a beautiful lively shade of rose, are half an inch to three-quarters of an inch across, and so plentiful as to almost hide the branches

P PSEUDO-CERASUS (the Japanese Cherry) —This is the tree whose flowering marks one of the epochs of the year in Japan   In the forests of North Japan this species becomes a large timber tree, but in England it is not often seen above 20 feet high, and it is the double-flowered varieties that are cultivated in England   They are of various shades of rosy white, and are known under such names as Cerasus Watereri, C Sieboldi, &c.   More so perhaps' than any other are these double-flowered Cherries worth extensive planting, never failing to flower, being of surpassing beauty and perfectly hardy   They should be grown on a cool, moist bottom, and the effect they produce in spring is all the greater if room can be afforded for a grove of a dozen or so trees with a backing of Holly or other evergreen

P SERRULATA —This cherry, which is a native of Japan, although scarcely so fine a tree as P pseudo-Cerasus, is nearly allied to

it, and it can be recognised by its peculiar mode of branching   The main stem is erect for a few feet, but then branches off almost horizontally into three or four divisions, and henceforth ceases to send up a defined lead It is picturesque, representing one of the modes of growth we have come to regard as essentially typical of Japanese tree vegetation, and it comes into flower about a fortnight later   The flowers, whilst scarcely so large as in the finest varieties of P pseudo-Cerasus, are beautiful, rose-tinted white, and always double   The single-flowered form is not in cultivation

P SIMONI —This has leaves of about the same size as the common Almond, but the tree itself is of more erect habit and frequently resembles the Lombardy Poplar in form of growth   The flowers are white, and appearing in February and March   Its fruit is deep purple and ripens early   China

P SPINOSA FLORE PLENO (the double Sloe or Blackthorn) —This flowers at the same time as the Sloe, its blossoms white, about half an inch in diameter and not perfectly double, the centre of the flower containing a cluster of stamens   The flowers are thickly crowded on the short spiny branches, the black colour of which serves to show off more vividly the beauty of the flowers   It is one of the most charming of March flowering shrubs

P TRILOBA FL -PL.—This, perhaps the most lovely of all the dwarf Prunus, is a native of China and was introduced by Fortune   The flowers are at their best in early April, and each one measures 1½ in to 2 in in diameter On first opening they are of a lovely shade of delicate rose, changing with age to an almost pure white   This species is perfectly hardy and will thrive as a bush in the open, although not so well as on a wall   The above remarks refer to the double-flowered variety, which for forty years has been in our gardens.   Within the last year or two, however, the single-flowered wild type has been introduced   It has smaller rosy white flowers and leaves of the same shape as Fortune's plant, but smaller —W J B

Pseudotsuga.   See PICEA.

PTERIS (*Brake*) —-The Bracken Fern (P aquilina), the only thoroughly hardy species of this genus, is generally so common as not to need cultivation   If, however, any one wishes to introduce it where it is scarce, he should bear in mind that to transplant it successfully large sods containing the strong creeping roots must be dug up, and planted in light soil, if peaty, so much the better   In very mild localities, such species as P. cretica and the elegant P scaberula, from New Zealand, sometimes thrive in sheltered nooks

PTEROCARYA (*Winged nut*) —Walnut-like trees of fine stately form of leaf and habit, *P caucasica* being hardy in our country, at least in the southern and warmer parts. There are good trees at Claremont and other places and one in Hyde Park. The foliage is very glossy and large, the tree is a vigorous grower and should not be planted near shrubs or other plants we wish to have a fair chance. The trees are natives of temperate

Pterocarya caucasica.

co untries in Asia and their number is likely to be added to as soon as more of China, Mongolia, and countries near are opened up. The Caucasian is the best known species—others are :—*rhoifolia* Japan, *stenoptera* China, and *Delavayi* Yun-Nan.

PTEROCEPHALUS.—*P. Parnassi* is a Scabious-like plant of dwarf compact growth, forming a dense rounded mass of

Pterocephalus Parnassi.

hoary foliage which in summer is studded with mauve-coloured flower-heads. It is a most desirable plant, thriving best in light warm soils, and is suited either for the rock-garden or the ordinary border. *Syn.* Scabiosa pterocephala. Greece.

PTEROSTYRAX.—*P. hispidum* is a deciduous Japanese shrub, and quite hardy enough for culture as a bush. It makes a capital wall shrub, being rapid in growth, handsome in foliage, and very beautiful in flower. The leaves are heart-shaped, about 6 in. long and 3 in. broad ; the small white flowers borne very freely in drooping clusters about the end of July. Another Japanese species, P. corymbosum, is less common, though desirable for walls. Its flowers, which are white or faintly tinged, are in crowded clusters. Both species are 8 to 12 ft. high in this country. They are known botanically as Halesia hispida and H. corymbosa, but ever since their introduction they have been known as Pterostyrax in gardens.

PUERARIA (*Kudsu*).—*P. thunbergiana* is a remarkable and climbing plant of almost tropical vigour, growing up poles, colonnades and walls to a great height in a very short time. It belongs to the pea family and is a plant the Japanese make a great economic use of in various ways, but our main concern with it here is for the flower garden and that has as yet been little tried in England. The flowers are a dull purple, and it is said to be hardy even in N. Germany.

PULMONARIA (*Lungwort*).—These are vigorous and hardy in any soil. Most of them grow well under the shade of trees, and all succeed best in shade. They form dense tufts of foliage, generally handsomely blotched and speckled with white, and make pretty groups in the spring garden, or in semi-wild places, but are worthy of the best places in the flower garden. There are about half-a-dozen kinds, all like each other. P. officinalis and P. angustifolia are native plants. P. officinalis (sometimes called P. saccharata) has rose flowers turning to blue, and P. angustifolia bears blue flowers. P. mollis is intermediate between the two, and P. grandiflora is somewhat similar to P. officinalis. P. azurea has rich blue flowers. Chiefly natives of Europe. P. dahurica is sometimes called Mertenzia dahurica.

PUNICA (*Pomegranate*).—Like the Myrtle, the Pomegranate, *P. granatum*, is grown as a wall shrub, the walls of some old houses being covered with it, and it makes a very beautiful covering with its dense mass of tender green foliage. The type has single flowers of a brilliant scarlet, but the best is the double-flowered sort (flore-pleno), which is also scarlet, and is that most commonly seen. There is also a yellow-flowered sort and a white or almost white kind (albescens)' with single and double forms, but these are rare. The flowers are borne freely on the young slender shoots of the previous year's growth, and in pruning these must be left untouched.

PUSCHKINIA (*Striped Squill*).—*P. scilloides* is one of the most beautiful of spring bulbous flowers. In its growth it is like some of the Scillas, but its flowers are delicate blue, each petal being

Puschkinia scilloides.

marked through the centre with a darker colour. The flower spikes are 4 or 5 in. high. There are two forms of the plant—the ordinary one and P. compacta. Compacta is so called from its denser and more numerous flowers, and is therefore the handsomer of the two. P. scilloides is also known as P. libanotica and P. sicula. The Puschkinia delights in a sunny border with a southern aspect near a wall, or an open border slightly raised will suit it. The soil should be light and friable, and about 1 ft. in depth ; and the bulbs planted about 4 in. deep. It will not thrive when mixed indiscriminately with plants of coarse growth, for their shade and consequent dampness injure the bulbs. During winter protect with a mulch, but this should be removed as soon as the severe cold is past. After the flowering season, which is late in spring, quite expose the soil so that it gets warm and dry, and to ripen the bulbs well. Shady situations in sub-alpine districts of Asia Minor.

PYRETHRUM (*Feverfew*).—Vigorous perennial or rock-plants, by far the most important of which is the Caucasian P. Roseum, which has yielded the innumerable varieties, both single and double, that have now become such popular border flowers. These varieties have much to recommend them ; they

are extremely showy, are very hardy and easy to grow, are little affected by sun or rain, and are invaluable as cut flowers for several months in summer and autumn. The blossoms are continually becoming more varied in colour and more refined in shape. Though Pyrethrums are in their fullest beauty in June, they are seldom altogether flowerless throughout the summer ; and a succession can easily be kept up by judicious stopping and thinning. They are also invaluable for autumn decoration, for if they are cut down after flowering in June they flower again in autumn. They are easily propagated by division or seed. The proper time for propagation is in spring. Take the plants up, shake off all soil, pull them to pieces, put them in small pots, and place them in a cold frame for a few weeks until they become established. Do not keep them too close, as they are apt to damp. When they are established they may be planted out. A good rich loam suits them best, though they will grow and flower freely in any good garden soil, and the more we incorporate well-rotted manure with the soil the better they grow and the more luxuriantly they flower. Mulching, especially in dry soils, is very advantageous, as it keeps the ground moist and cool. The varieties are so numerous that it is difficult to make a selection, and new sorts are continually being raised, but the following are some of the best : White and white-shaded— Boule de Neige, Delicatum, Madame Billiard, Nancy, Niveum plenum, Olivia, Argentine, Prince de Metternich, and Ne Plus Ultra. White with yellow centre— Bonamy, Impératrice Charlotte, La Belle Blonde, Virginale, and Voie lactée. Purple and red—Mrs. Dix, Rubrum plenum, Mons. Barral, Brilliant, and Wilhelm Kramper. Crimson—Michael Buckner, Miss Plinkie, Modèle, Multiflorum, Prince Teck, Progress, Emile Lemoine, and Marquis of Bute. Carmine and pink— Carmineum plenum, Charles Baltet, Floribundum plenum, Gloire de Stalle, Imbricatum plenum, Nemesis, Fulgens plenissimum, Haage et Schmidt, Iveryanum, J. N. Twerdy, and Rev. J. Dix. Yellow—Sulphureum plenum, Solfaterre. Lilac and rose—Comte de Montbrun, Delicatissimum, Dr. Livingstone, Gaiety, Galathée, Hermann Stenger, Lady Blanche, Lischen Minerva, Uzziel, and Roseum plenum. Most of these are double-flowered sorts ; but there is also a great diversity of colour among the single kinds, and they are quite as beautiful as the heavy-headed double flowers, and are more suitable for vases. Other species of garden value are—

P. Parthenium (*Feverfew*). — The golden-leaved variety of this plant (P. P. aureum or Golden Feather) is now common in every garden. Of this there are several forms. One is called laciniatum, and is very distinct from the older kind. These have their uses in geometrical borders, where they have a bright effect. Their culture is of the simplest description. Seed is sown in heat in spring, and the seedlings are pricked off in pans, and when large enough transferred to open borders, and there they withstand the winter unprotected. New plants should be raised every year, as after flowering the second year the old plants lose their neat compact growth.

P. Tchichatchewi (*Turfing Daisy*).— A Caucasian plant, retaining its verdure in dry weather on dry banks or slopes where few plants would flourish ; a dwarf creeper, quickly forming a carpet of green. The flowers have white rays and a yellow disc, and in forming turf of the plant in poor dry soils they should be removed, though for the rock-garden of the rougher kind or for borders the flowers have some claim to beauty.

P. uliginosum is one of the noblest of tall herbaceous plants, and forms dense tufts 5 to 7 feet in height. These are crowned by lax clusters of pure white flowers, each about twice the size of an Ox-eye Daisy. It is excellent for cutting, and its blossoms are produced late in autumn before the Chrysanthemums come in. It is a stately plant for a rich border, and thrives best in a deep, moist, loamy soil. It may be naturalised in damp places. Division. *Syn.*, P. serotinum. Hungary.

PYROLA (*Winter-green*).—Little evergreen plants of the northern woods and boggy or sandy places, very distinct and attractive both in leaf and flower.

P. rotundifolia (*Larger Winter-green*). —*P. rotundifolia* is a rare native plant, 6 to 12 in. high, inhabiting woods, shady, bushy, and reedy places. It has leathery leaves, and its erect stems bear long, handsome, and slightly-drooping racemes of pure white flowers, half an inch across, ten to twenty of which are borne on a stem. They have a sweet scent. P. r. arenaria is a very graceful plant, found wild on sandy seashores. It differs from the preceding in being smooth, deep green, and dwarfer, and in having as a rule several empty bracts below the inflorescence. Both the type and its variety are beautiful plants for the shady mossy flanks of the rock-garden in free sandy and vegetable soil.

They flourish more readily in cultivation than any other species of the family. In America there are varieties with flesh-coloured and reddish flowers, but none of these' are in cultivation. P. uniflora, P. media, P. minor, and P. secunda are also interesting British plants, and the first-named is very ornamental, besides being very rare. P. elliptica, a native of N. America, is also found in our gardens, though rarely. Any of the Pyrolas are worth growing in thin mossy copses on light sandy vegetable soil, or in moist and half-shady parts of the rock-garden or the fernery.

PYRUS (*Pear* and *Apple*).—Beautiful flowering trees and bushes of which there is now a bewildering number, since botanists have classed all Apples, Pears, and their allies under the one family. Here, however, it will be convenient to adhere to the old classification, which places Pears under Pyrus, Apples under Malus, Beams under Aria, and Mountain Ashes and Service Trees under Sorbus. No one is likely to confuse one with another, and their names are more easily remembered when so classified. These old genera are now placed as sections of Pyrus. The finest flowering trees are those included under the section Malus, the type of which is the common Crab Apple (M. communis). There is a beautiful flowering variety of the Crab Apple called the Paradise Apple, having large handsome flowers, but it is seldom planted for effect, although in common use as a stock for grafting. The Chinese and Japanese Crab Apples include the finest of our small trees that flower in early summer. The Chinese double-flowered Crab (P. M. spectabilis) is a lovely tree, 15 to 25 ft. high, with a wide-spreading head of branches abundantly wreathed with large semi-double delicate rose-pink flowers. It is not often met with, except in old gardens. The varieties of P. M. baccata or Berry Apple (so called from its small round fruits) are known as Siberian Crabs. They are graceful in growth, showy in flower, and have highly-coloured fruits, which add much to the beauty of the garden in autumn. The Japanese Crab (P. M. Toringo) has beautiful flowers and fruits. The flowers are white or pale pink, and the very small fruits are hung on long slender stalks. Of the Toringo Crab there are now several forms, differing in colour of flower and of fruit. It is a small tree, and is a large-spreading bush if the leaders are removed. The finest of the Eastern Crab Apples is the Japanese P. M. floribunda. Fully grown it makes a low tree with a dense wide-spreading head of slender branches, loaded every May with a profusion of flowers of a pale pink when expanded, and of a brilliant crimson in the bud, when they are most beautiful. No garden is well planted if this tree is wanting, as it is hardy, grows rapidly anywhere, and costs little to buy. There are a few varieties of it, one called Halleana having larger and more richly-tinted blossoms. The North American Sweet-scented Crab Apple (P. M. coronaria) is a lovely little tree with large pale pink deliciously-scented flowers. There are other ornamental Apples in the section Malus, but the foregoing include the finest and the most readily obtainable. The charming

Pyrus arbutifolia pumila.

Pyrus Maulei is allied to the handsome P. japonica. Of the true Pears as ornamental trees little can be said. They are a good deal like orchard and garden Pears in growth and flower, and their fruits are not remarkable. One or two, however, may be planted for ornament. One is P. Bollwylleriana, from Central Europe, which produces in spring an abundance of small white blooms in clusters ; and another, P. Salicifolia (the Willow-leaved Pear), which is well worthy of planting on account of its distinct and beautiful foliage, has leaves of silvery whiteness. P. olæagnifolia, or Oleaster-leaved Pear is another Eastern species with hoary leaves.

Of the *Sorbus* section the common Mountain Ash (P. Aucuparia) is a familiar example, but it is too common to need description. There is a rare kind with yellow berries (fructu luteo), another kind with weeping branches (pendula), a third of erect growth (fastigiata), and a fourth with variegated leaves. The last, however, is not very ornamental, as the variegation is seldom distinct. Other

species worthy of attention are P. S. americana, the American Mountain Ash, which is a good deal like our own Mountain Ash ; and P. S. hybrida, a tree of very distinct growth, with a dense pyramidal head. The leaves of P. S. hybrida are intermediate between those of P. S. Aucuparia and P. Aria (the White Beam). The true Service Tree, P. S. domestica, used to be more

The true Service Tree (Pyrus domestica).

frequently planted than now. It is a handsome tree with elegant foliage. Of the White Beam (P. Aria) there are some very handsome kinds. Even our native White Beam is ornamental. Like the Mountain Ash, it is also one of the best trees for planting in exposed places on poor soil, and no tree thrives so well on chalk. Its broad silvery foliage makes it show in the landscape, and it is a valuable park tree. Its allies and varieties include some beautiful trees, such as latifolia, with leaves which are broader than the type and quite as silvery. P. A. Hosti is a handsome tree, both in foliage and flower. Its leaves are large and silvery, and its delicate rose-pink flowers are in broad flat clusters. It is a Central European tree, perfectly hardy, and about 10 ft. high. The Himalayan Beam Tree, P. vestita (called also P. lanata and nepalensis) is extremely fine, but is not hardy everywhere. Its very large leaves are like those of the Loquat, and are of silvery whiteness. Where it thrives it is 20 to 30 ft. high.

PYXIDANTHERA (*Pine Barren Beauty*).—*P. barbulata* is a curious little American evergreen shrub, smaller than many Mosses, flowering in summer, rose-coloured in bud, white when open, the effect of the rosy buds and the white flowers on the dense dwarf cushions being singularly pretty : it is plentiful in the sandy dry "Pine barrens" between New Jersey and North Carolina and often found on little mounds in low, but not wet, places. It is a charming plant for the rock-garden, planted in pure sand and leaf-mould fully exposed to the sun   Division

QUAMOCLIT —*Q coccinea* is a pretty Convolvulus-like plant, with many small scarlet flowers and slender stems of rapid growth, attaining a height of 6 to 8 ft. in a few weeks   It may be treated either as a half-hardy annual, and sown in February or March under glass or in a hot-bed, but it requires a warmer climate than ours to do its best in   Q hederæfolia is another pretty species   It has scarlet flowers and lobed foliage, and requires the same treatment as Q. coccinea   Both are excellent plants for sheltered trellises, as they give abundance of flowers from July to September.

QUERCUS (*Oak*) —Noble evergreen and summer-leafing trees of northern and temperate regions, of which no book can give any but a feeble idea of their gift of beauty to the earth, and value to man , but if we think of our own stately Oak in the counties of Britain, and its varieties of form in different situations in our storm-tossed isle of such limited area, we may, perhaps, get some idea of the value of the several hundred known species of Oak   Of these, by far the most useful for our northern land are the summer leafing (or deciduous) Oaks, resting as they do from all evil influence during the trying season, and coming out in beautiful leaf, as our own Oak does, when the summer is nearly with us   The evergreen Oaks, though of vast importance in more temperate countries (I have passed through millions of acres of evergreen Oak in North Africa alone), are of less value in our cold climate, but we have one precious kind in the Ilex, and other kinds may be grown in the mild parts to a limited extent, especially in sea-shore districts where evergreen shelter is welcome.

From the point of view of effect, the most noble of the summer-leafing Oaks are the American Oaks, with their fine colour in autumn   No trees have been more and more talked of, yet why are they so rare in our gardens?   The answer is, I think, because of our ways of procuring them, by plants too old, from nurseries, and, most fatal of all, by the habit of grafting exotic kinds on the common Oak, and neglecting the natural modes of increase, in the case of Oaks, certainly by seed   If we were dealing with plants of a tender nature, for which some hardy stock would be necessary, there might be some reason for this, but it is not so, because these lovely American Oaks inhabit colder regions than our own

country, and they are absolutely different in character from ours, some of them living on dry, warm soils, whereas our Oak is usually best, and certainly the timber is best, on soils of a heavy nature   Therefore, those who wish to have the American Oaks in their beauty should work from seed sown in the place where we wish the trees to grow, or raised in nurseries and transplanted early, or purchase young and healthy plants from forest tree nurseries, and in that way secure the vigorous growth of the seedling tree   Communication is so easy with America now that there should be no difficulty in getting seeds by post, nor should there be any trouble in our nurserymen raising good stock from seed of all the more essential and well-known kinds   In getting acorns over from America or other countries, they should be sown as soon as possible after coming to hand, and it is best to have them sent packed tightly in moist earth

In the country seats of the United Kingdom there is much varied land in which these Oaks might find a place, at first for their beauty, as in the case of the scarlet and red Oaks, and eventually these great Oaks would have value as timber trees, more than some of the trees we give a place to   Therefore I think that in renewing and filling gaps in woodlands near the house, and also in planting new woods, it might often be well to plant a group or mass of these American Oaks

In such a large family as the Oak there are rare and delicate species which we need not concern ourselves with, at least before we have established about us in some effective ways the more stately and noble Oaks, nor need we be much concerned about hybrids which occur in nature between wild species, and also have been raised in gardens and much talked about   As a rule, hybrids in this family are not nearly so important as the wild trees, except, of course, such varieties as occur naturally when we raise the tree from seed, as in the case of the common European evergreen Oak, which gives a pretty variety from seed, as, indeed, our wild Oak does, of which we may see in any good Oak district, perhaps, trees in a dozen different states of leaf and colour in one day

It is well that some of the favoured shores and valleys of the world have Evergreen Oaks which we may grow in our country, the best known of these being the Ilex of Italy, which is, happily, hardy in our country   It is perhaps most beautiful in sea-shore districts, and many places, both in England and Ireland, have fine trees Old trees give excellent shade, and it is a very pretty shelter for the flower garden

With such a great shore-line, the opportunities for growing the evergreen oaks well are vastly greater than they would be in a Continental country of like temperature to ours They are lovely shelter trees as groups or groves for gardens swept by sea winds, as we may see at St Ann's, Holkar, in Norfolk, and Tregothnan, and they are just as good in inland places wanting shelter Sometimes after very hard winters the trees look as if they were killed, but afterwards throw off the injured leaves and grow happily again They should be transplanted with the greatest care when young, and the best way is often to raise plants from acorns, common where the tree grows well, and which may be often gathered in Italy and at home They should be sown as soon as possible after ripening

The following excludes kinds not likely, from their inhabiting warmer regions or other reasons, to be hardy and vigorous in our country —

SUMMER-LEAFING OAKS

Q ACUMINATA (*Chestnut Oak*) —A tall tree with a maximum height of over 150 ft , with grey flaky bark, and chestnut like leaves, shiny on the upper surface and greyish beneath This should be a very useful Oak in certain soils in Britain supposed to be inimical to our own Oak Eastern States and Canada, and westwards, in dry limestone soil

Q ALBA (*White Oak*) —A fine forest tree, sometimes 150 ft high with deeply lobed but not sharp-pointed leaves, and grey bark scaling off in plates A native of Canada and the more northern United States, its hardiness need not be doubted, and the wood is hard and tough and good

Q CERRIS (*Turkey Oak*) —This is a valuable tree for garden and park Though not unlike the common Oak in growth and branching, it is readily distinguished by its deeper green and finely cut foliage and by its mossy-cupped acorns It is also much more rapid in growth and will flourish in light and varied soils It retains its foliage longer than most other trees and some of its varieties are almost evergreen The chief of these is the Lucombe Oak a tree of graceful growth which rapidly ascends into a tall cone of foliage and retains its leaves through mild winters. The Fulham Oak is a similar tree of hybrid origin It is also partially evergreen and differs from the Lucombe Oak chiefly in its habit of growth being more spreading Other varieties of the

Turkey Oak are the Weeping, a decidedly pendulous branched variety and most desirable for a lawn, a variegated form, one of the best of these kinds as the leaves are clearly margined with creamy white, and the cutleaved, in which the leaves are finely cut, giving the tree an elegant feathery appearance The variety known as Q *austriaca sempervirens* is a form of the Turkey Oak sub-evergreen in character and of medium growth and useful for small gardens It is easy to attach too much importance to these varieties which rarely equal the wild tree in beauty or character, and which have the disadvantage of being increased by grafting, which is against their ever attaining the stature and dignity of the wild tree

Q COCCINEA (*The Scarlet Oak*) —A forest tree, in its native country growing to 160 ft high, and one of the best North American Oaks worthy of planting for ornament in this country. It is a beautiful tree at all seasons, but particularly so in the autumn when the rich scarlet and crimson hues of its foliage are very handsome There are varieties of it in nurseries called *macrophylla* with larger leaves than the type, and *pendula* which has a drooping habit of growth There is a variety known as *tinctoria*

Q CONFERTA (*Hungarian Oak*) —This is a noble tree in its own country and one of the quickest growing Oaks in cultivation It has much larger leaves than the common Oak and they are cut in much the same way Its growth is denser and less spreading as we see it here at present than in Hungary, but there are as yet no large trees of it It is without question a good Oak to plant as a tree of the future, as it is very hardy and grows well in almost all kinds of soil except the lightest and the heaviest Syn Q *pannonica*

Q MACROCARPA (*Bur Oak*) —A large forest tree of a maximum height of 160 ft with a trunk as much as 8 ft in diameter, and rather large, thin, deeply incised, but blunt lobed leaves shiny on the upper side, but whitish below The timber is good and tough A native of rich soils from Nova Scotia to Manitoba, and also southwards Syn Q *olivæformis*

Q MINOR (*Post Oak*) —A tall tree, sometimes in its best state 100 ft high, with rough grey bark and deeply incised but blunt pointed leaves The wood is very hard and durable North America, in the eastern states, and westwards and southwards

Q NIGRA (*Water Oak*) —A forest tree though not so tall as other Oaks—80 ft There is a variety of it in cultivation named *nobilis* which has leaves 9 ins or more in length of a rich green It makes a handsome small tree In wet and swampy ground, Eastern and Western United States, also southwards Syn Q *aquatica*

Q PALUSTRIS (*Pin Oak*) —A forest tree with a maximum height of 120 ft, and is so hardy and so handsome that it is quite an established tree in English nurseries It is one of the quickest growing Oaks and its chief beauty is the tender green, almost yellow, of the unfolding foliage in May, and rich autumn tints. It soon makes a fine tree and is one of the best to plant in moist ground or marshy places, as it grows naturally in such places. Leaves deeply cut, bright green and smooth. Northern United States and westward.

shade and fine beauty of form as at Shrubland and in many other places. Botanists give this and the other British Oak under the general term of *Q. Robur*, but they are wrong, as the Oaks are distinct in form and habit. Of the common Oak there are several varieties that

An Evergreen Oak.

Q. PEDUNCULATA (*British Oak*) is the most valuable of British trees and most beautiful in old age in many different states both in wood, park, chase, by rivers, and in pasture land, and one which I like well to see coming into the home grounds in its old state, giving noble

should be made use of in ornamental planting. Those with coloured foliage include the Golden Oak (*Concordia*) which has rich yellow foliage throughout the summer. It is a very slow growing variety and rarely seen larger than a dwarf scrubby tree. The purple leaved variety (*purpurascens*) is stronger growing and a desirable tree on account of the rich ruddy tinge of its foliage. It is also called *atropurpurea*. Of the varieties that differ from the type in growth the most distinct are *fastigiata* or *pyramidalis*) which is of much the same style of growth as the Lombardy Poplar, but does not grow so tall. The Weeping Oak (var. *pendula*) is as decided a weeping tree as the Weeping Ash and is a vigorous grower and a beautiful and graceful tree. There are several forms with cut leaves, the most distinct being those named *filicifolia* or the Fern leaved Oak, *heterophylla* and *scolopendrifolia* which latter has leaves like a miniature Harts Tongue fern. There are variegated forms of both the common type and of the Cypress Oak, but not so important for landscape effect as the varieties that take a natural colour, but we have never seen any variety of Oak as handsome as the common tree. It is frequently in forests over 100 ft. high, and occasionally over 150 ft., giving a great quantity of valuable timber. The leaves fall earlier than those of the Durmast Oak, and are more varied in yellowish and brownish colours at the commencement of growth.

Q. PHELLOS (*Willow Oak*).—A forest tree 80 ft. high, and unlike the other Oaks in foliage which is narrow and long like that of a Willow, whitish beneath which gives the tree a silvery appearance on a windy day. It is not a common tree though it was introduced from North America in the last century. It is of slow growth in cold places and soils and thrives well and grows rapidly on well drained light soils especially in a gravelly subsoil. United States.

Q. PLATINOIDES (*Swamp White Oak*).—A large forest tree with flaky green bark. and, in its best state, reaching a height of over 100 ft., with slightly lobed leaves, and the acorns on rather long stalks. It has good, tough, closely-grained wood. and is a native of moist and swampy soils in Canada and west to Michigan. Syn. Q. bicolor.

Q. PRINUS (*Rock Chestnut Oak*).—A large tree sometimes attaining a height of 100 ft. with the leaves somewhat chestnut like, and bearing an edible Acorn, in dry soil. Eastern States, and Ontario and southwards.

Q. RUBRA (*Red* or *Champion Oak*).—A noble forest tree with a maximum height of nearly 150 ft , and one of the finest of American trees, remarkable for the richness of its autumn tints. It is a fine park tree and also makes a beautiful shade tree for lawns. It grows best on a free and deep soil and is much more rapid in growth on moist than in dry soils. It has large foliage that hangs in heavy masses on the wide-spreading limbs. Nova Scotia, Canada and Eastern States.

Q. SESSILIFLORA (*Durmast Oak*) is the second species of British Oak and is often included with Q. *pedunculata* but is distinct from a planter's point of view, not being so long lived or quite so noble a tree. It is, nevertheless, one of the finest forest trees of northern countries, and has a straighter and more cylindrical stem and form of tree even than the common Oak, is of a deeper green, denser foliage, and giving better covert and more leaf soil. The leaves are a little longer than those of our other native Oak, sometimes, in mild winters, remaining on the tree until the others come. Its area of distribution is slightly different, growing less in plains and valleys than our other Oak, but inhabiting plateaux and slopes of hills and mountains, sometimes growing 3,000 or 4,000 ft. high, and also different from the common Oak in its thriving on gravelly, sandy and calcareous soil, while the common Oak is best in heavy soils. The qualities of the wood of the two kinds have been the subject of much dispute, and perhaps the discussion is often confused by the influence of soils, the wood of Q. *sessiliflora* is generally thought to be less tough and less resisting than that of the common Oak. It has a straighter fibre and finer grain. Like the other Oak this has several varieties of little value.

Q. VELUTINA (*Black Oak*).—A tall tree up to 150 ft., the outer bark a very dark brown with deeply cut leaves with sharp points. This fine tree is rare with us and worth a trial from seed sown where we wish it to grow, or from young seedling plants. Northern United States, Canada and westwards, and also in the southern states.   W. R.

EVERGREEN OAKS.

Q. ACUTA is a native of Japan, with dark leathery leaves about the size of those of the common Cherry Laurel. This has not been long enough in the country to enable one to judge the merits of an adult tree, but even as a bush it is a fine object. Q. *Buergeri robusta* is a vigorous large-leaved form.

Q. AGRIFOLIA, the Enceno of the Californian coast, is a distinct Oak rarely seen in gardens, in aspect not unlike some forms of Q. *Ilex*, but the leaves are of a different shade of green. Dr. Engelmann says it is "a large tree, with a stout, low trunk, often 8 to 12 ft., sometimes 16 to 21 ft., in circumference, and with a spread of branches of 120 ft."

Q. CHRYSOLEPIS (*Californian Live Oak*) is found along the coast ranges and along the western slopes of the Sierra Nevada, where it forms a tree 3 to 5 ft. in diameter of stem, or, at higher elevations, is reduced to a shrub. It has pretty spiny-toothed dark green leaves, somewhat golden on the under surface, and in its native country it is a beautiful evergreen tree.

Q. COCCIFERA.—A dense bush with small spiny dark green leaves, and very small acorns, often hardly larger than a Pea, which now and then ripen in Southern England. S. Europe.

Q. DENSIFLORA.—A tree 50 to 60 ft. high, in some positions often a shrub. At Kew this grows freely in rather sheltered places, and produces fine leathery leaves of a dark green colour, in outline somewhat like those of a small Spanish Chestnut. Mountains of California.

Q. GLABRA.—A Japanese Oak, with large handsome leaves, the acorns borne in upright spikes. Several varieties are mentioned in catalogues, but they are hardly distinct. At Kew the species makes a large bush and is thoroughly hardy.

Q. ILEX.—The best-known of Evergreen Oaks, and the most valuable for Britain. Old trees, which have been allowed plenty of space and have been allowed to grow naturally, resemble in form the Olive trees of the Italian coast and of the Riviera. It is one of the most variable of Oaks, but few of the named varieties—and there are many—are so beautiful as the wild kind.

Q. SUBER (*Cork Oak*).—The Cork Oak, which, except for the curious growth of its bark, hardly differs in effect from the Holm Oak. There are fine old trees of this at Mount Edgcumbe, Goodwood, and other places, though the Cork Oak is not hardy enough for our climate generally.

Q. VIRENS (*Live Oak*) is in its native country a tree of the first economic value, and deserves all the encomiums passed on it by Cobbett in his *Woodlands*. All the trees in England I have seen under this name are, however, forms of *Q. Ilex*, and I doubt there being any fine trees of the true *Q. virens* in cultivation in this country.—N.

RAMONDIA (*Rosette Mullien*).—*R. pyrenaica* is an interesting Pyrenean plant, with leaves in rosettes close to the ground, the flowers purple-violet colour, with

Ramondia pyrenaica.

orange-yellow centre, 1 to 1½ in. across, on stems 2 to 6 in. long, in spring and early summer. There has been a good deal of writing about its cultivation, but it is really not difficult; growing in cool peat borders on the lower ledges of the rock-

garden, or in moist chinks. It is found in the valleys of the Pyrenees, on the face of steep and rather shady rocks. There is a rare white variety which does well in borders of American shrubs in peat soil. There is one good and one or more pure white varieties, and some less known species of new kinds are talked of of, such as R. Heldreichi, R. serbica, and R. Nataliæ; the two last found in Servia. Seed and division. Gesneraceæ

RANUNCULUS (*Crowfoot Buttercup*). —Mountain, meadow, and marsh herbs, many of them weeds, while others are among the choicest of alpine flowers and perennials for borders. They are for the most part of the simplest culture; only R. asiaticus and its many varieties require special treatment.

R. aconitifolius.—A mountain pasture herb. The double-flowered variety which is known as Fair Maids of France is a pretty garden plant about 18 in. high,

Ranunculus aconitifolius fl.-pl. (Fair Maids of France).

for several weeks in early summer covered with small rosette-like white blossoms. It is a charming plant in deep moist soils, and the single wild plant worth a place in collections.

R. acris (*Bachelors' Buttons*).—The pretty double form of this plant is also a useful kind, its rich yellow blossoms borne in button-like rosettes: a border plant, and good in moist soil.

R. alpestris (*Alpine Buttercup*).—A native of the alpine regions of Central Europe, and found chiefly growing in calcareous soil: a handsome kind, forming small tufts of shining, dark-green, prettily cut leaves; flowers large pure white, with numerous yellow stamens in the centre, and borne singly on erect stems from 2 in. to 6 in. high in June and July. A good rock-garden plant in light, porous, moist soil.—C.

R. amplexicaulis (*White Buttercup*) is a lovely garden plant, about 1 ft. high, with slender stems, glaucous-gray leaves, and blossoms 1 in. across, pure white with yellow centres, blooming in April and May: a pretty border and rock-garden plant, doing best in a deep moist loam. Pyrenees and Alps of Provence.

R. asiaticus (*Turban Buttercup*).—An old garden plant, with neat double flowers of many colours, divided into various sections, such as the Dutch, Scotch, Persian, and Turkish, each representing a distinct race, and all beautiful. The culture of this Ranunculus is simple if a few essentials are observed. The situation should be open, but not exposed, and the soil a loam mixed with decayed stable manure equal to a third of its bulk. About a month previous to planting, the bed should be prepared to a depth of 15 in., and planting should take place the last half of February; in some seasons it may take place in October, though such an early date is not the best. Drills about 5 in. apart and 1½ deep should be made with a small hoe; the claws of the roots should be placed downwards and pressed firmly into the soil, which should be raked over the roots, and a top dressing of about 2 in. of good loam given. If the surface soil is light, it may be gently beaten with a spade in order to obtain a firm surface, and this may be repeated just before the foliage appears, say about a month or six weeks after the planting. As this Ranunculus delights in moist soil, water should be given if there is a scarcity of rain, and in no case should the roots be allowed to become dry. A light top-dressing of artificial manure or guano just as the foliage is above ground will do good. When the flowers are past and the leaves faded, the roots must be taken up, dried, and stored in a cool place in sand till the next planting season, for roots left in the ground are injured by rains and never strong. The Persian varieties are the finest as regards colour, compactness, and symmetry of growth; but the Turban varieties are of hardier constitution and of freer growth, and therefore are better suited for beds, lines, and masses. The Scotch and Dutch varieties are also fine for masses in beds, being all of highly effective colours. It is useless to enumerate the different varieties, as they are usually sold according to colour, and are mentioned in nearly every bulb catalogue. The large semi-double French (de Caen) and the Italian forms of this plant are good. The wild plant, which I gathered in Egypt both in the yellow and red forms, is a lovely wild flower, and as well worth growing as any of its garden varieties, but it is not hardy and soon perished on my cool stiff soil. To be grown it must be treated like its variety, *i.e.*, the roots taken up yearly.

R. bulbosus fl.-pl. is a showy plant, about 1 ft. in height, with, in early summer, numerous double yellow blossoms, growing well in any soil. Of R. repens there are two double varieties, one neat and the other untidy.

R. bullatus is a fine border plant, about 6 in. high, with large orange-yellow blossoms like those of the Marsh Marigold (Caltha palustris). It is not so hardy as the majority of the Crowfoots, and should therefore be placed in warm dry soil.

R. crenatus.—A native of alpine and siliceous mountains in Styria, the leaves entire and roundish; the flowers are large, white, with almost entire petals, two or three together at the extremity of stem, 3 or 4 in. high in April and May, in the rock-garden in deep sandy soil in our country, fully exposed to the sun.

R. glacialis (*Glacier Buttercup*). — This is the plant of the icy regions, being found near to the melting snow on the loftiest mountains. The whole plant involuntarily reminds one of melting ice. The thick fleshy leaves of a dark green, and deeply incised, the stem of a brownish-red tint, 3 or 4 in. long, prostrate on the ground, and bearing from one to four flowers, the petals of which are at first of a light pink colour, passing into a bright coppery - red — everything about this plant has a glacial aspect. It thrives

Ranunculus lingua.

on cool and moist but fully exposed ledge of the rock-garden, in deep gritty soil with white stones or sand on the surface to keep it cool. Alps and Pyrenees.

R. Lingua (*Great Spearwort*).—A native kind, and a noble waterside plant, its leaves rising boldly out of the water, and large yellow and attractive flowers. Thrives in muddy watersides, and the numerous and handsome flowers are good for cutting for the house.

R. Lyalli (*Rockwood Lily*).—A lovely New Zealand plant ; in moist places in the Southern Alps the plant has large rounded leaves and very large handsome waxy white flowers, not unlike those of Anemone japonica, with delicate yellow stamens in the centre. In some places in Britain this plant is not hardy, but in others it stands the winter well. A writer in *The Garden* says of a plant at Kew : " It is growing in a deep peaty bed, sheltered from the north and east, and has been without protection of any kind for over two years. To get the seed of this charming plant to germinate is difficult, as importations in recent years have failed, and like many other similar plants it seems to do best when let alone. It has flowered in a few gardens, and would seem to require cool rock-garden treatment so far as now known."—W. K.

R. parnassifolius (*Parnassia-leaved Buttercup*).—A singular-looking plant with thick, entire leaves, woolly on the edges, flowers large, of a pure white colour, borne two or three together on a prostrate stem in the month of May. In the Pyrenees and on the French Alps it is rare to find a flower of this handsome species which possesses the full number of petals. A rock-garden plant requiring the same treatment as the higher mountain species.

R. rutæfolius (*Rue-leaved Buttercup*) has Rue-like leaves and white flowers with dark yellow centres. Coming from the highest parts of the Alps, it requires the same treatment as the higher alpine plants, in a fully-exposed spot in moist soil with plenty of grit in it.

R. speciosus (*Large Double Buttercup*) is a showy plant, with compact rosette-like flowers of bright yellow in May, succeeding in any light soil. In a full collection, R. gramineus, chærophyllus, illyricus, and fumariæfolius may be included.

The above is but a selection from a very large family in nature, many of which are little known in gardens, and many of no garden interest.

RAPHIOLEPIS (*Japanese Hawthorn*). —*R. ovata* is a beautiful Japanese shrub, hardy in southern districts, and with a little winter-protection may even be planted in cold parts. Its thick evergreen leaves are of a dark colour, and its flowers,

which are large, white, and sweet-scented, are in clusters terminating the young branches. It is a low spreading bush, somewhat open and straggling, and should not be crowded with other shrubs. Some of the other species, such as R. indica and R. salicifolia, both from China, are not hardy enough for the open ground, but make good wall shrubs.

RESEDA (*Mignonette*).—The only species worth growing is *R. odorata*, and its varieties. Seed sown in the open ground in

Raphiolepis indica.

March or April produces in a few weeks flowering plants, which continue to bloom till late in autumn. If, fine masses be wished for, the seed should be sown in pans about the end of March, the seedlings placed singly in 3-in. pots, and planted out in good soil in an open position. A little attention should be given to thinning out the weak shoots and stopping the vigorous ones. Plants sown in autumn will survive mild winters and produce flowers in early summer, these being finer than those of spring-sown plants. There are now many varieties, as R. odorata grandiflora, R. o. pyramidalis grandiflora, the compact strong growing variety Machet, with bold spikes of reddish flowers and broad abundant leaves, and dwarf varieties. Machet is the kind grown so largely in pots for the London markets, and it is also a good kind for the open air.

Retinospora. See CUPRESSUS.

A name often wrongly given, and it would be difficult to exaggerate the evil effect in various ways of giving long Latin names to mere forms and " states " of twigs which may unhappily be propagated by cuttings or grafts, and the repeating for ever in nursery catalogues of doubtful generic names, of which a bad instance is that of this name, with which our catalogues have been crowded for years. As is not unusual among the conifers, mere states—of totally distinct trees, such as the *Arbor vitæ*—were catalogued ; and where it was given with somewhat better reason to distinct plants we now find that all given the name belong to a nobler race, the Cypresses. This name *Retinospora*, therefore, may be dropped out of use by those who care to simplify their words and collections of trees. One result of this confusion of mystifying names is that it very often keeps many willing planters

from finding the really great trees among the cloud of names

RHEUM (*Rhubarb*) — Herbaceous plants of great vigour and picturesque aspect, and their fine leaves are well seen by the margins of shrubberies and in places where luxuriant vegetation is desired They like deep and rich soil R Emodi is a fine-leaved plant, for groups in the pleasure-ground, but requiring good soil It grows about 5 ft high, and is imposing with its wrinkled leaves and large red veins R officinale, however, as regards foliage, is the most effective It is effective early in the year and should be placed near the shrubbery, on the turf, or in the wild garden In small glades with rich soil a bold effect might be produced by a good selection of Rhubarbs with Ferulas, Heracleums, Rhubarbs, Acanthuses, Yuccas, the common Artichoke, Gunnera scabra, and other vigorous hardy plants. R officinale is hardy and easily propagated. R palmatum is a slow-growing plant, and smaller than its variety, R p tanguticum, which increases rapidly, has fine foliage, and will be welcome to those who grow the other hardy species R nobile is distinct, forming a dense pyramid of foliage It is, however, one of the most difficult to cultivate, and in Europe has succeeded only in the Edinburgh Botanic Garden. Indian and Asiatic Mountains The garden Rhubarbs worth growing are R australe, R compactum, R rugosum, R hybridum, Victoria Rhubarb (with very large leaves and long red stalks), Myatt's Linnæus, and Prince Albert Scott s Monarch is the most ornamental of all the garden varieties

RHEXIA (*Meadow Beauty*) —R virginica is a beautiful dwarf bog plant with vivid, deep rosy flowers 6 or 8 in high, in sandy swamps in New England and the Eastern States, and is found as far west as Illinois and Wisconsin R Mariana is even scarcer in this country than R virginica, and less important The Rhexias must not be divided much, and healthy tufts should be obtained from their native localities, and planted in a sandy peat bed.

RHODANTHE (*Everlasting*) –Charming half-hardy annuals from Australia, valuable as border flowers and for winter bouquets They are all of slender growth, 1 to 1½ ft high, and have glaucous-grey foliage and pretty flowers The original species, R Manglesi has fine rose-coloured blossoms with yellow centres, and of which there is a double variety. R. maculata has a deep crimson ring encircling the eye of the flower , and there

is a pure white variety R atro-sanguinea differs considerably from R. maculata, being not only dwarfer, but more branched The flowers, of a bright magenta colour, are rather smaller than those of maculata, but average 1 in in diameter. It is rather less hardy than maculata, but sufficiently hardy for the open air All these kinds should be sown thinly in heat in pots in February or March In the southern counties they may also be sown in the open air in May on warm borders in good soil. In frames, freely watered, and placed in a temperature of 65° to 70°, the seeds quickly germinate, but if insufficiently watered, will remain dormant for several weeks. The seedlings should be pricked while young, as they do not transplant well when large. Plant them in a warm open position, and a well-manured light soil—if peaty, the better. They ought to be protected for a few days after transplanting

RHODODENDRON (*Rose Tree*) —A noble family of shrubs, so popular that they are often over-planted ; that is to say, we see Rhododendrons in large and often lumpy masses in many country places where no planting of any other kind worth speaking of is carried out. In districts where they do well, the soil and climate being suitable, monotonous effects arise through their over-use, against which all who care for beautiful gardens should protest The mild climate of our country and generally our rather mild winters allow many more kinds to grow with us than on the Continent of Europe generally, or in N America In severe winters some kinds are touched by frost even with us, and therefore we must be on our guard against planting other than the hardy varieties except in the south of England and Ireland The hardy American species should be grown more in lowland valleys, as I find that they stand winters which kill R. ponticum

The vast range in our country over which the plant will grow well, alike in Ireland, England, and Scotland, makes the possession of the finest kinds most important Among the numbers of kinds that have been raised by English nurserymen, a good many poor, dull, or ugly in colour have been sent out, and therefore it is important to get kinds good in colour and to group and arrange them better than has hitherto been done ; that is to say, not so much in flat areas and lumpy beds A far better way is to break them up into bold and simple groups, holding the colours more together and not scattering them about in spotty mixtures. It is important to get plants from layers where possible, and not grafted plants, as these are apt to perish and their places be taken by the common stock, of which we have already far too much. Hitherto it has been very difficult to get layered plants; but some of our best nurserymen see the change suggested here is a good one and are providing for it. It makes great difference in the end whether the kind has its own roots and

limeless soil, the difficulty is to prevent their growing so quickly as to smother each other. They are often too closely planted, and after a few years of rapid growth such plantations cannot show their beauty. It would be much better to plant all the choice kinds rather thinly. Where from previous thick planting the bushes are too close together, thin them promptly and severely, leaving the choicer kinds and the finest-formed bushes. In

Rhododendron Falconeri.

is spread about into many plants, or is on some wretched stock on which it perishes.

Rhododendrons are of free growth in almost any soils except those with lime in them. On many loamy soils free from lime the plants do perfectly well, although perhaps never so much at home as on a sandy peat. Over a large area of Ireland where the lime-stone prevails it is, I think, not worth try-ing to cultivate Rhododendrons and it is always better to grow things that do best on one's own soil. Given a peaty or

this way we get light and shade among the plants instead of allowing them to form one flat level mass. The excellent plan of placing lilies and the other fine handsome hardy flowers among Rhodo-dendrons and like shrubs tends to keep them more open and delightful in every way, their forms as well as flowers being better shown.

The plants, forming generally close balls of earth, are more easily transplanted than most shrubs. This is often done in late spring and summer, as for the London flower-shows, where numbers of the finest kinds are brought in spring and taken away in summer. In the case of all choice and rare varieties remove the seed-vessels after flowering, thus saving the strength of the plants for future good growth and flowers.

Hardy Rhododendrons seldom flower profusely in consecutive years, but fine displays biennially are usually made. Established plants can take care of themselves and in strong loamy soil artificial waterings are not required. In very dry summers mulching the roots of a few single plants that occupy a rather dry position is often necessary, but where the beds are on level ground they succeed without this attention. This is not so in all cases, as drought in the early autumn months often kills many of the large plants on shallow soils. Rhododendrons are, as a rule, safe from over-dryness at the root until August ; then, if the weather should be dry, a good soaking of water twice a week and a mulch over the roots of half-rotten manure, 3 or 4 in. in thickness, will maintain them in health. Some degree of shade is helpful to Rhododendrons, all the more so in dry soils and in the districts with a slight rainfall.

THE EVILS OF GRAFTING.—Apropos of this subject, Mr. Scrase Dickins, writes : "We have a large number of grafted Rhododendrons, planted over thirty years ago, from the base of which every year a thick growth of suckers springs up ; these require to be cleared off in the early summer, and again in the autumn, if the intended variety is to retain its claim to existence ; but the labour entailed is considerable, and many are overlooked or passed by for want of time. Occasionally one comes across a great bush of the common ponticum, with a small scraggy piece in the centre to show that once it was meant to be a hybrid variety of special beauty ; but the worst of the whole business seems to be that the older the plant the larger is the base from which the suckers spring, and consequently the larger is the number of suckers. With Ghent Azaleas the trouble is nearly as bad ; the common yellow form on which they are grafted, being a strong grower, soon makes short work in ejecting the less vigorous intruder. It is very unfortunate when, after a certain number of years, the labour and money spent in an endeavour to obtain some specially beautiful effect results in a commonplace arrangement of lilac and yellow. When the snow has prostrated large Rhododendrons, those that are on their own roots will often raise themselves in a thaw without help ; whereas those that are grafted will most likely have broken off short at the base. If the union between the stock and the scion is so imperfect as to give way under these provocations, it follows that the flow of sap and consequent development of the plant must be seriously interfered with. In some cases this may prove beneficial in restraining a coarseness of growth and inducing fertility, but it is the reason why we do not possess in our gardens finer examples of graceful and well-developed natural specimens. In order to gain new and improved varieties, it is necessary to raise a large number of seedlings. If nurserymen were to give their attention more generally to raising seedlings and layered plants, it might with reason be expected that they would raise a large number of new and improved varieties. If planters, looking forward to the future, as planters as a rule must do, would insist on being supplied by the nurserymen with own root plants only, then our successors would have finer examples to thank us for, and we should be increasing our store of what is beautiful among our treasures in garden and wood."

The following is a list of the best hardy varieties :—

Achievement.	Duchess of Connaught.
Adrian.	Duchess of Sutherland.
Agamemnon.	Duke of Connaught.
Album elegans.	Elfrida.
Album grandiflorum.	Everestianum.
Alexander Adie.	Fair Helen.
Alma.	Fimbriatum.
Amphion.	Fleur de Marie.
Archimedes.	Florence.
Atro-sanguineum.	Francis Dickson.
Auguste van Geert	Frederick Waterer.
Bacchus.	Garibaldi.
Barclayanum.	George Paul.
Baron Schrœder.	Gloire de Bellevue.
Beauty of Surrey.	Govenianum.
Bertram.	Guido.
Blandyanum.	Hamlet.
Bluebell.	Hannibal.
Boule de Neige.	Helen Waterer.
Bouquet de Flore.	Hendersoni.
Brayanum.	Hermit.
Broughtoni.	H. H. Hunnewell.
Bylsianum.	H. W. Sargent.
Caractacus.	Iago.
Catawbiense.	Ingrami.
Catawbiense album.	Jack Waterer.
Charles Bagley.	James Bateman
Charles Dickens.	James Macintosh.
Charles Thorold.	James Mason
C. S. Sargent.	James Nasmyth
Chionoides.	J. Marshall Brooks.
Cœrulescens.	John Spencer.
Concessum.	John Walter.
Congestum roseum.	John Waterer.
Coriaceum.	Joseph Whitworth.
Crown Prince.	Kate Waterer.
Cruentum.	Kate Alice Waterer.
Cynthia.	Kettledrum.
Delicatissimum.	Lady Annette de Trafford.
Delicatum.	Lady Armstrong.
Doncaster.	Lady Clementina Mitford.
Duchess of Bedford.	

Lady Clermont	Novelty
Lady Dorothy Neville	Odoratum.
Lady Eleanor Cathcart	Old Port
Lady Falmouth	Onslowianum
Lady Francis Crossley	Othello
Lady Grey Egerton	Paradox
Lady Godiva.	Perfection
Lady Olive Guinness	Perspicuum
Lady Tankerville	Pictum
Lalla Rookh	Picturatum
Limbatum	President van den Hecke
Lord John Russell	Prince Camille de Rohan
Lord Palmerston	Princess Christian
Lucidum	Princess Mary of Cambridge
Madame Carvalho	
Marchioness of Lansdowne	Punctatum
Marie Stuart	Purpureum elegans
Martin Hope Sutton	Purpureum grandiflorum
Mason s White Seedling	Purity
Maximum	Ralph Sanders
Maximum album	Raphael
Maximum Welsianum	Rosabel.
Maxwell T Masters	Roseum elegans
Melton	Roseum pictum
Memoir	R S Field
Meteor	Sappho
Michael Waterer	Scipio
Minerva	Sefton
Minnie	Seraph
Mirandum	Sherwoodianum
Miss Jekyll	Sigismund Rucker
Miss Owen	Silvio
Mont Blanc	Sir Charles Napier
Morion	Sir Isaac Newton
Mrs Arthur Hunnewell	Sir James Clark
Mrs Charles Leaf	Sir Thomas Sebright
Mrs Charles Thorold	Sir William Armstrong
Mrs Fitzgerald	Snowflake
Mrs Frank Phillips	Standard of Flanders
Mrs Fredk Hankey	St Simon
Mrs G H W Heneage	St Blaise
Mrs Harry Ingersoll	Stella
Mrs John Clutton	Sultana
Mrs John Kelk	Sunray
Mrs John Penn	Surprise
Mrs J P Lade	Sydney Herbert
Mrs John Walter	Sylph
Mrs John Waterer	The Cardinal
Mrs Mendel	The Moor
Mrs Milner	The Queen
Mrs R S Holford	The Warrior
Mrs Russell Sturgis	Titian
Mrs Shuttleworth	Torlonianum, a hybrid,
Mrs S Simpson	between Azalea and
Mrs Thomas Agnew	Rhododendron
Mrs Thomas Longman	Towardii
Mrs Thomas Wain	Vandyck
Mrs W Agnew	Vauban
Mrs William Bovill	Verschaffeltii
Neige et Cerise	Vestal
Nero	Victoria
Nigrescens	Vivian Grey
Norma	William Austin
Notabile	

RHODODENDRONS GROUPED FOR
EFFECT OF COLOUR —Reds, rose-colours,
and pinks with a few whites, viz Reds
—James Marshall Brooks, John Waterer,
Atro-sanguineum, Alexander Adie, Baron
Schræder Rose and rosy-pinks—Mrs
Penn, Ingrami, Cynthia, Bianchi, Fair
Rosamund Whites—Mrs John Clutton,
Minnie, Pictum, Fair Helen, Madame
Carvalho Rhododendrons of salmon-red
colour are best kept separate from others,
of these, good colourings are—Lady
Eleanor Cathcart and Mrs R S Holford
Purples must be kept away from reds, but
group well with any whites, some of the
best for colour are—Everestianum, Album

elegans fastuosum, Cyaneum, Lady Nor-
manton, Reine Hortense, Lucifer

DWARF KINDS.—There are some dwarf
kinds which may be associated with alpine
plants in the rock-garden—indeed, some
are but a span high One of the prettiest
of these is R Chamæcistus, which has tiny
leaves, and in early summer exquisite
purple flowers, of the same size as those of
Kalmia latifolia It is rarely seen in good
health in gardens, and is best in limestone
fissures, filled with peat, loam, and sand
mixed in about equal proportions A
native of calcareous rocks in the Tyrol,
and one of the most precious of dwarf
rock-shrubs The well-known R ferrugineum and R hirsutum both bear the
name of alpine Rose, and often terminate
the woody vegetation on the great
mountain chains of Europe They are
easily obtained from nurseries, and are
well suited for the large rock-garden,
where they attain, in deep peat soil, a
height of about 18 in R Wilsonianum,
R myrtifolium, R amœnum, R hybridum, R dauricum-atrovirens, R Govenia-
num, R odoratum, and R Torlonianum
are dwarf kinds, which may be used in
the rock-garden—the last two being sweet-
scented They should not be planted near
minute alpine plants

INDIAN RHODODENDRONS IN SOUTH-
ERN ENGLAND —The following is an
abstract from *The Garden* of a paper by
Mr W J Bean, of the Royal gardens at
Kew, of the Indian Rhododendrons in
the London district, and therefore of interest to growers in the home counties,
less favoured than many districts for the
growth of these fine shrubs

The altitudes at which these grow range
between 4,000 ft and 14,000 ft, but it is
at heights of 10,000 ft. and upwards that
the genus is most abundantly represented
Above 12,000 ft Sir J Hooker says that
three-fourths of the whole vegetation consists of Rhododendrons. The mean temperature at Darjeeling (in which neighbourhood most of the species are found)
does not widely differ from that of London,
but the extremes of heat and cold are
much greater here than there, and it is
only a few that can be said to thrive out
of doors really well and flower in the
London district, although many can remain healthy in foliage when grown in well-
sheltered spots. The greatest successes
with Himalayan Rhododendrons in the
British Isles have been obtained near the
sea in the south and south-western counties, where the temperature is equable
and moist. The districts in which they
are grown to greatest perfection are near

Swansea, in Wales, and about Falmouth, in Cornwall, and also in the· south of England and Ireland generally, the coast line all round the islands, too, being favourable. A soil which is naturally peaty is no doubt the best, but not essential ; they may be grown out-of-doors in loam either light or moderately stiff so long as lime is absent, and with plenty of leaf mould. They should always, if possible, be planted near trees—near enough to be screened from the sun for a few hours a day. /

The following is a list of species of some proved hardy in Britain in the southern counties and in good suitable soils.

R. FALCONERI.—A noble kind thriving in Cornish gardens, with oblong leaves about 10 ins. long, coated beneath with reddish down, dark green, slightly downy and curiously wrinkled above. The flowers are of a curious shade of creamy white tinged with lilac towards the base. *R. eximium* is a fine variety of this, differing in its bright pink flowers and the thicker reddish brown fluff on the upper surface of the leaves.

R. ARBOREUM.—The best known of the Himalayan species, and one of the most variable. The various forms may roughly be divided into two groups, the one with foliage that is silvery beneath, the other having the underside of the leaf covered more or less with a reddish tomentum. The leaves of all are from 5 ins. to 8 ins. long, the trusses rounded or sometimes almost conical, with the flowers closely packed, the colour of the bell-shaped corolla varying from rich crimson to almost white. The plants known under the following names belong to the arboreum group, some having been given specific rank : *Campbelliæ*, flowers rosy purple, leaves rusty beneath ; *limbatum*, flowers rosy purple, leaves silvery beneath ; *nilagiricum*, flowers rosy, leaves reddish beneath ; *Cinnamomeum*, flowers almost white ; *Windsori*, flowers and trusses smaller, rich crimson.

R. BARBATUM is described as being in a wild state 40 ft. to 60 ft. high ; I have seen it about 12 ft. high in Cornwall. The leaves are 5 ins. to 7 ins. long with flowers of a rich blood-red colour borne in a compact truss 4 ins. or more in diameter.

R. HODGSONI.—A spreading shrub or small tree, rarely more than 12 ft. high, the stout leaves upwards of 1 ft. long, covered beneath with a grey tomentum, the upper side a bright shade of green, and flowers are of a pale rosepurple. It is hardy in both the Welsh and Cornish gardens.

R. WIGHTI.—A small tree, found at elevations of 11,000 ft. to 14,000 ft., bearing yellow flowers 2½ inches across in large rounded trusses. The leaves are firm and stout, 6 ins. to 10 ins. in length, and when young quite white underneath, becoming grey with age.

R. NIVEUM.—One of the hardiest species, but far from the most showy, the young leaves being covered with a white tomentum, the upper surface afterwards becoming deep green and glabrous, the purplish lilac flowers close in a small head.

R. FULGENS.—One of the hardiest and rarest of Himalayan Rhododendrons, blooming out of doors early in March, and not always escaping the damaging spring frosts, but if it does, it is the most brilliantly coloured shrub flowering at that time. The flowers are in compact rounded trusses about 4 ins. across, a bright blood-red, the leaves coated beneath with a rusty felt. The true plant has been grown outside for many years in the Rhododendron dell at Kew, and it has never been injured by frost, nor does it ever fail to set abundance of bloom. Himalaya, at elevations of 12,000 ft. to 14,000 ft.

R. CAMPANULATUM.—Among the hardiest of the Himalayan species, flowering in April and forming a widely spreading bush. The leaves are coated beneath with a brightly coloured reddish felt, and the flowers are pale purple, changing to nearly white.

R. LANATUM.—The young branches, both surfaces of the leaves, and the petioles are covered with a dull white or tawny tomentum, the sulphur-yellow flowers are 2 ins. across.

R. AUCKLANDI.—This tender species attains the dimensions of a small tree, its stems being of a grey colour with the bark peeling off. A hybrid between it and *Hookeri* calied *kewense* (raised at Kew in 1874) has flowers of a pale flesh colour, not so large as those of *Aucklandi*, but more numerous in the truss. There is also a very pretty hybrid known as *Aucklandi hybridum* which is hardy in the London district ; its flowers are pure white. Syn. *R. Griffithianum.*

R. THOMSONI.—The flowers of this species of a fine red are borne in loose trusses, hardy in the London district and flowering in the early part of April ; the leaves 3 ins. to 4 ins. long, very dark green above. This is a plant of bushy habit ; the largest I have seen is growing at Tremough, near Falmouth—a magnificent garden for these Rhododendrons. It was 12 ft. high and 15 ft. through.

R. CAMPYLOCARPUM is closely allied to the preceding and it is of similar habit, but, the flowers are pale yellow, borne in a loose truss and scented like honey.

R. HOOKERI.—A native of Bhotan, and on the Oola Mountain this is said to form entire thickets accompanied by *Pinus excelsa*. The leaves are oblong or oval, 4 ins. long and glaucous beneath, the flowers of a bright red.

R. CINNABARINUM.—In "The Flora of British India" this name is made to include what have previously been known as *R. Roylei* and *R. blandfordiæflorum*. The species is, indeed, a most variable one, having flowers of a brick-red, rich crimson, or sometimes greenish colour. They are all distinguished by the long narrow corolla, resembling a Lapageria.

R. KEYSI.—A curious species, with flowers

more like those of a Correa, brick-red, about 1 in. long, the lobes of the tubular corolla being almost straight.

R. MADDENI.—A shrub 8 ft. to 10 ft. high with bright green lanceolate leaves. The corolla is pure white, bell-shaped, and about 3 ins. across the mouth. It is known also as *R. Jenkinsi. R. calophyllum* is practically the same thing, but a distinction is founded on the shorter calyx lobes and much smaller seed vessels.

many times larger, obovate, and 5 ins. long. Both have the margins ciliated. The flowers are in each variety white, although in the bud stage quite rosy pink. They are about 3 ins. wide and as much in depth. *R. Giòsoni* and *R. Johnstoni* are forms of this species, differing chiefly in the larger leaves.

R. anthopogon, flowers sulphur-yellow ; *R. glaucum*, flowers dull rose-purple ; and *R. pendulum*, flowers white, are small-leaved dwarf shrubs, chiefly of botanical interest.

Tree Rhododendron at Castlewellan, co. Down.

R. CILIATUM.—A bushy plant which thrives well in sheltered positions near London. Its leaves are densely covered with hairs when young, less so as they get older ; the flowers are borne loosely in small trusses, rosy white on opening, whiter with age. It has been used for hybridisation, and amongst others *R. præcox* and Rosy Bell have been raised from it.

R. FORMOSUM.—There are two very distinct varieties of this in cultivation ; the one has narrow leaves, in shape and size almost like those of an Indian Azalea ; the other has them

INDIAN RHODODENDRONS IN IRE-LAND.—There has been much interest taken in the Himalayan Rhododendrons, which, unfortunately, are not hardy enough for our country generally—certainly not for inland parts, though, no doubt, from time to time some of them, and also hybrids from them, will be found hardy here and there. Also there are many kinds very well worth growing in mild and favoured districts such as the south of England and Ireland. A correspondent in the south of Ireland, in Fermoy, sends to *The Garden* the following account of the kinds he has found to do well there—quite hardy without protection—and also of his failures :—

"As I have taken much pleasure in cultivating and hybridising Rhododendrons for about twenty-five years, especially with a view to acclimatise those of Sikkim and Bhotan, I think the results at which I have arrived may be interesting. In order to avoid occupying too much space, I shall first give the names, as furnished to me, of those varieties which I have found perfectly hardy trees without the slightest protection, although some of those which bloom early (about March) have their flowers occasionally spoiled by the spring frosts :—

"Alpinum ; Æruginosum ; Anthopogon ; Arboreum album ; Arboreum roseum, very beautiful ; Arboreum nepalense ; Barbatum, magnificent ; Calyculatum ; Camelliæflorum ; Campanulatum; Campbelli ; Campylocarpum ; Ciliatum ; Cinnamomeum ; Cinnabarinum ; Crispiflorum, not bloomed ; Eximium, fine, like Falconeri ; Falconeri, grand ; Fulgens ; Falconeri superbum, not bloomed ; Glaucum ; Hodgsoni, grand, has not yet bloomed ; Hookeri ; Keysi ; Lanatum ; Lancifolium, not bloomed ; Metternichi ; Massangei, beautiful bloom this year ; Niveum ; Nobile, a grand plant, never bloomed ; Ochraceum ; Roylei ; Virgatum ; Wallichi, I think same as Niveum ; Wighti.

"The following were more or less injured last spring (those marked * I have not yet succeeded in acclimatising) :—

"Argentum, much injured, growing well, not bloomed yet ; Aucklandi, much injured, growing well, bloomed well in 1878-79-80 ; Calophyllum, apparently killed, but growing well ; * Dalhousianum, I do not give this up ; * Edgeworthi, I do not give this up ; Formosum Gibsoni, much injured, but growing well ; Jenkinsi, much injured, doing well, never injured in twenty years previous ; Kendricki, I doubt its name ; Longifolium, much injured, growing well, has never bloomed ; Lindleyanum, much injured, growing well ; Maddeni, much injured, growing well (I see no essential difference between this and Jenkinsi ; centre of Jenkinsi flower, rose, of Maddeni, yellow) ; Nilghiricum not bloomed, much injured ; * Nuttali, many plants killed, I fear hopeless ; Thomsoni, much injured, but growing ; Windsori, very much injured, but growing well. The last two plants appear to me less hardy varieties of R. arboreum.

"I have not included any European hybrids in my list, of which, between Himalayan sorts alone, I know many, and have a great number of my own rearing also, and the reason I do not give up Dalhousianum and Edgeworthi is that I have seedlings from crosses of them which promise well to be hardy, one especially, between Edgeworthi and, I think, Calophyllum, which only lost its bloom-buds last spring, I am very proud of ; its fragrance is far beyond any I know—Rollisson's fragrantissimum and Lindleyanum being, so far, the best. I have named it the Empress of India in honour of our Queen.—H. H."

RHODODENDRONS IN SCOTLAND.—Indian Mountain Rhododendrons may not only be successful in the southern

parts of England and Ireland, but very fine flowers have been sent me from Scotland, (Stonefield, Tarbert, Argyleshire), kinds thriving there that do not always prove hardy in the south. Mr. D. Robertson, who sent the flowers, said the effect produced by them was very fine, and the following kinds have flowered in that place without any kind of protection :—*Falconeri, arboreum, arboreum album, niveum, cinnamomeum, Campbelli, campylocarpum, Thomsoni, barbatum, fulgens, Wallichi, ciliatum, Roylei, Edgeworthi, glaucum, Gibsoni, candelabrum, setosum,* and *pumilum.*

SPECIES OF RHODODENDRON.—According to the Kew list the following species of Rhododendron are in cultivation. About double the number are in some books, many of them of uncertain value, and there are vast regions of China and adjacent countries which are likely to yield valuable species :—

R. albiflorum, N. America ; *ovatum,* China ; *albrechti,* Japan ; *arborescens,* U. States ; *calendulaceum,* do. ; *dilatatum,* Japan ; *flavum,* Caucasus ; *indicum,* China and Japan ; *ledifolium,* do. ; *linearifolium,* Japan ; *nudiflorum,* Canada to Florida and Texas ; *occidentale,* California ; *rhodora,* N. America ; *rhombicum,* Japan ; *Schlippenbachii,* Mandshuria and Japan ; *serpyllifolium,* Japan ; *sinense,* China and Japan ; *vaseyi,* Mountains of Carolina ; *viscosum,* N. America ; *altaclerense,* garden origin ; *Anthopogon,* Alpine Himalaya, and N. Asia ; *arboreum,* Temperate Himalaya ; *blandianum,* garden origin ; *brachycarpum,* Japan ; *californicum,* California ; *campanulatum,* Alpine Himalaya ; *campylocarpum,* Sikkim ; *catawbiense,* Virginia to Georgia ; *caucasicum,* Caucasus ; *ciliatum,* Sikkim ; *cinnabarinum,* do. ; *collettianum,* Afghanistan ; *Cunninghami,* garden origin ; *dauricum,* Dahuria to Mandshuria and Sachalin ; *decorum,* Yunnan ; *Delavayi,* do. ; *ferrugineum,* Alps of Europe ; *arbutifolium, Hammondi, Wilsoni,* all garden origin ; *Fortunei,* China ; *fulgens,* Mountains of India ; *glaucum,* do. ; *halense,* Austrian Alps ; *hirsutiforme,* do. ; *hirsutum,* Alps of Europe ; *intermedium,* Tyrol ; *Kewense,* garden origin ; *Keysii,* Bhotan ; *lacteum,* Yunnan ; *lepidotum,* Temperate and Alpine Himalaya ; *Luscombei,* garden origin ; *Manglesii,* do. ; *maximum,* N. America ; *Metternichii,* Japan ; *myrtifolium,* garden origin ; *niveum,* Sikkim ; *nobleanum,* garden origin ; *parvifolium,* Siberia, China, &c. ; *ponticum,* Spain, Portugal, Asia Minor ; *præcox,* garden origin ; *pulcherrimum,* do. ; *punctatum,* N. America ; *racemosum,* Western China ; *roseum odoratum,* garden origin ; *russellianum,* do. ; *Smirnowi,* Caucasus ; *Smithii,* garden origin ; *Thomsoni,* Nipal and Sikkim, *Ungerni,* Caucasus ; *virgatum,* Sikkim ; *azaleoides, Cartoni, gemmiferum,* and *gowerianum,* all of garden origin.

RHODORA (*Canadian Rhodora*).—*R. canadensis* is a pretty deciduous bush, 2 to 4 ft. high, allied to the Rhododendron, a native of the swamps of Canada, hardy, and needing a moist light soil, though it prefers peat. In very early spring it has clusters of rosy-purple flowers before the leaves unfold.

RHODOTHAMNUS.—*R. chamæcistus* is a beautiful little alpine bush very rare in gardens and rather difficult to cultivate. It is less than 1 ft. in height with ovate leaves from a quarter of an inch to half an inch long, thickly clustered on the twigs, the margins set with slender hairs. It flowers towards the end of April and the beginning of May, and produces its blossoms in clusters at the ends of the

Rhodothamnus chamæcistus.

shoots. From two to four flowers are in the cluster, and each is about 1¼ inches in diameter, the free portions of the petals fully expanded. The colour is a pale clear pink with a ring of a deeper shade in the centre. A feature of the flower also is the long stamens. It is by no means rare in a wild state, being found in the Tyrol (often in large patches) as well as in Carniola. In cultivating this plant, full exposure of the foliage to sunlight, combined with cool, uniformly moist conditions at the roots are necessary. It should be planted in a sunny position in a crevice or small pocket between the stones, which keep the roots permanently moist and protected from the hot sun that the leaves enjoy. The compost should consist mainly of good loam, to which a small proportion of peat may be added, and which should be free from calcareous matter. Syn. *Rhododendron chamæcistus.*

RHODOTYPOS (*White Jew's Mallow*). —*R. Kerrioides* is a summer-leafing shrub from Japan, with a growth and foliage recalling the familiar old Jew's Mallow on cottage-walls, but with white flowers. It is of slender growth, but makes a vigorous bush when well grown, and is usually 5 or 6 ft. high, though against a wall it reaches a height of 10 or 12 ft. It flowers in May, and keeps in bloom a considerable time.

RHUS (*Sumach*).—Low trees shrubs or climbers with an acrid juice usually hardy and remarkable for their elegant

and picturesque growth, and often brilliantly coloured leaves in autumn. Such good qualities as they have are rarely shown in our gardens where they are indeed often absent save one or two of the commoner kinds, and these never grouped or shown in any right way, but perhaps half starved in the conventional muddle of the shrubbery. Several kinds are poisonous and should not be planted near the house or much in the garden, and, if so planted, should be handled with great care, as accidents in gardens are not rare from men handling them not suspecting danger, and their poisonous character is well known and feared in their native countries. The Sumachs are not difficult as to soil or cultivation, thriving in ordinary garden soils, and rather enjoying poor and dry soils, some of them being suitable, therefore, for grouping on dry banks where little else will grow. They may be increased by root cuttings, layers, and also by seed.

R. AROMATICA (*Fragrant Sumach*). — A hardy shrub with trifoliate leaves, a native of rocky woods in Canada and New England, and through Eastern America, especially along the mountains. It has pale yellow flowers in short dense clusters, formed in autumn but flowering in spring before the leaves appear. Syn. R. canadensis.

R. COPALLINA (*Mountain Sumach*).—A shrub or small tree with pinnate leaves turning a fine colour in autumn in its own country, as

Rhus copallina.

they probably would in ours in full sun in warm soil. New England, Canada, and southward and westward.

R. COTINOIDES (*American Smoke Tree*).—A small tree with oval leaves, and somewhat like our European kind to which it is related, but has larger and thinner leaves, taking also a fine colour in autumn, of a beautiful scarlet, suffused with orange and crimson. A native of Missouri, Indian territory and eastwards. It should be planted in dry, warm soil and sunny positions.

R. COTINUS (*Venetian Sumach*).—A beautiful and distinct shrub, long cultivated though not always well placed, the simple leaves taking a fine colour in autumn and the curious

The Venetian Sumach (Rhus cotinus).

inflorescence giving a very pretty effect. There is a purple variety which is an improvement, and a pendulous variety less important. The Venetian Sumach looks very well as a group in a sunny open situation. Southern and Central Europe, and the East.

R. GLABRA (*Scarlet Sumach*).—A distinct very hardy, bushy kind with smooth rather small leaves, thriving in any poor dry soil, the leaves taking a very brilliant colour in autumn. Var. *laciniata* is very distinct, the leaflets longer and of much greater breadth than in *R. Glabra* itself, but they are cut up into narrow pinnate segments, combining the beauty of the finest Grevillea with that of a Fernfrond. When unfolding they remind one of a finely-cut umbelliferous plant in spring ; when fully grown the midribs are red ; and in autumn the leaves glow off into a bright colour after the fashion of American shrubs. The wild plant is much rarer in cultivation than the cut-leaved variety.

R. OSBECKII.—A fine kind with pinnate leaves much finer than the others, striking foliage, also turning in good seasons and warm soils a good orange colour in autumn. This is one of the kinds that might be cut down annually where plentiful, so as to get the fine effect of the foliage on the young vigorous stems.

R. RADICANS (*Poison Ivy*).—A distinct woody climber very common in the North American hedgerows and copses and also up trees. Its leaves give it somewhat the character of a Virginian Creeper and some unprincipled nurserymen sent it out with a new name as *Ampelopsis Hoggi* under which it has been distributed in many gardens. It is a most poisonous plant in its own country and also in ours, accidents taking place from it in gardens, and the cause of the illness is not always known. If kept at all in the garden it should be in rough places where it would not have to be handled or pruned. Syn. R. Toxicodendron.

R. TYPHINA (*Stag's Horn Sumach*).—In its own country often a small tree or shrub, in ours generally a loose shrub common in gardens. The leaves often take a fine colour in autumn, and, as the plant is common it may be grown

Rhus typhina.

as a fine-leaved plant by cutting back a few plants every spring, and confining the growth to one or two shoots. It is a native of sandy or rocky soil from Nova Scotia and Canada southwards.

R. VERNIX (*Poison Sumach*).—This is a shrub or, in its own country, a small tree with pinnate leaves, and growing in swamps in southern Ontario and the coast district of the Eastern States. It is a very poisonous plant and must not, naturally, be brought much into the garden. The leaves are glossy and smooth, and turn a fine colour in autumn.

R. VERNICIFERA is the famous Lacquer Tree of Japan, but we have not yet proved that it will do in our country.

RIBES (*Currant*).—The favourite old Crimson-flowering Currant (R. sanguineum) is typical of the few species that can be called ornamental shrubs. This shrub is so common that I need only allude to the fine varieties of it that are to be obtained from the best nurseries.

Deeper and richer in colour is the variety atro-rubens (called also splendens), though the flowers and racemes are smaller The crimson-red of its blooms forms a striking contrast to the variety named albidum, whose flowers are almost white, though slightly suffused with pink. The double sort (flore-pleno) is an admirable shrub, with very double flowers, which last a long time in perfection, and, as they expand later than the common kind, prolong the season The variety glutinosum is distinguished by clammy foliage and large pale rosy-pink flowers

The Yellow - flowering, or Buffalo Currant (R aureum), deserves to be more commonly grown It is a different shrub from R sanguineum, having larger flowers of a rich yellow, which appear about the end of April or beginning of May, the leaves also are smaller, more deeply lobed, and of a paler green The variety praecox is so named because it flowers earlier than R aureum, and is most desirable on that account, and the variety serotinum, because it flowers late Serotinum is even finer than the type

R Gordonianum, a hybrid between R aureum and R sanguineum, is an old and tolerably common shrub—intermediate in growth as well as in flowers, which are an orange-red, it is distinct and showy It is also known as R Beatoni and R Loudoni Of the numerous other species there is none so fine as the Californian Fuchsia Currant (R speciosum), whose flowers so much resemble miniature Fuchsia-blossoms that in some places it goes by the name of R Fuchsioides Its deep red blooms have protruding stamens, and hang from the leaf-axils in clusters of two or three In growth and foliage it resembles a Gooseberry A densely-flowered bush is extremely pretty and lasts in perfection a long time Though quite hardy enough to be grown as a bush in the milder parts of England, it is usually seen against a wall, and there are few more elegant wall shrubs Grown thus it is 6 to 8 ft in height Most of the other varieties have inconspicuous flowers, but one or two are worth growing for the sake of their autumn foliage, which dies away in various shades of crimson The Missouri Currant (R floridum), also called R missourense, is one of the best of these It is a stock plant in some of the largest nurseries The Flowering Currants are really an important group of shrubs and deserve the best attention, and instead of being crammed in the usual shrubbery-mixture, should be grouped by themselves

RICHARDIA (*Calla*) —This name has been accepted by botanists for the last three-quarters of a century, although it is not yet generally used by gardeners

The genus consists now of various species They all have a perennial tuberous root-stock, not unlike that of Caladium, from which spring the annual leaves and scapes, the former with folding stalks, which form a kind of stem, bearing sagittate leaves, the latter erect, stout, and bearing a large spathe There is a noteworthy difference between R æthiopica and the others, the former having a rhizome and never naturally dying down

R. æthiopica (*Lily of the Nile*) was first introduced into Europe from S Africa in 1687 It is emphatically a Cape plant, and is not found within 1,000 miles or so of the Nile, although it is commonly known as the Lily of the Nile In some parts of this country, for instance Cornwall, it has become naturalised in shallow water, spreading and flowering with the same freedom as in the ditches and swamps of the Cape It varies considerably in the size of its spathes I have seen them 10 in long, and I am told that larger even than this have been grown by cultivators who cut off most of the leaf-blades when the spathes were developing The plant is useful in ponds and fountain basins in the warmer parts of our country. *Syn*, Calla

RICINUS (*Castor-oil Plant*) —*R communis* is a much-grown plant in warm countries, growing out-of-doors in the warm months in ours, and used for bold and noble beds near those of the more brilliant flowers, but it is not well to associate it closely with bedding plants, because of its strong growth and the shading of its leaves, it is a good plan to make a compact group of it in the centre of some wide circular bed and to surround this with a band of a dwarfer plant, say Aralia or Caladium, and to finish with flowering plants A bold centre may be thus obtained, while the effect of the flowers is enhanced It requires rich deep earth to form its finest leaves, and to raise the plants a brisk hotbed is needed in February or March, in which to plunge the pots in which the seeds should be sown The pots should be well drained, and the soil pressed down firmly with a little sifted soil placed over the seeds. When the plants are large enough, pot them singly into 4-in pots in soil composed of sandy loam and leaf-mould or rotted manure, keep them in a warm moist temperature, and give plenty of water at the roots; when the roots have reached the sides of the pots, place the plants in 6 or 8-in. pots. About the end of May gradually inure them to a cool temperature, and after a few weeks place them in a sheltered position out-of-doors. By the end of June they may be planted out in the beds; the more sheltered the situation the better. Dig out holes for them, placing in the bottom a few forkfuls of manure, and, if this be taken from a warm manure-bed, so much the better. Plant and water them with soft rain water, and mulch the surface with manure. During hot weather manure-water will be of use.

The best varieties are sanguineus, borboniensis, Gibsoni (a very fine dark variety), giganteus, Belot Desfougères (a very tall and branching kind), viridis (of a uniform lively green), insignis, africanus, africanus albidus, minor, hybridus, microcarpus, macrophyllus, atro-purpureus, and sanguinolentus, all of which are forms of R. communis, a native of the East Indies.

ROBINIA (*False Acacia*).—Beautiful flowering trees for lawn or shrubbery. The common Acacia or Locust Tree (R. Pseudoacacia) is of quick growth, hardy, and thrives almost anywhere. The ordinary form, with its white Pea-shaped blossom in full beauty about the end of July, is the most familiar. Of the numerous varieties the following are the best: Decaisneana, with delicate pink flowers;

Robinia pseudoacacia.

semperflorens, flowering throughout the summer, and having white blossoms and bright green foliage; and Bessoniana, the thornless branches of which form a dense globular head of deep green foliage, which is retained until very late in autumn, hence its great value as a town or a street tree; mimoscefolia, with finely-divided leaves; fastigiata, of upright growth; crispa, with curled foliage; monophylla, with leaves entire instead of pinnate; umbraculifera, with a spreading head; macrophylla, with large leaves; sophoræfolia, with leaves like the Japanese Sophora; and inermis, with a small head of spineless branches.

R. viscosa (*Clammy Locust*) is smaller than the ordinary False Acacia, but is elegant in foliage and beautiful in flower. The flowers resemble those of Decaisne's variety of the common Acacia, being of a pale pink colour, but the clusters are shorter and denser. It is a beautiful lawn tree, flowering while the tree is still small: fully grown it is of picturesque habit, from 30 to 50 ft. high, thriving best in a deep light soil in a sheltered spot.

R. hispida (*Rose Acacia*) is one of the finest of small trees, requiring little room and not fastidious as to soil. It is naturally straggling in growth, 5 to 15 ft. high; its foliage is much larger

Rodgersia podophylla.

than that of the other Robinias; the clear rose-pink flowers are also larger. A well-flowered specimen is a pretty sight. It flowers in June, but often continues at intervals till autumn. It may be known when not in leaf by the dense rusty hairs covering the young twigs. Its branches are brittle and apt to get broken by high winds, especially if it has been grafted high; therefore choose a spot sheltered from high winds. If the branches become heavy, especially in flower-time, support them by stakes. It may be grown as an espalier, like a fruit tree, and this will protect it from winds, are produced on tall branching spikes. R. podophylla is perfectly hardy, enjoying peaty soil and a shady situation. It is easily propagated by cutting the stoloniferous root-stock, and twenty plants can be obtained from a single root-stock in one year. Japan.

ROMNEYA (*White Bush Poppy*).—Among plants of recent introduction perhaps none surpass in stately beauty this fine Californian Poppywort, *R Coulteri*

Romneya Coulteri.

or it may be trained against a wall. There are several so-called varieties, but none is more beautiful than the type. The variety macrophylla (large-leaved) is of stronger growth and has finer foliage and flowers. N. America.

RODGERSIA. — *R. podophylla* is a handsome-leaved plant of the Saxifrage family, with bronze-green leaves measuring 1 ft. or more across and cleft into five broad divisions. The inconspicuous flowers

In favourable localities it has flowered freely on lengths of the current year's growth, fully 7 ft. high, when with some twelve or fifteen flowers in bloom at the same time, the plant has a charming effect. The flowers are of a peculiarly delicate texture, the petals somewhat transparent, and yet enduring in a good state for days; their fragrance delicate, something like that of a Magnolia. It is perennial, sub-shrubby, and the deeply-cut glaucous

3 D 2

foliage is retained throughout the winter It does not appear to flower on the last year's growth, though that growth remains in good condition The flowers are borne mainly on the points of the new shoots and on laterals nearest the points, more sparingly on the lower laterals. It is hardy in genial soils, enjoying best a warm loam Where it will not grow well in the open, it would do so in many places against a wall with a southern aspect It does best on warm soils in very different parts of the country, so that no one need doubt the fitness of this noble plant for English gardens.

The best winter protection for Romneya Coulteri is a mulch over the roots of some light and porous material Pine needles form the best covering, and, after these, rough cocoanut fibre. A straw mat may be placed round the branches during hard frosts, but should be removed as soon as the weather becomes less severe A point in starting is to get healthy plants in pots, planting in spring and not disturbing the roots much It may be increased by cuttings and seed

ROMULEA.—Bulbous plants of the Iris family. They are of dwarf growth, and have grassy foliage ; but though their blossoms are showy, they are not perfectly hardy, and they require to be grown either in frames or in very warm sheltered borders, in light soil The best known are R Bulbocodium, ramiflora, and Columnæ, natives of South Europe, and R rosea and R Macowani from the Cape of Good Hope The showy Crocus-like flowers of these open fullest in sunshine

ROSA (*Rose*)—The flower of flowers has been ill treated in its literature ! It would be difficult to imagine anything more confusing than the writings on the Rose and catalogues of the present day ! Almost useless groups, like the Boursault, are dignified as classes, while more important groups like the noble Teas often receive no due notice ; the confusion arising from the misleading term "hybrid perpetual" has effectually concealed the fact that the true perpetual bloomers are the Tea Roses, so keeping the noblest of all Roses out of gardens even in the southern counties For many years Roses far superior to the many so-called "perpetual" in point of continuity of bloom have been raised, and yet, as a result of that ill-chosen name, one may go into some of the largest gardens and hardly see a Rose in the Rose-garden in August The set idea of the Rose-garden itself, as laid down in all

the books, *i e.* a place apart where one can only see flowers at a certain season, was harmful, as it led to the absence of the Rose from the flower garden Instead of seeing the Rose in many different attitudes in a country place, we see a wretched mob of standards and half-standards rising out of the ground, generally in a miserable formal arrangement called the Rosery Instead of forming beautiful Rose-gardens, many growers have distinguished themselves by growing Roses on tall Briers and other stocks, from which they get perhaps one or two flowers bigger than their neighbours' to send to a Rose-show The Rose exhibitor's Rose-garden is even uglier than the so-called Rosery in the large country-seat, and thus the beautiful human and artistic side of the Rose-garden has been forgotten As, however, that important side of the Rose-garden is treated of in the first part of the book, it only remains here to deal with the kinds and groups most useful for the garden

TEA ROSES FOR THE FLOWER GARDEN —These are in many ways so superior to all other Roses, that we might place them first, yet there is room for a great extension of their culture in gardens, both large and small We find even standard works on Rose-growing speaking of the Teas as tender and needing protection Others say that only in a few instances can they be grown in the open ground ; and to have them in full beauty, to ensure a constant succession of flowers, and to produce them in all their loveliness and purity of colour, they must be grown under glass This is not so Tea Roses may be grown in many gardens where they cannot now be found, and I would urge all who love Roses to try them fairly, for none are more worthy The variety of lovely tints amongst Tea Roses, the delicate odour, the profusion of bloom, the long season over which it is borne, and their charming habit and foliage are great merits. Let us for ever give up the stupid notion of growing our Roses only in a Rosery, in some out-of-the-way spot The grand Tea Roses now under notice are worthy of the best position in the garden There are also many excellent kinds for clothing walls, fences, or any other erections about our homes, and we shall need much space if we want to grow all that are good Here I name all the best Tea Roses, and if we would make our gardens sweet from June to November, these are what we should plant Every kind is described from experience of it in a flower garden the climbing kinds wreathe the walls and the dwarfs are grouped in beds and borders solely for effect. None, with me, have ever been protected, but winter winds blow furiously over the garden, and on several occasions more than 20° of frost have been registered among the plants. They may be grown with every prospect of success over quite the southern half of England and in many other favoured spots. The dwarfer kinds prefer a soil more light and open than that usually chosen for other Roses. The plants should be either on the Brier Stock or on their own roots. The vigorous and perpetual blooming climbing kinds are the best Roses for walls and fences.

to buy strong plants of Tea Roses on their own roots, the trials were necessarily made with good plants grafted on the Dog Rose, but all my experience tends to show that with many of the best kinds I should have been more successful with plants raised from cuttings struck in the open air in October. A simple way is that pursued by cottage gardeners, of putting in cuttings in a bed in the open air without protection except inserting the cuttings slantwise, in which way they strike more surely. If Tea Roses were struck this way for a year or two, we should get a stock of healthy plants on their own roots, which we could soon compare fairly with the Roses on the various stocks of Manetti,

Rose, Celeste.

Many of the climbing Teas may be grown away from walls, which for such hardy vigorous kinds only furnish support, shelter not being needed. Plant in groups of from three to twelve plants where they have room to develop ; a stake here and there is all the support needed, and they will make huge bushes and bear flowers by the hundred.

TEA ROSES FOR ENGLISH GARDENS. —The following Tea Roses are the best of the varieties opening well in Britain, and the result of a trial of almost every obtainable kind, many thousand plants and for many years, all tried in the open air without protection of any kind at any season. As it is extremely difficult so far

Dog Rose, or other kinds. Where, however, we buy Roses worked very low, it is a simple way to get them on their own roots by burying the union of the stock and graft for an inch or two inches below the surface, scraping or cutting off a little of the bark of the Rose above the union. In this way the Roses often root above the stock, and we soon get the advantage of the plant on its own roots. The kinds that are best worth doing in this way are, we think, the Tea Roses and the allied monthly Roses, which give such continuous bloom throughout the summer in the flower garden. · The plan deserves trying, above all things in soil supposed not to be good for Rose culture—such as hot sands and other light soils, in which people often despair of Roses. I feel certain now that many of the kinds I have lost, or that bloomed feebly and died out, were the result of grafting, or arose from the stock itself and conflict of the saps of plants of quite different countries and natures. To be quite fair to all these beautiful Roses they should be tried in both ways, and not for one year only :—

Honourable Edith Gifford, Maman Cochet Blanche, Mme. Joseph Schwartz, Niphetos, Rubens, Mme. Carnot, Vicomtesse Folkestone, Jean Pernet, Mme. Chédane Guinoisseau, Mme. Edourd Helfenbein, Mme. Hoste, Yvonne Gravier,

the same Roses sometimes among the Noisettes, sometimes among the Teas. That matters little if we remember the good ones, and of those I have grown and found hardy and opening well, these are the best: Lamarque, Celine Forestier, Rêve d'Or, Bouquet d'Or, L'Ideale, W. A. Richardson, Mme. Alfred Carriere, Gloire de Dijon, Mme. Berard, Duchesse d'Auerstadt.

HYBRID PERPETUAL ROSES. — The general name " Perpetual." to all the varieties of this class is a misnomer, as many are not at all perpetual ; but some varieties, more especially some of our oldest Roses,

Buds of Tea Rose, Anna Olivier.

Docteur Grill, Emilie Dupuy, Mme. Charles, Marie Van Houtte, Anna Olivier, Archiduchesse Marie-Immaculata, Maman Cochet, Souvenir d'un Ami, G. Nabonnand, Grace Darling, Marie d'Orleans, Marquise de Viviens, Pauline Labonté, Baronne de Hoffmann, Mme. Lambard, Mme. Philippe Kunzt, Papa Gontier, Souvenir de David d'Angers, Princesse de Sagan.

CLIMBING ROSES OF THE TEA CHARACTER.—These are among the most precious of all plants : that their origin is somewhat obscure is clear from our finding

keep on blooming until November. Amongst the old H.P. kinds one may instance especially La France and Charles Lefebvre, and amongst newer varieties, Viscountess Folkestone and Victor Hugo as true perpetuals ; whereas Mrs. John Laing, Margaret Dickson, Gabriel Luizet, General Jacqueminot and many other H.Ps. do not usually bloom after the month of August. To this large class new varieties are continually being added, from which growers will select their favourite shades of colour. It is best not to follow any stereotyped selection, as frequently these are Roses chosen from anything but an artistic point of view, as to either colour or form

It has been a favourite practice in journals to make strict selections of the most popular Hybrid Perpetual Roses, but we do not follow it here, as it is best not to be narrow in one's selection where there are so many beautiful and well-known kinds It is otherwise with the Tea Roses, which have been unaccountably neglected as Roses for the open garden, even by the great Rose-growing nurserymen, and of these a careful selection has been given

HYBRID TEAS—The race of Hybrid Teas was obtained from crossing the beautiful Tea Rose and the Hybrid Perpetuals, and so we get a group intermediate in form and in colour, and often, as in the case of La France and its varieties, very charming They are also in some cases very enduring in bloom, which makes them more useful than the usual red Roses of our gardens. The ordinary culture of the Rose-garden suits them well, and the finer kinds should, if possible, be got on their own roots as well as grafted Among the kinds grown are Annette Gamon, Antoine Mermet, Augustine Guinoisseau (especially fine in the autumn), Camoens, Cannes la Coquette, Comte Henri Rignon, Countess of Pembroke, Duchess of Connaught, Duchess of Westminster, Esmeralda Gloire Lyonnaise, one of the best Roses for gardens, vigorous, with creamy-white, bold, handsome flowers, large and sweet ; the leaves have a distinct fragrance , Grace Darling, Jules Bassonville, Lady Alice, Lady Mary Fitzwilliam, La France, Madame Alexandre Bernaix, Madame André Duron, Madame Carle, Madame Etienne Levet, Madame Moser, Marquise de Salisbury, with glowing crimson flowers and deep green leaves , Michael Saunders, Pearl, Pierre Guillot, The Puritan, Waltham Climber, Viscountess Falmouth, Viscountess Folkestone

CLIMBING ROSES — If we look at southern Continental gardens, which have never received a tithe of the labour and care lavished on English gardens, but which enjoy the advantage of warmer climate and more constant sun, we shall see such arcades, bowers, pillars, and climbing masses of beautiful Roses on all sides as will put us out of humour with our own beautiful individual blooms, and will cause us to regret the absence from our gardens of these luxuriant

masses that neither receive nor indeed require or obtain any special care from one year's end to the other If it be unfortunately the case that Roses which produce such glorious effects in foreign gardens are not hardy enough for us, why not try to raise new varieties that will endure our cold and changeable season ? Surely in a family that ranges from Kamtschatka to India, we may find at least one species that shall be the parent of hardy climbing varieties, as beautiful in our climate as the Noisette and indica major are in the south of France and elsewhere We have R. sempervirens, and the several garden varieties, such as Félicité Perpetuée, that will climb a pillar or shade an arcade The Ayrshire Roses, R. arvensis and varieties of the Boursault Rose (R alpina), though very charming, bloom only in summer They are all quite hardy and of vigorous climbing growth, but they do not satisfy those who love the Hybrid Perpetual, the Noisette, or the Banksian Rose We have also the continuous blooming R rugosa, the semi-double yellow R Fortunei, and the beautiful R. sinica, the parent of the so-called large white Banksian Rose Fortunei Cannot some hybrids be raised from these and the sempervirens, alpina, or arvensis species ? Let us make use of what we have at hand , let us plant in the wilder parts such hardy climbers as are already mentioned, and make combinations of such red climbing Roses as can be found hardy. When a warm wall needs clothing, the Banksian Rose or the various hybrids of the Noisette and Tea Roses may be used, though they are liable to be cut down in cold situations and seasons For sweetness as well as continuity of bloom Lamarque's clusters of lemon-white flowers must stand first Maréchal Niel, though unrivalled for the splendour of its golden blooms, is only a shy bloomer in autumn Climbing Aimée Vibert, which is thoroughly hardy, should be in every garden. Its white clusters are so continuously abundant and its foliage so persistent that it ranks high as a garden Rose Rêve d'Or is a delightful climber, in a warm situation, and may be called a climbing Madame Falcot, so bright are its half-expanded buds

MONTHLY OR CHINA ROSES —Monthly or China Roses have bright and varied colours, free growth, hardy constitution, and are most constant bloomers They are the first to open in the early summer, and often continue to produce their buds and blossoms almost until winter has merged into spring again, a Monthly Rose bush in a warm nook being scarcely ever without at least a bud. They are perpetual and perennial in the fullest sense. They grow well either in light or heavy soil, preferring that which is light and warm, but not dry. Severe pruning is good for them, though on walls, when the earliest possible flowers are wished for, a few shoots may be left their full length. There are many varieties, all more or less distinct in colour or habit, from the

berg, Louis Phillippe, Nemesis, Prince Eugène, Prince Charles, St. Prix de Beuze, Laurette de Messimy, Eugène Resal, Confucius, Hermosa, Hebe, and Sanglant. Lemesle is one of the most handsome, deep pink with crimson reverse, which gradually creeps over and suffuses the whole flower ; the leaves of this variety have also great substance. Ducher and Rival de Poestum have white flowers. The latter is beautiful, the flowers abundant, not full, but of charming purity

Rose, Gloire Lyonnaise.

lovely dwarf kinds, up to the vigorous Crimson Cramoisie Grimpante, which will climb to the top of a two-storied house and bedeck it with rich crimson flowers during most of the year. The original single China Rose forms a bush 1½ to 2 ft. high ; its crimson blossoms, like brilliant butterflies hovering about, are lovely. Among the best are Alfred Aubert, Eugène Beauharnais, Cramoisie Superieur, Irene Watts, Marie Wolkoff, Nabonnand, Blanche de Chine, Fellem-

and form. Madame Laurette Messimy is perhaps the most distinct variety which has yet appeared, being unlike in colour any previously-known kind, of vigorous growth, and one of the most constant bloomers.— T. S.

MOSS ROSES.—These are divided into two sections—those which bloom only in summer—that is, during May, June, and July—and the so-called perpetual-flowering kinds. Among the early kinds, the old Common Moss Rose may be found, and beautiful it is. This charming Rose has been grown in English gardens for more than a century, and remains one of the best, although it is not seen nearly so much as it might be. In a few gardens I have seen this Rose grown as a standard, but it is not a success. Dwarfs or bushes on their own roots are much the best, sending out long vigorous shoots, if planted in rich soil, and these should be pegged down to the ground. Some of the other kinds may also be similarly grown with advantage.

In addition to the Common Moss, there is Little Gem, a charming miniature Rose, with small double crimson and well-mossed flowers. Crimson Globe has well-mossed buds, large, and of a deep crimson colour. Lanei, too, with large rosy-crimson buds, Crested Moss (pale rosy-pink), Marie de Blois (rosy-lilac), Celina (rich crimson), Reine Blanche (pure white), Luxembourg (crimson), Baron de Wassenar (bright red), and White Bath (paper-white), are all good, and there are many others. Other Moss Roses of note are classed separately as perpetual or autumn-flowering kinds, but there appears to be no need for this separation. Blanche Moreau, for example, is one of the best white Moss Roses, but only blooms once. Other so-called autumnal kinds are Madame William Paul, a fine variety with bright rose-coloured flowers, and Madame Moreau, rose-coloured, edged with white. Madame Edouard Ory, with large rosy-carmine flowers, and the Perpetual White Moss, which blooms in clusters, are also worth mentioning. Other good kinds are Salet, and Soupert and Notting (bright rose). The last-named is sweet-scented, but not quite so free in blooming as other varieties. Zenobia is of satiny-rose colour. Considering their charms, it is curious how seldom Moss Roses are well grown in private gardens. They are usually seen at their best in small gardens, where the owner is kind to his soil. Success with Moss Roses cannot be had except in good rich soil. The Moss Rose is a form of the Provence Rose, to which the same remarks as to cultivation apply.

SCOTCH ROSES.—Varieties of our hardy native Rose, they are as callous to frost and snow, wind and storm, as the proverbial Highlander in his plaid ; and, if only the ground be well broken and manured when the plants are first put in, they are better able to take care of themselves than any other Rose of garden origin. If carefully planted at first, they will need neither pruning nor protection, training nor top-dressing, they are not victims of green-fly or mildew, and they may be trusted to thrive for a considerable number of years without special attention. Scotch Roses are not particular as to soil ; and, if the soil is poor, a light mulching of short manure in November will keep them in good condition. Scotch Roses are only summer-flowering, but then their delightfully-fragrant flowers come so early that they are especially welcome.

There are, unfortunately, in cultivation many very dingy-coloured varieties, which have got these Roses a bad reputation from a decorative point of view, but when only delicately-coloured varieties are grown, nothing can be more charming than a mass of these dwarf, delightfully-fragrant, and very hardy Roses, the buds of which are in miniature the perfection of form—a quality which is maintained in the globular flowers of the more double varieties ; while in soils and situations where the cultivation of most other Roses would be hopeless, flourishing plants and flowers in abundance may be had of the Scotch Roses.—T. W. G.

POLYANTHA ROSES.—These are often of a dwarf bushy habit, rarely exceeding a foot in height. The flowers naturally are very small, but fragrant. Among the good varieties are Anne Marie de Montravel, pure white, very free ; Little Dot, soft pink ; Mignonette, pale rose, very pretty ; Perle d'Or, nankeen-yellow ; Paquerette, white ; Blanche Rebatel ; Clothilde Soupert ; Georges Pernet ; Gloire de Polyantha ; Golden Fairy ; Madame Allegatière ; Marie Pare ; Max Singer ; Souvenir d'E. Chatelaine.

There is, however, some danger in taking up seriously new classes of Roses of this kind, because there are very few that are not inferior in beauty to the lovely Tea and other Roses which are now obtainable. Roses that have not the finest forms, and are unfit for cutting for the house, are likely to take a back place.

THE BANKSIAN ROSE (Rosa Banksiæ), a native of China, was brought to England in 1807, and the best-known sorts are Alba Fortunei, white and yellow, and the Banksian Roses require a warm wall and dry border, with two or three years' growth to bloom in perfection. Merely cut out a few of the old already-bloomed shoots, and any late-growing sappy wood about July. They are very precious for covering house walls in many parts of England, but are not so good on wet and hilly shady places. Remove any growths that have been injured by severe frosts during the winter, but beyond that little spring pruning is needful.

NOISETTES.—Owing to some of the most important kinds in this group being often classed with the Teas, even in catalogues which class them as Noisettes, there is much confusion. We therefore omit Roses such as Bouquet d'Or, which we group among the Teas. They bloom long and well in clusters, grow freely, and are fragrant and useful for climbing or pillar Roses. The following are good vars. :—Aimée Vibert, Celine Forestier, Cloth of Gold, Cornelia Koch, Desprez à Fleur Jaune, Fellenberg, Grandiflora,

Madame Zoetmans, York and Lancaster (true).

THE PROVENCE ROSE or Cabbage Rose.—Of this the origin is not known, but growing abundantly in Provence, it has received that name, though the French themselves always call it *Rose à Cent-Feuilles.* "The rosarian should devote a small bed of rich soil, well manured, to the cultivation of this charming flower, growing it on its own roots, and pruning closely. The Double Yellow Provence Rose, of a rich, glowing, buttercup-yellow as to complexion, and prettily cupped as to form, full of petal, but of medium size, has almost disappeared from our gardens, and I have only seen it at the Stamford

Rose Harrisoni.

Isabella Grey, Jeanne d'Arc, Joseph Bernacchi, La Biche, Lamarque, Duchess of Mecklenburg, Madame Carnot, Madame Alfred Carriere, Madame Caroline Kuster, Madame Massot, Ophirie, Solfaterre, Triomphe de Rennes, Unique Jaune.

THE DAMASK ROSE (Rosa Damascena) is a native of Syria, whence it was brought to Europe about 1270 by Thibault IV., Count of Brie, returning from a crusade in the Holy Land. The Damasks have pale green leaves, green shoots, with numerous spines, are of free growth and hardy ; the flowers are pretty in form, and very fragrant. They need but little pruning. Among the kinds, besides the common one, are La Ville de Bruxelles, Leda, Madame Hardy, Madame Stoltz,

shows, sent there from Burleigh. Although common at one time in this country, it seems never to have been happy or acclimatised."—DEAN HOLE.

BOURBON ROSES are among the most useful of garden Roses. They seem somewhat capricious, with the exception of Souvenir de la Malmaison. Among the best kinds are—Armosa, Gloire de Rosomanes, Madame Isaac Pereire, Queen, Souvenir de la Malmaison, Empress Eugénie, Kronprinzen Victoria, Madame Baron Veillard, Marquis Balbaino, Mrs. Bosanquet, President de la Rocheterie.

ALBA ROSES.—The Alba Roses are, from their delicacy of colouring, interesting, and thrive under ordinary cultivation.

Noisette

R nitida

Bracted

Large flowered

Provence

Glossy

Small fruit

R sinica

Caucasian

Musk

Yellow Brier

Evergreen

Some Wild Roses and their hybrids

The moderate growers should be pruned closely, not the others Blanche Belgique, Belle de Segur, Celestial, Félicité, Madame Audot, Madame Legras, Maiden's Blush, Mrs Paul, and Lorna Doone are among the best kinds

EVERGREEN ROSES (R sempervirens) —These are Climbing Roses, with large clusters of from ten to fifty blooms each, and holding their dark green shining foliage through a great part of winter, they are free growers and quite hardy In pruning, the head should be thinned out, a few of the more pendent shoots being left their whole length

GALLICA ROSES — This is an old group, that used to be important, but is no longer so because of the other kinds that have been raised The many kinds may be distinguished by their stiff erect growth, and require close pruning whilst the flowers are fragrant and varied in hue The striped varieties of this section (Rosa Mundi, etc) are often called York and Lancaster The following are the best known —Boula de Nanteuil, Blanchefleur, Cynthie, D'Aguesseau, Duchess of Buccleuch, Kean, Œillet Parfait, Ohl, Perle des Panachees, Rosa Mundi, Village Maid.

AYRSHIRE ROSE (Rosa Arvensis vars) —These roses, of native origin, are of rapid growth, often running 15 or 20 ft in one season, and are of use in covering rough buildings, unsightly banks and trees They do not require rich soil, and should be pruned very little, or not at all Bennett's Seedling, Queen of Ayrshire, Queen of Belgians, Ruga, Dundee Rambler, Splendens, and Virginia Rambler, are the best-known sorts

BOURSAULT ROSE (Rosa Alpina) — This is a distinct species, but its varieties form a worthless group, which receives its name from M Boursault Most of the varieties are free from thorns and have long reddish shoots Amadis is most grown It is one of the groups of roses not worth keeping up

ROSE HEDGES — If the soil be naturally a good Rose soil, the work will be light In that case mark out the position of the hedge 2 ft wide, trench up that space 2 ft deep, adding as the work proceeds a quantity of well-rotted manure Where there is any doubt about the staple being of the right sort, remove it, and supply its place with a mixture of three parts loam and one of manure There are, however, many gardens the soil of which, with the addition of one barrowful of loam to every yard length of hedge, and about half that quantity of manure, will grow Roses well.

Plants on their own roots are indispensable, and if from 2 to 3 ft high so much the better, as they will form a hedge the sooner The time of planting must depend on the condition of the plants, but, if only small plants in pots are to be had it should be in April or May In any case it should be done when the soil is moderately dry, and some finely-sifted mould should be placed round the roots, the ground being made moderately firm Deep planting must be avoided The crown should be about 2 in under the surface, as the soil will afford it some protection during severe weather. As soon as the planting is done, give some support to the branches, a neat stake and a strong tie preventing them from being blown about by the wind Place a layer of short rotten manure over the roots This should be 3 in thick, and 1 ft wide on each side During the first two years little pruning will be necessary, but the second spring after planting, any strong shoots that exceed 3 ft in length should be cut back to that point In the ground place a few neat sticks, to which tie some of the lower branches to form the base of the hedge and bring it into shape After the second year the growth will gain more vigour and increase in length Cut down the strongest shoots to 4 ft the third year and from that time allow them to increase slowly in height so as to give the lower branches time to fill up the base Some supports will be necessary to keep the growth in shape The after-management consists in giving the roots a good dressing of rotten manure every winter. Rake away the soil from over the roots, lay the manure on them, and then replace the soil

WILD AND SINGLE ROSES.

There are many beautiful single Roses, and now that some interest has been awakened in them, we may expect to see them more freely planted There are vigorous climbers which, allowed to have their own way and a branched tree to support them, will climb to a great height, others, sturdy and bushy, are suitable for planting in bold groups and masses, and rare ones will merit special care They are free from the pests that infest the double Roses, and above all things when single Roses are present in the garden a roseless June will not happen even in the worst of seasons When Dog Rose and Sweet Brier toss from the hedges in early June our gardens might and should show some of the Wild Rose beauty, for the single Roses of many lands are at our disposal

Marsh

Many flowered

R alba

Alpine

R Lawrenciana

Long leaved China

Bramble leaved

Double Glossy

Hybrid China

Japanese

Damask

Some Wild Roses and their hybrids

R. ACICULARIS (*The Needle Rose*) is a beautiful Wild Rose, which when leafless might well be mistaken for the Japan Rose, it is so armed with the sharpest needle-pointed spines, and it has the same stout, vigorous bushy habit of growth as rugosa. In flower and fruit it is quite different, and is a bright flowered kind, but early and long blooming : and it is always one of the first to open. Its leaves are smaller than those of rugosa; the flower large, rich red, with a sweet scent. It also has a showy fruit, which differs from that of the Japan Rose, for, instead of being roundish and smooth, it is long and Pear-shaped, of a bright red colour, with its apex covered with spiny bristles. It is a native of Siberia, as hardy as any kind known, but as yet uncommon in gardens.

R. ALPINA (*Alpine Rose*) is really more worthy of a place in the garden than the varieties of which it is the parent—the Boursaults. It grows to a great size, with long, thornless shoots ; does not make such a colour display as most kinds, but t is welcome for its earliness, and a bowl of its rosy-red flowers is pretty in the house in May.

R. BRACTEATA (*The Macartney Rose*) is a little tender, but it is so beautiful that it repays a little extra care, and is pretty for a low wall, which in a sunny aspect is needed to bring it out in its full beauty. The plant is almost evergreen ; leaves dark green and shining ; the flowers large, milk-white, sweetly scented, of a pretty cupped form. China.

R. BRUNONIS (*White Indian Rose*), a very handsome Rose and almost worth growing for the sake of its foliage alone. It is perhaps a little tender, but vigorous ; any injury that happens from winter frosts is quickly effaced. July is its month of blooming, the flowers in clusters, pure white, with a yellow centre. Alone it is capable of covering a house, and it must have plenty of room. Better still to let it ramble over trees or shrubs, as it does at Kew near the Cactus house. A single Rose named Pissardi also belongs to the Musk Rose type, and has fragrant Dog Rose-like flowers. Under this same name, however, comes one from Germany with large rose-coloured blooms.

R. CAROLINA (*Carolina Rose*) is a very pretty Wild Rose, somewhat resembling R. lucida, but distinct, as it blooms during August, when most kinds are over, and it keeps flowering through September. It is a tall, upright grower, established bushes being 6 ft. high. Its wood is smooth, with few spines ; the leaflets are long and narrow, and the flowers come in clusters of a dozen or more among plenty of foliage, the buds when opening being rich crimson and the expanded flowers bright rosy-red sweet-scented. The leaves when handled have a distinct and pleasant fragrance.

R. INDICA (*Indian Rose*).—This species appeals to all who love Roses, as a parent of the best races. In it we see those excellent qualities, and continuous bloom, that have been kept through numerous generations, and contribute so much to the charm of the Tea and Monthly Roses of the present day. Of this species there are two or three forms in cultivation. At Cheshunt, Mr. Paul grows a lovely form, with flowers of a flesh-pink colour ; another variety has a large crimson-red flower. Like the Tea Roses, this species is ever growing and blooming from early summer till late autumn.

R. LUCIDA (*Glossy Rose*).—One of the best Wild Roses has leaves of a shining green colour, and just when our native and other early single Roses are passing away this comes into bloom in July and goes on for several weeks. Its flowers are large, opening flat, clear rosy-pink, sweet-scented, in clusters of from five to eight, but succeed one another, so that there is not usually more than one flower open at a time in a cluster. The heps are about as large as a Hazel-nut, deep red, and make a bright effect with the fading leaves, which assume autumn tints. The heps hang all the winter, the leafless wood becomes red, and through the dullest time of the year large groups of this Rose are pretty to see. A few plants soon spread into a thick mass as it runs freely underground, and it is so easily increased by its suckers, that it offers every facility for free planting.

R. LUTEA.—This very distinct Rose is better known through the forms derived from it than in its wild form, pretty as that is, and it would be charming to grow on warm banks. There are two garden varieties, commonly called Austrian Briers, one with yellow flowers, the other orange red, both beautiful for a sunny spot.

R. MACRANTHA is one of the early bloomers and a showy kind. The flowers are large and beautiful, chiefly white, but flesh-tinted round the edges and in the centre with a tuft of fine yellow stamens. In the open ground it makes a thick spreading bush, like R. arvensis of our hedges. Europe.

ROSA MOSCHATA NIVEA.—The old Musk Rose is supposed to have been introduced nearly 300 years ago, but the kind that bears the above name is of garden origin. It has a vigorous climbing habit, is hardy, not fastidious as to soil, with shoots like Willow wands, and sending up flowers in great clusters of thirty or more, and it is not uncommon to see from nine to twelve fully open at one time. The flowers individually are large, opening wide and flat, white, with a suffusion of pink towards the edges of the petals and a cushion of yellow anthers in the centre, which keep their colour whilst the flower lasts. The leaves have seven leaflets, are of a gray-green colour, and when young scented. The wood is chiefly smooth, but small spines are numerous towards the tips of the shoots. For cutting it is delightful, as the clusters have long stems, and in the house every bud opens in due course. The buds are of a lovely pink colour before they open.

R. NUTKANA, according to the *Garden and Forest*, is one of the most showy species of Western America, having the largest flowers and fruits. Its habit is described as stout, the leaves ample and broad, the flowers large, white, and the fruits bright scarlet, $\frac{1}{2}$ in. in diameter.

PAUL'S CARMINE is a garden variety, and a welcome addition to single Roses because of its bright carmine-red flowers. Its vigorous growth makes it useful for walls, fences, and on pillars it does well.

PAUL'S SINGLE WHITE is a vigorous Rose of garden origin, and as we happen to have it growing beside moschata nivea think it not nearly so good. It is rampant, hardy, and has large deep green leaves, the flowers in large clusters, scented, the buds of a tender pink colour, but the flowers do not open out like those of the Musk Rose, and the anthers turn black. It is nevertheless a useful single Rose if placed apart from the others, and it has one merit which they lack in flowering in succession. The vigorous shoots which grow up at the time

Asia, and, although often planted, is scarcely ever made enough of in country places. It is most useful for forming fences with Quick or even by itself on good banks, as it is so spiny that cattle, which do so much harm to almost every other kind of hedge plant, do not touch this, so that it swings careless in the field where they are. The plant ought to be grown by the thousand, and anybody with a few bushes of it can save the seed for this purpose. It is a delightful plant from the time its buds burst in early spring until the birds have eaten the brilliant berries in winter.

R. RUBRIFOLIA (*Red-leaved Rose*) should have a place for its lovely tinted leaves and shoots: it has a rambling or climbing habit, but also grows into a large self-supporting bush.

The Austrian Copper Brier.

of the first blooming usually produce a great cluster of flowers at the top when they have completed their growth.

R. POLYANTHA (*Bramble Rose*).—A rampant climber, which will quickly climb a tree, cover a building, or, away from any support, spread into an enormous bush. It has long, spineless shoots clothed with glossy green leaves, blooming early in June ; a mass of white flowers crowded in a pyramidal truss, with a powerful scent. The variety grandiflora is an improvement, but as yet it does not seem to have been much planted. It has all the vigour of the type, and flowers much larger. They cluster in an immense truss, are pure white and sweetly scented.

R. RUBIGINOSA (*Sweetbrier*).—Perhaps as pretty as any Wild Rose in flower, fruit, and delightful fragrance. It is a native Rose, but also distributed through much of Europe and

The flowers are red and small, the fruits purplish-red with soft flesh. Its chief charm, however, is in the colour of shoots and leaves. The young, strong shoots are purple-red overlaid with a pale gray bloom, whilst the leaves are of a peculiar glaucous colour brightly tinged with red. North America.

R. RUGOSA (*Ramanas Rose*).—A strong grower in any soil, it is one of the best, making a handsome bush when isolated, but large gardens should have great groups of it, and in leaf, flower, and fruit it is beautiful ; it is a long and persistent bloomer, and reaches the zenith of its beauty when the secondary flowers come with the glowing orange and red fruits that have succeeded the first flowers. Then a second crop of ripe fruit appears late in autumn, when the leaves turn yellow, showing the Rose in another pretty aspect. It makes a good hedge, and where pretty dividing lines are wanted, it is one of the best for the purpose. There are purple, pink, and white forms, this last being lovely, and quite the best single white Rose of the non-climbers. They are free enough to plant for covert. Rosa Regeliana and R. kamtschatica are forms of this species. Japan.

R. SPINOSISSIMA (*Burnet Rose*).—A pretty native Wild Rose, which will grow and flourish where many Roses fail in the lightest and

Sweetbrier. Rosa spinosissima.

hottest of soils. It is the parent of the Scotch Roses, some of which are so very pretty in like soils; the creamy white flowers of the wild plant are pretty and fragrant.

R. WICHURIANA.—A distinct and charming Rose, perfectly prostrate in habit, every branch lying flat on the ground, a rapid grower making shoots 12 ft. long in a season, the leaves lustrous green, and flowers standing a little above the mass of creeping stems, pure white, 1½ to 2 in. across. For rapidly covering sunny banks nothing could be more charming than this beautiful Japanese Rose, also for the bolder kind of rock-garden drooping over the larger rocks. It is hardy so far as recent winters entitle one to judge, and easily propagated by cuttings or division.

R. sinica is a large, single, white-flowered, climbing species from China or Japan. R. gigantea, the giant of single white Roses, lately introduced from India, is of doubtful hardiness, otherwise it would be a great addition. R. Beggeriana, a North American kind, of lowly growth, has white starry flowers. R. Woodsi, a garden form of R. blanda, has rosy-pink flowers, and continues blooming till stopped by sharp frost. R. pisocarpa, from California, makes a straggling bush, with flowers of medium size and bright red, are well worthy of a place in the rock-garden. R. berberifolia

Hardyi has flowers like those of a Cistus, rich yellow in colour, with a crimson blotch at the base of each petal, but wants heat and bright sun. Hebe's Lip is a garden form, but a pretty single Rose with a stout bushy habit of growth, and large, creamy white blossoms that have a distinct Picotee edge of red around the petals.

The above is a selection mostly of the best Wild Roses known to us for the garden or shrubberies and fences near the garden. There are many Wild Roses inhabiting northern and temperate countries, and many that have never been in cultivation that are very beautiful and deserving of it. It is to be hoped now that the increased cultivation of these beautiful things will lead to further knowledge of them.

WILD SPECIES OF THE ROSE IN CULTIVATION.—According to the Kew list the following wild species are in cultivation there, and the number deserves to be added to, as no doubt there are many wild kinds in the three continents of the northern world which have never been introduced.

R. acicularis, Siberia; *agrestis*, Europe; *alba*, Europe, &c. ; *alpina*, Europe ; *anemoneflora*, China ; *arkansana*, U. States ; *Banksiæ*, China ; *beggeriana*, Asia ; *blanda*, N. America ; *bracteata*, China ; *byzantina*, Eastern Europe ; *californica*, Western N. America ; *canina*, North Temperate Zone ; *carolina*, N. America ; *centifolia*, Orient ; *cinnamomea*, North Temperate Zone ; *damascena*, Eastern Europe, Orient ; *Engelmannii*, Western N. America ; *fedtschenkoana*, Central Asia ; *Fendlerii*, New Mexico ; *ferruginea*, Mountains of Europe ; *foliolosa*, N. America ; *fortuneana*, China ; *gallica*, S. Europe ; *gigantea*, Burmah ; *Hardii*, garden origin ; *hemisphærica*, Persia and Asia Minor ; *hibernica*, England and Ireland ; *hispida*, garden origin ; *humilis*, N. America ; *hybrida*, Europe ; *incarnata*, France ; *indica*, China ; *involucrata*, India ; *involuta*, Europe ; *lævigata*, China ; *laxa*, Siberia ; *leschenaultiana*, India ; *lucida*, N. America ; *lutea*, Orient ; *macrophylla*, India ; *micrantha*, Europe ; *microphylla*, China ; *mollis*, Europe ; *moschata*, S. Europe to India ; *multiflora*, China and Japan ; *nitida*, N. America ; *noisettiana*, garden origin ; *nutkana*, N. America ; *phænicea*, Orient ; *pisocarpa*, Western N. America ; *pomifera*, Europe ; *repens*, Europe ; *rubella*, Europe ; *rubiginosa*, Europe ; *rugosa*, Japan ; *sempervirens*, S. Europe ; *sericea*, India ; *setigera*, N. America ; *simplicifolia*, Orient ; *spinosissima*, Europe and Siberia ; *stylosa*, S. England ; *tomentosa*, Europe ; *watsoniana*, Japan; *webbiana*, Himalaya ; *wichuriana*, China and Japan ; *xanthina*, Persia, Afghanistan, &c.

ROSMARINUS (*Rosemary*).—A well-known shrub, *R. officinalis*, is not hardy enough everywhere, but in the embellishment of dry, warm, rocky banks it is useful ; all like its fragrance, and the flowers are pretty when the plant is grown on dry soils. Where it perishes in winter in the open ground it may be grown against a wall. Cuttings and seed.

RUBUS (*Brambles*). — Trailing and often prickly shrubs, some of the best from America ; the finest of these being the Rocky Mountain Bramble (R. deliciosus), quite unlike an ordinary Bramble, being without spines or prickles. It makes a rounded spreading bush about

4 ft. high, and, in June, bears snow-white flowers about the size of Dog Roses, and like them in form. It is hardy in most gardens where the soil is light, and in cold districts may be grown against a wall,

Rubus deliciosus.

which it quickly clothes with a beautiful growth, and flowers more abundantly than as a bush. Always select for it the sunniest and warmest place in the garden.

R. odoratus is 3 to 8 ft. high, with large-lobed leaves, and from June till August large clusters of rich purple flowers. It may be used in the rougher parts of the rock-garden, or in the wild garden, and is very hardy. Like the garden Raspberry, it sends up strong annual shoots, which in rich soils reach 6 ft. There is no finer shrub for planting under the shade of large trees and in rough places.

R. nutkanus.—This is found from North California to Nootka Sound, and is rather taller in growth than R. odoratus,

Rubus nutkanus (the Nootka Sound Raspberry)..

the flowers pure white. They are partial to a moist soil, as near the margins of

a pond or stream. They are among the best shrubs for the wild garden, where in a short time they spread into large masses if in good soil and partial shade. The Salmon Berry (R. spectabilis), from North-west America, has flowers of a bright red and very early. It is best in the rougher parts of the rock-garden or for the wild garden.

R. biflorus, or **R. leucodermis** (*White-washed Bramble*), from the Himalayas, has tall wand-like stems often 10 ft. or more in height, whitened with a mealy substance on the bark. Its white flowers are not showy, and are succeeded by edible-acid, Raspberry-like fruits. R. australis, from New Zealand, is without true leaves, and prickly. In warm situations on walls it grows several feet high. The beautiful R. rosæfolius (Rose-leaved Bramble), from the Himalayan region, is scarcely hardy enough for open-air except

Rubus laciniatus.

in favoured spots or against sunny walls. Its double variety (coronarius) has loose clusters of large white flowers, which are very double ; it is often grown as a greenhouse shrub. Among the best native Brambles are the beautiful double varieties of R. fruticosus, which flower late in summer. There are the double pink and the double white kinds, both known under various names ; but the names of double pink and double white are sufficient. As they are forms of distinct species or varieties, they differ in habit, the double pink being much the stronger and more free flowering. When well placed the double pink makes a wide-spreading mass like the common Bramble, and gives from the middle of August till autumn an abundance of bloom, every flower being a rosette of delicate pink petals. The double white is a form of R. tomentosus, and its flowers are larger than those of the double pink, but less

3 E

double. The double white and the double pink should be planted near each other, and will clothe banks or associate with bold rocks. Another fine Bramble is the Cut-leaved, or Parsley-leaved Bramble, which has a profusion of white blooms, succeeded by large delicious fruits. Some of the so-called American Blackberries,

Rubus cæsius (Dewberry).

such as the Lawton and Kittaninny, do not succeed in our country.

A few of the small kinds, such as R. arcticus (which grows a few inches high and bears numerous rosy-pink blossoms), the Cloud-berry, R. Chamæmorus (also dwarf and with white blossoms), the Dew-berry (R. Cæsius), and R. saxatilis, are pretty in partially-shaded spots in the rock-garden in moist peaty soil.

RUDBECKIA (*Coneflower*). — North American Composites, with showy yellow flower-heads, usually with a dark centre cone, making striking plants for the hardy border, flowering in late summer and autumn.

R. MAXIMA is a handsome plant 6 or 7 ft. high, having flowers densely set with broad golden rays produced in August and September. The large glaucous oval and entire leaf at once distinguishes it from others of the genus. A native of the warmer States of America, it thrives best in warm gardens and in hot summers, and from time to time it should be renewed from imported seeds.

R. PINNATA grows 4 ft. or 5 ft. high, flowering from July until hard frosts overpower it. It is not a long-lived plant, getting too hard and woody at the base to continue to break well, so it is better to keep a few seedlings on hand. Seed is abundantly produced and easily raised. Plants flower in the second year, and continue about five years more.

R. CALIFORNICA is the largest in size of flower and cone, the flower being often about 6 ins. across, and the cone 2 ins. high; leaves, flower-stalks, and root are equally robust. The

flowers come early in July; they have few and horizontal rays, and are solitary on the stalks, their size making up for their small number, and the whole plant having a majestic appearance. It is better for frequent division, exhausting the soil if left to itself for several years.

R. LACINIATA is the tallest of the cone flowers, 7 to 10 ft. high. The leaves, as the name implies, are unevenly divided into narrow ribbons, or cut into larger lobes, different individuals varying much in leafage. The flower is large, the rays curved downwards so as nearly to touch the stalk, and the cone is greenish. Plants live many years without spreading much, but are easily divided, and self-sown seedlings come up round if the seed escapes the green linnets and chaffinches, which delight to eat it.

R. NITIDA.—The general habit of this is that of *R. laciniata*, but the leaves are less incised than in any of that species; the flowers, though smaller in outline, are more regular and plentiful, and have broader and more golden rays. They begin to open when *R. laciniata* is over, and continue into November. It is a very handsome kind, vigorous and hardy, and grows 6 ft. or more high in good soil.

R. SUBTOMENTOSA.—In this the flowers show hardly any raised cone; the disc is very black, and the golden rays, about an inch long, continue horizontal, so that it would hardly be taken for a cone-flower. It grows 4ft. high, flowering late and very freely. Division. Young plants succeed best; when old they are apt, like *R. pinnata*, to get so hard at the base that large limbs suddenly lose their vital union with the root and wither before flowering.

R. PURPUREA.—In this distinct cone-flower the ray florets are of a reddish or rose-purple hue, and the flowers are fully 4 ins. across. When fully established the plants reach 3 to 4 ft. high, and are effective on account of their free-flowering and erect habit. The plant only rarely produces seeds, and these are generally slow to vegetate, so much so, that it is best rather to rely on careful division of the root to ensure maintaining a stock. Other kinds closely allied to this species are *R. pallida*, *R. angustifolia*, *R. purpurea intermedia*, a fine form with branching habit, and *R. p. serotina*.

R. SPECIOSA is given the unauthorised name of *R. Newmanni*, though I never could discover why. It is so well known that I need say little more than advise those who wish it to succeed in hot and dry summers to dress the surface with rich compost and to water it well, or it withers prematurely.

R. HIRTA is said by Asa Gray to be "annual or biennial," and it certainly requires frequent renewal from seed. Two-year-old plants begin to flower early in June, and continue gay through summer. It is well to select the largest and most golden flowers for seed. This species always attracts notice in my garden from the bright colour of the rays and the good contrast of the black cone.

Excepting *R maxima*, I have, in a long gardening experience, found no difficulty in maintaining a stock of all these cone-flowers *R pinnata*, *R laciniata*, *R hirta* ripen plenty of seed every year I never found ripe seed on any of the others, but they are all easily divided, the whole tribe likes a rich moist soil and a warm aspect   C WOLLEY-DOD

RUMEX (*Dock*) —The only one worth growing is our great native Water Dock (R Hydrolapathum), sufficiently striking for a place amongst ornamental subjects by the water-side Its leaves, sometimes 2 ft or more in length, form erect and imposing tufts ; while its flowering stem, frequently 6 ft in height, has a dense, pyramidal panicle of an olive-fawn or reddish colour In autumn the leaves change to a lurid red, a colour they retain for some time A root or two deposited in the mud near the bank of a pond or a slow stream will require no further attention

RUSCUS (*Butcher's Broom*) — These are distributed throughout Europe, North Africa, and temperate Asia All the hardy kinds may be planted under the drip and shade of trees where few other evergreens could exist Propagate by division of the roots The R aculeatus (Common Butcher's Broom) is a native of our copses and woods, with curious prickly leaves, or rather substitutes for leaves, and small greenish flowers which appear in April, and succeeded by bright red berries about the size of Peas This dense, much-branched Evergreen rarely grows more than 2 ft high, and its thick, white, twining roots strike deep into the ground The Alexandrian Laurel (R racemosus) is an elegant shrub with glossy dark green leaves Its stems are valuable for cutting from either in winter or at any other season It is one of the best plants for partial shade, and should have deep loamy soil, but thrives on chalk   S Europe R Hypophyllum, a very dwarf kind, and R Hypoglossum are not important

RUTA (*Rue*) —The common Rue (R graveolens) is not ornamental, but R albiflora is a graceful autumn-flowering plant about 2 ft high, with leaves resembling those of the common Rue, but more glaucous and finely divided The small white blossoms, borne profusely in large terminal drooping panicles, last until the frosts In some localities it is hardy, but, unless planted against a wall, should generally have slight protection in severe weather It is also known as Boenninghausenia albiflora Nepaul Another pretty plant is the Padua Rue (R patavina), 4 to 6 in high, with small golden-yellow

flowers of the same odour as the common Rue, and the plant is about as hardy as R albiflora

SABBATIA (*American Centaury*) — Pretty N American plants of the Gentian family. The species introduced are—S chloroides, with large pink flowers , S campestris, with light rose flowers ; and S. angularis, with purplish-red flowers   S chloroides, being found in bogs, requires a very moist spot ; S campestris, an open and drier place , S angularis, a sheltered situation and partial shade, in imitation of that afforded by the vegetation amongst which it grows wild The soil should consist of equal parts of good fibry loam and finely-sifted leaf-mould, with enough sand to make it open Seed, which should be sown in summer The seedlings should be potted off before they become in the least drawn, or they will make weak plants, and they should be wintered in a cold airy frame In spring repeatedly stopping the shoots will induce them to form bushy plants before flowering All are biennial and should be raised annually

SACCHARUM—*S ægyptiacum* is a vigorous perennial Grass, forming tufts of reed-like downy stems, 6 to 10 ft high, and clothed with graceful foliage It is suited for the margins of pieces of water and for pleasure-grounds, and requires a warm position In our climate it does not flower, but is a good plant from its leaves and habit Division in spring, and the offsets should be started in a frame or pit in May or June they may be planted out N Africa S Maddeni is a quick-growing hardy perennial, about 5 ft high, with graceful leaves, and is well worthy of growing with other large Grasses.

SAGINA (*Pearlwort*) -The only species worthy of culture is the Lawn Pearlwort (S glabra), a plant very generally known in consequence of being much talked of a few years since as a substitute for lawn Grass, though it has not answered the expectations formed of it It is none the less a pretty little alpine plant, forming on level soils carpets almost as smooth as velvet, and these in early summer are starred with pretty little white flowers It is multiplied by pulling the tufts into small pieces and then replanting them a few inches apart, when they soon meet and form a carpet Although S glabra does not generally form a permanent or satisfactory turf, yet by selecting a rather deep sandy soil a turf may be made, but it must be kept perfectly clean and well rolled, and this is rarely worth attempting When the plant begins to perish in flakes, it should be taken up and replanted.' Corsica. *Syn., Spergula pilifera.*

SAGITTARIA (*Arrowhead*).—Water plants of the Water Plantain family, the best known being our native Arrowhead, with its arrow-shaped leaves and tall spikes of white blossoms. Its double variety is handsome, and its blossoms last longer. There are one or two handsome double kinds, the origin of which is not clear, but they are worth growing in ponds; best in water 1 ft. deep, if their tubers are planted in mud.

SALISBURIA (*Maiden-hair Tree*).— *S. adiantifolia* is a beautiful tree in all stages and at all seasons, perhaps most attractive during the autumn, just before the leaves drop, since the foliage assumes then a bright yellow hue. Although it differs much from the Conifers, it belongs to that order, and is one of the few deciduous members of it. Probably its scarcity is accounted for by its not being readily propagated, and by its making slow progress during its earlier stages, since, on this account, it is not popular in nurseries. A rather deep, fairly moist soil of a loamy nature seems to meet its requirements, but it is not very particular as to soil, for a fine specimen grows on the shallow gravelly subsoil of Kew. Its fruits are said to be eaten in China and Japan, but they are rarely produced here. There are two or three varieties of the species, and, when raised from seed, as it always should be, there are individual differences. *Syn., Ginkgo biloba.*

SALIX (*Willow*).—Large and medium sized trees, shrubs, and even alpine trailers of northern and temperate countries, mostly hardy and of singular beauty and

Old Pollarded Willow in Suffolk, after Strutt.

interest for our gardens and home grounds, in which they are much neglected. Notwithstanding the number of trees in the country, I doubt if there is a more picturesque one than the Babylonian Willow, which is not common in many districts about London, although it is by the river and in the eastern counties. There are many, however, who plant this who do not care for handsome Willows of erect habit, but, as we think, with more beauty of colour, such as the scarlet-barked or cardinal Willow, and even the old yellow Willow. Of late years a number of other Weeping Willows have been propagated in Germany and elsewhere, so that we are no longer confined to the old Weeping Willow, which, occasionally, was apt to be cut down in hard winters. When the gardener plants a Willow, it is generally some curious one with a mop head, like the "American" Weeping Willow. Country gentlemen should therefore take the Tree Willows under their own care, and plant them in bold groups and colonies here and there, by water or in wet or marshy places. A marshy place planted with underwood formed of the yellow or red Willow would be charmingly picturesque in winter—indeed at all times, and there is no difficulty in getting any of these Willows by the hundred or thousand. In places which are much haunted by the rabbit, young Willows of these kinds go very rapidly, and, planted by streams in meadows where there are cattle, they are nibbled down, so that in certain districts a little care may be wanted to protect them. None of the Willows here mentioned should ever be grafted. I have skeleton Willows alongside some ponds, the sad remains of grafted Willows which were interesting and little-known kinds, all grafted on the common Sallow (*Salix caprea*). The grafted portion gradually died; the stump on which they are grafted remained sound, and from it have come the vigorous shoots of many Withies. Inasmuch as the whole country and the woods near have many of the same tree, which seeds everywhere near, this unsought plantation of a common tree by garden ponds, is far from a gain. "As easy to strike as a Willow," is a proverb among gardeners, and there is no good reason for grafting these plants. The graceful Willow, called in our gardens the American Willow, is invariably grafted on the Sallow, and if not watched and the suckers removed, will quickly perish; but if a shoot of this plant be hanging into water it quickly roots, showing how easily the trees could be increased if nurserymen would take the trouble to do it in the right way. The objection to the grafting is, first of all, the frequent death of the tree; secondly, falsified and weak growth, and, where it does not die, endless trouble ; thirdly, we lose some of the true uses of the tree, the habit not lending itself always to grafting on the standard form. Why should we not be able to use the Weeping Willows as rock or bank plants, not on standards, in which form the growth is often less graceful than on our own root trees? Though we think the finest Willows for effect in the landscape are the tree Willows, in all garden ground the Weeping Willows are likely to be the most planted, and we should guard against an excessive use of them in home landscape owing to this same weeping habit. One large isolated Weeping Willow, or a group of such trees on the margin of water, gives a much better effect than a number dotted about. Further, the Weeping Willow ungrafted when isolated has an advantage over many other weeping trees in its beauty of habit, all is grace and softness ; like a fountain of water, the branches rise lightly into the air to fall again gracefully. On the other hand, in most other weeping trees artificially made by grafting on standards there is none of this lightness of aspect and of form. Willows are admirably suited for giving us an abundance of shade where this is desired, and they are among the hardy trees that thrive in and near towns. Only the Willows most effective in the home landscape and in the home woods are named here. Some small and alpine Willows are interesting for the rock-garden, but they are more suited for botanical collections. The dwarf creeping kinds grown in gardens are— *S. herbacea, S. lanata, S. reticulata,* and *S. serpyllifolia,* all natives of the northern parts of Europe and America. They grow well among stones in ordinary garden soil. Sometimes certain of these dwarf forms are grafted generally on the sallow, on which their lives are very short, and it is impossible for us to judge of the value of such kinds as *S. repens var. argentea* and *pendula* and *S. cæsia var. Zabeli pendula,* when stuck on the ends of sticks of a wholly different nature.

S. ALBA (*White Willow*).—A graceful and stately tree of the marsh lands and river valleys throughout Europe and Asia, common in Britain, and often beautiful. It has several varieties, particularly a silvery one, and a red one (*britzensis*). Sometimes 80 ft. or more high, with a trunk diameter of 6 to 7 ft.

S. BABYLONICA (*Weeping Willow*). — A beautiful weeping tree, and the best known of the Willows of this character, though not the hardiest that we now know, and sometimes liable to be cut off in cold districts. There is a crisp-leaved variety. It is called Babylonian because it was thought to be the tree under which the Jews sat down to weep on the banks of the Euphrates River, but it is now known that the tree which grows on the banks of the Euphrates and resembles a Willow is a Poplar, having narrow Willow-like leaves. Japan and

The Weeping Willow.

China. *S. Salomoni* is a variety of this, and seems to be a free-growing and most graceful willow, but, with us, not old enough to show its true form. It is a very rapid growing tree, as, indeed, most willows are in river bank soils.

S. BLANDA (*Hybrid Weeping Willow*).— This is a vigorous and fine Weeping Willow, though not yet long enough in our country to show its true habit. It is thought to be a hybrid between the Babylon and Crack Willows having regard to its characteristics. The leaves, long even at the base of the branches, are 3 ins. to 5 ins. long by less than 1 in. across.

S. CAPREA (*Withy, Sallow, Goat Willow*). —The commonest Willow, often a round headed low tree, in our woodlands, and the one which bears the pretty catkins early in spring, and gathered at Easter, called Palm branches. It is used in nurseries throughout Europe as a stock to secure the greatest growth of various Willows, and usually with a fatal result to the life of each kind grafted on it. The Kilmarnock Willow is a weeping variety of this Willow. It is usually grafted, but in this case grafted on its own wild parent, so that the contest between stock and scion, that takes place among grafted Willows, does not occur to the same extent, though even in this case it would be best to increase the plant from cuttings or layers, at least for those who so desire it.

S. ELEGANTISSIMA.—A rapid growing and handsome weeping tree. Willows have a curious way of crossing and intercrossing, hybridising themselves in all sorts of ways, and it s difficult to account for the origin of this ; but from a garden point of view this is not of so much consequence. It is tall with long and pendent branches, a yellowish-green, often stained with russet, with a more spreading habit and a larger crown than *S. baby-lonica.*

S. FRAGILIS (*Crack Willow* ; *Withy*).—A fine and often picturesque tree of our river valleys, and a native of Northern Europe and Western Asia, including in it a variety of forms, among the best being the Basford Willow, and the broad-leaved form, *latifolia.* *S. Russelliana*, the Bedford Willow, is considered a hybrid between this and the White Willow. There is also an orange, twigged form of the Crack Willow (*S. decipiens*).

S. PENTANDRA (*Bay leaved Willow*).—A glossy leaved distinct looking Willow, sometimes almost a tree ; a native of Britain, mostly towards the north or west, and the latest flowering Willow.

S. PURPUREA (*Purple* or *Bitter Osier*).—A British Willow of some grace of habit, though not quite a tree, and most interesting from being the origin of the Willow called American by mistake. It is really a variety of this species, and a very beautiful weeping bush, which, however, is often lost by being grafted on the common withy, which soon kills the tree. This Willow and its varieties and hybrids are much grown in osier beds for basket making, though not so much as the osier. The pendulous form of the Purple Weeping Willow, commonly called the American Weeping Willow is not very high, but has pretty grey slender leaves, with long flexible twigs. It is usually grafted on and grown as a single, umbrella headed tree, although it is much prettier grouped or massed beside the water, and it is only then that one gets an expression of its extreme grace. This willow is grafted on the common sallow—a usually coarse growing willow of which the shoots spring from below the graft. If let alone for a year or two they would soon make an end of the Purple Willow ; but by continually removing them one may keep the tree alive. *S. purpurea scharfenbergensis* is allied to the above, but more elegant, and the branches tinged with a bright russet-brown. It is much to be recommended as a garden tree.

S. ROSMARINIFOLIA (*Graybush Willow*) is a graceful bushy Willow of a nice gray colour, especially for groups near water or in moist ground ; hardy and of easy culture. Europe.

S. VIMINALIS (*Osier*). — A distinct and native Willow, frequent in wet places in woods and osier beds, rarely planted in gardens, the leaves and branches are very fine in form. It is the Willow most used for basket making.

S. VITELLINA (*Golden Willow*) is sometimes classed with the White Willow by botanists, but from a planter's point of view it is a distinct tree, never so large as the White Willow, but effective in the colour of its yellow branches and twigs in the winter sun. While old trees of this often become good in form and occasionally pendulous, there is of recent years a distinctly pendulous variety, *S. pendula*, which is very graceful and precious

indeed, and quite hardy, which should never be grafted. Some of the red twigged willows, such as that called the Cardinal Willow,

Salix vitellina.

belong to *S. Vitellina.* The twigs are used to a great extent for packing in nurseries, and tying fruit trees in gardens.

SALPIGLOSSIS.—*S. sinuata* is a beautiful plant of the Solanum family, and one of the finest of half-hardy annuals ; it is slender, and has an erect stem, 1 to 2 ft. high, bearing large funnel-shaped blossoms that have dark veins on a ground which varies from white to crimson, yellow, orange, or purple, and intermediate shades. As the colour of the blossoms is so variable, the plant is known

Salpiglossis sinuata.

as S. variabilis, and its varieties have Latin names according to their tints. It is difficult to make a selection, but a packet of mixed seeds will produce a pretty variety of colours, and will yield a fine display, lasting from late summer till autumn. S. sinuata thrives in light, rich, sandy loam, and should be treated as a half-hardy annual. Chili.

· **SALVIA** (*Sage*).—The Sages are found in almost all sub-tropical and temperate countries, the showiest kinds in the mountains of Tropical America and Mexico, and hardy kinds in countries bordering on the Mediterranean Sea. Few of the Mexican species are really hardy, but many of them are among the best autumn and winter ornaments of the conservatory and the greenhouse, while, during summer, others are pretty in beds and borders. Few require special treatment, the herbaceous perennials being rapidly propagated by division or seed, and the half-shrubby species by cuttings of the young soft shoots in heat. The hardy perennial species require only a little care in the selection of a suitable situation and soil, but they are few in comparison with the half-hardy kinds. One of the handsomest of the hardy sorts is S. pratensis, a native species sporting into several varieties, which differ from each other in colour, and are called alba, rubra, bicolor, and S. sylvestris is even handsomer, and has long showy spikes of deep purple flowers. The well-known S. Sclarea and its variety bracteata are good plants for a mixed border, and so is S. Forskohlei, a species similar to them in habit and in colour. The finest of all is ˙S. hians, which is, however, rarely seen. Some of the forms of the common garden Sage (S. officinalis), especially the variegated-leaved kind, are pretty ; and so are the blue-flowered North American S. Pitcheri, and its white variety. The pretty purple red-topped Clary (S. Horminum) is a South European annual of easy culture. The tufts of coloured bracts which terminate its stems make it useful for cutting as well as for border decoration. The silvery Clary (S. argentea) is also an excellent border plant. It has silvery leaves, 6 to 12 in. long, which are handsome when well grown. S. candelabrum, a native of the south of Spain, is a half-shrubby species like the kitchen Sage, and has similar foliage, with ample panicles of rich violet and white flowers, borne on long stalks clear of the leaves. S. taraxacifolia is equally handsome.

Of the half-hardy species, S. patens is the most brilliant, being equalled by few flowers in cultivation. Although not hardy, except in some districts on light warm soils, it is easily preserved through the winter, and readily increased from cuttings. S. cacaliæfolia is a beautiful plant similar to S. patens, but of the same hardiness as those mentioned below. S. porphyranthera is a dwarf close-growing species with rich crimson flowers. It rarely fails in the open border. S. farinacea is a beautiful kind bearing light lavender blossoms with a white lip, and having a flower-spike covered with white powder. S. interrupta, a very fine species from Morocco, has large white and light blue flowers. S. Grahami, a very old Mexican kind, has a distinct habit and bears bright carmine blossoms. S. angustifolia and S. azurea are blue kinds,

Salvia patens.

worthy of open-air culture, as are also several of the sorts usually grown in greenhouses, such as S. Heeri, S. fulgens, S. gesneræfolia, S. elegans, S. tricolor, S. rutilans, S. splendens, and their varieties; for, though some of them do not flower till autumn, their use for indoor decoration is improved by their being planted out during summer.

In summer some tender kinds have a fine effect in the open border, and are all easily propagated by cuttings. In August and September they should be raised in a close cold frame, and in spring they should be treated like Heliotropes or Ageratums. When large plants are required, the old ones can either be potted, or put close together in deep boxes · and, if potted, they should be cut down to within 6 in. of the soil. Both old plants and potted cuttings are easily wintered in any dry place where frost is excluded. The tender Sages thrive in any good garden soil.

SAMBUCUS (*Elder*).—The common Elder (S. nigra) is not generally admired, but its cut-leaved, golden, and variegated varieties are often planted. A large Elder with branches sweeping the turf is no mean object on a lawn at midsummer, when covered with its flower-clusters, or when in berry. The golden Elder (foliis aureis) is becoming very common—too common, in fact,—for, like all conspicuous objects, it requires to be employed with caution, or a spotty effect will be produced. The same remark applies, but in a less degree, to the variegated golden-leaved and silver-leaved Elders. The Parsley-leaved or cut-leaved Elder (laciniata) is a most elegant shrub, and should be preferred to the common Elder, as it is ornamental even in a small state. It should be allowed to form itself into a small tree or a round symmetrical bush. A pretty shrub is the Scarlet-berried Elder (S. racemosa), which resembles the common Elder in habit, save that instead of bearing black berries it has clusters of brilliant scarlet fruits. Unfortunately, it is capricious in English shrubberies, and is seldom seen in perfection of berry. Its natural home is in alpine valleys, where in August and September it rivals the Mountain Ash in splendour. In hill districts it may be grown and fruited, but it must have a cool moist spot. Its cut-leaved variety (serratifolia) is an elegant shrub, with pinnate leaves deeply cut. S. Ebulus is a herbaceous Elder, having spreading foliage, cut into elegant leaflets, that may be planted in coverts, dry banks, and rough shrubberies ; scarcely suitable for border culture. It is hardy, and may be readily increased by division.

SAMOLUS.—S. *littoralis* is a pretty trailing plant, with long slender stems, small evergreen foliage, and numerous pink blossoms in summer. It is suitable for the bog-garden or for moist spots in the rock-garden, as it delights in plenty of moisture, and a peaty soil suits it best. New Zealand.

SANGUINARIA (*Bloodroot*). — S. *canadensis* is a pretty and distinct hardy plant, its thick creeping root-stocks sending up glaucous leaves about 6 in. high, the flowers, borne singly on stems as high as the leaves, are 1 in. across, white, with a tassel of yellow stamens in spring, in

Sanguinaria canadensis.

good-sized tufts, having a pretty effect. Sometimes the flowers are pinkish. It grows well in any border, but under the branches of deciduous trees on lawns it spreads about, and, without attention, becomes a charming wildling, in moist soil. It is strongest and best in moist peaty bottoms in woods or otherwise. It may be increased by division in autumn, but its fleshy stems must not be kept long out of the ground. Poppy family. Nova Scotia, Canada and westwards and southwards on the mountains.

SANTOLINA (*Lavender Cotton*). — Dwarf half-shrubby plants, of neat habit and pretty hoary foliage. One of the most distinct and useful of them is S. incana, a small gray shrub, with close habit and narrow leaves covered with dense white down. The pale greenish-yellow flowers are small, not showy, but the plant is useful from its form and silvery hue, for groups and edgings, growing readily in ordinary soil on the level border, or on slopes of the rock-garden. It is considered a variety of the better-known S. Chamæcyparissus (Lavender Cotton), which is pretty for banks and rock-gardens, forming silvery bushes 2 ft. high, but it is not suited for association with very dwarf alpine plants. Other species of Santolina suited for rock-gardens are S. pectinata and S. viridis, which form bushes something like the Lavender

Cotton S alpina is of more alpine habit, forming dense tufts close to the ground, from these arising slender stems bearing yellow button-like flowers   It grows in any soil, and may be used in the less important parts of the rock-garden Division Cuttings of the shrubby species strike readily in spring or autumn.

SANVITALIA.—*S procumbens* is a hardy annual from Mexico, with trailing branches and bright yellow flowers In the single-flowered kind the blossoms have a dark purple centre, but in the double (S. procumbens fl -pl), which is by far the showier, they are a bright yellow   S. procumbens flowers from July till late in September, and owing to its dwarf compact growth, it is useful for masses in beds or for the front rows of borders, or in suspended baskets, as the slender branches droop gracefully over   It may be sown in any ordinary garden soil—in autumn for spring flowering, or in March and April for summer flowering

SAPONARIA (*Soapwort*)—Perennial herbs and alpine plants or annuals of the pink family

S. cæspitosa is a neat little alpine perennial, good in the higher regions of the Central and Eastern Pyrenees, flowering in August, but in the lowlands its beautiful rose-coloured blossoms appear towards the end of June   It forms rosettes of linear leaves, thick, glabrous ; the flowers, forming a thick cluster, are supported by short stout stems   This graceful little plant is valuable for the rock-garden   A sandy soil suits it best, and it endures our winters

S calabrica is a pretty prostrate hardy annual, 6 to 9 in high, its slender stems covered with small pink blossoms all the summer   There is a white variety. It is much used for beds and edgings   Seeds may be sown in the open border in April, or earlier in heat if bloom is required early in the season, in rich sandy loam

S. ocymoides is a beautiful trailing rock-plant, with prostrate stems, its rosy flowers completely covering its leaves and branches in early summer   It is most valuable for clothing arid parts of the rock-garden, where a drooping plant is desired, as the shoots fall over the face of the rocks, and become masses of rosy bloom   It is also excellent for old walls, and the seed should be sown in mossy chinks where a little soil has gathered It thrives in ordinary soil, and is often a good dwarf border plant   Seeds and cuttings   Southern and Central Europe

S officinalis (*Soapwort*)—This is a handsome native plant about 2 ft high,

with large blossoms, usually rose-pink, the double variety being best   It is a rambling plant, and soon spreads rapidly, therefore it should not be planted in select borders, but is pretty for rough places in the pleasure-ground and wild garden, as it grows in any soil   Division

Sarana. See FRITILLARIA.

SARRACENIA (*Huntsman's Horn*) — This singular plant, *S. purpurea*, belongs to a family of Pitcher-plants, natives of North America, it being the hardiest, and handsome when well grown   Its curious leaves, hollowed like a horn, are blood-red in colour, and form a compact tuft 1 ft or more in height and the same in breadth ; the flowers, singular in shape, are not very showy   It is a good plant for the bog-garden or for damp spots in the rock-garden, in an open and fully-exposed position with the choicer bog-plants, in fibrous peat well mixed with Sphagnum Moss, which is common in marshy places   A layer of living Moss should be placed round the plant to keep it moist   The plant is hardy under these conditions, but precautions should be taken to prevent birds from disturbing the soil and exposing the roots   Some of the hybrids between it and others may be hardy   S flava, the hardiest species next to S purpurea, is rarely satisfactory in the open air

SASSAFRAS (*Ague Tree*)—*S officinale* is a distinct and remarkable tree, sometimes growing over 100 ft high, with a trunk 6ft or more in diameter, and a rough aromatic bark in sandy soils in New England, Canada, and westwards and southwards   The leaves are three-lobed, and vary much in shape   In our country this plant should have soils similar to those in which it grows in its own, as our cool summers are less likely to ripen the wood   *Syn , Laurus sassafras*

SAXIFRAGA (*Rockfoil*)—This genus includes, perhaps, more true alpine flowers than any other   In the Arctic circle, in the highest alpine regions, on the arid mountains of Southern and Eastern Europe and Northern Africa, and throughout the length and breadth of Europe and of Northern Asia, they are found in many interesting varieties of form and colour   One might expect them to be as difficult of cultivation as most alpine plants, but they are the easiest to grow of all   They were common in collections of alpine flowers where few other families were represented   Of late years many pretty species have been introduced, and the variety of the family is now so great that a very interesting garden might be made of Saxifrages alone For the purposes of cultivation some rough division is convenient, as Saxifrages are very different in aspect and uses. The most ordinary form is the Mossy or hypnoides section, of which there are many kinds in cultivation Their delicate Moss-like spreading tufts of foliage, so freshly green, especially in autumn and winter, when most plants decay, and their countless white flowers in spring, make them very precious They are especially suited for the tasteful practice of carpeting the bare ground beneath taller plants They are also admirable for the fresh green hue with which they clothe rocks and banks in winter Next to these we may place the very extensive silvery group These have their grayish leathery leaves margined with dots of white, so as to give to the whole a silvery character This group is represented by such kinds as S Aizoon and the great pyramidal-flowering S Cotyledon of the Alps Considering the freedom with which they grow in all cool climates, even on level ground, and their beauty of flower and foliage, they are perhaps the most precious group of alpine flowers we possess Anybody with a cottage garden can grow them The London Pride section is another of great beauty, the plants thriving under ordinary conditions in lowland gardens, and soon naturalising themselves in lowland woods and copses But the most brilliant, so far as flower is concerned, are found in the purple Saxifrage (S oppositifolia) group and its near allies Here we have tufts of splendid colour in spring with dwarfness and perfect hardiness The large leathery-leaved group, of which the Siberian S crassifolia is best known, is also of much importance, the plants thriving in ordinary soil and on the level ground There are various minor groups Such of the smaller and rarer alpine species as require any particular attention should be planted in moist sandy loam mingled with grit and broken stone, and made very firm Very dwarf and rather slow-growing kinds, like S cæsar and S aretioides, should be surrounded by half-buried pieces of stone, to prevent their being trampled on or overrun Stone will also help to preserve the ground in a moist healthy condition in the dry season, when the plants are most likely to suffer Very dry winds in spring sometimes have a bad effect when such precautions are not taken Established tufts are apt to throw out stem-roots into their own cushions, so to say These cushions are

frequently moist during the autumn and winter months. When the tufts are suddenly dried, the plants suffer if the ground-roots be dried too

The following are among the most important cultivated kinds, though the list excludes many species that are difficult to grow or to procure, and which are found only in very full collections

S. aizoides—A native plant, very abundant in Scotland, the north of England, and some parts of Ireland, and generally found in wet places and by the sides of mountain rills or streams At the end of summer or in autumn it has an abundance of flowers, $\frac{1}{2}$ in. across, bright yellow, dotted with red towards the base It forms dense masses of dwarf bright green leaves, and has leafy branched flower-stems, which distinguish it from other yellow Saxifrages Although a mountain plant, it is easy to grow in lowland gardens in moist ground Wherever a rill or streamlet is introduced into the rock-garden or its neighbourhood, S aizoides may be planted to form wide-spreading masses, as it does on its native mountains Easily propagated by division or by seed *Syn, S autumnalis.*

S. Aizoon is a good rock, border, and edging plant Plants established for two or three years form gray-silvery tufts, which do not flower so freely as the wild plants, but this need not be regretted, as it is the silvery mass, and not the flowers, that is sought This Rockfoil is often grown in pots, but it flourishes as freely as any native plant, and is best perhaps when exposed to the full sun There are several named varieties S pectinata, S Hosti, S intacta, S. rosularis minor, S australis, S. cartilaginea, and others are only slight variations from the type Division in spring.

S. Andrewsi—Among the green-leaved Saxifrages there is no better kind than this Its flowers are freely produced, prettily spotted, and larger than those of S umbrosa The plant is finer in the rock-garden than London Pride, grows as freely on any border soil, and merely requires to be replanted occasionally, when it spreads into very large tufts, or to have a dressing of fine light compost sprinkled over it annually The variety Guthrieana is distinct from the Pyrenees

S. aretioides.—A real gem of the encrusted section, forming cushions of silvery rosettes about $\frac{1}{2}$ in. high, and almost as small and dense as those of Androsace helvetica It has rich golden-yellow flowers, in April, on stems a little more than 1 in high, which remind one

of the flowers of Aretia Vitalliana S
arctioides requires a moist and well-
drained soil, and being so tiny, must be
protected from coarser neighbours. Seed
and careful division

S. Burseriana.—None of the Rockfoils
surpass S Burseriana in vernal beauty
It is almost Moss-like in habit, forms
broad patches, and spreads rapidly over
the earthy interstices of warm moist sandstone, if planted where it will not suffer
from stagnant moisture The blossoms
are borne singly on slender red stalks,
which rise 2 or 3 in above the general
surface of the plant, and are pure white,
the margins of the overlapping petals
elegantly frilled or crisped They appear
freely in January and February Before
they are expanded, their crimson-brown
unopened buds have a cheerful effect as
they emerge from the compact silvery
tufts of foliage, while interspersed among
full-blown flowers they enhance the
pearly whiteness of the petals S Burseriana soon forms good-sized tufts in the
open border or in the rock-garden, but
prefers a dry sunny situation and calcareous soil All lovers of hardy spring
flowers should possess it There are two
or three distinct forms which differ from
each other chiefly in habit, one being
much more tufted than the others There
is also a form with larger flowers than
those of the type, but not more desirable ,
it is called grandiflora Large panfuls of
this early Rockfoil are pretty in the
greenhouse Austrian Alps

S cæsia resembles an Androsace in
the neatness of its tufts On the Alps it
covers the rocks and stones like a silvery
Moss , and on level ground, where it has
some depth of soil, develops into beautiful
little cushions 2 to 6 in across It has
pretty white flowers in summer on smooth
thread-like stems, 1 to 3 in high Though
a native of the high Alps and Pyrenees, it
thrives in our gardens in very firm sandy
soil, if fully exposed and well watered in
summer It may also be grown in pots
or pans in cold frames near the glass, but,
being very minute, should always be kept
distinct from coarse neighbours, as even
the smallest weeds will injure or obscure it
Seeds or careful division Of similar
character are S calyciflora, S luteo-viridis,
S Kotschyi, S valdensis, S squarrosa,
and S diapensoides, all dwarf, and, for
the most part, difficult to grow, though
their beauty amply repays the trouble
bestowed on them They should be
grown in the same way as S cæsia

S. cæspitosa.—A dwarf kind forming dense carpet-like masses of foliage.
arranged in neat tufts, studded in summer
with white blossoms It succeeds in
almost any situation in any garden soil ,
is useful for margins to herbaceous borders,
and makes a beautiful covering for moist
banks It is one of the most variable of
all Saxifrages, and of its numerous varieties the most distinct are palmata and
grœnlandica

S. ceratophylla (*Stag's-horn Rockfoil*)
—An ornamental species of the mossy
section, with dark, finely-divided leaves
and numerous pure white flowers in loose
panicles in early summer. It quickly
forms strong tufts in any good garden
soil , and is adapted for any kind of rock-
garden, whether grown in level tufts on
the flat portions, or in sheets overhanging
the brows of rocks Spain Seed or division Similar to this species are S paniculata, ladanifera, Wilkommiana, geranio-
ides, irrigua, ajugæfolia, and aquatica

S. ciliata.—One of the broad-leaved or
Megasea section with large broad leaves,
covered with soft hair, and carried on creeping stems The flower-stems are 6 to 9 in
high, and bear numerous large flesh-
coloured flowers in spring A native of
North India, S. ciliata is suitable for open-
air culture in the south of England only,
but is so handsome and distinct that it
should be tried wherever it can be grown
A sheltered nook in the rock-garden, partially shaded, suits it best

S. cordifolia.—This Siberian plant
differs in aspect from the ordinary dwarf
Rockfoils, having ample heart-shaped
leaves on long and thick stalks Its clear
rose-coloured flowers are arranged in
dense masses, and in early spring half
concealed among the great leaves, as if
hiding from the cutting breath of March
S cordifolia and its varieties flower in
any soil and position ; but to encourage
early-flowering, place them in warm
sunny positions, where their fine flowers
may be induced to open well These
Saxifrages are perhaps more fitted for
association with the larger spring flowers
and herbaceous plants than dwarf alpines , and may be naturalised on bare
sunny banks, in wild sunny parts of the
pleasure-ground, or by wood walks They
may also be used with effect near cascades, or on rough rock- or root-work, or
on the rocky margins of streams or artificial water ; in fact, they are the fine-
foliaged plants of the rocks There are
several handsome varieties of S cordifolia, the finest of all the group being one
called purpurea

S. Cotyledon (*Pyramidal Saxifrage*) —
This beautiful kind embellishes with

its great silvery rosettes and elegant pyramids of white flowers many parts of the great mountain ranges of Europe, from the Pyrenees to Lapland. It is the largest of the cultivated Saxifrages, and also the finest, except S. longifolia, the linear leaves of which it does not possess. There is considerable difference in the size of the rosettes, which when grown in

the parent plant of the offsets as they appear. Many market growers have large stocks of this Rockfoil in pots. It is superb thus grown, but will succeed well in the rock-garden or ordinary border.

S. crassifolia.—A well-known Siberian species of the Megasea section, with large broad leaves. The flowers rise from the

Saxifraga pyramidalis (the great alpine Rockfoil).

tufts are generally much smaller than in isolated specimens. The flower-stem varies from 6 to 30 in. high, and about London, in common soil, often reaches 20 in. In cultivation the plant usually attains a greater size than on its native rocks. A variety more pyramidal and more robust is known in gardens under the erroneous name of S. nepalensis, and sometimes by the more appropriate one of S. pyramidalis. To get good specimens, denude

terminal shoots in showy pendent masses and are pale rose with a suspicion of lilac. The plant fulfils the same purposes as S. cordifolia. The chief varieties are ovata, which carries its deep rose-coloured flowers well above the foliage ; rubra, similar to the last, but with flowers of a deeper tinge of rose ; orbicularis, producing an abundance of light rosy flowers, well above the foliage, and sometimes considered a species, but in reality only a smaller form of ovata, with rather broader leaves and a more branching habit ; and media, a distinct variety, with large dark, shining green leaves and clusters of bright rosy-pink flowers on strong stems There is also a variety called aureo-marginata, with variegated foliage.

S. Cymbalaria.—Little tufts of this Rockfoil form in early spring masses of bright yellow flowers set in light green, glossy, ivy-like leaves, the whole not above 3 in. high. Instead of fading, it preserves its little rounded pyramids of golden flowers until autumn, when it is about 12 in. high. It is an annual or biennial, sows itself abundantly, and is suitable for moist spots on or near the rock-garden or on level ground, and in large pleasure-grounds ; is readily naturalised on the margins of a rocky stream and elsewhere.

S. flagellaris is distinct and free in growth Like its ally, S. Hirculus, it has large bright yellow blossoms. Each rosette throws off thread-like stolons, which root at the tips, and in moist, peaty, and gritty soil quickly form new rosettes One of the most arctic of plants

S. Fortunei has large panicles of white blossoms which rise in profusion from rosettes of dark green rounded leaves. It is a desirable plant, for it flowers in autumn and is not particular as to treatment.

S granulata (*Meadow Saxifrage*).— A lowland plant, with several small scaly bulbs in a crown at the root, and numerous white flowers three-quarters of an inch across. It is common in meadows and banks in England, its double form being very handsome , also useful as a border plant in the spring-garden or in the rougher parts of the rock-garden

S. hypnoides (*Mossy Saxifrage*) is a very variable plant as regards stems, leaves, and flowers, but usually forms mossy tufts of the freshest green, and no plant is more useful for forming carpets of glistening verdure in winter. For this reason it is suited for the low rocky borders frequent in town and villa gardens. It thrives in the rock-garden or on level ground, either in half-shady positions or when fully exposed to the sun. When so exposed it forms the fullest tufts, flowering profusely in early summer. It is also suitable for dwarf verdant carpets in the flower garden or the rock-garden with a view to placing plants above it Nothing can be easier to grow or to increase by division Under this species may be grouped S hirta, S affinis, S incurvifolia,

S. platypetala, S. decipiens, and several others, all showing differences which some think sufficient to mark them as species They are as free as S. hypnoides, and appear to suffer only from drought or drying winds If when first planted a few rather large stones are buried in the earth round each, the plants will soon lap over them and preserve the moisture in the tufts. S densa and S Whitlavi are the best free-growing species, and, being compact and always green, are suitable for a margin.

S. juniperina (*Juniper Saxifrage*) is one of the most desirable, with spine-pointed leaves densely set in cushioned masses. The yellow flowers appear in summer, and are arranged in spikes on a leafy stem. S juniperina thrives in moist, sandy, firm soil in the rock-garden, and in every collection of alpine plants ; should be grown in pots. Caucasus. Seed and careful division.

S. lantoscana.—One of the finest of the incrusted-leaved section. Though similar to the pyramidal variety of S Cotyledon, it is smaller, its leaves narrower and more crowded in the rosette, whilst its flower-spike, which is not erect but slightly drooping, is more densely furnished with flowers. It is easily grown in a fully-exposed position in a well-formed rock-garden, in a well-drained gritty soil It remains long in flower, and is one of the best of rock-garden plants.

S. ligulata (*Nepaul Rockfoil*).—This has broadly obovate leaves, bearing flowers in small cymose panicles. The flowers are white, with a rosy tint towards the margin of the petals , and the anthers before expansion are deep crimson Its tendency to early spring growth makes it liable to injury from frosts, which, occurring in three or four consecutive seasons, will ultimately prove fatal It should therefore be given a sheltered situation and a little shade also The varieties rubra and speciosa, particularly the latter, are in every way finer than the type S ligulata may be associated with others of the Megasea section

S. longifolia—This Pyrenean plant has single rosettes often 6, 7, and 8 in in diameter Its grayish leathery leaves are beautifully dotted with white on the margins, and in early summer it pushes up fox-brushlike columns of white flowers, from 1 to 2 ft. long, the stems covered with short, stiff, gland-tipped hairs. It is perfectly hardy, and may be grown in various ways On some perpendicular chink in the face of a rock-garden, where it can root deeply, it is very striking when the long outer leaves of the rosette spread away from the densely-packed centre. It may also be grown on the face of an old wall by first carefully packing a very small plant of it into a chink with a little soil. The stiff leaves will, when they roll out, adhere firmly to the wall in the form of a

sunny pit or frame, giving it plenty of water in spring, summer, and autumn. S. longifolia is propagated by seeds, which ripen from the bottom of the stem upwards, so that the lower seed-vessels should be cut off first, leaving the unripe capsules to mature. Visit the plant every day or two to collect the seeds as they ripen. S.

Saxifraga longifolia.

large silver star. S. longifolia will thrive on a raised bed or border if surrounded by a few stones to prevent evaporation and injury, also in a greenhouse or frame, and perhaps the best way to develop a weak young nursery plant into a sturdy rosette is to put it in a 6-in. pot well drained and filled with a mixture of sandy loam and stable manure. Place it in a

lingulata chiefly differs from this kind in having smaller flowers and shorter stems. It is a charming rock-plant, and will succeed in the same position as S. longifolia. S. crustata is considered a very small variety of S. longifolia, and should be associated with dwarfer plants.

S. Maweana is a handsome species of the cæspitosa section, and larger than any other in foliage and flowers. The latter, about the size of a shilling, form dense white masses in early summer. After flowering, this species forms buds on the stems, which remain dormant till the following spring. Though rare, it is of easy culture. Similar, but finer, is S. Wallacei, which is far more robust, earlier, and freer as regards flowering, but which does not develop buds during summer. It is a most desirable plant for the border or the rock-garden, and easily propagated. Potfuls of this are pretty as the flowers are large, and so free as to form a mass of white.

S. muscoides (*Mossy Saxifrage*).—A beautiful little plant, forming a dense bright green carpet like S. hypnoides and S. cæspitosa. There are several forms of it, but the best is atro-purpurea, which produces a dense mass of deep red-purple blossoms on stalks a few inches high. The varieties pygmæa and crocea are pretty, also the allied kinds S. exarata, S. pedemontana, S. Rhei, S. aromatica, and a few others ; they grow in almost any soil.

S. oppositifolia.—It is impossible to speak too highly of the beauties of this bright little mountain-plant, in colour and in habit so distinct from the familiar members of its family. The moment the snow melts, its tiny herbage glows into solid sheets of purplish-rose colour. Of the several varieties that known as splendens has flowers of far greater brilliancy, though slightly smaller than those of the type ; in bud especially the colour is almost carmine and exquisitely beautiful. In density of bloom it approaches the typical form, but rarely equals it. This variety was obtained many years ago on the mountains of Scotland. S. o. major has flowers twice the size of the type, clear rose, inclining to cherry, and has less of a purple tinge. In S. o. pyrenaica the shoots are twice as robust as those of any of the preceding kinds, and the flowers larger. Its finest form is S. o. p. maxima, which has lovely light rose blossoms as large as a shilling. S. o. alba has white flowers, in pleasing contrast to the other varieties. S. Rudolphiana has a more spreading habit of growth, and its rosy-purple flowers are sometimes borne singly, and sometimes (though rarely) in pairs. It is allied to S. biflora, the beautiful dwarf species of loose habit, the flowers of which, on clusters of two to four, vary from a bright rose to a deep blood-red, the petals narrow and wide apart. S. Kochi is similar in habit to this, and its rosy-purple flowers are in twos and fours at the extremities of the shoots. The foliage of

S. retusa is very short, firm, dense, and compact, the small flowers being borne in clusters at the extremity of erect stalks ; and their narrow petals are usually a pale rose colour, sometimes brighter. It blooms rather later than the varieties of S. oppositifolia. S. Wulfeniana is closely allied to S. Kochi. S. oppositifolia and its varieties succeed in deep, open, rich, loamy soil, and are finest in a fissure or on a ledge of the rock-garden, where the roots can ramble backwards or down to any depth. For the soil, a rich light loam mixed with fragments of limestone or grit, small fragments of any rock, and a little river sand

Group of Silvery Rockfoils.

will do. S. oppositifolia must have sunshine ; for though it will grow in the shade, it will not flower freely. The same treatment, with the addition of a little peat or vegetable mould, suits S. retusa and S. Wulfeniana. The Tyrolese species (S. biflora, S. Rudolphiana, and S. Kochi) are less easy to please. They grow wild on the moraines of glaciers, where light vegetable soil, sand, and débris of every kind blend with massive rocks, coating the surface, and filling the interstices where water drips or oozes around, and frequently flows in volume within 2 or 3 ft. so as to soak the bases of the rocks on which their rosy carpet is spread. They will grow in pots, but rarely with the same freedom as the varieties of S. oppositifolia.

S. peltata.—The shield-like leaves of

S. peltata make it unique among Saxifrages ; and on this account. some have referred the plant to a section under the name Peltiphyllum. From a thick and fleshy creeping root-stock rise stout erect leaf-stalks, at the ends of which grow the target-like leaves, 1 ft. or more in diameter. The white or pale pink flowers appear in spring, a little before the leaves, on stalks 1 to 2 ft. high, and in loose clusters, 3 to 6 in. in diameter. It is found in the neighbourhood and in the beds of quick-running streamlets throughout the Sierra Nevada of California, and is best in a deep moist border of peaty soil. Division or seeds.

S. purpurascens is the finest of the Megasea section. The stem is 10 to 12 in. high, and the flowers are produced in pendent masses of red and purple. Succeeds best in a moist peaty soil in a rather sheltered spot. High elevations about Sikkim.

S. Rocheliana (*Rochel's Saxifrage*).— A compact and dwarf kind, forming dense silvery rosettes of tongue-shaped leaves, with white margins and distinct dots. In spring appear large white flowers on sturdy little stems. There is no more exquisite plant for the rock-garden, pans, and for small rocky or elevated borders. Any good, free, moist, loamy soil suits it, and in London it thrives on borders, but should always be exposed to the full sun, associated with the choicest spring flowers and alpine plants. Austria. Seeds or careful division. S. coriophylla is similar but not so valuable.

S. sancta.—A beautiful species, forming a dense carpet-like mass of deep green foliage, studded in early spring with numerous bright yellow blossoms on stems an inch or so high. It seems to grow freely in any position in the rock-garden.

Saxifraga Wallacei.

S. sarmentosa (*Mother of Thousands*). —A well-known plant, with roundish leaves and numbers of creeping, slender runners, producing young plants Strawberry fashion. It grows freely in the dry air of a sitting-room, and may often be seen gracefully suspended in cottage-windows, but is most at home running wild on banks or rocks in the cool green-house or conservatory. In mild parts of England it lives in the open air, and may be used in graceful association with Ferns and other creeping plants. China. Flowers in summer. Closely allied is the delicate S. cuscutæformis with its thread-like runners similar to the stems of a Dodder, and distinguished from S. sarmentosa by smaller leaves and more uniform petals. It may be used in much the same way as S. sarmentosa, but being more delicate and fragile, requires more care. It is a beautiful plant for growing in Moss in a cool fernery, for it is perfectly at home, and the delicate markings of its

Saxifraga sarmentosa.

leaves show up against the green of its surroundings. The plants grown in gardens, as S. japonica and S. tricolor, are varieties of S. sarmentosa.

S. Stracheyi is a strong plant with leaves nearly as broad as long. Its flowers, produced on broad branching panicles, are of a light pink with a shade of lilac. It is hardier than its closest ally S. ciliata, blooms in March, and should be sheltered against bleak winds. It is suited for borders and rock-gardens.

S. tenella.—A handsome plant, forming tufts of delicate fine-leaved branches, 4 or 5 in. high, which root as they grow. The flowers, which appear in summer, are numerous, whitish-yellow, and arranged in a loose panicle. Similar in growth are S. aspera, S. bryoides, S. sedoides, S. Seguieri, S. Stelleriana, and S. tricuspidata, all suitable for clothing the bare parts of the rock-garden and slopes, but require moist soil and cool positions. Division in spring or the end of summer.

S. umbrosa (*London Pride*).—This almost universally-cultivated plant is abundant on the mountains round Killarney, though it has long been grown in our gardens. In old gardens it is much used for edging, and, being a pretty evergreen, should be freely used in the rough parts of rock-gardens, the fringes of cascades, etc. It is naturalised in several parts of England, and grows freely in dwarf herbage, or in rocky parts of woods. There are several varieties, for example, S. punctata, S. serratifolia, and Oglivieana, which is a most distinct form of this species, with pinkish blossoms in dense dwarf panicles not over 6 in. high. S. rotundifolia and similar kinds are related to S. umbrosa, but are unimportant. This plant and its forms will thrive in the cold shade of high walls where few other things will live.

There are other good kinds, but less important than the foregoing, such as S. mutata, S. florulenta, very difficult to grow, the London-Pride-like S. Geum, the native S. Hirculus, and the small gray tufted S. aspera.

GIANT ROCKFOIL HYBRIDS. — The Giant Saxifrages of our gardens, known as Megaseas, are so variously beautiful at all seasons that the wonder is they are not even more popular than they now are in all good gardens. From all the other Saxifrages they are known by their massive size and breadth of leaf, while, as a general rule, they are of evergreen habit, and so are effective at all times. Most of them are beautiful when in blossom during the earlier months of spring. Now and then, it is true, their flowers become nipped in the bud by spring frosts ; but even if this occasionally happens, general results are enough to justify their culture. Besides, it is so easy to pot up the plants in autumn and give them the shelter of a cold frame or an awning of mats, since plants so treated bloom freely and form handsome plants for cool greenhouse or conservatory decoration.

One of the best for pot and tub culture is M. crassifolia, which has large clusters of its peach or almond-tinted blossoms on tall stalks, its fragrance on a warm day being like that of Hawthorn. Another fine variety is cordifolia purpurea, which bears its pendulous bell-shaped flowers on vivid red scapes 18 in. or 2 ft. in height, the blossoms being darker in colour than those of crassifolia.

Other very fine species are purpurascens, Stracheyi, cordifolia, and ciliata, the last with large hairy leaves, but it is the most tender of the whole group, and its leaves succumb to the first sharp frosts. Its flowers are whitish with a rosy-red centre, and effective in warm sheltered

3 F

localities under cold frame culture in pots or tubs, as above recommended.

The following species and varieties are given in books: Megasea cordifolia, c. purpurea, crassifolia, ligulata, l. ciliata purpurascens, Stracheyi, S. alba, S. Milesi, hybrida splendens.

Numerous hybrids have been reared in this section of Saxifrage from time to time. One of the first which became popular in

Irish Rockfoil.

London nurseries about ten years ago is the seedling from cordifolia, now known as cordifolia purpurea, a noble plant, and luxuriant as seen at its best. Milesi is dwarf growing, and nearly if not quite deciduous, its presumed parentage being ciliata crossed with pollen of Stracheyi. As seen in its early bud stage of blossoming it is a distinct and beautiful plant, and is lovely grown in pots in a cold house or sunny frame. Its scapes are so short that its rose and white flowers are

apt to be splashed and spoiled by rains unless protected.

A very varied and robust series of hybrid Megaseas is that reared some years ago by Mr. T. Smith, of Newry. They are the result of crosses between cordifolia × purpurascens, and possess in some degree the good qualities of both parents. The plants are all robust, although varying much in colour of flower and in stature. Hybrida splendens is one of the finest in the group, but the following named kinds are also very remarkable in habit and in colour :—

M. CORDIFOLIA × PURPURASCENS VAR. BRILLIANT.—Leaves large, richly tinted in autumn and winter; flowers purple; calyces and pedicels crimson; fine.

M. CORDIFOLIA × PURPURASCENS VAR. CAMPANA.—Very neat dwarf crowded foliage; scape 1½ ft. with bell-shaped head of rosy-lilac flowers.

M. CORDIFOLIA × PURPURASCENS VAR. CORRUGATA.—Dwarf habit; large rough leaves; flowers pink.

M. CORDIFOLIA × PURPURASCENS VAR. DISTINCTION.—Dwarf crowded habit, with enormous head of pale pink flowers.

M. CORDIFOLIA × PURPURASCENS VAR. NANA.—A miniature of hybrida splendens.

M. CORDIFOLIA × PURPURASCENS VAR. PROGRESS.—A free growing plant, with tall scapes of rosy purple; bell-shaped blossoms, which are 1¼ in. across; extra fine.

M. CORDIFOLIA × PURPURASCENS VAR. STUDY.—Compact habit, with short stout scape of rose-coloured flowers.

One charm of these great Rockfoils is their rich autumnal and winter colouring. M. Stracheyi and M. purpurascens are especially good in this way, and many of Mr. Smith's hybrids are effective when planted in exposed positions; with other fine-leaved plants they show to advantage, some having leaves suffused with crimson, red, and soft yellow, while others are of the most vivid colour—crimson and brown. We have here a group of fine-leaved and flowering plants worthy of every attention, for we do not believe that the hybrids now known, fine as they are, will remain long the best now that it is seen that the species and varieties seed so freely and give such good results when crossed. The result promises to be a group of plants free from all cultural difficulties— plants that a cottager may grow in his garden, or a townsman in his window boxes, and handsome enough to be worthy of care and attention in the garden of a queen.—F. W. B.

SCABIOSA (*Scabious*).—Annual, biennial, and perennial plants, forming by far the largest proportion of the Teasel family cultivated in our gardens The old English name of Pincushion Flower, from the resemblance of the flower-heads to that useful article, is perhaps a little more appropriate than it is elegant, although it serves its purpose very well, and, indeed, we have been told these plants are known by no other name in the country Although comprising a large number of species, very few are found outside the botanic garden, and were all the known kinds hunted up, the sorts really worthy of the gardener's attention would certainly not amount to a dozen

S. atro-purpurea (*Sweet Scabious*), the most common Scabious, which when grown in distinct varieties, as it is now sold by our florists, adds much to the beauty of our mixed flower borders, as well as being largely used for greenhouse and conservatory decoration. The normal colour is said to be deep crimson, but under cultivation all shades of crimson, purplish-yellow, and white, may be seen Many varieties have double flowers and are preferred by some growers, but I think the single varieties are best, and they are also extremely useful for cutting Under the name Saudade the flower-heads of the Sweet Scabious (S atro-purpurea) are used for funeral wreaths by the Portuguese and other nations , indeed, the white varieties have attained such purity that they might well be employed in our own country, as they may be had at almost any season of the year by being sown and grown under glass Those desirous of having gay groups for the flower borders can order mixed packets from their seedsmen, and the seeds should be sown in the reserve ground along with other annuals in May, or even later, to bloom the following year If sown earlier, however, the Scabious will bloom the same year, for though considered a biennial by many growers we have always looked upon it as a hardy annual By sowing the seed in the open towards the end of March and thinning out as required, the plants will bloom well towards the latter end of summer To get earlier bloom, those sown the previous autumn may be transplanted in early spring to their flowering quarters , the succession will then be continued from early summer until late autumn South-western Europe

S. maritima (*Sea Scabious*) —A species similar to the above, equally beautiful, a hardy annual, and yielding abundance of purple-crimson flowers, which are invaluable for cutting.

S. caucasica (*Caucasian Scabious*) is the handsomest and most useful It flowers from early summer to late autumn, a true perennial on warm soils, but often perishes on cool soils It forms dense tufts, which yield large quantities of blue flower-heads, each usually from 3 to 4 in in diameter, on long foot-stalks, and are useful for cutting, as they last a long time in a warm room There is a white variety. Caucasus Division and seed

S. graminifolia (*Grass-leaved S*)—A graceful Scabious from 1½ to 2 ft high, with pale blue flowers and silvery white leaves , it is very useful for the rock-garden. Southern Europe June to October Division and seed

S. pterocephala (*Wing-headed S*), is a very dwarf-tufted hardy perennial, rarely exceeding 4 in or 6 in in height even when in flower , flower-heads pale purple in summer We find it very useful and less troublesome than most of the other species. Greece Division Syns , S Parnassi and Pterocephalus Parnassi

S. Webbiana is another useful species for the rock-garden or border, forming neat little masses of hoary leaves, which are attractive, especially when the plant is grown in poor soil. Its creamy yellow flowers, borne on long stalks, are pretty from July to August Division

Other kinds are succisa, arvensis, Portæ, suaveolens, Columbaria, gramuntia, but the above will be found a fair selection for most gardens In addition to the annual species given above, S stellata will no doubt find a place in many gardens It grows about 2 ft in height, the large florets spreading open like a star, of a pale purple colour, perhaps more curious than beautiful. A near ally of the above is S palæstina, a little taller, flowers larger, but paler , both are hardy annuals, but not to be compared with the Sweet Scabious and its varieties —D. K.

SCHISTOSTEGA (*Iridescent Moss*) — This Moss (*S pennata*) is so small that it would hardly be noticed by the naked eye but for the iridescent gleams of beautiful colour which it displays in suitable positions Some of the stones and sods on which it grows look as if sown with a mixture of gold and the material that forms the wings of green humming-birds It was supposed to require a particular kind of rock ; but its wonderful coruscations have lately been seen to spread over sods of turf and masses of peat, as well as over chips of rock brought from its native place Messrs Backhouse have it in perfection in the open air, in a quiet deep gorge of rocks, where it obtains sufficient moisture without being washed by rains

SCHIZANTHUS (*Fringe-flower*) — Pretty annuals of elegant growth, which bear in summer many showy and curiously-shaped blossoms There are in cultivation a few species, and these have yielded numerous varieties The hardy kinds are S pinnatus, 1½ to 3 ft high, and its rosy-purple and yellow blossoms are copiously spotted Its chief varieties are—papilionaceus (purple spotted), Priesti (white), atro-purpureus (deep purple with dark eye), and Tom Thumb (a dwarf compact variety) S porrigens is similar to S pinnatus, but has larger flowers The half-hardy kinds are S retusus (deep rose and orange flowers with crimson tips), Grahami (lilac and orange), and Hookeri (pale rose and yellow) These are also beautiful, and worthy of being grown well If treated as half-hardy annuals, the seed should be sown in heat in spring, but if treated as biennials, the seed should be sown in August, the plants preserved in the greenhouse till May, and then planted out Both kinds prefer a good, rich, sandy loam Chili

SCHIZOCODON —*S soldanelloides* was introduced by Captain Torrens, who in 1891 found the plants growing beside sulphur springs in the mountains of Japan, and, after carrying them hundreds of miles, succeeded at last in bringing home three or four living plants The flowers of the Schizocodon are like those of a large Soldanella, prettily fringed, deep rose in the centre, passing into blush or almost white towards the edges It evidently requires much the same treatment as Shortia Captain Torrens says — "The plant I found in an overhanging bank surrounded by Moss and moisture Since I brought it home I have kept it in a pot with peat and sand. It is a hardy plant, and I have had it out two winters in a cold frame, and it seems to have stood the climate well "

SCHIZOPETALON —*S Walkeri* is a curious Cruciferous half-hardy annual from Chili, about 1 ft. high, with slender stems, and numerous white almond-scented elegantly fringed blossoms If sown in April or May, in light, warm, rich soil in the open border, it flowers in July and August, and may also be sown in pots, but the ball of earth must not be broken as the plant does not well bear transplanting.

SCHIZOPHRAGMA (*Climbing Hydrangea*) —*S hydrangeoides* is a Japanese climbing shrub allied to the Hydrangea, with tall slender stems that send out roots which will fix it to a wall Its wood is of a

soft character, resembling that of the slow-growing Ivies, and it annually gives off fresh sets of roots along its branches, by means of which it clings to rocks, stone, stucco, bricks, and even wooden palings Its leaves are less in size than those of the common Hydrangea, of a lovely shade of green, which contrasts prettily with the reddish tinted young wood It is deciduous, of free growth, and flowers freely in sunny positions I know one case where it has been planted at a sunny corner of the house near French windows, up the sides of which there is lattice-work, and so charmed were the owners with the tender foliage, feathering the coign of the window, that they made more lattice-work in front of the window so that the creeper could extend and form a natural sunshade before the glass In a few years a plant had grown 11 ft high, and as much in width

SCHIZOSTYLIS (*Caffre Lily*) — *S. coccinea* is a handsome bulbous plant from Caffraria, with the habit of a Gladiolus, from 2 to 3 ft high The flowers appear late in the autumn on a one-sided spike opening from below upward, of a bright crimson colour, resembling in form those of Tritonia aurea, and should be well grown wherever cut flowers are desired in winter It is hardy, and in a mild autumn will flower out-of-doors, but should have some protection A good row planted close to a wall or fence, with some temporary protection against severe frosts, will give many spikes for cutting. S coccinea loves moisture both in the air and in the soil "When residing close to the sea in Dorset," says West Dorset, "I could grow this winter Flag splendidly in a shallow trench in good rich soil In summer it was deluged with water when the weather was dry, and in autumn a splendid crop of strong spikes of bloom resulted In North Hants, with a hot, dry, light soil, I never could grow it well, although I always kept it watered at the roots during summer "

SCIADOPITYS (*Umbrella Pine*) —A beautiful and distinct cone-bearing evergreen tree, very slow-growing in our country, but a hardy tree deserving the best care and positions with the choicest conifers When the trees are well established the growth is greater. It thrives best in moist soils and where the rainfall is copious, as in Cornwall Japan, Island of Nippon.

SCILLA —Beautiful spring flowers and bulbs, mostly natives of the colder parts of Europe or the Alps, and some precious for our gardens These all flower in spring, and are of the simplest culture.

In early autumn, when the plants are at rest, they should be planted a few inches deep in any good garden soil, not too heavy. When established, they need not be disturbed for years, except, perhaps, for a slight yearly top-dressing of manure. Some kinds, especially the many-coloured varieties of the Spanish Scilla, are suited for planting by the sides of woodland walks, or on the margins of shrubberies, and in the wild garden. Offsets may be taken from established clumps during summer.

Raising Scillas from seed is interesting, though slow. In some seasons the seeds are produced plentifully, and many varieties of merit, both as regards size and

S. bifolia.— Not so well known as S. sibirica, but quite as welcome, in the very dawn of spring, and indeed often in winter, this bears rich masses of dark blue flowers, and forms handsome tufts. The flowers are four to six on a spike ; and the plant varies from 6 to 10 in. high, according to the soil and warmth and shelter of the position. It thrives in almost any position in ordinary garden soil, the lighter the better, but must be left undisturbed to seed and increase as it likes. Although it blooms earlier than S. sibirica, it does not so well withstand the cold rains and storms of winter and spring, and therefore some tufts of it should be placed in warm sunny spots of the rock-garden or of the sheltered border. Southern and Central Europe. Of all Scillas, S. bifolia

Scilla hispanica.

colour, have been obtained in this way, but there is room for improvement. We retain the name Scilla as far prettier than the English one of " Squill."

The following are best kinds :—

S. amœna (*Star Hyacinth*). — This flowers in early spring, opening about three weeks after S. sibirica. It is less ornamental than any other kind, for its flowers have none of the grace of S. campanulata and the varieties of S. nutans, nor the dwarfness and brilliancy of S. sibirica. The leaves, usually about half an inch across, are about 1 ft. high, and easily injured by cold or wind, so that a sheltered position is best suited for the plant. It is not exactly suited for the choice rock-garden, though worth growing on sunny banks in semi-wild spots. Tyrol. Seeds or separation of the bulbs.

has produced the greatest number of varieties. Most of the forms known in gardens are better than the type. S. præcox is a stronger grower, the flowers larger, more abundant, and earlier. In purpureo-cœrulea the ovary and base of the segments are rosy-purple, gradually merging into blue, which becomes intense towards the tips, harmonising with the black and gold-banded anthers. It is a free flowerer, and the blooms individually are nearly as large as a shilling. In the Taurian variety, S. b. taurica, the flowers are much larger than in S. bifolia, and, with the exception of the white base, greatly resemble those of some of the forms of Chionodoxa Luciliæ. They vary from ten to twenty on each scape, and the leaves are larger and broader than those of S. bifolia. The white form of

S. b. taurica is very scarce. S. b. alba, a pretty ivory-white form, has flowers not larger than those of the type.

S. hispanica (*Spanish Scilla*).—One of the finest of early summer bulbs, and, though a more southern species than most of the others, coming from Portugal and Spain, is the most robust of the family. It is easily known by its strong pyramidal raceme of pendent, short-stalked, large, bell-shaped flowers, usually of a clear light blue. A variety major is larger in all its parts, and is a noble flower; while the white variety (alba) and the rose-coloured

Scilla nutans (Bluebell).

variety (rosea) are also welcome, the white kind being much grown for market. S. hispanica is never better seen than peeping here and there from the fringes of shrubberies and beds of Evergreens. The shelter it receives in such positions protects its large leaves from strong winds, but it is sturdy enough for any position. It deserves to be naturalised by wood-walks and in the grassy parts of the pleasure-ground. S. Europe. *Syn.*, S. campanulata.

S. italica (*Italian S.*)—This kind, with its pale blue flowers, intensely blue stamens, and delicious odour, is the most brilliant of the Scillas. It grows from 5 to 10 in. high, the flowers small and spreading in short conical racemes, which open in May. S. italica is hardy in almost any soil, but thrives best in warm and sandy places sheltered from east winds. Division should be done only once every three or four years, and the bulbs then planted in fresh positions. Italy and S. Europe.

S. nutans (*Wood Hyacinth* or *Bluebell*).—Though the Bluebell abounds in every wood and copse, its beautiful varieties are not too well known. Amongst the best are—the white variety, alba; the rose-coloured variety, rosea; the pale blue variety, coerulea; and a pleasing "French-white" variety. The variety bracteata has long bracts, and cernua is a Portuguese form with reddish flowers. S. patula is closely allied to the Bluebell, its flowers being of a pleasing violet-blue, but are not sweet or arranged on one side like those of the Bluebell. They are larger and more open, and have narrow bracts. All these kinds should be planted here and there in tufts among common Bluebells, along the margins of shrubberies, near the rock-garden, or for borders or woods.

S. sibirica (*Siberian S.*)—A minute gem among the flowers of earliest spring, and no rock-garden, or garden of any kind, is complete without the striking and peculiar shade of porcelain - blue which distinguishes this plant from all other Scillas. S. sibirica has many other names, but, unlike S. bifolia, it has sported into few varieties, S. amoenula being the chief, which, though not really distinct, is desirable, as it flowers a fortnight earlier than the type. Varieties with larger flowers, and with one on a stem instead of two or five, are preserved in herbariums and sometimes cultivated, but the difference between these and the type is trifling, arising often from the conditions in which the plants are placed. S. sibirica is hardy, and thrives best in a good sandy soil. Bulbs that have been used for forcing should never be thrown away; for they thrive well if allowed to fully develop their leaves and go to rest in a pit or frame, afterwards being planted out in open spots in warm soil, where in a year or two their usual vigour will be restored. They may then be lifted again and forced as before. It is unnecessary to disturb the tufts, except every two or three years for division, when they grow vigorously. S. sibirica flowers a little later than S. bifolia, but withstands the storms better, remaining also much longer in bloom In places where it does not thrive freely, whether from the coldness of the soil or from other causes, give it a sheltered position to prevent injury to its leaves The Siberian Squill may be used as an edging to beds of spring flowers or choice alpine shrubs.

OTHER CULTIVATED KINDS —Amongst Scillas not generally found in gardens, but hardy in dry situations, may be named S peruviana, a large species, with beautiful broad leaves, Yucca-like and very distinct , it stands well in sheltered nooks, or even in the open border in southern districts The numerous fine blue flowers are in a superb umbel-like pyramid, which lengthens during the flowering period. There are varieties, one named alba, and there are reddish varieties, such as elegans, also whitish and yellowish forms. Tufts of the Peruvian Scilla should be taken up every three or four years, when it is at rest Divide the bulbs and replant immediately The variety Clusi also succeeds S maritima is properly a greenhouse species, but in the places indicated for S peruviana it may be grown outside without hurt, though it rarely flowers S lilio-hyacintha is hardy, whilst S hyacinthoides, S. pratensis (amethystina), S obtusifolia (an Algerian species), autumnalis, Aristidis, patula, and its various forms, including cernua and others, differ little from one another

SCIRPUS   (*Bulrush*) — Sedge-like plants fringing lakes and ponds There are numerous native species that might be readily transplanted, and the best are S triqueter, S atrovirens, and S lacustris This is 3 to 8 ft high, and effective on the margins of lakes or streams with other tall plants

SCOLOPENDRIUM (*Hart's-tongue*). —*S vulgare* is one of the best known of hardy evergreen British Ferns, and broken into numberless interesting forms and varieties, some being very beautiful It prefers shade, and though sometimes met with on dry stone and brick walls, its favourite place is by the side of a stream in a shady ravine. Fine specimens have been seen between the joints of brickwork at the tops of old wells, the fronds developing fine proportions A suitable soil consists of equal portions of fibrous peat and loam, good sharp sand being added, together with broken oyster-shells or limestone. Scolopendriums should be associated with Lastreas, Polystichums, and Lady Ferns, or be placed in groups on the rock-garden with some flowering plant that will thrive in the same spot During hot dusty weather in summer a daily

afternoon syringing will much refresh and invigorate the plants. All the Hart's-tongues thrive in pots, and are useful for rooms and tables.

No fewer than 400 varieties of the Hart's-tongue were described thirty years ago, and since then this number has been much increased. Most of these, however, are deformities—vegetable cripples, so to speak A few of the characteristic forms of each group might be used where collections of hardy Ferns are being formed, being evergreen and diversified in form Of the following selection, commencing with simple forms and ending with much-divided ones, S. latifolium is a fine bold variety, having wavy spreading fronds, 8 to 10 in long, and 2 to 3 in broad S reniforme has oblong, roundish, or kidney-shaped fronds. S. cornutum is interesting, the point of the frond being prolonged into a horn-like appendage S marginatum is very distinct, with fronds crenated at the margin Some of the best forms of S pinnatifidum are attractive, and S. crispum is an old favourite, its fronds retaining the habit of the type, but the margin is frilled A form of it called grandidens has the margin deeply incised. Stansfieldi has curled incisions, and Wrigleyi is a luxuriant form with erect fronds upwards of 3 ft in length S. laceratum has broad flat fronds, deeply cut into lobes of variable length and breadth, whilst S sagittato-cristatum has fronds with wavy margins and crested lobes. S acrocladon has a narrow frond slightly widened at the base, and divided at the upper end into several wedge-shaped divisions, the upper margins deeply incised The fronds of S patulum are cut down near to the base into two or three divisions, each having a narrow wing and a broad terminal crest S digitatum has pleasing fronds 1 ft or more in length, with the divisions terminated by a forked and twisted crest S Kelwayi is a handsome form, the fronds terminating in a large crest 6 to 10 in broad S ramosa-marginatum resembles it in form of frond, but has a broad-winged stalk. Its crest is nearly flat and not unlike the tasselled frond-extremity of the maximum form of Pteris serrulata cristata The base of the frond of S corymbiferum is like the type, but the upper half has innumerable contorted and twisted incisions and looks like the leaf-ends of some of the ragged Kales S. Coolingi is very similar to S. corymbiferum, but the divisions form an intricate mass of slender segments, curled and twisted in various ways so as to form a globular head This kind of division represents the extreme form of variation. —J. M. S.

SCUTELLARIA (*Skullcap*).—Hardy perennials, several in cultivation, but few are good garden plants. These few are handsome flowers for the border, and on account of their dwarf neat growth may be given a place in a large rock-garden in an open sunny situation in any soil. S. macrantha, a native of Siberia, is the finest of all the species. It is an excellent alpine perennial, forming a hard woody root-stock, is 9 in. high, and produces an abundance of rich, velvety, dark blue flowers, much finer in colour than those of S. japonica. S. japonica is, however, a handsome plant. The alpine Skullcap (S. alpina) is a spreading plant with all the vigour of the coarsest weeds of its Natural Order, but neat in habit and ornamental in flower. The stems are prostrate, but so abundant that they rise in a full round tuft, 1 ft. or more high in the centre. The leaves are ovate, roundish or heart-shaped at the base, and have very notched and very short stalks, while the flowers are borne in terminal heads, short at first, but afterwards elongating. These flowers are purplish, or have the lower lip white or yellow. The variety bicolor, with the upper lip purplish and the lower white, is very pretty. S. lupulina is a very ornamental kind with yellow flowers. Pyrenees, Swiss and Tyrolese Alps, and many other parts of Europe and Asia. Division. Flowering free in summer. These kinds are admirably suited for borders, the margins of shrubberies, and the rougher parts of the rock-garden. S. japonica, S. orientalis, S. scordiifolia, S. altaica, S. galericulata, S. peregrina, and the British S. minor, an interesting little plant for the artificial bog, are among the best of the other cultivated kinds, but it is doubtful if they are worth a place in any but a very large collection. Division or seed.

SCYPHANTHUS (*Cup-flower*).—S. elegans is a beautiful slender climber, 5 to 8 ft. high, with forked stems, and valuable for trailing over a trellis or against a wall. Its leaves are deeply cut and enhance its graceful appearance. The flowers come singly in the forks of the branches. They are cup-like in shape, and are of a bright golden-yellow, with fine red spots inside. They appear profusely from August till October. S. elegans is easily cultivated in rich light soil, and should be treated as a half-hardy annual. Chili.

SEDUM (*Stonecrop*).—Rock and alpine plants which thrive in our gardens in nearly every soil. They may be grown in the ordinary border, in the rock-garden, on walls, and on ruins, and, indeed, in any place where the roots can obtain a foothold. Like the Saxifrages, they represent a great diversity of habit, some, like S. acre, being humble and creeping ; while others, like S. spectabile, are stately plants for the border. A great many are in cultivation, and we mention the most desirable of the hardy kinds, which are nearly all easily-cultivated perennials.

S. acre (*Wall Pepper*).—This little plant, with its small, thick, bright green leaves and its brilliant yellow flowers, grows abundantly on walls, thatch, rocks, and sandy places. The variegated variety (aureum) has shoots with tips of a yellow hue in early spring, and the tufts or flakes look quite showy. The silvery tones of the variety elegans are not so effective ; nor is the plant so vigorous as the variety aureum. This is beautiful in the winter garden ; its golden tips peep out in November, and only vanish with the heat of May. S. sexangulare is similar to S. acre.

S. Aizoon is 1 ft. or more in height, with erect stems terminated by dense clusters of yellow flowers. It is an old garden plant for the border or large rock-garden, and requires open positions and a light soil. Siberia and Japan. S. Maximowiczi and S. Selskyanum are similar.

S. Ewersi.—A neat little hardy plant, rarely more than 3 in. high, with broad glaucous silvery leaves and corymbs of purplish flowers. N. India and Asia.

S. glaucum.—A minute species of a grayish tone, forming dense spreading tufts of short stems, densely clothed with thick leaves and inconspicuous flowers. Other Sedums are nearly allied to it ; for instance, S. dasyphyllum, S. glanduliferum, S. farinosum, and S. brevifolium ; but though hardy on walls and rocks, they have not the vigour of many Stonecrops.

S. Lydium.—A pretty little plant from Asia Minor, scarcely an inch high, similar to S. glaucum, except that the tiny crowded leaves are greenish and tipped with red. For edgings, or slopes bordering footpaths it is not excelled, and likes plenty of moisture. It roots on the surface with great rapidity, and may, therefore, be speedily propagated. Very small pieces put in the soil in spring soon form a mass of rich verdure, scarcely an inch in height, and as level as a turf.

S. maximum, like S. Telephium, is variable, there being no fewer than a dozen named varieties. Of these by far the most important for the garden is hæmatodes, or atro-purpureum as it is commonly called, from the vivid purple of the stems and large fleshy leaves. It grows from 1 to 2 ft. high, and though the flowers are not showy, it is bold, stately, and admirably suited for massing. It should be planted in the poorest, stony, gravelly soil, and smoke will not injure it. On white calcareous rocks it is at home.

S. pulchellum (*Purple American Stone-crop*).—A pretty species, with purplish flowers, arranged in several spreading and recurved branchlets, bird's-foot fashion, with numerous spreading stems. It is

a curious crested variety, sometimes known as monstrosum or fasciatum. S. album, another native kind, has brownish-green leaves and white or pinkish flowers. Like the Stonecrop it occurs on old roofs and rocky places in many parts of Europe. All these kinds are worth naturalising on walls or old ruins, in places where they do not occur naturally, also on the margins of the pathways and the less important surfaces of the rock-garden.

S. sempervivoides (*Scarlet Stone-crop*).—This beautiful Stonecrop has ros-ettes of leaves like those of the common Houseleek, (Sempervivum tectorum). The brilliant scarlet flowers form a dense

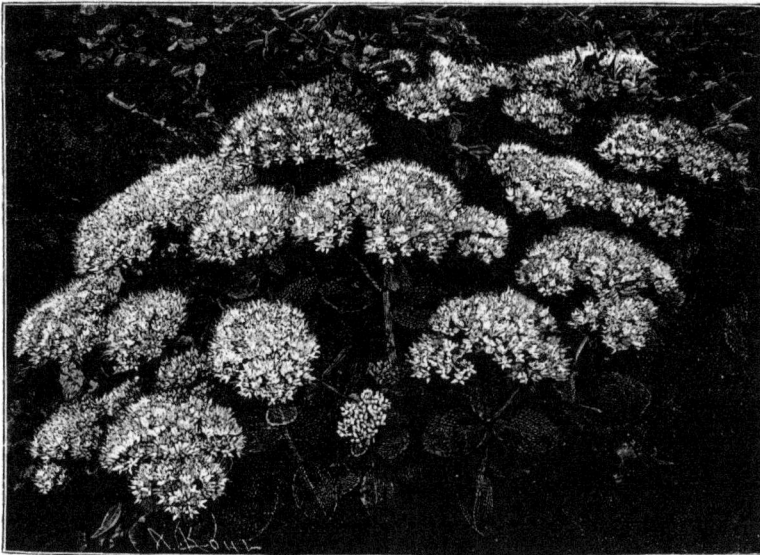

The Japanese Stonecrop (Sedum spectabile).

abundant in North America, and in France is a good deal used for edging. It is also appropriate for the rock-garden or the front margin of a mixed border, growing in any soil, and flowering in summer.

S. rupestre (*Rock Stonecrop*). — A densely-tufted native plant, with rather loose corymbs of yellow flowers, and numerous spreading shoots generally rooting at the base, but quite erect at the top. It is frequently used as an edging or border plant. There are several similar kinds, such as the glaucous-leaved S. pruinatum, commonly known as S. elegans ; S. Fosterianum, with light green leaves ; and S. reflexum, of which there are several varieties, including cristatum,

head similar to the well-known Rochea falcata. It is strictly biennial, as it flowers from seed freely in the second year, then dies, and is not hardy, but during summer grows freely on a dry bank. In winter it stands frost if the weather is dry, but frost and wet combined are fatal to it. Seeds germinate freely, and should be sown in January in gentle heat, plung-ing the pot in water before sowing, so that the soil may not get dry. As soon as large enough pot off singly. If well watered while growing, they ought, by the end of the summer, to be as large as a crown-piece. During autumn and winter the plants must only be just kept moist enough to prevent their leaves from shrivelling.

Erroneously called Umbilicus Semper-vivum, this being quite a distinct plant. Asia Minor and the Caucasus.

S. Sieboldi. — A well-known kind frequently grown in pots. Its roundish leaves are glaucous, and in late autumn often assume a lovely rosy-coral hue. They are in whorls of three on numerous stems, which in autumn bear soft rosy flowers which look pretty in pots, small baskets, or vases. The plant is hardy, and merits a place in the rock-garden, especially where its branches may fall without touching the earth and its graceful habit may be well seen ; but, except in favoured places, it does not make strong growth. There is a variegated variety,

autumn, makes a bright display, and is suited for edgings, the margins of mixed borders, and for the rock-garden. Other species are S. oppositifolium, S. trifidum, S. dentatum, and S. ibericum, the last-named kind having white flowers. Caucasus.

S. Telephium. — This is the most variable Stonecrop. No fewer than twenty forms have received names either as sub-species or as varieties, but our native form is as showy as any. It is 1 to 2 ft. high, the stout erect stems furnished with fleshy leaves, and in late summer and autumn bearing dense broad clusters of bright rosy-purple, but sometimes white, flowers. S. Telephium is distributed about the country, usually in hedgerows and thickets.

Sedum kamtschaticum.

more tender than the ordinary form. Japan. Division.

S. spectabile.—This is distinct and beautiful, erect, and with broad glaucous leaves. Its rosy-purple flowers appear in dense broad corymbs about the middle of August, and remain in perfection for two months or more. The glaucous foliage, even before the flowers come, is a pleasant relief to any high-coloured plant that may be near it. It withstands extreme cold, heat, or wet, and unlike most plants will grow and flower to perfection in shaded places, thriving in any soil. Japan.

S. stoloniferum (*Purple Stonecrop*).— The best of the Sedums with large flat leaves is the Purple Stonecrop. It flowers late in summer, and often through the

Like all other kinds about the same size, it is useful for dry borders and the rough parts of the rock-garden, but when well grown will flower the more vigorously. Cut blooms last a long time ; hence are often called Everlasting Livelongs.

The Sedums mentioned are the most distinct. The pretty S. cœruleum is an annual ; and S. carneum variegatum is not hardy enough for our winters. The Orange Stonecrop (S. kamtschaticum) has dark orange-yellow flowers in summer, and is hardy in almost any soil, but is best in warm rich loam. There are in cul-tivation many kinds of the easiest culture.

SELAGINELLA.—A few hardy kinds of this large family of Lycopods are valu-able for carpeting the fernery, or clothing shady spots in the rock-garden. These kinds are S. denticulata, S. helvetica, and S. rupestris, small trailing plants of a delicate green, mossy growth. S. Kraussiana, generally known in plant-houses as S. denticulata, is also hardy in many places, and in Ireland grows and thrives better than any of the kinds mentioned. All these plants require a well-drained peaty soil and shaded and sheltered position.

SEMPERVIVUM (*Houseleek*).—Succulent Rock and Alpine plants, of which the common Houseleek (S. tectorum), often seen growing in patches on old roofs and walls, is the most familiar. There is a strong family likeness throughout, and they form rosette-like tufts of fleshy leaves, which chiefly differ in the colour of the foliage, some deep red, others pale green. The flowers of most of them are of a reddish tinge, and several are yellow. All the hardy kinds will grow well in dry sandy parts of the rock-garden where few other alpines thrive ; or on old walls, ruins, and the like, merely requiring to be placed in chinks with a little soil. Most of them thrive on any border, if the soil be not too stiff and damp, but they prefer a dry elevated position, and full exposure to the sun. Nearly all are easily increased by offsets, which, as a rule, are abundantly produced. Of late years some of the larger kinds, such as S. calcareum, have been used for beds. Europe and W. Asia.

S. arachnoideum (*Cobweb Houseleek*). —One of the most singular of alpine plants, with tiny rosettes of fleshy leaves covered at the top with a thick white down, which intertwines itself all over the leaves like a spider's web. It is rarely seen in our gardens except in a frame, but thrives in moist sandy loam and exposed spots in sunny arid parts of the rock-garden. Its sheets of whitish rosettes look as if a thousand spiders had been at work upon them, and in summer send up pretty rose-coloured flowers. About London it sometimes suffers from sparrows plundering the "down." Division. Similar to this species are S. tortuosum (or Webbianum of gardens), S. Fauconneti, S. heterotrichum, and S. Laggeri, which have the rosettes of leaves united by a web of white threads.

S. arenarium (*Sand Houseleek*).— Grown in dense patches, this plant has a lovely effect. It is much smaller than its ally S. globiferum, and, unlike the latter species, the leaves of the rosettes are not incurved. The flowers are small, yellow, pretty, and the leaves usually rich crimson. S. Heufelli, a similar species, has in autumn almost chocolate-crimson foliage, the flowers being yellow. Other species of similar character are S. hirtum, S. Neilreichi, and S. soboliferum, which is often confused with S. globiferum.

S. calcareum (*Glaucous Houseleek*).— No finer Houseleek has ever been introduced than this, sometimes called S. californicum. It is as easily grown and as hardy as the common Houseleek (S. tectorum), and thrives in any soil. Planted singly, its rosettes are sometimes nearly 5 in. across, the leaves glaucous, and tipped at the points with chocolate. It is deservedly popular for edgings in the flower garden and also admirable for the rock-garden. Other cultivated kinds are S. glaucum, S. Camollei, S. Lamottei, S. Verloti, and S. juratense, and these are all desirable for a full collection.

S. fimbriatum (*Fringed Houseleek*).— One of the most profusely blooming kinds, the dark rose-coloured flowers appearing in summer on stems 6 to 10 in. high. The leaves, which are in small rosettes, are smooth on both sides, strongly fringed, and terminate in a long point, being marked at the end with a large purple spot. S. Funcki, S. Powelli, S. barbatulum, S. atlanticum, and S. piliferum are similar.

S. globiferum (*Hen-and-chicken Houseleek*).—This grows in firm dense tufts, its little round offsets being so abundantly thrown off that they are pushed clear above the tufts, and lie on the surface in small brownish-green balls. The small leaves of the young rosettes all turn inward and appear of a purplish colour, but in the full-grown rosettes are light green, the tips of the under side being of a decided chocolate-brown for nearly one-third of their length ; the flowers are small and yellow. This kind is well-suited for forming wide tufts in the rock-garden, and on banks below the eye. It grows freely in any soil, and is also known as S. soboliferum, but this is the name of another kind similar to S. arenarium.

S. montanum (*Mountain Houseleek*).— A dark green kind, smaller than the common Houseleek, the leaves forming neat rosettes, from which spring dull rosy flowers in summer. It is suitable for edgings or for the rock-garden, grows in any soil, and is easily propagated. Alps. S. assimile and S. flagelliforme are similar.

S. tectorum (*Common Houseleek*).— Though a native of rocky places in the great mountain ranges of Europe and Asia, the common Houseleek, having been cultivated from time immemorial on house-tops and on old walls, is well known to everybody. It may be used in flower-gardening, but it would be better to select some of the rarer species for edgings and other purposes It varies somewhat, and a glaucous form called rusticum is one of the most distinct. Other similar varieties are Royeni, Rœgnerianum, Sequieri, calcaratum, and Greenei Greenei resembles the common Houseleek, but is smaller.

S. triste is distinct from other House-leeks, as its rosettes of leaves are of a deep dull red, which makes it a handsome plant. It is about the size of S tectorum, and in light warm soil is quite as vigorous and rapid a grower Its singular colour makes it a valuable contrast to other plants, but at present it is not much known

Besides these kinds there are several tender species which are now largely used for summer gardening The most popular of these are—S. tabulæforme, a singularly handsome kind, with broad rosettes of leaves that lie flat on the soil , S Bolli, with leaves that form a dense cup-like tuft from 3 to 6 in across, and S arboreum, a tall, straggling plant, with stout branches terminated by a rosette of foliage. Propagated by quantity in heat in spring or autumn from offsets.

SENECIO (*Groundsel*) —Most of these Composites are troublesome weeds, but a few are worthy of cultivation The following are among the most desirable —

S. argenteus (*Silvery Groundsel*) —A minute but sturdy silvery-leaved plant, resembling on a small scale the popular Centaurea Ragusina. It is only 2 in high when fully developed, and its leaves are from ½ to 1½ in long. It will stand any weather, and live in sandy soil in any well-drained border. It is valuable for the rock-garden, and makes a beautiful dwarf edging. Similar to this, but inferior, are S incanus, S uniflorus, and S. carniolicus, which are good rock-garden plants Division

S. artemisiæfolius is a neat little perennial, with broad clusters of showy clear yellow flowers, on stems 1 to 1½ ft. high The deep green leaves are finely divided, and give the plant an elegant feathery appearance S abrotanifolius has similar foliage, but its orange-yellow flowers are larger and are fewer in number Both kinds are hardy European plants and thrive in ordinary soil either in the rock-garden or in the border.

S Doronicum is one of the showiest and most useful of Groundsels. It is 1 ft

to 3 ft. high, and in summer produces stout stalks of numerous large bright yellow flowers. It is perfectly hardy and is of easy culture in any soil Seed or division. Central Europe.

S. elegans (*Purple Jacobæa*) —This beautiful half-hardy annual has for generations been a favourite garden plant. It has a dwarf strain (nana), about 1 ft in height, and there are varieties with single and double flowers, the latter being the showiest and most desirable The colours of these varieties vary from white to deep crimson. S. elegans grows best in rich sandy loam It flowers from July to October, according to the time of sowing, and looks best in good-sized masses Cape of Good Hope

S. japonicus —This is one of the finest of the large kinds It is about 5 ft high, and its leaves are nearly 1 ft. across, and are divided into about nine divisions The flower-stems are slightly branched, the flower-heads are about 3 in. across, and the outer narrow florets are a rich orange colour S. japonicus is a hardy moisture-loving plant, and should have plenty of water in summer It should be grown in a rich and moderately stiff loamy soil, by a lake or a pond, so that its roots may have plenty of moisture Japan. *Syn*, Erythrochæte palmatifida

S. pulcher.—One of the handsomest of perennials, 2 to 3 ft high, and bearing in autumn rosy-purple flowers 2 to 3 in across, on tall stems S pulcher is hardy, but its beauty is somewhat impaired by the late season of its flowering. It succeeds best in a deep moist loam It rarely ripens seed in this country, but it may be freely propagated in spring by cuttings of the roots, 1 in long, and sown like seeds in a pan of light sandy earth, placed in a cool frame or put on a shelf in the greenhouse Buenos Ayres

S. saracenicus.—In moist situations in some parts of the west of England S. saracenicus grows wild, and attains a height of 4 to 5 ft It is a showy plant, suitable for the margins of ponds or streams in semi-wild places, where it spreads rapidly, and if associated with the Willow Herb (Epilobium angustifolium) produces a beautiful contrast, as the habit of the growth and the colour of the flowers of each are distinct and effective. Coarse species similar to this are S Dorio and S macrophyllus. These are suitable for the wild garden, but not for border culture

S. spathulæfolius is a rare hardy species, and an interesting and pretty plant. The pleasing orange-yellow flowers are about the size of a shilling, and are borne in terminal clusters 6 to 12 in. high, A similar species is the Piedmont Groundsel (S. Balbisianus), from elevated districts in Northern Italy, particularly Piedmont. It is 3 to 9 in. high, and has hoary rootleaves. The golden-yellow flowers, when contrasted with the foliage, have a remarkably bright appearance. S. spathulæfolius and the Piedmont Groundsel flourish in light rubbly soil and an exposed dry situation in a well-drained rock-garden.

SEQUOIA.—Enormous cone-bearing evergreen trees of the Pacific coast of North America, just hardy enough to be the object of numerous experiments in our country, far from successful either from an artistic or most other points of view. In some of the books it is said that these great trees are readily propagated by cuttings inserted under glass in autumn, but we would beg everybody never to plant any tree of the kind except from seed.

S. GIGANTEA (*Big Tree*).—A colossal tree in its own country, inhabiting mostly, in scattered groups or groves, the Californian Mountains for a distance of over 250 miles in length, existing trees being over 300 ft. high. No tree ever introduced has excited so much interest or been the subject of so much costly experiment in this country. It succeeds well in various districts, and even as far north as Scotland, but after it grows up the growth is very apt to be seared by harsh east winds. The tree is not good in form, while in very few cases it will ever attain the dignity of size that it does in its native country, one of the finest climates in the world. Even where the tree does well, the effect is never good in the home landscape. The variegated and golden forms are rubbish. *Syn.*, Wellingtonia gigantea.

S. SEMPERVIRENS (*Red Wood*).—A noble evergreen tree thriving somewhat better in our country than the Big Tree, but planted as it usually is by itself, it is often torn about by sleet storms in our climate, which is so very different to that of its native country. Still it grows rapidly in good free soils, and is worth trying grown in a wood or grove so that the trees may shelter each other. Sheltering groves or woods of it would give good timber in quick time, as it is a very rapid grower. The variegated forms are not worth planting. Coast range of Northern America. *Syn.*, Taxodium sempervirens.

SERAPIAS.—Terrestrial Orchids from S. Europe, worthy of a collection of hardy Orchids, as the flowers are always singular and in some kinds beautiful. The most desirable are S. cordigera, with large showy flowers, chiefly of a blood-red colour ; S. lingua, with peculiar brownish-purple flowers ; and S. longipetala, with large rosy-red flowers. These are all 9 to 12 in. high, and their flowers are densely arranged on broad erect stems. The plants succeed best in a soil composed of two parts of peat, one of loam, and one of sand and leaf-mould. The position should be partially shaded, and well sheltered from cold winds.

SESELI (*Gum Seseli*).—S. gummiferum is a handsome plant, 1½ to 3 ft. high, with elegantly-divided leaves of a peculiarly pleasing glaucous or almost silvery tone. Though a biennial, it is so distinct that some may like to grow it. The best position for it is on dry and sunny banks, or in raised beds or borders.

SHEFFIELDIA.—S. repens is a hardy little New Zealand creeper, with small leaves, small slender stems, and tiny white flowers which appear in summer. It is interesting for the rock-garden, and grows in any good well-drained soil. Primula Order.

SHORTIA.—S. galacifolia is an interesting and beautiful plant. It was first discovered over a hundred years ago by Michaux in the mountains of North Carolina, and rediscovered in 1877. It was found growing with Galax aphylla, and forms runners like this plant, being propagated by this means. The plant is of tufted habit, the flowers reminding one of those of a Soldanella, but large, with cut edges to the segments, like a frill, so to say, and pure white, passing to rose as they get older. There is much beauty, too, in the leaves, which are of rather oval shape, deep green, tinged with brownish-crimson, changing in winter to quite a crimson, when it forms a bright bit of colour in the rock-garden or border. A correspondent writing in *The Garden* says : " The cultural directions given in catalogues to keep the plant in a shady situation and grow it in Sphagnum and peat, deprive us of its chief charm—*i.e.*, the handsome-coloured leaves during the winter and spring months. Instead of choosing a shady spot I selected a fully exposed one, and here two plants have been for over a year, one in peat and the other in sandy loam. Both are vigorous." It succeeds well in various soils as described, and is hardy. It is also a delightful plant in a pot, as the flowers on their crimson stems are pretty, and one gets also the prettily tinted leaves. N. America.

SIBTHORPIA (*Moneywort*).—S. europæa is a little native creeper with slender stems and small round leaves. In summer it forms a dense carpet on moist soil, and should always be grown in the bog-garden. The variegated form is prettier but more delicate than the type, and rarely succeeds in the open, but thrives in a cool house or frame. Shady banks

Sibthorpia europæa variegata (Moneywort).

and ditches suit it. The flowers are inconspicuous.

SIDA.—S. dioica and S. Napæa are stout vigorous plants, suitable chiefly for the wild garden and shrubbery borders.

SILENE (*Catchfly*).—A large family containing few showy plants ; but among the perennials there are species of great beauty. Southern and Central Europe is the home of the Silene, though a few species extend westward to America, a few eastward to Siberia, and a sprinkling of them will be found on the southern shores of the Mediterranean and in Asia Minor. The following dwarf kinds are suitable chiefly for the rock-garden :—

S. acaulis (*Cushion Pink*).—A dwarf alpine herb tufted into light green masses like a wide-spreading Moss, but quite firm. In summer it becomes a mass of pink, rose, or crimson flowers barely peeping above the leaves. Many places on the mountains of Scotland, Northern Ireland, North Wales, and of the Lake District of England are sheeted over with its firm flat tufts of verdure, often several feet in dia-

meter. In cultivation it is as beautiful as when wild, and grows freely in almost any soil in the rock-garden, not shaded, or in pots and pans. There are several varieties : alba ; exscapa, with flower stems even less developed than in the type ; and muscoides, dwarfer still ; but none of them are far removed from the typical form or are of greater importance for the garden.

S. alpestris (*Alpine Catchfly*).—A very dwarf and compact alpine plant, hardy, and beautiful when in bloom. It succeeds in any soil and is 4 to 6 in. high. Its white flowers appear in May. It should be used abundantly in every rock-garden. Some forms are quite sticky with viscid matter, while others are free from it. S. quadridentata and quadrifida are similar. All the alpine Silenes are propagated either by division in spring or by seed.

S. Elisabethæ.—A remarkably beautiful alpine plant, the flowers looking more like those of some handsome but diminutive Clarkia than of the Silenes commonly grown. They are very large, bright rose with the claws or bases of the petals white. One to seven flowers are borne on stems 3 to 4 in. high. It is considered difficult to cultivate, but if strong plants are secured, is as easy to manage as the Cushion Pink. It is rare in a wild state, but occurs in the Tyrol and Italy, amidst shattered fragments of rock, and sometimes in flaky rocks without any soil. It thrives freely in a warm nook in the rock-garden, in a mixture of about one-third good loam, one-third peat, and one-third broken stones, and should be planted where its roots can penetrate 18 to 24 in. back, into congenial soil. Flowers rather late in summer. Seeds.

S. maritima.—The handsome double variety (S. maritima fl.-pl.) of this British plant is noteworthy, not only for its flowers, but for its dense spreading sea-green carpet of leaves, pleasing on the margins of raised borders, the front edge of the mixed border, or hanging over the faces of stones in the rougher parts of the rock-garden. The flowers appear in June, and those of the double variety rarely rise more than a couple of inches above the leaves, which form a tuft about 2 in. deep. There is a pretty rose-coloured variety, less rambling than the type.

S. pendula.—There are several varieties of this fine biennial, notably compacta, compacta alba, Bonnetti, ruberrima, and variegata, all improvements on the original. The compacta varieties are mostly used for spring-bedding, and form compact rounded tufts about 4 in. high. The other forms are 6 to 12 in. high. To obtain the finest plants for spring-flowering, seed should be sown in the reserve garden in autumn, and afterwards transplanted to permanent beds Flowers appear from May to August, according to the season of sowing. Italy and Sicily.

S. pennsylvanica.--The wild pink of the Americans is a dwarf and handsome plant, forming dense patches, and from April to June has clusters of six or eight purplish-rose flowers, about 1 in across, on stems from 4 to 7 in high It succeeds best in rather light sandy soil, but is not fastidious, and is a native of sandy, gravelly places in many parts of N America It will occasionally flower the first year from seeds, but it does not generally do so till the second season, and may also be readily increased by cuttings

S. Pumilio.—A beautiful species, resembling our own Cushion Pink in dwarf firm tufts of shining green leaves The leaves of S Pumilio, however, are a little more succulent and obtuse The rose-coloured flowers are also much larger, handsomer, and taller, though scarcely more than 1 in above the flat mass of leaves, so that the whole plant seldom attains a height of more than 3 in It thrives in rock-gardens as well as the Cushion Pink, and should be planted in deep sandy loam on a well-drained and thoroughly-exposed spot, sufficiently moist in summer, facing the south Place a few stones round the neck of the young plant to keep it firm and prevent evaporation Once it begins to spread, it will take care of itself There is a white variety which is not cultivated Tyrol

S. Schafta.—A much-branched plant from the Caucasus forming very neat tufts, 4 to 6 in high, covered with large purplish-rose flowers It is hardy As it flowers late (from July to September, or later), it should not be used where spring or early summer bloom is chiefly sought, but in summer is more suitable than most alpines for edgings to permanent beds, or for the front margin of the mixed border It grows, however, in the rock-garden in almost any position Seed or division of established tufts

S. virginica (*Fire Pink*)—A brilliant perennial, with flowers of the brightest scarlet, 2 in across, and sometimes more. The somewhat slender stalks lie flat on the soil and the flowers are borne a few inches above it The Fire Pink succeeds in a well-drained rock-garden, but requires careful attention, particularly in winter, as at that season excessive moisture is hurtful It is a native of open woods in America, from New York south-

wards, flowering from June to August. The best plants are obtained from seed, as it does not bear division well. S rupestris, a sparkling-looking white species, little more than 3 in high when in bloom, reminding one of a dwarf S alpestris, is better worthy of a place , and so is S. Hookeri, a dwarf and rare Californian species

SILPHIUM (*Rosin Plant*)—Stout NorthAmerican Sunflower-like perennials, of stately habit, and among those which suggested the idea of the "wild garden" to me There they are at home among the most vigorous growers, as they thrive and flower freely on the worst clay soils S. laciniatum is a vigorous perennial with a stout stem, often 8 ft in height, and fine yellow-coloured flowers, on drooping heads, which have the peculiarity of facing the east S perfoliatum (Cup Plant) is 4 to 8 ft in height, and has broad yellow leaves 6 to 15 in long and flower-heads about 2 in across S terebinthinaceum (Prairie Dock) has stems 4 to 10 ft. high, panicled at the summit, and bearing many small heads of light yellow flowers A variety (pinnatifidum) has leaves deeply cut or pinnatifid S terebinthinaceum has a strong turpentine odour Other species are S trifoliatum, S integrifolium, and S ternatum If planted in numbers in bold masses, these plants produce a stately effect in the wild garden, especially in autumn

SILYBUM (*Milk Thistle*)—S marianum is a robust and vigorous native biennial, 5 ft or more in height, well worth associating with other large fine-foliaged plants. Its large leaves are variously cut and undulated, and tipped and margined with scattered spines , they are bright glistening green, and variegated with broad white veins The Milk Thistle is easily raised from seed, and thrives in almost any well-drained soil The foliage is more vigorous if the flower-stems are pinched off as soon as they appear A few plants raised in the garden and planted out in rough and somewhat bare places or banks, will soon establish themselves S eburneum is much like the above, but with spines like ivory *Syn* , Carduus

SISYRINCHIUM (*Satin-flower*)—Iridaceous plants from North-West America, only one species of which is worth growing, namely S grandiflorum, a beautiful perennial that flowers in early spring, and with narrow, Grass-like leaves ; the flowers, borne on slender stems 6 to 12 in high, are bell-shaped and drooping, rich purple in the type and transparent white in the variety album No garden should be without them. They are charming for the rock-garden or borders, but like best a light peaty soil or sandy loam. Division.

SKIMMIA.—Beautiful dwarf evergreen shrubs from Japan, distinct, compact, and charming for peat beds or large rock-gardens.

The only ones worth cultivating are S. japonica and S. Fortunei. There has been much confusion between these two species, the plant universally known in gardens as S. japonica not being Japanese at all, but a native of China, its proper name being Skimmia Fortunei. The true S. japonica is a Japanese plant, introduced by Fortune. Unlike S. Fortunei, it is

berried species, plant specimens of the two sexes near to each other. Of S. Fortunei (the S. japonica of gardens) S. rubella is a seedling form. S. japonica argentea is a seedling or sport, only differing from the type in having the leaves bordered with white. S. Fortunei is much dwarfer than S. japonica, and does well as a pot-plant for window decoration.

SMILACINA (*Wild Spikenard*).—Graceful but not showy hardy perennials, somewhat resembling Solomon's Seal. They are easily managed plants, and the North American species will be found useful for mixed herbaceous borders, having rich green foliage and white feathery flower-heads in May and June.

Skimmia fragrans.

diœcious. Both sexes have received specific names. S. fragrans, for instance, is simply the male of the true S. japonica. The first plant of S. japonica which flowered in this country was named S. oblata, but has been proved to be identical with the one named S. japonica by Thunberg. That name has been transferred to it, and the one called S. japonica in gardens is now called S. Fortunei. The Skimmias thrive as well in strong clay as in poor sandy soil and peat. S. japonica is one of the very best town Evergreens we possess. Other forms of S. japonica are S. Foremani, S. Rogersi, S. oblata ovata, S. o. Veitchi, and S. fragrantissima. To produce beautiful

S. oleracea is a native of temperate Sikkim, and has been in cultivation for many years at Kew. It is somewhat difficult to manage where the plants are disturbed periodically, and is a slow grower, slow to increase, and a shy seeder. It is the most striking of the few species of this genus in cultivation, and in the south at any rate it will be found hardy, succeeding best in a rich peaty soil with a northern exposure. It is called Chokli-bi by the natives of Sikkim, where the young flower-heads, sheathed in their tender green covering, form an excellent vegetable.

S. racemosa and **S. stellata** are natives of North America, both white-flowered and hardy. They may be cultivated with ease in the mixed flower border, where in May and June they are very attractive.— D. D.

SMILAX (*Green Briar*).—Distinct and handsome climbing shrubs, nearly all evergreen. They are most suitable for walls, but several may be grown over large tree roots or may be trained over tree trunks, requiring in this case the most sheltered position that can be found. In some cases it is not the low winter temperature that kills, but rather the insufficiency of summer warmth that prevents development. All the kinds respond to good dry soil, and if the soil is not good it should be made so. If suitable cuttings can be got they will usually strike, but there is sometimes difficulty in rooting them. The plants may sometimes be divided, or pieces may be taken off, which readily make plants, and this is usually the surest method of propagation for hardy kinds. The following are the more hardy kinds of Smilax cultivated in this country :—

S. ASPERA.—A well-marked species, with angular and usually prickly stems, reaching a height of about 5 ft., or even 10 ft. In colour the leaves are dark green, with flecks of white on the upper surface, and the flowers whitish and fragrant. It is a native of South Europe and the Canaries, and has many varieties.

S. A. VAR. BUCHANANIANA. — With this variety I am acquainted only by a specimen at Kew. It has a long leaf, with numerous marginal setæ. I do not find the name in books, but the plant is distinct and is probably a native of India.

Smilax aspera.

S. A. VAR. MACULATA.—This is marked by a dense growth of slender stems, reaching a height of about 3 ft. and bearing leaves of small size, so dark as to be almost coppery in colour.

S. A. VAR. MAURITANICA has angular stems which reach a considerable height. The stems and branches have few prickles, and they are rare on the leaves. It is a handsome plant, native of the Mediterranean and the Canaries.

S. BONA-NOX (*Bristly Green Briar*).—The root-stocks have large tubers; the stems are slightly angled, the branches often four-angled, the leaves green and shining on both sides, and their margins are fringed with needle-like prickles. N. America.

S. CANTAB.—For many years this has been cultivated in the Cambridge Botanic Garden. It is evergreen, the strong shoots reaching a height of about 12 ft. or more, the stems round, armed with strong, straight green prickles; the branches slender, and usually without prickles. The male flowers are fragrant, in umbels of about eight to twelve. This plant is, perhaps, nearest to *S. rotundifolia* among the hardier kinds, but the leaves differ distinctly in shape.

S. GLAUCA.—The height of this plant is about 3 ft. It has stems, branches and twigs angled, armed with rather stout numerous or

A Smilax in fruit.

scattered prickles, or may sometimes be without any. The leaves are partially persistent, glaucous beneath and sometimes above. N. America.

S. HERBACEA.—I am not sure that this is worth cultivation outside of a botanic garden, but it is easily grown as an ordinary herbaceous plant and is sure to be interesting. The tubers are numerous, short and thick, the stems unarmed, usually branched, and bearing ovate leaves with numerous tendrils. Its herbaceous habit distinguishes it from all others in cultivation. N. America and Japan.

S. HISPIDA.—This is quite a distinct plant on account of the stems, which are usually thickly hispid with slender straight prickles. The leaves are thin and green on both surfaces, the margins usually toothed. N. America.

S. LAURIFOLIA.—A high climbing species, the stems round, armed with strong straight prickles, the branches angled, mostly unarmed. It is evergreen, and the plant is easily recognised by its leathery, bright green, three-nerved leaves, elliptic in shape. A fine specimen of this I have seen in Canon Ellacombe's garden at Bitton. N. America.

S. PSEUDO-CHINA.—The lower part of the stem is armed with straight, needle-like prickles, the upper part and the branches mostly unarmed. The leaves become leathery when old. They are ovate, often narrowed about the middle or lobed at the base, seven or nine-nerved and green on both sides, sometimes toothed on the margin. N. America and the West Indies.

S. ROTUNDIFOLIA (*Green Briar*).—A high climbing species with large, thin and nearly

3 G

round leaves   The stems, branches and young shoots often four-angled, the prickles are stout, scattered, and sometimes a little curved.   This is a handsome strong growing species, and I have had fine specimens from Mr. Burbidge, of the Trinity College Botanic Gardens, Dublin   N America.   *Syns S caduca* and *S. quadrangularis.*

S TAMNOIDES,—Under this name at Kew in the Bamboo Garden is a plant of very satisfactory qualities, growing freely and illustrating well how such a plant may be used to ramble over tree stumps and help to make a mass of picturesque vegetation   It has the habit of a free-growing *S. aspera*, and at the time of my visit was bearing numerous black berries

S. WALTERI has stems angled, prickly below, the branches usually unarmed   The berries are bright red, but I am not aware that they are produced in this country   N America   R IRWIN LYNCH.

SOLANUM (*Potato Tree*) — A family of many species that are graceful when young and free-growing, but too ragged for a tasteful garden , some kinds require a warmer clime than ours.   Most of the Solanums may be raised from seed or from cuttings, the latter making good plants by May. The kinds named may be associated with the larger-leaved plants, but do not as a rule attain the height and vigour of those of the first rank like Ricinus   As a rule, they require a temperate house in winter, and about the middle or end of May should be planted out in a warm sheltered position in rich light soil   The Potato tree (S crispum), a native of Chili, is the only ornamental Solanum hardy enough for the open air.   In the south and in coast districts it may be grown without any protection, but elsewhere it needs the shelter of a wall   When fully grown, it is 12 to 16 ft high, and in late summer has large clusters of fine purple-blue flowers, which, in the most favoured spots, are succeeded by small whitish berries   When grown against a wall, it should be pruned vigorously in autumn, or it will be injured by frosts , but when it thrives as a standard this is unnecessary   S jasminoides is the most beautiful of the family we know of in England, and a lovely hardy climber   With its delicate white and starry flowers and trusses, it is one of the most delightful things for planting against the walls of the house in borders of peat or other light soil   It is frequently grown in greenhouses, but thrives on walls in southern England and Ireland generally   Other Solanums of note are the South American S betaceum, quite a small tree with oval pointed leaves like those of the Beet,

and deep green colour.   It is suitable for grouping in round beds with dwarfer plants or shrubs at its base, but is much more suitable for isolation on slopes, etc. A rich soil is best   In the variety purpureum the leaves are green, tinged with violet, and in other varieties the flowers are tinged with purple, the fruits being striped with brown   S. crinitum, from Guiana, is fine in medium-sized groups in the south of England, and one may mention also the late mauve-flowered S lanceolatum , S. macranthum, which grows in one year nearly 7 ft. high, the elegant leaves deeply cut ; S robustum, and the ornamental S Warscewiczi, resembling S macranthum, but dwarfer, more thick-set, and with small white flowers   The stem is armed with slightly recurved strong spines.   It is one of the best and most handsome of the Solanums.

SOLDANELLA. — Diminutive and charming alpine flowers, at one time considered very difficult to grow, but not really so if grown in peaty or sandy and moist soil, and coarse vigorous plants are kept away from them   They should always be in the rock-garden, and also in the part of the regular garden devoted to dwarf-plants   So long as the idea prevailed that the rock-garden was to be a heap of burnt bricks and other like rubbish piled up so that the first dry wind thoroughly dried up every root and plant upon it, these things could not be grown   S alpina is one of the most interesting of the plants growing near the snow-line on many of the great mountain-chains of Europe   It is not brilliant, but has beautiful pendent pale bluish flowers, bell-shaped, and cut into narrow strips   Three or four are borne on a stem 2 to 6 in high, springing from a dwarf carpet of feathery roundish shining leaves   The plants thrive best in moist districts, and in dry ones evaporation may be prevented by covering the ground near them with Cocoa-fibre which is mixed with sand to give it weight   The most suitable position is a level spot in the rock-garden near the eye   S alpina is increased by division, though being usually starved and delicate from confinement in small worm-defiled pots, exposed to daily vicissitudes, it is rarely strong enough to be pulled to pieces   S. montana is allied to S alpina, having larger leaves and purer blue flowers   Like S alpina it inhabits several of the great Continental chains, and thrives under the same treatment   It is readily increased by division, but the cause that usually renders S alpina too weak to be divided, renders S. montana weak also. S. pusilla has kidney-shaped leaves, with the corolla not deeply cut into fringes. The very small S. minima, with its minute round leaves and its single flower, fringed for a portion of its length only, is rare. Both of these plants thrive under the same conditions as the others; but, being much smaller, require more care in planting, viz. in a mixture of peat and good loam with plenty of sharp sand, and associated with minute alpine plants. They require plenty of water in summer. S. Clusii and S. Wheeleri are similar to those mentioned above. (Primrose order.)

SOLIDAGO (*Golden Rod*).—These N. American Composites in borders exterminate valuable plants, and give a coarse, ragged aspect to the garden. They are also such gross feeders as to impoverish any good border. They hold their own, however, in a copse, or a rough open shrubbery among the coarsest vegetation. For a full collection the best are S. altissima, S. canadensis, S. grandiflora, S. nutans, S. multiflora, S. rigida, and S. Virgaurea.

SOPHORA (*New Zealand Laburnum*). —*S. tetraptera* is a large tree in its own country, and makes a charming wall-plant here. The variety grandiflora has larger flowers and is more robust, while the variety microphylla is remarkable for finely-divided leaves and smaller flowers. In sheltered gardens against walls in the southern and the mild parts all may be grown, though they may need extra protection in severe winters. Another species in cultivation

Sophora japonica

is S. chilensis, which also needs protection. *Syn.,* Edwardsia.

S. japonica (*Pagoda Tree*).—One of the finest of flowering trees, elegant in foliage, and, in September, covered with clusters of white bloom. It is one of the

largest of trees, and when old has a wide-spreading head with huge limbs. Its long pinnate leaves retain their deep-green colour until autumn. Where space is limited it may be kept in bounds by hard pruning. There are several varieties —a drooping kind, which is one of the best of all pendulous trees, and a variegated-leaved kind, which is not satisfactory, as the variegation is seldom good.

SPARAXIS.—Charming bulbous plants from the Cape of Good Hope, the many varieties coming chiefly from S. grandiflora and S. tricolor. They are about 1 ft. high, of slender growth, and bear large showy flowers which vary from white to bright scarlet and deep crimson, usually having dark centres. Sparaxis are valuable for early-summer flower, and should be treated like Ixias. S. pulcherrima (the Wand-flower), is so distinct that its claim to be a

Sparaxis pulcherrima (Wand Flower).

Sparaxis has often been made the subject of comment. Its tall and graceful flower-stems rise to a height of 5 or 6 ft., and wave in the wind, but, though slender, are so tough and wiry that they are never broken in a storm, like the much stouter and much stronger-looking stems of the Pampas Grass For six or seven weeks S pulcherrima has lovely Foxglove-shaped bells on almost invisible wire-like lateral foot-stalks Though the flowers of the type are usually rosy-purple, there are forms which are nearly white, and some of almost every intermediate shade, while others are beautifully striped S pulcherrima is finer and more elegant than *S Thunbergi*, which is stiffer and much dwarfer—its erect flower-stems being seldom more than 2½ ft high—and its flowers have very short stalks, whilst they are not pendulous The best position for S pulcherrima is in clumps among sheltering shrubs. In such a position it might be associated with Tritonia aurea, as the two plants flower together S pulcherrima is about as hardy as Tritonia, Montbretia Pottsi, and similar plants, and, though more difficult to establish, well repays a little care during the first year or two It has a great objection to removal, and, if necessary, this should be done as soon as the flowers begin to fade It succeeds in dry as well as damp positions, if it has a rich friable soil, or if when beginning to grow it is well watered

SPARTIUM (*Spanish Broom*) — *S junceum* is a South European shrub, blooming in July, August, and September, when shrubberies are usually flowerless It is thin-growing, 8 or 10 ft high, and its Rush-like shoots have so few leaves as to appear leafless It bears erect clusters of fragrant bright yellow flowers shaped like Pea-blossoms, is perfectly hardy, and useful for dry, poor soils, where, like the common Broom, it does well, coming freely from seed scattered broadcast where we wish it to grow.

SPECULARIA (*Venus's Looking-glass*) —These are similar to Campanulas, and often placed with them, though distinct enough for garden purposes S Speculum, with numerous open bell-like bright violet-purple flowers, is one of the showiest of our annuals Besides the large-flowered form called grandiflora, sometimes purple and sometimes white, there is a double-flowered kind which comes true from seed, also a dwarf compact form with violet-blue flowers S pentagonia is another favourite, its flowers larger, but less abundant than those of S Speculum, purple in colour, with a deep blue centre S. Speculum and S. pentagonia generally scatter seed, which germinates year after year, and no trouble is necessary, except to prevent the plants getting too plentiful. Both are hardy

SPHENOGYNE.—*S. speciosa* is a beautiful half-hardy Mexican annual Composite of slender, much-branched growth, about 1 ft high. The flowers, produced from July to September, are yellow with a brownish centre encircled by a conspicuous black ring, the centre being orange in the variety aurea. S. speciosa will succeed if sown in the open in spring, but it does better as a half-hardy annual, sown in early spring in heat, in any ordinary light soil. S anthemoides, introduced last century, and also called sometimes Arctotis anthemoides, differs from S. speciosa in having the underside of the florets purplish instead of yellow. Though a large and varied family, these are the only kinds to our knowledge in cultivation *Syn.*, Ursinia pulchra

SPIGELIA (*Worm Grass*)—*S Marilandica* is a beautiful native of North America, distinct from all other hardy plants It forms a dense tuft of slender stems about 1 ft high, each being terminated by long tubular flowers which are deep red outside and deep yellow inside The plant is rare in gardens, being considered difficult to cultivate In its native country it grows in sheltered situations, the roots finding their way deep down into a body of rich vegetable mould. These natural conditions should be imitated; and if the soil be not good, take it out 2 ft. in depth and fill up with a well-sanded mixture of loam, leaf-mould, and peat Partial shade in summer, with abundance of moisture in hot weather, is essential, whilst it is suitable for borders, the lower parts of the rock-garden, or for margins of beds of American plants

SPIRÆA (*Meadow Sweet*)—Beautiful plants in nature, and important for the garden, of easy culture, distinct habit, and often of fine form They grow well in rich soil in borders, and are also excellent for the margins of water There are also a number of shrubby species of the highest value.

S. Aruncus (*Goat's-beard*) is a vigorous perennial, 3 to 5 ft. high, beautiful in foliage and habit as well as in flower Its flowers are freely produced in summer in large gracefully-drooping plumes S. Aruncus is as good in midsummer as the Pampas Grass is in autumn It is valuable for grouping with other fine-foliaged herbaceous plants It thrives in ordinary soil, but succeeds best in a deep moist loam Division Various parts of Europe, Asia, and America

S. astilboides is a new species, and of unusual merit for borders It is a moisture-loving plant, and will be found more satisfactory in every way on the banks of a stream or pond. It is quite distinct, the inflorescence much branched, and the flowers of a creamy white closely packed on the stems.—K.

S. Filipendula (*Dropwort*).—A British species, 1 to 2 ft. high, with loose clusters of yellowish-white flowers, often tipped with

Spiræa Aruncus.

red. When the flower-stems are pinched off, it forms an effective edging plant, its Fern-like foliage being distinct. The double variety (S. Filipendula fl.-pl.) is useful in the mixed border. Division.

S. gigantea, recently introduced, may be described as a gigantic Meadow Sweet, growing from 6 to 10 ft. high, with huge palmate leaves and large fleecy bunches of white flowers terminating the tall stems. Its place is in rich bottoms or by water in deep soil.

S. lobata (*Queen of the Prairie*) is one of the handsomest of the hardy Spiræas, and from 18 to 36 in. high, with deep rosy carmine flowers in large terminal cymes. It does best in sandy loam in the mixed border, on the margins of shrubberies, or in beds among groups of the finer perennials. Similar to S. lobata are the handsome S. Humboldti and S. digitata. *Syn.* S. venusta.

S. palmata is a beautiful herbaceous species, and among the finest of hardy plants. It has handsome palmate foliage, and in late summer broad clusters of lovely rosy-crimson blossoms. When well-grown it is 4 ft. high, but often less, and being considered tender, is grown largely in pots ; but it is hardy, succeeding in moist deep loam well enriched by

decayed manure. It is a fine plant for many positions in large rock-gardens, in borders, or on the margin of shrubberies ; and may be naturalised, as it is quite vigorous enough to take care of itself. It looks best in masses. The variety elegans is said to be a hybrid ; the flowers pale pink, and altogether inferior to the best forms of S. palmata. A good effect is got by planting the species by the edge of streams or ponds : a mass of lovely colour is presented to the eye, and too-often bare spots are clothed with beauty.

S. Ulmaria.—This common British Meadow Sweet is seldom cultivated, but worse things are often seen in borders. It deserves a place, if only for the sake of variety, in the mixed border, on the margins of shrubberies, or in the rougher parts of pleasure-grounds, where it may be planted with other subjects which do not require much looking after. Almost any soil will suit it, but a moist one is best. The variegated-leaved form is ornamental, the creamy-yellow and green variegation being effective.

SHRUBBY MEADOW SWEETS.

S. ariæfolia (*Spray Bush*), a lovely shrub 8 to 10 ft. high, and I have seen it much higher grown on walls. It is of proved merit and hardiness, and we should seek to give full expression to its singular beauty by careful planting and grouping in the full sun— and taking care not to let it get destroyed in the horrible jumble that nurserymen and most other planters give us when they plant a "shrubbery." It is a kind often met with, but mostly in shrubbery thickets, while to show off its beauty to advantage it requires an open position. When isolated it forms a large bush of good form laden during summer with spray-like panicles of small whitish flowers.

S. cantoniensis (*Canton S.*) is a slender bush, about a yard high, bearing an abundance of small clusters of white flowers. There is also a beautiful less common double variety. The Plum-leaved Spiræa (S. prunifolia) is represented in gardens by the double variety (flore-pleno), a beautiful shrub, with flowers like tiny snow-white rosettes, in early summer wreathing every twig. S. media, better known in gardens as S. confusa, resembles S. cantoniensis, and therefore need not be included in a selection ; but its variety rotundiflora is pretty.

S. Douglasi and **S. Nobleana** are so similar in growth and flower that they may be conveniently coupled, though as they flower at different times it is well to have them both. They are of vigorous growth, and they bear dense erect clusters of deep red flowers. N. America. S. Douglasi succeeds in every part of the British Isles, but S. Nobleana is less hardy.

S. japonica (*Rosy Bush Meadow Sweet*) is easily recognised by its slender stems 3 or 4 ft. high, surmounted by broad flat clusters of deep pink flowers. The

japonica, very dwarf and compact, rapid in growth and hardy, about 2 ft. high, with broad clusters of deep rose-pink flowers. A fine new variety is A. Waterer. Even in such a beautiful family it outshines in brilliancy of colour. It is a variety of S. japonica, which for the last thirty or forty years has been known in gardens under other names, such as S. callosa, Fortunei, the name S. japonica having been errone-

Spiræa ariæfolia.

varieties splendens, rubra, superba, and atro-sanguinea are richer and deeper than the type, while the variety alba bears white flowers in small clusters. It is a variable species, and has numerous synonyms. All the varieties in catalogues ranged under the names S. callosa and Fortunei belong properly to S. japonica. S. bella is dwarfer and denser than S. japonica. S. Bumalda is a variety of S.

ously applied to a totally different plant, in fact—Astilbe or Hoteia japonica. The parent of A. Waterer is the variety of S. japonica named S. Bumalda, which is distinguished from the type by its dwarfer growth and persistent bloom throughout the summer and autumn. From S. Bumalda the A. Waterer variety does not differ except in brilliancy of colour.

S. Hypericifolia, from Asia Minor, is

the type of a small group, all elegant in growth and pretty in flower. The tall slender stems arch over gracefully, and in good soils and sheltered spots reach a height of 8 ft. In the flowering season the branches are wreathed with small clusters of small white flowers. S.

Spiræa japonica, A. Waterer.

flagelliformis and S. acuta are forms superior to the type.

S. Thunbergi (*Thunberg's Meadow Sweet*) is a favourite shrub for forcing into early flower. It is a dense bush, with small bright green leaves, and in early spring a profusion of tiny white blossoms. It is hardy, and especially suitable for planting in a bold rock-garden or on a raised bank among tree-stems. Few shrubs are so fine in autumn, its small leaves changing to brilliant crimson.

S. Lindleyana (*Plume Meadow Sweet*) is a noble shrub, sometimes 10 ft. high, its graceful foliage divided, and delicate green, the flower clusters large, white, and plume-like, being at their best about the middle of August. It thrives best in warm deep soil, not too light or too heavy, and should be sheltered from cold winds, which injure its young growth in spring. It has in some soils peculiar ways, and in others, especially of a chalky and warm nature, it blooms well enough to deserve the epithet superb. In cool soils it does not always attain such a grand flowering state. In too cool soils it seems to spread more at the root, but in all cases is beautiful for its foliage and habit. Himalaya. Division. The other pinnate-leaved Spiræas, such as S. sorbifolia and S. Pallasi, are less desirable.

There are so many confusing names applied to these plants, and so many useless varieties, that the following remarks by Mr. Goldring are worth attention :—
In a large genus like Spiræa numbering

half a hundred reputed species and encumbered with almost twice the number of names and synonyms, how perplexing it must be to single out the choice few required for the garden, and when there is absolutely no information given in nursery catalogues as to the respective merits of the kinds enumerated.

The bush Spiræas are all beautiful ; none are worthless in the sense that many other shrubs are, so that there is naturally a tendency among those who know them best to eulogise every kind ; but how few are the gardens where there is need for more than a dozen kinds in proportion to the host of other beautiful shrubs, unless it be in those where the object is to collect as many sorts as possible !

The fact is, we have now too great a number of Spiræas and too great a similarity among many of them, and flowering much about the same time. As an instance of this I count in a Continental catalogue no fewer than twenty varieties of the common North American S. salicifolia, and the synonyms of these number

Spiræa sorbifolia.

half as many. No collection of Spiræas need number more than a dozen kinds to represent the finest types of beauty of flower and growth. Good grouping of this select dozen kinds in a garden would produce better effect than the too common way of dotting about single plants of many kinds which, when crowded by other shrubs of diverse habit, never display that free growth which constitutes one of the charms of the shrubby Meadow Sweets.

My dozen would include the following kinds, which are placed according to their average heights, beginning with the tallest:—S. Lindleyana, ariæfolia, Douglasi, trilobata var. Van Houttei, prunifolia fl. pl., japonica superba, confusa, canescens var. flagellata, cantoniensis, bella, Thunbergi, and japonica Bumalda.

The above selection includes types of all the sections, and is sufficient for any garden in a general way, but should more be required, a second dozen may be selected to include the following :—S. opulifolia, salicifolia grandiflora, Nobleana, sorbifolia, japonica paniculata, cana, Blumei, japonica ruberrima, tomentosa, crenata, japonica alba, and bullata (crispifolia).

From these selections I have excluded

Douglasi, and others, and lesser groups of the dwarfer kinds, or these may form masses at jutting-out portions of a main tree and shrub group. The small kinds, such as Bumalda, should always be planted in a group. This does not necessarily imply that one must plant a hundred of a sort at the outset, but a definite plan should be made in one's mind as to where the bold groups of good colours shall be, and then a dozen plants can in the course of a few seasons be made to extend throughout the projected group by propagating.

Contrast a Spiræa—any of them—growing in a deep moist loam with one growing in a poor, gravelly, or sandy soil. One would scarcely at first think they were of the same kind. The fact is

Spiræa Bumalda.

that fine shrub Exochorda grandiflora, which is sometimes known as Spiræa grandiflora.

Let me plead on their behalf against the baneful practice of planting such graceful shrubs in the "mixed" shrubbery, where the delicate have to fight the strong, and where one seldom sees a healthy shrub. Such is not the place for these elegant plants, which being for the most part surface-rooters cannot bear to be encroached upon by ravenous Laurels and the like. The place for Spiræas is an open, sunny spot, away from the roots of big trees and shrubs, yet connected with the main masses of shrubbery by intelligent grouping. If a garden were large enough, I should always have isolated groups (good bold masses from 10 to 15 ft. across), of the taller-growing kinds, such as S. Lindleyana ariæfolia,

shrubs and ornamental trees require cultivating in order to get their beauty. Even if the soil is good and deep, the site for Spiræas and suchlike shrubs should be thoroughly and deeply trenched at the outset if good results are expected.

It should be remembered that Spiræas generally are lovers of moisture, and I have noticed where I have seen them growing wild in Japan and America that they like moist places. If they were not near streams or boggy places, they were growing best where plenty of moisture reached them. Some grow actually in boggy places, and the finest Spiræas I have seen in English gardens have been on the margins of lakes and streams. Wherever there are moist spots in a garden, such as near a pond, lake, or stream, there should groups of Spiræas be planted. Spiræa Lindleyana is a grand shrub for the water-side planted in bold groups, and masses of others might be made to fringe a lake or stream in a beautiful way.

For a full account of the Spiræas I refer the reader to *The Garden* (Vol. XII.), where the late Mr. Gordon described in detail about fifty kinds, and to the notes on Spiræas scattered through every one of the many volumes of *The Garden.*—W. G.

SPRAGUEA *S. umbellata* is a singular and pretty plant allied to Claytonia, 6 to 9 in. high, with fleshy foliage, and spikes of showy pinkish blossoms. If seeds are

perennial, about 1 ft. high, and if planted in a partially-shaded border succeeds in any soil. It has spikes of red flowers. Division.

STAPHYLEA (*Bladder Nut*).—Only S. colchica is important, this being a beautiful shrub with pinnate leaves, and in early summer large terminal clusters of snow-white flowers. It is hardy, and grows well in any good soil, preferring partial shade ; but it is commonly forced into flower for the greenhouse in early spring.

STATICE (*Sea Lavender*).—Plants of the Leadwort or Plumbago family, all dwarf perennials or annuals, chiefly natives of

Spiræa Lindleyana.

sown early in February in a warm frame, and the seedlings are afterwards pricked out singly in small pots, and planted out in May, the plants will bloom in August and September ; but if sown in May, the plants will not flower till the following summer. In light soils S. umbellata will resist an ordinary winter, but is best protected by a frame. Like most tap-rooted plants, it does not bear transplantation well, except while small. If seeds are plentiful they may be sown in the open ground ; but, as seeds are usually scarce, they should be sown in pots, in a moderate temperature. California.

STACHYS (*Woundwort*). — Few of these perennials are worth cultivating, the common S. lanata, the woolly-leaved plant, being used for edging, thriving in any soil. S. coccinea is a rather pretty

shore and mountain districts. Most of them bear large twiggy flower-stems covered with myriads of small flowers, which are for the most part dry and membraneous, and long retain their colour after being cut, so that they are frequently mixed with other everlasting flowers for vase decoration in winter. The larger species require least care when in an open exposed bed of sandy soil, while many of them are admirable for the rock-garden. The best of the larger kinds are S. Limonium, of which there are several varieties ; S. latifolia, the finest of all, with wide-spreading flower-stems with a profusion of small purplish-blue flowers ; and S. tatarica, a dwarfer species, with distinct red flowers. The smaller species, such as S. minuta, S. minutiflora, S. caspia, S. eximia, are good rock-plants. Among the half-hardy annuals and biennials the best are : S. Bonduelli (yellow), a biennial if protected in winter ; S. spicata, with spikes of small rosy flowers ; Thouini (violet), very free flowering ; and sinuata (purple and white), pretty, and easy to grow. There are several varieties of S. sinuata hybrida which have varied colours, and make pretty border flowers. All the annual and biennial Statices should be raised from seed in early spring, and planted out when large enough. The half-hardy biennials need protection during winter, and should not be planted out until the spring after they are raised.

STAUNTONIA.—*S. hexaphylla* is a fine evergreen twining pinnate-leaved shrub from China, hardy enough in the south and in the warmer parts of these islands for wall-culture. Its small flowers are whitish, fragrant, and produced in early summer. It must have a sheltered sunny wall, and during severe frosts be protected in a simple way.

Stenactis. See ERIGERON.

STEPHANANDRA.—Graceful shrubs allied to the Spiræas, these need good soil for one to see them at their best. They like a good loamy soil, well drained, but still moist, and are some of the most easily propagated of shrubs. Cuttings taken towards the end of the summer before the wood is too hard root readily ; they can also be increased by division. I have noticed that when plants of *S. flexuosa* which have been growing long in one spot are removed, quite a little thicket of young plants will spring from the roots left in the ground.

S. FLEXUOSA.—Although the earlier introduced of the two species, this has not long been in cultivation. It grows 3 ft. to 4 ft. high with us, but will probably get to be quite twice as high in more favourable climates. It forms a thick bush, suckering freely from the base like a Spiræa or a Kerria, and, like those plants, is improved by an occasional thinning out of the older growths. As it is chiefly for the graceful arching shoots clothed with the prettily cut foliage that it is grown, this shrub is seen to greatest advantage as an isolated bush or in a small group. Its branches are thin, wiry, and crooked, and it blossoms in June, the flowers being crowded on short branching panicles, small and greenish white. Japan and Corea. *Syn. Spiræa incisa.*

S. TANAKÆ.—From *S. flexuosa* this new species is readily distinguished by its coarser, more succulent growth and by its larger, but much less-divided leaves. The flowers are small and greenish, and, being less crowded on the longer, lax panicles, add even less to the attractiveness of the plant than do those of *S. flexuosa.* Japan. W. J. BEAN.

STERNBERGIA (*Lily-of-the-Field*).

—Pretty and interesting hardy bulbs, the flowers of much firmer texture, and able to withstand a far greater amount of bad weather than those of the autumn-blooming Crocus, and are thus better adapted for our climate. One source of failure with Sternbergias is moving them at the wrong time or before growth has fully developed. What they want is thorough ripening in summer and a slight protection, such as dry litter, during the winter. In sandy loams, and fully exposed to the sun, the bulbs will get the necessary ripening without being lifted, and the best plan will be to leave them undisturbed until they attain flowering size. We have them thriving on stiff soils and blooming freely every year, and for many years in the same border.

S. **colchiciflora.**—This is one of the old garden plants, having been cultivated by Clusius and Parkinson. It is described as fragrant, and perfuming, with its Jessamine-scented flowers, the fields of the Crimea about the Bosphorus. The leaves are narrow, and come with the fruit in spring : and the sulphur-yellow flowers appear in autumn at about the same time as those of S. lutea. It is found on dry exposed positions in the Cau-

Sternbergia lutea.

casus and Crimea, and is hardy in this country. S. dalmatica and S. pulchella are varieties.

S. **Fischeriana** is nearly allied, hardy, and has the habit of S. lutea, from which it differs chiefly in flowering in spring instead of autumn, and by its stalked ovary and capsule. Caucasus.

S lutea. — This is the great autumn or winter Daffodil of Parkinson, and a very pretty hardy plant, best on some gravelly soils The absence of seed on this bulb in a cultivated state is remarkable, seeing how plentiful it is and also how well it flowers in many parts of the country

My experience tells me that the bulbs must be large before they will flower freely, and imported bulbs are generally small, and will take a year or two to attain flowering size S lutea has five or six leaves, each about half an inch broad, about a foot long, and appearing at the same time as the flowers in autumn. It is supposed by some writers to be the Lily of Scripture, as it grows abundantly in the vales in Palestine S angustifolia appears to be a narrow-leaved form, very free-flowering, and growing rather more freely than S lutea.

S. græca, from the mountains of Greece, has very narrow leaves and broad perianth segments

S. sicula is a form with narrower leaves and segments than the type, while the Cretan variety has considerably larger flowers

S. macrantha.—This is a really handsome species, the leaves blunt and slightly glaucous, about an inch broad when fully developed about midsummer ; flowers bright yellow in autumn Asia Minor. —D D

As for some time these plants are not likely to be common, the rarest of them should have a place in our bulb borders, or on rocky borders in gritty or open soil, associated with the rarer Narcissi and the choicer hardy bulbs The effect of the oldest cultivated kind in masses near the shelter of walls in autumn is very fine

STIPA (*Feather Grass*)—None of the stipas is so elegant as the S European S pennata In bundles its beauty almost equals that of the tail of a bird of paradise S pennata is hardly to be distinguished from a strong stiff tuft of common Grass, except in May and June, when the tuft is surmounted by numerous gracefully-arching flower-stems, nearly 2 ft. high, and covered with long, twisted, feathery spikes It loves a deep sandy loam, and may be used either in an isolated position or in groups of small plants, but its flowers are too short-lived except for borders Division or seed S calamagrostis, S capillata, and S elegantissima are other good Feather Grasses

STOKESIA —*S cyanea* is a handsome hardy American perennial, 18 to 24 in high, and of stout free growth, with, in September, large showy blue flowers somewhat similar to those of a China Aster. It grows freely in good warm soils, but from its late flowering does not always expand its flowers well. In damp localities, place a hand-light over the plants at the flowering season, but so arranged as to allow free admission of air. S cyanea is useful for the conservatory in autumn and winter Division in spring Insert the slips a few inches apart in a warm border or a frame, in sharp sandy soil As soon as they get well rooted and begin to grow, transplant them A little river sand and leaf-mould should be mixed with the soil

STRATIOTES (*Water Soldier*) — *S. aloides* is an interesting native water-plant with a compact vasiform tuft of leaves, from the centre of which arises in summer a spike of unattractive blossoms In artificial lakes or ponds it will take care of itself

STRUTHIOPTERIS (*Ostrich Fern*) — The fronds of these fine hardy exotic Ferns are not unlike ostrich feathers They are of two kinds, fertile and sterile, the former being always grouped in the centre of the plant, and the latter forming a cordon round them Struthiopteris can be increased by division of the creeping underground stems, which run for some distance round well-established plants. Good well-drained peat and loam is necessary, and group the plants in bold slightly-sheltered spots, where their noble appearance will tell As they are deciduous, plant among and around them, for winter effect, some Polystichums or other robust evergreen Ferns, while, for effect at other seasons, some of our finer Lilies would form a useful mixture The kinds suited for gardens are S germanica and S pennsylvanica The former is one of the most elegant of hardy Ferns, having fronds nearly 3 ft. long, and well suited for the slopes of pleasure - grounds, cascades, grottoes, the rough rock-garden, and for the margins of streams and pieces of water, it will thrive either in the full sun or in the shade S pennsylvanica closely resembles it, but has narrow fertile fronds. Both kinds add much beauty of form to a garden, and should not be confined to a fernery

STUARTIA —Among the rarest and choicest of hardy - flowering deciduous shrubs They are allied to the Camellia, and S virginica and S pentagyna are both natives of N. America, being introduced during the last century The former is the best known, and fine specimens may be found in several old English gardens. It is a rounded and spreading bush, 6 to 10 ft. high, and in early summer, usually about May, bears creamy-white flowers with crimson-red stamens, about 3 in. across, in shape like those of a single Rose. In the neighbourhood of London and in gardens of Sussex and other coast counties S. virginica is perfectly hardy, the finest specimens we have seen being in a rather moist light soil in situations well exposed to the sun, but sheltered on the north and east by trees and shrubs. S. virginica and S. pentagyna (labelled in some gardens Malachodendron ovatum) are both of slow growth, but the latter is rather larger and taller than the former, and with similar white flowers. Its native habitat is said to be more northern than that of S. virginica, and it is therefore considered the hardier. S. pseudo-Camellia resembles the other two in growth, foliage, and habit, but its flowers are larger and whiter, and have yellow stamens instead of red. It has withstood full exposure for some years in the Coombe Wood Nursery in Surrey. These Stuartias are so beautiful when in bloom that they should be well grown, and though sometimes thought capricious, there must be numerous gardens where the exact conditions suited to them could be found.

STYLOPHORUM.—*S. diphyllum* is a handsome Poppywort, which somewhat resembles Celandine (Chelidonium majus), but is a much finer plant. Its foliage is grayish, and its large bright yellow flowers are freely produced in early summer. S. diphyllum is 1 to 2 ft. high. N. America. *Syns.*—S. ohioense and S. japonicum.

STYRAX (*Storax*).—The Styraxes are deciduous shrubs, the Japanese kinds being pretty when in flower, and, though rare in gardens, are likely to become generally cultivated. S. serrulata (also called S. japonica) is beautiful. It is now becoming common in some of the best nurseries, but has not been introduced long enough to show what size it will grow to in this country. Though in Japan it is said to be a tall tree, here it is known only as a dense shrub of neat habit. Its white flowers have a tuft of yellow stamens about three-quarters of an inch across, and are shaped like a shallow bell. They are profusely borne singly on thin stalks, on the under sides of the flattish branches, and, with the foliage, look pretty about midsummer. The variety S. virgata is also in cultivation. Both the type and the variety grow freely in the open border,

in a light position in good soil, and seem thoroughly suitable for the southern parts of England and warm districts. The N. American kinds, S. americana and S. pulverulenta, are not important, as they flower less freely, and are rarer. S. officinalis, which yields the Storax of commerce, is not so pretty as S. serrulata.

SWERTIA (*Marsh Swertia*). — *S. perennis* has slender erect stems, 1 to 3 ft. high, terminated by erect spikes of flowers, which are grayish-purple spotted with black, and produced in summer. It is not showy, but interesting for the bog-garden, or for moist spots near the rock-garden, and may be naturalised in damp places in peaty soil. Seed or division.

SYMPHORICARPUS (*Snowberry*).— The common Snowberry (S. racemosus) is a familiar shrub, but we would exclude it from a choice selection; also the Wolf Berry (S. occidentalis); and S. vulgaris, the Coral Berry, or Indian Currant, which has small purplish berries in clusters. The flowers of these kinds are not showy, their growth is not neat, and they smother choicer things. Their chief value is for pleasure-grounds, for undergrowth in woods, or for ornamental covert (as birds eat the berries), and they all flourish under almost any circumstances. A pretty variety of S. vulgaris has its foliage variegated with green and yellow. It is now common, and, being hardy and vigorous, is one of the best of variegated shrubs.

SYMPHYANDRA.— Campanula-like plants, S. pendula being a showy perennial from the rocky parts of the Caucasus, with branched pendulous stems and large cream-coloured bell-like flowers, almost hidden in the leaves. It is hardy, and rarely more than 1 ft. in height. It likes to be associated with most Bell-flowers, but is best seen at the level of the eye in the rock-garden; it is also a good border plant in ordinary garden soil. Seed. The Austrian S. Wanneri rarely exceeds 1 ft. in height, with deep mauve flowers borne freely on branching racemes. Like S. pendula, it prefers a light, warm, rich soil and a partially-shady situation. Both plants are short-lived, and duplicates should be kept at hand.

SYMPHYTUM(*Comfrey*).—These Borage-worts are chiefly bold, but somewhat coarse plants, suited for naturalising in rather open sunny places, since, when well developed, their foliage has a fine effect in masses. The largest and best kinds for the wild garden are S. asperrimum and S. caucasicum. The Bohemian Comfrey (S. bohemicum) is a handsome perennial, about 1 ft. high, with in early summer erect twin racemes of brilliant reddish-purple flowers. The variegated-leaved form of the common Comfrey (S. officinale) has striking variegation. S. officinale is effective in a garden of hardy flowers, although generally seen only in mixed collections of hardy variegated plants. Like S. bohemicum it succeeds in any ordinary garden soil in open sunny borders.

SYRINGA (*Lilac*).—Beautiful flowering shrubs, thriving well in Britain, though not so well in some cold soils and places where late frosts are frequent. Most of the common Lilacs may be classed in three species, viz. the common Lilac (S. vulgaris), the Chinese Lilac (S. chinensis), and the Persian Lilac (S. persica). There are several sorts of the first two. Of the white varieties the best are Marie Legrange, Alba grandiflora, Alba magna, and Alba virginalis. If only one white kind is selected, it should be Marie Legrange. The finest of the coloured sorts is Souvenir de L. Spath, which has massive clusters of large richly-coloured flowers. Charles the Tenth is a first-rate sort, and usually forced into early bloom, when its flowers are white. Other kinds of good colour are Alphonse Lavallée, Louis Van Houtte, Rubra de Marley, Le Gaulois, and Aline Mocquery. Some double sorts have recently come into cultivation, the chief ones being Lemoinei, Ranunculiflora, Renoncule, Hyacinthiflora plena, and Rubella plena. These have denser flower-clusters, and usually last longer than the single varieties. An indispensable Lilac is the small Persian (S. persica) which is distinct from the others, and, being dwarf and erect, is well suited for the outskirts of a group of Lilacs or a shrubbery. Its small flower-clusters are of a pale lilac, or are nearly white. The pretty variety, with deeply-cut leaves (laciniata), must not be overlooked. The Rouen or Chinese Lilac (S. chinensis), also known as S. dubia and S. rothomagensis, is intermediate between the common Lilac and the Persian Lilac, and, like the latter, is desirable. The large S. Emodi, from the Himalayas, is coarse in growth, and not remarkable for its flowers, which are pale purple. They come after those of the common Lilac are past. There is a variegated form. The Hungarian Lilac (S. Josikæa) is a pretty shrub, different from other Lilacs. It reaches a height of nearly 6 ft., and bears erect spikes of small pale mauve flowers. S. japonica, known also as S. amurensis and Ligustrina amurensis, bears in summer large dense clusters of creamy-white flowers, which

somewhat resemble those of the Japanese Privet. Though a native of Japan, it is suitable for English gardens. Though deep loamy soil best suits Lilacs, they will grow in almost any ground. Attention should be given to pruning, especially to removing root-suckers as they appear. The shrubs are often grafted on the Privet, but die on it. All who care for Lilacs should get plants from layers of all the finer sorts.

The species of syringa are *amurensis*, Manchoo ; *chinensis*, China ; *Émodi*, N. India ; *josikæa*, Transsylvania ; *oblata*, China ; *persica*, Persia, Caucasus ; *rotundifolia*, Manchoo ; *villosa*, China ; *vulgaris*, Transsylvania : *pubescens*, N. China ; *velutina*, China ; *yunnanensis*, W. China.

Very interesting as these species are from a botanical point of view little is yet known of their beauty in our country, and such of them as have been tried have less beauty than the finer hybrid forms of the old Lilac.

TAGETES.—The beautiful half-hardy French and African Marigolds have been for centuries favourite garden annual flowers. There are also perennial Tagetes, but they are not hardy enough to make satisfactory plants out-of-doors, though one or two, such as T. lucida and T. Parryi, are desirable. The annuals in cultivation are all natives of Mexico. The following are the best :—

T. erecta (*African Marigold*) is easily known by its stiff, erect habit, and massive double yellow blooms. A peculiarity of the African Marigold is that one-third of the seeds saved from the finest double flowers always produce single ones, while the rest are invariably double. A bed of them on the turf is finer when the deep orange and pale yellow forms are in association. Sow seed under glass in April, for then, even without bottom-heat, they will germinate freely. When the young plants are 3 in. in height, dibble them out again either into a frame or under hand-lights, as slugs are partial to the young plants. Where very large flowers are desired, the soil must be rich, and the buds on the branches should be thinned out.

T. patula (*French Marigold*) is a charming summer annual, the colours, not so limited as in the African Marigold, as there are many varieties striped, mottled, and coloured with yellow, orange, chestnut, and other hues. The older forms are coarser, spreading yet tall, and in good soil make huge plants, carrying scores of flowers of medium size, and if good, are double, rounded, sometimes partly reflexed, and invariably pretty. The striped forms can be kept true only by growing them free from other sorts, but even in the best strains the flowers vary. Sometimes one plant has striped

French Marigold, usually 12 to 15 in. high, with dense heads of perfect flowers. They make effective masses, and answer well as

Group of Tamarisk. From a photograph by G. Champion.

blooms, and at other times self-yellow or maroon flowers. The unpleasant odour unfits them for cutting. Of more recent introduction are the compact forms of the

edgings for beds of tall African Marigolds. Well harden them before being planted out, and put them singly, not in clumps.

T. signata is allied to the French

Marigold, but has much smaller flowers, either double or single. It was formerly largely used for summer bedding, its elegantly-cut leaves being perhaps its most pleasing feature. As it needs a little starving to induce it to bloom freely in beds and masses, the soil must be rather poor. Like all other Marigolds, it stands drought well. T. s. pumila is a dwarf form.

TAMARIX (*Tamarisk*). — Graceful hardy shrubs, often neglected owing to the too common habit of not grouping and making right use of each shrub in relation not only to soil, but also to exposure and position. Lost in the jumble of the shrubbery, these would never give any good effect, and would probably soon perish from the attacks of laurel, privet, elder, and other hungry rubbish of the conventional shrubbery, but their true use is for seashore gardens and for holding the soil of river banks. They are among the best shrubs, too, when we have to plant near the sea, the fine branches splitting up the winds. On shores they are often found all round the north of Africa and southern Europe, but they are also beautiful away from the shore if grouped properly in a full exposure. As to kinds, we are richer in names than in plants, a number of terms being nursery names for the few cultivated species and their varieties. Among hardy shrubs these are remarkably distinct in the feathery character of their growth. No other woody plants we can grow in the open air give the same fine effect as they do, and of the shrubs that can be grown on the seashore there is none so good.

T. chinensis is a recent introduction, and has been distributed from some nurseries as *T. japonica plumosa*. It is not quite so hardy as our native kind. It has very plumose branches, and is a most graceful shrub with pink flowers.

T. gallica (*French Tamarisk*). — Is found wild on the south-west coast of England, in France, and North Africa. It is a shrub 5 ft. to 10 ft. high, or in N. Africa a tree 30 ft. high or more. The flowers are pale pink, and borne on short cylindrical spikes in summer. *T. anglica* is one of the forms of this species, which vary according to the climate of which they are native. *T. africana* and *T. algeriensis* are names that have been given to the African forms of the species.

T. hispida (*Kashgar T.*).—According to M. Lemoine, this new species is from Central Asia. It is certainly distinct, the foliage being of a very glaucous hue. "The leaves are very small and imbricated on the stem, and its inflorescences are of a rosy carmine, brighter than in the other species in cultivation" (Lemoine). It flowers in autumn. *Syn.*, T. kaschgarica.

T. tetrandra is very like *T. gallica* in general appearance, but, as the name implies, it is distinguished by having four instead of five anthers. It is quite hardy, growing and flowering freely near London. The flowers are pinkish white. Caucasus.

Myricaria germanica is very nearly allied to Tamarix, and often figures in nursery catalogues under the latter name. It differs in having ten stamens to each flower. The branches are erect, rather sturdier than in the true Tamarisks, and the leaves are of a pale glaucous hue, the flowers white or rosy in June. It is a native of various parts of Europe and Asia. W. J. B.

TANACETUM (*Tansy*).—An elegant variety of the common Tansy, *T. vulgare*, much dwarfer in stature than the type, is the var. crispum. Its emerald-green leaves are smaller, and have a crisped appearance. It is quite hardy, will grow anywhere, and, if the shoots are thinned in spring to give them room to suspend their graceful leaves, the plant looks much better than if the stems are crowded. The flowers should be pinched off before they open.

T. Herderi, a silvery species, is a characteristic plant for the rock-garden ; the leaves abundant on thick forked stems, which rise a few inches from the surface. The bright yellow flowers have a good effect on the silvery foil. Division.

TAXODIUM (*Summer-leafing Cypress*). —*T. distichum* is a beautiful and stately tree, attaining in its own country,

Taxodium distichum.

Eastern America, Delaware to Florida, a maximum height of 150 ft. In our country it is a tree of proved hardiness and excellence, though neglected by planters since the Californian and other half hardy conifers became so popular. It is a native of swampy places in river banks and is best planted in like situations in our country. From the roots of old trees in such situations very curious excrescences arise in the shape of great growing knobs sometimes 3 or 4 ft. high and a foot through. A tree of such beauty and distinction should be grouped and massed in the many places in England where water enters into the home landscape, the fresh green of the summer leaves being a very welcome gain. There is a pendulous variety of it, but any other so-called varieties of it are better not taken any notice of. In planting this tree care should be taken to secure healthy young plants from seed only.

TAXUS (*Common Yew*).—This, one of the most beautiful of evergreen trees, has been much used in our flower-gardens for many years, clipped and distorted in what is called "topiary" work. Evelyn is said to have introduced the practice with the Yew, and we should be glad if it had no earlier authority, but probably it originated with very old gardens, in which the Yew tree stood by the door or gate and had to be clipped if it was not to overshadow the house or garden. In such a case clipping was necessary, but in modern gardens much clipping of a less profitable kind is often resorted to, so that the Yew is seldom seen in all its stately grace. As a hedge its use in gardens is frequent and often good, but its misuse is evident in many of the great gardens of the world, such as Versailles, where nothing is more ugly than the Yews cut hard against the sky-line, many of them distorted, diseased, and ugly from constant clipping for years. Their effect at Versailles is bad, either against the palace, the landscape, or the trees around. Although intimately connected with the flower garden, it need hardly be said that the Yew, being a gross feeder, should be kept as far as possible from the flowers of the garden. Indeed, in many cases hedges are used where walls would be better, as the walls have not the defect of robbing the good soil near. It is more as shelter, and as fine evergreen trees for groups seen from the flower garden, that the Yew is precious. As a shelter-belt there is perhaps no tree known to us quite so good in all stages of its life. Unlike many other fine evergreen trees, it is not at the mercy of heavy snowfalls and winds, and we have rarely seen it injured by them. A precious shelter from the north and east may be created round the flower garden, or any choice garden, by its means, if allowed to grow naturally and planted not too thick. Delightful ⸢shaded bowers may be formed under old Yew trees ; and alcoves and arches for seats under clipped Yews occasionally. Lines of hedging Yews should never be formed without good reason.

The Golden Yews and variegated kinds will form striking groups of colour ; but are better held together than dotted about at regular intervals, which is fatal to all artistic effect. The Golden Yew, and every Yew worth having of variegated sorts, is most striking in colour in bold picturesque groups. The Irish Yew, a plant of striking form, has been very much over-used by those who do not consider the effect of things on the landscape. I have seen houses with rows of Irish Yews on every side, destroying all possibility of good effect from other and far more beautiful trees, and all the variety and life that should be in an English garden. Variegated and other interesting forms often come from seed.

Of the recognised forms sold in nurseries not one of which is half so precious as the wild or common Yew, the following is an abstract of a classification by Mr. William Paul :—

VARIETIES OF SPREADING HABIT.— T. baccata, common Yew. T. b. fructuluteo (yellow-berried Yew) is one of the most elegant ; the fruit yellow instead of red ; growth vigorous. T. b. nigra is a striking plant of bold upright growth ; leaves bluish-green. It is effective in the landscape, forming a somewhat sombre, but massive tree. T. b. procumbens forms a spreading bush with bright green leaves, the plant having a reddish tint.

VARIETIES OF ERECT HABIT. — T. b. fastigiata (Irish Yew) is a plant of rigid growth, columnar in form ; leaves dark green. Seeds of this variety produce for the most part the common Yew, but some vary in form and tint. T. b. cheshuntensis is a graceful variety, of pyramidal growth, the leaves a glossy green. It is midway between the common and Irish Yew, but less formal than the latter and grows twice as fast. T. b. pyramidalis resembles cheshuntensis in form ; but the leaves are broader, and the bark of the young shoots is reddish. T. b. nidpathensis (Nidpath Yew) resembles cheshuntensis, but is of stiffer growth, being columnar rather than pyramidal, with a disposition to spread at the top. T. b. stricta is similar, but has smaller and paler green leaves, is almost as erect as the Irish Yew, and forms a dense tree. T. b. nana is a neat dwarf plant of compact upright growth, with leaves of a dark and more glossy green than the common Yew. It is equally suitable for a single tree on the lawn, for planting in masses, or for a dwarf hedge. T. b. erecta is similar, but of larger growth, with smaller leaves. T. b. erecta Crowderii is of compact pyramidal growth, and re-

variety, the branches shooting horizontally to some distance from the main stem, and drooping at their points. The foliage is ample and of a dull dark green. T. b. Jacksonii is a distinct weeping variety, with small light green curled leaves. T. b. recurvata is a handsome variety, with leaves of a pale green. The habit is diffuse and rather drooping, the leaves curled in the way of Picea nobilis.

The Irish Yew. One of the forms of the common Yew.

sembles erecta, but has smaller branches, and will probably not grow to so large a size. It is of more regular growth than erecta, and may perhaps be considered an improved variety of it. T. b. ericoides (empetrifolia) is a neat plant of dwarf growth, closely set with branches; the leaves small and the bark reddish.

VARIETIES OF WEEPING HABIT.— T. b. Dovastonii is a picturesque weeping

VARIETIES WITH VARIEGATED FOLI-AGE.—T. b. variegata (Golden Yew) is a well-known plant of great beauty, suited for planting in masses, and relieving the monotony of large surfaces of green. It is said, on good authority, that the Golden Yew is a male plant, but there are two or more varieties of too close an external resemblance to be distinguished; moreover, the offspring from seed retain

3 H

the variegation of the parent, though differing slightly among themselves. T. b. elegantissima is paler, more erect and uniform in growth than the last-mentioned. Both varieties, if grown entirely in the shade, quickly become green, but regain their golden appearance on re-exposure to the sun. T. b. fastigiata variegata (variegated Irish Yew) is a sport from the Irish Yew, with occasional silver leaves ; of slow growth, and hardly striking enough to become a general favourite. T. b. fastigiata variegata (Handsworth variety), one of the best variegated Yews, is most useful, growing freely and standing the sun well.

TCHIHATCHEWIA.—This beautiful alpine, *T. isatidea*, is a native of Asia Minor, hardy, and not particular as to soil or situation, but prefers growing among rocks. From a tuft of spathulate oblong leaves which is formed in the

first year, appear the flowers in the second season ; the leaves are dark green, thickly beset with shining silky hairs, from amongst which rises the thumb-thick flower-stalk showing a combined thyrsus of Syringa-like bright rosy lilac flowers, which are fragrant like vanilla. The bunch is over a foot across, and is in great beauty throughout the month of May.—M. L.

TECOMA (*Trumpet Creeper*).—Hand-

some and distinct climbing shrubs of much beauty of habit as well as of flower. They are not so often seen in our country as abroad, although well fitted for all the southern and warmer parts, and, in the case of one species and its varieties, hardy, flowering well against walls far north of London. *Syn.*, Bignonia.

T. RADICANS.—A native of North America, and an old garden favourite. Its long, wiry stems send out roots like Ivy, and cling to walls or any support. There is a variety named *major*, with larger flowers of a paler tint and more robust foliage. A strong plant will run up a wall 40 ft. high. It is useful also for covering arbours and pergolas. It is distinguished at the first glance from *T. grandiflora* by its more slender branches, smaller and hairy leaf, and its smaller flowers arranged in terminal corymbs. It is also hardier and has

Tecoma radicans.

several varieties :—*Flava speciosa*, flowers long, orange-red ; leaves distinct by their small, much indented folioles, with long narrow points. This form is dwarfer than the type and can be easily grown as a shrub. *Grandiflora atropurpurea*, flowers deep red-purple and large. A vigorous shrub, requiring much space to flower well. *Princei coccinea* is intermediate between the two species, of which it is perhaps a hybrid. The flowers are large, of a fine cochineal-red, and in large panicles. *T. hybrida*, this form, a cross between *T. grandiflora* and *T. radicans*, has small, hairy leaves and handsome orange flowers in panicles.

T. GRANDIFLORA.—This is a Chinese plant, not so hardy as the American Trumpet Creeper, but more showy in bloom, the drooping flowers orange-scarlet, in large clusters. Its foliage, too, is larger, but the plant to show its vigour and beauty should be planted in light soil and against a warm, sunny wall. It has produced the following varieties :—*Aurantia*, which forms a rounded bush if let alone, has fine foliage of a deep, shining green, with ribs covered with down. The flowers are orange-yellow, small for a variety of *T. grandiflora*, the lobes narrower and less open than in the type. In *Mme. Galen*, the handsomest of the race, the flowers are large, of a fine, deep salmon-red, orange-red outside. *Rubra*, flowers a fine deep red, leaves hairy on the lower side, a distinct and pretty variety. *Sanguinea Thunbergi* is probably only a

Tecoma grandiflora.

wild form of its parent, from which it is distinguished by its flowers, which are more highly coloured, the tubes shorter and lobes much reflexed. The branches and leaves are quite smooth. It is a vigorous, free-flowering shrub.

TECOPHYLÆA.—*T. cyanocrocus* is a beautiful spring-flowering bulbous plant from Chili, of dwarf growth, and bearing large open deep blue flowers. The variety Leichtlini has a white centre and a sweet perfume. This variety is not thoroughly hardy, except in very mild localities, but it succeeds well under frame-culture. About August, bulbs of flowering size should be planted 3 in. deep, in rich soil in a frame. If potted a depth of 2 in. is sufficient, and plunge the pots. They should be kept cool, and have as much air as possible. The lights must be taken off in February and March, when the weather becomes warm, and the pots should remain exposed until the flowers begin to expand. The plants may then be transferred to the greenhouse.

Telekia. See BUPTHALMUM.

TELLIMA.—Perennials of the Saxifrage order, from N. America, resembling Heucheras. T. grandiflora has leaves prettily coloured and veined like Heuchera Richardsoni, and spikes of small yellowish bell-like flowers, thriving in any soil. Division.

TEUCRIUM (*Germander*).—A few of these Labiates are of neat dwarf growth. T. Chamædrys (Wall Germander) is 6 to 10 in. high, with shining leaves and reddish-purple flowers in summer. It is found throughout Europe on walls and rocks, and is suitable for borders and naturalisation on ruins, stony banks, etc., in any light soil, whilst as an edging plant it is useful.

T. Marum (*Cat Thyme*) has somewhat the habit of the common Thyme, with bright red flowers in summer. Being a Spanish plant, it is likely to prove hardy only in the southern parts of these islands; then only on ruins, old walls, or in dry chinks in chalk or gravel pits. If planted out the soil should be brick rubbish, etc., with sand and a little poor dry loam. The Cat Thyme should be placed where cats cannot get to destroy it. Cuttings.

T. Polium (*Poly Germander*) is a curious dwarf whitish herb, 3 to 5 in. high, with small pale yellow flowers densely covered with short yellow down, and appearing in summer. It is suited for sunny spots in the rock-garden, and for light free soil, but is not hardy except in the milder southern districts and in favourable spots in the rock-garden, where it grows freely. Seed, cuttings, and division.

T. pyrenaicum (*Pyrenean Germander*) is a dwarf hardy perennial, 3 to 7 in. high, with purplish and white flowers in dense terminal clusters. The leaves, branches and stem are thickly covered with soft down. It is suitable for the rock-garden and for borders.

T. purpureum is a quaint, rigid, evergreen dwarf bush, 6 to 9 in. high, its erect twigs, studded with bright rosy purple flowers, giving a bit of good colour at a late and desirable season. Seed, cuttings, or division. T. hyrcanicum, T. lusitanicum, T. orientale, and T. multiflorum are also noteworthy.

THALIA.—*T. dealbata* is one of the most stately of water-side plants, and its glaucous foliage and elegant panicles of purple flowers are welcome along the margins of shallow ponds or streams, as it is hardy in sheltered positions in this country. It is best grown in pots or tubs pierced with holes, in a mixture of stiff peat and clayey soil, and river mud and sand. The plant attains fullest development in warm places in the southern counties, where alone it may be planted out. S. Carolina. Division.

THALICTRUM (*Meadow Rue*).— Perennial herbs with elegant foliage, but not showy flowers. A few of the smaller species rival in delicacy of form and colour some of the charming Maiden-hair Ferns, and may be associated with flowering plants, or those of fine or characteristic foliage. T. anemonoides (Rue Anemone) is usually only a few inches high, its white flowers being nearly 1 in. in diameter, and open in April and May. It is best suited for the rock-garden in deep moist soil and partial shade. The

3 H 2

double variety may be preferred to the type. N. America. T. minus forms compact slightly glaucous symmetrical tufts, 12 to 18 in. high. May be grown in any soil, but the slender flower-stems, which appear in May and June, should be pinched off. Not only in aspect does this bushy little tuft resemble the Maidenhair Fern, but its leaves when mingled with flowers are pretty ; stiffer, however, and more lasting than Fern fronds. T. minus would look well isolated in large tufts as an edging, in borders, or in groups of dwarf subjects. Division. T. adiantifolium is similar. T. tuberosum is about 9 in. high,

be associated with it and other border plants of the season. It grows best in good soil in an open situation, and is a native of California, also other parts of Western North America. T. fabacea occurs farther north, and should be propagated by seeds. T. barbata is a beautiful Himalayan species with purple flowers.

THLADIANTHA.—*T. dubia* is a handsome creeping perennial of the Gourd family, from N. China and India, with long climbing stems bearing many bright yellow flowers. In the neighbourhood of Paris it survives the winter in the open air.

with graceful foliage, and abundance of yellowish cream-coloured flowers. It is hardy in a deep peat soil. S-Europe. Beside these dwarf kinds there are about two dozen other species, ranging from 3 to 6 ft. in height. There is a great sameness among them, as all have finely-cut foliage. A good kind with fern-like foliage is T. aquilegifolium, which is about 4 ft. high, and grows vigorously in any soil. There are two or three varieties of it, one (atropurpureum) with dark purplish stems and leaves. All the Thalictrums do well naturalised.

THERMOPSIS.—Perennials, 2 to 3 ft. high, slender in growth, and with long terminal spikes of attractive yellow Lupine-like blossoms. T. montana is said to be a variety of the older T. fabacea or rhombifolia, but is distinct in aspect, of graceful growth, and as it flowers at the same time as the perennial Lupine, may

Thalictrum aquilegifolium.

THLASPI.—*T. latifolium* is a dwarf vigorous perennial from the Caucasus, 6 to 12 in. high, with large root-leaves, and flowers something like those of Arabis albida, but larger. Suitable for borders, the spring garden, beds, and naturalising with the dwarfer flowers of spring and early summer in ordinary garden soil. Division and seed. *Syn*, Iberidella.

THUNBERGIA.—*T alata* is a beautiful half-hardy annual, common in greenhouses, an elegant dwarf climber of the easiest culture, and in summer valuable for draping dwarf trellises The flowers of the type, a native of the East Indies, are yellowish-buff, but there are other varieties alba is pure white ; aurantiaca, bright orange ; Fryeri, orange with a white eye, Doddsi has variegated foliage ; and others with yellow and sulphur flowers T alata and its varieties grow 4 to 5 ft high, and from July till October their slender stems are covered with bloom Seeds should be sown in heat in early spring, and the seedlings potted separately when large enough In May plant them out in good light soil

THUYA (*Arbor-vitæ*). — Evergreen cone-bearing trees, some of much beauty, but the group is represented in gardens by numbers of worthless shrubs and mean trees, happily. the species are not so numerous as they seem from the many names that have been given to their mostly ugly varieties

T DOLOBRATA (*Japanese Arbor-vita*) —A distinct and beautiful evergreen tree, perhaps the most graceful of the group, fine in colour and very hardy Happily of this as yet few varieties have been found, these being worthless dwarf and variegated kinds The tree is said to attain its finest stature in mountain woods in Japan, and to grow well under-other trees, and it should be worth trying in like circumstances in our country It comes very freely from layers, in fact, the lower branches of the trees root themselves freely, and these over facile ways of increase make it all the more necessary that we should get healthy seedling trees, as suckers are not unlikely to take bushy rather than tree form *Syn*, Thuyopsis

T GIGANTEA (*Giant Arbor-vita*) —A tall and noble tree, fine in stature and form, hardy and healthy in our country, thriving in ordinary soils, and a free and rapid grower, even without the special attention in the way of soils such conifers often receive It attains in its own country a maximum height of 150 ft , and its wood is fine-grained and very useful N W America, finest on the Columbia river *Syn*, T Lobbi, T Craigiana, T menziesii

T JAPONICA (*Standish's Arbor-vita*) —A graceful evergreen tree of medium size attaining a height of over 50 ft , with branches of a slender pendulous character, of a fresh green colour, and a native of the mountains of central Japan It was introduced by Fortune, and sent out by the late John Standish, of Ascot,

but has not yet been much cultivated. The form usually grown is said not to be the true wild tree, a reason for getting seed from Japanese sources Happily this has not yet, like the others, sported into a mass of varieties. *Syn* , Thuyopsis Standishi

T OCCIDENTALE (*Western Arbor-vita*) —A rather poor hardy evergreen tree which has varied much in colour and foliage and form, ponderous Latin names having been applied to worthless varieties, over twenty being given in some catalogues It is sometimes used to get shelter fences and hedges rapidly, though by no means so good for that purpose as our own native shrubs like the Yew and the Holly, and it would be no great loss to omit it from the garden altogether ; all the more so, perhaps, as it is one of the cheap evergreens often used to form the muddle mixture of the common shrubbery

T. ORIENTALIS (*Chinese Arbor-vita*) —A low tree with little of the beauty of the Pine or Cypress, and which has, unfortunately, given rise to a crowd of varieties, variegated, silvery, golden, and other dense, monstrous and pendulous shapes, "mystified" by Latin names. Not only are they poor in themselves, but they keep the mind away from the central fact of the beauty, dignity and great value of the pine race These varieties have again synonyms and some of them under the wrong name of *Retinospora* get into cultivation

Thuyopsis See THUYA

THYMUS (*Thyme*) —Rock and alpine creeping plants suited for arid parts of the rock-garden and where many other plants will not thrive They spread quickly into wide dense cushions, and ought not to be placed near delicate or minute alpine plants. Nothing can be more charming than a sunny bank covered with the common wild Thyme (T. serpyllum) and the white variety T lanuginosus, though usually considered a very woolly variety of our common wild Thyme, is pleasing at all seasons, forming wide cushions in any soil, provided it be thoroughly exposed to the sun Another desirable plant is the variegated form of the Lemon-scented Thyme (T citriodorus aureus), which is more robust than the green-leaved kind, and retains its leaves through the winter The Golden Thyme is 9 in high, dense and compact, and used for edging It may be increased by cuttings, which strike readily in September, either in hand-glasses or in cold frames, and should be planted out in spring Those cuttings which are best variegated should be chosen, as others may revert to the normal green type Various other Thymes are worthy of the dry arid slopes of a large rock-garden, and of old ruins The minute, creeping, and Peppermint-scented T corsicus, with flowers so small as to be almost invisible, should be planted in every rock-garden, where .it will soon become one of the welcome weeds. Other kinds in cultivation are T. azoricus, T. azureus, T. bracteosus, T. Zygis, T. thuriferus, T. Chamædrys, and T. Mastichina.

TIARELLA (*Foam Flower*).—*T. cordifolia* is a hardy plant of rapid increase, flourishing in almost any soil and posi-

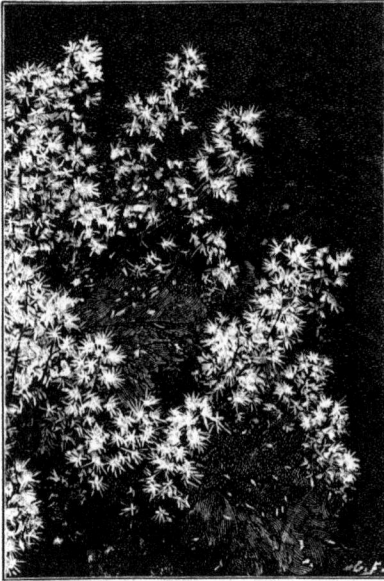

Tiarella cordifolia.

tion, of great beauty, bearing little starry flowers creamy-white, the buds delicately tinged with pink, a good mass of them seen a few yards off having a close likeness to a wreath of foam. The young leaves are tender green, spotted and veined with deep red, while the older ones at the base of the plant are of a rich red-bronze. All the care it needs is division every two years, the plants being at their best the second year after division.

TIGRIDIA (*Tiger Flower*). — *T. pavonia* are bulbous plants with very showy flowers, not hardy generally. In some of our most southerly counties they would be tolerably so in light soil and a warm position, but it is safer to treat them as one would the gandavensis Gladioli and tender bulbs of a similar nature. The annual lifting, storing, and spring planting are not great undertakings, and the bulbs are better for

having the bulblets of the past season's growth separated. In some warm gardens the bulbs are left in the ground all the winter, well protected with ashes, and the results are satisfactory. Choose the sunniest spot in the garden where there will be no cutting winds, as these spoil the great delicate flowers. Soil that is light and the subsoil gravelly are the most favourable conditions for these bulbs. A sandy loam lightened and enriched by leaf-mould is the best to ensure a strong and rapid growth. The bed should have at least 18 in. of good soil, and when this is dug up and allowed to settle, plant the bulbs the second or third week in April 3 in. deep and 6 in. apart, putting a little sharp sand round each before filling in the holes. If a dry time sets in when the foliage is half grown, the bed should be well watered occasionally. From about midsummer onwards till September, or even later, the plants will be in bloom, and the stronger the plants the more flowers will the sheaths yield. In October the foliage generally begins to turn yellow, a sign that the bulbs are ripening. Lift by November, bunch them, and hang in an airy shed till they are dry.

T. PAVONIA VAR. GRANDIFLORA.—Flowers larger and brighter in colour than the type as introduced from native localities and figured in early botanical books. Under this name I would include the names *speciosa, splendens, coccinea,* and *Wheeleri.*

T. P. CONCHIFLORA.—Flowers with outer segments yellow, heavily blotched with red at the bases, and with inner segments similarly variegated. The names *canariensis* or *conchiflora grandiflora* probably represent a form differing slightly as regards brilliancy of colour, but it is undoubtedly a seedling form of the original *T. conchiflora.*

T. P. ALBA.—Flowers with sepals and petals of ivory whiteness, heavily blotched at the bases with carmine-red

T. P. A. IMMACULATA.—This new variety is a sport from the ordinary white-flowered form of this beautiful summer-flowering bulb. Its name *immaculata* (without spots) has been given to it in allusion to the uniform snowy white colour of the flowers, which are in the interior entirely devoid of the conspicuous spots characteristic of the other varieties.

T. P. LILACEA.—Flowers with rosy carmine sepals and petals, the bases variegated with white, a cross between *T. Pavonia* and. *T. Pavonia alba.*

T. P. ROSEA.—Flowers with rose-coloured sepals and petals, the bases variegated with yellow, a cross between *T. Pavonia* and *conchiflora.*

These comprise the varieties and synonyms of the true *Tigridias,* unless the new *T. Pringlei* belongs to this section. The *Beatonias,* as the small-flowered *Tigridias* were once generically named, comprise a few species which, though interesting botanically, are not at present of horticultural importance. The species that are or have been in cultivation are *B. lutea* from Peru and Chili, *B. violacea, B.*

Tigridia pavonia alba immaculata.

Van Houttei, B. atrata, B. curvata, B. bucci-fera, and *B. Patscuaro*(?), all from Mexico. Of the new species it seems to me that we may expect most from *T. Pringlei,* which is said to grow 18 ins. high and to have large scarlet flowers.

TILIA (*Lime; Linden*).—Mostly summer leafing trees and of northern and temperate regions. The common Lime is cut into fantastic and often ugly shapes in French and Austrian and Dutch gardens. It was, no doubt, the readiest tree to hand in the old times when this fashion was more common ; but if we sought such effects now we have many trees that would be better for this purpose than the Lime, which, from its vigorous growth, takes much mutilation to keep it in the desired shape. By far the best effect of the tree is when it is allowed to take its natural shape, and its fragrance is often welcome on the lawn. The "pleached" alleys of old English gardens were often made of this tree, but it is much easier to get them now from various trees better in colour and leaf, such as the fine leaved

Acacias or graceful fruit trees like the Japanese and other crabs, which, while giving us the shade we seek, also give beautiful flowers in season. Some of the species of Limes are very handsome trees, hardy, fine in form and leaf, and good on lawn or in grove.

The species are *T. heterophylla* (N. America), *americana* (do.), *pubescens* (do.), *cordata* (Europe), *dasystyla* (Orient), *erichlora, mandshurica* (Japan), *Miqueliana* (Japan), *mongolica* (China), *petiolaris* (Hungary), *platyphyllos* (Europe), *Podhorsciana* (Podolia), *rubra* (Tauria), *semicuneata* (Siberia), *tomentosa* (Europe), *vulgaris* (do.). An interesting fact in connection with the Lime is, that while the common and well-known Lime of gardens is not a native of Britain, two other species less known are natives of Britain, viz., *platyphyllos* and *cordata.*

TRACHELIUM (*Blue Throatwort*).— *T. cœruleum* is a much-branched perennial, 1 to 2 ft. high, bearing in summer broad clusters of small blossoms, blue in the type and white and lilac in the varieties. It can be grown only in the warmest situations in dry borders, rocky banks, and old ruins or walls. It is an elegant plant for vases, etc. Mediterranean. Seed or cuttings.

TRADESCANTIA (*Virginian Spiderwort*). — Beautiful herbs, some quite hardy, of which *T. virginica* is by far the best, and with its varieties represents all the beauty of the family. It is 12 to 30 in. high, and has showy purple-blue flowers in summer. There are several varieties, one with double violet, and one each with single rose-coloured, lilac, and white blossoms. These grow in any soil and are suitable for the mixed border, margins of shrubberies, the rougher parts of extensive rock-gardens, and for the wild garden. Division.

Trichonema. See ROMULEA.

TRICUSPIDARIA.—*T. hexapetala* is a lovely flowering shrub from Chili, which has flowered in the gardens at Castlewellan several years, and appears to be hardy there. It is planted in a shady border near a large Yew hedge, in peat, leaf soil, and loam in equal proportions. It flowers twice a year, in the spring and in autumn, the colour of the flowers being a deep rich crimson. Being near the sea there is very little frost in ordinary winters, and the plant requires no protection, but in a less favoured climate it would be well to pot it and winter it in a cool greenhouse. *Syn.,* Crinodendron Hookerianum.

TRICYRTIS.—*T. hirta* is an interesting Japanese perennial, about 3 ft. high, with slender erect stems terminated by a few curiously-shaped pinkish blossoms, spotted with purplish-black. It is perfectly hardy, but flowers so late that it is invariably damaged by frosts. The variety nigra flowers three weeks earlier, and is therefore better, whilst the flowers are more attractive. T. pilosa is dwarfer, but is otherwise a similar plant, though

Tricuspidaria hexapetala. From a photograph sent by Lord Annesley.

rarer. They all thrive in a moist peat border, partially shaded, and if somewhat protected, so much the better.

TRIENTALIS (*Star-flower*).—*T. europæus* is a delicate and graceful plant found over Europe, Asia, and America, which inhabits shady, woody, and mossy places. It has erect slender stems, rarely more than 6 in. high, bearing from one to four flower-stems, each supporting a white or pink-tipped star-shaped flower. Healthy well-rooted plants are not difficult to establish among bog-shrubs in some half-shady part of the rock-garden, or in the shade of Rhododendrons and American shrubs, in peat soil. T. europæus is suitable for association with Linnæa, Pyrolas, and Pinguiculas, among mossy rocks. Flowers in early summer. Division.

TRIFOLIUM (*Trefoil*).—Among the few garden varieties are some dwarf and desirable creeping alpines, the best being T. uniflorum, a neat trailing plant

with pink and white flowers, larger than those of any other Trefoil, borne singly, and studded profusely over the plant. It delights in an exposed position on the rock-garden, with an open space on which to creep. T. alpinum is a stout spreading kind, 3 to 6 in. high, bearing large, but not brilliant flowers in summer, the upper petal flesh-coloured and streaked with purple. It is suitable for the rock-garden and margins of borders. T. rubens is a stout perennial, about 1 ft. high, with large dense heads of carmine flowers in early summer. It grows almost anywhere, but prefers dry, calcareous, marly or gravelly soil, therefore is specially suited for naturalisation on arid declivities with a southern aspect. T. pannonicum, with creamy-white flowers, is ornamental. Division or seed.

TRILLIUM (*Wood Lily*).—Perennials of low growth, which inhabit the woods of N. America. The finest is T. grandiflorum (White Wood Lily), one of the most beautiful hardy plants, 6 to 12 in. high, with on each stem a lovely white three-petalled flower, fairer than the white Lily, and almost as large. It is a free-growing plant of goodly size in a shady peaty border in open air ; but in a sunny or exposed position its large soft green leaves do not develop. Depressed shady nooks in the rock-garden or the hardy fernery suit it admirably. In the rosy variety the rosy hue is most pronounced in the young stage, and the leaf-stalks and the foliage are of a more bronzy shade of green than in the type. T. atro-pur-pureum, T. erythrocarpum, T. sessile, and T. pendulum are not equal to T. grandiflorum, but some of them are pretty, whilst all are interesting.

TRITELEIA (*Spring Star-flower*).—*T. uniflora* is a delicately-coloured, free-flowering, hardy, bulbous plant, 4 to 6 in. high ; the flowers white, with bluish reflections, and marked on the outside through the middle of the divisions with a violet streak, which is continued down the tube. They open at sunrise, and are conspicuously beautiful on bright days, but close in dull and sunless weather. The plant comes into flower with or before Scilla sibirica, and during April remains in effective bloom. T. uniflora flowers profusely in pots, and even in an unfavourable position in clay. There are several forms, which differ in the shade of their flowers. Associated with the best Scillas, Leucojum vernum, Iris reticulata, dwarf Daffodils, and the like, T. uniflora is delightful, and is equally useful for the rock-garden, borders or edgings. S. America. T. (Leucocoryne) alliacea is nearly allied, less pretty, and thrives under similar circumstances. For other species see BRODIÆA.

Tritoma. See KNIPHOFIA.

TRITONIA. — Graceful and rather brilliantly coloured plants from the Cape, but different from most S. African plants in their hardiness and vitality, sometimes in the poorest conditions of soil and exposure, growing indeed' like weeds, and so close that I have used them between shrubs to keep the ground clean and free from weeds ; and well they do it, giving very graceful bloom in masses towards the summer and autumn. In rich light loamy soils they give but little trouble ; in some clay soils where the drainage is less under control they are apt to fail, but we have seen them thrive admirably in

year, while the batch that had flowered and remained in the ground the winter previous would be the one to be lifted this coming autumn. In this way little loss would be sustained in a single year by deterioration, and the corms if harvested at the right time and well kept, *i.e.*, cool and dry, will more than repay the labour and trouble this lifting in alternate years involves. Even in those gardens where, so far as the soil and other local conditions are concerned, there is no real need to lift the roots, the above plan should be of value for the longer time of blooming it gives.

By reason of the somewhat numerous hybrids, chiefly of *T. Pottsi*, the numbers of beautiful things in this group are greatly increased, a few of the most worthy being Etoile de Feu, rich orange and yellow ;

Trillium grandiflorum (White Wood Lily).

poor clayey soil, not wet. In badly drained soils it is best perhaps to raise the bed by an addition of soil of a lighter nature than to undertake its improvement at the original level. All danger can be avoided by lifting, though some incline to the belief that the lifting is injurious. The success which has attended the planting of dry stock of these things during the early spring months—frequently as late as April—is the best proof that the harm resulting from drying such things is of very small moment. Where both systems can be pursued in any one garden it may safely be predicted that a long succession of bloom will be the result. The spring-planted stock of this year may remain through the coming winter in the soil to give an earlier bloom in the following

Gerbe d'Or, golden ; Soleil Couchant, a very free variety, golden yellow ; Transcendant, orange-vermilion shade, one of the most showy ; Aurore, orange-yellow, very large and effective ; and Phare, reddish crimson. These, together with *crocosmiæflora*, *Pottsi* and its variety *grandiflora*, make up a very beautiful set of equal hardiness and usefulness in the open garden. *Syn.*, Montbretia.

CULTURE IN THE WEST COUNTRY.— We have seen the Tritonias (of the *Montbretia* section) thrive for years and bloom every year freely on poor clay ; the better soils and more copious rainfall of the western side of the country make a difference, and this about their culture in a Cheshire garden may be useful to those who work under like conditions. "To make them do well, the chief point is to keep them thin, and so they must be divided every year. This may be done at any time in autumn before the ground is frozen up. My practice at Edge after digging them up—suppose there are twelve stalks, that is, twelve bulbs in each clump, with three or four young points to each bulb—is to have fifty or one hundred pots ready and to put three bulbs into each pot, filling up with any waste soil, drainage being superfluous. The less they grow before March the better. They must not be cut down till spring. When all the pots are full they are placed together in some sheltered waste spot out of doors and well watered—for if kept dry they die —then they are covered with a foot or two, according to weather, of dry leaves or other litter, enough to ensure their safety from frosts. By the end of March they are safe, and may then be planted out anywhere, letting the bulbs be at least 6 in. deep, either amongst herbaceous plants, which they like, or amongst low shrubs. I have some in beds of dwarf Roses, where they do and look very well. As they increase at least four-fold every year, the gardener must harden his heart and not be tempted to let them grow more densely, but, as he will find that most of his friends have as many as they want, throw the surplus on to the rubbish heap. I find one morning in each year enough to dig all up and fill a hundred pots, for the work may be done in the roughest and most hasty way without detriment to the welfare of the bulbs. Indeed, I have sometimes buried the clumps in a soil heap for winter, littering them over as described, and planting the bulbs out by threes in spring. The main objects are not to let them get frozen, and not to let them get dry or grow during winter. I generally also replant three bulbs where I dig up each clump. If the winter is mild, these survive and the pots are not wanted ; if they are killed, the pots take their place. They flower better if a spadeful of rich stuff is put in where each pot is planted. I recommend especially *Etoile de Feu,* scarlet, A 1 both in colour and habit ; *Aurore,* bright orange and very robust, growing more than a yard high ; *Drap d'Or,* bright yellow ; *Solfatare,* pale yellow ; *Feu d'Artifice* and *Bouquet Parfait,* mixed orange and yellow ; *Pottsi grandiflora,* scarlet outside, yellow inside, distinct and free flowering, with ornamental seed-heads."—C. WOLLEY-DOD, *Edge Hall.*

T. aurea. — This beautiful South African bulb often seen in a greenhouse is a useful plant for the open air. It grows about 2 ft. high, and has branched spikes of rich yellow flowers 2 in. across. Two fine forms of it are—maculata, with flowers deep orange colour stained with brown, 3 in. across, borne on spikes 4 ft. in height ; and imperialis, equally tall, with large flowers, narrower in the petal and of a brighter orange shade. In the garden T. aurea succeeds in any soil except clay, but prefers moist peaty beds associating well with and under conditions favourable to choice peat-loving shrubs. In the warmer parts of England and Ireland it may be left in the border all winter protected with a layer of leaves or under the shelter of a south wall. It spreads rapidly, becoming almost a weed in warm peaty borders. Though tolerably hardy, the lateness of flowering is an objection to leaving the bulbs out all the winter, and besides this, they are liable to be killed in severe winters unless well protected. It is better, therefore, to lift them about the middle of November. Anything like drying off or storing the roots in a dry place is fatal ; they should not be uncovered for a single day.

TROLLIUS (*Globe-flower*). — Handsome stout perennial herbs of erect habit, never requiring support. They may be grown in beds or borders, or naturalised by ponds, streams, or in any wet place, as they flourish well among the natural vegetation and give delightful effects. They are of a dense habit of growth, and both foliage and flowers rise from an underground crown. The roots are numerous and deep-searching, especially in a border where drainage removes the water-level to a considerable depth. The flowers vary from a pale yellow to a deep gold, almost bordering on vermilion. The Globe-flowers bloom in spring or in summer, and are at their best in April, May, and June. Occasionally old-established plants develop a few flowers in September and October ; but these flowers depend alike on the season and the strength of the plant itself. Division in September or March ; but if divided in March, a few bright dry days will injure the foliage, and the blossoms are certain to be puny and short-lived. Another way to propagate is by seeds, but Globe-flowers rarely vegetate in the year they are sown, coming up vigorously in the following spring, and, if carefully attended to, making fine flowering plants the second season ; not, however, attaining their full development until the fourth year or even later. They grow freely in any soil, and thrive in a good stiff loam overlying a cool moist sub-soil, but, if in a dry situation, should have plenty of manure partly to retain moisture.

T. acaulis.—A native of the higher Himalayan Mountains, and one of the most charming dwarf bog-plants, rarely exceeding 4 to 6 in. in height, its bright yellow flowers suffused with purple-brown on the outside. It is hardy, has been many years in cultivation, and will be found most useful for the low or moist spots in the rock-garden, growing best in a fine peaty soil.

T. asiaticus (*Orange Globe-flower*), which also includes chinensis, Fortunei, and other forms has rich orange-yellow flowers and bright orange red anthers, is hardy even in the most exposed positions, and differs from the European Globe-flowers chiefly in its less globular flowers, small finely-divided foliage and taller growth. China and Japan.

T. europæus (*Mountain Globe-flower*) grows about 15 in. high, has lemon-yellow flowers and is an extremely variable plant, so widely spread that almost every locality has its particular form. Raised from seed it also gives much variety, in habit, flowers, and foliage. T. europæus has various names in gardens, such, for instance, as pumilus, giganteus, dauricus, pallidus, americanus, albus, aurantiacus, and napellifolius. A few of these are distinct varieties, dauricus being noted for its large bloom and large much-divided leaves on long olive-green foot-stalks.

TROPÆOLUM (*Nasturtium*).—These are almost confined to the mountainous region from New Granada to Chili, seldom descending into the tropics, and, therefore, do not require great heat. This indeed is rather unfavourable to them, but, on the other hand, the first frost cuts most of them down to the ground. They love a half-shaded situation, and succeed in the open air in the summer. There are annual and perennial species, and the perennials may be divided into two groups, one with fibrous roots, and the other with tuberous roots. The rapid growth of the annuals T. majus and T. minus is proverbial, and their hardiness in a temperature above freezing-point, as well as their indifference to soil, should recommend them where anything unsightly is to be hidden. The following are the most fitted for the open air :—

T. aduncum (*Canary Creeper*).—Undoubtedly the favourite among Tropæolums, and almost unrivalled for elegance among yellow flowers. Its precise home is uncertain, as it occurs all over the west of S. America, from Mexico to Chili ; but it has doubtless spread from the Andes. It thrives in sun or shade, but is best in a position with a north aspect, festooning trellises, arbours, shrubs, etc. It rarely fails to produce a profusion of pretty yellow blossoms even in town gardens. Seeds should be sown in April in the open ground in sandy loam. *Syns.*, T. peregrinum and T. canariense.

T. Lobbianum.—This beautiful annual is of vigorous climbing growth, and easily known from the old T. majus by its more or less hairy foliage. The varieties of it differ chiefly in the colour of the blossoms which are mostly yellow, scarlet, and crimson. The plant will clothe unsightly spots, or provide temporary shelter during summer. Seeds should be sown about the middle of April. All the after-culture needed is guiding the leading shoots in the direction in which they are to grow. T. Lobbianum has a pleasing effect when sown here and there amongst shrubs in the back of a border. As the plants grow, they attach themselves to the bushes, and climbing over or through them, throw out wreaths of lovely blossoms which retain their beauty until cut down by frost. Temporary floral fences may also be made with this plant, all that is required being a row of Pea stakes for the shoots. It will also assume a pyramidal form by being allowed to overrun the dead tops of young Fir trees. In short, there is no end to the uses to which it may be put.

T. majus (*Large Indian Cress* or *Nasturtium*) differs from T. minus in being larger, and from T. Lobbianum in the absence of hairiness. There are many beautiful varieties of it, mostly hybrids. The climbing sorts are useful for the same purposes as T. Lobbianum, and require the same treatment, the most important varieties of T. majus being the dwarf or Tom Thumb strain, which includes many sorts. Few annuals come into flower more quickly than these dwarf Nasturtiums, and few bloom longer or more constantly. In poor soil the compactum forms bloom best. Their rich, bold colours are superb in masses, and they are never without flowers from first to last. Seeds or cuttings put in about the middle of September. A few dozen plants in store pots will yield a large number of cuttings in spring, these making the best plants for summer. The other Tom Thumb kinds may be sown in the open ground in spring, but the compactum race grows so freely, if raised in this manner, that it is best to sow under glass and then plant out. If sown under glass the plants bloom earlier, and are more compact. All who love rich masses of colour will find these dwarf Nasturtiums worth cultivating. The varieties are so numerous and beautiful, that it is difficult to make a selection ; and the catalogues of the seedsman abound with names of favourite sorts.

T. pentaphyllum.—A rapid growing climber, 6 to 10 ft. high, with yellowish-red flowers. It will cover pillars, walls, chains, bowers, and revels in sunshine, succeeding well on the south wall of a greenhouse or in any warm aspect. It does best in light and warm loams or calcareous soils. Division or seed. Chili.

T. polyphyllum.—This is one of the most valuable hardy plants ever introduced. While its foliage may form a dense carpet on a bank, its wreaths of flowers usually throw themselves into irregular windings and groupings. It is very distinct whether in or out of flower. Its

Tropæolum polyphyllum.

leaves are glaucous, almost Rue-like in tone, and cut into fine divisions or leaflets. In a warm rock-garden the stems creep about, snake-like, through the neighbouring vegetation, sometimes extending to a length of 3 or 4 ft. The flowers are deep yellow, and as profuse as the leaves. The plant is tuberous-rooted, and quite hardy in dry situations in the rock-garden, also on sunny banks, but should not often be disturbed. It springs up early, and dies down at the end of summer. Chilian Cordilleras.

T. speciosum (*Flame Nasturtium*).—

A splendid creeper, with long and elegant annual shoots, gracefully clothed with leaves from the axils of which spring such brilliant vermilion flowers, that a long shoot is startlingly effective, especially if seen wandering among Ivy leaves or in verdure of any kind. It has been long introduced from S. America, but, notwithstanding its graceful beauty and hardiness, is little known, especially in the south of England. It is impossible to find anything more worthy of a position where its shoots may fall over or climb up the face of some high rock or bank in the rock-garden ; while it is suited for an open spot in the hardy fernery, or for any other position where its peculiar beauty may be well seen. It is very beautiful when clambering through evergreen shrubs, and enjoys a deep, rich, and rather moist soil, in cool places, or near the sea. No pains should be spared to establish it in a vigorous condition.

A correspondent writes to *The Garden:* This beautiful climber evidently dislikes hot sun and a dry atmosphere, and the great portion of the failures in growing it are due to a want of a cool and comparatively moist atmosphere. Several years ago a friend who knew nothing of the nature of this plant received some roots from the fine old specimens that grow on Lismore Castle. By my advice some of the roots were planted against a west wall, in front of which grow some good-sized Nut-bushes and a few tolerably large Apple trees, so that in the hot summer weather the sun could only reach the plants for a couple of hours daily. The remaining roots were planted against a north wall, where scarcely any sun came, and at the west end of the dwelling-house, where the full force of the afternoon sun was felt. In all these cases the soil was alike. The plants behind the Nut-bushes and Apple trees grew remarkably well and bloomed as freely as could be expected in the first year of planting. On the north wall the growth was good, but the flowers were not so numerous ; but in the sunny position, although the roots made a growth of a foot or so, this growth gradually withered away as soon as the power of the sun made itself felt. There could be no better proof that the successful growth of the Flame-flower is simply a matter of position, and that, even in the southern counties, there are probably few gardens where the requirements of the plant may not be met.

When a position is selected, the soil should be made light, deep, and free by leaf-mould, peat, fibry loam, and sand, according to the nature of the ground. Mulch in summer with an inch or two of leaf-mould or manure to prevent excessive evaporation; and whatever' manure is used, it must be well decayed. The young plants should be planted in spring, the roots being inserted 6 or 8 in. in the

Tropæolum speciosum in Scotland.

soil and well watered. The Flame Nasturtium is best where the shoots may ramble among the spray of shrubs, Ferns, or trailers, but as it must be placed on a cleared spot, it is well to put a few branchlets over the roots for the young shoots to crawl over. It is much better to let them have their own wild way than to resort to any staking or support, except that of other subjects growing near. Division or seed. Seeds should be sown as soon as ripe, in a pan or box, in light loam, leaf-mould, and sand. Place in a pit or a frame, and keep the soil moist, but not wet, until the plants make their appearance in spring. The careful divi-

sion of the old roots is, however, much the best way to propagate.

T. tuberosum.—A distinct and beautiful tuberous-rooted climber from Peru, with slender stems 2 to 4 ft. high, and in summer a profusion of showy scarlet and yellow flowers on slender stalks. It should be grown in open spots in the poorest of soils, with its branches supported or allowed to trail along the ground. As it is not hardy in all soils, lift the tubers in autumn, store in a dry place, and plant out in spring.

TSUGA (*Hemlock Spruce*).—A distinct and graceful group of evergreen cone-bearing trees, remarkable for their fine form of leaf and graceful toss of branchlet, and also in their own country at least for picturesque and often stately form.

The one best known in Britain, so far, is the Canadian Hemlock Spruce, a tree of proved hardiness in our country, but rarely showing the dignity of form it does in its own, probably from the use of cutting plants. No tree of the pine race should be planted in any form but that of healthy seedlings. The splendid forms of these trees so promising for our

Hemlock Spruce.

country, coming as they do from moist cool regions, will be best secured by taking any necessary care to securing healthy seedling trees, never large ones.

The Japanese and Indian species of this family, *T. Sieboldi, Brunoniana,* and *diversifolia* are not proved to be of such distinct value as the American kinds. *Syn.*, Abies.

T. CANADENSIS (*Hemlock Spruce*). — A forest tree sometimes over 100 ft. high with a diameter of 4 ft. in the trunk, inhabiting very cold northern regions from Nova Scotia to Minnesota and southwards along the mountains. This tree has been much planted in England, but it has not so far seemed to attain the stature and form that it shows in Canada. The varieties of this, which are rather numerous, are of slight value. In my own planting of the Hemlock Spruce near water, while the growth is free, constant and unharmed by any winter, I am vexed to see every tree breaking from the bottom into half a dozen or more stems, splitting up the energies of the tree. I saw a very pretty hedge of the Hemlock near Philadelphia : it would prove, I think, a good evergreen hedge plant where the horribly dangerous poison of our own yew makes it impossible to use it as a hedge in any place to which horses or cattle have access.

T. CAROLINIANA (*Caroline Hemlock*). — A forest tree attaining a height of 70 to 80 ft., 4 ft. in diameter, and a very graceful and beautiful tree in a mature state. As yet a tree little planted in our country, but very promising at least for the southern parts of England and Ireland. Alleghany Mountains, ascending to over 4,000 ft. in North Carolina. *Syn.*, Abies Caroliniana.

T. MERTENSIANA (*Western Hemlock Spruce*). —A noble tree of fine and picturesque habit, allied to the Eastern Hemlock but a larger tree—sometimes 200 ft. high, with a trunk diameter of 10 to 12 ft. A native of Puget Sound, British Columbia to Alaska, and the coast region of Northern California, and coming from such fog-moistened region we look for a tree hardy enough for our island climate, and in this noble Hemlock we have it. The foliage, as graceful as a fern, is of a deep, lustrous green, and silvery white beneath. It is a hardy tree in this country, but it is best to plant it in the sheltered places in deep moist soil. *Syns.*, Abies mertensiana, and Albertiana.

T. PATTONIANA (*Alpine Hemlock*). — A beautiful and stately tree 100 to 150 ft. high, and from 6 to 10 ft. in diameter of trunk, with dark green foliage on slender branches that sway in the slightest wind. Alpine and subalpine forests in the Sierras of Northern California, the Cascades and Northern Rocky Mountains, often at great elevations. Hardy and at home in Britain. *T. Hookeriana* is a northern variety, smaller and sharply pyramidal in form.

T. TSUGA (*Japanese Hemlock Spruce*).— This tree, known also as *T. Sieboldi*, is as graceful in growth as the Canadian Hemlock Spruce and is quite as hardy. It takes more of the character of a large and dense spreading bush than of a tree, and is useful for grouping with other conifers.

TULIPA (*Tulip*).—Among the most beautiful of hardy bulbous flowers, the finest self Tulips being unsurpassed for brilliant effect in the garden. The main point is to obtain and plant the best kinds in quantity, for exquisite as a single flower of the striped or flaked Tulip may be, it is only the self-coloured species and varieties that give the best display. Tulips have been so long grown and are so variable in character that considerable confusion exists among them. The popular garden forms may, broadly speaking, be separated into two classes, early and late flowering. T. suaveolens from Southern Russia is now regarded as the type of the numerous early-flowering varieties, of which Duc van Thol is a familiar example ; but these, though commonly planted, are of less value for the garden than the finer later forms which open in May. These have all come from T. Gesneriana, and whilst possessing infinite variety of colour, all have the same fine form and stately character of the parent. These late Tulips coming in succession to the Daffodils are precious garden flowers of easy culture, but not grown to anything like the extent that they should be. For about three centuries they have been grown by the florists, who have raised numerous varieties, which form an enormous class divided into four sections— viz. breeders or self-flowers, bizarres, bybloemens, and roses. When a seedling flowers for the first time, it is usually a self, and in a few years (but occasionally not until thirty years) it will break into the flamed or feathered state. A feathered Tulip has the colour finely pencilled round the margin of the petals, the base of the flower being pure, and in a flamed flower stripes of colour descend from the top of the petals towards the base. In the bizarres the colours are red, brownish-red, chestnut, and maroon, the base being clear yellow ; in the bybloemens the colours are black and various shades of purple, the base being white ; and in the roses, rose of various shades and also deep red or scarlet, the base being white again.

We want however more Tulips of the same character as the florists' forms in self-colours. At present White Swan, Bouton d'Or, rich yellow, Golden Beauty, self yellow, and Golden Eagle, yellow, edged with red, are good kinds ; but little attention appears to have been given to the production of large, late, self-coloured Tulips. The Parrot Tulips, with curiously cut petals, are self-coloured and valuable in the garden, as they make a bright display.

Tulips are easily grown, the rich soil of old gardens suiting them best. They may be planted from October to the middle of November, and the old Tulip growers used to put a little sand at the base of each bulb, but this is not essential. It is well to lift the bulbs every two or three years, or they become too crowded and give small flowers. When the old flower stems are turning yellow, the bulbs may be taken up, dried, and stored till planting time or replanted at once if convenient, as nothing is gained by keeping them out of the ground a long

gated form, Aubretias, Hepaticas, Primroses, Cowslips, Silene pendula, Pansies and Violets, Saxifrages, Iberis corifolia, Ajuga reptans rubra, and many others make excellent carpets.

Among the wild Tulips there are beautiful kinds distinct from the garden varieties ; the larger kinds, noble flowers for free planting, and the smaller sorts gems of bright beauty for nooks in the rock-garden or in beds and borders of choice bulbs.

Old garden Tulips.

time. They can be increased by means of their little offsets. Some species rarely or never increase in this way, and recourse must be had to sowing seed, which if sown when ripe germinates the following spring, but the bulbs do not attain their full size for six or seven years. Beds of Tulips may be carpeted with small tufted or creeping plants, and there are many hardy flowering and pretty leaved plants suited for the purpose. The White Rock Cress (Arabis albida) and its varie-

T. ACUMINATA is curious, but its petals too long and thin to create a display.

T. ALBERTI, from Turkestan, is rather low-growing, with undulated leaves of a glaucous green colour trailing on the ground ; the flowers red, somewhat resembling those of T. Greigi in shape, but the petals are marked at the base with a blotch of yellow margined with black.

T. AUSTRALIS is variable in colour, but always pleasing, allied to T. sylvestris, not, however, so robust in habit, whilst the flower is more funnel-shaped, flushed on the outer side with red *Syn*, T Celsiana.

T BATALINI is a small-growing species, seldom exceeding 4 in in height, with leaves trailing on the ground, and rather large flowers (nearly 3 in in length) of a pale yellow colour

T. BIFLORA, from the Caucasus, a species known very long ago, is not very striking with its small pale yellow flowers, which, however, are borne in a cluster of three or four at the top of the flower-stem instead of being solitary, as is the case with the flowers of every other species of Tulip

T CLUSIANA, the dainty Lady Tulip, came from the Mediterranean region as long ago as 1636, has small flowers, and the whole plant is not more than 1 ft or so in height The flowers are white, with a flush of rose on the outer surface, and purplish-black at the base T stellata is a near ally It requires a deep vegetable soil and warm sheltered position

T DIDIERI, a May flowering kind from the Alps, grows tall, and has large bright red flowers with black blotches inside at the base A variety of T Didieri named Billetiana, equally handsome, has yellow flowers

T EICHLERI, a native of Georgia, is another superb and robust-growing species with large leaves and broad flowers of an intense scarlet-red colour, the petals roundish in shape, having at the base a black blotch margined with yellow

T ELEGANS, a graceful bright-coloured kind, opens late in April, the flowers bright red with yellow eye, the petals long, tapering to a point slightly reflexed

T FLAVA, a bright pleasing yellow, has a distinct bar of green down the centre of the petals, which also detracts from its beauty, but has one redeeming point—viz, its flowers continue quite a fortnight after those of all other Tulips are past.

T. FRAGRANS is a doubtful species, and given in some books as a synonym of T. sylvestris, our wild Tulip, from which it differs in its very sweet fragrance. In habit and size of flowers it is the same, the latter yellow, and very pretty. The warmest spots must be selected for this kind, which sometimes fails during the winter unless under especially favourable conditions

T. FULGENS, a form of T Gesneriana, has that graceful aspect characteristic of the race, the flowers rich crimson, borne on tall stems

T GESNERIANA —This the noblest and handsomest of all Tulips, the parent of

the large late-flowering race, should be grown in every garden, and being obtainable in quantity, planted in bold groups or broad masses

In Sussex I saw one or two very fine pictures made by planting the large crimson Tulipa Gesneriana in quantity. In one case a large oval Erica bed had been thickly planted with some few hundreds of this kind, and formed a solid shield-like mass of colour, more brilliant than a soldier's coat, and very picturesque it was as seen through the soft gray trunks of Scotch Fir trees

In another instance the bulbs had been planted in a solid, but not quite regular line, on a dry, rich and warm hedge-bank of turfy loam, and just through and above the great crimson blooms the common Quince had thrust its soft leafy branches, thickly set with small white or delicate rose-flushed flowers

It has an immense bright red flower borne on a tall stem, sweetly scented, with a black zone inside at the base, cut and taken whilst in the house, the flowers last admirably, and by artificial light at night, they open as widely as in the sun by day The finest form is that called spathulata. Eastern Europe and Asia The so-called " Darwin" Tulips are self-coloured forms of this species, and very handsome they are.—F. W B

T. GREIGI, which was introduced about the year 1871, has not yet received all the attention it deserves It is low-growing, the flower-stem seldom exceeding 8 in in height, the leaves marked with purplish blotches, and the large-sized flowers (from over 3 to nearly 4 in in length), of a dazzling vermilion-red colour faintly marked at the base with a dark spot It is hardy, comes into flower about the middle of April, and few things can equal the brilliant display produced by a bed of Tulipa Greigi in full bloom

T. KAUFMANNIANA, from Turkestan, is undoubtedly one of the finest known. It grows from 8 to 12 in high, has broad, flat leaves, flowers very large (nearly 4 in. in length), generally white, or pale creamy-yellow tinged with pink on the outside, the petals marked with a broad orange blotch This fine species is hardy, and comes into flower in April

T. KOLPAKOWSKYANA, also from Turkestan, is a brilliant species, not exceeding 1 ft in height, the flowers, which are large (3 in or more in length), are of a lively red colour, sometimes yellow with very small blotches or spots at the base.

T LANATA, a low-growing species with

red flowers, is remarkable for the little woolly point which forms the apex of each of the petals.

T. LEICHTLINI, from Cashmere, grows 1½ ft. high with a flower always erect, the three outer petals bright purple, with a broad white margin, the inner ones yellowish-white, much shorter than the outer, and obtuse at the apex.

T. LINIFOLIA has glaucous leaves deeply undulated and flowers of a dazzling red colour, with small black spots at the base. T. Dammanniana, a native of Syria, much resembles, but is somewhat more sensitive to cold than T. linifolia.

T. MACROSPEILA, closely allied to Gesneriana, flowers late in May, has large bright crimson flowers, with a distinct black yellow-bordered blotch at the base of each petal, and stamens also black about one third the length of the flower.

T. MACULATA is a well-marked form with a hairy stem and bright red flowers, having a black blotch at the base, flowering towards the latter end of May.

T. MONTANA, distributed over a considerable area in Armenia, Persia, and Afghanistan, is a small-sized species seldom exceeding 6 in. in height, with flowers resembling those of T. Oculussolis of the south of France, usually red, but sometimes yellow.

T. OCULUS-SOLIS is very distinct, its flowers brilliant scarlet, with an eye-like blotch at the base of each petal, of a shining black colour, bordered with yellow. T. præcox is apparently an early form of this, but more robust in growth.

T. ORPHANIDEA, from Greece, a fine species, is closely allied to T. sylvestris, and has large yellow flowers, tinged with red on the outside.

T. OSTROWSKYANA, one of the newer species from Turkestan, is allied to T. Oculus-solis, and has bright red flowers with black blotches at the base.

T. PULCHELLA, from the alpine regions of the Taurus range, has flowers of a purplish-red colour, with black and yellow markings.

T. RETROFLEXA, probably a hybrid between acuminata and Gesneriana, is a truly beautiful kind, growing 2 ft. in height ; with recurved flowers of a pure soft yellow, striking, distinct, and one of the easiest to grow.

T. SAXATILIS, a native of Crete, is a fine species, growing from 12 to 16 in. high, with flowers a peculiar mauve tint, passing to yellow at the base.

T. SYLVESTRIS, a British species everybody ought to grow, is pale yellow, with casual edgings of red, and frequently the

scapes carry two flowers, but the most valuable property of all is its aromatic perfume.

T. UNDULATIFOLIA, a native of Asia Minor, does not exceed 10 in. in height, has glaucous leaves deeply undulated at the margin, and flowers of a brilliant crimson-red, with black blotches margined with yellow at the base. It flowers in May and is closely allied to T. ciliatula.

T. VIOLACEA, a recent introduction, is also one of the first kinds to flower, and is of a deep self-red colour and welcome for its earliness.

T. VITELLINA has large finely-shaped flowers of a lovely delicate yellow tint, and open with the earliest of the Gesneriana section. It is a splendid Tulip, its dwarf sturdy habit fitting it to withstand heavy rains and winds.

Tulipa Species :—*Alberti*, Turkestan ; *altaica*, Siberian Alps ; *aristata*, China ; *australis*, Portugal, France ; *Beccariana*, Italy ; *Behmiana*, Turkestan ; *Biebersteiniana*, Caucasus ; *biflora*, do; *bithynica*, Asia Minor ; *bæotica*, Greece ; *Boroszcowi*, Turkestan ; *brachystemon*, do. ; *campsopetala*, (?) ; *caucasica*, Caucasus ; *chrysantha*, Persia, India ; *clusiana*, Europe ; *connivens*, Italy ; *cretica*, Crete ; *crispatula*, Persia ; *cuspidata*, Algeria, Persia ; *dasystemon*, Turkestan ; *Dideiri*, Europe ; *edulis*, China, Japan ; *Eichleri*, Turkestan ; *elegans* (?) ; *erythronioides*, China ; *etrusca*, Italy ; *foliosa*, Armenia ; *fragrans*, Algeria ; *fulgens* (?); *gallica*, France; *gesneriana*; E. Europe, East; *greigi*, Turkestan ; *Hageri*, Greece ; *heterophylla*, Alps ; *humilis*, Persia ; *hungarica*, Hungary ; *iliensis*, Turkestan ; *Kaufmanniana* do. ; *Kesselringi*, do. ; *Kolpakowskiana*, do. ; *Korolkowi*, do. ; *Kranseana*, do. ; *lanata*, Bokhara ; *linifolia*, do. ; *Lownei*, Syria ; *lurida*, Europe ; *maculata* (?) ; *maleolens*, Italy ; *Martelliana*, Europe ; *Montana*, East ; *oculus-solis*, S. Europe, East ; *orientalis*, S. Europe, Caucasus ; *Orphanidea*, Greece ; *Ostrowskiana*, Turkestan ; *oxypetala*, Tauria ; *Passeriniana*, Europe ; *patens*, Siberia ; *platystigma*, France ; *polychroma*, Persia ; *præcox*, S. Europe, Syria ; *primulina*, Algeria ; *pubescens* (?) ; *pulchella*, Cilicia ; *Regeli* (?) ; *retroflexa*, (?) ; *saxatilis*, Crete ; *scabriscapa*, Italy ; *serotina*, Italy ; *sogdiana*, Turkestan ; *sommierii*, Persia ; *strangulata*, Etruria ; *suaveolens*, S. Russia ; *systola*, Persia; *tetraphylla*, Turkestan; *thianschanica*, Cent. Asia ; *triphylla*, Turkestan ; *turkestanica*, do. ; *undulatifolia*, Asia Minor ; *uniflora*, Siberia ; *violacea*, Persia.

TUNICA.—*T. Saxifraga* is a small plant with a profusion of wiry stems that bear numerous elegant little rosy flowers. It forms tufts a few inches high, does best on poor soils, but thrives without particular care anywhere. It is a native of arid stony places on the Pyrenees and the Alps ; but it often descends into the lowlands, where it is found on the tops of walls. There can be no doubt that it will grow in such positions and on ruins in this country. It is a neat plant for the rock-garden and fringes of borders, and thrives like a weed between the stones in a rough stone wall. Seed.

TUSSILAGO (*Coltsfoot*).—*T. farfara*, the variegated form, is perfectly hardy, increases itself by running underground, like the Nettle or the Couch Grass, and, being of spreading habit, is not easily got rid of when established. It may be used with good effect in shady positions where

Tunica Saxifraga.

other plants will not thrive, and does well as an edging to a clump of Ferns, or as a groundwork to plants with graceful foliage.

TYPHA (*Reed Mace*).—*T. latifolia* is a native water-side plant, growing in tufts of two-rowed flat leaves, 18 to 24 in. long and 1 or 1½ in. wide. From the centre of each tuft springs a stem 6 or 7 ft. high, terminated in the flowering season by a close cylindrical spike 9 in. long, which is of dark olive, but changes to brownish-black as it ripens. *T. angustifolia* is like it except in the size of the narrower leaves and spike, and of the two is perhaps the more graceful, and *T. minor* is a smaller form of it. *T. minima* is the smallest of the hardy kinds, 12 in. to 18 in. in height, with slender rush-like leaves and dense or globose heads, those of the other kinds being much longer than they are broad.

ULEX (*Furze*).—The native Furze is so beautiful and is so well suited for clothing dry banks and the like, that it should be included among flowering shrubs. Where the common Furze grows wild, the double variety is well worth planting, as it is more effective in bloom than the single kind, and lasts longer. There is also a dwarf sort named nanus, which deserves a place, as it flowers at midsummer when its commoner relative is past flowering. This is also a native, and in places where it flourishes it makes a dense prickly bush 2 ft. high.

U. strictus (*Irish Furze*) is an uncommon variety of europæus, sometimes met with in botanical collections. As all the kinds of Furze are difficult to transplant when large, the best plan is to get small plants of the double and of the dwarf kinds, and to sow seed of the common single kind. In most nurseries the stock of double Furze is in pots, so that at any time the plants may be had and planted. There are few finer sights than a bank of double Furze in full bloom, and it fortunately may be grown in every garden. Vigorous pruning when its bushes become straggling is all the attention it needs. In severe winters all forms of these plants are liable to be cut down to the ground, but often start up as vigorous as before.

ULMUS (*Elm*).—Summer-leafing forest trees of northern and temperate regions and of importance in planting, though the dangerous habit of the common Elm of suddenly dropping heavy branches should make us cautious about planting it near houses. Some of the varieties and species that may be of interest in botanical collections are not worth a place in private grounds, and those planted should be of the most distinct and stately kinds only, as weedy-looking Elms, common in some districts, never give any but a poor effect. The common habit in many districts of forming avenues and shade trees of Elm only, might well be modified in favour of other trees of proved value, as the disfigurement which occurs after storms in Elm-planted villages and roadsides is deplorable.

U. AMERICANA (*Water Elm*).—A large and handsome tree inhabiting moist soil and banks of streams in Newfoundland and westwards and southwards, quite hardy, and useful in Britain. There is a weeping variety.

U. CAMPESTRIS (*Common Elm*).—This tree is common and naturalised in our river valleys, and is often blown down by storms in numbers. If we wish to shade our road or walks with trees we certainly should take the trouble to find those which anchor themselves securely, which this does not. There are many varieties, the Cornish, a pendulous one, and the usual variegated ones always more attractive in the nursery state than they are when they get older.

U. MONTANA (*Mountain* or *Wych Elm*).—A fine tree, distinct and handsome as a shade and lawn tree, and not so liable to cause accidents as the common Elm. There are rather numerous varieties, pyramidal upright growers, and, best of all, a weeping variety, a beautiful hardy and distinct tree thriving almost anywhere. There are many specimens in London gardens, and the trees being grafted on their own wild form, the junction is a sound and enduring one and the tree improves with age.

UMBILICUS.—Succulent plants similar to Houseleeks, Spinosus being a very singular-looking plant, with leaves forming a rosette something like that of a Sempervivum, each leaf bearing a spine at the apex. The yellow flowers appear early in summer, and form a cylindrical spike on the top of the flower-stem. It is a good plant for dry sunny spots in the rock-garden, and is tolerably hardy, but slugs destroy it whenever they have a chance. Siberia, China, and Japan.

U. Chrysanthus is about 4 in. high, with short panicles of yellowish flowers, and suitable for the same positions as spinosus.

U. Sempervivum forms a rosette-like tuft of succulent leaves, and produces in the second year of its growth a large cluster of pink flowers on a stem about 6 in. in height. It is useful for carpet-bedding, and when used for this purpose the flower-stems must be pinched out. Hardy in the rock-garden or in well-drained soils. Kurdistan.

UNIOLA.—*U. latifolia* is a handsome perennial Grass from N. America, 2 to 3 ft. high, with a large loose panicle, bearing large flattened spikelets. A clump, placed in rich garden soil, gathers strength from year to year, and when well established is a beautiful object.

UROSPERMUM.—*U. Dalechampi* is a rather handsome composite from S. Europe ; of dwarf tufted growth, with large heads of lemon-yellow blossoms. It thrives in an open position in any light soil, and is hardy.

UVULARIA (*Bellwort*). — Graceful perennials allied to Solomon's Seal, bearing yellow blossoms. There are four cultivated species, chinensis, grandiflora, puberula, and sessilifolia. Of these grandiflora is the finest, and the only one worth growing generally. It attains a height of 1 to 2 ft., and its numerous slender stems form a compact tuft, with flowers long and yellow, drooping gracefully, and pretty in early summer. It is a good peat border plant, thriving best in a moist peaty soil. North America, except chinensis. Division.

VACCINIUM (*Whortleberry*).—A few of the best Vacciniums may be planted for ornament in peat soil, though none are in the first rank of flowering shrubs. One of the most desirable is V. corymbosum, the Blue Berry of the North American swamps, a

Tussilago Farfara variegata (Variegated Coltsfoot).

rather large shrub, bearing a profusion of small pinkish flowers in dense clusters. The Pennsylvanian Blue Berry (V. pennsylvanicum) is, about October, usually a mass of scarlet and crimson. Though not remarkable for flower or berry, its decaying foliage assumes in autumn brilliant tints. Canadense, erythrinum, nitidum, and ovatum, with our native Vitis-idæa, Myrtillus, and uliginosum give interest to a plantation of peat-loving shrubs. V. Vitis-idæa (Red Whortleberry) is a dwarf British Evergreen, with Box-like foliage and clusters of small pale flowers, in summer, followed by berries about the size of Red Currants, borne on wiry stems 3 to 9 in. high. It forms a neat little bush in the rock-garden or in beds of peat soil. The Marsh Cranberry (V.' Oxycoccos) is a native of wet bogs in Britain, with slender creeping shoots and drooping dark rose flowers. It requires wetter soil than Vitis-idæa. The American Cranberry (V. macrocarpum), a much larger plant, deserves a place with bog shrubs ; it fruits profusely in beds of peat soil. V. hirsutum is showy late in summer when it becomes a brick-red colour in the leaves, which is most persistent, lasting many weeks.

VALERIANA (*Valerian*). — Hardy perennial and mountain plants, of which the only one worth cultivating in a general way is the golden-leaved variety of V. Phu—an effective plant in spring, when its foliage is young ; it is of neat tufted habit, and grows freely in any soil. A few dwarf alpine Valerians are sometimes grown, but they are not attractive. The flowers, too, are unpleasantly scented. Some of the larger species are pretty in rough places in moist land.

VALLOTA (*Scarborough Lily*).—V. *purpurea* is a handsome Amaryllis-like plant, hardy in mild climates. It requires a warm situation in light soil, for instance, at the foot of a south wall, and in such positions it often thrives better than in pots under glass, but the bulbs must be protected during severe frosts. The outdoor culture of this plant deserves more attention than it has hitherto had. Some flowers sent us by Mr. Kingsmill, grown in his garden, were superb. Offsets detached from the parent bulbs. Cape of Good Hope.

VANCOUVERIA.—V. *hexandra* is a most graceful and distinct plant, 10 to 18 in. high, with light fern-like leaves and slender spikes of pale flowers, and is a charming plant for the fernery and rock-garden, best in peaty soil. It is absolutely distinct in aspect from any other plant,

and grown in broad tufts and groups it is charming. Vancouver. Division.

VENIDIUM.—V. *calendulaceum* is a beautiful half-hardy Cape perennial of dwarf spreading growth, with in summer showy yellow Marigold-like blossoms. A good effect is gained by putting out several plants on a warm sunny border. Cuttings inserted in August root freely, and may be potted and kept in the greenhouse through the winter, when they must not have much water, or they will damp off. Seeds germinate freely in a hot-bed in early spring ; both should be planted out in May, in friable soil.

VERATRUM (*White Hellebore*).—V. *album* is a handsome erect pyramidal perennial, 3½ to 5 ft. high, with large plaited leaves and yellowish-white flowers in dense spikes on the top of the stem, forming a large panicle. The leaves are handsome, and most effective when the plant is in small groups, either in the rougher parts of the pleasure ground or by wood walks, thriving in peaty soil. The root is exceedingly poisonous. V. nigrum differs from V. album in having more slender stems, narrower leaves, and blackish-purple flowers. V. viride resembles V. album, except that its flowers are green. Division. France.

VERBASCUM (*Mullein*).—These are stately plants, mostly only of biennial duration, but the best are so handsome and

Verbascum olympicum.

long flowering as to be quite essential in the garden, where in many cases once introduced they take care of themselves and come year after year like the Foxglove. The finer kinds merit good treatment and free planting in bold groups.

V. Chaixi, or V. vernale (*Nettled-leaved Mullein*), is a perennial species, attains 10 ft. in height, and when well grown forms a most imposing group. The bright green leaves come up early ; the flowers are large, yellow, with purple filaments, and last a long time. It is a native of Europe. V. Crassifolium, a charming species, with yellowish tomentose

Verbascum phlomoides.

woolly leaves and robust spikes of large yellow flowers, is a native of Portugal. V. cupreum is nearly allied to V. phœniceum, hardy, a true perennial with copper-coloured flowers, quaint and interesting, flowering from May to August. V. nigrum, a native of Britain, is pretty, a true perennial like V. Chaixi in flower, but rarely more than 3 ft. high. A handsome form of it, now grown in gardens, with pure white flowers, is a good plant. South Europe.

V. olympicum is one of the grandest of the family, the flower-stems in strong specimens attaining 6 to 10 ft. in height,

the flowers rich yellow, the leaves woolly forming bold rosettes. A biennial from the Orient. V. phœniceum (Purple-leaved Mullein), one of the best perennials for

Verbascum phœniceum.

borders in small gardens, is very variable, there being white, violet, lilac, rose, and purple-flowered varieties, flowering from May to August. S. Europe.

V. phlomoides is the best of all Mulleins, varying in height from 5 to 9 ft. according to the richness of soil, its flowers rich yellow opening successionally over a prolonged period, the display lasting in beauty nearly the whole season through. It will grow in almost any soil, and should be grouped boldly in picturesque ways among shrubs and the larger hardy plants. S. Europe.

V. pyramidatum (*Pyramidal Mullein*), from Siberia, with candelabrum-like branches of bright yellow flowers, is a good plant, perennial on warm rich soils, and effective with its towering floweringstems and huge rosettes of crisped leaves.

Other Verbascums of interest are macrurum, longifolium, virgatum, Blattaria, niveum, Boerhavi, sinuatum, and orientale.

VERBENA.—Beautiful half hardy trailing plants which of late years have not been so popular in gardens, probably on account of the disease that attacks them. Verbenas bloom profusely out-of-doors till quite late in the autumn ; and if the lustre of the flowers happens to become dimmed by a storm, a burst of sunshine quickly restores their beauty. From the Continent have come many fine varieties, and some excellent kinds are the produce of English-saved seed. A pretty bed may be gained by mixing a few good varieties together. The Verbena should have a dry open border, and trench the ground, well dressing it with spent hot-bed manure and leaf-soil. Put out the plants about the end of May, and as they grow peg the shoots securely over the bed, keeping them well thinned. The best way of ensuring good cuttings for spring propagation is to keep a few store plants in pots all the summer, and in the autumn cut them pretty close. Give them a shift then into larger pots of rich soil. Soon afterwards set these store plants in a cool house, or a pit from which frost is excluded. Of late years Verbenas have been most successfully raised from seed sown about the middle of January, in light soil in a warm frame or pit. The seedlings should be pricked out, when a few weeks old, in 2½-in. pots, and when the plants are fully established, they should be placed near the glass in a pit which is well ventilated, in order to induce stout hardy growth. About the end of March the seedlings should be potted singly in 2½-in. pots, and a month later they should be transferred to 3-in. pots. About the middle of May the plants should be planted out about 2 ft. apart in a sunny border, and in a short time they will be aglow with flower. Verbenas raised from seed are valuable for garden adornment in summer, and need not be cut for propagation, while they run little risk of disease or of insects. Keeping the plants free from insects and disease in winter is a troublesome matter ; but with seedlings under fair conditions insects would be avoided, and the seedlings would certainly have a vigour that would get over the so-called disease. In any case it is an interesting fact that Verbenas in any number and of the greatest vigour may be raised from seed in the same year that they adorn the garden, or, in other words, may be treated as annual plants. The wonderful diversity and brilliancy of colour and the profusion of the flowers combine to place Verbenas grown from seed among the most valuable plants we possess. Verbena seed is sold in colours—scarlet, blue, white, carnation, flaked, and other forms, and all kinds come remarkably true. The scarlet kind is a fine reproduction of the old Defiance, and its growth and the quantity of its bloom are marvellous. The compact purplish-red kermesina is very pleasing and effective.

V. venosa is a perennial kind, 12 to 18 in. high, with heads of purple-violet blossoms, hardier than ordinary Verbenas, not so liable to mildew, and looks all the brighter for drenching rains. It is easily kept through the winter, and if its fleshy roots are stored thickly in boxes, plants may be propagated in spring from the young shoots thrown out. When the roots have to be lifted in autumn, place them at once in the boxes where they are to start, keeping them in a cool place until the time for putting them in heat. In herbaceous borders they may be allowed to remain for years, but should be protected through the winter.

VERBESINA.—*V. encelioides* is a half-hardy annual, 1 to 2 ft. high, with broad clusters of golden-yellow blossoms. California, Texas, and Mexico. V. gigantea from Jamaica is about 6½ ft. high. When young it is very pleasing, its round green stems being covered with large, winged, glistening, delicate green leaves. It is suitable for rich beds or groups, and should be planted out at the end of May or early in June. V. pinnatifida is a rough half-shrubby species, with larger leaves than those of V. gigantea. Both V. gigantea and V. pinnatifida require hothouse treatment in winter. Cuttings in early spring are best, and will be all the better for the most sheltered position, also the richest and lightest soil that can be given them.

VERNONIA (*Ironweed*). — Coarse North American Composites, of which some half-a-dozen species are in cultivation. They bloom so late that they are scarcely worth a place in the border; but V. præalta is a fine stately plant for the wild garden. Even if its flowers are injured or escape us, it may be grown in a copse, ditch, or open spot in a wood. Division.

VERONICA (*Speedwell*). — A large family of dwarf and shrubby plants, some trailing or carpeting in their growth, the flowers being generally of a blue shade, but often imperfect in colour, varying from rose to a dull white. Plants of the same species vary much in form, therefore the naming of the different Speedwells is difficult and perplexing. The shrubby New Zealand kinds are good in mild districts, where they do not get much hurt in ordinary winter, and for seaside gardens are especially valuable, as they with-

Shrubby Speedwell.

stand wind and spray better than most shrubs. V. speciosa is the commonest in seaside places. It is of dense growth, with broad leaves and erect feathery spikes of deep purplish-blue flowers. The variety imperialis has flowers of a rich red-purple, and in rubra they are inclined to red or to rose-pink. V. speciosa is but half-hardy, in cold localities requiring protection in winter, but is a good shrub for a light, airy, and cool greenhouse. V. salicifolia (the Willow-leaved Veronica), called also V. Lindleyana, is about 2 ft. high, with long narrow leaves, and spikes of white or purplish flowers. V. ligustrifolia has narrower leaves, and white flowers in feathery spikes. V. elliptica, known also as V. decussata, is something like V. speciosa, but smaller both in foliage and growth ; and V. Andersoni, said to be a hybrid, also resembles V. speciosa,

having spikes of bluish-violet flowers. The variegated form of Andersoni is a half-hardy bedding plant, but though fine in itself used too much in parks and gardens. Many well variegated things are spoilt through being planted anywhere and everywhere. All the foregoing are half-hardy, but suitable only for walls and warm spots in the mildest districts and at the seaside. Of the larger kinds only one is thoroughly hardy in all parts of England, V. Traversi, a neat shrub, forming a round-headed bush about 4 ft. high, in late summer very beautiful when crowded with spikes of pale mauve flowers. Among dwarfer kinds, V. verbenacea, V. fruticulosa, V. alpina, V. aphylla, V. Nummularia, V. Guthrieana, V. austriaca, V. incisa, V. bellidioides, and V. Dabneyi, are of good dwarf habit, and suited for a rock-garden. The pink variety of V. officinalis forms when established dense patches of pink-coloured blossoms, sometimes raised 3 in. above the ground. These mentioned are so hardy, that they may be divided or transplanted at all seasons. Such kinds as V. longifolia require frequent division to prevent too crowded growth. Most of the kinds ripen abundance of seed, and round them come up seedlings which vary in colour and form.

V. amethystina is 12 to 18 in. high, but rather too diffuse. It should be cut down in autumn, as otherwise it trails in an untidy way. In June it produces many terminal racemes of blossoms.

V. Chamædrys (*Germander Speedwell*) has been recommended for covering beds where late-flowering bulbs are grown. A curious variety, named pedunculata, is quite distinct and a neat plant.

V. gentianoides is one of the earliest of the Speedwells, and flowers in May. Three forms are common—the type with gray flowers, a variety with white flowers and bright glossy leaves like the Gentianella, and another with handsome variegated leaves. All are worth growing.

V. incana, also called V. candida, is a dwarf plant with silvery leaves, and dark rich purple flowers. It is used with good effect in bedding, its gray leaves being a contrast to most other foliage. V. neglecta is similar but inferior. Division.

V. longifolia is the commonest garden species, generally sold as V. spicata, and in four varieties—blue, white, rose-coloured, and purple. The variegation of the leaves is uncertain and irregular, but the habit of the plant is good. The rich colour of the flower, the length of the flower-spike, and the sturdy and compact growth of the plant make it handsome for the border. It grows well in any ordinary soil.

V. pectinata is a pretty trailing kind, with serrated downy leaves and blue or rose-coloured flowers. It is well suited for dry spots in the rock-garden, for the margins of borders, and for other places.

V. prostrata.—A very dwarf species, making spreading tufts. There are varieties with rose-coloured and white flowers which appear in early summer, the type being deep blue, hardy and pretty, blooming so freely that the leaves are often quite obscured by the flowers.

Veronica pinguifolia.

France, Central and Southern Europe, on stony hills and dry grassy places.

V. repens clothes the soil with a soft carpet of bright green foliage, covered, in spring, with pale bluish flowers. It thrives well on moderately dry soil, but delights in moist corners of the rock-garden.

V. rupestris trails neatly and closely, and flowers abundantly in June. To those who have seen large masses of it in rock-gardens it will want no further recommendation. There are several alpine species nearly allied to it.

V. satureiæfolia is one of the best of the Speedwells, though somewhat rare, with flowers about the size of those of V. saxatilis, of the same intense blue, and in abundant upright racemes.

V. saxatilis.—A native of alpine rocks in various parts of Europe, and also of a few places in the highlands of Scotland. It forms neat tufts 6 or 8 in. high, the flowers being little more than ½ in. across, of a pretty blue, striped with violet, and with a narrow but decided ring of crimson near the bottom of the cup, the base of which is pure white.

V. spicata is a dwarf native plant, not more than 5 or 6 in. high, useful for bare corners of rock-gardens, but seldom flowering before the end of July. V. corymbosa is a name given to varieties of two or three species, but the best seems to be a form of V. spicata. This is one of the best plants for rock-gardens, being profuse and continuous in bloom. V. hybrida is generally classed as a variety of it, but seems quite distinct, since it is far more robust, and its flowers vary in colour from dark purple to lavender and light rose. It grows wild in profusion on mountain limestone hills near Llandudno and in other parts of the north-western counties.

V. subsessilis is botanically considered a variety of V. longifolia, but for garden purposes is very distinct. It is the handsomest of the hardy Veronicas, and flourishes in spite of spring frosts and cold summers. Its large dense spikes of deep purple-blue flowers are effective, and it should always have a position among the choicest hardy flowers in a good deep loamy soil and open situation. Japan. Division or seed.

V. taurica.—A dwarf, wiry, and almost woody species from Tauria, forming neat dark green tufts, under 3 in. high; its fine Gentian-blue flowers borne abundantly. It is, perhaps, the neatest kind for forming spreading tufts in level spots of the rock-garden, or drooping from chinks, and for association with the dwarfest alpine plants. Division or cuttings.

V. Teucrium.—A Continental plant, the stems of which form spreading masses, from 8 to 12 in. high, covered in early summer with flowers of an intense blue, at first in dense racemes, but these afterwards become much longer. It is excellent for the rock-garden, or for borders, and grows freely in ordinary garden soil. Seeds or division.

V. virginica and other tall species are 3 to 4 ft. high, and flower in July, but are deficient in colour.

VESICARIA.—Hardy evergreen perennials, of which V. græca is the handsomest, and bears a strong resemblance to the better-known V. utriculata, long cultivated in gardens. The flowers open in succession for several inches on each stem. Rocky districts in Dalmatia and other places in South Europe. Cuttings or seed. Both V. græca and V. utriculata flourish in dryish soil, on dry sunny parts of the rock-garden.

VIBURNUM (*Guelder Rose*).—Handsome and vigorous shrubs of northern regions : of much beauty, of berry as well as flower : and with few exceptions of the easiest cultivation. They simply need a soil of fair quality and plenty of moisture. They can be easily propagated by cuttings and layers or seed—the best way.

Viburnum plicatum.

Some of the kinds are not worthy of a place in gardens, either from not being distinct from others, or from not showing their best characters in our country, and those admitted here are distinct and of value in our country. As N. Asia is very rich in these plants we may look for some good kinds from it, but it is best at first to limit the kinds to those giving really good effects.

V. CASSINOIDES.—Of the American Viburnum, this is one of the best, growing some 6 ft. high, with thick leathery leaves, 3 in. to 4 in. long, and yellowish white flowers, during the early part of June, in flat cymes 4 in. to 5 in. across, and handsome fruit, the berries changing first to rose colour and finally to bluish black. As they do not ripen simultaneously, fruits of both these colours, as well as green ones, occur on a cluster at the same time. Northern and Arctic America.

V. FURCATUM.—Is a rare and handsome species, a native of North Japan at low levels, and of the mountains of the more southern portions, and is one of the finest shrubs for autumn colour. The leaves, which are large and broad, turn brilliant scarlet and reddish purple before they fall, and it grows 12 ft. to 15 ft. in height. Japan.

V. LANTANA (*Wayfaring Tree*).—One of the two kinds native of Britain, and frequent in hedgerows and copses, especially in chalk or limestone soils. At its best it is almost a small tree, 12 ft. to 15 ft. high. The flowers are white during May and June on flat clusters at the ends of the branches. The fruit is red at first, ultimately black, and the leaves often die off a rich red. There is a variegated form of no particular value.

V. LANTANOIDES (*Hobble Bush* or *Moosewood*).—A North American kind, a large shrub, the leaves are almost round, and whilst averaging 3 in. to 4 in. across, are sometimes over 6 in. The truss has its outer flowers sterile, and they are 1 in. or more in diameter ; both they and the smaller ones that fill the centre are white. The fruit is at first coral-red, afterwards dark purple or almost black, and the foliage dies off a rich claret.

V. MACROCEPHALUM (*Great Snowball Bush*).—A Chinese species, not very hardy, but its flower-clusters are enormous. In some places it thrives against a wall, but is rarely seen in good health. Fortune mentions having seen it 20 ft. high in Chusan. The wild plant from which it has been derived is in cultivation, and is known as V. KETELEERI. This has the centre of the truss (which is much flatter than in *V. macrocephalum*) filled with fertile flowers, the outer ones only being sterile.

V. ODORATISSIMUM.—As a rule, when grown out of doors this is given a place on a wall, as it is not hardy in all winters. It is evergreen, its foliage being handsome. Each leaf 3 to 6 in. long, leathery, and of a lustrous dark green. The flowers are in corymbs, and although small and dull white, are charming for their fragrance. China. *Syn.* V. Awafuki.

V. OPULUS (*Guelder Rose*).—A handsome and often rather tall native bush, frequent in the underwoods of many districts. In the wild form the outer flowers only of the cyme are sterile, and these are about three-quarters of an inch across ; the centre is filled with small perfect flowers. In autumn this plant is valued for its clusters of fine red fruits and for the colour of its leaves. Of its best known varieties, is the VAR. STERILE (*the common Guelder Rose*). This has few or no perfect flowers, the whole truss consisting of the more showy barren ones. This causes it to lose its flatness and makes it much more rounded, which, together with the pure whiteness of the flowers, has led to its being popularly known as the Snowball Tree. A yellow fruited kind differs from the type in the fruits being yellow instead of red when ripe.

V. SIEBOLDI.—A handsome and distinct evergreen bush, with large glossy leaves and large heads of white flowers, in May and June in southern England. A promising kind, at least for districts where our evergreens usually escape the effects of hard winters.

V. TINUS (*Laurustinus*).—A beautiful and fragrant evergreen, thriving over a large area of Great Britain and Ireland, especially near the sea and on warm and gravelly soil, though now and then injured by severe winters even in the country south of London. In sunny positions it usually flowers freely, but not in shade, commencing to bloom in December, it will continue till the end of March. Although all its flowers are perfect, it does not ripen fruit regularly, but fruits occasionally occur, the colour being a dark blue. There are several varieties of the Laurustinus, one of which, the VAR. LUCIDUM, has fine large leaves, shining and almost smooth on both sides, and the flowers and flower-trusses also are larger. It is possibly not quite so hardy as some forms of Laurustinus, and should have a sheltered, sunny spot. Another variety is *Var. hirtum*, the distinguishing character of which is the hairiness of the leaves and branches, and *Var. purpurum* has the leaves suffused with a dull purple tinge. Laurustinus can be struck from cuttings.

V. PLICATUM (*Japanese Guelder Rose*).—A very sturdy, robust, flowering shrub. I have seen young, newly-rooted plants injured the first year after being put out, but when once established it will stand any frost up to 30° without lasting injury. It is a shrub of neat, yet graceful habit, well clothed with dark green, rather plaited leaves. It bears its fine trusses, 3 in. or more across, on short branches springing from the whole length of the previous year's growth, thus forming fine sprays of pure white blossom. *Syn.* V. Tomentosum Var. W. J. B.

VICIA (*Vetch*).—Perennial and annual plants, several of which are natives. V. Cracca, V. Orobus, V. sylvatica, V. Sepium, and V. argentea are the most desirable, but are not of great importance. V. argentea has elegant silvery leaves, but is rare in cultivation. Vicias grow freely in almost any soil, and are raised from seeds.

VIEUSSEUXIA (*Blue-eyed Peacock Iris*).—*V. glaucopis* is a beautiful bulbous plant 9 to 15 in. high, with flowers in early summer, about 2 in. across, pure white, with a beautiful porcelain-blue stain nearly ⅓ in. broad at the base of each of the three larger divisions. This stain is deep violet at the base, and margined with dark purple teeth. The plant should be grown on warm sheltered borders in sandy peat or sandy loam and leaf-mould. Increased by separation of the bulbs in autumn. Cape of Good Hope. *Syn.*, Iris Pavonia.

VILLARSIA (*Yellow Buckbean*).—*V. nymphæoides* is an interesting British water plant, with leaves like those of a Water-Lily, but smaller, and floating. Its yellow flowers are borne in summer singly, but are very numerous, and lasting through the summer. It is one of the best of water flowers. Division.

VINCA (*Periwinkle*). — Perennia. trailers, hardy and vigorous in almost any soil. The well-known V. major (common Periwinkle) is useful for banks on masses of rootwork, and also for rocky places or by wood walks and there are several variegated varieties, including a golden-leaved kind. The lesser Periwinkle (V. minor) is much smaller than V. major, and useful for the same positions, has several varieties well worthy of cultivation ; a white-flowered one (V. m. alba), a reddish one, and one or two double

Vinca major.

ones, and there are also several variegated forms. V. herbacea is much less frequently seen than our common Periwinkles, but is more worthy of culture on rocks, as it is not rampant in habit. It is a native of Hungary, flowers in spring and early summer, and its stems die down every year. V. acutiloba is a distinct and elegant Periwinkle, and flowers late in autumn and in winter, bearing delicate mauve blossoms. It is suitable for sunny banks and slopes and for warm borders.

VIOLA (*Violet*).—A beautiful and well-known family, many kinds of which are alpine flowers. Some Violets are among the most beautiful ornaments which bedeck the alpine turf; and even the common Violet itself may almost be claimed as an alpine plant, for it wanders along hedgerow and hillside, along copses and thin woods, all the way to Sweden. From all kinds of Violets the world of wild flowers derives a precious treasure of beauty and delicate fragrance ; and

no family has given our gardens anything more precious than the numerous
races of Pansies and the various kinds of
large, showy, sweet-scented Violets. Far
above the faint blue carpets of the various
scentless wild Violets in our woods and
heaths, our thickets and bogs, and above
the miniature Pansies that find their
home among our lowland field-weeds;
far above the larger Pansy-like Violas
(varieties of V. lutea) which flower so
richly in the mountain pastures of northern
England and even on the tops of stone
walls; above the large, free-growing
Violets of the American heaths and
thickets, we have true alpine Violets,
such as the yellow two-flowered Violet
(V biflora), and large blue Violets such
as the V. calcarata and V cornuta It
would be difficult to exaggerate the
beauty of these alpine Violets They
grow in a turf of high alpine plants not
more than an inch or so in height The
leaves do not show above this densely-
matted turf, but the flowers start up,
waving everywhere thousands of little
banners. Violets are of the easiest
culture, even the highest alpine kinds
thrive with little care, and V. cornuta and
V calcarata of the Alps and Pyrenees
thrive even more freely than in their
native uplands, the foliage and the stems
being much stronger Some of the many
stronger varieties of the Sweet Violet
might be naturalised with advantage
Slow-growing compact kinds, like the
American Bird's-foot Violet, enjoy, from
their stature and their comparative slowness of growth, a position in the rock-
garden or in the choice border, and in
such a position they are of easy culture
in moist sandy soil Violets of all kinds
are easily increased by cuttings from
stout short runners All runners that are
wiry and hard should be rejected, and
none should be taken from plants that
have grown in pots or under glass The
cuttings should be taken off the first
week in April if they are to bloom next
year. They should be put under hand-
lights on a shady border, and kept close
until they begin to grow, when the lights
may be tilted a little, and the space
gradually increased until at last the lights
may be wholly dispensed with By
September the plants will be ready for
transplanting, and may be placed in beds
4 ft wide, three rows 1 ft apart being
in one bed This space will afford room
to hoe between the rows while they are
growing They will soon spread and fill
the beds, but they must not remain more
than two, or, at the most, three years in

the same place, or the flowers will become
small and short stemmed If they are
more than two years in the same place,
they must receive liberal top-dressings of
rotten manure, or copious applications of
manure water. Another mode of propagation, which is perhaps attended with
less trouble, is to get a few large plants
as soon as they have done blooming, and
to tear them into as many pieces as
possible, each piece having a little bit of
root attached to it Little pieces without
roots may be placed under hand-lights
and treated like cuttings

The following are among the most
desirable for general cultivation —

V. biflora (*Two-flowered Yellow
Violet*). — This bright little Violet is a
lovely ornament on the Alps, and in many
parts it densely clothes every chink
between the moist rocks It even crawls
under great boulders and rocks, and lines
shallow caves with its fresh verdure and
its little golden stars, and is useful in
rock-gardens where rude steps of stone
give winding pathways It will run
through every chink between the steps.
Europe, N Asia, and America

V. calcarata (*Spurred Violet*) —This
plant resembles the well-known V cornuta
in flower and spur, but, instead of forming leafy tufts, it increases by runners
under the earth V calcarata is a pretty
plant on the Alps, usually found in high
situations, amidst dwarf flowers, and is so
plentiful that its large purple flowers
sometimes form sheets of colour, and it
is as charming in the rock-garden as in
its native wilds Its yellow variety (flava)
is the same as V Zoysi

V. cornuta (*Horned Pansy*).—A mountain Pansy, with sweet-scented flowers
pale blue or mauve, valuable but superseded by the many charming tufted
Pansies raised during recent years Alps
and Pyrenees Division, cuttings, or
seeds

V. cucullata (*Large American Violet*)
bears some resemblance to the common
Violet, though without its delicious scent
It belongs to a section which includes V
primulæfolia, blanda, obliqua, sagittata,
palmata, delphinifolia, canadensis, pubescens, striata, and others only fitted for
a place in botanical collections

V. gracilis is a remarkably pretty
dwarf species, never failing to produce
in spring an abundance of deep purple
blossoms in dense tufts It is hardy in
light soil Mount Olympus

V. lutea (*Mountain Violet*) — The
yellow form of this Violet is very neat
and compact, 2 to 6 in high From April

onwards it flowers abundantly, and its flowers are of a peculiarly rich and handsome yellow, the three lower petals being striped with thin lines of rich black.

V. Munbyana.—One of the prettiest of Violets, abundant in flower, free and robust in growth, and quite hardy. Generally it begins to bloom about the end of February, but it attains its greatest beauty in May. The deep purple-blue flowers resemble those of V. cornuta ; and there is also a yellow variety. Algeria.

V. odorata (*Sweet Violet*).—This well-known plant is in a wild state widely spread over Europe and Russian Asia, and is common in various parts of Britain, while it is grown in almost every garden, and enormous quantities of it are sold in London, Paris, and many other cities. Its delicious odour distinguishes it from other Violets. It may be grown where almost everything else but weeds would fail, forming carpets for open groves or the fringes of woods, of hedges, the open parts of copses, or for banks. Instead of being confined to a bed for cutting from, it should fringe shrubberies, rock-gardens, or ferneries. In such positions it requires no care, and rewards the planter by filling the cold March air with unrivalled sweetness. It will grow in almost any soil, but best on free sandy loam. It is well to naturalise the plant on sunny banks, fringes of woods, and on the warmer sides of bushy places to encourage a very early bloom.

The cultivation of the Sweet Violet is of great importance, not only for private gardens, but also to supply the vast demand for it in large cities. About Paris, the cultivation of Sweet Violets for the markets is largely carried on, and in some places three or four acres may be seen covered with these flowers. The ground is well exposed to the mid-day sun, and is rich, free, and warm. The plantations are made in spring, those required for the winter markets being grown in frames. Sweet Violets may be propagated to any extent by division, but strong, healthy, free-flowering plants are easily raised from seed, which should be sown as soon as possible after it is gathered. In cold dry parts, where Violets do not succeed well, and also where they are required in mid-winter, it is better to raise a number of healthy plants every year, and to put them in a light frame in a sunny position in autumn. With very little trouble we may have Violets long before they bloom in the open ground. Plants which are obtained by setting out runners in spring in rich soil, and receive in dry weather all the water they need, may be set in a cold frame early in autumn. Allow them to grow until the approach of winter, when fill the frames with leaves, put on the sashes with a shutter over these. The plants must have abundance of air on mild days, and water as they need it. A frame of three sashes, separated into three parts by boards, may be uncovered, one sash at a time, at intervals of two or three weeks, and thus a succession of flowers will be kept up. Violets do not like forcing, neither do they need it if their crowns are ripened early, and they are tempted by the protection of glass to open out genially and exhibit their fragrant blossoms.

In the open border Sweet Violets thrive on a moderately heavy rich soil ; if the soil happens to be light and gravelly, some stiff material and plenty of manure must be added to it ; and if poor and hard clay, it will be benefited by the sharp gritty matter and abundance of rotten manure. Violets require shelter, but not that of a wall ; and in town gardens or gardens surrounded by high walls they are seldom healthy. Their natural shelter is a hedgerow, in which they get currents of pure air, which are essential for keeping down red-spider and for maintaining the foliage in a healthy condition. Violets grow well on the north or north-east side of a Hornbeam hedge, if somewhat naked at bottom, so as to allow the sun to shine on their leaves early in spring, and afford a partial shade in summer. When the soil is deep and rich, however, Violets will bear a considerable amount of sunshine. It is well to have a few plants in different positions, so as to ensure a succession of bloom. On south borders Violets dwindle and die ; but a few roots on sunny banks will give some early pickings.

The insects that trouble the Violet most are green-fly and red-spider. The first is generally the result of a close unhealthy atmosphere, and is easily got rid of by gentle smokings. Red-spider is helped by strong sun and by dryness at the roots ; hand-dusting with sulphur is the best remedy, but it is easy to prevent ts occurrence by syringing the plants and their surroundings.

The varieties of the Violet are very numerous. We have the single white and the single rose, the double white, the Czar, (a very large and sweet variety), the Queen of Violets, Admiral Avellan, La Grosse Bleue, La France, California, Princess of Wales, Luxonne, Belle de Chatenay, White Czar, Lady Hume Campbell Marie

Louise, Victoria Regina, Wellsiana, and the perpetual blooming Violet—well known in France as La Violette des Quatre Saisons. It differs slightly from the Sweet Violet, but is valuable for flowering long and continuously in autumn, winter, and spring. It is the variety used by the cultivators round Paris. The double white, or, as it becomes in the open air, the rosy-white Belle de Chatenay, has a robust habit. Though not so pure as the old double white kind, it blooms more freely,

when grown in frames, or in beds in the open, where the thick growth keeps the flowers well up from the soil. Blandyana, another double, is a rather free bloomer with dark flowers.

V. pedata (*Bird's-foot Violet*).—The most beautiful of the American Violets, with handsome flowers 1 in. across, pale or deep lilac, purple or blue, the two upper petals being sometimes velvety and deep violet like the petals of a Pansy. The variety bicolor is prettier than the

Viola pedata (Bird's-foot Violet).

and is not so loose in its growth. The Neapolitan kind, V. o. pallida plena, will doubtless ever be a favourite, in spite of other and newer kinds, but it needs a frame in severe weather. Marie Louise is a fine kind, and is a great advance upon the Neapolitan kind; its flowers are larger, rather deeper, and more freely produced. The old double blue kind has very full and neat flowers, but its stems are short. It is, however, very beautiful

type; its flowers larger, and the petals are arranged flat like those of a Pansy, the two upper ones rich velvety purple, and the three lower delicate blush. V. pedata is free in growth in a light rich soil in partial shade, but the variety bicolor succeeds only in certain localities, and is rare even in its native soil. It is best adapted for the choice rock-garden, but may also be grown in borders where the soil is peaty, sandy, and moist.

V. reniformis (*New Holland Violet*).—
This mantles the ground with a mass of
small leaves, has numerous slender creeping stems, and bears throughout the
summer blue and white flowers of exquisite beauty, about 2 inches from the
ground. It is pretty for planting out over
a bed of peat or very light earth, where
taller plants are put out in a scattered

Viola reniformis (New Holland Violet).

manner during the summer, but being
very small and delicate, it should not be
used with coarse subjects. It must be
treated like a tender bedding plant—taken
up or propagated in autumn, and put out
in May or June. Australia. Division.
V. r. grandiflora is a larger plant in all its
parts. *Syn.*, Erpetion.

V. rothomagensis (*Rouen Violet*).—A
handsome plant belonging to the tricolor
group, dwarf, and with low creeping stems
which bear in spring numerous purple and
white blossoms. It is a free grower, but,
being a native of Sicily, is not so hardy as
some Violets, and should be grown in a
light soil and a warm border.

V. tricolor (*Heart's-ease*).—The Pansy
is usually classed under the head of V.
tricolor, though it is probably descended
from V. altaica—a species to which a
good many Pansies seem nearly allied.
But the Pansies are so numerous, so varied,
and, withal, so distinct from any wild
species of Violet, that little can be traced
of their origin. Of one thing we may be
certain : the parents of this precious race
were true mountaineers. Only alpines
could give birth to such rich and brilliant
colour and such noble amplitude of bloom.
Its season never ends ; it often blooms
cheerfully enough at Christmas, and is

sheeted with gold and purple when the
Hawthorn is white with blossoms. Such
a flower must not be ignored on our rock-
gardens, even though it thrives in almost
any soil and position. It may be treated
as an annual, a biennial, or a perennial,
according to climate, position, and soil.
One of the commonest of weeds in Scotland, the wild V. lutea, may be grown in
the south of England, if sheltered from
the midday sun. It thrives capitally with
a north or, better still, a north-east
exposure, if sheltered by tall trees or
buildings, so that it may get the cool sun
of the early morning only.

For borders one way is to grow the
plants from seed. The Belgian or fancy
Pansies are remarkable for the strange
and almost gorgeous variety of their
colours and the unusual size of many of
the blooms. They are more hardy as
seedlings, and more robust as plants, than
the other kinds, and yield a greater variety
of colours. The seed should be sown in
July or August, in pans of light leafy soil,
such as sand, leaf-mould, and mould from
rotted turf, and placed in a cool shady
place. When mixed seeds are sown, sow
each separately at a distance of 1½ in. or
so. As soon as the first seeds have germinated and the seedlings have three
pairs of leaves, they should be removed
without disturbing the weaker and more
backward ones, for amongst the seedlings
which are the last to appear will be found
the greatest proportion of finely-coloured
flowers. It is important to sow the seed
when fresh.

It is rarely convenient to plant the
seedlings at once where they are to
bloom, therefore they should be placed in
pots plunged in a cool place in the open
ground, and shifted to their final place
in time to get well-established before
winter sets in. They stand the winter
well, and the only danger lies in heavy
rain or sleet succeeded by sharp frosts.
A pot inverted over each plant to protect
the soil from too much wet would be
sufficient protection. It is not advisable
to move Pansies in spring unless they
have been kept in pots during winter, in
which case they may be planted, though
with as little root-disturbance as possible.

Pansies are divided into two sections
—the show or English kinds, and the
fancy or Belgian kinds. The first com-
prises five divisions : white and yellow
ground belted Pansies, white, yellow,
and purple Pansies. The selfs must be
clear decided colours, and should have a
black well-defined blotch under the
eye. The belted kinds should have a

white or yellow ground, together with centre blotch, and a broad margin of bronzy-red, chestnut, purple, or crimson, or other hue ; the colours must be dense, and the margins distinctly defined. The flowers of the show section should be rounded in form, stout of petal, and of good size, but size is of less importance than the quality of the markings. A fancy Pansy should have a large deep-coloured blotch, covering nearly the whole of the bottom petal and portions of the side petals. The rest of the flower may be white, yellow, buff, red, maroon, purple, crimson, and various other shades, but not so dense as the centre blotch. Some fancy Pansies are flaked or parti-coloured, but all good ones are showy and beautiful beyond the imagination of those who have only seen common strains. Named Pansies come fairly true from seed, but the only way to secure a stock of any particular variety is to take cuttings. When any plant or plants show flowers which it is desirable to perpetuate, the best way is to sacrifice the bloom for the year, pinch the bloom-buds off as fast as they show, feed the plant well with dressings of leaf-mould pricked in about the roots, and peg the first shoots down so as to leave the crown of the plant exposed, for fresh healthy shoots to rise from. A few shoots should be taken off when they have made three or four pairs of leaves, and be planted in light soil, sand, and leaf-mould, under a hand-glass, and kept moist and shaded. The pegged-down stems will produce shoots which may be taken off in the same way ; and when well rooted treated as seedlings.

A good plant combines a profusion of fine flowers with a dwarf, short-stemmed, stocky habit, and the plant when in bloom is a round green bush, with the flowers about ½ in. clear of the leaves. It is useless to save seed before a stock of first-class plants is obtained. July is early enough to sow the seed in the south of England, but farther north it may be sown earlier, until in Scotland it should be sown in the spring.

TUFTED PANSIES.—These are hybrids of Pansies and alpine Violets. The term "tufted" has been very properly used to distinguish plants of a spreading habit, like Pinks, Aubrietia, and Alpine Violets, from plants with simple erect stems, like, say, the Stock, Lupine, and Aster. Sometimes the two forms of habit occur in the same family ; for instance, there are Violas that are tufted and Violas that are not—the German, French, and other Pansies in our gardens do not spread at the root as the tufted Pansies do. Plants of this "tufted" habit are often a mass of delicate rootlets even above the ground, so that they are easily increased. Hence when older Pansies die after flowering, those crossed with the alpine species remain, like true perennials, and are easily increased. The term Pansies is a good one in all ways. Without an English name, we shall always have confusion with the Latin name for the name of wild species. To all of these belongs the old Latin name of the genus *Viola.* It is now agreed by botanists that all cross-bred garden plants — including tufted Pansies, of course—should have popular English, and not Latin, names. "Bedding Violas" is a vulgar compound of bad English and Latin ; whereas "tufted Pansies" is a good English name with a clear meaning.—*The Garden,* 16th Jan. 1892.

These are the flowers hitherto generally known as Violas and bedding Pansies, and Dr. Stuart, who has raised some of the best and truest of them, says :— "Botanically, Violets, Pansies, and Heart's-ease are all the same. Tufted Pansies are crosses from the garden Pansy and Viola cornuta, the latter being the seed-bearer. Pollen from V. cornuta applied to the Pansy produces a common enough form of bedding Pansy—never the tufty root-growth obtained when the cross is the other way. I have proved this by actual hand-crossing. Most strains of tufted Pansies are bred the wrong way, and in consequence lack the fibrous tufty root which makes the Violetta strain perennial."

Having settled the name, the next thing we have to do is select some of the most beautiful of these charming flowers, which are certainly more valuable for our flower gardens than the ordinary Pansy, fine and rich in colour as these are. They are so because the colours are simple and generally pure and true, and because they are most effective when used in groups, and then they are perennial, and may be easily increased and kept true.

The new race of Tufted Pansies raised by Dr. Stuart, of which Violetta was the first, is a precious addition to this large family, because the flowers are pure in colour and so sweetly scented. The older tufted Pansies were welcome, but all of them had wiry streaks about the eye, not a serious detraction, but it is a gain to have kinds that are quite rayless, as are all of Dr. Stuart's. Violetta the first has small flowers, but all the later varieties have large flowers, and in other respects they are equal to the older sorts, much more tufted in habit, and better garden-plants in every way. Among the best kinds are Albino, Blue Gown, Blush Queen, Bridal Wreath, George Muirhead, Queenie, Lucy Franklin, Flower of Spring, King of Whites, Sweet Lavender, and Sylvia. These in their several shades of colour are certainly some of the most beautiful flowers ever seen. The best of the older kinds with white flowers are Mrs. Kinnear, Countess of Hopetoun, Violetta, Mrs. Gray, and Marchioness of Tweeddale (with a delicate bluish shade). Near these creamy-whites come a group of creamy or pale yellow-coloured kinds, such as mentioned above, George Lord, Henry IV., and Devonshire Cream. Among yellows there is nothing better than Ardwell Gem,

A Tufted Pansy.

Pembroke, Molly Pope, Stephen, and Mrs. Greenwood. Perhaps the most precious of all are the lavenders and delicate blues, such as Ariel, Florizel, Azurea, Duchess of Sutherland, Formidable, and Bessie Clarke. Of the blues and rich dark purples we have Archie Grant, Blue King, Holyrood, Cliveden Purple, Lottie, and Max Kolb.

Although we like the colours simple and pure, there are other pretty ones of a different kind, such as Columbine, Blue Cloud, Duchess of Fife, Countess of Kintore, Skylark. In the south, however, they are uncertain, liable to vary much in colour, and never good in effect like the true selfs. Some kinds, like Violetta, are white, running off to delicate bluish or lilac hues. These delightful things are so easily raised and crossed, that it might

almost be well if each garden had its own colours, by the raising of a few kinds for itself, so as to have as much variety as possible.

These plants love a light and cool moist soil. In northern districts they are naturally more at home under ordinary conditions than in the south, and to bring them to perfection in the south, special treatment is necessary.

For early spring-flowering the cuttings should be rooted in July or August, and planted out in their places the first or second week in October. They commence blooming early in April. In heavy soils, that is, such as are liable to crack with drought, use abundance of leaf-soil, burnt ashes from the rubbish fires, and the like, to bring them into better working. Also select a dry time for digging, working in the above with plenty of short manure from an old Mushroom bed, and scattering an inch or so on the surface for the roots at planting time. Cuttings are better than divisions; particularly if they are made of the young shoots stripped from the old stool with a heel attached. To annually obtain a supply of these cuttings it will be necessary to plant out a reserve batch of plants for the purpose. About the second week in June, cut them back to within 2 in. of the soil. A month afterwards they will be bristling with young shoots. As soon as 3 in. long, scatter some fine soil and leaf-mould among the young growths, and keep well watered for a fortnight, by which time the majority will be making roots freely. A fortnight later they will be ready for planting in nursery-beds in a shady spot and in good soil. As growth is renewed, pinch out the top of each to encourage the quicker formation of shoots at the base. By October there will be some grand plants for putting into their permanent quarters, full of youth and vigour that will produce masses of flowers by-and-by.

Virgilia. See CLADRASTIS.

VISCARIA.—*V. oculata,* a showy and beautiful hardy annual from South Europe, is well suited for a border. Seed should be sown in spring or autumn, and the seedlings thinned out when large enough. V. oculata is 6 or 8 in. high, and bears a profusion of rose-coloured blossoms with a dark centre. The varieties cardinalis (bright crimson-purple), cœrulea (bluish), alba (white), Dunnetti (rose), splendens (scarlet), picta elegans (crimson purple, edged with white), and a dwarf variety, nana, about 9 in. high, are desirable.

VISCUM ALBUM (*Mistletoe*).—This half-shrubby parasite on trees is often welcome in the pleasure ground or orchard, and is not without beauty of colour, but where abundant it is very injurious to trees of all kinds, being a true parasite and living on the sap of its supporting tree. It grows on many trees, both evergreen and summer-leafing—orchard trees, limes, poplars, elms, willows, hornbeam, beech, acacia, horse-chestnut, firs—rarely on the oak in Britain. In districts where the plant is wild, the thrushes spread it about by wiping the seeds off their bills on the bark. In orchards or woods it is, where plentiful, very injurious to both fruit trees and

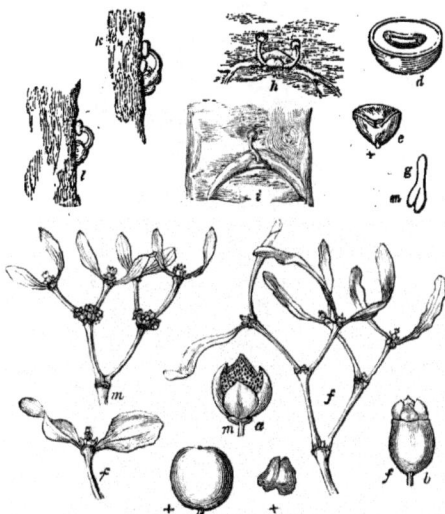

Mistletoe in various parts.

a, Male blossom. *b*, Female ditto. *d*, Berry cut through. *e*, Seed, showing embryos. *g*, Embryo magnified. *h*, Two embryos, with radicles germinating. *i*, Single radicle. *k*, Side view of two radicles. *l*, Section of the single radicle.

timber. As to the best way of increasing this plant, Mr. F. W. Burbidge writes :—

"I find growth of the seeds certain if they are placed on clean, fresh, smooth bark in April or May, and then covered with one thickness of black muslin or lawn, so that birds do not peck them away, as they do if unprotected. Many make the mistake of putting on the seeds at or about Christmas-time before they have ripened enough to grow. Do not cut slits in the bark in which to insert the seeds ; the best way is simply to apply it to the clean bark only.

"Apart altogether from its botanical interest or its antiquarian lore, the mistletoe, when well grown in dense masses on either apple or pear, really becomes an effective plant in either garden or in the winter landscape. The warm yellowish sap-green or olive-green leaf masses dangling from bare and leafless trunks or branches are distinct and effective, thickly set with the clustered berries that glisten in the sunshine."

VITEX (*Chaste Tree*).—*V. Agnus-castus* is a very old S. European shrub, with divided leaves, and in late summer, clusters of small pale lilac flowers. It grows 6 to 10 ft. high against a wall, but even thus protected is liable to be killed during a severe winter.

VITIS (*Vine*).—Woody climbing shrubs of much interest and garden value, owing to their luxuriant habit, grace, and handsome foliage, which in several instances affords the richest of colours—yellows, purples, and crimsons.

Whilst some are valuable for the walls of houses, others may be used for covering arbours, pergolas, the pillars of verandahs, old tree stumps or sloping banks. In the case of the stronger, taller-growing species they may be made to clamber over living trees. They are moisture-loving plants, and require liberal treatment. Where space is limited they can be kept at any required size by means of pruning, but the best effects are, of course, obtained where they can ramble without let or hindrance. Where they are intended to spread over living trees, they should always be planted sufficiently far away from the trunk to allow rain and light to reach them, and with good rich soil to start in. In the majority of the species increase can be accomplished by means of cuttings or by single "eyes" treated like those of the common Grape Vine, though some, however, can only be increased by seeds. Layering will occasionally prove successful with those that refuse to root from cuttings. Grafting should only be resorted to as a last resource.

In the following enumeration the names of Ampelopsis and Cissus are sunk under Vitis.

V. æstivalis (*Summer Grape*). — The leaves are of a deep green colour when old, but in a young state covered on the lower surface with a reddish down. The leaves of this measuring from 4 to 6 ins. across, the berries small—about the size of Black Currants—acid but edible. New England to Florida and westwards.

V. californica (*Californian Vine*).—This if the best of the American Grape Vines, (excluding the *Ampelopsis* section) for colour in autumn, and it is one of the strongest growers, climbing over lofty trees. Its leaves, which turn a deep crimson in autumn, are rounded and covered with down.

V. cordifolia (*Frost Grape*).—A vigorous Vine with thin, three-lobed leaves, measuring 3 to 6 ins. in diameter, the lobes ending in a long, fine point. The berries are black and only eatable, after frost. A moisture-loving Vine, affecting in a wild state the banks of streams. New England to Nebraska and southwards.

are grown in the United States. It often ascends high trees in its own country and may be planted in ours with this end in view. New England to Minnesota and southwards.

V. vulpina (*Southern Fox Grape*).—A distinct Vine, the leaves are small (2 to 3 ins. across) and rounded, smooth and shining on both surfaces, bright green. Other American Grape Vines worth growing, but possessing no particular value beyond those already described, are *V. rupestris, arizonica*, and *cinerea* (the downy Grape).

V. quinquefolia (*Virginian Creeper*).—

Vine growing on a gazeebo. From a photograph by Miss Willmott.

V. riparia (*Riverside Vine*).—In this the sweet, Mignonette-like perfume of the flowers of many American Vines is in this species especially apparent. The variety *palmata* has the branchlets and frequently the petioles of a red colour. Nova Scotia to Manitoba and southwards.

V. Labrusca (*Northern Fox Grape*).—Its leaves are amongst the largest, both they and the young branchlets being covered on the under surface with a rusty-coloured or sometimes whitish down. In a wild state the fruit has a musky flavour, but by cultivation it has been much improved, and numerous varieties

This is better known as *Ampelopsis quinquefolia*, its foliage changing in the fall of the year to various shades of crimson, scarlet, and purple. For covering arbours, walls, verandahs, or old tree stumps there is no climber which produces so luxuriant an effect in so short a time. Several varieties are in cultivation, viz., Major, incisa, hirsuta.

V. muralis (*Wall Vine*).—A name current in this country and on the Continent, whilst the same plant is known in America as *Vitis Englemanni*. It is a distinct form of the Virginian Creeper, possessing the same shaped leaves and developing equally, or even more, brilliant autumnal colours. This is self-supporting, and will attach itself firmly to, and climb to the tops of high walls—a useful quality.

Vitis Coignetiæ (*Crimson-leaved Vine*).—For many years a Vine clambering over a tall Pine in Mr. Anthony Waterer's nursery at Knap Hill has been at once a puzzle and a delight to all who have seen it. The foliage before falling turns a glorious crimson, making one of the most beautiful of autumn garden pictures. There is now every reason to believe that it is *Vitis Coignetiæ*, of which numerous plants have been lately raised in this country from seeds collected in Japan. The under-surface of the leaf is covered with a

V. inconstans.—As is the case with so many of the Vines, this shows great variety in the shape of the leaves, and this tendency to variation shows itself also in the colours the leaves put on in autumn. In the best forms the leaves assume various rich tints of purplish-red and crimson. There is also a form whose foliage has a bronzy hue more or less throughout the season, but especially when young. Cuttings. Japan. *Syns. Ampelopsis* Veitchi and A. tricuspidata.

V. Romaneti.—It has large leaves, differing from all the Vines in cultivation (except *Spinovitis Davidi*) in having the branches and petioles covered with bristles or stout hairs.

Vitis heterophylla variegata.

woolly-brown down, and in size of leaf and vigour of growth it is at least the equal of any other Vine.

V. heterophylla (*Hop-leaved Vine*).—A variety of this, known as humulifolia, is the most beautiful of the various forms of this species, and in autumn bears pretty turquoise-blue berries. This Vine requires in most places a position on a wall in order to induce it to fruit with proper freedom, and succeeds better in dry, poor soil. A variegated form is pretty, the foliage being mottled with white or faint pink. A sheltered, sunny position is necessary to develop the variegation to its full extent. China, Japan, and Corea.

Spinovitis Davidi is nearly allied to V. Romaneti, having the same bristly or even prickly character. Both this and V. Romaneti assume purplish-red autumn tints.

V. vinifera (*Common Grape Vine*).—Of the numerous varieties of the common Grape Vine the following may be alluded to : *Purpurea.*—This is one of the deepest purple-foliaged plants we possess. Although the colour becomes most intense in autumn the leaves have a bronzy-purple tinge from the first. Var. *apiifolia* is the Parsley-leaved Vine. Its leaves are very deeply cut, frequently into several leaflets, which are again deeply lobed. Besides these there are the

Miller's Grape, with smallish leaves covered with white down, and the "Teinturier" Grape, the leaves of which assume a beautiful claret colour before they fall, and among the large number of Vines grown in wine-making countries there are many worth growing for the beauty of their leaves.

Brief mention may be made of the following Asiatic species: *V. ficifolia*, a distinct plant with small round-lobed leaves like those of the Fig; *V. flexuosa*, *V. Thunbergi*, whose foliage turns red in autumn; and *V. serianæfolia*, an interesting species of the Ampelopsis group, with tuberous roots like a Dahlia, and

Claret-coloured Vine.

palmate or bipinnate foliage. All these are natives of China and Japan. V. himalayana is a North Indian species with striking trifoliate leaves.—W. J. B.

Vittadenia. See ERIGERON.

WAHLENBERGIA (*Tufted Hairbell*). —A charming group of alpines, closely allied to the Hairbells, and mostly inhabiting the mountains of Dalmatia and Asia Minor. They are all useful free-flowering alpines, and hardy, forming tufts which bear large heads of pretty, bell-shaped, upright flowers, of various shades of purple. The chief points in their culture are full exposure, plenty of sunshine, a free gritty soil, and raising the plants above the surrounding level, so that there is no possibility of stagnant moisture remaining near them.

All the species are true perennials, easily cultivated, vigorous, and free-flowering. They are difficult to increase by division on account of the long roots they make, but they ripen seed freely, which if sown directly it is gathered rarely fails to germinate. *Syn.* Edraianthus.

W. DALMATICA, a native of the mountains of Dalmatia, is a tufted species with narrow Grass-like leaves, 2 to 4 in. in length, and flower-stems at first drooping, afterwards erect, 4 to 6 in. high, with large flowers of a violet-blue colour, in clusters which appear in July and August.

W. GRACILIS. — This is a variable species from New Zealand, with square, hairy, much-branched stems, the leaves opposite, narrow toothed, and hairy, the flowers terminal, erect, but nodding while in bud, blue, large, and attractive, flowering all through the summer. W. stricta, littoralis, capillaris, and polymorpha are varieties of this kind.

W. GRAMINIFOLIA is the commonest and easiest to manage, forming tufts of long Grass-like leaves, bearing bunches of large purple flowers. It ripens seed freely, and that scattered about in the rock-garden usually germinates readily.

W. HEDERACEA (*Ivy-leaved Hairbell*).—A native plant closely allied to Campanula. It has creeping thread-like branches, which bear small leaves and light blue flowers. There is about it an interest and grace not found in other more robust members of the family, especially when seen interlaced with the pink Bog Pimpernel on British bogs. Worthy of a place for a moist spot in the rock or bog-garden, and easily increased by division. It is abundant in Ireland and the south and west of England.

W. KITAIBELI is a sturdy tufted species, with large purplish blue flowers and narrow toothed leaves.

W. PUMILIO forms a dwarf tuft of narrow, needle-like leaves of a bluish tint, half an inch or more in length, and has large flowers of a reddish-lilac or bluish colour, bell-shaped, numerous, and borne erect on short stems, coming in succession on the tuft for more than two months in May and June.

W. PUMILIORUM is the rarest, and although little different from W. Pumilio, it gives us another shade of colour, smaller and narrower leaves, a more straggling habit, and longer-tubed flowers   We find it an excellent hardy plant for the rock-garden, where on raised mounds of free gritty soil it grows and flowers vigorously.

W SAXICOLA —A beautiful species from the mountains of New Zealand, with leaves in close tufts and pretty flowers which first appear in June and keep coming in succession till November.   It is easily raised from seed and varies greatly from white to deep blue   The best forms can be increased by division   It makes a handsome rock plant, and, when left undisturbed and allowed to shed its seeds freely, gives the cultivator no trouble, but makes a highly attractive picture

W SERPYLLIFOLIA, with its small and Thyme-like leaves and abundance of purple-blue flowers, is effective on ledges in the rock-garden

W TENUIFOLIA is a dwarf compact growing species, with hairy stems, short slender leaves and small flowers, six to ten in a head, violet-blue or whitish-purple

WAITZIA.—Half-hardy annual Composites from Australia   Of the four kinds of Waitzias in cultivation all are valuable for their pretty flowers, which are useful for winter bouquets   W acuminata has a variety with purple flowers, and another with yellow flowers   W aurea has bright yellow flowers   W corymbosa has white and purple flowers, and the flowers of W grandiflora are like those of W aurea, but finer   All grow about 1 ft high, and require to be treated like other tender annuals, such as Rhodanthe   They succeed best in an open position in sandy peat   Seeds   The seedlings should be shifted into different-sized pots before planting out in May   Waitzias flower in August and September

WALDSTEINIA.—Dwarf Rosaceous plants, three of which, W geoides, W. fragarioides, and W. trifolia, are in cultivation   The last is the most attractive, but not one is ornamental enough for border culture, but only for dry banks and such places   Their yellow flowers appear in spring

WATSONIA (*Bugle Lily*). — Bulbous plants representing some of the most beautiful of the large Iridaceous family   Several of the finest were, long ago, favourites in gardens   Watsonias cannot be called hardy, but in the southern counties some of them succeed perfectly in open borders   There are only a dozen species and about as many varieties, half of which are varia-

tions from W. Meriana. All the species are natives of S Africa, but their headquarters are at the Cape   There is a great diversity of colours, and some of the trade lists even advertise a "mixed" selection representing "all colours "   The commonest species seem to be W Meriana, W coccinea, W iridifolia, W. rosea alba, W. humilis, W angusta (also known as W. fulgida), and W aletroides   All these kinds are true Watsonias, and have much more showy flowers than the other sections of the genus   The white Watsonia (W alba) is a lovely plant, flowering in early summer   With regard to culture, treatment similar to that recommended for the early Gladioli will suit them. Where they are grown in frames, a good deal of trouble is saved, and they give finer flowers as the young growths are protected when they most need it   Generally, however, it will be found best to grow the plants in warm situations in open borders of light rich soil. Of the varieties offered in trade lists, the following may be taken as representative   W. coccinea, fulgens, Meriana, alba, humilis, marginata, rosea, speciosa, fulgida, brevifolia, angustifolia, Grootvorst, Louis XVI , Wreede, Duchess, George IV , Chilea, Duc de Berri, and Blucher

WEIGELA (*Bush Honeysuckle*) —The Weigelas have long been in the front rank of flowering shrubs, and are deservedly popular, being elegant, rapid in growth, and beautiful in bloom   A multitude of varieties have sprung from W. floribunda, W grandiflora (known also as W. amabilis), W rosea, and W hortensis   These are natives of China and Japan, have been introduced within the last forty years, and so much hybridised that they are rarely found pure   The most valuable sorts have come from W. grandiflora, which has the largest flowers, while the smaller, but more numerously-flowered kinds, have originated from W rosea and W. floribunda   The varieties have been raised chiefly on the Continent, as may be inferred from their names   A selection of the best kinds should include the following   Abel Carrière, numerous small flowers of deep red , Isolinæ, large flowers of white or pale rose with yellow markings , Van Houttei, large and showy white and red flowers , Lemoinei, numerous small deep crimson - red flowers , Groenowegenei, one of the best, the flowers being large, of pink or pale rose, with a yellow blotch , striata, a pretty sort, having flowers striped with red and white , Stelzneri, with numerous deep red flowers , Lavalléi with numerous crimson red flowers ; hortensis nivea, more spreading than that of others, with larger and paler foliage, and large pure white flowers; and candida. If a large collection is needed, the following may be added to those already enumerated : Carminea, Emile Gallé, Docteur Baillon, Edouard André, Aug. Wilhelm, Diderot, Montesquieu, and Desboisi. The golden-leaved W. Looymansi aurea is a very fine ornamental shrub, usually retaining its bright golden foliage through the season. Its variegated-leaved form is also excellent. All sorts are of free habit if planted in good soil in an open position. They should never be crowded, but grown as

Weigela grandiflora.

isolated groups on lawns, or placed on the margins of shrubberies. Weigelas make large bushes, 6 to 10 ft. high and as much in diameter, and their graceful drooping branches are ornamental, even when leafless in winter. They should be top-dressed annually with good rich soil, and pruned, leaving the vigorous stems and the branches that yield the finest bloom. Weigelas are now classed botanically in the genus Diervilla, which also includes other species, such as D. sessiliflora and D. trifida, from N. America. Neither of these is to be recommended for general cultivation, though both are worth planting for the bright tints of their autumn foliage.
WHITLAVIA.—*W. grandiflora* is a

beautiful plant allied to the Nemophila, attaining a height of about 1 ft. of branched growth, with an abundance of showy bell-shaped blossoms of a rich deep blue. There is a white variety, and also one called gloxinioides with white and blue flowers. W. grandiflora is a hardy annual, and may be sown either in autumn or in spring in the open border, in good friable soil. California. Hydrophyllaceæ.

WIGANDIA. — These noble-leaved plants are natives of the Tropics, but they succeed in the open air in summer. The best is W. caracasana, from the mountainous regions of New Granada ; but even this will only succeed in the warmest and best sheltered southern gardens. W. caracasana may be used with superb effect either in a mass or as a single plant. It is propagated by cuttings of the roots, shoots, or from seeds, the young plants grown in a moist and genial temperature through the spring months, and kept near the light, so as to preserve the plant in a dwarf and well-clothed condition. It should be very carefully hardened off previous to being planted out at the end of May. The stems of W. macrophylla, from Mexico, are covered with short stinging hairs, bearing brownish viscid drops, which adhere to the hand like oil. W. imperialis, a new variety, is said to excel the others in its growth. W. Vigieri is another fine kind, of quick and vigorous growth, and of remarkable habit. Its leaves are 3 ft. 9 in. long (including the leaf-stalk), and are 22 in. across, and its stem, nearly 7 ft. high and 3 in. in diameter, bears a column of leaves. This plant is distinguished by its leaves and stem being covered in a greater degree with glossy, slender, stinging bodies, so thick as to give the stems a glistening appearance. W. urens is often planted, but is decidedly inferior to the foregoing, except in its power of stinging, in which it is not likely to be surpassed. All Wigandias have clusters of blue or violet blossoms, which are not often borne in the open air with us. In their native habitats they range from 3 to 12 ft. high, W. caracasana being the tallest.
WISTARIA (*Glycine*).—The noblest of all woody climbers ever introduced to Europe. Besides giving a beautiful covering for houses or other buildings, the common Wistaria is of great value used in various other ways. It can be grown on pergolas, on arbours, and even on trees. In Mr. Waterer's nursery at Knap Hill it has been trained up Laburnum

trees. In the end, no doubt, the Laburnums will get the worst of it, but meanwhile the two flower together, and the pale blue-purple racemes of the Wistaria and the golden ones of the Laburnum make a fine contrast. An old Oak that has seen its best days would be a suitable support for it. In getting this or any other climber to grow on living trees, the difficulty is at the start, chiefly because

The White Wistaria, Tresserve.

of the living roots of the tree on which it is to grow, and then the Wistaria should be planted well away from the trunk where sun and rain can reach it. A good plan is to sink a large tub with the bottom knocked out, and fill this with good rich loam and leafmould, and by the time the Wistaria has filled this with roots it will be able to hold its own.

It now and then makes very graceful

standards at least in the good situations in the south, and bowers and the most beautiful lacework of summer-houses may be formed with this climber alone. For example, a strong framework of tent shape might easily be covered with it. The timbers or irons of the roof might be close enough for the foliage of the Wistaria to cast a slight shade over the interior, and the motive for such a thing would be the grace and beauty of the shrub when in flower, garlanding it, and forming a temple of graceful bloom.

W. CHINENSIS.—The oldest kind introduced and so far the most beautiful. Its single and double white forms are beautiful, although neither of them flowers with anything like the freedom of the true plant. The double blue form is a poor thing, and in wet, stormy weather these double varieties are more liable to damage.

In the VAR. MACROBOTRYS the flowers are of a paler shade of blue-purple, and the racemes are longer, the flowers being farther apart. A variegated form is not worth a place.

W. BRACHYBOTRYS. — Although nearly seventy years since a Wistaria under this name was brought to Europe from Japan by Siebold, but little can be said of it. Judging by published figures, it appears to be no more than a dwarf variety of *W. chinensis*, with racemes of the same blue-purple flowers, only shorter, as the specific name suggests. Var. alba has been spoken highly of in the United States, but I have never seen it.

W. MULTIJUGA (*Japanese Glycine*).—A very beautiful plant with racemes often between 2 ft. and 3 ft. long, flowering a fortnight later than the Chinese Glycine, the blossoms much less closely packed on the spikes. The colour is not invariably the same in different plants, but it is always a variation of delicate lilac and white. The variety *alba* has flowers wholly white, and there are two forms of the plant in cultivation, one with shorter racemes.

W. JAPONICA.—The plant, a rare climber, sometimes met with under this name belongs to the closely allied genus *Millettia*. The flowers appear in small racemose clusters in June and July, and are white.

W. FRUTESCENS.—This is the only species found wild in the New World. It is a climber, but not a strong grower, the flowers pale blue-purple, arranged densely in racemes 3 ins. to 8 ins. long in June. There are two varieties in cultivation, one, magnifica, has racemes over 1 ft. in length ; the second is a white form. —W. J. B.

WOODSIA.—These pretty deciduous hardy Ferns are admirably suited for a northern position in the alpine or rock-garden. As they are impatient of sunshine, drainage should receive special attention, and they should have a mixture of fibry peat and loam, which has some broken-up sandstone mixed with it. It is a good plan to place Woodsias between little blocks of sandstone which just peep out of the soil. These blocks of stone could be covered with Sedums and other flowering rock plants. The best hardy species are W. ilvensis and W. alpina ; there is also a very beautiful North American kind named W. obtusa.

WOODWARDIA.—There are a few hardy species of these noble Ferns. All are handsome, have broad beautifully arching fronds, which are especially ornamental if seen a little above the level of the eye. Woodwardias thrive under the ordinary conditions of the hardy fernery, and succeed in a shady position if they have a light peaty soil that is moist in summer. The principal hardy kinds are W. areolata (angustifolia) and W. virginica, both from N. America ; W. japonica and W. orientalis, from Japan ; and W. radicans from Madeira. W. radicans is the tenderest, and requires a sheltered position, and perhaps protection in severe cold.

WULFENIA.—*W. carinthiaca* is a remarkably dwarf, almost stemless evergreen herb, 12 to 18 in. high, bearing in summer showy spikes of drooping purplish-blue flowers. Found only on one or two mountains in Carinthia. W. carinthiaca is a pretty plant for rock-gardens or borders, but should have a light moist sandy loam. W. Amherstiana from the Himalayas, similar to the Carinthian species, but more showy, rare, and we have seen it only in Kew Gardens. It is hardy, grows freely in any position in the rock-garden, but prefers a shady spot and light rich soil. Scrophulariaceæ.

XANTHOCERAS (*Chinese Chestnut*). —*X. sorbifolia* is a beautiful dwarf hardy tree, but not a rapid grower ; its leaves elegant, and its flowers, which are white and marked with red, borne in erect clusters, but to thrive it requires a climate warmer than that of Britain.

After having been for many years a rare plant in English gardens it is becoming more widely known and cultivated, and among the gardens where it succeeds well is that at Offington, Worthing, where it has ripened its fruits, which recall to us in form and size the fruits of the Horse Chestnut. The seedlings raised from English ripened fruits may give us fine varieties, as there is a great difference among individuals of this shrub as regards the size of flower and cluster as well as in the colour of the flowers. China. At Kew it thrives but indifferently compared with specimens I have seen in mild coast

gardens, but I imagine that against a wall it succeeds better, for at Kew it reaches the top of a 12 ft. wall, while as an open bush it is only half that height.

XERANTHEMUM.—*X. annuum* is a hardy annual, one of the prettiest of Everlasting flowers, growing about 2 ft. high, and, if sown in patches, yields abundant masses of white, purple, and yellow double, single, and semi-double blossoms. A packet of mixed seed sown in any ordinary garden soil in March will give a variety of colours. The principal kinds are —Album, white ; imperiale, dark violet-purple ; plenissimum, dark purple, double ; superbissimum, double, globe-flowered ; and Tom Thumb, a compact dwarf variety. The flowers are excellent for cutting, and, if dried in autumn, are useful for winter decoration. S. Europe. Compositæ.

XEROPHYLLUM (*Turkey's Beard*). —*X. asphodeloides* is a beautiful tuberous-rooted plant with the aspect of an Asphodel, forming a spreading tuft of grassy leaves, its tall flower-stem terminated by a raceme of numerous white blossoms. It grows well in a moist, sandy, peaty border, and in the drier parts of boggy ground. Pine barrens in N. America.

X. tenax.—This very beautiful species is found wild in various parts of North America, especially in Pine barrens, on the east and west sides of the continent. The flower-stems 2 to 5 ft. high, the raceme varying from 1 to 2 ft. long, the flowers crowded and attractive, the segments white with a violet centre. Division or seed. D. K.

YUCCA (*Adam's Needle*).—In its own peculiar habit and style of growth the Yucca has no rival among hardy plants. Though the stiffest of all garden plants, it has grace and elegance, under all conditions, if the plant is not cramped for room. Yuccas seem fitted for various uses, as a single plant may stand alone on a lawn, or in the centre of a bed, or numbers may be grouped with other plants, or form a bed by themselves. Yuccas look especially well on rock-garden banks. They are not very particular about soil, but do not flourish so well in sand, chalk, or peat. They are hardy save in very severe winters and on cool soils. All of the kinds mentioned below are so vigorous that it is almost impossible to kill them. Suckers, unless carefully taken, are apt to die down to the ground when first planted ; but if they are left alone they will renew their growth in a few months. There are several hardy species well suited for the flower-garden, and quite distinct from each other. The effect of well-developed Yuccas is equal to that of any hot-house plant that we can venture to place in the open air for the summer, while they are green and ornamental at all seasons. The free-flowering kinds, Y. filamentosa and Y. flaccida, may be associated with any of our nobler autumn-flowering plants, from Gladiolus to the great Statice latifolia. Even species that do not flower so often, like Y. pendula and Y. gloriosa, are magnificent if grown in the full sun and planted in good soil. Division of the stem and the rhizome. Yuccas should be

Yucca.

planted singly, beginning with healthy young plants, so as to secure perfect specimens.

Y. aloifolia.—A distinct species, with a stem which, fully developed, is as thick as a man's arm, and 6 to 18 ft. high. The numerous leaves of the plant are dark green, but have a slight glaucous bloom; ascend rigidly; are 18 to 21 in. long, broad at the middle, while their horny margin is rolled in for 2 or 3 in. below the point, and is finely toothed in the remaining portion. The flowers are almost white, and are borne in a vast pyramidal panicle. Y. aloifolia is hardy, but is not generally known to be so. It should be

tried on well-drained slopes in good sandy loam. The finest varieties are quadricolor and versicolor. Their leaves are variously edged with green, yellow, and red. They are hardy, but as they are yet far from common, it will be best to use them in the greenhouse or the conservatory, or to place them in the open air during summer. They look very pretty when isolated on the Grass, the pots being plunged to the rim. S. America and W. Indies.

Y. angustifolia.—This is the smallest of all the Yuccas. When in flower it is not more than 3 ft. high. Its long strips of leaves are nearly $1\frac{1}{2}$ ft. in length, but are not more than $\frac{1}{4}$ in. in width. They are thick and rigid, of a pale sea-green colour, and fringed with white filaments. Y. angustifolia bears a simple raceme of white flowers slightly tinged with yellow. Till it is more plentiful, it should be grown in warm borders, in well-drained sandy loam. It is excellent for rock-gardens. N. America.

Y. canaliculata.—The leaves of this Yucca are entire—*i.e.* neither toothed nor filamentose at the margin, and form a dense rosette on a stem 1 or 2 ft. high. Each leaf is 20 to 24 in. long, and 2 to $2\frac{1}{4}$ in. broad at the middle, strong, rigid, and deeply concave. The flowers are creamy-white, and borne in a large panicle 4 or 5 ft. high. It is well suited for isolation or groups, but, till more plentiful, should be encouraged in favourable positions and on warm soils. Mexico.

Y. filamentosa.—A well-known species, with apple-green leaves and a much-branched panicle, 4 to 6 ft. high. It varies very much when raised from seed. One variety (concava) has short, strong, broad leaves, which are more concave than those of the type; another variety (maxima) has narrow leaves which, though nearly 2 ft. long, are only $2\frac{1}{2}$ in. broad. It has a panicle 7 to 8 ft. high. Y. filamentosa flowers with much vigour and beauty. It has a fine variegated variety. All the varieties of Y. filamentosa thrive best in peaty or fine sandy soil. N. America.

Y. flaccida.—A stemless species, somewhat resembling Y. filamentosa, but smaller, has a downy branching panicle, 3 or 4 ft. high, and bears close rosettes of leaves 18 to 24 in. long, and about $1\frac{1}{2}$ in. broad at the middle. They are often fringed with filaments, the young ones nearly erect, and the old ones abruptly reflexed in the middle, and appearing almost broken. This gives such an irregular aspect to the tufts, that it is easily distinguished from any of the varieties of Y. filamentosa. Y. flaccida also flowers more regularly and abundantly than Y filamentosa, and is well suited for groups of the finer hardy plants, for borders, or to plant in large isolated tufts N America

Y. glaucescens. — A free-flowering kind, with a panicle 3 or 4 ft. high, and sea-green leaves, about 18 in long, with a few filaments on the margins The flowers are greenish-yellow, when in bud tinged with pink, which gives the whole inflorescence a peculiarly pleasing tone It is a very useful and ornamental sort, fine for groups, borders, isolation, or for placing among low shrubs N America

Y. gloriosa. — A large and imposing Yucca of distinct habit and somewhat rigid aspect Its flower-stem is over 7 ft high, much branched, and bears an immense pyramidal panicle of large almost white flowers Its numerous leaves are stiff and pointed It is one of the noblest plants in our gardens, and is suitable for almost any position It varies very much when grown from seed, and this is a good recommendation, as the greater variety of fine form we have the better Its chief varieties are Y g longifolia, plicata, maculata, glaucescens, and minor The soil should be a rich deep loam N. America

Y. pendula. — Perhaps the best species, considering its graceful habit, vigour and hardiness It grows about 6 ft high ; its leaves, at first erect and of a sea-green colour, afterwards become reflexed and change to a deep green Old and well-established plants standing alone on the Grass are pictures of grace and symmetry, from the lower leaves which sweep the ground to the central ones that point up as straight as a needle. It is amusing to think of people putting tender plants in the open air, and running with sheets to protect them from the cold and rain of autumn and early summer, while perhaps not a good specimen of this fine plant is to be seen in the place There is no plant more suited for planting near flower-beds or for associating with them N. America = Y recurva

Y. Treculeana. — This species is one of the most remarkable, both from its habit and from the dimensions of its leaves Like many Yuccas of its family, young specimens of Y. Treculeana differ considerably from those which have reached maturity Thus, while the leaves of young specimens are bent, and generally inflected, those of mature specimens are erect, rigid, long, and straight The stem of the plant is about 10 in in diameter, and furnished on all sides with leaves

about 4 ft long, straight, thick, and deeply channelled, very finely toothed on the edges, and end in a stiff sharp point The stout branched flower-stalk is about 4 ft. long, the branches erect, 12 to 20 in. long, bearing flowers with long narrow petals of a shining yellowish-white If placed singly it is excellent for banks and knolls, and is also suitable for the boldest groups. Texas

Any one wishing to have a distinct collection of Yuccas would find the kinds mentioned suitable, but there are several other species more or less desirable The dead flower-stems of Yuccas make capital supports for delicate creepers

ZAPANIA (*Creeping Vervain*) — Z *nodiflora* is a pretty, spreading trailer, with prostrate stems 2 or 3 ft in length, which late in summer bear small round heads of little purplish flowers Suitable for the rougher parts of the rock-garden, for borders or edgings in free warm soil. Asia and America *Syn* Lippia nodiflora.

ZAUSCHNERIA (*Californian Fuchsia*) — Z *californica* is a distinct and bright perennial hardy in warm soils in sheltered places, but in cold localities requiring a little winter protection, such as a covering of ashes It grows 12 to 18 in high, and yields an abundance of gracefully drooping bright vermilion flowers during summer and autumn. It flourishes in sandy loam in the rock-garden, and grows capitally on an old wall, but on heavy and moist soils does not thrive California Division or seed.

ZEA (*Indian Corn*) — Z *Mays* is one of the noblest of the Grasses that thrive in our climate, almost indispensable to our gardens, and has a fine appearance either isolated or associated with other fine-leaved plants Cuzko and Caragua are the largest of the green varieties, and gracillima the smallest and most graceful The variegated or Japanese Maize is a handsome variety that comes true from seed. It is useful for intermingling with arrangements of ordinary bedding plants for vases , and may be grown in light, rich, warm soil in the margins of beds of sub-tropical plants, or in any position where its variegation may be well seen, and where its graceful leaves are effective It has a habit of breaking into shoots rather freely near the base of the central stem, and this should recommend it for planting on the turf in an isolated manner, or in groups of three or five The seeds of the Maize should be sown on a gentle hot-bed in April, although seeds will occasionally succeed out-of-doors ' Gradually harden off the plants before they have made more than three or four little leaves, keeping them in a cool frame near the glass, so as to keep them sturdy, finally exposing them by taking off the lights This method is perhaps the more desirable in the case of the variegated Maize, which does not grow so vigorously as the green kinds In no case should the plants be drawn up long in heat, for if they are they will not thrive so well. The first few leaves of the variegated kind are green, but soon begin to manifest the striping The plants should be planted out about the middle of May

ZELKOWA (*Water Elm*) —Elm-like summer-leafing trees, distinct in form Several kinds are in cultivation, *acuminata* of Japan, *crenata* of the Caucasus (*Syn*, *Planera Richardi*). *Verschaffelti* of Eastern Asia, and *aquatica* of N. America. In Britain these trees take their place among the trees of a secondary nature, not being very remarkable for growth or flower, though the form of one kind (*crenata*) is distinct and good. *Syn.*, *Planera.*

ZENOBIA.—*Z speciosa* is one of the most beautiful shrubs in the Heath family, about a yard high, with small roundish leaves of a pale green. In the variety pulverulenta, the leaves are almost white, covered with a mealy glaucescence , flowers, white and wax-like in form, resembling those of Lily of the Valley, come in summer in beautiful loose drooping clusters A well-flowered specimen is most charming, and lasts for some weeks in beauty, thriving in a peaty soil or a sandy loam It comes from the Southern United States ; and is therefore not absolutely hardy In nurseries it is known as Andromeda cassiniæfolia and A. speciosa, and its variety Z pulverulenta as A dealbata and A pulverulenta

ZEPHYRANTHES (*Zephyr-flower*) — This beautiful flower has been termed the Crocus of America There are about fourteen species,—low-growing bulbous plants, with grassy leaves, which appear in spring with or before the Crocus-like flowers, which are white or rosy-pink, large and handsome Zephyranthes require rest during winter, and at that season are best kept dry. In spring they should be planted out in the full sun in sandy soil They do well in the greenhouse, four or six being planted in a pot. Offsets The valuable species are —

Z Atamasco (*Atamasco Lily*) —This handsome plant is a native of N America, where it is a conspicuous ornament of

damp places in woods and fields. Its glossy leaves appear at the same time as the blossoms, and slightly exceed them in height The white flowers are striped with rose, are about 3 in. long, and borne singly upon a scape 6 in high It flowers from May to July, grows well in the open border, and increases rapidly by offsets, which should be removed and divided in the spring of every third or fourth year Z. candida is similar, but less hardy.

Z. carinata. — This lovely plant has narrow leaves, and its flower-stem, which is about 6 in high, bears a delicate rosy flower, 2 or 3 in long It blossoms freely in the open border if kept dry in winter, and should be grown in light sandy loam S. America. Z. rosea, a beautiful species, with flowers of a bright rose, is a native of the mountains of Cuba

Z. tubispatha.—A handsome plant, bearing a white, slightly fragrant flower, 2 or 3 in long It is a native of Antigua, and of the Blue Mountains of Jamaica Though properly a stove plant, it will thrive and flower well in mild localities, if well protected in winter A pretty pink hybrid between this species and Z carinata is sometimes met with under the name of Z Spofforthiana Z Treatiæ, a new species resembling Z Atamasco, is too rare for us yet to speak of its culture.

ZIETENIA.—*Z lavandulæfolia* is a dwarf, creeping, half-shrubby perennial of a grayish hue, 6 to 12 in high, with purple flowers in summer, borne in whorls, forming a spike about 6 in long, with a slender downy stalk Suitable for the margins of borders and the rougher parts of the rock-garden, or for naturalisation in ordinary soil Division Caucasus

ZINNIA.—Half-hardy annual plants of splendid colour and thriving best in our country on good warm soils. They are among the most effective of summerblooming plants, and they flower well until autumn Their blooms are not easily injured by inclement weather, but retain all their freshness and gay colouring at a time when many bright flowers present but a sorry appearance In mixed borders, and in beds among sub-tropical plants, well-grown Zinnias are always attractive, but require a deep loamy soil and a warm open situation Seed should be sown in gentle warmth Nothing is gained by sowing before the middle or end of March, as, if the young plants have to stand for a considerable time before being planted, they are apt to become root-bound and stinted for nutriment, and to lose something of that fresh free growth which should be maintained until they come into flower. If the tissues once harden so much as to bring the young plants to a standstill, there will be little chance of rapid progress when they are set out in the open ground. Indeed, it is not advisable to plant them out much before the second week in June, as they are very sensitive to atmospheric changes, and are completely ruined by a few degrees of frost. Plant them in well-stirred, fairly-enriched soil and in full exposure, for they love to bask in the sun's fiercest rays, and demand merely a surface-covering, to protect the roots, and a constant supply of moisture. In a bed by themselves, they would be greatly improved if the soil were thrown out, and a good depth of fermenting manure were well trodden in, and the soil replaced. Both the single and double Zinnias are fine garden plants, and display a diversity and brilliancy of colour equalled by few plants. The double forms have of late been most in request, although both the double and single varieties have been greatly improved. There is one good characteristic about double Zinnias—they are not all so rank and unwieldy as the single types, dwarfing having gone hand-in-hand with multiplying petals in the flowers.

Selection has also done something to induce a better habit ; and it will be observed that particular types of flower often improve in habit and bloom at the same time. Some of the single Zinnias are very beautiful, for instance, the yellow, carmine, rosy-purple, scarlet, crimson, and orange kinds. Z. elegans is the species from which the numerous varieties mentioned in catalogues have been derived. Z. Darwini is a beautiful hybrid with very double flowers of various colours. Z. Haageana, known also as Z. mexicana, has a very neat habit, and rich orange-yellow blossoms ; it also occurs with double flowers.

ZYGADENUS. — Plants of the Lily family, of no great ornamental value, for their flowers are all greenish-yellow, but their distinct growth makes them worth cultivating in a botanical or a full collection. They are slender bulbous plants, with narrow grassy leaves, and tall branching flower-stems, 1 to 4 ft. high. Z. Fremonti (also known as Z. glaberrimus, Z. chloranthus, and Z. Douglasi) is the largest flowered species. The other kinds are Z. Nuttalli and Z. paniculatus. Zygadeni thrive best in a moist peaty border in a shady position protected from cold winds. California.

FLOWER GARDEN PESTS.

By no means the least of the difficulties that the cultivator of plants has to contend with is the number of different kinds of insects that feed on the objects of his care, at times rendering all his efforts of no avail. To keep a garden tolerably free from insect pests is never an easy task, and in some seasons an utterly impossible one, but a great deal may be done by a little well-directed care. Prevention is, of course, "much better than cure," and a great deal may be done in this way by never allowing any weeds to grow in a garden, as the insects that feed on them often prefer those in cultivation. A weedy, uncared-for corner in a garden is a regular nursery for all sorts of insects. Rubbish, stones and the refuse of a crop should never be allowed to lie about, as they form a welcome shelter to many kinds of pests. Anything taken from a plant that has been attacked by an insect or fungus should at once be burnt. Some plants suffer most from the attacks of insects when they are quite young; in such cases the plants should be pushed into vigorous growth as quickly as possible by suitable cultivation. Birds should be encouraged in gardens. Few persons realise the enormous number of insects killed by them, especially during the breeding season, when nearly all the young birds are fed on animal food. Toads also are most useful creatures in gardens, and should be encouraged far more than they are. All dead leaves should be collected and burnt, unless they are required for leaf-mould, when they should be made into a heap as soon as possible. Any leaves that do not fall with the others should be picked off and burnt, as they often contain chrysalides. When borders are being dug, a sharp look-out should be kept for chrysalides or cocoons which may be turned up. Any ground that is not in use should be kept well hoed and broken up. This will keep down weeds and expose any insects which may be in the soil to the birds. As soon as the attack of any insect is noticed, steps should at once be taken to check it, as in this case the old proverb, "A stitch in time saves nine," is especially true. If ants are seen running over plants, it is generally the case that the latter are infested by aphides or scale insects, and when ants make their nests at the roots of plants it will often be found that the roots are attacked by one of the root-feeding aphides.

Remedies will be applied in a more intelligent manner if those who use them are acquainted with a few elementary entomological facts; so it may be mentioned that a typical female insect when in a perfect state lays eggs; from these are hatched grubs, maggots or caterpillars, according to the kind of insect; these usually feed voraciously and increase rapidly; they change their skins several times, and when full grown become chrysalides; from these in due course the perfect insect emerges. Butterflies, moths beetles, bees, wasps, ants and some other kinds of insects undergo these changes, which are very marked. Others, such as crickets, grasshoppers, cockroaches, bugs, earwigs, green flies and scale insects, really go through the same changes, but they are much less apparent; the young just hatched from the egg very much resembles its parents. It is, of course, very much smaller and is never winged, but there is a general family resemblance between them. The young one as it grows at times changes its skin, and at a certain change the wings may be seen in a very rudimentary condition. The insect is then in the state that answers to the chrysalis state in the other insects, and on the next change of skin the insect appears in its mature condition. After attaining this period in its existence it never grows. A butterfly, bee, wasp, fly, or whatever the insect is, when in its perfect state never becomes any larger. All insects in their mature condition have a general similarity in their structure, although it may not always be easy to trace the three divisions in which they are formed, namely, head, thorax or forebody, and body, which in a wasp are particularly well marked.

The head is furnished with the organs of the mouth, the feelers or antennæ, and eyes To the forebody are attached the legs and the wings The body contains the breathing, digestive and other internal organs Every insect should have three pairs of legs and two pairs of wings, but in some kinds the latter are altogether wanting, or there is only one pair Insects do not breathe through openings in their heads, as the higher animals do, but, as a rule, through pores arranged along their sides, which lead into tubes that convey the air to all parts of the body

Insecticides act upon insects in different ways, some smother the insects by clogging their breathing apparatus, or by their action on their skins, others by poisoning their food Those first mentioned should be used in the case of insects which feed by suction, the others when the insects have biting mouths. Insecticides, as a rule, have no effect on the eggs, so that it is always best in the case of insects that breed very rapidly to use them again in the course of a few days, and perhaps even a third time, so as to make sure that the pest has been exterminated. There are now several kinds of spraying machines and spraying nozzles in the market With them the insecticides can be used much more economically than with an ordinary syringe, and they can be applied with greater ease to the undersides of the leaves where the insects are as a rule

INSECTICIDES

Carbolic acid (crude) 1 pint, soft soap 1 quart, water 1 gallon, or carbolic acid 1 part, water 50 to 100 parts

Paraffin 1 wineglassful, soft soap 1 pint, mixed very thoroughly together with a little hot water, and then add one gallon of water This must be kept well stirred.

PARAFFIN EMULSION — Soft soap 1 quart, well mixed in 2 quarts of boiling water, while hot add 1 pint of paraffin oil, churn or pump the mixture through a garden engine for 5 or 10 minutes, then dilute ten or twelve times with water, and add a quarter of a pint of turpentine Or condensed milk 1 to 1½ pints, water 3 pints, mix together and add 1 gallon of paraffin, churn until it forms a butter, dilute with ten or twelve times its bulk of water

QUASSIA EXTRACT — Boil 6 ozs of quassia chips in a little water for half an hour, strain off the liquor and add it to 4 ozs of soft soap and mix thoroughly in 5 gallons of water ; if it is to be used to

kill red spider, add half a pound of flowers of sulphur.

TOBACCO WATER —Boil 1 oz of strong tobacco in half a gallon of water and strain when cold

SOLUBLE PARAFFIN —Half a pint to 2 gallons of water for mealy bug, quarter of a pint to 2 gallons of water for aphides or red spider

The water used with insecticides should always if possible be soft water , if this be impossible add a little soda

PLANTS AND THEIR PESTS

Anemone	See	snake millipedes and wireworms
Aster	,,	common dart moth
Auricula	,,	common dart moth
Balsam	,,	common dart moth
Carnations	,,	aphides, bulb mite, Carnation fly, froghopper, earwig, red spider, thrips, and wireworms
Chrysanthemum	,,	aphides, froghopper, earwigs, Marguerite Daisy fly, plant bugs
Cyclamen	,,	aphides, black Vine weevil, slugs, wireworms
Dahlias	,,	common dart moth, earwigs, thrips
Ferns	,,	black Vine weevil, froghopper, plant bugs, various caterpillars
Fuchsia	,,	aphides, red spider
Gladiolus	,,	red spider, wireworms
Hyacinth	,,	bulb mites, Narcissus fly
Lilies	,,	aphides, bulb mites, wireworms, snake millipedes.
Mignonette	,,	white Cabbage butterfly
Narcissus	,,	bulb mite, Narcissus fly, snake millipedes
Pæonies	,,	Rose beetle
Pansies	,,	slugs, snails, snake millipedes
Phlox	,,	froghopper, thrips.
Rose	,,	aphides, bell moths, Rose beetle, Rose gall fly, red spider, scale insects, sawflies
Stocks	,,	snake millipedes
Verbascums	,,	Mullein moth

ANTS (Lasius niger) —Ants are not injurious directly to flowering plants in any way, but they are so at times by making their nests at the roots of plants. When this is the case it will generally be found that the plant is infested at the roots by one of the root-feeding aphides, and that the ants chose the locality on that account, so that they might benefit by the sweet substance secreted by the aphides. When a plant is overrun by ants it is an almost certain sign that it is infested by aphides or scale insects Ants may be destroyed by pouring boiling water, paraffin oil, carbolic or sulphuric acid, diluted with ten or twelve times their bulk of water, into their nests If in a position in which it is undesirable to use any of these, a garden pot with the holes at the bottom closed and partially filled with leaves should be inverted over the entrance to the nest, and the ground round the nest kept well watered ; the ants will soon leave the damp earth and move their nest into the dry pot. In about a fortnight the pot may be removed and its contents thrown into a pail of boiling water.

APHIDES (the family to which the green-fly and other nearly allied insects belong) may be destroyed in various ways, but whatever means are used no time should be lost in applying them as soon as the insects are noticed, as the latter increase and multiply in the most rapid manner. Spraying or syringing the plants is one of the most effectual methods of killing these pests. For this purpose use the extract from 6 oz. of quassia chips, 4 oz. of soft soap,well mixed and added to 5 gallons of water ; paraffin emulsion, or a quarter of a pint of soluble paraffin in two gallons of water. They may also be destroyed when the plants are wet by dusting them with snuff, powdered tobacco,or Pyrethrum powder (commonly known as insect powder),or they may be killed by tobacco smoke. This can be effected out of doors by covering the plant with some tolerably air-tight cloth and applying the smoke with a fumigator. When pruning Roses in the spring or autumn, the shoots cut off should always be burnt, as they may have some eggs of these insects on them.

BELL MOTHS OR ROSE TORTRICES (Tortricidæ).—The caterpillars of several members of this family attack the leaves and flower-buds of Roses, rolling up and feeding on the leaves, and eating the young petals, or making holes in the buds. From the sheltered positions that they occupy,in-secticides are almost useless ; pinching the curled leaves is the easiest way of killing them, if you can be quite sure that the intended victim has not dropped out before your fingers closed on the leaf ; or a basket may be held under the leaf or bud, which should be cut off so that it falls into the basket. The leaves and buds should then be burnt or crushed.

THE BULB MITE (Rhizoglyphus echinopus).—This little mite feeds on the bulbs of Hyacinths, Daffodils, and probably on those of other bulbous plants. It also attacks the stems of Carnations. It is impossible to make any insecticide reach them while the bulbs are in the soil, and even when taken up, as the mites work between the scales of the bulbs, it is only after many hours soaking that they can be reached. For this purpose use the extract from 4 oz. of quassia chips mixed in 2 gallons of water, or 3 lb. of sulphide of potassium dissolved in one gallon of water. The bulbs should be allowed to soak in one of these mixtures for twenty-four hours,

and even then it may not be successful, as it is very difficult to make fluid pass freely between the scales of the bulbs, as there is often air imprisoned there. Immersing the bulbs in water at a temperature of 120° Fahr. for a quarter of an hour would, I believe, kill them ; the mites when taken from the bulbs and placed in water at 115° Fahr. died in less than five minutes. The mites are only about one-twentieth of an inch in length, and are of a milk-white colour, and may be easily mistaken for grains of sand, but they may readily be detected with a good pocket lens.

THE CARNATION FLY (Hylemyia nigrescens).—The grubs of this fly feed on the pith of the stems of Carnations, doing much injury to the plants. The grubs, each about three-eighths of an inch in length, are nearly white with dark heads. There is no remedy but burning the affected plants.

THE COCKCHAFER OR MAY BUG (Melolontha vulgaris).—This insect is injurious to plants both as a beetle and as a grub ; the cockchafers feed on the leaves of various trees, and the grubs on the roots of most plants. It appears to be useless to try and kill the grub with any insecticide, but strong salt and water, or gas liquor diluted with ten times its bulk of water, renders the soil distasteful to them. The only practical way of destroying them is to open the ground round a plant which is attacked and find the grub. When full grown the grubs are each about two inches long and half an inch in diameter. They usually lie in a curved position, are whitish in colour, but the tail, which is the thickest part of the body, is bluish. As they take three years to come to maturity, one grub will do an enormous amount of damage in the course of its life. The cockchafers may be shaken or beaten off the trees in the middle of the day, when they are generally sluggish, and crushed or collected as they lie on the ground.

DADDY-LONGLEGS OR CRANE FLY (Tipula oleracea).—The grubs of this insect are among the most mischievous of our garden pests, as they destroy the roots of turf and many other plants they will eat right through the tap-root, and then go on to another plant and do the same. They are greyish brown grubs; when full grown they are each about one and a half inches long and about a quarter of an inch in diameter, thickest near the tail,and tapering towards the head. They are commonly known by the name of leather jackets. They are very difficult to kill, and when below the surface of the ground, as they usually are, no insecticide can be made to reach them with fatal effect   Watering very thoroughly with strong liquid manure, such as a solution of guano, salt, or nitrate of soda, has been found beneficial, as it is distasteful to the grubs and stimulates the plants   They may be trapped by burying slices of Turnips, Mangold, Carrots, or Potatoes about an inch below the surface , each slice should have a small skewer stuck into it, so that it may be more easily found   The traps should be examined every morning

THE COMMON DART MOTH (Agrotis segetum) —The caterpillars of this very common moth live on the roots of many different plants grown in gardens   Their favourites are Auriculas, Dahlias, China Asters, and Balsams They usually feed on the crowns or just below them, and often bite right through the roots   They feed at night, lying hidden under stones, clods, or some similar shelter during the day Warm soap and water applied to the roots of the attacked plants until the cracks and holes in the ground are filled will bring the caterpillars to the surface, but turning up the ground with a spud and picking out the pests is the most practical way of killing them   A full-grown caterpillar is from one and a half inches to two inches in length, and are of a smoky yellow colour with various small black spots and paler longitudinal stripes

THE EARWIG (Forficula auricularis) feeds on many kinds of flowers, but is particularly fond of those of the Dahlia, Chrysanthemum and Carnation   The only way of destroying them is by trapping them, or, as they are night feeders, by catching them on the flowers after dark The best traps are the hollow stems of Sunflowers or Broad Beans, from which they may be blown into a basin of boiling water, or water on which a little paraffin is floating, small garden pots filled with dry Moss or hay, or pieces of paper crumpled up   Or pieces of sacking or canvas, tied so that they hang in folds, or folded and laid upon the ground at the foot of the plants, are also very useful traps   In fact anything in which they can hide during the day is useful

THE FROG-HOPPER (Aphrophora spumaria) —The well-known little masses of froth so often seen on plants, and commonly called cuckoo spit or frog spittle, are formed by this insect when in its immature state, as a covering to itself, and the amount of sap withdrawn from the plant for the sustenance of the insect and the formation of the froth is very considerable and the cause of much injury to the plant   Honeysuckles, Lavender, Lilies,

Carnations, Phloxes and grasses are among the plants which suffer most from their attacks   The best way to destroy this insect is to remove it with a small, stiffish brush, which should then be dipped in a pan of water, or the shoots and leaves may be drawn through the fingers, which should be dipped in water, to remove the froth and insects, before cleansing another leaf   Syringing is not of much use, as probably only the froth would be washed off

THE MARGUERITE DAISY FLY (Phytomyza affinis) —The grubs of this insect burrow in the leaves of these Daisies, and also in those of Chrysanthemums, Cinerarias, and other composite plants, and feed on their inner substance   When many leaves are attacked in this way, the plants are not only rendered unsightly by the discolouring and blistering of the leaves, but they suffer very considerably in health   The best way of destroying this insect is by cutting off the infested leaves and burning them, or, if the attack has only just commenced, by pinching the leaves at the part where the grubs are Syringing with insecticides is not of much use, as they would not reach the grubs, but they would have the effect probably of preventing the flies from laying their eggs on the leaves, if they could be applied at the right time

THE MULLEIN MOTH (Cucullia verbasci) —The caterpillars of this moth feed on the leaves and flowers of the Mulleins, and when abundant quite ruin the appearance of the plants.   When full-grown they are about two inches long and of a greenish-white colour, with a yellow band across each joint, on which are several large black spots, so that they are conspicuous insects and may easily be picked off by hand

PLANT BUGS (Hemiptera) —These insects are often injurious to the foliage and buds of plants, the buds of Chrysanthemums being frequently injured by them These insects, of which there are many species, are provided with a long beak, with which they suck the juices of the leaves and buds.   They vary much in size , the species that attacks Chrysanthemums is about one-eighth of an inch in length, the head and forebody are black, and the wings brownish yellow   The perfect insects run and fly readily, so that it is not easy to kill them, but in their immature condition they have no wings, and may be killed by syringing or spraying the plants with paraffin emulsion or quassia extract and soft soap

RED SPIDER (Tetranychus telarius) —

This most annoying pest is often very destructive to the foliage of plants, particularly to those which are dry at the roots The best way of destroying them is by spraying or syringing with one of the following mixtures 1 lb of flowers of sulphur and 2 lbs of fresh lime, boiled in 4 gallons of water, then add 1½ lb of soft soap, and, before using, 3 more gallons of water, or the extract from 6 oz of quassia chips, 4 oz of soft soap, and half a pound of flowers of sulphur, well mixed, added to 5 gallons of water, paraffin emulsion, or 2 oz or 3 oz. of Gishurst compound in 1 gallon of water

THE ROSE BEETLE OR GREEN ROSE CHAFER (Cetonia aurata) —This handsome metallic green beetle is unfortunately very injurious to the flowers of the Rose, Pæony, Candytuft, Lilac, Elder, and several other trees and plants Their grubs also are destructive to the roots of many plants They are very much like those of the cockchafer, and are frequently mistaken for them, and are each about 1½ inches in length and scarcely half an inch in diameter, of a dirty white colour The tail, which is the thickest part of the insect, is bluish They lie in a curved position some 2 inches or 3 inches below the surface, so that no insecticide can reach them Watering very freely with liquid manure or soapsuds is distasteful to them and may make them shift their quarters The beetles are each about three-quarters of an inch in length, and are so conspicuous that they may easily be picked off the flowers

THE ROSE GALL-FLY (Rhodites rosæ) —These gall-flies lay their eggs in the young shoots, and in the midribs of the leaves of Briers, the young grubs from which form the curious mossy galls formerly known as "bedeguars," sometimes 2 inches or 3 inches in diameter, often seen on Briers, and at times on other Roses The best way of destroying this insect is to cut off and burn the galls

THE ROSE SAWFLIES (Hylotoma rosarum and others) —The grubs of these insects feed on and do much damage to the foliage of Roses Some (the species just named among them) eat away the leaves, leaving only the thicker ribs; others feed only on the upper surface of the leaves, and do not touch the lower skin or the veins; another species rolls up the leaves into tubes about the size of a quill pen and feeds within this shelter, another lives on the pith of the young shoots The grubs mostly become chrysalides in the earth, so that after a bad attack it is best to remove the earth from under the bushes to the depth of about 3 inches and burn it, or bury it not less than 1 foot below the surface. The grubs should be picked off by hand, or the bushes may be syringed or sprayed with paraffin emulsion, or quassia extract and soft soap, or Paris green In the autumn cut off and burn any shoots that appear to be withered, as they may contain chrysalides

SCALE INSECTS (Coccidæ) —These insects infest Roses, Cotoneasters, &c To destroy them spray or syringe with paraffin emulsion, or quassia extract and soft soap; then, if possible, any of the insects that are on the stems or shoots should be scraped off In the course of a few days spray again to make sure of killing any of the young that escaped the first application

THE GARDEN SNAIL (Helix aspersa) —There is practically nothing to be done in the way of killing them but hand-picking Thrushes are very fond of them

SLUGS —There are several kinds of slugs that infest gardens, the commonest is Limax agrestis, its ravages being only too well known Small heaps of bran, each placed on a small piece of slate or board, make good traps Dusting with fresh lime is very useful, and large numbers may be killed of an evening if the plants that are attacked and the ground round them are searched with the aid of a lantern If the slug be stabbed or cut through with a sharp-pointed knife at the shield (that part just behind the head) the creature dies immediately

SNAKE MILLIPEDES (belonging to the genera Julus, Blanjulus, and Polydesmus) —These creatures are among the most annoying pests in gardens, as they are so difficult to destroy They feed on the roots of Lilies and other bulbs, Anemones, Pansies, Stocks and various plants in the flower garden Few insecticides have any effect on them, as their skins are so horny and smooth, but a strong solution of salt or nitrate of soda will kill them if it can be made to reach them They may be trapped by laying bricks, slates, tiles, pieces of board, turf or Cabbage leaves about, as the millipedes are fond of creeping under such things. They may be distinguished from the centipedes—with which they are often confused, and which are of great use in gardens—by the slowness of their movements, while the centipedes are very active There is, however, one exception, the luminous centipede, a long, thread-like creature, 2 inches to 2½ inches in length, which, in spite of its extraordinary number of legs, moves with the greatest deliberation. The snake millipedes, according to the species, when full-grown each measures from half to 1 inch in length, and are composed of a great number of joints. With the exception of the "flattened snake millipede," they are nearly cylindrical in form.

THRIPS (Thrips adonidum).—This insect is more injurious to plants grown under glass than to those in the open air; but Phloxes, Carnations, Dahlias, and some other plants often suffer from their attacks. Syringing or spraying with paraffin emulsion, quassia extract and soft soap, Gishurst compound, or tobacco water are the best remedies for outdoor use.

VARIOUS CATERPILLARS.—Besides the caterpillars already mentioned, most plants in the flower garden are liable to be attacked by the caterpillars of various moths, which it is hardly necessary to enumerate. Suffice it to say that they are best destroyed by hand-picking.

THE WHITE CABBAGE and TURNIP BUTTERFLIES (Pieris brassicæ and P. rapi).—In the flower garden the caterpillars of these butterflies are very injurious to the leaves of Tropæolums of various kinds and Mignonette. The plants should be carefully looked over, and the caterpillars picked off. If very numerous, syringe or spray with paraffin emulsion.

WIREWORMS (the grubs of various species of "click beetles," Elateridæ).—These well-known pests are by no means easy to get rid of, and as they are over two years in coming to maturity, if left alone they have plenty of time to do a great amount of harm. They attack various flowering plants, but they are particularly fond of Carnations and plants of that nature. Those belonging to the largest species when full-grown are three-quarters of an inch in length, and much resemble a piece of brass or copper wire of that length, and they are almost as tough. No insecticide is of much use, and trapping them is the best way of destroying them. Slices of Carrots, Turnips, Potatoes, or Rape-cake buried about an inch below the surface make good traps. Each should have a small skewer stuck into it to show where it was buried. They should be examined every morning. Most birds are fortunately very fond of them.

WOODLICE, if found to congregate at the base of a wall or in other positions, may be killed by pouring boiling water over them. They may be trapped by laying bricks, tiles, or pieces of slate or board near their haunts, which they will creep under. Toads kill great numbers of them. Or they may be poisoned by laying pieces of Potato about which have been boiled in water in which some arsenic has been placed.   G. S. S.

Eden Hall, Cumberland,

INDEX.

R CLAY AND SONS, LTD, BREAD ST HILL, E C, AND BUNGAY, SUFFOLK

Ingram Content Group UK Ltd.
Milton Keynes UK
UKHW020206160323
418650UK00005B/60